The town plans

All plans in the book are based on up-to-date aerial photography and information supplied by local authorities. The central area of each town is shown on a detailed large-scale plan. In addition, each of the major conurbations has a route map of the surrounding area, referred to in the text by the prefix "R".

Note: All parking shown on the town parks. Where there is no plan, car parks text. All other parking listed in the text limited periods only.

Town plans

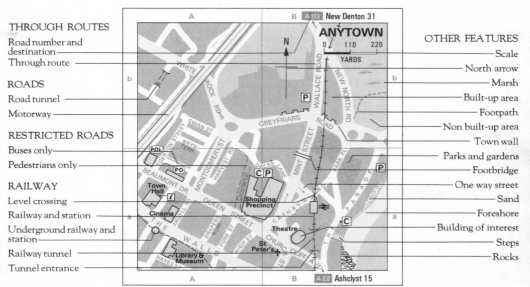

THROUGH ROUTES
Road number and destination
Through route

ROADS
Road tunnel
Motorway

RESTRICTED ROADS
Buses only
Pedestrians only

RAILWAY
Level crossing
Railway and station
Underground railway and station
Railway tunnel
Tunnel entrance

OTHER FEATURES
Scale
North arrow
Marsh
Built-up area
Footpath
Non built-up area
Town wall
Parks and gardens
Footbridge
One way street
Sand
Foreshore
Building of interest
Steps
Rocks

Route maps

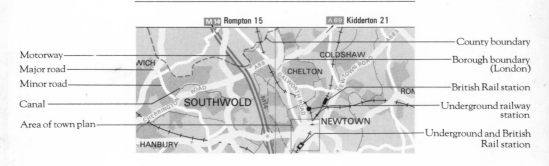

Motorway
Major road
Minor road
Canal
Area of town plan

County boundary
Borough boundary (London)
British Rail station
Underground railway station
Underground and British Rail station

Symbols

P	Car park
C	Public convenience
🚻	with facils. for disabled
i	Tourist Information
POL	Police Station
PO	Post Office
AA	AA Service Centre
🚢	Car ferry
🗼	Lighthouse
H	Casualty hospital (route map)
✈	Airport
⠮	Ruin
†	Church

NT	National Trust
🏛	House
🏵	Museum and Art Gallery
⚒	Industrial monument
🏰	Abbey
🏯	Castle
🛠	Windmill
❋	Botanical garden
🐘	Zoo
⛳	Golf course
⬭	Stadium
◎	Lifeguard
🌊	Swimming pool (indoor)

🌊	Swimming pool (outdoor)
⛵	Sailing and Boating
🛶	Canoeing
🏏	County Cricket
⚽	Association Football
🏉	Rugby Union
🏉	Rugby League
🎾	Championship Tennis
🐕	Greyhound racing
🐎	Show jumping
🐎	Horse racing
🏍	Motorcycle racing
🏃	Athletics

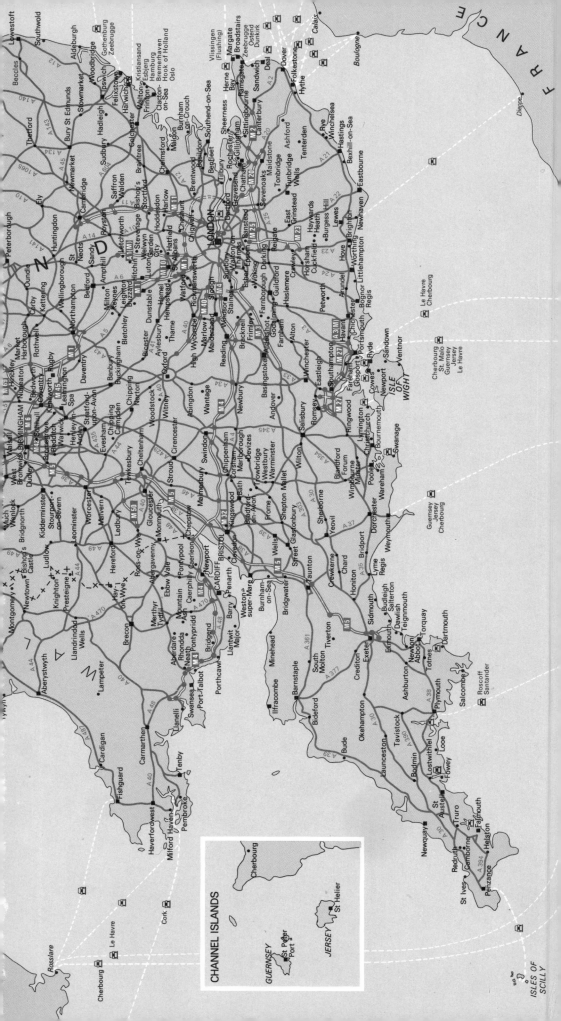

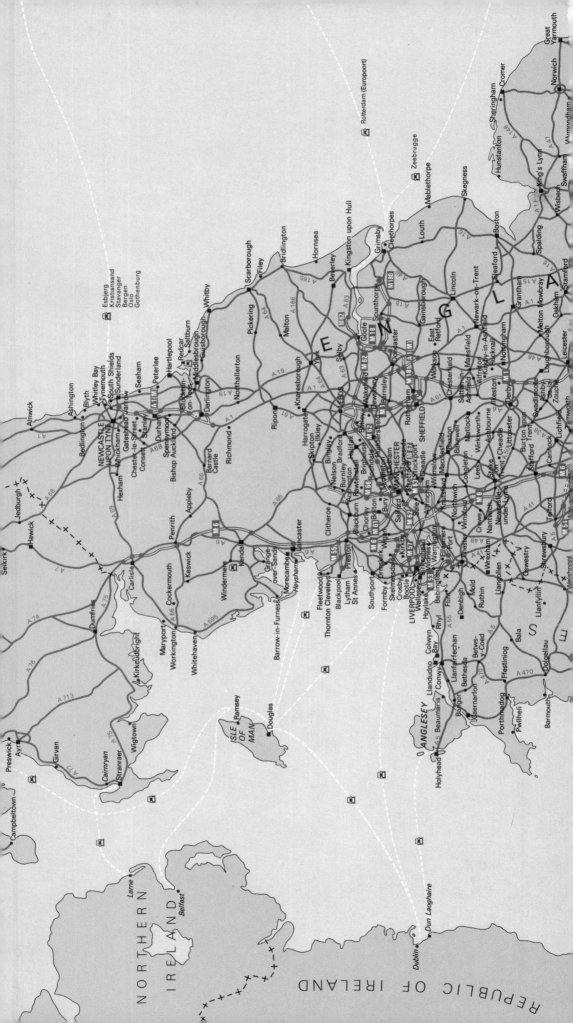

AA

BOOK OF BRITISH TOWNS

AA

BOOK OF BRITISH TOWNS

Published by Drive Publications Limited
for the Automobile Association
Fanum House, Basingstoke, Hants RG21 2EA

Book of British Towns
was edited and designed by The Reader's Digest Association Limited
for Drive Publications Limited
Berkeley Square House, London W1X 5PD

Printed in Great Britain

Cover photograph: Tewkesbury Abbey and town

CONTRIBUTORS

The publishers would like to thank the following people for major contributions to this book

Authors

Philip Llewellin
Ann Saunders

Photographers

Malcolm Aird
Clive Coote
Christopher Drew
Ric Gemmell
Neil Holmes
Ian Howes
Colin Molyneux
Julian Plowright
Mike St Maur Sheil
Patrick Thurston
Trevor Wood

Artists

David Baird
Patricia Calderhead
Michael Craig
Colin Emberson
Shirley Felts
Nick Hall
Hayward and Martin

Guided tour maps

Peter Morter

A comprehensive
guide to nearly 700
cities and towns
in Britain

CONTENTS

Glossary of architectural and historical terms

A

Aberdare Mid Glamorgan

At the head of the Cynon Valley, Aberdare stands on a broad plain with Graig Mountain – the southern edge of the Brecon Beacons National Park – forming a scenic backdrop. The town was once a coal-mining centre, producing the best steam-coal in the world, but the collieries are now closed.

The town centre, Victoria Square, is a mixture of modern and Victorian architecture, dominated by a bronze statue of Griffith Rhys Jones who led the South Wales Choral Union to victory in the first choir contest held at London's Crystal Palace, in 1872.

St John the Baptist Church, in the High Street, dates from about 1200. St Elvan's Church was built in 1851; its spire is a prominent landmark.

GRIFFITH RHYS JONES, *leader of a great Welsh choir.*

Information Tel. 875161.
Location On the A4059, 20 m. NW of Cardiff.
Parking Ynys; High Street; Green Fach; Gadly's Pit; Cross Street.
District council Borough of Cynon Valley (Tel. 875161).
Population 36,600.
E-C Thur.
Police Cross Street (Tel. 872456).
Casualty hospital Aberdare General Hospital (Tel. 872411).
Post office High Street.
Theatres Coliseum, Trecynon (Tel. 3033); Little Theatre, Gadlys (no telephone).
Cinema Rex, High Street (Tel. 872104).
Public library Green Fach.
AA 24 hour service Tel. Cardiff 394111.

ABERGAVENNY *The houses huddle together on the valley floor beneath the surrounding mountains.*

Aberdeen see page 10

Abergavenny Gwent

A ring of mountains rising to nearly 2,000 ft surrounds Abergavenny, which lies in the valley of the River Usk on the eastern edge of the Brecon Beacons National Park. The town is a base for exploring the Beacons. It is also the centre of a prosperous farming area, and its cattle market is one of the largest in South Wales.

The Church of St Mary, in Monk Street, was originally the chapel of an 11th-century Benedictine priory. Only the tithe barn and prior's house remain of the priory buildings, but the church has traces of medieval architecture and contains some 14th-century choir stalls, tombs dating from the 13th to 17th centuries and a Norman font.

The ruins of an 11th-century castle are a reminder of Abergavenny's part in Welsh history. It was the scene of a massacre in 1175 when the Norman William de Braose gained a savage revenge against the Welsh who had murdered his uncle. He invited the local chieftains to a Christmas dinner and, while they were eating, had them slaughtered.

The castle was destroyed in 1645 on the orders of Charles I to prevent Cromwell's forces from using it.

Information Tel. Pontypool 2311; Abergavenny 3254 (summer).
Location On the A40, 9 m. N of Pontypool.
Parking Fairfield; Castle Street; Town Hall (cp); Bus Station (cp); Tiverton Place; The Priory.
District council Monmouth (Tel. Pontypool 2311).
Population 9,400.
E-C Thur. **M-D** Tues., Fri.
Police Tudor Street (Tel. 2273).
Casualty hospital Brecon Road (Tel. 2091).
Post office St John's Square.
Cinema Coliseum, Lion Street (Tel. 3033).
Public library Baker Street.
Places to see Castle and Museum, Castle Street.
Shopping Cross Street; Frogmore Street; High Street.
Trade and industry Printing and bookbinding; light engineering.
AA 24 hour service Tel. Newport 62559.

ABERDEEN
Grampian

The granite capital of Britain's oil industry

Salt-rimed trawlers now share Aberdeen's busy harbour at the mouth of the River Dee with supply ships carrying oil-drilling equipment, and local accents mingle with those of other lands. The geographical position of Scotland's "Granite City" combines with its seafaring and commercial traditions to make it the ideal base for servicing the North Sea drilling rigs and production platforms. The oil boom, however, has done little to alter the deeply etched character of the city; it is just another chapter in a long, eventful and proud story.

Aberdeen, known to the Romans as Devana, was granted its first royal charter by King William the Lion in 1179. By the end of the 13th century it was a flourishing port, sending fish, wool, hides and timber to other parts of Britain and across the North Sea to Europe. Its early history is also stained with blood. Between 1297 and 1336, during the long and bitter Anglo-Scottish wars, Aberdeen was attacked three times and finally burned to the ground by England's Edward III. From the ashes arose what became known as New Aberdeen.

Modern Aberdeen has developed since the end of the 18th century alongside such evocative reminders of the past as the 16th-century Provost Ross's House, the ancient bridge Brig o' Balgownie, 14th-century St Machar's Cathedral, and 15th-century King's College. Several architects, notably Archibald Simpson, the son of a local merchant, became enchanted by the neo-Classical style, and translated it into a wealth of handsome buildings of grey granite flecked with mica that glitters like silver when caught by the sun.

Union Street, the broad arrow-straight main artery, opened in 1805, runs inland for almost a mile from the 17th-century **Mercat Cross**, which was built near the site of a long-

FORTIFIED CATHEDRAL *The two squat towers of St Machar's Cathedral were fortified when they were built in the turbulent 14th century.*

vanished castle. Building the street was a major feat of civil engineering that involved the partial levelling of a hill and throwing the graceful, 130 ft span of Union Bridge over a deep, steep-sided valley.

Trophy winner

The valley's western bank now forms **Union Terrace Gardens**, a tranquil park-in-miniature in the city centre, with Aberdeen's crest picked out in flowers at one end. The many public parks display Aberdeen's passion for flowers. The city has won the Britain in Bloom trophy nine times and has become famous for its roses; 4 million bloom throughout the city every year.

The city that grew up after the fire of 1336 slowly spread northwards, towards the River Don, and merged with Old Aberdeen, although the union did not become official until 1891. Old Aberdeen has remained an enchanting backwater where old houses and shops of pink granite line cobbled streets and narrow "wynds", or alleys, contrasting sharply with the modern university buildings little more than a stone's throw away.

PLACES TO SEE

1 Marischal College
2 Anthropological Museum
3 Art Gallery and Museum
4 Cruickshank Botanic Garden
5 James Dun's House
6 Provost Ross's House
7 Provost Skene's House
8 Brig o' Balgownie
9 St Machar's Cathedral
10 King's College
11 Mercat Cross
12 Gordon Highlanders' Museum
13 Union Terrace Gardens
14 St Nicholas's Kirk

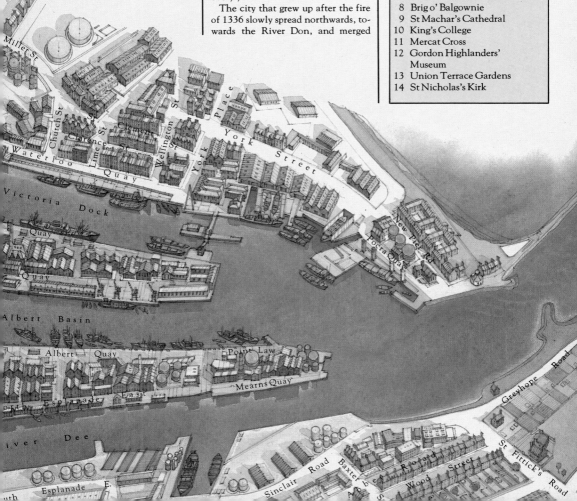

In the old city stands twin-towered **St Machar's Cathedral**. It is approached along the Chanonry, a sleepy little street in which stands Aberdeen's oldest inhabited house – The Chaplain's Court, built in 1519. Legend tells how Machar, a follower of St Columba, was sent to the mainland from the holy island of Iona in the 6th century. He was told to keep travelling eastwards until he found a place where a river, as it neared the sea, flowed in the shape of a bishop's crozier.

Riverside cathedral

His journey ended, and a church was established where the Don sweeps in crozier-like curves around what is now Seaton Park. Much of the cathedral dates from the 14th and 15th centuries, but the towers' spires were added by Bishop Dunbar between 1518 and 1532. He was also responsible for the heraldic ceiling of panelled oak with its 48 shields depicting the arms of the pope, numerous kings and bishops, and many other notables.

Another outstanding building in the old city is **King's College**, the university of Old Aberdeen. It was founded in 1494 by Dunbar's predecessor, Bishop Elphinstone, who also planned the old bridge that still takes traffic over the Dee. He created the university so that those who had previously been "rude and barbarous" could win "the pearl of knowledge which shows the way to living well and happily".

MERCAT CROSS *Aberdeen's "new" cross was built in 1686 for £100.*

King's College Chapel, completed in 1505, forms one side of a grassy quadrangle and has an unusual crown-topped tower in honour of James IV of Scotland, the university's co-founder and first patron. The tower looks down on Bishop Elphinstone's elaborate tomb.

New Aberdeen's **Marischal College** was founded 99 years after King's, enabling the citizens to boast that they had as many universities as the whole of England at that time. In 1860 the two colleges were united to form the modern university.

One of Old Aberdeen's most attractive buildings, the Wallace Tower, now a private house, has an unusual history. It was built in 1616 and re-mained in the city centre until 1963, when it was carefully dismantled, stone by stone, to make way for a redevelopment scheme. It now stands 2 miles away, on a steep bank overlooking Seaton Park, where a wooded riverside walk leads to the picturesque bridge, **Brig o' Balgownie**, with its clusters of immaculate 16th-century cottages. The bridge, one of the oldest in Britain, was begun about 1285 and completed at the command of Robert Bruce in about 1320.

In the heart of the modern city it is also easy to leave the present behind without straying far from Union Street. One of the most interesting links with the past is **Provost Skene's House**, in Flourmill Lane. Adorned with a pair of jaunty turrets, it dates from the 16th century and commemorates Sir George Skene, Provost of Aberdeen from 1676 to 1685. The restoration work started in 1951, and Queen Elizabeth the Queen Mother was among those who urged that it be rescued rather than razed to make way for new buildings.

The house has been decorated and furnished in several appropriate styles. In the Georgian Room, complete with a cut-glass decanter and brimming glasses, is a portrait of the Duke of Cumberland, the soldier son of George II. He spent several weeks at the house in 1746 while on his way to meet Bonnie Prince Charlie's army of Highlanders, which he defeated at Culloden with great slaughter.

The top floor has become a folk museum, with exhibits ranging from spinning-wheels and domestic utensils to muskets and a huge two-handed sword almost 6 ft long. The house's most remarkable feature is the chapel, where the restorers uncovered a ceiling of religious paintings believed to date from the early 17th century. Some are badly damaged, but among those preserved are two picturing the birth and death of Christ that are among the most important of their kind in Scotland.

City's oldest street

Overlooking a corner of the harbour in cobble-stoned Shiprow, possibly the oldest street in Aberdeen, is **Provost Ross's House**, which dates from 1593. It was built by the father of George Jamesone, Scotland's first great portrait painter, but is named after its most illustrious owner, John Ross, Provost of Aberdeen in the 18th century. Like Provost Skene's House, it was in an advanced state of decay before being rescued in the 1950s to become a National Trust for Scotland property. The house was closed in 1981 to prepare for its opening as Aberdeen Maritime Museum the next year.

Towers and steeples embellish Aberdeen's skyline. One of the most notable is the spire of **St Nicholas's Kirk**, the city's main church, which replaced the original spire destroyed by fire in 1874. Its replacement, built two years later from 2,000 tons of

PROVOST ROSS'S HOUSE *Built in 1593, the second oldest house in the city centre is named after an 18th-century owner.*

granite, soars 195 ft. A row of lofty pillars and an ancient burial ground shield the church from Union Street, and like Union Gardens it is a pool of tranquillity in the busy city centre. It has the largest carillon of any church in Britain, and the city carilloneur rings the bells frequently in summer. The 48 bells span four chromatic octaves; 14 of the bells can be rung automatically by a revolving drum fitted with wooden pegs, like a giant musical-box. Visitors may see the bells after some recitals.

Great sculptors

The **art gallery**, opened in 1885, stands behind the church in Schoolhill. Sculptures by Sir Henry Moore and Dame Barbara Hepworth dignify the light and spacious entrance hall, while the rooms display works by such artists as Monet, Degas, Renoir, Reynolds, Romney and Epstein. The gallery incorporates a domed war-memorial room that includes a Greek warrior's helmet from the 6th or 7th centuries BC.

The 18th-century **James Dun's House**, on the opposite side of Schoolhill, is part of the gallery. Recently restored, it won a European Architectural Heritage Year award in 1975. Many of its exhibits are aimed at children, and there is a room where

UNIVERSITY FOUNDER *William Elphinstone (1431–1514), Bishop of Aberdeen, has two memorials – one in the cathedral, the other outside King's College Chapel.*

KING'S COLLEGE *A beautiful stone crown surmounts the tower of the 15th-century college, since 1860 part of the modern university.*

youngsters may try their hand at drawing and painting.

The **anthropological museum** of Marischal College, with exhibits gathered since the 1830s, is a tight-packed wonderland for lovers of the unusual. Delicate embroidery from China, Roman glassware, Tibetan gods and dragon-shaped candlesticks from Peking's Summer Palace mingle with Egyptian mummies, Ashanti tom-toms, Japanese armour, Ethiopian battle-axes and Fijian whale-tooth necklaces. One puzzling exhibit is a kayak – a sealskin canoe, almost 18 ft long – found drifting off the mouth of the Don in 1700; its mysterious Eskimo occupant died of exhaustion soon after being rescued.

The **Gordon Highlanders' Museum**, on the western outskirts of the city, has many relics of the famous Scottish regiment, first raised by the Duke of Gordon in 1794.

Aberdeen's reputation as a busy cargo and fishing port and business centre, together with the rather stern "Granite City" image, tends to obscure the fact that it is also a holiday resort. Golf has been played in Aberdeen since the 17th century, and spacious links form a green barrier between the town and the sandy beaches stretching for almost 2 miles between the Don and Dee.

OUTDOOR DRAUGHTS *Four large boards provide unusual amusement in peaceful Union Terrace Gardens, in the city centre.*

Information St Nicholas House, Broad Street (Tel. 23456).
Location On the A92, 57 m. NE of Dundee.
Parking See map.
District council City of Aberdeen (Tel. 23456).
Population 208,900.
E-C Wed., Sat. (no E-C in city centre). **M-D** Fri.
Police (Cb) Queen Street (Tel. 29933).
Casualty hospital Aberdeen Royal Infirmary, Foresterhill (Tel. 681818).
Post office (Aa) Crown Street.
Theatres HM Theatre **(Ab)** (Tel. 28080); Aberdeen Arts Centre (23456).
Cinemas ABC **(Bb)** (Tel. 51477); Capitol (23141); Odeon (26050).
Public library (Ab) Rosemount Viaduct.
Shopping Union Street; George Street; St Nicholas Street; Holburn Street; Thistle Street; Chapel Street; Rose Street; New Market; Rosemount; Dyce Shopping Centre.
Events Aberdeen Festival (June); Aberdeen Highland Games (June); International Football Festival (July); International Festival of Music and Performing Arts (Aug.).
Sport Scottish League football, Aberdeen FC, Pittodrie Park.
Car ferry To Shetland (Tel. 29111).
AA 24 hour service Tel. Aberdeen 51231.

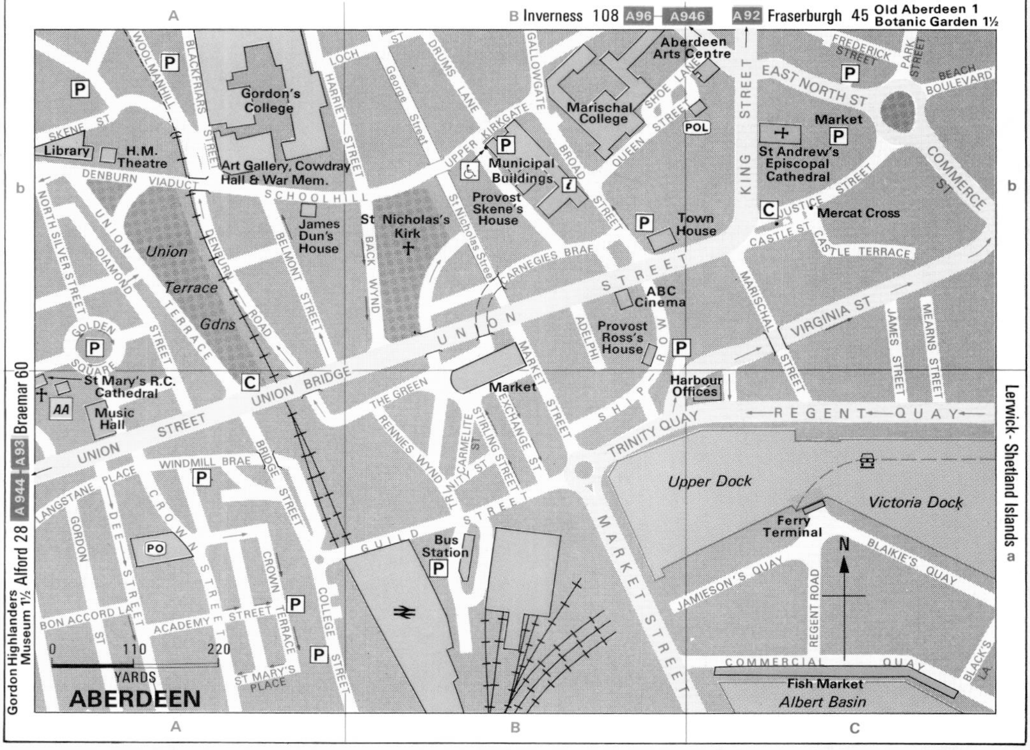

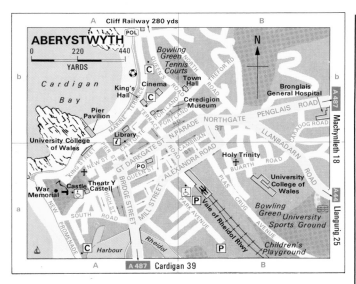

ABERYSTWYTH

Cliff Railway 280 yds

Cardigan Bay

Bowling Green Tennis Courts

King's Hall · Cinema · Town Hall · Ceredigion Museum

Bronglais General Hospital

Pier Pavilion

Library

University College of Wales

Holy Trinity

University College of Wales

War Memorial · Castle · Theatr Y Castell

Bowling Green · University Sports Ground

Children's Playground

Harbour

A 487 Cardigan 39

A 487 Machynlleth 18

A 44 Llangurig 25

Vale of Rheidol Riwy

Rheidol

Aberystwyth Dyfed

The principal seaside resort of west Wales, Aberystwyth is also the home of the University College of Wales and the National Library of Wales. The town grew up behind a castle built on a promontory beside the Rheidol estuary, and a stone jetty makes this a safe haven for fishing-boats and pleasure-craft. At the north end of the promenade is a cliff railway to the summit of Constitution Hill.

In term time there are some 3,200 students in the town – more than a quarter of the total population. Most of the college buildings are on high ground inland, as is the National Library. This houses more than 2 million books and about 3·5 million documents, including the 12th-century Black Book of Carmarthen, the oldest manuscript in Welsh.

Aberystwyth is also the terminus of the Vale of Rheidol Railway, a narrow-gauge, single-track line that runs 12 miles inland through spectacular scenery.

Information Tel. 617911.
Location On the A487, 39 m. NE of Cardigan.
Parking Bath Street; Park Avenue (2) (all car parks).
District council Ceredigion (Tel. 617911).
Population 8,700.
E-C Wed. **M-D** Mon. (cattle).
Police (Ab) Victoria Terrace (Tel. 612791).
Casualty hospital (Bb) Bronglais General, Penglais Road (Tel. 3131).
Post office (Aa) Great Darkgate Street.
Theatres King's Hall **(Ab)**, Marine Terrace (Tel. 617911); Theatr Y Werin, University Campus (4277);

Castle Theatre, St Michael's Place (3177).
Cinema Commodore **(Ab)**, Bath Street (Tel. 612421).
Public library (Ab) Corporation Street.
Places to see Aberystwyth Castle **(Aa)**, New Promenade; Ceredigion Museum **(Ab)**, Terrace Road; National Library of Wales, Penglais Road.
Shopping Great Darkgate Street; Pier Street; Terrace Road.
AA 24 hour service
Tel. Cardiff 394111.

Abingdon Oxfordshire

Until 1870 Abingdon was the county town of Berkshire; in that year Reading "took over" the county. Then in 1974 Abingdon was removed from Berkshire and added to Oxfordshire. All this has made no difference to the look of the town, which is one of the most attractive in England.

Abingdon grew up at the gates of an abbey founded in 675. Abbey and town prospered with the medieval wool trade. Most of the abbey was destroyed at the Dissolution in 1538, and little remains but the 15th-century gatehouse and a few buildings in Thames Street. The oldest of these, the 13th-century Checker, may have been the abbey exchequer.

The Guildhall, originally an outbuilding of the abbey, was bought by the corporation in the 16th century and later used as a courtroom and school. It is now a council office.

RIVERSIDE CHURCH *The spire of St Helen's Church looks down on the mellow old houses that line the River Thames at Abingdon.*

The County Hall, in the Market Place, is one of the grandest in the country. It was built in 1678–82 by Christopher Kempster, one of Sir Christopher Wren's masons at St Paul's. It is now a museum.

Bridge Street runs from the Market Place past the old county gaol to the bridge which has carried traffic over the Thames for more than 500 years.

The part-13th-century Church of St Helen, which stands near the river south-west of the bridge, is unusual in being wider than it is long. Its churchyard is flanked on three sides by almshouses dating from the 15th and 18th centuries.

Still an agricultural market town, in recent years Abingdon has also become a dormitory for the scientists of the Atomic Research Establishment at Harwell.

Information Tel. 22711.
Location On the A34, 6 m. S of Oxford.
Parking West St Helen's Street; Stert Street; Oxford Road (all car parks).
District council Vale of White Horse (Tel. 20202).
Population 22,700.
E-C Thur. **M-D** Mon.
Police Bridge Street (Tel. 20303).
Casualty hospital John Radcliffe, Headington, Oxford (Tel. Oxford 64711).
Post office High Street.
Theatres Little Theatre, Old Gaol Sports Centre (4 days) (Tel. 22806); Unicorn Theatre, Thames Street (25334).
Cinema Little Theatre.
Public library The Charter.
Places to see County Hall, Market Place; Abingdon Abbey, Thames Street; Guildhall, Bridge Street.
Shopping Bury Street.
AA 24 hour service Tel. Oxford 40286.

Accrington Lancashire

Smooth red bricks spread the name of Accrington throughout Victorian Britain. Hard and durable, the bricks were often used for public buildings. Accrington was also well known for cotton and linen fabrics.

The Haworth Art Gallery in Manchester Road contains collections of early-English water-colours and a large collection of Tiffany glass.

Information Tel. 384131.
Location On the A680, 5 m. E of Blackburn.
Parking Union Street (car park).
District council Borough of Hyndburn (Tel. 384131).
Population 35,900.
E-C Wed. **M-D** Tues., Fri. and Sat.
Police Manchester Road (Tel. 382141).
Casualty hospital Blackburn Royal Infirmary, Bolton Road, Blackburn (Tel. Blackburn 63555).
Post office Abbey Street.
Cinema Unit Four, Broadway (Tel. 33231).

ALDEBURGH MOOT HALL *The timber-framed hall is still used for council meetings – as it has been for 400 years. It also houses the local museum.*

Public library St James's Street.
Shopping Broadway; Abbey Street; Whalley Road; Blackburn Road.
AA 24 hour service Tel. Manchester (061) 485 6299.

Airdrie Strathclyde

Like Rome, Airdrie is built on seven hills. This has helped it to retain the atmosphere of a country market town, in spite of a long industrial history. There are wide views from Airdriehill, the town's highest point.

Information Tel. 62453.
Location On the A89 and A73, 11 m. E of Glasgow.
Parking Hallcraig Street; Wellwynd; Broomknoll Street; Victoria Place; Gartlea Road; Anderson Street; Stirling Street; Manse Place; North Bridge Street; Mill Street; Clark Street (all car parks).
District council Monklands (Tel. Coatbridge 24941).
Population 36,900.
E-C Wed. **M-D** Tues., Fri.
Police Anderson Street (Tel. 62222).
Casualty hospital Monks Court Avenue (Tel. 69344).
Post office Buchanan Street.
Theatre Arts Centre, Anderson Street (Tel. 55436).
Public library Wellwynd.
Shopping Graham Street; Stirling Street; South Bridge Street.
Sport Scottish League football, Airdrieonians FC, Broomfield Park.
AA 24 hour service Tel. Glasgow (041) 812 0101.

Aldeburgh Suffolk

In the 16th century Aldeburgh was one of the leading ports on the east coast, and had a flourishing ship-building industry. Aldeburgh men served with Drake in the *Greyhound* and *Pelican*, both built in the local yards. Ship-building declined when the lower reaches of the River Alde silted up and became unable to take larger ships. It is now a haven for yachtsmen.

Information Tel. 3637.
Location On the A1094, 6 m. SE of Saxmundham.

Parking Oakley Square; Thorpeness Road; Slaughden Road (Fort Green) (all car parks).
District council Suffolk Coastal (Tel. Woodbridge 3789).
Population 2,900.
E-C Wed.
Police King's Road, Leiston (Tel. Leiston 830377).
Casualty hospital General, Ivry Street, Ipswich (Tel. Ipswich 212477).
Post office High Street.
Cinema The Aldeburgh, High Street (Tel. 2996).
Public library Victoria Road.
Places to see Moot Hall, Market Cross; Church of St Peter and St Paul; Martello Tower, Slaughden.
Event Aldeburgh Festival (June).
AA 24 hour service Tel. Norwich 29401.

ALDEBURGH FESTIVAL

Every June, music-lovers from all over the world gather at Aldeburgh for the largest music festival in England. Founded in 1948 by the composers Benjamin Britten and Eric Crozier and the singer Peter Pears, it takes place in the Snape Maltings, the 15th-century Church of St Peter and St Paul and the Jubilee Hall in Aldeburgh. Additional performances are held in the villages of Orford, Blythburgh and Framlingham. Other events are held at Snape throughout the year.

The Maltings, Snape, are 19th-century malting buildings, rebuilt in 1970 to include a concert hall.

Sir Peter Pears sings as he conducts at Snape.

Aldershot Hampshire

A little more than a century ago, Aldershot was a quiet hamlet surrounded by heathland. Then in 1854 the War Department bought 10,000 acres for a camp that was to become the home of the British Army.

Museums devoted to the history of airborne forces, army engineers, medical and nursing corps and other regiments are open to the public.

In Manor Park stands the Heroes Shrine, dedicated to the dead of the Second World War.

BRONZE DUKE *The statue of the Duke of Wellington on Round Hill, Aldershot, once stood in London.*

Information Tel. 22456.
Location On the A323, 8 m. W of Guildford.
Parking High Street; Birchett Road; Victoria Road; Wellington Avenue; Princes Gardens; The Grove; Little Wellington Street (all car parks).
District council Borough of Rushmoor (Tel. Farnborough 44451).
Population 32,700.
E-C Wed. **M-D** Thur.
Police Wellington Avenue (Tel. 24545).
Casualty hospital Frimley, Portsmouth Road, Camberley (Tel. Camberley 62121).
Post office Station Road.
Theatre West End Centre, Queens Road (Tel. 21158).
Cinemas ABC 1, 2 and 3, High Street (Tel. 20355); Palace, Station Road (22042).
Public library High Street.
Shopping High Street; Union Street; Wellington Street.
Sport FA League football, Aldershot FC, High Street.
AA 24 hour service
Tel. Guildford 72841.

Alfreton Derbyshire

A Saxon called Alfred – not Alfred the Great – gave his name to Alfreton. Nothing remains from those earliest days, but the church dates from the 12th century, and the charter for the weekly market, which is still held, was granted in 1252.

Information Tel. 2292.
Location On the A61, 10 m. S of Chesterfield.
Parking Rodger's Lane (2); Hall

Street; Market Place; Church Street (all car parks).
District council Amber Valley (Tel. Ripley 42331).
Population 23,100.
E-C Wed. **M-D** Tues., Fri., Sat.
Police Hall Street (Tel. 3413).
Casualty hospital Slack Lane, Ripley (Tel. Ripley 43456).
Post office High Street.
Cinema Empire, High Street (Tel. 3146).
Public library Severn Square.
AA 24 hour service
Tel. Nottingham 787751.

Alnwick Northumberland

For 200 years Alnwick (pronounced Annick) was virtually the capital of northern England. From their castle beside the town the Percy family, Earls of Northumberland, held the border against the Scots and ruled much of northern England. The original castle, built in the 11th century, fell into decay when the border wars ended. Restored in the 18th century to the design of Robert Adam, it contains paintings by Titian, Tintoretto, Van Dyke and Canaletto, and is open to the public.

The only surviving gateway to the original town walls is the Hotspur Tower, built in 1450 by the 2nd Earl of Northumberland, the son of Harry Hotspur who died at the Battle of Shrewsbury in 1403.

The Percy Tenantry Column was erected in 1816 by local tenant farmers, in gratitude to the 2nd Duke of Northumberland, who reduced their rents at a time of depression.

DUCAL BEAST *The Percy lion surmounts Alnwick's Tenantry Column.*

Information Tel. 603120.
Location Off the A1, 30 m. S of Berwick-upon-Tweed.
Parking Bondgate Without; Pottergate; Lagny Street; Dispensary Street (all car parks).
District council Alnwick (Tel. 603221).
Population 7,200.

E-C Wed. **M-D** Sat.
Police Prudhoe Street (Tel. 602777).
Casualty hospital South Road (Tel. 602661).
Post office Fenkle Street.
Cinema The Playhouse, Bondgate Without (Tel. 602122).
Public library Green Batt.
AA 24 hour service
Tel. Newcastle upon Tyne 610111.

Alton Hampshire

The town dates back to Roman times, but it lies on a far older route – a Bronze Age trackway later known as the Pilgrim's Way. The long main street follows the ancient route and is a blend of Georgian and later buildings.

In 1643, during the Civil War, Alton was the scene of a bitter struggle between the Roundheads and Royalists. The battle ended in the parish church of St Lawrence, where Charles I's supporters fell, fighting to the end. The main door of the church still has musket balls embedded in the surrounding stonework.

Information Tel. 83147.
Location On the A31, 10 m. SW of Farnham.
Parking Ladyplace; High Street; Inner Relief Road (2); Mount Pleasant Road; Vicarage Hill; Turk Street; Market Square; Church Street (all car parks).
District council East Hampshire (Tel. Petersfield 665311).
Population 14,600.
E-C Wed. **M-D** Tues.
Police Orchard Lane (Tel. 82244).
Casualty hospital Basingstoke and District, Aldermaston Road, Basingstoke (Tel. Basingstoke 3202).
Post office High Street.
Cinema Palace, Normandy Street (Tel. 82303).
Public library Vicarage Hill.
Places to see Curtis Museum, High Street; Allen Gallery, Church Street.
Shopping High Street; Market Square.
AA 24 hour service
Tel. Basingstoke 56565.

Altrincham G. Manchester

For some 500 years Altrincham was a quiet market town on the edge of the rich Cheshire Plain. Then, in the late

---

JANE AUSTEN'S HOUSE

In the village of Chawton, 1 mile south of Alton, is an 18th-century red-brick house, the home of Jane Austen from 1809 until just before her death at Winchester in 1817. Here she wrote the final drafts of her six novels, *Sense and Sensibility* (1811), *Pride and Prejudice* (1813), *Mansfield Park* (1814), *Emma* (1815-16), *Northanger Abbey* and *Persuasion* (1817).

The drawing-room contains the novelist's work-table and first editions of her books, and in other rooms are letters and personal possessions. In the wash-house stands Jane's donkey-cart.

18th-century Industrial Revolution, it became a producer of woollen and cotton yarn. With the decline of textile industries in this century, Altrincham has become mainly residential, for workers in other parts of Greater Manchester.

Information Tel. Manchester (061) 928 6464.
Location On the A56, 9 m. SW of Manchester.
Parking Denmark Street; Regent Road; High Street; Oakfield Road; Lloyd Street (all car parks).
District council Borough of Trafford (Tel. 061 872 2101).
Population 39,600.
E-C Wed. **M-D** Tues., Fri. and Sat.
Police Dunham Road (Tel. 061 872 5050).
Casualty hospital Wythenshawe Hospital, Southmoor Road (Tel. 061 998 7070).
Post office Stamford New Road.
Theatre Garrick Playhouse, Barrington Road (Tel. 061 928 1677).
Cinema Studio 1, Stamford Street (Tel. 061 928 0331).
Public library Stamford New Road.
Shopping Market Street; Stamford New Road; Grafton Mall; Petro's Shopping Precinct.
AA 24 hour service Tel. 061 485 6299.

Ampthill Bedfordshire

Many fine Georgian houses in Ampthill town centre have been given a new lease of life thanks to Professor Sir Albert Richardson (1880-1964). Sir Albert, an architect and President of the Royal Academy from 1954-6, lived in the 18th-century Avenue House, and encouraged extensive restoration work.

In Ampthill Park a cross marks the site of a 15th-century castle which fell into ruin in the 17th century. It was there that Henry VIII sent his first wife, Catharine of Aragon, while arranging the divorce that led to the break with Rome. The 300 acre park is open to the public.

Information Tel. 402051.
Location On the A418, 8 m. S of Bedford.
Parking Church Street; Bedford Street; Woburn Street (all car parks).
District council Mid Bedfordshire (Tel. 402051).
Population 5,770.
E-C Tues. or Sat. **M-D** Thur.
Police Woburn Street (Tel. 404422).
Casualty hospital Kempston Road, Bedford (Tel. Bedford 55122).
Post office Church Street.
Public library Saunders Piece.
AA 24 hour service Tel. Hatfield 62852.

Andover Hampshire

Since 1961 the quiet market town of Andover has become a manufacturing centre, with light industries such as printing and engineering.

A Georgian Guildhall commands the High Street, and there are timber-framed 16th-century cottages in Chantry Street. St Mary's is a fine example of Victorian Gothic church architecture.

Information Tel. 3621.
Location On the A343, 17 m. NE of Salisbury.
Parking West Street; East Street (2); Chantry Street (2); South Street; Bridge Street (all car parks).
District council Test Valley Borough (Tel. 52328/9).
Population 31,000.
E-C Wed. **M-D** Thur., Sat. (stalls).
Police South Street (Tel. 4311).
Casualty hospital Andover Hospital, Charlton Road (Tel. 61155).
Post office Bridge Street.
Cinema Savoy, London Street (Tel. 52624).
Public library Chantry Way.
Shopping High Street; Bridge Street.
AA 24 hour service Tel. Basingstoke 56565.

Appleby-in-Westmorland Cumbria

The largest horse-fair in Britain is held at Appleby each June, when gipsies from all over Britain gather to buy and sell horses.

For the rest of the year Appleby is a quiet market town and tourist centre. It lies at the foot of the Pennines and is a good base both for hill-walking and exploring the Eden Valley.

The town grew up round a Norman castle built to take advantage of the river's natural defence. Lady Anne Clifford rebuilt the castle in the 17th century, retaining its Norman keep, and restored the parish church, which contains her tomb.

APPLEBY FAIR *Gipsies flock to the town every June to trade at Britain's largest horse-fair.*

Information Tel. 51177.
Location On the A66, 13 m. E of Penrith.
Parking Chapel Street (2); The Sands; Boroughgate (all car parks).
District council Eden (Tel. Penrith 64671).
Population 2,380.
E-C Thur. **M-D** Sat.
Police The Sands (Tel. 51331).
Casualty hospital Cumberland Infirmary, Carlisle (Tel. Carlisle 23444).
Post office Market Square.
Public library Low Wiend.
Places to see Moot Hall, Market Square; Shire Hall, The Sands.
Town trails Available at Moot Hall.
Event Appleby Fair (2nd Wed. in June).
AA 24 hour service Tel. Carlisle 24274.

ARBROATH SMOKIES *Haddock smoked and flavoured over an oak fire are a prized Scottish delicacy.*

Arbroath Tayside

In 1320, Robert Bruce signed Scotland's Declaration of Independence at Arbroath Abbey. The town, made a royal burgh in 1599, is now a resort, fishing port and industrial town.

The abbey was founded by King William the Lion in 1178, and his remains are buried before the high altar. The south transept contains the "O of Arbroath", a circular window once lit as a mariners' beacon. The abbot's house is now a folk museum.

Arbroath "smokies" – haddock smoked over an oak fire – have won international acclaim.

Information Tel. 72609.
Location On the A92, 18 m. NE of Dundee.
Parking High Street; Bridge Street; Helen Street; West Abbey Street (all car parks).
District council Angus (Tel. Forfar 65101).
Population 24,000.
E-C Wed.
Police Springfield Terrace (Tel. 72222).
Casualty hospital Arbroath Infirmary, Rosemount Road (Tel. 72584).
Post office Hill Street.
Theatre Webster, High Street (Tel. 74637).
Cinema Palace, James Street (Tel. 73069).
Public library Hill Terrace.
Places to see Abbey and Museum; Signal Tower Museum.
Shopping High Street; West Port.
Event Agricultural Show (July).
Sport Scottish League football, Arbroath FC, Gayfield Park.
AA 24 hour service Tel. Aberdeen 51231.

Ardrossan Strathclyde

This town grew up in the 19th century on two bays separated by a narrow peninsula, crowned by the ruins of a 13th-century castle.

To the north, on a shingle coast, was developed a port, which now operates passenger services to the Isle of Arran, the Isle of Man and Belfast, and is an oil terminal.

Later, the southern bay, with a long, sandy beach, became the starting point of a holiday resort, with safe bathing, sea-angling and boating.

The adjoining towns of Saltcoats and Stevenston, to the south and east, are also resorts. During the 16th century, Saltcoats was a salt-producing area. Its harbour was built in the 17th century to export coal to Ireland.

Information Tel. Largs 673765.
Location On the A78, 12 m. W of Kilmarnock.
Parking South Beach Road; South Crescent Road (both car parks).
District council Cunninghame (Tel. Irvine 74166).
Population 11,400.
E-C Wed.
Police Green Street, Saltcoats (Tel. Saltcoats 68236).
Casualty hospital North Ayrshire District General, Crosshouse, Kilmarnock (Tel. Kilmarnock 21133).
Post office (Ba) Glasgow Street.

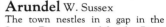

Theatre Ardrossan Civic Centre **(Bb)**, Glasgow Street (Tel. 68396).
Public library (Aa) Princes Street.
Shopping Glasgow Street; Princes Street.
Trade and industry Engineering; shipping; petroleum products.

Car ferries To Isle of Arran (Brodick) and Isle of Man (Douglas) (Tel. Gourock 34568).
AA 24 hour service Tel. Glasgow (041) 812 0101.

Arundel W. Sussex

The town nestles in a gap in the Sussex Downs carved by the River Arun. For centuries the gap has been guarded by Arundel Castle, home of the Dukes of Norfolk, Earls Marshal of England for 500 years.

The castle was begun in the reign of Edward the Confessor and completed by Roger Montgomery, Earl of Shrewsbury, after the Norman Conquest. In 1643 Cromwell's troops destroyed most of the castle with cannons fired from the tower of St Nicholas's Church.

The castle was rebuilt in the 18th century, but the original keep and 13th-century barbican were preserved. Considerable restoration was carried out in 1890 by the 15th Duke of Norfolk. The rooms contain 15th-century furniture, paintings by Van Dyck, a collection of armour and a magnificent library.

The parish church of St Nicholas dates from 1380. Its chancel was sold to the Duke of Norfolk by Henry VIII in 1544 and is now the Fitzalan Chapel, containing monuments to the family. Arundel's Roman Catholic cathedral of Our Lady and St Philip was built in 1868-73 to the design of Joseph Hansom, the inventor of the Hansom Cab.

Below the castle the streets run down to the riverbank. The Arun flows to the sea less than 5 miles away. In Norman times the town was a port.

The town is mostly Victorian, but there are many 18th-century houses

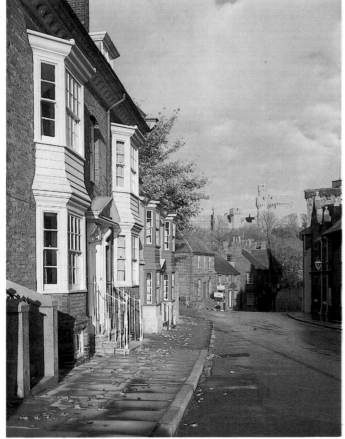

STATELY HOMES IN A SUSSEX TOWN *Fine Georgian houses and the noble ramparts of the castle give Arundel an air of quiet dignity.*

and an 18th-century coaching inn, the Norfolk Arms, stands in the High Street. A unique attraction is the Museum of Curiosity, an exhibition of stuffed animals and birds arranged in tableaux by Walter Potter, a Victorian naturalist and taxidermist. Arundel Museum and Heritage Centre is devoted to the town's historical heritage.

Information Tel. 882419.
Location On the A27, 11 m. E of Chichester.
Parking Crown Yard; Mill Road; River Road (car parks); High Street.
District council Arun
(Tel. Littlehampton 6133).
Population 2,240.
E-C Wed.
Police The Causeway
(Tel. 882676).
Casualty hospital St Richard's, Spitalfield Lane, Chichester
(Tel. Chichester 788122).
Post office High Street.
Public library School Lane.
Places to see Arundel Castle, Mill Road; Museum of Curiosity, High Street; Arundel Museum and Heritage Centre, High Street; Toy Museum, High Street; Wildfowl Trust, Mill Road.
Town trails Available from Tourist Information Centre, 61 High Street.
Shopping High Street; The Square.
Sport First-class cricket, Castle Ground.
AA 24 hour service
Tel. Brighton 695231.

Ashbourne Derbyshire

Hills rising to 600 ft surround Ashbourne, which is on the fringe of the Peak District National Park. Henmore Brook, a tributary of the River Dove, runs through the town.

The main thoroughfare, Church Street, is dominated by the 212 ft spire of the 13th-century Church of St Oswald. Inside the church there are many fine monuments. The street has stone and brick buildings dating from the 16th to 19th centuries, including the Old Grammar School founded by Elizabeth I in 1585. Opposite the school is The Mansion, where Dr Samuel Johnson often stayed with his friend, Dr John Taylor. Both buildings are now boarding houses for the new grammar school in Green Road.

A Georgian inn, the Green Man and Black's Head, has its sign on an arch across St John's Street.

Bonnie Prince Charlie stayed at Ashbourne Hall in 1745 before marching on Derby, and again on his retreat. Part of the hall is now the public library. It stands opposite the Memorial Gardens, which contain a memorial bust of Catherine Booth who, with her husband, William, founded the Salvation Army. She was born in Ashbourne in 1829.

Ashbourne's more robust citizens take part in a unique football game every Shrove Tuesday and Ash Wednesday. The teams are the Up'ards and Down'ards, those living on opposite sides of Henmore Brook. The game dates from medieval times, and it is a free-for-all with few set rules and no limit on the number of players. The goals are 3 miles apart, and were formerly marked by old millwheels, which a scorer touched with the ball. The millwheels are both destroyed, and now the Down'ards goal (Clifton) is marked by a stone plaque, and at the Up'ards goal there is the spindle of its original millwheel, erected vertically. Play starts at 2 p.m. and continues until a goal is scored, or until 10 p.m.

Information Tel. 43666.
Location On the A52, 13 m. NW of Derby.
Parking Market Place; Victoria Square; Cattle Market; Cockayne Avenue; Shawcroft (all car parks).
District council West Derbyshire
(Tel. Matlock 3461).
Population 5,960.
E-C Wed. **M-D** Thur., Sat.
Police Station Street (Tel. 42101).
Casualty hospital St Oswald's, Bellevue Road (Tel. 42121).
Post office Compton.
Public library Cockayne Avenue.
Shopping Compton; St John's Street; Market Place; Church Street; Dig Street.
Event Royal Shrovetide Football Match (Shrove Tuesday and Ash Wednesday).
Trade and industry Knitwear; light engineering; textiles.
AA 24 hour service
Tel. Nottingham 787751.

Ashburton Devon

In medieval times Ashburton was a market for the thriving local wool industry and a stannary town, where tin from the Dartmoor mines was brought for weighing and assessing. It stands within the bounds of Dartmoor National Park, on the south-eastern edge of the rugged moorland plateau.

Until 1894 Ashburton was governed by the officers of the Lord of the Manor, the Portreeve, the Bailiff and the Court Leet. These offices date back more than 600 years and are still kept in being, though today their functions are purely social and traditional. Officers under the Court Leet include the Ale Tasters and Bread Weighers. Once a year they go in procession to each inn and bakery in the town and carry out the ale-tasting and bread-weighing ceremony.

Ashburton's streets have much charm, with buildings from the Elizabethan, Georgian and Victorian periods. In North Street, a shop with a Norman granite arch was once the Mermaid Inn. The Parliamentarian general Sir Thomas Fairfax used it as his headquarters in 1646.

St Andrew's Church dates from the 15th century, and is built of Devon limestone and granite. Its impressive tower rises to 92 ft. The interior of the church has many notable features. The west window is thought to be by C. E. Kempe (1837-1907), and the two candelabra in the nave are 18th-century Italian brasswork. Under the tower is an oak chest made in 1482 with a lock that is still operated by the original key.

The Old Grammar School was housed in St Lawrence's Chapel until 1938. The chapel tower is all that remains of the original 14th-century building. The rest of the structure dates from about 1593.

On the Old Totnes Road, an ancient granite cross in a grassy plot stands beside a tiny spring. This is St Gudula's Well, the water from which was believed to benefit the eyes.

Holne village, 3 miles west of Ashburton, was the birthplace of Charles Kingsley (1819-75), author of *The Water Babies*.

The Benedictine abbey at Buckfast stands on a site thought to have been occupied in the 6th century. The present abbey church of St Mary was built by the monks between 1906 and 1938. The monks form an industrious community, producing stained-glass windows, honey and a tonic wine.

HOUSE OF CARDS *Slates cut with the designs of playing cards decorate a house in Ashburton. The house was built in the 17th century as a gaming club.*

Information Tel. 52142.
Location On the A38, 20 m. SW of Exeter.
Parking Kingsbridge Lane (cp).
District council Teignbridge
(Tel. Newton Abbot 67251).
Population 3,560.
E-C Wed. **M-D** Tues.
Police Eastern Road
(Tel. 52210).
Casualty hospital Ashburton and Buckfastleigh, Eastern Road
(Tel. 52203).
Post office St Lawrence Lane.
Public library Town Hall, North Street.
Places to see Ashburton Museum, West Street; Buckfast Abbey, 2½ m. S off A38.
Town trails Available from local shops.
Shopping North Street; West Street; East Street.
Event Ale-tasting and bread-weighing ceremony, during Carnival Week (June/July).
Trade and industry Agriculture; stone quarrying.
AA 24 hour service
Tel. Exeter 32121.

Ashby-de-la-Zouch Leics.

The Norman suffix which distinguishes Ashby from other towns of the same name comes from the La Souche family, lords of the manor from about 1160. They built a stone hall which was extended into a castle in the 15th century by the 1st Lord Hastings. The castle, now a ruin, has a turbulent history; in the 17th century Royalist forces were besieged there by Parliamentarians for more than a year.

In Sir Walter Scott's novel *Ivanhoe*, Ashby Castle is the setting for the tournament in which Ivanhoe and the Black Knight took part.

Information Tel. Coalville 35951.
Location On the A50, 17 m. NW of Leicester.
Parking North Street; South Street; Brook Street.
District council North West Leicestershire
(Tel. Coalville 36371).
Population 11,500.
E-C Wed. **M-D** Sat.
Police South Street, 9 a.m.–7 p.m.
(Tel. 412173); Ashby Road, Coalville (Tel. Coalville 36300).
Casualty hospital Burton on Trent
(Tel. Burton on Trent 66333).
Post office Market Square.
Public library Kilwardby Street.
Places to see Ashby Castle.
Shopping Market Street.
Event Statutes Fair (Sept.).
Trade and industry Biscuits; soap; crisps.
AA 24 hour service
Tel. Leicester 20491.

Ashford Kent

Ashford has been a market centre for the cattle and sheep farmers of the Weald of Kent and Romney Marsh since the Middle Ages. Its industry developed after the railway works were established in the 19th century.

There are Tudor and Georgian houses in the town centre. The 15th-century parish church of St Mary was built on the site of a Saxon chapel.

Godinton Park is a Jacobean mansion set in formal gardens. Wye College Museum at Brook, housed in a 13th-century tithe barn, exhibits old farm implements and machines. There is also a display of hop growing in an old oast-house.

Information Tel. 24411.
Location On the A28, 14 m. SW of Canterbury.
Parking Vicarage Lane; New Street; Elwick Road (2); Edinburgh Road; Godinton Road (2); Station Road (all car parks).
District council Ashford
(Tel. 34241).
Population 40,000.
E-C Wed. **M-D** Sat.
Police Tufton Street (Tel. 25789).
Casualty hospital William Harvey, Kennington Road (Tel. 33331).
Post office Tufton Street.
Cinema The Cinema, Beaver Road
(Tel. 20124).

Public library Church Road.
Places to see Heritage Centre, Hythe Road; Intelligence Corps Museum, Templer Barracks; Godinton Park, 1½ m. W on A20; Wye College Museum, Court Lodge Farm, Brook, 4 m. NE.
Shopping High Street; Bank Street; Tufton Centre.
AA 24 hour service
Tel. Maidstone 55353.

Ashington Northumberland

Coal-mining has been Ashington's staple industry for years, but the town is also the site of one of the largest aluminium smelting plants in Europe.

Ashington is laid out in modern housing estates, intersected by numbered avenues. There are only two public houses, but more than 40 working-men's clubs.

Newbiggin-by-the-Sea, 3 miles east, has a sandy beach, and there is attractive scenery to the south along the banks of the River Wansbeck.

Information Tel. 814444.
Location On the A197, 6 m. E of Morpeth.
Parking Lintonville Road; Backwoodhorn Road North; Kenilworth Road; John Street (all car parks).
District council Wansbeck
(Tel. 814444).
Population 23,700.

E-C Wed. **M-D** Fri.
Police Station Road (Tel. 814511).
Casualty hospital West View
(Tel. 812541).
Post office Station Road.
Cinema Wallaw, Woodhorn Road
(Tel. 812231).
Public library Kenilworth Road.
Places to see Woodhorn Church Museum.
AA 24 hour service
Tel. Newcastle upon Tyne 610111.

Ashton-under-Lyne
see Tameside

Aylesbury Buckinghamshire

Most of Aylesbury's older buildings are in the area around the Market Square, a broad expanse of cobblestones with a Victorian Gothic clocktower in the centre. There are several ancient inns, among them the 15th-century King's Head, which is now owned by the National Trust. It is a typical coaching hostelry with a large stable yard and medieval gateway. A wooden-framed window in the lounge bar contains 20 panes of 15th-century stained glass, and the inn has a chair reputedly used by Oliver Cromwell when he stayed there in 1651 after his victory at the Battle of Worcester.

Aylesbury's links with the Par-

OLD AND NEW *Modern office blocks overshadow the ancient Market Square in Aylesbury. The clock in the centre of the square was put up in the 19th century.*

liamentary cause in the Civil War are also commemorated in the Market Square, where there is a bronze statue of John Hampden (1594-1643), the local man who played a key part in the events leading up to the Civil War. He opposed Charles I by refusing to pay Ship Money, a tax levied to strengthen the navy. Hampden was mortally wounded in a fight with Cavalier troops at Chalgrove Field in 1643.

Aylesbury is the county town of Buckinghamshire. The red-brick County Hall, at one end of the square, was built about 1720, and contains the Assize courtroom and County Council chamber.

There are several 17th and 18th-century buildings in Church Street, including the old grammar school opened in 1720. This is now part of the County Museum, which also incorporates Ceely House, an 18th-century mansion next door. The museum contains a gallery devoted to Buckinghamshire rural life, and a display of old costumes.

Aylesbury's parish church of St Mary dates from the 13th century, but was heavily restored in the 1860s by Sir Gilbert Scott. The central tower is Norman and is surmounted by a small spire, a copy of the 17th-century original. The stained-glass windows are Victorian, and there is a carved 12th-century font.

An alabaster monument in the church commemorates the wife and three children of Sir Henry Lee, an ancestor of the American Civil War general, Robert E. Lee. An inscription on the monument asks for crimson flowers to be placed on Lady Lee's tomb, and the request has been honoured ever since her death in 1584.

From the Norman Conquest until 1845 the parish of Aylesbury belonged to the Bishops of Lincoln, and its vicars were appointed by a prebendary, or honorary canon, of Lincoln Cathedral.

The former vicarage, next to the church, is now called Prebendal House. It is a three-storey, 18th-century building in large grounds, and was for a time the home of John Wilkes (1727-97), MP for Aylesbury for seven years from 1757. In his stormy career as a satirist and publisher, Wilkes was twice expelled from the House of Commons for his attacks on George III and his government. In 1977, Lady Rosebery moved to Prebendal House after the sale of her family home, Mentmore, near Leighton Buzzard.

The road at the top of Church Street is called Parsons Fee because the land around it once belonged to the Prebendal Farm. In it there are timber-framed buildings, and the farmhouse, mainly 17th century but with some 16th-century sections.

The farmhouse has been renamed after St Osyth, who, according to legend, was martyred by the Danes in the 7th century. Osyth was born at Quarrendon, in the parish of Ayles-

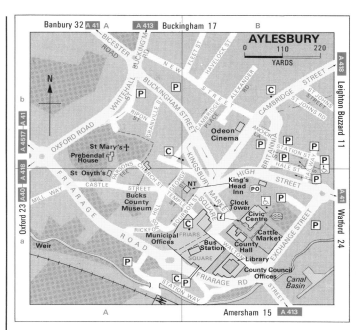

AYLESBURY

Information Tel. 5000.

bury, and founded a priory near Colchester in Essex.

Aylesbury has given its name to the surrounding vale, watered by the River Thame and one of the richest dairy-farming regions in England. Although the town itself is a developing industrial centre, it keeps its links with the land chiefly through the twice-weekly livestock market, at which cattle, sheep and pigs are sold. The market, one of the country's leading ones, has been held since before 1204, and now occupies a permanent site in Exchange Street.

The Vale of Aylesbury, beneath the Chilterns, has many unspoiled villages and tracts of woodland where snowdrops, primroses and bluebells bloom in spring.

At Wing, 7 miles north-east on the A418, there is a Saxon church with many rare features, including a galleried crypt. The village has several 16th and 17th-century buildings. The mansion of Ascott, in Wing, is a half-timbered hunting lodge built in 1870, and contains a picture collection, French and English furniture, and Chinese porcelain.

Whitchurch, 4 miles north on the A413, is a village of half-timbered and thatched cottages. On Market Hill there are the earthworks and moat of Bolebec Castle, built in 1147 and pulled down after the Civil War.

AYLESBURY DUCK *The Aylesbury breed of duck is prized for its meat. Thousands were raised locally in the 18th century.*

Information Tel. 5000.
Location On the A413, 17 m. SE of Buckingham.
Parking Friarage Road; Exchange Street; Anchor Lane; Station Street; Station Way; Buckingham Street; Whitehall Street; Civic Centre (all car parks).
District council Aylesbury Vale (Tel. 5900).
Population 48,200.
E-C Thur. **M-D** Wed., Fri., Sat.
Police Walton Grove (Tel. 5010).
Casualty hospital Stoke Mandeville Hospital, Mandeville Road (Tel. 84111).
Post office (Ba) High Street.
Cinema Odeon **(Bb)**, Cambridge Street (Tel. 82660).
Public library (Ba) Walton Street.
Places to see County Museum **(Aa)**, Church Street.
Shopping High Street; Friars Square.
Event Festival of Arts (Spring).
Trade and industry Light engineering; printing; dairy products.
AA 24 hour service Tel. Oxford 40286.

JOHN HAMPDEN *The Buckinghamshire MP was a leading opponent of Charles I.*

AYR Strathclyde

The holiday town at the heart of the Burns country

Traditional seaside amusements abound in this lively resort overlooking the Firth of Clyde. It owes much of its popularity to 2½ miles of sandy beach and an attractive fishing harbour, from which the ocean-going paddle-steamer *Waverley* provides excursions. But it is best known for its many connections with Scotland's national poet, Robert Burns, who was born at Alloway 3 miles away. There is good shopping, and the town's surviving links with the past offer a fascinating panorama of its long history.

The only substantial remain of the 12th-century Church of St John the Baptist is St John's Tower. It was in the church that Robert Bruce called a Scots parliament in 1315 to decide his successor to the Scottish throne. In 1652, Cromwell's army incorporated the church in a fort which they built. Its remains can be seen near by.

As compensation for the take-over of the Church of St John, in 1654, Cromwell supplied money to build the **Auld Kirk**. It still retains its original canopied pulpit, and has three galleries – known as the Merchants', Sailors' and Traders' lofts. In the lichgate are some iron grave-covers used in the days of body-snatchers.

Ayr's oldest domestic building, **Loudoun Hall**, has title deeds that go back to 1534, when it was the town house of the hereditary Sheriffs of Ayrshire. During the 18th century the building was allowed to decline,

STUDY IN GOLD AND BLACK *Fishing vessels ride in silhouette as the sun sets over Ayr harbour.*

and later narrowly escaped demolition as a slum. But in 1938 restoration was started, and today the Hall, looking as it did in the 16th century, is open to the public each summer.

The **Town Buildings** were designed by Thomas Hamilton of Edinburgh in 1828. They are notable for the magnificent 126 ft high steeple, one of the finest in Britain; its upper part consists of an octagonal turret with tall, narrow windows. The Town Buildings were once Ayr's administrative centre, and are now a local-government department.

The Twa Brigs

Where the River Ayr cuts through the centre of the town it is spanned by two bridges close to one another – the Twa Brigs. The oldest of these, the 13th-century **Auld Brig,** was immortalised by Scotland's greatest poet, Robert Burns (1759-96), in his poem *The Brigs of Ayr* as "a poor, narrow footpath of a street. Where two wheel-barrows tremble when they meet".

The Auld Brig was restored in 1910,

and now carries pedestrians only. New Bridge was built in 1788 and rebuilt in 1878.

The **Tam o' Shanter Inn,** a thatched building in the High Street, now houses a Burns museum. Over the door is a painting showing Tam o' Shanter, hero of Burns's famous poem of the same name, mounting his grey mare, Meg, before setting out on his journey to Kirkoswald.

Every June, Ayr celebrates the journey with Burns Ride. A procession follows Tam o' Shanter's route and ends at the Auld Brig o' Doon.

Tam's escape

At the southern end of Ayr, the River Doon meanders through green fields, housing estates and woodland, reaching the sea at Doonfoot. Close to the Alloway road the **Auld Brig o' Doon,** a graceful 13th-century arch, spans the river flanked by gardens and tree-lined walks. It was here that, in the poem, Tam o' Shanter finally eluded the witches who pursued him after he had interrupted their orgy at **Alloway Kirk.** Close to the bridge are

TAM O' SHANTER MUSEUM *The inn of Burns's day now commemorates the poet's work.*

BURNS'S BIRTHPLACE

Three miles outside Ayr, at Alloway, is the heart of Robert Burns country. Here, Scotland's national poet was born on January 25, 1759, in the low, thatched, whitewashed "auld clay biggin" his father William had built two years earlier. The cottage, where Burns lived for seven years until his family moved to nearby Mount Oliphant, is an object of pilgrimage for the poet's admirers all over the world. It retains some of its original furniture, including the bed in which Burns was born and the chair supposedly used by the original of Tam o' Shanter, hero of his best-known poem. An adjoining museum contains original manuscripts, books, paintings and other mementoes of the poet's life.

A portrait of Burns in stained glass from the birthplace collection.

At the Land o' Burns Centre, next to Alloway Kirk, there is an audio-visual presentation representing the life and times of the poet. The Burns monument, not far from Alloway Kirk, contains life-size sculptures of Tam o' Shanter and other Burns characters.

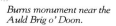

Burns monument near the Auld Brig o' Doon.

set fire to a barn with 500 soldiers inside. The neo-Gothic **Wallace Tower** incorporating a statue of him was erected in 1832.

Information Tel. 68077.
Location On the A70, 13 m. SW of Kilmarnock.
Parking Barns Crescent; King Street; Carrick Street; Kyle Street; North Harbour; Wellington Square; Cromwell Road North (all car parks).
District council Kyle and Carrick (Tel. 81511).
Population 48,700.
E-C Wed. **M-D** Tues., Thur.
Police (Bb) King Street (Tel. 66966).
Casualty hospital County **(Ca)**, Holmston Road (Tel. 81991).
Post office (Bb) Sandgate.
Theatres Gaiety **(Ba)** (Tel. 264639); Civic **(Ca)** (263755).
Cinema Odeon **(Ba)** (Tel. 264049).
Public library (Bb) Main Street.
Places to see Tam o' Shanter Museum **(Ba)**, High Street; Museum and Art Gallery, Rozelle Park; Burns Cottage, Alloway; Land o' Burns Centre, Alloway; Loudoun Hall **(Bb)**, Boat Vennal; St John's Tower **(Ab)**, off Citadel Place; Wallace Tower **(Bc)**, High Street.
Town trails Available from the Librarian, Public library.
Shopping High Street; Main Street; Sandgate; Beresford Terrace.
Events West of Scotland Agricultural Show (Apr.); Burns Ride and Burns Festival (June).
Sport Horse racing, Craigie Road; Scottish League football, Ayr United FC, Tryfield Place.
AA 24 hour service
Tel. Glasgow (041) 812 0101.

the ruins of the kirk, whose church-yard contains the grave of Robert Burns's father. Near by is the cottage where Burns was born.

On the other side of the road, set in beautiful gardens, is the Burns monument which was designed by Thomas Hamilton Junior in the form of a Grecian temple, and erected in 1823. Inside are relics, including two Bibles said to have been exchanged between Burns and "Highland Mary" – his sweetheart, Mary Campbell – and the wedding ring of Jean Armour, whom he married in 1788.

John McAdam (1756-1836), the road-builder and inventor of the road-making process which bears his name, was born at Ayr, and is commemorated by a monument in Wellington Square.

In 1297, when Ayr was in the hands of English soldiers, the Scottish patriot William Wallace is said to have

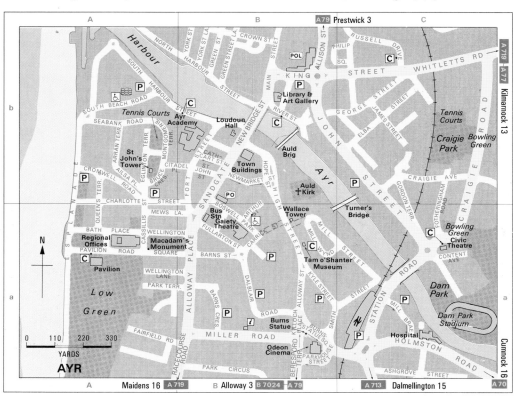

B

Bakewell Derbyshire

Romans and Saxons were attracted to this valley below the Peak District hills by its 12 wells producing chalybeate (iron bearing) water at a constant 15°C (59°F). Most wells have now dried up or have been filled in, but each July the well sites are dressed – decorated with flower petals and foliage – a custom which may go back to pagan times. The brownstone buildings of Bakewell (originally *Badecanwiellon*, "Badeca's Springs"), date mainly from the 17th and 18th centuries, and include the Bath House of 1697.

Bakewell tart or pudding was created by mistake when a cook at the Rutland Arms Hotel spread an egg mixture on jam in an open tart.

Information Bridge Street (Tel. 3227).
Location On the A6, 25 m. NW of Derby.
Parking Market Place; Granby Road; New Street; Smith Woodyard; Coombs Road (all car parks).
District council West Derbyshire (Tel. Matlock 3461).
Population 3,950.
E-C Thur. **M-D** Mon.
Police Granby Road (Tel. 2504).
Casualty hospital Cottage Hospital, Butts Road (Tel. 2834).
Post office Bridge Street.
Public library New Street.
Places to see The Old House Museum, off Church Lane.
AA 24 hour service
Tel. Nottingham 787751.

Bala Gwynedd

At the northern end of Lake Bala – Llyn Tegid in Welsh – the town of Bala straddles the tree-lined highway which leads to the peaks of the Snowdonia National Park. The lake is the largest in Wales, 4 miles long and three-quarters of a mile wide.

During the summer months trains run on the Bala Lake narrow-gauge railway, following the lake shoreline.

Information Tel. Dolgellau 422341.
Location On the A494, 18 m. NE of Dolgellau.
Parking Station Road; The Green; Plasey Street; Lake foreshore (all car parks); High Street.
District council Meirionnydd (Tel. Dolgellau 422341).
Population 1,850.
E-C Wed. **M-D** Thur. (livestock).
Police Pensarn Road (Tel. 520424).
Casualty hospital War Memorial Hospital, Wrexham (Tel. Wrexham 51041).
Post office High Street.
Public library Ysgol-y-Berwyn.
AA 24 hour service
Tel. Llandudno 79066.

Banbury Oxfordshire

A cross and a nursery rhyme have made Banbury one of the best-known towns in England. It dates back to Saxon times, and in the 13th century was noted for its woollen cloth.

The "fine lady" of the nursery rhyme may have been Lady Godiva or Elizabeth I, but more likely she was a local girl who rode in a May Day procession. Jonathan Swift took the name Gulliver, for his book *Gulliver's Travels*, from a tombstone in Banbury churchyard. The tombstone can still be seen.

Information Tel. 59855.
Location On the A423, 23 m. N of Oxford.
Parking Castle Street; Horsefair; South Bar; North Bar; Bolton Road; Bridge Street; Calthorpe Street; Windsor Street; George Street; Market Place (all car parks).
District council Cherwell

BANBURY CROSS *Built in 1859, the cross replaces the medieval one destroyed by Puritans in 1602.*

(Tel. Banbury 52535).
Population 35,800.
E-C Tues. **M-D** Thur., Sat.
Police (Ab) Warwick Road (Tel. 52525).
Casualty hospital Horton General, Oxford Road (Tel. 4521).
Post office (Ab) High Street.
Cinema Classic **(Ab)**, Horsefair (Tel. 62071).
Public library (Aa) Marlborough Road.
Places to see Museum **(Aa)**.
AA 24 hour service
Tel. Oxford 40286.

Banchory Grampian

Standing beside the River Dee, and sheltered by tree-clad hills, the burgh of Banchory is a quiet holiday resort. The town, as it appears today, dates from the beginning of the 19th century. The River Feugh enters the Dee at Banchory, and the 18th-century Bridge of Feugh spans a rugged gorge in which salmon can be seen leaping.

East of the town stands the 16th-century Crathes Castle. An ivory horn, said to have belonged to Robert Bruce, hangs in the Great Hall.

Information
Tel. Stonehaven 62001.
Location On the A93, 11 m. NW of Stonehaven.
Parking Dee Street; High Street (2) (all car parks).
District council Kincardine and Deeside (Tel. Stonehaven 62001).
Population 4,600. **E-C** Thur.
Police High Street (Tel. 2252).
Casualty hospital Aberdeen Royal Infirmary, Foresterhill, Aberdeen (Tel. Aberdeen 681818).
Post office High Street.
Public library Bellfield Park.
Places to see Crathes Castle, 3 m. E on the A93.
AA 24 hour service
Tel. Aberdeen 51231.

FOURTEENTH–CENTURY BRIDGE *The bridge over the River Wye at Bakewell was built 600 years ago. It is still in use, carrying cars and lorries.*

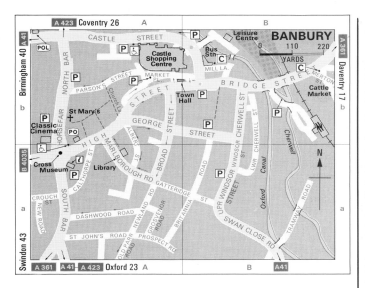

Banff Grampian

The county town of Banff stands at the mouth of the River Deveron, where it flows into the Moray Firth. Banff was made a royal burgh by Robert II in 1372. But it only really began to flourish in the 18th century, after the harbour was built. Several fine buildings survive from this period. Duff House was designed by William Adam in the Baroque style and was finished in 1740.

The town is now a quiet holiday resort, with sandy beaches flanked by many miles of breathtaking coastal scenery.

Information Tel. 2789/2419.
Location On the A98, 47 m. NW of Aberdeen.
Parking St Mary's, Low Street; Bridge Road; Deveronside (all car parks).
District council Banff and Buchan (Tel. 2521).
Population 4,050.
E-C Wed. **M-D** (fish) Macduff and Whitehills harbours, weekdays, 8 a.m.
Police High Shore (Tel. 2555).
Casualty hospital Chalmers Hospital, Clunie Street (Tel. 2567).
Post office Carmelite Street.
Public library High Street.
Places to see Duff House; Museum, High Street (library).
Trade and industry Marine engineering; fishing; boat building.
AA 24 hour service
Tel. Aberdeen 51231.

Bangor Gwynedd

The history of Bangor goes back to the 6th century, when a Celtic monastery was founded there. A bishopric established at about the same time is one of the oldest in Britain. The cathedral, founded in the 12th century, is dedicated to St Deinol, the first Bishop of North Wales, who was consecrated about 546. The present building was restored by Sir George Gilbert Scott in the 19th century.

The University College of North Wales stands on rising ground to the west of the city centre.

Bangor's Town Hall dates from Tudor times, and was originally the bishop's residence. Between the Town Hall and the cathedral is the *Gardd Yr Esgob* (the Bishop's Garden) which includes a unique "Biblical Garden". All the trees, shrubs and flowers mentioned in the Bible, and capable of surviving in the local climate, are planted on each side of a footpath called the "Bible Walk".

Penrhyn Castle, a splendid example of Victorian mock-Norman architecture, contains stuffed birds and animals, a slate bedstead weighing 4 tons, and more than 1,000 dolls. In the grounds are a fine collection of exotic plants, a natural-history display and an exhibition of railway relics, including steam locomotives.

BIBLE GARDEN
A fig tree illustrates the story of Adam and Eve.

Information Tel. 2463.
Location On the A55, 51 m. W of Chester.
Parking Dean Street; Glanrafon; Kyffin Square; Waterloo Street; High Street; Garth Road (all car parks).
District council Borough of Arfon (Tel. 2463).
Population 12,200.
E-C Wed. **M-D** Fri., Sat.
Police Garth Road (Tel. 52222).
Casualty hospital Holyhead Road (Tel. 53321).
Post office Deiniol Road.
Theatre Gwynedd, Deiniol Road

(Tel. 51708).
Cinemas Plaza, High Street (Tel. 2059); City, High Street (53406).
Public library Ffordd Gwynedd.
Places to see Art Gallery and Museum, Old Canonry; Penrhyn Castle, 1 m. E on the A5.
AA 24 hour service
Tel. Llandudno 79066.

Banstead Surrey

In medieval times Banstead was a market for wool and mutton from the sheep which grazed on the downs. Today it is a residential area, but there are still stretches of open downland – many of them commons – between the built-up areas.

Information
Tel. Burgh Heath 53430.
Location On the A217, 3 m. E of Epsom.
Parking High Street; The Horseshoe.
District council Borough of Reigate and Banstead (Tel. Reigate 42477).
Population 43,200.
E-C Wed.
Police High Street (Tel. Burgh Heath 57251).
Casualty hospital Redhill General, Earlswood Common, Redhill (Tel. Redhill 65030).
Post office High Street.
Public library The Horseshoe.
AA 24 hour service
Tel. Guildford 72841.

Barking see London

Barmouth Gwynedd

An impressive combination of sea, sand and mountains turned the port of Barmouth on the Mawddach estuary into a holiday resort in the 19th century. A 2 mile long promenade runs behind a sandy beach to the tiny harbour, today a haven for lobster boats and pleasure craft. Dinas Oleu, 4¼ acres of land on the hill above the town, was the National Trust's first property. It was given to the Trust by a local landowner, Mrs C. T. Talbot, in 1895.

Information Tel. 280787.
Location On the A496, 10 m. W of Dolgellau.
Parking Marine Parade; Harbour; North Promenade; Promenade (cps).
District council Meirionnydd (Tel. Dolgellau 422341).
Population 2,500.
E-C Wed.
Police Station Road (Tel. 280222).
Casualty hospital Dolgellau and District (Tel. Dolgellau 422479).
Post office King Edward Street.
Theatre Dragon Theatre, Jubilee Road (Tel. 280651).
Public library Station Road.
Places to see Lifeboat Museum, Harbour.
AA 24 hour service
Tel. Cardiff 394111.

Barnard Castle Durham

The ruined castle from which the town takes its name perches on a cliff above the River Tees. The castle was rebuilt in 1112 by Bernard Baliol, and has a 14th-century rounded keep.

There are many fine 17th and 18th-century houses and inns in the town centre. Charles Dickens stayed at the King's Head while writing *Nicholas Nickleby* in 1838.

The Bowes Museum in Newgate houses 10,000 exhibits, including furniture, porcelain and paintings by Goya and El Greco.

RIVER GUARD *The ruins of Barnard Castle look down on the River Tees.*

Information Tel. Teesdale 38481.
Location On the A66, 31 m. W of Middlesbrough.
Parking Galgate (cp); Horse Market; Market Place.
District council Teesdale (Tel. 38481).
Population 5,000.
E-C Thur. **M-D** Wed.
Police Harmire Road (Tel. 37328).
Casualty hospital Darlington Memorial Hospital, Hollyhurst Road (Tel. Darlington 60100).
Post office Galgate.
Public library Hall Street.
Places to see Bowes Museum, Newgate; Castle ruins.
AA 24 hour service
Tel. Newcastle upon Tyne 610111.

Barnet see London

Barnsley S. Yorks.

The coal that made Barnsley rich has been mined for about 500 years. Now all the pits near the town are closed.

Barnsley's origins go back to Norman times, when the land in the area belonged to the priories of Pontefract and Monk Bretton. The ruins of Monk Bretton Priory, 2 miles northeast of the town, include a 13th-century chapter house and a church.

Information Tel. 6757.
Location On the M1 and A61, 17 m. N of Sheffield.
Parking High Street; Graham's Orchard; Foundry Street; Queens Road; Regent Street; Westgate; Churchfield; York Street; Silver Street; Metropolitan Centre (all car parks).
District council Metropolitan Borough of Barnsley (Tel. 203232).
Population 73,600.
E-C Thur. **M-D** Mon. (cattle); Tues., Wed., Fri. and Sat.
Police Churchfield (Tel. 6161).
Casualty hospital District General, Gawber Street (Tel. 86122).
Post office Pitt Street.
Theatre Civic Hall, Eldon Street (Tel. 6757).
Cinema Odeon, Eldon Street (Tel. 5494).
Public library Shambles Street.
Places to see Monk Bretton Priory.
Shopping Metropolitan Centre; Peel Centre; Queen Street; Eldon Street.
Sport FA League football, Barnsley FC, Oakwell Ground.
AA 24 hour service
Tel. Sheffield 28861.

Barnstaple Devon

History records that Barnstaple was granted a charter in AD 930, and it claims to be the oldest borough in England. It minted its own coins in the 10th century, and the town has had mayors since 1300.

At one time it was a cloth-manufacturing town, ship-building centre and a port for trade with America. The silting up of the Taw estuary in the 19th century ended the port's importance, and today Barnstaple is an agricultural centre.

The town's architecture is mostly Georgian. The finest example is Queen Anne's Walk, a colonnaded arcade where merchants and ship-owners traded; the Tome Stone, where bargains were sealed, can still be seen.

The 14th-century St Anne's Chapel, now a museum of local antiquities, was once a grammar school where John Gay (1685-1732), author of *The Beggar's Opera*, was a pupil.

Information Tel. 72511.
Location On the A39, 40 m. NW of Exeter.
Parking North Walk (cp); Pannier Market; Queen Street (cp); The Square; Vicarage Street (cp); Seven Brethren Bank (cp).
District council North Devon (Tel. 72511).
Population 19,000.
E-C Wed. **M-D** Tues., Fri.
Police (Aa) Civic Centre (Tel. 73101).
Casualty hospital Raleigh Park (Tel. 72577).
Post office (Bb) Boutport Street.
Theatre Queen's Hall **(Bb)**, Boutport Street (Tel. 3239).
Cinemas Classic **(Bb)**, Boutport Street (Tel. 2550); Regal, The Strand (2002).
Public library (Ba) The Square.
Places to see North Devon Athenaeum **(Ba)**; St Anne's Chapel

CASTLE QUAY, BARNSTAPLE *The quays on the River Taw are quiet now, but they bustled with trade until the estuary silted up in the last century.*

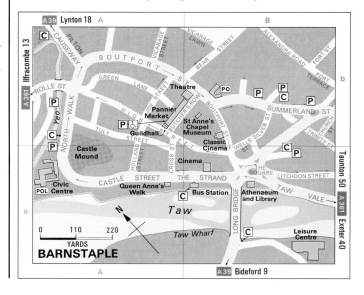

BARNSTAPLE

(Bb); The Guildhall (Ab), High
Street; Queen Anne's Walk.
Town trails Available from Civic
Centre.
Shopping Holland Walk; Butcher's
Row; High Street; Boutport Street.
AA 24 hour service Tel. 45691.

Barrow-in-Furness
Cumbria

Britain's nuclear submarines are built
at Barrow-in-Furness, a 19th-century
town on the western tip of a peninsula
jutting into Morecambe Bay. The
red-sandstone ruins of the 12th-
century Cistercian Furness Abbey
stand 2 miles north-east.

There are fine sandy beaches and a
nature reserve on Walney Island,
which is linked to Barrow by a bridge.

Information Tel. 25795.
Location On the A590, 15 m. SW of
Windermere.
Parking Preston Street; Market
Street; Upper Forsham Street;
Strand; Hall Street; Grellin Street
(all car parks).
District council Borough of Barrow-
in-Furness (Tel. 25500).
Population 61,700.
E-C Thur. **M-D** Wed., Fri. and Sat.
Police Market Street (Tel. 24532).
Casualty hospital School Street
(Tel. 24201).
Post office Abbey Road.
Theatre Civic Hall, Duke Street
(Tel. 25795).
Cinema Astra, Abbey Road
(Tel. 25354).
Public library Ramsden Square.
Places to see Museum; Piel Castle;
Furness Abbey.
Shopping Dalton Road; Cavendish
Street.
Trade and industry Ship-building;
engineering; paper.
AA 24 hour service
Tel. Carlisle 24274.

Barry S. Glamorgan

Barry grew up as a port in the 1880s to
serve the needs of the South Wales
coal industry. By 1900, it was exporting 6 million tons of coal a year.

Depression hit the town hard during the 1930s, and the port switched
to handling other commodities.

Pebble Beach, across the Old Harbour, ends at a valley which runs
inland to the 225 acre Porthkerry
Country Park.

Information Tel. 730333.
Location On the A4055, 10 m. SW
of Cardiff.
Parking Barry Island; Knap;
Porthkerry Country Park; Memorial
Hall; Court Road (all car parks).
District council Vale of Glamorgan
(Tel. 730333).
Population 43,800.
E-C Wed.
Police Gladstone Road
(Tel. 734451).
Casualty hospital Cardiff Royal
Infirmary, Newport Road (Tel.

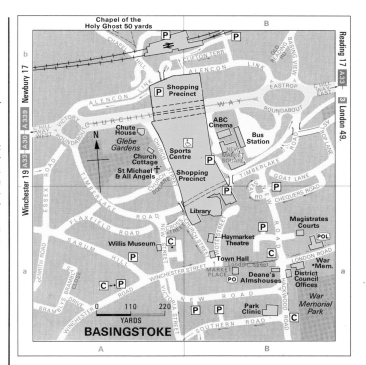

Chapel of the
Holy Ghost 50 yards

BASINGSTOKE

Cardiff 33101).
Post office Holton Road.
Cinema Theatre Royal, Broad Street
(Tel. 735019).
Public library King's Square.
Shopping High Street; Holton Road;
Broad Street.
AA 24 hour service
Tel. Cardiff 394111.

Basildon Essex

Until the railway arrived in the 19th
century, Basildon was a village of
fewer than 200 people, whose cottages clustered around the 14th-
century Holy Cross Church. As a new
town, it will eventually have a population of more than 130,000.

Pitsea Hall, Pitsea, was built in the
late 16th century, and the gabled
Great Chalvedon Hall, in the same
suburb, is several years older.

Information Tel. 22881.
Location On the A127, 26 m. E of
London.
Parking Great Oaks (2);
Southernhay (2); Towngate (all car
parks).
District council Basildon
(Tel. 22881).
Population 93,900.
M-D Tues., Fri. and Sat.
Police Great Oaks (Tel. 26011).
Casualty hospital Basildon Hospital,
Nethermayne (Tel. 3911).
Post office East Square.
Theatre Towngate Theatre,
Towngate (Tel. 23953).
Cinema ABC 1, 2 and 3, Great Oaks
(Tel. 27431).
Public library Fodderwick.
Shopping Town Square; Market
Square; East Gate Shopping Mall;
East Walk.
AA 24 hour service
Tel. Chelmsford 61711.

NUREMBERG CLOCK-WATCH
*The 16th-century timepiece
is in Basingstoke Museum.*

Basingstoke Hampshire

Several ancient
buildings survive amid
the brick and concrete
of modern Basingstoke,
a rapidly developing
commercial and
industrial centre.

The parish church of St Michael
has traces of Norman architecture.
The 16th-century stained glass in the
windows of the south aisle was
brought from the 13th-century
Chapel of the Holy Ghost, now a
ruin, near the railway station.

Information Tel. 56222.
Location On the A33, 19 m. NE of
Winchester.
Parking Timberlake Road; Sarum
Hill; Winchester Road; Red Lion
Lane; Vyne Road (all car parks).
District council Basingstoke and
Deane (Tel. 56222).
Population 67,400.
M-D Wed., Sat.
Police (Ba) London Road
(Tel. 3111).
Casualty hospital Aldermaston Road
(Tel. 3202).
Post office (Ba) London Street.
Theatre Haymarket **(Ba)**, Wote
Street (Tel. 65566).
Cinemas ABC **(Bb)**, Lower Wote
Street (Tel. 22257); Mercury
President, Aldermaston Roundabout
(20212).
Public library (Ba) Town Centre.
Shopping Town Centre.
Trade and industry Miscellaneous,
including heavy industry, electronics
and pharmaceuticals.
AA 24 hour service Tel. 56565.

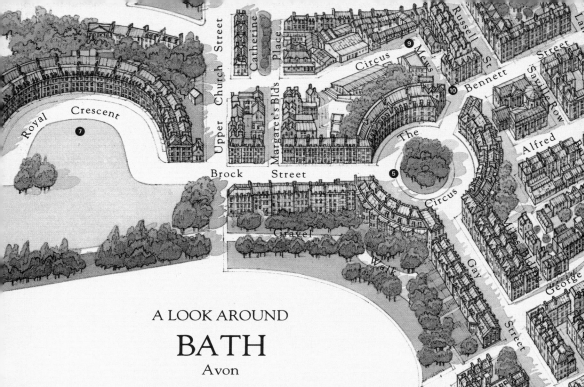

A LOOK AROUND

BATH
Avon

The golden city where an age of elegance lives on

Well-preserved Roman remains and a unique wealth of Georgian architecture combine to make Bath one of the most fascinating cities in the country. It is also one of the easiest to explore, with a compact centre of broad main streets linked by quaint, narrow, traffic-free lanes running between picturesque shops and pubs bright with flowers. Elegant crescents and terraces of pale gold stone greet the eye at every turn.

According to legend, the city's origins go back to 860 BC when Prince Bladud, father of the King Lear immortalised by Shakespeare, caught leprosy, was banished from the royal court and became a swineherd. His pigs also suffered from a skin disease, but they were cured after wallowing in pools of warm mud. The prince followed them in, and he, too, was eventually cured. He returned to the court, and, after becoming king, founded a settlement on the site of the healing pool.

The therapeutic value of the spa was quickly recognised by the Romans after they invaded Britain in AD 43. Elaborate baths were built near a temple dedicated to Sulis Minerva; Sul was an ancient Celtic god, and Minerva was the Roman goddess of healing. Known as *Aquae Sulis* (Waters of Sul), the settlement flourished until the 5th century, when the legions were recalled to Rome.

Workmen's find

The Roman remains vanished slowly beneath centuries of accumulated debris. But in 1727, long after the city had been re-established as a spa, workmen digging a sewer in Stall Street, at the western end of the baths, unearthed a gilded bronze head of Minerva. More discoveries were made in the 1750s, but it was not until the end of the last century that the **Great Bath** of the Roman era was uncovered. Still lined with the lead put in place by Roman craftsmen almost 2,000 years earlier, it is fed by springs that well up from unknown sources far below the surface. Each day they produce 250,000 gallons of water at a constant 49°C (120°F).

With the exception of Hadrian's Wall, the bathing complex is Britain's greatest memorial to the Roman era. Many relics of Roman times, and others relating to Bath's history in general, are preserved in a museum adjoining the baths.

The exhibits include the bust of Minerva, astonishingly well-preserved despite its long burial, and the nightmarish head of a gorgon, discovered in 1790, that originally decorated the temple's pediment.

The city's history in the years after the Romans left is shrouded in mystery, but by the 9th century an abbey had been built by the Saxons. In AD 973 it witnessed the crowning of Edgar, the first king of all England, and the ritual followed then became the basis for all future coronations.

HEART OF THE CITY *Roman figures look down on the Great Bath in the shadow of the abbey.*

CLASSIC FRIEZE *Symbols of the arts and sciences adorn John Wood's Circus.*

An olive tree and crown surmounted by a mitre, carved on the abbey west front, commemorate Bishop Oliver King who restored the abbey.

PLACES TO SEE

1 Great Bath
2 Abbey
3 Pump Room
4 Queen Square
5 The Circus
6 Sally Lunn's House
7 Royal Crescent
8 Pulteney Bridge
9 Carriage Museum
10 Assembly Rooms
11 Holburne of Menstrie Museum
12 American Museum

The present **abbey** was created by Oliver King, Bishop of Bath and Wells between 1495 and 1503. He had a dream, later immortalised in stone at the western end of the abbey, in which angels climbed up and down ladders to Heaven and a voice urged "a king to restore the church". He took this to mean that he should restore the abbey.

King's abbey was badly damaged during the Dissolution of the Monasteries in the 1530s, but was restored the following century. The interior is notable for its soaring traceries of fan-vaulting and for hundreds of memorial tablets.

City of crooks

Bath began to regain fame as a spa in the early 17th century when Anne of Denmark, wife of James I, took the waters in the hope of curing dropsy. She was followed by other royal visitors, but despite the benefit of royal patronage, 17th-century Bath left many things to be desired. It became notorious for pickpockets, duels, crooked gamblers and quack doctors. The great transformation started in the 1700s with the arrival of the dandy Richard "Beau" Nash (1674-1762), who soon became the city's Master of Ceremonies and made it respectable. The original **Pump Room**, the spa's social centre, was built during Nash's long reign, but the present building dates from 1796.

Today sedan chairs stand in the room where soft, sedate music is still played while visitors sip their tea and eat Bath buns. It was here that Dickens's character Sam Weller drank

A FRAGMENT OF AMERICA IN A CORNER OF ENGLAND

At Claverton Manor, just outside Bath, is the American Museum founded in 1961 by two Americans, Dallas Pratt and John Judkyn, to increase Anglo-American understanding. The museum has 18 rooms set out with American furniture dating from the late 17th to the mid-19th centuries.

In addition there are galleries of silver, glass and pewter, and a collection of American quilts. One section of the museum is devoted to the arts and customs of the American Indians. Another depicts the opening up of the American West.

In the grounds, a Conestoga wagon and the observation platform from an American train show two methods of transport that helped to open up the West.

The manor, standing close to the River Avon, was designed in 1820 by Sir Jeffry Wyatville, architect to George IV, and is built of Bath stone.

WEATHERVANE made about 1820 of gold-leaved metal.

health-giving water from the fountain, and said it tasted like warm flat-irons. Above the Pump Room's entrance the motto "Water is best" is carved in Greek.

Nash made Bath synonymous with high fashion, good taste, order and discipline – an outlook that was shared by other men who left more tangible memorials of the city's golden age. One was Ralph Allen (1693-1764), who revolutionised the nation's postal services, making a huge fortune in the process. He bought the Combe Down quarries 2 miles south of the city to provide the architects and builders with the raw materials that they used to create a city of classical beauty.

Many artists in stone have left their mark on Bath, but the most prolific was John Wood the Elder, who was born in or near Bath and was baptised there in 1704.

When Wood arrived in Bath in 1727, the city was still essentially

medieval. His first great project, **Queen Square**, was started in 1728, but work on his masterpiece, The Circus, did not start until 1754, the year of his death. Its circumference is divided into three arcs, containing 33 houses. The frontages are ennobled by Doric, Ionic and Corinthian columns, and 528 motifs symbolising the arts, sciences and occupations form a frieze above the ground-floor windows.

Old houses saved

Many old houses were demolished under Wood's rebuilding scheme, but some were saved, including the house in **Lilliput Alley** where, as legend has it, Sally Lunn lived. She is said to have sold buns in the streets of Bath, and a type of bun is named after her.

Wood's son, John Wood the Younger, was born in 1727 and carried on his father's work. His greatest contribution to Bath's heritage was the **Royal Crescent**, a majestic sweep of 30 houses faced with 114 huge Ionic columns. The first house in the crescent is now the property of the Bath Preservation Trust. It has been restored, redecorated and filled with Georgian furnishings, so that visitors can see something of the life-style of upper-class Bath around 1800.

Many houses throughout the city bear plaques recording famous residents of the past. These included characters as diverse as John Wesley, the founder of Methodism, Lord Nelson, Thomas Gainsborough, and the Emperor Napoleon III of France.

Until the end of the last century,

COMFORTS OF BATH *The popularity of Bath's spa attracted considerable attention during the 18th century, and prompted the satirist Thomas Rowlandson to produce this caricature of visitors "taking the cure". The bath they used was much smaller than the Roman bath, which was not discovered until 1878.*

FASHION SHOW *A dress of the 1740s in the Costume Museum.*

Bath's streets echoed to the clatter of horses, and more than 30 relics of those days are preserved by the **Carriage Museum** in Circus Mews. The **Museum of Costume**, one of the largest of its kind in the world, is housed in the restored **Assembly Rooms** built by Wood the Younger in 1769-71. Its collections include clothing of many periods, from Tudor times to the latest fashions. The **Holburne of Menstrie Museum** contains fine silver, porcelain and paintings of the 18th century (Gainsborough, J. M. W. Turner and George Stubbs), and also 20th-century craftwork belonging to the Crafts Study Centre.

The Octagon, in Milsom Street, built as a chapel in 1767, now houses the Royal Photographical Society's National Centre of Photography. Burrows Toy Museum is now in York Street.

PULTENEY BRIDGE *Named after William Pulteney, 1st Earl of Bath, the bridge was designed by Robert Adam in 1770. It was inspired by the Pontevecchio in Florence, and is lined with shops on both sides.*

Information Tel. 62831.
Location On the A4, 13 m. SE of Bristol.
Parking Avon Street; Broad Street; Charlotte Street; Ham Gardens; Kingsmead; Manvers Street; Walcot Street; Sawclose (all car parks).
District council City of Bath (Tel. 61111).

Population 80,000.
E-C Mon. or Thur. **M-D** Wed.
Police (Ba) Manvers Street (Tel. 63451).
Casualty hospital Royal United, Combe Park (Tel. 28331).
Post office (Bb) New Bond Street.
Theatre Royal **(Bb)**, Sawclose (Tel. 62821).
Cinemas Beau Nash **(Bb)**, Westgate

Street (Tel. 61730); Little Theatre **(Bb)**, St Michael's Place (66822); Gemini 1-2, Monmouth Street (61506).
Public library (Bb) Bridge Street.
Shopping Milsom Street; Union Street; Stall Street; Southgate; Marchants Passage.
AA 24 hour service Tel. 24731.

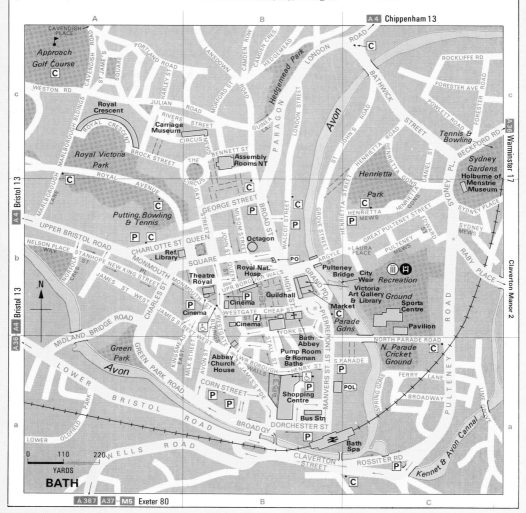

Batley W. Yorks.

New industries are gradually replacing the blankets, carpets and other heavy-woollen goods that have been made at Batley for centuries.

The parish church of All Saints, which dates back in part to the 15th century, has a fine carved screen.

Between Batley and neighbouring Birstall lies 40 acre Wilton Park, with lakes and sheltered walks. Bagshaw Museum, set in the park, is devoted to archaeology, local history and the heavy-woollen industry.

Information Tel. 473141.
Location On the A652, 9 m. SW of Leeds.
Parking Market Place; Hanover Street; Wards Hill; Henrietta Street; Shay Farm (all car parks).
District council Kirklees Metropolitan Council (Tel. Huddersfield 22133).
Population 42,500.
E-C Tues. **M-D** Fri., Sat.
Police Market Place (Tel. 474161).
Casualty hospital Batley General, Carlinghow Hill (Tel. 473333).
Post office Market Place.
Public library Market Place.
Places to see Art Gallery; Bagshaw Museum.
Shopping Commercial Street.
AA 24 hour service
Tel. Leeds 38161.

Beaconsfield
Buckinghamshire

In coaching days, Beaconsfield was a staging post on the London to Oxford road. Several of the coaching inns still survive, including the Royal White Hart and the Saracen's Head.

The majority of houses in the main street date from the 16th and 18th centuries. The parish church of St Mary and All Saints, a building of flint and Bath stone, has a 15th-century pinnacled tower; the rest of the church was restored in 1868.

Close to the station is Bekonscot Model Village, where visitors can walk among the miniature houses, shops and churches built to a scale of 1 in. to 1 ft.

Information Tel. 5173.
Location On the A40 and M40, 6 m. SE of High Wycombe.
Parking Penn Road; Warwick Road; Burkes Road (cps). Old Town: London End; Windsor End; Wycombe End; Aylesbury End (all car parks).
District council South Buckinghamshire (Tel. Slough 33333).
Population 10,900.
E-C Wed.
Police Tatling End, Gerrard's Cross (Tel. 82222).
Casualty hospital High Wycombe General, Marlow Hill (Tel. High Wycombe 26161).
Post office Station Road.
Cinema Chiltern, Station Road (Tel. 3248).

Public library Reynolds Road.
Places to see Bekonscot Model Village, Ledborough Lane.
AA 24 hour service
Tel. Reading 581122.

Bearsden Strathclyde

Some of the best-preserved sections of the Antonine Wall, Scotland's major Roman work, can be seen at Bearsden. The wall was built in AD 143, during the reign of Emperor Antoninus Pius, as a frontier stretching from the Clyde to the Forth.

The town is a northern suburb of Glasgow, and borders on the Kilpatrick Hills. It is sometimes called New Kilpatrick.

Information
Tel. 041 942 2262.
Location On the A809, 6 m. NW of Glasgow.
Parking Kirk Road; Douglas Place; Drymen Road.
District council Bearsden and Milngavie (Tel. 041 942 2262).
Population 27,900.
E-C Tues.
Police Main Street, Milngavie (Tel. 041 956 1113).
Casualty hospital Western Infirmary, Dumbarton Road, Glasgow (Tel. 041 552 4513).
Post office Roman Road.
Cinema Rio, Milngavie Road (Tel. 041 942 0112).
Public library Drymen Road.
Places to see Antonine Wall; Roman Bath House.
AA 24 hour service
Tel. 041 812 0101.

Beaumaris Gwynedd

After his conquest of Wales in the 13th century, Edward I built a castle on the eastern shore of the Isle of Anglesey at a place he called Beau Marais, meaning "fair marsh". The town that grew up around the castle became the island's capital, but now is a quiet place of half-timbered houses and Victorian terraces.

The castle was designed by the king's military architect, James of St George. Although never completed, it represents medieval fortified building at its finest. The six-sided outer walls, surrounded by a moat, are strengthened with drum towers at the angles. The inner stronghold is square, with a drum tower at each corner and a massive gateway on both the north and the south sides.

Opposite the castle is the 17th-century County Hall, where the county assizes were held until 1971. On the wall of the flagstoned court hangs a branding iron once used to brand prisoners convicted of theft.

The Bull's Head, built in 1472, contains a door said to be the largest simple hinged door in Britain – 13 ft high and 11 ft wide. The 14th-century Church of St Mary and St Nicholas retains some of its original stained glass.

Information Tel. 712626.
Location On the A545, 3 m. NE of Bangor.
Parking The Green (cp); Castle Street.
District council Isle of Anglesey (Tel. Llangefni 722920).
Population 2,000.
E-C Wed.
Police New Street (Tel. 810222).
Casualty hospital Caernarvon and Anglesey General, Bangor (Tel. Bangor 53321).
Post office Church Street.
Public library Old David Hughes School.
Places to see Castle; Gaol, Steeple Lane; County Hall; Tudor Rose, Castle Street.
AA 24 hour service
Tel. Llandudno 79066.

Bebington Merseyside

The Unilever complex of chemical, soap, detergent and food companies is the mainstay of Bebington, a town on the Wirral Peninsula. In Port Sunlight, the model village built for Unilever employees, is the Lady Lever Art Gallery, which includes fine collections of paintings and sculpture.

Information Tel. Liverpool (051) 645 2080.
Location On the M53, 3 m. S of Birkenhead.
Parking Woodhead Street; Barlow Avenue; Grove Street; Roland Avenue; Kingsway; Civic Way (all car parks).
District council Borough of Wirral (Tel. 051 638 7070).
Population 64,100.
E-C Wed.
Police Civic Centre (Tel. 051 647 7900).
Casualty hospital Clatterbridge Road (Tel. 051 334 4000).
Post offices Cross Lane and New Ferry.
Public library Civic Way.
Shopping Bebington Road; Church Road; Bromborough Precincts.
AA 24 hour service
Tel. 051 709 7252.

Beccles Suffolk

Fires destroyed most of the old town in the 16th and 17th centuries, and Beccles re-emerged as a handsome place of red-brick Georgian houses.

TOWN SIGN
Elizabeth I hands Beccles' charter to the portreeve.

BECCLES

The River Waveney on which it stands, is popular with boating enthusiasts.

The 97 ft high, stone-faced tower of the 14th-century parish church of St Michael stands apart from the rest of the building. Many of the town's surviving older buildings show Dutch influence, particularly the gabled Roos Hall dating from 1583. It was once the home of Sir John Suckling, an ancestor of Lord Nelson.

Information Tel. Lowestoft 65989.
Location On the A1116, 10 m. W of Lowestoft.
Parking Hungate Lane; Blyburgate; Puddingmoor; The Quay (all car parks).
District council Waveney (Tel. Lowestoft 62111).
Population 8,900.
E-C Wed. **M-D** Fri.
Police Hungate (Tel. 713011).
Casualty hospital District General, Lowestoft Road, Gorleston (Tel. Great Yarmouth 600611).
Post office Smallgate.
Public library Blyburgate.
Shopping Blyburgate; Exchange Square.
AA 24 hour service Tel. Norwich 29401.

JOHN BUNYAN
A statue of the author of Pilgrim's Progress stands on St Peter's Green.

Bedford Bedfordshire

The Saxons built a fortified settlement at Bedford in 915, the Danes pillaged it in 1010, and Henry II granted it a charter in 1166. Today Bedford is the county town, and an educational centre noted for the Harpur Trust schools. These are financed by income from the lands of a 16th-century Bedford-born Lord Mayor of London, Sir William Harpur.

There are four old churches in the town; St Mary's and St John's, both 14th century; St Paul's, built in the 14th and 15th centuries; and St Peter's, part Saxon, part Norman. In front of St Peter's Church stands a statue of John Bunyan. Born in the nearby village of Elstow in 1628, Bunyan wrote *Pilgrim's Progress* while imprisoned in Bedford gaol for his Nonconformist religious beliefs. The Bunyan Meeting House displays relics of the writer's life, and the County Library contains his works, including a rare copy of his first book, *Some Gospel Truths Opened*, which was published in 1656.

Information Tel. 67422 or 215226.
Location On the A6, 52 m. N of London.
Parking Ashburnham Road; Horne Lane; St Paul's Square; Goldington Road; Brace Street; Allhallows; Lurke Street; Batts Ford; Commercial Road; Duck Mill Lane; St Cuthbert's Street; Derby Place (all car parks).
District council North Beds. Borough Council (Tel. 67422).
Population 74,200.
E-C Thur. **M-D** Wed., Sat.
Police (Ab) Greyfriars (Tel. 68221).
Casualty hospital Bedford General, South Wing, Kempston Road (Tel. 55122).
Post office (Bb) Dane Street.
Theatre Civic **(Bb)**, St Paul's Square (Tel. 52691).
Cinema Granada **(Bc)**, St Peter's Street (Tel. 45952).
Public libraries Harpur Street **(Bb)**; Cauldwell Street **(Ba)**.
Places to see Bedford Museum **(Bb)**, The Embankment; Bunyan Museum **(Bb)**, Mill Street; Cecil Higgins Art Gallery **(Bb)**; St Peter's Church and Bunyan Statue.
Shopping Church Square; East and West Arcades; Harpur Centre; Howard Centre; Silver Street.
Sport Rugby Union, Bedford RFC, Goldington Road.
AA 24 hour service Tel. Hatfield 62852.

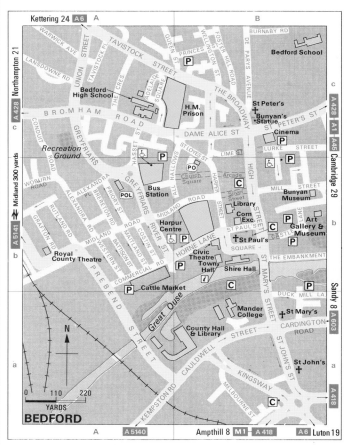

Bedlington Northumberland

The centre of the town is a mixture of architectural styles from the 16th century onwards, with stone-built houses, trees and greens lining the wide main street. Bedlington's iron-works pioneered the making of rolled-iron rails – it was here that the rails were made for the world's first public railway: the Stockton and Darlington, opened in 1825.

Information Tel. Ashington 814444.
Location On the A192, 4 m. SE of Morpeth.
Parking Vulcan Place; Town Centre Relief Road (both car parks).
District council Wansbeck (Tel. Ashington 814444).
Population 26,700.
E-C Wed.
Police Front Street West (Tel. 822001).
Casualty hospital Ashington, West View, Ashington (Tel. Ashington 812541).
Post office Front Street.
Public library Glebe Road.
Trade and industry Engineering.
AA 24 hour service
Tel. Newcastle upon Tyne 610111.

Bedworth Warwickshire

The town of Bedworth developed during the 18th century when French Protestant ribbon-weavers, driven abroad by religious persecution, settled there. No traces of the ribbon trade remain, but some local families have French surnames.

The oldest buildings in Bedworth date from the 18th century. The parish Church of All Saints is a good example of the Victorian Gothic revival.

Information Tel. Nuneaton 384027.
Location On the A444, 6 m. N of Coventry.
Parking Mill Street (2); Park Road (2); Coventry Road; High Street; Rye Piece; King Street; George Street; Chapel Street (all car parks).
District council Nuneaton and Bedworth Borough (Tel. Nuneaton 326211).
Population 41,900.
E-C Wed. **M-D** Tues., Fri. and Sat.
Police Leicester Road (Tel. 314038).
Casualty hospital Manor Hospital, Manor Court Road, Nuneaton (Tel. Nuneaton 384201).
Post office King Street.
Public library High Street.
Shopping High Street; Hypermarket; Mill Street; All Saints Square.
Trade and industry Coal-mining; engineering; textiles.
AA 24 hour service
Tel. Birmingham (021) 550 4858.

Benfleet, South Essex

A narrow creek divides South Benfleet from Canvey Island, on the northern side of the Thames Estuary. Two causeways link the island with the mainland, and in summer Benfleet's streets are busy with traffic heading for the island. The beaches are concentrated along its southern shore. To the west is Bowers Marsh, the haunt of many wild birds and a favourite place for birdwatchers and wildfowlers. The sheltered waters of Benfleet Creek itself are favoured by yachtsmen.

Information Tel. 2711.
Location On the A13, 7 m. W of Southend-on-Sea.
Parking School Lane; Richmond Avenue; West Green; Constitution Hill (all car parks).
District council Castle Point (Tel. South Benfleet 2711).
Population 85,500 (inc. Canvey Island).
E-C Wed.
Police High Road (Tel. 56221).
Casualty hospital Basildon General, Nethermayne, Basildon (Tel. Basildon 3911).
Post office High Road.
Public library High Road.
Shopping High Road.
AA 24 hour service
Tel. Chelmsford 61711.

Berkhamsted Hertfordshire

It was at Berkhamsted that William the Conqueror accepted the throne from the Saxon leaders in 1066. Soon afterwards work started on a castle in the Chiltern valley. Kings and queens, princes, court favourites and distinguished foreigners stayed there, and the Black Prince was especially fond of his Berkhamsted home. King John of France was imprisoned at Berkhamsted after his capture at the Battle of Poitiers in 1356.

In medieval times the demands of a great castle made Berkhamsted a thriving market town. Today there is still a market in the wide, almost straight High Street, part of a Roman road later known as Akeman Street.

Castle Street, 900 years old, is largely dominated by Victorian and later additions to Berkhamsted School, a Tudor foundation with a 16th-century red-brick schoolhouse. This faces the large parish Church of St Peter, begun in 1222, and which contains an east window dedicated to William Cowper, the poet and hymn writer, who was born at Berkhamsted Rectory in 1731. Berkhamsted has been the home of several famous writers, including Graham Greene, whose father was headmaster of Berkhamsted School.

The canal-builders of the 19th century used the floor of the valley to take the Grand Union Canal on its way from London to Birmingham. The building of the railway in 1837 led to a spurt in the town's growth, and so did the electrification of the line in more modern times.

Information Tel. 2441.
Location On the A41, 13 m. E of Aylesbury.
Parking Lower King's Road; St John's Well Lane; Water Lane; High Street (all car parks).
District council Dacorum (Tel. Hemel Hempstead 3131).
Population 15,400.
E-C Wed. **M-D** Sat.
Police High Street (Tel. 71551).
Casualty hospital Hemel Hempstead General, Hillfield Road, Hemel Hempstead (Tel. Hemel Hempstead 3141).
Post office High Street.
Cinema Rex 1 & 2, High Street (Tel. 4154).
Public library King's Road.
Places to see Berkhamsted Castle, Brownlow Road.
Trade and industry Chemicals; furniture; wood products.
AA 24 hour service
Tel. 01 954 7373.

Berwick-upon-Tweed
Northumberland

Few towns in Britain have as turbulent a history as Berwick. Lying on the River Tweed, which forms part of the border of England and Scotland, it was fought over incessantly by the Scots and English during the 12th to 15th centuries, and changed hands 14 times before finally becoming English territory in 1482.

Such an eventful history has moulded the shape and character of Berwick. It was strongly fortified in the Middle Ages, though there are only slight remains of the medieval wall. Elizabeth I had a new wall built on the northern and eastern sides of the town. They were built to the latest Italian design which gave fine cover for all parts of the wall.

The medieval wall, following the line of the river, was rebuilt between 1760 and 1770 and is still well preserved. A walk along the top gives good views of the harbour and town.

There is little left of Berwick Castle. It was built around 1150, but the Victorians almost completely demolished it to make way for a railway station, leaving only part of the wall and a tower. The station is connected to one of Berwick's three bridges, the Royal Border Bridge built by Robert Stephenson in 1850. Its 28 arches stand 126 ft above the water.

The Old Bridge was built of sandstone in 1624 and has 15 arches. It connects the town with Tweedmouth and is still open to motor traffic. The road from the south is carried into

BATTLE FLAG *A tattered relic of the First World War hangs in the museum of the King's Own Scottish Borderers.*

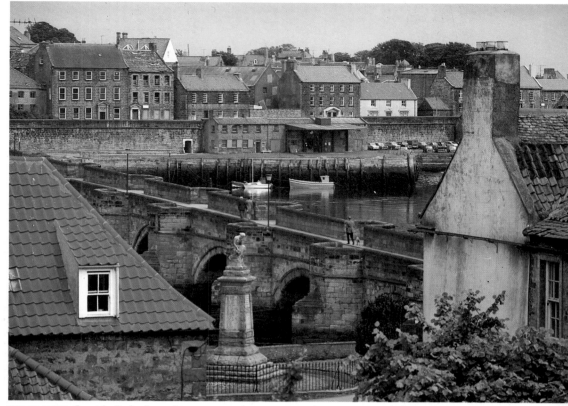

BORDER TOWN *Berwick, England's northernmost town, has guarded the north bank of the River Tweed since the 12th* *century. At one time its only link with the south was the 17th-century bridge built by order of James I.*

Berwick across the Royal Tweed Bridge, built in 1928.

Within its walls, Berwick retains an old-world charm with grey-stone buildings, red-tiled roofs and cobbled streets. The Town Hall was built in the 1750s in Classical style and has a portico of four Tuscan columns, a bell-tower and a 150 ft steeple. The top floor was once a gaol.

Berwick Barracks houses the museum of the King's Own Scottish Borderers. The building was erected in 1717-21 after the townspeople protested against billeting soldiers in their homes. Opposite the barracks is the parish church of Holy Trinity, one of only two Anglican churches built during the Commonwealth (1649-60). The other is at Staunton Harold, Leicestershire.

The museum and art gallery in Marygate has a collection of pictures, brass, bronze, ceramics and glass. The Berwick Room contains items of local history, including medieval coins minted at Berwick.

Information Tel. 6332.
Location On the A1, 63 m. NW of Newcastle upon Tyne.
Parking Parade; Marygate; Chapel Street; Foul Ford; Magdelene Fields; Bridge Street; Sandstell Road; Pier Road; Sandgate; Castlegate; Railway Street (all car parks).
District council Borough of Berwick-upon-Tweed (Tel. 6332).
Population 12,100.
E-C Thur. **M-D** Wed., Sat.

Police (Ba) Church Street (Tel. 7111).
Casualty hospital Infirmary, Violet Terrace (Tel. 7484).
Post office (Ba) Wool Market.
Cinema Playhouse **(Aa)**, Sandgate (Tel. 7769).
Public library (Bb) Marygate.
Places to see Museum and Art Gallery **(Bb)**, Marygate; Museum of the King's Own Scottish Borderers **(Bb)**, The Barracks.
Shopping Marygate; Hide Hill; Bridge Street; Castlegate.
Events Riding of the Bounds (May); Tweedmouth Feast (July).
Sport Scottish League football, Berwick Rangers FC, Sheffield Park.
AA 24 hour service
Tel. Newcastle upon Tyne 610111.

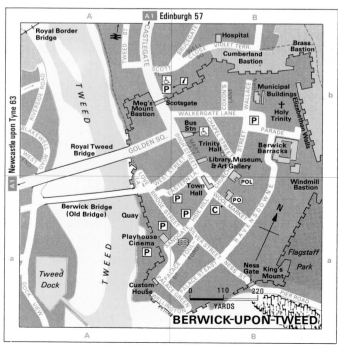

BETHESDA *The little town, named after its Nonconformist chapel, lies in the shadow of its slate quarry, the largest in the world.*

Bethesda Gwynedd

Carved into the side of the Fronllwyd Mountain is the world's largest slate quarry, and facing it is the quarryman's town of Bethesda. The town takes its name from its Nonconformist chapel, and has grown with the development of the quarry which was started in 1765. The quarry is 1,200 ft deep and covers an area of 560 acres. It is noted for its red, blue and green slate of exceptional quality.

A peculiar feature of the quarry is its sensitivity to earth tremors. The slate seams following the line of the disturbance give off a clicking sound.

Information Tel. Bangor 2463.
Location On the A5, 5 m. SE of Bangor.
Parking Victoria Place (cp).
District council Arfon Borough (Tel. Bangor 2463).
Population 4,060.
E-C Wed.
Police High Street. (Tel. 600222).
Casualty hospital Caernarfon and Anglesey General, Holyhead Road, Bangor (Tel. Bangor 53321).
Post office High Street.
Public library High Street.
Places to see Slate quarry (by prior arrangement only; Tel. 600656).
AA 24 hour service
Tel. Llandudno 79066.

Betws-y-Coed Gwynedd

The resort of Betws-y-Coed grew up in the last century to serve tourists attracted to one of the most beautiful areas of Snowdonia. The name means "chapel in the woods", and the resort nestles among the hills of the Gwydyr Forest in a valley where three rivers meet. The rivers – the Conwy, Llugwy and Lledr – tumble down to the town over waterfalls. The most spectacular are the Swallow Falls on the Llugwy, 2 miles west, and the Conwy Falls, 2 miles south. An elegant iron bridge built in 1815 by Thomas Telford spans the Conwy, and a picturesque 15th-century stone bridge crosses the Llugwy. The artist David Cox

(1783-1859), whose paintings popularised Betws-y-Coed, painted the original sign for the Royal Oak, which is now inside the hotel.

Information Tel. Llandudno 76413.
Location On the A5, 17 m. S of Conwy.
Parking Royal Oak; Pont-y-pair (both car parks).
District council Aberconwy (Tel. Llandudno 76572).
Population 660.
E-C Thur.
Police Holyhead Road (Tel. 222).
Casualty hospital Caernarfon and Anglesey General, Holyhead Road, Bangor (Tel. Bangor 53321).
Post office Holyhead Road.
Places to see Ugly House, 2 m. W; Swallow Falls; Conwy Falls; Fairy Glen; Conwy Valley Railway Museum, Old Goods Yard.
AA 24 hour service
Tel. Llandudno 79066.

Beverley Humberside

In the 15th century Beverley was a town with four gateways. Today only the north gate, or North Bar, remains, dividing the main road through the town into North Bar Without and North Bar Within. The gate was erected in 1409.

The northern approach to the town is the most impressive. Here many fine 18th-century and early-19th-century houses line North Bar Without.

On the left of the broad North Bar Within, which leads to the centre of the town, stands one of Beverley's two great churches – the parish church of St Mary, built between 1120 and 1525. Originally started as a chapel to Beverley Minster, it represents the finest in English Gothic architecture. Particularly notable are the central pinnacled tower, the chancel with its ceiling of 40 panels representing the kings of England up to Henry VI, and the fine carved misericords.

The other great church is Beverley Minster, in the south of the town. The fourth church built on the site, it dominates the surrounding buildings with its twin western towers. It was founded in the 8th century by John of Beverley, who was buried there in 721 and canonised in 1037. Most of the architecture is medieval, and like St Mary's contains some of the best work of the period – from the Early English east end, begun about 1220, to the Perpendicular west towers, completed about 1420.

Beverley Minster's most outstanding feature is the Percy Tomb, a shrine to the Percy family who owned land in the area. The canopy of the shrine dates from the 14th century and is richly ornamented with carvings of angels, fruit, leaves and symbolic beasts. There are magnificent wood and stone carvings throughout the building, among them the fantastic rural scenes on the misericords.

The interior of the Minster was extensively restored during the 18th century, and outstanding work from this period includes the font canopy of 1726, the lead statues of St John of Beverley and King Athelstan dating

BEVERLEY MINSTER *A landmark for miles around, Beverley's 13th–15th-century church is a masterpiece of Gothic workmanship. The two towers and the north porch, in the centre of the building, date from 1390-1420.*

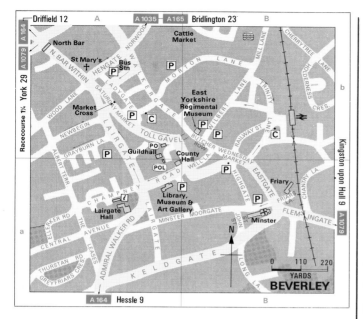

Map labels:
Driffield 12 · A 1035 · A 165 · Bridlington 23 · York 29 · A 164 · A 1079 · Racecourse 1¼ · North Bar · Cattle Market · MILL LANE · CHERRY TREE LANE · St Mary's · Bus Stn · HODERNESS · N BAR WITHIN · HENGATE · NORWOOD · LADYGATE · MORTON LANE · TRINITY · WILBERT LANE · RAILWAY ST · CRES · b · Market Cross · WOOD LANE · NEWBEGIN · SATURDAY MARKET · TOLL GAVEL · East Yorkshire Regimental Museum · BUTCHER ROW · WEDNESDAY MARKET · EASTGATE · Kingston upon Hull 9 · GRAYBURN LA · Guildhall · PO · POL · County Hall · WELL LA · HIGHGATE · Friary · CHANTRY LA · A 1079 · ALBERT TERR · Library, Museum & Art Gallery · FRIARS · FLEMINGATE · Lairgate Hall · CHAMPNEY · MINSTER · MOORGATE · ST JOHN ST · Minster · CELLOKER RD · THE AVENUE · KELDGATE · N · THURSTAN RD · GREYFRIARS CRES · ADMIRAL WALKER RD · LONG LA · 0 110 220 YARDS · BEVERLEY · A 164 · Hessle 9 · A

from 1781, and some early-18th-century carved panels on the inside of the west door.

Between St Mary's Church and the Minster lie Wednesday Market and Saturday Market. Wednesday Market is an attractive small square with Georgian houses. Leading from it is Butcher Row; Number 11 houses the East Yorkshire Regiment Museum.

The central feature of Saturday Market is the Market Cross, which dates from 1714. It bears four shields with the arms of Queen Anne, Beverley Borough, and the Hotham and Warton families who all contributed to the building costs.

Lairgate Hall, once the home of an 18th-century Member of Parliament for the town, was built about 1700. The entrance hall has an Adam decorated ceiling. The drawing-room has hand-painted Chinese wallpaper, and the ceiling is decorated with musical motifs.

Beverley is fortunate in having its own "green belt", an open area of common land surrounding it on three sides and known as the Beverley Pastures. The lands were granted to the town by the Church and lords of the manor in the Middle Ages. The last to be granted – Westwood in 1380 – is the site of Beverley racecourse, where meetings have been held since 1767.

Although Beverley is more than 10 miles from the sea, it once had a shipyard where trawlers were built. The yard stood on the River Hull which runs east of the town before flowing into the Humber at Kingston-upon-Hull. A branch of the Hull, the Beverley Beck, leads almost to the town centre and provides access to the Humber for boating enthusiasts.

Information Tel. Hull 882255.
Location On the A1079, 9 m. N of Hull.
Parking Wilbert Lane; Morton Lane; Saturday Market; Grayburn Lane; Spencer Street (all car parks).
District council East Yorkshire Borough of Beverley (Tel. Hull 882255).
Population 16,400.
E-C Thur. **M-D** Tues., Wed. (livestock), Sat. (produce).
Police (Ab) Register Square (Tel. Hull 881111).
Casualty hospital Hull Royal Infirmary, Anlaby Road, Hull (Tel. Hull 28541).
Post office (Ab) Register Square.
Public library (Aa) Champney Road.
Places to see Art Gallery and Museum (**Aa**); Lairgate Hall; East Yorkshire Regimental Museum (**Bb**); Old Dominican Friary (**Ba**).
Town trails Available from Tourist Information Office, The Hall, Lairgate.
Shopping Saturday Market; Toll Gavel; Butcher Row; Wednesday Market.
Trade and industry Leather tanning; rope-making; light industries.
Sport Horse racing, Ripon Road.
AA 24 hour service Tel. Hull 28580.

PERCY TOMB *A richly carved canopy surmounts the tomb of a 14th-century noblewoman in Beverley Minster.*

Bewdley
Hereford & Worcester

A handsome three-arched bridge designed by Thomas Telford in 1798 leads over the Severn to Bewdley, which clings to a hillside above the west bank of the river at the southeastern corner of the Wyre Forest.

In Elizabethan times Bewdley was a prosperous trading and woollen town, but its waterfront has long since been quiet. The town museum, housed in the Shambles – the former butchers' market – has displays devoted to local trades of the past, including charcoal-burning and ropemaking. Several craftsmen have studios in the museum and sometimes demonstrate their crafts.

The Church of St Leonard's, Ribbesford, has a carved early-Norman doorway and a bell that may date back to 1225. St Anne's parish church is a classical building of the 1740s.

Tickenhill Manor, an 18th-century house on a hill above the town, contains 15th-century roof timbers. It replaces the Royal Manor where, in 1499, Prince Arthur, heir to Henry VII, was married by proxy to Catherine of Aragon. He died in 1502 and his widow married his brother, the future Henry VIII.

Bewdley is the southern terminus of the Severn Valley Railway, which operates a steam service to Bridgnorth during the summer.

SEVERN VALLEY RAILWAY *Steam trains still carry passengers on the picturesque Bridgnorth to Bewdley line.*

Information Tel. 400157/403573.
Location On the A456, 4 m. W of Kidderminster.
Parking Load Street; Westbourne Street; Dog Lane (all car parks).
District council Wyre Forest (Tel. Stourport 77211).
Population 8,700.
E-C Wed. **M-D** Sat.
Police Kidderminster Road (Tel. 402222).
Casualty hospital Kidderminster General, Bewdley Road, Kidderminster (Tel. Kidderminster 3424).
Post office Load Street.
Public library Load Street.
Places to see Severn Valley Railway; West Midlands Safari Park, 1 m. E on Kidderminster Road; Museum.
AA 24 hour service Tel. Birmingham (021) 550 4858.

Bexhill-on-Sea E. Sussex

The German architect Erich Mendelsohn in partnership with Serge Chermayeff designed the town's showpiece, the De la Warr Pavilion, built in 1935. It houses a terrace bar, ballroom, theatre and concert hall.

Bexhill has a gently shelving beach of shingle, which gives way to firm sand at low tide. Bathing is safe.

Just east of the town, at Little Galley Hill, a submerged forest can be seen at low tide. This was part of the land bridge that linked Britain to the Continent 10,000 years ago.

Information Tel. 212023.
Location On the A259, 5 m. W of Hastings.
Parking Marina; Eversley Road; De la Warr Road; Beeching Road (cps).
District council Rother (Tel. 216321).
Population 35,500.
E-C Wed. **M-D** Tues.
Police Cantelupe Road (Tel. 213630).
Casualty hospital Cambridge Road, Hastings (Tel. Hastings 434513).
Post office Devonshire Square.
Theatre De la Warr Pavilion, Marina (Tel. 212022).
Cinema Curzon Leisure Centre, Western Road (Tel. 210078).
Public library Western Road.
Places to see Natural History Museum; Bexhill Manor Costume Museum.
Shopping Devonshire Road; Western Road; Sackville Road; Sea Road.
AA 24 hour service
Tel. Brighton 695231.

Bicester Oxfordshire

Every soldier in Britain is kitted out from Bicester. When the army established its ordnance depot there in 1941 it changed the old-world character of the market town, but it remains a well-known hunting centre, with a hunt dating back to the late 1700s.

The parish church of St Edburg incorporates work from every period of English architecture up to the 15th century.

Rousham House, at Steeple Aston, 6¼ miles west, is one of the finest Jacobean mansions in England. It was built by Sir Robert Dormer in 1635. The magnificent gardens, laid out in 1738, are the only surviving landscape designed by William Kent.

Information Tel. 2915.
Location On the A41, 13 m. NE of Oxford.
Parking Sheep Street; Manorsfield Road; Chapel Lane; Victoria Road; Market Place (all car parks).
District council Cherwell (Tel. Banbury 52535).
Population 14,400.
E-C Thur. **M-D** Fri.
Police Queen's Avenue (Tel. 2022).
Casualty hospital John Radcliffe II, Headington (Tel. Oxford 64711).
Post office Sheep Street.

BIDEFORD QUAY *Gone are the days when the mile-long quayside on the River Torridge bustled with activity, but coasters still unload timber there.*

Public library Old Place Yard.
Places to see Rousham House, 6¼ m. W.
AA 24 hour service
Tel. Oxford 40286.

Bideford Devon

When Sir Richard Grenville fought the Spaniards in the Azores in 1591, his ship *Revenge* was crewed by Bideford men. This was during the town's hey-day as a port, shipbuilding centre and export outlet for the cloth weavers of Devon.

Bideford, straddling the River Torridge, remained the principal port for North Devon until the late 18th century. Today, its tree-lined quay is still used by coasters and small ships from the Continent.

Bideford Bridge has 24 arches, each a different width. The 677 ft long bridge was built about 1460.

In the town, narrow streets climb steeply from the Quay, which is also the main thoroughfare and has many fine old houses. From the Quay a walk along the riverside to Appledore passes a Georgian mill, now a concrete works. Bridgeland Street was laid out in about 1690 and has changed little since then.

On the river's eastern bank, known locally as "East-the-Water", is the 17th-century Royal Hotel, where Charles Kingsley wrote part of his tale of Elizabethan seamen, *Westward Ho!* (1855). The hotel has a floridly decorated plaster ceiling of the period.

The popularity of Kingsley's novel led to the development in the 1860s of a seaside resort of the same name 2 miles north of Bideford. Its long, sandy beach is one of the best in Devon. Westward Ho! is the site of the United Services College where Rudyard Kipling was a pupil and which he used as the basis of his school story *Stalky and Co.* (1899).

At the mouth of the Torridge lies the village of Appledore, famous for its shipyards. The village has pictures-que, narrow streets with bow-fronted Georgian cottages and elegant houses once owned by merchants and sea captains.

Information Tel. 6711.
Location On the A39, 43 m. NW of Exeter.
Parking The Quay; The Pill; Bridge Street.
District council Torridge (Tel. 6711).
Population 12,200.
E-C Wed. **M-D** Tues., Sat.
Police New Road (Tel. 6896).
Casualty hospital North Devon District Hospital, Raleigh Park, Barnstaple (Tel. Barnstaple 72577).
Post office The Quay.
Cinema The Strand, Kingsley Road (Tel. 2070).
Public library The Quay.
Places to see Burton Art Gallery.
Town trails Available from the Town Hall.
Shopping The Quay; High Street; Mill Street; Bridgeland Street.
Event Regatta (Sept.).
Trade and industry Agriculture; ship-building; glove-making.
AA 24 hour service
Tel. Exeter 32121.

Biggar Strathclyde

Nineteenth-century Biggar lives on in the Gladstone Court Museum, in which shops, a bank and a schoolroom are preserved just as they were 150 years ago.

Mary Fleming, one of the four Marys chosen as ladies-in-waiting to Mary, Queen of Scots, lived in Biggar, and each June she is remembered in the ceremony called the Crowning of the Fleming Queen. Her home, Boghall Castle, is now a ruin.

The churchyard of St Mary's – one of the last churches built in Scotland before the Reformation – contains graves of the Gladstones, ancestors of the 19th-century Liberal Prime Minister, William Ewart Gladstone.

BINGLEY FIVE-RISE *The Leeds and Liverpool Canal rises 60 ft at Bingley up one of the most impressive groups of locks on the canal system.*

Birkenhead Merseyside

It was the opening of the Laird ship-building yards in 1824 and the docks in 1847 that turned Birkenhead from a quiet hamlet into a busy and populous town. The best examples of its Victorian architecture include Hamilton Square, laid out in 1826, and the Town Hall of 1887.

The Williamson Art Gallery has a large collection of English watercolours. A ceramics section includes Della Robbia pottery and Liverpool porcelain.

Information
Tel. Liverpool (051) 652 6106.
Location On the M53, 16 m. NW of Chester.
Parking Greenfield Street; Atherton Street; Duncan Street; William Street; Claughton Road; Oliver Street; Wilbraham Street; Hinson Street (all car parks). On-street disc parking in central area.
District council Borough of Wirral (Tel. 051 636 7070).
Population 123,900.
E-C Thur. **M-D** Wed., Fri. and Sat.
Police (Bb) Chester Street (Tel. 051 647 7900).
Casualty hospital Park Road North (Tel. 051 652 6134).
Post office (Ba) Argyle Street.
Theatre Little Theatre **(Aa)**, Grange Road West (Tel. 051 647 6593).
Cinemas ABC **(Bb)**, Argyle Street (Tel. 051 647 8726); Classic **(Bb)**, Conway Street (051 647 6509).
Public library (Aa) Borough Road.
Places to see Williamson Art Gallery.
Shopping Grange Road; Grange Precinct.
Trade and industry Docks, ship-building and repairing; flour milling.
AA 24 hour service
Tel. 051 709 7252.

Information Tel. 20104.
Location On the A702, 18 m. W of Peebles.
Parking High Street; Carwood Road (both car parks); School Green.
District council Clydesdale (Tel. Lanark 61331/61511).
Population 1,960.
E-C Wed. **M-D** Thur., Sat.
Police Edinburgh Road (Tel. 20100 or Lanark 2455).
Casualty hospitals Minor injuries: Kelho Hospital, Johns Loan (Tel. 20077); major accidents: Law Hospital, Carluke (Tel. Wishaw 72621).
Post office High Street.
Theatre Corn Exchange Theatre, High Street.
Places to see Gladstone Court Museum, High Street.
Event Crowning of the Fleming Queen (June).
AA 24 hour service
Tel. Edinburgh (031) 225 8464.

Bingley W. Yorks.

The Airedale terrier, originally used for hunting otters, was first bred in the old wool town of Bingley – hence the dog's other name, the Bingley terrier.

Among many fine Georgian houses in the town is Myrtle Grove, where John Wesley once stayed. He described it as a "little paradise". It is now council offices. Ireland Bridge, over the River Aire, dates from 1686.

East Riddlesden Hall, north-west of the town, is a 17th-century manor house now owned by the National Trust. Its first owners, the Murgatroyd family, were renowned locally for their profanity and debauchery. It is said that the River Aire changed course to avoid their house.

Information Tel. Bradford 29577.
Location On the A650, 6 m. NW of Bradford.
Parking Wellington Street; Chapel Lane; Ferncliffe Road; Queen Street (all car parks).
District council City of Bradford (Tel. Bradford 29577).
Population 28,000.
E-C Tues. **M-D** Wed., Fri.
Police Main Street (Tel. 562262).
Casualty hospital Bradford Royal Infirmary, Duckworth Lane, Bradford (Tel. Bradford 42200).
Post office Shopping Precinct, Myrtle Walk.
Theatre Little Theatre, Main Street (Tel. 564049).
Public library Myrtle Walk.
Places to see East Riddlesden Hall, 3 m. NW on A650; Bingley Five-Rise locks on the Leeds and Liverpool Canal.
Shopping Main Street; Bradford Road; Chapel Lane; Myrtle Walk.
Trade and industry Light engineering; joinery; textiles.
AA 24 hour service
Tel. Bradford 724703.

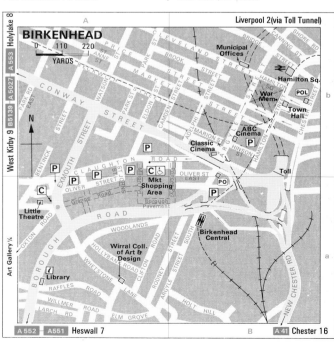

BIRMINGHAM W. Midlands

The space-age city that sprang from a revolution

Britain's second-largest city was spawned by the Industrial Revolution, and grew during the 19th century into one of the world's great workshops. Hundreds of trades flourished, especially in metalwork. Birmingham made everything from jewellery to guns, from buttons to steam engines. Products stamped "Made in Birmingham" became essential to life – and death – in nearly every country in the world. The city itself developed into a grimy area with ugly factories and workshops, and rows of back-to-back houses that became slums almost as soon as they were built. By the end of the century improvements were being made, but progress was slow until after the Second World War. Then came a period of rapid change. Bomb-damaged areas were cleared and much of the old ugliness was swept away.

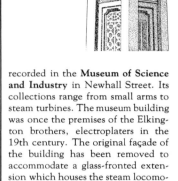

BIG BRUM
The clock-tower on the Council House has been affectionately given this name by Birmingham's residents.

The centre of old Birmingham is the **Bull Ring**, where a market which has been held since the 12th century still thrives six days a week. Beside the traditional open-air market is a covered market hall, built on different levels.

Subways and an outdoor escalator connect the Bull Ring to the main shopping area, which includes an enclosed complex of shops built over the ultra-modern New Street Station.

The **Town Hall** in Victoria Square was designed by Joseph Hansom (1803-82), inventor of the Hansom Cab. It was opened in 1834 and is modelled on the Temple of Castor and Pollux in Rome. The City of Birmingham Symphony Orchestra has made the Town Hall its home, and weekly recitals are given on the fine organ.

Across the square from the Town Hall stands the **Council House**, home of the city council, which was built in the 19th century in the Italian Renaissance style. The **Central Museum and Art Gallery** next to the Council House has an impressive collection of Pre-Raphaelite paintings and works by Van Gogh, Botticelli, Gainsborough and Constable.

Gold and silver

The museum's collection of gold and silver is a reminder that Birmingham has been a centre for the precious-metals trade for nearly 200 years.

There are more fine paintings, including works by Rubens and Degas, at Birmingham University's **Barber Institute of Fine Arts**. The institute, on the university campus at Edgbaston, about 3 miles from the city centre, also has medieval ivories and antique bronzes and furniture.

Birmingham's industrial history is recorded in the **Museum of Science and Industry** in Newhall Street. Its collections range from small arms to steam turbines. The museum building was once the premises of the Elkington brothers, electroplaters in the 19th century. The original façade of the building has been removed to accommodate a glass-fronted extension which houses the steam locomotive *City of Birmingham*.

The engine stands on a section of track and can move, powered by an electric motor, to demonstrate the working parts.

Sarehole Mill, an 18th-century water-mill on the River Cole in the southern suburb of Hall Green, has been restored and is now a branch of the City Museum. The mill was once leased by the engineer Matthew Boulton for rolling sheet steel, before he opened his Soho foundry where he and James Watt perfected the steam engine.

Birmingham has more miles of waterways than Venice. Its canal system was built in the 18th and 19th

CAMBRIAN WHARF *Narrow-boats and cabin cruisers can moor close to the city centre at Cambrian Wharf, which is part of the Birmingham canal system. Birmingham's waterways have been carefully preserved, and this 19th-century dock contrasts sharply with the city's modern buildings and the slender Post Office Tower on the skyline.*

centuries to provide water transport into the heart of the city, and consists of several converging waterways. The Birmingham Canal, built by James Brindley in 1769, brought coal from the Wednesbury coalfields and meets the Worcester-Birmingham Canal and the Birmingham-Fazeley Canal to the east of the city. The Grand Union runs up from London and connects with the Birmingham-Fazeley at Graveley Hill, while the Digbeth Branch Canal links the two waterways at Aston and Bordesley.

Much of this intricate network of canals has been preserved. The **Gas Street Basin** has moorings for narrow-boats and modern cabin cruisers, and there are several canalside walks such as Brindley Walk, Summer Row and Kingston Row.

Boat trips on the canals are run from the Gas Street Basin and from Kingston Row.

Aston Hall, 2½ miles north of the city centre, is a Jacobean house which remains almost exactly as it was when built between 1618 and 1635.

The house, which stands in pleasant parkland, contains a magnificent balustraded staircase, a panelled gallery, and a kitchen set out with period cooking equipment.

The rooms are furnished in 17th and 18th-century styles, and there are some good examples of English Japanwork, a form of lacquer-ware that was made in the Midlands during the late 17th and early 18th centuries.

Blakesley Hall, in the eastern suburb of Yardley, is a 16th-century, timber-framed yeoman's house with several rooms containing original

THE ROTUNDA *The cylindrical office block in the Bull Ring has become the symbol of the new Birmingham.*

wall-paintings and exhibited as period rooms.

The rest of the house has displays of rural crafts, kitchen utensils and domestic equipment. The garden has been set out with lawns, yew trees and fruit trees in the style common to a house of that period.

Birmingham has 6,000 acres of parks and open spaces. **Cannon Hill**, the largest of the city's parks, includes a nature centre. The centre covers 5 acres in which plants and animals can be studied in their natural surroundings. There are also displays of farming activities. The **Botanical Gardens** at Edgbaston, which were laid out in 1831, contain not only collections of trees, shrubs, alpine plants and cacti, but also cockatoos, monkeys and bush babies.

Cathedrals and churches

St Philip's, in Colmore Row, is Birmingham's **Anglican cathedral**. It was consecrated in 1715, but did not become a cathedral until 1905. The designer Thomas Archer had lived in Rome, and the Baroque style of the building reflects the Italian influence. Edward Burne-Jones (1833-98) the painter, was baptised in St Philip's for which he later designed

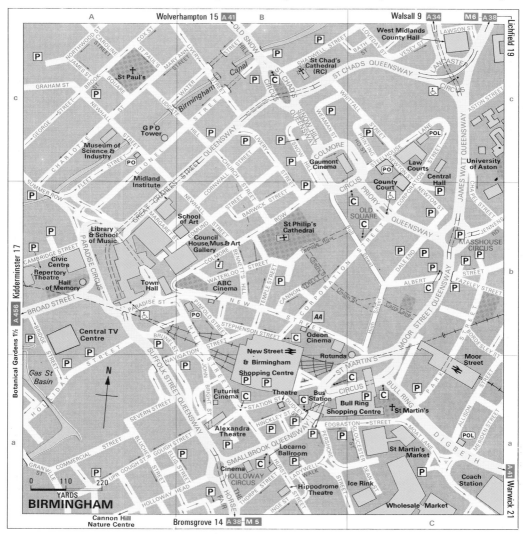

four great stained-glass windows. The cathedral is surrounded by acres of well-kept gardens where city workers relax in summer.

The **Roman Catholic cathedral**, St Chad, was completed in 1841, making it the first Roman Catholic cathedral to be built in England since the Reformation. It was designed by Augustus Pugin, who helped to design the Houses of Parliament.

But Birmingham's most famous church is St Martin's in the Bull Ring. It dates from the 13th century, though it was extensively restored in Victorian times.

The oldest building in the city centre, other than St Martin's, is the **Old Crown House**, an inn standing in High Street, Deritend. It is a half-timbered building of the late 15th century, and was originally part of a large medieval courtyard house. In addition to the inn it includes two shops.

Birmingham's newest venture, the

giant **National Exhibition Centre**, is 8 miles east of the city centre off the M42, close to Birmingham Airport. The centre is a complex of halls, conference rooms, lecture theatre, restaurants and hotels. It stands at the hub of Britain's motorway system – there is parking for 15,000 cars – and has its own railway station, Birmingham International.

Seven halls of various sizes make up the exhibition area. The two hotels can accommodate 1,200 people. The centre is used for all types of exhibitions, particularly those connected with engineering, and is now the venue for the International Motor Show.

The old market town of **Sutton Coldfield** was incorporated into Birmingham in 1974. Its showpiece is the 2,400 acre **Sutton Park**, which has remained virtually unaltered since it was given to the town in 1528. It is an area of heath and woodland interspersed with streams and

CATHEDRAL WINDOW *One of four windows in St Philip's Anglican cathedral by Sir Edward Burne-Jones, who was born in Birmingham in 1833.*

NATIONAL EXHIBITION CENTRE *The 310 acre site is at Bickenhill, 8 miles east of the city centre. The centre is on the M42 motorway, close to its junction with the M6. It has its own railway station and is alongside Birmingham Airport.*

THE CHOCOLATE FACTORY IN A GARDEN

When George Cadbury provided houses for his workers he had no desire to become a landlord, so he handed over the village to an independent body, The Bournville Village Trust.

In 1879 the chocolate manufacturers George and Richard Cadbury set up a factory on the southern outskirts of Birmingham, by a tiny stream, the Bournbrook. They called the factory Bournville, a name derived from this, and later the name was used for a blend of chocolate.

Around the factory the Cadburys built houses for their employees, set in tree-lined avenues and amid lawns and gardens. Two 14th-century houses – Selly Manor and Minworth Greaves – were transported to the site to give it a rural atmosphere; they are now museums containing domestic equipment.

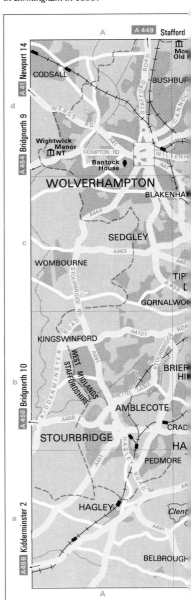

lakes, all preserved in their natural state. The man who secured the park for the town was John Veysey, Bishop of Exeter. He died in 1554 at the age of 102, and is buried in the parish church. There he now lies in mitred effigy on his tomb.

Information

Tel. Birmingham (021) 235 3411.
Location On the A41, 118 m. NW of London.
Parking See map.
District council Metropolitan City of Birmingham (Tel. 021 235 9944).
Population 920,400.
E-C Wed. (in suburbs). **M-D** Mon. to Sat.
Police (Cc) Steelhouse Lane (Tel. 021 236 5000).
Casualty hospital Accident Hospital, Bath Row (Tel. 021 643 7041).
Post office (Bb) Victoria Square.
Theatres Alexandra **(Ba)**, Suffolk Street (Tel. 021 643 1231); Repertory **(Ab)**, Broad Street

(021 236 4455); Hippodrome **(Ba)**, Hurst Street (021 622 2576).
Cinemas ABC 1, 2 and 3, Bristol Road (Tel. 021 440 1904); ABC **(Bb)**, New Street (021 643 4549); Futurist **(Ba)**, John Bright Street (021 643 0292); Gaumont **(Bc)**, Colmore Circus (021 236 3014); Odeon Queensway **(Ba)**, Holloway Circus (021 643 2418); Odeon **(Bb)**, New Street (021 643 6101).
Public library (Ab) Paradise Circus.
Places to see City Museum and Art Gallery **(Bb)**, Chamberlain Square; Museum of Science and Industry **(Ac)**, Newhall Street; Cannon Hill Park Nature Centre **(RCb)**, Pershore Road; Barber Institute of Fine Arts, The University **(RCb)**, Edgbaston; Birmingham Railway Museum **(RDb)**, Warwick Road, Tyseley; Aston Hall **(RDb)**, Trinity Road; Blakesley Hall **(RDb)**, Blakesley Road; Selly Manor **(RCa)** and Minworth Greaves, Maple Road; Botanical Gardens **(RCb)**,

Westbourne Road, Edgbaston; Weoley Castle **(RCa)**, Alwold Road; Sarehole Mill **(RDa)**, Cole Bank Road.
Town trails Available from City Information Office **(Bb)**, 110 Colemore Row.
Shopping Bull Ring and Birmingham Shopping Centres; New Street; Corporation Street; High Street; Bull Street.
Trade and industry Car manufacture; engineering; brass founding; metal manufacture; jewellery; chocolate.
Sport FA League football: Aston Villa FC **(RDb)**, Villa Park; Birmingham City FC **(RDb)**, St Andrews. Rugby football, Birmingham RFC, Foreshaw Heath Lane. Speedway and Greyhound racing, Perry Barr Stadium **(RCc)**, Walsall Road. Warwickshire County Cricket Club **(RDb)**, Edgbaston.
AA 24 hour service Tel. 021 550 4858.

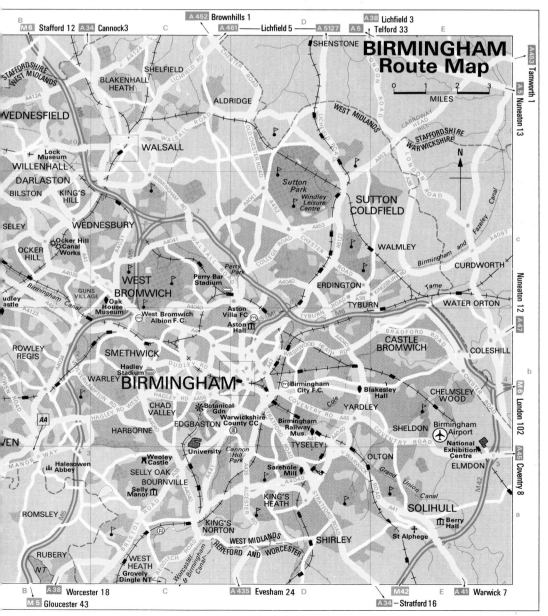

Bishop Auckland Durham

An 18th-century gatehouse leads from the market square to Bishops Park and Auckland Castle, seat of the Bishops of Durham for more than 600 years. The castle was built in the 13th century around a Norman manor house. With its gardens and courtyards it covers 5 acres, and it is separated from the rest of the park by a screen of stone arches and a 15th-century gate.

Information Tel. 605981.
Location On the A689, 11 m. SW of Durham.
Parking North Bondgate; Tenters Street; Finkle Street; Southgate Street; Kingsway; Market Place (all car parks).
District council Wear Valley (Tel. Crook 3121).
Population 32,600.
E-C Wed. **M-D** Thur., Sat.
Police Woodhouse Close Estate (Tel. 603566).
Casualty hospital Lady Eden, Cockton Hill Road (Tel. 604040).
Post office Tenters Street.
Cinema Odeon, Tenters Street (Tel. 602552).
Public libraries Woodhouse Lane; Kingsway.
Shopping Newgate Street; Bondgate.
Trade and industry Engineering; textiles; agriculture.
AA 24 hour service
Tel. Newcastle upon Tyne 610111.

Bishopbriggs Strathclyde

Modern housing developments have joined three small villages together to form the new Bishopbriggs, a town since 1964. Most of its residents came originally from nearby Glasgow.

There are pleasant walks beside the Forth and Clyde Canal, now used only by anglers and canoeists.

Information
Tel. Glasgow (041) 772 3210.
Location On the A803, 3 m. N of Glasgow.
Parking Kenmure Drive (cp); Springfield Road; Emerson Road.
District council Strathkelvin (Tel. 041 772 3210).
Population 22,800.
E-C Wed.
Police Kirkintilloch Road (Tel. 041 772 1113).
Casualty hospital Stobhill Hospital, Springburn (Tel. 041 558 0111).
Post office The Cross Court.
Theatre Fort Theatre, Kenmure Avenue (Tel. 041 772 7054).
Public library Kirkintilloch Road.
Shopping Kirkintilloch Road; Churchill Way.
AA 24 hour service
Tel. 041 812 0101.

Bishop's Castle Salop

The Bishop of Hereford built a castle on the site in 1127, to protect his sheep pastures against Welsh raiders from across the border close by. The castle has been reduced to a few stones around a bowling-green.

Bishop's Castle is 500 ft above sea-level, and is ringed by hills rising to 1,000 ft and more. It has three well-preserved Tudor houses – Blunden Hall, the Old Market Hall and the House on Crutches, with its upper storey supported by posts. The 17th-century Three Tuns Inn is one of Britain's few public houses where the landlord still brews his own ale.

Information Tel. Ludlow 2381.
Location On the A488, 8 m. NW of Craven Arms.
Parking Station Street (cp); Market Square; High Street; Church Street.
District council South Shropshire (Tel. Ludlow 2381).
Population 1,199.
E-C Wed. **M-D** Fri., Sat.
Police Grange Road (Tel. 481).
Casualty hospital Copthorne Hospital, Mytton Oak Road, Shrewsbury
(Tel. Shrewsbury 52244).
Post office Church Street.
Public library Old Chapel Yard.
AA 24 hour service
Tel. Birmingham (021) 550 4858.

Bishop's Stortford
Hertfordshire

The Norman Bishops of London had a castle called Waytemore in what is now the Castle Gardens. King John destroyed most of the castle, but there are still traces of the central mound. The open space once enclosed by the outer walls has been laid out as a park.

Stortford, the shopping and market centre of a large rural area, began to develop its industries in 1769, when

---

EMPIRE-BUILDER

Cecil Rhodes (1853-1902), son of a vicar of Bishop's Stortford, made his fortune from diamonds and gold in southern Africa. There he annexed vast tracts for Britain in the 1880s, founding the colony of Rhodesia (now Zambia and Zimbabwe). The vicarage where he was born is a museum of his life and times.

Cecil Rhodes, founder of Rhodesia.

---

the River Stort was made navigable.

A Tudor house in the High Street is now an outfitter's shop, which has been run by the same family since 1601.

Information Tel. 55261.
Location On the M11, 16 m. NE of Hertford.
Parking South Street; The Causeway; Basbow Lane; Apton Road; Crown Terrace; Adderley Road (all car parks).
District council East Hertfordshire (Tel. 55261).
Population 22,800.
E-C Wed. **M-D** Thur.
Police Basbow Lane (Tel. 53312).
Casualty hospital Herts and Essex General, Haymead Lane (Tel. 55191).
Post office South Street.
Public library The Causeway.
Places to see Rhodes Memorial Museum, South Road.
Trade and industry Agriculture; malting; light engineering.
AA 24 hour service
Tel. Chelmsford 61711.

Blackburn Lancashire

The reminders of Blackburn's immediate past as a cotton town are disappearing. Most of the old mills have turned to new industries, though full-scale models of the machinery they used can be seen in the Lewis Textile Museum.

Blackburn Cathedral is 19th century, but there has been a church in the area since AD 596. Even earlier, the Romans built an outpost near by to guard their road across the moors, and relics of their occupation are on show in Blackburn Museum.

Corporation Park was landscaped by the Victorians around a steep-sided valley.

Information Tel. 55201.
Location On the A666, 24 m. NW of Manchester.
Parking Brown Street; Church Street; Starkie Street; Regent Street; Limbrick; Penny Street; Princes Street (all car parks); Barton Street; Fieldon Street; Fleming Square.
District council Borough of Blackburn (Tel. 55201).
Population 88,200.
E-C Thur. **M-D** Wed., Fri. and Sat.
Police (Ab) Northgate (Tel. 51212).
Casualty hospital Royal Infirmary, Bolton Road (Tel. 63555).
Post office (Bb) Ainsworth Street.
Cinemas Unit Four (Ab), King William Street (Tel. 51779); Palace (Ba), Boulevard (58992); Unit Four, Plane Tree Road (52325).
Public library (Ab) Town Hall Street.
Places to see Cathedral (Ba); Lewis Museum of Textile Machinery (Ab), Exchange Street; Blackburn Museum and Art Gallery (Ab), Library Street.
Shopping Precinct Shopping Centre, King William/Ainsworth Street; Market and Market Hall.

BACK TO BACK *Neat terraces of mill-workers' houses are typical of Blackburn and other Lancashire towns.*

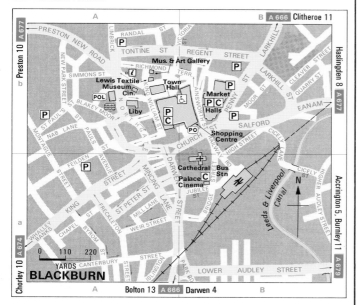

Some earlier buildings did survive the blaze – the Ryves Almshouses of 1682, and Old House (1660).

Blandford is the "Shottsford Forum" of Thomas Hardy's Wessex novels. Edmund Spenser mentioned the town in *The Faerie Queene,* published in 1590.

Information Tel. 54111.
Location On the A354, 17 m. NE of Dorchester.
Parking West Street; Church Lane; Market Place (all car parks); East Street; Salisbury Street; Sheep Market Hill; The Tabernacle; The Plocks.
District council North Dorset (Tel. 54111).
Population 3,910.
E-C Wed. **M-D** Thur., Sat.
Police Salisbury Road (Tel. 52101).
Casualty hospital Poole General, Longfleet Road, Poole (Tel. Poole 5100).
Post office The Tabernacle.
Public library The Tabernacle.
Trade and industry Agriculture; brewing; agricultural engineering; animal food processing.
AA 24 hour service Tel. Bournemouth 25751.

Bletchley Buckinghamshire

Bletchley was a small village until its railway junction was built in the 1830s. After that, it developed rapidly into the most important industrial town in north Buckinghamshire. It is now part of the new town of Milton Keynes (see p. 290).

Woburn Abbey, east of Bletchley, was built in the 18th century for the Dukes of Bedford. The house contains fine paintings, silver, porcelain and furniture, while the estate has been developed to attract visitors, and now includes a game reserve.

Information
Tel. Milton Keynes 678361.
Location On the A5, 13 m. NW of Dunstable.
Parking Leisure Centre; Brunel Centre (both car parks).
District council Borough of Milton Keynes (Tel. 679200).
Population 42,500.
E-C Wed. **M-D** Thur., Sat.
Police Sherwood Drive (Tel. Milton Keynes 71166).
Casualty hospital Stoke Mandeville, Mandeville Road, Aylesbury (Tel. Aylesbury 84111).
Post office Queensway.
Theatre Jennie Lee Theatre, the Leisure Centre, Princes Way (Tel. Milton Keynes 77251).
Cinema The Studio, Queensway (Tel. Milton Keynes 73121).
Public library Westfield Road.
Places to see Woburn Abbey, 6 m. E, off A5.
Shopping Queensway.
Trade and industry Engineering; computers; plastics.
AA 24 hour service Tel. Hatfield 62852.

Trade and industry Textiles; engineering.
Sport FA League football, Blackburn Rovers FC, Ewood Park; Greyhound racing, Hill Street.
AA 24 hour service Tel. Manchester (061) 485 6299.

Blackpool see page 46

Blairgowrie Tayside

The climate and soil around Blairgowrie combine to give conditions ideal for growing raspberries, and the area yields three-quarters of the Western world's commercial crop.

Since 1928 the burgh has included Rattray, linked to its larger neighbour by a 19th-century bridge across the Ericht, a fast-flowing salmon and trout stream. North of the town the river rushes through a 200 ft deep gorge, overlooked by the 17th-century mansion of the Rattray family.

Information
Tel. 2960/3701 (summer); 2258 (winter).
Location On the A93, 20 m. NW of Dundee.
Parking Croft Lane; Leslie Street; Lower Mill Street; Mill Street; The

Croft; Upper Mill Street (all car parks).
District council Perth and Kinross (Tel. Perth 21161).
Population 6,000.
E-C Thur.
Police Croft Lane (Tel. 2222).
Casualty hospital Perth Road (Tel. 2047).
Post office Perth Street.
Cinema Quinn's, Reform Street (Tel. 3105).
Public library Leslie Street.
Event Sheepdog Trials (July).
AA 24 hour service Tel. Dundee 25585.

Blandford Forum Dorset

The town's name would be Chipping Blandford if Latin-speaking officials had not changed it in the 13th century. They translated the Saxon prefix *Cheping* (market) into *forum* in their tax records, and this version has survived.

Few towns in the south of England can match the centre of Blandford for elegance. It was rebuilt in classical Georgian style after a fire in 1731, according to designs prepared by the local architects John and William Bastard. The Church of St Peter and St Paul, which they built in 1739, is one of the finest of its period.

BLACKPOOL Lancashire

Playground of the North

There is no place in the world quite like Blackpool. Its publicists have described it variously as the Fun City, Playground of the North and the Entertainment Capital of Europe – and they back their claims by pointing to its 7 miles of sandy beaches, three piers, two towers, 40 acre amusement park, and a host of ballrooms, discos, bingo halls, amusement centres and every other conceivable form of entertainment. It is Britain's largest holiday resort, and 6 million holidaymakers go there every year – almost half of them for at least the tenth time. Blackpool is a modern town which, from its earliest years, has shown a flair for originality and enterprise that has kept it at the forefront of British holiday towns.

At the beginning of the 19th century, Blackpool was a little-known fishing village on the north-west coast with a population of fewer than 500. The arrival of the railways in 1846 linked the resort with the industrial towns of Lancashire and Yorkshire. This gave the inhabitants of these towns the chance to get away from their smoke-laden environment and seek fresh air and relaxation on the coast.

Soon, however, the visitors began to demand organised entertainment. Blackpool was quick to oblige, and it was in the latter part of the 19th century that it developed some of its best-known attractions. Most seaside resorts of that period had a pier, some had two – Blackpool decided to have three, each with sun-decks and a theatre. And while piers in other parts of the country have fallen into disuse, Blackpool's North, Central and South piers have been maintained and modernised – though still managing to retain some of their Victorian elegance.

Blackpool Tower is as much a northern institution as Lancashire hot-pot or Yorkshire pudding. It was built between 1891 and 1894 in imitation of the Eiffel Tower in Paris. But, at 518 ft, it is little more than half the height of the French original. Even so, for many years it was Britain's tallest structure. Between its feet was built the Tower Circus and Ballroom, decorated in the exuberantly lavish style of the Paris Opera.

Butterflies

The Tower buildings have recently been modernised and redesigned, and now boast a circus, modern aquarium, tropical aviary and butterfly hall.

The **Winter Gardens** complex has a ballroom, built in 1896; it is noted for its 12 huge glass chandeliers. The Opera House, in the complex, is one of Britain's largest theatres, with seating for nearly 3,000.

Apart from the **Town Hall**, which was built at the turn of the century, these Victorian buildings are almost all that remain from Blackpool's early years of development.

One other reminder of Blackpool's Victorian hey-day is its tramway system. The original trams have long since gone out of service, some to transport museums, but modern, comfortable vehicles now run the full length of the Promenade – Britain's last surviving commercial tramway.

At the heart of the Promenade is the **"Golden Mile"**, a bustling boulevard of amusement arcades, hot-dog stalls and candy-floss stands, while at the southern end is the vast Pleasure Beach with its Monorail, Big Wheel, Grand National roller-coaster, and numerous other thrill-a-minute rides, such as the Starship *Enterprise* and Europe's first 360° "super dooper looper". It also has Blackpool's second tower, the 158 ft **Space Tower**, which an observation car ascends to give a panoramic view of the coastline.

Quieter side

But behind the noisy, garish façade there is a quieter Blackpool. Only minutes from the Golden Mile is **Stanley Park**, with its boating lake, Italian gardens and rose beds. On the other side of East Park Drive is the Zoo Park, where more than 400 different animals and birds live in moated enclosures. In the nearby Woodland Gardens there are shady walks among the trees – an oasis of peace and tranquillity away from the bustling crowds and the blare of amplified music. There are also pleasant walks to Anchorsholme, 4 miles to the north.

For art-lovers the **Grundy Art Gallery** in Queen Street has a fine collection of 19th and 20th-century paintings by British artists.

Blackpool has the longest season of all seaside resorts, extended by its conferences and exhibitions in the spring and autumn – and by its autumn spectacular, the **Illuminations**. From early September until late October, 5 miles of the Promenade are transformed into a glittering display of coloured lights and tableaux. At this time, too, the trams come into their own – taking on many exotic shapes, including a moon rocket, a Santa Fé express, pleasure boat and hovertrain.

New attractions

And Blackpool is still developing; every year new attractions are added to keep the town ahead of its rivals, and to live up to its motto – Progress.

Three major developments are now taking place: a shopping precinct for pedestrians only, a £4½ million seafront leisure complex, and an entertainment and shopping centre with covered car parks.

Information Tel. 21623/25212.
Location At the end of the M55, on the A584, 17 m. W of Preston.
Parking Sheppard Street; Coronation Street; West Street; Promenade; Bond Street; Bonny Street; General Street; Warbeck Hill Road; Seed Street; Swainson Street; Watson Road; Princes Way (all car parks).
District council Borough of Blackpool (Tel. 25212).

AWAY FROM IT ALL *Blackpool is not all funfairs and coloured lights. At the northern end of the beaches there are shallow cliffs sloping down to a quiet promenade and firm, tide-washed sands.*

BLACKPOOL ILLUMINATIONS *The best-known seaside landmark in the country, the 518 ft high tower – built in the 1890s – is at the centre of the illuminations that in September and October glitter along the seafront.*

Population 147,900.
E-C Wed. (small shops only).
Police Bonny Street **(Ab)** (Tel. 293933).
Casualty hospital Victoria Hospital, Whinney Heys Road (Tel. 34111).
Post office (Ac) Abingdon Street.
Theatres North Pier **(Ac)** (Tel. 20980); South Pier, Promenade (43096); Central Pier **(Ab)** (20423); Tower Circus, Promenade (27776); Opera House **(Ac)** (27786); Ice Drome, Pleasure Beach (41707); Grand **(Ac)** (28372).
Cinemas Studio 1, 2, 3, 4 **(Ac)**, Promenade (Tel. 25957); Odeon 1, 2, 3 **(Ac)**, Dickson Road (23565); Princess **(Ac)**, Promenade (20467); Royal Pavilion **(Aa)**, Rigby Road (25313); ABC 1, 2, 3, Church Street (24233); Tivoli, Clifton Street (27460).
Public library (Ac) Queen Street.
Places to see Tower buildings **(Ab)**, Central Promenade; Grundy Art Gallery, Queen Street; Zoo Park, Model Village, East Park Drive; Waxworks, Central Promenade.
Shopping Hounds Hill Centre; Talbot Road; Topping Street; Lytham Road; Bond Street; Dickson Road.
Events Veteran/Vintage Car Run (May/June); Milk Race Finish (June); Dog Show (June).
Trade and industry Tourism; catering; food manufacturing; light engineering; helicopter repair/servicing.
Sport FA League football, Blackpool FC, Bloomfield Road; Rugby League, Blackpool Borough, Borough Park; Greyhound racing, Princess Street; County cricket, The Oval, Stanley Park.
AA 24 hour service
Tel. Blackpool 44947.

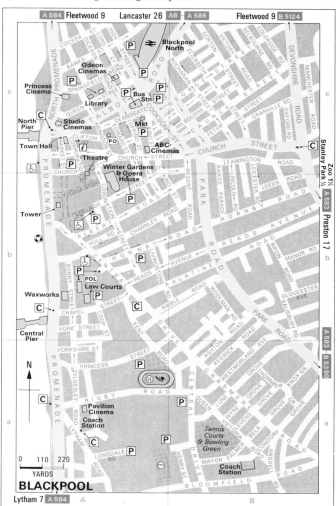

Blyth Northumberland

A 3 mile long beach of white sand stretches south of Blyth harbour and attracts holidaymakers to the town. Coal-carrying and ship-building, which made Blyth prosperous in the 19th century, have declined, but fishermen and yachtsmen still use the harbour, which has a growing import and export trade. Blyth lighthouse, which is still in use, is not on the shore – it stands inland behind a row of houses near the quayside.

Information
Tel. Seaton Delaval 370780.
Location On the A193, 20 m. N of Tynemouth.
Parking Thoroton Street; Trotter Street; Beaconsfield Street; King Street; Percy Street (all car parks).
District council Borough of Blyth Valley (Tel. Seaton Delaval 370780).
Population 36,500.
E-C Wed. **M-D** Fri., Sat.
Police Bridge Street (Tel. 4422).
Casualty hospital Ashington Hospital, West View, Ashington (Tel. Ashington 812541).
Post office Bridge Street.
Cinema Wallaw, Union Street (Tel. 2504).
Public library Bridge Street.
Shopping Bridge Street; Regent Street; Waterloo Road.
Trade and industry Textiles; cosmetics; tractors and electronic equipment.
AA 24 hour service
Tel. Newcastle upon Tyne 610111.

Bodmin Cornwall

Because the Crown Court sits in the town, Bodmin claims to be the capital of Cornwall – a claim denied by Truro, seat of the county council.

BODMIN BOWL *Stone angels support the unusual font in St Petroc's.*

Bodmin's streets, with their brownstone and granite-faced buildings, still retain the charm of a typical Cornish country town. The 15th-century parish church is the largest in Cornwall, and is dedicated to the county's patron saint, Petroc. The casket that once held his remains is enshrined in the south wall. The church also contains a Norman font and some fine slate memorials.

The county gaol was the scene of some 50 executions between 1785 and 1909 – carried out in public until 1862. H. C. McNeile, "Sapper", the creator of Bulldog Drummond, was born there in 1888, while his father was governor of the naval prison. During the First World War the Domesday Book, Crown Jewels and other national treasures were kept in the prison.

Largely rebuilt after a fire in 1881, Lanhydrock House, a National Trust property to the south-east, retains its original 17th-century gatehouse and north wing. Pencarrow House to the north-west is a Georgian mansion full of 18th-century treasures and has an Italian garden.

Information Tel. 4159.
Location On the A30, 31 m. W of Plymouth.
Parking Berrycombe Road; Bell Lane; Turf Street; Mount Folly; Fore Street (all car parks).
District council North Cornwall (Tel. 4471).
Population 12,100.
E-C Wed. **M-D** Sat.
Police Priory Road (Tel. 2262).
Casualty hospital East Cornwall, Rhind Street (Tel. 2244).
Post office St Nicholas Street.
Cinema Palace, Fore Street (Tel. 2632).
Public library Lower Bore Street.
Places to see Regimental Museum of the Duke of Cornwall's Light Infantry, Lostwithiel Road; Lanhydrock House, 2½ m. SE; Pencarrow House, 2½ m. NW.
AA 24 hour service
Tel. Plymouth 669989.

Bognor Regis W. Sussex

George V convalesced at Bognor in 1929 following a serious illness, and afterwards the town was granted the title *Regis* (of the king) by royal command. This episode realised the dream of Sir Richard Hotham, who transformed Bognor from a fishing hamlet to a resort in the 1790s. Sir Richard built several fine residences in the hope that they would attract royalty, but only the Prince of Wales made a visit in the 1790s – a brief one to one of his mistresses who was staying in Bognor.

Five miles of firm, flat sand and safe bathing have made the town a popular family resort. Lawns and rock pools line the Esplanade, and Hotham Park has both untouched wooded glades and formal gardens.

Hotham Park House was the home

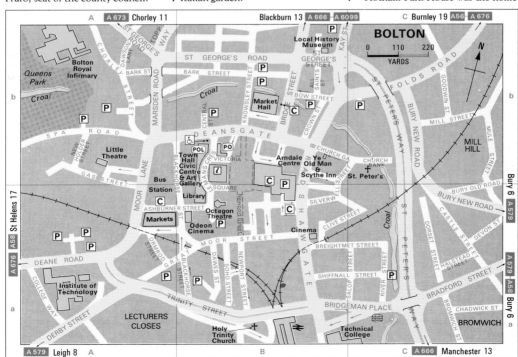

HALL I' TH' WOOD *The 15th to 17th-century house at Bolton was once the residence of Samuel Crompton, inventor of the spinning mule.*

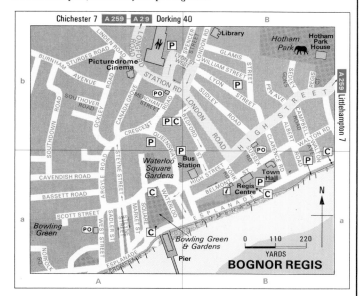

District council Bolton Metropolitan Borough (Tel. 22311).
Population 146,700.
E-C Wed. **M-D** Tues., Thur., Sat.
Police (Bb) Howell Croft North (Tel. 22466).
Casualty hospital Royal Infirmary, Chorley New Road **(Ab)** (Tel. 22488).
Post office (Bb) Victoria Square North.
Theatres Octagon **(Ba)**, Howell Croft South (Tel. 20661); Little Theatre **(Ab)**, Hanover Street (24469).
Cinemas Odeon **(Ba)**, Ashburner Street (Tel. 24096); Studios 1 & 2 **(Ba)**, Bradshawgate (25597).
Public library Le Mans Crescent **(Ba)**.
Places to see Museum and Art Gallery **(Bb)**; Hall i' th' Wood Museum; Smithills Hall Museum, Smithills Dean Road; Textile Museum, Tonge Moor Road; Museum of Local History **(Bb)**.
Shopping Deansgate; Newport Street; Arndale Centre; Churchgate; Bradshawgate; Knowsley Street; Town Hall Precinct; Oxford Street; Corporation Street; Market Street.
Trade and industry Engineering; textiles; chemicals.
Sport FA League football, Bolton Wanderers FAC, Burnden Park.
AA 24 hour service
Tel. Manchester (061) 485 6299.

Bo'ness Central

The steam age had its beginnings in 1764 in the thriving port of Bo'ness (the name is a contraction of Borrowstounness). In that year James Watt (1736-1819) developed the condensing steam engine, working in a cottage on the estate of Kinneil House, a 16th-century mansion.

The Antonine Wall, a Roman fortification running from the Forth to the Clyde, ended at Bo'ness.

The Scottish Railway Preservation Society has restored the railway station at the old harbour, and two locomotives, the 1891 *Maude* and 1928 *Morayshire*.

Information Tel. Falkirk 24911.
Location On the A904, 17 m. W of Edinburgh.
Parking Seaview Place; Union Street (both car parks).
District council Falkirk (Tel. 24911).
Population 16,000.
E-C Wed.
Police Union Street (Tel. 2877).
Casualty hospital Royal Infirmary, Falkirk (Tel. Falkirk 23011).
Post office East Pier Street.
Public library Scotland Close.
Places to see Scottish Railway Preservation Society, The Old Harbour; Kinneil House and Museum, Kinneil Estate.
Shopping East Pier Street; North Street; South Street; Grangepans.
AA 24 hour service
Tel. Edinburgh (031) 225 8464.

that Sir Richard built for himself. He lived there until his death in 1799, and is buried in the churchyard of St Mary Magdalene at South Bersted, the medieval core of Bognor.

William Blake, the visionary poet and artist, lived at nearby Felpham from 1800 to 1803. Enchanted with the village, he wrote, "Heaven opens here on all sides her golden gates".

Information Tel. 823140.
Location On the A259, 7 m. SE of Chichester.
Parking High Street (2); Lyon Street (2); Belmont Street (2); Market Street; London Road; Silverston Avenue; Gloucester Road (all car parks).
District council Arun (Tel. Littlehampton 6133).
Population 39,500.
E-C Wed. **M-D** Sat.
Police London Road (Tel. 820211).
Casualty hospital St Richard's, Spitalfield Lane, Chichester (Tel. Chichester 788122).
Post office (Bb) High Street.
Theatre and cinema Regis Centre **(Ba)**, Belmont Street (Tel. 865915).
Cinema Picturedrome **(Ab)**, Canada Grove (Tel. 823138).
Public library (Bb) London Road.
Shopping London Road; High Street.
AA 24 hour service
Tel. Brighton 695231.

Bolton Greater Manchester

The growth of the cotton industry brought prosperity to Bolton, birthplace of Samuel Crompton (1753-1827), inventor of the spinning mule. His birthplace is at Firwood Fold, and some 3 miles away, off Crompton Way, is Hall i' th' Wood where he lived for a time.

Crompton's original spinning mule of 1779 is now in the Tonge Moor Textile Museum, along with James Hargreaves's spinning jenny and Richard Arkwright's water frame.

At the end of the Civil War, the 7th Earl of Derby was executed in Bolton by Cromwell; the 13th-century Ye Old Man and Scythe Inn is where he is said to have spent his final hours.

The town's art gallery has an impressive collection of 18th and 19th-century English water-colours, local textiles and English pottery. Smithills Hall, a 14th-century manor house, contains Stuart furniture.

Information Tel. 22311.
Location On the A666, 17 m. NW of Manchester.
Parking Deane Road; Bow Street; Bark Street; Falcon Street; Folds Road; Dawes Street; Coronation Street; Flax Place; Central Street; Chorley Street; Spa Road; River Street (all car parks).

Bootle Merseyside

Salmon and otters thrived in the streams of Bootle when it was a village 200 years ago. Now 1½ miles of docks, the most extensive on the River Mersey, have taken the place of the streams. These can be visited by permit from the Mersey Docks and Harbour Company at Pier Head, Liverpool.

Information Tel. Liverpool (051) 922 4040.
Location On the A565, 7 m. N of Liverpool.
Parking New Strand Car Park; Stanley Road; Washington Parade; Pembroke Road; Oriel Road; Trinity Road.
District council Borough of Sefton (Tel. Liverpool (051) 922 4040).
Population 62,500.
E-C Wed.
Police Marsh Lane (Tel. 051 709 6010).
Casualty hospital Walton, Rice Lane, Walton, Liverpool 9 (Tel. 051 525 3611).
Post office Stanley Road.
Public library Stanley Road.
Places to see Docks.
Shopping New Strand Shopping Centre; Stanley Road.
AA 24 hour service Tel. Liverpool (051) 709 7252.

Boston Lincolnshire

Ten years after the *Mayflower* took the Pilgrim Fathers to America, another band of Puritans set out from Boston and founded the settlement of the same name in what is now Massachusetts, USA. Their pioneering efforts contributed to the Lincolnshire town's decline as a major sea port, for as a transatlantic trade grew, ports on the west coast, such as Bristol and Liverpool, took trade away from those in the east.

Since the 19th century, however, Boston's docks have recaptured some of their earlier importance. Timber, grain and animal foodstuffs are unloaded beside the River Witham, while other cargo vessels take aboard coal and cattle.

The town abounds in medieval architecture. The most outstanding example is the 14th-century St Botolph's Church, whose 272 ft tower, known as the Boston Stump, is a prominent landmark. From the top, one-third of the county can be seen, including Lincoln, 32 miles northwest. The church has a medieval painted ceiling, and its misericords date from 1390.

The cells in which the Pilgrim Fathers were imprisoned in 1607, after their first attempt to escape to America, can still be seen in the 15th-century Guildhall, now the Borough Museum. The adjoining Fydell House was built in 1726 by William Fydell, three times Mayor of Boston. It has an American Room set aside for the use of visitors from Boston, USA.

BOSTON STUMP *The lofty lantern tower of St Botolph's Church, Boston, was once a beacon for Fenland travellers and navigators on The Wash.*

The Blackfriars Theatre was built in the 13th century as the refectory of a Dominican friary, and was converted to its present use in 1965.

IN FASHION *The restored 15th-century Pescod Hall, Boston, is now a boutique.*

Information Tel. 62354 (summer); 64601 (winter).
Location On the A16, 32 m. N of Peterborough.
Parking Bargate Green; Market Place; Cattle Market; Bargate Bridge; Botolph Street; Buoy Yard; Doughty Quay; Lincoln Lane; County Hall Yard; Municipal Buildings (all cps).
District council Borough of Boston (Tel. 64601).
Population 26,400.
E-C Thur. **M-D** Wed., Sat.
Police (Ab) Lincoln Lane (Tel. 66222).
Casualty hospital Sibsey Road (Tel. 64801).
Post office (Ab) Wide Bargate.
Theatre Blackfriars **(Ba)**, South Street (Tel. 63108).
Cinema Classic **(Ba)**, South Square (Tel. 62961).
Public library County Hall.
Places to see The Guildhall **(Ba)**; Fydell House **(Ba)**.
Shopping Market Place; West Street; Strait Bargate; Wide Bargate.
Trade and industry Shipping; agriculture.
AA 24 hour service Tel. Lincoln 42363.

Bournemouth see page 52

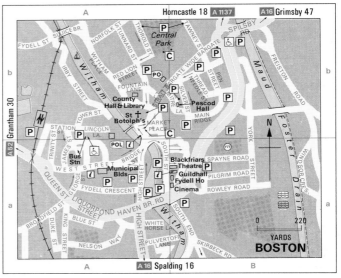

Bracknell Berkshire

The Bronze Age barrow on Bill Hill and the modern buildings of Bracknell town centre span between them 4,000 years of history.

The mainly 19th-century market town of Bracknell was designated a new town in 1949. Its history is depicted in a 98 ft long relief mural on the Honeywell building in the central shopping precinct, Charles Square.

The imposing 18th-century Italianate mansion of South Hill Park, south of the town, was the home of George Canning (1770-1827), Prime Minister in 1827. It is now an arts centre.

Information Tel. 23149.
Location On the A329, 11 m. E of Reading.
Parking The Old Manor; Market Street; Albert Road; The Ring.
District council Bracknell (Tel. 24642).
Population 48,750.
E-C Wed. **M-D** Fri., Sat.
Police Broadway (Tel. 21311).
Casualty hospital Heatherwood, London Road, Ascot (Tel. Ascot 23333).
Post office High Street.
Theatre South Hill Park Arts Centre (Tel. 27272).
Cinemas ABC 1 and 2, High Street (Tel. 52821); South Hill Park Arts Centre (27272).
Public library Town Square.
Places to see South Hill Park, Ringmead.
Shopping Broadway; Crossway; High Street; Charles Square.
Trade and industry Engineering; electronics; chemicals; computers; precision tools; food processing.
AA 24 hour service
Tel. Reading 581122.

Bradford-on-Avon Wilts.

Houses of yellow Bath stone nestling in a wooded dell give Bradford an unspoiled charm. The town flourished as a cloth-weaving centre from the Middle Ages onwards, and its prosperity is reflected in its many fine buildings. The Hall in Woolley Street, built by a local clothier in 1610, is an outstanding example of Jacobean architecture.

A six-arched bridge spans the River Avon. The two central arches are from the 14th century, while the rest were rebuilt 300 years later. The small, domed building at one end of the bridge was once a chapel, and in the 17th century became a lock-up.

Barton Farm, off the Frome Road, has one of the largest tithe barns in England. It was built shortly after 1300 and is 168 ft long and more than 30 ft wide.

Bradford's tiny Church of St Laurence is Saxon, and parts of it may be 1,250 years old. It originally served a monastery which was later sacked by the Danes, and the church itself was hidden for centuries among other buildings. In 1856 the local vicar rediscovered it and it was restored to its original function. The church is only 25 ft 2 in. long and 25 ft 5 in. high. It is one of the few Anglo-Saxon churches to survive intact.

Great Chalfield Manor, 2½ miles to the north-east, dates from about 1480 and consists of a house, church and other buildings surrounded by a moat. The great hall contains a mural of the first owner, Thomas Tropenell.

South-west of the town, Westwood Manor is 15th century and has modern gardens with hedges trimmed into various designs.

ABBOT'S CHURCH *Aldhelm, Abbot of Malmesbury, founded St Laurence's, Bradford-on-Avon, about AD 700.*

Information Tel. Trowbridge 63111.
Location On the B3107, 6 m. E of Bath.
Parking Bridge Street; St Margaret's Street; Station Road; Market Street (all car parks).
District council West Wiltshire (Tel. Trowbridge 63111).
Population 8,750.
E-C Wed.
Police Avonfield Avenue (Tel. 2222).
Casualty hospital Berryfield Road (Tel. 2975).
Post office The Shambles.
Public library St Margaret's Street.
Places to see Town Bridge Lock-up; Tithe Barn, Barton Farm; Great Chalfield Manor, 2½ m. NE on the B3103; Westwood Manor, 1½ m. SW.
Town trails Available from the library.
Trade and industry Rubber manufacture; light engineering; printing; electronics.
AA 24 hour service
Tel. Bristol 298531.

Bradford see page 54

PILGRIMS' HALT *During the Middle Ages, pilgrims on their way from Malmesbury to Glastonbury paused to pray in the chapel on the bridge at Bradford-on-Avon.*

BOURNEMOUTH Dorset

A seaside town invented by the Victorians

The Victorian love-affair with the seaside changed Bournemouth from a desolate heath to a bustling resort in less than 50 years. Rich men built their villas on the pine-clad slopes of the Bourne valley, speculators erected hotels on the high cliff-tops, and by 1900 the town's population had risen from 695 (in 1851) to 59,000. Bournemouth has a mild climate, sandy beaches and fine coastal views, and the town's planners have landscaped the natural beauty of the valley and the Bourne stream to make spacious parks and gardens. Behind the gardens spreads a modern town of shops, hotels, theatres and cinemas, giving way to shaded streets where Victorian villas still stand among scented pines.

A Dorset squire named Lewis Tregonwell founded Bournemouth in 1811, when he built a summer home on the site of what is now the Royal Exeter Hotel. It was the only building, apart from an inn, on the wild stretch of heathland that followed the sweeping curve of Poole Bay from Hengistbury Head in the east to Durlston Head in the west. The coastline could have been made for the holidaymaker: it is rugged and split by deep ravines, called chines, that open out to the sea.

In 1837 Sir George Tapps-Gervis, a local landowner, conceived the idea of establishing a resort on the land east of Tregonwell's estate, sheltered from storms by the Purbeck Hills, Hengistbury Head, and the Isle of Wight. In the same year Westover Villas, Westover Gardens and the Bath Hotel were all built.

A jetty was built in 1856, but was replaced in 1859. This second structure was itself replaced by an iron pier in 1880 which forms part of the present pier. In 1866 The Arcade was built on the site of a rustic bridge crossing the Bourne stream.

The railway came to Bournemouth in 1870, bringing more visitors, but the town had little to offer in the way of entertainment until the first **Winter Gardens** were built in 1875.

This building was used as a concert hall until 1935, when it was dismantled and replaced by an indoor bowling-green – the first in the country. The building was taken over by the Royal Air Force during the Second World War, and after the war it was discovered that the hall had good acoustic properties. The Winter Gardens then became the permanent home of the Bournemouth Symphony Orchestra.

Inland gardens

Fifty years after the opening of the Winter Gardens Bournemouth had another major centre of entertainment – the **Pavilion**. This was opened in 1929 and includes a 1,500-seat theatre, ballroom and restaurant with terraces overlooking the **Lower Gardens** through which flows the Bourne stream.

The Lower Gardens lie in a valley, bordered on one side by footpaths winding among pine trees. The gardens follow the Bourne, to form the

BOURNEMOUTH BEACH *Summer crowds flock to the long, sandy beaches and the sunny climate of the south coast's largest resort.*

Central Gardens and Upper Gardens, from which a short walk leads to Meyrick Park – a pine-clad estate of 154 acres.

Five of Bournemouth's churches are listed as being of architectural or historical interest, the only one of great antiquity being St Andrew's, at Kinson, which has a 12th-century tower and 14th-century chancel.

St Peter's, in Hinton Road, was completed in 1879 in the Gothic style and has a square tower and a spire. In the churchyard is the Shelley Tomb, burial place of Mary Shelley (1797-1851) the author of the novel *Frankenstein* and wife of the poet Percy Bysshe Shelley.

The **Russell-Cotes Art Gallery and Museum** specialises in Victoriana. The building itself is an interesting example of Victorian architecture with a large conservatory, bow-fronted upper windows and pinnacled roof.

The **Rothesay Museum** has Italian paintings and pottery, English furniture, African objects, and arms and armour. The **Big Four Railway Museum** has a large collection of locomotive nameplates and other railway relics. The **British Typewriter Museum** has nearly 400 machines on display.

Information Westover Road (Tel. 291715).
Location On the A35, 31 m. SW of Southampton.
Parking Bath Road South (cp); Upper Hinton Road (cp); Exeter Road; West Overcliff Drive; Avenue Road; Madeira Road; Richmond Hill (cp); West Hill (cp); Richmond

LISTEN TO THE BAND *Holidaymakers relax in the sunshine in Bournemouth's Lower Gardens, part of the 2,000 acres of parkland in the town.*

Gardens (cp); Glen Fern (cp); Lansdowne Road (cp).
District council Borough of Bournemouth (Tel. 22066).
Population 144,800.
E-C Wed. or Sat.
Police (Cc) Madeira Road (Tel. 22099).
Casualty hospital Poole General, Longfleet Road, Poole (Tel. Poole 5100).
Post office (Bb) Post Office Road.
Theatres Pavilion **(Bb)**, Westover Road (Tel. 25861); Winter Gardens **(Aa)**, Exeter Road (26446); Pier **(Ba)** (20250).
Cinemas Playhouse, Westover Road (Tel. 23257); ABC 1, 2 and 3 **(Bb)**, Westover Road (20250); Gaumont **(Bb)**, Westover Road (22402); Continental, Wimborne Road (529779); Galaxy **(Bb)**, Westover Road (23277).

Public library Lansdowne.
Places to see Russell-Cotes Art Gallery and Museum **(Cb)**, Russell-Cotes Road; Rothesay Museum, Typewriter Museum **(Ba)**, Bath Road; Big Four Railway Museum **(Bc)**, Old Christchurch Road.
Town trails Available from Bournemouth Teachers' Centre, 40 Lowther Road, Bournemouth BH8 8NR.
Shopping Old Christchurch Road; The Arcade; Commercial Road; The Square; Westover Road.
Events Music Festival (Easter); Hard Court Tennis Championships of Great Britain (May); Regatta (Aug.).
Sport FA League football, Bournemouth FC, Dean Court; Hampshire County cricket, Dean Park.
AA 24 hour service Tel. Bournemouth 25751.

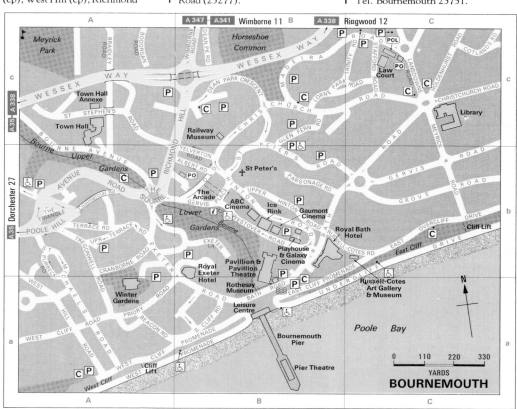

BOURNEMOUTH

BRADFORD West Yorkshire

City where wool means wealth

The Industrial Revolution stamped its mark heavily on Bradford – a mark that was both ugly and impressive. Rows of slum houses surrounded its smoke-grimed wool mills, yet at its heart prosperity blossomed in the shape of flamboyant buildings that proclaimed the Victorians' pride and confidence in their city. Bradford is busily engaged in erasing the worst excesses of industrial blight, and a bright, modern city is emerging from the debris of the past.

MANNINGHAM MILL *Samuel Cunliffe Lister, later Baron Masham, built the mill during the Victorian era of prosperity in Bradford.*

Bradford City Hall, built in 1873, curves decorously around one side of Town Hall Square. Two Bradford architects, Lockwood and Mawson, designed the building and lavished upon it every facet of the then fashionable Gothic revival. Arched windows, pinnacles and stone embossments adorn the frontage, and at second-floor level stand 35 statues of kings and queens.

A 200 ft clock-tower soars above the Hall in imitation of the tower of the Pallazzo Vecchio in Florence.

Local stone was used to build the Town Hall, now cleaned and restored to its original sandy colour. Similar stone was used to build the nearby Law Courts in 1972.

The **Wool Exchange** in Market Street, where wool merchants from all over the world used to gather, was also designed by Lockwood and Mawson. It was built in 1864 with tall, arched porches that lead to an interior decorated with pink-granite columns.

St George's Hall, in Bridge Street,

is one of the oldest buildings in the city centre. Lockwood and Mawson designed it in 1851, when the Classical revival was still at its height, and gave it an impressive façade of giant Corinthian columns. It was built as a concert hall and, apart from a period in the 1930s when it served as a cinema, has always been one of the principal music centres in northern England. Bradford music-lovers are quick to point out that the composer Frederick Delius (1862-1934) was born in the city.

Medieval cathedral

Although Bradford is largely a Victorian city, its **cathedral** dates from the 15th century. It was then the parish church of St Peter, and its size reflects the prosperity Bradford enjoyed as a wool town in the late Middle Ages.

The cathedral stands on a rise above the city centre, in Church Bank, and is a sturdy building of millstone grit with a massive tower. It was raised to cathedral status in 1919, and a Lady Chapel and Chapter House were added between 1954 and 1965.

Museums

Bradford's Art Gallery and Museum is housed in the **Cartwright Memorial Hall**. It was built in 1904 in memory of Edmund Cartwright (1743-1823), a native of Nottinghamshire, who contributed to Bradford's prosperity with his invention of the power loom. Among the exhibits are paintings by Gainsborough, Reynolds and Stanley Spencer.

Local history is displayed in **Bolling Hall**, a manor house, the earliest part of which is a 15th-century tower. Additions were made during the following centuries, and the view as seen from its terraced garden is a curious mixture of styles, including Elizabethan and Georgian. Inside, the rooms are furnished to show the development of English furniture from the 16th to the 19th centuries.

Bradford's links with the past are displayed in the Industrial Museum, housed in **Moorside Mills**. The building is a typical worsted spinning mill of the 19th century; it dates from 1875, and was in use until 1970. The museum traces the history of the wool trade from its origins, and includes a 10 ft diameter water-wheel, steam engines, turbines and textile machinery. There is also a transport section with tram-cars and steam locomotives.

Behind the museum is **Moorside House**, the home of successive managers of Moorside Mills until 1929. It has been decorated and furnished in Victorian and Edwardian style to recreate a typical middle-class home of the period.

Brontë country

At **Keighley**, 10 miles north-west of the city centre, is **Cliffe Castle**. This is not a medieval fortress, but a Victorian mansion adapted to display the geology, archaeology and social history of the district. Its grounds include an aviary, conservatory and gardens.

Keighley itself is a large town now absorbed into Bradford and similar in character, having grown up during the 19th century. It was here that Charlotte Brontë came to shop, often walking the 4 miles from Haworth where she lived with her sisters, Anne and Emily.

The Brontë sisters lived at the **Haworth Parsonage** with their father, Patrick, and their brother, Patrick Branwell Brontë. There they wrote the novels that have become literary classics: Emily's *Wuthering Heights*, Anne's *Tenant of Wildfell Hall* and Charlotte's *Jane Eyre* – all three published in 1848.

The Haworth Parsonage is now preserved as a Brontë Museum.

Many visitors travel to Haworth on

BRADFORD'S MEN O' BRASS

Brass bands are a northern institution, and none has been more successful than Black Dyke Mills, the company band of John Foster & Son, worsted-yarn spinners. Founded in 1853 the band has won the British Open Brass Band Championship 22 times. The band was awarded the freedom of Bradford in 1976 for service to the city.

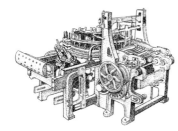

WOOL COMB *The Holden Comb, displayed in the Bradford Industrial Museum, was used in the manufacture of worsted cloth.*

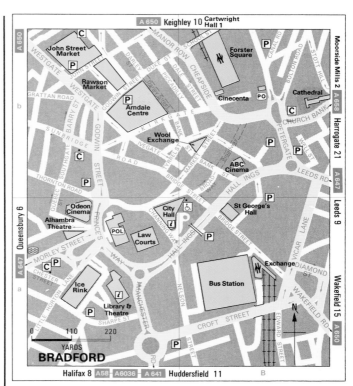

the Worth Valley Railway, which runs steam trains from Keighley to Oxenhope via Haworth.

Model village

About 3 miles to the north of Bradford is **Saltaire**, founded by Sir Titus Salt (1803-76) in 1851. The village grew around Salt's huge mill, which he built to manufacture alpaca cloth.

The mill was the biggest in Yorkshire, and Salt provided 800 houses, a public dining hall, schools and a church for his employees. It was a model village, one of the first in the world.

Sir Titus Salt lies in the mausoleum of the Congregational church he built. It stands opposite the mill and has an impressive, colonnaded front porch. Above is a domed, circular tower decorated with ironwork.

Information Tel. 29577.
Location On the A650, 9 m. W of Leeds.
Parking Rawson Road; Mill Street; Well Street; Charles Street; Hall Ings (2); Nelson Street; William Street; Westgate; Godwin Street; Valley Road; Little Horton Lane; George Street; Bridge Street (all car parks).
District council Bradford (Tel. 29577).
Population 280,700.
E-C Wed. **M-D** Daily.
Police (Aa) The Tyrls (Tel. 23422).
Casualty hospital Duckworth Lane (Tel. 42200).
Post office (Bb) Forster Square.
Theatres Alhambra **(Aa)**, Morley Street (Tel. 27007); Playhouse, Chapel Street (20329); St George's Hall **(Ba)**, Hall Ings (32513); Library Theatre **(Aa)**, Prince's Way (23975).
Cinemas ABC **(Bb)**, Broadway (Tel. 23678); Cinecenta **(Bb)**, Cheapside (23177); Odeon **(Aa)**, Prince's Way (26716); Film Theatre, Chapel Street (20329).
Public library (Aa) Prince's Way.

Places to see Cartwright Hall, Lister Park; Bolling Hall, off Wakefield Road; Industrial Museum, Moorside Road; Cliffe Castle, Keighley; Brontë Museum, Haworth.
Town trails Available from City Hall, Town Hall Square.
Shopping Market Street; Westgate; Manningham Lane; Darley Street; Broadway; John Street.
Event Lord Mayor's Parade (June).
Trade and industry Woollen textiles; engineering; printing; electrical engineering; electronics.
Sport FA League football, Bradford City FC, Manningham Lane; Rugby League, Bradford Northern, Odsall Stadium, Rooley Avenue; Cricket, Yorkshire County Cricket Club, Park Avenue.
AA 24 hour service Tel. 724703.

BRONTË MUSEUM *The Haworth Parsonage contains manuscripts and personal relics of the Brontë sisters.*

THE LITTLE ENGINE WITH THE BIG PULL

The Jowett Car Company was founded in 1910 by Benjamin and William Jowett who, at the turn of the century, ran a cycle works in Bradford. The first Jowett car had a flat, twin-cylinder engine of less than 1 litre capacity. But it had enormous pulling power, which made the car an instant success.

After the Second World War, Jowett produced the renowned Bradford van, still using the twin-cylinder engine. A four-cylinder version was fitted to a saloon car, the Javelin, and a two-seater sports car, the Jupiter.

Jowett Cars ceased production in 1954, because of financial difficulties, but several cars are on display in the Industrial Museum.

The "flat" engine, depicted in the badge, powered the sleek Javelin of the late 1940s.

Braintree Essex

Textiles have brought prosperity to Braintree for over 400 years. At first the trade was in woollen cloth, and when this declined around 1800 the Courtauld family introduced silk-weaving, which continues today.

Braintree is on the old Roman road from St Albans to Colchester, and the Church of St Michael includes Roman bricks. Braintree Market, first chartered in 1199, is still held.

Information Tel. 43140.
Location On the A120, 11 m. NE of Chelmsford.
Parking Blyths Meadow; Sandpit Road; Station Approach; Manor Street (all car parks).
District council Braintree (Tel. 23131).
Population 22,000.
E-C Thur. **M-D** Wed., Sat.
Police Fairfield Road (Tel. 21211).
Casualty hospital Chelmsford and Essex, New London Road, Chelmsford (Tel. Chelmsford 83331).
Post office Fairfield Road.
Cinema Embassy, Fairfield Road (Tel. 20378).
Public library Coggeshall Road.
Places to see Heritage Centre, Town Hall.
AA 24 hour service Tel. Chelmsford 61711.

Brechin Tayside

Red-sandstone buildings line the steep streets of Brechin, which stands on a hill beside the South Esk river. Beyond the city rises the backcloth of the East Grampian range.

The 13th-century cathedral which made Brechin a city was partly demolished in 1807, but it has some original fabric and a spire of 1360.

Next to it stands an even older structure, an 87 ft high round tower built in the 10th century as a watch-tower and place of safety for the priest and church treasures. The only other tower of this type on the Scottish mainland is at Abernethy; round towers are otherwise found only in Ireland. Near by are ruins of the Maison Dieu, a 13th-century hospital.

Edzell Castle, 6 miles north, is remarkable for a walled garden, which survives largely as it was laid out in 1604. Shrubs and lawns have been clipped to spell out mottoes.

Information Tel. Montrose 2000.
Location On the A935, 9 m. W of Montrose.
Parking Bank Street; Braik's Close; Market Street; Maisondieu Lane; Church Street; City Road (all car parks).
District council Angus (Tel. Forfar 65101).
Population 7,000.
E-C Wed.
Police Clark Street (Tel. 2222).
Casualty hospital Stracathro Hospital by Brechin

(Tel. Edzell 312).
Post office Clerk Street.
Cinema King's, High Street (Tel. 2140).
Public library St Ninian's Square.
Places to see Museum; Round tower.
Sport Scottish League football, Brechin City FC, Glebe Park.
AA 24 hour service Tel. Dundee 25585.

Brecon Powys

Above the town rise the triple peaks of the Brecon Beacons – Pen Y Fan (2,907 ft), flanked by Cribin (2,608 ft) and Corn Dū (2,863 ft) – the highest mountains in South Wales. Brecon, the administrative centre for the 40 mile long Brecon Beacons National Park, lies on its northern edge, at the junction of the rivers Usk and Honddu.

Known also as Brecknock, Brecon is one of the oldest Welsh towns: it was granted its first charter in 1246. Another charter of 1366 gave it the right to hold a fair, and pleasure fairs are still held in the streets for three days every May and November.

The town centre is an interesting assortment of medieval, Georgian, Jacobean and Tudor architecture. A tower and battlemented wall are all that remain of the Norman castle.

The priory church of St John, dating from the 13th and 14th centuries, was designated a cathedral in 1923. Its side chapels are dedicated to various trades, such as tailoring, weaving, fulling and shoe-making.

On the western bank of the Usk stands Christ College, founded in 1541 and turned into a public school in 1853. It incorporates the remains of a 12th–14th-century friary, and its chapel is one of the oldest places of worship still in use in Wales.

The Brecknock Museum in Glamorgan Street is devoted to local history and folklore and has a collection of love-spoons, carved from wood by young men as gifts for the girls they were courting. The 24th Regiment (South Wales Borderers) Museum displays 13 of the regiment's 23 VCs.

The single bridge spanning the Usk at Brecon provides good views of the Usk Valley and the Beacons. East of the town is the terminus of the Monmouthshire and Brecon Canal, built between 1797 and 1812.

Information Tel. 4437.
Location On the A470, 18 m. N of Merthyr Tydfil.
Parking Free Street; George Street;

BENEATH THE BEACONS *The tower of St Mary's Church soars above the roofs of Brecon, only to be dwarfed by the Brecon Beacons.*

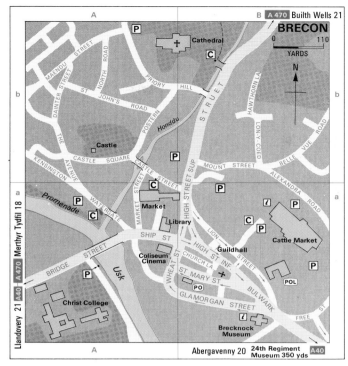

Map labels: A470 Builth Wells 21, BRECON, 0 110 YARDS, N, Cathedral, Castle, Castle Square, Promenade, Merthyr Tydfil 18, A470 A40, Llandovery 21 A40, Market, Library, Ship St, Coliseum Cinema, Christ College, Usk, Guildhall, High St, Cattle Market, Brecknock Museum, Abergavenny 20, 24th Regiment Museum 350 yds, A40, Honddu, Struet, POL, PO, Bridge Street, Glamorgan Street, Bulwark, Free St

Ship Street; Bridge Street; The Struet (all car parks).
District council Brecknock Borough (Tel. 4141).
Population 6,500.
E-C Wed. **M-D** Tues. and Fri.
Police (Ba) Lion Street (Tel. 2331).
Casualty hospital War Memorial, Cerrigcochion Road (Tel. 2443).
Post office (Ba) St Mary Street.
Cinema Coliseum 1, 2 and 3 **(Aa)**, Wheat Street (Tel. 2501).
Public library (Aa) Ship Street.
Places to see Brecknock Museum; 24th Regiment Museum **(Ba)**.
Shopping Bulwark; High Street.
AA 24 hour service
Tel. Cardiff 394111.

Brent see London

Brentwood Essex
Deer roam by the lakes in the 428 acre park at South Weald, part of Brentwood's attractive "green belt".

The town – now a dormitory for London – grew up in the late 12th century, around a forest clearing, as a convenient stopping place for pilgrims from East Anglia and the Midlands on their way to St Thomas Becket's shrine at Canterbury. The town later developed as a staging-post with good inns. Then, in the 1840s, its modern growth began with the coming of the railway.

Information Tel. 228060.
Location On the A128, 12 m. SW of Chelmsford.
Parking Coptfold Road; Hart Street; Weald Road; North Road; High Street (all car parks).
District council Brentwood (Tel. 228060).

Population 55,800.
E-C Thur.
Police London Road (Tel. 220202).
Casualty hospital Harold Wood, Gubbins Lane, Harold Way (Tel. Ingrebourne 45533).
Post office High Street.
Cinema Focus 1 and 2, Chapel High Precinct (Tel. 227574).
Public library Coptfold Road.
Shopping High Street; Chapel High Precinct; King's Road.
Events Sports Festival (May); Tattoo (May).
AA 24 hour service
Tel. Chelmsford 61711.

Bridgend Mid Glamorgan
A ruined Norman castle on a wooded hill above the River Ogmore commands the site where Bridgend developed. The town straddles the river at a point where three valleys meet – the Ogmore, Garw and Llynfi. Near by are two other Norman castles – Coity, 1½ miles to the north-east, and Ogmore, 2 miles south. Between them the three castles dominated this fertile corner of the Vale of Glamorgan. Bridgend has been for centuries the market town for the area. Now it is an industrial centre as well. Ewenny Priory, 1½ miles south, is a fine example of a Norman defensive church. The priory walls, encircling 5 acres, still stand.

Information Tel. 62141.
Location On the A4063, 19 m. W of Cardiff.
Parking Brackla Street; Angel Street; The Rhiw, Tondu Road; Brewery Lane (all car parks).
District council Borough of Ogwr (Tel. 62141).
Population 15,700.

E-C Wed.
Police Brackla Street (Tel. 55555).
Casualty hospital General, Quarella Road (Tel. 62166).
Post office Dunraven Place.
Cinema Embassy, Tondu Road (Tel. 3429).
Public library Wyndham Street.
Places to see New Castle; Coity Castle, 1½ m. NE; Ogmore Castle, 2 m. S; Ewenny Priory, 1½ m. S.
Shopping Adare Street; Caroline Street; Rhiw Arcade; Nolton Street.
Trade and industry Agriculture, iron-founding.
AA 24 hour service
Tel. Cardiff 394111.

Bridge of Allan Central
In Victorian times Bridge of Allan was developed as a spa. It is now a holiday and residential resort and a touring centre for the glens and hills of central Scotland.

The 220 ft high Wallace Monument, 2 miles to the south-east, commemorates Sir William Wallace (1272-1305), martyr-hero of Scotland's long struggle for independence from England.

WALLACE MONUMENT *The tower, near Bridge of Allan, commemorates the Scottish patriot.*

Information Tel. Stirling 3111.
Location On the A9, 3 m. N of Stirling.
Parking Fountain Road; Allanvale Road (both car parks); Henderson Street.
District council Stirling (Tel. Stirling 3131).
Population 4,670.
E-C Wed.
Police Henderson Street (Tel. 832222).
Casualty hospital Royal Infirmary, Livilands Gate, Stirling (Tel. Stirling 3151).
Post office Fountain Road.
Public library Fountain Road.
Places to see Wallace Monument.
Shopping Fountain Road; Henderson Street.
Event Strathallan Highland Games (Aug.).
AA 24 hour service
Tel. Glasgow (041) 812 0101.

BRIDGNORTH *St Leonard's Church overlooks High Town, and the gabled Bishop Percy's House.*

LEANING *Bridgnorth castle keep has stood like this for 300 years.*

Bridgnorth Salop

The main part of Bridgnorth stands on a high ridge above the River Severn, and is known as High Town. Below the ridge, and across the river, is Low Town. The two "towns" are linked by a six-arched road-bridge dating from 1823.

Bridgnorth's High Street, where weekly markets are held, is dominated by the 17th-century Town Hall, standing in the centre of the road. The lower storey of the building consists of open arches.

Little remains of Bridgnorth Castle, but the ruined Norman keep leans at 17 degrees – three times further than the leaning tower of Pisa. It subsided after being undermined by the Parliamentarians in 1646.

Bridgnorth's oldest house is Bishop Percy's House, an attractive timbered building of 1580 and the birthplace in 1729 of Thomas Percy, who became Bishop of Dromore. The house stands on Cartway, which leads down from the High Street to the river and has caves along its sides cut into the sandstone cliff. The caves were used as dwellings until Victorian times.

St Mary Magdalene's Church was built in 1792 to the design of the engineer Thomas Telford (1757-1834), better known for his bridges, roads and canals.

There are several flights of stone steps linking High Town and Low Town, and also a cliff railway which has a gradient of 2 in 3. Bridgnorth is the headquarters of the Severn Valley Railway, which runs steam trains to Bewdley daily during the summer.

Information Tel. 3358.
Location On the A442, 14 m. SW of Wolverhampton.
Parking Innage Lane; Whitburn Street; Severn Street; Listley Street (2) (all car parks).
District council Bridgnorth (Tel. 5131).
Population 11,000.
E-C Thur. **M-D** Sat.
Police Wenlock Road (Tel. 2246).
Casualty hospital Northgate (Tel. 2641).
Post office West Castle Street.
Cinema Majestic Screen 1 & 2, Whitburn Street (Tel. 61815).
Public library Listley Street.
Places to see Castle; New Road; Town Hall, High Street; Bishop Percy's House, Cartway; Severn Valley Railway, Hollybush Road.
AA 24 hour service
Tel. Stoke-on-Trent 25881.

Bridgwater Somerset

A quiet quay on the River Parrett serves as a reminder that this town was a busy port until it became overshadowed by the port of Bristol. Modern shops now line the quay, and it is no longer used by any ships.

On the waterfront the Water Gate is all that remains of a 13th-century castle, destroyed along with much of the town by Cromwell's army during the Civil War (1642-9). Ironically, Bridgwater gave Cromwell his great admiral, Robert Blake (1599-1657). Blake's reputed birthplace is now a museum.

The 14th-century Church of St Mary also survived the Civil War, and from its tower the rebel Duke of Monmouth surveyed Sedgemoor in 1685 before his defeat by the Royalists. The church has a 175 ft spire and a fine Jacobean wooden screen.

Castle Street, built by the Duke of Chandos in about 1720, has some good Georgian architecture, and The Lions on West Quay is an outstanding house of that period.

The four-day St Matthew's Fair in September and the Guy Fawkes Carnival are big events in Bridgwater.

Information Tel. 424391.
Location On the A38, 9 m. NE of Taunton.
Parking Mount Street; Clare Street; Rope Walk; Dampiet Street; Barclay Street; Northgate; Market Street; Watsons Lane; Broadway (cps).
District council Sedgemoor (Tel. 424391).
Population 26,100.
E-C Thur. **M-D** Wed.
Police Northgate (Tel. 58161).
Casualty hospital Taunton and Somerset District, East Reach (Tel. 73444).
Post office Cornhill.
Theatres Bridgwater Arts Centre, Castle Street (Tel. 422700); Town Hall, High Street (424391).
Cinemas Classic, Penel Orlieu (Tel. 422383); Palace, Penel Orlieu (422368).
Public library Binford Place.
Places to see Admiral Blake Museum, Blake Street.
Town trails Included in Bridgwater Town Guide, on sale at Public Library and newsagents.
Shopping Eastover; Fore Street; High Street; St John's Street.
Trade and industry Footwear; packaging materials; shirts.
AA 24 hour service
Tel. Bristol 298531.

Bridlington Humberside

This lively seaside resort, with a busy harbour, is built round an old town.

Flat, sandy beaches stretch for miles on each side of the harbour, from which cobles – open-decked fishing-boats – run fishing trips.

The Priory Church has the remains of a 14th-century nave. The priory gatehouse also survives and is now the Bayle Museum, displaying weapons, jewellery, dolls' furniture and maps.

Sewerby Hall, a Georgian mansion owned by the borough, houses an art gallery and museum that contains relics of the record-breaking woman pilot Amy Johnson (1903-41). The hall stands in 50 acres of parkland which contain a zoo.

Information Tel. 73474 and 79626 (Easter to Oct.); 78255 (Oct. to Easter).
Location On the A165, 30 m. N of Hull.
Parking Alexandra Drive; The Promenade; Prospect Street; Limekiln Lane; Station Approach; South Cliff Road; Belvedere Road (all car parks).
District council Borough of East Yorkshire (Tel. 79151).
Population 29,300.
E-C Thur. **M-D** Wed., Sat.
Police Ashville Street (Tel. 72222).
Casualty hospital Quay Road (Tel. 73451).
Post office Quay Road.
Theatres 3B's, Promenade (Tel. 72634); Spa Theatre, Spa Royal Hall, Spa Promenade (78258).
Cinema Winter Gardens, Promenade (Tel. 73012).
Public library King Street.
Places to see Priory Church; Bayle Gate Museum; Art Gallery and

Museum, Sewerby Hall.
Town trails Available from Tourist Information Office, Garrison Street.
Shopping The Promenade; King Street; Quay Road; Chapel Street.
AA 24 hour service Tel. Hull 28580.

Bridport Dorset

Rope and nets of all kinds have been made at Bridport for nearly 1,000 years. In the past the bulk of the rope output was for the rigging of sailing ships. But ropes for gallows were also made there, and the hangman's noose was nicknamed the "Bridport dagger". The town is still the biggest net-making centre in Europe.

The long gardens at the rear of the houses were used as rope-walks, places where the flax strands were laid out and twisted into shape.

Information Tel. 24901 (summer); Dorchester 67992 (winter).
Location On the A35, 15 m. W of Dorchester.
Parking South Street; East Street; West Street; Rope Walk; Rax Lane (all car parks); South Street.
District council West Dorset (Tel. Dorchester 5211).
Population 6,900.
E-C Thur. **M-D** Wed., Sat.
Police St Andrew's Road (Tel. 22266).
Casualty hospital Melcombe Avenue, Weymouth (Tel. Weymouth 72211).
Post office West Street.
Cinema Palace, South Street (Tel. 22167).
Public library East Street.
Places to see Museum and Art Gallery, South Street.
Shopping East Street; West Street; South Street.
AA 24 hour service Tel. Yeovil 27744.

Brighouse W. Yorks.

In the early 18th century Brighouse was one of several small woollen textile communities in the Calder Valley. When the Calder and Hebble Canal was cut in 1759, Brighouse became a canal "port" and the focal point of the district. By the 19th century not only wool, but cotton and silk were spun at Brighouse.

Information Tel. 71457.
Location On the A629, 4 m. SE of Halifax.
Parking Park Street; Bethel Street; Mill Royd Street; Mill Lane; Briggate; Churchfields Road; Dale Street; Bank Street; Bethel Church (cps).
District council Metropolitan Borough of Calderdale (Tel. Halifax 65701).
Population 35,200.
E-C Tues. **M-D** Wed., Sat.
Police Bradford Road (Tel. 714492).
Casualty hospital Free School Lane, Halifax (Tel. Halifax 57222).
Post office Park Street.
Public library Halifax Road.

Places to see Smith Art Gallery, Halifax Road.
Shopping Commercial Street; Bethel Street; King Street; Bradford Road; Wellington Arcade.
Trade and industry Textiles; clothing manufacture; engineering.
AA 24 hour service Tel. Bradford 724703.

Brighton see page 60

Bristol see page 62

Broadstairs Kent

A Victorian charm that dates from its development as a seaside resort still lingers at Broadstairs. It has strong associations with Charles Dickens who worked on some of his most famous novels there. The clifftop mansion, Bleak House, where he wrote much of *David Copperfield*, and the seafront house that is the original of Betsey Trotwood's home in that novel, are now Dickens museums. In June, during the week-long Dickens Festival, townspeople in costume bring the novelist's most famous characters to life in processions through the narrow streets.

A lighthouse on the North Foreland, built in 1683 but with modern additions, is the most recent of a series of beacons that have guided shipping since Roman times.

Information Tel. Thanet 68399.
Location On the A255, 2 m. N of Ramsgate.
Parking High Street; Albion Street; St Peter's Park Road; Harbour Street; Vere Road (all car parks).
District council Thanet (Tel. Thanet 25511).
Population 23,400.
E-C Wed.
Police (Aa) Gladstone Road (Tel. Thanet 25566).
Casualty hospital Kent and Canterbury Hospital, Ethelbert Road, Canterbury (Tel. Canterbury 66877).
Post office (Aa) High Street.
Theatre The Pavilion on the Sands **(Ba)** (Tel. Thanet 64682).
Public library (Aa) High Street.
Places to see Bleak House **(Ba)**, Fort Road; Dickens House Museum **(Ba)**, Victoria Parade; North Foreland Lighthouse.
Shopping High Street; The Broadway; Albion Street; York Street.
AA 24 hour service Tel. Thanet 81226.

Bromley see London

BROADSTAIRS *Viking Bay is sheltered by the curving arm of its 16th-century pier. Above stands the fort-like Bleak House where Charles Dickens stayed while writing David Copperfield.*

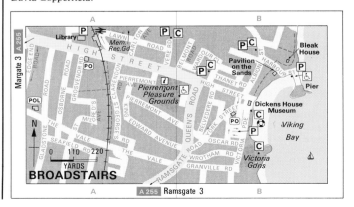

BRIGHTON E. Sussex

The town a doctor prescribed for a prince

"Doctor Brighton", "London-by-the-sea", England's most fashionable resort has had many nicknames during its 200 years history. Princes, politicians and playboys have patronised it, landladies and lovers have immortalised it – and Brighton embraces them all in a unique blend of outrageous architecture, quaint streets and ultra-modern entertainment centres.

ROYAL PAVILION *Brighton's Oriental extravaganza was built in 1787 and 1815 for the Prince Regent.*

One man started it all – Dr Richard Russell, a resident of nearby Lewes. In 1750 he published a book extolling the beneficial effects of the sea air and bathing at Brighthelmstone, as the village was then called. When the Prince of Wales and his circle decided to sample these in 1783, the reputation of the resort was made.

Brighton's outstanding landmark, the **Royal Pavilion**, was built for the Prince of Wales by Henry Holland in 1787. Holland reconstructed the original seaside villa as a classical building with a rotunda and dome. In 1815, by which time the Prince of Wales had become Regent, John Nash, architect of Regent's Park in London, added a larger onion-shaped dome, tent-like roofs, pinnacles and minarets, in the style of an Indian mogul's palace. The Chinese interior is lavishly decorated; the banqueting hall, for example, has a be-dragoned chandelier hanging from a ceiling moulded like the fronds of a palm tree.

PALACE PIER *Brighton has two piers – the West Pier, opened in 1866, and the Palace Pier, which was completed 33 years later. West Pier is no longer open to the public, but Palace Pier offers a wide range of amusements.*

Gold and silver

The splendid furnishings can be seen throughout the year, and each summer there is a special Regency Exhibition. The banqueting table is set with silver, gold plate, glass and porcelain of the period, and the music-room, with its elegant furniture and Aubusson carpet, is prepared as for a chamber concert.

The town displays other evidence of its hey-day at this period in its many outstanding examples of Regency architecture: **Royal Crescent**, built in 1799; **Regency Square**, laid out in 1818; and **Clifton Terrace**, not constructed until 1850 but elegantly Regency in style.

The oldest quarter is **The Lanes**; narrow, twisting, brick-paved passages lined by 17th-century fishermen's cottages that are now mostly antique shops. In the centre is Brighton Square, with its pavement cafe.

Brighton has 3 miles of seafront, from which hotels and terraced boarding houses look down on shingle beaches, three outdoor and two indoor swimming-pools and children's boating and paddling-pools. Swimming is safe from the foreshore in all but rough weather.

The marina, the largest in Europe, covers 126 acres, 35 of them artificially created land. It provides moorings for more than 2,000 boats and incorporates a yacht club and sports centre. It contrasts strikingly with the old **Palace Pier**, opened in 1901, which offers cockles and whelks, "what-the-butler-saw" machines and other amusements of a bygone age.

Entertainment at the resort caters for practically every taste. **The Dome** – an Indian-style building opposite the Royal Pavilion and once George IV's stables – puts on orchestral, pop and military-band concerts, variety shows and wrestling. The Riding School near by is now the Corn Exchange. The **Theatre Royal**, established in 1807, presents high-quality productions, many of which later go on to London's West End.

High life

Further entertainment is provided by cinemas, discotheques, ballrooms, cabarets and other night spots. On the outskirts of Brighton, the **Gardner Arts Centre**, part of Sussex University campus, presents drama, opera, dance and music.

In spring, the Brighton Festival is a spectacular showcase for the arts, at which world-famous musicians, singers, actors and dancers perform. On a less exalted level, there is also a seafront art exhibition in summer.

Amusements for children abound. The 1½ mile long **Volks Railway** provides a ride along the seafront from Palace Pier to Black Rock. Opened in 1883, it was Britain's first public electric transport. One of its stops is at **Peter Pan's Playground**, which has talent shows as well as the usual children's swings and roundabouts.

Preston Manor, a 13th-century house rebuilt in 1738 and set among magnificent rose gardens and lily ponds, is permanently laid out with its 18th-century furnishings, including rare silver and porcelain.

Housed in what were originally stables for the Royal Pavilion, **Brighton Museum and Art Gallery** includes Flemish, Dutch and English Old Master paintings, furniture, glass, bronze, pottery, old musical instruments, and collections devoted to Sussex life through the ages.

A museum of a different kind is the **Booth Museum of Natural History**, which contains among other collections most species of birds found in the British Isles, displayed in model panoramas of their natural habitats. The gallery of animal skeletons includes those of rare and extinct species. There is also a collection of nearly 1 million butterflies.

Brighton Aquarium and Dolphinarium was established in 1872. It has daily dolphin shows in summer, and displays a large variety of marine, tropical and freshwater fish.

The town has two churches of interest. **St Peter's** parish church, a much-pinnacled piece of Gothic Revival, was built between 1824 and 1828 by Sir Charles Barry, architect of the Houses of Parliament. **St Nicholas's Church** dates from the 14th century and contains a splendidly carved Norman font and interesting monuments and tombs. Among those buried in the churchyard is

Martha Gunn, "queen" of the dippers – the attendants who looked after women bathers in the 18th century. Also buried there is Captain Nicholas Tattersell, who took Charles II to safety in France after the Battle of Worcester in 1651.

Sussex University, set in the 200 acres of Stanmer Park on the outskirts of the town, is a cluster of striking red-brick and concrete buildings designed by Sir Basil Spence, architect of Coventry Cathedral, and opened in the early 1960s.

The town is a major centre for conferences and exhibitions. These are held at a 5,000-seat multi-purpose complex that is the largest in Britain, and also at the Dome, Corn Exchange, Metropole Exhibition Centre and Royal Pavilion.

The town is the finishing point for several well-known events, including the RAC Veteran Car Run that starts from Hyde Park in London on the first Sunday in November. It commemorates the "Emancipation Run" of 1896, when the speed limit was raised to 14 mph. Only vehicles built before 1904 can take part, and some competitors wear period costume, as befits the occasion. Somewhat faster machinery can be seen each September at the Speed Trials, when racing and sports-cars race in pairs along Madeira Drive.

Other events include the Stock Exchange Walk in May and the Historic Motor Cycle Run in March.

Horse racing is provided at Brighton Racecourse, which has several meetings between April and October. The track featured dramatically in Graham Greene's thriller *Brighton Rock*.

REGENCY SQUARE *Elegant balconies, bow windows and railings grace this fine example of Regency architecture.*

Information Tel. 23755 and (summer only) 26450.
Location On the A23, 53 m. S of London.
Parking Regency Square; North Road; Church Street; Regency Road (2); New England Street (3); Belmont Street; St Peter's Street; Blackman Street; Whitecross Street/Market Street; Redcross Street; Pelham Street; Kingswood Street; John Street; High Street; St James's Street; Dyke Road; Churchill Square; St Mark's Place; Cannon Place; Ship Street; Black Lion Street (all car parks).
District council Borough of Brighton (Tel. 29801).
Population 146,100; total with Hove 212,700.
E-C Wed. in St James's Street area; Thur. in London Road and Western Road areas. **M-D** Sat. (antiques).
Police (Cb) John Street (Tel. 606744).
Casualty hospital Royal Sussex County Hospital, Eastern Road (Tel. 606611).
Post office (Ba) Ship Street.
Theatres Theatre Royal **(Bb)**, New Road (Tel. 28488); Gardner Centre, University of Sussex, Lewes Road (685861).
Cinemas ABC Film Centre **(Ba)** (Tel. 27010); Cinescene (738059); Continentale (681348); Duke of York's (602503); Odeon Film Centre **(Ba)** (23317).
Public library Church Street.
Places to see Aquarium and Dolphinarium **(Ca)**, Marine Parade; Booth Museum of Natural History, Dyke Road; Museum and Art Gallery **(Bb)**, Church Street; Palace Pier; Preston Park Engineerium, The Droveway; Royal Pavilion **(Ba)**, Church Street; Volks Railway, Madeira Drive; The Lanes.
Shopping Churchill Square; London Road; Western Road; North Street; East Street; The Lanes. Hove: Blatchington Road; George Street.
Events Historic Motor Cycle Run (Mar.); Historic Commercial Vehicles Run (May); Arts Festival (spring); Veteran Car Run (Nov.); Brighton Marina Regatta (Aug.).
Trade and industry Tourism; conference and exhibition trade; manufacture of polishes, perfume, typewriters, sponges, electrical equipment.
Sport FA League football, Brighton and Hove Albion FC, Old Shoreham Road; Sussex County Cricket Club, Eaton Road; Horse racing, Elm Grove.
AA 24 hour service Tel. 695231.

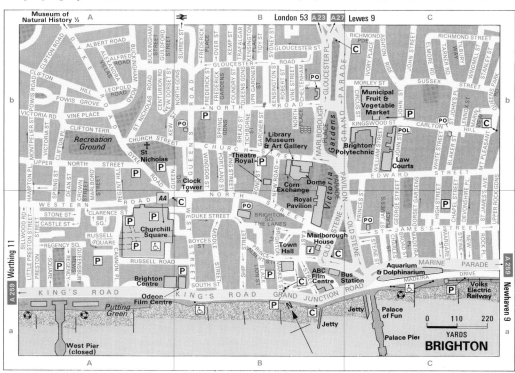

BRISTOL Avon

England's gateway to the New World

Birthplace of America, because discoverers and thousands of early settlers sailed from it . . . city of churches, because it contains so many splendid old places of worship . . . city of flowers, because colourful, massed displays beautify so many of its aspects – Bristol is all these, but, above all, it is a city of contrasts: side by side with modern shopping, office and entertainment complexes and multi-storey car parks stand old docks, almshouses and inns steeped in history.

Bristol was originally known as *Bricgstoc* (the place of the bridge). Permanent settlement probably began in Anglo-Saxon times. Unearthed coins show that by the reign of Ethelred the Unready (978-1013) Bristol had its own mint.

The settlement grew up around its harbour on the River Avon, and its importance as a port increased after the Norman Conquest. A castle was built on the narrow neck of land east of the town, between the rivers Avon and Frome, and it became the Key to the West.

The trade of Bristowe (as it became known in the Middle Ages) increased rapidly during the 12th and 13th centuries, and as a result its area doubled and its wharfage increased. During the 14th century it became a major wool-exporting port, sending cargoes to Ireland and the Baltic countries.

Mythical lands

In the late 15th century, Bristol's sailors brought home stories from Iceland of mythical lands to the west which had been discovered 500 years before by Leif Ericson; stories of Helluland, Markland and Wineland the Good, richly endowed tracts of what is now North America.

Stimulated by these tales, and driven by the economic need for new markets and fishing grounds, Bristol's merchants dispatched ships in search of them. The most renowned voyager, John Cabot, set sail in 1497 with his son Sebastian in the *Mathew*.

He landed on the North American coast near modern Newfoundland, believing it at first to be Asia. His achievement is commemorated by the 150 ft **Cabot Tower** on Brandon Hill, erected 400 years later.

In 1552 the Society of Merchant Venturers was founded, to exploit Cabot's discovery and extend trade to other parts of the world. The port flourished, shipping wool and leather and importing wines, tobacco and cocoa beans – commodities that led to the setting up of some of Bristol's major manufacturing industries.

Less happily, during the 17th century the city also prospered on the slave trade; the abolition of this in the 19th century was a serious setback to the port, particularly as Liverpool was beginning to offer strong trading competition.

An opportunity for Bristol to develop as a transatlantic port came with the launching of Isambard Kingdom Brunel's steamships *Great Western* in 1837 and *Great Britain* in 1843. Both ships were built at Bristol, but later were forced to ply from Liverpool because of the high dock charges imposed by the Bristol Docks Committee.

The *Great Britain* was the first screw-propelled passenger ship to

enter the Atlantic service, and sailed until 1886 when she was abandoned as a hulk in the Falkland Islands. In 1970 the ship was brought back to Bristol on a specially constructed raft, and is now being restored to her original condition in the dock where she was built.

Gothic station

Brunel had a long association with Bristol. In 1830 he redesigned the docks, and in 1841 completed the Great Western Railway's line from London. He also designed Temple Meads Station, whose Gothic-style frontage still stands.

In 1836, Brunel was commissioned to build a suspension bridge to span the **Avon Gorge** at Clifton. Only the

BARGAIN COUNTER *The nails in Corn Street were used by merchants when striking a bargain. The money was paid on the nail head.*

CHRISTMAS STEPS *Completed in 1669, the ancient thoroughfare is lined with antique shops and bookshops. At the top is the tiny 15th-century Chapel of the Three Kings of Cologne, which is only 18 ft by 22 ft.*

CLIFTON SUSPENSION BRIDGE *Delicately spanning the rocky, wooded, 250 ft deep Avon Gorge like a spider's web, the bridge was designed by the engineering genius Isambard Kingdom Brunel and completed in 1864. It incorporates 1,500 tons of steel.*

buildings that had survived the war.

Bristol's churches range from the graceful **St Mary Redcliffe** to the humble Wesley's Chapel. St Mary's was built in the 13th to 15th centuries and has a 285 ft spire. The interior contains magnificent roof bosses and much stained glass. **Wesley's Chapel**, dating from 1739, was built by John Wesley (1703-91), the founder of Methodism. It is the oldest Methodist chapel in the world.

Bristol Cathedral, which stands on College Green, was founded in the 1140s as the church of an Augustinian abbey, and became a cathedral in 1542. The Norman chapter house, the finest in England, the great gatehouse, the entrance to the abbot's lodging, the walls of the south transept and the east walk of the cloister all survive from the original 12th-century building.

The carving of the Elder Lady Chapel is comparable to that in Wells Cathedral, and the 14th-century choir with its aisles of equal height and lack of flying buttresses is unique in this country. A nave to match this choir was built in the 19th century.

Crusoe connection

The cathedral contains fine 16th-century misericords (the hinged seats in the choir stalls) and many fascinating tombs and monuments. Some candlesticks of 1712 are thanksgiving gifts from the privateers who rescued Alexander Selkirk from a desert island in 1709. Selkirk was the man on whom Daniel Defoe based the character of Robinson Crusoe.

Other churches of note are **Christ Church**, with its wooden figures that strike bells at each quarter of the hour; the 14th-century **St John the Baptist's**, built above a medieval vaulted gateway; and the ruined Perpendicular **Temple Church**, which has a leaning tower.

The Norman **Church of St Nicholas** is now a museum and contains church vestments, plate and an altar-piece by Hogarth taken from St Mary Redcliffe.

The **City Museum and Art Gallery** stand next to Bristol University. The museum has local archaeological and geological relics, and the art gallery displays paintings by Sir Thomas Lawrence – a Bristol man – and collections of ceramics and glass.

Blaise Castle House Museum is an 18th-century mansion containing an

abutments were built before work stopped through lack of funds, but in 1864, five years after Brunel's death, the Institute of Civil Engineers finished the **Clifton Suspension Bridge** as a tribute to their former colleague.

Close to the suspension bridge, on the Clifton side, is **The Observatory**. Once a snuff-mill, it now contains a camera obscura which gives panoramic views of the city. A passageway beneath the observatory leads to the **Giant's Cave**, which opens out on to a ledge on the side of the gorge high above the river. The gorge is limestone, and is about 250 ft deep with rocky outcrops.

Bristol Zoo, on Clifton Down, has a notable collection of rare animals, including the only white tigers in Europe.

Clifton is a residential suburb of Bristol, spreading across the Downs above the city and known for its

Regency crescents and Georgian terraces. **Royal York Crescent**, overlooking the gorge, is claimed to be the longest in Europe.

During the Second World War, Bristol suffered extensive bomb damage and lost many old churches and historic buildings. From these ruins soaring new structures of glass and concrete rose to mingle with the old

---

BRISTOL-BUILT SUPERPLANE

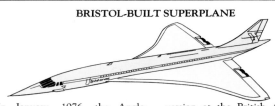

In January, 1976, the Anglo-French Concorde became the first supersonic passenger aircraft to enter regular commercial service. The plane, assembled in its British version at the British Aerospace (BAC) works at Filton, Bristol, cruises at 1,320 mph – nearly one-and-three-quarters the speed at which sound travels.

exhibition of West Country life; it takes its name from a Gothic castle of the same period in the grounds, where there are also a water-mill, thatched dairy and the remains of an Iron Age hill-fort.

On display at **Kings Weston Roman Villa**, in Long Cross, are the mosaics, bath suite and foundations of a Roman country house of the 3rd and 4th centuries AD.

Bristol University was opened in 1925. Its 215 ft tower, an almost exact replica of the "Boston Stump" at Boston, Lincolnshire, is a city landmark.

Paying on the nail

In the old part of Bristol stands the **Exchange**, built by John Wood of Bath in the 18th century. Outside, on the pavement, are the "nails", four bronze pillars on which merchants completed their money transactions – which gave rise to the saying "to pay on the nail". The nearby **Guildhall** was erected in 1843 and stands on the site of the original medieval building.

One of Bristol's oldest streets is King Street, a cobbled thoroughfare with many old houses and Britain's

GEORGIAN ELEGANCE *These fine houses in Sion Hill, Clifton, line the Avon Gorge, looking out over the suspension bridge. They were built in the years after 1780 when Clifton was developed as a residential suburb.*

oldest working theatre, the **Theatre Royal**, opened in 1766. It is the home of the Bristol Old Vic, and now incorporates the adjacent Cooper's Hall.

Another old thoroughfare, Christmas Steps, rebuilt in 1669, is where a number of antique dealers and booksellers trade.

The **Llandoger Trow** (1664), an old inn in King Street, was once the drinking den of pirates and is believed to be the original of Long John

Silver's haunt "The Spy Glass" in Robert Louis Stevenson's *Treasure Island*.

Several old houses in Bristol are open to the public: the 16th-century **Red Lodge**, which was altered in the 18th century and has carvings and furnishings from both periods; **Chatterton House**, the birthplace of the poet Thomas Chatterton (1752-70); and the **Georgian House**, with 18th-century furniture and fittings.

The whole of Bristol celebrated when the Great Britain *was launched by Prince Albert in July 1843. It is now back in the city where it was made.*

Great Britain's *ornate prow.*

When Isambard Kingdom Brunel's *Great Britain* was launched in 1843 the 322 ft long ship was the largest in the world. The use of iron for the hull and a screw propeller for the drive had previously been tried only on much smaller vessels. The ocean-going career of the *Great Britain* lasted until 1886, when she was abandoned in the Falkland Islands after being almost wrecked in a storm.

BRISTOL'S SHAME *A negro servant's tombstone recalls that Bristol once prospered from the slave trade.*

The administrative centre of Bristol is the **Council House** which was opened in 1956. Built in Georgian style, it curves around one side of College Green and terminates in two pavilion entrances – each topped by a golden unicorn representing those that support the City Arms. In the centre arch stands the symbolic figure of an Elizabethan seaman, looking towards the old City of Bristol and the harbour beyond.

Information Tel. 293891.
Location On the A4, 13 m. NW of Bath.
Parking Bond Street; Park Row; Victoria Street; Prince Street; Redcliffe Way; Nelson Street; Fairfax Street; Rupert Street (all car parks); Anchor Road; Dale Street, off Wellington Road; Berkeley Place; Penn Street; Queen Charlotte Street.
District council City of Bristol (Tel. 26031).
Population 388,000.
E-C Wed., Sat. **M-D** Mon. to Sat.
Police (Cc) Bridewell (Tel. 22022).
Casualty hospital (Cc) Bristol Royal Infirmary, Marlborough Street (Tel. 22041).
Post office (Cb) Small Street.
Theatres Little Theatre **(Bb)**, Colston Street (Tel. 291182); Theatre Royal and New Vic **(Cb)**, King Street (24388); Hippodrome **(Bb)**, St Augustine's Parade (299444).
Cinemas ABC **(Bb)**, New Bristol Centre, Frogmore Street (Tel. 22848); Europa Cinemas **(Dc)**, Lower Castle Street (291810); Odeon Film Centre **(Cc)**, Union Street (276141); Studios 1, 2, 3 and 4 **(Cc)**,

All Saints Street (25069).
Public library (Bb) College Green.
Places to see Cabot Tower **(Ab)**, Brandon Hill; City Museum and Art Gallery **(Ac)**, Queen's Road; Georgian House **(Bb)**, Great George Street; Red Lodge **(Bb)**, Park Row; SS *Great Britain* **(Aa)**, Gasferry Road; St Nicholas Church and City Museum **(Cb)**, St Nicholas Street; Zoological Gardens, Clifton Down; Kings Weston Roman Villa (key obtainable from Blaise Castle House); Blaise Castle House Museum, Henbury; Bristol Industrial Museum, Princes Wharf; Cathedral **(Bb)**; Wesley's Chapel **(Cc)**.
Shopping Broadmead; Union Street; Fairfax Street; The Horsefair; The Haymarket; Queen's Road; Park Street.
Trade and industry Aerospace engineering; tobacco; printing; food-processing.
Sport FA League football: Bristol City FC and Bristol Rovers FC, Ashton Gate; Greyhound racing, Bristol Stadium, Eastville.
Motorail Temple Meads Station.
AA 24 hour service
Tel. Bristol 298531.

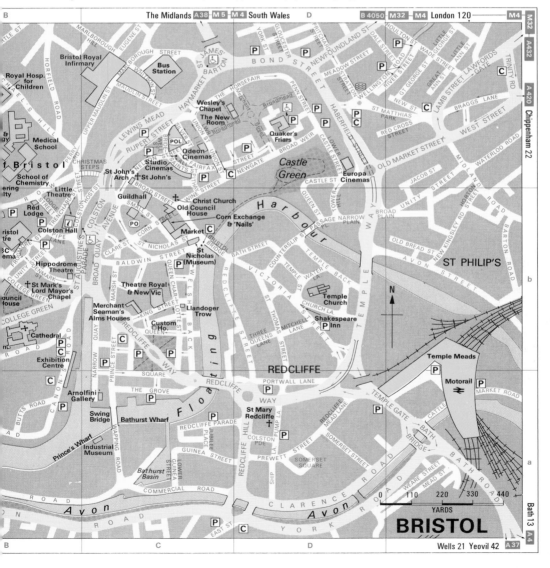

Bromsgrove H. & W.

When nails were made by hand, Bromsgrove was the nail-making capital of the world. But when machines took over in the 19th century, the trade declined. The town was also – and still is – the market for the fruit farms and market gardens of the surrounding countryside. The 14th-century Church of St John the Baptist has fine medieval and Tudor tombs of the Talbot and Stafford families. In the tower is a carillon which plays a different tune every day of the week. The Avoncroft Museum of Buildings was founded when Bromsgrove's oldest building – a 15th-century house – was threatened with demolition in 1962. It was dismantled and reassembled at the museum, where many other ancient buildings have since been brought for preservation.

HOW OUR ANCESTORS LIVED *The open-air Avoncroft Museum of Buildings includes replicas of Iron Age huts.*

Information Tel. 31809.
Location On the A38, 14 m. SW of Birmingham.
Parking Churchfields; Recreation Road; Parkside; Windsor Street; Stourbridge Road; School Drive; Hanover Street; St John's Street (all car parks).
District council Bromsgrove (Tel. 72337).
Population 43,700.
E-C Thur. **M-D** Tues., Fri. and Sat.
Police The Crescent (Tel. 71611).
Casualty hospital The Cottage Hospital, New Road (Tel. 73351).
Post office High Street.
Public library Stratford Road.
Places to see Avoncroft Museum of Buildings; Norton Museum, Birmingham Road.
Trade and industry Agriculture; light industry; drop-forging; car-making.
AA 24 hour service
Tel. Birmingham (021) 550 4858.

Buckhaven & Methil
Fife

The growing importance of coal in the 19th century turned Buckhaven and Methil, then separate seaside villages, into mining towns. They were united in 1891.

Methil's 17th-century harbour grew into Scotland's major coal port; but the coal dock was closed in 1977.

Information Tel. Kirkcaldy 261144.
Location On the A955, 10 m. NE of Kirkcaldy.
Parking Wellesley Road; Birch Grove; Byron Street; College Street; East High Street; Kirkland Walk;

Logie Street; Methil Brae; Ossian Crescent.
District council Kirkcaldy (Tel. Kirkcaldy 261144).
Population 17,700.
E-C Thur.
Police Sea Road (Tel. 712881).
Casualty hospital Victoria, Hayfield Road, Kirkcaldy (Tel. Kirkcaldy 261155).
Post office Wellesley Road.
Public library Wellesley Road.
Shopping College Street; Wellesley Road; Randolph Street.
AA 24 hour service
Tel. Dundee 25585.

Buckingham Bucks.

Alfred the Great made Buckingham the shire town in 886. So it remained until 1725, when a great fire destroyed much of the town and the county government was transferred to Aylesbury. However, set in a loop of the River Ouse and surrounded by rich farmland, Buckingham is still a market and business centre.

Reconstruction after the fire of 1725 gave the town a predominantly Georgian face, though some earlier buildings survive. Among them is a 13th-century chantry chapel, rebuilt in 1475 as the Royal Latin School. Dominating Market Hill is the castle-like Old Gaol, built in 1748.

Information Tel. 2295.
Location On the A422, 11 m. W of Bletchley.
Parking Bridge Street.
District council Aylesbury Vale (Tel. Aylesbury 5900).
Population 6,630.
E-C Thur. **M-D** Tues., Sat.
Police Moreton Road (Tel. 2222).
Casualty hospital Buckingham Hospital, High Street (Tel. 3243).
Post office High Street.
Cinema Chandos, Chandos Road (Tel. 3196).
Public library Verney Close.
Shopping High Street; Market Square.
Trade and industry Motor accessories; carpets; light engineering.
AA 24 hour service
Tel. Oxford 40286.

Bude Cornwall

Sir John Betjeman, the Poet Laureate, described Bude as the "least rowdy" resort in the county. It overlooks hard, golden sands and is flanked by spectacular cliffs. In the 19th century the town was notorious for its wreckers, who plundered the ships that came to grief off the coast – more than 80 between 1824 and 1874.

Its Atlantic-pounded beaches make it a surfers' paradise, and Australians have called it the "Bondi of Britain".

The town developed when a canal was built in 1819-23 for carrying fertiliser inland and for exporting local produce. The canal is now used for pleasure-boating and fishing.

Bude Castle, a castellated stone mansion that houses council offices, was built about 1830 by the inventor Sir Goldsworthy Gurney, the first man to make a long journey in a mechanical vehicle – a steam carriage – from London to Bath and back.

At Bude's twin town of Stratton, which probably dates from Roman times, steep streets of Georgian and earlier houses climb to St Andrew's Church, built in 1348. The Tree Inn was the home of the 17th-century "Cornish Giant" Anthony Payne, 7 ft 4 in. tall. He was a retainer of the Royalist leader Sir Bevil Grenville, who won a Civil War battle at nearby Stamford Hill in 1643.

Information Tel. 4240 (summer); 3576 (winter).
Location On the A39, 27 m. SW of Bideford.
Parking The Crescent; The Wharf; Crooklets Beach; Summerleaze Beach; Howell's Bridge, Stratton (all car parks).
District council North Cornwall (Tel. Bodmin 4471).
Population 6,780.
E-C Thur.
Police Lansdown Close (Tel. 2131).
Casualty hospital Stratton Cottage Hospital, Hospital Road, Stratton (Tel. Bude 2161).
Post office Belle Vue.
Cinema Headland Leisure Centre, Crooklets Road (Tel. 2016).
Public library The Castle.
Places to see Ebbingford Manor; Bude Historical and Folk Exhibition, The Wharf; Militaria Museum, The Wharf.
Shopping Princes Street; Lansdown Road; Queen Street; Belle Vue.
AA 24 hour service
Tel. Exeter 32121.

Budleigh Salterton Devon

Little has changed since Budleigh Salterton developed as a resort in the early 19th century. Fishermen's capstans still occupy the same positions on the beach of pearl-grey pebbles; and the sea wall that the Victorian painter Sir John Millais depicted in *The Boyhood of Raleigh* still stands.

Sir Walter Raleigh was born in 1552 at Hayes Barton, a farmhouse 3 miles north of the town, near East Budleigh village. The church there contains a memorial to his family.

The high red cliffs that rise over 400 ft at West Down Beacon afford superlative views – south to Torbay, and inland to Dartmoor and Exmoor.

The Fairlynch Arts Centre and Museum is housed in an 18th-century thatched house that has a smugglers' cave and lookout tower.

Information Tel. 5275.
Location On the A376, 4 m. E of Exmouth.
Parking Station Road; Brook Road; Granary Lane; Fore Street (all car parks).
District council East Devon

BUDLEIGH SALTERTON *A beach of smooth, round pebbles slopes down to the sea at a resort that retains the quiet charm it had in the 19th century.*

(Tel. Sidmouth 6551).
Population 4,440.
E-C Thur.
Police Fore Street (Tel. 2431).
Casualty hospital East Budleigh Road (Tel. 2020).
Post office High Street.
Public library Station Road.
Places to see Fairlynch Arts Centre and Museum.
Shopping High Street; Fore Street.
AA 24 hour service
Tel. Exeter 32121.

Burgess Hill W. Sussex
Apart from the "New Towns", Burgess Hill is the fastest-growing town in south-east England. The brick and tile-making which have flourished since 1714 have been joined by many other industries, and the town is noted as a shopping centre. Nearby Ditchling Beacon is, at 813 ft, one of the highest points on the South Downs and is crowned by Iron Age earthworks.

Information Tel. 41252.
Location On the A273, 9 m. N of Brighton.
Parking Crescent Way; Civic Way; Queen's Crescent; Cyprus Road; Church Road (all car parks).
District council Mid Sussex (Tel. Haywards Heath 58166).
Population 23,500.
E-C Mon., Wed. **M-D** Wed., Sat.
Police The Brow (Tel. 2211).
Casualty hospital Cuckfield Hospital, Ardingly Road, Haywards Heath (Tel. Haywards Heath 50661).
Post office Station Road.
Cinema Orion, Cyprus Road (Tel. 2137).
Public library The Martlets.
Shopping Church Road; Station Road; The Martlets.
AA 24 hour service
Tel. Brighton 695231.

Burnham-on-Crouch
Essex
At the height of the summer sailing season, 2,000 or more yachts and other craft crowd the anchorage at Burnham-on-Crouch. The town, which lies on the north bank of the Crouch 6 miles from the sea, has five yacht clubs and has been described as the Cowes of the East Coast.

The Quay and High Street combine Georgian and Victorian architecture, and there are many typical Essex weather-boarded cottages.

Information Tel. Maldon 54477.
Location On the B1010, 20 m. SE of Chelmsford.
Parking Millfield; The Promenade; Ship Road (all car parks).
District council Maldon (Tel. Maldon 54477).
Population 6,290.
E-C Wed.
Police Station Road (Tel. Maldon 782121).
Casualty hospital Chelmsford and Essex, New London Road, Chelmsford (Tel. Chelmsford 83331).
Post office High Street.
Cinema Rio, High Street (Tel. Maldon 782027).
Public library Station Road.
Trade and industry Boat-building.
AA 24 hour service
Tel. Chelmsford 61711.

Burnham-on-Sea Somerset
The story of modern Burnham began in the early 19th century when its curate built a lighthouse, exacted a toll from passing ships and used the money to sink two wells on the foreshore to make Burnham a spa. Although the waters were unpleasant, and the spa was never prosperous, this laid the foundations of the town as a resort. Burnham's appeal now rests on its 7 miles of sandy beach, with its wooden "lighthouse on legs".

The fine medieval Church of St Andrew has superb carvings by Grinling Gibbons (1648-1720). Sir Christopher Wren designed them for an altar in James II's chapel in Whitehall Palace.

Information Tel. 782377, Ext. 44.
Location On the B3139, 8 m. N of Bridgwater.
Parking Pier Street; Berrow Road; Lynton Road (all car parks).
District council Sedgemoor (Tel. 782377).
Population 14,900.
E-C Wed.

Police Highbridge Road (Tel. 782288).
Casualty hospital Weston General, The Boulevard, Weston-super-Mare (Tel. Weston-super-Mare 25211).
Post office Victoria Street.
Theatre Princess Hall, Princess Street (Tel. 784464).
Cinema Ritz, Victoria Street (Tel. 782871).
Public library Adam Street.
Shopping High Street; Victoria Street.
Event Illuminated Carnival Procession (Nov.).
AA 24 hour service
Tel. Bristol 298531.

ROYAL GIFT *The kneeling angel in St Andrew's Church, Burnham-on-Sea, was the gift of George IV.*

Burnley Lancashire
Heavy industry now dominates what was once the largest cotton-weaving centre in the world. Towneley Hall, a considerably rebuilt 14th-century house situated in a 246 acre park, has period rooms furnished in 17th-century style. Its 18th-century entrance hall is perhaps the finest early-Georgian interior in the country. The Hall is an art gallery and museum.

Information Tel. 25011.
Location On the A56, 22 m. N of Manchester.
Parking Bankhouse Street; Finsley Gate; King Street; Cow Lane; Market; Brown Street; Yorke Street; Centenary Way; Church Street; Hall Street (all car parks).
District council Burnley Borough Council (Tel. 25011).
Population 69,900.
E-C Tues. **M-D** Mon., Wed., Thur. and Sat.
Police Parker Lane (Tel. 25001).
Casualty hospital General Hospital, Casterton Avenue (Tel. 25071).
Post office Hargreaves Street.
Cinemas Studios 1, 2 and 3, Market Square (Tel. 24478); Unit Four, Rosegrove (22876).
Public library Grimshaw Street.
Shopping St James's Street; Market Walk; The Mall; Howe Walk; Fleet Walk; Keirby Walk.
Sport FA League football, Burnley FC, Turf Moor.
AA 24 hour service
Tel. Manchester (061) 485 6299.

Burton upon Trent Staffs.

Benedictine monks discovered that Burton's water was ideal for brewing. The monastery has gone, but Burton is still renowned for its beer.

The Bass Museum in Horninglow Street tells the story of brewing, and its displays include a model of a Victorian brewery. Visitors can book there to tour the modern brewery.

The Church of St Modwen, built in 1726, is dedicated to an Irish princess who preached in the area in the 9th century.

Information Tel. 45369.
Location On the A38, 28 m. SW of Nottingham.
Parking High Street; Station Street; Union Street; Lichfield Street; New Street; Fleet Street; Cross Street; Milton Street (all car parks).
District council East Staffordshire (Tel. 45369).
Population 47,900.
E-C Wed. **M-D** Thur., Sat.
Police Horninglow Street (Tel. 65011).
Casualty hospital Burton District, Belvedere Road (Tel. 66333).
Post office New Street.
Theatre Little Theatre, Guild Street (Tel. 42588).
Cinema Odeon 1, 2 and 3, Guild Street (Tel. 63200).
Public library High Street.
Places to see Bass Museum of Brewing, Horninglow Street.
Shopping Central Precinct; High Street; Bargates.
Trade and industry Brewing; engineering; hosiery.
AA 24 hour service Tel. Stoke-on-Trent 25881.

Bury Greater Manchester

A statue in front of the 19th-century Church of St Mary in the Market Place commemorates Sir Robert Peel (1788-1850), Prime Minister and founder of the modern police force, who was born in Bury. John Kay, who in 1733 patented the flying shuttle which revolutionised the cotton industry, lived at Ramsbottom, 2 miles to the north.

The Transport Museum has a collection of items connected with steam railways. There are Bronze Age relics in the town museum, and paintings by Constable, Turner and Landseer in the art gallery.

The Borough of Bury has been extended to include the towns of Prestwich, which has several 18th and 19th-century merchants' houses, and Radcliffe, where there are the ruins of a fortified house beside the church.

Information
Tel. Manchester (061) 764 6000.
Location On the A56, 9 m. N of Manchester.
Parking Rochdale Road; Bolton Street (2); Cecil Street; Cross Street (2); Lord Street; Parsons Lane; Spring Street; The Rock; Georgiana Street (all car parks).

District council Metropolitan Borough of Bury (Tel. 061 764 6000).
Population 67,500.
E-C Bury, Tues. Prestwich and Radcliffe, Wed. **M-D** Bury, Wed., Fri. and Sat. Radcliffe, Tues., Fri. and Sat.
Police Irwell Street (Tel. 061 764 8111).
Casualty hospital Bury General, Walmersley Road (Tel. 061 764 2444).
Post offices Bury, Crompton Street; Prestwich, Kingswood Road; Radcliffe, Dale Street.
Cinemas Classic 1 & 2, Market Street (Tel. 061 764 4133); Mayfair, Bury Old Road, Whitefield (061 766 2369).
Public library Manchester Road.
Places to see Transport Museum, Castlecroft Road; Art Gallery and Museum, Moss Street; Lancashire Fusiliers Museum, Bolton Road.
Shopping Bury, The Rock; The Precinct; The Market.
Trade and industry Paper; engineering; textiles.
Sport FA League football, Bury FC, Gigg Lane.
AA 24 hour service Tel. Manchester (061) 485 6299.

Bury St Edmunds Suffolk

The ancient market and cathedral town takes its name from the martyred Saxon king, St Edmund, whose bones were brought to the local monastery 33 years after his death at the hands of the Danes in AD 870.

King Canute raised the monastery to the status of an abbey in 1032, and during the Middle Ages it was a shrine and centre of learning, producing illuminated manuscripts which are among the most treasured possessions of museums all over the world. In 1214, King John's barons swore on the high altar to force the king to accept the Magna Carta, an event recalled in the town's ancient motto,

"Shrine of a King, cradle of the Law".

Fire destroyed the abbey in 1465, but it was rebuilt with such splendour that John Leyland, antiquary to Henry VIII, wrote in 1538: "A man who saw the abbey would say verily it were a city; so many gates . . . so many towers and a most stately church." One year later, it was torn apart when Henry VIII ordered the Dissolution of the Monasteries.

The best-preserved remains are two gatehouses, one of the 12th century and the other of the 14th century. Little is left of the great abbey church, and the west front, stripped of its facing, has houses built into it. But the 13th-century Abbot's Bridge still spans the River Lark.

On the edge of the former abbey precincts are two churches, the 15th-century St Mary's, which has a hammer-beam roof decorated with angels, and the slightly later St James's, which has been the cathedral since 1914.

Angel Hill is a spacious square surrounded by fine buildings, among

NORMAN TOWER *The 12th-century bell-tower of Bury St Edmunds Cathedral was originally the main abbey gate.*

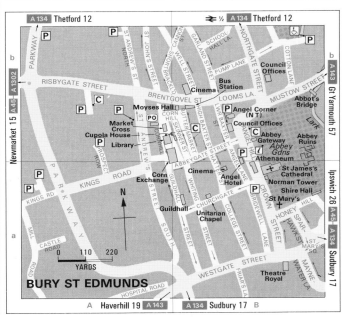

BURY ST EDMUNDS

them the Athenaeum, an 18th-century assembly hall where Charles Dickens gave readings. The novelist stayed at the ivy-clad Angel Hotel in 1859 and 1861. On the north side of the square is Angel Corner, a Queen Anne mansion which contains the Gershom-Parkington collection of clocks and watches, one of the largest in Britain.

Moyses Hall, in the Butter Market, was built in 1180 and is claimed to be the oldest Norman house in East Anglia. It is now a museum, and the exhibits include Bronze Age weapons and a 13th-century monks' chronicle. The 15th-century Guildhall, with its central tower, has a 13th-century gateway.

The building called Market Cross, off Cornhill, was designed by Robert Adam in 1771, and now contains an art gallery.

Information Tel. 63233 or 64667 (summer only).
Location On the A143, 23 m. NW of Ipswich.
Parking St Andrew's Street South; St Andrew's Street North; Ram Meadow, off Cotton Lane; Parkway (all car parks).
District council Borough of St Edmundsbury (Tel. 63233).
Population 28,900.
E-C Thur. **M-D** Wed., Sat.
Police Raingate Street (Tel. 2992).
Casualty hospital West Suffolk Hospital, Hardwick Lane (Tel. 63131).
Post office (Ab) Cornhill.
Theatre Theatre Royal **(Ba)** (Tel. 5469).
Cinemas Studios 1 and 2 **(Ba)** (Tel. 4477); Focus **(Bb)** (4259).
Public library (Ab) Cornhill.
Places to see Abbey ruins **(Bb)** and cathedral **(Ba)**; Gershom-Parkington collection of clocks and watches, Angel Corner **(Bb)**; Market Cross Art Gallery **(Ab)**, off Cornhill; Moyses Hall Museum **(Bb)**, Butter Market; Suffolk Regiment Museum, Outer Risbygate Street.
Town trails Information Office, Abbey Gardens (summer only).
Shopping Cornhill; Abbeygate Street; Butter Market.
AA 24 hour service Tel. Cambridge 312302.

Buxton Derbyshire

Warm mineral-charged springs, bubbling up from between 3,500 ft and 5,000 ft underground, have drawn visitors to Buxton for at least 2,000 years. The Romans knew about them, and the pleasant-tasting water – unusual in a spa – is still drunk and bathed in today.

The springs' medicinal properties were popularised during the late 18th century by the 5th Duke of Devonshire. He built the elegant Doric-style Crescent facing St Ann's Well, and a huge riding school and stables which later became the Devonshire Royal Hospital. Its 156 ft wide dome, added

in 1879, was until recently the widest dome in the world.

Although Buxton is, at 1,000 ft, one of Britain's highest towns, it is sheltered by a ring of even higher hills. On the shoulder of one, Grin Low, stands a late-19th-century folly; a tower built by Solomon Mycock and known as Solomon's Temple. From it, there is a panoramic view of the grey-roofed resort.

The Buxton Museum in Terrace Road houses a collection of Blue John ware made from a rare multi-coloured, translucent stone that used to be mined locally.

Information Tel. 5106.
Location On the A515, 12 m. E of Macclesfield.
Parking Wye Street off Spring Gardens; Burlington Road; Market Place; Market Street (all car parks).
District council High Peak (Tel. 2061).
Population 20,800.
E-C Wed. **M-D** Tues., Sat.
Police Silverlands (Tel. 2811).
Casualty hospitals Buxton Hospital, London Road (Tel. 2293); Stockport Infirmary, Wellington Road South, Stockport (Tel. Manchester (061) 480 7441).
Post office (Bb) The Quadrant.
Theatre Opera House **(Ab)**, The Pavilion Gardens (Tel. 71010).
Cinema Ciné One and Two, Spring Gardens (Tel. 6322).
Public library (Bb) The Crescent.
Places to see The Crescent **(Bb)**; Poole's Cavern; Buxton Museum **(Ba)**, Terrace Road; Micrarium **(Bb)**, St Ann's Well, The Crescent.
Town trails Information Office, The Crescent.
Shopping Spring Gardens; Market Place.
Events Antiques Fair (May); Well-Dressing Carnival (July); Opera Festival (July/Aug.).
AA 24 hour service Tel. 061 485 6299.

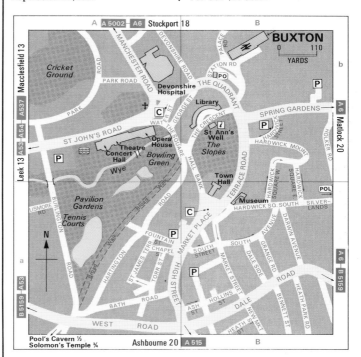

CHALLENGE TO BATH *The Crescent at Buxton was laid out in the 18th century, when the Derbyshire spa tried to rival fashionable Bath.*

C

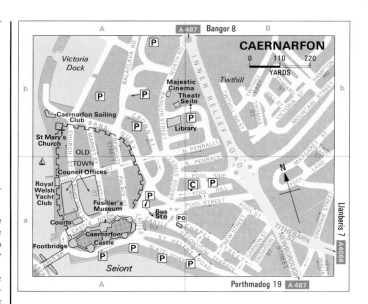

Caerleon Gwent

The Romans laid out a fortress beside the River Usk about AD 74, as the headquarters of the 2nd Augustan Legion. The area it covered is now the centre of Caerleon.

Broadway, which starts opposite the Legionary Museum of Roman relics in the High Street, follows the route of the original Roman road through the fort. At its far end, remnants of the fortress wall and defensive ditch run to right and left. Across the ditch, on the left, there are the remains of an amphitheatre where the Romans watched gladiators fight, and the legionaries trained. It seated 6,000 people, the whole garrison.

Caerleon's position near the border of Wales made it strategically important, and it was fought over by Saxons, Vikings, Normans and Welsh. The Normans built a castle shortly after the Conquest, but all that is left is the mound on which it stood.

According to the 12th-century chronicler Geoffrey of Monmouth, King Arthur had his court at Caerleon. In 1865, Alfred, Lord Tennyson stayed at the 16th-century Hanbury Arms beside the river while working on his Arthurian poem *Idylls of the King*.

Until late in the 19th century, Caerleon was a trading centre through which iron ore and tin were shipped from the area to Bristol.

Information Tel. Cwmbran 67711.
Location On the B4236, 3 m. N of Newport.
Parking Common; Broadway (2); High Street (all car parks).
District council Newport (Tel. Newport 65491).
Population 6,700.
E-C Thur., Sat.
Police Goldcroft Common (Tel. 420222).
Casualty hospital Royal Gwent, Cardiff Road, Newport (Tel. Newport 52244).
Post office High Street.
Public library Cold Bath Road.
Places to see Roman Amphitheatre and Barracks, Broadway; Legionary Museum, High Street; Castle, Castle Street.
Town trails Available from Legionary Museum.
Event Fair (May).
AA 24 hour service Tel. Newport 62559.

Caernarfon Gwynedd

Edward I's impressive castle stands guard over the Menai Strait, with the old town of Caernarfon clustered beneath its ramparts. The 9 ft thick, multi-coloured walls and 150 ft high octagonal towers were built between 1283 and 1330 as the pivotal point from which the English controlled North Wales.

Edward's son, later Edward II, was born in Caernarfon in 1284, and in 1301 he was presented to the Welsh as the first English Prince of Wales. Nearly seven centuries afterwards, in 1969, Prince Charles was invested with the same title at a ceremony in the castle.

The Queen's Tower, named after Eleanor, wife of Edward I, contains the museum of the Royal Welsh Fusiliers Regiment, and the items displayed on its three floors include eight Victoria Crosses and other medals.

The old town shelters behind its own walls, which extend from those of the castle to enclose a maze of narrow streets crowded with ancient houses, shops and inns. The 14th-century Church of St Mary incorporates a corner of the defences.

At Llanbeblig Hill, half a mile south-east of Castle Square beside the A4085 to Beddgelert, are the remains of the Roman fort of Segontium, begun about AD 78. Its museum has a collection of equipment and personal items left by the legionaries. Near by, in South Road, is a second, smaller, fort which superseded the first one towards the end of the Roman occupation. Both were abandoned shortly before the Romans left Britain at the start of the 5th century.

Llanbeblig Church was built in the 13th century opposite the site of the Roman burial ground. It is dedicated to St Peblig, traditionally believed to have been the uncle of the Roman emperor Constantine the Great. The church has a tower with stepped

WALLS OF CAERNARFON *In 1294, the Welsh sacked Edward I's town and castle. The walls were repaired and strengthened the following year. After nearly 700 years they still show a formidable face to the world.*

MAN-MADE LAKE *The waters of the vast moat which surrounds Caerphilly's 13th-century castle are held back by a medieval dam nearly 400 yds long.*

battlements, a fine oak roof and a 16th-century altar tomb.

Twthill, a rocky outcrop half a mile north-east of the old town, offers superb views of Snowdonia, the Menai Strait, Anglesey and the castle. Bronze Age settlers lived behind a wooden stockade which they built on top of the hill.

In 1963 Queen Elizabeth II made Caernarfon a Royal Borough, and since the reorganisation of local government in 1974 it has been a Royal Town. It is the headquarters of two sailing clubs, the Royal Welsh Yacht Club and the Caernarfon Sailing Club. There is sea-fishing in the Menai Strait. Salmon and trout can be caught in the Seiont.

Information Tel. 2232.
Location On the A487, 8 m. SW of Bangor.
Parking Slate Quay; Pool Side; Crown Street; Bangor Street; Pavilion Road; St Helens Road (all car parks).
District council Arfon Borough (Tel. Bangor 2463).
Population 9,500.
E-C Thur. **M-D** Sat.
Police Castle Ditch (Tel. 3333).
Casualty hospital C. & A. Infirmary, Holyhead Road, Bangor (Tel. Bangor 53321).
Post office (Aa) Castle Square.
Theatre Theatre Seilo **(Ab)**, Bangor Street (Tel. 4073).
Cinema Majestic, Bangor Street (Tel. 2516).
Public library Bangor Street.
Places to see Caernarfon Castle **(Aa)**, including Royal Welsh Fusiliers Regimental Museum; Old Town **(Aa)**; Segontium Roman Fort Museum, Llanbeblig Road; Twthill **(Bb)**, open space; Maritime Museum **(Ab)**, Victoria Dock.
Shopping High Street; Bridge Street.
Events Festival Week (July); Menai Strait Regatta (Aug.).
Trade and industry Asbestos fibre goods; engineering.
AA 24 hour service
Tel. Llandudno 79066.

Caerphilly Mid Glamorgan

Until about 1910 Caerphilly was best known for the crumbly cheese which bears its name. The cheese is no longer made locally; most now comes from Somerset.

Caerphilly Castle, which with its moat and outer defences occupies 30 acres in the town centre, is the largest in Wales and, after Windsor, the largest in Britain.

Gilbert de Clare, Earl of Gloucester, started to build the castle in 1268, near the site of a Roman fort. The Welsh under Prince Llywelyn ap Gruffydd destroyed the first foundations in 1270, but the second attempt at construction, begun in 1271, was successful.

In 1646, during the Civil War, the Royalists tried to blow up the castle to stop the Roundheads from using it, and badly damaged one of the round towers. But this still stands, leaning about 12 ft off perpendicular.

Caerphilly, which lies in the coalfield of the Rhymney Valley, was once known as "the Welsh Swindon" because of its large locomotive and carriage workshops, opened in 1902 and closed in 1964.

In the hills around the town, which rise to heights of 800 ft and more, the Welsh defied the Norman invaders for 200 years after 1066. Caerphilly Mountain, 1 mile south on the A469, lies in an area of open countryside which is now a Country Park.

From its summit, there is a commanding view over Cardiff and the Bristol Channel to Somerset and North Devon beyond. A nature trail starts on its slopes, crossing Caerphilly Common on the ridge marking the Rhymney Valley's southern edge.

At Watford, a southern suburb of Caerphilly, a cottage called Waunwaelog stands on the site of the house in which David Williams (1738-1816) was born. Williams, a pamphleteer, founded the Royal Literary Fund to "aid distressed talents".

Information Tel. 863378 (summer): Hengoed 812241 (winter).

Location On the A469, 6 m. N of Cardiff.
Parking Crescent Road; Castle Street; Station Terrace; Bedwas Road (all car parks).
District council Rhymney Valley (Tel. Hengoed 812241).
Population 42,700.
E-C Wed. **M-D** Daily.
Police Park Lane (Tel. 882222).
Casualty hospital Cardiff Royal Infirmary, Newport Road, Cardiff (Tel. Cardiff 492233).
Post office Twyn.
Cinema Castle, Market Street (Tel. 868083).
Public library Morgan Jones Park.
Places to see Caerphilly Castle and Museum.
Shopping Cardiff Road; Piccadilly Square; Carrefour Hypermarket.
AA 24 hour service
Tel. Cardiff 394111.

Callander Central

The small Scots burgh of Callander, at the junction of the rivers Teith and Lemy, became familiar to millions of television viewers as the "Tannochbrae" of the *Dr Finlay's Casebook* series. It is a holiday resort, with a golf course and good salmon and trout fishing, and a base for touring the Trossachs and Loch Katrine to the west.

Callander was laid out in the 18th century, and its focal point is the well-proportioned Ancaster Square in front of the Church of St Kessog. According to tradition, Kessog, a missionary from Ireland, first preached the Gospel beside the Teith 14 centuries ago. The spot is marked by a flagpole.

There are several scenic walks around the town, including two that lead to Callander Crags half a mile north, which rise 1,000 ft above sea-level, and one to the waterfall of Bracklinn, 1½ miles north-east. Ben Ledi, 2,875 ft, 3 miles north-west on the edge of the Trossachs, has rocky climbs for mountaineers.

Information Tel. 30342/30624.
Location On the A84, 16 m. NW of Stirling.
Parking Station Road; Leny Road; Bracklinn Road (all car parks); Ancaster Square; Cross Street; North and South Church Street.
District council Stirling (Tel. Stirling 3131).
Population 2,520.
E-C Wed.
Police South Church Street (Tel. 30222).
Casualty hospital Stirling Royal Infirmary, Livilands Gate, Stirling (Tel. Stirling 3151).
Post office Main Street.
Public library South Church Street.
AA 24 hour service
Tel. Glasgow (041) 812 0101.

Camberley see Frimley

Camborne-Redruth
Cornwall

More than 100 old tin mines lie scattered in the countryside around the twin towns of Camborne and Redruth, once the heart of Cornwall's mining industry. Today, silent engine-rooms and smokeless chimney-stacks stand over the derelict shafts.

The rapid expansion of tin and copper-mining throughout the 19th century was made possible largely by Richard Trevithick (1771-1833), who was born near Camborne. He invented a high-pressure steam engine that made it possible to pump water out of pits from greater depths than ever before – an advance that revolutionised deep-shaft mining throughout the world.

The Dolcoath pit at Camborne became the biggest, deepest and richest in Britain, dropping 3,300 ft through extensive deposits of copper and tin. The pit operated until the 1920s, when cheap ore from Malaya virtually killed off the industry.

Behind Druid's Hall in Redruth is the former home of the Scottish inventor William Murdock (1754-1839), who made the first house to be lit by gas, in 1792.

At Pool, between Camborne and Redruth, is the School of Mining, which has a fine collection of geological specimens in its museum. The National Trust owns the Cornish mine engines at Pool where the original 19th-century beam pumping and winding engines are on show. On Carn Brea, the hill which separates Camborne from Redruth, are the remains of Neolithic and Iron Age settlements, and a medieval castle.

Information Tel. 712941.
Location On the A3047, 14 m. NE of Penzance.
Parking Camborne: Rosewarne Road. Redruth: West End; Green Lane; Fore Street (all car parks).
District council Kerrier (Tel. 712941).
Population 46,500.
E-C Thur. **M-D** Fri.
Police South Terrace, Camborne (Tel. 714881).
Casualty hospital Royal Cornwall, Infirmary Hill, Truro (Tel. Truro 74242).
Post offices Chapel Street, Camborne; Fore Street, Redruth.
Cinemas Cameo, Rofkear Terrace, Camborne (Tel. 712020); Regal, Fore Street, Redruth (216278).
Public libraries The Cross, Camborne; Clinton Road, Redruth.
Places to see Roman villa, Magor; Carn Brea; Camborne Museum (at public library); Cornish Mine Engines, Pool; School of Mines Museum, Trevenson, Pool.
Shopping Camborne: Trelowaren Street. Redruth: Fore Street.
Trade and industry Mining; engineering; textiles.
AA 24 hour service Tel. Truro 76455.

Cambridge see page 74

Camden see London

Campbeltown Strathclyde

A grey-stone fishing town, Campbeltown nestles beneath green hills and around its harbour on Campbeltown Loch. At its peak, at the end of the last century, it had 34 distilleries and a fleet of 646 herring-boats. Today only two distilleries remain, the fleet is small, and the town has become a quiet resort for golfers, anglers and ramblers. The island of Davaar, at the mouth of the loch can be reached by a causeway at low tide, and has a cave with a remarkable painting of the Crucifixion.

Information Tel. 2056.
Location On the A83, 38 m. S of Tarbert.
Parking Burnside Street; Main Street; Hall Street; High Street; Bolgam Street (all car parks).
District council Argyll and Bute (Tel. Lochgilphead 2127).
Population 6,100.
E-C Wed. **M-D** Mon.
Police Castlehill (Tel. 2253).
Casualty hospital Cottage (Tel. 2077).
Post office Castlehill.
Cinema Picture House, Hall Street (Tel. 2264).
Public library Hall Street.
AA 24 hour service Tel. Glasgow (041) 812 0101.

Cannock Staffordshire

Plantagenet kings hunted in the leafy Cannock Chase, which now forms an oasis of heath and forest land, roamed by herds of fallow deer.

Cannock retains its charm, yet it has kept up to date. West Cannock No. 5 Colliery is one of the most modern in the country, and the town is the home of Compower (the National Coal Board's Computer Centre). The M6 has brought a new vitality to Cannock, and boosted the town's engineering, brick and tile-making industries.

Information Tel. 2019.
Location On the M6, 8 m. NE of Wolverhampton.
Parking Beecroft Road; Hunter Road; Church Street; Allport Street; Mill Street; Manor Avenue; Backcrofts (all car parks).
District council Cannock Chase (Tel. 2621).
Population 59,200.
E-C Thur. **M-D** Tues., Fri. and Sat.
Police Wolverhampton Road (Tel. 4545).
Casualty hospital Stafford Infirmary, Foregate Street, Stafford (Tel. Stafford 58251).
Post office Church Street.
Cinema Classic, Walsall Road (Tel. 2226).

Public library Manor Avenue.
Shopping Stafford Road; Walsall Road; High Green; Market Hall Street; Wolverhampton Road.
Trade and industry Electrical engineering; brick and tile manufacture.
AA 24 hour service Tel. Stoke-on-Trent 25881.

Canterbury see page 78

Cardiff see page 82

Cardigan Dyfed

The estuary of the River Teifi shelters Cardigan, which was a prosperous port until the 19th century when the river silted up and the arrival of the railways took away its trade. Today Cardigan is best noted for its access to fine salmon and sea-trout angling in the Teifi, one of the loveliest rivers in Wales.

The 17th-century bridge across the river was originally Norman. It was rebuilt in 1640, and again after damage by Cromwell's troops a few years later. The Roundheads also destroyed most of the castle, whose ruins overlook the bridge. The castle, which was built about 1160, is now privately owned.

Part of the town's market is held in the pillared basement of the Guildhall.

Information Tel. 613230.
Location On the A487, 39 m. SW of Aberystwyth.
Parking Quay Street; Bath House Road; Fiedfair; behind Guildhall (all car parks).
District council Ceredigion (Tel. Aberystwyth 7911).
Population 4,200.
E-C Wed. **M-D** Mon., Sat.
Police Priory Street (Tel. 612209).
Casualty hospital Cardigan and District Memorial, Pont-y-Cleifion (Tel. 612214).
Post office High Street.
Cinema Pavilion, Napier Gardens (Tel. 613671).
Public library Guildhall.
Places to see Castle; Cardigan Wildlife Park, 3 m. S.
Shopping High Street; Pendre; Priory Street.
Events Civic Week (July/Aug); Agricultural Show (July).
AA 24 hour service Tel. Swansea 55598.

ANCIENT BOATS
Ancient Britons built coracles by stretching hide over a wickerwork frame. Coracles are now covered by canvas sealed with pitch. Fishermen still use them on the River Teifi at Cardigan.

Carlisle Cumbria

Its position near the border with Scotland made Carlisle a strategically important city from early times, and this long history is reflected in the ancient remains that mingle with its modern industrial development.

There was probably a settlement in prehistoric times at Carlisle. In AD 78 the Roman leader Agricola chose it as the site of a fort on the fortified east-west road called the Stanegate. However, this defensive line began to be replaced in 122 by the more formidable Hadrian's Wall. Stretches of the wall can still be seen east of the city. Agricola's fort on the Stanegate was superseded by the town of Luguvalium, and now lies buried beneath the city centre.

CARLISLE CROSS
The town's Great Fair, granted by charter in 1352, is proclaimed from the steps of the cross.

From Norman times Carlisle continually changed hands between England and Scotland, a struggle that finally ended only in 1745, when English troops drove out Bonnie Prince Charlie's men.

The red-sandstone cathedral is the second smallest in England, only Oxford Cathedral is smaller. It began in 1123 as a Norman priory church, in 1133 its eastern end was made a cathedral, while its nave served as the parish church of St Mary. It was rebuilt after fire had damaged it in 1292. The Early English choir is dominated by the beautiful east window, one of the finest in the country, with 14th-century stone tracery.

Much of the nave was destroyed during the Civil War, but it continued to be used as a church until 1870. In 1797 the novelist Sir Walter Scott was married there. The cathedral became a memorial chapel for the Border Regiment in 1949.

Carlisle Castle was founded by William Rufus in 1092, and strengthened in the following century by David I of Scotland. Over the centuries it was to bear the brunt of the many conflicts that raged in and around the city. The chief remains today, within the still-intact outer walls, are the 12th-century keep, the 14th-century main gate and part of Queen Mary's Tower.

In the central market place stands the Guildhall, a wooden-framed building with overhanging upper floors, probably dating from the 14th century. Also in the market place, in front of the 18th-century Old Town Hall, is Carlisle Cross, erected in 1682.

The main surviving part of the medieval city wall is on the west side of the city. It includes the Sallyport, a secret gateway out of the city. Near by stands the recently restored medieval tithe barn.

After centuries as a garrison town, Carlisle began to prosper as a textile centre from the end of the 18th century. This prosperity led to the development of fine roads of Georgian and Victorian houses, such as Abbey Street and Victoria Place.

Carlisle Museum and Art Gallery is mainly housed in Tullie House, a graceful Jacobean mansion built in 1689. The museum includes a fine Roman collection.

Information Tel. 25517.
Location On the A6, 58 m. W of Newcastle upon Tyne.
Parking Lower Viaduct; Upper Viaduct; Cecil Street; Civic Centre; Town Dyke Orchard; Bitts Park; William Street; Devonshire Walk; The Sands, near Eden Bridge (all car parks).
District council Carlisle City Council (Tel. 23411).
Population 71,500.
E-C Thur. **M-D** Daily except Thur. afternoons and Sunday.
Police (Bb) Rickergate (Tel. 28191).
Casualty hospital Cumberland Infirmary, Port Road (Tel. 23444).
Post office (Ba) Warwick Road.
Theatres West Walls (Aa), West Wall (Tel. 33233); Stanwix Arts Theatre, Brampton Road (25333).
Cinemas Lonsdale (Ba), Warwick Road (Tel. 25586); Studios 1, 2, 3 and 4, Botchergate (21144).
Public library (Ab) Castle Street.
Places to see Carlisle Castle,

VICTORIAN DIGNITY *The textile boom of the 19th century saw the development of fine residential terraces in Carlisle.*

including Border Regiment Museum (**Ab**); Tullie House Museum and Art Gallery (**Ab**), Castle Street; Guildhall Museum, Green Market; Cathedral Museum, Prior's Tower.
Shopping English Street; Castle Street; Fisher Street; Scotch Street; Devonshire Street; Lowther Street; Botchergate.
Sport FA League football, Carlisle United FC, Brunton Park. Rugby League Football, Carlisle RFC, Warwick Road.
AA 24 hour service Tel. 24274.

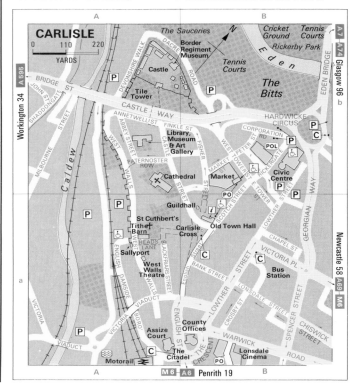

CAMBRIDGE Cambridgeshire

A centre of learning for 700 years

Cambridge was a regional centre for more than 1,000 years before the university was established. The town began when the Romans built a camp on a small hill beside the River Cam, which they called the Granta. By the 5th century it had become a Saxon market town. In the 9th, it was a Danish army base and in the 11th, a Norman military stronghold. It was not until the 13th century that the first students appeared – and with them Cambridge took on the character which still exists today.

The university is the heart of Cambridge. Its colleges, churches and museums cover much of the city centre. Even the industry which has expanded the outer city into a modern manufacturing centre owes much to the university. Printing and science-based trades such as instrument-making and electronics are among the largest employers.

Any unguided tour of the old city should be planned in advance. Trumpington Street, which enters Cambridge from the south, is a suitable place to start.

Hobson's choice

The deep gutters which line Trumpington Street survive from a 17th-century scheme for bringing water into the city. **Hobson's Conduit,** an ornate fountain-head on the west side of the road, is named after Thomas Hobson (1544-1631), a livery-stable owner who contributed to the scheme. He is immortalised in the expression "Hobson's choice", after his custom of offering his patrons a horse of his own choice or none at all.

Also in Trumpington Street is the **Fitzwilliam Museum**, which was founded in 1816 by Viscount Fitzwilliam. One of the world's greatest museums, its exhibits include Egyptian, Greek and Roman antiquities; illuminated manuscripts; ceramics; coins; arms and armour; and an outstanding collection of paintings, including works by Rembrandt, Titian, Constable and Turner.

Beyond the museum lies the university's oldest college, **Peterhouse**, endowed by Hugh de Balsham,

Bishop of Ely, in 1284. The first students had settled in Cambridge 75 years earlier, after fleeing from riot-torn Oxford in 1209.

Peterhouse is one of 12 colleges founded between the 13th and 15th centuries. Since then, another 19 have been established. The members of these 31 colleges compose the university today.

Pembroke College, a little way up the street from Peterhouse, was founded in 1347 by the Earl of Pembroke's widow, Lady Mary de Valence. Some of the medieval building survives. The chapel, built in 1666, was the first completed design of Sir Christopher Wren.

On the corner of Silver Street, which leads from Trumpington Street to the river, is **St Catharine's College** which was founded in 1473. None of the original buildings remain, but there is a handsome open court, built between 1674 and 1780.

Queens' College, in Silver Street, is named after the two queens who founded it in the mid-15th century: Henry VI's wife, Margaret of Anjou, and Edward IV's wife, Elizabeth Woodville. Most of the original 15th-century building survives. The Dutch theologian Erasmus stayed at the college in 1511 and imported his own wine rather than drink the local beer.

Inquisitive Victorians

Leading from Queens' over the river is the wooden Mathematical Bridge, erected to the design of William Etheridge in 1749 without metal fastenings. It was dismantled by inquisitive Victorians to see how it was

made, but they could only put it together again with iron bolts.

Opposite St Catharine's, in Trumpington Street, is **Corpus Christi College**, founded by the townspeople in 1352. On one wall of the Old Court is a tablet commemorating two of the college's most famous students, the Elizabethan dramatists Christopher Marlowe and John Fletcher. A 16th-century passage links the college's Old Court to the city's oldest building, the Saxon **Church of St Bene't**, which dates from the early 11th century.

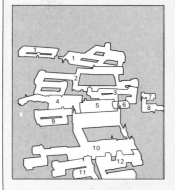

A KEY TO THE UNIVERSITY

The ancient heart of Cambridge is where most of the university buildings are concentrated. The key, left, identifies those buildings which can be seen in the aerial view of the city, right.

1 St John's	7 St Michael's
2 Trinity	Church
3 Gonville and	8 Great St
Caius	Mary's Church
4 Trinity Hall	9 Clare
5 Old Schools	10 King's
6 Senate	11 Queens'
House	12 St Catherine's

Beyond Bene't Street, Trumpington Street gives way to King's Parade, with **King's College** set back to the west. Founded in 1441 by Henry VI, it is best known for its chapel which was built between 1446 and 1515. It is one of the supreme achievements of the Gothic style of architecture. The 16th-century stained-glass windows are a glory of coloured light; and the wooden screen and the choir stalls are richly carved. Behind the altar is Rubens' masterpiece the *Adoration of the Magi*.

Further up King's Parade is the 18th-century **Senate House**, where the Senate, the university's "parliament", meets fortnightly to supervise the running of the university. Successful students gather there at the end of June to receive their degrees.

University church

On the opposite side of the road is **Great St Mary's Church**, the official university church. Visitors can climb the 17th-century tower, which provides sweeping views of the town and surrounding countryside. St Mary's clock chimes a tune specially written for it in 1793 which was later copied for Big Ben in London.

Next to the Senate House is **Gonville and Caius** (pronounced Keys) **College**, founded in 1348 by the priest Edmund Gonville and further endowed in 1557 by Dr John Caius, a former student who became physician to Edward VI and Mary I. Ancient Gonville Court is disguised by an 18th-century façade. Dr Caius added a second court with the gates to symbolise his students' progress. Two can still be seen: "Virtue" leads into Caius' Court, and "Honour" marks

the way out for successful students.

Backing the river behind these buildings on the left of King's Parade are **Clare College** and **Trinity Hall.**

Clare, now a mixed college, was built between 1638 and 1715. Graceful wrought-iron gates give access to the oldest bridge in the city, built in 1640. This leads to the Masters' and Fellows' gardens across the river. They are open to the public on most weekday afternoons.

Trinity Hall was founded in 1350 as a training college for priests. It has an Elizabethan library, where the books are chained to the shelves.

King's Parade gives way to Trinity Street, on the left of which is **Trinity College,** established by Henry VIII in 1546 and now the university's largest college. Thomas Nevile, Master of the college in Elizabeth I's time, built the Great Court, the largest university quadrangle in the world.

Famous graduates

The college chapel, which was built between 1555 and 1567, contains memorials to Isaac Newton, Francis Bacon, Lord Macaulay, Lord Tennyson and other former Trinity undergraduates who made their mark on the world.

Beyond Trinity is **St John's College.** It is entered through a Tudor gateway surmounted by gilded heraldry, including the arms of Henry VII's mother, Lady Margaret Beaufort, who founded the college in 1511.

THE QUIET WAY *A punt on the gently flowing River Cam offers a leisurely trip past the Backs, and views of the colleges.*

FOLK MUSEUM

The everyday life of Cambridgeshire over the last 400 years is recorded by the Folk Museum. The story is told in a series of rooms, each devoted to a theme such as domestic life, trades and occupations, children's toys and rural life. Exhibits peculiar to the Fenland crafts include equipment for catching eels, and overshoes for both men and horses to prevent them sinking into the mud. One display, on relationships between the town and university, exhibits the standard weights and measures used by the university to check up on local traders.

Overshoe for Fenland horse

Eel-catcher's wicker trap

Three-pronged gleve for spearing eels

The Hall has a fine Tudor roof and is hung with portraits of famous men who studied at the college, including William Wordsworth, William Wilberforce and Lord Palmerston.

Behind St John's the river is spanned by the charming New Bridge, built in 1831. It is known as the Bridge of Sighs because it resembles the Venetian bridge of that name.

To the north, across Magdalene (pronounced Maudlin) Street, is **Magdalene College.** This was founded in 1542. The diarist Samuel Pepys was a student there, and he left his library of 3,000 books, including the shorthand manuscripts of his diaries, to the college.

Southwards, Magdalene Street becomes Bridge Street where the **Round Church,** one of the few circular churches in England, stands.

Set well back from Jesus Lane, a turning off Bridge Street, is **Jesus College.** It was founded in 1497 by John Alcock, Bishop of Ely, on the site of a 12th-century convent, whose chapel, cloister and other buildings were retained.

Cromwell's head

Bridge Street continues into Sidney Street, with **Sidney Sussex College** on the left. This was founded in 1596 by Lady Frances Sidney, widow of the Earl of Sussex. Oliver Cromwell was a student there in 1616. What is believed to be his embalmed head was buried in the ante-chapel in 1960.

Further down the street, in the angle with Hobson Street, is **Christ's College,** which originated in the mid-15th century as a teachers' college known as God's House; it was reformed in 1505 by Lady Margaret Beaufort, whose arms and statue are displayed on the main gate. In the chapel there is an oriel window through which Lady Beaufort joined the services from her rooms in the Master's Lodge. John Milton, earlier a student at the college, is reputed to have written his poem *Lycidas* under the ancient mulberry tree in the grounds.

Further down the main thoroughfare, where it becomes St Andrew's Street, is **Emmanuel College,** founded in 1584 by Sir Walter Mildmay,

RARE CHURCH *The Round Church built in 1130 is one of only four in England.*

Chancellor of the Exchequer to Elizabeth I. Sir Christopher Wren designed the chapel and its colonnade in 1666.

The **Scott Polar Research Institute** in Lensfield Road was founded as a memorial to Captain Scott and his companions, who perished in Antarctica in 1912, after reaching the South Pole. Letters, diaries and photographs from their journey are on display, together with records and souvenirs of other polar expeditions.

Across the river, behind the colleges, are **the Backs** – lawns and gardens sloping down to the river's edge.

Downstream from the Backs is Midsummer Common, where the Midsummer Fair has been held since the Middle Ages. At the opening the mayor distributes pennies to children. The stretch of river by the common is where the colleges and local clubs go for rowing practice. The river is not wide enough for conventional racing, and the university eight practises for the Boat Race against Oxford at Ely where conditions are similar to those on the Thames.

Information Tel. 358977; 353363 (weekends).
Location 60 m. N of London on A10.
Parking New Square; Corn Exchange Street; Park Street; Gonville Place; Adam and Eve Street; Saxon Street (all car parks).
District council Cambridge City Council (Tel. 358977).
Population 90,400.
E-C Mon., Thur. **M-D** Mon. to Sat.
Police Parkside (Tel. 358966).
Casualty hospital Addenbrookes New Hospital, Hills Road (Tel. 45151).
Post office (Cb) St Andrew's Street.
Theatres ADC **(Bc)** (Tel. 59547); Arts **(Bb)** (352000).
Cinemas ABC 1 and 2 **(Cb)** (Tel. 354572); Arts **(Bc)** (352001);

Victoria 1 and 2 **(Bb)** (352677).
Public library (Bb) Lion Yard.
Places to see The colleges are open to the public on most days during daylight, though there may be restrictions in term time; Fitzwilliam Museum **(Ba)**; Folk Museum **(Ad)**; Scott Polar Research Institute **(Ca)**; Sedgwick Museum of Geology **(Cb)**; University Library **(Ab)**; University Museum of Archaeology and Ethnology **(Bb)**; University Museum of Classical Archaeology **(Ba)**; University Museum of Zoology **(Bb)**; Whipple Science Museum **(Bb)**; Kettles Yard Art Gallery **(Ad)**.
Shopping King's Parade; Magdalene Street; Regent Street; Sidney Street; Trumpington Street; Lion Yard.
Events Rag Week (Feb.); Music, Dance, Speech and Drama Festival (Apr.); May Week (June); Midsummer Fair (June); Arts Festival (July); Folk Festival (July).
AA 24 hour service Tel. 312302.

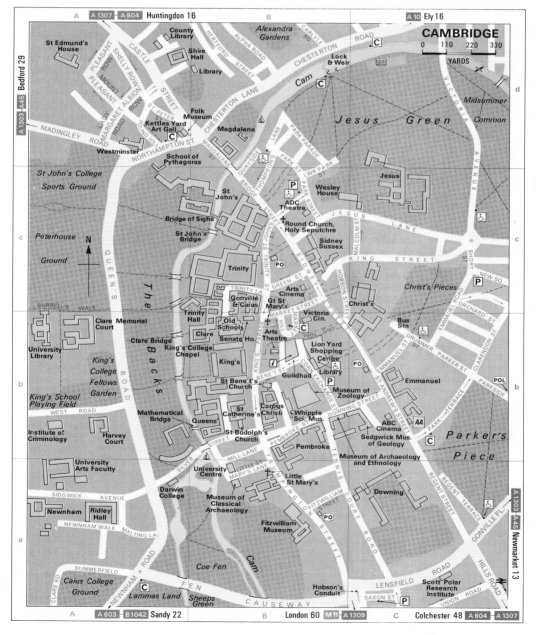

A LOOK AROUND
CANTERBURY
Kent

Home of England's Mother Church

The birthplace of English Christianity, because it was from here, in the 7th century, that St Augustine and his followers spread the Gospel . . . one of Europe's most celebrated places of pilgrimage since the martyrdom of Thomas Becket in 1170 . . . the seat of the Primate of All England – Canterbury has an unchallengeable right to the title she claims for herself in the city motto, "Hail, Mother of England". Still half-surrounded by massive medieval walls standing on Roman foundations, watched over by the cathedral's majestic tower, the city retains even today some of the atmosphere known to the medieval pilgrims and celebrated in Chaucer's *Canterbury Tales*.

Canterbury's roots go back to prehistoric times, when Iron Age people founded a settlement beside the River Stour. But the city's story really starts after the Roman invasion of AD 43. Durovernum Cantiacorum, as it was then known, became a trading centre on what was the most direct route between London and the mainland of Europe. Other roads linked the town to coastal forts at Lympne, Richborough and Reculver. Fordwich, a few miles downstream, provided a link with the English Channel.

Visible remains of the Roman settlement, which is now as much as 12 ft below ground in places, include the foundations of Britain's largest Roman theatre, a mosaic pavement and part of a central-heating system. Gold, silver, pottery, bottles, coins, brooches, statuettes of gods and many other Roman relics are displayed in the **Royal Museum**.

St Martin's, a few hundred yards east of the city wall, may also date from Roman times and is said to be the oldest church in England. Letters on a spoon and a bowl in the Royal Museum support the theory that Christianity had reached Canterbury during the Roman occupation.

In 597 St Augustine arrived on his mission from Rome, and six years later became the first Archbishop of Canterbury. The extensive ruins of **St Augustine's Abbey**, which he founded, include the tombs of early saints and the unique uncompleted rotunda started by Abbot Wulfric in the 11th century. In its early years the abbey was regarded as the greatest centre of learning in England.

Archbishop killed

Canterbury's position on flat land and within easy reach of the Channel, made it a tempting target for raiders and invaders. In 851 the city was captured by Vikings, and in 1011 it fell to the Danes, who burned the cathedral and murdered Archbishop Alphege, after whom one of Canterbury's churches is named.

The Normans surrounded the city with a tower-studded wall, and built a castle on its southern boundary. The ruined keep is all that remains of the stronghold, but about a mile of the wall has survived more or less intact.

The Normans began their legacy to the city, **the cathedral**, in 1070. The work was started by Archbishop Lanfranc, who shipped in stone from France. Some of this early fabric survives, including part of the crypt – the largest Norman crypt in the world – and parts of the cloister walls.

From 1174 William of Sens and William the Englishman constructed the early-Gothic choir and eastern end of the cathedral, built as a shrine to St Thomas the Martyr – St Thomas Becket. A beautiful new nave, which soars to a vault 80 ft high, was completed in 1400, and the magnificent central tower was finished a century later. It is known as Bell Harry Tower, after the original bell given by Friar Henry of Eastry in 1316 and replaced in 1726. The most recent

THOMAS BECKET *Among the cathedral's glories are its medieval Miracle Windows. One of the finest is this portrait of Archbishop Becket, whose martyrdom in 1170 made Canterbury a place of pilgrimage.*

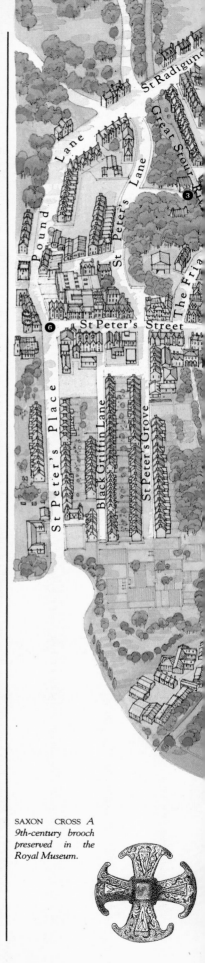

SAXON CROSS *A 9th-century brooch preserved in the Royal Museum.*

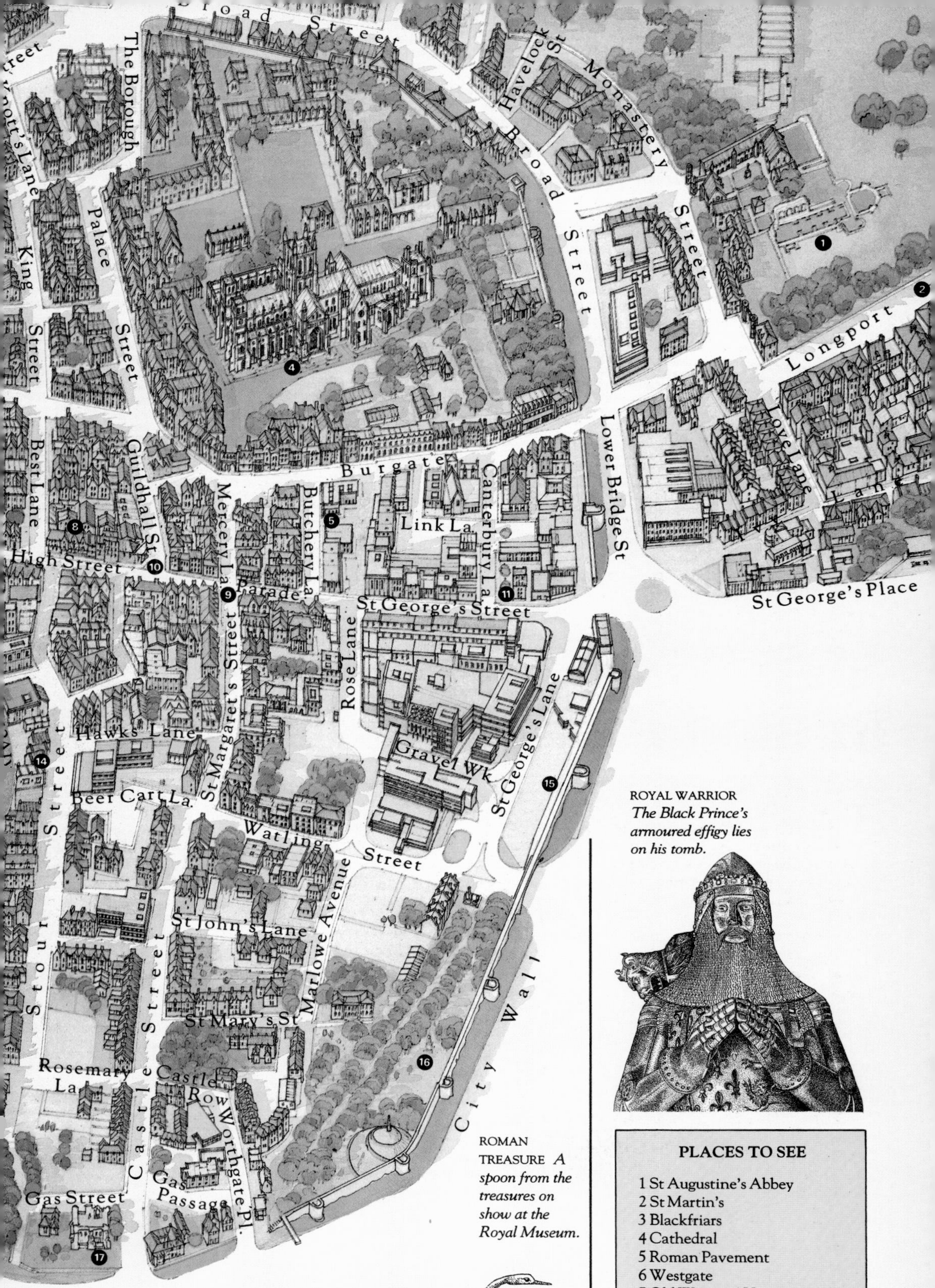

Broad Street
The Borough
Havelock St
Monastery Street
Broad Street
Palace Street
King Street
Longport
Lower Bridge St
Love Lane
Burgate
Butchery La.
Canterbury La.
Link La.
Best Lane
Guildhall St
Mercery La.
High Street
Parade
St George's Street
St George's Place
Rose Lane
St Margaret's Street
Hawks Lane
Gravel Wk
St George's Lane
Beer Cart La.
Stour Street
Watling Street
Marlowe Avenue
St John's Lane
Castle Street
St Mary's St
City Wall
Rosemary La.
Castle Row
Worthgate Pl.
Gas Passage
Gas Street

ROYAL WARRIOR *The Black Prince's armoured effigy lies on his tomb.*

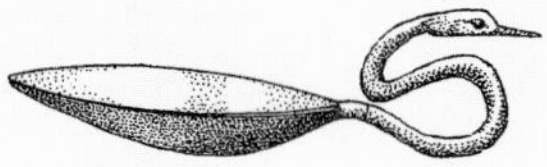

ROMAN TREASURE *A spoon from the treasures on show at the Royal Museum.*

PLACES TO SEE

1 St Augustine's Abbey
2 St Martin's
3 Blackfriars
4 Cathedral
5 Roman Pavement
6 Westgate
7 Old Weavers' House
8 Royal Museum
9 Mercery Lane
10 Queen Elizabeth's Guest Chamber
11 St George's Tower
12 Eastbridge Hospital
13 Greyfriars
14 Poor Priests' Hospital
15 City Walls
16 Dane John Gardens
17 Castle

addition, dating from 1831 to 1840, is the north-west tower.

The cathedral is renowned for its stained glass – the oldest substantial collection in the country, much of it dating from the 12th century. Some of the earliest windows trace Christ's descent from Adam; other windows known as the Poor Man's Bible, depict scenes from the Old and New Testaments; and the Miracle Windows illustrate the life and death of St Thomas. This priceless collection of glass, spanning 800 years, accounted for more than one-third of the cathedral's £3.5 million restoration appeal launched in 1975.

Henry IV (1367-1413) and his

CANTERBURY CATHEDRAL *The Mother Church of English Christianity rises above the rooftops, dominated by its magnificent Bell Harry Tower.*

PILGRIMS' STEPS *Over 300 years the feet of pilgrims to St Thomas's Shrine in Trinity Chapel, Canterbury Cathedral, gradually wore these stairs away.*

APT SIGN *A monk marks the cathedral bookshop in the precincts.*

wife, Joan of Navarre, are buried in the cathedral, together with more than 50 archbishops; but the most famous tomb is that of Edward the Black Prince (1330-76), one of the most splendid memorials in England.

It was the murder of Thomas Becket that made the cathedral a magnet for pilgrims. Becket was made Archbishop of Canterbury in 1162. He soon quarrelled with Henry II, who wanted to control the power of the Church, and went into exile. Then, at the end of 1170, he returned to Canterbury. On December 29 of that year, four French knights, hoping to please the king, cut the priest down inside the cathedral. Becket was later canonised, and in 1174 Henry did public penance for the killing.

Pilgrims from all over Britain and Europe were soon travelling to the saint's jewel-encrusted shrine. Chaucer's *Canterbury Tales* record the journey of a typical group of pilgrims. The shrine survived until 1538, when Henry VIII, declaring the martyr a traitor, ordered it to be stripped of its treasures and destroyed. A century later the cathedral suffered at the hands of Cromwell's men, but repairs were carried out soon after the Resto-

ration of the Monarchy in 1660.

Poor pilgrims rested at the Hospital of St Thomas the Martyr, also known as **Eastbridge Hospital**, which became an almshouse after the destruction of the shrine. Built about 1175 it spans a branch of the Stour, and its cool, dimly lit rooms provide a restful contrast to the bustle of shoppers and traffic in the nearby High Street.

Greyfriars, tucked away on a secluded backwater of the River Stour, is the remains of the first Franciscan settlement in England.

Medieval city

Blackfriars, founded by Dominicans about 1240, flanks the river and is now a Christian Science church. Buildings like these, together with narrow alleyways such as **Mercery Lane**, convey vivid impressions of what Canterbury must have been like in the Middle Ages.

The Old Weavers' House, one of the most eye-catching in the city, rises straight out of the Stour. This timber-framed building, now a shop, was built in 1507 and takes its name from Flemish and Huguenot weavers who settled in Canterbury to escape religious persecution during the 16th and 17th centuries. Raw materials were brought up the river by barge, and the little jetty behind the building is still in use, as the departure point for pleasure-boats. Old bobbins, threads and coins were discovered when the house was restored early this century. A resident weaver using an early-Victorian loom maintains a link with the building's past.

The Flemish refugees were wel-

comed by Elizabeth I. She gave them permission to ply their trade in Canterbury and offered them a special place of worship in the cathedral – a privilege which their successors still enjoy. Elizabeth visited Canterbury in 1573 when, with a possible marriage in mind, she entertained the French Duke of Alençon in what was then the state-room of the 15th-century Crown Inn, which is now a restaurant known as **Queen Elizabeth's Guest Chamber**.

In the **Dane John Gardens** a grassy mound, believed to be prehistoric, overlooks a memorial to Christopher Marlowe, the Elizabethan dramatist, author of *Tamburlaine* and *Dr Faustus*. Born the son of a Canterbury shoemaker in 1564, he was baptised in **St George's Church**, whose flint-studded tower survived the bombing of the building in 1942. Marlowe was stabbed to death in a drunken brawl at Deptford in 1593.

The 14th-century **Westgate**, the finest fortified city gate in England,

A CRICKETER REMEMBERED *A bronze memorial to the great Kent and England batsman Fuller Pilch (1803-70) stands in St Lawrence cricket ground.*

KENTISH GALLANTRY
This gold medal in the Buffs Museum was presented to Captain Latham for outstanding courage against the French in the Spanish campaign of 1811.

provides memorable views over the rooftops to the cathedral. It was built by Archbishop Sudbury who, like several of Canterbury's prelates, met a violent end; in 1381, the year after the gateway was finished, he was murdered in London by Wat Tyler's rebels.

Westgate was used as a prison for many years, and has been a museum since 1906. Such whimsical exhibits as a penny-farthing bicycle and an even cruder "boneshaker" of 1868

share the rooms with old weapons, shackles, the timbers of the old gallows, and other grisly relics. There is a fine view of the city and cathedral from the roof of the gate.

In Stour Street, part of what was originally the 14th-century **Poor Priests' Hospital** houses the **Museum of Canterbury**. The museum of The Buffs, the Royal East Kent Regiment, raised in 1572, is in the Royal Museum. The Buffs were based in Canterbury from 1873 until 1960, and seven years later they became part of the then newly formed Queen's Regiment.

During the Second World War, Canterbury was bombed as a reprisal for British air-raids on Cologne in Germany. Miraculously the cathedral escaped damage, but many old buildings were destroyed. In their places have arisen buildings which contrast vividly with their medieval surroundings, yet keep the city abreast of the 20th century. In 1965 the opening of the University of Kent gave new vigour to Canterbury's traditional role as a seat of learning.

OLD WEAVERS' HOUSE *Flemish weavers found refuge in this 16th-century merchant's house whose bay windows overlook the River Stour.*

Information Tel. 66567.
Location On the A2, 15 m. NW of Dover.
Parking Broad Street; St George's Place; St Peter's Place; Watling Street; St Radigund's Street; North Lane; Northgate; Rosemary Lane; Longport; Abbot's Place; Queningate; Castle Street (all car parks).
District council City of Canterbury (Tel. 51755).
Population 34,400.
E-C Thur. **M-D** Mon. (cattle)

and Wed.
Police (Ba) Old Dover Road (Tel. 55444).
Casualty hospital Kent and Canterbury, Ethelbert Road (Tel. 66877).
Post office (Ab) High Street.
Theatre Gulbenkian, Giles Lane (Tel. 69075).
Cinema ABC **(Ba)**, St George's Place (Tel. 62022).
Public library (Bb) High Street.
Shopping Guildhall Street; High Street; St Peter's Street; St

George's Street; St George's Lane; Burgate; Rose Lane; Longmarket; Butchery Lane; Sun Street; Mercery Lane; Palace Street.
Events Hospital Fair (June); King's School Week of Drama (July); Cricket Week (Aug.).
Trade and industry Agriculture and leather goods.
Sport Kent County Cricket Club, Old Dover Road.
AA 24 hour service
Tel. Thanet 81226.

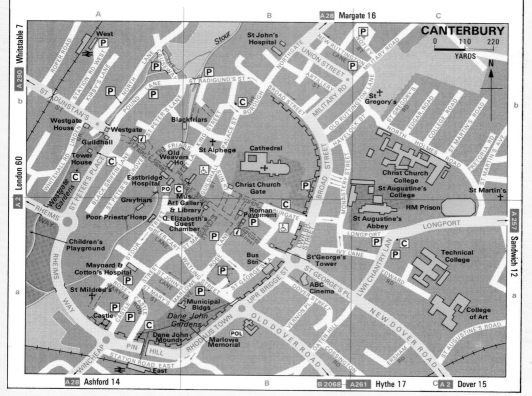

CARDIFF S. Glamorgan

Capital city which grew on coal

When, in 1955, Queen Elizabeth II made Cardiff the official capital of Wales, she was honouring 150 years of growth which had transformed a tiny, decayed old town on the estuary of the River Taff into the elegant, modern heart of a country.

Cardiff grew on coal. In its hey-day, as the biggest coal-shipping port in the world, it handled more than 6 million tons a year. Now this role is over, but Cardiff's importance as a civic, industrial and commercial centre, seaport and university city has never been greater.

RUGBY FERVOUR *A Welsh supporter carries his flag on the way to a rugby international in Cardiff.*

The Romans built a fort beside the River Taff in AD 75 to control the Welsh tribesmen. Then, in AD 300, they extended it as a defence against pirates raiding from across the Irish Sea. The city's Welsh name of Caerdydd, meaning "city of Dydd", may refer to a Roman, Aulus Didius.

Legend says that Lancelot sailed from Cardiff after King Arthur banished him, but it is unlikely that he stayed at the fort. It was almost certainly deserted from the time the Romans left until after the Norman invasion, when William the Conqueror offered his knights whatever land they could win in Wales if they would subdue the local tribes.

Robert FitzHamon led an expedition to conquer and settle in what is now Glamorgan. In 1093 he built a fort on a moated hillock which can still be seen in a corner of Cardiff Castle grounds.

Haunt of pirates

The town grew up around the fort, and in 1581 it was given its first royal charter by Elizabeth I. At that time Cardiff was a haunt for pirates raiding in the Bristol Channel, who thrived with the backing of local officials. The town held out for Charles I in the Civil War, but it was taken by Parliamentary troops and afterwards became a small, peaceful country community of farmers and fishermen.

Coal from the valleys to the north fuelled Cardiff's expansion at the dawn of the 19th century. In 1794 a riverside dock was linked by canal to Merthyr, then the largest town in Wales and centre of the chief iron and coal-producing region of Britain.

Enterprising marquis

Much of Cardiff had passed by marriage into the hands of the Bute family in 1776. It was the energy of the 2nd Marquis of Bute that finally launched the city into the industrial age. In 1839 he began building more docks, and these were soon linked by rail to pits and ironworks inland.

The quayside to the east of the Taff swarmed with seamen from all parts of the world. They drank in taverns with exotic names like The Bucket of Blood and The House of Blazes. The area itself became known as **Tiger Bay**, one of the toughest seaports in the world. Today, Tiger Bay has been developed into a modern city suburb with an up-to-date dock.

The 3rd Marquis of Bute rebuilt **Cardiff Castle** in the 1870s, on the site of its Norman and Roman predecessors. It has an ornate clock-tower, roof gardens and, inside, an ante-room in Moorish style and a cathedral-like dining-room.

Cardiff's shopping arcades also date from the second half of the last century. Two of the finest are the **Morgan Arcade**, which is Italian in style and has gabled glass roofs and elegant balustrades, and the three-storey **Castle Arcade**.

The **Civic Centre** in Cathays Park has grown up over the past 80 years. Its buildings include the City Hall, with domes, clock-tower and marble halls, the Law Courts and the **National Museum of Wales**. The museum has collections of archaeological remains, industrial items, animals and birds. Its art department has paintings by Welsh artists, including Richard Wilson (1714-82) and Augustus John (1878-1961), as well as a fine collection of paintings by 19th-century French impressionists.

Llandaff, once a separate community but now part of Cardiff, is one of the oldest Christian settlements in Wales. The cathedral, which stands on the site of a 6th-century wooden church, has been sacked by pagans, burned by the Welsh, battered by gales and bombed by the Germans. It was rebuilt and reopened in 1957. Jacob Epstein's aluminium statue of Christ in Majesty dominates the nave.

Rugby fervour

The towering **National Stadium**, beside the River Taff, becomes a cauldron of Celtic fervour when the Welsh rugby football team plays its home matches there. It holds nearly 50,000 people, whose singing before, during and after the game demonstrates Welsh choral talents.

The Cardiff Rugby Club, alongside the National Stadium, has produced some fine players, including the Wales and British Lion half-backs Gareth Edwards and Barry John, and the three-quarter Gerald Davies. The clubhouse, open to visitors by request on weekdays, has a trophy-room with photographs and other items spanning more than 100 years of rugby.

HEART OF CARDIFF *The Civic Centre was built from 1897 onwards on land presented to the city by the Marquis of Bute. It contains some of Cardiff's most handsome buildings, including the City Hall (centre) and the stately Law Courts (left).*

Across the river, in **Sophia Gardens**, the only first-class county cricket side in Wales, Glamorgan, has its ground. It lies in the shadow of the **National Sports Centre**, which has an artificial ski-slope and an Olympic-size swimming-pool.

Information Tel. 27281.
Location On the A48, 153 m. W of London.
Parking North Road (2); Dumfries Place; Knox Road; North Edward Street; Greyfriars Road; Westgate Street; Wood Street; Mill Lane; Castle Mews; Homfray Street; Churchill Way; Newport Road; West Canal Wharf; Bridge Street; Rodney Street (all car parks).
District council City of Cardiff (Tel. 31033).
Population 260,500.
E-C Wed. **M-D** Mon. to Sat.
Police (Bb) Cathays Park (Tel. 44111).
Casualty hospital Cardiff Royal Infirmary, Newport Road (Tel. 492233).
Post offices Westgate Street **(Ba)**; Bute Docks; Churchill Way **(Ca)**; The Hayes **(Ba)**.
Theatres New **(Cb)** (Tel. 32446); Sherman **(Cc)** (396844); Chapter Arts Centre, Market Road, Canton (25776).
Cinemas ABC 1, 2, 3 **(Bb)** (Tel. 31715/34680); Odeon **(Bb)**, Queen

Street (27058); Plaza, North Road (25824); Globe, Albany Road (493044); Monico Twin, Rhiwbina (62426).
Public library (Ba) The Hayes.
Places to see Cardiff Castle **(Bb)**, Castle Street; National Museum of Wales **(Bb/Cb)**, Cathays Park; National Maritime and Industrial Museum, Bute Street; Folk Museum, St Fagans; Welsh Arts Council Gallery **(Ca)**, Charles Street.
Town trails Apply to Victorian Society, 1 Priory Gardens, Bedford

Park, London W4.
Shopping Queen Street; St John Street; High Street; St Mary Street; Duke Street; Castle Street; Working Street; The Hayes; St David's Centre
Events Llandaff Festival (June).
Trade and industry Iron and steel; engineering; paper.
Sport Rugby football, Cardiff Arms Park; FA League football, Cardiff City FC, Ninian Park; Glamorgan County Cricket Club, Sophia Gardens.
AA 24 hour service Tel. 394111.

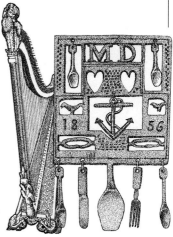

FOLK HERITAGE OF A NATION

Ancient buildings from all over Wales have been reassembled stone by stone at the Welsh Folk Museum at St Fagans, 4 miles west of Cardiff. They include a 15th-century farmhouse and an 18th-century wool-mill. Each building is furnished and equipped with items of the appropriate period. A large section of the museum is devoted to folklore, and weavers and basket-makers ply their traditional crafts in the grounds.

The 19th-century love-spoon was a token of devotion, and a test of carving skill. The Welsh harp was made in 1851.

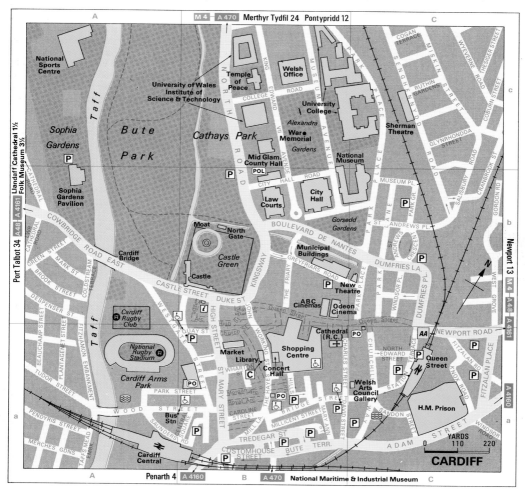

Carmarthen Dyfed

A modern county hall and the gatehouse of a ruined Norman castle stand side by side in Carmarthen, which shares with Caerleon the title of the oldest town in Wales.

The first settlement on the site, strategically placed on a bluff above the upper tidal reaches of the River Towy, was probably a Celtic hill-fort. The Romans replaced it with a wooden fort about AD 75. No trace of either now remains above ground, but a Roman amphitheatre which seated 5,000 people has been discovered off Priory Street. Roman relics can be seen at the Carmarthen Museum at Abergwili, just east of the town on the A40 Llandeilo Road.

In Welsh folklore, King Arthur's wizard, Merlin, is supposed to have been born near the town in AD 480. The decayed stump of an oak is said to carry his spell: "When Merlin's oak shall tumble down, Then shall fall Carmarthen town." It can be seen in the foyer of St Peter's Civic Hall, in King Street.

During the Middle Ages, the town had a priory where the Black Book of Carmarthen, the oldest known manuscript in the Welsh language, was written. The book is now preserved in the National Library of Wales at Aberystwyth.

The town was given a royal charter in 1201 by King John, and about 1451 held one of the earliest recorded Eisteddfods of Welsh bards.

On the river, an even more ancient tradition still survives: salmon-netting from coracles. These frail craft are made with a wickerwork ash frame covered with tarred calico. Similar craft covered with hide were used by the ancient Britons. The coracles work in pairs, with a net strung between to catch the salmon.

Information Tel. 31557.
Location On the A40, 27 m. NW of Swansea.

Parking Priory Street; St Peter's Street; John Street; Fair Lane; Morfa Lane; Lammas Street; Morley Street; Blue Street (all car parks).
District council Carmarthen (Tel. 4567).
Population 12,300.
E-C Thur. **M-D** Mon., Wed. and Sat.
Police Friar's Park (Tel. 6444).
Casualty hospital West Wales General Hospital, Glangwili (Tel. 5151/4191).
Post office (Bb) King Street.
Cinema Lyric **(Bb)**, King Street (Tel. 6207).
Public library (Bb) St Peter's Street.
Places to see Carmarthen Museum, Abergwili; Roman amphitheatre, off Priory Street; Dylan Thomas's Boathouse, Laugharne, 13 m. SW on A4066.
Town trails Available from Council Offices, Spilman Street.
Shopping King Street; Lammas Street; Guildhall Square; Dark Gate Precinct; Red Street Precinct; John Street Precinct.
Events Carnival (June); Regatta (June); United Counties Show (Aug.).
AA 24 hour service Tel. Swansea 55598.

Carnoustie Tayside

Golf has been played at Carnoustie (pronounced Car-noos-tee) for more than 400 years, and its championship course is one of the best known in the world. The town is also a seaside resort with sandy beaches stretching 5 miles to Buddon Ness at the mouth of the River Tay.

Information Tel. 52258.
Location On the A930, 13 m. NE of Dundee.
Parking Park Avenue; Links Avenue; (both car parks).
District council Angus (Tel. Forfar 65101).

Population 8,400.
E-C Tues.
Police Burnside Street (Tel. 52222 and Forfar 62551).
Casualty hospital Infirmary, Rosemount Road, Arbroath (Tel. Arbroath 72584).
Post office Queen Street.
Public library High Street.
Shopping Dundee Street; High Street.
AA 24 hour service Tel. Dundee 25585.

Chalfont St Giles Bucks.

Old-world cottages and a church grouped around a green give Chalfont St Giles a charm that has often attracted film producers from the nearby Pinewood Studios. A sign erected on the green depicts St Giles, the patron saint of lepers, cripples and animals.

The cottages are mostly half-timbered, and at one end of the main street is Milton's Cottage – the blind poet's refuge from the Great Plague in 1665. Here he finished *Paradise Lost* and began *Paradise Regained*, the first editions of which are displayed in the cottage.

The parish church of St Giles is approached through an archway set in a row of 16th-century gabled houses, and is 12th century with 13th – 15th-century additions. Among the church treasures are a Purbeck marble font, medieval wall-paintings and a Jacobean alms-box.

Chalfont's Elizabethan manor house, The Vache, is now a training college for the National Coal Board. The house takes its name from a Norman family. One of the lords of the manor, George Fleetwood, was a signatory to Charles I's death warrant.

Information Tel. Chesham 783231.
Location On the A413, 3 m. SE of Amersham.
Parking High Street (car park).
District council Chiltern (Tel. Amersham 4433).
Population 10,000.
E-C Thur.
Police Chiltern Avenue, Amersham (Tel. Amersham 3033).
Casualty hospital High Wycombe General, Marlow Hill (Tel. High Wycombe 22161).
Post office High Street.
Public library High Street.

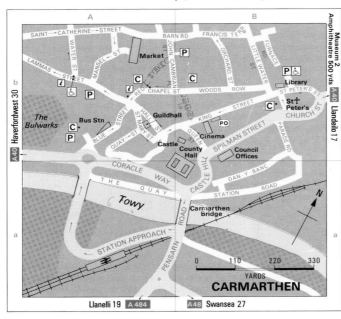

MILTON'S COTTAGE *The poet moved to Chalfont St Giles with his family in 1665 to escape the plague in London.*

Places to see Milton's Cottage,
Deanway; The Vache, Vache Lane.
Shopping High Street.
AA 24 hour service
Tel. Reading 581122.

Chard Somerset

Two streams flow along Chard's High
Street, one going northwards to the
Bristol Channel and the other south
to the English Channel.

Chard had a thriving wool industry
for nearly 600 years. Then, in the
19th century, local people turned to
making the netting from which
machine-made lace is produced. One
local man, John Stringfellow, had
even more progressive ideas. In 1849
he made a steam-powered model aircraft which flew for 120 ft before it
crashed. It is now in the Victoria and
Albert Museum, London.

The Choughs Hotel in High Street
is one of several interesting buildings,
including the 15th-century church, a
16th-century court house and a 17th-
century grammar school. The town
was the birthplace of Miss Margaret
Bondfield (1873-1953), the first
woman Cabinet Minister. She was
Minister of Labour in the Labour
Government of 1929-31.

Information Tel. 4414.
Location On the A30, 17 m. SW of
Yeovil.
Parking Bath Street; Boden Street;
Combe Street; Fore Street (all car
parks).
District council Yeovil
(Tel. Yeovil 5171).
Population 9,300.
E-C Wed.
Police Silver Street (Tel. 3131).
Casualty hospital Taunton and
Somerset, East Reach, Taunton

(Tel. Taunton 73444).
Post office Fore Street.
Public library Boden Street.
Shopping Fore Street; High Street;
Holyrood Street.
AA 24 hour service
Tel. Yeovil 27744.

Chatham Kent

Elizabeth I established Chatham as a
naval town when she ordered the
building of Chatham Dockyard, and
here were built many of the ships that
routed the Spanish Armada in 1588.
One of the fleet's commanders, Vice
Admiral Sir Francis Drake, had
learned his seamanship on the Medway when he was an apprentice.

Charles I expanded the dockyard in
the early 17th century as rivalry with
the Dutch for expanding trade routes
simmered towards war. But the dockyard's defences were weak, and in
1667 the Dutch admiral Micheil de
Ruyter sailed up the Medway, bombarded the docks and towed away the
Royal Charles, the pride of the fleet.
This ignominious defeat led to the
strengthening of Chatham's defences, and it became a strong military as well as a naval town.

In January 1771 a 12-year-old boy
arrived at Chatham to join the
Raisonnable, moored in the estuary.
His name was Horatio Nelson, newly
appointed as "Captain's servant" to
his uncle, Sir Maurice Suckling. On
the way to his ship the young Nelson
probably saw his future flagship,
HMS *Victory,* moored in the Medway. She had been launched at
Chatham in 1765, but did not go into
service until 1778.

As the Naval Establishment at
Chatham expanded, the local work
force was augmented, and one man

who was transferred to the Navy Pay
Office in 1816 was John Dickens,
who brought with him his son
Charles. They lived at number 11
Ordnance Terrace, and when Charles
Dickens wrote *Pickwick Papers* he de-
scribed Chatham as a noisy, smelly
and dirty place littered with drunks.

Several of the buildings he knew
still exist. In the High Street is Sir
John Hawkins's Hospital, founded by
the Elizabethan naval commander in
1592 as almshouses for mariners and
shipwrights. The present buildings
date from 1790.

Many of the old Victorian buildings
in the town have gone. They have
been replaced by modern shops, car
parks and offices. The old Gun
Wharf has been laid out as riverside
gardens.

Information Tel. Medway 43666.
Location On the A2, 8 m. N of
Maidstone.
Parking Cross Street; Medway Street;
James Street; Whiffens Avenue; Old
Road; Best Street; Church Street;
Union Street; High Street; The
Brook; Rhode Street; Globe Lane;
Dock Road (all car parks).
District council Borough of
Rochester upon Medway
(Tel. Medway 77890).
Population 61,900.
E-C Wed.
Police (Bb) The Brook
(Tel. Medway 41266).
Casualty hospital Gillingham
Hospital, Windmill Road,
Gillingham (Tel. Medway 46111).
Post office (Aa) Railway Street.
Cinema ABC **(Ba)**, High Street
(Tel. Medway 42522).
Public library (Ab) Riverside.
Places to see Medway Heritage
Centre, Dock Road.

MEDWAY HOUSE *Figureheads from old sailing ships line the
approach to the official residence of Chatham's Admiral of the
Port. The Queen Anne-style house is the administration
centre for the dockyard. The imposing figurehead with up-
raised arm once looked out from the bows of the* Chasseur,
which was bought from the French in 1855.

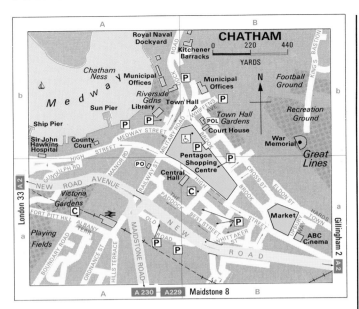

Shopping Pentagon Shopping
Centre, The Brook; High Street.
Trade and industry Printing; marine
engineering.
AA 24 hour service
Tel. Maidstone 55353.

Cheadle Staffordshire

The 200 ft steeple of Cheadle's
Roman Catholic church, designed in
1846 by A. W. N. Pugin, one of the
architects of the Houses of Parliament, is a distinctive landmark for
miles around.

There are several 16th-century,
half-timbered houses in the High
Street, and a 17th-century cross in
the Market Place. Hawksmoor, 2
miles east off the road to Oakamoor,
is a 250 acre nature reserve and bird
sanctuary where curlews nest. In the
reserve is a hut once used by charcoal
burners.

Information Tel. 2157.
Location On the A521, 8 m. NW of
Uttoxeter.
Parking Chapel Street; Tape Street
(both car parks).
District council Staffordshire
Moorlands (Tel. Leek 385181).
Population 10,000.
E-C Wed. **M-D** Tues., Fri. and Sat.
Police High Street (Tel. 2265).
Casualty hospital North
Staffordshire Royal Infirmary,
Hartshill, Stoke-on-Trent.
(Tel. Stoke-on-Trent 49144).
Post office High Street.
Public library Leek Road.
Places to see St Giles's Roman
Catholic church; Hawksmoor Nature
Reserve and Churnet Valley, 2 m. E.
Shopping High Street.
AA 24 hour service
Tel. Stoke-on-Trent 25881.

Cheadle & Gatley
Greater Manchester

Cheadle and Cheadle Hulme are
linked with Gatley in a mainly resi-

dential district of Greater Manchester.

Most of Cheadle's older buildings
date from the 19th century, when
merchants and industrialists moved
there from Manchester, Salford and
Stockport. The red-brick, Gothic
Town Hall, started in 1847, was originally built as a merchant's house.

The Church of St Mary was rebuilt
between 1530 and 1558, but has some
earlier tombs, including one sur-

mounted by the alabaster figures of
two knights which dates from the
15th century.

There are several fine timber-
framed mansions in the area, including Bramall Hall, 1 mile south-east of
Cheadle Hulme off the A5102 to
Stockport, a Tudor mansion set in
landscaped grounds. The furnishings
include a 16th-century tapestry.

Information
Tel. Manchester (061) 486 0283.
Location On the A34, 3 m. W of
Stockport.
Parking Massie Street; Mary Street;
Station Road; Gatley Road; Church
Road (all car parks).
District council Metropolitan
Borough of Stockport
(Tel. 061 480 4949).
Population 58,700.
E-C Wed.
Police Station Road, Cheadle Hulme
(Tel. 061 480 7979).
Casualty hospital Stockport
Infirmary, Wellington Road South,
Stockport (Tel. 061 480 7441).
Post office Old Rectory Gardens,
Wilmslow Road, Cheadle.
Cinema Tatton, Gatley
(Tel. 061 428 2133).
Public library Ashfield Road.
Places to see Bramall Hall, 1 m. SE
off the A5102.
Shopping High Street; Wilmslow
Road; Church Road, Gatley.
Trade and industry Chemicals;

GOTHIC EXTRAVAGANCE *The architect A. W. N. Pugin (1812-52) covered almost
every available surface in the Roman Catholic church of St Giles at Cheadle
(Staffordshire) with lavish decorations to enrich his Gothic design.*

brick-making; engineering.
AA 24 hour service
Tel. 061 485 6299.

Chelmsford Essex

The county town of Essex is set in heavily cultivated farmland dotted with unspoiled villages. Although Chelmsford has lost much of its rural peace through the demands of industry, its roots are still in the soil. Its livestock market, which began about AD 1200, is one of the most important in East Anglia.

The Romans built a small town, which they called Caesaromagus, halfway along the road from London to Colchester in the 1st century AD. Traces of it have been found in the Moulsham area of Chelmsford. The present town grew from the medieval manors of Moulsham and Celmeresfort, which were linked in about 1100 by a wooden bridge across the River Can. The present bridge was designed in 1787 by John Johnson, who also built the classical Shire Hall in the High Street. Bridge and Hall are among Chelmsford's oldest buildings, for many earlier ones have been pulled down since 1800, as the town has grown.

Johnson helped to restore the Church of St Mary, St Peter and St Cedd, at the top of the High Street, which has been Chelmsford Cathedral since 1914. It is basically a 15th-century parish church with many old tombs and monuments. But there are some striking later additions, such as the 20th-century figure of St Peter on the South Chapel, which depicts the saint dressed as a modern fisherman and holding a Yale key.

All Saints' Church, in the Springfield district, has a Norman base to its tower and fragments of Roman tiles and bricks built into its walls.

The construction of the Chelmer and Blackwater Navigation in 1797, and the arrival of the railway in 1843, made Chelmsford a suitable centre for industrial development.

The growth of the town's industry is traced in the Chelmsford and Essex Museum in Oaklands Park, which also has a collection of birds, fossils, costumes, paintings and drawings.

Writtle, 2 miles west of Chelmsford on the A122, is an attractive village with two greens.

Information Tel. 61733.
Location On the A12, 37 m. NE of London.
Parking Parkway; Baddow Road; Glebe Road; Railway Street; Townsfield Road; Rainsford Road; Bellmead; Victoria Road; Coval Lane (all car parks).
District council Chelmsford (Tel. 61733).
Population 58,100.
E-C Wed. **M-D** Tues., Fri. and Sat.
Police (Bb) New Street (Tel. 64041).
Casualty hospital Chelmsford and Essex Hospital **(Ba)**, New London

CHELMSFORD CATHEDRAL *Chequered flintwork on the east end and south porch of the cathedral is typical of Essex churches of the 15th century.*

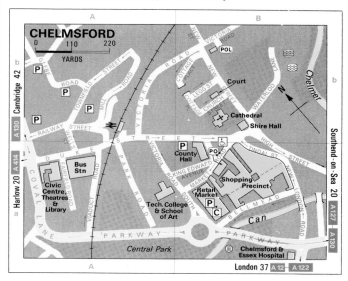

Road (Tel. 83331).
Post office (Ba) Market Road.
Theatres Civic Theatre and Cramphorn Theatre **(Aa)**, Fairfield Road (Tel. 61659); Chancellor Hall, Market Road (65848).
Cinema Pavilion, Rainsford Road (Tel. 61945).

Public library (Aa) Duke Street (Tel. 61733).
Places to see Cathedral **(Bb)**; Chelmsford and Essex Museum, Moulsham Street.
Shopping High Street and central shopping precinct.
AA 24 hour service Tel. 61711.

RADIO PIONEER

The world's first radio factory was set up in Hall Street, Chelmsford, in 1899, by Guglielmo Marconi (1874-1937). From a later factory, in New Street, he started transmitting Britain's first radio programmes of music, news and talks in 1920. This was two years before the for-

mation of the British Broadcasting Company which became the British Broadcasting Corporation in 1927.

W. T. Ditcham making the world's first news broadcast on February 23, 1920.

The site in Chelmsford where the world's radio industry was born.

CHELTENHAM Gloucestershire

The festival town that grew around a Cotswold spring

The inland resort of Cheltenham lies in the heart of the Cotswolds and is a beautifully planned town graced by Regency architecture and wide, tree-lined avenues. As well as the attraction of its spa, Cheltenham has always offered a wide range of entertainments. Its festivals of music and literature are renowned throughout the world, and its many sporting events include the Cheltenham Gold Cup steeplechase and a Cricket Festival.

The original medicinal spring from which Cheltenham grew was discovered by accident in a field early in the 18th century. One of its owners, Captain Henry Skillicorne, a retired privateer, deepened and enclosed the well in 1738, built an assembly room and laid out walks and rides, thus founding the spa. His epitaph in St Mary's parish church is one of the longest in Britain.

Throughout the 18th century many more springs were found, and other pump rooms built. In 1788 the town suddenly became fashionable when George III and his family took the waters there. However, it was the Duke of Wellington who finally made the spa's reputation; he had a liver disorder which the waters relieved. He took the waters in 1816, and it is from around that time that the large-scale development of the town took place.

Regency gem

The **Pittville Pump Room**, the finest gem of the spa's Regency architecture, was built for Joseph Pitt, MP, in 1825-30. Set in a spacious park, it consists of a great hall surmounted by a gallery and dome, with a colonnade of Ionic columns based on the Temple on the Ilissus at Athens. Waters are still dispensed from a restored fountain surrounded by columns. The beautiful grounds contain sweeping lawns and several lakes surrounded by trees.

The waters, which today can be taken at the **Town Hall** as well as Pittville, are the only natural, drinkable alkaline waters in Britain. Their medicinal properties are attributed to the magnesium and sodium sulphates and the sodium bicarbonate that they contain.

After the Pittville Pump Room, the town's best known examples of Regency building are Montpellier Walk and the **Rotunda**. The Rotunda was built behind an existing pump room to provide a bigger drinking hall. It is now the hall of a bank. The Walk is lined with female figures, modelled on those of the Erechtheion Temple at Athens.

Lining the broad, tree-lined **Promenade** is a fine terrace incorporating Ionic columns and a pediment at the entrance. The building is now the town's municipal offices.

The town is rich in examples of the beautiful ironwork that marked the Regency period. Some is so delicately cast that it resembles fine lacework. Outstanding examples can be seen on the verandahs and balconies opposite the Imperial Gardens of The Promenade, in London Road and St George's Road.

Rose window

The only medieval building still standing is St Mary's parish church. This retains traces of early-12th-century Norman work, but is best known for its 14th-century window tracery, including that of an uncommon rose window in the north transept. The church also contains some fine Victorian stained glass.

The **Art Gallery and Museum** contains major collections of paintings, and also work by 17th-century Dutch artists, porcelain, pottery, furniture, costume, and archaeological collections.

Cheltenham holds more festivals than any other town in Britain. The Cheltenham International Festival of Music gives first performances of new works by British composers, and since 1945, when the festival began, more than 350 such works, by Benjamin Britten, Malcolm Arnold, Sir Arthur Bliss and many others, have been presented. Contemporary music from

PITTVILLE PUMP ROOM *Once a rendezvous for the nobility and gentry.*

ROOMS WITH A VIEW *Verandahs and balconies overlook tree-lined avenues and gardens in Cheltenham. These elegant terraces are characteristic of the Regency period during which the town grew with the popularity of the waters.*

ARTISTRY IN IRON *Regency craftsmen excelled in decorative cast-iron work, and many houses in Cheltenham have balconies fronted with intricate designs.*

NEPTUNE *Fountain in The Promenade based on the Trevi Fountain, Rome.*

abroad is also played. The larger concerts are held in the Town Hall, which has a concert hall seating more than 1,000.

Competitors from all over Europe attend the Festival of Literature in autumn, and the town's oldest festival, that of Music, Speech, Drama and Dancing, held every spring.

Cheltenham is well known as a centre of education. There are two public schools for boys, Cheltenham College and Dean Close, and also one for girls – Cheltenham Ladies' College.

The Cricket Festival, first held in 1877 in honour of W. G. Grace, takes place each August on Cheltenham College's fine ground.

Information Municipal Offices, The Promenade (Tel. 22878).
Location On the A40, 8 m. NE of Gloucester.
Parking Rodney Road; St George's Road; Bath Road; Winchcombe Street; High Street; St James's Street; St James's Square; Sherborne Place; Grosvenor Terrace; Portland Street (all car parks).
District council Borough of

Cheltenham (Tel. 21333).
Population 73,200.
E-C Wed. **M-D** Thur.
Police Lansdown Road (Tel. 21321); St George's Road **(Aa)** (28282).
Casualty hospital General, Sandford Road (Tel. 21344).
Post office (Ba) The Promenade.
Theatres Everyman **(Ba)**, Regent Street (Tel. 25544); The Playhouse **(Ba)**, Bath Road (22852).
Cinema Odeon **(Bb)**, Winchcombe Street (Tel. 24081).
Public library (Bb) Clarence Street.
Places to see Art Gallery and Museum **(Bb)**, Clarence Street; Holst Birthplace Museum **(Bb)**, Clarence Road; Pittville Pump Room, Pittville Gardens; Montpellier Rotunda and Montpellier Walk **(Aa)**.
Town trails Details available from

Information Centre, The Promenade.
Shopping The Promenade; High Street; Montpellier Walk; Clarence Street.
Events Festival of Music, Speech, Drama and Dancing (May); International Festival of Music (July); Cheltenham Horse Show (July); Antiques Fair (Sept.); Festival of Literature (Oct.).
Trade and industry Manufacture of aircraft parts, clocks, watches, hydraulic and electrical equipment, chemical products, pharmaceuticals; woodwork.
Sport Cricket Festival, Cheltenham College (Aug.); National Hunt Racing, Prestbury Park (Sept.-Apr.).
AA 24 hour service
Tel. Gloucester 23278.

GUSTAV HOLST

The composer Gustav Holst (1874-1934) was born at 4 Clarence Road, Cheltenham. Holst, who is best known for his orchestral suite *The Planets*, was descended from a Swedish family long settled in England. His birthplace is now a museum devoted to his life and work.

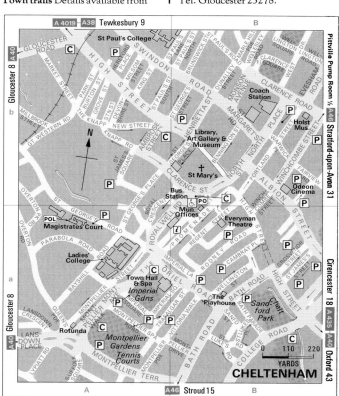

Chepstow Gwent

The River Wye loops a broad, protective arm around this ancient fortress town on the Welsh-English border. The Normans built its castle on limestone cliffs at the water's edge, and it proved impregnable until Cromwell's guns tore holes in its walls during the Civil War.

The castle has four courtyards, dominated by a 40 ft high keep and surrounded by walls strengthened by towers. Marten's Tower, added during the 13th century, was for 12 years, until his death in 1680, the prison of Henry Marten, one of those who signed Charles I's death-warrant.

In the 13th century, Chepstow was bounded by the 6 ft thick Portwall, guarding the side of the town not protected by the river. Much of the wall is preserved, and the town gate leads to steep and twisting medieval streets. The graceful iron bridge spanning the river was built in 1816 by the Scottish engineer John Rennie (1761-1821).

Information Tel. 2214.
Location On the A48, 17 m. E of Newport.
Parking Bank Street; Nelson Street; Severn Bridge Car Park; Church Road.
District council Monmouth (Tel. Pontypool 2311).
Population 9,300.
E-C Wed.
Police Moor Street (Tel. 3993).
Casualty hospital Mount Pleasant, Mounton Road (Tel. 2232).
Post office Station Road.
Public library Upper Nelson Street.
Places to see Chepstow Castle; Chepstow Museum, Bridge Street; Town walls.
Shopping High Street.
Sport Racecourse on the A466.
AA 24 hour service Tel. Newport 62559.

CHEPSTOW *Gateway to a border town.*

Chertsey see Runnymede

Cheshunt Hertfordshire

The urban sprawl of Cheshunt lies in the Lea valley, with marshlands to the east and wooded parks to the west.

Old inns, 17th and 18th-century buildings and modern office blocks line the main street of Cheshunt, which narrows at the southern end where an Eleanor Cross stands. The cross, from which Waltham Cross takes its name, is one of 12 built in 1291 to mark the resting places of Queen Eleanor's coffin on its journey to Westminster Abbey for burial. Only two others survive – at Hardingstone and Geddington.

Information
Tel. Waltham Cross 27933.
Location On the A10, 14 m. N of London.
Parking High Street; Windmill Lane; College Road; Turners Hill; Boffs Lane (all car parks).
District council Broxbourne (Tel. Waltham Cross 27933).
Population 49,700.
E-C Thur.
Police Turners Hill (Tel. Waltham Cross 27377).
Casualty hospital Enfield District Hospital, The Ridgeway, Enfield (Tel. 01 366 6600).
Post office Old Pond.
Cinema Embassy, High Street, Waltham Cross (Tel. Lea Valley 761044).
Public library Turners Hill.
Shopping Old Pond.
AA 24 hour service Tel. Hatfield 62852.

Chester see page 92

Chesterfield Derbyshire

There were Saxon and Roman settlements on the site of Chesterfield, which lies on the fringe of the rugged Peak District. The town is recorded in the Domesday Book, and a hint of its medieval past remains in the names of the town-centre streets, such as Knifesmithgate and Glumangate – a gluman or gleeman was a minstrel.

Chesterfield's parish church of St Mary and All Saints is the town's most notable landmark. Its twisted, leaning spire can be seen for miles. The central tower and the spire were built in the 14th century.

There is a local legend that the builders intended the 228 ft high spire to be twisted, but it is more likely that the heat of the sun expanded the lead plates, warping the wooden frame into its distorted shape. The church has a Norman font, a Jacobean pulpit, Victorian stained glass and a modern altar.

There are few historic buildings in Chesterfield, although a fine 18th-century terrace still lines Saltergate,

and the Royal Oak Inn in The Shambles dates from Tudor times. The Market Place has been renovated, with shopping facilities in the 19th-century Market Hall. A heritage centre has been set up in the medieval Peacock Inn.

The Cock and Pynot Inn at Old Whittington, on the north side of the town, was the meeting place of the 4th Earl of Devonshire and his fellow plotters, who helped bring about the downfall of James II in 1688. The inn is now called Revolution House, and is a museum of local history.

Hardwick Hall, 7 miles south of Chesterfield, was built at the end of the 16th century by Elizabeth, Countess of Shrewsbury – Bess of Hardwick – ancestress of the Dukes of Devonshire. Inside are fine Elizabethan furniture, tapestries and portraits.

Bolsover Castle, 6 miles east of the town, was built in the 17th century on the site of a medieval fortress.

Information Tel. 207777.
Location On the A61, 12 m. S of Sheffield.
Parking Saltergate; Soresby Street; Rose Hill West; Rose Hill East; Spa Lane; Devonshire Street; Park Road; New Beetwell Street (all car parks).
District council Borough of Chesterfield (Tel. 77232).
Population 70,500.
E-C Wed. **M-D** Mon., Fri. and Sat.
Police (Ba) Beetwell Street (Tel. 31155).
Casualty hospital (Bb) Royal, Holywell Street (Tel. 77271).
Post office (Aa) West Bars.
Theatre Civic **(Ba)**, Corporation Street (Tel. 32471).
Cinema ABC **(Bb)**, Cavendish Street (Tel. 73333).
Public library (Ba) Corporation Street.
Places to see Revolution House, Old Whittington; Peacock Heritage

RAILWAY PIONEER

George Stephenson moved to Chesterfield in 1837, eight years after his steam locomotive *Rocket* had revolutionised railway transport. He married the daughter of a local farmer and lived at Tapton House, north of the town, until his death in 1848. He is buried in the chancel of Chesterfield's Holy Trinity Church.

Tapton, home of a railway genius.

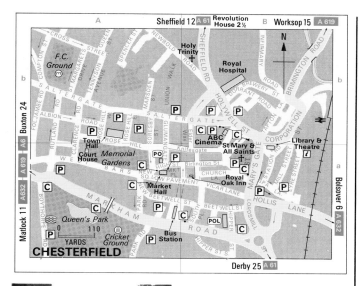

CROOKED SPIRE *Chesterfield's odd landmark has lasted for 600 years.*

Centre; Lecture Hall (**Aa**), New Square; Bolsover Castle, 6 m. E, off A632; Hardwick Hall, 7 m. S.
Shopping The Pavements; Knifesmithgate; Burlington Street.
Trade and industry Engineering; glass; potteries.
Sport FA League football, Chesterfield FC, Saltergate.
AA 24 hour service
Tel. Sheffield 28861.

Chester-le-Street Durham

The Romans founded Chester-le-Street in the 1st century AD as a base on their main road north. It is thus one of the oldest towns in Britain. When the legions left in the 5th century, the settlement sank into obscurity until monks from Lindisfarne built a shrine there in 883 for the body of St Cuthbert. The saint remained at Chester-le-Street for 112 years before being removed to Durham.

Throughout the Middle Ages, the town was a stopping post on the Great North Road. Its modern development sprang from the exploitation of the Durham coalfield. Only one mine remains in the neighbourhood, and the town is now a business centre.

In the 14th century, Lord Lumley, Chancellor to Richard II, built Lumley Castle on the eastern outskirts of the town. Although modernised in the 18th century, the castle still retains a medieval look. Lambton Castle, seat of the Earls of Durham, was designed by the Italian architect Bonomi in 1794. Lambton Lion Park, near the castle, is open to the public in the summer.

Information Tel. 882521.
Location On the B6313, 8 m. S of Newcastle upon Tyne.
Parking South Burns; Front Street; North Burns; Mains Park Road; Church Chare; Chare; Cone Terrace; Cricket-Ground (all car parks).
District council Chester-le-Street (Tel. 882521).
Population 26,500.
E-C Wed. **M-D** Tues. and Fri.
Police Newcastle Road (Tel. 884311).
Casualty hospital Dryburn Hospital, North Road, Durham (Tel. Durham 64911).
Post office Front Street.
Public library Station Road.
Places to see Lambton Lion Park, 2 m. E.
Shopping Front Street.
Trade and industry Coal-mining; light engineering.
AA 24 hour service
Tel. Newcastle upon Tyne 610111.

Chichester see page 94

Chigwell Essex

Charles Dickens used a Chigwell inn, the King's Head, as the model for the Maypole Inn in *Barnaby Rudge*.

Chigwell School in High Road was founded in 1629 by Samuel Harsnett, Archbishop of York. Among its former pupils was William Penn, the Quaker who gave his name to the State of Pennsylvania in America.

The town was also the home of Captain Eliab Harvey, who fought alongside Nelson at Trafalgar. Two chairs in the garden of Rolls Park (private), his family home, are said to have been made from the timbers of his ship, the *Temeraire*, immortalised by the artist J. M. W. Turner in his picture the *Fighting Temeraire*.

Information Tel. 01 508 5566.
Location On the A113, 14 m. NE of London.
Parking Victory Hall, Hainault Road (car park); Brook Parade.
District council Epping Forest (Tel. Epping 77344).
Population 51,300.
E-C Thur.
Police Brook Parade (Tel. 01 501 2231).
Casualty hospital King George, Eastern Avenue, Newbury Park (Tel. 01 554 8811).
Post office Brook Parade.
Public library Hainault Road.
Shopping Brook Parade; Manor Road; Grange Hill.
AA 24 hour service
Tel. Chelmsford 61711.

Chippenham Wiltshire

A market town since the 14th century, Chippenham still has one of the largest cattle markets in England. One of its oldest buildings, the 15th-century Yelde Hall in Market Place, has a wooden turret and twin gables. The Hall is now a museum of local history.

Just outside Chippenham, the Georgian church at Hardenhuish (pronounced Harnish) was built in 1781 by John Wood the Younger, designer of Bath's Royal Crescent.

Lacock Abbey, in the National Trust village of Lacock, 3 miles south of Chippenham, was the home of William Fox-Talbot, the father of modern photography. In 1833 he made the first photographic prints there. There is a museum of photography in the grounds.

Information Tel. 4188.
Location On the A4, 13 m. NE of Bath.
Parking Gladstone Road; River Street; Westmead Lane; Monkton Hill; Sadler's Thread; Park Lane (all car parks).
District council North Wiltshire (Tel. 4188).
Population 19,300.
E-C Wed. **M-D** Fri.
Police Wood Lane (Tel. 4455).
Casualty hospital London Road (Tel. 51144).
Post office Market Place.
Cinema Studios One and Two, Marshfield Road (Tel. 2498).
Public library Timber Street.
Places to see Yelde Museum, Market Place; Fox-Talbot Museum, Tythe Barn, Lacock, and Lacock Abbey, both 3 m. S.
Trade and industry Electrical engineering; dairy products.
AA 24 hour service
Tel. Bristol 298531.

CHESTER Cheshire

A city stranded by the sea

The best-preserved walled city in England, and one of the richest in architectural and archaeological treasures, Chester has a distinctive dignity. With its medieval, galleried streets and houses of plaster and age-blackened wood, no town conjures up more vividly the atmosphere of old England.

EASTGATE *Part of the city walls since the 10th century, Eastgate Tower was rebuilt in 1897 and crowned with a clock.*

The site, on a sandstone spur north of the River Dee, was first settled in the middle of the 1st century by the Romans. The 20th Legion, one of three in Britain, was stationed here and the site was chosen because of its strategic position between recently conquered Wales and the north of England.

The Romans called their fortress Deva, but Chester's modern name comes simply from the Latin *castra* (a fortified camp). The Romans also built the largest amphitheatre so far discovered in Britain. It measures 314 ft by 286 ft and lies east of Newgate.

The city's **Grosvenor Museum** in Grosvenor Street has a large collection of Roman remains.

Conquered by William

It is believed that the 20th Legion withdrew from Chester in the late 3rd century, and little is known about the city in the Dark Ages. Probably there was a small community living there until, in the late 7th century, Chester became part of the Saxon Kingdom of Mercia. At the beginning of the 10th century the Roman defences were strengthened, but in 1069 the city was laid waste by William the Conqueror. He gave control of the city to Hugh of Avranches and made him Earl of Chester. Since 1301 this title has usually been held by the male heir to the throne, as Prince of Wales and Earl of Chester. It is now held by Prince Charles.

Chester grew into a trading centre and port. More towers were added to the walls, among them the **Water Tower** in the city's north-west corner, built in 1322.

Inside the walls, building was also going on. **The Rows** – streets in which shops open on to balustraded walkways – date from medieval times. The distinctive style of The Rows is thought to have developed because the early inhabitants built their homes both in front and on top of the old Roman buildings. Today these galleried arcades, which are reached by steps from the road, form traffic-free shopping centres that dominate Watergate Street, Eastgate Street and Bridge Street. Several half-timbered houses, notably **Bishop Lloyd's House**, **God's Providence House** and **Old Leche House**, have rich carvings cut deep into age-blackened wood. The **British Heritage Exhibition** in Vicar's Lane contains a life-size replica of part of The Rows as they were in the 19th century, complete with sounds and smells.

Chester Castle began as a timber building about 1069. Henry III added stone ramparts and towers, but the outer walls were mostly torn down in the late 18th century to make way for a group of buildings designed by the architect Thomas Harrison. This group includes the castle's Grand Entrance, and the city's Crown Court.

Mystery Plays

The cathedral, at the heart of the city, was built on the site of a Benedictine monastery and is mainly 14th century. It was a Benedictine abbey until its dissolution in 1540, and it became a cathedral in 1541. A grotesque figure, known as the **Chester Imp**, leers out from the north side of the clerestory in the cathedral nave – a reminder of the nightmarish way in which the medieval Church sought to drive off evil spirits.

The Chester Mystery Plays are another surviving link with the abbey. These were performed on carts which travelled through the streets within the city walls and stopped at certain sites. The plays, banned by Tudor Puritans, were revived this century and are now performed every five years on a different site each year, but always within the walls.

In the 15th century, Chester's prosperity began to be affected by the silting up of the River Dee. But a new channel cut in 1735 and the Chester Canal built in 1770 helped revive trade. There are a number of fine Georgian houses in the city which bear witness to considerable wealth during this period. During the Napoleonic Wars, Chester's shipyards built ships for the Royal Navy, and in 1810 it was noted that more ships were being built than at Liverpool. Leadworks also contributed to the city's wealth, and the still surviving Shot Tower, built in 1800, is probably the oldest in Britain.

Backed the loser

During the Civil War the city chose to back the losing side, the Royalists. From **King Charles's Tower**, in September 1645, Charles I is said to have watched the defeat of his forces at the Battle of Rowton Moor. After the battle, the king fled to Wales; but the beleaguered citizens held out for five months more, until starvation forced them to submit. King Charles's Tower today contains an exhibition portraying life in the city in those grim years.

Another reminder of Chester's violent past is the **Bridge of Sighs**, which crosses the canal outside Northgate. It was so called because it is said that condemned felons used it on the way from the medieval dungeons in the rock beneath the gate to hear their last church service in the Chapel of Little St John.

In the south-east corner of the walls, however, is a rather more light-hearted legacy: six short flights of stone stairs known as the **Wishing Steps**. They were built in 1785 and, according to tradition, a would-be

THE ROWS *Chester's medieval streets, dating from at least the 14th century, are lined by double-tiered balustraded walkways. These are reached by steps from street level and give access to shops.*

wisher must run to the top, back to the bottom and then up again, without drawing breath.

Information Tel. 40144.
Location On the A56, 25 m. S of Liverpool.
Parking Garden Lane; Delamare Street; St Anne Street; Steam Mill Street; Castle Drive; Cuppin Street; Weaver Street; Princess Street; Trinity Street; Frodsham Street; Pepper Street; New Crane Street (all car parks).
District council City of Chester (Tel. 40144).
Population 88,400.
E-C Wed.
Police (Ba) Castle Esplanade (Tel. 315432).
Casualty hospital Royal Infirmary **(Ab)**, St Martin's Way (Tel. 315500).
Post office (Bb) St John Street.
Theatres Gateway **(Bb)**, The Forum (Tel. 40393); Little, Gloucester Street, Newtown (22674).
Cinemas ABC **(Cb)**, Foregate Street (Tel. 22931); Odeon **(Bc)**, Northgate Street (24930).
Public library (Bb) St John Street.
Places to see Chester Heritage Centre **(Bb)**, Bridge Street Row **(Bb)**; Cathedral **(Bb)**; Grosvenor Museum **(Bb)**, Grosvenor Street; Guildhall Museum **(Bb)**, Watergate Street; Zoo, Upton; Roman amphitheatre **(Cb)**, Vicar's Lane; Stanley Palace, Watergate Street;

CHESTER CATHEDRAL *The magnificently carved stalls in the choir date from the late 14th century, when the cathedral was extensively rebuilt.*

The Rows **(Bb)**; Castle, Cheshire Regiment Museum and city walls; King Charles's Tower Museum; British Heritage, Vicar's Lane.
Shopping Grosvenor Precinct; The Forum; The Rows.

Sport Chester Races (May, July, Sept.); FA League football, Chester FC, Sealand Road; Greyhound racing, Sealand Road.
AA 24 hour service
Tel. Liverpool (051) 709 7252.

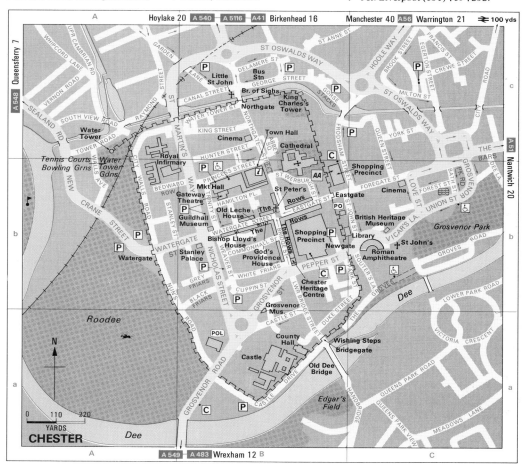

CHICHESTER W. Sussex

The city beneath the Downs

The centre of Chichester closely reflects the layout of the city built by the Romans from the 1st century AD, and its four main streets, crossing at right-angles, follow the lines of the original Roman street plan. Chichester was then known as *Noviomagus* (the new city of the plain). Now it is one of Britain's oldest towns, a careful blend of ancient and modern.

Chichester lies in one of the most attractive corners of Britain. The wooded South Downs, glorious stretches of unspoiled countryside, roll almost to the fringe of the city, hiding in their folds tiny villages of thatched cottages, half-timbered houses and centuries-old churches. To the south lies the rest of the coastal plain, the sea, and Chichester Harbour, a yachtsman's delight with its 27 sq. miles of navigable water.

MARKET CROSS *Bishop Edward Story gave the elaborate market cross to Chichester in 1501.*

There was a settlement in Chichester even before the Emperor Claudius led the Romans to Britain in AD 43. Invading Belgae from northern France had persuaded a local tribe, the Regni, to leave their hill-top settlement at nearby Trundle and form an alliance in a new tribal capital at the head of the navigable part of the harbour. Their leader when the Romans arrived was Cogidubnus. He offered no resistance, and won the remarkable privilege for a barbarian of being appointed Imperial Legate.

Roman town

The Romans used Chichester as a base camp when they first arrived in Britain, but later it was laid out as a market town and administrative centre. Today, Chichester is still that – market town for the extensive farming community on the coastal plain and the slopes of the South Downs, and county town of West Sussex.

In about AD 200 the city walls were built. They formed an 11-sided polygon with gates at the end of each main street, North, South, West and East. The walls were altered considerably in later centuries. Large stretches remain, but most of what can be seen is medieval. After the Romans left, the city fell into the hands of the Saxons, and it is from this vigorous race that Chichester gets its modern name. The Saxon chief Aella, who landed about 477, gave the settlement to his son, Cissa, who called it Cissa's *Ceaster* (castle).

Christianity reached the Sussex coastal plain in 681 when St Wilfrid, banished from the See of York, landed at Selsey and set up the diocese of the South Saxons. But it was the Normans who turned Chichester into a cathedral city. William the Conqueror gave it to Roger de Montgomery, Earl of Arundel, and in 1075 the See was transferred from Selsey. It

was a wise move. The original cathedral now lies under the waves off Selsey Bill.

Work on **Chichester Cathedral** was started in 1091 by Bishop Ralph de Luffa on the site of an old collegiate church. It has twice been damaged by fire and was desecrated by the Puritans, but the cathedral remains substantially as it was built in the 12th and 13th centuries. It has a soaring nave and a graceful spire 277 ft high, visible for miles at sea.

The separate bell-tower was built in the 15th century, and stands near the north porch. The cathedral has a contemporary altar tapestry designed by John Piper in 1966, and in the Sailors' Chapel is the pennant flown by Sir Francis Chichester on his epic solo voyage around the world in *Gipsy Moth IV* in 1966-7.

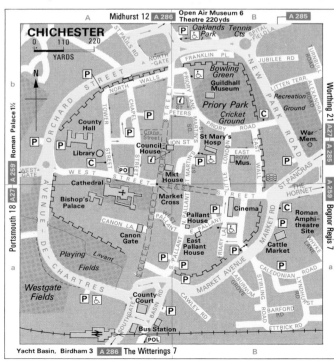

The winged sea-horse motif forms part of a mosaic floor which was made about AD 150.

Chichester has a peaceful history, and for centuries its farmers and merchants have prospered. Wool was its major product in the 14th century, and there was a large export trade from the port. Later, cloth, and then wheat, became in turn the city's most important commodities. The market cross, which stands at the city centre, was the gift of Bishop Edward Story in 1501. It is 50 ft high and one of the finest in England.

Much of Chichester today is Georgian, and there are some beautiful merchants' houses in **West Street** and the **Pallants**.

Buried palace

In 1960 workmen laying a water-pipe for some new houses on the western outskirts of the city uncovered a mosaic floor. They had accidentally made one of the most exciting archaeological discoveries for decades – the site of **Fishbourne Roman Palace**. Years of patient excavation have now revealed it as the largest single Roman building yet found in Britain. In size and grandeur it would have competed with the palaces of Imperial Rome itself.

Fishbourne was a Roman supply base after Claudius's invasion. Wooden storehouses have been discovered, as well as evidence of a harbour. The palace was not built until about AD 70, and may well have been the residence of Cogidubnus, the local king.

The whole of the north wing and parts of the west and east wings have been excavated. A modern building now encloses the whole north wing, and finds from the site are in a museum alongside. The central gardens of the palace have been re-planted in the original, formal style. There is clear evidence that the palace was burned down in 270.

The history of Sussex is also preserved at a unique open-air museum in the nearby village of **Singleton**. Buildings from the past that have been threatened by decay or demolition have been painstakingly re-erected in a wooded valley.

With the development of the extensive yacht basin at nearby **Birdham**, Chichester has become one of the busiest yachting centres in the British Isles.

In 1962 **Chichester Festival Theatre** was opened just outside the old city walls. It is a modern building of hexagonal design with a traditional apron stage, and is one of the best-equipped theatres in the country. Its presentation of classical and contemporary theatre has won it an international reputation.

Four miles from the city is **Goodwood House**, an 18th-century mansion built on the site of a former royal hunting lodge, and the seat of the Dukes of Richmond and Gordon. The house is rich in paintings and furniture.

Goodwood, a racecourse in a setting of unrivalled beauty, was laid out in the grounds by the third Duke of Richmond in 1801.

FESTIVAL THEATRE *Lord Olivier was the theatre's first artistic director.*

Information Tel. 784255.
Location On the A27, 18 m. E of Portsmouth.
Parking Orchard Street; St Martin's Street; Northgate; East Pallant; New Park Road; Market Avenue; Avenue-de-Chartres; Caledonian Road; Market Road; Chapel Street; South Pallant; St John's Street (all car parks).
District council Chichester (Tel. 784255).
Population 24,200.
E-C Thur. **M-D** Wed.
Police Kingsham Road (Tel. 784433).
Casualty hospital St Richard's, Spitalfield Lane (Tel. 788122).
Post office (Ab) West Street.
Theatre Chichester Festival, Oaklands Park (Tel. 781312).
Public library (Ab) Tower Street.
Places to see District Museum **(Bb)**, Little London; St Mary's Hospital Almshouses, St Martin's Square; Pallant House Gallery **(Ba)**, North Pallant; Goodwood House, 4 m. NE off A285; Guildhall Museum **(Bb)**; Roman Palace, Salthill Road, Fishbourne; Weald and Downland Open Air Museum, Singleton.
Shopping North Street; East Street; South Street; West Street.
Events Gala Week (July); Festival (July); Sloe Fair (Oct.).
Sport Horse racing, Goodwood (May, July, Aug., Sept.).
AA 24 hour service Tel. Brighton 695231.

CHICHESTER CATHEDRAL *The graceful spire of the 12th–13th-century cathedral, seen from the gates of the Deanery, soars to a height of 277 ft. The spire was rebuilt in the 1860s after the original collapsed in a gale.*

Chipping Campden Glos.

The name Chipping, also found in other Cotswold towns, is Old English for market or trading centre. In the 14th and 15th centuries Chipping Campden was a wool town, where merchants bought fleeces in the 14th-century Woolstaplers Hall, now a museum of photographic and medical equipment.

The mainly 15th-century Church of St James is one of the finest "wool" churches in the Cotswolds, and contains many fine monumental brasses.

Old Campden House was burned down by Royalists during the Civil War to prevent it falling into the hands of Cromwell, and only a fragment remains. The stable block was converted into the Dower House after the Civil War. North-east of the town, the magnificent gardens of Hidcote Manor and Kiftsgate Court are open to the public.

Dover's Games, held annually, are a re-creation of the classical Olympic Games. They were founded in the 17th century, and include the rural sport of shin-kicking.

Information
Tel. Evesham 840289.
Location On the B4035, 12 m. S of Stratford-on-Avon.
Parking Market Square; High Street (both car parks).
District council Cotswold (Tel. Cirencester 5757).
Population 1,960.
E-C Thur.
Police High Street
(Tel. Evesham 840500 or 840611).
Casualty hospital Cheltenham General, Sandford Road, Cheltenham (Tel. Cheltenham 21344).
Post office High Street.
Public library High Street.
Places to see Woolstaplers Hall Museum; Car Collection, High Street; Market Hall; Hidcote Manor, 4 m. NE; Kiftsgate Court, 3 m. NE.
Event Dover's Games (May or June).
AA 24 hour service
Tel. Gloucester 23278.

Chipping Norton Oxon.

The wide market place of this old wool-trading town is still the centre of its communal life. Tweed was made here until 1980 and the largest building in the town is a Victorian tweed-mill. The parish church is also large – one of the largest in Oxfordshire – and has many fine brasses. Near by are almshouses dating from 1640. The White Hart Hotel in the High Street was a staging post in the 18th century, and contains much furniture of that period. Three miles north are the Rollright Stones, a Bronze Age circle of 1800-550 BC.

Information Tel. 41320.
Location On the A361, 20 m. NW of Oxford.
Parking New Street; Cattle Market; Albion Street (all car parks).
District council West Oxfordshire (Tel. Witney 3051).
Population 5,000.
E-C Thur. **M-D** Wed.
Police London Road (Tel. 2021).
Casualty hospital John Radcliffe II, Headington, Oxford
(Tel. Oxford 64711).
Post office West Street.
Theatre and cinema Spring Street (Tel. 2350).
Public library Goddard's Lane.
Places to see Guildhall; Rollright Stones, 3 m. N on A34.
Shopping Market Place.
AA 24 hour service
Tel. Oxford 40286.

Chorley Lancashire

A busy market-town atmosphere helps Chorley to avoid the grimness that often besets industrial towns. Chorley, standing at the foot of the Pennines, grew on cotton weaving and calico printing. The 14th-century parish church of St Laurence recalls Chorley's pre-industrial past as a trading centre for the surrounding farmland. So, too, does Astley Hall, a splendid Jacobean mansion rebuilt on the foundations of an Elizabethan hall. The long gallery contains a massive table for playing shovel-board, and there are fine collections of paintings and pottery.

Henry Tate (1819-99), the sugar magnate and founder of the Tate Gallery, was born at Chorley and began his career there as a grocer's assistant.

ASTLEY HALL *Extensive parkland borders this fine Jacobean mansion at Chorley, dating from 1666.*

Information Tel. 65611.
Location On the A6, 11 m. NW of Bolton.
Parking Cattle Market; Hughlock Hindle; West Street; Farrington Street; Queens Road; Albion Street; Pall Mall; Fleet Street; Halliwell Street; Clifford Street (all car parks).
District council Borough of Chorley (Tel. 65611).
Population 34,600.
E-C Wed. **M-D** Tues., Fri. and Sat.
Police St Thomas's Road
(Tel. 62831).
Casualty hospital Preston Royal Infirmary, Deepdale Road, Preston (Tel. Preston 54747).
Post office Union Street.
Theatre Little Theatre, Dole Lane (Tel. 75123).
Cinema Studios 1, 2, 3 and 4, Bolton Road (Tel. 70244).
Public library Avondale Road.
Places to see Astley Hall.
Shopping Market Street; Chapel Street; High Street; Cleveland Street; Fazakerley Street.
Event Carnival (July).
AA 24 hour service
Tel. Manchester (061) 485 6299.

Christchurch Dorset

In Saxon times Christchurch was a walled town, one of Alfred the Great's strongholds against the Danes. Today it is a holiday resort, but the town centre still retains the Saxon street plan.

The magnificent 12th-century priory church is one of the longest parish churches in England. The carved choir stalls are older than those in Westminster Abbey.

Near by are the ruins of a Norman castle and its constable's house. Place Mill, mentioned in Domesday Book, still stands on Christchurch Quay.

Information Tel. 471780 or 486321.
Location On the A35, 6 m. E of Bournemouth.
Parking Quay Road; Christchurch Quay; Wick Lane (2); Bargates (2); Soper's Lane; Willow Way; Stoney Lane South; Wortley Road; Avon Run Road; Sandhills; Mayors Mead; Bridge Street; Mudeford Quay;

TIME-WORN STONES *Chipping Campden's Market Hall was built in 1627. Its mellow arches look out on a scene little changed since medieval times.*

Southcliffe Road; Highcliffe Cliffs (all car parks).
District council Borough of Christchurch (Tel. 486321).
Population 32,800.
E-C Wed. **M-D** Mon.
Police Barrack Road (Tel. 486333).
Casualty hospital Poole General, Longfleet Road, Poole (Tel. Poole 5100).
Post office Arcade, High Street.
Public library Druitt Buildings.
Places to see Castle ruins; Priory church; Place Mill; Red House Museum and Art Gallery; Tucktonia Model Britain, Stour Road.
Shopping High Street; Castle Street; Bargates.
AA 24 hour service
Tel. Bournemouth 425204.

Cirencester Gloucestershire

Cirencester (pronounced Syrensester) was in Roman times the second largest town in Britain after London. It was founded about AD 75 to house the local British tribe, the Dobunni, and its Roman name was Corinium Dobunnorum. By the 2nd century it had become a 240 acre fortified town of colonnaded streets and sumptuous buildings, and the crossroads of three major routes, including the Fosse Way. In the 6th century the Roman town was destroyed by the Saxons, who later built a new town on its site.

ABBEY GROUNDS *A Norman arch is all that is left of Cirencester Abbey.*

Cirencester had another period of greatness in the Middle Ages, when it became the largest wool market in England. But the cloth trade declined during the Industrial Revolution, and since then the town has developed as an agricultural centre.

The architectural glory of Cirencester is the Church of St John Baptist, in the Market Place. The Normans built it as a small parish church, but in the 14th and 15th centuries it was enlarged – almost to cathedral size – at the expense of the town's wealthy wool merchants. The rebuilding created the most magnificent "wool" church in the country. Its outstanding features include the soaring west tower and the fan tracery of the unique three-storey south porch. The peal of 12 bells is the oldest in the country.

Also in the Market Place are the Corn Hall, a Victorian building with finely detailed decoration, and next

to it the King's Head, an inn with an 18th-century façade.

Surrounding the Market Place is a network of fascinating old streets. Among them are Spitalgate, with the remains of a 12th-century almshouse, the Hospital of St John; Coxwell Street, an unspoiled row of wool-merchants' houses and workmen's cottages; Thomas Street, which contains the Weaver's Hall, continuously occupied since it was founded in 1425 for poor weavers; and Dollar Street, containing bow-windowed shops with dim interiors, some dating back to the 17th century.

North of the parish church are the grounds of the now-vanished abbey, through which the River Churn winds into a lake graced by swans.

Little visible evidence of the Roman occupation survives in the town, but the Corinium Museum houses one of the country's most impressive collections of Roman remains, including some beautiful mosaic floors, sculpture and domestic objects. Some of the highlights are a reconstruction of a town-house dining-room, built around a mosaic of the four seasons, and a cut-away view of a central-heating system.

Information Tel. 4180.
Location On the A419, 19 m. SE of Gloucester.
Parking Dugdale Road; Beeches Road; Southway; Ashcroft Road; Market Place; The Waterloo; Tetbury Road (all car parks).
District council Cotswold (Tel. Cirencester 5757).
Population 15,600.
E-C Thur. **M-D** Mon., Fri.
Police (Ba) Northway (Tel. 2121).
Casualty hospital (Aa) Cirencester Memorial, Sheep Street (Tel. 5711).
Post office (Aa) Castle Street.

MARKET PLACE *Cirencester's great "wool" church has looked down for centuries on the colourful trading scene beneath.*

Theatre Beeches Barn Theatre **(Bb)**, Beeches Road (Tel. 3669).
Cinema Regal, Lewis Lane (Tel. 2358).
Public library (Bb) The Waterloo.
Places to see Corinium Museum **(Aa)**, Park Street; Abbey Butterflies, West Market Street.
Town trails Available from Information Centre, museum and shops.
Shopping Market Place; Dyer Street; Cricklade Street; Castle Street.
AA 24 hour service
Tel. Gloucester 23278.

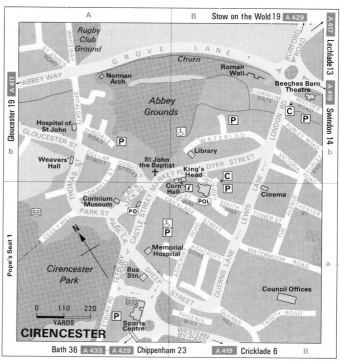

CIRENCESTER

Clackmannan Central

The town climbs from the banks of the Black Devon river up a steep hill crowned by a 14th-century, 79 ft tower, reputedly built by Robert Bruce.

Beside the 16th-century Old Tolbooth is the Mannan Stone. A legend says that Robert Bruce left a *pannan* (glove) at the *clach* (stone), and that this is how the town got its name. The stone is a block of rough-hewn whinstone, more than 9 ft tall and 15 ft around the base.

Information Tel. Kincardine 30096 or Alloa 722160.
Location On the A907, 12 m. W of Dunfermline.
Parking Main Street (car park). Unrestricted street parking.
District council Clackmannan (Tel. Alloa 722160).
Population 3,240.
E-C Tues.
Police Drysdale Road (Tel. Alloa 723255).
Casualty hospital Clackmannan County Hospital, Ashley Terrace, Alloa (Tel. Alloa 213141).
Post office Drysdale Street.
Public library Castle Street.
Places to see Robert Bruce's Tower; Old Tolbooth; Mannan Stone.
Shopping Main Street; Lochies Road.
AA 24 hour service
Tel. Glasgow (041) 812 0101.

Clacton-on-Sea Essex

A century ago the quiet east-coast village of Great Clacton awoke to the then novel craze for sun, sea and sand, and became Clacton-on-Sea. It is now a typically boisterous English seaside resort with pier, funfair, pavilion, holiday camp, and other traditional amusements.

Moot Hall was built as a dower house in 1490 at Bury St Edmunds. It was moved to Clacton in 1910 and is

CLACTON *Every inch of the modern pier is crammed with amusements, and only the lifeboat uses it as a jetty. But the original pier of 1871 was a landing-stage for Clacton's first trippers, arriving by steamer from London.*

now a private house. The Martello Towers on the seafront are two of many built around the south and east coasts when Napoleon was threatening to invade Britain at the beginning of the 19th century.

Great Clacton's church dates from Norman times. Although restored, it retains a 15th-century tower.

Information Tel. 25501.
Location On the A133, 16 m. SE of Colchester.
Parking Old Road; Wash Lane; Agate Road; West Road; Ipswich Road; Hazelmere Road; York Road; Caernarvon Road; Wellesley Road (all car parks).
District council Tendring (Tel. 25501).
Population 43,500.
E-C Wed. **M-D** Tues., Sat.
Police (Aa) West Avenue (Tel. 22314).
Casualty hospital Clacton and District **(Aa)**, Freeland Road (Tel. 21145).
Post office Station Road.
Theatres West Cliff **(Aa)**, Tower Road (Tel. 21479); Princes **(Bb)**, Town Hall (22958).
Cinema Mecca 1 and 2 **(Ab)**, Pier Avenue (Tel. 21188).
Public library (Bb) Station Road.
Shopping High Street; Station Road; Pier Avenue.
AA 24 hour service
Tel. Chelmsford 61711.

Cleethorpes Humberside

Only 100 years ago Cleethorpes was a tiny fishing village, its boats overshadowed by the giant fishing fleets of nearby Grimsby. Now, however, it is one of the North's favourite East Coast resorts, with as many as a million visitors a year. Many of Grimsby's rich fishing families built fine houses in Cleethorpes.

The attractions that draw the holidaymakers include wide promenades, a 300 ft long pier, and a boating lake, but most of all the sands. The beaches of Cleethorpes stretch for 3 miles, and the land shelves so gently that the North Sea retreats over a mile at each tide.

Information Tel. 67472.
Location On the A18, 2 m. S of Grimsby.
Parking Alexandra Road; Grant Street; Thrunscoe; Anthony's Bank (all car parks).
District council Borough of Cleethorpes (Tel. 66111).
Population 35,400.
E-C Thur.
Police Princes Road (Tel. 67131).
Casualty hospital Grimsby General, West Marsh, Grimsby (Tel. Grimsby 59901).
Post office High Street.
Theatre Pier Pavilion (Tel. 61022).
Cinema ABC, Grimsby Road (Tel. 61713).
Public library Isaac's Hill.
Shopping St Peters Avenue; High Street.
AA 24 hour service
Tel. Hull 28580.

Clevedon Avon

The Victorian influence can be seen everywhere in Clevedon; in its houses, hotels and gardens, and the pier – now partly collapsed – which is claimed to be the finest Victorian pier in England.

There are two good medieval buildings, the parish church and Clevedon Court. St Andrew's Church is partly Norman, and stands on a headland. Clevedon Court was built about 1320, and is one of the few surviving manor houses of the period. In 1709 the house was bought by Abraham Elton, a wealthy Bristol merchant. Sir Arthur Elton transferred the house to the National Trust in 1961.

Information Tel. Weston-super-Mare 26838.

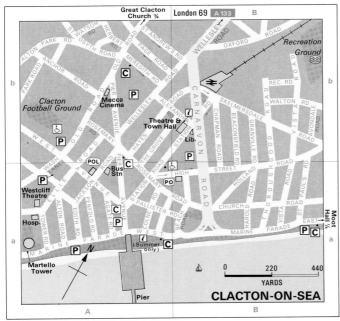

CLACTON-ON-SEA

Location On the B3130, 13 m. W of Bristol; just off M5 (Junction 20).
Parking Station Road; Old Station Yard; Salthouse Fields; Elton Road; Marson Road (all car parks); Gardens Road; Hillside Road.
District council Woodspring (Tel. Weston-super-Mare 31701).
Population 17,900.
E-C Wed.
Police Queens Road (Tel. 873461).
Casualty hospital Clevedon Hospital, Old Street (Tel. 872212).
Post office Albert Road.
Cinema Curzon, Old Church Road (Tel. 872158).
Public library Linden Road.
Places to see Clevedon Court, ½ m. E, on B3130; Craft Centre, Moor Lane; Walton Castle, Castle Road.
Shopping Six Ways; The Triangle; Hill Road; Alexandra Road.
AA 24 hour service
Tel. Bristol 298531.

Clitheroe Lancashire

A ruined Norman castle with the smallest keep in England stands on a limestone knoll above Clitheroe. Its last resident was Henry, Earl of Lincoln, who died in 1311. Roundheads destroyed the castle in 1648.

The town retains much of its ancient character, and a winding main street climbs to the castle between rows of sombre, limestone buildings flecked with white-fronted Georgian houses. The old town well, in Wellgate, is still in working order.

Information Tel. 25566.
Location On the A59, 18 m. NE of Preston.
Parking North Street; Holden Street; Queensway; Whalley Road; Station Road; Chester Avenue (all car parks).
District council Borough of Ribble Valley (Tel. 25111).
Population 13,500.
E-C Wed. **M-D** Tues., Sat.
Police King Street (Tel. 23818).
Casualty hospital Royal Infirmary, Bolton Road, Blackburn (Tel. Blackburn 63555).
Post office King Street.
Cinema Civic Hall, York Street (Tel. 23278).
Public library Church Street.
Places to see Castle ruins and Museum, Castle Street.

Shopping Castle Street; Moor Lane; Market Place.
AA 24 hour service
Tel. Manchester (061) 485 6299.

Clydebank Strathclyde

Some of the world's finest ships were built at Clydebank, which has echoed to the sound of the riveter's hammer since 1871. The town was rebuilt after the Second World War, and in the 1970s the shipyards turned to a new industry – building rigs for the North Sea oilfields.

Information Tel. Glasgow (041) 941 1331; (041) 221 6136.
Location On the A814, 7 m. W of Glasgow.
Parking Miller Street; Belmont Street; Gordon Street; Gordon Road; Argyle Road (all car parks).
District council Clydebank (Tel. 041 941 1331).
Population 40,900.
E-C Wed. **M-D** Wed., Sun.
Police Montrose Street (Tel. 041 941 1113).
Casualty hospitals Gartnavel General, Great Western Road (Tel. 041 338 8122); Glasgow Western Infirmary, Dumbarton Road (041 552 4513).
Post office Chalmers Street.
Theatre Repertory, Agamemnon Street (Tel. 041 952 4644).
Cinema ABC, Graham Avenue (Tel. 041 952 1229).
Public library Dumbarton Road.
Places to see Clydebank District Museum, Hall Street.
Shopping Clyde Shopping Centre, Kilbowie Road.
Sport Scottish League football, Clydebank FC, Kilbowie Park.
AA 24 hour service
Tel. 041 812 0101.

Coatbridge Strathclyde

Locally mined coal, a canal to Glasgow, and Scotland's first railway combined to make Coatbridge prosperous in the 18th and 19th centuries. Then ironstone was found there, and the town became the centre of the Scottish iron industry.

Information Tel. 24941.
Location On the A89, 9 m. E of Glasgow.
Parking Dunbeth Road; King Street;

Baird Street; Central Station; Gartsherrie Road; Espreside Street; Dundyvan Road; Academy Street; Hutton Street; St John Street; Church Street; Murryhall Street; Kildonan Street; Whifflet Street; Bank Street (all car parks).
District council Monklands (Tel. 24941).
Population 48,200.
E-C Wed.
Police Whittington Street (Tel. 20155).
Casualty hospital Monkland, Manor Drive, Airdrie (Tel. Airdrie 69344).
Post office Bank Street.
Cinema ABC, Ellis Street (Tel. 23450).
Public library Academy Street.
Shopping Main Street; Whifflet Precinct.
Sport Scottish League football, Albion Rovers FC, Cliftonhill.
AA 24 hour service
Tel. Glasgow (041) 812 0101.

Cockermouth Cumbria

At one end of Cockermouth's broad, tree-lined main street stands a Georgian house – the birthplace in 1770 of William Wordsworth, the Lakeland poet.

Wordsworth is remembered in the 19th-century All Saints Church by a stained-glass window. Part of the church rooms are on the site of the grammar school attended by Wordsworth and Fletcher Christian, leader of the *Bounty* mutiny in 1789.

WORDSWORTH'S BIRTHPLACE *The poet lived at this house in Cockermouth until 1778.*

Information Tel. 823741 (822634 summer).
Location On the A595, 13 m. NW of Keswick.
Parking Riverside; South Street; Memorial Gardens, Market Street; Station Road (all car parks).
District council Allerdale (Tel. 823741).
Population 7,100.
E-C Thur. **M-D** Mon.
Police Main Street (Tel. 823212).
Casualty hospital West Cumberland, Hensingham, Whitehaven (Tel. Whitehaven 3181).
Post office Station Street.
Public library Main Street.
Places to see Wordsworth's Birthplace.
Event Agricultural Show (Aug.).
AA 24 hour service
Tel. Carlisle 24274.

SHIPS THAT WERE THE ENVY OF THE WORLD

In the hey-day of the ocean liners, Clydebank ships were the Rolls-Royces of the sea – luxurious, reliable and fast. From the *Servia* of 1881 to the modern *Queen Elizabeth* *II* they showed a creamy wake to their rivals, and when a ship fit for a queen was required, Clydebank built the Royal Yacht *Britannia*.

Three Queens – Elizabeth II *(top),* Elizabeth *and* Mary.

COLCHESTER Essex

Where the Romans first settled in Britain

Harmoniously mingling the ancient and the new, England's oldest-recorded town stands on the River Colne in the midst of rolling country. Inside the town are 180 acres of public gardens and parks, so that almost every street offers a view of greenery. Colchester abounds in historic buildings, remains and museums, but its major industries, its university, and many cultural and sporting activities ensure that it also teems with modern life.

HARVESTING OYSTERS *Colchester is renowned for these shellfish, cultivated on beds in the River Colne; oyster feasts date back to the 17th century.*

There was a settlement on the site as early as the 7th century BC, and by the 1st century AD Camulodunum, as it was called, had become the capital of the king of south-east England, Cunobelin – Shakespeare's Cymbeline. Camulodunum was protected on the west by dykes and ramparts, stretches of which can still be seen – particularly Grime's Dyke, Triple Dyke and Bluebottle Grove.

The Romans overran the capital when they invaded Britain in AD 43, and established their own first colony in Britain near by seven years later. In AD 60, however, Britons led by Queen Boudicca sacked the city and destroyed its temple. The colony lost its original importance, but in the 2nd century the Romans rebuilt it as a major town. Its main streets have become those of modern Colchester, and the walls, including the monumental West or **Balkerne Gate**, still surround the old quarter of the town.

When the Romans left Britain in the early 5th century, the Saxons occupied the town and coined its modern name, which means "the Roman fortress on the River Colne". By Norman times it had become a large borough, and in the 11th century a powerful castle was built over the base of the Roman temple. All that remains is the massive keep, the largest ever built in Europe, now the **Castle Museum.**

The castle keep was even more forbidding before it was reduced from four storeys to two in the 1680s. It closely resembles the White Tower of London, but its ground plan is half as large again. A staircase leads to four vaults – the substructure of the Roman temple of Claudius, built between AD 50 and 60. The Castle

Museum includes one of the finest Roman collections in the country, outstanding finds from a 1st-century-AD Iron Age burial mound, and splendid medieval exhibits.

In the Middle Ages the town's livelihood depended on its market, fishery and cloth-making. The cloth trade declined in the 1550s, but two decades later 500 Flemish Protestant refugees gave it new life. The half-timbered and plastered houses of Stockwell Street are now known as the **Dutch Quarter**, even though some of them date back to well before the 16th century.

The Civil War brought severe destruction to the town, when the Parliamentarians besieged it for 11 weeks; and many historic buildings bear the scars of the conflict.

By the early 19th century the cloth trade had disappeared. But it was soon supplanted by an engineering industry which revived the town's fortunes.

All that now stands of the Benedictine **St John's Abbey**, founded in 1096, is its imposing 15th-century gatehouse. Two storeys high, it is

PLACID WATERS *The River Colne skirts the northern edge of Colchester, and the North Bridge stands on the site of a Roman bridge. In medieval times there was a suburb beyond the river, and a few houses still remain.*

100

battlemented and flanked by octagonal turrets. Another 11th-century monastic building, **St Botolph's Priory**, has lain in ruins since it was battered down by Roundhead's fire in 1648. The ruins consist only of the west front, with its fine doorway, and part of the nave.

Saxon church

Holy Trinity Church is the only Saxon building in Colchester and is largely built from Roman materials. The west wall of the nave goes back even beyond Saxon times to an unknown date. A notable feature is the triangular-headed door in the west wall. The church is now a museum displaying rural crafts.

Beside Bourne Pond stands **Bourne Mill**, built in 1591 of stone from St John's Abbey. Its most striking feature is its stepped, curved, pinnacled gables. Originally a fishing lodge, it was converted into a mill in the early 19th century. It is now owned by the National Trust and is open to visitors by appointment.

The **Town Hall**, which was completed in 1902, dominates the broad High Street. Its tall clock-tower is topped by a figure of St Helena, holding a sceptre and cross and facing towards Jerusalem. She is said to have been the daughter of the mythical King Cole of Colchester, who is commemorated with his fiddlers three in the nursery rhyme. One of the bells in the tower dates from about 1400.

In the main room, the **Moot Hall**, the Oyster Feast, for the mayor and corporation, is held each October.

Almost as overpowering as the Town Hall is a gigantic water-tower called **Jumbo**. Built in 1882, it is named after the huge African elephant then in London Zoo.

In East Street stands **Siege House**, one of several 15th-century houses in the town. During the Civil War siege of 1648 its timbers were riddled with Royalist bullets, and the holes can still be seen.

Fine Georgian house

The **Holly Trees Museum** is in a fine Georgian house built in 1716-19. It contains collections of 18th and 19th-century domestic, craft and military objects.

The Minories, another Georgian house, with an early-16th-century wing, is an art gallery that contains work by Constable. It also houses a collection of Georgian furniture, pictures, china and silver.

The **Natural History Museum** was formerly All Saints' Church. It illustrates the county's wildlife, and includes an aquarium and a diorama of land reclamation from the sea.

Colchester's harbour, the **Hythe** – which may have been used by the Romans – declined with the arrival of the railways in the 19th century. Since the Second World War, however, it has become busier, and now more than 2,000 ships in the coastal trade use it each year.

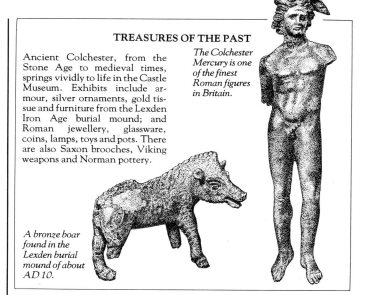

TREASURES OF THE PAST

Ancient Colchester, from the Stone Age to medieval times, springs vividly to life in the Castle Museum. Exhibits include armour, silver ornaments, gold tissue and furniture from the Lexden Iron Age burial mound; and Roman jewellery, glassware, coins, lamps, toys and pots. There are also Saxon brooches, Viking weapons and Norman pottery.

The Colchester Mercury is one of the finest Roman figures in Britain.

A bronze boar found in the Lexden burial mound of about AD 10.

Roses, as well as oysters, have long been associated with the town. Cant's well-known horticultural nurseries were first established in 1766. Each July a great rose show is held.

The **University of Essex**, founded in 1961, stands in Wivenhoe Park and can be visited by arrangement.

Information Tel. 46379 or 76071.
Location On the A134, 18 m. SW of Ipswich.
Parking Southway; Osborne Street; Priory Street; Shewell Road; Balkerne Hill; Nunns Road; Culver Street; High Street (east end); Queen Street (all car parks).
District council Borough of Colchester (Tel. 76071).
Population 81,900.
E-C Thur. **M-D** Sat.
Police (Ba) Queen Street (Tel. 74444).
Casualty hospital Essex County Hospital, Lexden Road (Tel. 77341).
Post office (Aa) Head Street.
Theatres Mercury **(Aa)** (Tel. 73948); University (term-time) (861946); St Mary's Arts Centre, Church Walk (77301).
Cinema Odeon **(Aa)**, Crouch Street (Tel. 72294).
Public library (Ba) Trinity Street.
Places to see Castle, including museum **(Bb)**; Dutch Quarter **(Ab)**; Holly Trees Museum **(Bb)**; Minories Art Gallery **(Ba)**; Roman Walls **(Aa)**; Natural History Museum **(Ba)**; Rural Crafts Museum **(Ba)**; Bourne Mill; St Botolph's Priory **(Ba)**; St John's Abbey Gate **(Ba)**; Siege House; Town Hall **(Bb)**.
Shopping High Street; Head Street; Lion Walk Precinct; Queen Street; Eld Lane; Crouch Street; North Hill.
Events Rose Show (July); Tattoo/Festival (Aug., alternate years); Oyster Feast (Oct.).
Trade and industry Engineering; agriculture; warehousing.
Sport FA League football, Colchester United FC, Layer Road.
AA 24 hour service
Tel. Chelmsford 61711.

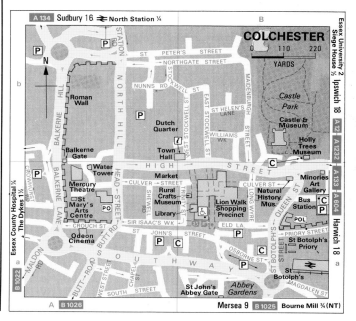

COLCHESTER

HILLS AND SEA *The iron tracery of Colwyn Bay's pier frames a view of the bay and its long promenade and sandy beach. Beyond is Old Colwyn.*

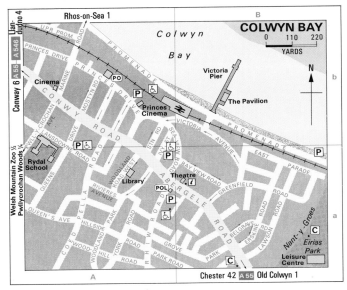

and a penguin pool with underwater windows for observing the birds as they swim and feed.

Information Tel. 30478.
Location On the A55, 6 m. SE of Llandudno.
Parking Douglas Road; Lansdowne Road; Ivy Street; Princes Drive (all car parks).
District council Borough of Colwyn (Tel. 55271).
Population 26,300.
E-C Wed.
Police (Aa) Rhiw Road (Tel. 30266).
Casualty hospital Glan Clwyd Hospital, Bodelwyddan (Tel. St Asaph 583910).
Post office (Ab) Princes Drive.
Theatres Prince of Wales **(Ba)**, Abergele Road (Tel. 2668); Harlequin, Cayley Promenade, Rhos-on-Sea (48166).
Cinemas Astra **(Ab)**, Conwy Road (Tel. 30803); Princess **(Ab)**, Princes Drive (2557).
Public library (Aa) Woodland Road West.
Places to see Welsh Mountain Zoo.
Shopping Station Road; Penrhyn Road; Abergele Road.
AA 24 hour service
Tel. Llandudno 79066.

Congleton Cheshire

Standing in a bend of the River Dane, Congleton probably takes its name from the Celtic word *congl* (a bend).

Its earliest inhabitants may have been New Stone Age people who built the Bridestones, a chambered tomb whose remains are still visible beside the road to Leek. There are also clues to Bronze Age settlement, but very little evidence of subsequent occupation until Norman times.

The parish church of St Peter, built in 1740-2 on the site of an earlier church, has a fine untouched Georgian interior which includes galleries with box-pews, and 18th-century monuments and coats of arms.

One of the finest Tudor houses in England, Little Moreton Hall, stands surrounded by a moat, 4 miles south-west of Congleton. The black-and-white, half-timbered building has remained virtually unchanged since 1580.

Five miles south of the town is Mow Cop, a rise which provides good views of the countryside and is topped by a folly – a mock ruined castle – built about 1750 by Randle Wilbraham.

"SNAKE" BRIDGE *This canal bridge near Congleton allowed the barge horse to cross without unhitching.*

Colwyn Bay Clwyd

Until the middle of the last century Colwyn Bay was an obscure village snuggling in the shelter of the North Wales hills. Then, in the 1840s, the railway line to Holyhead was built. It skirted the bay; and soon retired people and prosperous families from industrial Lancashire were moving into the area to take advantage of its sandy beaches and mild winters.

The town's growth quickened after 1865, and by 1900 it had a population of 8,000. Now, Colwyn Bay is a year-round and almost entirely modern resort. It lies behind 3 miles of sandy beach – part of an 18 mile stretch of coastline which is made up of long beaches punctuated by the occasional headland.

Rhos-on-Sea, once a separate village, is now a breezy suburb at one end of the red-roofed sprawl of buildings; Old Colwyn is at the other. A continuous promenade links the two, running past neat suburban streets which slope up towards sheltering woods on the hillsides.

On the foreshore at Rhos-on-Sea is the tiny St Trillo's Chapel, which is built entirely of rough, mortared stone – the roof included – and is only about 9 ft high. It is believed to have been built in the 6th century over a Holy Well, which for centuries supplied water for local baptisms.

The boundary between Old Colwyn and Colwyn Bay is marked by a small river, the Nant-y-Groes, which runs through the Nant-y-Glyn valley. Two miles up the valley, at Bryn-y-Maen, is Christ Church, known, because of its size, as The Cathedral on the Hill. There is a panoramic view of the bay from the church tower.

There is an open-air theatre at Eirias Park; and the Pwllycrochan woods behind the town have been laid out with a network of leafy walks.

On a nearby hillside is the unusual Mountain Zoo. It has daily displays of hunting by free-flying falcons,

Information Tel. 71095.
Location On the A54, 8 m. SW of Macclesfield.
Parking Albert Street; Antrobus Street; Chapel Street; Bank Street; Market Street; Mill Street; Park Street; West Street (all car parks).
District council Borough of Congleton (Tel. Sandbach 3231).
Population 23,800.
E-C Wed. **M-D** Sat.
Police Market Square (Tel. 71144).
Casualty hospital Macclesfield Infirmary, Cumberland Street, Macclesfield (Tel. Macclesfield 21000).
Post office Mill Street.
Public library Market Square.
Places to see The Bridestones, 4 m. E; Little Moreton Hall, 4 m. SW off A34; Mow Cop, 5 m. S.
Shopping Mill Street; Duke Street; Bridge Street; High Street; Lawton Street; Swan Bank.
Trade and industry Textiles; light engineering; sand quarrying.
AA 24 hour service
Tel. Manchester (061) 485 6299.

Consett Durham
Iron and steel have been the backbone of Consett's economy since the discovery of iron-ore in the area in 1839. The town's architecture is mostly 19th century, but with a modern shopping centre.

Just outside the town, at Shotley Bridge, is Cutler's Hall – a reminder that in the 17th century Shotley Bridge was noted for its colony of German sword-makers, who tempered and smoothed their products in the River Derwent. Stones bearing the grooves left by the smoothing process can still be seen in the river.

Information Tel. 505211.
Location On the A692, 14 m. SW of Newcastle upon Tyne.
Parking Market Square (not Fri. and Sat.); Albert Road; Green Street (all car parks).
District council Derwentside (Tel. 502211).
Population 33,400.
E-C Wed. **M-D** Fri., Sat.
Police Parliament Street (Tel. 504204).
Casualty hospital Shotley Bridge General Hospital, Shotley Bridge (Tel. 503456).
Post office Victoria Road.
Cinema Empire, Front Street (Tel. 506651).
Public library Victoria Road.
Shopping Middle Street; Front Street.
AA 24 hour service
Tel. Newcastle upon Tyne 610111.

Conwy see page 104

Corby Northamptonshire
Although Corby is a new town, it centres on a village whose history goes back to Roman times. Locally mined iron-ore gave the town its importance. The ore was used in Roman times and the Middle Ages. Today, it is still being exploited by the British Steel Corporation.

The town has a large shopping precinct, civic centre, and a 200 acre wooded park in the middle of the built-up area.

To the north of Corby, Rockingham Castle stands on the summit of a hill above the River Welland. The castle was built in the time of William the Conqueror, and its Norman gatehouse and Hall entrances are well preserved. The rest of the building has Elizabethan, Restoration and 19th-century architecture.

The village of Rockingham, on the slope below the castle, is built almost entirely in local ironstone and has many 17th and 18th-century houses.

Information Tel. 2551.
Location On the A43, 22 m. NE of Northampton.
Parking Everest Lane; George Street; Cardigan Place; Anne Street (all car parks).
District council Corby (Tel. 2551).
Population 47,800.
E-C Wed. **M-D** Fri., Sat.
Police Elizabeth Street (Tel. 62661).
Casualty hospital Kettering General, Rothwell Road, Kettering (Tel. Kettering 81141).
Post office Corporation Street.
Theatre Civic Theatre, George Street (Tel. 3482).
Cinema Focus Cinema 1 & 2, Queens Square (Tel. 65381).
Public library Queens Square.
Places to see Rockingham Castle, 2 m. N on the A6116.
Shopping Town-centre shopping precinct.
AA 24 hour service
Tel. Leicester 20491.

Corsham Wiltshire
Warm, cream-coloured Bath stone characterises the small Cotswold town of Corsham, whose High Street contains Flemish-style cottages dating back to the 15th century.

St Bartholomew's Church was extensively restored in 1874, but still displays much work from Norman times. Corsham Court is a splendid Elizabethan mansion with Georgian additions by Nash and a park landscaped by "Capability" Brown.

The town lies at the eastern end of Box Tunnel, the 1.8 mile long railway tunnel built by Isambard Kingdom Brunel in 1836-41. It is said that the sun shines through the tunnel at sunrise on one day each year – April 9, Brunel's birthday.

Information Tel. Chippenham 4188.
Location On the B3353, 9 m. NE of Bath.
Parking Newlands Road (4); Pickwick Road (all car parks).
District council North Wiltshire (Tel. Chippenham 4188).
Population 10,000.
E-C Wed.
Police Priory Street (Tel. 712172).
Casualty hospital Chippenham, London Road, Chippenham (Tel. Chippenham 51144).
Post office High Street.
Public library Pickwick Road.
Places to see Corsham Court.
Shopping The Precinct, High Street.
AA 24 hour service
Tel. Bath 24731.

ROCKINGHAM CASTLE *Elizabeth I granted the castle to an ancestor of the present owner, after it had served as a royal fortress for five centuries. King John was a frequent visitor, and his iron treasure-chest is still there.*

CORSHAM COURT *A 16th-century manor with magnificent Georgian staterooms added in 1760. The gallery is lined with damask, dating from 1769.*

Coventry see page 108

A LOOK AROUND
CONWY
Gwynedd

A fortress city by the sea

Rearing against a background of wooded hills, Conwy's eight-towered, 13th-century castle is the greatest of all the fortresses Edward I built to subdue and control the Welsh. The town walls, defended by towers set at 50 yd intervals, are the finest of their age in Britain. Conwy itself is a town of narrow streets plagued by traffic congestion. Thomas Telford's mock-medieval, 19th-century suspension bridge over the river was superseded in the 1950s by a larger road bridge.

LLYWELYN THE GREAT *A richly decorated statue in Lancaster Square commemorates the Welsh prince who founded Conwy in the 12th century.*

PLACES TO SEE
1 Castle
2 Plas Mawr
3 Aberconwy
4 Suspension bridge
5 Tubular bridge
6 Smallest house
7 Abbey church
8 Town walls
9 The Quay
10 Llywelyn monument

Edward I started to build the castle in 1283, after his armies had crushed the power of the Welsh princes. Faced with the formidable problem of controlling his new domain, he solved it, at great speed and enormous expense, by binding the coast with a great chain of fortifications stretching from Flint to Aberystwyth. These fortresses rank among the best examples of medieval military architecture in the world. Conwy was an obvious site to choose. It is built on a steep and rocky ridge that overlooks the broad, current-swept estuary. Together they form a formidable natural defence.

When Edward I arrived in Conwy in 1283 it was the site of a Cistercian abbey, which had been richly endowed by the Welsh warrior prince Llywelyn ap Iorwerth (Llywelyn the Great, 1173-1240), and was destined to be his burial place.

Edward moved the monks 8 miles inland, to Maenan, to make way for his castle and new town. Only the **abbey church** was kept. It is still in use, seven centuries later. Original workmanship survives in the east wall of the chancel and the west wall of the tower. The interior is notable for a richly carved 15th-century rood screen.

The church has a very peaceful atmosphere thanks to being set back from the main streets and reached by narrow lanes that open out into a grassy churchyard.

Castle builder

To construct the **castle** and town walls, builders were recruited from all over England to work under James of Saint George, the greatest military architect of his day. Translated into present-day figures, the total cost of the castle and walls was about £2 million.

Long and narrow, with a tidal stream forming an extra line of defence to the south, the great stronghold makes perfect use of its rocky site. The interior was divided into two distinct sections, so that if attackers managed to cross the main drawbridge, on the landward side, the garrison could withdraw behind an inner ward, raising another drawbridge behind them. Water came from a well, 91 ft deep. Human skeletons believed to date from the Civil War were found in the well during excavations in 1939.

James of Saint George's masterpiece was soon put to the test. In 1294 the Welsh under Madog ap Llywelyn captured English-held castles at Denbigh and Caernarfon. Edward hurried to North Wales, but withdrew to Conwy after his supply train was ambushed at Penmaenmawr. He was cooped up in the castle for 14 days, at the start of 1295, before

ABBEY CHURCH *Set back from the main streets and reached by narrow lanes, the 12th-century church is an oasis of peace in the busy town.*

Madog's revolt was finally put down.

In 1401, Owain Glyndwr made what was to be the last great effort to regain Welsh independence. Gwilym and Rhys ap Tudor, members of the Anglesey family that was to produce the Tudor dynasty, managed to capture the castle without bloodshed. Henry Hotspur marched from Denbigh with 500 troops, surrounded the castle and eventually reached an agreement with the Tudors. The Welsh seized nine of their own number while they were sleeping and handed them over for execution. In return, the rest were pardoned and allowed to go free after handing over their weapons.

Films and novels about medieval campaigns invariably give the impression that castles had huge garrisons, but troops were expensive and, under the feudal system, generally served for 40 days a year. Conwy's first constable had only 30 troops under his command. The total rose to 75 when Glyndwr was posing a constant threat, but had dwindled to only six by 1418, when North Wales was at peace again.

In 1627, when it was sold to Lord Conwy for £100, the castle was in such a derelict state that it could not be entered in safety; but its days of military importance had not ended. When the Civil War broke out it was repaired, provisioned and garrisoned by Conwy-born John Williams, Archbishop of York and, at that time, one of Charles I's most loyal and ardent supporters.

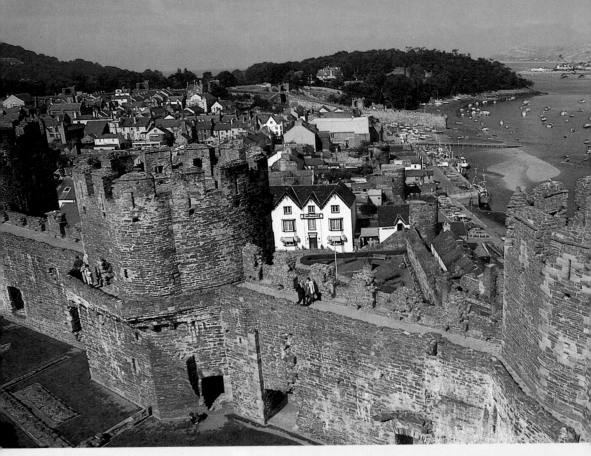

MEDIEVAL TOWN *Conwy still shelters beneath the castle built by Edward I 700 years ago to command the estuary of the Afon Conwy.*

CRAMPED QUARTERS *The smallest house in Britain stands on Conwy quayside. It is 10 ft high – and the last man to live there was 6 ft 3 in. tall.*

PLAS MAWR *The 16th-century mansion, seen from one of its two courtyards, is one of the finest Elizabethan town houses in Wales.*

In August 1646, Parliamentary troops under Major-General Thomas Mytton laid siege to the castle, but it did not surrender until three months later. It was later "slighted", to make it militarily useless, and its lead and timber were removed and sold. John Wesley, visiting Conwy in the 18th century, described the castle as "the noblest ruin I ever saw".

Ancient gates

The **town walls**, almost 6 ft thick and 35 ft high, extended right down to the shore. They were built in such a way that attackers who managed to scale them could be isolated by a series of small drawbridges. There were three main, twin-towered, gates, two of which are still in everyday use.

In some places the wall is sandwiched between shops, pubs and cottages. The most remarkable of these buildings is a tiny dwelling on the quayside that is the **smallest house in Britain**. It has a 6 ft frontage, is only 10 ft high and consists of two rooms linked by an almost vertical staircase.

In contrast is **Plas Mawr**, on the corner of Crown Lane and High Street. Built in 1576, it is one of the finest Elizabethan town houses in Wales. The interior has a great wealth of ornate plasterwork, much of which was not revealed until the late 19th century, having been covered up, it is believed, to escape destruction by Puritans in the Civil War.

Since 1887 the house has been the headquarters of the Royal Cambrian Academy of Art.

Aberconwy, a National Trust property at the junction of High Street and Castle Street, is said to be the oldest house in Wales. The earliest parts may be 14th century, but most of the building dates from 1500. **Parlwr Mawr**, the birthplace and home of Archbishop Williams, stood in Chapel Street until 1948. The site is marked by slate tablets commemorating the coronation of George VI and giving Welsh translations for the days of the week and other words in common use.

The Quay, built in 1833, is one of Conwy's most attractive areas, overlooking a sandy, natural harbour bright with boats. In 1725 Daniel Defoe hailed it as a "noble harbour which infinitely outdoes Chester or Liverpool itself". It was busy until the end of the 19th century with fishing boats and ships exporting slate and copper. Pleasure craft now heavily

QUAYSIDE RELIC
An old ship anchor, dredged up from the sea-bed off Prestatyn, is preserved on Conwy Quay.

MIGHTY FORTRESS *Beyond the town's three bridges rises the crenellated bulk of Edward I's military masterpiece, 13th-century Conwy Castle.*

mock-medieval details to harmonise with the castle.

The tubes, each 424 ft long and weighing almost 1,300 tons, were assembled on site, floated out on huge rafts and then slowly raised into position. Stephenson had to use tubes because the railway track ruled out a suspension bridge, and the rapidity and depth of the current ruled out a conventional bridge supported by piers on the river bed.

Stephenson rested the tubes' eastern ends on rollers and gun-metal balls to allow for expansion and contraction, knowing that iron grows or shrinks by 1/10,000th of its length for every 15°F change in temperature.

THREE BRIDGES *Conwy's road and rail links span a tide-swept estuary.*

ABERCONWY – *one of the oldest houses in Wales.*

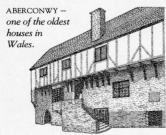

outnumber the fishing boats, but fresh fish is sold from a stall on the quay, and mussels are also landed. The river used to be famous for freshwater pearls, one of which was presented to Queen Catherine, wife of Charles II.

Conwy was not easy to reach by road until the early 19th century, when bridges replaced the dangerous and inefficient ferry. In 1802 the engineer John Rennie proposed spanning the estuary with a vast high-level bridge, but because this would have passed right through the castle the plan was rejected. Instead, the design of Thomas Telford was accepted. His graceful **suspension bridge**, opened in 1826, was used until the present road bridge was completed in 1958.

In many ways, the **railway bridge** built by Robert Stephenson 20 years later is a much greater technical achievement than Telford's. A vital link on the railway line between Chester and Holyhead, it consists of two iron tubes, rectangular in section, supported by towers rich in

Information Tel. 2248 or Llandudno 78881.
Location On the A55, 6 m. W of Colwyn Bay.
Parking Castle Square; Conwy Quay; Mount Pleasant; Rose Hill Street; Llanrwst Road (all car parks).
District council Aberconwy (Tel. Llandudno 76276).
Population 13,000.
E-C Wed. **M-D** Tues.

Police (Aa) Lancaster Square (Tel. 2222).
Casualty hospital Llandudno General (Tel. Llandudno 77471).
Post office (Aa) Bangor Road.
Cinema (Bb) Palace (Tel. 2376).
Public library (Bb) Castle Street.
Shopping Castle Street; High Street; Lancaster Square.
AA 24 hour service Tel. Llandudno 79066.

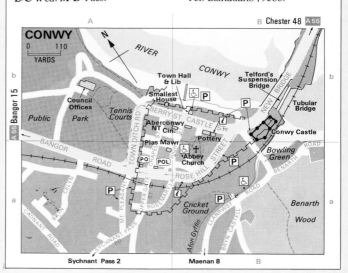

COVENTRY W. Midlands

The city of Lady Godiva and the motor car

The modern cathedral beside the ruins of its medieval predecessor is the symbol of Coventry's resilience. In 1940, a single air-raid levelled 40 acres of the city centre, but now only the newness of most of its buildings hints at the scale of that night's destruction. Coventry has been skilful in keeping its many industries at a distance. The central area, much of it closed to cars, is dotted with parks. Green open spaces ring the suburbs, and southwards there are the meadows and woods of Warwickshire and the Shakespeare country.

Leofric, Earl of Mercia, started Coventry's development as a centre of commerce and industry in 1043, when he chose the small Saxon township as the site for a Benedictine monastery. He gave the monks land on which to raise sheep, laying the basis for the wool trade which made Coventry prosperous for 500 years.

Yet the earl is cast as the villain in the city's best-known legend, that of Lady Godiva's naked ride. The story, in which Godiva pleaded with Leofric, her husband, to cut the taxes on the people of Coventry, was first recorded a century after her death.

Earl's challenge

Leofric told Godiva she could ride naked through the streets before he would grant her request. She did so, having sent messengers to tell people to stay indoors with their shutters closed, and the earl relented. Peeping Tom, who peered through a window at Godiva and was struck blind, was added to the tale in the mid-17th century. Figures of Godiva and Tom re-enact the legend hourly on the clock in the arch over Hertford Street. There is a modern **statue of Godiva** on horseback in Broadgate.

By 1400, Coventry ranked with Bristol, York and Plymouth as one of the four leading provincial centres of England. Part of its wealth came from cloth and thread, dyed blue by a special process which kept the colour from fading. "True as Coventry blue", later "true blue", entered the language as a byword for reliability.

In 1642 the city refused admission to Charles I, and throughout the Civil War it was a Parliamentary stronghold. Royalists captured in the Midlands were imprisoned in the 14th-century **Church of St John** in the Bablake area – "sent to Coventry", in the words of an account written in 1647. The phrase came to mean "banned from society".

After the restoration of the monarchy in 1660, Coventry was ordered to knock down its city walls. The citizens left the 12 gates, two of which still stand at either end of **Lady Herbert Garden**.

Trade slump

Over the next 200 years, clockmaking and silk-weaving became Coventry's main industries, but in the 19th century imports of silk from France and watches from Switzerland brought a slump in both. As a result, hundreds of local families emigrated to America.

Those who stayed turned to new occupations – cycle-making and engineering. In 1896, Daimler and Humber opened the city's first car factories, and other motor firms soon joined them.

In 1914, and again in 1939, the engineering skills which Coventry

CHRIST IN GLORY *Graham Sutherland designed the new cathedral's altar tapestry, seen through a window which reflects the old cathedral.*

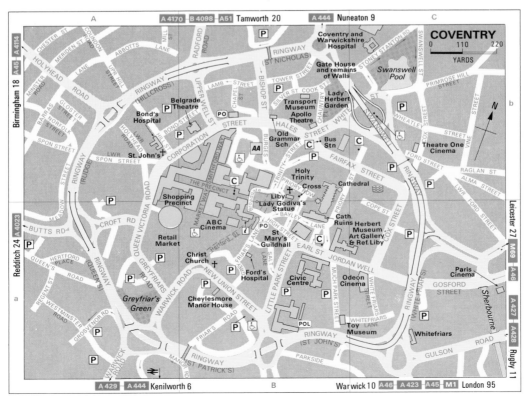

LINK WITH THE PAST *A canopied porch connects the ruins of Coventry's medieval cathedral, preserved as a reminder of Second World War bombing, to its modern successor, designed by Sir Basil Spence and consecrated in 1962.*

DESTROYED BY BOMBS
Coventry's parish church of St Michael was made a cathedral in 1919. It was built in the 14th and 15th centuries and destroyed by German bombs in 1940.

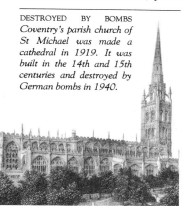

A LEGEND IN SILK

A clothed Lady Godiva rides a white horse through Coventry in a 19th-century, woven-silk picture. Such pictures, called Stevengraphs after Thomas Stevens, a local man who was one of the first to make them, were made by Coventry silk-workers when imported French ribbons threatened their livelihood as ribbon makers.

had developed were applied to the machinery of war. Its factories were an inevitable target for enemy bombers in the Second World War.

The bombing raid of November 14, 1940, was the most concentrated ever suffered by a British city. Out of 1,000 buildings in the central area only 30 were undamaged, and most were devastated. **St Michael's Cathedral** was destroyed, apart from its spire and outer walls. These are now linked to the new cathedral.

Some of Coventry's other historic buildings fared better. The 14th-century **Guildhall of St Mary** (The Guildhall), with its minstrel galleries and tapestries, is still used for civic banquets. **Whitefriars**, part of a 600-year-old Carmelite monastery, is now owned by Coventry's Herbert Museum. Medieval buildings from various parts of the city have been reassembled in **Spon Street**, and Coventry has two fine Tudor almshouses – **Bond's Hospital** and **Ford's Hospital**.

Information Tel. 51717, 20084.
Location On the A46, 18 m. SE of Birmingham.
Parking Fairfax St; Grove St; Gosford St; Lower Ford St; Cox St; Tower St; Much Park St; Friars Rd; Wheatley St; Greyfriars Rd (2); Greyfriars Lane (2); Little Park St; Bond St; New Union St; Croft Rd; Hill St; Grosvenor Rd; Queen's Rd; Warwick Rd; Corporation St; Friars Lane (2) (all car parks).
District council City of Coventry (Tel. 25555).
Population 312,600.
E-C None. **M-D** Wed., Fri. and Sat.
Police (Ba) Little Park Street (Tel. 555333).
Casualty hospital Coventry and Warwickshire Hospital **(Cb)**, Howard Street (Tel. 24055).
Post offices Hertford Street **(Ba)**; Corporation Street **(Bb)**.
Theatres Belgrade **(Bb)**, Corporation Street (Tel. 20205); Apollo, Hales Street (23141).
Cinemas Odeon **(Ca)**, Jordan Well

(Tel. 22042); ABC **(Ba)**, Hertford Street (23600); Paris **(Ca)**, Far Gosford Street (26526); Theatre One **(Cb)**, Ford Street (24301).
Public libraries Bayley Lane (reference) **(Ba)**; Trinity Church Yard (lending) **(Bb)**.
Places to see Lady Godiva's Statue **(Ba)**, Broadgate; Coventry Cross **(Bb)**; Cathedral **(Bb)**; Herbert Art Gallery and Museum **(Ba)**, Jordan Well; Old Grammar School; The Guildhall **(Ba)**, Bayley Lane; Bond's Hospital **(Ab)**, Hill Street; Ford's Hospital **(Ba)**; Museum of British Road Transport **(Bb)**, Cook Street.
Town trails Available from City Information Centre, 36 Broadgate.
Shopping Broadgate Precinct.
Trade and industry Engineering; textiles; telecommunications.
Sport FA League football, Coventry City FC, Highfield Road; Rugby Union, Coventry RFC, Coundon Road.
AA 24 hour service Tel. Birmingham (021) 550 4858.

Cowes Isle of Wight

Twenty-one brass cannon point out across the Solent from the ramparts of Cowes Castle, home of the Royal Yacht Squadron. Once the guns of the sailing ship *Royal Adelaide*, they are now used to start the races which have made Cowes the headquarters of yachting in Britain.

YACHTING CAPITAL *Cowes is the "Ascot" of yacht racing, and the world's yachtsmen take part in the races during Cowes Week.*

A yachting regatta was first held at Cowes in 1776, but it was the royal patronage of the 19th century that gave the port its international reputation for the sport.

The Yacht Club, formed in 1815, became the Royal Yacht Club when its most notable member, the Prince Regent, became George IV in 1820. Its name was changed in 1833 to the Royal Yacht Squadron, whose 300 members share, among other privileges, the freedom of all foreign ports. In 1944 the building became chief operations centre for the D-Day landings.

Cowes is really two towns, one on each side of the River Medina, linked by a floating bridge. West Cowes is all yachts and fashion. East Cowes is all boatyards and industry. Ships were being built there in the 16th century when Henry VIII had castles built on either side of the estuary to protect the Solent. Only the west castle, the Royal Yacht Squadron's home, remains. Wooden battleships of Nelson's day rolled down the slipways at East Cowes, and so did iron destroyers of both World Wars. In the 1950s the hovercraft made its first test runs off the mouth of the Medina.

Thomas Arnold, the headmaster of Rugby school, and immortalised in Thomas Hughes's *Tom Brown's Schooldays*, was born in the town in 1795.

A mile-long, tree-lined road leads from the centre of East Cowes to Osborne House, a favourite residence of Queen Victoria. It is packed with relics of the queen and her husband.

Information Tel. Newport 524343.
Location On the A3020, 5 m. N of Newport.
Parking Cross Street; Brunswick Road; Terminus Road; Park Road. East Cowes: Esplanade; Well Road (all car parks).
District council Borough of Medina (Tel. Newport 522493).
Population 19,700.
E-C Wed.
Police (Aa) Birmingham Road (Tel. 295241).

Casualty hospital St Mary's, Newport Road, Newport (Tel. Newport 524081).
Post office (Ab) High Street.
Public library (Aa) Beckford Road.
Places to see Osborne House; Barton Manor Gardens; Maritime Museum **(Aa)**; Norris Castle, 1 m. NE.
Shopping High Street; Shooters Hill; Birmingham Road.
Events Regattas (every weekend from end Apr. to end Sept.); Round the Island Yacht Race (June); Dinghy Week (July); Cowes Week (first week in Aug.).
Trade and industry Ship-building; plywood; sail and rope-making.
Car ferry To Southampton (Tel. 292101).
AA 24 hour service Tel. Newport 522653.

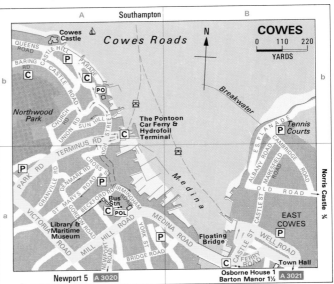

OSBORNE HOUSE, VICTORIA'S FAVOURITE HOME

In 1845 Osborne House, near Cowes, was acquired as a summer retreat for the royal family. The existing house was enlarged to designs prepared by Prince Albert and the architect Thomas Cubitt, and Queen Victoria was delighted with it. After Albert's death in 1861 the queen spent most of her time there, turning it into a shrine to her husband's memory, and she died there in 1901. Her son, Edward VII, who did not wish to live at Osborne, gave the estate to the nation.

Beyond a fountain in the grounds – which contain every species of tree grown in Britain – rises the Italianate elegance of Osborne House, which is still furnished as Queen Victoria left it in 1901.

Crawley W. Sussex

The new town – one of the first built after the Second World War – has swallowed up the old coaching and market community that was the original Crawley. Set in magnificent wooded countryside, the town offers many fine walks. The largest of its parks, Tilgate, has three lakes for sailing, rowing and fishing.

Information Tel. 28744.
Location On the A23, 7 m. NE of Horsham.
Parking Haslett Avenue; The Boulevard; High Street; Parkside; Orchard Way; Queensway (all car parks).
District council Borough of Crawley (Tel. 28744).
Population 72,800.
E-C Wed.; no E-C Town centre.
M-D Thur. and Sat.
Police Exchange Road (Tel. 24242).
Casualty hospital West Green Drive (Tel. 27866).
Post office The Boulevard.
Theatre Ifield Barn Theatre, Rectory Lane (Tel. 25036).
Cinema Embassy 1, 2 & 3, High Street (Tel. 27497).
Public library Northgate Avenue.
Shopping The Broadway; The Boulevard; Queen's Square; The Martlets.
Trade and industry Miscellaneous light industries.
AA 24 hour service Tel. 25685.

Crediton Devon

According to many historians, Crediton was the home of the most influential Englishman ever. He was born with the name of Winfrith in about AD 674. But the world knows him better as St Boniface, one of the first Christian preachers in northern Europe.

Thanks to his work, Crediton was made the seat of the first Bishop of Devon and Cornwall, and became the site of the cathedral-size church that still dominates the town.

Many of the town's early buildings were destroyed by fire in 1743 and 1769, but the 13th-century Chapter House next to the church survives. It contains a collection of armour and weapons from the Civil War, and the room where the church's 12 governors have met since 1547.

Information Tel. 3755.
Location On the A377, 8 m. NW of Exeter.
Parking St Saviours Way; Market Street (both car parks).
District council Mid Devon (Tel. 3755).
Population 6,200.
E-C Wed.
Police St Martins Lane (Tel. 2223).
Casualty hospital Royal Devon and Exeter, Barrack Road, Wonford, Exeter (Tel. Exeter 77833).
Post office Market Street.
Public library Belle Parade.
Places to see Chapter House.

DEVON SAINT
A statue of St Boniface is at Crediton.

Shopping High Street; Union Road; Market Street.
Trade and industry Manufacture of pharmaceuticals, cider, foodstuffs.
AA 24 hour service Tel. Exeter 32121.

Crewe Cheshire

The railway reached Crewe in 1837 when a line linking Warrington and Birmingham passed through the town. The age of steam turned this little market centre serving the cattle farmers of the South Cheshire plain into the first great railway town.

Locomotives were rolling out of the sheds in 1843, and for 100 years Crewe was famous for its engines.

Information Tel. 583191.
Location On the A532, 15 m. NW of Stoke-on-Trent.
Parking West Street; Crewe Street; Oak Street; Delamere Street; Chester Street; Flag Lane (all car parks).
District council Borough of Crewe and Nantwich (Tel. 583191).
Population 47,800.
E-C Wed. **M-D** Mon. (a.m.), Fri. and Sat.
Police Civic Centre (Tel. 55111).
Casualty hospital Leighton, Middlewich Road (Tel. 55141).
Post office Weston Road.
Theatre Lyceum, Heath Street (Tel. 55620).
Cinemas Focus, Delamere Street (Tel. 56707); Ritz, Co-operative Street (215225).
Public library Civic Centre.
Shopping Victoria Shopping Centre; Market Street; Edleston Road; Earle Street.
AA 24 hour service Tel. Manchester (061) 485 6299.

Crewkerne Somerset

There was a settlement at Crewkerne in Roman times, and the Saxons had a royal mint in the town. Crewkerne is the market centre for surrounding farms, and also once had an ancient industry, sail-making – sailcloth for Nelson's ships was made there.

On the 4th and 5th of September each year the market square is the scene of a street fair which dates back to Saxon times. Another ancient tradition, Punkie Night, is observed at Hinton St George, a village north of the town, on the last Thursday in October. Village children parade through the streets carrying lanterns carved out of mangel-wurzels (punkies), commemorating the time when the wives of the village searched for their missing husbands in the same way.

Information Tel. Yeovil 5272.
Location On the A30, 9 m. SW of Yeovil.
Parking Abbey Street; West Street; South Street (all car parks); Gouldsbrook Terrace; Market Square; Court Barton.
District council Yeovil (Tel. Yeovil 5171).
Population 5,300.
E-C Thur.
Police South Street (Tel. 73431).
Casualty hospital Yeovil District, Higher Kingston (Tel. Yeovil 5122).
Post office Market Square.
Cinema Palace, West Street (Tel. 74782).
Public library Falkland Square.
Shopping Market Street.
Events Fair (Sept.); Punkie Night (Oct.).
AA 24 hour service Tel. Yeovil 27744.

Criccieth Gwynedd

David Lloyd George (1863-1945), the Liberal Prime Minister who led the country during the First World War, was raised from early boyhood in this tranquil seaside resort. His grave is here too – on the bank of the River Dwyfor at Llanystumdwy, 1¼ miles west.

Criccieth is built around two curves of beach in the northernmost corner of Cardigan Bay. But, since both beaches face south below the windbreak of Snowdonia, winter can be as mild in Criccieth as in South Devon.

A humped headland dividing the town's two beaches is the site of a castle built in 1230.

Information Tel. Porthmadog 2981.
Location On the A497, 14 m. W of Ffestiniog.
Parking High Street; Esplanade; Marine Parade (all car parks).
District council Dwyfor (Tel. Pwllheli 3131).
Population 1,600.
E-C Wed.
Police Caernarfon Road (Tel. 2721).
Casualty hospital Madoc Memorial, Porthmadog (Tel. Porthmadog 2255).
Post office High Street.
Public library High Street.
Places to see Lloyd George Museum, Llanystumdwy; Castle.
Shopping High Street.
AA 24 hour service Tel. Llandudno 79066.

Crieff Tayside

The name Crieff may derive from *craobh*, the Gaelic word for "tree", and refer to the town's old gallows tree whose timbers are still preserved in the Town Hall.

Outside the Town Hall stands the 17th-century octagonal cross of the Burgh of Regality of Drummond, as Crieff was once known.

In the High Street, near the Old Tolbooth, built in 1665, are iron stocks that were used until 1816. Across the road is a market cross of red sandstone, probably dating back to the 10th century and carved with interlacing patterns.

The burgh was granted its charter in 1218, and later it became the main centre for Strathearn. In 1716 the Jacobites put the town to the torch and virtually destroyed it. Rebuilding began in 1731, and Crieff developed as an industrial centre, based on tanning and bleaching.

The 19th century saw the establishment of the hydro and rapid expansion. Crieff became a fashionable holiday resort, and also the "Gateway to the Highlands".

Crieff stands on the lower slopes of the 911 ft high Knock, the summit of which has an indicator to the surrounding views – some of the finest in Scotland.

Three miles south-east, in the hamlet of Innerpeffray, is the oldest public library in Scotland, built between 1705 and 1751. Its rare books include a pocket Bible carried by the Marquis of Montrose during his last battle at Carbisdale in 1648.

Drummond Castle, 2 miles south of Crieff, was founded in 1491. It was badly damaged during the Civil War, and partly demolished in 1745 to prevent its occupation by Hanoverian troops. Only the square tower of the original building remains. This contains a good collection of old armour.

Some 3½ miles south-east of Crieff, off the B8062, are the remains of a Roman signal station and Roman road, built during the great advance of the legions towards the Grampians in the 1st century. The road linked the forts at Inchtuthil, and Bertha (just north of Perth) with the fort at Ardoch, 7 miles south of Crieff, and then went on to the Antonine Wall.

Information Tel. 2578 (Apr. to Oct.); Dundee 23281.
Location On the A85, 17 m. W of Perth.
Parking King Street; Leadenflower Street; Burrell Street (all car parks); Meadow Place; Lodge Street; Addison Terrace; High Street; James Square; Galvelmore Street.
District council Perth and Kinross (Tel. Perth 21161).
Population 5,800.
E-C Wed.
Police (Aa) King Street (Tel. 2247); Barrack Street, Perth (Tel. Perth 21141).
Casualty hospital Perth Royal Infirmary, Tullylumb, Perth (Tel. Perth 23311).
Post office (Ba) High Street.
Cinema Crieff Cinema (Ba), High Street (Tel. 2311).
Public library (Ab) Comrie Street.
Places to see Tolbooth, High Street; Drummond Castle, 2 m. S; Innerpeffray Library, 3 m. SE; Roman signal station and Roman road, 3½ m. SE off B8062; ruins of Ardoch Roman Fort, 7 m. S.
Shopping High Street; King Street; James Square.
Event Highland Games (3rd Sat. in Aug.).
Trade and industry Tourism; whisky distilling; craft work, including glass and pottery.
AA 24 hour service
Tel. Glasgow (041) 812 0101.

Cromer Norfolk

The narrow streets of old Cromer form a maze round the 14th-century Church of St Peter and St Paul, and lead down to the shore where crab fishermen prepare bait beside their boats drawn up on the beach. The old town is the centre of Norfolk's crab industry. The new town which developed round it is a holiday resort with access to miles of sandy beaches.

But the sand which attracts the holidaymakers is a peril to seamen. Offshore are dangerous sand-banks, known as "The Devil's Throat", which have made the Cromer lifeboat one of the busiest in Britain. The former lifeboat house is now a museum that commemorates, among others, the local hero Henry Blogg, lifeboat coxswain from 1909 to 1947. A bronze bust of him stands in North Lodge Park.

Felbrigg Hall, 2½ miles south-west of the town, is early 17th century with 18th-century furnishings. The church in Felbrigg Park contains fine 14th-century brasses, as well as

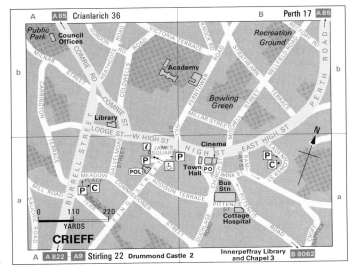

LIFEBOAT HERO *Henry Blogg of Cromer won decorations including the George Cross for saving life at sea.*

monuments by Grinling Gibbons and Joseph Nollekens.

Information Tel. 512497.
Location On the A148, 25 m. N of Norwich.
Parking Cadogan Road; The Meadow; Runton Road (all car parks).
District council North Norfolk (Tel. 513811).
Population 6,200.
E-C Wed.
Police Holt Road (Tel. 51221).
Casualty hospital District, Mill Road (Tel. 513571).
Post office (Ba) Church Street.
Theatre Pier Pavilion **(Aa)** (Tel. 512495).
Cinema Regal **(Ba)** (Tel. 513735).
Public library (Aa) Prince of Wales Road.
Places to see Lifeboat Museum **(Ba)**.
Shopping Church Street; Mount Street.
AA 24 hour service Tel. Norwich 29401.

Crosby Merseyside

In the 10th century Great Crosby and Little Crosby were probably Viking villages; both have now become suburbs of Liverpool. All that remains of their ancient past is the Whitlock-Blundell family, who claim descent from a fair-haired Saxon warrior called Blondell who fought at the Battle of Hastings; the family still lives at Crosby Hall.

Information
Tel. Liverpool (051) 928 6487.
Location On the A565, 8 m. N of Liverpool.
Parking Islington; Moor Lane; Richmond Road; off Houghoumont Avenue (all car parks).
District council Sefton (Tel. 051 922 4040).
Population 53,600.
E-C Wed.
Police Crosby Road North (Tel. 051 709 6010).

Casualty hospital Walton, Rice Lane, Walton, Liverpool 9. (Tel. 051 525 3611).
Post office Lorne Road.
Theatre Civic Hall (Tel. 051 928 1919).
Cinema Classic (Tel. 051 928 2108).
Public library Crosby Road North.
Shopping Moor Lane; St John's Road; South Road; Waterloo.
AA 24 hour service Tel. 051 709 7252.

Cuckfield W. Sussex

Elizabethan and Georgian shops, inns and houses line Cuckfield's High Street, which was once part of the London to Brighton coach road.

The parish church of The Holy Trinity dates from the 13th and 14th centuries. The west tower has a broach spire. Restoration in the 19th century included much stained glass; two windows are by C. E. Kempe (1837-1907).

Cuckfield Park is an Elizabethan manor house. Inside are fine panelling and ceilings. At Handcross, 3 miles to the north-west, is Nymans, a 30 acre garden with fine topiary work.

Information
Tel. Haywards Heath 58166.
Location On the A272, 17 m. N of Brighton.
Parking Broad Street (car park); High Street; London Road.
District council Mid Sussex (Tel. Haywards Heath 58166).
Population 28,200.
E-C Wed.
Police Boltro Road, Haywards Heath (Tel. Haywards Heath 51555).
Casualty hospital Cuckfield Hospital, Ardingly Road, Cuckfield (Tel. Haywards Heath 50661).
Post office High Street.
Public library High Street.
Places to see Cuckfield Park; Nymans Garden, 3 m. NW.
Shopping High Street; London Road.
AA 24 hour service Tel. Crawley 25685.

Cumbernauld Strathclyde

No traffic lights or wardens, a vast multi-storey shopping, business and entertainment complex under one roof, and every single house possessing a garage or car-parking space. It sounds like a town of the future, but in the new town of Cumbernauld, the future already exists.

Information Tel. 22131.
Location Just off the A80, 12 m. NE of Glasgow.
Parking St Mungo's Road; Tryst Road (both car parks).
District council Cumbernauld and Kilsyth (Tel. 22131).
Population 44,300.
E-C Wed.
Police Grieve Road (Tel. 23341).
Casualty hospital Monkland, Manor Drive, Airdrie (Tel. Airdrie 69344).
Post office Town Centre.
Theatre Cumbernauld Theatre, Braehead Road (Tel. 32887).
Public library Allander Walk.
Shopping Town centre.
Trade and industry Electronic and mechanical engineering; distributive trades; plastics manufacturing.
AA 24 hour service Tel. Glasgow (041) 812 0101.

Cupar Fife

Castlehill, the focal point of Cupar, was the site of the ancient stronghold of the Thanes of Fife. In 1535 it was the scene of a remarkable event when Sir David Lindsay gave the first performance of his nine-hour play, *Ane Satyre of the Three Estaits*, an attack on the Church of Scotland. The site is now occupied by a community centre, part of which was built as a theatre by French prisoners during the Napoleonic Wars (1793-1816).

On a hill to the south is Scotstarvit Tower, which dates from 1579. It was once the home of Sir John Scot (1585-1670), the pioneer map-maker and scholar. Near by is Hill of Tarvit, a mansion built in 1906. It contains French and English furniture, Dutch paintings and Flemish tapestries.

Information Tel. St Andrews 72021.
Location On the A91, 10 m. W of St Andrews.
Parking Burnside Street; Bonnygate; Kirk Wynd; Short Lane; Water End Road; Bobber Wynd (all car parks).
District council North-east Fife (Tel. 53722).
Population 7,350.
E-C Thur. **M-D** Tues.
Police Carslogie Road (Tel. 52226).
Casualty hospitals Minor injuries: Adamson Hospital, Bank Street (Tel. 52901). Major casualties: Victoria Hospital, Dunnikier Road, Kirkcaldy (Kirkcaldy 261155).
Post office Crossgate.
Public library Crossgate.
Places to see Hill of Tarvit mansion and Scotstarvit Tower, 2½ m. S.
AA 24 hour service Tel. Dundee 25585.

CUCKFIELD PARK *A gatehouse of mellow Elizabethan brick leads to the manor house which was built by a Sussex ironmaster. In Tudor times the Sussex Weald was the centre of the British iron industry.*

D

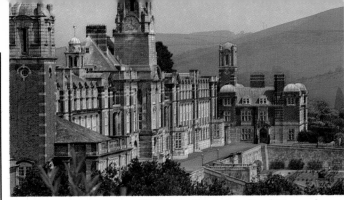

DARTMOUTH NAVAL COLLEGE *The future officers of the Royal Navy and many foreign navies are trained at Britannia College, completed in 1905. Notable cadets have included the Duke of Edinburgh and Prince Charles.*

Darlington Durham

Darlington's modern history began on September 27, 1825, when George Stephenson's locomotive, *Locomotion No. 1*, pulled the carriages on the world's first public passenger railway, from Shildon to Darlington and then to Stockton. The engine is now in the Railway Museum at the restored North Road Station, built in 1842.

Off the market-place stands the parish church of St Cuthbert, probably begun in 1192 by Hugh Pudsey, Bishop of Durham, on the site of a Saxon church. It is an outstanding example of the Early English style.

Information Tel. 62034.
Location On the A66, 11 m. W of Stockton-on-Tees.
Parking Russell Street; Parkgate; Park Place; Barnard Street; Northumberland Street; Upper Archer Street; Bells Place; Beaumont Street West; Kendrew Street; Commercial Street; East Row; East Street; Garden Street; Feethams (all car parks).
District council Darlington Borough Council (Tel. 60651).
Population 85,400.
E-C Wed. **M-D** Mon., Sat.
Police (Ba) Park Place (Tel. 67681).
Casualty hospital Memorial,

Hollyhurst Road (Tel. 60100).
Post office (Bb) Northgate.
Theatre Civic **(Ba)**, Parkgate (Tel. 59411).
Cinema ABC, Northgate (Tel. 62745).
Public library (Bb) Crown Street.
Places to see Railway Museum, North Road Station; Museum **(Ba)**, Tubwell Row; Art Gallery **(Bb)**, Crown Street; Roman remains, Piercebridge, 5 m. W.
Town trails Available from Chief Planning Officer, Town Hall.
Shopping Northgate; High Row; Bondgate; Blackwellgate; Tubwell Row; Skinnergate; Priestgate.
Sport FA League football, Darlington FC, Feethams.
Trade and industry Railway equipment; heavy engineering.
AA 24 hour service Tel. Middlesbrough 246832.

Dartford Kent

History has marched for more than 2,000 years across the ford on the River Darent that gave Dartford its name. Ancient Britons, Romans, Saxon pilgrims, Wat Tyler's rebels and Tudor kings all passed that way.

The town is still a vital road and rail communications centre. The Dartford Road Tunnel, linking Essex and Kent was opened in 1963.

Information Tel. 27266.
Location On the A2, 19 m. E of London.
Parking Market Street; Overy Street; Kent Road; Orchard Street; Instone Road; Home Gardens; Heath Street; Springvale; Wellcome Avenue; Trevithic Drive (all car parks).
District council Dartford (Tel. 27266).
Population 42,000.
E-C Wed. **M-D** Thur., Sat.
Police Instone Road (Tel. 27202).
Casualty hospital West Hill (Tel. 23223).
Post office Hythe Street.
Public library Market Street.
Shopping High Street; Lowfield Street; Hythe Street; Spital Street.
Trade and industry Paper-milling; chemical works; engineering.
AA 24 hour service Tel. 01 954 7373.

Dartmouth Devon

The River Dart is a lively scene as naval vessels mingle with pleasure yachts and coastal trawlers, and ferries froth between Dartmouth and Kingswear. Above, on the steep, wooded western flank of the Dart valley, rise the buildings of this ancient port, crowned by the bulk of Britannia Royal Naval College. At the harbour entrance stands the 15th-century Dartmouth Castle.

The port has seen many historic sailings. The Crusades of 1147 and 1190 assembled and set out from Dartmouth, and in 1944 an American fleet left to take part in the D-Day invasion of Normandy. Relics of these and other episodes in maritime history are on display in the town museum.

Thomas Newcomen, inventor of the first effective steam engine, was born in the town in 1663. One of his original engines, possibly the oldest steam engine in the world, is preserved in Royal Avenue Gardens.

Information Tel. 2281/2.
Location On the A379, 30 m. E of Plymouth.

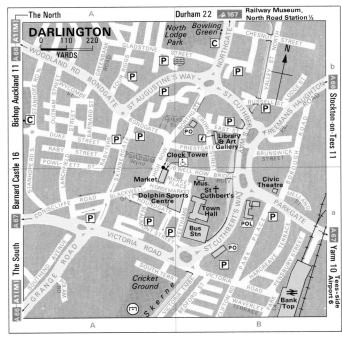

DARLINGTON

Parking Mayor's Avenue; Market
Square; The Quay; Police Station
Square (all car parks).
District council South Hams
(Tel. Totnes 864444).
Population 6,300.
E-C Wed., Sat. **M-D** Tues., Fri.
Police Mayor's Avenue (Tel. 2288).
Casualty hospital South
Embankment (Tel. 2255).
Post office Victoria Road.
Cinema Royalty, Mayor's Avenue
(Tel. 2355).
Public library Newcomen Road.
Places to see Dartmouth Castle,
Castle Road; Bayard's Castle,
Bayard's Cove; Museum, Butterwalk;
Newcomen Engine, Royal Avenue
Gardens; Agincourt House, Lower
Ferry.
Event Royal Regatta (Aug.).
Town trails Available from local
shops.
Trade and industry Boat-building.
Car ferries Dartmouth-Kingswear
and Higher Ferry (Tel. 3144); Lower
Ferry (Kingswear 5342).
AA 24 hour service
Tel. Torquay 25903.

Daventry Northamptonshire

The tall masts of a BBC radio-
transmitting station tower above a
Stone Age fort and Roman excavations on Borough Hill, just outside
Daventry. The town was a market
centre for the surrounding agricultural district in the Middle Ages, and
still holds twice-weekly markets.

Information Tel. 71100.
Location On the A45, 13 m. W of
Northampton.
Parking Bowen Square; New Street;
Sheaf Street; North Street; Golding
Close; St James's Street (all car
parks).
District council Daventry
(Tel. 71100).
Population 16,200.
E-C Thur. **M-D** Tues., Fri.
Police New Street (Tel. 2241).
Casualty hospital Northampton
General, Billing Road
(Tel. Northampton 34700).
Post office Sheaf Street.
Cinema Regal, New Street
(Tel. 2674).
Public library Ashworth Street.
Places to see Stone Age fort and
Roman excavations, Borough Hill.
Trade and industry Electronics; light
engineering.
AA 24 hour service
Tel. Northampton 66241.

Dawlish Devon

Oddly, for a seaside resort, the layout
of central Dawlish ignores the sea
completely. Instead, most of its Regency and Victorian houses face inland towards the burbling Dawlish
Water, where black swans swim.

Powderham Castle, 4 miles north,
is the 14th-century home of the Earls
of Devon. It stands in a deer park by
the Exe estuary.

Information Tel. 863589, summer;
Teignmouth 6271, winter.
Location On the A379, 13 m. S of
Exeter.
Parking Dawlish Warren; Barton
Hill; Strand; Playing Fields Road (all
car parks).
District council Teignbridge
(Newton Abbot 67251).
Population 10,800.
E-C Thur.
Police West Cliff Road
(Tel. 862331).
Casualty hospital Royal Devon,
Exeter (Tel. Exeter 77833).
Post office Brunswick Place.
Theatre Shaftesbury, Brunswick
Place (Tel. 863061).
Public library The Strand.
Places to see Powderham Castle,
4 m. N off the A379.
Town trails Available from Council
Offices, Kingsteignton Road,
Newton Abbot.
AA 24 hour service
Tel. Torquay 25903.

Deal Kent

The old part of this holiday resort
runs parallel to the beach, with narrow streets running down to the seafront. At the southern end stands
Deal Castle, built by Henry VIII in
1540 and shaped like a Tudor rose –
an arrangement that gave the fort's
145 cannons maximum fire-cover.

The Time Ball Tower on the seafront was built in 1854. It provided
Greenwich Mean Time to passing
ships by dropping a large black ball
down a shaft on top of the tower at
precisely 1 p.m. each day. The time
ball stopped working in 1927 when
most ships were fitted with radio.
Deal's 1,000 ft long pier, opened in
1957, is one of the most modern in
Britain.

Walmer Castle, 2 miles south of the
town, was built at the same time and
to the same pattern as Deal Castle.

Information Tel. 61161.
Location On the A258, 8 m. NE of
Dover.
Parking West Street; Stanhope
Road; Oak Street; Union Road.
District council Dover
(Tel. Dover 206090).
Population 25,900.
E-C Thur. **M-D** Sat.
Police (Aa) London Road
(Tel. Dover 201010).
Casualty hospital Victoria Hospital,
London Road (Tel. 2122).
Post office (Bb) Stanhope Road.
Theatre Astor **(Bb)**, Stanhope Road
(Tel. 4931/61161).
Cinema Classic **(Aa)**, Queen Street
(Tel. 4479).
Public library (Ba) Broad Street.
Places to see Deal Castle **(Ba)**;
Walmer Castle and Wellington
Museum, 2 m. S off the B2057;
Maritime Museum **(Bb)**; Deal
Museum **(Bb)**, Town Hall.
Shopping High Street.
AA 24 hour service
Tel. Thanet 81226.

BEACHED *Deal has no harbour, so
fishermen pull their boats ashore.*

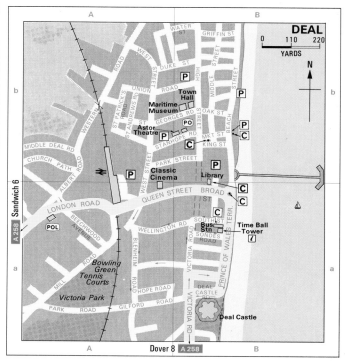

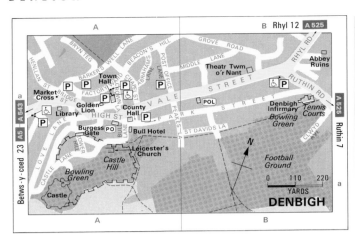

DENBIGH

Denbigh Clwyd

The ruined castle at Denbigh, and the town around it, overlook the rich pastures of the Vale of Clwyd. The castle was built in 1282 by Henry de Lacy, Earl of Lincoln for Edward I, who is said to be represented by an ancient stone figure above the gatehouse.

Close to the castle gate stood the cottage where H. M. Stanley, the journalist and explorer, was born in 1841. It was Stanley who found Dr Livingstone in the heart of Africa, and greeted him with the words – "Dr Livingstone, I presume?"

The town contains many buildings of historic interest, including the 16th-century County Hall and the Golden Lion Inn with a 15th-century timber-framed archway.

Information Tel. Ruthin 2201.
Location On the A525, 7 m. NW of Ruthin.
Parking Barkers Well Lane; Vale Street; Ruthin Road; Post Office Lane.
District council Glyndwr (Tel. Ruthin 2201).
Population 9,000.
E-C Thur. **M-D** Wed.

FAVOURITE'S HALL *Denbigh's County Hall was founded in 1572 by Elizabeth I's favourite, the Earl of Leicester, who was also Lord of Denbigh.*

Police (Ba) Vale Street (Tel. 2474).
Casualty hospital (Ba) Infirmary, Ruthin Road (Tel. 2624).
Post office (Aa) High Street.
Theatre Theatr Twm Or Nant **(Ba)**, Station Road (Tel. 4878).
Public library (Aa) Lenten Pool.
Places to see Castle **(Aa)**, Tower Hill; Town Walls and Leicester's Church **(Aa)**.
Town trails Available from County Planning Officer, Clwyd County Council, Shire Hall, Mold.
Trade and industry Agriculture; quarrying; timber; clothing; printing.
AA 24 hour service
Tel. Llandudno 79066.

Derby Derbyshire

Rolls-Royce engines and Royal Crown Derby porcelain are just two of the modern products for which England's newest city is renowned. Derby was created a city by Queen Elizabeth II during a silver jubilee visit in 1977, but its history goes back to Roman times. The Romans built a fort there in the 2nd century AD.

In Norman times Derby became a busy market town. Later it developed as a manufacturing centre – making woollen cloth, beer and soap. Then, in 1717, England's first silk-mill was established in the town. The mill, in Full Street, is now a museum of industrial archaeology. Its gates, which were made in 1725, are still there – one of the finest examples of wrought-iron work in Britain. The prosperous years of the 18th century were interrupted just once – when Bonnie Prince Charlie's Highland army entered the town on December 4, 1745. But they stayed only two days before retreating north to eventual defeat at Culloden.

The porcelain industry began in 1756, when William Duesbury set out to create china of unrivalled beauty. George III became a patron, and granted Duesbury the right to put a crown on his wares; and in 1890 Queen Victoria commanded that they be marked "Royal Crown Derby".

During the 19th century, huge railway workshops were developed at Derby. In recent times they have pro-

BADGE OF MERIT *Rolls-Royce moved to Derby in 1907.*

duced the Advanced Passenger Train. In 1907 Derby became the home of Rolls-Royce Ltd – makers of motor cars and aero engines. A statue of Sir Henry Royce, engineer-founder of the firm, stands in the Arboretum, which was opened in 1840 as Britain's first public park.

Derby Cathedral was the parish church of All Saints until 1927. The soaring, 178 ft high pinnacled tower is the earliest part, built in 1525. St Mary's Chapel, on St Mary's Bridge over the River Derwent, dates from the 14th century. It is one of the few surviving bridge chapels.

Derby Museum and Art Gallery includes work by the Derby-born painter Joseph Wright (1734-97), a master of candlelight and firelight scenes.

Information Tel. 31111.
Location On the A52, 11 m. NE of Burton upon Trent.
Parking Darwin Place; The Cock Pitt; Full Street; Bradshaw Way; Eagle Centre; Bold Lane; Chapel Street; Ford Street; London Road; Burton Road; Liversage Street; Kensington Street (all car parks).
District council City of Derby (Tel. 31111).
Population 215,700.
E-C Wed. **M-D** Tues., Thur., Fri. and Sat.
Police (Bb) Full Street (Tel. 40224).
Casualty hospital Royal Infirmary, London Road (Tel. 47141).
Post office (Ba) Victoria Street.
Theatre Derby Playhouse **(Ca)**, Eagle Centre (Tel. 363275).
Cinemas ABC **(Ba)**, East Street (Tel. 43964); Odeon, London Road (44744); Metro, Green Lane (40170).
Public library (Aa/Ba) The Wardwick.
Places to see Art Gallery and Museum **(Aa/Ba)**, The Strand; Royal

PRINCE'S ROOM

Derby Museum has a room of relics of Bonnie Prince Charlie, whose army took the town in 1745. Other exhibits include paintings by Wright, and Crown Derby porcelain.

Crown Derby chocolate cup with cover and stand of about 1795.

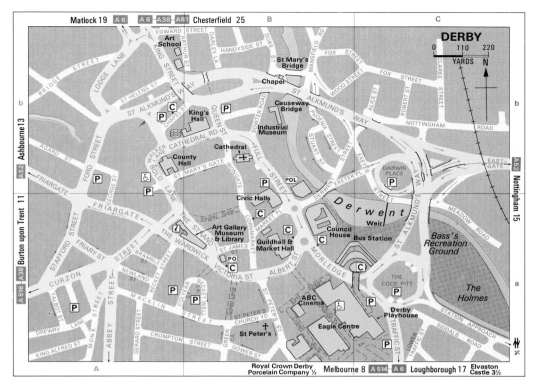

Ashbourne 13 **A52** | Burton upon Trent 11 **A38** | **A516** | Nottingham 15 **A52**

Royal Crown Derby Porcelain Company ½ | Melbourne 8 **A514**—**A6** Loughborough 17 | Elvaston Castle 3½

Crown Derby Porcelain Company, Ormaston Road; Industrial Museum **(Bb)**, The Silk Mill, Full Street; Elvaston Castle, Elvaston Park.
Shopping Eagle Centre; St Peter's Street; Victoria Street; Sadler Gate; Cornmarket; Irongate; Main Centre.
Trade and industry Engineering; porcelain; paper; paint; textiles.
Sport FA League football, Derby County FC, The Baseball Ground, Osmaston Road.
AA 24 hour service Tel. Nottingham 787751.

Devizes Wiltshire
A castle built in the 12th century by Roger, Bishop of Salisbury, and sited between two manors gave the town its name. It comes from the Latin *ad divisas* (at the boundaries). The ancient remains are now private.

On a hillside near Devizes a flight of 29 locks, the longest in Britain, carries the Kennet and Avon Canal over the 230 ft high Caen Hill.

Information Tel. 71279 (summer); 4911.
Location On the A361, 19 m. E of Bath.
Parking Sheep Street; Maryport Street; High Street; New Park Street; Station Road; Commercial Road (all car parks).
District council Kennet (Tel. 4911).
Population 10,600.
E-C Wed. **M-D** Tues., Thur., Sat.
Police New Park Street (Tel. 2141).
Casualty hospital Devizes Hospital (Tel. 3511).
Post office Maryport Street.
Cinema Palace, Market Place (Tel. 2971).
Public library Sheep Street.

Places to see Museum, Long Street.
Town trails Available from Tourist Information Centre, Devizes Wharf, Couch Lane.
Shopping Market Square; The Brittox.
Trade and industry Agriculture; brewing; light engineering.
AA 24 hour service Tel. Bath 24731.

Dewsbury W. Yorks.
St Paulinus, who came to Britain with Augustine, is said to have preached the Gospel at Dewsbury early in the 7th century. Among Saxon relics in the parish church is part of a cross dating from the 7th century or soon after. Dewsbury lies beneath the Pennines, in the Calder Valley. It grew from village to town with the expanding woollen industry of the 18th and 19th centuries.

Information Tel. 465151.
Location On the A638, 10 m. S of Bradford.
Parking Wood Street; Railway Street; Wellington Road; Bradford Street; Cliffe Street (all car parks).
District council Kirklees (Tel. Huddersfield 22133).
Population 48,300.
E-C Tues. **M-D** Wed., Sat.
Police Aldams Road (Tel. 466181).
Casualty hospital Batley General, Carlinghow Hill, Batley (Tel. Batley 473333).
Post office Leeds Road.
Cinema Classic, Market Place (Tel. 464949).
Public library Wellington Road.
Places to see Museum and Art Gallery, Crow's Nest Park.
Shopping Westgate; Northgate;

Market Place; Foundry Street.
Trade and industry Heavy woollens; engineering; chemicals.
AA 24 hour service Tel. Leeds 38161.

Dingwall Highland
Macbeth, immortalised by Shakespeare, is said to have ruled Ross-shire from the castle at Dingwall before he seized the Scottish throne from Duncan in AD 1040.

At that time the town was called Inverpeffer, which is still its name among Gaelic speakers. It was given its present name by Norsemen who captured the castle in Duncan's reign. By 1700 the castle was a ruin, and only traces of the tower remain.

Dingwall is a holiday centre and a base for touring the Highlands.

Information Tel. 63381.
Location On the A9, 21 m. NW of Inverness.
Parking Cromartie; Warden's Lane; Mayfield; High Street; Grant Street (all car parks).
District council Ross and Cromarty (Tel. 63381).
Population 4,960.
E-C Thur. **M-D** Wed.
Police High Street (Tel. 62444).
Casualty hospital Ferry Road (Tel. 63313).
Post office High Street.
Cinema Picture House, High Street (Tel. 62263).
Public library Tulloch Street.
Places to see Macdonald Monument; Town House Museum, High Street.
Shopping High Street.
Event Highland Games (July).
AA 24 hour service Tel. Aberdeen 51231.

Dolgellau Gwynedd

The town's name is pronounced Dolgethlaye. Experts disagree about what it means in English, but the most romantic translation is "cottages in a meadow".

Gold was discovered in the district in 1844, and mines were worked until 1966. Queen Elizabeth II's and the Princess of Wales' wedding rings are made from gold they yielded. Their recorded history is traced in a display at the Maesgwm Visitor Centre, set in a forest 8 miles north of Dolgellau on the A470.

Dolgellau is a popular resort for anglers and hikers visiting the 840 sq. miles of Snowdonia National Park. There are several well-maintained paths for walkers near the town. The Pony Path leads to the top of Cader Idris, the 2,927 ft mountain, 2 miles to the south of the town; the Precipice Walk circles a high ridge 2 miles to the north.

To the east of Dolgellau the Cambrian Mountains are crossed by a 1,790 ft high pass – *Bulch-y-Groes* – which is the highest road in Wales. The name means "Pass of the Cross", because travellers reputedly made the sign of the cross in prayer before tackling the daunting climb.

Information Tel. 422888.
Location On the A487, 34 m. N of Aberystwyth.
Parking The Marian; Arran Road (both car parks).
District council Dolgellau (Tel. 422341).
Population 2,300.
E-C Wed. **M-D** Fri.
Police Barmouth Road (Tel. 422222).
Casualty hospital Hospital Drive (Tel. 422479).
Post office Meyrick Street.
Public library Arran Road.
Shopping Bridge Street; Eldon Square.
Event Autumn Fair (Sept.).
Trade and industry Forestry; hill farming.
AA 24 hour service
Tel. Llandudno 79066.

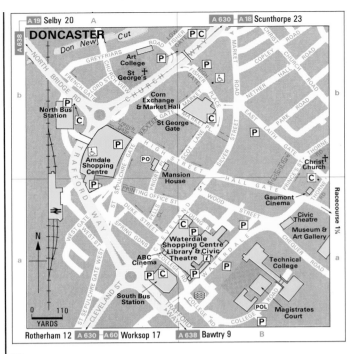

Doncaster S. Yorks.

Doncaster, in the heart of the Yorkshire coalfield, is best known for its railway works and other heavy industries, its butterscotch and its racecourse. But it is also the centre of an arable farming area, a hub of the inland waterway system, and a settlement tracing its history back to Roman times.

The 170 ft, many-pinnacled tower of St George's Church is visible from most parts of the town. The church was designed by Sir George Gilbert Scott and completed in 1858 to replace a medieval one gutted by fire five years earlier.

The 18th-century Mansion House contains an ornate banqueting hall, and a wide staircase with a hand-wrought iron balustrade.

Doncaster Racecourse is the home of the St Leger Stakes, which is run there every September. The race has been run since 1776, and is four years older than the Derby.

Doncaster Museum has a display of Roman ornaments, Saxon weapons and 300-million-year-old fossils.

Information Tel. 20321.
Location On the A630, 22 m. NE of Sheffield.
Parking Greyfriars Road; Trafford Way; Waterdale (2); West Laith Gate; High Fisher Gate; East Laith Gate; College Road; Low Fisher Gate; Young Street; Waterdale; Wood Street (all car parks).
District council Doncaster Metropolitan Borough (Tel. 20321).
Population 81,600.
E-C Thur. **M-D** Tues., Fri. and Sat.
Police (Ba) College Road (Tel. 66744).
Casualty hospital Doncaster Royal Infirmary, Thorne Road (Tel. 66666).
Post office (Ab) Priory Place.
Theatre Civic Theatre **(Ba)**, Waterdale (Tel. 64983).
Cinemas Gaumont **(Ba)**, Thorne Road (Tel. 62523); ABC **(Aa)**, College Road (67934).
Public library (Ba) Waterdale.
Places to see Museum and Art Gallery **(Ba)**, Chequer Road; Cusworth Hall Museum, 1½ m. NW.
Town trails Available from Museum, Chequer Road.
Shopping Arndale Centre; St Sepulchre Gate; Baxtergate; High Street; Waterdale.
Trade and industry Coal-mining; engineering; commerce.
Sport FA League football, Doncaster Rovers FC, Bawtry Road; Flat and steeplechase horse racing, Leger Way.
AA 24 hour service
Tel. Sheffield 28861.

DOLGELLAU BRIDGE *The graceful, seven-arched bridge over the River Wnion was built in 1638. Its name – Bontfawr – means "Big Bridge".*

Dorchester see page 120

WHITE HORSE, DORKING *The 15th-century coaching inn was called the Cross House until 1750. Charles Dickens stayed there.*

1874. Five of the original 16 locomotives pull red-and-cream carriages at a leisurely pace along the 15 mile route.

DOUGLAS I.O.M *Horse-drawn trams have run on the promenade since 1876.*

Dorking Surrey

Some of the finest scenery in Surrey surrounds Dorking, which lies where the Roman Stane Street once intersected the prehistoric track known in the Middle Ages as the Pilgrims' Way.

Dickens stayed at the old coaching inn, the White Horse, parts of which date back to the 15th century.

Great hills surround the town. The 965 ft Leith Hill, to the south-west, is the highest point in south-east England. From the top of the tower that crowns it, 12 counties can be seen. Leith Hill Place was the home of Ralph Vaughan Williams, the composer.

Burford Bridge Hotel, beside the River Mole, was called the Hare and Hounds in the 19th century. It was there that Nelson parted from Lady Hamilton before the Battle of Trafalgar in 1805.

Information Tel. 885001.
Location On the A24, 13 m. E of Guildford.
Parking High Street (4); Church Street; Reigate Road; South Street; North Street; Mill Lane; West Street (all car parks).
District council Mole Valley (Tel. 885001).
Population 22,400.
E-C Wed. **M-D** Fri.
Police Moores Road (Tel. 882284).
Casualty hospital Redhill General, Earlswood Common, Redhill (Tel. Redhill 65030).
Post office High Street.
Public library Pippbrook.
Places to see Leith Hill Place.
Town trails Available from the Museum, West Street.
Shopping High Street; South Street.
Trade and industry Agriculture; brick-making.
AA 24 hour service
Tel. Guildford 72841.

Dornoch Highland

Miles of sandy beaches, backed by grass-covered links, stretch out from Dornoch. The links are the home of the third oldest golf-course in the world – first mentioned in 1616.

Dornoch, one of the oldest cities in Scotland, has broad streets flanked by buildings of honey-coloured sandstone. The cathedral, founded in 1224, contains memorials to the Earls of Sutherland.

Information The Square (Tel. 400).
Location On the A949, 22 m. SE of Lairg.
Parking Meadows (cp); The Square; High Street.
District council Sutherland (Tel. Golspie 392).
Population 830.
E-C Thur.
Police The Square (Tel. 222).
Casualty hospital Golspie Memorial Hospital (Tel. Golspie 3157).
Post office St Gilbert Street.
Public library High Street.
Places to see Earls Cross (on the links); Witch's Stone; Skelbo Castle, 5 m. NW.
Shopping High Street; Castle Street.
Event Highland Games (Aug.).
Trade and industry Tourism; agriculture.
AA 24 hour service
Tel. Aberdeen 51231.

Douglas Isle of Man

In June and September the roar of TT and Grand Prix motor-cycles brings hordes of enthusiasts to Douglas, capital of the Isle of Man. The town is the seat of the Tynwald, the parliament founded by Vikings 1,000 years ago. The steam railway between Douglas and Port Erin was opened in

Information Tel. 4323.
Location On the A11, 10 m. NE of Castletown.
Parking Shaw's Brow; Victoria Street; Church Street; Villiers; Chester Street; Market Street (all car parks).
District council Corporation of Douglas (Tel. 23021).
Population 19,300. **E-C** Thur.
Police Glencrutchery Road (Tel. 26222).
Casualty hospital Noble's **(Aa)**, Westmorland Road (Tel. 3661).
Post office (Ba) Regent Street.
Theatre (Bb) Gaiety (Tel. 5191).
Cinemas Regal **(Ba)** (Tel. 5355); Picture House **(Ba)** (6814); Strand **(Ba)** (4086).
Public library (Aa) Ridgeway Street.
Places to see Manx Museum **(Ab)**; Manx Cattery; Laxey Wheel; Manx Electric Railway.
Shopping Duke Street; Strand Street; Castle Street; Victoria Street.
Trade and industry Finance; shipping.
Car ferry To Liverpool, Heysham, Fleetwood, Llandudno, Ardrossan, Belfast and Dublin (Tel. 3824).
AA 24 hour service
Tel. Liverpool (051) 709 7252.

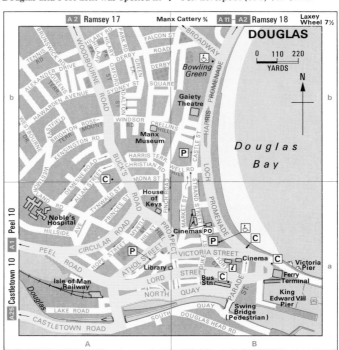

DORCHESTER Dorset

The capital of Hardy's Wessex

Dorset's county town was largely rebuilt after a series of fires in the 17th and 18th centuries destroyed most of its medieval buildings. The site has been occupied since prehistoric times, but it was the Romans who founded the town in AD 70, calling it Durnovaria.

Dorchester was a Saxon mint in the 10th century, a hunting centre under the Normans, and a Roundhead stronghold during the Civil War of 1642-9. In the early 17th century a group of local Puritans founded Dorchester in Massachusetts.

ANCIENT SEAL *Dorchester's original seal, which dates from 1610 when the town received its first charter.*

Two miles south-west of Dorchester are the massive earthworks of **Maiden Castle**, which extend over 120 acres. Its history goes back to 2000 BC, when Stone Age farmers lived there. In the Bronze Age a vast barrow, or funeral mound, about one-third of a mile long was built on the site, which was abandoned until 300 BC. Iron Age men then expanded it into a township and later fortified it with a series of ditches and ramparts. It was this fort, estimated to have housed 5,000 people, that the Roman 2nd Legion of Vespasian overwhelmed in AD 43.

Maumbury Rings, in the southern part of the town, were built by Stone Age men as a Sacred Circle, but the Romans turned it into a vast amphitheatre where 10,000 spectators could watch gladiatorial combats.

Public executions

In the Middle Ages it was used for bear-baiting, and as late as 1767 "Hanging Fairs" – public executions – were held there. These were often attended by crowds as large as those which watched the gladiators fight in Roman times.

The **Old Crown Court,** in High West Street, was in 1834 the scene of a noted trial, that of the six Tolpuddle Martyrs who were sentenced to seven years' transportation after forming the Friendly Society of Agricultural Labourers – a major stage in the development of the trade-union movement in Britain. The court is now a public memorial to the Martyrs, who were pardoned in 1836 after prolonged local agitation.

Grey's Bridge, on the London road, carries a plate which warns that any person damaging the bridge was liable to be transported for life – an example of the severe justice existing in the 19th century.

Dorset poet

St Peter's was one of three churches in Dorchester to survive the fire of 1613. It is mainly 15th century with a 12th-century doorway and a 14th-century Easter sepulchre. In the churchyard stands a statue to the poet William Barnes, who lived in Dorchester from 1837 until his death in 1886. Barnes, who was Rector of Winterborne Came, just south of the town, wrote poetry in the Dorset dialect.

In 1685, following the Monmouth Rebellion, Judge Jeffreys held a "Bloody Assize" in Dorchester. Afterwards the heads of some of the men who were executed were impaled on the church railings, where they were left for several years as a warning of the penalty for treason.

Judge Jeffreys is believed to have held his court in a room which still exists at the rear of the **Antelope Hotel** in South Street. He lodged in a house in High West Street, and this is said to be haunted still by his ghost.

Napper's Almshouses, also known as Napper's Mite, were founded in 1610 by Sir Robert Napper, a Dorset judge who was elected MP for Dorchester in 1586. The building provided lodgings for "ten poor men", but now consists of shops and a cafe.

The **Hangman's Cottage** is a 16th-century thatched building close to the River Frome. It still looks much as it did when its occupant was one of the busiest men in Dorchester. It is a private residence.

Several mosaic floors still survive in the **Roman House**, which is next to the County Hall at Colliton Park.

THE MEN OF TOLPUDDLE

Trade unions were not illegal in 1834, but the six Tolpuddle farmworkers – the Martyrs – were charged with swearing unlawful oaths when taking part in their society's initiation ritual.

There were many celebrations in Dorset after local agitation had secured the Martyrs' release.

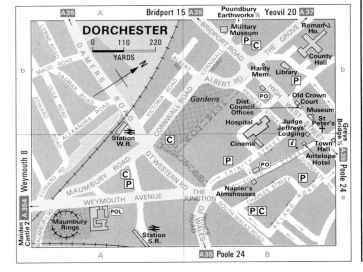

John Stanfield and James Loveless, two of the Tolpuddle six.

FAR FROM THE MADDING CROWD, WHERE THOMAS HARDY LIVED AND WORKED

The novelist Thomas Hardy was born at Higher Bockhampton, 2½ miles from Dorchester, in 1840. Trained as an architect, he designed a house for himself at Max Gate in Dorchester. He went there 11 years after completing two of his novels, *Far from the Madding Crowd* and *Under the Greenwood Tree* at his cottage birthplace.

Most of Hardy's novels were set in Dorset, and many places took on new names in his stories – Tolpuddle became Tolchurch, Lulworth became Lulstead, and in *The Mayor of Casterbridge* (Dorchester) many of the town's streets and inns provided settings for his characters.

Thomas Hardy died at Max Gate on January 11, 1928. He is buried in Westminster Abbey, but his heart lies beneath a yew tree in Stinsford churchyard.

This life-size statue of Hardy stands in The Grove, Dorchester.

The foundations, which have lasted nearly 2,000 years, can also be seen.

Poundbury Earthworks, northwest of the town, date from the same period as Maiden Castle, but are much smaller, covering about 20 acres. The site is surrounded by a single, low rampart. It, too, was captured by the Romans who built an aqueduct which runs along the north side of the fort.

Dorset's history, from the Stone Age to the 20th century, is traced in the **Dorset County Museum**. Geology, natural history, archaeology and local history are covered, and there are important finds from Maiden Castle.

The museum's Thomas Hardy Memorial Collection includes some of the novelist's manuscripts and personal possessions, housed in a reconstruction of his study. The museum also has relics of William Barnes, and paintings by local artists.

Regimental history

Dorset Military Museum, which is housed in The Keep – the entrance to the former Dorset Regiment barracks – records the history of all the Dorset regiments from 1661. The display includes pictures, uniforms, medals, and weapons, including the sword and saddle used by Cornet Glyn in the Heavy Brigade Charge at Balaclava. An unusual exhibit is a desk from Adolf Hitler's Berlin Chancellery. It was presented by the Russians to the Dorset Regiment in 1945.

Information Tel. 67992.
Location On the A35, 29 m. W of Bournemouth.
Parking Charles Street (2); Durngate Street; Bridport Road; Weymouth Avenue (all car parks).
District council West Dorset (Tel. 65211).
Population 14,000.
E-C Thur. **M-D** Wed., Thur.

Police (Aa) Weymouth Avenue (Tel. 63011).
Casualty hospital Weymouth and District, Melcombe Avenue, Weymouth (Tel. 72211).
Post office (Ba) South Street.
Cinema Plaza **(Ba)**, Trinity Street (Tel. 62488).
Public library (Bb) Colliton Park.
Places to see Old Crown Court **(Bb)**, Maiden Castle, Maiden Castle Road; Maumbury Rings **(Aa)**, Weymouth Avenue; Poundbury Earthworks, Poundbury Road; Roman House **(Bb)**, Colliton Park; Dorset County Museum **(Bb)**, High West Street; Dorset Military Museum **(Bb)**, Bridport Road.
Shopping South Street; High West Street; High East Street.
Events Carnival (July).
Trade and industry Brewing; agriculture; agricultural engineering.
AA 24 hour service Bournemouth 25751.

JUDGE JEFFREYS' LODGINGS *James II's Lord Chancellor stayed here while holding his "Bloody Assize", when he sentenced 74 men to death for their part in the Duke of Monmouth's rebellion at Sedgemoor on July 6, 1685.*

DOVER Kent

The threshold of Shakespeare's "Sceptred Isle"

The 500 ft high chalk cliffs of Dover are cross-Channel passengers' first or last sight of England's shores, and have always had a symbolic significance for the English. They are the portals of the traditional gateway to England from the Continent; a port that has been in Britain's first line of defence ever since the Romans came.

Dover stands where the once-broad River Dour breaks through the cliffs. The town has changed shape and size many times over the centuries. The first small Stone Age settlement was established about 2000 BC. In Iron Age times, about 200 BC, a large defensive earthworks was built, which is now largely masked by the medieval castle. When the Romans settled, about AD 125, they developed the natural harbour formed by the tidal River Dour estuary. On each of the flanking headlands the Romans built a huge octagonal **stone pharos**, or lighthouse. One still stands in the castle grounds, and is the tallest surviving Roman building in the country.

In 1971 excavations in New Street uncovered a **Roman house** built in the 2nd century, with wall-paintings unmatched in Britain for their extent, design and colour. These are the oldest paintings discovered in Britain, and consist of rectangular panels separated by painted columns.

The walls of the house survive to a height of 9 ft in places, and beneath the pink mortar floors is a complete

heating system. On the west side of the house is part of the wall of a Roman fort.

By the 6th century, Anglo-Saxons had built a community of wooden huts next to the harbour. This settlement gradually flowered into a fine late-Saxon and medieval town, whose seamen, like those of today, carried passengers and goods to the Continent.

Saxon church

The Saxons built several churches, of which **St Mary-in-Castre**, in the castle grounds, still survives. Built in the late 10th and early 11th centuries, it was extensively restored in the 19th century.

Because of fierce Saxon resistance, the Normans destroyed much of the town when they invaded. William I later rebuilt it. It was in the 1180s that Henry II began building the keep of the present **castle** on commanding heights above the town and within the area of the old Iron Age fort. Built in the centre of an inner bailey, the keep is one of the most imposing and impregnable works in Europe. The banqueting halls, chapels and splendid collection of weapons are open to the public. The fortifications of the surrounding outer bailey were completed in the 12th century, making the castle one of the earliest concentric fortresses in England.

Continuously garrisoned since it was built, the castle proved its worth in the early 13th century when Hubert de Burgh held it for King John against invading French forces. The French honeycombed the cliff beneath the castle with underground

passages, which can still be explored. They were used as air-raid shelters in the Second World War.

In the castle grounds stands a decorated brass cannon, known as **Queen Elizabeth's Pocket Pistol**. A local rhyme declares: "Use me well and keep me clean – I'll send a ball to Calais Green" – but its proven range in the early 17th century was only 2,000 yds.

On East Cliff promenade are memorials to two men who set out from Dover on epic journeys – Captain Webb, who in 1875 became the first man to swim the Channel, and C. S. Rolls, who in 1910 made the first two-way flight across the Channel.

To the east, St Margaret's Bay, the nearest cove to France, is the most popular starting point for modern cross-Channel swimmers. On the clifftop above the bay is a memorial to the sailors of the **Dover Patrol** who lost their lives in the two World Wars. The Dover Patrol consisted of fishing trawlers converted into minesweepers, whose task was to keep the lanes to the Channel ports open.

On the other side of the town the 350 ft high, sheer face of Shakespeare Cliff rears above the shore. It is so called because this is the cliff referred to by Edgar in *King Lear* when he cries:

"How fearful
And dizzy 'tis to cast one's eyes
    so low!"

The town hall and the museum are housed in **Maison Dieu House**. Built in 1203, this was originally a hospice that cared for travellers and those in need and was founded by Hubert de Burgh, Constable of Dover Castle. The museum includes collections of Bronze Age, Iron Age and Roman finds, pottery, glassware, furniture, clocks and watches, and natural-history specimens. One room is devoted to the history of Dover.

Busy port

The port owes its importance to its closeness to the French coastline. It is only 21 miles from Calais and 25 miles from Boulogne. Lying in one of the world's largest artificial harbours – about 850 acres in area and

FRONT-LINE PORT *Dover Castle stands above the docks, where cross-Channel ferries serve continental travellers.*

FIRST CROSS-CHANNEL FLIGHT

On July 25, 1909, the French aviator Louis Blériot (1872-1936) piloted his monoplane from the French coast to North Fall Meadow, Dover – behind the castle – and so became the first man to fly the Channel. The distance covered was 26 miles, and the flight lasted 36½ minutes. Blériot's plane is now preserved in the Science Museum in London.

A granite aircraft silhouette commemorates Blériot's achievement.

protected by massive breakwaters – it consists of two complexes: the docks to the west of the town, which deal with train ferries, and the modern car-ferry terminal and hoverport to the east. Handling about 12 million travellers each year, Dover is the busiest passenger port in Britain.

Dover's proximity to the French coast led to the building of cavernous brick shelters on the western heights during the Napoleonic Wars, to house British troops in case Napoleon invaded. **Crabble Mill**, built in 1812 as a water-mill, was used to provide flour for them. It ceased to function in about 1890, but was recently restored to working order.

The Admiralty Pier, more than 4,000 ft long, claims to offer the longest marine-pier walk in the world.

The surrounding countryside is a walker's paradise. The way to Kingsdown, over the clifftops to the east, offers superb views of the Channel; and for long-distance walkers there are the 20 mile Pilgrims' Way to Canterbury and the North Downs Way to Surrey.

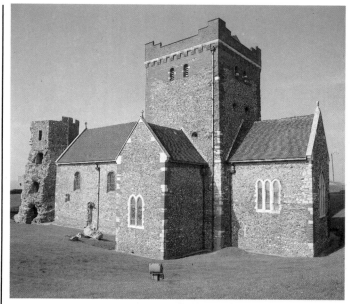

SAXON CHURCH, ROMAN LIGHTHOUSE *St Mary-in-Castre Church, built largely from Roman stone in the 10th and 11th centuries, is next to the octagonal Roman pharos, or lighthouse, which served it as a bell-tower.*

Information Town Hall, Priory Road (Tel. 206941).
Location On the A2, 15 m. SE of Canterbury.
Parking Ladywell; Norman Street; Church Street; Woolcomber Street; Castle Hill Road; Townwall Street; St James Lane; Bulwark Street; Old Folkestone Road; Buckland Bridge; Hawkesbury Street; Crafford Street (all car parks).
District council Dover (Tel. 206090).

Population 32,800.
E-C Wed. **M-D** Sat.
Police (Ab) Ladywell (Tel. 201010).
Casualty hospital Coombe Valley Road (Tel. 201624).
Post office (Aa) Biggin Street.
Cinema ABC **(Ba)**, Castle Street (Tel. 206750).
Public library (Aa) Biggin Street.
Places to see Castle **(Bb)**; Roman lighthouse **(Cb)**; Roman Painted House **(Aa)**, York Street; Blériot Memorial **(Cb)**; Maison Dieu **(Aa)**;

Crabble Mill; Chapel of St Edmund, Priory Street.
Shopping Biggin Street; High Street; Cannon Street; Castle Street; Pencester Road.
Trade and industry Paper-making; iron-founding; chair-making.
Car ferry To Boulogne, Calais, Dunkirk, Ostend, Zeebrugge (Tel. 205108). Hovercraft to Calais, Boulogne (Tel. 208288).
AA 24 hour service Tel. Thanet 81226.

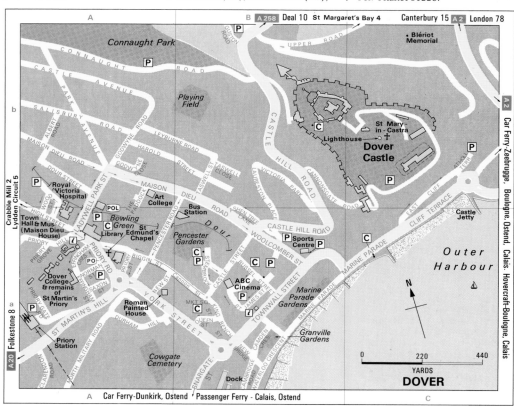

Dudley West Midlands

There is iron in the soul of Dudley. Once the "capital of the Black Country", it has been a centre for iron-working since the Middle Ages.

The castle, which has dominated the town from its 180 ft high hill since the 13th century, was the home of John Dudley, Duke of Northumberland. In 1553 he made his daughter-in-law, Lady Jane Grey, Queen of England – but her reign lasted only nine days and she and her husband were executed in February 1554. Old limestone pits near the castle now house Dudley Zoo.

The Dudley Canal Trust organises regular trips for visitors through another legacy of Dudley's industrial past: the 1¾ mile canal tunnel which runs 200 ft below the town centre from Park Head to Tipton Green. Trips start at the Black Country Museum off Tipton Road, and *Electra*, the world's first electrically powered narrow boat, may be booked to take parties right through the tunnel. Traditional narrow boats had to be "legged": the crew lay on their backs and propelled the 20 ton boats through the tunnel by pushing with their feet along the tunnel walls.

The Central Museum in St James's Road has a collection of local fossils, many of them from Wren's Nest Hill, a geological nature reserve 1 mile north-west of the castle.

Information Tel. 50333.
Location On the A459, 6 m. S of Wolverhampton.
Parking Flood Street; King Street (2); St James's Road; Wolverhampton Street; Stafford Street; Tower Street; Steppingstone Street; Trident Centre (all car parks).
District council Dudley (Tel. 55433).
Population 187,200.
E-C Wed. **M-D** Daily, except Sun.
Police New Street (Tel. 56900).
Casualty hospital Guest, Tipton Road (Tel. 56966).
Post office Wolverhampton Street.
Cinema Plaza, Castle Hill (Tel. 55518).
Public library St James's Road.
Places to see Castle and Zoo, Castle Hill; Wren's Nest Hill Geological Nature Reserve; Central Museum and Art Gallery; Black Country Museum; Broadfield House Glass Museum, Kingswinford, 5 m. SW.
Shopping High Street; Birdcage Walk; Churchill Precinct; Trident Centre; Fountain Arcade.
AA 24 hour service
Tel. Birmingham (021) 550 4858.

Dufftown Grampian

There is a saying in Dufftown that Rome was built on seven hills and Dufftown on seven stills; for this little town at the junction of the Fiddich river and Dullan Water is the capital of the malt-whisky distilling industry.

There were illicit stills in the district until 1934, when the last arrest for illicit distilling was made. Dufftown was built in 1817, laid out in the shape of a cross, by James Duff, the 4th Earl of Fife.

For centuries before, there had been a stronghold at this strategic meeting point of the glens. The ruins of 13th-century Balvenie Castle, one of the largest and best preserved castles in northern Scotland, lie 1 mile north of the town. Mary, Queen of Scots stayed there in 1562 during her campaign against the Gordons.

South of Dufftown stands the 12th-century church at Mortlach. A stone in the churchyard commemorates a victory over the Danes in 1010.

Information Tel. 20501.
Location On the A941, 16 m. SE of Elgin.
Parking Albert Place (cp).
District council Moray (Tel. Elgin 3451).
Population 1,650.
E-C Wed.
Police Hill Street (Tel. 20222).
Casualty hospital Stephen Cottage, Stephen Avenue (Tel. 20215).
Post office Albert Place.
Public library Balvenie Street.
Places to see Tower Museum; Balvenie Castle; Mortlach Church; Glenfiddich Distillery.
Shopping Balvenie Street; Conval Street; Fife Street; Church Street.
Event Gala week and Highland Games (July).
AA 24 hour service
Tel. Aberdeen 51231.

Dumbarton Strathclyde

St Patrick is said to have been born at Dumbarton and carried away to Ireland by raiders. A sundial in the ruins of the town castle recalls another historic departure, that of Mary, Queen of Scots, who was six years old when she sailed to live in France in 1548 after a brief stay at the town.

In the 5th century there was a castle on the twin peaks of the 240 ft high rock which stands beside the junction of the Leven and the Clyde. William Wallace was imprisoned in Dumbarton Castle for a short time after his capture by the English in 1305. The Wallace Tower and some 17th and 18th-century fortifications are all that remain of the castle.

Ship-building flourished at Dumbarton in the 19th century, when the town grew rapidly. The clipper ship *Cutty Sark* was built at a Dumbarton yard in 1869. It is now preserved beside the Thames at Greenwich.

Information Tel. 65100.
Location On the A814, 15 m. NW of Glasgow.
Parking Dalreoch Station; Church Street; High Street (all car parks).
District council Dumbarton (Tel. 65100).
Population 23,600.
E-C Wed.
Police Crosslet (Tel. 63311).
Casualty hospital Vale of Leven, Alexandria (Tel. Alexandria 54121).
Post office (Ab) Town Centre.
Theatre Denny Civic **(Bb)**, Town Centre (Tel. 65538).
Cinema Rialto **(Bb)**, College Street (Tel. 62763).
Public library (Bb) Strathleven Place.
Places to see Castle, Castle Road; Glencairn Greit House **(Aa)**.
Town trails Available from Public library.
Shopping High Street; Town Centre.
Trade and industry Whisky distilling; light industry.
Sport Scottish League football, Dumbarton FC, Miller Street.
AA 24 hour service
Tel. Glasgow (041) 812 0101.

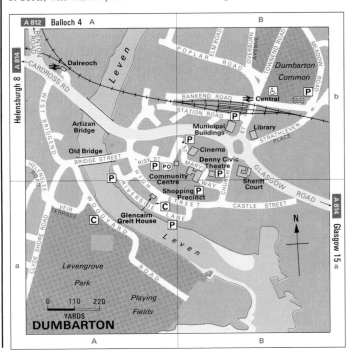

EARL OF DUNBAR'S MONUMENT *King James I's Minister for Scotland is remembered in Dunbar's parish church.*

DUNBAR HARBOUR *A fleet of small fishing craft rides at anchor in one of the two harbours of this historic cobble-quayed Scottish town.*

Dumfries see page 126

Dunbar Lothian

A turbulent past hides behind the peaceful air of ancient Dunbar. The town stands on the Scottish coast on the direct route between England and Edinburgh, and for centuries the Scots and English fought to gain control over it. Eleven hundred years ago the town was sacked by the Scottish king, Kenneth McAlpin (Kenneth I), the first man to rule both the Scots and the Picts.

Generals marching north preferred the coastal route because they could keep their men supplied by sea, and in 1296 Dunbar's defenders were routed by the troops of Edward I.

In 1338 Black Agnes, Countess of March and Dunbar, wrote one of the most stirring pages of Scottish history with her vigorous defence of the castle. Her husband was away, but she held off an attack led by the Earl of Salisbury for six weeks. She was relieved by a raiding party from the sea.

The bloodiest battle of Dunbar was fought in 1650, when the Covenanters, outnumbering Cromwell's Roundheads by two-to-one, had them apparently trapped in the town. But the Scots recklessly left a strong position on Doon Hill to prepare for a battle on the plain. In a surprise dawn attack Cromwell defeated the Scots.

Five years later Cromwell, perhaps remembering Dunbar as his greatest victory, granted £300 towards the cost of a new harbour at the town.

Now only a small fishing fleet remains, and the picturesque harbour with the ruined castle beside it forms an attractive centrepiece to the resort.

Information Tel. 63353.
Location On the A1087, 28 m. E of Edinburgh.
Parking Bayswell Road (2) (both car parks).
District council East Lothian (Tel. Haddington 4161).
Population 4,600.
E-C Wed.
Police Castellau (Tel. 62718 and Haddington 4101).
Casualty hospital Belhaven, Beveridge Row (Tel. 62246).
Post office High Street.
Public library Castellau.
Places to see Myreton Motor Museum, Castle Park.

Shopping High Street.
Event Vintage vehicle rally (Aug.).
AA 24 hour service
Tel. Edinburgh (031) 225 8464.

Dunblane Central

The small but ancient city of Dunblane is dominated by its 13th-century cathedral, which stands on high ground above the turbulent Allan Water. Some fine late-19th-century woodcarving can be seen in the cathedral choir, and the south side with its tall 12th-century tower and lofty windows in the choir has a majestic quality. The roof of the nave collapsed in the 16th century, and was restored in 1893. Six beautifully carved 15th-century stalls flank the west door.

Opposite the cathedral is The Dean's House, a museum containing local historical relics. The surrounding narrow streets have some fine houses, dating from the 17th century.

The Leighton Library was built in 1687, to house the books which Bishop Leighton bequeathed to the town's clergy in the 17th century. The shaded riverside path where he often strolled is called Bishop's Walk.

Information Tel. 824428 or Stirling 3131.
Location On the A9, 6 m. N of Stirling.
Parking The Haining; Mill Row (both car parks).
District council Stirling (Tel. Stirling 3131).
Population 6,820.
E-C Wed.
Police Perth Road (Tel. 822222).
Casualty hospital Stirling Royal Infirmary, Livilands Gate, Stirling (Tel. Stirling 3041).
Post office Stirling Road.
Public library High Street.
Places to see Cathedral; Dean's House Museum; The Cross.
Shopping Stirling Road; High Street.
Event Agricultural Show (July).
AA 24 hour service
Tel. Glasgow (041) 812 0101.

DUMFRIES Dumfries & Galloway

Scotland's fair "Queen of the South"

Old red-sandstone buildings, spacious parks and the broad waters of the River Nith have earned for Dumfries the title "Queen of the South". The town lies a few miles inland from where the Nith flows into the Solway Firth. The town is the market centre for a large agricultural area, beyond which lie the hills, forests and moors of Galloway. In addition, it has several thriving industries, including the manufacture of high-quality hosiery and knitwear, for which it has been noted since the early 1800s. It is the largest town in south-west Scotland.

The town was created a royal burgh by William the Lion in 1186, and received its first-known charter from Robert III in 1393. It was in Dumfries that the Scottish patriot Robert Bruce committed the first act of rebellion against Edward I, in 1306, which led to the Wars of Independence.

Bruce slew the king's representative, Sir John Comyn, on the altar of the Greyfriars Monastery, and later declared himself King of Scotland. On the west side of Castle Street, a plaque on a wall marks the spot where the monastery stood; the present Greyfriars Church was built in 1868.

Bruce's first victory in the war against Edward was the capture of Dumfries Castle. Only traces of the castle remain, at **Castledykes**, and the site is now a wooded parkland with a sunken garden.

The most prominent building in Dumfries is the **Midsteeple**, built in 1707 to serve as a courthouse and prison. The old Scots "ell" measurement (37 in.) is carved on the front of the building, and a table of distances to other towns includes Huntingdon, in England. This is because the Scots cattle-drovers of the 18th century took their animals to Huntingdon to sell in the English markets.

Another embellishment on the façade of the Midsteeple is a relief-map of the town showing it as it was in the time of Robert Burns. It was unveiled in 1959 to mark the bi-centenary of the birth of Burns, who died in Dumfries in 1796. The poet's funeral took place from the Midsteeple.

Burns moved to Dumfries in 1791, and the house in which he died, now

TOWN PEEPSHOW *Dumfries spreads out round the River Nith in the view below, which was taken from the camera obscura in Dumfries Burgh Museum. The museum (left) is housed in a restored 18th-century windmill.*

called **Burns House**, is a museum containing many of his relics. Near the house is St Michael's churchyard, where Burns, his wife Jean Armour and five of his children lie buried in the Mausoleum. Burns spent many evenings at the **Globe Inn** in the High Street. The chair in which he usually sat is preserved, and on a pane of glass in an upper room are two verses of poetry scratched by the poet with a diamond.

The Scottish playwright Sir James Barrie also had associations with Dumfries. He was a pupil at the Academy, and it was in the nearby gardens that he first conceived the idea for his play, *Peter Pan.*

The parish church of St Michael dates from 1744, but its completion was delayed when Bonnie Prince Charlie visited the town in 1745. Finding little support in Dumfries for his claim to the English Crown, he stripped the lead from the church roof, and added it to his other booty of £1,000 in cash and 1,000 pairs of shoes for his soldiers. A brass plate in the church marks the pew where Robert Burns sat.

Windmill museum

Dumfries Burgh Museum was founded in 1835, and was also used as an observatory. The building is a mid-18th-century windmill, and at the top is a camera obscura which was installed in 1836. This device is a darkened room into which views of the town are reflected on to a table through a periscope arrangement to give a moving panorama of the world outside. The museum has a comprehensive display of local history, and a portrait gallery of local people who have achieved international fame.

Another museum, in the **Old Bridge House**, has six rooms depicting life in several periods; a 16th–18th-century room, a dental surgery of 1900, a Victorian child's room, an 1850 kitchen, a 1900 town kitchen and an 1870 bedroom. The museum is at one end of the medieval stone bridge that crosses the River Nith. Known as the Old Bridge, or Devorgilla Bridge, it has six arches and is on the site of a previous wooden bridge erected by Lady Devorgilla, wife of John de Baliol, founder of Balliol College, Oxford.

Just downstream from the Old Bridge is the **Caul,** an 18th-century weir built to provide power for riverside grain mills. Today it is one of the sights of the town, when, on summer evenings, salmon can be seen leaping it to get upstream to spawn.

Royal tomb

On the west side of the river are the remains of **Lincluden College,** a collegiate church dating from the early 15th century. The remains include some of the finest stonework of the period surviving in Scotland. There are many elaborate heraldic carvings and the tomb of Princess Margaret, daughter of Robert III of Scotland.

Six miles south of Dumfries lies **Sweetheart Abbey,** founded by the Lady Devorgilla in memory of her husband. When he died in 1269 she had his heart embalmed. At her own death, 21 years later, the heart was buried with her body in front of the abbey altar. It was this devotion to her husband that is said to have given the word "sweetheart" to the English language.

Every year, on a Saturday in June, Dumfries celebrates the granting of its Royal Charter with the Guid Nychburris (pronounced Neebors) Festival. The original ceremony is re-enacted, and ends with the crowning of the Queen of the South, a girl chosen from one of the local schools.

During the festival a shooting competition takes place for the Siller (Silver) Gun. This prize, a miniature firearm, was first presented in 1617 by James I (VI of Scotland) and is now in the Burgh Museum. The winner now receives a replica.

Information Tel. 3862.
Location On the A75, 35 m. NW of Carlisle.
Parking Whitesands; Burns Street; Nith Street; High Street; Irish Street; Charlotte Street; Gordon Street; George Street; Loreburn Street; Munches Street; Glasgow Street; Shakespeare Street; Brooms Road (all car parks).
District council Nithsdale (Tel. 3166).
Population 29,000.
E-C Mon., Thur. **M-D** Wed.
Police (Bb) Loreburn Street (Tel. 2112).
Casualty hospital Bankend Road (Tel. 3151).
Post office (Bb) Great King Street.
Theatre Theatre Royal **(Ba)**, Shakespeare Street (Tel. 4209).
Cinema ABC **(Ba)**, Shakespeare Street (Tel. 3578).
Public library (Bb) Catherine Street.

COUNTRY POET *Burns's statue in Dumfries High Street shows him seated on a tree stump with his dog at his feet.*

Places to see Burns House **(Aa)**, Burns Street; Dumfries Burgh Museum **(Aa)**, Church Street; Old Bridge House Museum **(Ab)**; Devorgilla Bridge **(Ab)**; Lincluden College, 2 m. NW; Sweetheart Abbey, 6 m. S; Shambellie House Museum of Costume, New Abbey, 8 m. SW.
Shopping High Street; English Street; Buccleuch Street; Friars Vennel.
Sport Scottish League football, Queen of the South FC, Palmerston Park.
AA 24 hour service Tel. Dumfries 69257.

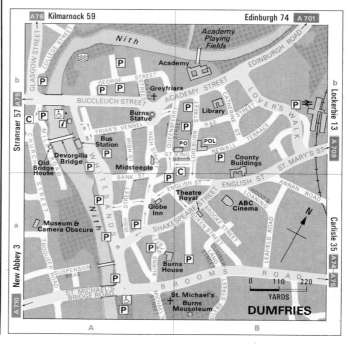

DUNDEE Tayside

A thriving city on the "Silvery Tay"

Jute, jam and journalists brought wealth to Scotland's fourth-largest city in the 19th century. It still produces all three, together with motor tyres, carpets, business machines, ships, whisky and Dundee cakes.

The Firth of Tay, spanned by road and rail-bridges, provides a natural deep-water harbour, one of the best on Britain's North Sea coast. It is an expanding base for the off-shore oil industry, and an all-cargo port.

The 19th-century jute-mills and tenements which were characteristic of pre-war Dundee have mostly been pulled down and replaced by modern buildings.

Three of the best-known comics.

Dundee was an established settlement when the Romans invaded this part of Scotland in the 1st century AD, and there are still traces of its early Celtic inhabitants. A pre-Roman hill-fort stands on the Law, the 571 ft volcanic crag on whose lower slopes part of the city is built. And in Camperdown Park an earth house was found – a stone-roofed underground dwelling of Iron Age date – now filled in.

But the city has few ancient buildings. For 300 years from the 14th century it was fought over by English and Scots, and few buildings survived for long. The growth of industry, whaling in the 18th century and jute manufacture in the 19th century, brought rapid building and further destruction.

Dundee has been a royal burgh since 1190, and in the 12th century it had both a castle and a monastery, which have long since disappeared. By tradition William Wallace (*c.* 1272-1305) was educated at the monastery school. In 1288 he began a lifetime of struggle against the English when he killed the son of the English Constable of Dundee. A wall plaque in Castlehill, showing where the castle once stood, commemorates Wallace. It also recalls the birth, in a later house on the site, of Admiral Adam Duncan (1731-1804), who defeated the Dutch at the Battle of Camperdown in 1797.

The land once occupied by the monastery is called The Howff, or meeting-place, because the trade guilds once met there. It was given to Dundee in 1565 by Mary, Queen of Scots to use as a cemetery, and contains monuments from the 16th, 17th and 18th centuries.

The 15th-century Old Steeple is all that remains of the Church of St Mary. It is being turned into a museum.

Castle in a park

Dudhope Castle, in a park beside Lochee Road, was built in the 13th

CITY ON THE TAY *St Paul's Cathedral towers over Dundee's High Street. The busy city and port is on the north bank of the* *Firth of Tay, and is linked to the south by a railway bridge and a 1.4 mile dual-carriageway road bridge with 42 spans.*

NOTED FARE *Keiller's rich Dundee fruit cakes and marmalade are two of the city's most celebrated products.*

century for the Scrymageur family, hereditary Constables of Dundee. The house, rebuilt in the 16th century, and the office of Constable passed to John Graham of Claverhouse (c. 1649-89), the "Bonnie Dundee" who brutally suppressed the Covenanters, Scottish Presbyterians. It is now used for meetings.

Camperdown House has a golf museum which illustrates the history of the sport over the past 300 years.

Dundee University, founded in 1881, was at first affiliated to St Andrew's University but is now independent.

The City Museum contains the oldest known astrolabe, an instrument used in navigation, which dates from 1555. The Barrack Street Museum is a museum of the environment, commerce and maritime history. The whaling trade, ecology and the local community are recorded in the museum at Broughty Castle, 4 miles to the east in the seaside village of Broughty Ferry, which is now a suburb of the city.

"GREAT BAD VERSE"

William McGonagall (1830-1902), self-styled poet and tragedian.

According to *Punch*, William McGonagall was the "greatest Bad Verse Writer of his age". He worked in Dundee as a weaver and many of his poems were inspired by local landmarks. The Dundee firm of David Winter still prints his works.

In Caird Park, ruins are all that remain of the 16th-century Mains of Fintry Castle, once the seat of the Graham family. Claypotts Castle, 3 miles to the east, was also one of their strongholds.

Dundee's docks cover an area of 35 acres, and are expanding. The shipyards which built the polar-exploration vessels *Terra Nova*, for Shackleton, and *Discovery*, for Scott, are still busy, and in the dock area the *Unicorn*, a wooden frigate launched in 1824, has become a floating museum.

Information Tel. 23141 or 27723.
Location On the A92, 21 m. NE of Perth.
Parking South Tay Street; Gellatly Street; Dock Street; Cowgate; West Port (2); King Street; Catherine

Street; James Street; Roseangle; Seafield Road; Sinclair Street; Union Place; Commercial Street; Earl Grey Place; Bell Street; Leisure Centre (all car parks).
District council City of Dundee (Tel. 23141).
Population 180,000.
E-C Wed. **M-D** Tues., Thurs.
Police (Ab) West Bell Street (Tel. 23200).
Casualty hospitals Dundee Royal Infirmary **(Ab)**, Barrack Road (Tel. 23125); Ninewells Hospital, Ninewells (60111).
Post office (Bb) Meadowside.
Theatres Dundee Repertory **(Aa)**, South Tay Street (Tel. 22200); Little **(Bb)**, 58 Victoria Road (25835); Whitehall, Bellfield Street (22200).
Cinemas ABC **(Ba)**, Seagate (Tel. 26865); Victoria **(Bb)**, Victoria Road (26186); Steps Film Theatre **(Bb)**, Wellgate Centre (24938).
Public library (Bb) Wellgate Centre.
Places to see Dundee Museum and Art Gallery **(Bb)**; Barrack Street Museum **(Bb)**; Broughty Castle Museum; Camperdown House (The Spalding Golf Museum); Mills Observatory; Dudhope Castle **(Ab)**; HMS *Unicorn* **(Ca)**; Claypotts Castle; Fintry Castle; The Howff **(Ba, Bb)**; The Old Steeple **(Ba)**, Nethergate.
Shopping North Tay Street; Market Gait; Nethergate; High Street; Murraygate; Meadowside; Euclid Crescent; Ward Road; Overgate.
Event Highland Games (July).
Sport Scottish League football, Dundee United FC, Tannadice Park, and Dundee FC, Dens Park.
AA 24 hour service Tel. 25585.

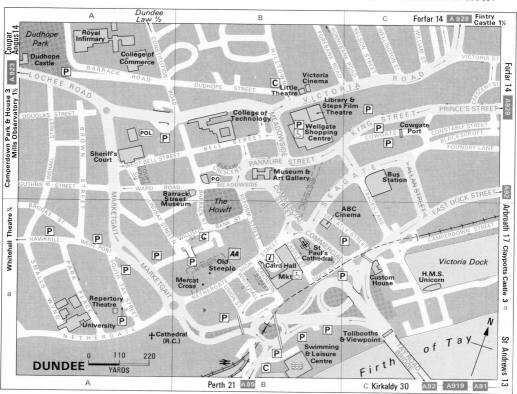

DUNDEE

Dunfermline Fife

For six centuries Dunfermline was Scotland's capital, and seven Scottish kings are buried there – Malcolm III, Edgar, Alexander I, David I, Malcolm IV, Alexander III and Robert I (Robert Bruce). Malcolm III built a palace there in 1070, and in that year he married a Saxon princess, Margaret, in a small church near the palace. Margaret became a strong influence in Scottish religious life, and eventually replaced the old Celtic religion with her own Roman Catholic belief. At the place of her marriage she founded a Benedictine abbey – the first in Scotland.

Dunfermline Abbey still has a late-Norman nave, and the original foundations of Margaret's abbey can be seen through grilles set in the nave floor. The tower was restored early in the 19th century, and its parapet has the words "King Robert the Bruce" in stone lettering extending around four sides. Robert Bruce was buried in the abbey in 1329, and his tomb is marked by a brass plate given by the Earl of Elgin – a descendant of Bruce – in 1889.

At the east end of the nave is the shrine of St Margaret, who was canonised in 1250. Margaret was also responsible for a new palace, on a grander scale than Malcolm's. The palace was rebuilt in 1315 after having been destroyed on the orders of Edward I. It was the birthplace of James I of Scotland in 1394 and Charles I in 1600. It is now a ruin, but the 205 ft long west wall, supported by eight buttresses, still remains.

Dunfermline was almost completely destroyed by fire in 1624, and many of its ancient buildings were lost. One that survived was the 16th-century Abbot's House, which has been carefully restored.

In the 18th century the town became a prosperous textile centre, and in the late 19th century 3,000 hand-loom weavers were engaged in producing the fine linen for which Dunfermline was noted.

The millionaire industrialist and philanthropist Andrew Carnegie, who was born in Dunfermline, gave Pittencrieff Park to the town. The 17th-century mansion in the park contains a costume museum. A circle of stones in the park marks the site of Malcolm III's palace. Dunfermline Museum, in Viewfield Terrace, has exhibits of fine damask linen and other relics of the weaving trade.

Information Tel. 20999; 36321 (summer).
Location On the A907, 17 m. NW of Edinburgh.
Parking Chalmers Street; Walmer Drive; Carnegie Drive; Viewfield Terrace; St Margaret Street; Abbey View; Bruce Street (all car parks).
District council Dunfermline (Tel. 22711).
Population 41,830.
E-C Wed. **M-D** Sun. morning.
Police (Bb) Carnegie Drive

(Tel. 26711).
Casualty hospital (Ba) Dunfermline, Reid Street (Tel. 23131).
Post office (Ab) Queen Anne Street.
Theatre Carnegie Hall **(Bb)**, Eastport (Tel. 23796).
Cinema The Cinema **(Bb)**, Eastport (Tel. 21934).
Public library Abbot Street.
Places to see Abbey and Abbot's House **(Ab)**; Royal Palace, Kirkgate; Pittencrieff House **(Ab)**, Pittencrieff Park; Museum **(Bb)**, Viewfield Terrace; Carnegie's Birthplace **(Aa)**, Moodie Street.
Shopping High Street; Bruce Street.
Sport Scottish League football, Dunfermline Athletic FC, Halbeath Road; Rugby Union football, Dunfermline RFC, McKane Park.
AA 24 hour service
Tel. Edinburgh (031) 225 8464.

GIVER OF MILLIONS

Andrew Carnegie (1835-1919) emigrated to America in 1848, and by 1881 had made his fortune in the iron and steel business. One of his first acts on becoming a millionaire was to present his home town, Dunfermline, with a library. In 1901 he retired from business and devoted his life to distributing his wealth. Carnegie endowed nearly 3,000 towns in the USA, Canada and Britain with libraries. In all, he is estimated to have given away more than £70 million in his lifetime.

Andrew Carnegie's birthplace was a weaver's cottage.

Dunoon Strathclyde

The Firth of Clyde and the rounded hills of the Cowal peninsula make a peaceful setting for Dunoon, a resort for the people of Glasgow since the mid-19th century. Its two excellent bays provide good sailing for yachtsmen.

Above the steamer pier the scanty remains of a 13th-century castle lie in the attractive Castle Gardens. These provide a fine view across the Firth, and make an excellent spot for ship-watching. The present "castle", known as Castle House, dates from 1822.

The gardens contain a statue of "Highland Mary" – Robert Burns's sweetheart, Mary Campbell, who was born at Auchnamore Farm on the outskirts of Dunoon.

Information Tel. 3785.
Location On the A815, 39 m. S of Inveraray.
Parking Bride Road; Hanover Street; Argyll Street; Moir Street; Kirk Street; Victoria Road; Auchnamore Road (all car parks).
District council Argyll and Bute (Tel. Lochgilphead 2127).
Population 7,950.
E-C Wed.
Police Argyll Road (Tel. 2222).
Casualty hospital General, Sandbank Road (Tel. 4341).
Post office Argyll Street.
Theatre Queen's Hall, Argyll Street (Tel. 3935).
Cinema Studios A & B, John Street (Tel. 4545).
Public library Tulloch Library, Castle House.
Places to see Ruins of 13th-century castle, Castle Gardens.
Shopping Argyll Street; West Bay Shopping Centre.
Event Cowal Games (Aug.).
Car ferries To Gourock (Tel. Gourock 33755). Hunter's Quay to McInroy's Point (4452).
AA 24 hour service
Tel. Glasgow (041) 812 0101.

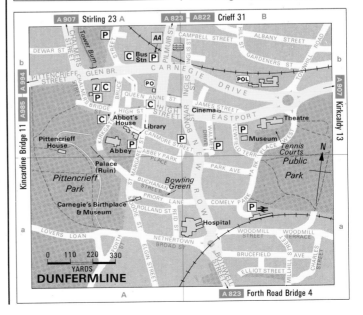

DUNFERMLINE

Duns Borders

A stone at the summit of Duns Law, a 700 ft hill beside the small market town of Duns, marks the spot where the Covenanters, under General David Leslie, set up their standard in 1639. This marked the beginning of the fight for Scottish religious liberty, first against Charles I and later against Cromwell.

Earlier, in 1551, after Berwick had become a part of England, Duns became the county town of Berwickshire. However, it has remained little more than a village, with a market for the sheep farmers of the surrounding hills.

A museum in the former Burgh Chambers displays the trophies won by racing driver Jim Clark (1936-68), who was born at nearby Chirnside. Clark won the world championship in 1963 and 1965. He died in a motor-racing crash in 1968.

Information Tel. 2331.
Location On the A6105, 15 m. W of Berwick-upon-Tweed.
Parking Market Square (off South Street, Easter Street); Newtown Street (both car parks).
District council Berwickshire (Tel. 2331).
Population 2,250.
E-C Wed.
Police Newtown Street (Tel. 2222).
Casualty hospital The Knoll, Station Road (Tel. 3373).
Post office South Street.
Public library Newtown Street.
Places to see Jim Clark Room, Burgh Chambers; Duns Castle, 1½ m. NW.
Shopping South Street; Market Square; Murray Street; Castle Street.
Event Festival week (July).
AA 24 hour service
Tel. Edinburgh (031) 225 8464.

Dunstable Bedfordshire

The Romans established a posting station, where travellers could rest and change horses, at Dunstable, which they called Durocobrivae. It was sited where the Roman road, Watling Street, crossed the prehistoric Icknield Way. When the Romans left in the 5th century the small settlement crumbled. Then, in the 12th century, Henry I built the Augustinian priory around which the present market town grew.

All that remains of Henry's priory is the parish church of St Peter. It was founded in 1132, and has a fine Norman nave and a west front which was restored in 1903.

Dunstable Downs, about 1 mile south, has been the home of the London Gliding Club since the 1930s. In Whipsnade Zoo, on the edge of the downs, many animals roam freely in spacious paddocks. Near by is Whipsnade Tree Cathedral, the creation of a local landowner who planted trees in the outline of a cathedral after the First World War. The "cathedral" is owned by the National Trust.

HISTORIC PRIORY *Archbishop Cranmer pronounced the divorce of Catherine of Aragon from Henry VIII in Dunstable's Church of St Peter in 1533.*

Information Tel. 603326.
Location On the A5, 5 m. W of Luton.
Parking Queensway Hall; Church Street; Vernon Place; Bullpond Road; West Street; Matthew Street; Regent Street (all car parks).
District council South Bedfordshire (Tel. 603166).
Population 30,900.
E-C Thur. **M-D** Wed., Sat.
Police West Street (Tel. 603141).
Casualty hospital Luton and Dunstable, Dunstable Road, Luton (Tel. Luton 53211).
Post office (Ab) High Street North.

Theatre Queensway Hall **(Bb)**, The Civic Centre, Vernon Place (Tel. 603326).
Public library (Bb) Vernon Place.
Places to see Whipsnade Zoo, 3 m. S off B4540; Whipsnade Tree Cathedral, 4 m. S on B4541; Sewell Cutting Nature Reserve, French's Avenue.
Shopping High Street; The Quadrant; Ashton Square.
Trade and industry Motor accessories; commercial vehicles; printing.
AA 24 hour service
Tel. Hatfield 62852.

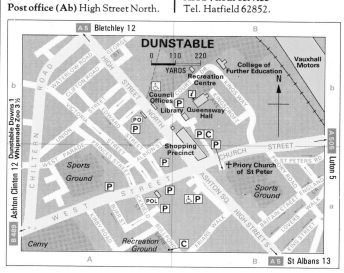

A LOOK AROUND
DURHAM
Durham

The city whose bishops ruled as princes

The heart of Durham is a lofty sandstone outcrop, almost made an island by a tight-necked loop of the meandering River Wear. It has the relaxed but fascinating atmosphere of a history-steeped market town. Seen from the riverside footpath, with its elegant bridges, picturesque old mill and numerous grassy picnic places, the city centre is almost completely hidden by trees. The great cathedral towering above them could easily be set in a forest far from other works of men. Few towns or cities in Britain can boast such delightful views.

Nearly 1,000 years ago a party of monks were seeking a resting-place for the remains of St Cuthbert, one of the founders of Christianity in northern England. They wanted a site that would be safe from the raiding Vikings who had driven them from their original home on the holy island of Lindisfarne. They chose a rocky outcrop above the River Wear, and there, in 995, they built a simple wooden church to shelter their saint. A stone church soon followed, to be replaced in its turn by the present **cathedral**, which was started by a Norman bishop, William of Calais, in 1093.

Additions and alterations were made by later generations – the most dramatic being the central tower, completed in 1470 after the original had been struck by lightning – but the building's character has remained essentially and indomitably Norman. Its main doorway has a grotesque sanctuary knocker dating from the 12th century.

The knocker recalls the freedom from arrest which medieval fugitives from the law obtained in the cathedral and its precincts. Entries in the Sanctuary Book reveal that 331 fugitives, including 283 murderers, were admitted between 1464 and 1525. Exhibits in the **cathedral museum** include a letter sent by Edward IV in 1473, requesting the return of an escaped prisoner convicted of treason. The fugitive's fate is not recorded.

The museum also has St Cuthbert's

IMMUNITY *The sanctuary knocker symbolised freedom for fugitives.*

beautiful gold pectoral cross and the remains of his original coffin, carved by the monks of Lindisfarne after he died in 687.

More than 300 steps lead to the top of the central tower, but the climb is richly rewarded. There are superb views of the cathedral, the castle, the mainly Georgian suburbs beyond the river, and the countryside rolling westwards to the Pennines. **College Green**, south of the cloisters, is particularly attractive in early summer, when its lawns are carpeted with pink and white blossom.

Stolen relics

Durham's bishops held the title "Prince-Bishop", a status that did not end until 1836, although for many years it had been little more than a courtesy title. The last holder was Bishop William van Mildert, co-founder of **Durham University**. His statue, book in hand, stands in the cathedral's Chapel of the Nine Altars, close to the tomb of St Cuthbert.

The Venerable Bede – whose work the *Ecclesiastical History of the English People* established him as the father of English history – is buried at the opposite end of the cathedral. Bede died at Jarrow in 735, but his bones were stolen 300 years later and taken to Durham by the cathedral's sacrist – the keeper of sacred relics – an enthusiastic but obviously far from scrupulous collector of the remains of England's northern saints.

MOUNTED LORD *The statue of Lord Londonderry (1778-1854), one of Wellington's cavalry generals, looks out over the Market Place.*

"GREY TOWERS OF DURHAM" *The first line of Sir Walter Scott's poem accurately describes the cathedral – the finest Norman building in the world. It has stood on its rock above the city for nearly 900 years.*

Inside the cathedral massive columns, carved with geometric patterns typical of Norman craftsmanship, seem to spring from the rock on which the building stands. The true scale of the interior is difficult to appreciate until people appear on a gallery crossing the north transept

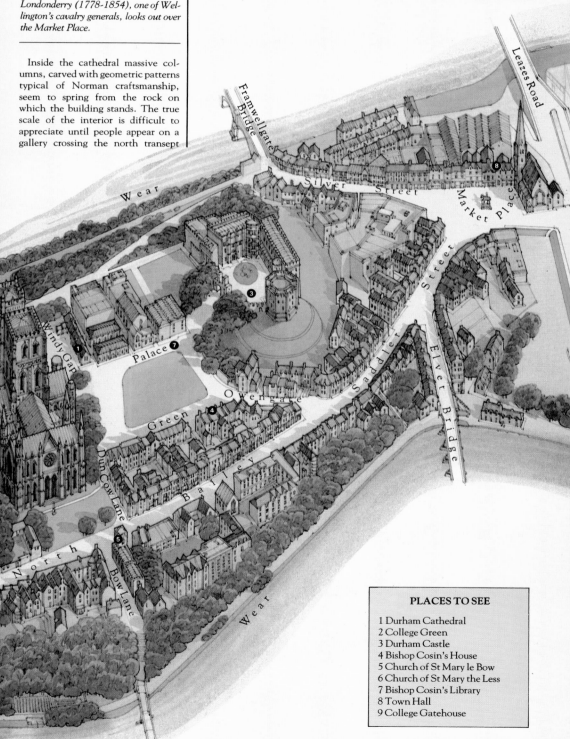

PLACES TO SEE

1 Durham Cathedral
2 College Green
3 Durham Castle
4 Bishop Cosin's House
5 Church of St Mary le Bow
6 Church of St Mary the Less
7 Bishop Cosin's Library
8 Town Hall
9 College Gatehouse

and are dwarfed by a window some 60 ft high. It looks across the nave to one of the cathedral's most unusual features, an extravagantly decorated clock with four faces that give information about the moon and stars as well as telling the time. The oldest parts date from the late 15th century, and the clock was lucky to survive a period in 1650 when the cathedral served as a prison for 4,000 Scots captured at the Battle of Dunbar. They destroyed most of the woodwork to make fires during the winter.

Durham University – founded in 1832 and the oldest in England after Oxford and Cambridge – remains centred on the cathedral area, and occupies many fine old buildings in the highest part of the city. Some of the most attractive flank the grass of **Palace Green**.

Defied Scots

John Cosin was Durham's bishop from 1660 to 1672. The house he built still stands and is notable for the elaborately decorated portico over the doorway. The equally old Grammar School next door is now used for university lectures. **Bishop Cosin's Library** is near the castle's main gate. The original librarian, appointed to catalogue Cosin's books, is said to have tired of his task after reaching the fourth letter of the alphabet, and to have eloped with the bishop's daughter.

Durham Castle is unique among England's northern strongholds because it never fell to the Scots. The Norman chapel, its stones carved with elaborate scenes and individual figures, is the castle's oldest part. In 1952, after a break of 400 years, the chapel was re-opened for religious use. Outstanding examples of post-Conquest stone-carving may also be seen in the Norman Gallery, and at the archway entrance to Tunstal's Gallery, named after a 16th-century bishop.

The castle, now a university residence, has been inhabited without a break for more than 900 years. Today's students follow in the footsteps of the prince-bishops, for it was their palace from 1072 until 1837.

Bishop Cosin left many memorials in Durham, one of the most noteworthy being the castle's **Black Staircase**, between the **Great Hall** and **Tunstal's Gallery**. It is 57 ft high and built mainly of oak, with carved panels of softer wood.

Many rooms in the castle are still used for their original purposes. **Fox's Kitchen** dates from the 15th century – parts may be 300 years older – and is still used to cook more than 300 meals every day. The castle keep catches the eye more than any other part of the building. It is a replica of the original and was built in 1840 to provide rooms for students.

After years of increasing noise, congestion and exhaust fumes, the city centre's network of narrow streets has regained much of its old charm thanks to a new, by-passing bridge and a convenient multi-storey car park. The **Market Place** is overlooked by a handsome equestrian statue of the 3rd Lord Londonderry, founder of Seaham Harbour.

The statue is close to the **Town Hall**, built by public subscription and opened in 1851. It has a hammerbeam roof, similar to the one in London's Westminster Hall. There are also relics of "Count" Joseph Boruwlaski, born in Poland in 1739, who spent the last 17 of his 98 years in Durham. An accomplished violinist, he was nicknamed "Lord Tom Thumb" as he was only 3 ft 3 in. tall. The Town Hall's designer was P. C. Hardwick (1792-1870), who also designed the Great Hall at Euston Station.

Rebuilt churches

The Church of St Mary le Bow in North Bailey was rebuilt in 1685, after its tower fell and destroyed the nave. The original tower formed part of the city's fortifications; the present tower was erected in 1702. St Mary the Less in South Bailey dates from the 12th century but was completely rebuilt in 1847. A carving of Christ in Glory in the chancel is said to be early Norman.

The city started spreading beyond the river in the 18th century, and is now surrounded by pleasant suburbs and university buildings set among pools, trees, lawns and flower beds. The **School of Oriental Studies**, on Elvet Hill, houses the **Gulbenkian Museum**, probably Britain's finest collection of oriental art and archaeology.

Displayed in a large, multi-level hall flanked by smaller rooms are

TOM THUMB *A statue of Durham's celebrated midget is in the Town Hall.*

colourful Tibetan paintings, known as "tankas", exquisite carvings from Japan and China, Assyrian reliefs of 1500 BC and relics from ancient Egypt. There are Indian paintings, still vivid after 500 years, Islamic pottery, a Tibetan magician's apron fashioned from human bones, and a 50 ft long series of carved teak panels from a Burmese palace.

Although it was a military base from Norman times until the 17th century – ancient seals portray prince-bishops in full armour with drawn swords – Durham has a peaceful history. The city was a venue for several Anglo-Scottish peace conferences, the most notable bringing King Stephen of England and David I of Scotland together in 1139. The one major battle in the district was fought in 1346. Philip VI of France, engaged in a losing war against Edward III, urged his Scottish allies to invade England. They were defeated at Neville's Cross, now in the city's western suburbs, by an army raised by Edward's wife, Queen Philippa.

Her commanders included Lord Ralph Neville of Raby Castle, 16 miles south-west of Durham. On his death, in 1367, he became the first layman to be buried in the cathedral. He is commemorated by the magnificent **Neville Screen** that stands be-

NORMAN STONEWORK *Delicately carved arches rest on decorated pillars in the cathedral's nave.*

hind the main altar. These religious links with one of England's most famous warrior-families underline the dual role played by the city for much of its long life.

FAIR TRADING *Copper tubs used to measure grain in the 19th century are on show in the Town Hall.*

In recent years Durham has expanded to take in several surrounding villages and much farmland. It has become a major tourist centre for visitors to the North of England. Despite its growth, the city has not become industrialised, but it is a mecca for North-East miners. Once a year, on a day in July, they gather in thousands in the city for the world-famous Durham Miners' Gala.

Grouped in their lodges, the miners march behind banners and brass bands through the city's narrow streets to the old racecourse. There, they mix a long day of revelry with rousing speeches from their leaders.

MINERS' REGALIA *Bands play and banners wave when the miners march through Durham on their Gala Day.*

Information Tel. 67131.
Location On the A177, 16 m. S of Newcastle upon Tyne.
Parking Freemans Place; Claypath, off Hallgarth Street; Old Elvet; Leazes Bowl; Millburngate; Palace Green; Framwelgate (all car parks).
District council City of Durham (Tel. 67131).
Population 26,400.

E-C Wed. **M-D** Sat.
Police (Cb) Court Lane (Tel. 64222).
Casualty hospital Dryburn Hospital (Tel. 64911).
Post office (Cc) Claypath.
Cinema Classic, North Road (Tel. 48184).
Public library (Bc) South Street.
Places to see Castle **(Bc)**, Palace

Green; Durham Light Infantry Museum, Framwelgate; Gulbenkian Museum **(Ba)**, Elvet Hill; Cathedral Dormitory Museum.
Shopping North Road; Silver Street.
Event Miners' Gala (July).
Trade and industry Agriculture; coal-mining; carpets.
AA 24 hour service
Tel. Newcastle upon Tyne 610111.

DURHAM

[Map of Durham]

E

Ealing see London

Eastbourne E. Sussex

The town's history as a resort dates from 1780, when four of George III's children spent their summer holidays there. In the following century two local landowners, the 7th Duke of Devonshire and John Davies Gilbert, developed the town, building the broad roads and seafront parades.

On the seafront, to the west of the pier, is the Wish Tower, originally a Martello Tower built during the threat of Napoleonic invasion and now a museum of the period. The old Eastbourne lifeboat station, below the Wish Tower, was opened in 1937 as the country's first lifeboat museum.

The Towner Art Gallery, in a former manor house built about 1760, includes works by British painters of the 19th and 20th centuries.

Among the town's many fine parks and gardens are: the Carpet Gardens along the seafront; Hampden Park, 2 miles inland; and the Italian Gardens at the foot of Beachy Head, west of the town. There towering cliffs rear up from the sea to 575 ft, dwarfing the 142 ft lighthouse at their base.

Information Tel. 27474.
Location On the A22, 25 m. E of Brighton.
Parking Grand Parade; Ashford Road; Arndale Centre; Trinity Place; Royal Parade (all car parks).
District council Borough of Eastbourne (Tel. 21333).
Population 77,600.
E-C Wed.
Police (Ab) Grove Road (Tel. 22522).
Casualty hospital General, King's Drive (Tel. 21351).
Post office (Ab) Upperton Road.
Theatres Congress **(Ba)**, Carlisle Road (Tel. 36363); Devonshire Park **(Ba)**, Compton Street (21121); Winter Garden **(Ba)**, Compton Street (25252); Royal Hippodrome **(Bb)**, Seaside Road (24336).
Cinemas ABC **(Bb)**, Pevensey Road (Tel. 23612); Curzon **(Bb)**, Langney Road (31441); Tivoli **(Bb)**, Seaside Road (21031).
Public library (Ab) Grove Road.
Places to see Redoubt Museum and Aquarium; Lifeboat Museum **(Ba)**; Wish Tower Museum **(Ba)**; Towner Art Gallery, Borough Lane.

Shopping Terminus Road; Langney Shopping Centre; Arndale Centre.
AA 24 hour service
Tel. Brighton 695231.

East Grinstead W. Sussex

An unbroken line of fine old houses and shops stands on the south side of East Grinstead High Street. Among the most notable are: Amherst House (mid-14th century); Cromwell House (1599); Sackville House (15th century); and Dorset House (1705). Opposite is Sackville College, an almshouse founded in 1609.

Information Tel. 28442.
Location On the A22, 9 m. E of Crawley.
Parking Railway Approach; Vicarage Walk; Tower, off Moat Road; Christopher Road; King Street; Queens Road; De la Warr Road (all car parks).
District council Mid Sussex (Tel. Haywards Heath 58166).
Population 22,300.

E-C Wed. **M-D** Sat.
Police East Court (Tel. 21155).
Casualty hospital Queen Victoria, Holtye Road (Tel. 24111).
Post office London Road.
Theatre Adeline Genee, Lingfield Road, Dormans Park (Tel. Dormans Park 532).
Cinema Classic 1, 2 and 3, King Street (Tel. 21688).
Public library London Road.
Places to see Museum, East Court.
Shopping London Road; High Street; Queens Walk.
AA 24 hour service
Tel. Crawley 25685.

East Kilbride Strathclyde

What was in 1946 an agricultural village of only 2,500 inhabitants is today the largest New Town in Scotland.

But the past is still in evidence. In the centre of the town is the parish church, rebuilt in 1774. The tower, built in 1818, has an open belfry. The restored tower and dungeon of Mains Castle, built in about 1500 for the

WHERE THE BRASS BANDS PLAY *Eastbourne's Bandstand Arena on the Grand Parade seats 3,500 people. Concerts take place throughout the summer season.*

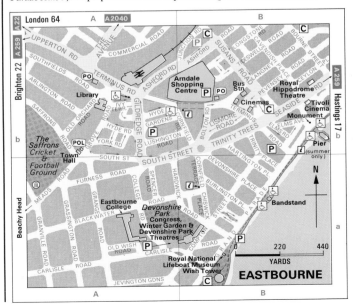

SUSSEX STYLE *The buildings in East Grinstead High Street are typical Sussex houses of the 15th and 16th centuries.*

Lindsay family, lie 1 mile to the north.

The grave of Jean Cameron, persecuted for supporting Bonnie Prince Charlie in 1745, is in Glen Dessary, a street named after her birthplace.

The Hunter Museum at Long Calderwood commemorates the Hunter brothers, William and John, 18th-century pioneers of surgery who were born in East Kilbride.

Information Tel. 34811.
Location On the A749, 9 m. S of Glasgow.
Parking Torrance Road; Eaglesham Road; Rothesay Street (4); Alexandra Street; Andrew Street; Victoria Place; Alexandra Court; The Murray (4); Calderwood; Westwood (3); Greenhills (all car parks).
District council East Kilbride (Tel. 28777).
Population 76,000.
E-C Wed.
Police Andrew Street (Tel. 21361).
Casualty hospital Hairmyres, Eaglesham Road (Tel. 20292/6).
Post office Cornwall Street.
Theatre Village Theatre, Maxwell Drive (Tel. 48669).
Cinema The Cinema, Town Centre (Tel. 31020).
Public library Alexandra Arcade.
Places to see Mains Castle, Market Hill Road; Castlehill House, Carmunnock Road; Torrance House, off Strathaven Road; Hunter Museum, Long Calderwood.
Shopping Princes Street; Princes Square; Plaza, St Leonard's and Greenhills Shopping Centres.
Trade and industry Engineering; textiles.
AA 24 hour service Tel. Glasgow (041) 812 0101.

Eastleigh Hampshire

The town developed around the railway engineering works built there in 1889. Eastleigh Borough forms a loop around the City of Southampton, and stretches from Southampton Water to the Test Valley in the north. Within its confines are the yachting centres of Hamble and Bursledon.

Information Tel. 614646 or 616027.
Location On the A333, 6 m. N of Southampton.
Parking Southampton Road; Factory Road; Romsey Road; High Street; Market Street (all car parks).
District council Borough of Eastleigh (Tel. 614646).
Population 53,100.
E-C Wed. **M-D** Thur., Sun.
Police Leigh Road (Tel. 612291).
Casualty hospital Southampton General, Tremona Road, Shirley (Tel. Southampton 777222).
Post office High Street.
Public library Leigh Road.
Shopping Market Street; High Street; Leigh Road; Chandlers Ford.
AA 24 hour service Tel. Southampton 36811.

East Retford
Nottinghamshire

The town contains a variety of fine Georgian and Victorian buildings including the former coaching inns of the Great North Road, almshouses and other early charitable foundations. All Hallows and St Michael's churches date from the 14th century and St Swithun's from the 15th century. Retford is a good centre for touring nearby villages from which the Pilgrim Fathers originated.

Information Tel. Worksop 475531.
Location On the A638, 19 m. NW of Newark.
Parking Chancery Lane; West Street; Bridgegate; Canal Street; New Street; Exchange Street; Churchgate; Chapelgate (all car parks).
District council Bassetlaw (Tel. Worksop 475531).
Population 19,300.
E-C Wed. **M-D** Thur., Sat.
Police Exchange Street (Tel. 701222).
Casualty hospital Retford and District, North Road (Tel. 702545).
Post office Exchange Street.
Theatre Little Theatre, Wharf Road (Tel. 702002).
Cinema Majestic, Coronation Street (Tel. 702741).
Public library Churchgate.
Shopping Carolgate; Bridgegate; Market Place.
AA 24 hour service Tel. Nottingham 787751.

Ebbw Vale Gwent

A valley in the South Wales coalfields gives Ebbw Vale its name. It is best known for its 2½ mile long steel-sheet and tinplate works. The only surviving colliery is highly mechanised, and many of the former coal-tips have been removed or landscaped.

Aneurin Bevan was Labour MP for Ebbw Vale in 1929–60, and there is a monument to him near his birthplace, Tredegar, 2 miles west.

Information Tel. 303401.
Location On the A465, 20 m. N of Newport.
Parking Tredegar Road; Armoury Terrace; The Walk (all car parks).
District council Borough of Blaenau Gwent (Tel. 303401).
Population 24,400.
E-C Wed. **M-D** Mon. to Sat. (indoor), Fri. (outdoor).
Police Bethcar Street (Tel. 303921).
Casualty hospital Nevill Hall, Brecon Road, Abergavenny (Tel. Abergavenny 2091).
Post office Bethcar Street.
Public library Bethcar Street.
Shopping Market Street; Bethcar Street; Church Street.
AA 24 hour service Tel. Newport 62559.

Elgin Grampian

Its ruined 13th-century cathedral, once known as the Lantern of the North, is Elgin's best-known landmark.

Much of the cathedral's original work still exists, including the transepts and choir. The detached octagonal chapter house was reconstructed in the 15th century. The 15th-century nave contains an ancient Celtic cross-slab carved with Pictish symbols, which was unearthed in the High Street.

In the precincts, a wing of the early-15th-century Bishop's Palace still stands.

The High Street contains several notable buildings. Braco's Building is a three-storeyed house dating from 1694, with stepped gables and a stone-slab roof; Gray's Hospital, founded in 1815, has an octagonal-based dome. The Moray Society Museum, which contains collections of prehistoric weapons and fossils, is housed in a mid-19th-century Italianate house. Outside the museum is the Little Cross, a 1733 replacement of one erected in 1402 to mark the limits of the cathedral sanctuary.

Information Tel. 3388.
Location On the A96, 36 m. W of Banff.
Parking Lossie Green; Lossie Wynd; Trinity Road; Greyfriars Street; Ladyhill Road; St Giles Road; Batchen Lane; Moray Street; North Port (all car parks).
District council Moray (Tel. 3451).
Population 19,300.
E-C Wed.
Police Moray Street (Tel. 3101).
Casualty hospital Dr Gray's, Pluscarden Road (Tel. 3131).
Post office High Street.
Cinema The Playhouse, High Street (Tel. 2680).
Public library Cooper Park.
Places to see Museum, High Street; cathedral and Bishops' Palace, both ruins.
Shopping High Street; South Street; Commerce Street; Batchen Street.
AA 24 hour service Tel. Aberdeen 51231.

EDINBURGH

Lothian

Scotland's capital, where history and beauty unite

JOHN KNOX'S HOUSE *Scotland's great religious reformer is said to have lived here when he was minister of St Giles' from 1561 to 1571.*

Edinburgh is one of the world's most attractive capitals, rich in vivid reminders of the past and abundantly endowed with memorable buildings. They range from a great crag-perched castle to elegant Georgian houses and the ultra-modern Meadowbank Sports Centre where the 1970 Commonwealth Games were held. Many other cities can boast long, stirring histories and a wealth of noble architecture, but few can match Edinburgh's dramatic grandeur or equal the way in which its busy streets are balanced by a profusion of parks, leafy squares and immaculate gardens bright with flowers. The open countryside, so typical of Scotland, never seems far away. There is even a clear river, the Water of Leith, where anglers catch trout within 500 yds of Princes Street with its big stores and crowds of bargain-hunting shoppers.

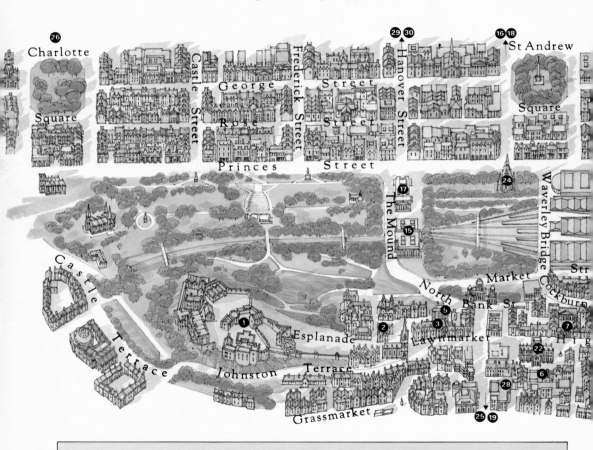

PLACES TO SEE

1 Castle	12 Wax Museum	22 St Giles' Cathedral
2 Outlook Tower	13 Huntly House Museum	23 Royal Observatory
3 Gladstone's Land	14 Museum of Childhood	24 Sir Walter Scott Monument
4 Whitehorse Close	15 National Gallery of Scotland	25 Greyfriars Bobby
5 Lady Stair's House	16 Scottish National Portrait	26 No. 7 Charlotte Square
6 Parliament House	Gallery	27 Nelson Monument
7 City Chambers	17 Royal Scottish Academy	28 National Library of Scotland
8 John Knox's House	18 Museum of Antiquities	29 Royal Botanic Garden
9 Acheson House	19 Royal Scottish Museum	30 Scottish National Gallery of
10 Palace of Holyroodhouse	20 Register House	Modern Art
11 Canongate Tolbooth	21 Transport Museum	31 National Monument

EDINBURGH'S OLD NEW TOWN *Princes Street runs arrow-straight at the foot of Castle Rock. The street was completed in 1805 to form part of the new town started 38 years earlier. The Gothic clock-tower in the foreground surmounts the North British Hotel. Beyond are the spires of St Mary's Episcopal cathedral.*

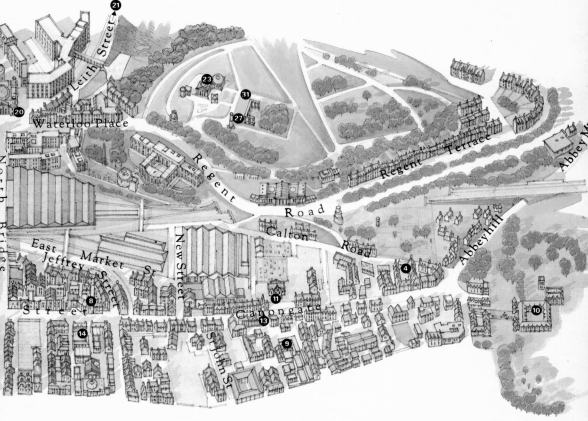

Ice Age glaciers shaped the ancient volcanic mass of **Castle Rock** into the almost-perfect defensive site on which Edinburgh Castle now stands. The rock was fortified in prehistoric times, and later by the Picts.

Dominating Edinburgh, the **castle** played a key role in Scotland's history until the middle of the 18th century. It was attacked for the last time in 1745 when the city, but not the castle, fell to Bonnie Prince Charlie's Jacobite army. The royal apartments include the tiny bedroom where

Mary, Queen of Scots gave birth in 1566 to the son who succeeded her as James VI of Scotland and afterwards became James I of England. In the adjoining Crown Room are displayed the Scottish Regalia. The three most important pieces, known as the Honours of Scotland, are the Crown, the Sceptre and the Sword of State.

Inside the castle is Mons Meg, a huge 15th-century cannon, 13 ft 4 in. long. According to old records it could hurl an iron ball 1,408 yds, and a stone one twice as far if charged

with 105 lb. of gunpowder. The cannon has not been fired since the 17th century, when it burst while saluting a royal birthday. A shot still sounds from the castle, however – every day from Monday to Saturday. It signals one o'clock in the afternoon, and at the same time a time-ball is raised and lowered over the Nelson Monument on Calton Hill.

Edinburgh extends eastwards from the castle, down what is now known as the Royal Mile. At the far end stands the **Palace of Holyroodhouse**,

139

ROYAL RESIDENCE *James IV made Holyroodhouse a royal palace when Edinburgh became Scotland's capital at the end of the 15th century. Mary, Queen of Scots lived there for six years of her reign.*

with the turf of Arthur's Seat and volcanic cliffs of Salisbury Crags forming a magnificent background. David I of Scotland is said to have been hunting near the hill in 1128 when he was attacked by a stag and, grappling with the animal, grasped a cross that miraculously appeared between its antlers. A dream later told him to found an abbey dedicated to the cross – the holy rood – and its ruins still stand beside the palace. A royal burial vault contains the remains of several Scottish kings and queens.

Scene of murder

James IV built the forerunner of the present palace at the end of the 15th century. It was there, in 1566, that a gang of nobles led by Mary's husband, Lord Darnley, murdered her secretary, David Riccio. Darnley, who suspected Riccio of being the queen's lover, was murdered himself the following year. A brass plaque in Queen Mary's supper room marks the spot where Riccio fell. The palace was damaged by fire during the Commonwealth, but, at the Restoration, Charles II ordered it to be rebuilt.

Many aspects of Scotland's past may be seen during a walk down Castlehill, High Street and Canongate, which together form the Royal Mile. One curious relic is a cannon ball lodged below the window of a house at the top of Castlehill. It is said to

CHILDISH THINGS *Historical toys and costumes are displayed on four floors of the Museum of Childhood.*

have been fired from the castle when the city was in Jacobite hands. The **Outlook Tower**, on the opposite side of the street, has a camera obscura in which a fascinating all-round view of Edinburgh is projected on to a white, concave table.

Several of the Royal Mile's buildings are open to visitors, including **Gladstone's Land** built in 1620 by Thomas Gladstone, a city burgess. **Lady Stair's House**, built in 1622, contains a museum dedicated to Scotland's greatest literary figures, Sir Walter Scott, Robert Burns and Robert Louis Stevenson.

Heart of Midlothian

St Giles' Cathedral, in High Street, is Edinburgh's main church. Pillars supporting the crown-topped tower are probably 12th-century work, but most of the building dates from between 200 and 300 years later. The most recent addition is a tiny chapel, built in 1911 and dedicated to the Most Ancient and Most Noble Order of the Thistle, Scotland's highest order of chivalry. Near the cathedral's west door, a heart-shaped design among the cobbles marks the site of the city's old tolbooth, or prison. It was demolished in 1817, but *The Heart of Midlothian* has been immortalised as the title of one of Scott's novels. Also of interest near the cathedral are the **Parliament House** – last used as such in 1707 – the Mercat Cross, where royal proclamations are still read, and a statue of Charles II, erected in 1685 and the oldest statue in Edinburgh.

The Royal Mile has several museums, but the city's main local-interest museum is in **Huntly House**. Exhibits include the National Covenant, a huge document with more than 3,000 signatures, drawn up by Presbyterians in 1638 when many Scots feared that Charles I was preparing the way for a return to Catholicism. The document was signed in Greyfriars Kirk, where the Covenanters' memorial stands in a corner of the quiet graveyard.

During the 18th century Edinburgh began to expand, and a plan for a new town, by a 23-year-old architect, James Craig, was approved after a competition in 1767. His town to the north of the drained North Loch,

below the Castle Rock, is a network of broad streets, squares and circuses overlooked by classical façades of pale stone. Craig's work was further enhanced by such men as Robert Adam, who planned **Charlotte Square** in 1791. Part of one of the square's houses – No. 7 – has been furnished and decorated in period style, and gives a vivid impression of what life was like "upstairs and downstairs" during George III's reign.

Information Tel. Edinburgh (031) 226 6591.
Location On the A1, 45 m. E of Glasgow.
Parking Castle Terrace; Leith Street; Tollcross; Lothian Road; Morrison Street; Greenside Place; Maugh Street; Weir Nicolson Street; Pleasance; Weir Adam Street; Salisbury Street (all car parks).
District council City of Edinburgh (Tel. 031 225 2424).
Population 419,200.
E-C Tues., Wed. or Sat.

In 1822 George IV became the first monarch to visit Edinburgh for almost 200 years. The visit was organised by Sir Walter Scott, whose memorial towers above Princes Street Gardens. It is 200 ft high and has niches containing statues of 64 characters from Scott's works.

Edinburgh's many art galleries, libraries and museums include the **Scottish National Portrait Gallery**, in Queen Street, where one room has a 16th-century painted ceiling discovered by chance in a ruined Fife castle in 1957. Characters portrayed in the gallery include kings, queens, Bonnie Prince Charlie, Flora Macdonald, Robert Burns and many more. The collection was started in 1882 to "illustrate Scottish history by likenesses of the chief actors in it". It succeeds brilliantly, putting faces to most of the characters whose stories are interwoven with that of Edinburgh itself.

GREYFRIARS BOBBY
For 14 years a dog watched over his master's grave at Greyfriars Kirk.

Police High Street
(Tel. 031 667 3361).
Casualty hospital (Ca) Royal Infirmary, Lauriston Place
(Tel. 031 229 2477).
Post office (Cc) Waterloo Place.
Theatres Adam House **(Cb)**, Chambers Street (Tel. 031 225 3744); King's Theatre **(Ba)**, Leven Street, Tollcross (031 229 1201); Royal Lyceum **(Ab)**, Grindlay Street (031 229 9697); Playhouse, Greenside Place (031 557 2590); Church Hill Theatre, Morningside Road (031 447 7597).

Cinemas Calton Studios, Calton Road (Tel. 031 557 2159); ABC **(Aa)**, Lothian Road (031 229 3030); Odeon **(Da)** (031 667 3805); Caley **(Ab)**, Lothian Road (031 229 7670); Cameo **(Aa)** (031 229 6822); Edinburgh Film Theatre **(Ab)**, Lothian Road (031 228 6382); Dominion, Newbattle Terrace (031 447 2660).
Public library (Cb) George IV Bridge.
Shopping Princes Street; Tollcross; St David Street; St James Centre; Hanover Street; George Street;

Frederick Street; Castle Street; Queensferry Street; West End; Shandwick Place; Lothian Road; Earl Grey Street; Brougham Street.
Events Royal Highland Show (June); International Festival (Aug./Sept.).
Sport Scottish League football: Heart of Midlothian FC, Tynecastle Park; Hibernian FC, Easter Road Park.
Motorail Waverley Bridge (Tel. 031 226 6591).
AA 24 hour service
Tel. 031 225 8464.

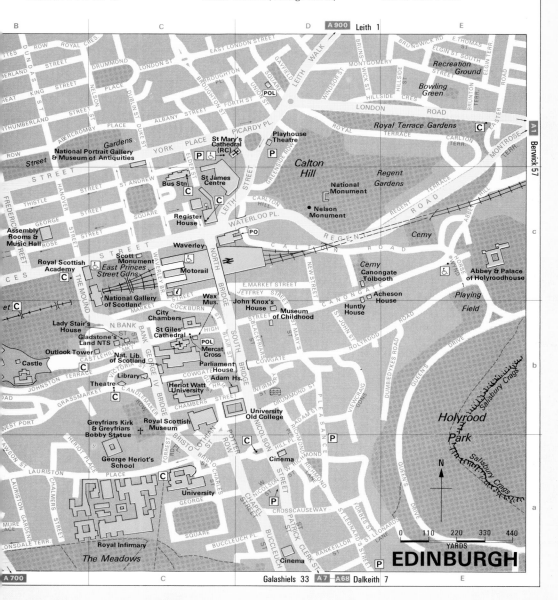

EDINBURGH

Ellesmere Port Cheshire

The Shropshire Union Canal, of which Thomas Telford's Chester and Ellesmere Canal, built in the 1790s, is part, led to the growth of Ellesmere Port. The system linked the Midlands and Potteries industries with the Mersey, where Telford built a tidal basin. Today's thriving port and industrial centre grew around the basin and nearby villages. Telford's disused upper basin and warehouses now house the Boat Museum.

Information
Tel. Liverpool (051) 355 3665.
Location On the M531, 7 m. N of Chester.
Parking Wellington Road; Princess Road; Station Road; Whitby Road; Granage Road; Chester Road (all car parks).
District council Borough of Ellesmere Port and Neston (Tel. 051 355 3665).
Population 63,300.
E-C Wed. **M-D** Tues., Fri. and Sat.
Police Stanney Lane (Tel. 051 355 4066).
Casualty hospital Chester Royal Infirmary, Martins Way, Chester (Tel. Chester 315500).
Post office Marina Walk.
Public library Civic Way.
Places to see Boat Museum, Dock Yard Road (Easter–Oct.).
Shopping Marina Walk; Whitby Road; Rivington Road; Marina Drive; Market Square.
Trade and industry Car manufacturing; oil refining; chemicals.
AA 24 hour service
Tel. Liverpool (051) 709 7252.

Ely Cambridgeshire

The name of this city in the fens derives from the Saxon *Elig*, meaning "eel island", because of the large numbers of eels caught there. It remained an island until the 17th and 18th centuries, when the fens were drained.

An abbey was founded there in the 7th century by St Etheldreda, a daughter of the King of the East Angles, and around it grew the town of Ely. Hereward the Wake defended it against William the Conqueror in 1071, before being defeated and until driven from the island. Ten years later William appointed a fellow Norman, Simeon, to be Abbot of Ely, and he planned a new cathedral – the Church of the Holy and Undivided Trinity.

Simeon's cathedral was not completed until 1189, and in 1252 the choir and presbytery were rebuilt to make a more fitting setting for St Etheldreda's Shrine. Most of the cathedral's original Norman work survives in the west front, nave and transepts. The nave is one of the longest in England – 248 ft – and its wooden ceiling is 72 ft high. The ceiling was painted in the 19th century by the artists H. L. Styleman-L'Estrange

FENLAND GLORY *Ely Cathedral's west tower soars to 217 ft behind the central tower with its octagonal lantern.*

and T. Gambier-Parry. The transepts have lavishly decorated roofs with carved angels as hammer-bearers.

In 1322 the original central tower collapsed and was replaced by a unique octagonal tower conceived by one of the monks, Alan of Walsingham, and built by William Hurley who was Edward III's carpenter. The tower has a fan-vaulted timber roof which supports a wooden lantern, weighing 400 tons and standing 94 ft above the floor.

Among other cathedral buildings are the Porta, a 14th-century gatehouse which was the main entrance to the Benedictine priory, and the 13th-century St Mary's Church. The house which is now the vicarage was the home of Oliver Cromwell from 1636 to 1647.

King's School was founded in AD 970, and is one of England's oldest schools. Edward the Confessor, while Prince Edward, entered the school in 1010, and granted a charter to the town when he became king.

Goldsmiths' Tower and Sacrist's Gate, in the High Street, were built in 1325 by Alan of Walsingham. Part of the building houses Ely Museum, which displays local relics. A grassy mound in Cherry Hill Park is all that remains of Ely's 12th-century castle.

Information Tel. 3311/2894.
Location On the A10, 16 m. N of Cambridge.
Parking Newnham Street; Broad Street; Barton Road; Butcher's Row; Ship Lane (all car parks).
District council East Cambridgeshire (Tel. 3311).
Population 10,300.
E-C Tues. **M-D** Thur.
Police Nutholt Lane (Tel. 2392).
Casualty hospital Royal Air Force Hospital, Lynn Road (Tel. 5781).
Post office Market Place.
Public library Palace Green.
Places to see Ely Museum, High Street (weekends only).
Town trails Available from Tourist Information Centre, St Mary's Street.
Shopping Market Street; High Street; Market Place; Forehill; Lynn Road.
AA 24 hour service
Tel. Cambridge 312302.

Enfield see London

Epsom Surrey

Horse races have been held on the slopes of Epsom Downs for centuries. Its racecourse is the home of the world-famous race, the Derby.

In the 18th century, Epsom salts, in the waters of a local spring, made the town a fashionable spa. Many graceful buildings from this period survive.

Information Tel. 26252.
Location On the A24, 17 m. SW of London.
Parking High Street; Upper High Street; Hook Road; Depot Road (all car parks).
District council Epsom and Ewell (Tel. 26252).
Population 69,200.
E-C Wed. **M-D** Sat.
Police Church Street (Tel. 40411).
Casualty hospital Epsom District,

HOW THE WORLD'S GREATEST HORSE RACE WAS BORN

A riotous party of wealthy sportsmen met in a Surrey country house in 1778 and founded a race for three-year-old fillies, to be run at Epsom in May 1779. It was called The Oaks, after their host's house, and was such a success that a second race – for three-year-old colts and fillies – was arranged for May 1780. This race they named after their host – Lord Derby. The first Derby was won by a horse called Diomed.

Epsom Downs on Derby Day is a sea of cars as hundreds of thousands of spectators flock to the world's greatest horse race.

Dorking Road (Tel. 26100).
Post office High Street.
Cinema ABC 1 and 2, Kingston Road, Ewell (Tel. 01 393 2211).
Public library Waterloo Road.
Shopping High Streets (Epsom and Ewell).
Event Derby Week (June).
AA 24 hour service
Tel. 01 954 7373.

Esher Surrey

There are two centres to Esher – the High Street, which carries the busy Portsmouth Road, and the old village green, flanked by old houses and the parish church of Christ Church. The church dates from the middle of the 19th century. Sandown House, now the council offices, is late 17th century but has a Victorian façade.

Claremont School for girls, to the south-east of the town, is bounded by 50 acres of National Trust parkland. The school is housed in a mansion built for Clive of India by the architect "Capability" Brown in 1768. It is occasionally open to the public.

Information
Tel. Walton-on-Thames 28844.
Location On the A307, 4 m. SW of Kingston-upon-Thames.
Parking Sandown Park; King George's Hall, in High Street; Highwayman's Cottage, in High Street; Heather Place; Berguette, in Claremont Lane.
District council Borough of Elmbridge
(Tel. Walton-on-Thames 28844).
Population 61,400.
E-C Wed.
Police High Street (Tel. 67261).
Casualty hospital Kingston Hospital, Galsworthy Road, Kingston-upon-Thames (Tel. 01 546 7711).
Post office High Street.
Cinema Embassy, High Street
(Tel. 63362).
Public library Old Church Path, High Street.
Places to see Claremont, ½ m. SE on A244.
Shopping High Street.
Sport Steeplechasing and Flat Racing, Sandown Park Racecourse.
AA 24 hour service
Tel. 01 954 7373.

Eton Berkshire

If Henry VI had not lost his throne, the greystone building that is now Eton College chapel would have been only the choir of an immense church. But Henry's ambitious plan was dropped after he was deposed in 1461.

Nevertheless, the chapel still soars imposingly above the public school, which the king founded in 1440.

The town owes its existence to the school. The High Street has the college at its northern end, and the bulk of Windsor Castle across the Thames to the south. The two towns are linked by an iron bridge built in 1824. It is now only a footbridge.

COLLEGE CREW *Rowing is a major sport at Eton College. The* Eton Boating Song *is sung on Founder's Day.*

Information Tel. Windsor 52010.
Location On the B3022, 2 m. S of Slough.
Parking Eton Court (cp); High Street; South Meadow Lane.
District council Royal Borough of Windsor and Maidenhead
(Tel. Maidenhead 33155).
Population 3,500.
E-C Wed.
Police Windsor Road, Slough
(Tel. Slough 31282).
Casualty hospital Wexham Park Hospital, Wexham Street, Slough
(Tel. Slough 34576).
Post office High Street.
Public library High Street.
Places to see Eton College.
Town trails Available from The Victorian Society, 1 Priory Gardens, Bedford Park, London W4.
Shopping High Street.
Event College Founder's Day (June).
AA 24 hour service
Tel. Reading 581122.

Evesham H. & W.

At the centre of Evesham stands the 110 ft high, 16th-century Bell Tower; it is part of a now-ruined Benedictine abbey. The tower is flanked by the 12th-century All Saints Church and the 16th-century Church of St Lawrence. Abbot Reginald's Gateway, a 12th-century timber-framed building, leads to the two churchyards.

On Green Hill there is an obelisk in memory of Simon de Montfort, the father of the House of Commons, who was killed in battle by the forces of Prince Edward, later Edward I, on August 4, 1265. In Vine Street the 14th-century Abbey Almonry has a museum of local history. The old town stocks are preserved on the green outside the museum.

Information Tel. 6944 (summer).
Location On the A44, 15 m. SW of Stratford-upon-Avon.
Parking Bewdley Street; Burford Road; Merston Green; Oat Street (all car parks).
District council Wychavon
(Tel. 45151).
Population 15,300.
E-C Wed. **M-D** Sat.
Police Abbey Road (Tel. 2511).

Casualty hospital Evesham General, Briar Close (Tel. 41141).
Post office High Street.
Cinema Regal, Port Street
(Tel. 6002).
Public library Market Place.
Places to see Abbey ruins, Abbey Park; Abbey Almonry Museum, Vine Street; All Saints Church, off Market Place.
Shopping High Street; Bridge Street; Port Street, Bengeworth.
Trade and industry Fruit growing, market gardening.
AA 24 hour service
Tel. Birmingham (021) 550 4858.

Exeter see page 144

Exmouth Devon

A terrace of elegant Georgian houses, called the Beacon, is an early example of Exmouth's development as a seaside resort, which began in 1792. A 2 mile long seafront stretches from the docks at the mouth of the River Exe to the red cliffs of Orcombe Point. Behind the wide Esplanade there are pleasant gardens set out with lawns and flower beds.

HOUSE OF SHELLS *The A La Ronde house near Exmouth, built in 1798, is decorated inside with shells and feathers.*

Information
Tel. 3744 (summer).
Location On the A376, 11 m. S of Exeter.
Parking Church Street; Queen's Drive; Royal Avenue (2); Maer Road (2) (all car parks).
District council East Devon
(Tel. Sidmouth 6551).
Population 28,800.
E-C Wed.
Police North Street (Tel. 4651).
Casualty hospital Claremont Grove
(Tel. 4381).
Post office Chapel Street.
Cinema Savoy, Rolle Street
(Tel. 72866).
Public library Exeter Road.
Places to see Lifeboat Museum, The Esplanade; A la Ronde, Summer Lane (1 m. N); The Great Exmouth 00 Model Railway, The Esplanade.
Shopping Rolle Street; Magnolia Shopping Centre, Chapel Street; High Street; Church Street; The Strand.
Event Carnival (July).
AA 24 hour service
Tel. Exeter 32121.

EXETER Devonshire

A cathedral city in the heart of Devon

In the midwinter of 1068, William the Conqueror was laying siege to Exeter, the only town in England still holding out after his victory at Hastings two years earlier. After 18 days the two sides made peace, and Exeter opened its gates to the Normans. William promised not to take revenge on the defenders, though, unknown to him, the townsfolk had been sheltering a special refugee – Gytha, the mother of the defeated King Harold. As William marched in through the East Gate, Gytha and her followers slipped quietly away to safety through the West Gate. Courage and defiance have helped Exeter on many other occasions, none more so than one night in 1942 when German bombers devastated the city.

Exeter entered the history books about AD 80 as Isca Dumnoniorum, a Roman town built on the site of a fortress occupied by the 2nd Augusta Legion between AD 50 and AD 75.

The Romans built a wall around 93 acres of the town about AD 200. Since then, Saxons, Danes and Normans have occupied it, each adding to or taking away from the fortifications. Today, the remains of the Roman wall can still be seen, most easily in Southernhay. At **Rougemont**, the northernmost corner of the wall is a tower added in the late 12th century.

Near it is the gatehouse of the castle built by William the Conqueror.

Twin Norman towers rise above the transepts of **Exeter Cathedral**, which was rebuilt in its present form between 1270 and 1360. The west face has the largest surviving array of 14th-century sculpture anywhere in Britain. Inside, the longest stretch of 13th-century Gothic vaulting in the world decorates the ceiling. The 59 ft high oak Bishop's Throne in the cathedral dates from 1313.

Royal patronage

The **Guildhall**, claimed to be the oldest municipal building in the country, has been on its present site since at least 1160. The roof was restored in 1469 during the Wars of the Roses, and carries prominently the Bear and Ragged Staff badge of Warwick the Kingmaker, arch-enemy of Edward IV. Despite the carvings, the citizens were able to persuade the new king that they had really been loyal to him throughout. So successful was this bogus persuasion that Edward gave the city the right to use a sword as part of its regalia. Henry VII is also said to have given Exeter the same right in gratitude after the citizens had resisted the rebellion in 1497 of Perkin Warbeck. Warbeck was a 23-year-old impostor from Flanders who claimed to be the son of Edward IV and the younger of the two Yorkist princes in the Tower. Both swords are now in the Guildhall.

Exeter's canal

Much of medieval Exeter's prosperity came from the trade that passed through its port on the river. But, in 1290, the flow of goods was diminished by the Countess of Devon, Lady Isabel. She built a weir across the Exe, 3 miles south of the city. The resulting dispute gave rise to a legal case that lasted almost 300 years. When the case was finally decided, the city won the right to remove the weir, but by then trade had been seriously affected, so, in 1564, the city commissioned England's first ship canal. The 5½ mile long channel brought some trade back to Exeter. Today, however, it is mostly used by pleasure boats, and the canal basin is the site of the **Maritime Museum**.

The past that survived

Many of the city centre's ancient buildings were destroyed by German bombers in 1942. But much survived the air-raids. **St Mary Steps Church**, on Stepcote Hill, has a clock in its wall in which the hours are struck by three figures, known locally as Matthew the Miller and his two sons.

Underground aqueducts, some dating from the 13th century, which carried the city's water supply, can also be visited. Other parts of the city – in particular the old gates – were demolished deliberately after 1769 as Exeter expanded. A large model in the **Royal Albert Memorial Museum** shows how cramped the city was by then, and helps to explain the odd shapes of the ground plans of many of the old buildings.

Information Tel. 77888.
Location On the A38, 44 m. NE of Plymouth.
Parking Southernhay; North Street; Smythen Street; Paul Street; Magdalen Street; Leighton Terrace; Bampfylde Street; King William

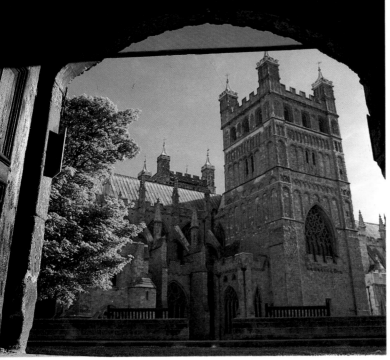

THE CATHEDRAL OF ST MARY AND ST PETER *Two Norman towers, as massive as castle keeps, flank the nave – a unique arrangement in England. The cathedral was rebuilt in the 13th century, and has changed little since.*

STONE ART *A 14th-century figure from the west front of Exeter Cathedral.*

144

Street; Trinity Green; Dix's Field;
Richmond Road (all car parks).
District council Exeter City
(Tel. 77888).
Population 95,600.
E-C Wed. **M-D** Daily.
Police (Cb) Heavitree Road
(Tel. 52191).
Casualty hospital Royal Devon and
Exeter, Wonford (Tel. 77833).
Post office (Bb) Bedford Street.
Theatres Northcott, University
Estate (Tel. 54853); Barnfield
Theatre **(Cb)**, Barnfield Road
(70891).
Cinemas ABC **(Bc)**, London Inn
Square (Tel. 75274); Odeon **(Cc)**,
Sidwell Street (54057).
Public library (Bb) Castle Street.
Places to see Underground
aqueducts, Princesshay **(Bb)**;
Guildhall **(Bb)**, High Street;
Rougemont Castle **(Bc)**; Rougemont
House Museum **(Bc)**, Castle Street;
Royal Albert Memorial Museum and
Art Gallery **(Bb)**, Queen Street;
Maritime Museum, The Quay;
Tucker's Hall, Fore Street; St
Nicholas Priory, off Fore Street.
Town trails Available from
Information Centre, Dix's Field.
Shopping Bedford Street; Guildhall
Precinct; High Street; Paris Street;
Sidwell Street; South Street;
Princesshay.
Event Devon County Show (May).
Trade and industry Light industries;
engineering.
Sport FA League football, Exeter
City FC, St James's Park; Greyhound
racing and speedway racing, County
Ground, Church Road.
AA 24 hour service
Tel. Exeter 32121.

MARINERS' MEETING PLACE *Mol's Coffee House, in the cathedral close, dates from
Elizabethan times. The Armada Room on the first floor was a meeting place of
sea-captains. It is now an art-dealer's shop.*

MARITIME MUSEUM *The Exeter Ship Canal provides an appropriate setting for this
fine collection of vessels. Floating exhibits include a replica of a State Barge, made for
the film* A Man for All Seasons, *and a steam tug.*

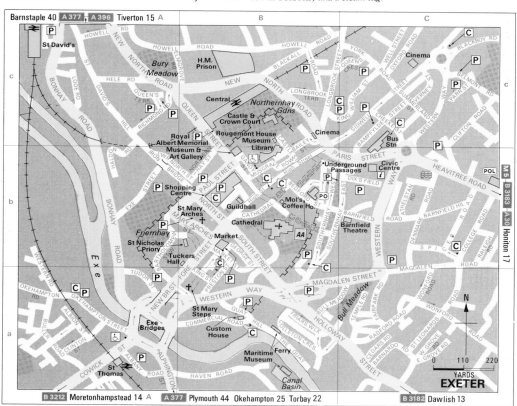

F

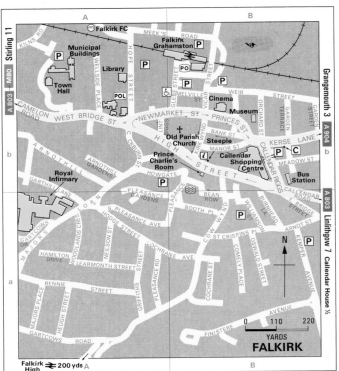

Falkirk Central

The original parish church at Falkirk, built in the 11th century, was known as the "faw", or spotted, kirk, because of its mottled stonework. It was from this that the town got its name.

The historic centre of Falkirk is the Steeple, the third to occupy the site since the 16th century. It was built in 1814 and has an octagonal tower on a square base. In the 19th century one floor was used as a gaol. Today it houses the local information centre.

There have been two battles at Falkirk. In 1298 the Scottish patriot William Wallace was defeated by Edward I, and in 1746 Bonnie Prince Charlie routed the English forces under General Hawley. The second battle is commemorated by a monument in Greenbank Road; and still standing in the High Street is the house, No. 121, where Prince Charles spent the night after the battle. It was rebuilt in 1900 and is now occupied by a firm of bootmakers. The room used by the prince can be seen by visitors.

General Hawley spent the night before the battle at Callendar House, which stands in parkland to the east of Falkirk town centre. The oldest part of the house is thought to date from the 14th century. Mary, Queen of Scots was a frequent visitor. In 1650 Oliver Cromwell attacked the house and put its defenders to the sword, because they broke an undertaking not to molest his troops.

Falkirk has been an iron-working town for more than 200 years. The Carron Ironworks, 2 miles north, began in 1760, with the manufacture of carronades – cannons used on many warships of the time, including Nelson's *Victory*. A 20 ton cast-iron gate, probably the largest ever made, stands in Gowan Avenue. It was cast by the Grahamston Iron Company for the Edinburgh International Exhibition of 1886.

In Wallace Street there is a railway museum run by the Scottish Railway Preservation Society. Two canals – the Union, and the Forth and Clyde – served the town before the railway was built, and although these are now derelict there are pleasant walks along the towpaths.

Information Tel. 24911.
Location On the A803, 23 m. NE of Glasgow.

Parking Howgate; Market Square; Melville Street; Weir Street; Meek's Road; Baxter's Wynd; Booth Place; Cockburn Street; Durrator Road; Eastburn Drive; Garrison Place; Hope Street; Williamson Street (all car parks).
District council Falkirk (Tel. 24911).
Population 36,900.
E-C Wed.
Police (Ab) West Bridge Street (Tel. 34212).
Casualty hospital (Aa) Royal Infirmary, Majors Loan (Tel. 24000).
Post office (Bb) Garrison Place.
Cinema ABC 1, 2 & 3 **(Bb)**, Princes Street (Tel. 23805).
Public library (Ab) Hope Street.
Places to see Falkirk Museum **(Bb)**, Orchard Street; Prince Charlie's Room **(Bb)**, High Street; Callendar House and park, off Callendar Road; Railway Museum, Wallace Street.
Shopping High Street; Callendar Riggs Shopping Centre.
Trade and industry Iron-founding; aluminium rolling.
Sport Scottish League football, Falkirk FC, Brockville Park.
AA 24 hour service Tel. 25454.

Falmouth Cornwall

In the age of sail, a regular instruction to English merchant ships bound for Europe after the long voyage from the Indies or Americas was: Falmouth for orders. At this port in the southernmost part of England they would be told where their cargoes could find the best markets in Britain or on the Continent.

Occasionally, messengers and ambassadors travelling to London would

PENDENNIS CASTLE *Henry VIII built the fort to guard Falmouth harbour.*

be dropped at the port, for they could reach the capital faster by horse than by the longer sea route via the North Foreland and the Thames with its tides and westerly winds.

The port stands at the entrance to Carrick Roads, a magnificent natural harbour formed at the junction of several estuaries.

The castles of Pendennis and St Mawes, which face each other across the roads, were built by Henry VIII. The protection they gave against marauders was vital to the rise of Falmouth as a port.

Pendennis Castle was the last Royalist stronghold in England to surrender to Cromwell in the Civil War. There is a fine view of the town from the castle ramparts. Near the Custom House Quay is the King's Pipe, a brick chimney where, for years, smuggled tobacco was burned when seized by excisemen.

In 1688 the first Royal Mail Packet Station in England was set up at Falmouth. It became the communications centre of the British Isles. Small sloops darted across the oceans, carrying post, royal messages and bullion to America, Africa, India and the Mediterranean. The packet service brought great prosperity, and when it

THE BOSUN'S LOCKER *On Falmouth waterfront a striking figurehead stands outside a ships' chandlers, or candle store. In the days of sail, merchant ships replenished their stores at the port before making the long haul across the oceans.*

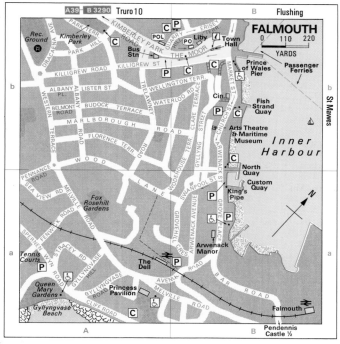

Fareham Hampshire

The Georgian houses that line the High Street are relics of when Fareham was a fashionable residence for naval officers. It lies on a quiet backwater of Portsmouth Harbour, and was once a major commercial harbour and naval base.

Portsdown Hill provides one of the finest panoramic views in southern England: it takes in the English Channel, Spithead, the Solent and Portsmouth Royal Naval base.

Information Tel. 285432.
Location On the A27, 12 m. E of Southampton.
Parking The Market; Bath Lane; Osborn Road; High Street; Trinity Street; West Street; Hartlands Road; Quay Street; East Street; Civic Way (all car parks).
District council Borough of Fareham (Tel. 236100).
Population 88,300.
E-C Wed. **M-D** Mon.
Police Quay Street (Tel. 236211).
Casualty hospital Queen Alexandra Hospital, Cosham (Tel. Cosham 379451).
Post office West Street.
Cinema Embassy, West Street (Tel. 280102).
Public library Osborn Road.
Places to see Portchester Castle, 3 m. E; Titchfield Abbey, 3 m. W.
Shopping West Street.
Trade and industry Agriculture; electrical and aerospace equipment.
AA 24 hour service
Tel. Southampton 36811.

Farnborough Hampshire

Since 1905, Farnborough has been the home of the Royal Aircraft Establishment – the laboratory of British military aviation and the site of the biennial International Air Show.

St Michael's Abbey was built in 1881 by the Empress Eugenie, wife of Napoleon III of France, after their exile to England in 1871. Napoleon, Eugenie and their son, the Prince Imperial, are buried in the crypt.

Information Tel. 513838.
Location On the A325, 11 m. NW of Guildford.
Parking Kingsmead; Westmead; Pinehurst (all car parks).
District council Rushmoor (Tel. 44451).
Population 45,500.
E-C Wed. **M-D** Tues.
Police Pinehurst Avenue (Tel. 40661).
Casualty hospital Frimley Park District, Portsmouth Road, Camberley (Tel. Camberley 62121).
Post office Queensmead.
Public library Pinehurst Avenue.
Places to see St Michael's Abbey.
Shopping Kingsmead; Queensmead; Camp Road.
Event Biennial International Air Show (Sept.).
AA 24 hour service
Tel. Guildford 72841.

was transferred to Southampton, Falmouth's fortunes declined.

They were revived in 1863, when the railway reached Falmouth. Holidaymakers soon followed, and the town is now one of the leading resorts on the Cornish Riviera.

Information Tel. 312300.
Location On the A39, 10 m. S of Truro.
Parking Town Quarry; The Moor; The Dell; Church Street; Grove Place; Swanpool; Gyllyngvase; Castle Drive (all car parks).
District council Carrick (Tel. Truro 78131).
Population 18,500.
E-C Wed.
Police Commercial Road, Penryn (Tel. Penryn 72231).

Casualty hospital City, Infirmary Hill, Truro (Tel. Truro 74242).
Post office (Bb) The Moor.
Theatres Falmouth Arts **(Bb)**, Church Street (Tel. 314566); Princess Pavilion **(Aa)**, Melville Road (311277).
Cinema Grand **(Bb)**, Market Street (Tel. 312412).
Public library (Bb) Municipal Buildings, The Moor.
Places to see Pendennis Castle; St Mawes Castle; Military Vehicle Museum, Lamanva; Maritime Museum **(Bb)**; Arwenack Manor **(Ba)**.
Shopping High Street; Killigrew Street; Church Street; Market Street; Arwenack Street.
AA 24 hour service
Tel. Truro 76455.

GEORGIAN FAÇADES *Many houses in Farnham's Castle Street have Georgian fronts on medieval buildings, identified by the steeply pitched roofs.*

Farnham Surrey

Bronze Age merchants travelling across southern England to trade with the tribes of the east passed through a prehistoric settlement at Farnham. The town grew with the development of agriculture in medieval times.

The manor was given to the Bishops of Winchester in 688 by King Caedwalla of Wessex. Soon after the Norman Conquest, a Norman bishop, Henry of Blois, built a castle there on the London to Winchester road. It became the Palace of the Bishops of Winchester. The 12th-century stone keep, the walls and a fine Tudor tower still stand.

William Cobbett, the radical politician and author of *Rural Rides*, was born at the Jolly Farmer Inn, now the William Cobbett, in Bridge Square.

Charles I stayed at Vernon House, now the town library, in West Street on his way to London and execution in 1649. Jonathan Swift wrote *A Tale of a Tub* while at Moor Park, just outside the town.

Information Tel. Godalming 4104.
Location On the A31, 10 m. W of Guildford.
Parking Dogflud Way (2); The Hart (2), off West Street; South Street; Victoria Road; Waggon Yard, off Downing Street (all car parks).
District council Waverley (Tel. Godalming 4104).
Population 35,300.
E-C Wed. **M-D** Fri.
Police Longbridge (Tel. 716262).
Casualty hospital New Royal Surrey County, Gill Avenue, Egerton Road, Guildford (Tel. Guildford 71122).
Post office West Street.
Theatre Redgrave, Brightwells (Tel. 715301).
Cinema Studios 1 & 2, East Street (Tel. 721142).
Public library West Street.
Places to see Farnham Castle and Fox's Tower; Museum, West Street; Ashgate Art Gallery, Waggon Yard, Farnham Maltings, Bridge Square.
Shopping West Street; The Borough; Downing Street; Woolmead.
AA 24 hour service
Tel. Guildford 72841.

Farnworth see Manchester

Felixstowe Suffolk

The Victorians discovered the charm of Felixstowe towards the end of the 19th century, and its architecture ranges from the sedate hotels and houses of that period to modern seafront pavilions and amusement centres.

Felixstowe lies in a gently curving bay between the estuaries of the rivers Deben and Orwell, and its 2 mile long beach – a mixture of shingle, pebbles and sand – is backed by a wide promenade, lawns and floral gardens. One of its oldest buildings is a Martello Tower, built about 1810 as defence against the threat of invasion by Napoleon.

At the southern end of the town, overlooking Harwich Harbour, is the third largest container port in the United Kingdom. On Landguard Point, a narrow peninsula of shingle which protects the harbour entrance, there is a 16th-century fort.

Information Tel. 2126/2122.
Location On the A45, 12 m. SE of Ipswich.
Parking Langer Road (2); Undercliff Road West (4); Sea Road; Garrison Lane; Cliff Road (2); Highfield Road; Cobbold Road; Ranelagh Road; Golf Road (all car parks).
District council Suffolk Coastal (Tel. Woodbridge 3789).
Population 20,900.
E-C Wed. **M-D** Thur.
Police (Bb) High Road West (Tel. 2178).
Casualty hospital Felixstowe General, Constable Road (Tel. 2214).
Post office (Bb) Hamilton Road.
Theatres Spa Pavilion **(Ba)**, Promenade (Tel. 3303); Concert Hall, Pier Pavilion **(Ba)** (2605).
Cinema Lucky Seven Twin Cinema **(Bb)**, Crescent Road (Tel. 2787).
Public library (Bb) Crescent Road.
Places to see Martello Tower, Promenade; Model Railway.
Shopping Hamilton Road; Orwell Road; Crescent Road.
Car ferries To Zeebrugge (79461); to Gothenburg (78777).
AA 24 hour service
Tel. Norwich 29401.

Ffestiniog Gwynedd

The Vale of Ffestiniog is a slate-quarrying district, and the town of Blaenau Ffestiniog grew around the industry.

The Festiniog Railway, perhaps the best-known of Britain's narrow-gauge lines, was built in 1836 to carry slate from the quarries. It runs from Blaenau Ffestiniog to the harbour at Porthmadog, a distance of 13 miles, through some of the finest scenery in North Wales. It now operates a passenger service from March to November. The slate quarries are now mostly tourist attractions.

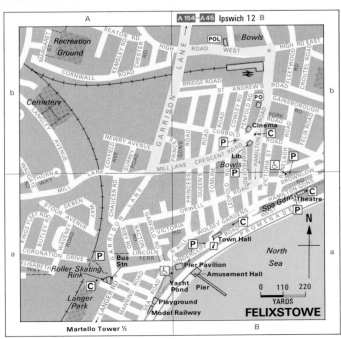

FELIXSTOWE

ANCIENT CRAFT *Workers split slate stone to make roofing slates near Blaenau Ffestiniog, in a quarry that produces some of the best slates in the world.*

Fishguard Dyfed

Trains packed with travellers for the ferry to Ireland roll into Fishguard's Goodwick terminal. But this busy traffic detracts nothing from the beauty of Fishguard and its sweeping bay. Tree-lined slopes drop to a quaint old harbour.

A rocky bay beneath Carregwastad Point was the scene of the last invasion of Britain. French troops under an American, Colonel William Tate, landed in 1797 to rouse the population against George III. The attack ended in fiasco. The invaders meekly lined up on Goodwick sands and laid down their arms after, it is said, they had mistaken Welsh women wearing traditional red cloaks for British soldiers. A stone marks the French landing place at Carregwastad.

Information Tel. 873484 (summer).
Location On the A40, 15 m. N of Haverfordwest.
Parking Fishguard: West Street; Hamilton Street (both car parks); Wallis Street; West Street. Goodwick: The Parrog; Station Hill (both car parks); Main Street.
District council Preseli (Tel. Haverfordwest 4551).
Population 4,900.
E-C Wed. **M-D** Thur.
Police (Ba) Brodog Lane (Tel. 873225).
Casualty hospital Withybush General Hospital, Fishguard Road, Haverfordwest (Tel. Haverfordwest 4545).
Post office (Ba) West Street.
Cinema (Ba) Studio Cinema, West Street (Tel. 873421).
Public library (Ba) High Street.
Shopping Fishguard: High Street; Market Square; West Street; Main Street. Goodwick: Main Street.
Car ferry To Rosslare (Tel. 872881).
AA 24 hour service Tel. Cardiff 394111.

GREAT LITTLE TRAIN *A steam engine of the Festiniog Railway.*

Information Tel. 415.
Location On the A470, 14 m. SW of Betws-y-Coed.
Parking Diffwys Square; Pengwern Square.
District council Meironnydd (Tel. Dolgellau 422341).
Population 5,400.
E-C Thur.
Police Park Square, Blaenau Ffestiniog (Tel. 252).
Casualty hospital Wynne Road, Blaenau Ffestiniog (Tel. Ffestiniog 256).
Post office High Street, Blaenau Ffestiniog.
Public library Meiron Terrace.
Places to see Slate Mines, Blaenau Ffestiniog; Festiniog Railway.
Shopping High Street, Blaenau Ffestiniog.
AA 24 hour service Tel. Llandudno 79066.

Filey N. Yorks.

Six miles of sand stretch south from Filey. The beaches, which offer safe bathing, are bounded to the north by the mile-long natural breakwater of Filey Brigg. The breakwater is included in a nature trail. The Romans had a signal station on Carr Naze above the Brigg.

Modern Filey is a holiday resort with elegant hotels and a busy shopping centre. The northern part of the town is the old fishing port, where flat-bottomed craft known as cobles are launched from the beach.

Filey is the starting point of the 93 mile Cleveland Way long-distance footpath, which follows the coast before cutting inland across the North Yorkshire Moors.

Information Tel. 512204 (summer); Scarborough 72261 (winter).
Location On the A1039, 8 m. SE of Scarborough.
Parking West Avenue; Station Avenue; Country Park (all car parks).
District council Borough of Scarborough (Tel. Scarborough 72351).
Population 5,700.
E-C Wed.
Police Murray Street (Tel. Scarborough 512222).
Casualty hospital Scarborough Hospital, Scalby Road, Scarborough (Tel. Scarborough 68111).
Post office Murray Street.
Theatres Sun Lounge, The Crescent (Tel. Scarborough 512079); Brig Theatre, Station Avenue (513207).
Cinema Grand, Union Street (Tel. Scarborough 512129).
Public library West Avenue.
Places to see Folk Museum, Queen Street.
Nature trail Tourist Information Centre, John Street.
Shopping Murray Street; Union Street; Belle Street; John Street.
Events Festival (June/July); Fishing Festival (Sept.).
AA 24 hour service Tel. York 27698.

FISHGUARD & GOODWICK

Map: Fishguard and Goodwick street plan. Features include Car Ferry Terminal & Harbour Station, Goodwick, East Breakwater, Fishguard Harbour, Saddle Point, Castle Point, Goodwick Moor, Goodwick Brook, French Walk, Penyraber, Fishguard, scale 0–220–440 yards. Roads: A40 (Haverfordwest 15), A487 (St David's 16, Cardigan 18), Quay Road, Wern Road, High Street, West Street, Main Street, Clive Road, Heol Dyfed, Heol Dewi, etc. Library, Town Hall marked.

FLEETWOOD'S LIVELIHOOD *Trawlers at the dockside and piles of nets on the quay testify to Fleetwood's dependence on the fishing industry. The trawler fleet operates as far afield as Greenland.*

Fleetwood Lancashire

A fleet of modern, deep-sea trawlers steams regularly into Fleetwood. It comes from the rich fishing grounds off Greenland and the waters north of Scotland, and brings with it good-quality cod and haddock. Fleetwood is the third-largest fishing port in England – but the industry is declining. Catches in recent years have been almost halved to 25,000 tons a year since Iceland extended its fishing limit from 50 to 200 miles in 1975.

Fleetwood is bounded by the sea on three sides. It has 4 miles of fine sands, good bathing and splendid views across Morecambe Bay. The peaks of the Lake District can be seen in clear weather. The town also has the largest model-yacht pond in Europe, where an International Model-yacht Regatta is held.

Information Tel. 71141.
Location On the A585, 9 m. N of Blackpool.
Parking The Esplanade (2); Princes Way; Custom House Lane; Laidley's Walk; Queen's Terrace (all car parks).
District council Borough of Wyre (Tel. Poulton-le-Fylde 882233).
Population 28,400.
E-C Wed. **M-D** Mon., Tues., Fri., Sat. (summer only), Tues. and Fri.
Police North Church Street (Tel. 6611).
Casualty hospital Victoria Hospital, East Park Drive, Blackpool (Tel. Blackpool 34111).
Post office Ash Street.
Theatre Marine Hall, The Esplanade (Tel. 71141).
Cinema Regent Triple, Lord Street (Tel. 3667).
Public library Poulton Road.
Shopping Lord Street; Poulton Road.
Car ferry Isle of Man Terminal, Queens Terrace (Tel. 6263).
AA 24 hour service
Tel. Manchester (061) 485 6299.

Flint Clwyd

The castle at Flint, probably begun by Edward I in 1277, is unusual in having its strongest tower, or donjon, separate from the main structure. Donjon and castle are linked only by a drawbridge. Possibly this was to protect the supply ships that tied up at the castle at a time when the River Dee ran between the two structures. The river has since silted up. In 1399 the castle witnessed the surrender of Richard II to Henry Bolingbroke, who succeeded him as Henry IV. Much of the castle was destroyed during the Civil War.

Information Tel. Holywell 710710.
Location On the A548, 12 m. NW of Chester.
Parking Church Street; Sydney Street; Chapel Street; Castle Road; Feather Street (2); Earl Street (all car parks).
District council Borough of Delyn (Tel. Holywell 710710).
Population 16,400.
E-C Wed. **M-D** Fri.
Police Chapel Street (Tel. 2222).
Casualty hospital Flint Cottage, Cornist Road (Tel. 2215).
Post office Church Street.
Public library Church Street.
Places to see Castle; Old Town Hall; Cornist Hall.
Shopping Market Square; Chapel Street Precinct; Church Street.
AA 24 hour service
Tel. Liverpool (051) 709 7252.

Folkestone Kent

Business and pleasure mix happily in Folkestone, one of England's most cheerful holiday towns. In summer, day trippers throng the quay of the pretty cliffside harbour to catch the cross-Channel steamers to Boulogne, Calais and Ostend. The crowded ferries pick their way through rows of fishing boats as they start their journeys. Since a new passenger terminal was opened in 1968, Folkestone has handled more passengers than any other south-coast port except for its near neighbour, Dover.

The old town behind the harbour has lost none of its quaintness because of this developing commerce. Narrow, cobbled, pub-lined streets still lead down to the wharves where the fishing boats land their daily catches.

Until the last century Folkestone had never been anything more than a fishing village, supplying mackerel in season for the London market. In 1843 the railway reached the town, and soon afterwards the holidaymakers arrived, attracted to the safe, sandy beach that lies in the shelter of East Cliff.

To the west of the town is a broad, clifftop walk, The Leas. It stretches 1½ miles and is laid out with lawns, flower beds and a bandstand. There is a magnificent view of the Channel, and on a clear day the coast of France can be seen 26 miles away. From the promenade, paths wind through banks of tamarisk trees to the beach 200 ft below. At the eastern end of The Leas a lift, built in 1890 and driven by water pressure, carries thousands of passengers each year to and from the marine gardens below.

The parish church of St Mary and St Eanswythe was founded in 1135. It was rebuilt in 1216 after being burned by a raiding party from France. A window commemorates William Harvey, born in Folkestone in 1578, the man who discovered how the blood circulates.

Information Tel. 57388.
Location On the A20, 8 m. SE of Dover.
Parking Middleburgh Square; Gloucester Place; Rendezvous Street; Tontine Street; Shellons Street; Forresters Way; Tram Road; Dover Road; Lower Sandgate Road; Marine Parade (all car parks).
District council Shepway (Tel. 57388).
Population 43,700.
E-C Wed. **M-D** Mon.
Police (Ab) Shorncliffe Road (Tel. 54611).
Casualty hospital William Harvey, Willesborough, Ashford (Tel. Ashford 33331).
Post office (Bb) Bouverie Square.
Theatres Leas Cliff Hall **(Aa)**, The Leas (Tel. 53193); Leas Pavilion **(Ba)**, The Leas (52466); Marine Pavilion **(Ca)**, Marine Parade (53708); Little Theatre, Sandgate High Street (38460).
Cinema Curzon 1, 2 and 3 **(Bb)**, George Lane (Tel. 53335).
Public library (Bb) Grace Hill.
Places to see Art Gallery **(Bb)**, Grace Hill; Art Centre; New Metropole; The Leas.
Shopping Sandgate Road; Tontine Street; Guildhall Street; Old High Street; Sandgate High Street.
Event International Folklore Festival (June, Biennial).

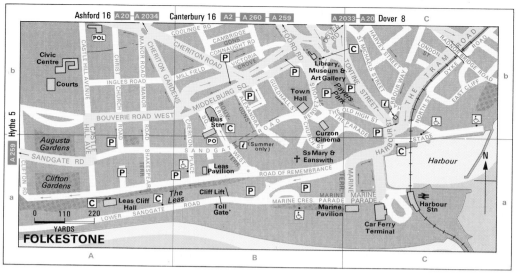

FOLKESTONE

THE LEAS *Folkestone's clifftop lawns are a favourite spot with holidaymakers. Military bands play on the ornate bandstand during the summer.*

Sport Horse-racing, Folkestone Racecourse.
Car ferry To Ostend, Calais, Boulogne (Tel. 53949).
AA 24 hour service Tel. Thanet 81226.

Forfar Tayside
The former county town of Angus is a tourist centre, with golf, sailing on Forfar and Rescobie lochs, trout fishing and, in the winter, ski-ing at Glenshee.

Malcolm III of Scotland is said to have held a parliament at Forfar in 1057. The castle he built was razed in 1308 by Robert Bruce, and a 17th-century octagonal turret marks the site.

The town was sacked by Cromwell's troops during the Civil War, and there are few obvious signs of its history before the 17th century. But the museum in the Meffan Institute preserves Stone Age and Bronze Age relics found in the area, and a medieval witch bridle used to gag those about to be burned.

Forfar lies in the Vale of Strathmore, famous for strawberries and raspberries which are canned in the town. Nurseries on the valley slopes grow trees and plants for sale to gardeners all over Britain, and there are jute mills and factories making agricultural machinery.

The ruined Restenneth Priory, 2 miles to the north-east, has a 15th-century spire and the remains of 12th-century walls. An infant son of Robert Bruce is buried there.

Information Tel. 63468.
Location On the A94, 12 m. N of Dundee.
Parking West High Street; Craig O'Loch Road; Myre; East Greens; Market Muir; Myre Road; Old Halkerton Road; St James's Road; The Vennel (all car parks).
District council Angus (Tel. 65101).
Population 12,250.
E-C Thur. **M-D** Mon., Fri.
Police West High Street (Tel. 62551).
Casualty hospital Forfar Infirmary,

SILENCER *A witch bridle, or gag, displayed in Forfar's museum.*

Arbroath Road (Tel. 64551).
Post office West High Street.
Cinema Regal, East High Street (Tel. 62222).
Public library West High Street.
Places to see Museum; Glamis Castle, 6 m. SW; Angus Folk Museum; Restenneth Priory ruins, 2 m. NE.
Shopping Castle Street; East High Street; West High Street.
AA 24 hour service Tel. Dundee 25585.

Formby Merseyside
More than a mile of sand dunes separate Formby from its beach. A fishing village once stood on the shore, but has long since been buried under the sands left by the receding sea.

The beach is one of the finest on the north-west coast, stretching almost 9 miles to Southport in the north. The National Trust controls 400 acres of the dunes west of the town, and there is a National Nature Reserve at Ainsdale, 3 miles north.

In the late 19th century an attempt was made to establish Formby as a seaside resort, but bathing is unsafe in the fast incoming tide, and the plan failed. Formby remained as it is today, a residential area for Liverpool.

Information Tel. 75078.
Location On the B5424, 15 m. S of Southport.
Parking Three Tuns Lane; Back Chapel Lane; Halsall Lane; Victoria Road (all car parks).
District council Sefton (Tel. Liverpool (051) 922 4040).
Population 25,800.
E-C Wed.
Police Church Road (Tel. 72212).
Casualty hospital Walton General, Rice Lane, Walton, Liverpool 9 (Tel. 051 525 3611).
Post office Brows Lane.
Public library Duke Street.
Shopping Church Road; Chapel Lane.
AA 24 hour service Tel. 051 709 7252.

Forres Grampian

The ancient burgh of Forres was the site of King Duncan's court in the 11th century, and is mentioned in Shakespeare's *Macbeth*. Sueno's Stone is a 23 ft high, carved sandstone monument thought to commemorate the victory of the King of Denmark's son, Sweyn, or Sueno, over Duncan's grandfather Malcolm II in 1008.

The Falconer Museum includes a fine collection of local fossils. Darnaway Castle, 3 miles south-west, built in 1810, incorporates a 15th-century hall where Mary, Queen of Scots held court in 1564. It is not open to the public.

Information Tel. 72938.
Location On the A96, 12 m. W of Elgin.
Parking High Street; Cumming Street; Leys Road; Orchard Road; Tulloch Park; Leask Road (all car parks).
District council Moray (Tel. Elgin 3451).
Population 7,950.
E-C Wed.
Police High Street (Tel. 72224).
Casualty hospital Leanchoil, St Leonards Road (Tel. 72284).
Post office High Street.
Public library High Street.
Places to see Falconer Museum, Tolbooth Street; Nelson Tower, Cluny Hill; Sueno's Stone, Findhorn Road; Brodie Castle, 2½ m. W off A96.
Shopping High Street; Tolbooth Street.
Event Highland Games (July).
AA 24 hour service
Tel. Aberdeen 51231.

Fort William Highland

The fort from which this town takes its name was built in 1690 by order of William III to keep the rebellious Scottish clans in order. The garrison repelled attacks by Jacobite rebels during the uprisings of 1715 and 1745. The fort was dismantled in 1855.

Fort William lies at the head of Loch Linnhe, and is a tourist centre for the Western Highlands and a base for climbers of Ben Nevis (4,406 ft), Britain's highest mountain. A footpath from Achintee Farm – 2½ miles from the town – leads to the summit. The precipitous north face is a challenge to experienced rock climbers.

Each year, Fort William is the start and finish of the gruelling Ben Nevis Race. The competitors run over a 12 mile course – to the top of Ben Nevis and back. The record, set in 1976 by David Cannon, is 1 hour 26 minutes 55 seconds.

The West Highland Museum in Fort William contains many relics of the Jacobite risings, including a bed in which Bonnie Prince Charlie slept. There is also a "secret" portrait of the prince which is revealed only when reflected in a cylindrical mirror.

Inverlochy Castle, 2 miles to the north-east, dates from the 13th century and is a square building with round corner-towers. The largest of the towers, Comyn's Tower, has 10 ft thick walls.

At Banavie, 3 miles north, is Neptune's Staircase, eight linked locks on the Caledonian Canal. The locks take the canal down 90 ft in less than 2 miles between Loch Lochy and Loch Linnhe. Thomas Telford (1757–1834) built the 60 mile canal to link the North Sea to the Atlantic.

Information Tel. 3581.
Location On the A82, 49 m. NE of Oban.
Parking High Street (4); North Service Road; A82 trunk road (3); Nevis Terrace; Cameron Square (all car parks).
District council Lochaber (Tel. 3881).
Population 4,000.
E-C Wed. (except summer).
Police High Street (Tel. 2361).
Casualty hospital Belford Road (Tel. 2481).
Post office High Street.
Public library Parade Road.
Places to see Fort ruins; West Highland Museum, Cameron Square; Inverlochy Castle, Inverlochy, 2 m. NE.
Shopping High Street.
Events Highland Games (July/Aug.); Ben Nevis Race (Sept.).
AA 24 hour service
Tel. Glasgow (041) 812 0101.

Fowey Cornwall

Ships from many nations visit Fowey (pronounced Foy) to collect china clay from the jetties about 1 mile upstream. The town sprawls along the water's edge. The main street is narrow and has a one-way traffic system along its full length.

Fowey has all the charm of a typical Cornish coastal town, as well as being a commercial port. Behind the Quay is Trafalgar Square with its 18th-century Town Hall. The Council Chamber, now Fowey Museum, is medieval. Noah's Ark, a house in Fore Street dating from the 14th century, now contains a museum of Cornish domestic life.

Off Fore Street is Place, a 15th-century house. In the 19th century a granite tower was added, which is higher than that of the nearby Church of St Fimbarrus. The Haven, a house overlooking the river, was the home of Sir Arthur Quiller-Couch (1863-1945) who wrote about Fowey in his novels, calling it "Troy".

Information Tel. 3320.
Location On the A3082, 9 m. E of St Austell.
Parking Tower Park; Caffa Mill Pill; Park Road; Albert Quay; Central, off Hanson Drive (all car parks).
District council Restormel (Tel. St Austell 4466).
Population 2,400.
E-C Wed.

PIRATES' DEN *In the 14th and 15th centuries, ships from Fowey, the "Fowey Gallants", constantly raided the French coast – and continued to do so even after Edward IV had made peace with the French. Today, ships enter the deep Fowey estuary to load with china clay from the jetties along the river. In summer the harbour throngs with yachts and cabin cruisers.*

Police Vicarage Meadow
(Tel. 3438).
Casualty hospital City Hospital,
Infirmary Hill, Truro
(Tel. Truro 74242).
Post office Fore Street.
Public library Church Avenue.
Places to see Fowey Museum, Town
Hall; Aquarium, the Quay; Noah's
Ark Folk Museum, Fore Street.
Event Royal Regatta and Carnival
Week (Aug)
Car ferry To Bodinick
(Tel. Polruan 453).
AA 24 hour service
Tel. Truro 76455.

Fraserburgh Grampian

Fish and tourism are Fraserburgh's
chief industries.

The town was created in the 16th
century by Alexander Fraser, 7th
Laird of Philorth, who built the original harbour. The castle, on Kinnaird
Head, was started by his grandson
in 1569. Only the central tower
remains. It was adapted in 1787 to
accommodate Kinnaird Head lighthouse.

On rocks at the foot of the castle
stands the oddly named Wine Tower,
virtually unchanged since it was built
in the 16th century and the oldest
building in Fraserburgh.

At one time this attractive little
town was one of Scotland's busiest
herring ports. But the decline of the
great herring shoals means that now
mostly white fish is landed at the
port.

Information Tel. 2315 or Banff
2789.
Location On the A92, 26 m. E of
Banff.
Parking Saltoun Square; Hanover
Street (both car parks).
District council Banff and Buchan
(Tel. Banff 2521).
Population 12,300.
E-C Wed. **M-D** (Fish) Mon. to Sat.
Police Kirk Brae (Tel. 3121).
Casualty hospital Lochpots Road
(Tel. 3151).
Post office Commerce Street.
Public library King Edward Street.
Places to see Kinnaird Head
lighthouse.
Shopping High Street; Broad Street;
Castle Street shopping precinct.
Trade and industry Fishing; fish
processing; marine engineering.
AA 24 hour service
Tel. Aberdeen 51231.

Frimley and Camberley
Surrey

Until the 19th century Frimley was a
small village, and Camberley did not
exist. Then, in 1812, the Royal Military Academy (Sandhurst) moved to
Camberley, to be followed in 1857 by
the Army Staff College. Some of the
academy buildings – a group in Classical style by James Wyatt – front on to
the London Road. York Town, the
oldest part of Camberley, was laid out

in a grid pattern in the early 19th
century. Its large houses were built to
accommodate academy staff.

The composer Sir Arthur Sullivan
(1842-1900) lived in the town as a
boy when his father was a bandmaster
at Sandhurst.

Information Tel. Camberley 63184.
Location On the A30, 15 m. NW of
Guildford.
Parking Frimley: Station Road.
Camberley: Knoll Road; Portesbery
Road; Upper Charles Street; Lower
Charles Street; Pembroke Broadway
(all car parks).
District council Surrey Heath
(Tel. Bagshot 72324).
Population 51,650.
E-C Wed.
M-D Camberley: Thur., Fri., Sat.
Police Portesbery Road, Camberley
(Tel. 27131).
Casualty hospital Frimley Park
Hospital, Portsmouth Road,
Camberley (Tel. 62121).
Post office London Road,
Camberley.
Theatre Civic Hall, Knoll Road,
Camberley (Tel. 23738).
Cinema Classic, London Road,
Camberley (Tel. 63909).
Public library Knoll Road,
Camberley; Beech Road, Frimley
Green.
Places to see Royal Military
Academy, Sandhurst (by
appointment only); Surrey Heath
Museum, Knoll Road, Camberley.
Shopping High Street, Frimley; High
Street, Camberley.
AA 24 hour service
Tel. Guildford 72841.

Frinton and Walton Essex

Two contrasting seaside resorts exist
side by side on the East Coast.
Frinton-on-Sea is sedate, with no
pubs within the gates and no organised entertainment. Walton-on-the-
Naze has a pier, amusement arcades
and bustling crowds. But both have
fine sandy beaches.

Frinton developed as a resort at the
end of the last century, and has preserved an air of Victorian gentility.
Walton's popularity began nearly 100
years earlier, and its Marine Parade
was completed in 1832. The Naze, or
Ness, is a headland jutting into the
sea. Behind it is a 1,900 acre National
Nature Reserve – a haven for birds.

Information Tel. Frinton 5542
(summer); Clacton 25501 (winter).
Location On the B1036, 8 m. NE of
Clacton-on-Sea.
Parking Frinton: The Leas and
Esplanade. Walton: Church Road;
Station Street; Mill Lane; Bathhouse
Meadow; The Naze (all car parks).
District council Tendring
(Tel. Clacton-on-Sea 25501).
Population 14,600.
E-C Wed. **M-D** Mon., Thur.
Police Pole Barn Lane, Frinton
(Tel. 4166). Martello Road, Walton
(Tel. Frinton 5622).

Casualty hospital Clacton and
District, Freeland Road, Clacton
(Tel. Clacton-on-Sea 21145).
Post offices Connaught Avenue,
Frinton; High Street, Walton.
Public libraries Connaught Avenue,
Frinton; High Street, Walton.
AA 24 hour service
Tel. Chelmsford 61711.

Frome Somerset

The River Frome (pronounced
Froom) meanders through the centre
of the town, below steep, narrow
streets lined with medieval and
Tudor buildings. Cheap Street is flagstoned, with a central watercourse.

Fine buildings in the town include
the Blue House almshouses of 1726,
close to the bridge. Rook Lane Congregational Chapel in Bath Street was
built in 1707, and is a fine example of
an early nonconformist church.

Longleat House, 4 miles south-east,
is one of the finest Elizabethan mansions in England and is the home of
the Marquess of Bath.

Information Tel. 65757.
Location On the A361, 15 m. S of
Bath.
Parking North Parade; Christchurch
Street West; South Parade; Cork
Street (2); Saxonvale Broadway;
Bridge Street (all car parks).
District council Mendip
(Tel. Wells 73026).
Population 14,500.
E-C Thur. **M-D** Wed., Sat.
Police Oakfield Road (Tel. 62211).
Casualty hospital Victoria Park Road
(Tel. 63591).
Post office Market Place.
Theatre Merlin, Bath Road
(Tel. 65949).
Cinemas Grand, Christchurch Street
West (Tel. 62795); Westway
Entertainment Centre, Westway
(65685).
Public library Scott Road.
Places to see Frome Museum;
Longleat House, 4 m. SE; Nunney
Castle, 3½ m. SW.
Shopping Westway and Kingsway
precincts; Market Place; Badcox.
AA 24 hour service
Tel. Bath 24731.

THE BLUE HOUSE *For generations this
gracious 18th-century house in Frome
Market Place has been an almshouse for
elderly women.*

G

Gainsborough Lincolnshire

Since the late 17th century Gainsborough has been a town of warm red brick. It retains only one earlier building, the 15th-century Old Hall. Richard III visited the Hall on his way back to London from his second coronation in York in 1484. The Pilgrim Fathers also met at the Old Hall in the late 16th century. Gainsborough is a busy port on the River Trent and handles coasters, lighters and a liner service to Rotterdam.

Information Tel. 5411.
Location On the A159, 19 m. NW of Lincoln.
Parking Roseway; Casket Street; North Street; Lord Street; Ropery Road; Hickman Street (all car parks).
District council West Lindsey (Tel. 5411).
Population 18,700.
E-C Wed. **M-D** Tues., Sat.
Police Morton Terrace (Tel. 2244).
Casualty hospital Ropery Road (Tel. 4751).
Post office North Street.
Public library Cobden Street.
Places to see Old Hall, Parnell Street.
Shopping Market Square; Church Street; Silver Street.
AA 24 hour service
Tel. Lincoln 42363.

Galashiels Borders

The town stretches for more than 2 miles along the banks of the River Gala, and is the centre of Scotland's tweed-manufacturing industry.

Galashiels was granted a charter in 1599, and the event is celebrated each summer with the "Braw Lads" Gathering, when the granting of the charter is re-enacted.

The town's motto – "Sour Plums" – is displayed on the Municipal Buildings. It refers to an incident in 1337 when some English soldiers were slain while picking wild (sour) plums.

Information Tel. 55551.
Location On the A7, 16 m. NW of Jedburgh.
Parking Livingstone Place; Scott Crescent; Gala Terrace; Elm Row; Lawyers Brae; Paton Street; Ladhope Vale; Bridge Street; Cornmill Square; Union Street; High Street; Station Yard.
District council Ettrick and Lauderdale (Tel. Galashiels 4751).
Population 12,300.
E-C Wed. **M-D** Fri.
Police Bridge Street (Tel. 2222).
Casualty hospital Peel Hospital, Clovenfords, by Galashiels (Tel. 2295).
Post office Channel Street.
Cinema Kingsway Entertainment Centre, Market Street (Tel. 2767).
Public library Lawyers Brae.
Shopping Channel Street; Bank Street; High Street.
Event "Braw Lads" Gathering (June/July).
AA 24 hour service
Tel. Edinburgh (031) 225 8464.

Gateshead Tyne & Wear

A gleaming skyline of concrete and glass rises above the slopes of the River Tyne, where Gateshead stretches for almost 13 miles along the river bank. Little of historic Gateshead remains – much of it was destroyed by a great fire in 1854. But St Mary's Church, which was rebuilt in 1855, retains its 12th-century south doorway and north chancel wall, 15th-century roof and 17th-century carved pews.

Blaydon is part of the Gateshead borough; the song *Blaydon Races* was written by a Gateshead music-hall performer, Geordie Ridley, in 1862.

Information Tel. 773478.
Location On the A69, 1 m. S of Newcastle upon Tyne.
Parking West Street; Church Street; Wylam Street; Regent Court; Cross Keys Lane (all car parks).
District council Metropolitan Borough of Gateshead (Tel. 771011).
Population 74,600.
E-C Wed.
Police High West Street (Tel. 770234).
Casualty hospital Sheriff Hill (Tel. Low Fell 878989).
Post office West Street.
Theatre Gateshead Little Theatre, Saltwell View (Tel. 781499).
Cinema The Classic, Durham Road (Tel. 876938).
Public library Prince Consort Road.
Places to see Shipley Art Gallery, Prince Consort Road.
Shopping Trinity Square; High Street; Jackson Street; Coatsworth Road.
Trade and industry Engineering; light industries.
Sport Athletics, Gateshead International Stadium.
AA 24 hour service
Tel. Newcastle upon Tyne 610111.

Gillingham Kent

Pronounced Jillingham, this town on the River Medway contains most of Chatham's Royal Dockyard. Henry VIII founded the dockyard, and by the late 17th century it had become the finest in the country. In 1765 Nelson's *Victory* was launched from the slipways. Charles Dickens, who spent much of his childhood in Chatham, described the dockyard area in *Pickwick Papers*.

On Watling Street is a memorial to Will Adams, a local ships' pilot who in the early 17th century landed by chance in Japan and went on to become a local ruler and a founder of the country's navy.

The Royal School of Military Engineering is at Gillingham, and the Royal Engineers Museum displays relics of General Gordon, including the folding chair he used at Khartoum. (See also Chatham, p. 85.)

COAT OF ARMS *The royal emblem above the dockyard gate at Gillingham.*

Information Tel. Medway 51066.
Location On the A2, 9 m. N of Maidstone.
Parking Arden Street; Randolph Road; Mill Road; Dalton Street; James Street; Railway Street (all car parks).
District council Gillingham Borough Council (Tel. Medway 50021).
Population 93,700.
E-C Wed.
Police Birling Avenue, Rainham (Tel. Medway 34488).
Casualty hospital Windmill Road (Tel. Medway 46111).
Post office Green Street.
Public library High Street.
Places to see Royal Engineers Museum, Pasley Road.
Shopping High Street; Canterbury Street.
Trade and industry Marine engineering; market gardening.
AA 24 hour service
Tel. Maidstone 55353.

Girvan Strathclyde

The town, which grew up round a small fishing port at the mouth of the River Girvan, is now the home of one of Scotland's best-known distilleries. It is also a seaside resort looking out across the Firth of Clyde.

About 10 miles offshore is Ailsa Craig, a 1,110 ft high rock, uninhabited except for its lighthouse keepers and thousands of seabirds. It is one of the main breeding sites of the gannet. Trips can be arranged from Girvan.

Information Tel. 2056.
Location On the A77, 21 m. S of Ayr.
Parking Harbour; The Flushes; Dalrymple Street; Ainslie Park (all car parks).
District council Kyle and Carrick (Tel. Ayr 81511).
Population 7,770.

E-C Wed.
Police Montgomerie Street
(Tel. 3587).
Casualty hospital The Avenue
(Tel. 2571).
Post office Dalrymple Street.
Cinema Vogue, Dalrymple Street
(Tel. 2101).
Public library Montgomerie Street.
AA 24 hour service
Tel. Glasgow (041) 812 0101.

Glasgow see page 156

Glastonbury Somerset

Two great English legends are linked with Glastonbury. Joseph of Arimathea, the man who gave his tomb to Christ, is said to have come from the Holy Land to convert the British, choosing Glastonbury as his base. The legend says that he placed the Holy Grail – the cup used by Christ at the Last Supper – beneath a spring known as Chalice Well on Tor Hill, east of the town.

Joseph is said to have built a chapel at Glastonbury, and in about 700 an abbey was founded there which was to become one of the richest and most famous in England. It was rebuilt several times and constantly added to throughout the Middle Ages, and was barely complete when Henry VIII dissolved the monasteries in 1539.

A few gaunt remains are all that is left of the abbey, memorials to the cradle of Christianity in England.

Tor Hill is also associated with King Arthur: it is claimed to be the legendary Avalon, to which his body was taken after death.

Legend gives way to fact in Glastonbury's bustling streets, it is a market town with local industries in the sheepskin and leather trades.

Information Tel. 32954 (summer); or Wells 73026.
Location On the A39, 15 m. E of Bridgwater.
Parking Archers Way; Northload Street; Magdalene Street; George Street; Silver Street; Norbins Road; Butt Close (all car parks).
District council Mendip
(Tel. Wells 73026).
Population 6,700.
E-C Wed. **M-D** Tues.
Police (Ab) Benedict Street
(Tel. 32112 or Frome 62211).
Casualty hospital Bath Road, Wells
(Tel. Wells 73154).
Post office (Bb) High Street.
Public library (Ab) Northload Street.
Places to see Abbey ruins **(Bb)**; Abbot's Kitchen **(Aa)**; St Joseph's Chapel **(Ab)**; Gatehouse Museum **(Ab)**; Rural Life Museum, Bere Lane; Tribunal Museum **(Ab)**, High Street.
Town trails Available from the Tourist Centre, 7 Northload Street.
Shopping High Street.
Events Miracle Plays (July/Aug.).
AA 24 hour service
Tel. Bristol 298531.

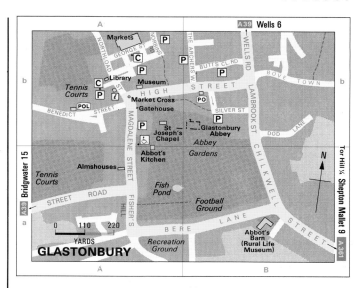

CENTREPIECE *Glastonbury's Victorian market cross stands in the town centre. The shop on the left has an early-19th-century bow window.*

Glossop Derbyshire

A winding road over the Pennines known as Snake Pass leads to Glossop, which lies below the moors of the Peak District. The north-eastern part of the town is known as Old Glossop, a largely 17th-century village centred on the parish church. There are some imposing mills in the town, relics of the 19th-century cotton boom which brought prosperity to Glossop.

North-west of the town are the remains of a Roman fort called Melandra. Excavations have revealed ramparts, a bath-house and gateway foundations. Steam locomotives can be seen working at the Dinting Railway Centre, 1 mile west of Glossop.

Information Tel. Chinley 50711.
Location On the A57, 14 m. E of Manchester.
Parking Victoria Street; Edward Street; Norfolk Square; Chapel Street (all car parks).
District council Borough of High Peak (Tel. Chinley 50711).
Population 25,300.
E-C Tues. **M-D** Fri., Sat.
Police Ellison Street (Tel. 3141).
Casualty hospital Darnton Road, Ashton-under-Lyne
(Tel. Manchester (061) 330 4321).
Post office Victoria Street.
Public library Victoria Hall.
Shopping High Street.
AA 24 hour service
Tel. 061 485 6299.

GLASGOW Strathclyde

Scotland's second "capital" in the west

Scotland's largest city was founded in 543 when St Mungo built a church in what was then called Glasgu (meaning "beloved green place"). The establishment of a cathedral in the 12th century and Scotland's second university in the 15th century brought renown to the city, and in 1454 it was made a royal burgh. Glasgow's commercial prosperity dates from the 17th century when Port Glasgow, further down the River Clyde, began importing tobacco, sugar, cotton and other goods from the Americas. During the Industrial Revolution, ship-building and heavy engineering made the city one of the great industrial centres of the world. It grew rapidly, spawning acres of cheap housing that soon became notorious slums. Today these are being cleared, and much of the old city has disappeared.

END OF THE LINE *One of the city's early tramcars is on display in the Transport Museum. It is one of the largest museums of its kind.*

The most notable building in Glasgow is the **cathedral**, the only complete medieval cathedral on the Scottish mainland. The cruciform structure with its low central tower and spire was begun in the 12th century, on or near the site of the church built by St Mungo. The choir and crypt were finished the following century, and the building was completed at the end of the 15th century. During the Reformation, the city's last Roman Catholic Archbishop, James Beaton, fled to France with most of the cathedral treasures, and the townspeople marched on the building to cleanse it of all traces of "idolatry". They ruthlessly destroyed altars, statues, vestments and the valuable library. The present furnishings are mostly 19th century, and many of the windows have been renewed with modern stained glass.

The cathedral's most outstanding feature is the fan vaulting around St Mungo's tomb in the crypt. There is much fine work in the choir, including a 15th-century stone screen. The cathedral is best viewed from the nearby Necropolis, a cemetery laid out in 1833, which contains the ornate tombs of city merchants.

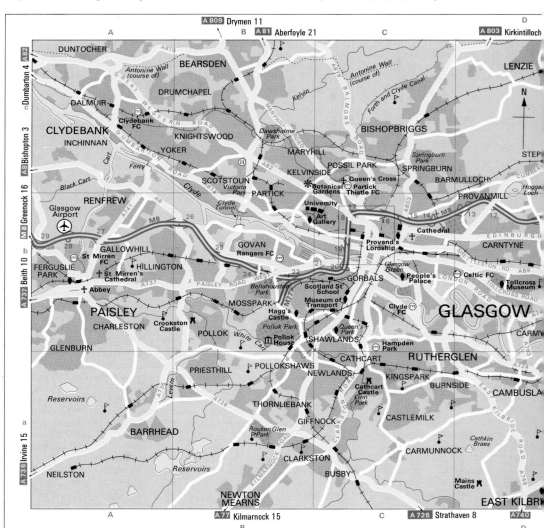

Across Cathedral Square stands **Provand's Lordship**, the oldest house in Glasgow. Built in 1471 for a priest, it is at present closed for repairs but will reopen as a museum devoted mainly to 17th and 18th-century furniture and domestic articles.

The centre of the city is **George Square**, which was laid out at the end of the 18th century and named after George III. It probably has more statues than any other square in Scotland. They include those of Queen Victoria, Prince Albert, Sir Walter Scott, Robert Burns, William Gladstone, Sir Robert Peel, James Watt, and the soldier Sir John Moore.

Seats of learning

Flanking the square are Victorian buildings, notably the **City Chambers** designed in Italian Renaissance style by William Young. The building has an imposing arcaded entrance hall, elaborately decorated with mosaics, marble and other stones. A marble staircase leads to a great banqueting hall decorated with murals showing the city's history.

In George Street, near the square, is the **University of Strathclyde**, which specialises in applied science and business studies. It was established in

1964, but its origins stem from the Andersonian Institution, founded in 1795. John Logie Baird, the pioneer of television, studied at the institution. On the central campus is a modern sculpture group inspired by the standing stones at Callanish, on the Isle of Lewis.

On the north side of nearby St George's Place the Athenaeum building is the home of the Royal Scottish Academy of Music and Drama. The inaugural meeting of the Athenaeum was held in 1847 under the chairmanship of Charles Dickens.

Hutcheson's Hospital, home of the Glasgow Educational Trust, was built by David Hamilton in 1803 in neo-Classical style with a traditional Scottish "town house" steeple. The founders of this charitable institution, which provided almshouses and schools for the city, were George and Thomas Hutcheson, 17th-century lawyer brothers. Their statues, which were sculpted by James Colquhoun in 1649, look down towards the site of the original almshouse which stood in Trongate. The narrow streets of this part of Glasgow formed the old merchants' city, and in Virginia Street is a relic of their trade, the Tobacco Exchange; the little window over the door inside its entrance is believed to have been the auctioneer's box.

Facing the west end of Ingram Street is the **Royal Exchange**, which is now occupied by Stirling's Library. The exchange was built in 1775 as a private residence by William Cunningham. It passed in 1817 to the Royal Bank and ten years later to the Royal Exchange, when the splendid portico was added to the front. The interior has a handsome coffered ceiling, and massive Corinthian columns flank the main hall.

Cross and steeples

Glasgow Cross, a centre of trade and administration in earlier days, was formerly regarded as the city centre. In it stands the **Tron Steeple**, which forms an arch over a footpath. The steeple is the only surviving part of St Mary's Church, built in 1637. The church was accidentally burned down by drunken members of the Glasgow Hellfire Club in 1793. After a meeting, they went to the church to warm themselves by the fire, which they built up until it got out of control.

The nearby 126 ft high **Tolbooth Steeple** is the only remnant of the tolbooth erected in 1626. It is one of only three crowned steeples in Scotland. Carved strapwork containing emblems of St Mungo and royalty decorates the lintels. The prison which once stood here was described by Sir Walter Scott in *Rob Roy*. The Mercat Cross next to the steeple is a 1929 replica of the medieval original.

Southward lies the **Merchants' Steeple**, built into the old Fish Market building of 1872. The steeple, which has charming details in Gothic and Renaissance style, rises in four

diminishing square towers to 164 ft, and is all that remains of the old Merchants' House built in 1651-9.

Also in this area of the city is Glasgow Green, where Bonnie Prince Charlie reviewed his troops in 1745 after their retreat from England. In the main carriageway of the green stands the **People's Palace**, opened in 1898; this is a museum that records the history and life of the city. Also on the green is a 144 ft high monument to Lord Nelson, erected in 1806.

The former carpet factory adjoining the green is a late-19th-century reproduction in colourful bricks and tiles of the Doge's Palace in Venice.

Old university

In 1451 William Turnbull, Bishop of Glasgow, was authorised by Pope Nicholas V to found a university in the city. At first there was only one faculty – arts – and lectures were held in the cathedral crypt and a neighbouring monastery. In the 17th century the university moved to new buildings in the High Street. These became too small, and in 1870 came a second move to the present site, Sir George Gilbert Scott's pinnacled Gothic buildings on **Gilmorehill**. The tower of the main building dominates the site and provides a magnificent view of the city and surrounding hills.

The Lion and Unicorn balustrade on the stone staircase opposite the Principal's Lodging is a relic of the old High Street colleges, as is the stonework of the lodge gateway. The imposing Bute Hall, which is used for graduation and other university ceremonies, was added in 1882.

WITH CHILDREN IN MIND

The 16th-century Hagg's Castle is now a children's museum. It shows what life was like during the last 400 years, with displays and practical demonstrations. There is a Victorian nursery equipped with toys.

GLASGOW Route Map

0   1   2

MILES

E

A80 — M80 — Stirling 18

MUIRHEAD

GARTCOSH

Provan Hall NTS

EASTERHOUSE

COATBRIDGE

A89 — Airdrie 3

A8 — Edinburgh 35 — b

North Calder

Calderpark

TANNOCHSIDE

A721 — Coatbridge — a

UDDINGSTON

A725

BOTHWELL

Livingstone Memorial

BLANTYRE

Calder

Hamilton Academicals FC

M74 — Carlisle 84 / Lanark 17 — A72

HAMILTON

E

The splendid **Hunterian Museum** forms part of the university, to which it was bequeathed by Doctor William Hunter in 1783. It was opened in 1807 as the city's first museum. Its collections include illuminated manuscripts, notably the York Psalter of about 1175; early printed books; and Roman relics from the Antonine Wall. It also has one of Britain's largest collections of coins.

The **Hunterian Art Gallery** contains paintings by Rembrandt, Rubens, Chardin and Whistler, and an interior reconstruction of a Charles Rennie Mackintosh house.

Across the River Kelvin from the university, in Kelvingrove Park, the **Glasgow City Art Gallery and Museum** houses the finest municipal collection of British and European paintings in Britain, enriched in 1944 by the Burrell Collection. Works on display include Giorgione's *The Adulteress Brought Before Christ*, Rembrandt's *Man in Armour*, Salvador Dali's *Christ of St John of the Cross*, and some outstanding examples of French Impressionist, Post-Impressionist, and Dutch and modern Scottish schools. There is much fine sculpture, with pottery, porcelain, silverware, costumes and tapestry. There is also a collection of arms and armour that includes the earliest complete suit of armour to be seen in Britain, made in Milan in the 15th century.

Spanish paintings

The city has several other fine museums. Three miles south-west of the city centre is **Pollok House**, designed by William Adam and completed in 1752. Standing in extensive wooded parklands, where Highland cattle graze, it contains one of the best collections of Spanish paintings in Britain, including works by Goya, El Greco and Murillo. There are also six paintings by William Blake, a fine panel by Luca Signorelli and works from other schools. The house also contains fine silver, porcelain, glass and furniture.

The **Transport Museum** in Albert Drive houses collections of trams, motor cars, horsedrawn vehicles, bicycles, historic Scottish locomotives, and a collection of model ships.

The **Mitchell Library**, founded in 1874, is the largest public reference library in Scotland. It has nearly a million volumes, and valuable collections which include books on Robert Burns, Scottish poetry, Celtic literature and the history of the city.

Glasgow's other outstanding buildings include works by two of the city's finest architects of recent times, Alexander "Greek" Thomson (1817-75) and Charles Rennie Mackintosh (1868-1928). Thomson was known as "Greek" because of his many designs in the classical Grecian style. His **St Vincent Street Church** (1859) has magnificent Ionic porticoes, an elaborate tower that is a local landmark, and a spacious interior with two tiers of columns decorated in red, blue, white and gold. Other fine examples of his work are **Great Western Terrace** (1870), and the **Egyptian Halls** in Union Street. Another outstanding building in Ionic style, the **Caledonia Road Church** (1857), has been a ruin since a fire in 1965.

Mackintosh's masterpiece is the **Glasgow School of Art**, built be-

GEORGE SQUARE *The grey stones of the City Chambers fail to dull the charm of the square, bright with lawns and flower beds. The square is noted for its statues, which include Queen Victoria, Prince Albert and James Watt.*

tween 1897 and 1909 after he had won a competition to design it. His other surviving works in the city include **Scotland Street School** (1904), the *Daily Record* building (1901), **Martyrs Primary School** (1895) and **Queen's Cross Church** (1897).

For such a built-up area, Glasgow has a surprisingly large number of fine open spaces. **Rouken Glen** is nearly 230 acres, much of it woodland, with a burn forming a spectacular waterfall near the boating pond. The glen contains much wildlife, and foxes can be regularly seen in daylight.

Kelvingrove Park, on the banks of the Kelvin, was laid out by Sir Joseph Paxton, designer of London's Crystal Palace. It was twice used for international exhibitions (1888 and 1901).

The **Botanic Gardens**, also beside the River Kelvin, were founded in 1817. They contain outstanding collections of orchids and begonias, and the Kibble Palace, originally used for concerts and meetings, has a collection of rare tree ferns.

Ivy-clad ruins

Linn Park includes the grounds of 14th-century Cathcart Castle, now demolished. There is a children's zoo in the park.

FLOWING BOWL *An 18th-century Delft punchbowl, made for the Saracen's Head Inn, bears the Glasgow arms.*

Victoria Park has a grove of fossil tree stumps discovered in 1887. The trees stand in the position in which they grew 230 million years ago.

Bellahouston Park was the setting for the Empire Exhibition of 1938, and a cairn erected by visiting clans and societies is still there. The park contains a sunken garden and an athletics centre.

Queen's Park is named after Mary, Queen of Scots, whose reign ended when she lost the Battle of Langside there in 1568. A memorial outside the park marks the battle site. Today the park is noted for its floral displays and superb views. South-east of the park is **Hampden Park** football ground which, with a possible capacity of 135,000, is Britain's biggest football stadium. However, crowd capacity is now limited to 88,000 for safety. The "Hampden roar", at Scottish internationals and local-derby encounters between two of Glasgow's teams, Rangers and Celtic, can be heard miles away.

There are ten nature trails – through Kelvingrove, Linn, Pollok, Rosshall, Springburn, Tollcross and Dawsholm parks, Rouken Glen, Cathkin Braes and Hogganfield Loch Island, which has a nature reserve.

Below the streets

Glasgow's modernised underground was reopened by the Queen in 1979 and is one of the most modern in the world. Trains run regularly from 6.30 a.m. until 10.45 p.m.

Glasgow is the home of two fine orchestras, the Scottish National Orchestra, which gives Saturday-night concerts at the City Hall, and the BBC Scottish Symphony Orchestra. The city is also the home of Scotland's only opera house, the **Theatre Royal**.

A strange relic of the city's past is the disused tunnel under the Clyde, between Finnieston on the north bank and Mavisbank Quay on the other. Opened in 1895, it was part of the Harbour Tunnel, which also included two vehicle passages. The six entrances were circular brick towers, still standing.

Glasgow's central position in the Clyde valley, surrounded by developing coalfields and with deep-water

docks 20 miles from the sea, led to its rapid development in the Industrial Revolution. And in this, Glasgow men played their part.

James Watt (1736-1819) developed the steam engine after studying at the university. James Neilson (1792-1851) created the hot-air blast that transformed smelting, and George Burns (1795-1890) helped found the Cunard shipping line.

Several other famous men were connected with the city. Adam Smith (1723-90), founder of economics, wrote *Wealth of Nations* while he was Professor of Moral Philosophy. The writer James Boswell (1740-95) was at the Old College, and explorer David Livingstone (1813-73) studied medicine at the university. The hero of Corunna, Lieutenant-General Sir John Moore (1761-1809), was born in Glasgow. So was the discoverer of antiseptics, Joseph Lister (1786-1869).

It is many years since salmon were caught in the Clyde, but two appear as supporters of the city's coat of arms. Each fish has a ring in its mouth, and they recall an old legend of adultery. It is said that the Queen of Strathclyde was given a ring as a present from her husband – but she gave it to her lover.

The king found the lover wearing the ring as he slept beside the river. He took the ring and threw it in the

---

A PIONEER OF STYLE

Charles Rennie Mackintosh's buildings were created at the turn of the century, and his combination of art-nouveau curves and sturdy angularity contrasted sharply with the ornate Victorian style of the day.

When he designed a house he included all its fittings and furniture, right down to the clocks and cutlery. He had a preference for black-and-white interiors, as can be seen in his School of Art building.

One man's work – Mackintosh's designs included part of the Glasgow Herald building, high-backed chairs and the door of the Willow Tea Room.

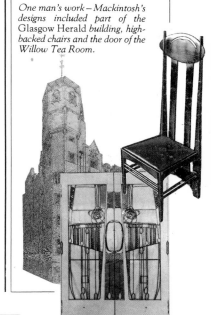

---

water. Then he asked his wife to show it to him. The queen prayed to St Mungo, and at once her servants found the ring . . . in the mouth of a salmon they caught in the river. The king had to accept her pleas of innocence.

Information Tel. Glasgow (041) 221 7371/2 and 6136/7.
Location On the M8, 45 m. W of Edinburgh.
Parking Oswald Street; Cambridge Street; Waterloo Street; Mitchell Street; Port Dundas Road; Bath Street; Shuttle Street; North Frederick Street; Hope Street (2); North Hanover Street; Cadogan Street; Montrose Street; Elmbank Cross; Bishop Street; Albion Street; Howard Street (3); McAlpine Street (all car parks).

District council City of Glasgow (Tel. 041 221 9600).
Population 771,440.
E-C Tues. or Sat. **M-D** Sat., Sun.
Police Central Station, Jocelyn Square (Tel. 041 552 2474); Strathclyde Regional **(Ab)**, Pitt Street (041 204 2626).
Casualty hospital Royal Infirmary, Castle Street (Tel. 041 552 3535).
Post office (Cb) George Square.
Theatres Theatre Royal **(Bc)**, Hope Street (Tel. 041 332 1234); Apollo Centre **(Bb)**, Renfield Street (041 332 9221); Citizens' Theatre, 119 Gorbals Street (041 429 0022); King's Theatre **(Ab)**, Bath Street (041 248 5153); Pavilion Theatre **(Bb)**, Renfield Street (041 332 0478); Mitchell Theatre **(Ab)**, Granville Street (041 248 5153); Glasgow Theatre Club, The

Tron, 50 Parnie Street (041 552 4267).
Cinemas ABC Film Centre **(Ac)**, Sauchiehall Street (Tel. 041 332 1592/9513); Classic Grand **(Ba)**, 18 Jamaica Street (041 248 4620); Curzon Continental **(Ac)**, Sauchiehall Street (041 332 1298); Glasgow Film Theatre **(Bc)**, 12 Rose Street (041 332 6535); Scala **(Bb)**, 155 Sauchiehall Street (041 332 1228); Odeon Film Centre **(Bb)**, 56 Renfield Street (041 332 8701); Regent **(Bb)**, 72 Renfield Street (041 332 3303).

RIVER OF STEEL *Shipyards line the River Clyde, snaking its way towards the heart of the city and the rolling hills of the Clyde Valley beyond.*

Public library Stirling's Library **(Cb)**, Queen Street.

Places to see Art Gallery and Museum **(RBb)**, Kelvingrove Park; City Chambers **(Cb)**, George Square; Museum of the Royal Highland Fusiliers **(Ac)**, Sauchiehall Street; People's Palace **(RCb)**, Glasgow Green; Provands Lordship **(RCb)**, Castle Street; Pollok House **(RBb)**, Pollokshaws Road; Transport Museum **(RCb)**, Albert Drive; Provan Hall **(RDb)**, Auchinlea Road; Hunterian Museum and Art Gallery, Glasgow University; Hagg's Castle **(RBb)**, St Andrews Drive; Crookston Castle **(RBb)**, Brockburn Road.

Shopping Argyle Street; Jamaica Street; Trongate; High Street; Queen Street; Buchanan Street; Argyll Arcade; Union Street; Renfield Street; Sauchiehall Street; Renfrew Street.

Events Glasgow Highland Gathering (May); Horse Show and Country Fair (June); Folk Festival (July).

Sport Scottish League football: Celtic FC **(RDb)**, Celtic Park; Rangers FC **(RBb)**, Ibrox Park; Queen's Park FC **(RCb)**, Hampden Park; Partick Thistle FC **(RCc)**, Firhill Park.

AA 24 hour service
Tel. 041 812 0101.

THE BURRELL COLLECTION

The Dictionary of National Biography describes Sir William Burrell (1861-1958) as an art collector, a fitting title for a man who sold a thriving shipping company in order to devote half his life to art. Burrell began collecting in the 1880s, and in 1917 bought Hutton Castle near Berwick-upon-Tweed to house his treasures. In 1944 he gave his collection to Glasgow, the city of his birth, and £450,000 for the building of a museum.

The Burrell Collection contains some 8,000 items, including French paintings, medieval tapestries and English stained glass. It is estimated to be worth about £40 million. Many items are on loan to museums, but when the new museum opens in Pollok Park it will bring the collection under one roof.

The Rehearsal, *by Degas, was one of Sir William Burrell's earliest acquisitions.*

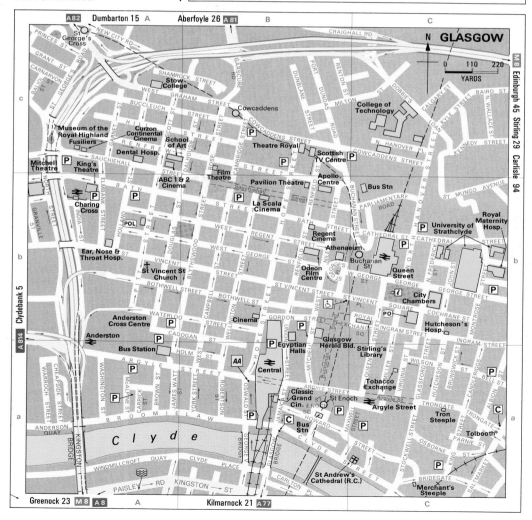

Gloucester Gloucestershire

In Roman times Gloucester was a fortified port on the River Severn, called Glevum. It was built for the invasion of Wales during the 1st century AD. Glevum's gates lie roughly beneath Northgate, Southgate, Westgate and Eastgate Streets. Except for a small part of the Roman wall, the only visible remains of the Roman settlement – coins, pottery, and other objects – are in the City Museum. This also contains one of the finest examples of Celtic bronze craftsmanship in Britain – the Birdlip Mirror, made about AD 25.

The glory of the city is its cathedral, one of the most beautiful buildings in Britain. Its Norman core, built between 1089 and 1260, has a massive nave lined with piers which support a triforium and clerestory in Romanesque style. The transepts and choir, remodelled in the mid-14th century to house the tomb of Edward II, are among the earliest examples of Perpendicular architecture. The choir is dominated by the east window, which depicts the Coronation of the Virgin. It is a memorial to those who died at the Battle of Crécy in 1346. It is the largest stained-glass window in Britain, measuring 72×38 ft.

The 14th-century cloisters are perhaps the most perfect in Britain, mainly because of the exquisite fan tracery of the roof.

After the cathedral crypt, the oldest building in Gloucester is St Oswald's Priory. An arch incorporated in its north nave arcade may date from the 10th century.

The Church of St Mary de Crypt is Norman in origin, with 15th-century additions and several 17th and 18th-century monuments.

Bishop Hooper's Lodging in Westgate Street is a 15th–16th-century timber-framed house in which the bishop, who was a Protestant, is supposed to have spent the night before his martyrdom in 1555.

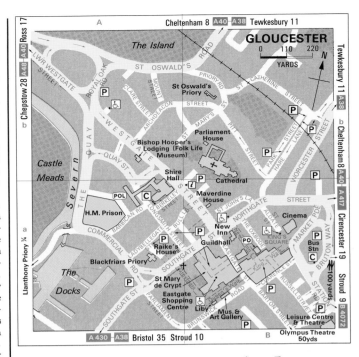

Gloucester's port was overtaken by Bristol in the Middle Ages. To revive the city's fortunes, artificial docks and a canal connecting them with the mouth of the Severn were begun in the late 18th century and opened in 1827. Nine of the original warehouses are still in use, and the canal now accommodates ships of nearly 1,000 tons.

Information Tel. 421188.
Location On the A40, 8 m. SW of Cheltenham.
Parking Nettleton Road; Northgate Street; St Michael's Square; Hare Lane; Bruton Way; Worcester Street; St Catherine Street; Royal Oak Road (all car parks).
District council City of Gloucester (Tel. 22232).
Population 92,100.

MURDERED KING *Edward II was slain in 1327 at Berkeley Castle. His tomb is in Gloucester Cathedral.*

E-C None. **M-D** Mon., Thur., Sat.
Police (Aa) Bearland (Tel. 21201/3).
Casualty hospital Royal, Great Western Road (Tel. 28555).
Post office (Ba) King's Square.
Theatres Cambridge Theatre **(Ba)**, Station Road (Tel. 36498); Olympus, Kingsbarton Street (25917).
Cinema ABC 1, 2 and 3 **(Ba)**, St Aldate Street (Tel. 22399).
Public library (Ba) Brunswick Road.
Places to see Blackfriars Priory **(Aa)**, Blackfriars; City Museum and Art Gallery **(Ba)**, Brunswick Road; Bishop Hooper's Lodging; Folk Life Museum **(Ab)**, Westgate Street; Llanthony Priory, Hempsted Lane; Raikes' House **(Aa)**, Southgate Street; Gloucestershire Regimental Museum, Custom House, Commercial Road.
Town trails Available from Information Centre, College Street.
Shopping Northgate Street; King's Square; Worcester Street; Westgate Street; Southgate Street; Eastgate Street; The Oxbode; St Aldate Street; Eastgate and King's Walk Shopping Centres.
Events Cheese Rolling Ceremony (May); Festival (July); Skiing Championships (May, Oct.).
AA 24 hour service Tel. 23278.

GLOUCESTER'S GLORY *The Normans built the original abbey church at Gloucester, and medieval craftsmen set about beautifying it in the 13th century. The magnificent pinnacled tower was added in the 15th century.*

OCTAGON *Arcades beneath Godalming's eight-sided Old Town Hall were once used by market stallholders.*

Godalming Surrey

Several old coaching inns in Godalming's High Street are reminders that the town was once a staging point on the London to Portsmouth road. The King's Arms Royal Hotel bears the date 1753, but is older – Peter the Great of Russia dined there in 1689.

The Old Town Hall in the High Street is now used as a museum of local history. It was built in 1814 and, in spite of its name, it is more recent than most of the surrounding buildings, which date from the 16th to 18th centuries.

Charterhouse School is just outside the town. It was founded in London in 1611, and moved to Godalming in 1872. The buildings are dominated by the 150 ft Founder's Tower.

Winkworth Arboretum, 3 miles south-east, has a collection of rare trees.

Information Tel. 4104.
Location On the A3100, 4 m. S of Guildford.
Parking Queen Street; Crown Court; The Burys; Mint Street; Mead Row (all car parks).
District council Waverley (Tel. 4104).
Population 18,200.
E-C Wed. **M-D** Fri.
Police The Wharf (Tel. 4343).
Casualty hospital New Royal Surrey County, Gill Avenue, Egerton Road, Guildford (Tel. Guildford 71122).
Post office High Street.
Public library Bridge Street.
Places to see Museum, Old Town Hall, High Street; Charterhouse School.
Town trails Available from Museum.
Shopping High Street.
AA 24 hour service Tel. Guildford 72841.

Goole Humberside

Ships using the busy port of Goole travel inland 50 miles from the North Sea. The port is on the Yorkshire Ouse, and developed when the Aire and Calder Canal was opened in 1826, linking it with Knottingley and the Yorkshire coalfields.

The town grew around its docks, and the only building earlier than 1820 is the Georgian Lowther Hotel.

Information Tel. 2187.
Location On the A161, 20 m. NE of Doncaster.
Parking Boothferry Road; Church Street; Aire Street; Estcourt Street; Gordon Street (all car parks).
District council Boothferry (Tel. 5141).
Population 17,100.
E-C Thur.
M-D Wed., Fri. and Sat.
Police Estcourt Terrace (Tel. 2131).
Casualty hospital Bartholomew, Bartholomew Avenue (Tel. 4121).
Post office Victoria Street.
Public library Market Square.
Places to see Goole Museum.
Shopping Boothferry Road; Pasture Road.
Sport Rugby Union, Goole RUFC, Murham Avenue.
AA 24 hour service Tel. York 27698.

Gosport Hampshire

Portsmouth Harbour and the waters of Spithead and the Solent flank Gosport. The town has many naval establishments, including HMS *Alliance*, the Royal Navy Submarine Museum, and HMS *Dolphin*, the submariners' school on Haslar Lake. Part of the school is in Fort Blockhouse, on a site fortified since the 15th century. There are shingle bathing beaches at Stokes Bay and at Lee-on-the-Solent, 3 miles west of Gosport town centre.

Information Tel. 84242.
Location On the A32, 13 m. W of Portsmouth.
Parking Clarence Road; Fort Road; South Street; Mumby Road; Stokes Bay Road; Church Path; Haslar Road; Haslar Sea Wall; Jamaica Place; White's Place; Beach Road; Green Lane (all car parks).
District council Borough of Gosport (Tel. 84242).
Population 77,300.
E-C Wed.
M-D Tues.
Police South Street (Tel. 84666).
Casualty hospital Royal Naval Hospital, Haslar Road (Tel. 84255).
Post office High Street.
Cinema Ritz Cinema, Walpole Road (Tel. 83822).
Public library High Street.
Places to see Gosport Museum, Walpole Road; HMS *Alliance*; HMS *Dolphin*; Fort Brockhurst.
Shopping High Street; Forton Road; Stoke Road; Brockhurst Road.
AA 24 hour service Tel. Southampton 36811.

Grangemouth Central

Oil refineries created Grangemouth long before the first great finds of the North Sea made this a major industry in Scotland. Refining began in 1924, and the growth of petrol and chemical processing has doubled the popu-lation since then. North Sea oil has brought another boom.

Grangemouth's strategic position on the Firth of Forth, halfway between Glasgow and Edinburgh, has made it the busiest port on Scotland's east coast.

Information Tel. Airth 422 (summer).
Location On the A904, 24 m. W of Edinburgh.
Parking Kersiebank Avenue; Abbotsgrange Road; Talbot Street; Union Road (all car parks).
District council Falkirk (Tel. Falkirk 24911).
Population 21,600.
E-C Wed.
Police Bo'ness Road (Tel. 482232).
Casualty hospital Royal Infirmary, Majors Loan, Falkirk (Tel. Falkirk 24000).
Post office York Square.
Public library Bo'ness Road.
Places to see Grangemouth Museum.
Shopping York Square; La Porte Precinct; Charlotte Dundas Court.
AA 24 hour service Tel. Edinburgh (031) 225 8464.

Grange-over-Sands
Cumbria

A year-round mild climate was the basis of the transformation of this one-time fishing village into a Victorian seaside resort. The town is backed by woodland and overlooks the expanse of Morecambe Bay. A mile-long promenade curves around the shore, fringed by beautiful gardens with rare trees and shrubs. The Lakeland Rose Show is held in nearby Cark-in-Cartmel each July.

At Lindale-in-Cartmel, about 2 miles north, is an iron monument to the 18th-century ironmaster John Wilkinson, who spent his youth in the district and went on to cast the pieces for the world's first iron bridge – at Ironbridge, Shropshire.

Cartmel Priory, to the east of Grange, was founded in 1188 and escaped destruction at the time of the Dissolution of the Monasteries. It has magnificent stained glass.

Information Tel. 4331.
Location On the B5277, 14 m. SW of Kendal.
Parking Hampsfell Road; Berners Close; Kents Bank Road; Main Street (all car parks).
District council South Lakeland (Tel. Kendal 24007).
Population 3,650.
E-C Thur.
Police Hampsfell Road (Tel. 2242).
Casualty hospital North Lonsdale, School Street, Barrow-in-Furness (Tel. Barrow-in-Furness 24201).
Post office Main Street.
Public library Grange Fell Road.
Places to see Cartmel Priory, 2 m. E.
Shopping Main Street; Kents Bank Road.
AA 24 hour service Tel. Carlisle 24274.

Grantham Lincolnshire

North from London, south from York, traffic has surged through Grantham for centuries. Coaching inns played a vital part in the development of the town. The Angel and Royal in the High Street is one of the oldest in Britain. It stands on the site of an even older inn where King John held court in 1213. The George, near by, which dates from the 18th century, was described by Charles Dickens in *Nicholas Nickleby*.

One of the finest buildings in the town is the 15th-century grammar school, now King's School. Its classrooms produced a towering genius in Sir Isaac Newton. He carved his name on a window-ledge where it can still be seen.

It was at his parents' home in nearby Woolsthorpe that Newton formulated his theory of gravity, which gave rise to the legend of the apple falling in the orchard. A bronze statue of Newton stands in front of Grantham's Guildhall.

Near the grammar school stands the dominating feature of the town, the 13th-century Church of St Wulfram. Its massive tower and richly decorated spire climb 281 ft towards the sky. Above the south porch is a room containing a chained library, given to the church by a local rector in 1598.

One of its 83 volumes is dated 1472.

In the centre of Grantham are 25 acres of open gardens and parkland surrounding Grantham House, which is now owned by the National Trust. This fine house was built in the late 14th century, but it was considerably enlarged and altered in the 16th and 18th centuries.

Information Tel. 66444 (summer).
Location On the A607, 25 m. S of Lincoln.
Parking Watergate; Union Street; Conduit Lane; Greenwood's Row; Dysart Road; Welham Street (all car parks).
District council South Kesteven (Tel. 5591).
Population 30,100.
E-C Wed. **M-D** Sat.
Police (Ba) Stonebridge Road (Tel. 2501).
Casualty hospital Grantham and Kesteven General, Manthorpe Road (Tel. 5232).
Post office (Ba) St Peter's Hill.
Public library (Ba) St Peter's Hill.
Places to see Museum **(Ba)**, St Peter's Hill; Grantham House **(Bb)**.
Shopping High Street; Watergate; Westgate.
Trade and industry Engineering.
AA 24 hour service
Tel. Nottingham 787751.

QUIET DIGNITY *A by-pass has brought peace to Grantham's streets.*

LIVING SIGN *A busy hive of bees marks Grantham's Beehive Inn.*

Grantown-on-Spey
Highland

A local landowner, Sir James Grant, laid out Grantown on the wooded banks of the River Spey in 1776. He planned it as a centre of the Highland linen industry, but it has become one of Scotland's leading inland holiday resorts. It is a town of broad streets, and most of its older buildings are of granite. The Old Spey Bridge, now closed to traffic, was built in 1750 to carry a military road.

The Spey and its tributary, the Dulnain, are world-renowned salmon and trout streams, and the slopes of the Cairngorm Mountains outside the town draw skiers and mountaineers from all over Britain.

In winter, Grantown is the setting for bonspiels, or curling tournaments. Castle Roy, 4 miles to the south, is now a ruin. It was built in the 13th century.

Information Tel. 2773.
Location On the A95, 27 m. NE of Kingussie.
Parking High Street (two car parks); The Square; Church Lane; Burnfield Avenue.
District council Badenoch and Strathspey (Tel. Kingussie 555).
Population 1,870.
E-C Thur.
Police Castle Road (Tel. 2922).
Casualty hospital Ian Charles Hospital, Castle Road (Tel. 2528).
Post office High Street.
Public library High Street.
Places to see Castle Roy, 4 m. S.
Shopping High Street.
AA 24 hour service
Tel. Aberdeen 51231.

Gravesend Kent

The half-mile-wide reach of the Thames at Gravesend is reputed to be the busiest waterway in the world. Thousands of ships are logged through this gateway to London yearly.

The main office of the Customs and Excise, the Port of London's Health Authority, and the Trinity House pilot's base are all at Gravesend.

Information Tel. 64422.
Location On the A226, 15 m. NW of Maidstone.
Parking Rathmore Road; West Street; Horn Yard; The Market; Bentley Street; Stuart Road; Milton

INDIAN PRINCESS *In 1608 a 13-year-old Red Indian princess, Pocahontas, saved a Virginian colonist from execution by her father's braves. She later visited James I. She died in a boat off Gravesend, and her statue stands near St George's Church where she is buried.*

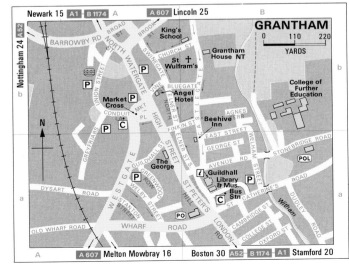

GRANTHAM

Newark 15 A1 B 1174 A | A 607 Lincoln 25 | B

0 110 220 YARDS

King's School
Grantham House NT
St Wulfram's
College of Further Education
Angel Hotel
Market Cross
Beehive Inn
The George
Guildhall Library & Mus.
Bus Stn
PO

Nottingham 24 A52
BARROWBY RD
BROAD ST
BROOK ST
NORTH STREET
SWINEGATE
CHURCH ST
WATERGATE
UNION STREET
CONDUIT
HIGH STREET
VINE ST
BLUEGATE
ELMER STREET
FINKIN ST
AGNES
AVENUE RD
EAST STREET
GEORGE ST
WELHAM STREET
STONEBRIDGE ROAD
POL
GREYFRIARS
GUILDHALL STREET
WESTGATE
DYSART ROAD
WELBY STREET
GREENWOOD
STANTON STREET
ST PETER'S HILL
ST CATHERINE'S ROAD
DUDLEY ROAD
Witham
OLD WHARF ROAD
WHARF ROAD
LONDON RD
CAMBRIDGE ST
OXFORD ST
COLLEGE ST

A 607 Melton Mowbray 16 | Boston 30 A52 B 1174 A1 Stamford 20

Place; Lord Street; Anglesea Centre;
Parrock Street (all car parks).
District council Borough of
Gravesham (Tel. 64422).
Population 53,000.
E-C Wed. **M-D** Sat.
Police Windmill Street (Tel. 64346).
Casualty hospital West Hill,
Dartford (Tel. Dartford 23223).
Post office Milton Road.
Theatre Woodville Halls, Civic
Centre (Tel. 534244).
Cinema ABC 1, 2 and 3, King Street
(Tel. 52470).
Public library Windmill Street.
Shopping High Street; Anglesea
Centre; King Street; Milton Road;
Queen Street; Windmill Street.
AA 24 hour service
Tel. Maidstone 55353.

Great Yarmouth
see page 166

Greenock Strathclyde
James Watt, the pioneer of the steam
engine, was born in Greenock in
1736 – so, too, was the pirate Captain
Kidd, in 1645. The town's Municipal
Buildings, opened in 1886, are in the
Classical style and are surmounted by
a 245 ft high tower.

Information Tel. 24400.
Location On the A8, 23 m. NW of
Glasgow.
Parking Hunter Place; Cathcart
Street (2); Station Avenue; George
Square; Bruce Street; Kilblain Street;
Sir Michael Street (all car parks).
District council Inverclyde
(Tel. 24400).
Population 59,200.
E-C Wed.
Police Rue End Street (Tel. 24444).
Casualty hospital Inverclyde Royal,
Larkfield Road (Tel. 33777).
Post office Cathcart Street.
Theatre Arts Guild, Campbell Street
(Tel. 23038).
Cinema ABC 1, 2 & 3, West
Blackhall Street (Tel. 23552).
Public library Clyde Square.
Places to see McLean Museum and
Art Gallery, Union Street.
Shopping Hamilton Way; Hamilton
Gate; West Blackhall Street;
Cathcart Street.
Sport Scottish League football,
Morton FAC, Cappielow Park.
AA 24 hour service
Tel. Glasgow (041) 812 0101.

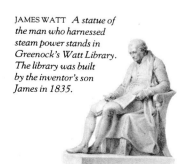
JAMES WATT *A statue of
the man who harnessed
steam power stands in
Greenock's Watt Library.
The library was built
by the inventor's son
James in 1835.*

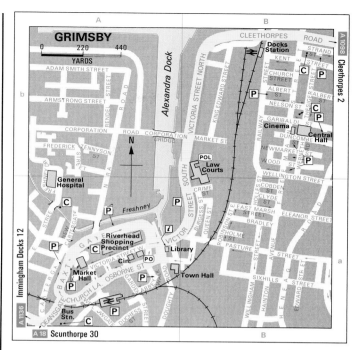

Greenwich see London

Grimsby Humberside
A thousand years ago a Danish fisherman named Grim landed on the south
shore of the Humber estuary, built
houses with his ship's timbers and
began selling fish to the locals.

That was the beginning of Grimsby. Today around 238 fishing vessels
sail from its docks, and up to 150,000
tons of fish pass through its markets
each year.

Flemish ships were landing herrings
at Grimsby early in the 15th century,
and sailing smacks from the town
fished on the rich grounds off Iceland. But in the 16th century the
harbour silted up and Grimsby went
into decline.

Lincolnshire landowners came to
the rescue in the 18th century and
formed the Grimsby Haven Company; and in 1801 the old dock was
re-opened. Forty-seven years later the
Manchester, Sheffield and Lincolnshire railway reached the town, providing a fast link with the country's
major cities.

Although Grimsby received its first
charter from King John in 1201, most
of the town behind the docks dates
from the 19th century. The Town
Hall of 1863 dominates Town Hall
Square.

Information Tel. 53123.
Location On the A18, 22 m. SE of
Hull.
Parking Albion Street; Baxtergate;
Cartergate; Abbey Walk; Duchess
Street; Market Hall; Kent Street;
Nelson Street; Orwell Street;
Victoria Street; Wellington Terrace;
Werneth Road (all car parks).
District council Borough of Great
Grimsby (Tel. 59161).
Population 92,100.

SEA ROVERS *Grimsby's tough Seine-net
vessels which brave the stormy North
Sea.*

E-C Thur. **M-D** Tues., Fri. and Sat.
Police (Bb) Victoria Street
(Tel. 59171).
Casualty hospital General, Central
Parade (Tel. 59901).
Post office (Aa) Victoria Street.
Cinemas Focus, Victoria Street
(Tel. 42576); ABC **(Bb)**, Freeman
Street (42878); Whitgift Film
Theatre, Crosland Road (53123).
Public library (Aa) Town Hall
Square.
Places to see Dock Tower; Fish
Docks; Welholme Galleries,
Welholme Road.
Shopping Victoria Street; Riverhead
Centre; Freeman Street; Cleethorpe
Road.
Trade and industry Fishing; food
processing; chemicals; light
engineering; plastics.
Sport FA League football, Grimsby
Town FC, Blundell Park,
Cleethorpes.
AA 24 hour service
Tel. Hull 28580.

GREAT YARMOUTH Norfolk

The golden fringe of the Norfolk Broads

Where the River Yare flows out of Breydon Water it meets the River Bure and turns south, leaving a 3 mile long spit of land between the river and the North Sea. Great Yarmouth grew on this spit, facing inwards towards the river which formed a safe, natural anchorage. As a port it flourished for more than 1,000 years. Then, in the 19th century, when the Victorians discovered the delights of the seaside, Great Yarmouth extended its boundaries to take in the miles of golden sand on the seaward side of the spit, and began to cater for holidaymakers. It is now one of Britain's major seaside resorts.

NELSON MEMORIAL *Great Yarmouth's column is 144 ft high – 41 ft less than the one in London.*

The old part of Great Yarmouth is linked to the mainland by the Haven Bridge. South of the bridge the quay presents one of the finest waterfronts in England, with a mixture of buildings – Tudor, Georgian and Victorian – that were once the homes of rich merchants. Close to the bridge is the 19th-century Gothic **Town Hall.** Number 4 South Quay, **Elizabethan House,** contains a museum of domestic life in the 19th century.

Behind South Quay are narrow courts and alleys called **The Rows.** Their alignment has remained unaltered since medieval times, and they form the basis of old Yarmouth's grid pattern of streets. There were originally 145 Rows, running east to west with three intersecting streets running north to south. The area was badly damaged during air-raids in the Second World War, but several Rows remain and some of the older buildings have been restored. The **Old Merchants' House** in Row 117 is a 17th-century dwelling and has a display of local woodwork and metalwork from the 17th to 19th centuries. Numbers 6, 7 and 8 in Row 111 are typical small houses of the 17th century. The **Tolhouse,** in Tolhouse Street, dates from the late 13th century and is said to be the oldest civic building in Britain. Its dungeons are open to the public and there is a museum of local history.

Ancient town walls

The quay to the north of Haven Bridge runs to the north-west tower of the town walls. The walls were built in the late 13th century and protected the town on its northern, eastern and southern sides. The south-east tower

ALL THE FUN OF THE FAIR *As dusk falls, the lights of Great Yarmouth's pleasure beach paint multi-coloured patterns against the sky.*

GIRL WHO LOVED HORSES
Anna Sewell (1820-78), the author of *Black Beauty*, was born in a 17th-century house in Church Plain. It is now a museum.

has also survived, and several parts of the wall are well preserved.

Great Yarmouth's market place is one of the largest in England, and twice weekly is crammed with stalls selling a variety of merchandise. At the north-east corner is the **Fishermen's Hospital,** founded in 1702.

The parish church of St Nicholas dates from the 12th century, but was gutted by fire during the Second World War. It has been restored with a neo-Gothic interior, and the Norman tower and Early English west end have been preserved. At the opposite end of the market place, and beyond the town centre, is St George's Church, built in 1713. It is now used as an arts centre for exhibitions and concerts.

Two piers

Yarmouth's 5 miles of sandy beach is the town's major attraction for holidaymakers, and organised entertainment of every kind can be found. There are two piers – the Wellington and Britannia – each with a theatre. Gardens, sports and leisure centre, ornamental boating-lakes and a vast pleasure beach are among the many attractions along the length of the promenade. The **Maritime Museum** for East Anglia on Marine Parade is an exhibition of shipping, ship models, life-saving apparatus and general marine equipment.

At the southern end of the town there is a monument to Lord Nelson. It was erected in 1819 on what was then a remote spot, but it is now surrounded by factories.

Officially part of Great Yarmouth, **Caister,** 3 miles to the north, is the site of a 15th-century moated castle which was built by Sir John Fastolf – the original of Shakespeare's Falstaff. The castle has a 100 ft high tower, and contains a veteran and vintage car museum.

Continental link

Great Yarmouth is nearer to Rotterdam in Holland – 114 miles – than it is to London – 135 miles – and so has become an important link in trade with Europe. The harbour entrance is guarded by two piers, one on each side of the mouth of the Yare, where the river turns sharply to enter the sea at right-angles. This arrangement was suggested by Joas Johnson, a Dutch engineer in the 1560s, to speed the flow of the river and prevent silting at its mouth.

Although it is separated from Great Yarmouth by the River Yare, **Gorleston** is still part of the borough. The town is similar in character to Yarmouth, though on a smaller scale, and its beach is backed by cliffs.

Information Tel. 2195.
Location On the A12, 20 m. E of Norwich.
Parking Great Yarmouth: South Market Road; Howard Street South (2); St Francis Way; North Quay; Northgate Street; North Drive;

OLD AND NEW *Wellington Pier, the older of the town's two piers, dates from 1853. Its elaborately decorated Pavilion was added in the 20th century.*

South Beach Parade (2); Salisbury Road; Beaconsfield Road; North Denes Road; St Peter's Plain; Church Plain (2); Market Place; Marine Parade (4). Gorleston: High Street. Caister: Beach Road (all car parks).
District council Borough of Great Yarmouth (Tel. 3233).
Population 48,300.
E-C Thur. (Gorleston, Wed.). **M-D** Wed., Sat.
Police (Ab) Howard Street North (Tel. 2222).
Casualty hospital Great Yarmouth and Waveney District, Lowestoft Road (Tel. 60611).
Post office (Ab) Regent Street.
Theatres ABC **(Ab)**, Regent Road (Tel. 3191); Britannia **(Bb)**, Britannia Pier (2209); Wellington **(Ba)**, Wellington Pier (2244); Windmill **(Ba)**, Marine Parade (3504); Hippodrome **(Ba)**, Marine Parade (4172).
Cinemas ABC **(Ab)**, Regent Road

(Tel. 3191); Cinemas 1 & 2 **(Bb)**, Marine Parade (2043); Regent **(Bb)**, Regent Road (2354).
Public library (Aa) Tolhouse Street.
Places to see Tolhouse Museum **(Aa)**, Tolhouse Street; Greyfriars Cloisters **(Ab)**, Greyfriars Way; Elizabethan House **(Ab)**, South Quay; Maritime Museum **(Ba)**, Marine Parade; Caister Castle and Motor Museum, Caister; St George's Art Centre, King Street.
Shopping Town centre; Market Place; King Street; Regent Road.
Events Carnival (Sept.); English Bowling Association Open Bowls Tournament (Aug.-Sept.); National Raft Race (Aug.).
Sport Flat racing, Yarmouth Racecourse (June-Sept.); Greyhound racing, Yarmouth Stadium.
Car ferry To Scheveningen, Holland (Tel. 56133).
AA 24 hour service
Tel. Norwich 29401.

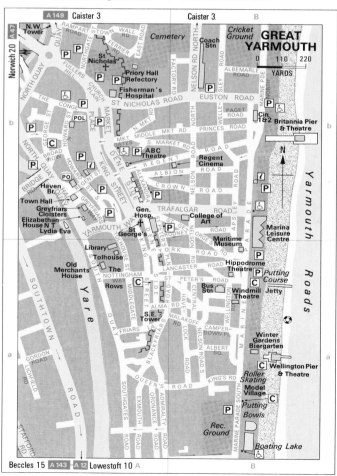

Guildford Surrey

Surrey's county town has a High Street that has maintained a mellow Georgian character in an age of redevelopment. The street runs down steeply to the River Wey. Though the frontages are mostly Georgian, several conceal older buildings at the rear. The most impressive of these is the Guildhall, which has a 17th-century façade added to a Tudor building.

A clock bearing the date 1683 projects over the street from the front of the Guildhall. The building itself has an elegant balcony, tall windows and a hexagonal bell-turret. A set of standard measures, presented to the town by Elizabeth I, are preserved in the old courtroom. It is one of the few complete sets still existing.

Halfway up the High Street is the Hospital of the Blessed Trinity, more commonly known as Abbot's Hospital. It was built in 1619 by George Abbot, Archbishop of Canterbury, as an almshouse for old people, and is still in use today. Parts of the building are open to the public. Between Abbot's Hospital and the Guildhall is

Guildford House, which was built in 1660 and is now the town's art gallery. The Royal Grammar School at the top of the High Street was founded in 1507 and endowed by Edward VI in 1552. It has a notable chained library.

A short distance from the High Street is the ruined Guildford Castle, built in the 12th century by Henry II. The castle stands on a mound, and a good view of the town can be had from the top of the keep. The castle museum of local history and archaeology has a collection of items connected with Charles Lutwidge Dodgson (Lewis Carroll), the author of *Alice in Wonderland*, who died in Guildford in 1898 and is buried in Mount Cemetery.

Guildford's most imposing building is the cathedral, which occupies a commanding position on Stag Hill. Building started in 1936, but the Second World War delayed progress and the cathedral was not consecrated until 1961. It was designed by Sir Edward Maufe in a simplified Gothic style, with a red-brick exterior.

Guildford Cathedral is one of only three Anglican cathedrals to be built in Britain since the Reformation. The others are at Liverpool and Truro.

The Civic Hall, which seats 1,040 for concerts, is the home of the Guildford Philharmonic Orchestra. Theatrical entertainment is provided at the Yvonne Arnaud Theatre, opened in 1965 and named after the actress and concert pianist who died in 1958.

The theatre is pleasantly situated on the river bank, a short distance from the Town Bridge. Close to the bridge is the Crane and Cranehouse with a tread-wheel that once operated a crane which was used to load and unload barges. It is believed to date from the 18th century.

The University of Surrey occupies two sites, one on Stag Hill near the cathedral and the other north-west of the town. The River Wey, once a commercial waterway with locks built in 1653, is now used by pleasure craft.

Loseley House, 2½ miles to the south-west of Guildford, was built in 1562 and is noted for its fine panelling and fireplaces. The Elizabethan Sutton Place, 3½ miles north-east, has attractive gardens open to the public. Clandon Park, 3 miles east, was designed in the Palladian style by Giacomo Leoni in the 1730s. It contains fine furniture and porcelain.

Information Tel. 67314.
Location On the A3, 13 m. W of Dorking.
Parking Bedford Road; Bright Hill; Civic Hall; Foxenden Quarry; York Road; Guildford Park Road; Laundry Road; Millbrook; Mary Road; North Street; Upper High Street; Sydenham Road; Tunsgate (all car parks).
District council Guildford Borough Council (Tel. 71111).
Population 56,700.
E-C Wed. **M-D** Wed., Fri., Sat.
Police (Ab) Margaret Road (Tel. 31111).
Casualty hospital New Royal Surrey County, Gill Avenue, Egerton Road (Tel. 71122).
Post office (Ab) North Street.
Theatres Yvonne Arnaud (**Aa**), Millbrook (Tel. 60191); Civic Hall, London Road (67314).
Cinemas Odeon, Epsom Road (Tel. 504990); Studios 1 & 2 (**Ab**), Woodbridge Road (64334).
Public library (Bb) North Street.
Places to see Castle (**Ba**), Castle Street; Museum (**Ba**), Quarry Street; The Guildhall (**Bb**), High Street; Guildford House (**Bb**), High Street.
Town trails Available from Tourist Information Centre, Civic Hall.
Shopping High Street; North Street; Tunsgate; Friary Centre.
Event Surrey County Agricultural Show (Spring Bank Holiday).
AA 24 hour service Tel. 72841.

HIGH STREET *Guildford's Guildhall adds charm to an elegant street.*

Guisborough Cleveland

The architectural gem of Guisborough, the ancient capital of Cleveland, is the ruined Augustine Priory of St Mary. It was founded in 1119 by Robert de Brus, an ancestor of Scotland's Robert Bruce. All that now stands are the magnificent 13th-century east end, the 12th-century gatehouse and octagonal dovecot.

The town grew extensively in the last century as a centre of the ironstone industry. It is the market town for the surrounding area and a good base for exploring the North Yorkshire Moors and Cleveland Hills.

Information Tel. Eston Grange 468141.
Location On the A171, 9 m. SE of Middlesbrough.
Parking Fountain Street; Westgate; Northgate (all car parks).
District council Borough of Langbaurgh (Tel. Eston Grange 468141).
Population 19,900.
E-C Wed. **M-D** Thur., Sat.
Police Church Lane (Tel. 33531).
Casualty hospital Middlesbrough General, Ayresome Green Lane, Middlesbrough (Tel. Middlesbrough 83133).
Post office Westgate.
Cinema Fairworld Film Centre, Chaloner Street (Tel. 34360).
Public library Westgate.
Places to see Augustine Priory, Westgate; Captain Cook Museum, Great Ayton.
Town trails Available from Saltburn YHA, Riftswood Hall, Victoria Road, Saltburn.
Shopping Westgate.
AA 24 hour service Tel. Middlesbrough 246832.

Hackney see London

Haddington Lothian

No less than 129 buildings in the small town of Haddington are listed as historically interesting by the Council for British Archaeology. Top of their list is the 14th-century parish church of St Mary, which is richly embellished with gargoyles.

In Sidegate is Haddington House, built in the early 17th century, and in Lodge Street is Carlyle House, a fine early-18th-century building in the Classical style. The graceful Town House, in wide, tree-lined Court Street, was built in 1748 partly by William Adam, father of Robert and William.

Alexander II of Scotland was born at Haddington in 1198, as was Samuel Smiles (1812-1904), author of *Self-Help*.

Information Tel. 4161.
Location On the A6093, 17 m. E of Edinburgh.
Parking Newton Port; Hardgate; Poldrate (all car parks).
District council East Lothian (Tel. Musselburgh 3711).
Population 8,100.
E-C Thur. **M-D** Fri.
Police Court Street (Tel. 4101).
Casualty hospital Roodlands General, Hospital Road (Tel. 3182).
Post office Court Street.
Public library Newton Port.
Places to see Kinloch House, Market Street.
Town trails Available from Dept of Physical Planning, East Lothian District Council, Haddington.
Shopping High Street; Market Street; Sidegate; Court Street.
AA 24 hour service Tel. Edinburgh (031) 225 8464.

Hadleigh Suffolk

The 15th-century, timber-framed Guildhall with its two overhanging storeys is a splendid monument to the wool and cloth trades that gave Hadleigh its prosperity from medieval times. It stands in Church Square beside a High Street that is a pageant of local architecture with buildings of brick, timber and plasterwork.

Guthrum, King of the Danes, is reported to have been buried in St Mary's Church after his defeat by Alfred in the 9th century. But the unnamed tomb said to be Guthrum's is at least five centuries too late.

Information Tel. 822801.
Location On the A1071, 10 m. W of Ipswich.
Parking Magdalen Road (two car parks).
District council Babergh (Tel. 822801).
Population 5,880.
E-C Wed. **M-D** Fri.
Police High Street (Tel. 823404).
Casualty hospital Ipswich General, Ivry Street, Ipswich (Tel. Ipswich 212477).
Post office Church Street.
Public library George Street.
Places to see Guildhall, Church Square.
Shopping High Street.
AA 24 hour service Tel. Norwich 29401.

ANCIENT BURGH *The slender spire of Haddington's Town House soars above this Scottish town, a royal burgh since the 12th century. A walk around its historic streets is aided by information boards placed at points of interest.*

RELIGIOUS REFORMER

John Knox (1505-72), founder of the Presbyterian Church in Scotland, was born in or near Haddington. His influence rested on tracts such as *Blast of the trumpet against the monstrous regiment of women*, and on his fiery preaching.

REMINDER *Piece Hall, where the wool merchants of Halifax traded, has a weathervane in the shape of a sheep.*

MONEY GIANT *The Halifax Building Society, the largest in the world, is housed in an ultra-modern office block, which was opened by the Queen in 1974.*

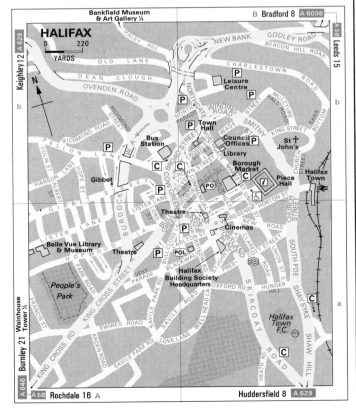

Halifax W. Yorks.

Two fine buildings sum up the story of Halifax. One is the wool-trade's ancient Piece Hall, the other is the ultra-modern headquarters of the Halifax Building Society.

Piece Hall, which was rebuilt in the 1770s and recently restored, is the only surviving manufacturers' hall in Britain. There, weavers took their pieces, or lengths of cloth, to be sold.

Surrounding the Hall's massive central quadrangle, where an open-air market is now held, are arched and colonnaded galleries which gave access to the rooms of 315 merchants. These rooms have now been transformed into a textile museum, shops and a gallery of modern art.

The Halifax Building Society, which was founded in 1853, is housed in a gleaming glass-and-concrete office block built over enormous fireproof vaults, which hold house deeds of the thousands of home-buyers who have mortgages with the society.

Near by is the parish church of St John, a 15th-century Perpendicular building incorporating the remains of Norman and Early English churches.

A notable landmark of the town is the Wainhouse Tower. This 253 ft high octagonal structure was originally designed as a dyeworks chimney, but was never used. When it was completed in 1875 it was recognised as a folly – and a masterpiece of stonemasonry. At the top there is a viewing balcony reached by a spiral staircase of more than 400 steps.

On the eastern edge of the town is Shibden Hall, a 15th-century mansion, now the Folk Museum of West Yorkshire. On view are 17th-century furniture, early agricultural implements and a bar parlour from an early-19th-century public house.

Bankfield Museum is principally concerned with textiles. It has a fine collection of costumes, brocades, and textile machinery.

In Gibbet Street stands a reconstruction of the Halifax Gibbet, used from the 13th century until the mid-17th century to execute criminals. Gibbet is a misnomer, as the instrument is a form of guillotine, not a gallows. The last blade used in it is on display at Bankfield Museum.

It is only a short journey from the

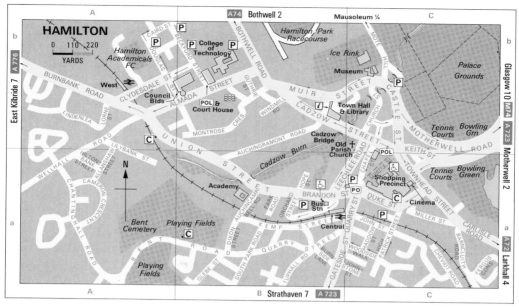

HAMILTON

0 110 220
YARDS

(map of Hamilton with labels: Bothwell 2, Mausoleum ¼, Hamilton Park Racecourse, College of Technology, Hamilton Academicals FC, Ice Rink, Museum, Palace Grounds, West, Clydesdale, Council Blds, Almada Street, Pol & Court House, Montrose Cres, Muir Street, Windmill Rd, Cadzow Street, Castle Street, Town Hall & Library, Church St, Tennis Courts, Bowling Grn, Cadzow Bridge, Cadzow Burn, Old Parish Church, Keith St, Motherwell Road, Academy, Leechlee Rd, Chapel St, Shopping Precinct, Pol, Tennis Courts, Bowling Green, Bent Cemetery, Playing Fields, Brandon St, Bus Stn, Cinema, Duke St, Miller St, Carlisle Road, Central, Playing Fields, Kemp Street, Quarry Street, John St, Meadowside Walk, Woodside, Patrick St, Burn Blantyre Lane, Gateside, Chevoit Road, Fergus Gdns, Strathaven 7, A723, East Kilbride 7, A726, Glasgow 10, M74, A723, Motherwell 2, A72, Larkhall 4, Burnbank Road, Lindenlea, Lorne, Hilton Bank Street, Allanshaw Street, Wellhall Road, Chantinghall Road, Cameron Crescent, Lilybank St, Union Street, Dixon, South Park Road, Glebe St, Quarry, Orchard, Park, John St, Brandcluth Road)

bustle of the town to the depths of the Yorkshire Dales or the moors, which north of Halifax rise to 1,400 ft.

Information Tel. 65701 or 68725.
Location On the A58, 8 m. NW of Huddersfield.
Parking Culver Street; Lower Cross Street; Kent Street; Gibbet Street (all car parks).
District council Calderdale (Tel. 65701).
Population 87,500.
E-C Thur. **M-D** Fri., Sat. and Sun.
Police (Ba) Harrison Road (Tel. 60333).
Casualty hospital Halifax Royal Infirmary, Free School Lane (Tel. 57222).
Post office (Bb) Commercial Street.
Theatres Civic **(Ba)**, Wards End (Tel. 51156); Playhouse **(Aa)**, King Cross Street (65998).
Cinemas ABC **(Ba)**, Wards End (Tel. 52000); Astra 1 and 2 **(Ba)**, Wards End (61849).
Public library (Aa) Lister Lane.
Places to see Piece Hall **(Bb)**; Wainhouse Tower; Bankfield Museum; Shibden Hall; Halifax Gibbet **(Ab)**.
Shopping Southgate; Commercial Street; Union Street.
Sport FA League football, Halifax Town FC, Skircoat Road.
AA 24 hour service
Tel. Bradford 724703.

Hamilton Strathclyde
Modern high-rise developments have failed to dominate Hamilton's most notable landmark – the Mausoleum of Alexander, 10th Duke of Hamilton (1767-1852), said to have cost the duke £40,000. It includes the black-marble sarcophagus of an Egyptian princess in which the duke's remains were interred, but these now lie in Bent Cemetery.

South of the town lies the ruined Cadzow Castle, built in the 12th cen-

DUKE'S TOMB *The last resting place of the 10th Duke of Hamilton was designed in the style of Roman architecture by David Bryce. It was completed in 1854.*

---

tury. A royal residence until the time of Robert Bruce (1306-29), it passed to the Hamilton family. Mary, Queen of Scots stayed there in 1568.

Another ducal property, Chatelherault Lodge, was built in 1732 by William Adam, who also designed the Old Parish Church in Cadzow Street. Netherton Cross, a Celtic stone cross of the 6th century, stands in the churchyard.

Information Tel. 282323.
Location On the A723, 10 m. SE of Glasgow.
Parking Brandon Street (2); Duke Street; Leechlee Street; Edinburgh Road; Miller Street; Graham Street (all car parks).
District council Hamilton (Tel. 282323).
Population 49,700.
E-C Wed. **M-D** Wed.
Police (Ca) Campbell Street (Tel. 286303).
Casualty hospital Stonehouse (Tel. Stonehouse 793521).
Post office (Ca) Brandon Street.
Cinema Odeon **(Ca)**, Townhead Street (Tel. 283802).
Public library (Bb) Cadzow Street.
Places to see Hamilton District Museum and Museum of the

Cameronians **(Ca)**, Muir Street.
Shopping Regent Way Shopping Precinct; Quarry Street.
Sport Horse racing, Hamilton Park; Scottish League football, Hamilton Academicals FC, Douglas Park.
AA 24 hour service
Tel. Glasgow (041) 812 0101.

Hammersmith see London

Haringey see London

Harlow Essex
In 1947 Harlow became one of eight new towns designed to siphon off people and industry from London. But several reminders of its long history survive in the rural parishes that surround The High, its modern centre. St Mary's Church, Latton, retains a Norman doorway and window and has a fine 15th-century triple arch. The parish church of Great Parndon is basically 15th century.

Information Tel. 446622.
Location On the A11, 20 m. W of Chelmsford.
Parking Linkway; Post Office Road; Terminus Street; College Gate; Wych Elm (all car parks).
District council Harlow (Tel. 446611).
Population 79,200.
E-C Wed. **M-D** Thur., Fri. and Sat.
Police Crown Gate (Tel. 29500).
Casualty hospital Princess Alexandra, Hamstel Road (Tel. 26791).
Post office The High.
Theatre Playhouse Theatre and Arts Centre, The High (Tel. 31945).
Cinema Odeon, The High (Tel. 26989).
Public library The High.
Shopping The High.
AA 24 hour service
Tel. Chelmsford 61711.

HARROGATE North Yorkshire

Fairs and flowers on the edge of the moors

In 1571 a man named William Slingsby drank from a spring near Knaresborough and noticed that the water tasted like that of spas he had visited on the Continent. Several years later a physician, Timothy Bright, declared that the spring had healing properties. During the 18th and 19th centuries, more springs were discovered – they were rich mostly in iron or sulphur – and Harrogate was developed to become one of Britain's most celebrated spas, offering cures for everything from gout to nervous tension. But as medical science discovered and developed new drugs, so the demand for "the cure" declined. Harrogate has adapted to the change by becoming a major conference and exhibition centre. Much of the town's architecture is Victorian, and represents some of the best of that period. It is built mostly with dark Yorkshire stone, and its sombre dignity is offset by gardens, parks and stretches of grassland that give the town a spacious air.

ROYAL PUMP ROOM *Harrogate's most celebrated building is built on the site of a sulphur-well.*

The **Royal Pump Room** occupies the site of Harrogate's most celebrated mineral spring, a sulphur-well known originally as "The Stinking Spaw". An octagonal building was erected over the spring in 1804, but long before then people had used its waters to treat all sorts of ills. At the height of its popularity, which extended well into the 20th century, more than 1,000 glasses of sulphur water were served in a single morning. The pump room now houses a museum of local history. But the original well-head in the basement can be visited, and the water can be tasted.

The **Royal Baths**, which were opened in 1897, grew to be one of the largest hydrotherapy establishments in the world, offering treatments for rheumatic complaints ranging from sulphur baths to hot, sulphur-mud poultices. After 1949 the cure was obtainable under the National Health Scheme. The baths were closed down in 1969, but the elegant assembly rooms are still used for meetings and conferences.

Harrogate's main entertainment and conference centre, the **Royal Hall**, was built in 1903 and was originally called the Kursaal. It seats 1,350 and is Edwardian in style, with a horseshoe-shaped balcony and ornate ceiling. The adjacent exhibition centre is a series of single-floor halls covering an area of 100,000 sq. ft.

Garden of wells

Valley Gardens is a sheltered park lying in a natural dell which projects like a wedge into the town, with its tip pointing towards the Royal Pump Room and Baths. Along one side is the **Sun Colonnade**, a glass-covered walkway 600 ft long. It leads to the Sun Pavilion, a glass-domed building with suntrap lounges, tea-rooms and a concert hall.

A green-domed building with a glass-roofed terrace houses the **Magnesia Well**, discovered in 1895. In this part of the garden are 36 mineral

SUNSHINE ROOM *After taking the waters at the Royal Pump Room, visitors to Harrogate could dine beneath the glass-domed roof of the Sun Pavilion. The pavilion still provides light refreshments, and concerts are held in the concert hall.*

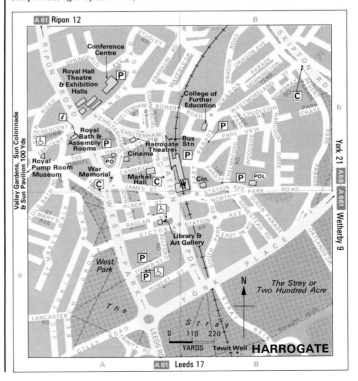

Church Square. It was built in 1786 with additions in 1842 and is in the Gothic style, with an embattled tower.

Ripley and its castle

To the north of Harrogate is the village of **Ripley**, remodelled in 1827 by Sir William Amcotts to resemble a French village in Alsace Lorraine. In the cobbled square are the old stocks and the village cross, and close by is Ripley Castle where the Ingilby family has lived for generations. The castle dates mostly from the 16th century, although the gatehouse, now a museum, may date from 1450.

In 1644 the Ingilby men rode out to join the Royalist forces at Marston Moor and, after defeat by Oliver Cromwell, returned to find that Cromwell had spent the night at the castle in the presence of Lady Ingilby, who had armed herself with a pair of pistols concealed in her apron pocket.

Ripley Church bears reminders of the battle. Its walls are scarred with bullet holes made when Cromwell's troopers executed several Ripley men who had been captured at Marston Moor. The church contains tombs of the Ingilby family from the 14th century onwards.

Information Tel. 65912.
Location On the A61, 17 m. N of Leeds.
Parking Harlow Moor Drive; Valley Drive; Princess Square; Railway Station; Ripon Road; East Parade; King's Road; Royal Baths; Tower Street; Union Street (all car parks). Disc parking is operative in the town centre – discs available from shops, banks and Information Centre.
District council Borough of Harrogate (Tel. 68954).
Population 66,400.
E-C Wed. **M-D** Daily.
Police North Park Road (Tel. 55541/5).
Casualty hospital Lancaster Park Road (Tel. 885959).
Post office Cambridge Road.
Theatres Royal Hall, Ripon Road (Tel. 50349); Harrogate Theatre, Oxford Street (502116).
Cinemas Odeon, East Parade (Tel. 503626); ABC, Cambridge Road (68350).
Public library Victoria Avenue.
Places to see Art Gallery, Victoria Avenue; Royal Pump Room Museum, Crescent Road; Ripley Castle, 2 m. N on A61.
Town trails Available from Tourist Information Centre, Royal Baths Assembly Rooms, Crescent Road.
Shopping James Street; Oxford Street; Cambridge Street; Parliament Street; Montpellier Parade; Crescent Road; King's Road; Town Centre.
Events Spring Flower Show (Apr.); Halle Festival of Music (July); Harrogate Festival (Aug.).
Trade and industry Rubber; chemicals; dairy products.
AA 24 hour service Tel. Leeds 38161.

wells – all within the space of 1 acre. Water from here was pumped to the Royal Baths Hospital, which stands on the fringe of the gardens.

Horticultural gardens

A short distance from Valley Gardens are pine-woods, and beyond are the trial gardens of the Northern Horticultural Society – **Harlow Car Gardens**. They consist of 60 acres of ornamental, woodland and rock gardens with greenhouses, trial beds and lily ponds. Harlow Hill Tower, built in 1829, is 90 ft high.

Rudding Park is a Regency house just outside Harrogate to the south-east, and is surrounded by superb gardens with English and French roses, rhododendrons and azaleas as the main attractions.

A stretch of common land, called **The Stray**, covers more than 200 acres, and was declared "open and unenclosed" by an Act of Parliament in 1770. It borders the southern edge of the town centre, and joins with West Park and Church Square to embrace the town in a broad sweep of tree-lined lawns and pleasant walks.

At the western end of The Stray is the **Tewit Well**, the spring discovered by William Slingsby and now covered by a pillared dome. A footpath, called Slingsby Walk, leads across The Stray to Wedderburn House, built in 1786 and once the home of Alexander Wedderburn, Lord Loughborough, who planted many of the trees in The Stray.

Another well, St John's, is at the eastern end of The Stray. It was discovered in 1631 by Dr Michael Stanhope, who wrote of its salt-free iron properties in a book, *Cures without Care*. **St John's Well** took its name from a church which has now been replaced by Christ Church, in

Harrow see London

Hartlepool Cleveland

The old walled town of Hartlepool was once Durham's chief port, with Georgian and Victorian houses clustered around the 12th-century Church of St Hilda. It still has a busy fish dock and market, but little remains of the past except the church. The rest of the town is thoroughly modern, with its chemical works and nuclear power station.

Information Tel. 66522.
Location On the A689, 9 m. N of Middlesbrough.
Parking Middleton Grange Shopping Centre (3); Church Square; Church Street; Stockton Street; Park Road; York Road; Tower Street (all car parks).
District council Borough of Hartlepool (Tel. 66522).
Population 90,300.
E-C Wed. **M-D** Thur.
Police (Ab) Raby Road (Tel. 74137).
Casualty hospital St Hilda's, Friar Street (Tel. 66155).
Post office (Aa) Middleton Grange Shopping Centre.
Theatre Forum, Billingham (Tel. Middlesbrough 552663).
Cinema Fairwold **(Ab)**, Raby Road (72114).
Public library (Aa) Clarence Road.
Shopping Middleton Grange Centre.
Sport FA League football, Hartlepool United FC, Clarence Road.
AA 24 hour service
Tel. Middlesbrough 246832.

Harwich Essex

A medieval atmosphere still lingers in the narrow streets of Harwich, once a walled town. Edward III's fleet gathered in the natural anchorage to the north before sailing in 1340 to Sluys and victory in the first sea battle of the Hundred Years' War.

Number 21 King's Head Street was the home of Captain Christopher Jones, master of the *Mayflower*, in which the Pilgrim Fathers sailed to America in 1620. On Harwich Green can be seen what is probably the only tread-wheel crane in the world. It was built in 1667 to lift naval stores.

To the south is the seaside resort of Dovercourt, with long sandy beaches.

Information Tel. 6139 (summer only), or Clacton-on-Sea 25501.
Location On the A604, 19 m. NE of Colchester.
Parking Wellington Road; Parkstone Quay; Harwich Quay. Dovercourt: Milton Road; Lower Marine Parade (all car parks).
District council Tendring (Tel. Clacton-on-Sea 25501).
Population 15,000.
E-C Wed. **M-D** Fri.

Police (Aa) High Street (Tel. 2456).
Casualty hospital Harwich and District and Fryatt Memorial, 419 Main Road, Dovercourt (Tel. 2446).
Post offices Kingsway **(Ab)**, Dovercourt. Church Street **(Ba)**, Harwich.
Public library (Aa) Kingsway, Dovercourt.
Places to see Tread-wheel crane **(Ba)**, Harwich Redoubt **(Ba)**.
Town trails Available from Mrs Winifred Cooper, 5 Church Street, Harwich, Essex CO12 3DR.
Shopping Kingsway and High Street, Dovercourt. Church Street and Market Street, Harwich.
Car ferries To Hook of Holland, Hamburg and Esbjerg.
AA 24 hour service
Tel. Chelmsford 61711.

Haslemere Surrey

For centuries craftsmen worked their skills in iron, glass, leather and wood to provide a prosperous trade in this tiny country town. But the Industrial Revolution swept them all away and Haslemere became a residential centre.

One craft remains in the town. The Dolmetsch family make harpsichords, lutes and other early instruments, and give recitals on them.

Information Tel. Godalming 4104.
Location On the A286, 14 m. SW of Guildford.
Parking High Street; Chestnut Avenue; Weydown Road; Tanners Lane; Lion Green; Wey Hill (all car parks).
District council Waverley (Tel. Godalming 4104).
Population 13,900.
E-C Wed.
Police West Street (Tel. 4655).
Casualty hospital New Royal Surrey County, Gill Avenue, Egerton Road, Guildford (Tel. Guildford 71122).
Post office West Street.
Cinema Rex, Shottermill (Tel. 2444).
Public library Wey Hill.

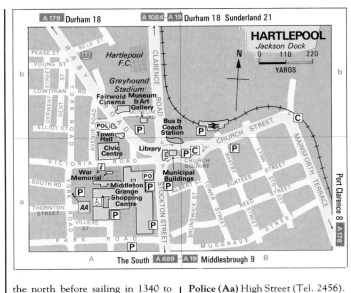

Places to see Educational Museum,
High Street; Dolmetsch Museum,
Jesses, Grayswood Road.
Shopping High Street; West Street.
AA 24 hour service
Tel. Guildford 72841.

Hastings E. Sussex

The Battle of Hastings in 1066 actually took place at Battle, 6 miles inland. William stepped ashore at Norman's Bay, a beach to the west of
Hastings, and the massive Conqueror's Stone, now near the pier, is
supposed to have been the dining
table for his first meal in England.

Today, Hastings offers all the traditional amusements of the seaside, yet
retains the character of its past.

The ruined castle on the hill was
built a year after the Conquest. The
chief remains are parts of the north
and east walls, a gatehouse, a tower,
an arch and the dungeons.

On show in the Town Hall is the
243 ft long Hastings Embroidery,
created in 1966 by the Royal School
of Needlework to mark the 900th
anniversary of the Norman invasion.
Inspired by the Bayeux Tapestry, it
depicts 81 events of British history
since 1066.

The old part of the town, with its
twisting, narrow streets and timbered
houses, contains the Fishermen's
Museum, which houses the last of the
town's sailing luggers.

Hastings has two fine churches. St
Clement's, which dates from the late
14th century, and the 15th-century
Church of All Saints.

The Roman Catholic church, St
Mary Star-of-the-Sea, was built in

HASTINGS OLD TOWN *The 14th-century St Clement's Church and houses from medieval to Victorian times nestle between East and West Hill.*

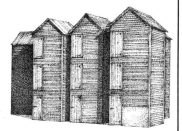

HIGH AND DRY *Fishing nets are dried in 16th-century huts at Hastings.*

1880-3 by the poet Coventry Patmore
(1823-96) as a memorial to his wife.

In Queen's Road is a plaque to John
Logie Baird, who in 1924 made the
world's first television transmission in
his rooms there.

Near the castle are St Clement's
Caves, which were once smugglers'
store-chambers.

Information Tel. 424242.
Location On the A21, 5 m. E of
Bexhill.
Parking Cornwallis Street;
Robertson Terrace; White Rock;
Eversfield Place; Middle Street;
Priory Street; Castle Hill Road;
Pelham Place; St Margaret's Road.
District council Borough of Hastings
(Tel. 424182).
Population 74,800.
E-C Wed.
Police (Aa) Bohemia Road
(Tel. 425000).
Casualty hospital Cambridge Road

(Tel. 434513).
Post office (Ba) Cambridge Road.
Theatres White Rock Pavilion **(Aa)**
(Tel. 421840); Stables Theatre **(Ca)**,
The Bourne (423221).
Cinema Classic 1 and 2 **(Ba)**,
Queen's Road (Tel. 420517).
Public library (Aa) Claremont.
Places to see Castle **(Ba)**; Museums
(Aa); Battle Abbey.
Town trails Available from
Information Centre, Robertson
Terrace.
Shopping London Road; Robertson
Street; Cambridge Road; Queen's
Road; Castle Street; George Street.
Events National Town Criers
Championship (Aug.); International
Chess Congress (Dec./Jan.).
Trade and industry Electrical and
electronic engineering.
Sport Cricket, Sussex CC, Queen's
Road.
AA 24 hour service
Tel. Brighton 695231.

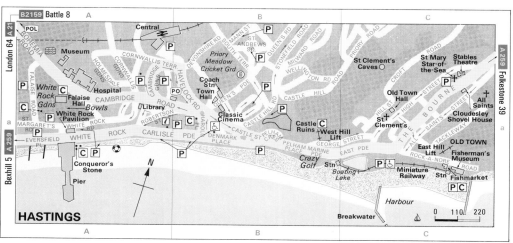

HASTINGS

HATFIELD HOUSE

The imposingly large, E-shaped mansion was built in 1607-12 for Robert Cecil, 1st Earl of Salisbury, to replace the 15th-century Royal Palace where Queen Elizabeth lived as a child. The house has a magnificent hall and decorated wooden staircase, contains fine portraits and relics of Elizabeth. The carved figures of Elizabeth and her courtiers are in a summer-house.

Hatfield Hertfordshire

There are two distinct parts to Hatfield: the charming old coaching town east of the railway, and the post-war new town to the west. Old Hatfield is dominated by 17th-century Hatfield House, home of the Cecil family and one of the finest mansions in England. Near it stands the 13th-century Church of St Ethelreda, which has a chapel for the Cecil family.

There are a number of fine half-timbered and Georgian buildings in the old town, including the 17th-century Eight Bells Inn.

Information Tel. Welwyn Garden City 31212.
Location On the A414, 5 m. N of St Albans.
Parking Great North Road; Batterdale; Queensway; Link Drive; High View; The Common; The Broadway (Old Town) (all car parks).
District council Welwyn Hatfield (Tel. Welwyn Garden City 31212).
Population 25,100.
E-C Thur. **M-D** Wed., Sat.
Police St Albans Road East (Tel. 67373).
Casualty hospital Queen Elizabeth II, Howlands, Welwyn Garden City (Tel. Welwyn Garden City 28111).
Post office Town Centre.
Theatre The Forum, Lemsford Road (Tel. 71217).
Public library Queensway.
Places to see Hatfield House; Old Palace; Museum, Old Mill House, Mill Green; Northaw Great Wood.
Shopping Town Centre; Market Place.
AA 24 hour service
Tel. 62852.

Havant Hampshire

Roman roads and ancient trackways converge on Havant, which has been a major road junction since prehistoric times. The remains of a Roman villa were discovered south of the town in 1926.

Havant was a parchment-making centre until well into this century, and provided the material on which the Treaty of Versailles was written in 1919.

Information Tel. 474174.
Location On the B2149, 10 m. W of Chichester.

Parking West Street; Elmleigh Road; Civic Centre Road; North Street (2); Park Road South; Park Way; Leigh Park Community Centre; Dunsbury Way; Park Road North (all car parks).
District council Borough of Havant (Tel. 474174).
Population 116,600.
E-C Wed.
Police Civic Centre Road (Tel. 486464).
Casualty hospital Queen Alexandra Hospital, Cosham (Tel. Cosham 379451).
Post office East Street.
Theatre Havant Arts Centre, East Street (Tel. 472700).
Cinema Empire, East Street (Tel. 483179).
Public library North Street.
Shopping North Street; West Street; East Street; Market Parade.
AA 24 hour service
Tel. Southampton 36811.

Haverfordwest Dyfed

From 1545 until 1974 Haverfordwest was also a county in its own right. It is a market town of narrow streets on two hills overlooking the River Cleddau, and is dominated by the ruins of a Norman castle. This was built about 1100, as part of a chain of fortifications erected across Pembrokeshire by Norman invaders against the Welsh to the north.

The castle was strengthened in the 13th century with walls 6-12 ft thick.

Cromwell ordered it to be destroyed after the Civil War, but much of it was left intact. What remained became the County Gaol, of which the new (1820) building now houses the former County Museum and Records Office.

Information Tel. 3110.
Location On the A40, 15 m. S of Fishguard.
Parking St Thomas's Green; Riverside; Castle Lake; Scotchwells; Queen's Square (all car parks).
District council Preseli (Tel. 4551).
Population 9,900.
E-C Thur. **M-D** Sat.
Police (Aa) Milford Road (Tel. 3355).
Casualty hospital Withybush Road, Fishguard Road (Tel. 4545).
Post office (Bb) Quay Street.
Cinema Palace (Aa), Upper Market Street (Tel. 2426).
Public library (Ab) Dew Street.
Places to see Castle and museum (Ab); Foley House (Bb); Augustinian priory (Ba).
Shopping Bridge Street; High Street.
AA 24 hour service
Tel. Cardiff 394111.

Havering see London

Hawick Borders

Knitting has made Hawick prosperous. It began as a cottage industry 200 years ago when a local magistrate introduced the first successful stocking frame. Mills were built in the 19th century, and the town's knitted products have since been exported all over the world.

Information Tel. 2547 (summer).
Location On the A7, 14 m. W of Jedburgh.
Parking Victoria Road/Albert Road; Garfield Street (3); Mart Street; O'Connell Street (all car parks).
District council Roxburgh (Tel. 5991).
Population 16,400.
E-C Tues. **M-D** Sat.

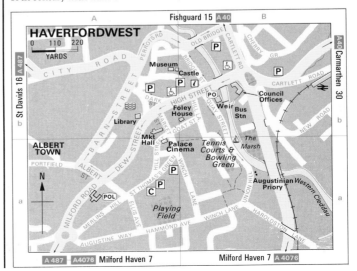

Police Wilton Hill (Tel. 5051).
Casualty hospital Hawick Cottage Hospital, Buccleuch Road (Tel. 2162).
Post office (Ba) North Bridge Street.
Cinema Marina **(Aa)**, Towerdykeside (Tel. 2445).
Public library (Ba) North Bridge Street.
Shopping High Street; Bridge Street; Howegate.
AA 24 hour service
Tel. Edinburgh (031) 225 8464.

Hay-on-Wye Powys

Fierce marcher lords, Anglo-Norman feudal rulers of the Welsh border areas, rode out from the old castle of Hay whenever the borders were disputed. The 12th-century castle is now mostly ruined.

Modern Hay stands high above the southern bank of the River Wye, a pretty town of old buildings and narrow streets. It has the world's largest second-hand bookshop, which has spread to more than six buildings.

Information Tel. 820391.
Location On the B4350, 17 m. NE of Brecon.
Parking Oxford Road; Memorial Square (both car parks).
District council Brecknock (Tel. Brecon 4141).
Population 1,300.
E-C Tues. **M-D** Thur.
Police Heol-y-Dwr (Tel. 820318).
Casualty hospital Brecon War Memorial, Cerrigcochion Road, Brecon (Tel. Brecon 2443).
Post office High Town.
Public library Chancery Lane.
Shopping Castle Street; High Town; Broad Street; Lion Street; Market Street.
AA 24 hour service
Tel. Newport 62559.

Haywards Heath
W. Sussex

The town of Haywards Heath grew around a station on the London to Brighton Railway in the mid-19th century. The station was built to serve the neighbouring communities of Cuckfield and Lindfield, both of which refused to accommodate the railway. The cattle market, begun in 1867, is now the largest in Sussex.

Information Tel. 58166.
Location On the A272, 13 m. SE of Horsham.
Parking Church Road; Franklynn Road; Haywards Road; Gower Road; Oaklands Road; Harlands Road; Commercial Square (all car parks).
District council Mid-Sussex (Tel. 58166).
Population 25,491.
E-C Wed. **M-D** Tues., Sun.
Police Boltro Road (Tel. 51555).
Casualty hospital Cuckfield, Ardingly Road, Cuckfield (Tel. Haywards Heath 50661).
Post office Boltro Road.

Public library Boltro Road.
Shopping Broadway; South Road; Commercial Square; Boltro Road; Sussex Road.
AA 24 hour service
Tel. Crawley 25685.

Hebden Bridge W. Yorks.

In the early 16th century a stone bridge was built over the River Hebden as part of a packhorse route. Around it there grew the nucleus of present-day Hebden Bridge. The establishment of textile mills brought prosperity in the late 18th century.

Every Good Friday, Hebden Bridge holds the ancient "pace-egg play", when a colourful procession parades the streets.

Information Tel. 3831.
Location On the A646, 8 m. W of Halifax.
Parking St Georges Square; Albert Street; New Road; Bridge Gate; Hanging Royd Lane (all car parks).
District council Borough of Calderdale (Tel. Halifax 65701).
Population 8,700.
E-C Tues. **M-D** Thur.
Police Hope Street (Tel. 2307).
Casualty hospital Halifax Royal Infirmary, Free School Lane, Halifax (Tel. Halifax 57222).
Post office Holme Street.
Cinema Picture House, New Road (Tel. 2807).
Public library Cheetham Street.
Places to see Old Packhorse Bridge; Old Grammar School Museum, Heptonstall.
Town trails Available from South Pennine Information Centre, Westbourne House.
Shopping Bridge Gate; Crown Street; St George's Square; Albert Street; Market Street.
AA 24 hour service
Tel. Bradford 724703.

HEBDEN BRIDGE *Mills occupied the valley floor, so Victorian "up-and-down" houses of several storeys were built flush against the hillside.*

Helensburgh Strathclyde

Sir James Colquhoun designed Helensburgh in 1780, and named it after his wife. It was built as a resort on the north bank of the Clyde.

In Hermitage Park there is a memorial to John Logie Baird (1888-1946), the television pioneer who was born in Helensburgh. Also in the park is the flywheel of the *Comet*, Britain's first commercially successful steamboat. Henry Bell (1767-1830), who was the town's provost, was the mastermind behind the *Comet* in 1812, and a granite obelisk to his memory stands on the waterfront. The tower of the 13th-century Ardencaple Castle is in the west part of the town. Hill House was designed by Charles Rennie Mackintosh (1868-1928), and contains much beautiful furniture.

Information Tel. Dumbarton 65100.
Location On the A814, 8 m. NW of Dumbarton.
Parking Sinclair Street; Princes Street West; Clyde Street; Maitland Street (all car parks).
District council Dumbarton (Tel. Dumbarton 65100).
Population 13,300.
E-C Wed.
Police East King Street (Tel. 2141).
Casualty hospital Victoria Infirmary, Granville Street (Tel. 2158).
Post office Princes Street West.
Cinema La Scala, James Street (Tel. 2615).
Public library John Street.
Places to see Ardencaple Castle tower; Hill House, Upper Colquhoun Street.
Shopping Clyde Street; Sinclair Street; Princes Street.
AA 24 hour service
Tel. Glasgow (041) 812 0101.

Helston Cornwall

In the 13th century Helston was a port, until sand and shingle silted up the harbour mouth. It was also a stannary town, or tin-mining administrative centre, until the industry died out earlier this century. Helston Museum, in the Old Butter Market building, illustrates the industry with tools, mineral specimens, plans and photographs. The archaeological sec-

CORNISH CHAMPION

Bob Fitzsimmons (1862-1917), who was the world heavyweight boxing champion from 1897 until 1899, was born in Helston. He won the title from "Gentleman Jim" Corbett of the USA by a knock-out in the 14th round.

At 11 st. 2 lb. Bob Fitzsimmons was the lightest man ever to hold the heavyweight title.

TUDOR TOWN *Oak from the Forest of Arden was used in many of the 16th-century timber-framed houses in the long main street of Henley-in-Arden.*

tion has finds from all over the Lizard Peninsula, including a Bronze Age axe. Other exhibits include man-traps, a butcher's travelling shop and a horse-worked cider-mill.

Helston is a typical Cornish town, built of granite and slate. A maze of narrow roads and alleys, lined with quaint old shops and houses, spreads out from the main thoroughfare, Coinagehall Street, which curves steeply down to the Cober river.

The town's well-known Furry Dance dates back to pre-Christian times. Every May, on or near the 8th between 7 a.m. and 5 p.m., dancing takes place through the greenery-decorated streets. The origin of the dance's name is obscure; it might be a corruption of the Roman "Flora", or derived from the Celtic *feur* (fair).

Helston's parish church of St Michael was built in the mid-18th century. It has Elizabethan brasses in the porch, and a vast brass chandelier made in 1762. In the churchyard is the grave of Henry Trengrouse (1772-1854), who developed a rocket life-saving apparatus for sailors. His original apparatus is in the museum.

The Old Grammar School in Wendron Street numbered among its pupils the novelist Charles Kingsley, author of *The Water Babies*.

Information Tel. 2921.
Location On the A394, 13 m. E of Penzance.
Parking Trengrouse Way; Market off Porthleven Road; Tyacke Road; St John's Road (all car parks).
District council Kerrier (Tel. Camborne 712941).
Population 10,700.
E-C Wed. **M-D** Sat.
Police Godolphin Road (Tel. 2414).

Casualty hospital West Cornwall, St Clare Street, Penzance (Tel. Penzance 2382).
Post office Coinagehall Street.
Cinema Flora, Wendron Street (Tel. 2459).
Public library Trengrouse Way.
Places to see Museum, Butter Market; Cornish Seal Sanctuary, Gweek, 4 m. E.
Shopping Coinagehall Street; Meneage Street.
Event Furry Dance (May).
AA 24 hour service
Tel. Truro 76455.

Hemel Hempstead Herts.

The "new town" of Hemel Hempstead began in the 1950s, based on a small community in the Gade valley and on the edge of the Chiltern Hills. The modern town centre runs parallel to the River Gade, and at its northern end reverts to the charm of the old High Street with bow-fronted shop windows and the Norman parish church of St Mary. At Piccotts End, 1 mile north, is a 15th-century house with wall-paintings of the period.

The Grand Union Canal runs to the south and there are several old inns along the towpath. The town is proud of its many open-air sculptures, the most prized being the statue of the French novelist Honoré de Balzac (1799-1850), by the French sculptor Auguste Rodin (1840-1917).

Information Tel. 64451.
Location On the A41, 7 m. W of St Albans.
Parking Hillfield Road; Selden Hill; Moor End Road (2); King Harry Street; High Street; Wolsey Road; Bridge Street (2) (all car parks). Waterhouse Street.

Ring local **AA 24 hour service** for latest information on hotels, restaurants and all-night petrol stations

District council Dacorum
(Tel. 3131).
Population 77,600.
E-C Wed. **M-D** Thur., Fri. and Sat.
Police Combe (Tel. 64881).
Casualty hospital Hemel Hempstead
General, Hillfield Road (Tel. 3141).
Post office Marlowes.
Theatres Pavilion, Marlowes
(Tel. 64451); Old Town Hall Arts
Centre, High Street (64451).
Cinema Odeon, Marlowes
(Tel. 64013).
Public library Coombe Street.
Shopping High Street; Marlowes.
AA 24 hour service
Tel. 01 954 7373.

Henley-in-Arden Warks.

In Tudor times this town stood in the
thickly wooded Forest of Arden. The
trees were felled for fuel to smelt iron
before the advent of coal, and only
sparse clumps of trees remain. But
some forest survives in the many
Tudor buildings along the main street
of Henley-in-Arden. The 15th-
century Guildhall is still used by the
ancient manor court, which appoints
constables and other local officers.

Near by are the remains of a
medieval market cross. The parish
church of St John the Baptist is 15th
century, and has fine stone carvings.

Information
Tel. Stratford-upon-Avon 293127.
Location On the A34, 9 m. NW of
Stratford-upon-Avon.
Parking High Street (street parking,
east side).
District council Stratford-upon-
Avon (Tel. 67575).
Population 1,640.
E-C Thur. **M-D** Mon., Wed., Sat.
Police High Street (Tel. 2691).
Casualty hospital Stratford-upon-
Avon General Hospital, Alcester
Road, Stratford-upon-Avon
(Tel. Stratford-upon-Avon 5831).
Post office High Street.
Public library High Street.
Places to see Guildhall; Gorcott
Hall, 5 m. NW.
Shopping High Street.
Event Mop Fair (Oct.).
AA 24 hour service
Tel. Birmingham (021) 550 4858.

Henley-on-Thames
Oxon.

The tortuous course of the River
Thames straightens for about 1 mile
at Henley, and along this stretch of
water is held the annual rowing regatta that has become a major international rowing event. But long before
oarsmen began to compete at Henley
there was a town here, thriving on the
fertile land and using the river for the
carriage of grain and timber.

There has been a bridge spanning
the river at Henley for centuries, but
the present five-arched bridge was
built in 1786. The keystones have
stone carvings representing Father
Thames and the goddess Isis. Close by

DOWN BY THE RIVERSIDE *The wide stretch of the Thames at Henley provides ample
room for all types of craft, from rowing-boats to motor-cruisers.*

is the parish church of St Mary, with a
16th-century square tower topped at
each corner by an octagonal turret.
Both the tower and the wall of the
south aisle contain distinctive flint-
and-stone chequerwork. The interior
was restored in the 19th century, but
the 14th or 15th-century nave arcades are still visible.

Henley has more than 300 buildings
listed by the Department of the Environment as "of special architectural
or historic interest". They include the
14th-century Chantry House, connected to the church by a porch, and
the Speaker's House, home of William Lenthall, Speaker of the House
of Commons from 1640 until 1653.
Lenthall was a signatory to the death
warrant of Charles I, and became
known as the Regicide Speaker.

Henley's main street has many
Georgian frontages built on to older
buildings. A good example of this is
the Catherine Wheel Hotel. There
are many old coaching inns in the
town, including the Red Lion, where,
at one time or another, Charles I,
Boswell and George III all stayed.

HENLEY ROYAL REGATTA

A regatta was first held at Henley
in 1839, and in 1851 Prince Albert became Patron of the Regatta
and endowed it with the title
"Royal". It became a social occasion, and much of the "garden-
party" atmosphere of Victorian
and Edwardian times still surrounds the event.

*A crew
carry their
boat ashore.*

Another inn, the Bell, is now three
private dwellings called Elm House,
Rupert's Elm and Rupert's Guard.
During the Civil War, Prince Rupert
stayed at the inn and while there
hanged a Roundhead spy from an elm
tree, the trunk of which still stands in
front of the buildings.

The offices of the Henley Brewery
in New Street date from the 18th
century. In the same street is the
Kenton Theatre, built in 1805.

Three miles north-west of Henley is
Grey's Court, a 16th-century mansion built on the site of the 14th-
century castle. Its name derives from
Lord de Grey, who fought at Crécy
and was one of the original Knights of
the Garter. Little remains of de
Grey's medieval castle except the
Great Tower and three smaller
towers. The present house contains
some 18th-century plasterwork and
furniture. The grounds include a
well-house and donkey-wheel.

Information Tel. 2626.
Location On the A423, 8 m. N of
Reading.
Parking Greys Road; Kings Road
(both car parks).
District council South Oxfordshire
(Tel. Wallingford 35351).
Population 11,000.
E-C Wed. **M-D** Thur.
Police Kings Road (Tel. 4602).
Casualty hospital Townlands, York
Road (Tel. 2544).
Post office Reading Road.
Theatre Kenton Theatre, New Street
(Tel. 5698).
Cinema Regal, Bell Street
(Tel. 4806).
Public library Ravenscroft Road.
Places to see Grey's Court, 3 m. NW
on road to Peppard.
Shopping Hart Street; Duke Street;
Bell Street.
Events Henley Royal Regatta (July);
Henley Town Regatta (first Sat. in
Aug. or last Sat. in July).
AA 24 hour service
Tel. Reading 581122.

Hereford H. & W.

This cathedral city on the banks of the River Wye was founded about AD 700. The oldest area of the city was bounded by a ditch which stretched south of the river to enclose Bishop's Meadow. The fortifications were intended to protect Saxon Hereford from the Welsh. In the 11th century the walls were built and were extended northwards 200 years later. A well-preserved section still stands, near the 15th-century Wye Bridge.

There has been a cathedral at Hereford since the city was founded. Most of the present building dates from the 12th century, and the central tower and choir stalls from 200 years later. The cathedral contains a world map drawn on vellum about AD 1300, and a chained library of 1,500 books – the world's largest.

The Coningsby Hospital, founded in 1614, incorporates a 12th-century dining-hall of the Knights of St John.

More recent relics, including the GWR locomotive *King George V*, are in the Bulmers Railway Centre.

Information Tel. 68430.
Location On the A49, 13 m. S of Leominster.
Parking West Street; Maylord Street; Symonds Street; Blackfriars Street; Greyfriars Avenue; Gaol Street; Bath Street (all car parks).
District council City of Hereford (Tel. 68121).
Population 47,700.
E-C Thur. **M-D** Wed.
Police (Bb) Gaol Street (Tel. 6422).
Casualty hospital (Ba) Nelson Street

HISTORIC CITY *Hereford and its cathedral have stood beside the River Wye for more than 1,000 years.*

(Tel. 2561).
Post office (Ab) Broad Street.
Theatre Nell Gwynne **(Ab)**, Edgar Street (Tel. 59252).
Cinema Focus **(Bb)**, High Town (Tel. 2554).
Public library (Aa) Broad Street.
Places to see Booth Hall **(Bb)**, off High Town; Churchill Gardens Museum, Venns Lane; Coningsby Hospital and Black Friars Monastery **(Bb)**, Widemarsh Street; Museum and Art Gallery **(Aa)**, Broad Street;

Old House **(Bb)**, High Town; Bulmers Railway Centre, Whitecross Road; Waterworks Museum, Broomy Hill; Cider Museum, Grimmer Road.
Shopping Eign Gate; Widemarsh Street; High Town; Commercial Street.
Sport Horse racing, Hereford Racecourse, off Newtown Road. FA League football, Hereford United FC, Edgar Street.
AA 24 hour service
Tel. Worcester 51070.

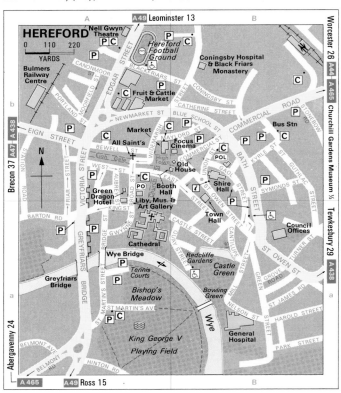

Herne Bay Kent

The Victorians developed Herne Bay as a seaside resort. The town is still mainly a holiday centre, but good road and rail links with London have helped it to grow as a residential area for commuters. There are 7 miles of shingle beach, and excellent bathing, sailing and sea-angling.

Information Tel. 66031.
Location On the A299, 9 m. N of Canterbury.
Parking Western Esplanade; Central Parade; Beacon Hill; William Street (all car parks).
District council City of Canterbury (Tel. Canterbury 51755).
Population 27,500.
E-C Thur. **M-D** Sat.
Police Gordon Road (Tel. 63831).
Casualty hospital Kent and Canterbury General, Ethelbert Road, Canterbury (Tel. Canterbury 66877).
Post office Cavendish Road.
Theatre The King's Hall, East Cliff (Tel. 4188).
Cinema Classic, Avenue Road (Tel. 4930).
Public library High Street.
Places to see Regulbium Roman fort, 3 m. E; Museum.
Shopping High Street, Mortimer Street.
AA 24 hour service
Tel. Thanet 81226.

Hertford Hertfordshire

Elizabeth I spent many happy days as a child in the castle at Hertford. The Normans built the stone keep beside the River Lea on a site first fortified by the Saxons in 911 at the start of their campaign to reconquer the Danelaw. The castle became a royal palace, but was demolished by James I; the gatehouse now houses council offices. The town has been the county town of Hertfordshire since before 1066.

Information Tel. 54977.
Location On the A414, 10 m. W of Harlow.
Parking Gascoyne Way; St Andrew's Street; Old London Road; Railway Street (all car parks).
District council East Herts. (Tel. Bishop's Stortford 55261).
Population 21,400.
E-C Thur. **M-D** Mon. (cattle); Sat.
Police Ware Road (Tel. 57711).
Casualty hospital Queen Elizabeth II, Howlands, Welwyn Garden City (Tel. Welwyn Garden City 28111).
Post office Fore Street.
Cinema County, Ware Road (Tel. 53461).
Public library Old Cross.
Places to see Museum and Art Gallery, Bull Plain; Castle.
Shopping Maidenhead Street; Fore Street; Ware Road; St Andrew's Street.
AA 24 hour service
Tel. Hatfield 62852.

Hexham Northumberland

For 13 centuries the sheep and cattle farmers of Northumberland have driven their beasts to the Tuesday market beside Hexham Abbey. The open parkland of the Sele, the old monastic enclosure in the town centre, the charming 16th and 17th-century houses, and the magnificent views across the River Tyne belong to a rural age long past in most of Britain.

The town's first church was built on the site of Hexham Abbey by St Wilfrid in 674. The present crypt is all that remains of St Wilfrid's Church. It is possibly the best example of an Anglo-Saxon crypt still in existence. In the chancel stands St Wilfrid's Chair, which was used to crown the Kings of Northumbria.

Across the market place from the abbey stands a massive 14th-century tower of the former Moot Hall.

ABBEY CARVING
One of several 15th-century stone caricatures that decorate the Leschman Chantry in Hexham Abbey.

Information Tel. 605225.
Location On the A69, 20 m. W of Newcastle upon Tyne.
Parking Gilegate; Loosing Hill; Wentworth Nurseries (all car parks).
District council Tynedale (Tel. 604011).
Population 9,600.
E-C Thur. **M-D** Tues.
Police Shaftoe Leazes (Tel. 604111).
Casualty hospital General, Corbridge Road (Tel. 602421).
Post office Battle Hill.
Cinema Forum, Market Place (Tel. 602896).
Public library Beaumont Street.
Places to see Moot Hall, Market Place; Manor Office, Hallgate.

Shopping Battle Hill; Fore Street; Priestpopple; Hallstile Bank.
AA 24 hour service
Tel. Newcastle upon Tyne 610111.

High Wycombe Bucks.

The beech trees of the Chiltern Hills around High Wycombe supplied the timber that made the town the centre of the English furniture-making industry. There are prehistoric earthworks on Desborough Hill, and a 2nd-century AD Roman villa was found on The Rye.

The octagonal Market House and the Guildhall were designed by Robert Adam, and are only two of several fine buildings in the Georgian High Street. West Wycombe Park was the home of Sir Francis Dashwood (1708-81), founder of the Hell-Fire Club which held orgies in the nearby ruins of Medmenham Abbey.

Benjamin Disraeli, 1st Earl of Beaconsfield (1804-81), the Victorian Prime Minister, lived at Hughenden Manor near by.

Information Tel. 26100.
Location On the A40, 19 m. NE of Reading.
Parking Dovecote Road; Easton Street; Newland Street (all car parks).
District council Wycombe (Tel. 26100).
Population 68,400.
E-C Wed. **M-D** Tues., Fri., Sat.
Police (Aa) Queen Victoria Road (Tel. 23131).
Casualty hospital General (Aa), Alexander Road (Tel. 26161).
Post office (Ba) Queen Victoria Road.
Cinema Palace (Ab), Frogmore (Tel. 23647).
Public library (Aa) Queen Victoria Road.
Places to see Hughenden Manor, 1½ m. N; Chair Museum, Priory Avenue; West Wycombe Park.
Shopping The Octagon; High Street.
AA 24 hour service
Tel. 01 954 7373.

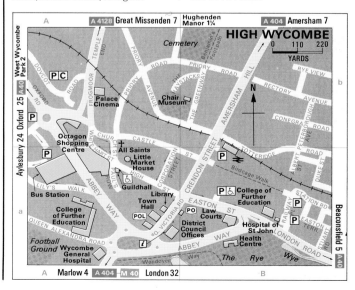

Hillingdon see London

Hinckley Leicestershire

The town has a long history of hosiery (to which it has added shoe-making), and it was here in 1640 that one of the first British stocking frames was installed by William Iliffe.

At Bosworth Field, 5 miles north, Richard III was killed in 1485, during the last great battle of the Wars of the Roses.

Information Tel. 30852/635106.
Location On the A47, 13 m. SW of Leicester.
Parking Stockwell Head; Mount Road; Lower Bond Street; The Borough; Druid Street; Church Walk; Brunel Road; Mansion Street (all car parks).
District council Borough of Hinckley and Bosworth (Tel. 38141).
Population 55,300.
E-C Thur. **M-D** Mon., Sat.
Police Upper Bond Street (Tel. 637881).
Casualty hospital Hinckley and District, Mount Road (Tel. 610722).
Post office Station Road.
Theatre Concordia, Stockwell Head (Tel. 615005).
Cinema Classic, Trinity Lane (Tel. 637523).
Public library Lancaster Road.
Places to see Battlefield Centre, Bosworth Field; Twycross Zoo.
Shopping Castle Street; Regent Street; Market Place.
AA 24 hour service
Tel. Leicester 20491.

Hitchin Hertfordshire

Attractive old medieval houses, inns and almshouses cluster together in the centre of Hitchin. St Mary's Church is the largest in the county and abounds in 15th-century craftsmanship. Hitchin Priory, built in the 18th century, includes fragments of a 14th-century monastery.

STEEL PIONEER

Sir Henry Bessemer (1813-98), a native of Hitchin, revolutionised British industry with the invention in 1856 of a process for converting molten pig iron into steel.

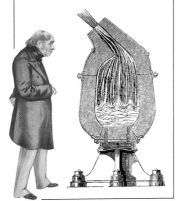

Information Tel. Letchworth 6500.
Location On the A505, 5 m. SW of Baldock.
Parking Bancroft; Old Park Road; Portmill Lane; St Mary's Square; Walsworth Road; Charlton Road; High Street; Queen Street; Bedford Road (all car parks).
District council North Hertfordshire (Tel. Letchworth 6500).
Population 30,300.
E-C Wed. **M-D** Tues., Sat.
Police Grove Road (Tel. 59636).
Casualty hospital Lister, Coreys Mill Lane, Stevenage (Tel. Stevenage 4333).
Post office Hermitage Road.
Public library Paynes Park.
Places to see St Mary's Bancroft Museum; Skynner Almshouses.
Shopping Arcade Precinct; High Street; Bancroft; Hermitage Road.
AA 24 hour service
Tel. Hatfield 62852.

Hoddesdon Hertfordshire

This old town has several reminders of its past. The Chapel of St Katherine dates from medieval times; Hogges Hall retains some 15th-century beams, and Rawdon House, with its fine gabled front, dates from 1622.

About 1 mile east of the town centre are the remains of moated Rye House, where in 1683 was hatched a plot to assassinate Charles II and his brother, the Duke of York, later James II. The plot failed, and the conspirators were executed.

Information Tel. 68331.
Location On the A1170, 4 m. SE of Hertford.
Parking Burford Street (2); Brocket Road (2); High Street; Cock Lane; Charlton Way; Conduit Lane (all car parks).
District council Borough of Broxbourne (Tel. Waltham Cross 27933).
Population 29,900.
E-C Thur. **M-D** Wed.
Police High Street (Tel. 68444).
Casualty hospital Enfield District General, Chace Wing, The Ridgeway, Enfield (Tel. 01 366 6600).
Post office High Street.
Public library High Street.
Places to see Rye House ruins.
Shopping High Street; Tower Centre; Fawkon Walk.
AA 24 hour service
Tel. Hatfield 62852.

Holyhead Gwynedd

The town is on Holy Island, and is reached from Anglesey by the Stanley Embankment, built by Thomas Telford in 1822. Further south is Four Mile Bridge which, with the Stanley Embankment, encloses a tidal lake known as the Inland Sea.

Holyhead, the largest port in Wales, has long been the main port for the sea route to Dublin. Boats came to the harbour as early as 2000 BC, trading in axes with Ireland.

The 6 ft thick walls of Caer Gybi Roman fort, which dates from the 3rd or 4th centuries, enclose the parish church of St Cybi, which dates from the 13th century.

At the entrance to the harbour is Salt Island, where salt was extracted from the sea during the 18th century. Near by is the Customs House of 1830. The harbour is protected by a 1⅓ mile long, Z-shaped breakwater, the longest in Britain. The automated lighthouse retains its original brass clockwork machinery of 1837.

At Ty Mawr, on the south-west slope of 710 ft high Holyhead Mountain, are the remains of dwellings which were occupied in the 3rd and 4th centuries. North and west the mountain drops down to the sea in sheer cliffs. At the foot is South Stack Island, which is joined to the mainland by an iron bridge. Its lighthouse was built in 1808 by Daniel Alexander, designer of Dartmoor Prison in Devon. Thousands of seabirds, including puffins and fulmars, nest on the island, and seals breed on its beaches.

HIGH LIGHT *South Stack lighthouse throws its beam 197 ft above high water and can be seen for 20 miles.*

Information Tel. 2622 (Apr.–Oct.); Colwyn Bay 56881 (Nov.–Mar.).
Location On the A5, Isle of Anglesey.
Parking Newry Street; Swift Square; Trearddur Square; Promenade (all car parks).
District council Isle of Anglesey (Tel. Llangefni 722920).
Population 10,500.
E-C Tues. **M-D** Fri., Sat.
Police (Ab) Newry Street (Tel. 2323).
Casualty hospital Stanley Sailors **(Bc)**, Salt Island (Tel. 2384).
Post office (Ab) Boston Street.
Cinema Empire 1 and 2 **(Ab)**, Stanley Street (Tel. 3754).
Public library (Ab) Newry Street.
Places to see South Stack lighthouse; Admiralty Arch **(Bc)**, Salt Island; Caer Gybi fort **(Ab)**.
Shopping Market Street; Stanley Street.
Events National Cycle Race (June or July); National Sailing Championship Racing (end July–Sept.); Regatta (Aug.).
Trade and industry Manufacture of clocks, toys, agricultural implements.

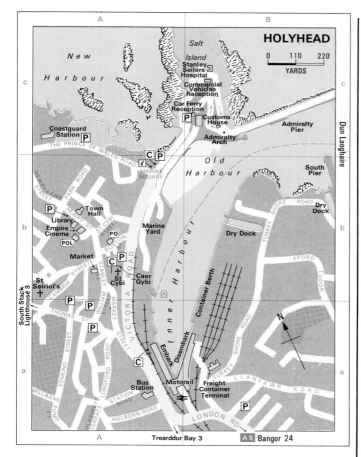

HOLYHEAD

0   110   220
YARDS

New Harbour

Salt Island

Stanley Sailors Hospital

Commercial Vehicles Reception

Car Ferry Reception

Customs House

Admiralty Pier

Coastguard Station

THE PRINCE OF WALES ROAD

Admiralty Arch

Old Harbour

South Pier

MARINE SQUARE

Town Hall

Library
Empire Cinema

POL

Market

Marine Yard

Dry Dock

Dry Dock

St Seiriol's

St Cybi

Caer Gybi

PO

Inner Harbour

Container Berth

TURKEY SHORE ROAD

FFORD

South Stack Lighthouse 3

Bus Station

Motorail

Freight Container Terminal

Embark

Disembark

Trearddur Bay 3   A5 Bangor 24

Dun Laoghaire

LLANFAWR ROAD

LONDON RD.

HOLBORN ROAD

Car ferry to Dun Laoghaire (for Dublin) (Tel. 2304).
AA 24 hour service
Tel. Llandudno 79066.

Honiton Devon

The long main street of Honiton is lined by Georgian shops and houses, built after fires had destroyed most of the town in the 18th century.

Honiton lace is world-famous. Queen Charlotte wore a dress of Honiton lace at her wedding to George III in 1761. Honiton and Allhallows Museum contains a valuable collection of the lace.

Information Tel. 3716.
Location On the A30, 17 m. NE of Exeter.
Parking Dowell Street; New Street; Silver Street; King Street (all car parks).
District council East Devon (Tel. Exmouth 4356).
Population 6,600.
E-C Thur. **M-D** Tues., Sat.
Police High Street (Tel. 2171).
Casualty hospital Royal Devon and Exeter Hospital (Wonford), Barrack Road, Exeter (Tel. Exeter 77833).
Post office High Street.
Public library New Street.
Places to see Honiton and Allhallows Museum, High Street; The Pottery, High Street.
Shopping High Street; New Street.
AA 24 hour service
Tel. Exeter 32121.

Hornsea Humberside

The sea is eating away at the long stretch of coast north of Spurn Head, and only huge concrete walls hold back the erosion. Hornsea, a pleasant holiday town, stands on a ¾ mile strip of land between the sandy beach and 324 acre Hornsea Mere, the largest natural freshwater lake in Yorkshire. Sailing and fishing are allowed on the mere. Most of its wooded banks and islands make up a protected nature reserve, where herons, grebe, swans, geese, cormorants and teal can be seen.

Thousands of visitors call each year at Hornsea Pottery, where potters can be watched at work.

Information Tel. 2919.
Location On the B1242, 12 m. NE of Hull.
Parking Newbegin (2); Fair Place; Sands Lane; Marine Drive; South Promenade; Morrow Avenue (all car parks).
District council Holderness (Tel. Skirlaugh 62333).
Population 7,200.
E-C Wed.
Police Parva Road (Tel. 2133).
Casualty hospital Hornsea Cottage Hospital, Eastgate (Tel. 3146).
Post office Newbegin.
Public library Newbegin.
Places to see Hornsea Pottery Leisure Park; Museum of Village Life, Burn's Farm, Newbegin.
Town trail Available from all newsagents.

Shopping Newbegin Shopping Centre; Market Place.
Event Carnival (July).
AA 24 hour service Tel. Hull 28580.

Horsham W. Sussex

In 1844 a man named Johnson sold his watch to raise 30 shillings to buy Ann Holland, who was offered for sale by her husband in Horsham Market Square. She lived with Johnson for a year, had a child and then disappeared.

Massive building stones, known as Horsham slabs, were once quarried locally. Other industries include brewing and engineering.

The parish church of St Mary was built by the Normans and enlarged over the centuries. It contains a tablet to the memory of the poet Percy Bysshe Shelley, who was born at Warnham, 2 miles north-west. The gardens of Field Place, Shelley's family home, are open to the public once a year.

Information Tel. 64191.
Location On the A281, 14 m. S of Dorking.
Parking Worthing Road; Albion Way (both car parks).
District council Horsham (Tel. 64191).
Population 25,400.
E-C Mon., Thur. **M-D** Fri., Sat.
Police Hurst Road (Tel. 4242).
Casualty hospital Cuckfield Hospital, Ardingley Road, Cuckfield (Tel. Haywards Heath 50661).
Post office The Carfax.
Theatres The Capitol, Swan Walk (Tel. 60679); Christ's Hospital, Arts Centre (Tel. 2709).
Public library North Street.
Places to see Knepp Castle, 6 m. S; Horsham Museum, The Causeway; Wainham Museum, 2 m. N.
Shopping East Street; West Street; Carfax; Swan Walk; The Bishopric.
AA 24 hour service
Tel. Crawley 25685.

THE CAUSEWAY *This quiet road of old buildings includes the Tudor Causeway House, now Horsham Museum.*

Hounslow see London

Hove E. Sussex

Regency terraces with bow fronts and tall pilasters, broad lawns and a refined air separate Hove from its more boisterous seaside companion, Brighton. The town developed as a residential area following the Prince Regent's visits to Brighton.

In the graveyard of All Saints Church is the tomb of Sir George Everest (1790-1866), Surveyor-General of India, after whom the world's highest mountain is named.

ELEGANT HOVE *Brunswick Square is typical of Hove's Regency architecture.*

Information Tel. Brighton 775400.
Location On the A259, 2 m. W of Brighton.
Parking King Alfred Sports Centre; Norton Road; Haddington Street; Malvern Street; Stirling Place (cps).
District council Borough of Hove (Tel. Brighton 775400).
Population 66,600.
E-C Wed., Thur.
Police Holland Road (Tel. Brighton 778922).
Casualty hospital Sussex County, Brighton (Tel. Brighton 606111).
Post office Church Road.
Theatre Old Market Arts Centre, Upper Market Street (Tel. Brighton 779821).
Cinema Embassy, Western Road (Tel. Brighton 735124).
Public library Church Road.
Shopping Western Road; Church Road; George Street.
Sport County cricket, Eaton Road; FA League football, Brighton and Hove Albion FC, Old Shoreham Road.
AA 24 hour service
Tel. Brighton 695231.

Hoylake Merseyside

Ancient coins found on the shore show that Hoylake was settled in pre-Roman times. Later it became a major port, but its sheltered anchorage, Hoyle Lake, silted up and disappeared

in the 18th century. Near by are the Royal Liverpool Links, where the Open Championship has been held.

Information
Tel. Liverpool (051) 632 3401.
Location On the A55, 11 m. W of Liverpool.
Parking Market Street; Charles Road (both car parks).
District council Metropolitan Borough of Wirral (Tel. 051 638 7070).
Population 32,900.
E-C Wed.
Police Queen's Road (Tel. 051 709 6010).
Casualty hospital Clatterbridge General, Clatterbridge Road, Babington (Tel. 051 334 4000).
Post office Station Road.
Cinema Classic, Alderley Road (Tel. 051 632 1345).
Public library Market Street.
Shopping Market Street.
AA 24 hour service
Tel. Liverpool (051) 709 7252.

Hucknall Nottinghamshire

The poet Lord Byron is buried in Hucknall parish church. His body was brought back to the family vault from Greece, where he died of fever in 1824 during the Greek struggle for independence from Turkey. Four miles north of Hucknall lies Newstead Abbey, Byron's family home (open to the public).

POET'S NICHE *A statue of Byron overlooks the market square in Hucknall.*

Information Tel. Mansfield 559111.
Location On the A611, 7 m. N of Nottingham.
Parking South Street; Piggins Croft; Titchfield Street; Station Road; Market Place (all car parks).
District council Ashfield (Tel. Mansfield 559111).
Population 28,100.
E-C Wed. **M-D** Fri.
Police Watnall Road (Tel. Nottingham 633081).
Casualty hospital Mansfield General, West Hill Drive, Mansfield (Tel. Mansfield 22515).
Post office High Street.
Cinema High Street (Tel. Nottingham 636377).
Public library Market Place.
Shopping High Street; Market Place.
AA 24 hour service
Tel. Nottingham 787751.

CHIMNEYSCAPE *A forest of stacks rises from the mills of Huddersfield.*

Huddersfield W. Yorks.

Wool has been spun and woven in and around Huddersfield for centuries. It was a cottage craft in the villages on the Pennine moors until the 18th century. Then textile mills were built in the town where they could be powered by water from the streams feeding the River Colne. Steam power followed, then two canals to carry fuel to the mills. As the town grew, the residential area spread up the hillside.

The railway station, built for a line opened in 1847, is an outstanding example of Victorian railway architecture. It has a Corinthian portico of six fluted columns flanked by pilastered wings.

Huddersfield has several good Victorian Gothic buildings, among them St Peter's Church, built in 1838, and the clock-tower, completed in 1902.

In Ravensknowle Park is a partial re-erection of the Cloth Hall, built as a centre for the cloth industry in 1776 and dismantled in 1930.

Also in the park is the Tolson Memorial Museum, whose exhibits range from archaeological relics to a collection of horse-drawn vehicles. Local history is displayed in the Colne Valley Museum at Golcar, on the western outskirts of the town. Exhibits include a restored weaver's cottage of the 1860s, with living-room, workshop and working looms, and a gas-lit clog-maker's shop.

An art gallery in the public library houses a permanent collection of paintings and sculptures by L. S. Lowry, Stanley Spencer, Turner, Gainsborough, Constable and Henry Moore. The imposing 19th-century Town Hall is the home of the internationally known Huddersfield Choral Society.

Information Tel. 22133.
Location On the A62, 16 m. SW of Leeds.
Parking Alfred Street; Upperhead Row; Pine Street; Railway Station Forecourt; Sergeantson Street;

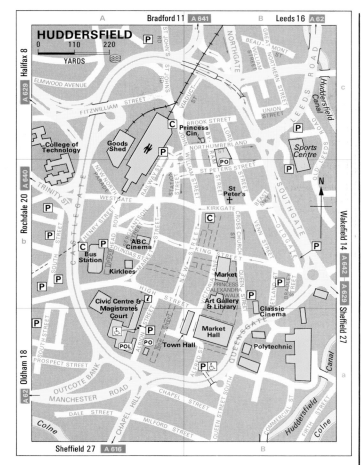

HUDDERSFIELD

Bradford 11 A 641 · Leeds 16 A 62 · Halifax 8 A 629 · Rochdale 20 A 640 · Oldham 18 A 62 · Wakefield 14 A 642 · A 629 Sheffield 27 · Sheffield 27 A 616

Huntingdon Cambs.

Associations with the Cromwell family abound throughout the town. Hinchingbroke House, now a school, was originally a 13th-century nunnery that passed to the Cromwell family during the Dissolution of the Monasteries. Sir Richard, great-grandfather of Oliver, built a Tudor country house around its walls, and his son, Sir Henry, entertained Queen Elizabeth there in 1564.

Oliver Cromwell (1599-1658) was born in a house whose site is now occupied by the Huntingdon Research Centre. The George, a former coaching inn of which records date back at least to the time of Henry VIII, once belonged to Cromwell's grandfather.

All Saints Church, where he was baptised and his father was buried, dates from the 14th and 15th centuries but has been much altered and restored.

The town forms a single unit with Godmanchester, to which it is linked across the River Great Ouse by a beautiful 14th-century bridge.

Information Tel. 52181.
Location On the A14, 16 m. NW of Cambridge.
Parking St Germain Street; Trinity Place; Ingram Street; Great Northern Street; St Benedict's Court (all car parks).
District council Huntingdon (Tel. 56161).
Population 17,500.
E-C Wed. **M-D** Sat.
Police Hinchingbroke Park (Tel. 56111).
Casualty hospital Huntingdon County, Brampton Road (Tel. 53681).
Post office Chequers Court.
Public library Princes Street.
Places to see Cromwell Museum; Hinchingbroke House, ½ m. SW.
Shopping St Benedict's Court; High Street; Chequers Court.
AA 24 hour service
Tel. Cambridge 312302.

Queen Street; Bradley Street; Oldgate; Sports Centre (all car parks).
District council Kirklees (Tel. 22133).
Population 123,900.
E-C Wed. **M-D** Mon., Thur.
Police (Aa) Castlegate (Tel. 22122).
Casualty hospital Huddersfield Royal Infirmary, Lindley (Tel. 22191).
Post office (Bc) Northumberland Street.
Cinemas ABC 1 and 2 **(Ab)**, Market Street (Tel. 24130); Classic **(Ba)**, Queensgate (30874); Princess **(Bc)**, Northumberland Street (32235); Venn Street Arts Centre (22133).
Public library (Bb) Princess Alexandra Walk.
Places to see Railway station **(Ab)**; Art Gallery **(Bb)**, Princess Alexandra Walk; Tolson Memorial Museum; Cloth Hall; Castle Hill; Colne Valley Museum, Golcar.
Town trails Available from I. Crouch, Department of Geography and Geology, The Polytechnic, Queensgate.
Shopping New Street; New Street Precinct; Princess Alexandra Walk; Brook Street Market.
Trade and industry Woollen textiles; chemicals; engineering.
Sport FA League football, Huddersfield Town FC, Bradley Mills Road; Rugby League, Huddersfield RLC, Fartown.
AA 24 hour service
Tel. Leeds 38161.

Hunstanton Norfolk

The largest of west Norfolk's seaside resorts faces to The Wash. Long stretches of sand are backed by striped cliffs formed from layers of white and red chalk and a type of brown sandstone called carr stone. The cliffs, which stretch north from the pier, are a source of many unusual fossils. Hunstanton St Edmund is predominantly Victorian, with large turreted houses like French châteaux.

Information Tel. 2610.
Location On the A149, 16 m. N of King's Lynn.
Parking Seagate Road; Beach Terrace Road; Boston Square; Lighthouse Close; St Edmund's Terrace (all car parks).
District council Borough of King's Lynn and West Norfolk (Tel. King's Lynn 61241).
Population 4,100.   **E-C** Thur.
Police King's Lynn Road (Tel. 2666).
Casualty hospital Queen Elizabeth Hospital, King's Lynn (Tel. King's Lynn 66266).
Theatre Princess Theatre (Tel. 2252).
Post office High Street.
Public library Westgate.
Places to see Lavender distillery, Heacham, 2 m. S; Holme Nature Reserve, 3 m. NE.
Shopping High Street; Westgate; Greevegate-Northgate Precinct.
AA 24 hour service
Tel. Norwich 29401.

OLIVER CROMWELL

The leader of the Parliamentarians during the Civil War and Lord Protector of England from 1653 until his death in 1658 was educated at Huntingdon Free School, which later became the Grammar School and is now a museum devoted to his life.

Cromwell's seal is one of many relics preserved in the museum.

MARTELLO TOWERS *On Hythe beach stand some of the circular forts built in the late 18th century as a precaution against invasion by Napoleon.*

I

Huntly Grampian

The powerful Gordon clan, who gave their name to the "Gay Gordons" dance, made Huntly their chief seat in the 14th century. The derelict castle outside the town was the home of the clan chieftains, the Marquesses of Huntly, until 1752 when they abandoned it. The castle has an imposing south front, with a row of oriel windows in place of the traditional battlements.

The Stan'in' Stanes of Strathbogie (now reduced to two) in the town square were originally a Druid circle, but came to symbolise the power of the Gordons.

Information Tel. 2280.
Location On the A97, 21 m. SW of Banff.
Parking The Square; Eastpark Street; Nelson Street; George V Avenue (all car parks).
District council Gordon (Tel. Inverurie 20981).
Population 4,000.
E-C Thur. **M-D** Wed.
Police Castle Street (Tel. 2246).
Casualty hospital Jubilee, Bleachfield Street (Tel. 2114).
Post office The Square.
Cinema The Playhouse, Gordon Street (Tel. 2895).
Public library The Square.
Places to see Museum, The Square; Huntly Castle ruins.
Shopping Gordon Street; Duke Street.
Trade and industry Knitwear; agriculture; oil-related engineering.
AA 24 hour service Tel. Aberdeen 51231.

Hyde see Tameside

Hythe Kent

The seafront at Hythe is that of a traditional English seaside resort. But inland the town has a quiet charm, with mellow old houses, inns and hilly streets and the still waters of the Royal Military Canal. The canal, a defensive measure built in Napoleonic times, is now used for boating and a spectacular water carnival every other year.

Hythe is one of the Cinque Ports –

Dover, Hastings, Romney and Sandwich are the others – charged with the defence of the south coast from the 12th to the 14th centuries. The parish church of St Leonard, with its 13th-century chancel, is one of Kent's most impressive churches.

The town is the northern terminus of the smallest public railway in the world, the Romney, Hythe and Dymchurch, opened in 1927.

Information Tel. 66152.
Location On the A259, 13 m. SW of Dover.
Parking Prospect Road; Military Road; Mount Street; Portland Road (all car parks).
District council Shepway (Tel. Folkestone 57388).
Population 12,700.
E-C Wed.
Police Prospect Road (Tel. 68223).
Casualty hospital William Harvey, Ashford (Tel. Ashford 33331).
Post office High Street.
Cinema Classic Entertainment Centre, Prospect Road (Tel. 66292).
Public library Stade Street.
Places to see Romney, Hythe and Dymchurch Light Railway; Martello Towers.
Shopping High Street; Bank Street.
Event Venetian Fete (every other Aug.).
Trade and industry Surgical instruments.
AA 24 hour service Tel. Thanet 81226.

Ilfracombe Devon

The largest holiday resort on the North Devon coast grew up around an ancient fishing harbour during the 19th century. The town is built in terraces on steep hills which rise from the shore. Its many coves and bays are sand and shingle, with rocky outcrops. Exmoor lies within easy reach. A medieval chapel to St Nicholas, patron saint of sailors, stands on a rock at the harbour entrance.

Chambercombe Manor, 1 mile to the south-east, is a 15th-century house with a secret room and a 12th-century cider press. The 18th-century Bicclescombe Mill still works.

Information Tel. 63001.
Location On the A399, 13 m. N of Barnstaple.
Parking Brookdale Avenue; Wilder Road (2); Bath Place; Jubilee Gardens; The Pier; Cove; High Street; Oxford Grove (all car parks).
District council North Devon (Tel. Barnstaple 72511).
Population 10,100.
E-C Thur.
Police (Aa) Princess Road (Tel. 63633).
Casualty hospital North Devon District, Raleigh Park, Barnstaple (Tel. Barnstaple 72577).
Post office (Aa) High Street.
Theatre Victoria Pavilion **(Bb)**, The Promenade (Tel. 62228).
Cinemas Clifton 1 and 2 **(Aa)**, High Street (Tel. 62626); Embassy **(Aa)**, High Street (63484).
Public library (Aa) Brookfield Place.
Places to see Chambercombe Manor;

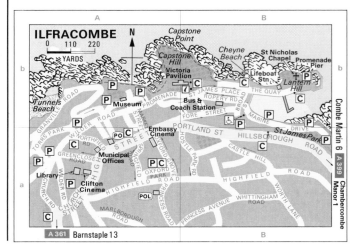

ILFRACOMBE

Bicclescombe Mill.
Shopping High Street; Church
Street; Wilder Road; The Quay.
AA 24 hour service
Tel. Barnstaple 45691.

Ilkeston Derbyshire

The hilltop town of Ilkeston has been
for centuries the market centre for
the Erewash Valley. As well as weekly
markets, a three-day fair has been
held annually for more than 700
years. Ilkeston's parish church of St
Mary was built in about 1150 and has
an intricately carved, 14th-century
stone screen. Frame knitting of stockings flourished in the 18th century. In
the 19th century canals and railways
brought cheap fuel, transforming the
trade into a factory industry now replaced by other textile industries.

Information Tel. 301104.
Location On the A609, 7 m. W of
Nottingham.
Parking East Street; Market Place;
Stanton Road; Market Street;
Pimlico; Albion Place; Station Road;
Wilton Place; North Street; Durham
Street (all car parks).
District council Erewash Borough
Council (Tel. Long Eaton 60121).
Population 33,000.
E-C Wed. **M-D** Thur., Sat.
Police Wharncliffe Road
(Tel. 324311).
Casualty hospital General, Heanor
Road (Tel. 301133).
Post office South Street.
Cinema Scala, Pimlico
(Tel. 324612).
Public library Market Place.
Shopping Bath Street; South Street;
Market Place.
Event Annual Charter Fair (Oct.).
AA 24 hour service
Tel. Nottingham 787751.

Ilkley W. Yorks.

In the old folk-song any young man
courting on Ilkley Moor baht 'at
(without a hat) risked catching a fatal
chill. The town stands on the edge of
the moor, whose mineral springs
prompted the Victorians to make Ilkley a spa. The hydros have disappeared, and Ilkley is now a residential
town and tourist centre for the Yorkshire Dales. Scattered over the moors
are Bronze and Iron Age relics.

Information Tel. 608505.
Location On the A65, 15 m. N of
Bradford.
Parking Brook Street; Station Road;
Railway Road; Wells Road; Leeds
Road (all car parks).
District council City of Bradford
Metropolitan Council
(Tel. Bradford 29577).
Population 24,100.
E-C Wed.
Police Riddings Road (Tel. 601060).
Casualty hospital Airedale General,
Skipton Road, Steeton, Keighley
(Tel. Steeton 52511).
Post office Chantry Drive.

Theatre Ilkley Playhouse, Weston
Road (Tel. 609539).
Public library Station Road.
Places to see Manor House Art
Gallery and Museum; Roman fort.
Town trails Available from public
library.
Shopping Brook Street; The Grove.
AA 24 hour service
Tel. Leeds 38161.

Inveraray Strathclyde

When the sun is out, the 18th-
century whitewashed buildings of Inveraray are a dazzling sight against the
blue waters of Loch Fyne.

The town, a royal burgh until 1975,
is the oldest in Argyllshire, dating
back beyond historical records. But
no trace of ancient buildings survives,
because a new town replaced the old
in the late 18th century.

The most notable building is the
18th-century castle, seat of the Dukes
of Argyll, chiefs of the Campbell
clan. North of it towers the hill of
Duniquaich, crowned by a tower.

The parish church, built 1794-
1806, is unusual: a central dividing
wall was erected so that Gaelic and
English services could be held simul-
taneously; the Gaelic part is now the
church hall. In the main street is a
500-year-old cross in Celtic style.

The Old Town House was originally built as a customs house in 1753.
This was a year after the unfair trial
and hanging of James Stewart for the
murder of Colin Campbell, the story
of which is told by Robert Louis
Stevenson in *Kidnapped*.

Information Tel. 2063 (summer
only).
Location On the A83, 25 m. NE of
Lochgilphead.
Parking Church Square; Front Street
(both car parks).
District council Argyll and Bute
(Tel. Kilmory 2127).
Population 690.
E-C Wed. (not in summer).
Police The Police Station
(Tel. 2222).
Casualty hospital Vale of Leven,
Alexandria
(Tel. Alexandria 54121).
Post office Main Street.
Places to see Castle; Old Town
House; Dunderave Castle, 5 m. NE;
Auchindrain Farming Township
Museum, 6 m. SW.
Shopping Main Street; Shore Street.
Event Highland Games (July).
AA 24 hour service
Tel. Glasgow (041) 812 0101.

WARLIKE TRADITION *Muskets, swords,
dirks and shields are displayed in the
armoury of Inveraray Castle, stronghold
of the chiefs of the Campbell clan.*

INVERARAY CASTLE *Campbell chiefs built the neo-Gothic castle between 1744 and
1794 to replace a 15th-century stronghold. It contains portraits by Gainsborough,
Raeburn and Landseer, superb French tapestries, and Louis XIV furniture.*

INVERNESS Highland

The capital of the Highlands

The name of this ancient Scottish town is Gaelic for "river mouth of the Ness", upon which it stands. To the north, south and west the town is ringed by mountains, while to the east lies the Moray Firth. The town is a busy communications centre at the eastern end of the Caledonian Canal. It is also a thriving market town and business centre.

Inverness is one of the oldest settlements in Scotland, as the many prehistoric burial cairns, carved stones and other memorials in the area show. Well-known remains include Clava Cairns, Bronze Age burial mounds, 7 miles east of the town.

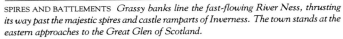

JACOBITE RELICS *Inverness Museum contains many relics of the clans who followed Bonnie Prince Charlie.*

The earliest mention of the town is in a contemporary biography of the 6th-century St Columba, who is said to have visited the Pictish King Brude at his fortress beside the Ness.

In the old castle of Inverness, that stood east of the present one, King Duncan was murdered by Macbeth in 1039 – a crime dramatised by Shakespeare. All that remains of the castle today is the site, Auld Castlehill.

David I (1124-53) created Inverness a royal burgh, built another castle that was to stand for six centuries, and made the town a seat of justice. It eventually came to symbolise law and order to the unruly clans, who over the centuries stormed and pillaged it time and time again.

After the Jacobite Rising of 1715, the old castle was enlarged and strengthened by General Wade, who called it Fort George, after George I.

In the 1745 Rising, Bonnie Prince Charlie occupied Inverness. The castle garrison surrendered to him after a two-day siege, and he ordered the castle to be blown up. The following year, after the rout of the Jacobite army at Culloden, the Duke of Cumberland, known as "the Butcher", descended on the town and wreaked vengeance upon it. Many houses were ransacked, churches were destroyed and prisoners were shot.

In 1817 a new market made Inverness the centre of the Highland wool and sheep trade, and the coming of the railways in 1855 opened up the town to the south.

Little of this past can be seen today. The present **castle,** replacing the two former buildings on the same site, dates from 1834-46. It is a courthouse and administrative centre.

On the castle esplanade is a memorial to **Flora Macdonald,** who helped Bonnie Prince Charlie escape to the Isle of Skye after the Battle of Culloden. The statue shows her looking south-west towards his hiding place. Inscribed on the monument are the words of Dr Johnson, who said: "The Preserver of Prince Charles Edward will be mentioned in history, and if courage and fidelity be virtues, mentioned with honour."

Gaelic culture preserved

The most interesting old house in the town is **Abertarff House** in Church Street. Built about 1593, it contains the last remaining example of the old turnpike stair, a kind of spiral staircase once common in the homes of wealthy townspeople. The house is the headquarters of *An Comunn Gaidhealach*, the association which preserves Gaelic language and culture. It contains an exhibition depicting the history of the Gael.

The **Town House,** a group of Gothic-style offices built in 1878-82,

---

SPIRES AND BATTLEMENTS *Grassy banks line the fast-flowing River Ness, thrusting its way past the majestic spires and castle ramparts of Inverness. The town stands at the eastern approaches to the Great Glen of Scotland.*

was the venue of the first British Cabinet meeting ever held outside London, in September 1921. The meeting was called by the Prime Minister, Lloyd George, who was on holiday in Scotland. A document in the council chamber bears the signatures of the ministers who attended.

Seat of wisdom

In front of the Town House and partly sunk below ground level is the *Clach-na-cuddain* (Stone of the tubs), so called because townswomen of old would rest at the stone when carrying home their tubs of water. According to tradition, the stone was the seat of a seer who predicted that so long as it was preserved Inverness would flourish.

Near by, in **Castle Wynd,** is an art gallery and the town's museum, which contains relics of the Jacobites and the Highland way of life.

The clock-tower is all that survives of a five-sided citadel built by Cromwell's army after 1652. It was demolished in 1662 after the restoration of Charles II. Some of the stones were used for Dunbar's Hospital, in Church Street, built in 1688 as an almshouse, but partly used as a grammar school.

The parish church has a 14th-century vaulted tower. Bullet marks on a stone in the churchyard are grim reminders of the execution of prisoners after the Battle of Culloden.

At the corner of Church Street stands a 130 ft high steeple, built in 1791 as part of the town prison. Dangerous prisoners were once kept in a small cell beneath the bells.

Beauty in stone and in cloth

St Andrew's Cathedral, built 1866-9, has a richly decorated interior, with illuminated windows and carved pillars. The font is a copy of one in Copenhagen Cathedral, Denmark.

In Friar's Street, one broken sandstone pillar is all that survives of a Dominican priory built in 1233.

At a workshop in Dores Road, tartan and tweed-spinning and weaving by hand can be watched.

One mile west of the town is Tomnahurich cemetery, claimed by some as the most beautiful cemetery in the world, commanding from its 220 ft summit magnificent views of Inverness and the surrounding landscape.

The Ness Islands, less than a mile up-river from the town centre, which are linked to the shore by bridges, are illuminated on summer evenings.

At Craig Phadrig, 1½ miles west of the town on a 556 ft hill, is a grassy mound – all that remains of a "vitrified fort" of the 4th century BC. The fort was an enclosure built of granite blocks which have been vitrified – fused into a glass-like mass by fire. How prehistoric man produced the intense heat required – at least 1,300°C – remains a mystery.

Field of slaughter

At **Culloden** battlefield, 6 miles east of the town, the graves of the 1,200 fallen members of the clans are marked. It was here, on April 16, 1746, that the Jacobites under Prince Charles Edward Stuart were defeated by the British in one of the bloodiest battles fought on Scottish soil. A small, thatched cottage called Old Leanach remains almost exactly as it

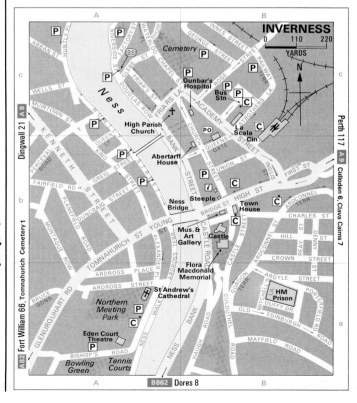

DESERT FIGHTER *The Cameron Highlanders fought in the 19th-century campaigns in Egypt.*

was when the battle raged around it.

A path from the cottage leads through the Field of the English, where the 76 men of the Duke of Cumberland's forces who died in the battle are said to be buried.

Information Tel. 34353.
Location On the A9, 16 m. SW of Nairn.
Parking Chapel Street; Rose Street; Bishop's Road (2); Riverside Street; Strothers Lane; Castle Street; Station Yard; Station Square (all car parks).
District council Inverness (Tel. 39111).
Population 39,700.
E-C Wed. **M-D** Tues.
Police Raigmore (Tel. 39191).
Casualty hospital Raigmore Hospital, Perth Road (Tel. 34151).
Post office (Bb) Queensgate.
Theatre Eden Court **(Aa),** Bishop's Road (Tel. 221718).
Cinema La Scala **(Bc),** Academy Street (Tel. 33302).
Public library Farraline Park.
Places to see Abertarff House **(Bb),** Church Street; Castle **(Bb),** Castle Street; Cromwell's clock-tower, off Shore Street; Museum and Art Gallery **(Bb),** Castle Wynd; Clava Cairns, 7 m. E; Culloden battlefield, 6 m. E on B9006.
Shopping Union Street; High Street; Bridge Street; Church Street; Academy Street; Castle Street; Eastgate; Queensgate; Baron Taylor Street.
Event Highland Games (July/Aug.).
Trade and industry Engineering; tourism; weaving.
Motorail Tel. Inverness 32651.
AA 24 hour service Tel. Aberdeen 51231.

TOWN HOUSE *The British Cabinet met here in 1921. It included two future prime ministers, Stanley Baldwin and Winston Churchill.*

Inverurie Grampian

Wide streets of granite buildings criss-cross the royal burgh of Inverurie, a good centre for exploring the wooded valleys of Aberdeenshire and for salmon and trout fishing in the River Don. In the cemetery is a 50 ft high sand-and-gravel mound called the Bass, the site of a Norman castle.

Information Tel. 20981; also Banff 2419/2789.
Location On the A96, 17 m. NW of Aberdeen.
Parking Market Place (2); Victoria Street; Western Road (all car parks).
District council Gordon (Tel. 20981).
Population 7,700.
E-C Wed. **M-D** Thur.
Police High Street (Tel. 20222).
Casualty hospital Aberdeen Royal Infirmary, Foresterhill, Aberdeen (Tel. Aberdeen 23423).
Post office West High Street.
Cinema Victoria, West High Street (Tel. 21436).
Public library Market Place.
Places to see Museum; Brandsbutt Stone; Pitcaple Castle, 5 m. NW.
Shopping Market Place; High Street.
AA 24 hour service Tel. Aberdeen 51231.

Ipswich Suffolk

The county town of Suffolk was successively a Stone Age, Iron Age, Roman and Anglo-Saxon settlement known as Gippeswic. King John granted the town its first charter in 1200, and for the next four centuries it flourished as a port trading Suffolk cloth with the Continent. Today the port, on the estuary of the River Orwell, handles over 2½ million tons of cargo each year.

Much of the town's past is revealed in the collection at Ipswich Museum. It includes Saxon weapons and jewellery retrieved from a local cemetery, and replicas of the Mildenhall and Sutton Hoo treasures.

Christchurch Mansion, a red-brick Tudor country house, has rooms furnished and decorated in the styles of the 16th to 19th centuries. It also contains paintings by Constable, Gainsborough and Munnings.

The Ancient House in the Butter Market is a 15th-century building with richly carved plasterwork.

Cardinal Wolsey was born in the town about 1475, probably in Silent Street. In 1528 he founded a college in the town. However, it was abandoned when he fell from power, and all that remains today is the red-brick gateway in College Street.

CHRISTCHURCH MANSION *This 16th-century Ipswich house is now a museum.*

RICH CARVING *Charles II's coat of arms forms a centrepiece in the ornate plasterwork on the Ancient House, a 15th-century extravaganza in the Butter Market.*

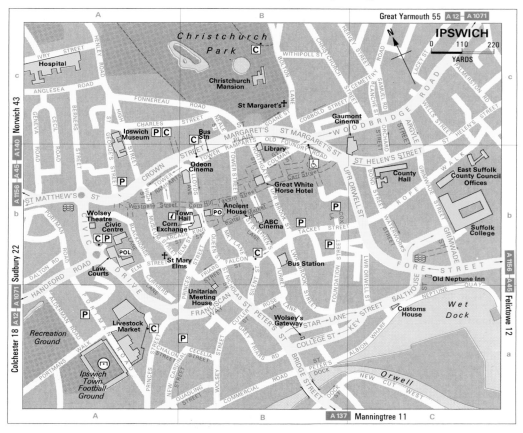

Information Tel. 58070.
Location On the A12, 12 m. NW of Felixstowe.
Parking St George's Street; Charles Street; Civic Drive; Tacket Street (2); Portman Road; Portman's Walk; Chalon Street (all car parks).
District council Borough of Ipswich (Tel. 211211).
Population 120,400.
M-D Tues., Thur., Fri., Sat.
Police (Ab) Civic Drive (Tel. 55811).
Casualty hospital Ipswich General (Ac), Ivry Street (Tel. 212477).
Post office (Bb) Cornhill.
Theatre Wolsey (Ab), Civic Drive (Tel. 53725).
Cinemas ABC 1, 2 and 3 (Bb), Butter Market (Tel. 53353); Gaumont (Cc), St Helen's Street (53641); Odeon 1, 2 and 3 (Bb), Lloyds Avenue (52082); Ipswich Film Theatre, King Street (215544).
Public library (Bb) Northgate Street.
Places to see Christchurch Mansion and Wolsey Art Gallery (Bc); Ancient House (Bb); Ipswich Museum (Ac); Town Hall (Bb).
Shopping Westgate Street; Tavern Street; Carr Street; Upper Brook Street; Butter Market; Queen Street.
Sport FA League football, Ipswich Town FC (Aa), Portman Road; Speedway, Foxhall Stadium.
AA 24 hour service Tel. Norwich 29401.

Irvine Strathclyde

The ancient burgh of Irvine was the main port for Glasgow before the River Clyde was deepened in the 18th century. It is Britain's first "new town" by the sea. Robert Burns lived in Irvine from 1781 to 1782.

Information Tel. Largs 673765.
Location On the A78, 7 m. W of Kilmarnock.
Parking Harbour Road (2); East Road (2); Friar's Croft (3); High Street; Castle Street; Quarry Road; Kirkgate (all car parks).
District council Cunninghame (Tel. 74166).
Population 32,000.
E-C Wed.
Police High Street (Tel. 74911).
Casualty hospital North Ayrshire District General, Crosshouse, Kilmarnock (Tel. Kilmarnock 21133).
Post office High Street.
Theatres Harbour Arts Centre, Harbour Street (Tel. 74059); Magnum Theatre/Cinema, Harbour Street (78381).
Public library Cunninghame House, off Fullarton Street.
Shopping Eglinton Street; High Street; Bridgegate.
AA 24 hour service Tel. Glasgow (041) 812 0101.

Islington see London

ST PAUL'S, JARROW *The Saxon church was part of a monastery where Bede, the first English historian, died in 735.*

Jarrow Tyne & Wear

The town entered the history books during the depression of the 1930s, when its workers marched to Westminster to demand employment. Jarrow is in the Tyneside ship-building area, and has produced many of the Royal Navy's finest warships, including the battleship HMS *Resolution* which served in the two World Wars.

In earlier times, Jarrow was the home of the Venerable Bede (673-735) whose *Ecclesiastical History* was the first written record of the English people. Jarrow's parish church of St Paul stands beside the site of the monastery where Bede lived and worked. Part of the church dates from Bede's time, and inside is preserved a Saxon chair traditionally known as Bede's chair.

Information Tel. 892106.
Location Off A185, 3 m. W of South Shields.
Parking Chapel Road (3); Cambrian Street (all car parks).
District council South Tyneside (Tel. South Shields 554321).
Population 27,100.

E-C Wed.
Police Clervaux Terrace (Tel. 894281).
Casualty hospital Ingham Infirmary, Westoe Road, South Shields (Tel. South Shields 560221).
Post office Monkton Road.
Public library Cambrian Street.
Places to see St Paul's Church; Bede Monastery Museum, Jarrow Hall.
Shopping Viking Precinct; Arndale Centre; Bede Precinct; Elliston Street; Grange Road.
Trade and industry Light engineering, chemicals.
AA 24 hour service Tel. Newcastle upon Tyne 610111.

Jedburgh Borders

For many centuries Jedburgh was a battleground in the wars between the Scots and the English. Its castle, built in the 12th century, changed hands many times – and in 1409 the Scots destroyed it because of its value to the English. The site is now occupied by the former County Prison, erected in 1823 but still known as "The Castle". It contains a museum displaying penal methods of the 19th century.

Jedburgh Abbey was founded in the 12th century. Like the castle, it came under attack during the various English invasions and in 1523 it was bombarded and burned. The tower rises to 86 ft above the roofless nave.

Queen Mary's House is a picturesque building of rough-hewn stone which contains a small bedroom supposedly occupied by Mary, Queen of Scots during her stay at Jedburgh in 1566. The house is now a museum containing relics associated with the queen.

Information Tel. 3435/3688.
Location On the A68, 14 m. E of Hawick.
Parking Canongate; Lothian Park; Murray's Green (all car parks).
District council Roxburgh (Tel. Hawick 5991).
Population 4,050.
E-C Thur.
Police Castlegate (Tel. 2264).
Casualty hospitals Health Centre, Queen Street (Tel. 3361). Evenings and weekends: Cottage Hospital, Castlegate (3212).
Post office High Street.
Public library Castlegate.
Shopping Market Place; High Street.
Event Handball (Shrove Tuesday).
Trade and industry Woollens; hosiery; tanning.
AA 24 hour service Tel. Edinburgh (031) 225 8464.

JEDBURGH ABBEY *The 12th-century, red-sandstone abbey is partially ruined, but still dominates the town with its grandeur.*

K

Keighley see Bradford

Kelso Borders

For centuries Kelso was a strategic point in the Border wars between the Scots and the English. The 12th-century abbey, destroyed by the Earl of Hertford in 1545, was the largest of the Border abbeys. Its ruins still display fine Norman and early-Gothic work.

The town's focal point is its wide, cobbled market square, bounded by imposing buildings of the 18th and 19th centuries. Floors Castle, home of the Duke of Roxburgh, was designed by Sir John Vanbrugh in 1718.

Information Tel. 3464.
Location On the A699, 11 m. NE of Jedburgh.
Parking The Knowes (2); Abbey Court; East Bowmont Street (all car parks).
District council Roxburgh (Tel. Hawick 5991).
Population 5,000.
E-C Wed.
Police Simon Square (Tel. 3434).
Casualty hospital Cottage Hospital, Jedburgh Road (Tel. 2591).
Post office Horsemarket.
Cinema Roxy, Horsemarket (Tel. 2609).
Public library Bowmont Street.
Places to see Kelso Abbey; Floors Castle; Turret House.
Town trails Available from Tourism Division, Borders Regional Council, Newtown, St Boswells.
Shopping Horsemarket; The Square.
Trade and industry Agricultural implements; electronics; plastics.
Sport National Hunt racing, Kelso Racecourse, Berrymoss.
AA 24 hour service
Tel. Edinburgh (031) 225 8464.

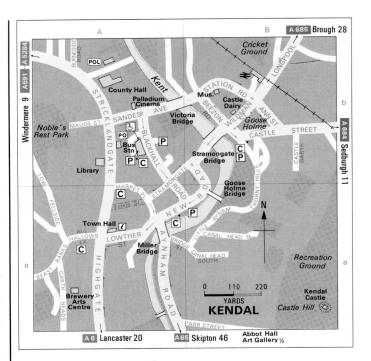

KENDAL

Kendal Cumbria

The "Auld Grey Town" – so called because of its many limestone buildings – lies at the foot of softly rounded fells just outside the Lake District National Park. In 1331 Flemish weavers settled in Kendal and established a woollen-weaving industry.

The ruined Norman castle was the birthplace of Catherine Parr, Henry VIII's sixth wife, who outlived him. Her prayer book, bound in silver, is in the town hall and can be seen by appointment. The town hall also contains paintings by George Romney (1734-1802), who was apprenticed in Kendal.

Abbot Hall Art Gallery, an 18th-century mansion, has paintings by Romney, Reynolds, Turner and Raeburn, and sculptures by Barbara Hepworth and Hans Arp. The stables house the Museum of Lakeland Life and Industry.

Information Tel. 23649.
Location On the A6, 8 m. SE of Windermere.
Parking Stricklandgate (2); Blackhall Road (2); New Road; Kirkland (3); Lowther Lane (all car parks).
District council South Lakeland (Tel. 24007).

Population 23,400.
E-C Thur. **M-D** Wed., Sat.
Police (Ab) Busher Walk, Stricklandgate (Tel. 22611).
Casualty hospital Westmorland County, East View (Tel. 22641).
Post office (Ab) Stricklandgate.
Cinema The Palladium **(Ab)**, Sandes Avenue (Tel. 20152).
Public library (Ab) Stricklandgate.
Places to see Castle **(Ba)**; Castle Dairy **(Bb)**; Abbot Hall Art Gallery and Museum; Lakeland Museum of Natural History, Station Road.
Shopping Highgate; Stricklandgate; Finkle Street.
AA 24 hour service
Tel. Carlisle 24274.

Kenilworth Warwickshire

The imposing red-sandstone ruins on the edge of the town are the remains of 12th-century Kenilworth Castle, the setting of Sir Walter Scott's novel *Kenilworth*.

The National Agricultural Centre, home of the annual Royal Show, lies 2 miles east, at Stoneleigh Abbey.

Information Tel. 52595.
Location On the A429, 5 m. SW of Coventry.
Parking Warwick Road; Abbey End; Station Road; Barrowfield Road (all car parks).
District council Warwick (Tel. Leamington Spa 27072).
Population 19,300.
E-C Mon., Thur.
Police Smalley Place (Tel. 52121).
Casualty hospital Warwick Hospital, Lakin Road, Warwick (Tel. Warwick 495321).
Post office Warwick Road.
Theatres Talisman, Barrow Road (Tel. 56548); Priory, Rosemary Hill (55301).
Public library Smalley Place.

KELSO BRIDGE *John Rennie built the five-arched bridge over the River Tweed in 1803 as a model for London's Waterloo Bridge, which he completed in 1817.*

Places to see Kenilworth Castle.
Shopping Talisman Square; The Square; Warwick Road.
Events Royal Show (July); Town and Country Festival (Aug.).
AA 24 hour service
Tel. Birmingham (021) 550 4858.

Kensington see London

Keswick Cumbria

This quiet Lake District town beside Derwentwater has been a holiday centre since Victorian times. The Fitz Park Museum contains original manuscripts by Wordsworth, Ruskin and other writers associated with the district.

The Moot Hall in the main street was built in 1813 on the site of a 16th-century original. The poet Robert Southey (1774-1843) is buried in the churchyard at Great Crosthwaite, north-west of the town.

Information Tel. 72803.
Location On the A66, 22 m. NW of Windermere.
Parking Bell Close; Central Car Park; Lake Road; Heads Road (all car parks).
District council Allerdale (Tel. Cockermouth 823741).
Population 5,640.
E-C Wed. **M-D** Sat.

MOOT HALL *Keswick's decorative civic centre was built in 1813.*

Police Bank Street (Tel. 72004).
Casualty hospital Mary Hewetson, Crosthwaite Road (Tel. 72012).
Post office Bank Street.
Theatre Century, Lakeside, Lake Road (summer only) (Tel. 74411).
Cinema Alhambra, St John Street (Tel. 72195).
Public library Heads Road.
Places to see Fitz Park Museum and Art Gallery, Station Road; Castlerigg Stone Circle, 1¼ m. E; St Herbert's Island; Lingholm Gardens, 3 m. SW.
Town trails Available from Information Officer, Lake District Special Planning Board, Bank House, High Street, Windermere, Cumbria.
Shopping Bank Street; Market Place; St John Street.
Event Festival (June).
Trade and industry Pencil-making; granite and slate quarrying.
AA 24 hour service
Tel. Carlisle 24274

Kettering Northamptonshire

Boot and shoe-making transformed Kettering from a market town into an industrial town a century ago. Boughton House, 3 miles north-east, a home of the Duke of Buccleuch, houses a collection of paintings, tapestries and other treasures.

Information Tel. 82143.
Location On the A43, 14 m. NE of Northampton.
Parking London Road; Lower Street; Commercial Road; Sheep Street; Tanners Lane; Queen Street (cps).
District council Borough of Kettering (Tel. 85211).
Population 45,400.
M-D Fri., Sat.
Police London Road (Tel. 83433).
Casualty hospital Kettering and District General, Rothwell Road (Tel. 81141).
Post office Lower Street.
Cinema Studios 1 and 2, Russell Street (Tel. 512794).

Public library Sheep Street.
Places to see Boughton House; Wicksteed Park, London Road.
Shopping Gold Street; High Street; Silver Street; Market Street; Market Place; Sheep Street; Newland Street; Newborough Centre.
Event Kettering Feast (July).
AA 24 hour service
Tel. Northampton 66241.

Kidderminster
Hereford & Worcester

Nineteenth-century carpet-mills still dominate the former carpet capital of England, and the industry still flourishes. All that remains of the medieval town is the Church of St Mary and All Saints, which retains a 13th-century chancel.

Information Tel. 752832.
Location On the A456, 17 m. SW of Birmingham.
Parking Blackwell Street; Bromsgrove Street; Castle Road; Market Street; Pitts Lane; Prospect Lane; Pike Mills; Churchfields (all car parks).
District council Wyre Forest (Tel. Stourport 77211).
Population 51,300.
E-C Wed. **M-D** Thur., Sat.
Police Mason Road (Tel. 65122).
Casualty hospital General, Bewdley Road (Tel. 3424).
Post office (Ab) Bull Ring.
Cinema ABC **(Ba)**, Oxford Street (Tel. 2612).
Public library (Aa) Market Street.
Places to see Art Gallery and Museum **(Aa)**, Market Street; Rowland Hill Statue **(Aa)**, Town Hall; Carpet factories.
Shopping Swan Shopping Centre; Oxford Street; Vicar Street; High Street; Worcester Street; Coventry Street; Blackwell Street; Bull Ring; Rowland Hill Centre.
AA 24 hour service
Tel. Birmingham (021) 550 4858.

FATHER OF THE POST

Sir Rowland Hill (1795-1879), founder of the modern postage system, was born in Kidderminster. He first proposed a prepaid penny stamp on letters in 1837, and three years later the first Penny Blacks were issued. In 1854 Hill became the first Secretary to the Post Office.

Sir Rowland Hill and the first postage stamp – the original Penny Black.

KIDDERMINSTER

Kilmarnock Strathclyde

John Walker, a grocer of King Street, Kilmarnock, perfected a blend of whisky in 1820, and the Johnnie Walker whisky-bottling plant is now the largest in the world.

Kilmarnock also has associations with Robert Burns (1759-96), whose first collection, *Poems Chiefly in the Scottish Dialect*, was published there in 1786 by John Wilson.

The Laigh Kirk, setting for Burns's poem *The Ordination*, was rebuilt shortly after the poet's death, but the tower he knew still stands. A Victorian tower in Kay Park commemorates the poet, and commands fine views of the town and district. Its spiral stair climbs past two rooms containing books and portraits of Burns; the museum is open to the public.

The Dick Institute Museum, donated by a Kilmarnock businessman, James Dick, houses a collection of Scottish arms and armour, an art gallery featuring Scottish painters, and a children's museum.

The beautifully restored Dean Castle, with its 14th-century keep, contains collections of European arms and armour and early musical

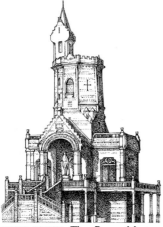

POET'S TOWER *The Burns Museum contains portraits of Scotland's greatest poet and copies of his works.*

instruments. A nature trail wanders around the 100 acre castle park.

Dundonald Castle, to the south-west, stands on a high hill, surrounded at the foot by modern houses. The oblong tower-house was rebuilt by Robert II, Scotland's first Stuart monarch, who died there in 1390.

In the parish of Kilmaurs north of Kilmarnock are the ruins of Rowallan Castle, ancient home of the Mure family.

A few miles east of Kilmarnock are the textile towns of Galston, Newmiln and Darvel. Dutch and Huguenot immigrants settled there in the 17th century.

Information Tel. 21140.
Location On the A71, 13 m. NE of Ayr.
Parking Foregate (3); Loanhead Street; Sturrock Street (2); Queen Street; Portland Street; St Andrew's Street; St Marnock Street; West Langlands Street (all car parks).
District council Kilmarnock and Loudoun (Tel. Kilmarnock 21140).
Population 48,250.
E-C Wed. **M-D** Thur., Fri., Sat.
Police (Aa) St Marnock Street (Tel. 21188).
Casualty hospitals (Ab) Infirmary, Hill Street (Tel. 22441); North Ayrshire District General, Crosshouse (21133).
Post office (Aa) John Finnie Street.
Cinema ABC 1, 2 and 3, Titchfield Street (Tel. 25234).
Public library (Ba) Elmbank Avenue.
Places to see Dick Institute Museum (**Ba**), Elmbank Avenue; Burns Museum (**Bb**), Kay Park; Dean Castle, Dean Road; Dundonald Castle, 4 m. SW, on A759.
Shopping King Street; Titchfield Street; Burns Precinct; John Finnie Street.
Sport Scottish League football, Kilmarnock FC, Rugby Park.
AA 24 hour service
Tel. Glasgow (041) 812 0101.

King's Lynn Norfolk

In the 12th century Lynn was part of the lands of the Bishop of Norwich, and was known as Bishop's Lynn. It became royal property when Henry VIII seized the town during the Dissolution of the Monasteries (1538-9).

The Saturday Market centres on the Church of St Margaret, built by Bishop de Losinga about 1101. Fifty years later, Bishop Turbus built the Chapel of St Nicholas which is near the Tuesday Market.

Two of King's Lynn's most imposing buildings are the Trinity Guildhall and Town Hall. Both are built in a striking, flint-chequered design, but nearly 500 years separate them; the Guildhall was built in the early 15th century, and the Town Hall in 1895 to match its neighbour.

In the 14th century Lynn ranked as the third port of England, and by the 18th century was prospering on the export of corn. This age of prosperity is reflected in the houses built by wealthy merchants and in the elegant Customs House, built in 1683. The son of the Deputy Collector of Customs, born in 1757, gave his name to an island and a city 5,000 miles away. His name was George Vancouver, and he navigated the west coast of North America in 1791.

Between the 17th and 19th centuries King's Lynn was also a glass-making centre. At a modern factory visitors can watch glassware being made by hand.

Information Tel. 63044.
Location On the A17, 14 m. NE of Wisbech.
Parking Baker Lane; St James Street; Blackfriars Street; Ferry Street; Chapel Street; Railway Road; Oldsunway; Albert Street; Austin Street; Austin Fields; Tuesday Market Place; Saturday Market Place (all car parks).
District council Borough of King's Lynn and West Norfolk (Tel. 61241).
Population 33,300.
E-C Wed. **M-D** Tues., Sat.
Police (Ba) St James Road (Tel. 61311).
Casualty hospital Queen Elizabeth, Gayton Road (Tel. 66266).
Post office (Ba) Baxter's Plain.
Theatre Fermoy Centre (**Ab**), King Street (Tel. 3578).
Cinemas Pilot (**Ab**), Pilot Street (Tel. 2760); Majestic (**Ba**), Tower Street (2603); Fermoy Centre (**Ab**) (3578).
Public library (Ba) The Millfleet.
Places to see Art Gallery, Fermoy Centre (**Ab**); Wedgwood Glass Factory, Oldmedow Road; Clifton House (**Aa**), Queen Street; Trinity Guildhall (**Aa**), St James Street; Museum (**Bb**), Market Street; Guildhall of St George, Fermoy Centre (**Ab**); Hampton Court (**Aa**), Nelson Street.
Shopping High Street; Norfolk Street; New Conduit Street; Broad Street.

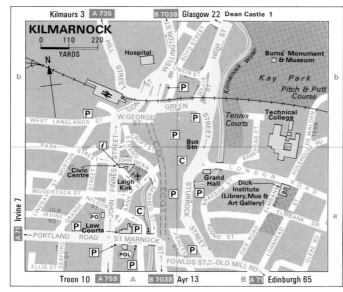

ANCIENT HOUSE *Behind the 18th-century doorway of Clifton House, King's Lynn, are rooms dating back to the 14th and 15th centuries.*

miners, were forced to sell their boots elsewhere.

Kingswood was a stronghold of Nonconformism in the 17th and 18th centuries, and John Wesley was among the revivalists who preached from Hanham Mount. A symbolic beacon, 80 ft high, stands on the site.

Information Tel. 563480.
Location On the A420, 3½ m. NE of Bristol.
Parking Bank Road; Kings Chase; Hall's Road; High Street (all car parks).
District council Kingswood (Tel. Bristol 615161).
Population 31,600.
E-C Wed.
Police High Street (Tel. 672151).
Casualty hospital Frenchay Hospital, Frenchay Park Road (Tel. 565656).
Post office Hanham Road.
Public library High Street.
Places to see John Wesley's Beacon, Hanham Mount.
Shopping High Street; Regent Street; Kings Chase.
Trade and industry Footwear; clothing; light engineering.
AA 24 hour service Tel. Bristol 298531.

Kinross Tayside

Anglers flock to Kinross for the famous salmon trout of Loch Leven. Standing on an island in the loch are the ruins of the 15th-century Loch Leven Castle where Mary, Queen of Scots was imprisoned by the nobles of Scotland and forced to abdicate in 1567. She escaped the following year and fled to England, where she was kept in prison for nearly 20 years until her execution in 1587.

The fine 17th-century Kinross House is set in magnificent grounds between the town and the lakeside. The house was built by Sir William Bruce, the architect who, in the 1670s, restored the Palace of Holyroodhouse in Edinburgh.

Still attached to the town cross are the old "jougs" – an iron collar in which wrongdoers were once held.

Information Tel. Perth 23281.
Location On the M90, 12 m. N of Dunfermline.
Parking Curate Wynd (cp).
District council Perth and Kinross (Tel. Perth 24241).
Population 3,450.
E-C Thur.
Police High Street (Tel. 63571).
Casualty hospital Perth Royal Infirmary, Tullylumb, Perth (Tel. Perth 23311).
Post office High Street.
Cinema County Cinema, Station Road (Tel. 62425).
Public library High Street.
Places to see Kinross House; Loch Leven Castle; St Serf's Priory; Marshall Museum.
Shopping High Street.
AA 24 hour service Tel. Edinburgh (031) 225 8464.

Trade and industry Glassware; engineering; agriculture.
AA 24 hour service Tel. 3731.

Kingston upon Hull
see page 196

Kingston upon Thames
see London

Kingswood Avon

A royal forest that covered the whole of south Gloucestershire gave Kingswood its name. Now only a protected stretch of the Avon Valley remains.

Three centuries of expanding industry have turned a once-tiny village into a spreading development of some 31,600 people on the edge of Bristol. It began with coal-mining in the 17th century, and for 200 years the pits were worked. But when they closed, the Kingswood cottagers, who had made hob-nailed boots for the

KING'S LYNN

KINGSTON UPON HULL Humberside

The king's town which grew into a great port

Britain's third-largest seaport, after London and Liverpool, and the country's busiest deep-sea fishing base was founded in the 12th century by Cistercian monks from Meaux Abbey, 8 miles away. They chose the site at the junction of the Hull and Humber rivers for a quay from which wool produced on the abbey estates could be shipped to Europe. In 1293 Edward I acquired the settlement from the abbey and laid out a new town – Kingston (king's town) upon Hull. Wool is still shipped through Hull docks, but in the other direction. It is brought from New Zealand and Australia to supply the mills of the textile towns in West Yorkshire.

CAPTAIN COOK *Silver plate, a gun and other relics of the great explorer are displayed in Trinity House.*

REFORMER'S BIRTHPLACE *William Wilberforce, who was primarily responsible for the abolition of slavery in the British Empire, was born at 25 High Street. The house is now a museum chiefly devoted to his work.*

The oldest part of Hull is the medieval area between Queen Victoria Square and the River Hull, bounded by the River Humber to the south and Queen's Gardens to the north. Most of the old town has now disappeared, but the 14th-century **Church of the Holy Trinity** in Market Place was restored in 1869 and again in 1907.

The church contains the tomb and effigy of William de la Pole (d. 1366), who in his lifetime was the most prominent merchant in England. He was appointed Hull's first mayor in 1331, and did much to assure the port's prosperity.

New era of prosperity

De la Pole's descendants became the Earls of Suffolk, and the family is commemorated in the church's **Broadley Chapel**, restored in 1863. There is a statue of William de la Pole by the **Victoria Pier**.

The **Church of St Mary** in Lowgate dates from the 14th century, but it has been rebuilt in 19th-century neo-Gothic style. The east window contains some medieval glass.

The **White Harte Inn**, in an alley off Silver Street, was in the 17th century the home of the Governor of Hull, Sir John Hotham. Here, in a room now called the "Plotting Parlour", Hotham and his associates

agreed to follow Parliament's instructions and to close the town gates to Charles I at the beginning of the Civil War.

The king sought entrance through the **Beverley Gate**, but had to withdraw. The gate stood in Whitefriargate, which is now a pedestrian shopping precinct. The site is marked by a plaque.

The port of Hull entered a new era of prosperity when the first of a long line of docks was opened in 1778. The site was filled to make the Queen's Gardens.

The 18th-century buildings which still survive include **Trinity House**, next to Whitefriargate, and **Maister's House**, in the High Street.

Trinity House is the home of the Guild of Pilots, which no longer controls pilotage in the Humber but administers marine charities and runs a navigation school.

Maister's House replaced an earlier building destroyed by fire in 1743. The Maisters were a wealthy family of merchants, and the house has a magnificent hall and staircase. The building is used for offices, but the hall may be visited during office hours.

William Wilberforce (1759-1833), the anti-slavery campaigner, was born in Hull. His birthplace is now a museum, and he is also commemor-

ated by a statue on a 90 ft column in front of the College of Technology at the eastern end of Queen's Gardens.

Traditions of the sea

At the other end of the gardens is **City Hall**, built at the beginning of the century, and the city's main centre for concerts and exhibitions. Also facing the square is the **Ferens Art Gallery**, which has works by Canaletto and *Portrait of a Young Woman* by Frans Hals, also marine paintings and modern sculptures.

Hull is steeped in the traditions of the sea, and its museums give a vivid picture of its maritime links, past and present. The **Town Docks Museum**, largely devoted to whaling, is in Queen's Dock Avenue.

The **Transport and Archaeology Museum**, at 36 High Street, contains a plank-built boat found at North Ferriby, near Hull, and dating from 1000-800 BC, more than 1,000 years older than any similar vessel yet discovered in Europe. The museum also has a collection of vehicles, including motor cars, coaches and trams.

Information Tel. 223344.
Location On the A1079, 38 m. SE of York.
Parking Albion Street; Dock Street;

QUEEN OF THE AIR

Hull was the birthplace of Amy Johnson (1903-41), the aviation pioneer, whose greatest achievement was her solo flight to Australia in 1930 – the first by a woman. She disappeared over the Thames Estuary while ferrying a plane for the RAF. A statue of her stands in Prospect Street, Hull.

RECORD LENGTH *Opened in 1981, the Humber Bridge has the longest single span in the world – 4,626 ft.*

TOWN DOCKS MUSEUM *The former Dock Office contains a gallery devoted to Hull's history as a whaling centre, including early harpoons and a collection of scrimshaw – engraved whalebone.*

Casualty hospital Anlaby Road (Tel. 28541).

Post office (Cb) Lowgate.

Theatres Humberside Theatre **(Ab)**, Spring Street (Tel. 23638); New **(Bb)**, Kingston Square (20463).

Cinemas ABC **(Ab)**, Ferensway (Tel. 23530); Cecil 1, 2 and 3 **(Ab)**, Anlaby Road (24981); Hull Film Theatre **(Ab)**, Albion Street (25017).

Public library (Ab) Albion Street.

Places to see Ferens Art Gallery **(Bb)**; Trinity House **(Ba)**; Maister's House **(Cb)**; Wilberforce House **(Cb)**; Town Docks Museum **(Bb)**; Transport and Archaeology Museum **(Cb)**.

Shopping Jameson Street; George Street; Prospect Street; Ferensway; Paragon Street; King Edward Street; Whitefriargate; Carr Lane.

Sport FA League football, Hull City FC, Boothferry Road. Rugby League, Hull Kingston Rovers, Craven Park; Hull FC, The Boulevard.

Car ferry To Rotterdam and Zeebrugge (Tel. 795141).

AA 24 hour service Tel. 28580.

Ferensway; George Street; Mason Street; Myton Street; Osborne Street; John Street; Pryme Street; St Stephen's Square; Salthouse Lane; Sewer Lane; Wright Street (all car parks).

District council City of Kingston upon Hull (Tel. 223111).

Population 268,300.

E-C Thur. **M-D** Tues., Fri. and Sat.

Police (Bb) Queen's Gardens (Tel. 26111).

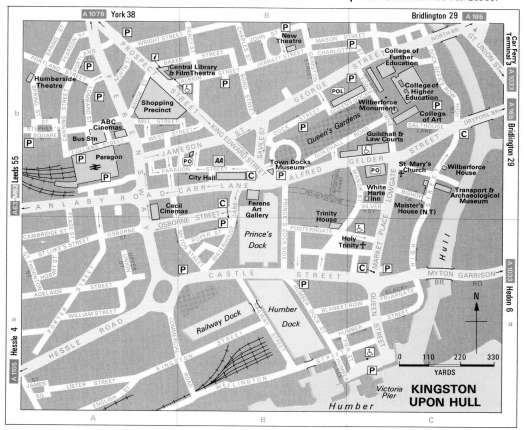

KINGSTON UPON HULL

Kirkby Merseyside

Christian Vikings from Ireland built a church near the site of Kirkby's St Chad's as early as 870. The later church, a Norman foundation rebuilt in neo-Gothic style in 1871, still has its tub-shaped Norman font. Another relic from the past is the curious square red-stone dovecot of 1703 in Whitefield Drive. Kirkby, a village in 1945, grew almost to its present size by 1961, following development as a "new town".

Information
Tel. Liverpool (051) 548 6555.
Location On the A506, 8 m. NE of Liverpool.
Parking Webster Drive; St Chad's Drive; Irlam Drive; Hall Lane; Cherryfield Drive (all car parks).
District council Borough of Knowsley (Tel. 051 548 6555).
Population 50,900.
E-C Wed. **M-D** Tues., Sat.
Police St Chad's Drive (Tel. 051 546 5111).
Casualty hospital Walton General, Rice Lane, Walton, Liverpool 9 (Tel. 051 525 3611).
Post office Newtown Gardens.
Public library Newtown Gardens.
Shopping Broad Lane; County Road; St Chad's Parade.
AA 24 hour service
Tel. 051 709 7252.

Kirkby-in-Ashfield Notts.

Small grassy hills where sheep graze rise up round Kirkby-in-Ashfield, a mining town near the Derbyshire border. The hills are a lesson on what can be done to repair the ravages of mining – they are old colliery spoil heaps, reclaimed for pasture.

Newstead Abbey, 5 miles southeast of the town, was the family home of Lord Byron (1788-1824). It was built in 1170 by Henry II, and became the home of the Byron family in 1540, after the Dissolution. The house is set in 9 acres of gardens, noted for rare trees and shrubs, and contains a museum with many relics of the poet.

Information Tel. Mansfield 755755.
Location On the B6018, 13 m. NW of Nottingham.
Parking Ellis Street; Market Place (both car parks).
District council Ashfield (Tel. Mansfield 755755).
Population 24,500.
E-C Wed. **M-D** Fri., Sat.
Police Urban Road (Tel. Mansfield 752224).
Casualty hospital Mansfield General, West Hill Drive, Mansfield (Tel. Mansfield 22515).
Post office The Precinct.
Public library The Precinct.
Places to see Newstead Abbey.
Shopping The Precinct.
Trade and industry Coal-mining; hosiery.
AA 24 hour service
Tel. Nottingham 787751.

CHURCH ON A HILL *The steep lane of Kirk Wynd climbs up to Kirkcaldy's parish church. The tower and belfry date from 1244.*

Kirkcaldy Fife

A mile-long esplanade stretching along the Firth of Forth has given Kirkcaldy the name "Lang Toun".

Several houses near the harbour date from the late 15th century, and in Sailors' Walk some 17th-century houses have been restored. The Adam Smith Centre, which includes a theatre and hall, commemorates the Scottish economist and author of *The Wealth of Nations* (1776), who was born in Kirkcaldy in 1723.

Another celebrated son of Kirkcaldy was the architect Robert Adam (1728-92). A tablet marks the site of the old Burgh School in Hill Street which he and Adam Smith attended as pupils.

Kirkcaldy Museum has a large collection of Wemyss Ware, a distinctive pottery made in the town during the early part of this century. The Art Gallery has a fine collection of Scottish art, and the Industrial Museum illustrates horse-drawn transport, crafts and the linoleum industry. A linoleum factory built in 1847 established the town as the world's leading manufacturer of this material, and floor-coverings still play a large part in Kirkcaldy's industry.

Ravenscraig Castle, on a rocky headland at the north-eastern end of the town, was built by James II in 1459. It is said to be the first Scottish fortress designed for defence by artillery. The castle fell into disuse after the 17th century, but the Department of the Environment has restored it.

Information Tel. 261144.
Location On the A92, 14 m. E of Dunfermline.
Parking Esplanade; Charlotte Street; High Street; Thistle Street; Hunter Street; Oswald's Wynd (all car parks).
District council Kirkcaldy (Tel. 261144).
Population 46,300.
E-C Wed.
Police (Bb) St Brycedale Avenue (Tel. 252611).
Casualty hospital Victoria, Dunnikier Road (Tel. 261155).
Post office (Ab) Hunter Street.
Theatre Adam Smith Centre **(Ab)**, Bennochy Road (Tel. 260498).
Cinema ABC, High Street (Tel. 260143).
Public library (Ab) War Memorial Gardens.
Places to see Ravenscraig Castle; Industrial Museum; Museum and Art Gallery **(Ab)**.
Shopping High Street; Mercat; The Postings.
Event Scottish Motor-cycle Road Race (June).
Sport Scottish League football, Raith Rovers FC, Stark's Park.
AA 24 hour service
Tel. Edinburgh (031) 225 8464.

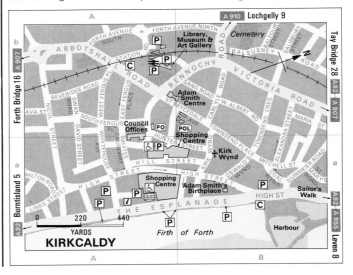

KIRKCALDY

Kirkcudbright D. & G.

The town's name (pronounced Kirk-oobrie) is probably a corruption of Kirk-cuthbert, after St Cuthbert, who converted much of southern Scotland to Christianity. The present Church of St Cuthbert was built in 1838. In the burial ground of an earlier church on the edge of the town is the tomb of Billy Marshal, who is said to have married 17 times and to have fathered four children after the age of 100. He died in 1792, aged 120.

The town lies on the estuary of the Dee and is the centre of the Kirkcudbright Stewartry, so called because the district was administered by kings' stewards during the 14th and 15th centuries. McLellan's Castle is an excellent example of a 16th-century fortified and castellated mansion.

High Street Tolbooth – built about 1600 – has a weather-vane shaped like a 17th-century sailing ship.

Information Tel. 30494.
Location On the A762, 28 m. SW of Dumfries.
Parking Harbour Square (cp).
District council Stewartry (Tel. 30291).
Population 2,700.
E-C Thur.
Police High Street (Tel. 30600).
Casualty hospital Kirkcudbright Cottage Hospital, St Mary's Place (Tel. 30755).
Post office Harbour Square.
Public library High Street.
Places to see Stewartry Museum; McLellan's Castle; Tolbooth.
Shopping St Mary Street; St Cuthbert Street.
AA 24 hour service
Tel. Glasgow (041) 812 0101.

AMERICAN NAVAL HERO

In 1779, during the American War of Independence, John Paul Jones (1747-92), in command of a few American and French ships, won a dramatic victory against a powerful British force off the English coast and became an American hero. Jones was born plain John Paul at Arbigland, 20 miles east of Kirkcudbright. He added the Jones when he joined the US Navy in 1775.

Jones was a hero to Americans, but the British saw him as a pirate.

Kirkintilloch Strathclyde

The Romans founded the town as a station on the Antonine Wall, which they built to keep out warlike tribes from the north. The wall, which ran from the Forth to the Clyde, was built about AD 140 and abandoned about 50 years later. Kirkintilloch was made a burgh of barony in the 12th century.

The Church of St Mary, built in 1644 on the site of an earlier chapel, has been restored and is a museum.

Information
Tel. Glasgow (041) 221 6136.
Location On the A803, 8 m. NE of Glasgow.
Parking Townhead; Shamrock Street; Queen Street; Broadcroft; Regent Street; Union Street; Freeland Place; Industry Street (all car parks).
District council Strathkelvin (Tel. 041 776 7171).
Population 27,300.
E-C Wed.
Police Townhead (Tel. 041 776 1113).
Casualty hospital Stobhill Hospital, Balornock Road, Glasgow (Tel. 041 558 0111).
Post office Kerr Street.
Public library Camphill Avenue.
Shopping Cowgate; Townhead.
Events Highland Games (second Sat. in Aug.); Strathkelvin Arts Festival (Feb.).
AA 24 hour service
Tel. 041 812 0101.

Kirkwall Orkney

The capital of the Orkney Islands was once known as Kirkjuvagr (church bay). This was a reference to the 11th-century Church of St Olaf, of which only a doorway remains. Today this town of narrow streets and grey-stone houses on Mainland island is a busy port. Its centre-piece is the Cathedral of St Magnus, founded in 1137 by Earl Rognvald, the Norse ruler of Orkney, and dedicated to his uncle and predecessor, Earl Magnus. The canonised relics of both men are sealed within two pillars. When the remains of St Magnus were disinterred in 1919, the skull was found to have an axe-wound, just as described in the *Orkneyinga Saga*.

The pillars of the cathedral are massive, except in the 13th-century extensions to the choir, and support Romanesque arches. The late-12th-century chapels have Gothic arches.

The 125 ft tower looks down on the Bishop's Palace, and the Earl's Palace. The first was built about the same time as the cathedral. It was here that King Haakon of Norway died in 1263 after his abortive invasion of Scotland. The palace was reconstructed in the mid-16th century by Bishop Reid, who added the great defensive round tower at the north-west corner.

The Earl's Palace, perhaps the finest piece of Renaissance architecture in Scotland, was built about 1600 for the Earl of Orkney, Patrick Stewart. In 1611 he was imprisoned following complaints about his tyrannical rule. Then in 1614 he was executed for inciting his son to rebellion. The now-roofless palace has decorated turrets, and a great hall that must once have been one of the noblest state-rooms in Scotland.

Opposite the cathedral is Tankerness House, a 16th-century merchant's house, now a museum depicting the folk-history of the Orkneys over 4,000 years. The public library, founded in 1683, is claimed to be the oldest in Scotland.

Kirkwall's oldest surviving custom, dating from Viking times, is The Ba' Game, a loose form of rugby which is played on Christmas Day and New Year's Day.

"THE MARVEL OF THE NORTH"
Kirkwall's red-and-yellow sandstone St Magnus Cathedral was founded in 1137, when Norsemen ruled the Orkneys.

Information Tel. 2856.
Parking Great Western Road; Junction Road; Gunn's Close; Shore Street; Thoms Street (all car parks).
Council Orkney Islands (Tel. Kirkwall 3535).
Population 4,800.
E-C Wed. **M-D** Mon.
Police Watergate (Tel. 2241).
Casualty hospital Balfour, New Scapa Road (Tel. 2763).
Post office Junction Road.
Theatre Orkney Arts, Mill Street (Tel. 2047).
Cinema Phoenix, Junction Road (Tel. 3340).
Public library Laing Street.
Places to see St Magnus Cathedral; Bishop's Palace; Earl's Palace; Tankerness House Museum.
Town trails Available from Scottish Tourist Board, 23 Ravelston Terrace, Edinburgh EH4 3EU.
Shopping Bridge Street; Albert Street; Broad Street; Victoria Street.
Events The Ba' Game (Christmas Day and New Year's Day).
Trade and industry Whisky distilling; silvercraft; milk processing.
Car ferries To Lerwick (Tel. 2044); to Aberdeen (Aberdeen 29111).

Kirriemuir Tayside

Sandstone cottages line the narrow streets of Kirriemuir, a little town on the beautiful southern slopes of the Braes of Angus. This is popular tourist country and, in season, trout fishermen head for the rich streams that flow into the Esk. Kirriemuir still has some jute-weaving, and there are also grain mills.

Information Tel. 2357.
Location On the A926, 17 m. N of Dundee.
Parking Bellies Brae; Reform Street; Kirk Wynd; Pierhead (all car parks).
District council Angus (Tel. Forfar 65101).
Population 5,300.
E-C Thur.
Police Reform Street (Tel. 2222).
Casualty hospital Dundee Royal Infirmary, Barrack Road, Dundee (Tel. Dundee 23125).
Post office Reform Street.
Public library Town Hall, Reform Street.
Places to see Inverquharity Castle; Barrie's Birthplace; Camera Obscura, Hill Road.
Shopping High Street; Bank Street.
AA 24 hour service
Tel. Dundee 25585.

BARRIE'S THRUMS

Kirriemuir has been immortalised as Thrums in the tales of Sir James Barrie (1860-1937), who also wrote *Peter Pan*. Barrie, the son of a jute-weaver, was born at 9 Brechin Road, which is now preserved as a memorial to him.

Number 9. A memorial to Barrie.

Knaresborough N. Yorks.

The ruins of a 14th-century castle, partly demolished by the Roundheads in 1646, crown the old town of Knaresborough. The twin towers of the main gate, the king's chamber and the dungeon survive, and are open to the public.

The chemist's shop in the market square has been in continuous use since 1720, and claims to be the oldest in England.

The prophetess Mother Shipton was reputedly born in the cave near the Dropping Well in 1488. Another cave, St Robert's, also on the banks of the Nidd, sheltered the 12th-century hermit and healer, St Robert.

Off Abbey Road is the Chapel of Our Lady of the Crag, a shrine which was cut from the rock about 1408.

Information Tel. Harrogate 866886 (summer).
Location On the A59, 3 m. NE of Harrogate.

STEEP GORGE *The hill on which Knaresborough Castle stands overlooks the steep gorge of the River Nidd, spanned by a lofty railway viaduct.*

Parking Castle Yard; Chapel Street; York Place; Conyngham Hall; Waterside (all car parks).
District council Borough of Harrogate (Tel. Harrogate 68954).
Population 13,400.
E-C Thur. **M-D** Wed.
Police Castlegate (Tel. Harrogate 862222/3).
Casualty hospital Harrogate District, Lancaster Park Road, Harrogate (Tel. Harrogate 885959).
Post office High Street.
Public library Market Place.
Places to see Castle; Dropping Well; Court House Museum.
Town trails Available from Tourist Information Kiosk, Market Place, or Harrogate Tourist Information Centre, Royal Baths Assembly Rooms, Crescent Road, Harrogate.
Shopping Market Place; High Street.
AA 24 hour service
Tel. York 27698.

TURNED TO STONE *The limestone in the water of The Dropping Well in Knaresborough petrifies porous materials.*

Knighton Powys

The old Welsh name of Knighton was Trefyclawdd (Town on the Dyke). This referred to Offa's Dyke, which runs through the town and was built in the 8th century by King Offa of Mercia (d. 796) to keep the Welsh out of his kingdom.

There are earthwork remains of a 12th-century castle on the hill which is private ground. The Swan Hotel and a number of other buildings in Town Clock Square are 17th century.

Information
Tel. Llandrindod Wells 2600.
Location On the A488, 17 m. W of Ludlow.
Parking Market Street; Norton Arms; Bowling Green Lane; Victoria Road (all car parks).
District council Radnor (Tel. Llandrindod Wells 3737).
Population 2,700.
E-C Wed. **M-D** Thur.

Police Ludlow Road (Tel. 310).
Casualty hospital Llandrindod Wells, Temple Street, Llandrindod Wells (Tel. Llandrindod Wells 2951).
Post office Wylcwm Street.
Public library West Street.
Places to see Offa's Dyke; Offa's Dyke Heritage Centre, West Street.
Shopping Broad Street; High Street.
Trade and industry Agricultural engineering; tyres.
AA 24 hour service
Tel. Newport 62559.

Knutsford Cheshire

The town derives its name from the Danish King Canute, or Knut, who is said to have forded the local stream. Knutsford's May Day celebrations are among the oldest and most colourful in the country, and feature a procession, crowning ceremony and maypole dance.

Two miles north of Knutsford is Tatton Park, one of the finest Georgian mansions in Britain. It contains priceless paintings, period furniture and silver.

Information Tel. 2611.
Location On the A50, 17 m. SW of Manchester.
Parking Tatton Street; Princess Street; Silkmill Street; Old Market Place; King Street; Stanley Road (all car parks).
District council Borough of Macclesfield (Tel. Macclesfield 21955).
Population 13,700.
E-C Wed. **M-D** Fri., Sat.
Police Toft Road (Tel. 3404).
Casualty hospital Wythenshawe, Southmoor Road, Manchester 23 (Tel. Manchester (061) 998 7070).
Post office King Street.
Theatres Little, Queen Street (Tel. 3000); Civic Hall, Toft Road (3005).
Cinema Civic Hall, Toft Road (Tel. 3005).
Public library Brook Street.
Places to see Tatton Park, 2 m. N.
Shopping King Street, Princess Street.
Trade and industry Photographic paper; engineering; plastics.
AA 24 hour service
Tel. 061 485 6299.

L

Lambeth see London

Lampeter Dyfed

A market has been held in Lampeter since 1284. It is also a centre for the breeding and sale of disease-resistant cattle. The remains of a castle said to have been built in the reign of Stephen (d. 1154) lie in the grounds of St David's College, founded in 1822 and now part of the University of Wales.

Information Tel. 422426.
Location On the A482, 29 m. S of Aberystwyth.
Parking The Common; The Rookery.
District council Ceredigion (Tel. Aberystwyth 617911).
Population 2,000.
E-C Wed. **M-D** Alternate Tues.
Police Temple Terrace (Tel. 422526).
Casualty hospital Aberaeron Cottage Hospital, Princes Avenue (Tel. Aberaeron 570225).
Post office College Street.
Theatre Felinfach, Arts Centre (Tel. Aeron 470697).
Public library Town Hall.
Places to see Castle ruins.
Shopping High Street; College Street; Harford Square; Bridge Street.
Event Rhys Thomas James Eisteddfod (Aug.).
AA 24 hour service Tel. Swansea 55598.

Lanark Strathclyde

The town is the market centre for some of the best farmland in southern Scotland. The ruins of the 12th-century Church of St Kentigern stand in the churchyard. One of its bells, now in the Town Steeple and still in use, was made in 1110 and is the oldest in Britain.

New Lanark, 1 mile south, was founded in 1784 by the philanthropist David Dale. His son-in-law, the reformer Robert Owen, developed many welfare schemes for workers in its cotton-spinning factories. It is now a conservation area.

The area is much as it was in Owen's day. Dale's original cotton mill stands by the River Clyde, and behind it on the slope of a hill are the workers' distinctive tenement blocks. The houses have four storeys at the front and two at the back.

Information Tel. 61331, Ext. 88.
Location On the A73, 25 m. SE of Glasgow.
Parking St Patrick's Road; Castlegate; Broomgate; North Vennel (2); Greenside Lane; South Vennel/Wellgate; Kildare Road; Wellgatehead; South Vennel (2); Bannatyne Street (all car parks).
District council Clydesdale (Tel. 61311).
Population 9,500.
E-C Thur. **M-D** Mon., Tues., Thur.
Police Westport (Tel. 2455).
Casualty hospital Law, Law by Carluke (Tel. Wishaw 72621).
Post office St Leonard Street.
Public library Hope Street.
Places to see Industrial Archaeology Museum; New Lanark.
Shopping High Street; Bannatyne Street; Wellgate; Bloomgate.
Trade and industry Agricultural engineering; tanning; textiles.
AA 24 hour service Tel. Glasgow (041) 812 0101.

Lancaster Lancashire

The Romans built a camp (*castrum*) by the River Lune, and from this Lancashire's county town takes its name. The Normans erected a castle on the site of the camp in the 11th century. The gateway, towers and banqueting halls were added in the 14th century, and Elizabeth I further strengthened the defences. Since the 18th century it has housed a prison and the county courts.

The 14th–15th-century parish church of St Mary has a Saxon doorway. Below Castle Hill the streets and alleyways nestle around the Market Square, where Charles II was proclaimed king in 1651.

From Castle Hill a road leads to St George's Quay, on the banks of the River Lune. The 18th-century Cus-

MORRIS MEN *A 17th-century panel preserved in Lancaster Museum.*

tom House is a reminder that Lancaster was once a busy port, handling a greater tonnage of shipping than Liverpool.

On the eastern side of the town stands the domed Ashton Memorial, built in 1909 by Lord Ashton in memory of his wife. It is sometimes called the Taj Mahal of the North.

The cathedral was built in 1859. It is chiefly noted for its frescoes and carved altar.

Information Tel. 2878.
Location On the A6, 23 m. N of Preston.
Parking Damside Street; Stonewell; North Road; St Leonard's Gate (2); Thurnham Street (all car parks).
District council City of Lancaster (Tel. Morecambe 417120).
Population 46,300.
E-C Wed. **M-D** Daily, except Wed. and Sun.
Police (Aa) Thurnham Street (Tel. 63333).
Casualty hospital Royal Lancaster Infirmary **(Aa)**, South Road (Tel. 65944).
Post office (Aa) Market Street.
Theatre Duke's Playhouse **(Ba)**, Moor Lane (Tel. 66645).
Cinema Studios 1 and 2 **(Aa)**, King Street (Tel. 64141).
Public library (Ab) Market Square.
Places to see Castle **(Ab)**; Ashton Memorial; City Museum **(Aa)**.
Town trails Available from Lancaster City Museum.
Shopping King Street; Market Street; St Leonard's Gate.
Trade and industry Linoleum; rayon.
AA 24 hour service Tel. Manchester (061) 485 6299.

Launceston Cornwall

The hilltop remains of a Norman castle and a medieval town gate are reminders that Launceston once guarded the main route from Devon into Cornwall. Close to the castle, the 16th-century Church of St Mary Magdalene has one of the most lavishly carved exteriors of any church in England. Narrow streets, with Georgian houses, surround the church and The Square, the town centre.

Information Tel. 3693 or 3306.
Location On the A30, 19 m. SW of Okehampton.
Parking Rear of Town Hall; off Westgate Street; Castle Street; Tower Street; Race Hill (all cps).
District council North Cornwall (Tel. Bodmin 4471).
Population 6,200.
E-C Thur. **M-D** Tues., Sat.
Police Moorland Road (Tel. 4211).
Casualty hospital College Road (Tel. 2455).
Post office Westgate Street.
Cinema Tower, Market Street (Tel. 2072).
Public library Bounsalls Lane.
Places to see Castle, Western Road; Lawrence House Museum, Castle Street.
Shopping Church Street; The Square; Southgate Street; Westgate Street; Broad Street; High Street.
Event Torchlight carnival (Nov.).
AA 24 hour service
Tel. Plymouth 69989.

Leamington Spa Warks.

Queen Victoria bestowed the title of "Royal" upon Leamington in 1838, at the height of its fame as a spa.

Salty, underground springs feed baths in the Pump Room, where about 50,000 people a year receive treatment for rheumatic ailments. Visitors can taste the waters from a fountain in the Pump Room Annexe.

The north bank of the River Leam has many fine Georgian, Regency and early-Victorian houses, laid out in terraces and squares.

Information Tel. 311470.
Location On the A452, 2 m. E of Warwick.
Parking Russell St; Bedford St (2); Park St; Satchwell St; Newbold Terrace; Court St; Guy Place (2); Avenue Rd (all car parks).
District council Warwick (Tel. 27072).
Population 43,000.
E-C Mon., Thur. **M-D** Wed., Fri.
Police (Ba) Hamilton Terrace (Tel. 32121).
Casualty hospital Warwick Hospital, Lakin Road, Warwick (Tel. Warwick 495321).
Post office (Ba) Victoria Terrace.
Theatres Loft Theatre **(Ba)**, Victoria Colonnade (Tel. 26341); Royal Spa Centre **(Ba)**, Newbold Terrace (34418/9).
Cinemas Clifton, Spencer Street (Tel. 25979); Regal **(Aa)**, Portland Place (26106).
Public library (Aa) Avenue Road.
Places to see Art Gallery and Museum **(Aa)**, Avenue Road; Royal Pump Room **(Ba)**, Lower Parade.
Town trails Available from the Tourist Information Centre **(Ba)**, Jephson Lodge, Lower Parade.
Shopping Parade; Warwick Street.
Events Competitive Festival (June); Folk Dance Festival (June).
AA 24 hour service
Tel. Birmingham (021) 550 4858.

Leatherhead Surrey

The name Leatherhead has nothing to do with leather or heads. It comes from two Saxon words meaning "public ford" – the town was a crossing place on the River Mole, where it carves its way through the North Downs. Leatherhead has remained a key road centre in England ever since.

Some of its finest buildings, including the early-16th-century Running Horse Inn in Bridge Street, are relics of the coaching days. Sir Anthony Hawkins (1863-1933) who, under the name Anthony Hope, wrote *The Prisoner of Zenda* and created the Kingdom of Ruritania, is buried in the parish churchyard.

Information Tel. 74411.
Location On the A243, 5 m. N of Dorking.
Parking Bridge Street; Upper Fairfield Road; Station Road; Randalls Road; Church Road; Church Street; Leret Way (all cps).
District council Mole Valley (Tel. Dorking 885001).
Population 40,500.
E-C Wed.
Police 44 Kingston Road (Tel. 72255/6).
Casualty hospital Epsom District, Dorking Road, Epsom (Tel. Epsom 26100).
Post office North Street.
Theatre/Cinema Thorndike, Church Street (Tel. 75461/2).
Public library Church Street.
Shopping High Street; Church Street; Bridge Street.
AA 24 hour service
Tel. Guildford 72841.

Ledbury H. & W.

The poet John Masefield (1878-1967), who was born in Ledbury, described it as "pleasant to the sight, fair and half-timbered houses, black and white".

Ledbury has changed little since those lines were written. Tudor houses line Church Lane, leading to the Church of St Michael and All Angels, rebuilt in the 13th and 14th centuries. The 17th-century market house stands in the High Street, and near by is the splendid 16th-century Feathers Inn.

Information Tel. 2461.
Location On the A449, 8 m. SW of Great Malvern.
Parking Bye Street (2 car parks).
District council Malvern Hills (Tel. Malvern 2700).
Population 4,810.
E-C Wed. **M-D** Wed.
Police Worcester Road (Tel. 2222).
Casualty hospital Worcester Royal Infirmary, Castle Street, Worcester (Tel. Worcester 27122).
Post office The Homend.
Public library Barrett Browning Institute.
Places to see Old Grammar School Museum, Church Lane; Butcher Row House, Church Lane; Eastnor Castle,

LEAMINGTON SPA

Kenilworth 5 — A 452 — A 46 Coventry 10 — A 445 Rugby 15

Warwick 2 — A 445

0 — 110 — 220 YARDS

Southam 7

Banbury 20 — A 41 — A 452

TUDOR WALK *Ledbury's Church Lane has changed little since Tudor times. The 13th-century church tower with its 18th-century spire rises to 202 ft.*

2 m. E on A438.
Shopping High Street; The Homend.
AA 24 hour service
Tel. Worcester 51070.

Leeds see page 204

Leek Staffordshire

The centre of Leek is an area where fine 18th-century houses mingle with the 17th-century inns. Older still is the Abbey Inn, built from the stones of a ruined medieval abbey.

James Brindley (1716-72), who developed the canal system in Britain, built Brindley Mill, recently restored and opened as a textile museum.

Information Tel. 385509.
Location On the A53, 10 m. NE of Stoke-on-Trent.
Parking Brook Street; Stockwell Street; Vicarage Road; Derby Street; High Street; Silk Street; Leonard Street (all car parks).
District council Staffordshire Moorlands (Tel. 385181).
Population 19,700.
E-C Thur. **M-D** Wed.
Police Leonard Street (Tel. 384411).
Casualty hospital North Stafford Royal Infirmary, Princes Street, Stoke-on-Trent (Tel. Stoke-on-Trent 46100).
Post office St Edward Street.
Cinema Grand 1, 2 and 3, High Street (Tel. 385852).
Public library Stockwell Street.
Places to see Art Gallery, Stockwell Street; Brindley Mill, Mill Street.
Shopping Smithfield Precinct; Derby Street; Market Square; St Edward Street; High Street; Haywood Street.
AA 24 hour service
Tel. Stoke-on-Trent 25881.

Leicester see page 208

Leighton Buzzard
Bedfordshire

Leighton (the "Buzzard" probably derives from an ancient family) takes in Linslade and is sometimes known as Leighton-Linslade.

Many fine old buildings line the streets leading to the 600-year-old Market Cross, a five-sided structure.

Information Tel. 371202.
Location On the A418, 11 m. NE of Aylesbury.
Parking West Street; North Street; Church Square; Hockliffe Street; High Street; Lake Street; Baker Street (all car parks).
District council South Bedfordshire (Tel. Dunstable 603166).
Population 29,800.
E-C Thur. **M-D** Tues., Sat.
Police Hockliffe Road (Tel. 372222).
Casualty hospital Royal Bucks. Hospital, Aylesbury (Tel. Aylesbury 84111).
Post office Church Square.
Theatres Civic Centre, West Street (Tel. 371202); Library Theatre, Lake Street (378310).
Public library Lake Street.
Shopping High Street; Bossard Centre; Peacock Market.
AA 24 hour service
Tel. 01 954 7373.

Leominster H. & W.

From the 13th to the 18th centuries, the fine-spun wool known as Lemster Ore assured the prosperity of this attractive town in the valley of the River Lugg. The locally bred Ryelands sheep produced exceptionally good wool, and helped to establish the great herds of Australia.

Leominster (pronounced Lemster) has many fine old buildings – medieval in the High Street, Tudor in Drapers' Row, Jacobean in Pinsley Road and Georgian in Broad Street and Etnam Street. The priory church of St Peter and St Paul is 12th century.

SHREW TAMER *Until 1809, Leominster's nagging wives were punished by ducking. The stool is in the church.*

Information Tel. 2291.
Location On the A49, 13 m. N of Hereford.
Parking Corn Square; Broad Street; West Street; Etnam Street; Dishley Street; Bargates (all car parks).
District council Leominster (Tel. 2291).
Population 9,100.
E-C Thur. **M-D** Fri.
Police Ryelands Road (Tel. 2345).
Casualty hospital South Street (Tel. 2646).
Post office Corn Square.
Public library South Street.
Places to see Museum, Etnam Street; Berrington Hall, 3 m. N, on A49.
Shopping Corn Square; High Street; South Street.
AA 24 hour service
Tel. Worcester 51070.

Lerwick Shetland

Fishermen of all nations use Lerwick, capital of the Shetlands, as a base and refuge when storms drive them from the fishing grounds in the North Sea. The narrow streets of the town run uphill from the sheltered harbour. There are many 17th-century buildings, including merchants' houses round the quays which have lodberries – loading bays – built out over the water.

The Shetlands were inhabited during the Iron Age by Picts, who built farmsteads with fortified towers called brochs. The remains of one broch survive at Clickimin, a suburb of Lerwick. Between the 8th and 15th centuries the islands were ruled by Norsemen, from whom most of the present inhabitants are descended.

The islands are famous for their knitwear, made by crofters from the soft fleeces of local sheep. During the summer there are demonstrations of spinning and knitting at the Isleburgh Community Centre.

Information Tel. 3434.
Location On Mainland, largest of the Shetland Islands.
Parking Church Road; Hill Lane; Seafield; Fort Road; Commercial Road (all car parks).
District council Shetland Islands (Tel. 3535).
Population 7,200.
E-C Wed. (all day).
Police Market Street (Tel. 2110).
Casualty hospital South Road (Tel. 2751).
Post office Commercial Street.
Theatre Garrison Theatre, Market Street (Tel. 2114).
Cinema North Star, Harbour Street (Tel. 2923).
Public library Lower Hillhead.
Places to see Fort Charlotte, Harbour; Broch of Clickimin; Museum, Lower Hillhead.
Shopping Commercial Street.
Events Up-Helly-Aa Festival (Jan.); Folk Festival (Apr./May).
Car ferries To Aberdeen (Tel. 4848 or 5252).

WHEN WINTER ENDS

In the Middle Ages the pagan Norsemen of Shetland celebrated the end of Christmas with the Up-Helly-Aa Festival in January.

After a torchlight procession, a replica Viking ship is burned.

LEEDS W. Yorks.

The city that clothes the world

In the Middle Ages, Leeds was a wool centre. It still is. Sheep on the Yorkshire moors provided the wool for the cottage-craft industries of spinning and weaving. The introduction of machinery in the late 18th century started the mill system around which the city grew. By the mid-19th century Leeds had moved into the field of ready-made clothing, and by the end of the century was the world centre for the trade. In 1883 Joseph Hepworth pioneered chain-store tailoring, and by 1921 Montague Burton's mill was the largest clothing factory in the world.

The rapid growth of the city led to poor living conditions; cellar dwellings existed into the 20th century, and back-to-back houses still exist. But after the First World War, large-scale slum demolition and the building of suburban housing estates began to change the face of Leeds, and since the Second World War there has been a major redevelopment of the city centre. In 1974 Leeds spread its boundaries to include ten other boroughs and urban districts.

JOSEPH PRIESTLEY (1733-1804) The man who discovered oxygen was a minister at Mill Hill Chapel, Leeds. His statue is in City Square.

The impressive frontage of **Leeds Town Hall** occupies one side of Victoria Square. Broad steps, flanked by four stone lions, lead up to a colonnaded entrance, above which is a frieze depicting the fine arts, poetry, music, industry and science.

The classical lines of the building are emphasised by Corinthian columns extending along all sides and on the 255 ft clock-tower. The Town Hall was opened in 1858 and was designed by Cuthbert Brodrick, a Hull architect who was only 29 years old when his plans were accepted. Brodrick also designed the casing for the Town Hall organ which, when it was installed in 1859, was one of the largest in Europe. It stands 50 ft high, weighs nearly 70 tons and has 6,500 pipes.

Over the years the biscuit-coloured stonework of the building became blackened by grime, but cleaning work costing £30,000 has restored the original colour and has revealed some fine carvings and ornamentation.

Statues and nymphs

In contrast to the soft tones of the Town Hall, the **Civic Hall** is a dazzling showplace of white Portland stone. It was built in 1933 and has a porticoed and colonnaded front overlooking well-kept flower beds in Calverley Street. Two pinnacled towers are surmounted by gilded owls.

The oldest building in City Square is the 19th-century Mill Hill Chapel; the newest is the pale-blue office block of the Norwich Union Insurance Group. Facing Mill Hill Chapel is the GPO building, erected in 1896. But the square is most notable for its five statues, four of them memorials to men associated with Leeds and the largest a statue of the Black Prince. This bronze figure was the work of Sir Thomas Brock (1847-1922), who also designed the Victoria Memorial that stands opposite Buckingham Palace.

The square also has eight nymphs, sculptured by Alfred Drury (1856-1944) whose other works include the figures at the entrance to the Victoria and Albert Museum in London.

Leeds has several shopping arcades,

MILL TOWN *A slender chimney symbolises the industrial beginnings of Leeds.*

built mostly in the late-Victorian period. The finest is the County Arcade. Its lofty glass roof has ornate ironwork arches, and the heavily decorated parapets above the shopfronts are supported on marble columns. Thornton's Arcade is narrower and more austere, with Gothic arches under the glass roof and rows of cathedral-like windows above the shops. At one end of the arcade there is a clock with a moving tableau of figures from Sir Walter Scott's *Ivanhoe*. The mechanism was designed by Sir Edmund Beckett (1816-1905) who also designed the mechanism of London's "Big Ben".

Versatile architect

There are also modern arcades, such as the Bond Street Centre, where plate-glass, chromium and plastics are the predominant materials.

Cuthbert Brodrick, architect of the Town Hall, also designed the oval-shaped **Corn Exchange** at the top of Duncan Street in 1861. Its domed roof allowed the entry of light by which the traders could see the quality of the grain being offered. Some of the benches used to display the samples can still be seen. The building is now used for shows and exhibitions.

The **Mechanics Institute** is another building by Brodrick, opened in 1865. The versatile architect used French styling for the institute, in contrast to the Gothic and Classical styles of his other work in the city. The front entrance is a cavernous arch surmounted by carvings representing the arts and sciences. The institute was built as a training school for young mechanics. It now houses the circular Civic Theatre.

St Anne's Roman Catholic Cathedral in Cookridge Street was built to the design of J. H. Eastwood. It has a reredos by Edward Pugin (1834-75). The 19th-century parish church of St Peter stands in Kirkgate on the site of a medieval church, and contains a Saxon cross. Holy Trinity Church is the only surviving 18th-century church in Leeds; its slender spire, added in 1841, soars above Boar Lane. St John's Church, in New Briggate, was built in 1634 and has some fine woodwork of the period.

The ruins of **Kirkstall Abbey** are on the banks of the River Aire, 3 miles north-west of the city centre. Cistercian monks founded the abbey in 1152, and their exploitation of iron-ore, tanning and pottery, spinning and weaving laid the foundations for industries that developed in the town in the Middle Ages. The last abbot, John Ripley, converted the abbey gatehouse to a private dwelling, and it now contains a folk museum displaying costumes, dolls and toys, musical instruments and domestic relics.

Lord Darnley, who married Mary, Queen of Scots in 1565, was born in **Temple Newsam House** in 1545. It is now owned by the Leeds Metropolitan District Council and houses a

PRIDE OF A CITY *Leeds Town Hall is a monument to the civic pride of the Victorian era. It was opened in 1858 by Queen Victoria.*

museum with collections of 17th and 18th-century silver, furniture, ceramics, sculptures and paintings. The house stands in parkland 5 miles south-east of the city. "Capability" Brown (1715-83), the landscape gardener, laid out the magnificent grounds.

Waterways east to west

Leeds is served by two waterways – the Leeds and Liverpool Canal and the Aire and Calder Navigation. The canal was built between 1770 and 1816, and is 127 miles long. It is the only surviving navigable waterway crossing the Pennines, and at one point is 487 ft above sea level. At Bingley the canal rises 60 ft through five locks (see Bingley p. 39).

At the Leeds end the canal connects with the Aire and Calder Navigation, which links the city with the port of Goole 34 miles distant on the River Humber. The River Aire was first made navigable into the heart of Leeds in 1700. A little later the River Calder, a tributary of the

Aire, was made navigable to Wakefield.

Leeds' two waterways, therefore, traverse the country from east to west. The Leeds and Liverpool Canal is used commercially only for transporting coal to Wigan power station, from a colliery at Leigh, but the Aire and Calder Navigation has busy two-way traffic – coal barges to Goole and oil barges from Immingham on the Humber.

At Middleton, south of the city, there is a railway line which is claimed to be the oldest in the world. It was laid down in 1758 between Leeds and Middleton Colliery, a distance of 3½ miles, and until 1812 the trucks were horse-drawn. Then Matthew Murray, an engineer from Newcastle, designed a steam engine which became the first commercially successful steam locomotive to run on rails. It worked on a cog-and-rack principle, and a section of the original track is in the Leeds Museum. Murray built four of these engines.

The **Middleton Colliery Railway** runs at weekend afternoons during the summer months, using industrial steam locomotives and rolling-stock.

Leeds is the cricket capital of Yorkshire. The Headingley ground, home of Yorkshire County Cricket Club, is also a traditional venue for Test Matches. Leeds United Football Club play at Elland Road stadium.

Morley, 5 miles to the south of Leeds, is where Herbert Asquith, Prime Minister at the outbreak of the First World War, was born in 1852. A bust of Asquith stands in the ves-

CORN EXCHANGE *Light streams through the north-facing windows in the huge dome, giving it an air of almost fragile delicacy.*

tibule of **Morley Town Hall**, built on the lines of Leeds Town Hall and opened by Asquith in 1895. A plaque identifies the house where he was born – Croft House in Church Road – which is a private residence. The small museum in Morley's library contains his oak cradle.

Three miles to the west of Leeds is the mill town of Pudsey. On the edge of the town is Fulneck, where Moravian religious refugees settled in 1742, naming their settlement after a town in Germany. The **Fulneck Moravian Museum** contains Victorian exhibits.

Cricketing heroes

But cricket enthusiasts know Pudsey as the birthplace of two Yorkshire batsmen – Herbert Sutcliffe and Len Hutton. Sutcliffe played for Yorkshire and England in the 1920s and scored 50,138 runs, including 149 centuries, during his career. Len Hutton is best known for his Test score of 364 against Australia in 1938 – a record that still stands. He was knighted on retiring in 1956.

At the extreme north-west edge of the Leeds Metropolitan District is Otley, lying at the foot of the 900 ft Chevin which gives magnificent views over Wharfedale. Otley is a market town and has a Victorian maypole at Cross Green, a medieval bridge and several old inns.

All Saints parish church is late Norman, with 14th and 15th-century features. In the churchyard is a memorial to more than 30 men who died while constructing the Bramhope Railway Tunnel, through the Chevin, between 1845 and 1849.

Thomas Chippendale, the furniture designer, was born in Otley in 1718. His birthplace has gone, but a plaque marks the spot. The painter J. M. W. Turner often visited Otley and painted many scenes in the area.

French-style gardens

Eight miles north of the city is **Harewood House**, the home of the Earl of Harewood, built in 1759-71 by John Carr of York for Edwin Lascelles, the 1st Earl of Harewood. Robert Adam decorated the interior, and in 1843 Sir Charles Barry carried out alterations and added the Italian-style terrace. The grounds were laid out by "Capability" Brown and now include a bird garden.

Bramham Park, 10 miles east of Leeds city centre, was begun in 1698 by the 1st Lord Bingley, Lord Chamberlain to Queen Anne. The mansion contains furniture, pictures and porcelain of the period.

The gardens and grounds are laid out in the manner of the Palace of Versailles, in France, with beech hedges and broad walks.

Information Tel. 31301.
Location On the M1, 9 m. E of Bradford.
Parking Portland Street; Little Queen Street; Park Street; Portland Crescent; Mark Lane; Grafton Street; Templar Street; Duke Street; Swinegate; Pitt Row; Woodhouse Lane; Merrion Centre; Albion Street; Sovereign Street; New York Street; York Street; Eastgate; Neville Street (all car parks).
District council Leeds Metropolitan (Tel. 462041).
Population 448,500.
M-D Tues.
Police (Bb) Millgarth (Tel. 35353).
Casualty hospitals (Cc) General Infirmary, Calverley Street (Tel. 32799, even dates); St James's Hospital, Beckett Street (33144, odd dates).
Post office (Cb) City Square.
Theatres Leeds Playhouse **(Bc)**, Calverley Street (Tel. 42111); City Varieties Music-Hall **(Db)**, The

ROBIN HOOD'S CLOCK *Robin Hood and Gurth the Swineherd strike the quarters, Richard Coeur de Lion and Friar Tuck strike the hours in Thornton's Arcade. The tableau is a scene from Sir Walter Scott's Ivanhoe.*

THE GOOD OLD DAYS OF MUSIC-HALL

Leeds is the home of one of the last remaining music-halls in Britain – the City Varieties Music-Hall, built in 1850. It claims to be the only theatre in the world where old-time music-hall is regularly played.

The artists and audience wear Edwardian clothes during performances. The entertainer Bruce Forsyth is seen here with the chairman Leonard Sachs.

LEEDS

Headrow (30808); Civic Theatre
(Cc), Cookridge Street (455505);
Grand Theatre **(Db)**, New Briggate
(450891).
Cinemas Odeon 1, 2 and 3 **(Db)**,
Eastgate (Tel. 30031); Plaza **(Db)**,
New Briggate (456882); Tower **(Db)**,
New Briggate (458229); ABC 1 and 2
(Db), Vicar Lane (451013).
Public library (Cb) Calverley Street.
Places to see City Museum and Art
Gallery **(Cb)**, Calverley Street;
Kirkstall Abbey and Abbey House
Museum, 3 m. NW on A65; Temple
Newsam House, 5 m. SE off A63;
Harewood House, 8 m. N on A61.
Town trails Available from Leeds
Civic Trust, Claremont, 23
Clarendon Road, Leeds LS2 9NZ.
Shopping Central Shopping
Precinct; Merrion Shopping Centre;
Kirkgate Market; Briggate; Harrison
Street; The Headrow; Vicar Lane.
Events Leeds Gala (Aug.); Music
Festival and International Piano
Competition (Sept.).
Sport FA League football, Leeds
United FC, Elland Road. Rugby
League: Leeds, St Michael's Lane;
Bramley, Town Street, Bramley; New
Hunslet, Elland Road. Yorkshire
County CC, Headingley; Greyhound
racing, Elland Road.
AA 24 hour service Tel. 38161.

VICTORIAN SHOPPING CENTRE *Shoppers in Thornton's Arcade have been protected from the weather since 1878 by the lofty, nave-like roof. The arcade is one of several built in Leeds during the late 19th century.*

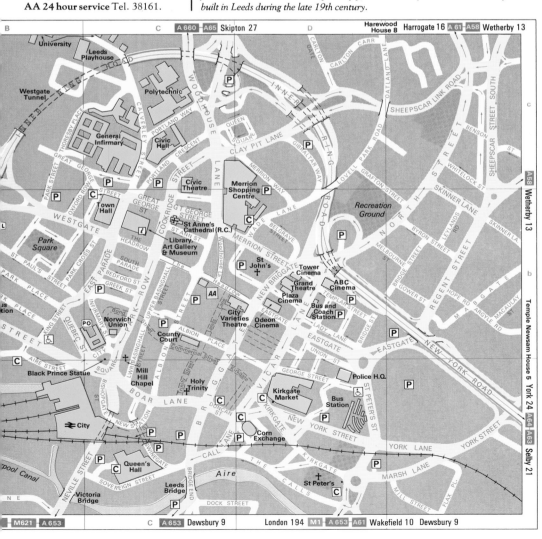

LEICESTER Leicestershire

A modern city which treasures its past

Hundreds of acres of red-brick Victorian terraces and modern housing estates bear witness to the expansion which has transformed the compact county town of the early 19th century into the sprawling industrial city of today. Leicester's growth gathered momentum from 1832, when the railway linking it to the Leicestershire coalfield was opened. Hosiery and footwear were the main industries, and still thrive, though engineering is now the largest source of employment. Leicester gained city status in 1919. St Martin's Church became a cathedral in 1926, and the former University College, founded in 1921, was made a full university in 1957.

For all its modernity, Leicester has a long history which can be traced in its many museums, and in the ancient buildings around the city centre.

It was known to the Romans as *Ratae Coritanorum* (capital of Coritani), and is mentioned under the name of Ledecestre in the Domesday Book of 1086.

The Jewry Wall, close to St Nicholas Circle, is all that remains above ground level of the Roman town. It formed part of a complex which included a public bath and shops. The site has been excavated, and the Jewry Wall Museum contains the Roman finds, as well as relics from other parts of the city.

Simon de Montfort

In the 13th century, the Earldom of Leicester was held by Simon de Montfort, leader of the barons' revolt against Henry III which brought into being the first English parliament. He is commemorated in the 20th-century De Montfort Hall, the city's main centre for concerts.

Leicester stands in farming country, and has had a livestock market for centuries. The general market, held in the square near Gallowtree Gate, is equally old.

By the wall is the Church of St Nicholas, one of the oldest churches in England. It is Saxon in style and may have been built in the 7th century. Stones from Roman buildings were used in the tower.

Leicester Castle was a Saxon stronghold which the Normans began to rebuild in 1068, and the remains of the original Norman motte, or central mound, can be seen. The 12th-century great hall is concealed within 18th-century brickwork. It is now used as the Crown Court.

The castle church of St Mary de Castro was started about 1107 and extended several times during the following 200 years. Near the altar there are five stone sedilia – seats for the clergy – which date from 1180 and are regarded as the finest of their kind in England.

The Newarke (new work) adjoins the castle on the south side. It was built during the 14th century and formerly enclosed a church which has now disappeared. The entrance gateway at the corner of Oxford Street was once used as the town's armoury and contains a museum tracing the history of the Leicestershire Regiment. The 16th-century Chantry House forms part of the Newarke

Houses Museum of social history. The exhibits include a life-size mid-Victorian street scene.

Leicester Cathedral, off the High Street, was built in the 14th century, but extensively altered in the 19th. There was a bishopric of Leicester until 874. It was revived in 1926.

Wolsey's grave

The medieval town had an Augustinian abbey, founded in 1143. Its ruins lie in Abbey Park, 1 mile north of the city centre. Cardinal Wolsey died at the abbey in 1530, and a slab marks the presumed site of his grave.

Leicester's other religious buildings include All Saints Church, in Highcross Street, which dates from around 1300, and St Margaret's Church, in Churchgate, which is 15th century.

Several attractive 18th-century buildings survive in Leicester, among them Belgrave Hall, a Queen Anne house off Thurcaston Road, 2 miles north of the city centre. It is now a museum of furniture. Farm implements and old coaches are displayed in the stables.

There are Georgian town houses in Friar Lane and New Street. New Walk, running from the city centre for 1 mile to Victoria Park, is a tree-lined traffic-free residential avenue laid out in 1785.

The Museum and Art Gallery is in New Walk, in a building designed in 1849 by J. A. Hansom, who patented the horse-drawn cab which bears his name. The museum specialises in natural history, geology, painting and sculpture.

STRANGE PROPHECY *A tablet on Bow Bridge records a supposedly prophesied accident that befell Richard III on his way to his death at the Battle of Bosworth in 1485.*

MEDIEVAL COUNCIL CHAMBERS *The 14th-century, timber Guildhall is one of Leicester's few medieval buildings. From the late 15th to the 19th century it was the meeting place of the mayor and corporation.*

LEICESTER LANDMARK *The city's best known building, its Victorian clock-tower, bears statues of Simon de Montfort and other city benefactors.*

TREASUREHOUSE OF MACHINES

The centrepiece of the Leicester-shire Museum of Technology is its quartet of late-19th-century beam pumping engines which can be seen working at specified weekends. But it also contains the finest collection of hosiery machinery in the world and extensive collections of horse-drawn vehicles, light aircraft, type-writers and optical instruments.

An 84 ton steam shovel is one of the museum's working exhibits.

These beam-engines once operated a pump-house on the museum site.

Information Tel. 556699.
Location On the A50, 12 m. S of Loughborough.
Parking Haymarket Centre; Lee Street; Queen Street; Dover Street; Wellington Street; Abbey Street; St Peter's Lane; Rutland Street; East Street; Hamshaw House; Clinton Street; Newarke Street; Fox Street; Conduit Street; New Walk Centre; St Nicholas Circle (2) (all car parks).
District council City of Leicester (Tel. 549922).
Population 279,800.
E-C Thur. 6-day trading in centre.
M-D Wed., Fri. and Sat.
Police (Cb) Charles Street (Tel. 20845).
Casualty hospital (Ba) Royal Infirmary, Infirmary Square (Tel. 541414).
Post office (Bb) Bishop Street.
Theatres Haymarket Theatre and Studio Theatre **(Bc)**, Belgrave Gate (Tel. 539797); Little **(Bb)**, Dover Street (551302); Phoenix Arts **(Ba)**, Newarke Street (554854).
Cinemas ABC 1, 2, 3 **(Ac)**, Belgrave Gate (Tel. 24346); Cinecenta **(Ac)**, Abbey Street (25892); Odeon **(Bc)**, Queen Street (22892).
Public library (Bb) Bishop Street.
Places to see Castle **(Aa)**; Corn Exchange **(Bb)**; Guildhall **(Ab)**; Newarke Houses Museum **(Aa)**; Jewry Wall Museum **(Ab)**; Museum of Technology; Museum and Art Gallery **(Ca)**, New Walk; Leicestershire Regimental Museum **(Ba)**; Newarke Magazine Gateway **(Ba)**; Museum of Costume **(Ab)**, Roger Wygston's House, St Nicholas Circle. All closed Friday.
Town trails Tourist Information Centre, Bishop Street.
Shopping Haymarket; Haymarket Centre; Charles Street; Humberstone Gate; Gallowtree Gate; Granby Street; Belvoir Street; King Street; Hotel Street; Belgrave Gate.
Event Abbey Park Show (Aug.).
Trade and industry Hosiery; boots and shoes; engineering; electronics.
Sport FA League football, Leicester City FC, Filbert Street; Rugby football, Leicester RFC, Welfor Road; County cricket, Grace Road; Speedway and Greyhound racing, Parker Drive Stadium.
AA 24 hour service Tel. 20491.

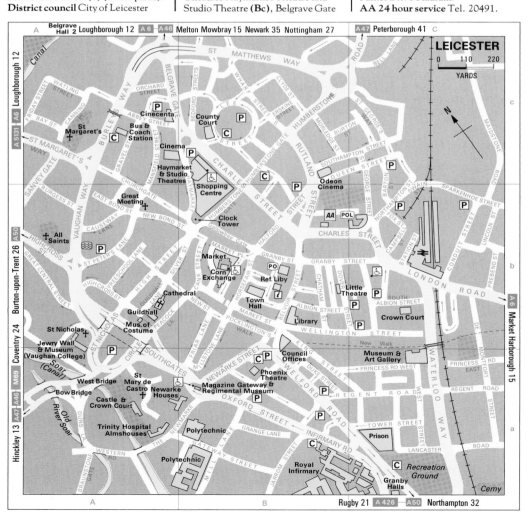

GARDEN CITY *The house and gardens of Letchworth spread out in an informal pattern that conceals the careful plan to which they were built.*

Letchworth Herts.

The world's first Garden City was started at Letchworth in 1903, and was built according to principles laid down by Sir Ebenezer Howard (1850-1928), a pioneer of modern town planning. Howard's ideal was extended in 1963 when the residents acquired the land on which the town stands. Letchworth's development is illustrated in the museum in Norton Way South.

Information Tel. 6500.
Location On the A505, 3 m. NE of Hitchin.
Parking Arena Parade; Birds Hill; Hillshott; Station Place; Station Way; Rowlands Way; The Wynd; Town Hall (all car parks).
District council North Hertfordshire (Tel. 6500).
Population 31,800.
E-C Wed.
Police Nevells Road (Tel. 5522).
Casualty hospital Lister Hospital, Corey's Mill Lane, Stevenage (Tel. Stevenage 4333).
Post office Broadway.
Cinema Broadway, Eastcheap (Tel. 4721).
Public library Broadway.
Places to see Museums, Norton Way South and Broadway.
Shopping Leys Avenue; Arena, Eastcheap; Commerce Way; Central Approach; The Arcade; Station Road.
Trade and industry Engineering; parachutes; printing.

AA 24 hour service
Tel. Hatfield 62852.

Lewes E. Sussex

A high street of Georgian shops and houses leads to the lofty mound on which stands the Norman castle of Lewes. The castle was built to guard a gap in the South Downs, carved by the River Ouse, and the town grew up on the hillside between the castle and the river. The steep streets of the old town are linked by narrow passageways called twittens.

The castle keep and barbican still stand. Near by is the 16th-century Barbican House, now an archaeological museum. Southover Grange, an Elizabethan house to the south of the castle, was the boyhood home of the diarist John Evelyn (1620-1706). The house is built of Caen stone taken from the neighbouring Priory of St Pancras after the Dissolution of the Monasteries in 1537. Some carved stonework from the priory is preserved in Anne of Cleves House, which was given by Henry VIII to his fourth wife after their divorce in 1540. It is now a folk museum.

Information Tel. 6151.
Location On the A27, 9 m. NE of Brighton.
Parking Cliffe High Street; East Street (2); The Causeway; High Street; West Street; North Street; South Street (2); Mountfield Road (all car parks).

District council Lewes (Tel. 71600).
Population 13,800.
E-C Wed. **M-D** Tues.
Police (Bb) West Street (Tel. 5432).
Casualty hospital Royal Sussex County, Easton Road, Brighton (Tel. Brighton 609411).
Post office (Ab) High Street.
Public library (Bb) Albion Street.
Places to see Castle (Ab); Priory ruins (Aa); Barbican House Museum (Ab); Ann of Cleves House (Aa); Southover Grange (Aa); Glynde Place, 3 m. N.
Town trails Available from M. Barnard, County Planning Department, East Sussex County Council, Southover House, Lewes, East Sussex, BN7 1YA.
Shopping High Street.
AA 24 hour service
Tel. Brighton 695231.

Lewisham see London

Lichfield Staffordshire

Dr Samuel Johnson (1709-84) was born and educated at Lichfield. His literary achievements as essayist, critic and compiler of a pioneering *Dictionary* (1755) were considerable, but he is best remembered as the wit and champion of common sense portrayed by his biographer James Boswell (1740-95). Statues of both men stand in Market Square.

Johnson's birthplace, facing the statue, is a museum dedicated to his life and work. Dame Oliver's School and the grammar school, where he was taught, both survive. The grammar school, now merged into a comprehensive school, also included among its pupils the essayist Joseph Addison (1672-1719) and the Shakespearian actor David Garrick (1717-79). At the Swan Inn, near by, Johnson used to meet his friends.

Another notable citizen of Lichfield was Elias Ashmole (1617-92), who founded the Ashmolean Museum, Oxford, in 1677. It is Britain's oldest public museum.

Lichfield Cathedral, built in the 13th century, has three spires. The central one is a replacement of a spire

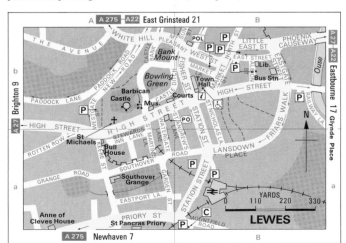

LEWES

JOHNSON

DR JOHNSON *The celebrated man of letters, wit and embodiment of British common sense gazes in effigy at his birthplace in Lichfield's Market Square.*

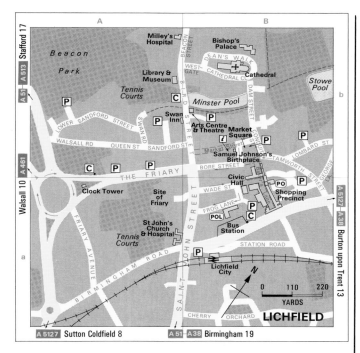

LICHFIELD

Stafford 17 · A513 · A51
Walsall 10 · A461
A5127 · A38 · Burton upon Trent 13
A5127 Sutton Coldfield 8
A51 · A38 Birmingham 19

0 110 220 YARDS

TRIPLE LANDMARK *The Ladies of the Vale, the three graceful spires of Lichfield Cathedral, beckon the traveller to the city from afar.*

1242, is considered one of the finest examples of Gothic architecture in Scotland. Since 1964 the tower has been topped by a controversial aluminium crown.

The ruins of Linlithgow Palace stand on a knoll overlooking the loch. Begun in 1425 for James I of Scotland, the palace was the birthplace of James V in 1512 and Mary, Queen of Scots in 1542. In 1746 the palace was gutted by a fire, probably caused by the Duke of Cumberland's troops on their way back from defeating the Highland clans at Culloden.

Information Tel. 3121 or 4600 (summer).
Location On the A706, 18 m. W of Edinburgh.
Parking The Vennel; Lochside; High Street (west) (all car parks).
District council West Lothian (Tel. Bathgate 53631).
Population 9,500.
E-C Wed.
Police Court Square (Tel. 3235).
Casualty hospital Falkirk and District Royal Infirmary, Majors Loan, Falkirk (Tel. Falkirk 23011).
Post office High Street.
Public library The Vennel.
Places to see St Michael's Church; Palace.
Town trails Available from West Lothian District Council.
Shopping High Street.
Trade and industry Paper-making; distilling.
AA 24 hour service
Tel. Edinburgh (031) 225 8464.

Littlehampton W. Sussex

Holidaymakers have taken over Littlehampton, an ancient port at the mouth of the River Arun. The resort offers flat, sandy beaches, a growing marina, free fishing on the river towpath, and boat trips. The Sussex Downs are a short walk away inland. A few of the dockyard's old wharves still cling to the river banks.

Information Tel. 6133.
Location On the A259, 7 m. E of Bognor Regis.
Parking Ring Road (3); Beach Road; Windmill Road; Sea Road; Surrey Street; River Road; Norfolk Road (all car parks).
District council Arun (Tel. 6133).
Population 22,200.
E-C Wed. **M-D** Fri., Sat.
Police East Street (Tel. 6161).
Casualty hospital Littlehampton and District, Fitzalan Road (Tel. 7101).
Post office Arcade Road.
Theatre Windmill, The Green (Tel. 21681).
Cinema Palladium, Church Street (Tel. 6644).
Public library Maltravers Road.
Places to see Maritime Museum, River Road.
Shopping Surrey Street; High Street; Beach Road.
AA 24 hour service
Tel. Brighton 695231.

---

that was destroyed during the Civil War. The west front contains more than 100 statues. Well-preserved 14th–16th-century houses and a 17th-century Bishop's Palace line the close.

The ruined Franciscan friary dates from 1229. Milley's Hospital, founded in 1424 and rebuilt in 1504, has a fine gateway.

Information Tel. 52109.
Location On the A5127, 19 m. N of Birmingham.
Parking Sandford Street; Bird Street; Lombard Street; Tamworth Street; Frog Lane; The Friary (2) (all car parks).
District council Lichfield (Tel. 54181).
Population 25,600.
E-C Wed. **M-D** Fri., Sat.
Police (Ba) Frog Lane (Tel. 51111).
Casualty hospital Victoria, Friary Road (Tel. 55321).
Post office (Ba) Bakers Lane.
Theatre Lichfield Arts Centre **(Bb)**,

Bird Street (Tel. 22223).
Public library (Ab) Bird Street.
Places to see Cathedral and Bishop's Palace **(Bb)**; Samuel Johnson's birthplace **(Bb)**; Friary ruins **(Aa)**; Letocetum Roman city, 2 m. SW.
Town trails Available from Tourist Information Centre **(Bb)**, Breadmarket Street.
Shopping Baker's Lane; Market Street; Bore Street; Bird Street; Tamworth Street.
Events Festival (June); Abbots Bromley Horn Dance (Sept.).
AA 24 hour service
Tel. Stoke-on-Trent 25881.

Lincoln
see page 212

Linlithgow Lothian

Through its port at Blackness, Linlithgow enjoyed a monopoly of trade along the nearby Forth shore in the 15th and 16th centuries.

St Michael's Church, founded in

A LOOK AROUND
LINCOLN
Lincolnshire

The city above the plain

Three honey-coloured towers rise majestically above Lincoln Cathedral, and at their feet medieval buildings spill down the sides of a limestone ridge to the banks of the River Witham, 200 ft below. The city stands over the flat, Lincolnshire plain like a speckled cushion supporting a golden crown, and seen from afar the cathedral has a dream-like quality, its colour seeming to vary with every subtle change of light. Yet this masterpiece of medieval craftsmanship is young compared with the city's Newport Arch – the only Roman gateway in Britain still used by traffic.

OBSERVATORY TOWER *A 19th-century amateur astronomer added the turret to Lincoln Castle. Its top provides wide views of the city and plain.*

The strategic ridge on which the cathedral and Norman castle stand was the site of a Roman fortress – the base from which the 9th Legion kept the peace in eastern England. A city, Lindum Colonia, succeeded the fortress around AD 100. Apart from the unique Newport Arch, other Roman survivals include the substantial foundations of the **East Gate**, the **Lower West Gate** (excavated only in the 1960s and 1970s), a length of the wall and ditch that surrounded the city, and, in Bailgate, stones marking positions of columns that supported a noble façade almost 100 yds long.

But the most remarkable of all the Roman works in Lincoln is the 11 mile long Fossdyke Navigation, the oldest canal in the country, dug more than 1,800 years ago to link the Witham and the Trent. It is still in use and, in recent years, has made Brayford Pool a popular and colourful base for pleasure craft.

After the Romans withdrew from Britain, Lincoln was colonised by the Anglo-Saxons and, later, the Danes. By the time of the Norman Conquest it was one of the three or four largest cities in the country, a formidable military base and the centre of a rich farming area with excellent land and water communications. The wool trade, in particular, produced great wealth, and the local cloth has been immortalised in the Lincoln green said to have been worn by Robin Hood and his men.

In 1068 the Normans built **the castle,** incorporating some of the Roman defences. It was often attacked, captured and regained, and featured prominently in King John's struggle with the barons. It was stormed for the last time in 1644, during the Civil War, when the occupying Royalists surrendered to the Roundheads.

Third-largest cathedral

The castle has a large bailey and two artificial mounds. **Observatory Tower** stands on the smaller, while the other is occupied by **Lucy Tower** – named after Countess Lucy who died about 1139 – which formed the keep, or main strongpoint.

The cathedral is the third-largest medieval cathedral in Britain, after St Paul's and York Minster. The craftsmen who built it, shaped a miracle in wood, stone and glass. Its origins can be traced back to a century before the Battle of Hastings, when Lincoln was part of a huge diocese administered by a bishop from Dorchester-on-Thames, now a village a few miles from Oxford. Shortly

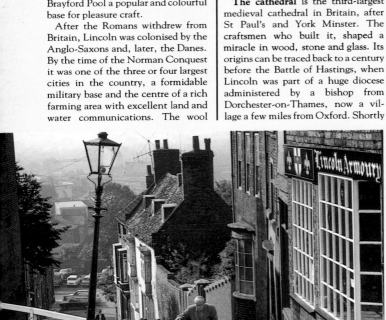

STREETS OF ANTIQUITY *Medieval houses, now mostly antique shops, line the cobbled and flagstoned pavements winding down from Castle Square.*

PLACES TO SEE

1 Aaron the Jew's House
2 Bishop's Palace
3 Cardinal's Hat
4 Castle
5 Cathedral
6 Roman East Gate

7 Exchequer Gate
8 Roman Lower West Gate
9 City and County Museum
10 Museum of Lincolnshire Life
11 Newport Arch
12 Potter Gate

13 Priory Gate
14 St Mary's Guildhall
15 Stonebow and Guildhall
16 Usher Gallery
17 Jew's House
18 Dernstall House

GOTHIC SPLENDOUR *Lincoln Cathedral, with its fine west front, was one of the earliest Norman churches in Britain. The* central tower at the eastern end of the nave has a 5 ton bell called Great Tom of Lincoln.

TRANQUILLITY *Swans glide down the Witham as it flows through the city.*

LORD TENNYSON *The poet's statue stands near the east end of cathedral.*

mainly to create a worthy setting for Bishop Hugh's shrine after he was made a saint. The choir is backed by the largest and earliest eight-light window in England. The nave is a glorious structure, flanked by limestone or Purbeck marble pillars consisting of clustered columns, with floral capitals.

The present central tower was completed in 1310 and crowned with an immense spire that reached about 540 ft above ground level. The spire fell during a ferocious storm in 1547; and smaller spires on the western towers were demolished at the start of the 19th century.

The 12th-century Bishop's Palace was enlarged by Bishop Hugh of Avalon, and by Bishop Hugh of Wells in the 13th century. The Civil War wrought considerable damage, but the ruins include a remarkable barrel-vaulted 12th-century hall.

Oldest domestic buildings

Narrow cobbled streets, flanked by many shops selling antiques, books and souvenirs, run steeply down from Castle Square to the lower part of the city. The square itself – closed on one side by the 14th-century **Exchequer Gate** leading to the cathedral – is notable for the exceptionally fine 16th-century merchant's house with two timber-framed storeys and three gables overhanging the bow-windowed ground floor.

Aaron the Jew's House, on Steep Hill, was built at the end of the 12th century and is one of the oldest domestic buildings still in use in Britain. Lower down Steep Hill, where it joins The Strait, is the **Jew's House,** another miraculous survivor from the 12th century. Its neighbour, the Jew's Court, may be of the same date.

The short walk from Castle Square to the city centre spans 400 years. **Dernstall House** and the **Cardinal's Hat,** two 15th-century black-and-

after the Norman Conquest the bishop's seat was moved to the thriving city of Lincoln, where an Anglo-Saxon minster had previously existed.

The new bishop was Remigius, almoner of Fécamp Abbey in Normandy. He had supported William the Conqueror's invasion with a ship and soldiers, and was England's first Norman bishop. The royal charter confirming his appointment can still be seen in the cathedral. It reveals that the king also gave Remigius land "free of all customary payments, for the building of the mother church of the whole Bishopric".

Work started on the Norman church about 1072, and was finished 20 years later. The new building, more than 100 yds long, was marked by a spectacular western façade, facing the castle and framed by twin towers. It is one of the cathedral's great glories, and may have been designed to symbolise heaven's gate.

The original cathedral had a timber roof, but this was destroyed by fire in 1141 and rebuilt in stone. Bishop Alexander undertook the work, and also embellished the west front with carved figures. These include representations of Noah, the ark, and Daniel in the lions' den. Bishop Alexander had a great reputation as a builder, but his stone roof proved too heavy for its supports when an earthquake shook Lincoln in 1185. The cathedral collapsed, although the west front and its towers remained sufficiently intact to be incorporated in the new building.

Glorious nave

The task of reconstruction fell to Bishop Hugh, a Carthusian monk from Avalon. He started in 1192, working from the eastern end, building five chapels behind the high altar, then slowly working back towards the great façade left by Remigius. The five chapels lasted for less than a century, because the cathedral's eastern end was rebuilt to form the outstandingly beautiful Angel Choir,

LINCOLNSHIRE LIFE

The Museum of Lincolnshire Life displays the agricultural, social and industrial history of the county. A small section is devoted to the activities of the traditional folk-hero, the Lincolnshire Poacher.

A Lincolnshire haywain of the 19th century is among the exhibits in the Transport and Industry Gallery.

white buildings reflect the city's economic life. The Cardinal's Hat, a former inn, was probably given its curious name in honour of Cardinal Wolsey, Bishop of Lincoln in 1514-15.

In the High Street is an impressive 500-year-old Tudor gateway called the **Stonebow**. In keeping with ancient traditions, the city council still meets in the **Guildhall**, above the gate, and members are summoned by the tolling of the Mote Bell, cast in 1371 and the oldest of its kind in Britain. The civic regalia in another room includes a 14th-century sword, believed to have been presented to Lincoln by Richard II, and a model of "Little Willie", the world's first tank, built in Lincoln in 1915.

The **City and County Museum**, housed in a two-storey church, contains several magnificent suits of armour, a prehistoric boat found buried near the Witham, and natural-history exhibits. The building itself dates from about 1250, and is the oldest Franciscan church in England.

The **Usher Gallery** contains a remarkable collection of antique watches, exquisite miniatures, Sir Jacob Epstein's handsome bust of Paul Robeson and more than 50 paintings by Peter de Wint, the Staffordshire-born artist who worked in Lincoln. One room is devoted to Alfred, Lord Tennyson, the 19th-century Poet Laureate whose father was a Lincolnshire rector.

At the southern end of the High Street, easily overlooked, **St Mary's Guildhall** has stood since the late 12th century. Its handsome gateway is rich in dog-tooth carvings.

Information Tel. 29828.
Location On the A46, 17 m. NE of Newark-on-Trent.
Parking Westgate (3); St Paul's Lane; Castle Hill; Flaxengate (2); St Rumbolds Street; Saltergate (2); Beaumont Fee; Orchard Street; Lucy Tower Street; Waterside South; Melville Street; St Mary Street; Brayford Street; Tentercroft Street (all car parks).
District council City of Lincoln (Tel. 32151).
Population 76,600.
E-C Wed. **M-D** Thur., Fri., Sat.
Police Newland (Tel. 29911).
Casualty hospital County, Sewell

Road (Tel. 29921).
Post office (Bb) Guildhall Street.
Theatre Royal **(Bb)**, Clasketgate (Tel. 25555).
Cinemas ABC **(Bb)**, Saltergate (Tel. 23062); Odeon, High Street (20951).
Public library (Bb) Free School Lane.
Places to see Aaron the Jew's House **(Bc)**; Cardinal's Hat **(Bb)**; Castle **(Bc)**; Cathedral **(Bc)**; Roman East Gate **(Bc)**; Exchequer Gate **(Bc)**; City and County Museum **(Bb)**; Jew's House **(Bb)**; Museum of Lincolnshire Life; Newport Arch; Potter Gate **(Cc)**; Priory Gate **(Cc)**;

St Mary's Guildhall; Stonebow and Guildhall **(Bb)**; Usher Gallery **(Bb)**; Royal Lincolnshire Regiment Museum.
Town trails Available from Tourist Information Centre, Castle Hill.
Shopping High Street; Stonebow Centre; Saltergate; Sincil Street; Silver Street; Bailgate.
Events Music Festival (end Feb. to early Mar.); St Matthew Passion (Mar.); Water Festival (June); Lincolnshire Show (June).
Sport FA League football, Lincoln City FC, Sincil Bank.
AA 24 hour service
Tel. Lincoln 42363.

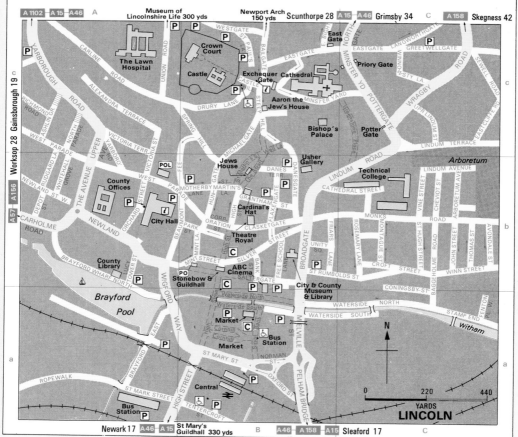

LIVERPOOL Merseyside

A busy port and city on the Lancashire coast

There was a settlement on the north bank of the River Mersey in the 1st century, close to a muddy creek, or "lifrugpool". By 1200 a fishing village had grown up, and in 1207 King John granted "Livpul" a charter to encourage the development of a port. Modern Liverpool's growth began in the late 17th and early 18th centuries, with the West Indies sugar trade and the slave trade. The coming of the steamship in the 1840s made the port busier than ever. It became a terminal for the Cunard and White Star liners, and for merchant ships from all parts of the world, with 7 miles of docks along its waterfront.

The steamships took emigrants to Australia, Canada and America, and they brought in thousands of Irish refugees from the potato famines of the 1840s. Many got no further than Liverpool and, as other nationalities followed, the city began to take on the cosmopolitan character which it still retains. Today the mighty transatlantic liners have gone, but Liverpool is still Britain's second largest port after London.

CITY CREST *The Liver (pronounced Lyver) bird is said to get its name from the piece of seaweed – laver – in its beak.*

Liverpool's **Anglican cathedral,** the largest Anglican cathedral in the world, is 671 ft long and stands on a wooded slope to the east of the city. The central tower is 331 ft high, and spans the full width of the building. It is built of red sandstone to a Gothic design by Sir Giles Gilbert Scott. The foundation stone was laid in 1904 by Edward VII, but, interrupted by two World Wars, the building was finally completed in 1978.

TWENTIETH-CENTURY GOTHIC *The red sandstone Liverpool Cathedral was started in 1904 and is a modern expression of medieval Gothic.*

Prime Minister

Just north of the cathedral is Rodney Street, one of the finest groups of Georgian houses in northern England. William Ewart Gladstone (1809–98), who was Prime Minister four times in the reign of Queen Victoria, was born at No. 62.

The city's **Roman Catholic cathedral** stands about half a mile further north, also on high ground. The original plan was for a building that would be second only to St Peter's in Rome. But soaring costs and war-time interruptions caused a change of plan. The present building, designed by Sir Frederick Gibberd in 1960, was consecrated in 1967. It is cylindrical in shape, with a conical roof topped by a tapering, coloured-glass tower.

CITY WATERFRONT *Three landmarks dominate Liverpool pierhead – the Royal Liver Building, the Cunard Building and the Dock Board Offices.*

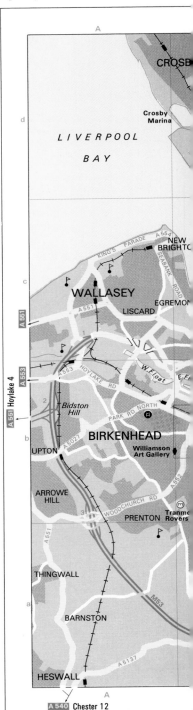

A detached bell-tower stands at one side of the main building, and is balanced by the Chapel of the Sacrament at the other side.

One of the most imposing buildings in Liverpool, **St George's Hall**, was designed by Lonsdale Elmes, who was only 24 when the foundation stone was laid in 1838. Elmes died at the age of 33, and the building was finished seven years later in 1854.

St George's Hall is said to be the finest example of the Greco-Roman style in Europe. Sixteen Corinthian columns, each about 60 ft high, make up the front portico, which is approached from Lime Street.

SPACE-AGE GLORY *Liverpool's Roman Catholic cathedral was built during the 1960s. Its lantern tower has stained glass by two modern designers, John Piper and Patrick Reyntiens.*

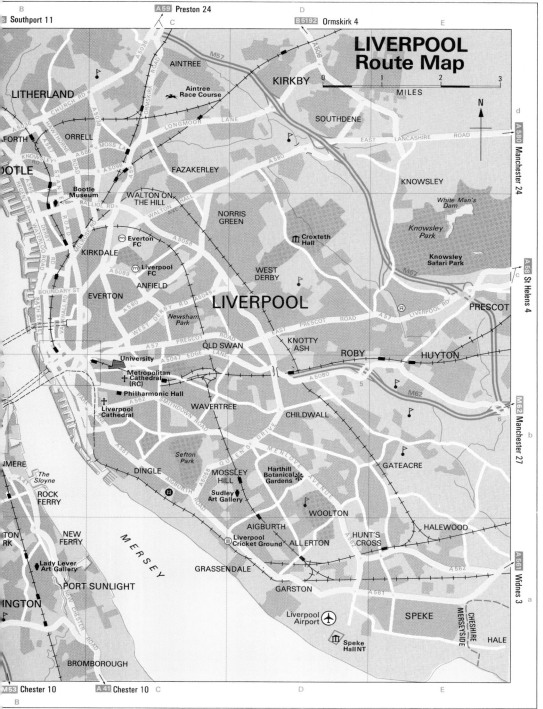

LIVERPOOL
Route Map

LIVERPOOL SCENE *The statues at the back of St George's Hall look across the city towards the twin towers of the Royal Liver Building. On each tower a Liver bird perches 300 ft above the city it symbolises.*

The main hall can accommodate 1,750 people. Its sunken floor is made up of 20,000 tiles mixed with bands of stone to produce a mosaic effect.

Liverpool's **Town Hall** was completed in 1754 to the design of John Wood, the architect who gave the city of Bath much of its elegance. The figure of Minerva by Felix Rossi was added to the dome in 1802.

Many priceless treasures are displayed in the building, and the visitors' book contains signatures of royalty, British and foreign statesmen, soldiers, diplomats and personalities of the theatre covering several generations.

The chandeliers in the large ballroom were made in 1820. Each one is 28 ft long, contains 20,000 pieces of crystal and weighs more than a ton.

Lord Mayor's gift

Sir Andrew Barclay Walker, Mayor of Liverpool in 1873, provided the money to build the **Walker Art Gallery** which contains the largest collection of paintings in Britain outside London. Among the famous works on display are: *And when did you last see your father?* by W. F. Yeames, Rubens' *Virgin and child with St Elizabeth and the child Baptist*, Martini's *Christ discovered in the Temple* and a Holbein portrait of Henry VIII. Other paintings include works by Hogarth,

Reynolds, Turner and George Stubbs, who was born in Liverpool. Also on view are sculptures by Rodin, Renoir, Le Hongre and Epstein.

The **Merseyside County Museum** in William Brown Street contains an aquarium and transport gallery in the basement, while the ground floor is devoted to the development of the City and the Port.

The first floor covers the history of the Ship and on the third floor is the Time Keeping Gallery with a fine collection of watches, clocks and a reconstruction of a Chinese water-clock. Also on the third floor is a public planetarium.

Speke Hall, near the south-east border of the city and close to the airport, was started in 1490 by Sir William Norris. The house was completed in 1610 in its present form of four wings surrounding a cobbled courtyard. The house escaped 18th-century modernisation, and looks today much as it did towards the end of the reign of Elizabeth I. With its black-and-white half-timbering it is one of the best houses of the period in existence.

Much of the interior furnishing reflects the tastes of Richard Watt, a wealthy merchant who acquired the house in 1797, and his successors in the 19th century. The kitchen includes an array of copperware, a col-

lection of smoothing irons and some early vacuum cleaners.

The first Mersey road tunnel, the **Queensway Tunnel**, was opened in 1934 by George V. It is nearly 2 miles long and runs between Liverpool and Birkenhead. When opened, it was the world's longest underwater tunnel. The **Kingsway Tunnel** is 1½ miles long and links Liverpool with Wallasey. It was opened by the Queen in 1971.

TITANIC *The memorial on Liverpool pierhead to the engine-room staff of the* Titanic, *now commemorates all engineers lost at sea since the* Titanic *sank in 1912.*

THE ART OF STUBBS

George Stubbs (1724–1806), the great animal painter, was born in Ormond Street, Liverpool. His birthplace has vanished, but the city treasures eight of his works in the Walker Art Gallery.

Horse frightened by a lion, from the Walker Art Gallery.

WHERE THE BEATLES BEGAN

In the early 1960s a favourite nightspot in Liverpool was a club called the Cavern. There, four young Liverpudlians called The Beatles introduced a new beat which was to have the greatest influence on pop music since ragtime.

John Lennon, Paul McCartney, George Harrison and Ringo Starr.

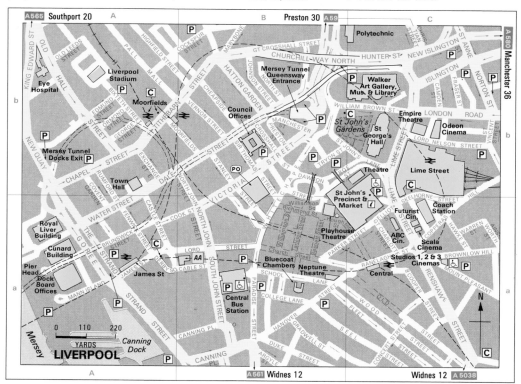

Information

Tel. Liverpool (051) 709 3631.
Location On the A57, 36 m. W of Manchester.
Parking St John's Lane; New Quay; Paradise Street; Mount Pleasant; College Lane; Cleveland Square; Byrom Street; Vauxhall Road; Manchester Street (all car parks).
District council City of Liverpool (Tel. 051 227 3911).
Population 510,300.
E-C Wed. **M-D** Daily.
Police Canning Place (Tel. 051 709 6010).
Casualty hospital Royal Liverpool Teaching Hospital (Tel. 051 709 0141).
Post office (Bb) Whitechapel.
Theatres Royal Court **(Cb)**, Roe Street (Tel. 051 709 7411); Playhouse **(Ba)**, Williamson Square (051 709 8363); Empire **(Cb)**, Lime Street (051 709 1555); Neptune **(Ba)**, Hanover Street

(051 709 7844); Everyman, Hope Street (051 709 4776).
Cinemas Odeon 1, 2, 3, 4 and 5 **(Cb)**, London Road (Tel. 051 709 0717); Scala **(Ca)**, Lime Street (051 709 1084); Studio 1, 2 and 3 **(Ca)**, Brownlow Hill (051 709 7847); ABC **(Ca)**, Lime Street (051 709 6277); Futurist **(Ca)**, Lime Street (051 709 3186).
Public library (Cb) William Brown Street.
Places to see St George's Hall **(Cb)**, Lime Street; Town Hall **(Ab)**, Castle Street; Walker Art Gallery **(Cb)**, William Brown Street; Merseyside County Museum **(Cb)**, William Brown Street; Sudley Art Gallery **(RDb)**, Mossley Hill Road; Speke Hall **(RDa)**, 7 m. S off A561; Knowsley Safari Park **(REc)**; Croxteth Country Park, Muirhead Avenue, 5 m. E.
Town trails Available from City Information Office, St John's

Centre, 1st Floor, and City PR Office, Municipal Buildings, Sir Thomas Street.
Shopping London Road; Lord Street; Church Street; Williamson Square; Tarleton Street; Basnett Street; Parker Street; Elliot Street; Ranelagh Street; Great Charlotte Street; Bold Street.
Events Lord Mayor's Parade (June).
Trade and industry Engineering; chemicals; flour milling; tobacco; oilseed processing; shipping.
Sport FA League football: Liverpool FC **(RCc)**, Anfield Road; Everton FC **(RCc)**, Goodison Park. Steeplechasing, Aintree Racecourse **(RCd)**. Wrestling/Boxing, Liverpool Stadium, Bixteth Street.
Car ferries To Isle of Man (Tel. 051 236 3214); to Belfast (051 236 5464); to Dublin (051 227 5151).
AA 24 hour service Tel. 051 709 7252.

BIRD'S-EYE VIEW *The longest cable-car in Britain carries passengers 5,320 ft to the top of the Great Orme headland at Llandudno.*

Llandrindod Wells Powys

Bubbling saline streams and bottomless sulphur wells drew health-seeking Victorians to Llandrindod Wells in their thousands. Taking the waters has been replaced by modern medicine, but spacious Edwardian Llandrindod still draws the tourists. Perhaps its restful atmosphere is as good a cure for the ills of the 20th century as the waters were for gout and rheumatism in the past.

Information Tel. 2600/3737.
Location On the A483, 20 m. N of Brecon.
Parking High Street; Princes Avenue; Beaufort Road; Alexander Terrace; Station Terrace; West Street.
District council Radnor (Tel. 3737).
Population 4,200.
E-C Wed. **M-D** Fri.
Police High Street (Tel. 2227).
Casualty hospital Tremont Road (Tel. 2951).
Post office Station Crescent.
Theatres Albert Hall, Ithon Road; Grand Pavilion, off Spa Road (Tel. 2600 for both theatres).
Public library Beaufort Road.
Places to see Castell Collen Roman fort; old bicycle collection, Automobile Palace.
Shopping Temple Street; Middleton Street; Park Crescent.
Event Wales Semi-national Eisteddfod (Oct.).
AA 24 hour service Tel. Cardiff 394111.

Llandudno Gwynedd

The largest resort in Wales lies on a curving bay, flanked on the west by the Great Orme, a massive limestone headland nearly 700 ft high, and on the other side by the Little Orme, a smaller headland. It is a well-planned town with a wide promenade and main streets, the legacy of two men, Edward Mostyn and Owen Williams, who in 1849 set about transforming Llandudno from a mining and fishing village into a flourishing resort.

The Great Orme provides views of Snowdonia, the Isle of Man and the Lake District. Near the summit stands St Tudno's Church. The oldest part, the north wall of the nave, dates from the 11th or 12th centuries.

Happy Valley, one means of access to the Great Orme, is a garden lover's delight, containing rare plants, shrubs and trees. Other ways of reaching the summit include the Great Orme tramway, a railway nearly a mile long, and a cable-car lift.

Information Tel. 76413.
Location On the A546, 5 m. N of Conwy.
Parking Conwy Road; Back Madoc Street; Clarence Road; Happy Valley Road; Maelgwyn Road; Great Orme summit; West Parade; York Road (all car parks). The Parade.
District council Aberconwy (Tel. 76276).
Population 19,000.
E-C Wed. (not summer). **M-D** Daily, except Wed. afternoon.
Police (Ba) Oxford Road (Tel. 78241).
Casualty hospital Maesdu, West Shore (Tel. 77471).
Post office (Ba) Vaughan Street.
Theatres Arcadia, The Parade (summer only) (Tel. 76570); Astra Theatre/Cinema **(Aa)**, Gloddaeth Street (76666); Pier Pavilion **(Ab)** (75649).
Cinemas Palladium **(Aa)**, Gloddaeth Street (Tel. 76244); Savoy **(Ba)**, Mostyn Street (76394).
Public library (Ba) Mostyn Street.
Places to see Doll Museum **(Aa)**; Mostyn Art Gallery, Vaughan Street **(Ba)**; Rapallo House Museum, Craig y Don.
Shopping Mostyn Street; Gloddaeth Street; Madoc Street.
Events International 14s Sailing Championships (July); Carnival (Aug.).
Sport North Wales League Cricket, The Oval.
AA 24 hour service Tel. 79066.

THE ORIGINAL ALICE

A little girl on holiday at Llandudno in 1862 inspired a children's classic. Alice Liddell, daughter of an Oxford don, so loved the stories told by a family guest, Charles Lutwidge Dodgson, that he decided to write one down. In 1865, under the name Lewis Carroll, he published the story as the immortal *Alice in Wonderland.* Six years later he published *Alice through the Looking Glass.*

Alice Liddell and the White Rabbit on the West Shore at Llandudno.

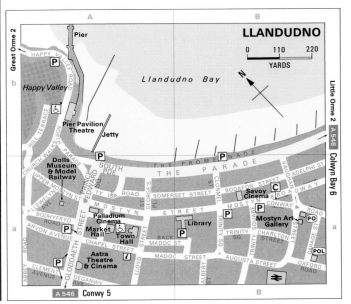

LLANDUDNO

Llanelli Dyfed

The coal trade was thriving in Llanelli in the 17th century, but it was the late-18th-century introduction of the pit engine for working deep seams that led to its growth. Tinplating began in 1850 and still thrives.

The town's Rugby Union football team, one of the strongest in Wales, is celebrated for its "anthem" – *Sospan Fach* (Little saucepan).

Information Tel. 3538.
Location On the A484, 12 m. W of Swansea.
Parking Water Street; Thomas Street; Vauxhall; Island Place; Murray Street (all car parks).
District council Borough of Llanelli (Tel. 58181).
Population 24,000.
E-C Tues. **M-D** Thur., Sat.
Police Waunlanyrafon (Tel. 2222).
Casualty hospital Llanelli General, Marble Hall Road (Tel. 4351).
Post office John Street.
Theatre/Cinema Entertainment Centre (3 cinemas, 1 theatre) (Tel. 4057).
Public library Vaughan Street.
Places to see Llanelli Museum, Parc Howard.
Shopping Stepney Street; Vaughan Street; Park Street.
Events Festival of Music and Drama (Mar. – Apr.).
Trade and industry Tin plate manufacturing; petrochemicals; tin reclamation.
Sport Rugby football, Llanelli RFC, Stradey Park.
AA 24 hour service Tel. Swansea 55598.

Llanfairfechan Gwynedd

Snowdonia towers above Llanfairfechan, a resort facing the vast expanse of the Lavan Sands in Conwy Bay. The beach close to the promenade is safe, but it is dangerous to venture far out on to the sands which are swept by a swift, incoming tide.

There are many beautiful walks, including one to the Aber Falls, 4½ miles south-west, where the Afon Goch plunges 150 ft from jutting rocks. The Afon Llanfairfechan descends 1,500 ft in 3 miles, then runs through the town to join the sea.

Information Tel. Conwy 2248.
Location On the A55, 8 m. E of Bangor.
Parking Village Road; Station Road; Promenade (all car parks).
District council Aberconwy (Tel. Llandudno 76276).
Population 3,800.
E-C Wed.
Police Village Road (Tel. 680555).
Casualty hospital Caernarfon and Anglesey General, Holyhead Road, Bangor (Tel. Bangor 53321).
Post office Village Road.
Public library Village Road.
Places to see Aber Falls, 4½ m. SW.
Trails Available from the library, Village Road.

Shopping Village Road; Station Road.
Event Carnival (July).
AA 24 hour service Tel. Cardiff 394111.

Llanfyllin Powys

The green valleys and rolling hills to the north of Llanfyllin are a delight for pony-trekkers, and the inns and hotels around the little town make it an ideal centre for touring. There is good fishing 9 miles west in Lake Vyrnwy, one of the largest man-made lakes in Wales.

Information Tel. 285 or Welshpool 2828.
Location On the A490, 12 m. NW of Welshpool.
Parking High Street (cp).
District council Montgomery (Tel. Welshpool 2828).
Population 1,200.
M-D Thur., summer only.
Police High Street (Tel. 222).
Casualty hospital Oswestry and District, Upper Brook Street, Oswestry (Tel. 4511).
Post office High Street.
Public library High Street.
Shopping High Street.
Events Music Festival (July); Agricultural Show (Aug.).
AA 24 hour service Tel. Cardiff 394111.

Llangollen Clwyd

The International Eisteddfod at Llangollen has attracted thousands of competitors and visitors from all parts of the world every July since 1947. The town is also a touring centre set in a mountain-bordered vale of the Dee. The stone bridge over the Dee was built in 1345-6, and is known as one of the Seven Wonders of Wales.

A narrow canal winds round the hillside above the town. It joins the main line of the Shropshire Union Canal, 4 miles east of the town beside the Pontcysyllte Aqueduct. The aqueduct, which carries the canal 120 ft above the Dee Valley, was built between 1795 and 1805 by Thomas Telford.

Plas Newydd (New Place) is a large, attractive 18th-century timbered house. From 1780 until 1831 it was the home of the celebrated "Ladies of

EISTEDDFOD *Up to 10,000 musicians and dancers, many in national costume, compete at Llangollen every July.*

Llangollen", Lady Eleanor Butler and Miss Ponsonby, who entertained Sir Walter Scott, the Duke of Wellington, Wordsworth and others when the town was a staging post on the London to Holyhead road.

North-west are the ruins of Valle Crucis Abbey, a Cistercian monastery founded in 1200. Near by is Eliseg's Pillar, a mutilated 9th-century cross.

The rocky fragments on the hilltop 1 mile north-east of Llangollen are the weathered ruins of the 8th-century fortress of Castell Dinas Bran.

Information Tel. 860828.
Location On the A5, 13 m. NW of Oswestry.
Parking Market Street; Brook Street (both car parks).
District council Glyndwr (Tel. Ruthin 2201).
Population 3,050.
E-C Thur. **M-D** Tues.
Police Parade Street (Tel. 860222).
Casualty hospital Llangollen Cottage Hospital, Abbey Road (Tel. 860226).
Post office Berwyn Street.
Public library Parade Street.
Places to see Plas Newydd; Valle Crucis Abbey ruins, 1½ m. NW.
Town trails Available from Tourist Information Centre, Town Hall, Parade Street.
Shopping Berwyn Street; Castle Street.
Event Eisteddfod (July).
AA 24 hour service Tel. Llandudno 79066.

Llantwit Major S. Glam.

In the 4th century St Illtud, a Celtic missionary, founded a monastery at Llantwit Major. It became a major seat of learning in the Celtic Church, and St David, patron saint of Wales, studied there. It lays claim to being the first British university.

Nothing is left of the monastery, but the parish church of St Illtud stands on or near the spot. It is actually a part-Norman church joined to a 13th-century one by a tower.

Information Tel. 3707.
Location On the B4265, 21 m. SW of Cardiff.
Parking Col-Hugh Beach; Town Hall; Shopping Precinct rear Station Road (all car parks).
District council Vale of Glamorgan (Tel. Barry 730333).
Population 6,500.
E-C Wed.
Police Wesley Street (Tel. 2268).
Casualty hospital Cardiff Royal Infirmary, Newport Road, Cardiff (Tel. Cardiff 492233).
Post office Wine Street.
Public library Boverton Road.
Shopping Commercial Street; The Precinct; Church Street.
Events Carnival (May/Aug.).
AA 24 hour service Tel. Cardiff 394111.

THE MAKING OF LONDON

The capital where history never stops

The River Thames flows from the heart of England to the east coast, and London grew up at the lowest convenient crossing place. Spits of gravel on the north and south banks provided firm ground for the Romans to build a bridge, soon after their invasion of Britain in AD 43. They gave their settlement a Celtic name, *Llyn-din* (river place), later called Londinium.

There is insufficient evidence to assume that a pre-Roman settlement existed at the spot, although the Thames Valley was certainly inhabited from the earliest times. A Stone Age workshop has been uncovered in Acton; the site of an Iron Age temple lies beneath one of the runways at Heathrow Airport; and many pre-Roman objects have been recovered from the Thames. But London began with the Romans. It was not only the capital of Roman Britain, but also the sixth-largest city in the Roman Empire.

SEAT OF GOVERNMENT *The Houses of Parliament were built by Sir Charles Barry and A. W. Pugin in 1840-60.*

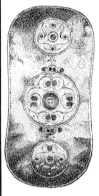

CELTIC ART *Red-glass studs adorn this bronze shield found in the Thames at Battersea. It dates from the 1st century AD.*

The Romans laid out a network of military roads converging upon the bridge-head at London, while the Thames itself provided a waterway for merchants trading with the Continent or the inland districts.

By AD 60 there was a sizeable town there. But in that year Queen Boudicca (Boadicea) and her Icenian followers wiped it out. The ashes of their destruction are still found when deep foundations are dug for new buildings. But such were the natural advantages of the site, that when the Romans regained control the settlement was re-established.

Londinium flourished, and within a generation had become the administrative centre for the province. This, apart from the original choice of the site, was probably the most significant event in London's early history.

Civic buildings were erected within massive walls – portions of which can be seen beside the Tower and near St Giles, Cripplegate. Other pointers to the size and magnificence of the city have been discovered: a carved altar to Diana on the site of the Goldsmith's Hall; a temple to Mithras in Queen Victoria Street, now reconstructed near by; and the footings of a fort gateway near Wood Street.

An immense basilica and the forum – the main market and meeting place – lie beneath Leadenhall Market. Cannon Street Station covers the site of the Governor's palace. Also in Cannon Street is **London Stone**, possibly the stump of a column which served as the central milestone for the whole of Roman Britain. The stone is set in the wall of the Bank of China.

When the Romans withdrew from Britain in AD 410, life limped on in the walled city for the next two centuries. Then, in 604, St Augustine ordained Miletus, the first Saxon Bishop of London, and before the end of the century a mint had been re-established. Early in the 8th century the Venerable Bede described the city as "the mart of many nations resorting to it by land and sea".

King Alfred rebuilt the fortifications in 886 against Viking attacks, and from that point on London grew in political and military importance and in trade and wealth. After the Norman Conquest in 1066, William I made a separate peace with the citizens of London, promising that they could retain their laws and customs undisturbed. But at the same time he began to build the **Tower of London** just outside the city – a stern reminder of the king's authority.

Divided city

By the end of the 11th century a significant new development had occurred. King Canute (1016-35), England's only Danish king, had built a palace to the west of the city. Edward the Confessor (1042-66) chose to live there, too, and beside the palace he built a church, his Minster in the west, which gave the name Westminster to the small enclave that grew up around the royal buildings.

From that time onwards, London had two centres – Westminster where royal, and later political, power was established, and the City, centre of mercantile wealth.

Neither could hope to flourish

WHITE TOWER *The oldest part of the Tower of London, the White Tower, was built by William the Conqueror to overawe the citizens of London. It became known as the White Tower when it was whitewashed in 1241.*

CITY PRIDE *A gaslit alley leads to the river, with the dome and towers of St Paul's beyond.*

---

without the other, and the Strand, running alongside the Thames, linked the two.

Throughout the Middle Ages the two centres kept pace. William Rufus (1087-1100) enlarged the palace; the City won the right to elect its own Lord Mayor in 1191; Henry III began to rebuild the abbey in about 1245, while his son Edward, the future Edward I, strengthened the defences of the Tower.

Buildings in the City and in Westminster vied in size and beauty. **St Paul's Cathedral** grew to be the largest in England – and by the 14th century was 585 ft long with a 489 ft tower and spire. Richard II's mason and master carpenter gave **Westminster Hall** its magnificent hammerbeam roof in 1397, and the City responded by building the **Guildhall**, completed in 1440.

Westminster Abbey grew ever more magnificent. In 1503 Henry VII began a new Lady Chapel, which was completed in 1512 by Henry VIII, who called it Henry VII's Chapel. Its roof is a riot of filigree fan-vaulting arching above the tomb of its founder and his queen.

Population explosion

During the 16th century London's population increased from about 50,000 to some 200,000, and in 1580 Elizabeth I issued a proclamation against expansion outside the walls of London. It did no good. Aristocratic landowners developed new estates in Bloomsbury and Covent Garden – their names are perpetuated in many of the streets.

The Great Fire of 1666 laid waste to 13,200 houses in the City, causing almost overnight development outside. Inside the City the fire brought about stricter building regulations, calling for the use of stone, brick and slate. From these regulations the pattern of long terraces of houses and symmetrical squares emerged, though not in the City itself.

In the 18th century the hill-top villages north of the City – Islington, Hampstead and Highgate – began to spread down their slopes, while London stretched out eager tentacles along the main roads towards them.

South of the Thames, development gave rise to a need for more bridges. Westminster Bridge, begun in 1736, was completed in 1750, Blackfriars Bridge followed in 1769 and the rest spanned the river during the next century.

Victorian times

The railways and Queen Victoria arrived almost together. London's first railway station, Euston, was opened on July 20, 1837, one month after the accession of Queen Victoria. In 1863 the Metropolitan Railway, forerunner of the capital's underground railway system, opened its first section. It ran between Paddington and Farringdon Street in a shallow tunnel.

By the end of the 19th century London had become the financial centre of the world, and the outer suburbs began to expand to accommodate the city workers. The Metropolitan Railway slid its lines across the fields westwards to Wembley, Harrow and beyond. "Live in Metroland" became their slogan.

During the First World War, London had its first taste of aerial bombardment from German airships. Twenty-five years later the first bomb of the Second World War fell in Fore Street on August 27, 1940.

Before the war ended, 164 of the City's 677 acres had been laid waste, and Westminster fared little better. Rebuilding began with high-rise offices and blocks of flats, and the City skyline became a panorama of concrete-and-glass monoliths, softened by the graceful dome of St Paul's Cathedral which had miraculously survived the bombing.

In 1965 a new administration, the Greater London Council, was set up to govern London. The capital's 616 sq. miles and 7,300,000 inhabitants were split up into 32 boroughs – each of them larger and wealthier than most of Britain's other cities. The City remains, as it always has, separate and self-governing.

London has renewed itself since the Second World War with as much vitality as it did after the Great Fire, not only in the City but throughout the whole area – Middlesex, parts of Essex, Kent, Surrey and Hertfordshire – which makes up Greater London. The outward signs of that renewal lie in the buildings, both the new ones that have risen from the ashes and the old ones which have been refurbished.

London may be old, but it does not stagnate. Each generation adapts to change without losing the charm and character moulded into the capital's 2,000 years of history.

GARDEN SUBURB *Hampstead, once a village, retains a rural atmosphere.*

THE GROWTH OF LONDON

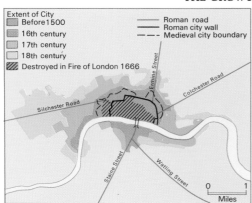

Extent of City
- Before 1500
- 16th century
- 17th century
- 18th century
- Destroyed in Fire of London 1666

— Roman road
— Roman city wall
--- Medieval city boundary

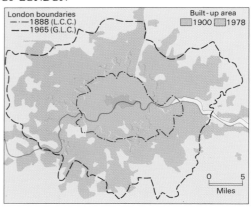

London boundaries
- —·—1888 (L.C.C.)
- ——1965 (G.L.C.)

Built-up area
- 1900 □ 1978

In less than 2,000 years, London has grown from the 1 sq. mile of the Roman city to its present size of 616 sq. miles. Its growth is marked by a successive series of boundaries, spreading like the rings of a tree trunk. The maps show an expansion that was linked to the capital's increasing influence of wealth and political power.

THE CITY

The square mile where London's history began

The pulse of Britain's financial and commercial power throbs within the City of London; a power so great that throughout the world this complex of banks and business houses is known as simply "The City". From Norman times it has been proudly independent, and is a county in itself governed by the Corporation of London, presided over by the Lord Mayor of London and possessing its own police force.

CITY ARMS *A winged griffin supports a shield bearing the Cross of St George and St Paul's sword.*

The City was granted the right to elect its own mayor by Prince John in 1191. The first lord mayor was Henry FitzAlwyn, who held the office in 1192-1212, but London's best-known lord mayor was Richard Whittington – immortalised in the fairytale as the man who "turned again" to become thrice Lord Mayor of London, in 1397-8, 1406-7 and 1419-20.

A stained-glass window in **St Michael, Paternoster Royal**, restored after wartime bombing, shows Whittington arriving in London with his cat. This part of the Whittington legend did not appear until 1605, when an engraver, Renold Elstrack, portrayed him with his hand upon a cat. It is said that the portrait originally showed a skull, and that Elstrack changed it to a cat as a result of public protests. The picture is now in the National Portrait Gallery.

Lord Mayor's Show

On the second Saturday in November the new lord mayor starts his one-year term of office by driving in his golden coach to the Law Courts in the Strand. Here, he is sworn in by the Judges of the Queen's Bench and then returns to the Guildhall for a banquet traditionally attended by the Prime Minister.

This procession, the Lord Mayor's Show, is the City's biggest annual display of pomp and pageantry. The magnificent coach is part of a parade made up of marching bands, horse-drawn coaches and decorated floats depicting a theme chosen by the new lord mayor.

Within the City the lord mayor takes precedence over everyone except the monarch. When the monarch enters the City in state the lord mayor greets him or her at Temple Bar, the historic boundary between the City and Westminster, and offers the City's Pearl Sword; the Sovereign touches the hilt and returns the weapon. This ancient ceremony symbolises the City's loyalty, and the monarch's trust in the City.

Mansion House and Guildhall

The **Mansion House** was built in 1739-53 to the design of George Dance the Elder (1700-68) – until then each lord mayor lived in his own house. It is an imposing building in Palladian style, and contains a glittering collection of gold and silver plate, which is added to yearly when the retiring lord mayor presents a piece to commemorate his year of office.

The **Guildhall** is where the lord mayor presides over the City's governing body, the Court of Common Council. The original Guildhall was started in 1411, but the Great Fire of 1666 destroyed most of the building. It was restored in 1669, probably by Wren. George Dance the Younger (1741-1825) gave it a new front in 1788. Sir Giles Scott (1880-1960) re-roofed the Great Hall in 1953 after it had been severely damaged by bombing in the Second World War.

Above the Great Hall, decorating the Musicians' Gallery, are carved wooden figures of the giants Gog and Magog, "survivors" of a legendary race of giants that were said to have ruled Britain. They are 9 ft 3 in. tall and were carved by David Evans after the Second World War to replace an earlier pair that were destroyed during an air-raid in 1940.

Livery Companies

The City of London's Livery Companies are guilds representing 84 trades or professions. Some of the guilds date from medieval times and others, such as the Guild of Air Pilots and Air Navigators, were formed in this century.

Fires, bombs and changes of fortune have reduced the number of livery halls to 36 – and each contains its own treasures. The **Barbers Hall**, in Monkwell Square, possesses a Holbein portrait of Henry VIII, the **Fishmongers Hall** at London Bridge has the dagger with which their Master, Sir William Walworth, stabbed Wat Tyler in 1381 and ended the Peasants' Revolt.

The halls are not normally open to the public, but party visits can be arranged through the City Information Centre.

Ancient customs

The Livery Companies exist to maintain the professional standards of their trades, and several have ancient customs which they still observe. One traditional custom follows the election of the Vintners' Master and Warden.

The ceremony takes place in July, and after the election the company parades to St James's, Garlickhythe, preceded by wine porters who sweep the way clear with birch brooms.

Finance and commerce

The City is a world centre of finance. It is the home of the **Bank of England**, founded in 1694. The present building was built between 1924

THE BARBICAN *Blocks of flats among the office blocks around St Giles, Cripplegate, are intended to increase the City's population, for although 500,000 people work in the City only about 4,000 live there.*

and 1939 to the design of Sir Herbert Baker (1862-1946). Beside it stands the **Royal Exchange**, founded in 1571 by Sir Thomas Gresham and made "Royal" by Elizabeth I. The present Royal Exchange, completed in 1844, is the third building to stand on the site. It was the work of Sir William Tite (1798-1873).

The mysterious world of "bulls and bears" goes on inside the **Stock Exchange**, which was founded in 1773. It is now housed in a modern stone-and-glass building surmounted by a 350 ft tower.

Lloyd's shipping underwriters began in 1691 in Edward Lloyd's eating house at 16 Lombard Street. It became the world's biggest insurance

GOLDEN COACH *The Lord Mayor of London arrives at the Law Courts with a guard of Pikemen and Musketeers of the Honourable Artillery Company.*

corporation, and now occupies offices built in the neo-Classical style of the 1950s. In the Room, the hall where the underwriters do business, is the Lutine Bell. It came from a French frigate, the *Lutine,* which sank in 1799 with a cargo of gold bullion. The bell is rung to announce news of an overdue vessel: once for a loss, twice for an arrival.

Street of ink

From Temple Bar to Ludgate Circus runs Fleet Street, named after the river that flows beneath the City and empties into the Thames at Black-friars. Here, and in the surrounding streets, are the newspaper offices; the **Daily Mirror** in Fetter Lane, and in Fleet Street itself the dignified **Daily Telegraph** and the modern, black-and-chrome **Daily Express** besides a host of provincial and international newspaper offices.

Beyond Ludgate Circus, Ludgate Hill climbs to **St Paul's Cathedral** – Wren's masterpiece built between 1675 and 1708, and two centuries later the symbol of London's defiance in the air-raids of the Second World War.

City from the ashes

In 1666 fire raged through the City, feeding ravenously on the timber-and-plaster buildings in its path. It started in a baker's shop in Pudding Lane – the **Monument** to the fire stands 202 ft from the spot, the exact height of the column. When the fire abated, four-fifths of the City had been destroyed.

Sir Christopher Wren was the chief architect of the City's recovery. He built 51 new churches, and replaced the medieval St Paul's Cathedral that had perished in the flames. His design was influenced by St Peter's, Rome, particularly in the great dome with its lantern and cross 365 ft above the streets.

Inside the dome are paintings by Sir James Thornhill (1675-1734). Stairs lead up to the Whispering Gallery, which picks up whispers round the base of the dome, and to the Golden Gallery, 218 ft above the nave. The crypt of St Paul's has the tombs of Nelson and Wellington.

The nave contains many monuments, but none more apt than that

to Wren himself. An epitaph below the dome and engraved in Latin ends with the words *"Si monumartum requiris circumspice"* (If you seek a monument, look around you).

City Information Centre, St Paul's Churchyard (Tel. 606 3030).
Places to see Central Criminal Court (**6De**), Old Bailey. Open to public when court is sitting.
Guildhall (**6Ee**), Gresham Street.
Dr Johnson's House (**6Cd**), Gough Square.
Middle Temple Hall (**6Cd**), Fountain Court. Elizabethan hall, part of the Temple of the Knights Templar founded in 1180.
Monument (**6Ed**), Fish Street.
Prince Henry's Room (**6Cd**), Fleet Street. Sixteenth-century tavern with Jacobean ceiling bearing the Prince of Wales feathers and the initials PH.
Royal Exchange (**6Ed**), Threadneedle Street.
Stock Exchange (**6Ed**), Throgmorton Street.
Temple Church (**6Cd**), Inner Temple. Twelfth-century church of the Knights Templar.
Temple of Mithras (**6Ed**), Queen Victoria Street. Second-century stone temple reconstructed in the forecourt of Bucklersbury House.
Events Lord Mayor's Show. Procession from Mansion House to Law Courts (second Sat. in Nov.).
City of London Festival. Even-numbered years (July).
Opening of Law Courts (Oct.).
Christs Hospital "Bluecoats" march (Sept.).

GIANTS *The Guildhall's Gog and Magog.*

STREETS AND BUILDINGS

The threads and fabric of a historic tapestry

London's street pattern is a chaotic legacy from the Middle Ages. Narrow alleys twist and turn and seem to lead nowhere; broad avenues run arrow-straight into elegant squares; nothing is consistent. Yet every bend may reveal some new vista: a gracious Georgian crescent or a brooding Gothic terrace; a towering skyscraper or a gabled Tudor mansion. It is this tangled web of streets and buildings that knits together London's history in bricks and stone.

The Roman street pattern has been almost obliterated in London. Only **Wood Street** remains; it was once the main road to a fort. The other Roman roads vanished in the confusion of the centuries after the Romans had left, and the medieval street pattern that developed survives to this day. In places it is no more than a maze of alleys and passages threading their way among, and sometimes through, the modern tower blocks of the City.

The City's streets survived even the Great Fire of 1666, for rebuilding began on the sites of the previous buildings almost before the ashes were cold. The opportunity to replan the City was lost, and only two new streets were made – **Queen Street** and **King Street**.

Sixteen knights abreast

According to the laws of Henry I, a street had to be wide enough for two loaded carts to pass, or for 16 knights to ride abreast. Roads led out into the countryside, so the City of London has only streets.

Their names sprang mainly from their function, destination or characteristics. The citizens could buy their needs in shopping places such as Bread Street and Milk Street. They worked in areas such as Carter Lane and Distaff Lane, or plied their trades in Petticoat Lane, Apothecary Street and similar thoroughfares.

The origins of some street names are more obscure. Undershaft was the site of a maypole whose shaft was taller than the nearby church of St Mary Axe, which became known as the church "under the shaft". Pudding Lane has a less-savoury origin, it was named after the "puddinges and other filth of beastes".

Palaces in the Strand

Outside the City, Westminster huddled around its abbey, with only the **Strand** linking the two communities. At one time the Strand ran along the shore, or strand, of the Thames. But in medieval times land was reclaimed from the river and bishops built their palaces along the thoroughfare. Their presence is recalled by street names such as York Buildings and Durham House Street.

Most of the surrounding land belonged to Norman families or the Church. But, when Henry VIII dis-

WAYMARK *This milestone in Kensington Road stood in a country lane when Kensington and Hounslow were villages, separated from London by fields and farms.*

solved the monasteries in the 1530s, friaries like Blackfriars, Whitefriars and Crutched Friars disappeared and their lands were given to loyal courtiers. The new owners, who were often not on good terms with their neighbours, built streets that ended abruptly at a boundary hedge or wall.

Years later, when neighbouring landlords agreed to interconnect their properties, a sharp kink was often needed in order to link adjacent streets. In some cases the neighbours never did get together, with the result that some London streets end infuriatingly in cul-de-sacs or turn at a right-angle to follow a long-forgotten boundary. A good example of this is **Farm Street**, in Mayfair, which turns abruptly to follow the fringe of the Berkeley Estate, and is totally isolated from Mount Street on the edge of the neighbouring Grosvenor Estate.

London's first square

Elizabeth I and the Stuarts forbade the extension of the City, but illegal building continued. Forty years after the Great Fire, London was built up as far west as Green Park, taking in Soho, St James's and part of Bloomsbury.

The medieval manor of Blemund'sbury had been bought by the Earl of Southampton in 1545 – his descendants, the Dukes of Bedford, partly own it today – and both names are honoured in Southampton Row and Bedford Square. The 4th Earl of Southampton developed the site in 1661 by building **Bloomsbury Square**, the first site in London to be officially named a square.

Finest period

In the 18th century, Britain moved into its finest architectural period under the reign of the Georges. The Georgian architects built fine houses, orderly streets and handsome squares for the landowners. The Grosvenor family, the Berkeleys, and the Curzons owned the land west of Bond Street, an area which included Brook Field where an annual May Fair was held.

The fair was notorious as "a place of lewdness – a public nuisance and inconvenience", but in the 1750s Mayfair became a place of respectable elegance. The landowners gave their names to its squares and streets, naming one square after the House of Hanover that then ruled the country.

North of Oxford Street the land was developed by Sir Henry William Portman, the Duke of Portland and the Harley and Cavendish-Bentinck families. In Marylebone almost every street is named after some member of these families.

FASHIONABLE SUBURB *Hampstead attracted many artists and writers during the 18th and 19th centuries. At Number 2 Lower Terrace, the house with a blue door, lived the painter John Constable in 1821.*

Behind the rows of terraced houses were the mews, narrow rows of coach-houses where horses and carriages were kept and where the coachmen lived. The name derived from the days of falconry – a place where a falcon could moult, or mew. The Royal Mews, where Trafalgar Square now stands, was converted into stables when falconry lost its popularity, but the name was retained and came to mean "stabling".

Expansion into the suburbs

London continued to expand in the late 18th and early 19th centuries, absorbing large country estates and swallowing villages. At West Hampstead much of the land belonged to the Powell-Cottons, a big-game-hunting family who also owned land in Kent. Their country seat was at Quex Park in the Isle of Thanet, and many of Hampstead's streets are named after their properties near Quex – such as Acol, Minster, Kingsgate and Manstone. Somali Road and Gondar Gardens are named after the Powell-Cotton shooting estates in Ethiopia.

Hampstead itself was a village that crept down the hill to meet the advancing capital, and eventually became part of it. More than any other, however, the village of Hampstead managed to maintain its rural character, aided by the expanse of Hampstead Heath. In the 18th century it became a fashionable place to live, and landowners built mansions to attract new residents. One part of the heath called Hatches Bottom was a disease-ridden swamp; in about 1800 the land was drained and built on, and the name was changed to Vale of Health.

Country houses survive

London's expansion in the 18th century left a pattern of streets and squares lined with solid, middle-class homes for those who could afford to move out of central London. Those who could not, stayed in the overpopulated areas to the east. But some relics of the days when wealthy men built their homes in the country re-

SOMERSET HOUSE *Sir William Chambers (1726-96) built the house in 1776-86 to accommodate government offices. It stands on the site of a palace begun by the Duke of Somerset in 1547.*

main. In Islington, Canonbury House survives, it was built in the 16th century by Sir John Spencer, Lord Mayor of London in 1594-5. Highgate still retains Cromwell House, built in about 1637 for the Sprignell family of London merchants.

The village of Chelsea fared less happily. The home of its best-known citizen, Sir Thomas More's Beaufort House, was demolished in 1740. Henry VIII's Manor House, where Katherine Parr once lived, went in 1760.

Chelsea became an extension of Mayfair, due largely to the Cadogan family who were descendants of Sir Hans Sloane (1660-1753), physician to George II. The family names feature prominently in the district, for example Sloane Square, Cadogan Square and Caversham Street – the 3rd Earl Cadogan was Baron Oakley of Caversham.

Chelsea's oldest building is the 15th-century **Crosby Hall**, yet it has been in the borough only since 1908. It was originally the great hall of a mansion built by Sir John Crosby, a wool merchant, and stood in Bishopsgate in the City. The Duke of Gloucester, afterwards Richard III, is said to have occupied the hall at one time. The building was dismantled and re-erected on its present site in Cheyne Walk to form part of the headquarters of the Federation of University Women. It is open to the public at weekends.

As London spread its bounds it engulfed many agricultural and rural industrial areas, some relics of which can still be seen. At Dulwich there is a mill pond, and although the mill has long-since disappeared, some weatherboarded cottages of the same period still survive.

In a garden just off Brixton Hill stands a windmill. It is the nearest surviving windmill to the centre of London – little more than 3 miles from Charing Cross. The mill was built in 1816 and was restored in 1964.

Another windmill stands further afield, at Upminster in Essex. The mill dates from the late 18th century, but Upminster's oldest agricultural relic is its medieval tithe barn in Hall Lane.

Cannons in the streets

In Victorian times, London was a leisurely place where pedestrians strolled rather than hurried to their destinations. They had time to look around and, much as the Victorians decorated and furnished their houses, so they furnished the streets.

Every large house had a coal-cellar, and the coal-hole covers set in the pavements were often cast-iron works of art. The passage of thousands of feet has worn many of them smooth, but in some of the quieter streets and squares their bold patterns can still be seen.

Some of London's commonest street furnishings are the bollards, usually set into the pavement at the corners of narrow streets to protect the buildings from passing traffic. Discarded ships' cannons proved ideal for this purpose, although by the end of the 19th century the supply had begun to run out and later "cannons" were merely replicas.

Street lights were almost always ornately decorated, there are some fine examples along the **Victoria Embankment** where dolphins and cherubs abound. In some cases the lamps themselves are interesting.

At the south corners of **Trafalgar Square**, two lamps are said to be from Nelson's flagship, HMS *Victory*. A street lamp erected in Savoy Place in about 1900 still burns gas, but it is the gas drawn off from the sewers beneath.

ORNAMENTS AND ODDITIES ABOVE THE STREETS

The keen observer has only to raise his eyes to find a wealth of curious sights above the streets of London. Here are the works of stonemasons and sign-makers over the centuries. Stone carvings adorn churches and department stores, trade signs thrust out above shopfronts, and ornate clocks give the time of day. Some are old, some new, but most go unnoticed, except by those who have the time to stand and stare.

Snarling dog on the Guildhall roof.

Mr Fortnum and Mr Mason stand by the clock above their Piccadilly shop.

Sunny sign for an insurance company in Basinghall Street.

Before the Great Fire there were 108 churches in the City, but only 20 survived the flames. It was decided to rebuild 51, and this monumental task was entrusted to Sir Christopher Wren.

Wren's masterpiece was St Paul's Cathedral, but each church was designed with the same painstaking care so that no two were alike. Nearly every one was crowned with a tower or steeple, and sometimes both.

Wedding-cake steeple

After St Paul's, **St Bride** is perhaps the best-known of Wren's churches. It stands in Fleet Street just inside the City boundary, and its white, wedding-cake steeple rises to 226 ft – the tallest of Wren's steeples. In the crypt are the remains of a Roman wall and a museum.

Legend surrounds **St Mary-le-Bow**, in Cheapside, built on the site of a Norman church and noted for its bells. It is said that the sound of Bow bells persuaded Dick Whittington to "turn again" to become thrice Lord Mayor of London.

The Great Bell of Bow was originally a curfew bell which was sounded in medieval times to wake the local cockneys, hence the saying that a cockney is someone born within the sound of Bow bells. When Wren rebuilt the church the bell was rehung, and continued to sound until 1874.

During the Second World War nearly all Wren's churches were destroyed or damaged. Most were reconstructed, and of the 39 churches in the City, 23 are by Wren. The towers of six others still stand.

Sir Christopher Wren died in 1723, and by this time his mantle had fallen on two men – Nicholas Hawksmoor,

BARRISTERS' WALK *Lincoln's Inn is one of four Inns of Court, with Gray's Inn, Middle Temple and Inner Temple.*

Wren's assistant, and a young Scotsman named James Gibbs. In 1714-17 Gibbs built **St Mary-le-Strand**, his first London church, and in 1719 he added a steeple to Wren's **St Clement Danes**. His best-known London church is **St Martin-in-the-Fields**, built in 1722-6 at the edge of a site that nearly 100 years later became Trafalgar Square.

Hawksmoor built only one church in the City, St Mary Woolnoth, in Lombard Street in 1716-27. He built three in Stepney: St Anne, Limehouse; Christ Church, Spitalfield; and St George-in-the-East, Cannon Street Road.

Hawksmoor's **St George Church** in Bloomsbury is one of the most dramatic churches in London. It has an impressive portico of Corinthian columns and a distinctive stepped spire. The church was completed in 1731, four years after the death of George I. Hawksmoor honoured the king by placing a statue of him on top of the spire.

Palace builder

Inigo Jones (1573-1652) transformed English architecture and introduced a Classical style whose influence was to last for nearly 300 years. In 1617 he began to build the Queen's House at Greenwich, and in 1619 was commissioned by James I to build the **Banqueting House** for Whitehall Palace. Charles I commissioned the magnificent ceiling paintings by Rubens in 1629. Twenty years later the king stepped through a window of the hall on to the scaffold where he was executed.

Jones was also responsible for **Covent Garden**. The scheme was promoted in 1630 by the Earl of Bedford, and Jones based his design on the style of an Italian piazza. His **St Paul's Church** on the western side of the square was damaged by fire in 1795, and the present building, a close replica, was built in the same year.

Covent Garden became known for its fruit and vegetable markets and for its Opera House, all of which came long after Jones's death. The market was established in 1670, but the buildings associated with it were added in the 19th century. E. M. Barry (1830-80) built the Opera House in 1857 and the Floral Hall in 1858.

In 1974 the market was moved to new premises in Nine Elms, and Covent Garden has become a tourist attraction with continental-style restaurants, bars and clubs.

Street named after a game

London's West End began with St James's, a development built on land behind St James's Palace by Henry Jermyn in the late 17th century. Its grandest street was Pall Mall, built on the site of a long green where Charles I had played "paille maille", a fashionable game that was the forerunner of croquet. When Charles II was re-

WESTMINSTER CATHEDRAL *The Roman Catholic cathedral was completed in 1903. Its tower is 284 ft high.*

stored to the throne he replaced the old pall-mall green with a new one running parallel to it – now called The Mall. The Duke of York's Steps lead down from Waterloo Place, in Pall Mall, to link the two thoroughfares.

London's club life is centred in Pall Mall, the home of The Athenaeum and other clubs. The Mall is the capital's ceremonial way, a tree-lined avenue forming Buckingham Palace's "front path", down which monarchs drive on state occasions.

On the north side of St James's is Piccadilly. It is said to take its name from the "piccadillies" – a kind of border for ruffs and collars – sold there in Elizabethan times by a man named Robert Baker. It attracted the socially élite of the day, including the Earl of Burlington whose **Burlington House** is now the Royal Academy of Arts.

The 3rd Earl of Burlington's grand-

EAST MEETS WEST *The Central London Mosque, built in 1977, stands in Regent's Park.*

son built the **Burlington Arcade**, alongside the house, in 1819 – to stop people throwing rubbish into his garden, it is said.

Piccadilly Circus formed part of a grand scheme devised by one of London's foremost builders – John Nash (1752-1835). He was a friend of the Prince Regent whose palace, Carlton House, had been built for him by Henry Holland on the north edge of St James's Park. The prince also owned land just over a mile to the north, Regent's Park, and he commissioned Nash to build a triumphal way that would link the two properties. Nash's Regent Street ran north of Carlton House – this part is now called Lower Regent Street – to Piccadilly Circus, and then turned in a handsome colonnaded curve towards Oxford Circus. In Langham Place, Nash built **All Souls Church** before linking up with Portland Place, and at the top end of this he built twin crescents of elegant terraced houses overlooking the park beyond.

A grand archway

Nash went on to build **Carlton House Terrace**, which replaced Carlton House. He enlarged **Buckingham Palace** and gave it a grand archway, called the **Marble Arch**, which was moved in 1851 to Cumberland Gate, Hyde Park, where it still stands.

In 1829 Nash laid out **Trafalgar Square**, named to commemorate Nelson's naval victory over the French in 1805. But he did not live to see its completion. The 185 ft high **Nelson's Column** was erected in 1842. The bronze lions at its base are by Sir Edwin Landseer (1802-73).

Two years after Nash's death Queen Victoria came to the throne, and a new era was ushered in that brought the first major change in architectural styles since the days of Inigo Jones.

Temples to steam

Britain was in the grip of the Industrial Revolution, and when the railways came to London the Victorians built stations that were virtual temples to steam.

Philip Hardwick (1792-1870) built **Euston Station** in 1837 and graced its entrance with a Doric Arch. Less than a mile down the road Lewis Cubitt (1799-1883) built **King's Cross Station** in 1851-2 and gave it a yellow-brick façade, large arched windows and a square clock-tower.

Between these two stations came Scott's gigantic **St Pancras** in 1868, deliberately designed to overshadow its neighbours. Sir George Gilbert Scott (1811-78) was a disciple of the 19th-century Gothic revival in architecture, and he lavishly adorned St Pancras Station with pinnacled towers, pointed arches and cloverleaf windows. Behind the building, which included a hotel, is the trainshed designed by W. H. Barlow (1812-1902) with its 243 ft span roof – the largest single-span roof in the world when it was built.

The Victorian Gothic style was predominant in London's buildings until the end of the century, and can still

LAST STRAW *Camels support a seat on Victoria Embankment.*

COMMUNICATIONS CENTRE *Aerials and reflectors bristle around the top of the Post Office Tower.*

be seen in many civic, public and commercial buildings. One of its strongest supporters was Prince Albert, and after his death in 1861 a fitting **memorial** to him was designed by Sir George Gilbert Scott. A 15 ft bronze statue of the prince sits beneath a 175 ft high Gothic canopy and looks across Kensington, the borough that he made into London's centre for the arts and sciences.

Prince Albert's other London monument is the **Royal Albert Hall**, opposite the memorial. It was designed by Captain Francis Fowke (1823-65) in the form of a circular building enclosing an oval amphitheatre. A terracotta frieze around the building illustrates the Triumphs of Arts and Sciences. The vast interior has three tiers of boxes with a gallery and balcony above, and seats 6,000 people. It was opened in 1871.

Into the 20th century

The trend in architecture during the first 20 years of the 20th century was largely a continuation of the Victorian style. In 1912 the London County Council began to build a new **County Hall**, designed by their architect Ralph Knott, on a riverside site facing the Victoria Embankment. Its 750 ft long façade is a curving colonnade built of Portland stone. The building was opened in 1922 and was extended in 1939, 1957 and 1963. It can be visited, and the interior is notable for its facings of Italian, Belgian and Ashburton marbles and the committee rooms panelled in English oak.

No less impressive is the former headquarters of the Port of London Authority in Trinity Square. It, too, was built between 1912 and 1922, to a design by Sir Edwin Cooper (1874-1942), and has a portico of Corinthian columns and a 170 ft tower. The PLA headquarters is now at St Katharine Dock.

In the 1930s the shape of things to come began to emerge in a few scattered buildings. On the Embankment the square-shouldered **Shell-Mex House** arrived in 1931, and the plain lines of London University's **Senate House** arose in Bloomsbury in 1934. A new exhibition hall was built at

Earls Court, and was the largest reinforced-concrete building in Europe when it was opened in 1937. The arena seats 20,000 spectators.

After the Second World War London, and particularly the City, underwent its biggest redevelopment since the Great Fire. Out of the devastation there arose concrete-and-glass skyscraper blocks, towering above St Paul's Cathedral which had miraculously survived the bombing.

London had reached its acceptable bounds, and building land was a rare and precious commodity. So commercial buildings reached for the sky, matched by high-rise blocks of flats in the East End.

The Shell Centre on South Bank was built in 1957-62, and is 351 ft high. A year after its completion, Millbank Tower topped it by 36 ft and in 1969 the **Post Office Tower** dwarfed them both – at 580 ft it was the tallest building in Britain. The latest contender for the title of London's tallest building is the 600 ft **National Westminster Bank** building in Bishopsgate.

The face of London changes, as it must if the capital is to remain alive. But its past is still there for all to see – in streets and buildings that portray almost 2,000 years of history.

THE FALSE FACES OF LONDON

Some London buildings are not what they seem. In Green Lanes, Stoke Newington, what appears to be a Gothic castle, with tower and keep, is really a waterworks pumping station built in 1854. Another Gothic edifice, in Lincoln's Inn, looks like a large Victorian dolls' house. It is merely a tool shed.

But London's most elaborate sham is in Leinster Gardens, pictured below. The blankly staring windows in mock-Georgian houses give the game away: behind the façade are not spacious rooms but the track of the Metropolitan Railway.

The sham frontage avoids an ugly gap between the houses.

WHERE THEY LIVED IN LONDON

The homes of London's celebrated citizens

All the world, it seems, once lived in London – and the homes of those who made their mark on the capital are tangible links with the past. Many are humble dwellings, the birthplaces of those who achieved greatness or had greatness thrust upon them. Some are the stately homes of the aristocracy, and others purely the resting places for those to whom London was a workshop for their skills or a showplace for their talents. Peers and prime ministers, writers and artists, scientists and soldiers, reformers and revolutionaries – London has been home to a fascinating variety of people.

There can be no more distinctive address in London than the house once occupied by the **Duke of Wellington.** His home, **Apsley House,** was known as "No. 1 London". Apsley House stands at Hyde Park Corner, and at one time was the first house past the turnpike that stood there – hence its unique address. Wellington bought it in 1817, two years after his victory over Napoleon at Waterloo, and set about altering Robert Adam's design of 1778. The duke and his architect, Benjamin Wyatt (1775-1850), faced the exterior with Bath stone and added a pedimented portico. In 1829 the house was extended to include the Plate and China Room and the Waterloo Gallery.

Every year, on June 18, the anniversary of the Battle of Waterloo, the duke entertained his generals with a reunion banquet held in the Waterloo Gallery. They dined at a table set with a 26 ft long silver centrepiece, given to the duke by the Regent of Portugal in 1816 in gratitude for delivering his country from the French in 1808.

Gift to the nation

In 1947 the 7th Duke of Wellington presented Apsley House to the nation. Visitors can see the magnificent centrepiece in the dining room, and in the Plate and China Room is the silver Waterloo Medal, the first-ever campaign medal. There are ten field-marshals' batons of seven different armies, swords, daggers and snuff-boxes.

Art treasures abound, including four paintings by Velasquez and Corregio's *The Agony in the Garden,* said to be Wellington's favourite. Portraits of Wellington himself include one by Goya painted after the duke's victory over Joseph Bonaparte at Vittoria in 1813. X-ray examinations of the portrait have shown that the head was originally that of Joseph Bonaparte – hastily painted over by Goya after the subject's downfall.

In contrast to the display of finery is the duke's dressing case, which he took on all his campaigns. It shows that Wellington was a man of simple requirements when in the field, needing only razors, nail scissors, toothbrushes and a hairbrush.

High life of the Lauderdales

Stately homes abound in and around London, and some are as fine today as when they were first built. **Ham House,** home of the **Duke and Duchess of Lauderdale** in the 17th century, is one of these. The duke acquired the house in 1672 by marrying its owner, Elizabeth, Countess of Dysart. It was a modest house by the standards of the time, and the duke and duchess set about enlarging and redecorating it as a suitable place to entertain guests. Charles II and his queen, Catherine of Braganza, were frequent visitors – the duke was one of Charles's ministers and his close confidant.

The Lauderdales were a well-matched pair. Both were ambitious and greedy, and their love of high living was reflected in the flamboyant style they lavished upon Ham House.

A south wing was added and filled with furniture imported from Holland. The Italian artist Antonio Verrio (1639-1707) was employed to paint the ceilings, and the finest craftsmen of the day embellished the rooms with grained panelling and parquetry floors. Silver-mounted fire-tongs, shovels and bellows in the fireplaces represented the height of ostentation.

Original furniture

The Duke of Lauderdale died in 1682 and left no heir. The duchess lived until 1697 and the house passed to the children of her first marriage to Sir Lionel Tollemache. In 1948 their descendants presented Ham House to the National Trust.

In their lifetime the Duke and Duchess of Lauderdale were great hoarders, a habit continued by the duchess's descendants for the next two-and-a-half centuries. Ham House, therefore, is unique in containing more original furniture and furnishings than any other mansion in the country. The walls are hung with tapestries, damasks and velvets, and the silver fire utensils stand by the chimneypieces. In the Round Gallery are portraits by Sir Peter Lely

HAM HOUSE *The splendour of this Jacobean house has remained since the Duke and Duchess of Lauderdale enlarged it in the 1670s. The stone figure in the forecourt is* Father Thames, *by John Bacon (1777-1859).*

TREES FROM A BASKET

Marble Hill House, by the Thames.

In the 18th century Lady Suffolk, who lived in Marble Hill House, received a gift of figs from Turkey in a willow basket. Her neighbour, the poet Alexander Pope, planted a wand from the basket in his garden and from it grew Britain's first weeping willow tree.

HISTORIAN'S HOME *Thomas Carlyle lived in this red-brick house for 47 years. While there he wrote* The French Revolution – *twice. The original manuscript was accidentally burned by the servant of Carlyle's friend, John Stuart Mill.*

DICKENS HOUSE *The great novelist's signature is one of his relics preserved in the museum.*

(1618-80), one of which shows the extraordinary couple whose extravagances have left a clear picture of what life was like in a mansion during the 17th century.

Marks of distinction

Since 1866 the homes of distinguished people have been marked by plaques put up by the Royal Society of Arts, then the London County Council and now by the Greater London Council. The first plaque was put up on **No. 24 Holles Street,** now demolished, where the poet **Lord Byron** was born in 1788.

A few of the early plaques were brown, but most of these have now been replaced by the familiar blue, circular plates of which there are now more than 450.

The plaques are made of glazed stoneware and in the past have been manufactured by Minton and Doulton. The Historic Buildings Board of the GLC decides whether a plaque should be erected, but suggestions from any individual are considered. Apart from their fame, the subjects of a blue plaque need only one other qualification – they must have been dead for at least 20 years.

Chelsea's celebrated residents

The largest group of people honoured by blue plaques are the writers and poets, and **Chelsea** was a favourite spot with several of them. The essayist and poet **Leigh Hunt** (1784-1859) lived at 22 Upper Cheyne Row. Number 93 Cheyne Walk was the birthplace of the novelist **Mrs Gaskell** (1810-65), and **George Eliot** (1819-80) died at 4 Cheyne Walk, having lived there for only three weeks.

Chelsea's most celebrated resident was, perhaps, **Thomas Carlyle** (1795-1881). Carlyle lived at **24 Cheyne Row** for nearly 50 years, and while there published *The French Revolution* and *Frederick the Great.* His house is much the same as it was when he lived there with his wife Jane.

Carlyle's attic study contains his writing desk, pewter inkstand and reading lamp. The house is open to the public. The house at **33 Ampton Street,** Camden, where Carlyle lived for a while, has a blue plaque.

A writer of importance

A table once owned by Thomas Carlyle eventually found its way to **34 Tite Street,** Chelsea, and on it **Oscar Wilde** (1856-1900) began his writing career, hoping that the table would be an incentive to his work. Wilde moved to Tite Street with his newly married wife in 1884. His first play, *Lady Windermere's Fan,* was produced in 1892, followed by *A Woman of No Importance* in 1893 and *The Importance of Being Earnest* in 1895.

Wilde's house, still a private residence, has changed little since he lived there – a modest Victorian dwelling contrasting with the flamboyant life-style of its most famous occupier.

A Dickens museum

Few authors moved around the country as did **Charles Dickens** (1812-70). Portsmouth – his birthplace – Chatham, Broadstairs and Great Yarmouth all have associations with him, and his home in London at **48 Doughty Street,** Holborn, has been preserved as a museum. Dickens lived there from 1837 until 1839, and during that time completed *Pickwick Papers* and wrote *Oliver Twist, Nicholas Nickleby,* and began *Barnaby Rudge.* The museum contains a collection of Dickens relics, including parts of the manuscripts of *Oliver Twist* and *Nicholas Nickleby.*

Dickens House is the only residence of the novelist in London to have survived. It is owned by the Dickens House Trust and has a fine collection of Dickens' relics.

Birds of a feather

Some houses in London were the homes, at different times, of more than one celebrated person. In **Red Lion Square,** at No. 17, lived three painters: **Dante Gabriel Rossetti** (1828-82), **William Morris** (1834-96) and **Sir Edward Burne-Jones** (1833-98). Prime ministers seem to have liked **No. 10 St James's Square** – it was the home of **William Pitt** (1708-78), **Edward Stanley** (1799-1869) and **William Gladstone** (1809-98).

No fewer than seven notable men lived in **19-20 Bow Street: Henry Fielding** (1707-54), novelist; **Sir John Fielding** (d. 1780), magistrate and Henry's half-brother; **Grinling Gibbons** (1648-1720), wood-carver; **Charles Macklin** (1697-1797), actor; **John Radcliffe** (1652-1714), physician; **Charles Sackville** (1638-1706), poet; and **William Wycherley** (1640-1716), dramatist.

Homes of a diarist

Samuel Pepys (1633-1703) is best remembered for his diary, but he also had a distinguished career as Secretary to the Admiralty. He survived false charges of betraying naval secrets to the French in 1679, and that year moved to **12 Buckingham Street** where he lived until 1688. The house became the Admiralty Office, and Pepys moved to 14 Buckingham Street, where he remained until he retired to Clapham in 1701.

The house at No. 12 is much as it

THE GIRL NEXT DOOR *Keats House was semi-detached when the poet lived there. He occupied the right-hand half, and next door lived Fanny Brawne with whom Keats fell in love.*

HOUSE OF WORDS *Dr Johnson compiled his Dictionary at 17 Gough Square. His portrait there, by James Barrie, is on loan from the National Portrait Gallery.*

was in Pepys's day, but No. 14 has been rebuilt. This second house was also the residence of two notable men, the painters **William Etty** (1787-1849) and **Clarkson Stanfield** (1793-1867).

Conversations at an inn

Dr Samuel Johnson (1709-84) is probably quoted more often than any other man with the exception of Shakespeare. The Doctor's remark "when a man is tired of London, he is tired of life" certainly applied to himself, for he never tired of visiting the City's inns, and particularly the **Cheshire Cheese** in Fleet Street. It was here that he spent much of his time with his friends James Boswell, Dr Oliver Goldsmith and Sir Joshua Reynolds. Johnson would enthral the company with his brilliant conversation, and many of his best-known remarks were made at the dinner table and were recorded by Boswell, his biographer.

Somewhere between his lengthy visits to the Cheshire Cheese, Johnson managed to produce his *Dictionary* at his house in **Gough Square.** He lived there during the years 1748-59, and chose it for its well-lit garret and its closeness to the printer of the *Dictionary* and the Cheshire Cheese.

The Dictionary Attic has been restored, and is believed to be much as it was when Johnson and his six copyists worked there. Downstairs the rooms are small and contain relics of Johnson and some of his friends – Boswell's beer mug and Sir Joshua Reynolds' cup and saucer – as well as books, prints and letters.

Hampstead's tragic poet

The white-stuccoed **Wentworth Place,** in Hampstead, is a pleasant-looking house. Here lived one of literature's most tragic figures – the poet **John Keats.** He died of consumption at the age of 25. Keats lived at Wentworth Place from 1818, staying with his friend Charles Armitage Brown.

ARTIST'S RETREAT *William Hogarth spent most of his time at his house in Chiswick after 1749. The mulberry tree in the garden still flourishes.*

One of his best-known poems, *Ode to a Nightingale,* was written in the garden of the house. Much of Keats's poetry was inspired by his neighbour, Fanny Brawne, to whom he became engaged. But in 1820 his health was failing and his doctors advised him to go abroad. Accompanied by Brown, the poet went to Italy and died in Rome on February 23, 1821.

Keats House, as Wentworth Place is now called, contains many relics of the poet, including locks of his hair, letters and first editions of his works. There are also personal items of Fanny Brawne.

Attractions of a village

The genteel and rural atmosphere of Hampstead attracted many artists and writers. In the summer of 1915 the novelist **D. H. Lawrence** (1885-1930) moved there with his wife, Frieda, and lived at **1 Byron Villas** in the Vale of Health. The Lawrences were great friends of the writer **Katherine Mansfield** (1888-1923)

WINDOW MEMORIAL *Sir Alexander Fleming, discoverer of penicillin, is portrayed in stained glass in St James's Church, Paddington.*

TURN STONE *Dick Whittington is said to have "turned again" at this spot on Highgate Hill – to become thrice Lord Mayor of London.*

who lived at **17 East Heath Road** with John Middleton Murry. For a time, Lawrence and Murry edited a critical magazine called *Signature*.

On the night of September 8, 1915, Lawrence witnessed the first Zeppelin raid on London from the slopes of Hampstead Heath, and recalled the incident in his novel *Kangaroo* published seven years later.

The landscape painter **John Constable** (1776-1837) also found Hampstead to his liking. While living at **40 Well Walk** he wrote of the village's scenes, "as long as I am able to hold a brush I shall never cease to paint them".

"A little country box"

If the artist **William Hogarth** (1697-1764) is to be believed, life in London during the 18th century consisted mainly of drunkenness and debauchery. His engravings were fine works of art and became very popular. He invented the use of a series of pictures to illustrate a theme, usually pointing a moral, two examples being *The Harlot's Progress* and *The Rake's Progress*. Much of his work was copied by others, and this led to the introduction of the Copyright Act of 1735 for the protection of artists and writers.

At the height of his career, Hogarth moved to a house in **Chiswick** which he called "a little country box by the Thames". He lived there from 1749 until his death 15 years later. Today, London's 20th-century life rushes past the door on the Great West Road, but inside the house can be seen several of Hogarth's satires including *The Election, Marriage à la Mode,* and *The Harlot's Progress*.

Man of ideals

Life in 19th-century London, and in the rest of the country, had improved since Hogarth's time, but not sufficiently for the liking of **William Morris**. He was a man of ideals and of many talents, and in 1883 he joined the Democratic Federation which under his leadership adopted Socialism as its doctrine.

Morris was born in Walthamstow, and the house in Forest Road is now the **William Morris Gallery** (see Museums and art galleries, p. 241). Apart from becoming a social reformer, Morris was a successful poet, artist and businessman. In partnership with several friends, including the painters Edward Burne-Jones and Dante Gabriel Rossetti, he set up a decorating and furnishing business in Red Lion Square – some of Morris's wallpaper designs are still in use today. The partnership was dissolved in 1874.

From 1878 until his death, William Morris lived in **Kelmscott House,** Hammersmith, in Upper Mall. There he founded the Kelmscott Press, for which he designed type founts and ornamental letters. The house, not open to the public, dates from about 1780.

PAPER ART
Wallpaper designs by William Morris and a bust of the artist are among the exhibits at the William Morris Gallery.

Homes of the innovators

Many scientists and inventors lived and worked in London, and the work of several was made possible by the "father" of electricity, **Michael Faraday** (1791-1867). A blue plaque on **No. 48 Blandford Street,** St Marylebone, records that Faraday was an apprentice there. The premises were occupied by a bookseller, and Faraday's training as a bookbinder gave him access to educational works which sparked his interest in science.

Also in St Marylebone lived the American painter **Samuel Morse** (1791-1872) who invented the telegraphic code named after him. Fittingly, Morse's home at **141 Cleveland Street** now lies in the shadow of the Post Office telecommunications tower.

The Italian pioneer of wireless communication, **Guglielmo Marconi** (1874-1937), lived in London for only a few months, but it was at **71 Hereford Road,** Paddington, that he convinced officials of the General Post Office that his revolutionary invention worked.

Thirty years after Marconi's invention, telecommunication was taken a stage further by **John Logie Baird** (1888-1946) when he demonstrated television to members of the British Institution in a room (now part of a restaurant) at **22 Frith Street,** Soho. The inventor of the ciné film, **William Friese-Greene** (1855-1921), lived at **136 Maida Vale.** He first used his process successfully in 1889.

Empire builders

In May 1900, London went wild with jubilation – Mafeking had been relieved, after a 217 day siege by the Boers. The defence had been led by one of London's greatest sons, **Robert Baden-Powell.** The hero of Mafeking was born in Paddington in 1857. On his return from South Africa, Robert Baden-Powell lived at **9 Hyde Park Gate.** He devoted himself to social work, and in 1907 he founded the Boy Scout Movement. Most of his later years were spent abroad, and he died and was buried in Kenya in 1941.

More than a century before Baden-

Powell, **Robert Clive** (1725-74) was establishing the British Empire in India. Clive first went to India as a clerk for the East India Company, but later joined the army and was responsible for several brilliant campaigns which led to complete British control of the country.

At the peak of his career, Clive of India was accused of corruption while in India – charges which Parliament found groundless. But the publicity depressed him and he took large doses of opium, to which he was addicted.

He died at his home at **45 Berkeley Square,** but the manner of his death is uncertain. It has been said that he committed suicide by taking an overdose of opium, but Dr Samuel Johnson, who apparently believed in Clive's guilt, said that Clive "acquired his fortune by such crimes that his consciousness of this impelled him to cut his own throat".

Home from the sea

High above a plate-glass shop window in Bond Street a plaque records that "**Admiral Lord Nelson** (1758-1805) lived here in 1798". Nelson lived in a number of houses in London, but **103 New Bond Street** is the only one surviving. He lived there while recovering from the loss of his right arm in the battle at Santa Cruz.

One of Nelson's contemporaries was **Captain William Bligh** who lived at **100 Lambeth Road.** Bligh achieved dubious fame in 1788 when the crew of his ship, HMS *Bounty,* mutinied, led by the mate Fletcher Christian. Bligh and 18 loyal crew members were set adrift in an open boat and eventually landed at Timor almost 4,000 miles away. On his return to England he continued his naval career, and in 1805 was appointed Governor of New South Wales, Australia. He returned to London in 1811 and died in 1817. His tomb can be seen in St Mary's Churchyard, Lambeth.

Reformers and revolutionaries

Men from abroad who changed the world's history have often found London a refuge. The German philosopher and architect of Communism, **Karl Marx** (1818-83), spent the last 27 years of his life in London. Between 1851 and 1856 he lived at **28 Dean Street,** Westminster. Marx was buried in Highgate Cemetery, and a huge bust marks his tomb.

Lenin – Vladimir Ilich Ulianov – (1870-1924), the Russian who put Marx's theories into practice and founded the USSR, lived at **16 Percy Square,** Finsbury in the early 1900s. While there he published the revolutionary newspaper *Iskra* (The Spark) which was smuggled into Imperialist Russia.

The Indian leader **Mahatma Gandhi** visited London in 1931, and lodged at the humble Kingsley Hall. The blue plaque on the building in Powis Road is the only one in Poplar.

WESTMINSTER

A royal city and home of the Mother of Parliaments

For nearly 1,000 years Westminster has been the seat of Britain's government, and for most of that time the home of its monarchs. Within this small, historic city a constitutional monarchy was shaped, and the world's first parliament was born. Around its palace and abbey sprang up the offices of the Crown, from where the nation's life is controlled.

ABBEY NAVE *The choir screen in Westminster Abbey contains a monument to Sir Isaac Newton (1642-1727).*

ROYAL TOMB *Lions and angels guard the effigies of Henry VII and Elizabeth of York in the king's chapel.*

E dward the Confessor, England's king from 1042 until 1066, chose Westminster as the site for his royal palace. A pious man, Edward ordered the building of a great church beside his palace – a church more magnificent than any other in the kingdom.

Westminster Abbey was consecrated in December 1065, though still incomplete, and eight days later its creator was dead. The crown passed to Edward's brother-in-law, Harold, but his reign ended with his death on the battlefield at Hastings, and England had a new king – William the Conqueror.

William's coronation took place in the abbey, and every monarch since has been crowned there, except for two: Edward V who was murdered in the Tower of London in 1483, and Edward VIII who abdicated in 1936.

A king's shrine

Nothing of Edward the Confessor's abbey remains above ground. Henry III rebuilt it, in 1245, in the style of the great churches of France as a place for grand occasions, and as a fitting resting place for Edward who had been made a saint in 1161.

St Edward's Shrine stands in the centre of the Confessor's Chapel. The base of the shrine is the original tall plinth of Purbeck marble. The

JEWEL TOWER *Edward III's treasure-house at Westminster.*

PLACES TO SEE

TRAFALGAR SQUARE *The fountains were remodelled by Sir Edwin Lutyens in 1939, and are floodlit at night.*

upper part – the feretory – contains Edward's remains and is a wooden structure of arches and pilasters. It was made in 1557 to replace the original, which was destroyed during the Dissolution of the Monasteries in 1540.

Around the shrine are the tombs of five kings and three queens: Henry III; Edward I and his wife, Eleanor; Edward III and Philippa; Richard II and Anne; and Henry V.

Also in the chapel is the Coronation Chair. It was made in 1300 for Edward I, and in its base is the Stone of Scone – the traditional coronation seat of Scottish kings which Edward captured in 1296. According to the legend, this was the stone upon which Jacob laid his head and dreamed of angels ascending a ladder.

The chair is placed before the High Altar for the coronation ceremony, on a platform built on a mound which Henry III had raised for this purpose. His son, Edward I, was the first king to be crowned in the rebuilt abbey, in 1272. The Coronation Chair was first used in 1307 for the crowning of Edward II.

Tombs of the Tudors

In 1503 Henry VII, the first Tudor king, had a chapel built in the abbey. The glory of Henry's chapel is its roof, a soaring vault of elaborately carved arches with huge, fan-shaped pendants suspended like ornate stalactites. In the nave the walls are enriched with the brilliantly coloured banners of the Knights Grand Cross of the Order of the Bath, whose chapel it has been since 1725.

Behind the altar is the tomb of Henry and his queen, Elizabeth of York. The magnificent tomb was the work of the 16th-century Italian sculptor Pietro Torrigiani, and is topped by the gilded effigies of the king and queen.

In the north aisle stands the tomb of Henry VII's grand-daughter Elizabeth I; a marble effigy of the queen lies beneath a massive canopy supported by ten black columns. In the same tomb lies Elizabeth's sister, Mary, who has no monument.

Beyond Henry VII's chapel is another small chapel dedicated to the men of the Royal Air Force who died in the Battle of Britain. The stained-glass window contains the badges of 68 squadrons that took part in the battle in September 1940.

In the abbey's south transept is Poet's Corner. Here are buried Chaucer, Dryden and Tennyson, and many others. There are also monuments to poets buried elsewhere, including Shakespeare, Burns and Wordsworth.

The **Abbey Museum** is in the 11th-century undercroft. Here are funeral effigies of kings, queens and nobles, made to be carried at the funeral and to lie in state. The oldest is that of Edward III, whose distorted mouth shows that the face was made from a death mask after he had died from a stroke. Anne of Bohemia, wife of Richard II, is represented only by a wooden head; Charles II is a full-length figure dressed in his Garter robes.

One splendid effigy is that of Lord Nelson. It was bought by the abbey in 1806 to attract visitors away from his tomb in St Paul's Cathedral.

England's first parliament

Edward the Confessor's Palace of Westminster was too humble a dwelling for William the Conqueror, who was accustomed to the more majestic palaces of France. He rebuilt it, and in 1097 his son, William Rufus, added **Westminster Hall**. Almost two centuries later, in 1265, the hall was the scene of England's first parliament, when Henry III's barons, knights and citizens forced the king to reform his government to include representatives of the people.

In 1394, Richard II ordered his master mason, Henry Yevele, and the carpenter Hugh Herland to re-roof the hall. The result was one of the finest hammer-beam roofs in Europe. The oak beams rise to 90 ft at the centre of the Gothic arches, and the supporting beams are carved with flying angels.

Beneath these massive timbers some of the most significant scenes in England's history have been enacted. Richard's roof was barely complete before he was deposed by Parliament, meeting in the hall. Four centuries later, in 1649, Charles I was tried there for treason "in the name of the people". Oliver Cromwell was installed as Lord Protector in the hall in 1653. In 1661 his body was exhumed and his head was impaled on a pole on the roof, where it stayed for 23 years.

MEMBERS' VIEW *When Members of Parliament attend the State Opening of Parliament they stand behind the Bar of the House of Lords, facing the gilded throne from which the Queen makes her speech.*

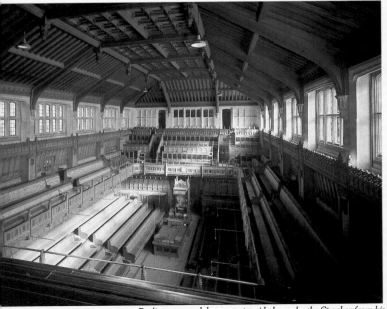

HOUSE OF COMMONS *Parliamentary debates are presided over by the Speaker from his canopied chair; the Government sits on his right, the Opposition on his left. Public and press galleries overlook the chamber.*

Westminster Hall survived a number of fires that ravaged the Palace of Westminster, the worst of which was in 1834. A competition for a new palace, or **Houses of Parliament** as it had by then come to be called, was won by Charles Barry (1795-1860). His commission was to build in a Gothic or Elizabethan style. He chose Gothic. With his assistant, Augustus Welby Pugin (1812-52), Barry produced a building that was majestic yet restrained.

The symmetrical ground plan was Barry's, with the two debating chambers – the House of Lords and the House of Commons – and the lobbies running in line along the centre.

At the western end of the building is the **Victoria Tower**, 336 ft high, and at the eastern end is the 316 ft Clock Tower. The great bell in the Clock Tower was named **Big Ben**, after Sir Benjamin Hall the Commissioner for Works. The 14 ton bell, which has a 4 ft crack, strikes the hours and has been heard the world over since it was first broadcast in 1923. A light in the top of the tower remains lit when the Commons is sitting.

The Houses of Parliament were completed in 1868, but neither of the designers lived to see their work completed. Augustus Pugin died insane in 1852, the year in which Barry was knighted for his achievement.

Each November the Queen attends the House of Lords for the State Opening of Parliament, and sits on a gilded throne designed by Pugin.

A vanished palace

Whitehall Palace once ran almost the full length of Whitehall and alongside the River Thames. It was the residence of Tudor and Stuart kings and queens, but when fire destroyed it in 1698 only the **Banqueting House** and **Henry VIII's Wine Cellar** survived. The reigning monarch, William III, preferred his palace at Kensington, so Whitehall Palace was not rebuilt. Instead, the street became the centre for government offices, most of which date from the 18th century or later. Squeezed between the Treasury building and the Home Office is **Downing Street**, built by Sir George Downing in the 1680s. The house at number 10 is the official residence of the Prime Minister. It was given to Sir Robert Walpole by George II in 1732.

HORSE GUARDS *The frontage facing Horse Guards Parade was designed by William Kent about 1745-8.*

At the southern end of Whitehall is the **Cenotaph**, designed by Sir Edwin Lutyens (1869-1944) in 1919 to commemorate the dead of the First World War. It now also serves that purpose for those who died in the Second World War.

Opposite the Old War Office is **Horse Guards**. The entrance is guarded by mounted sentries of one of the two Household Cavalry Regiments: the Life Guards, or the Blues and Royals. Behind the white 18th-century building is **Horse Guards Parade**, a vast parade ground where the Queen takes the salute at the Trooping the Colour ceremony on her official birthday.

After the destruction of Whitehall Palace the royal residence moved to **St James's Palace** in The Mall. Henry VIII had it built in 1532, and it was the birthplace of Charles II, James II, Mary II, Queen Anne and George IV. Charles I spent his last night in the guardroom before going to the scaffold in Whitehall.

The palace ceased to be a royal residence when George III bought Buckingham House in 1762, but it remains a royal palace, and foreign ambassadors are accredited to the Court of St James. Several apartments are occupied by those working in the royal households.

When George IV succeeded his father, the brick-built Buckingham House – built for the Duke of Buck-

NUMBER TEN *The home of the Prime Minister in Downing Street.*

HUB OF GOVERNMENT *The domes and spires of Whitehall tower above the trees in St James's Park.*

ingham in 1703 – did not appeal to him, so he engaged his favourite architect, John Nash, to alter it. Nash clad the building in Bath stone, but George IV died before it was completed, as also did his successor, William IV.

The first monarch to occupy Buckingham Palace was Queen Victoria. She moved in three weeks after her accession in 1837. The Queen had the deep forecourt enclosed by a new frontage in 1847, and Nash's Marble Arch, which he had built as a grand entrance, was moved to become the north-east entrance to Hyde Park.

In 1912 the frontage was heightened and refaced in Portland stone to blend with the **Victoria Memorial** which stands opposite at the top of the Mall. The seated figure of Victoria was the work of Sir Thomas Brock (1847-1922). The marble base and surround was by Sir Aston Webb (1849-1930), and the complete edifice, topped by a gilt figure of Victory, stands 82 ft high.

ROYAL HOMES OUTSIDE WESTMINSTER

Kensington Palace was the residence of William III and his wife Mary. The house was built in 1605 and enlarged by Sir Christopher Wren for William and Mary in 1689.

An orangery built in the gardens for Queen Anne was probably the work of Sir John Vanbrugh (1664-1726). Grinling Gibbons (1648-1720) was responsible for much of the palace's interior – his magnificent wood carvings appear in several rooms. William Kent (1684-1748) lavishly decorated the walls and ceilings with paintings for George I.

The **Tower of London** was built by William the Conqueror in the 11th century to overawe the citizens of London. Later it became a royal residence, sometimes not by choice. Henry III lived there, and had the Keep whitewashed, after which it became known as the White Tower. Richard I, Edward I, Edward III, Richard II and Henry

VIII all made additions to the walls and towers.

Edward IV added a sinister chapter to the Tower's history when he set up a permanent execution scaffold, and in the 15th and 16th centuries the fortress increased its reputation as a grim prison. The Garden Tower became known as Bloody Tower after the murder of the princes in 1483.

James I was the last monarch to use the Tower as a residence. The chief occupants today are the Yeoman Warders in their Tudor costumes, and the ravens – without which, it is said, the Tower will fall.

The Crown Jewels are displayed in the Jewel Tower. They include the Imperial State Crown, which contains 3,000 jewels, and the Royal Sceptre which has the largest cut diamond in the world – the 530 carat Star of Africa. This was in turn cleaved from the largest diamond ever found – the 3,106 carat Cullinan.

MUSEUMS AND ART GALLERIES

London's treasure-houses of art and antiquity

Napoleon said that the British are a nation of shopkeepers; he could have said also that they are a nation of collectors. The affluence of the 18th century produced men who acquired art treasures from all over the world. Many of these collections formed the basis for the museums and art galleries founded by the Victorians, who left a priceless legacy to the 20th century. Nowhere can that legacy be enjoyed more than in London.

Behind the Classical façade of the **British Museum** lies one of the world's most fabulous treasure stores. The museum was founded in 1753 with a collection of books and antiquities donated by Sir Hans Sloane (1660-1753), physician to George II, on condition that £20,000 was paid to his daughter. The money was raised by a public lottery. The collection expanded in 1757 when George II presented the museum with the Royal Library, a collection of books amassed by the Kings and Queens of England since Tudor times.

Among the museum's best-known antiquities are the Elgin Marbles, Greek sculptures from the Parthenon in Athens brought to London in the 19th century by Lord Elgin. In the Egyptian Gallery is the Rosetta Stone dating from 196 BC. The stone bears inscriptions in Egyptian and Greek, which enabled scholars to decipher Egyptian hieroglyphic script.

The Waddesdon Bequest Room contains a collection of gold and silverware of the Renaissance period. It was donated by Baron Ferdinand de Rothschild whose home was at Waddesdon Manor, near Aylesbury.

Principal art gallery

On the north side of Trafalgar Square the domed and porticoed **National Gallery** is England's principal art gallery and one of the finest in Europe. It is also one of the youngest, having been founded in 1824 with only 38 paintings. The present building was designed in 1834 by William Wilkins (1778-1839). He incorporated part of Carlton House, the Prince Regent's London home, in the façade.

Leonardo da Vinci's cartoon of *The Virgin and Child with St Anne*, Botticelli's *Mars and Venus* and Raphael's *Madonna and Child* are among the works by Italian artists. Dutch masters include 20 Rembrandts – notably *A Woman Bathing in a Stream* – Vermeer's *A Young Lady standing at a Virginal* and Van Gogh's *Sunflowers*.

Round the corner from the National Gallery, in St Martin's Place, is the **National Portrait Gallery**, a collection of more than 9,000 portraits of notable men and women of British history.

English paintings and modern European and American art can be seen in the **Tate Gallery** overlooking the

THE PORTLAND VASE *A Roman glass vase, which belonged to the Dukes of Portland, is in the British Museum.*

Thames at Millbank. The gallery was commissioned by Sir Henry Tate, the sugar refiner, in 1897. Works by Turner, Blake and Constable figure prominently among the oil-paintings, and the sculpture collection includes figures by Rodin, Epstein, Henry Moore and Barbara Hepworth.

Two other notable art collections in Central London are the **Wallace Collection** in Manchester Square and the **Courtauld Institute** in Woburn Square. The Wallace Collection was bequeathed to the nation by Lady Wallace in 1897, and contains pictures by British and European artists, miniatures, sculptures, furniture, armour and ceramics.

Samuel Courtauld, the industrialist, and Lord Lee of Fareham jointly founded the Courtauld Institute, which is London University's Faculty of the History of Art. It contains Impressionist and Post-Impressionist paintings, Old Masters, sculpture and furniture. The galleries are entered from Woburn Square.

Story of London

London's own museum, which presents the city's history from Roman times, is in London Wall. Now called the **Museum of London**, it was formed by uniting the London and Guildhall museums and was opened in 1976. The collection of exhibits is arranged to tell the story of London in chronological order. There are religious sculptures found beneath the

floor of the Temple of Mithras, the filigree stock of a Jacobean jeweller, old inn signs, Samuel Pepys's set of chessmen, and models of trams which were still running in London as recently as 1952.

Carriages and steam

Two vastly contrasting museums can be seen west of central London: the **Gunnersbury Park Museum** and the **Kew Bridge Pumping Station**. Gunnersbury Park was the home of the Rothschild family. The house is a Regency mansion, and contains exhibits of local archaeology as well as the 19th-century carriages used by the Rothschilds.

The Kew Bridge Engines Trust preserves, in working order, five of the steam engines which for more than 100 years drove huge pumps to supply water to west London.

On the northern outskirts of the capital is **Church Farm House**, standing at the top of a hill in Hendon. The house dates from the 17th century and became a museum in 1955. The ground floor, which includes a well-equipped kitchen, is arranged as it would have been in the 18th and early 19th centuries.

At the foot of the hill a vast housing estate now covers what was once the home of the Royal Air Force – Hendon Aerodrome – and in one corner is the **Royal Air Force Museum**. The oldest aircraft on display is a 1909 Bleriot, and the history of the RAF is represented by machines ranging in size from the flimsy First World War fighter planes to the Lancaster bomber of the Second World War.

Bequest to the nation

Hampstead is best known for the Heath, a large wedge of parkland which includes Parliament Hill and Kenwood. At the north-east corner is Kenwood House. It was built in the 17th century but given its present character by Robert Adam after 1764. In 1925 the house was bought by Lord Iveagh, and on his death in 1927 the estate was left to the nation. It is now known as the Iveagh Bequest.

The house contains 18th-century furniture, but the main attraction is the fine collection of paintings. One of the many self-portraits by Rembrandt is here, believed to have been painted in about 1663 when the artist was 57. There is a wealth of work by Van Dyck, Vermeer, Cuyp and Hals as well as English 18th-century paintings by Reynolds, Romney and Gainsborough.

Hampstead is also the home of one of London's more unusual museums – **Fenton House**. The building dates from 1693 and was the home of an

18th-century merchant, Philip Fenton. It now houses a fine collection of 18th-century porcelain, and some musical instruments, including a pair of 1664 virginals and a harpsichord of 1612.

Stamps and wallpaper

Tottenham would seem an unlikely setting for a house named after a Scottish king, but **Bruce Castle** was built there in 1514 on land once owned by Robert Bruce, Robert I of Scotland. When Bruce won the Scottish throne in 1306, the manor of Tottenham was confiscated by Edward I, but the name was retained.

The house was enlarged in the 17th and 18th centuries and became a school run by the Hill family, one of whom was Rowland Hill (1795-1879) who introduced the "penny" post. Bruce Castle now contains a display of postal history.

The boyhood home of William Morris (1834-96) in Forest Road, Walthamstow is now the **William Morris Gallery.** Morris was a poet, artist and designer of textiles and wallpapers. Many of his tapestry and wallpaper designs are on view.

In Romford Road the **Passmore Edwards Museum** is notable for its fine collection of Bow porcelain. The building is late Victorian and was built with the aid of John Passmore Edwards (1823-1911), the publisher and philanthropist. It is a centre for the study of geology, archaeology, local history and related subjects. The natural-history gallery has live animals and an aquarium. Almshouses dating from the 18th century have been utilised for the **Geffrye Museum** in Shoreditch. The rooms are furnished and decorated in styles dating from the Elizabethan period until 1939.

The **Bethnal Green Museum** is for and about children. There is a collection of toys and dolls' houses, and the museum is being developed as a Museum of Childhood.

Maritime history

Viewed from the north, from across the river, the tall masts of the clipper ship *Cutty Sark* signpost the site of the **National Maritime Museum** at Greenwich.

The museum was opened in 1937 to illustrate the maritime history of Great Britain, which it does with the aid of models, paintings, uniforms and navigational instruments. Two galleries are devoted to the life and times of Nelson. Relics of the great admiral include the coat he wore at Trafalgar.

The *Cutty Sark*, built in 1868, was one of the last of the clippers which brought tea to England from China. Below decks is a collection of ships' figureheads.

A museum which caters for children is the **Horniman Museum** in Forest Hill. It deals with the study of man and his environment, showing primitive tools, weapons, utensils and art. A zoology section illustrates animal evolution, movement and defences. There is also a large collection of musical instruments.

English and European art

The **Dulwich College Picture Gallery**, completed in 1814 to the design of Sir John Soane (1753-1837), was one of England's first purpose-built art galleries. Among its collection of English and European paintings are several by Poussin and Rubens with Rembrandt's *Girl at a Window*, Watteau's *Plaisirs du Bal* and Hogarth's *Fishing Party*.

The **South London Art Gallery** has a permanent collection of 20th-century prints, and works by British artists from 1700 to the present day.

The **Cuming Museum** in Southwark concentrates on the archaeology of the Southwark area. Its exhibits include fragments of a Roman boat, shaped stones from the palace of the Black Prince at Kennington and the pump from the old debtors' prison at Marshalsea. There is also a collection of objects associated with London superstitions.

The domed building housing the

THE VIRGIN OF THE ROCK *Leonardo da Vinci's painting is one of the finest treasures in the National Gallery's collection of more than 4,500 works of art. The gallery includes some of the finest works by European artists.*

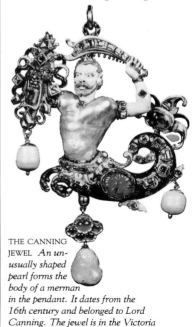

THE CANNING JEWEL *An unusually shaped pearl forms the body of a merman in the pendant. It dates from the 16th century and belonged to Lord Canning. The jewel is in the Victoria and Albert Museum.*

Imperial War Museum in Lambeth was once a lunatic asylum. It was built in 1815 as the Bethlehem Hospital for the Insane, or Bedlam, and became the home of the museum when it moved from South Kensington in 1936.

The museum is concerned with all aspects of warfare in which Britain has been involved since 1914. The major exhibits are weapons, vehicles, aircraft and equipment of the two World Wars. There is a large collection of paintings by war artists.

South Kensington is London's "museumland". In the 19th century an area of land between Kensington Gardens and Cromwell Road was developed as a cultural centre, spurred by the enthusiasm of Prince Albert and paid for with the proceeds of the Great Exhibition of 1851 which he had fostered.

Within this huge complex of colleges and institutes there are four large museums: the Natural History Museum, the Victoria and Albert Museum, the Geological Museum and the Science Museum.

Queen's command

The first museum on the site was the South Kensington Museum, opened in 1857. Queen Victoria directed that the title be changed to the **Victoria and Albert Museum** when a new building was commissioned in 1899, but she did not live to see it completed. Aston Webb (1849-1930) was its designer, and he produced one of south-west London's most imposing buildings; a work in Classical style, with an octagonal central tower of columns and flying buttresses and an impressive arched entrance facing Cromwell Road. Edward VII opened it in 1909.

The Victoria and Albert is a museum of fine and applied arts of all countries, styles and periods. Its exhibits range from arms and armour to water-colours and woodwork. Among the museum's treasures are Raphael's cartoons depicting scenes from the New Testament, painted as designs for a set of tapestries now in the Vatican in Rome, and Holbein's miniature of Anne of Cleves. A collection of English, French and Italian furniture includes the 16th-century Great Bed of Ware (see Ware) which could sleep eight people.

The **Natural History Museum**,

which is part of the British Museum, moved to its present site in 1880. The architect was Alfred Waterhouse (1830-1905). His Romanesque design gives the building a sombre dignity compared with its more elegant neighbour, the Victoria and Albert Museum. The 675 ft long frontage includes two massive towers 192 ft high, and the deep entrance porch is approached by wide, stone steps.

Bones of mammoths

The size of the Natural History Museum reflects the importance the Victorians placed on the subject. Permanent exhibitions on human biology, ecology, evolution, and dinosaurs are to be found among the collections

CLOCKWORK PIG *A 19th-century German toy in the Bethnal Green Museum. When wound, the pig rears up.*

KEW BRIDGE PUMPING STATION *One of the five Cornish beam-engines that pumped water for west London until 1944. The engines were built between 1820 and 1869, and can be seen working on their original site.*

HORNIMAN MUSEUM *Art nouveau in south-east London. The façade mosaic is by Robert Anning Bell (1863-1933).*

which include birds, insects and butterflies. In the Fossil Galleries can be seen some of the bones of mammoths discovered in Kent and Essex.

The Whale Gallery includes a 91 ft long model of a blue whale, the largest animal alive on earth.

When the Victoria and Albert Museum was opened, its science collection was already housed in a building across the road, and this collection became known as the Science Museum. The present building consists of a large block opened in 1928, and extensions added in 1963.

Science on display

Of all the South Kensington museums the **Science Museum** comes closest to being a living display. The main hall is flanked by the nodding beam-engines of James Watt, and beyond is the Transport Gallery with Stephenson's *Rocket*, a 1905 Rolls-Royce car and giant locomotives of the last days of steam on the railways. The upper galleries contain collections on subjects ranging from clocks to printing machines, ships to medicine and photography to television.

HARP-LUTE *This unusual instrument, made in Liverpool in the early 19th century, is in Fenton House.*

The Aeronautics Gallery contains a comprehensive display of aircraft and engines. Throughout the museum are working models that can be operated by the press of a button, and special demonstrations are featured at certain times of the day.

Earth's history

The last of South Kensington's major museums is the **Geological Museum**, which opened its doors in 1935. It is devoted to the study of earth's history and geological science. In the main hall a revolving globe shows the world modelled in relief. The central area of the hall is occupied by a display of gemstones. Dioramas – illuminated moving scenes – illustrate the actions of earthquakes, volcanoes, the sea and glaciers.

The hall itself demonstrates some of the uses of minerals, with an entrance arch in Devon and Irish marbles, a fountain in Peterhead granite and a vase carved from Siberian quartz. Displays include The Story of the Earth, Treasures of the Earth, and Britain before Man.

The first-floor gallery is devoted to the regional geology of Britain. There are collections of minerals and fossils and an exhibit showing the geology of Stonehenge.

On the second floor, economic geology is demonstrated with fuel, building and atomic materials.

POSTING CHARIOT *This 1820 carriage is in the Gunnersbury Park Museum.*

London's museums and art galleries

Artillery Museum (4Ce), The Rotunda, Woolwich Common. Firearms.
Barnet Museum (1Ee), Wood Street, Barnet. Local history.
Bethnal Green Museum of Childhood (2Ab), Cambridge Heath Road. Toys, games, dolls.
British Museum (6Be), Great Russell Street, Westminster. Greek, Roman, Egyptian, Western Asiatic, prehistoric and Romano-British antiquities.
Bruce Castle Museum (2Ac), Lordship Lane, Tottenham. Local history, Middlesex Regiment. Postal history display.
Church Farm House Museum (1Dc), Greyhound Hill, Hendon. Local history.
Clock Museum (6Ee), Guildhall Library, Aldermanbury.
Courtauld Institute Gallery (6Be), Woburn Square, Westminster. Impressionist and Post-Impressionist paintings.
Cuming Museum (6Db), Walworth Road, Southwark. Local history.
Dulwich College Picture Gallery (4Ad), College Road, Dulwich. Old Masters including British, French, Spanish and Dutch.
Fenton House (1Ec), Hampstead Grove, Hampstead. Musical instruments and porcelain.
Geffrye Museum (2Ab), Kingsland Road, Shoreditch. Period rooms from 1600 to 1939.
Geological Museum (5Dc), Exhibition Road, South Kensington. Geology and mineralogy.
Guards Museum (6Ab), Wellington Barracks, Birdcage Walk, Westminster. History of Guards regiments.
Guildhall Art Gallery, King Street, Cheapside, City.
Gunnersbury Park Museum (1Da), Gunnersbury Park, Ealing. Local archaeology and topography. Transport items of Rothschild family.

Hayward Gallery (6Cc), South Bank, Westminster. Temporary exhibitions of British and foreign art.
HMS Belfast (6Fc), Symons Wharf, Vine Lane. Naval museum.
Horniman Museum (4Ad), London Road, Forest Hill. Ethnographical, natural history and aquarium.
Imperial War Museum (6Db), Lambeth Road. Weapons and materials of 20th-century warfare.
Iveagh Bequest, Kenwood **(1Ec)**, Hampstead. English and Dutch paintings.
Livesay Museum (4Ae), Old Kent Road, Southwark. Local history.
London Transport Collection (1Ca), Covent Garden. Transport relics.
Museum of London (6De), London Wall, City. Social history of London.
Museum of Mankind (6Ad), Burlington Gardens, Westminster.
Musical Museum (1Ca), High Street, Brentford. Organs, mechanical pianos, music boxes.
National Army Museum (5Eb), Royal Hospital Road, Chelsea. History of British army, 15th to 20th centuries.
National Gallery (6Bd), Trafalgar Square, Westminster. British and foreign paintings.
National Maritime Museum (4Be), Romney Road, Greenwich. Nautical exhibits.
National Museum of Labour History (2Ba), Limehouse Town Hall.
National Portrait Gallery (6Bd), St Martin's Place, Westminster. Portraits of British personalities.
National Postal Museum (6De), King Edward Street, City. British and foreign postage stamps.
Natural History Museum (5Cc), Cromwell Road, South Kensington. Fossils, animals, plants.
Passmore Edwards Museum (2Bb), Romford Road, Stratford. Bow porcelain, antiquities of Essex.
Public Record Office Museum (6Cd), Chancery Lane, Holborn. National archives, including Domesday Book.
Rangers House (4Be), Chesterfield

Walk, Blackheath. Old-Master paintings and Stuart portraits.
Royal Academy of Arts (6Ad), Burlington House, Piccadilly. Special exhibitions of paintings, archaeology, sculpture.
Royal Air Force Museum (1Dc), Aerodrome Road, Hendon. Collection of aircraft and equipment of RFC and RAF.
Royal Mews (5Fc), Buckingham Palace Road, Westminster. State coaches.
Science Museum (5Dc), Exhibition Road, South Kensington. Collection of exhibits portraying the sciences and development of engineering.
Sir John Soane's Museum (6Ce), Lincoln's Inn Fields, Holborn. The home of Sir John Soane, containing his collections of art and antiquities.
South London Art Gallery (4Ae), Peckham Road, Peckham. Paintings and 20th-century prints.
Tate Gallery (6Ba), Millbank, Westminster. British and foreign art.
The Queen's Gallery (6Ab), Buckingham Palace Road, Westminster. Royal collection of art.
Thomas Coram Foundation for Children (1Fb), Brunswick Square, Westminster. British paintings, especially Hogarth.
Victoria and Albert Museum (5Dc), Cromwell Road, South Kensington. Sculpture, miniatures, silver, costumes, furniture, ceramics, English and European masters.
Wallace Collection (5Ee), Manchester Square, Westminster. British and European paintings, ceramics, sculpture, furniture.
Wellcome Institute of the History of Medicine (1Fb), Euston Road, Camden. History of Medicine.
Wellington Museum Apsley House **(5Ed)**, Hyde Park Corner. Home of the Duke of Wellington. Exhibits include relics of the duke.
Whitechapel Art Gallery (2Aa), High Street, Whitechapel. Exhibitions of modern art.
William Morris Gallery (2Bc), Lloyd Park, Walthamstow. Textiles and wallpapers designed by Morris.

THE GREEN CAPITAL

London's heritage of parks and open country

London's wealth of open spaces makes it unique among the world's capitals. Parks, gardens and squares break up the mass of tightly packed buildings in its centre, and vast woods and heathland stretch the length and breadth of Greater London. These open spaces are part of the capital's heritage – the parks of kings, the gardens of the nobility, and the common lands which held out against the land-hungry speculators and stemmed the tide of urban development.

ONE MAN'S VIEW *At Speakers' Corner, in Hyde Park, orators air their views with impassioned speeches, amid equally impassioned heckling.*

Much of London's parkland stems from royal whims: a duke's desire for a palace; one king's love of hunting; and another's craving for a relief from his asthma. The open spaces they preserved are now the Royal Parks, still owned by the Crown but which all are privileged to enjoy.

Royal enclosure of **Greenwich Park** goes back to 1433, after the building there of Bella Court Palace by Humphrey, Duke of Gloucester, in 1428. It was at a gatehouse that once stood at the park's entrance that, it is said, Sir Walter Raleigh threw down his cloak so that Elizabeth I should not walk in the mud.

The Queen's House, built by Inigo Jones in 1616, stands in the grounds of the National Maritime Museum, and behind it the park sweeps up to Blackheath. Avenues of trees criss-cross wide lawns, and the park has an ornamental pond, three bird sanctuaries and two herds of deer, one of red deer, the other of fallow deer.

Thieves and highwaymen

Henry VIII's passion for hunting led eventually to the formation of London's three best-known parks – Hyde Park, St James's Park and Regent's Park. In the 16th century the king stocked them with deer, and royal hunts continued to be held there long after his death. The last deer hunt in Hyde Park was held in 1768. Each park subsequently became identified with particular monarchs.

In 1635 Charles I opened **Hyde Park** to the public, and it became a fashionable pleasure ground. The Serpentine Lake and the Long Water were added by Queen Caroline, wife of George II.

In the 18th century Hyde Park was the haunt of thieves and high-waymen, many of whom ended their days on the Tyburn gallows where Marble Arch now stands at the north-east corner of the park. It was a place, too, where duellists settled their differences; today it is better known for the verbal exchanges between the orators and their hecklers at **Speakers' Corner**.

The arguments have changed since the first speaker mounted his soap box in 1872, but little else in the park has. Hyde Park is still a place to stroll, or even to ride – Rotten Row, a soft-earth bridle-path, has been there since the days of William III when it was the *route du roi* (the royal way).

St James's Park has several royal associations. James I kept a menagerie there, and his son Charles I walked through the park on his way to the scaffold in Whitehall in 1649. Charles II redesigned the park in the French style, after his restoration to the throne in 1660, and opened it to the public. One of the attractions was an aviary along the road now called Birdcage Walk, which runs from Buckingham Palace to Whitehall.

The Tsar of Russia presented Charles with a pair of pelicans to add to the collection of wildfowl on the ornamental lake. Since then pelicans have been a familiar sight in the park.

In 1667, Charles II bought **Green Park** as an extension to St James's Park. The king was fond of walking, and Constitution Hill, which runs alongside Green Park, is said to be so called because he often took his "constitutional" there. Green Park differs from other Royal Parks in that it has no flower beds or water. But it lives up to its name with wide expanses of

DUTCH TREAT IN KENSINGTON *Tulips and pleached limes surround the sunken garden in the grounds of Kensington Palace. The garden was laid out in 1909 in Dutch style, on the site of a garden designed by Queen Anne.*

grass and stately groups of shady trees.

Regent's Park was originally called Marylebone Park, and was opened to the public in 1838. It was named after the Prince Regent, later George IV, who was responsible for the building of the elegant houses by John Nash (see Streets and Buildings, p. 230) around its fringe.

At the northern end of Regent's Park is the **London Zoo**, founded in 1828, lying on both banks of the Regent's Canal. Boat trips along the canal start from the Paddington basin, known as Little Venice, and give a picturesque view of the park and zoo with trees overhanging the water's edge.

In the Inner Circle of the park are the rose beds of Queen Mary's Garden and the Open-Air Theatre, which gives productions of Shakespeare's plays during the summer. There is boating on the artificial lake, created by Nash, which is also a bird sanctuary with a collection of waterfowl.

Palace in a garden

When William III came to the throne in 1689 he bought Nottingham House, which stood at the western end of Hyde Park, because he feared that the damp atmosphere of the riverside Whitehall Palace would make his asthma worse.

The house became Kensington Palace (see Royal London, p. 239), and its grounds now form **Kensington Gardens**. The Broad Walk passes the Round Pond, where model-boat enthusiasts gather, and the Flower Walk is planned so that blooms can be seen at most times of the year.

The Albert Memorial dominates the southern end of Kensington Gardens, and in the north-eastern corner is a statue of James Barrie's *Peter Pan* by Sir George Frampton (1860-1928). Close by is a children's playground and the Elfin Oak, carved with figures of pixies and fairies.

Natural beauty

The biggest of the Royal Parks is **Richmond Park**, 2½ miles across from north to south and from east to west. It was created by another hunting monarch, Charles I, in 1637. Here, in surroundings as varied as any part of the English countryside, roam two herds of the Queen's deer – the magnificent red deer and the dainty fallow deer.

Natural beauty is the keynote of Richmond Park. Great stretches of bracken give way to woodland, and in the Isabella Plantation a stream runs through masses of flowering shrubs.

South-west of Richmond Park, the River Thames cradles **Hampton Court Park** and **Bushy Park** in a broad loop. Bushy Park comprises areas of cropland and grazing for cattle. In Hampton Court Park there is a large expanse of open parkland known as Home Park, and also formal lawns and gardens designed to enhance the great palace from which the park takes its name.

ROYAL HUNTING GROUND *Kings and their courtiers once hunted in Richmond Park. Now the herds of fallow deer can graze safely beneath the trees.*

The **Royal Botanic Gardens** at Kew were begun at the request of Princess Augusta, wife of Frederick, Prince of Wales, in 1751.

The Palm House is a vast "greenhouse" of glass and iron, 362 ft long and 62 ft high at the centre. It was designed by Decimus Burton (1800-81) in 1844, and took four years to build. The distinctive Pagoda is purely a giant 163 ft high garden ornament, erected in 1761.

London's lungs

The eight Royal Parks form only a small part of London's open spaces – the Greater London Council controls about 30, and the 32 borough councils tend many more. These "lungs" of London are spread generously across its face, providing welcome relief from the noise and grime of the streets. There are squares, gardens and, around central London's perimeter, wide expanses of commons and heathland.

The commons and heaths cover some 3,500 acres, and about one-third of this area is taken up by **Wimbledon Common** and its neighbour, **Putney Heath**. Together with the adjacent Richmond Park they form a sizeable spread of open country south-west of the city. A windmill, built in 1817, stands on Wimbledon Common. It is open to the public at weekends during the summer.

Clapham Common is a triangular, tree-lined wedge of green lying in the path of traffic heading south from Chelsea Bridge. Funfairs are held on the common, and in August each year it is the site of the Greater London Horse Show.

Historic heath

Further east is **Blackheath**, perhaps London's most historic open space. Here the rebel leader Wat Tyler gathered his forces in 1381, and the priest John Ball preached his sermon: "When Adam delved and Eve span, who was then the Gentleman?"

In 1415 Londoners greeted Henry V on the heath after his victory at Agincourt, and in 1660 Charles II was met

LAKESIDE CONCERT *Orchestras play by the placid water in Kenwood on summer evenings.*

there by the citizens of London on his way to being restored to the throne. His grandfather, James I, is said to have introduced the game of golf to England on Blackheath in 1608.

In 1588 a beacon flared on Blackheath, warning the country of the approach of the Spanish Armada. Its light would have been seen on London's highest ground 10 miles to the north – **Hampstead Heath**. The heath is 437 ft above sea-level, and a flagstaff stands on the spot believed to be the site of Hampstead's beacon.

Hampstead Heath is known to Londoners as "Appy ampstead", a nickname it earned through the vast Bank Holiday funfairs that centre on the Vale of Health. East of the vale, grass and woodland stretch across to Highgate, taking in Kenwood, where open-air orchestral concerts are held in the summer. Below Kenwood is Parliament Hill. A tumulus at the top of the hill is said to be the burial place of Queen Boudicca.

LONDON: THE GREEN CAPITAL

From Ware in Hertfordshire the River Lea flows south to meet the Thames at Tower Hamlets, carving a valley of marshes down the eastern side of London. The whole of the **Lea Valley** is being developed into a regional park and recreation area extending to 10,000 acres.

Hackney Marsh is already an established sports area with more than 100 football pitches. There are plans to

PARK SCULPTURE *Modern sculptures are sometimes exhibited in Battersea Park. Henry Moore's* Three Standing Figures, *created in 1948, is on permanent view beside the lake.*

cater for almost every kind of recreation, with the emphasis on water sports to make full use of the river and its reservoirs. This new and ambitious project, however, should not detract from the attractions of Victoria Park on the boundary of Hackney and Tower Hamlets. The park was opened in 1845 and is London's oldest municipal park. At one time it was a favourite place for public debates, and became known as "the forum of the East End". It is a park for individual rather than competitive pastimes, with fishing, boating and swimming in the artificial lake.

Easter parade

South London had to wait until 1858 for its first municipal park, which was laid out at Battersea beside the Thames. **Battersea Park** became the site of the 1951 Festival of Britain Pleasure Gardens, a huge complex of sideshows, pavilions, tree walks and a funfair.

Interest in the amusement park dwindled over the years and it was closed in 1975, but the open-air con-

MONSTERS IN SE19 *Life-sized models of prehistoric monsters lurk in the Crystal Palace undergrowth.*

cert pavilion still has regular light music and jazz performances in the summer. On Easter Sunday each year there is a carnival parade through the park, with decorated floats and marching bands.

Until a disastrous fire in 1980, **Alexandra Park** at Wood Green was dominated by Alexandra Palace, built in 1873. It served in turn as a concert hall, exhibition centre and television studio. The world's first television service began there in 1936.

The palace is being rebuilt as a major leisure, art, conference and exhibition centre. Meanwhile, Alexandra Pavilion, a massive temporary structure near by, fulfils these roles. The grounds include a children's zoo, play park and a ski slope.

Palace of glass

South London had its own "palace" in 1851, when the huge glass-and-steel **Crystal Palace** was moved from the Great Exhibition site in Hyde Park to Sydenham. The building was the work of Joseph Paxton (1801-65), and for 85 years it towered above spacious parkland set with ornamental lakes, gardens and trees. The palace was destroyed by fire in 1936 and the grounds fell into disrepair, but in 1952 the park was revitalised when it was designated as the site for a National Sports Centre.

Several parks have been made from the grounds and gardens of once-private houses. Some, like **Gunnersbury Park** and **Osterley Park**, were still in private hands well into the 20th century – Gunnersbury was opened to the public in 1925, and Osterley became National Trust property in 1949.

Stately gardens

Syon Park Gardens belong to the Duke of Northumberland, who opened both house and grounds to the public in 1969. The 48 acres of gardens were originally laid out by the landscape gardener "Capability" Brown (1715-83).

Hurlingham House near Putney Bridge was the 18th-century home of Dr Cadogan, physician to the London Foundling Hospital in 1754. Part of the estate later became polo grounds, in use until 1939. The then London County Council acquired these in 1952, and later opened them to the public as **Hurlingham Park**. The house and remaining grounds, now the Hurlingham Club, are private.

WATER TAXI *Converted narrow-boats on the Regent's Canal give an unusual view of London Zoo. The giant aviary was designed by Lord Snowdon. It stands 80ft high, and visitors can walk through it on an elevated walkway.*

One of London's earliest riverside parks was **Ranelagh Gardens**, opened in 1742. The gardens were part of the home of Richard, Earl of Ranelagh who died in 1712.

In Georgian times Ranelagh Gardens were the scene of boisterous entertainments, much to the annoyance of people at the nearby Royal Hospital, Chelsea, and were closed in 1805. They now belong to the hospital and are open to the public.

A botanical laboratory

Near the Royal Hospital, on Chelsea Embankment, is the **Physic Garden**. It was founded in 1673 by the Worshipful Society of Apothecaries as a botanical laboratory; the seeds that founded America's cotton industry were sent from the Physic Garden in 1732. The garden is not open to the public.

Kensington's **Holland Park** was the site of a great Jacobean manor, which was almost totally destroyed by bombing in the Second World War. The house belonged to the Earls of Holland, and from 1874 the Earls of Ilchester. It was acquired by the London County Council after the war. The remains of the manor were partly restored and are used as dormitories by the nearby George VI Youth Hostel for students of all nations.

Beside the house is a Dutch garden, laid out in 1812. Avenues of lime trees cross the park, and peacocks parade on the lawns. Open-air concerts are held in front of the house during the summer.

Statues and fountains

London's squares were built by the 17th and 18th-century developers, who erected fine houses and gave their residents a view of lawns and trees in the centre. Today, many of the houses are occupied by businesses and embassies, and the gardens are tiny atolls in a sea of swarming traffic.

Each square is different in character: **Berkeley Square** has giant plane trees and a Georgian shelter, which

GARDEN ORNAMENT
The Pagoda in Kew Gardens is purely ornamental. It was built by William Chambers in 1761 for Princess Augusta, who founded the botanical gardens at Kew.

CITIZENS' FOREST *Epping Forest belongs to the City of London, and Londoners have enjoyed its peaceful glades for more than 100 years.*

conceals a water tank; a statue of President F. D. Roosevelt stands opposite the American Embassy in **Grosvenor Square**; in **Belgrave Square** a dozen or so embassies surround dignified gardens.

Leicester Square is brash and noisy, even though traffic is now banned from its centre. But there are seats and flower beds among the plane trees – and a statue of Shakespeare, looking a little bewildered in this world of cinemas and discotheques. A few minutes' walk away is **Trafalgar Square**, its paved expanse carpeted by pigeons, or sometimes by the wind-blown spray from the two giant fountains.

The City of London has no parks within its square mile. Instead, open spaces have been created wherever possible amid the jungle of tall buildings. The churchyard of St Botolph's Church, Aldersgate, is now a leafy garden. Workers from the nearby Post Office building have made it their lunchtime haven, and it has become known as **Postman's Park**. In **Finsbury Circus** is a garden which has the only bowling-green in the City.

No place for adults

There are gardens just outside the City, on the Embankment just beyond the Temple and in Lincoln's Inn Fields where bands play in the summer. And no more than a mile from the City boundary is a park which no man, or woman, may enter unless accompanied by a child. This no-grown-ups-land is **Coram's Fields** in Guilford Street, on the site of the old Foundling Hospital built in the 1740s by Thomas Coram (1668-1751). The playground was opened in 1936 and includes tennis courts and play equipment for the under tens.

Just north of the City, in City Road, is **Bunhill Fields**, the burial ground of Nonconformists from 1665 until 1853. It is said to take its name from Bone Hill, so called because bones from the charnel-house of St Paul's were deposited there in the 16th century. Among the tombs are those of John Bunyan (1628-88), William Blake (1757-1827) and Daniel Defoe (1661-1731).

Susanna Wesley (1669-1742), mother of John Wesley, is buried in Bunhill Fields, but her son lies in the graveyard behind the chapel opposite the burial ground. In the Quaker cemetery, now a garden, in Bunhill Row, is the grave of George Fox (1624-91), the founder of the Society of Friends.

The City's playgrounds

The City's biggest playgrounds are the 7,000 acres of commons, woods and parks, most of which the City Corporation acquired at the end of the 19th century "for the recreation and enjoyment of the public". The largest is **Epping Forest** on the borders of Essex. It is 13 miles long, yet nowhere more than 2 miles wide. Elizabeth I hunted there; her **Tudor Hunting Lodge** at Chingford is now a museum of the forest's history.

Westward, near Slough, is **Burnham Beeches**. As its name implies, the forest is noted for its beech trees, which look their best in spring and autumn. And in Surrey, four tracts of open land combine to make up the 430 acres of **Coulsdon Commons**. **Highgate Wood**, **Queen's Park**, **Kilburn**, **West Ham Park** and **West Wickham Park** are also owned by the City of London. Together they make a giant contribution to the wealth of open spaces that make London the biggest country town in the world.

THE RIVER THAMES

London's highway to the sea

London owes its existence to the River Thames. The stone for the Roman city came up the river in barges; the Saxons built quays; and over the centuries the city became a port – the largest in the world by the 19th century. The river became a highway, and a setting for pageantry. Watermen plied between its banks, and royalty and City dignitaries sailed in ornate barges to attend state occasions. The railways ended the river's role as the main local highway, and gradually the docks spread down the river, leaving the upper reaches largely to pleasure boats and yachtsmen who can now sail on the river in safety.

A vessel sailing up the Thames from the estuary reaches the outskirts of London at Crayford Ness, a small promontory on the south bank. Here the river bends to the left, leaving behind the flat Aveley Marshes on the north bank where the bones of a mammoth, now in the Natural History Museum, were found.

Beyond the industrial sprawl of Erith the river bends again and enters Erith Reach, and another mammoth comes into view – the vast complex of the Ford Motor Company at Dagenham which dominates the north-bank waterfront.

Across the river the marshes return, at Erith and Plumstead, where the new town of Thamesmead is rising from the flat landscape.

Barking Power Station provides a landmark, and just up river is the Northern Outfall Sewer. Its pumping station at **Abbey Mills** is a model of Victorian industrial architecture. Sir Joseph Bazalgette (1819-91) built it in 1868 – a Gothic temple to Hygeia, the Greek goddess of health, adorned

with decorative cast-iron work. The original beam-engines have been removed, but visitors wishing to study the building can now do so by prior arrangement with the Metropolitan Public Health Division of the Thames Water Authority.

Worst disaster

Where the river bends left at the start of Gallions Reach there occurred the worst disaster on British inland waters. In 1878 the paddle-steamer *Princess Alice* was cut in two by a collier heading down river. The paddle-steamer sank in less than five minutes and more than 600 people died. The tragedy led to the tightening up of navigation rules on the river.

Increasingly high tides have threatened London in recent years, and at Woolwich a flood barrier is being built. The barrier consists of massive steel gates, 200 ft wide and 66 ft deep and weighing 3,300 tons, that will rise from the river bed when tidal floodwaters threaten.

Woolwich is also the crossing point for the Free Ferry, which dates from the 14th century. Its modern diesel-powered vessels can each carry 200 tons of vehicles and 1,000 passengers.

During the two World Wars, thousands of workers used the ferry to get to the nearby **Royal Arsenal**, which grew from the Brass Gun Foundry built in 1716. The Victorians enlarged it to cover 1,200 acres. The arsenal closed in 1963, and the land is being incorporated in Thamesmead.

At one time Woolwich was also a naval establishment. The Royal Naval Dockyard was founded there in the 16th century, and flourished during the reign of Henry VIII. It was closed in 1869.

On the opposite bank wharves and warehouses fringe three huge docks – the Royal Albert, Royal Victoria and King George V. The **Royal Victoria Dock** was built in 1850-5 and was the first in Britain to have hydraulically operated gates. The mile-long **Royal Albert Dock** followed in 1880, and the 38 ft deep **King George V Dock** was opened in 1921.

Isle of Dogs

Looping around a thumb of land, the river takes in the waters of the River Lea, flowing from the north, before entering Blackwall Reach. Here the Blackwall Tunnel burrows beneath the river. The **India Docks** and the **Millwall Docks**, a complex built in the 19th century on marshland, cut across a bulge of land known as the Isle of Dogs. These five docks have closed, although ships enter them occasionally.

At the southern tip of the isle is a small park called **Island Gardens**. It was opened in 1895, and from it can be seen one of London's finest vistas – the stately waterfront of Greenwich on the other side of the river.

The Tudors had a palace at Greenwich, Henry VIII was born there as were his daughters Mary and Elizabeth. James I had a new house built in 1616 for his queen, Anne of Denmark, and entrusted the work to Inigo Jones (1573-1652). Jones designed the house in the style of the Italian architect Palladio (1508-80), and the elegant white-stone building

SILENT GUNS *HMS* Belfast *lies in retirement in the Pool of London. At one time this part of the river teemed with cargo ships, making their way to and from the busy wharves through the raised arms of Tower Bridge.*

ROYAL NAVAL COLLEGE *The lines of Sir Christopher Wren's Greenwich masterpiece can be appreciated best from across the river.*

became known as the **Queen's House**. East and west wings were added in 1807, and in 1937 it became part of the National Maritime Museum.

In 1694 Sir Christopher Wren designed a **Royal Hospital for Seamen** at Greenwich. It stands at the water's edge, a glistening-white group of buildings in the Classical style with two domed towers. In 1873 the hospital was transformed into the Royal Naval College. Wren's Painted Hall forms a pair with the chapel, and was completed in 1704. The ceilings and upper walls were painted in Baroque style by James Thornhill (1675-1734). In 1805 the hall was the setting for the lying in state of Admiral Lord Nelson before his burial in St Paul's Cathedral.

Meridian line

Wren also built the **Old Royal Observatory** in Greenwich Park on the instructions of Charles II for "the finding out of the longitude of places for perfecting navigation and astronomy".

The Greenwich Meridian dividing the Eastern and Western Hemispheres (longitude 0°) runs through the observatory and is marked by a brass plate outside the Meridian Building. The building contains a collection of telescopes and other instruments; the Royal Observatory is now at Herstmonceux in Sussex.

Flamsteed House, near the Meridian Building, was the home of the first Astronomer Royal, John Flamsteed (1646-1719). A red ball on the Meridian Building roof is lowered from the top of its mast at 1300 hours Greenwich Mean Time each day as a time check for vessels on the Thames.

A dry dock near Greenwich Pier contains the clipper ship *Cutty Sark*, built in 1869; below decks is a collection of ships' figureheads. Close by is the yacht *Gipsy Moth IV* in which Sir Francis Chichester sailed singlehanded around the world.

The river bends sharply northwards after Greenwich, with the now-closed Surrey Commercial Docks to the west and the Millwall foreshore to the east. Here, Isambard Kingdom Brunel built his giant steamship *Great Eastern*; the stumps of the launching slipway can still be seen at low tide.

At Rotherhithe the river twists back to its east-west course and is underpassed by a road tunnel opened in 1908. Another tunnel, linking Rotherhithe with Wapping on the north bank, was built by Marc Brunel and his son Isambard. Called the Thames Tunnel it took 18 years to build and, when opened in 1843, was the world's first underwater pedestrian tunnel. It is now part of London's underground railway system.

On both sides of the river ancient taverns stand close to the waterfront. Several date from the 16th, 17th and 18th centuries, including the **Prospect of Whitby** in Wapping Wall, **The Grapes** in Narrow Street, the **Mayflower** in Rotherhithe Street and **The Gun** in Coldharbour.

Pool of London

From Wapping to Southwark the river straightens for some 2 miles, a stretch known as the Pool of London. Disused warehouses, derelict cranes and deserted wharves line the banks, for most of the trade handled by this once-busy section of the river has moved downstream to Tilbury.

On the north bank one disused dock has now taken on a new guise. It is **St Katharine Dock**, built in 1828 by Thomas Telford (1757-1834) and now developed as the World Trade Centre, incorporating a marina, residential area and exhibition centre. One warehouse has been converted to luxury flats above a shopping arcade and another timber-framed warehouse dating from the 18th century is now an inn. The two basins throng with private yachts and cabin cruisers, and one part has historic ships including the *Discovery*, Captain R. F. Scott's 1901-4 polar-expedition vessel, Thames sailing barges and a lightship.

Tower Bridge is London's river gateway. It was built in 1894 by Sir John Wolfe-Barry (1836-1918), and between its Gothic towers the roadway is carried on two bascules which lift to allow ships to pass through, a

IVORY HOUSE *The old ivory warehouse in St Katharine Dock makes a fitting background for a Thames sailing barge preserved in the yacht marina.*

sight which is becoming rarer as fewer ships use the Pool of London. Beside the bridge is the **Tower of London**, built by William the Conqueror just outside the city walls to overawe the citizens of London. Beside the Tower a row of 6-pounder guns points across the river. The guns were captured from the French at Waterloo. In their sights, beside the south bank, lies the Second World War cruiser HMS *Belfast*, now a naval museum.

Traitors' heads

The Pool of London ends at **London Bridge**. Until 1749, when the first Westminster Bridge was built, London Bridge was the only bridge over the river in London. The Saxons certainly had a wooden structure there, and there was a Roman bridge nearby. In 805 the Danes destroyed the bridge. Rebuilt, it collapsed in 1091 and a replacement burned down in 1136. Between 1176 and 1203 a stone bridge was built – the first in Europe since Roman times – and the rhyme "London Bridge is falling down" originates from this period.

It was a remarkable achievement – 905 ft long and supported on 19 piers. Shops, houses and a chapel were built on the bridge. Less attractive adornments were the heads of traitors impaled on the spikes above the fortified

SWAN UPPING *Marking the swans on the Thames is a tradition dating from the Middle Ages, when the birds were a table delicacy.*

gates, a grisly custom that continued until the 17th century.

In 1831 the medieval bridge was demolished and replaced by a granite, five-arched bridge designed by John Rennie the Elder (1761-1821). Rennie's London Bridge stood for nearly 150 years, but by 1973 it could not meet the demands of modern traffic.

A new bridge was designed by the City Engineer, Harold Knox King. It was built of concrete with an elegant flat-arched profile carried on slender piers. Meanwhile, an American company bought the old bridge and shipped it stone by stone to Lake Havasu City, Arizona.

River traditions

London Bridge is the starting point for one of London's traditional sporting events – the Doggett's Coat and Badge Race. The race is a single sculls event for young Thames watermen and lightermen who race from London Bridge to Chelsea Bridge. The race was founded in 1716 by a London theatre manager, Thomas Doggett, to mark the second anniversary of George I's accession. The winner receives an orange-coloured coat, and a silver arm badge embossed with the white horse of Hanover.

The race is started by the Barge Master of the Fishmongers Company. Two other City Livery Companies with ties to the river are the Vintners and Dyers who share the ownership of swans on the river with the Queen. Each July the Companies' Swanmasters go out in boats to take part in **Swan Upping** – marking the birds to identify ownership. The birds are marked by cutting nicks in their bills – one nick for the Dyers, two for the Vintners. The Queen's birds are left unmarked.

Rose window

Close to London Bridge is one of London's oldest buildings. The four pinnacles of the 15th-century tower of **Southwark Cathedral** can be seen from the river, and in nearby Clink Street, named after the prison that once stood there, are the remains of the 12th-century Palace of the Bishops of Winchester. A 14th-century rose window high in a gable still has its delicate tracery intact.

Road traffic crosses the river on **Southwark Bridge**, and a little further upstream a railway bridge carries the Southern Region into Blackfriars Station. Then comes Blackfriars Bridge, another road crossing. From its northern end the Victoria Embankment runs directly alongside the river to Westminster Bridge. The embankment was completed in 1870 to the design of Sir Joseph Bazalgette whose memorial near the foot of Northumberland Avenue bears the inscription *Flumini vincula posuit* – He put chains on the river.

Floating Livery Hall

Three ships are moored at the Victoria Embankment. *President* and *Chrysanthemum* are First World War sloops used by the London division of the Royal Naval Reserve. The *Wellington* is the floating Livery Hall of the Master Mariners Company.

Sir Giles Scott's elegant **Waterloo Bridge**, built in 1945, heralds the modern complex of the **South Bank Arts Centre** – Festival Hall, Hayward Gallery, National Film Theatre and the National Theatre. Their strikingly modern lines contrast with the demure Victorian embankment across the water, with its dolphin-entwined lamp-posts and the pink-granite finger of **Cleopatra's Needle** poking up from the trees. The 69½ ft tall obelisk was erected at Heliopolis in Egypt in about 1500 BC, and came to Britain as a gift from that country in 1878.

Gothic frontage

Trains thunder across **Hungerford Bridge**, where the river bends again and gardens and car parks on the south bank give way to the curved front of **County Hall**, headquarters of the Greater London Council. But this short stretch of river is commanded by the Gothic frontage of the Palace of Westminster, the **Houses of Parliament**, into which the simple lines of **Westminster Bridge** seem to blend.

Lambeth Bridge, steel-built and painted brown, springs from the south bank just beyond **Lambeth Palace**, official residence of the Archbishops of Canterbury since the 12th century. Then, suddenly, old London has passed by for a while, and concrete and glass take over again.

RIVERSIDE HOMES *Houseboats at the water's edge on Chelsea Reach. The pylons of Albert Bridge rise above the iron arches of Battersea Bridge.*

Vauxhall Bridge, with its sculptures of London scenes, and **Chelsea Bridge**, one of three suspension bridges on the river, have between them the new Covent Garden Market at Nine Elms and Battersea Power Station, both on the south bank. Then antiquity returns with the **Royal Hospital**, lying behind the **Chelsea Embankment**.

Charles II founded the hospital in 1682, as a home for veteran soldiers. The designer was Sir Christopher Wren.

On the opposite bank the lawns and trees of **Battersea Park** run all the way to Albert Bridge, the second of the Thames suspension bridges. In the park is the Festival Pleasure Garden, which was part of the 1951 Festival of Britain.

Battersea, Wandsworth and Putney bridges straddle the river as it swings in a broad loop, with the 18th-century **Hurlingham House** standing in Hurlingham Park at the apex of the bend.

Just before the tightly curving Chiswick Reach, Sir Joseph Bazalgette's **Hammersmith Bridge** of 1887 hangs by its suspension cables from gilded iron pylons topped with elaborate turrets. Chiswick lies within another loop of the river, and here is some of the most picturesque scenery on London's river. Georgian houses stand in **Chiswick Mall** and **Strand on the Green**, and between them is **Chiswick House**. It was built in 1725 for Lord Burlington, an admirer of the Italian architect Palladio, and is modelled on the Villa Capra near Vicenza in Italy.

Longest arch

Chiswick Bridge, built in 1933, has the longest concrete arch of any bridge on the Thames. Its central span measures 150 ft.

Once again the river swings south, with **Kew Gardens** on the Surrey side and **Syon Park** on the Middlesex

STILL LIFE *The figures clinging to a lamp-post in Cheyne Walk, Chelsea, were captured in cast-iron nearly a century ago.*

BRIDGE SCULPTURE *The model of St Paul's Cathedral on Vauxhall Bridge is called "Little St Paul's on the water" by Thames watermen.*

STRAND ON THE GREEN *A peaceful stretch of the river at Chiswick, but the houses have raised doorways to guard against high tides.*

side. Kew Bridge is officially named King Edward VII Bridge, after the monarch who opened it in 1903. Sir John Wolfe-Barry designed it – a fine stone structure with three spans.

Where Kew ends, Richmond begins. **Richmond Park** was enclosed in 1637 by Charles I and stocked with deer for hunting. Shooting of deer in the park stopped in 1904, and now the herds roam freely and safely.

Twickenham Bridge takes a busy main road across the river here, but Richmond itself is served by one of the most attractive of all London's bridges. **Richmond Bridge** spans the river in five graceful arches constructed of stone, and was built by James Paine (1725-89) in 1774-7.

Island tea dances

Approaching Twickenham, the river passes **Marble Hill House**, built by George II for his mistress Henrietta Howard in the 1720s. Near by are York House, built about 1700, and the Octagon built by James Gibbs (1682-1754), whose other works include St Martin-in-the-Fields in Trafalgar Square.

The river divides at Twickenham, around **Eel Pie Island** where Edwardians gathered at the hotel for its tea

dances. Opposite the island is St Mary's Church – designed by John James (died 1746) in 1714 – where the poet Alexander Pope (1688-1744) lies buried.

On the Surrey bank the 17th-century **Ham House** contains a collection of period furniture.

At Teddington the river ceases to be tidal. Here the water roars impressively over a weir, which can be crossed by a footbridge. **Teddington Lock** is the largest on the Thames, 650 ft long and 25 ft wide, able to accommodate a tug and six barges.

Last stretch

The Thames runs southwards again, and then twists to the north in a broad curve that cradles **Hampton Court** in its crook. The waterside affords the best view of the palace, built by Cardinal Wolsey in the 16th century but more strongly associated with Henry VIII who made it his own after the downfall of the cardinal.

The last stretch of the Thames within the Greater London boundaries runs past Hampton Green and then Bushey Park, with its 17th-century mansion, now the offices of the National Physical Laboratory. Then, characteristically, the river

bends again to meander on through fields and valleys to its source at Thames Head in Gloucestershire.

PLACES TO SEE

Abbey Mills Pumping Station **(2Bb)**, Abbey Lane, Stratford, E15.
Chiswick House **(1Da)**, Burlington Lane, Chiswick.
Cutty Sark **(4Be)**, Greenwich Pier.
HMS *Discovery* **(6Fd)**, Maritime Trust National Collection of Historic Ships, St Katharine Dock, E1.
Ham House **(3Cd)**, Riverside, Richmond.
Hampton Court Palace **(3Cc)**, Riverside, Hampton Court.
Kew Gardens **(3De)**, Kew Bridge Road, Kew.
Lambeth Palace **(6Cb)** (Great Hall), Lambeth Palace Road, Lambeth.
Marble Hill House **(3Cd)**, Riverside, Twickenham.
Old Royal Observatory **(4Be)**, Greenwich Park, Greenwich.
Royal Naval College **(4Be)**, Riverside, Greenwich.
Syon House **(1Ca)**, Syon Park, Brentford.
Events University Boat Race, Putney to Mortlake (Mar.).
Chelsea Flower Show, grounds of Royal Hospital, Chelsea (May).
Swan Upping, on the river (July).
Doggett's Coat and Badge Race, London Bridge to Chelsea Bridge (July).

SHOPS AND MARKETS

Where to go for the best, the bargain and the bizarre

London's multitude of shops caters for every human need. But London is set apart from other shopping centres – by the specialists of the bespoke trades whose skills attract people from all parts of the world. Their craftsmen will make virtually anything to the customer's specification – from a dinner service in gold plate to an umbrella. The made-to-measure specialists include shoemakers, hatters, tailors and even gunsmiths, who will fit a gun to a customer, just as a tailor fits a suit.

Antiques

The world trade in antiques is centred in London. Finely restored furniture can be bought at Mallett or Partridge, both in New Bond Street, W1. Grays Market with Grays Mews, Davies Street, W1, is one of the world's largest antique centres, with some 400 dealers under two roofs. Browse in Mount Street, W1, for English furniture or Oriental pieces. Jellinek and Sampson in Brompton Road, SW3, specialise in pottery, The Map House in Beauchamp Place, SW3, has antique maps and atlases, Keith Harding in Hornsey Road, N7, deals in musical boxes, mechanical singing birds and clocks, and Spink of King Street, SW1, sell coins and works of art. Strike One, Camden Walk, N1, is the place to go for old clocks. Bargain hunt in Chelsea Antiques Market, Kings Road, SW3, and in Portobello Road, W11.

Art dealers

Most galleries are in Mayfair and St James's. Agnew's and Colnaghi's, both in Old Bond Street, W1, deal in old masters. The Fine Art Society, New Bond Street, W1, handle 19th and 20th-century British paintings and water-colours. Contemporary art dealers include Brook Street Gallery, Bruton Place, W1; Crane Kalman, Brompton Road, SW3; Lefevre, Bruton Street, W1; and Marlborough Fine Art, Albemarle Street, W1.

Auctions

Sales are held daily at Sotheby's, New Bond Street, W1, the world's oldest auctioneers, founded in 1744. Glass, books, silver, art and furniture are sold. Christie's, King Street, SW1, specialise in fine art. Phillips, Blenheim Street, W1, have a monthly wine sale. Bonham's Chelsea Galleries, Lots Road, SW10, sell inexpensive furnishings every Tuesday.

Books

Foyle's, with 4 million volumes, is at the heart of London's book trade in Charing Cross Road, WC2. There are bargains near by at second-hand and paperback dealers. Hatchard's, in Piccadilly, W1, opened in 1767 and is London's oldest bookshop. Dillon's, Malet Street, W1, deal in textbooks, and Quaritch, Lower John Street, W1, in antique books and first edi-

tions. Best for youngsters is the Children's Book Centre, Kensington High Street, W8.

Carpets

Fine Wilton and Axminster carpets are stocked at Afia, Baker Street, W1. London's largest selection of plain carpets is at Resista Carpets, Fulham Road, SW6. Liberty's, in Regent Street, W1, specialise in Oriental rugs and carpets, but the biggest store of Oriental carpets is at The International Oriental Carpet Centre in Highbury Road, NW5, a bonded warehouse open by appointment only. Phone 01-267 3346 to be put in touch with a broker.

China and glass

Most department stores stock china and glass. In Regent Street, W1, are the specialist shops, Lawleys; Rosenthal, who sell their own china; and Gered, who deal in Wedgwood. Modern designs are stocked at Habitat, King's Road, SW10, and the Reject China Shop, Beauchamp Place, SW1, handle seconds. Thomas Goode, South Audley Street, W1, sell china and crystal. Their priceless Minton elephants flanking the doorway were produced for their display at the Paris Exposition of 1889. Howard Phillips, Henrietta Place, W1, is a treasure house for collectors of old glass.

DRESSING UP *A bizarre range of animal costumes can be hired from The Theatre-Zoo, 28 New Row, WC2.*

SPARKLING DISPLAY *Antique silver of every type fills Shapland's shop window in High Holborn.*

QUIET ELEGANCE *The shops in Woburn Walk, WC1, a pedestrian backwater behind St Pancras Church, which have changed very little since they were built in 1822.*

STREET MARKETS

Early start – antique dealers in the New Caledonian Market start trading before daybreak in the winter.

London's market stalls were there long before the first shop. Their history is enshrined in Cheapside – from the Saxon *céap* (market) – once the city's main market place. Today there are dozens of markets in all parts of the capital. Most of them are general markets selling everything from clothing to vegetables, and catering for local shoppers. However, there are some specialist markets – particularly for antiques. These are listed below with a few of the larger general markets.

Camden Passage, N1, antiques, Wed. and Sat. New Caledonian Market, Tower Bridge Road, SE1, antiques, Fri. 7 a.m. to 1 p.m. Petticoat Lane (Middlesex Street), E1, everything, Sun. morning. Portobello Road, W11, antiques, daily. Leather Lane, Holborn, EC1, everything, Mon. to Sat. lunchtimes.

Clothing

London has an almost endless number of shops selling clothing. Many tend to be located together in the following streets. **Women's clothing:** Beauchamp Place, SW3; Brompton Road, SW1; Kensington High Street, W8; King's Road, SW3; Knightsbridge, SW1; New Bond Street, W1; Oxford Street, W1; Regent Street, W1; Sloane Street, SW1; South Molton Street, W1. **Men's clothing:** Carnaby Street, W1; Jermyn Street, SW1; King's Road, SW3; New Bond Street, W1; Old Bond Street, W1; Oxford Street, W1; Piccadilly, W1; Regent Street, W1; Savile Row, W1; St James's Street, SW1. **Children's clothing:** A range of good-value children's clothes is available at Marks and Spencer and Mothercare, Oxford Street, W1, and the big department stores. Trendy styles are stocked at Meeny's, and Small Wonder, in Kings Road, SW3; Zero Four, South Molton Street, W1, has hand-knitted clothes. Rowes, New Bond Street, W1, are tailors to the royal children.

Food

London's specialist shops stock rare foods from all parts of the world. Delicacies, exotic foods and magnificent hampers are available at Fortnum and Mason, the royal grocers in Piccadilly, W1. The meat department at Harrods, Knightsbridge, SW1, is unrivalled, and the store stocks 500 cheeses. Ceres in Portobello Road, W11, sell 100% wholewheat bread. Cranks, Marshall Street, W1, has a wide range of health foods. Justin de Blank, Elizabeth Street, SW1, stock high-quality but expensive French cheeses. Soho is crammed with delicatessens: Lina, Brewer Street, W1, for salamis, fresh ravioli and pasta. Excellent vegetables sell cheaply each day at Berwick Street Market, W1. John Baily, Mount Street, W1, are England's oldest poulterers. All their birds are free range and unfrozen. Richards, Brewer Street, is a traditional fishmonger. John Lane, Walkers Court, Berwick Street, W1, sell frogs' legs, snails, haggis and meats. Selfridges, Oxford Street, W1, stock haggis, and Prestat, South Molton Street, W1, chocolate truffles.

Furniture and furnishings

The traditional centre of the furniture trade is Tottenham Court Road, W1, where Habitat, Heal's, and Maple & Co., Ltd are all located. Furnishers also group together in King's Road, Chelsea, SW3. Stores include the Designers' Guild and Osborne and Little.

Guns

Made-to-measure guns can be ordered at Holland and Holland, Bruton Street, W1. James Purdey and Sons, of South Audley Street, W1, hand-build about 100 guns a year.

Hi-fi, radio and video

Enthusiasts can browse among specialist shops in Tottenham Court Road, W1. Lion House Hi-Fi is ideal for do-it-yourself fans, Laskys offer a wide choice. The Video Palace, Kensington High Street, W8, has a large selection.

Jewellery

The gem centre of London is Hatton Garden, EC1, but jewellery shops are scattered throughout the city. Cartier, New Bond Street, W1, is expensive and exclusive. Andrew Grima, Jermyn Street, SW1, makes pieces for the Royal Family. S. J. Phillips, New Bond Street, stock fine antiques.

Left-handed shop

Scissors, knives, potato peelers, can openers and irons are sold at Anything Left Handed, Beak Street, W1.

Music and musical instruments

Chappell & Co., Ltd (founded in 1811) in New Bond Street, W1, sell everything musical except records.

Boosey & Hawkes Ltd (founded 1930) in Regent Street, W1, sell sheet music and specialise in brass instruments; they also have a large record library. J. & A. Beare, Broadwick Street, W1, are violin dealers. Paxman Ltd, of Long Acre, WC2, make French horns. T. W. Howarth & Co., Chiltern Street, W1, sell flutes, and the Flutemakers Guild, Shacklewell Road, N16, both make and sell them.

Shoes

John Lobb, St James's Street, SW1, made Queen Victoria's shoes. Lobb's hand-made shoes, designed on personal lasts, take three months to finish and are priced accordingly.

Silver

The London Silver Vaults Ltd in Chancery Lane, WC2, accommodate dozens of dealers in antique and modern silver in underground strongrooms. There are other silver dealers in Chancery Lane, in nearby Hatton Garden, EC1, and other streets.

Sports goods

Lillywhites Ltd, of Piccadilly Circus, W1, stock clothing and equipment for every type of game and sport from archery to yachting. Specialist shops include: Arthur Beale, 194 Shaftesbury Avenue, WC2, yacht chandlers. Hardy Bros Ltd, 61 Pall Mall, SW1, fishing tackle. Blacks Camping and Leisure, 53 Rathbone Place, W1, camping and sports goods.

Toys

The six floors of Hamleys, Regent Street, W1, are filled with games, toys, models and sports kit. Historic and traditional toys can be seen and bought at Pollock's Toy Museum, Scala Street, W1. James Galt, Great Marlborough Street, W1, specialise in educational toys such as climbing frames and bricks.

Wines

The trade is centred on St James's. Port and claret can be bought at Berry Bros, and Rudd's in St James's Street, SW1, in a panelled office unchanged since 1730. Christopher and Co., Ormond Yard, SW1, are London's oldest wine merchants. Loeb, Jermyn Street, W1, specialise in German wines.

KEEPING DRY W. E. Gladstone shopped at James Smith, New Oxford Street, WC1, Europe's biggest and oldest umbrella and stick shop. You can still buy a swordstick.

ENTERTAINMENT

Lively London – a town for all seasons

ONE-MAN BAND *An enterprising street busker, ready to entertain the theatre queues.*

Dr Johnson said, "there is in London all that life can afford". If he were alive today the great conversationalist would probably feel that in London there is more than life can afford, so enormous and varied is the range of entertainment available. From a raucous sing-song in a smoke-laden pub to the glitter of a first night at the opera, there is always something going on.

There are more than 50 theatres in London, mostly concentrated in a part of the West End that has become known as "theatreland". They range in size from the tiny May Fair, seating 310, to the giant Coliseum with its capacity of 2,352. The oldest is Drury Lane, which opened as the Theatre Royal in 1663, although the present building dates from 1812. The newest is the National Theatre, opened in 1976 and combining three theatres under one roof – the Olivier, Lyttelton and Cottesloe.

Productions are diverse enough to suit all tastes: opera and ballet at the Coliseum and Covent Garden; musicals at Drury Lane and the Palace; variety at the Palladium; Shakespeare at the Old Vic. Revues are a London stage tradition, some lavishly produced in large theatres like the Victoria Palace and the Piccadilly, others more modest affairs in the intimate atmospheres of the May Fair, Savoy and Fortune.

Changing roles

Other London theatres have changed their roles, but still offer entertainment. For example, the old Hippodrome, in Cranbourn Street, is now the Talk of the Town, a theatre-restaurant where dinner and a stage show are offered. The Lyceum, just off the Strand, has been a dance hall since the Second World War.

One building whose designer never envisaged it as a place of entertainment is the Round House in Chalk Farm Road, NW1. It was built as an engine shed in 1847, and in 1967 was reconstructed as an arts centre. New works and unconventional productions of established works are featured.

Cinema clubs

The National Film Theatre on the South Bank, and the Institute of Contemporary Arts in The Mall feature vintage, foreign and specialist films. Both are cinema clubs, and membership can be obtained at the door, or from The British Film Institute, 81 Dean Street, W1, and the ICA, Nash House, The Mall, SW1.

Musical highlight

London's two principal concert halls, the Royal Albert Hall and the Royal Festival Hall, hold regular concerts which include performances by symphony orchestras, brass bands and ballet companies. One musical highlight is the season of Promenade Concerts at the Albert Hall during July, August and September. Performances are by the BBC Symphony Orchestra and visiting orchestras. The last night of the "Proms" is traditionally a festive occasion.

Solo recitals and chamber-music concerts are held at the Wigmore Hall, Queen Elizabeth Hall and Purcell Room. The restored 18th-century St John's Church in Smith Square, SW1, is also a setting for small orchestral concerts and recitals.

Two large concert halls in the suburbs are the Fairfield Halls at Croydon, and the Wembley International Conference Centre.

Rock and jazz

The main venue for rock and "pop" concerts is the Rainbow Theatre at Finsbury Park. Jazz clubs come and go, but there are three well-established clubs – the 100 Club at 100 Oxford Street, W1, Ronnie Scott's Club in Frith Street, W1, and the Bull's Head public house at Barnes. The Jazz Centre Society organises concerts, particularly at the Shaw Theatre where the Camden Jazz Festival is held in March.

Annual events

From January to December the London entertainment calendar is sprinkled with events. In January, boating enthusiasts flock to the Boat Show at Earls Court, where the indoor swimming-pool becomes a miniature harbour displaying the latest in yachts and cabin cruisers.

February brings the dog-breeding world to Earls Court and Crufts Show, the premier event in the canine year. In March the Ideal Home Exhibition at Earls Court displays everything from tin-openers to new houses.

Also in March, antique collectors gather at the Chelsea Antiques Fair in the Old Town Hall in King's Road. In May, Chelsea puts on its Flower Show at the Royal Hospital.

Earls Court stages the Royal Tournament in July, a colourful display by the three Services with events such as the Navy's field-gun competition and the musical ride of the Royal Horse Artillery.

Horses also take the stage in July at the Royal International Horse Show at the Wembley Arena.

Sounding brass and galloping hooves thrill their respective devotees in October, when brass bands compete for the National Championship at the Albert Hall and the horses return to Wembley for the Horse of the Year Show.

As Christmas approaches, the pantomime season starts, and at Wembley pantomime on ice provides a lavish spectacle.

ARTS CENTRE *The National Theatre is the latest addition to the South Bank complex, joining the Royal Festival Hall and the National Film Theatre.*

Information

The daily press gives details of events taking place in and around London. Further information, and where to obtain tickets, can be had from the British Tourist Authority (Tel. 499 9325) or the London Tourist Board (Tel. 730 0791). When dialling from outside London, prefix telephone numbers with 01.

West End theatres and concert halls

33 **Adelphi:** 836 7611
26 **Albany:** 836 3878
19 **Aldwych:** 836 6404
11 **Ambassadors:** 836 1171
21 **Apollo:** 437 2663
45 **Arts Theatre:** 836 2132
3 **Astoria:** 437 6239/437 5757/734 4291
13 **Cambridge:** 836 6056
32 **Coliseum:** 240 5258
37 **Comedy:** 930 2578
28 **Criterion:** 930 3216
17 **Duchess:** 836 8243
31 **Duke of York's:** 836 5122
15 **Fortune:** 836 2238
30 **Garrick:** 836 4601
22 **Globe:** 437 1592
38 **Haymarket:** 930 9832
39 **Her Majesty's:** 930 6606
20 **Lyric Theatre:** 437 3686
36 **May Fair:** 629 3036
43 **National Theatre** (Olivier, Lyttelton, Cottesloe): 928 2252
5 **New London:** 405 0072
10 **Palace:** 437 6834
2 **Palladium:** 437 7373
7 **Phoenix:** 836 8611
27 **Piccadilly:** 437 4506
9 **Prince Edward:** 437 6877
29 **Prince of Wales:** 930 8681
42 **Queen Elizabeth Hall** and **Purcell Room:** 928 3002
23 **Queen's Theatre:** 734 1166
41 **Royal Festival Hall:** 928 3191
14 **Royal Opera House,** Covent Garden: 240 1066

8 **Royalty:** 405 8004
12 **St Martin's:** 836 1443
35 **Savoy:** 836 8888
4 **Shaftesbury:** 836 4255
18 **Strand:** 836 2660
24 **Talk of the Town:** 734 5051
16 **Theatre Royal,** Drury Lane: 836 8108
34 **Vaudeville:** 836 9988
40 **Whitehall:** 930 6692
44 **Windmill Theatre:** 437 6312
25 **Wyndham's:** 836 3028

West End cinemas

6 **ABC 1 & 2,** Shaftesbury Avenue: 836 8861
2 **Academy 1:** 437 2981
2 **Academy 2:** 437 5129
2 **Academy 3:** 437 8819
17 **Centa Cinema:** 437 3561
21 **Cinecenta:** 930 0631
15 **Classic Royal:** 930 6915
18 **Classic Eros:** 437 3839
26 **Classic Moulin Cinema Complex:** 437 1653
1 **Classic:** Oxford Street: 636 0310
7 **Columbia:** 734 5414
3 **Dominion:** 580 9562
11 **Empire:** 437 1234
4 **Essential:** 439 3657
5 **Filmcenta:** 437 4815
12 **Jacey,** Leicester Square: 930 1143
22 **Leicester Square Theatre:** 930 5252
19 **London Pavilion:** 636 1655
27 **National Film Theatre:** 928 3232/3
20 **Odeon,** Haymarket: 930 2738/2771
25 **Odeon,** Leicester Square: 930 6111
16 **Odeon,** St Martin's Lane: 836 0691
23 **Plaza 1, 2, 3 & 4:** 437 1234
13 **Prince Charles:** 437 8181
8 **Rialto:** 437 3488
10 **Ritz:** 437 1234
9 **Scene 1, 2, 3 & 4:** 439 4470
24 **Soho Cinema:** 734 4205
14 **Warner West End:** 439 0791

Theatres, cinemas and halls outside the West End are shown on the London maps, pp. 260-71. Each place can be located by the reference in brackets after its name.

Theatres

Ashcroft – Fairfield Halls (**4Ab**), Croydon: 688 9291
Greenwich (4Be): 858 7755
Hampstead (1Eb): 722 9301
Jeannetta Cochrane (6Ce) Theobalds Road, WC1: 242 7040
Kings Head (2Ab): 226 1916
Mermaid (6Dd): 236 5568
Old Vic (6Cc): 928 7616
Open Space (6Ae) 303/307 Euston Road, NW1: 387 6969
Rainbow Theatre (1Fc): 263 3148
Round House (1Eb): 267 2564
Royal Court (5Eb): 730 1745
Sadler's Wells (2Ab): 837 1672
Theatre Royal, Stratford (**2Bb**): 534 0310
Theatre Upstairs – Royal Court – (**5Eb**): 730 2554
Victoria Palace (5Fc): 834 1317
Westminster (5Fc): 834 0283
Young Vic (6Dc): 928 6363

Cinemas

Biograph (5Fc): 834 1624
Coronet (5Bd): 727 6705
Curzon (5Fd): 499 3737
Gala Royal (5De): 262 2345
Odeon Marble Arch (**5Ee**): 723 2011/2
Paris Pullman (5Cb): 373 5898

Concert Halls and Exhibition Centres

Earls Court (5Bb): 385 1200
Fairfield Halls (4Ab) Croydon: 688 9291
Olympia (5Ac): 603 3344
Royal Albert Hall (5Cc): 589 8212
Wembley Arena (1Dc): 902 1234
Wembley Conference Centre (1Dc): 902 8833
Wigmore Hall (5Fe): 935 2141

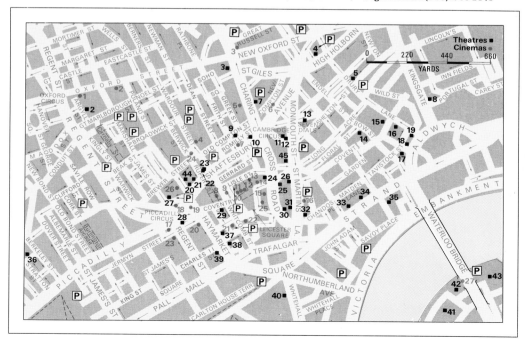

SPORT IN LONDON

The sporting life of the nation's capital

History records that football was played in London in the 12th century. First-class cricket came a little later, in 1719, when the first county match was played at Lamb's Conduit Field, Bloomsbury, between London and Kent. The Greater London Council helps to maintain this tradition in its 47 parks and open spaces, most of which have an area set aside for recreation. Hackney Marsh, for example, has more than 100 football pitches.

London has three major open-air stadiums – White City, Wembley and Crystal Palace – and there are indoor arenas at the Royal Albert Hall, Earls Court and the Wembley Arena. Between them they stage some of the greatest sporting events in Britain, and in the past have been involved with events that made sporting history.

The White City Stadium was built in 1908 as part of the Franco-British Exhibition, and in the same year was the venue for the 4th Modern Olympic Games. It became London's principal athletics stadium and remained so for nearly 60 years, staging international events that made national heroes of men like Sidney Wooderson in the 1930s and Chris Chataway in the 1950s.

In 1927 London's first greyhound meeting was held at the White City, and in the 1930s a speedway track was added. These two sports are the only events now held there regularly; greyhound racing's most important event, the Greyhound Derby, is held there each June.

Cup Final stadium

Wembley Stadium, properly called the Empire Stadium, was opened in 1923. Although part of the large complex housing the British Empire Exhibition of 1923, the stadium was designed specifically as a permanent home for the Football Association Cup Final, which until then had been played at various grounds in the country. The arena was designed to hold 127,000 spectators, but for the first Cup Final held there in 1923 nearly 200,000 people crammed into the stadium.

The match, between Bolton Wanderers and West Ham United, was delayed for 40 minutes because spectators had over-run the pitch, and the game was played with crowds lining the touchline. Since then the accommodation has been limited to 100,000. In 1962 the roofing was extended and Wembley became the largest stadium in Britain in which all the spectators are under cover.

Like the White City, Wembley also became a dog track – the Greyhound St Leger is held there each September – and a speedway circuit. Speedway club racing is no longer featured, but the stadium is sometimes the venue for the World Speedway Rider's Championship.

In 1948, Wembley staged the 14th Olympic Games, and from time to time the central turf has been used for show-jumping, baseball, hockey, hurling and championship boxing tournaments. But Wembley's principal function is still as a football stadium – the home of the FA Cup Final and England's home ground in international matches. Since 1929 it has also been the venue for the Rugby League Challenge Cup Final.

All-weather track

Athletics meetings moved from the White City in 1964 to the National Sports Centre at Crystal Palace. The stadium holds 17,000 spectators, and the modern rubber-and-tarmac track allows meetings to take place in all weathers. An Olympic-size swimming-pool stands near the athletics track.

At one time London's largest pool was the Empire Pool, Wembley, now called the Wembley Arena; when it was opened in 1934, it was the largest in the world, catering for 8,000 to 11,000 spectators. The swimming events in the 1948 Olympics were held there, but the pool is now covered and the arena is used for boxing, show-jumping, ice-skating,

international six-day cycle racing, indoor tennis and badminton.

In the winter, thousands of amateur footballers take the field at weekends, but on Saturday afternoons soccer fans flock to see their favourite professional teams play at London's 12 football stadiums. The largest is Highbury Stadium, home of Arsenal FC, with a capacity of 60,000.

Soccer – association football – has been played in London since the middle of the last century; Fulham FC is the oldest London club, founded in 1880. Support for each club reaches fever pitch during the season, and stretches well beyond the area in which the teams are based.

For those who prefer to see the ball carried rather than kicked, top-class rugby football is played at several grounds. Rugby's "Mecca" is Twickenham, headquarters of the Rugby Football Union and home ground of the Harlequins and the England team. The big international matches, seven-a-side games and the annual Oxford v. Cambridge University match attract more than 70,000 supporters.

Longest racecourse

Oxford and Cambridge Universities also give vent to their sporting rivalry once a year on London's longest racecourse – the River Thames. The University Boat Race is held in early spring, and is rowed over a 4¼ mile course from Putney to Mortlake. The race has been held on the Thames since 1829, and has become a traditional event. Thousands of spectators, most of whom take no interest in rowing for the rest of the year, line the banks to watch the two crews of eight oarsmen and a cox battle against each other, the weather and the river's tricky cross-currents. The same course, rowed in the opposite direction, is used for the Head of the River Race, in which more than 100 crews compete.

National summer game

In the spring the sports fans' fancy turns to thoughts of cricket and tennis – and in London that means Lord's, The Oval and Wimbledon. Lord's Cricket Ground is the headquarters of the game throughout the world. Test Matches, Middlesex county matches and one-day tournaments are held there. The Oval, Kennington, is the home of the Surrey County Cricket Club, and the traditional venue for the final Test in each series.

In June and July the world's top tennis players compete at Wimbledon for the All-England Lawn Tennis Championships. The championships were started in 1877 and have become a social as well as a sporting event.

There are 16 grass courts at Wimbledon and 10 hard courts. The centre court, scene of the finals in the championships, has a spectator capacity of about 14,000. Number 1 court seats about 7,500 spectators.

HIGH ENDEAVOUR *Pole-vaulting is a spectacular field event at the National Sports Centre.*

LORD'S – THE HALLOWED CAPITAL OF CRICKET

Lord's Cricket Ground owes its name to Thomas Lord, who, in the 1780s, was groundsman for the White Conduit Cricket Club at Islington. In 1787 Lord found a new ground at Marylebone, and the club became the Marylebone Cricket Club (MCC). In 1809 the club moved, to North Bank. This time Lord took his turf with him. But the new ground was in the path of the Regent's Canal. So, in 1813, Lord moved his turf to St John's Wood where it has remained ever since.

The club ground which became the cricket capital of the world.

Thomas Lord. His turf lives on.

SPORTING VENUES

Association Football

Arsenal FC **(2Ab)**, Avenall Road, Highbury.
Brentford FC **(1Ca)**, Griffin Park, Brentford.
Charlton Athletic FC **(4Ce)**, The Valley, Charlton.
Chelsea FC **(5Ba)**, Stamford Bridge, Fulham Road.
Crystal Palace FC **(4Ac)**, Selhurst Park, Sydenham.
Fulham FC **(1Da)**, Craven Cottage, Stevenage Road.
Millwall FC **(4Be)**, The Den, New Cross.
Orient FC **(2Bb)**, Leyton Stadium, Brisbane Road.
Queen's Park Rangers FC **(1Da)**, Loftus Road, Shepherd's Bush.
Tottenham Hotspur FC **(2Ac)**, White Hart Lane, Tottenham.
West Ham United FC **(2Ca)**, Boleyn Ground, Upton Park.
Wimbledon FC **(3Ed)**, Plough Lane.

Rugby Union

Blackheath RFC **(4Ce)**, Rectory Field, Blackheath.
Harlequins RFC **(3Cd)**, Twickenham.
London Irish RFC **(3Bc)**, The Avenue, Sunbury-on-Thames.
London Scottish RFC **(3Cd)**, Richmond Athletic Ground.
London Welsh RFC **(3Dd)**, Old Deer Park, Kew Road, Richmond.
Richmond RFC **(3Cd)**, Richmond Athletic Ground.
Rosslyn Park RFC **(3Dd)**, Upper Richmond Road, Richmond.
Saracens RFC **(1Fd)**, Green Road, Southgate.
Wasps RFC **(1Cc)**, Repton Avenue, Sudbury.

Cricket

Blackheath **(4Ce)**, Rectory Field.
Ilford **(2Cc)**, Valentine's Park, Cranbrook Road, Ilford.
Kennington **(6Ca)**, The Oval.
Lord's **(1Eb)**, St John's Wood, Marylebone.
Romford **(2Ec)**, Gallows Corner Sports Ground, Gidea Park.

Athletics

East London Stadium **(2Bb)**, Victoria Park, Tower Hamlets.
National Sports Centre **(4Ac)**, Crystal Palace Park, Sydenham.
New River Sports Centre **(2Ac)**, White Hart Lane, Tottenham.
West London Stadium **(1Db)**, Wormwood Scrubs.

Tennis

All-England Tennis Club **(3Ed)**, Church Road, Wimbledon.
Hurlingham Park **(1Ea)**, Fulham.
Queen's Club **(1Ea)**, Palliser Road, Barons Court.

Greyhound racing

Catford Stadium **(4Bd)**, Dogget Road, Catford.
Hackney Wick Stadium **(2Bb)**, Waterden Road, Hackney.
Harringay Stadium **(1Fc)**, Green Lanes, Haringey.
Walthamstow Stadium **(2Bc)**, Chingford Road, Walthamstow.
Wembley Stadium **(1Dc)**, Wembley.
White City Stadium **(1Db)**, Wood Lane, Shepherd's Bush.
Wimbledon Stadium **(3Ed)**, Plough Lane, Wimbledon.

Speedway racing

Hackney Wick Stadium **(2Bb)**.
White City Stadium **(1Db)**.
Wimbledon Stadium **(3Ed)**.

Boxing

Royal Albert Hall **(5Cc)**, Kensington.
Wembley Arena **(1Dc)**, Wembley.

LONDON'S BOROUGHS

Finding your way round the capital

The huge task of governing the capital is shared by the Greater London Council, the City and the 32 London boroughs—each of which is bigger than most of Britain's cities. Between them the London authorities administer 610 sq. miles with a population of about 6,700,000, at a total annual cost of more than £5,000 million.

BARKING
Information Civic Centre, Wood Lane, Dagenham (Tel. 592 4500).
Police (2Cb) Ripple Road (Tel. 594 9111).
Casualty hospital (2Cc) King George's, Eastern Avenue, Newbury Park, Ilford (Tel. 554 8811).
Public library Axe Street, Barking.

BARNET
Information Town Hall, The Burroughs, Hendon, NW4 (Tel. 202 8282).
Police (1Ed) 26 High Street (Tel. 440 5212).
Casualty hospital (1Ed) Barnet General, Wellhouse Lane, Barnet (Tel. 440 5111).
Public library The Burroughs, Hendon, NW4.

BEXLEY
Information Civic Offices, Broadway, Bexleyheath (Tel. 303 7777).
Police (4Dd) Broadway, Bexleyheath (Tel. 304 3021).
Casualty hospital (4Dc) Queen Mary's, Frognal Avenue, Sidcup (Tel. 302 2678).
Public library Townley Road, Bexleyheath.

BRENT
Information Brent Town Hall, Forty Lane, Wembley (Tel. 903 1400).
Police (1Cb) 603 High Road, Wembley (Tel. 900 7212).
Casualty hospital (1Dd) Edgware General, Burnt Oak, Broadway, Edgware (Tel. 952 2381).
Public library High Road, Willesden Green, NW10.

BROMLEY
Information Town Hall, Bromley (Tel. 464 3333).
Police (4Bc) Widmore Road, Bromley (Tel. 697 9212).
Casualty hospital (4Bc) Bromley General, Cromwell Avenue (Tel. 460 9933).
Public library High Street, Bromley.

CAMDEN
Information Town Hall, Euston Road, NW1 (Tel. 278 4366).
Police (1Fb) Holmes Road, Kentish Town, NW5 (Tel. 725 4212).
Casualty hospital (1Fb) University College Hospital, Gower Street, WC1 (Tel. 388 0321).
Public library Euston Road, NW1.

CROYDON
Information Taberner House, Park Lane, Croydon (Tel. 686 4433).
Police (4Ab) Park Lane (Tel. 680 6212).
Casualty hospital (4Ac) Mayday, Mayday Road, Thornton Heath (Tel. 684 6999).
Public library Mint Walk.

EALING
Information Town Hall, Ealing, W5 (Tel. 579 2424).
Police (1Cb) Uxbridge Road, W5 (Tel. 900 7212).
Casualty hospital (1Ca) King Edward Memorial, Mattock Lane, W13 (Tel. 567 6666).
Public library Walpole Park, W5.

ENFIELD
Information Civic Centre, Silver Street, Enfield (Tel. 366 6565).
Police (2Ad) Baker Street, Enfield (Tel. 367 2222).
Casualty hospital (2Ae) Enfield District General, The Ridgeway, Enfield (Tel. 366 6600).
Public library Cecil Road, Enfield.

GREENWICH
Information Cutty Sark Gardens, SE10 (Tel. 858 6376).
Police (4Ce) Market Street, SE18 (Tel. 853 8212).
Casualty hospital (4Cd) Brook General, Shooters Hill Road, SE18 (Tel. 856 5555).
Public library Woolwich Road, SE10.

HACKNEY
Information Town Hall, Mare Street, Hackney, E8 (Tel. 986 3123).
Police (2Ab) Mare Street (Tel. 488 5212).
Casualty hospital (2Bb) Hackney Hospital, Homerton High Street, E9 (Tel. 985 5555).
Public library Mare Street, E8.

HAMMERSMITH AND FULHAM
Information Town Hall, King Street, W6 (Tel. 748 3020); 2-6 Fulham Broadway, SW6 (385 1212).
Police (1Da) 226 Shepherd's Bush Road, W6 (Tel. 741 6212).
Casualty hospital (1Ea) Charing Cross Hospital, Fulham Palace Road, W6 (Tel. 748 2040).
Public library Shepherd's Bush Road, W6.

HARINGEY
Information Civic Centre, High Road, N22 (Tel. 881 3000).
Police (1Fc) High Road, Wood Green, N22 (Tel. 888 1113).
Casualty hospital (1Ec) Whittington Hospital, Highgate Hill, N19 (Tel. 272 3070).
Public library Wood Green.

HARROW
Information Civic Centre, Station Road, Harrow (Tel. 863 5611).
Police (1Cc) Northolt Road, South Harrow (Tel. 900 7212).
Casualty hospitals (1Dd) Edgware General, Burnt Oak, Edgware (Tel. 952 2381); (Cc) Northwick Park Hospital, Watford Road, Harrow (864 5311).
Public library Gayton Road.

HAVERING
Information Town Hall, Romford (Tel. Romford 46040).
Police (2Ec) Main Road, Romford (Tel. Romford 23311).
Casualty hospital (2Ec) Oldchurch Hospital, Oldchurch Road, Romford (Tel. 46090).
Public library St Edwards Way, Romford.

HILLINGDON
Information High Street, Uxbridge (Tel. Uxbridge 50706).
Police (1Ab) 49 Windsor Street, Uxbridge (Tel. 900 7212).
Casualty hospital (1Ab) Hillingdon Hospital, Pield Heath Road, Hillingdon (Tel. Uxbridge 38282).
Public library High Street, Uxbridge.

HOUNSLOW
Information Civic Centre, Lampton Road (Tel. 570 7728).
Police (1Ca) 5 Montague Road, Hounslow (Tel. 572 7333).
Casualty hospital (1Ca) West Middlesex Hospital, Twickenham Road, Isleworth (Tel. 560 2121).
Public library Treaty Road.

ISLINGTON
Information Borough Information Office, Highbury Corner, N1 (Tel. 226 1234).
Police (1Fb) King's Cross Road, WC1 (Tel. 837 4233).
Casualty hospital (1Fc) Royal Northern Hospital, Holloway Road, N7 (Tel. 272 7777).
Public library Fieldway Crescent, N5.

KENSINGTON AND CHELSEA
Information Town Hall, Hornton Street, W8 (Tel. 937 5464); Old Town Hall, King's Road, SW3 (352 1856).
Police (5Db) Lucan Place, SW3 (Tel. 741 6212).
Casualty hospital (5Ca) St Stephen's Hospital, 369 Fulham Road, SW10

(Tel. 352 8161).
Public library Hornton Street, W8.

KINGSTON-UPON-THAMES
Information Guildhall, High Street
(Tel. 546 2121).
Police (3Cc) High Street
(Tel. 546 7777).
Casualty hospital (3Dc) Kingston
Hospital, Galsworthy Road
(Tel. 546 7711).
Public library Fairfield Road.

LAMBETH
Information Town Hall, Brixton
Hill, SW2 (Tel. 274 7722).
Police (4Ad) Brixton Road, SW9
(Tel. 733 5678).
Casualty hospital (6Cb) St Thomas's
Hospital, Lambeth Palace Road, SE1
(Tel. 928 9292).
Public library Brixton Road,
Brixton, SE5.

LEWISHAM
Information Borough Mall,
Lewisham Centre, SE13
(Tel. 318 5421).
Police (4Bd) Ladywell Road, SE13
(Tel. 697 9212).
Casualty hospital (4Bd) Lewisham
Hospital, Lewisham High Street,
SE13 (Tel. 690 4311).
Public library Lewisham High Street,
SE13.

MERTON
Information Town Hall, The
Broadway, Wimbledon, SW19
(Tel. 946 8070).
Police (3Ec) Queens Road, SW19
(Tel. 947 4141).
Casualty hospital (3Ec) St Helier
Hospital, Wrythe Lane, Carshalton
(Tel. 644 4343).
Public library Wimbledon Hill Road.

NEWHAM
Information Town Hall, East Ham,
E6 (Tel. 472 1430).
Police (2Cb) High Street South, East
Ham, E6 (Tel. 552 5311).
Casualty hospital (2Bb) Queen
Mary's Hospital, West Ham Lane,
E15 (Tel. 534 2616).
Public library High Street South,
East Ham, E6.

REDBRIDGE
Information Town Hall, High Road,
Ilford (Tel. 478 3020).
Police (2Cb) High Road, Ilford
(Tel. 553 3400).
Casualty hospital (2Cc) King
George, Eastern Avenue, Newbury
Park, Ilford (Tel. 554 8811).
Public library Oakfield Road, Ilford.

RICHMOND-UPON-THAMES
Information 58-60 York Street,
Twickenham, and Old Richmond
Town Hall, Hill Street, Richmond
(Both Tel. 892 0032).
Police (3Cd) Red Lion Street
(Tel. 940 9595).
Casualty hospital (3Dc) Kingston
Hospital, Galsworthy Road,

Kingston-upon-Thames
(Tel. 546 7711).
Public library Little Green,
Richmond.

SOUTHWARK
Information Town Hall, Peckham
Road, SE5 (Tel. 703 6311).
Police (6Dc) 323 Borough High
Street, SE1 (Tel. 407 8044).
Casualty hospital (6Ec) Guy's, St
Thomas Street, SE1 (Tel. 407 7600).
Public library Lordship Lane, SE22.

SUTTON
Information Civic Offices, St
Nicholas Way, Sutton
(Tel. 661 5000).
Police (3Eb) Carshalton Road,
Sutton (Tel. 680 6212).
Casualty hospital (3Ec) St Helier
Hospital, Wrythe Lane, Carshalton
(Tel. 644 4343).
Public library St Nicholas Way,
Sutton.

TOWER HAMLETS
Information 88 Roman Road, E2
(Tel. 980 3749).
Police (6Fd) Leman Street, E1
(Tel. 488 5212).
Casualty hospital (2Aa) London
Hospital, Whitechapel Road
(Tel. 247 5454).
Public library Bancroft Road.

WALTHAM FOREST
Information Town Hall, Forest Road,
E17 (Tel. 527 5544).
Police (2Bd) King's Head Hill, E4
(Tel. 529 8666).
Casualty hospital (2Bc) Whipps
Cross Hospital, Whipps Cross Road,
Leytonstone, E11 (Tel. 539 5522).
Public library High Street,
Walthamstow, E17.

WANDSWORTH
Information Town Hall,
Wandsworth High Street, SW18
(Tel. 874 6464).
Police (3Ed) Wandsworth High
Street, SW18 (Tel. 870 9011).
Casualty hospital (3Dd) Queen
Mary's, Roehampton Lane, SW15
(Tel. 789 6611).
Public library West Hill, SW11.

WESTMINSTER
Information City Hall, Victoria
Street, SW1 (Tel. 828 8070).
Police (6Bb) New Scotland Yard,
Broadway, SW1 (Tel. 230 1212).
Casualty hospital (6Bb)
Westminster, Dean Ryle Street,
Horseferry Road, SW1
(Tel. 828 9811).
Public library Marylebone Road.

TOURIST INFORMATION
The London Tourist Board can help
find accommodation, obtain theatre
tickets and answer general enquiries.
The board maintains Tourist
Information Centres at:
Victoria Station, near platform 15.
Heathrow Central Station at London
Airport.
26 Grosvenor Gardens, SW1.
Tower of London, by the main gate.
The board also operates a telephone
information service on 730 0791
from 9 a.m. to 6 p.m. daily
throughout the year. In addition, the
Post Office offers a recorded service
on 246 8041. This gives a daily
selection of the main events and
places of interest in and around
London.
Note *When dialling from outside
London, prefix seven-figure telephone
numbers with 01.*

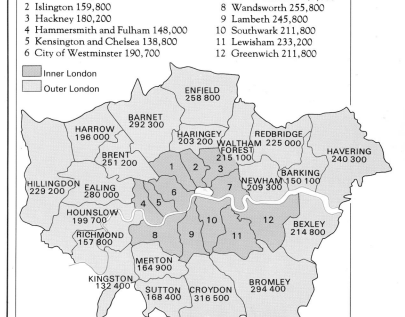

POPULATION IN LONDON BOROUGHS
1 Camden 171,600
2 Islington 159,800
3 Hackney 180,200
4 Hammersmith and Fulham 148,000
5 Kensington and Chelsea 138,800
6 City of Westminster 190,700
7 Tower Hamlets 143,000
8 Wandsworth 255,800
9 Lambeth 245,800
10 Southwark 211,800
11 Lewisham 233,200
12 Greenwich 211,800

Inner London
Outer London

ENFIELD 258 800
BARNET 292 300
HARROW 196 000
HARINGEY 203 200
WALTHAM FOREST 215 100
REDBRIDGE 225 000
HAVERING 240 300
BRENT 251 200
BARKING
NEWHAM 150 100
NEWHAM 209 300
HILLINGDON 229 200
EALING 280 000
HOUNSLOW 199 700
BEXLEY 214 800
RICHMOND 157 800
MERTON 164 900
KINGSTON 132 400
SUTTON 168 400
CROYDON 316 500
BROMLEY 294 400

GREATER LONDON NORTH-WEST

Hemel Hempstead 4 A411   St Albans 4 A405 M1   St Albans 4 A5183

Amersham 5 A404

Beaconsfield 7 A40

A40

M40

M 40

A412

A4007

A4

RADLETT
Letchmore Heath
WATFORD
Whippendell Wood
Cassiobury Park
Watford FC
Chorleywood Common
Chess
CHORLEYWOOD
CROXLEY GREEN
OXHEY
BUSHEY
Aldenham Country Park
RICKMANSWORTH
Grand Union Canal
BATCHWORTH
Moor Park Mansion
SOUTH OXHEY
Oxhey Woods
Grim's Dyke House
Bentley Priory (RAF)
STANMORE
AA
MOUNT PLEASANT
HAREFIELD
HERTS BUCKS
NORTHWOOD
HERTFORDSHIRE
GREATER LONDON
HATCH END
HARROW WEALD
PINNER GREEN
Grand Union Canal
Colne
Bayhurst Wood Country Park
PINNER
Headstone Manor
WEALDSTONE
KENTO
H A R R O W
EASTCOTE
HARROW
HARROW ON THE HILL
Northwick Park Hospital
Denham Place
DENHAM
WEST RUISLIP
RUISLIP
Harrow School
POL
ICKENHAM
Swakeleys
H I L L I N G D O N
SUDBURY
WEME
NEW DENHAM
POL
UXBRIDGE
NORTHOLT
A4090
POL
Brunel University
Hillingdon Hospital
COWLEY
PERIVALE
GREENFORD
E A L I N G
IVER
WOOD END
Hayes Botanic Gardens
HAYES
King Edward Memorial Hosp.
Pitshanger Manor
HANWELL
POL
YIEWSLEY
Grand Union Canal
Southall Park
SOUTHALL
Rochester House
Musical Museum
WEST DRAYTON
Southall Manor
BRENTFOR
NORWOOD GREEN
Osterley Park
Osterley Park NT
Brentfor FC
HARMONDSWORTH
HARLINGTON
NORTH HYDE
M4
HESTON
OSTERLEY
Syon House
W. Middlesex Hospital
Heston Service Area
CRANFORD
POL
HOUNSLOW
ISLEWORTH
Old Deer Park
Heathrow Airport
GREATER LONDON
SURREY
HOUNSLOW

0   1   2   3   4
MILES

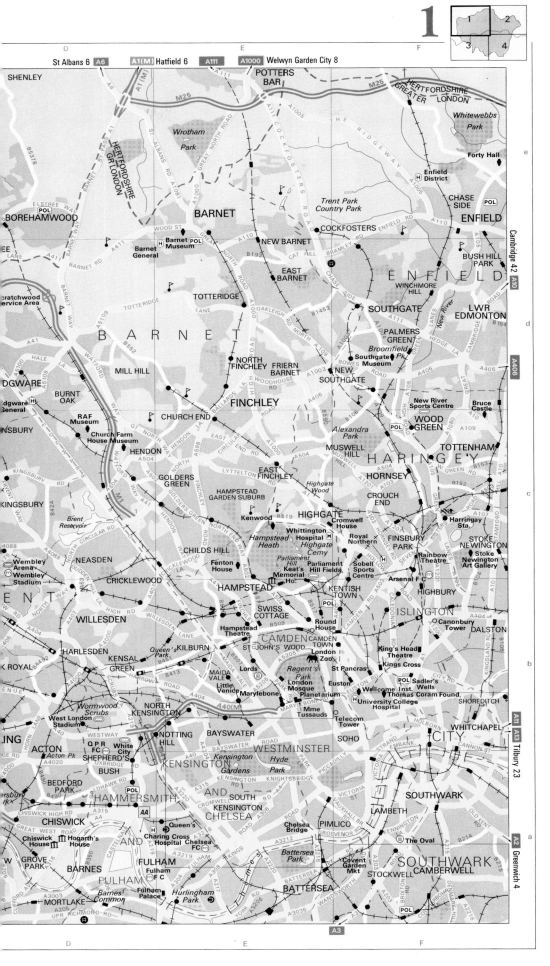

1

St Albans 6 `A6` `A1(M)` Hatfield 6 `A111` `A1000` Welwyn Garden City 8

SHENLEY

POTTERS BAR

HERTFORDSHIRE GREATER LONDON

Whitewebbs Park

Forty Hall

Wrotham Park

Enfield District

CHASE SIDE

POL

Trent Park Country Park

ENFIELD

BOREHAMWOOD

POL

E L S T R E E   W A Y

BARNET

New Barnet Museum

COCKFOSTERS

Barnet General

NEW BARNET

BUSH HILL PARK

EAST BARNET

WINCHMORE HILL

E N F I E L D

Cambridge 42 `A10`

TOTTERIDGE

SOUTHGATE

LWR EDMONTON

B A R N E T

PALMERS GREEN

Southgate Museum

Broomfield Pk

`A406`

Scratchwood Service Area

NORTH FINCHLEY

FRIERN BARNET

NEW SOUTHGATE

DGWARE

MILL HILL

FINCHLEY

WOOD GREEN

Bruce Castle

New River Sports Centre

POL

NSBURY

BURNT OAK

CHURCH END

TOTTENHAM

dgware General

RAF Museum

HENDON

MUSWELL HILL

H A R I N G E Y

Church Farm House Museum

HORNSEY

KINGSBURY

GOLDERS GREEN

EAST FINCHLEY

Highgate Wood

CROUCH END

Alexandra Park

Harringay Sta.

Kenwood

HIGHGATE

Cromwell House

FINSBURY PARK

STOKE NEWINGTON

Brent Reservoir

CHILDS HILL

Hampstead Garden Suburb

Whittington Hospital

Highgate Cemy

Royal Northern

Stoke Newington Art Gallery

NEASDEN

Fenton House

Parliament Hill

Keat's Memorial Ho.

Parliament Hill Fields

Sobell Sports Centre

Rainbow Theatre

Wembley Arena Wembley Stadium

Hampstead Heath

HIGHBURY

ENT

CRICKLEWOOD

HAMPSTEAD

KENTISH TOWN

Arsenal F C

WILLESDEN

SWISS COTTAGE

Round House

ISLINGTON

Canonbury Tower

DALSTON

HARLESDEN

KENSAL GREEN

Hampstead Theatre

CAMDEN TOWN

CAMDEN

King's Head Theatre

KILBURN

St.JOHN'S WOOD

London Zoo

Kings Cross

L ROYAL

Queen's Park

MAIDA VALE

Regent's Park

St Pancras

Sadler's Wells

Lords

London Mosque Planetarium

Euston

Wellcome Inst. Wells

Thomas Coram Found.

SHOREDITCH

Little Venice

Marylebone

University College Hospital

Wormwood Scrubs

NORTH KENSINGTON

Mme Tussauds

Telecom Tower

West London Stadium

WHITCHAPEL

`A11` `A13` Tilbury 23

ING

ACTON

Q.P.R. F C

White City

NOTTING HILL

BAYSWATER

SOHO

CITY

SHEPHERD'S BUSH

KENSINGTON

Kensington Gardens

Hyde Park

WESTMINSTER

BEDFORD PARK

POL

HAMMERSMITH

AND

SOUTH KENSINGTON

KNIGHTSBRIDGE

SOUTHWARK

CHISWICK

AA

CHELSEA

LAMBETH

Chiswick House

Hogarth's House

Queen's

Charing Cross Hospital

Chelsea FC

Chelsea Bridge

PIMLICO

Covent Garden Mkt

The Oval

Greenwich 4 `A2`

GROVE PARK

BARNES

FULHAM

Fulham F C

Battersea Park

SOUTHWARK

CAMBERWELL

STOCKWELL

MORTLAKE

Barnes Common

Fulham Palace

Hurlingham Park

BATTERSEA

POL

`A3`

GREATER LONDON NORTH-EAST

0   1   2   3   4
MILES

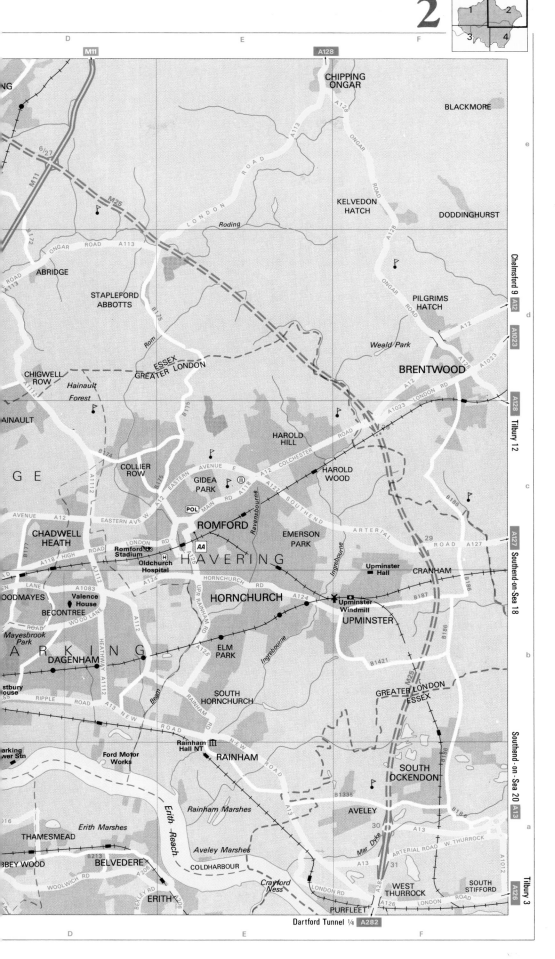

2

D   E   F

M11   A128

CHIPPING
ONGAR

BLACKMORE

e

6/27

KELVEDON
HATCH

DODDINGHURST

Roding

ONGAR   ROAD   A113

Chelmsford 9   A12

ABRIDGE

STAPLEFORD
ABBOTTS

PILGRIMS
HATCH

d

A1023

Rom

Weald Park

ESSEX
GREATER LONDON

BRENTWOOD

CHIGWELL
ROW

Hainault
Forest

A1023   LONDON RD

A128   Tilbury 12

AINAULT

HAROLD
HILL

COLCHESTER

c

G E

COLLIER
ROW

GIDEA
PARK

HAROLD
WOOD

A127

ARTERIAL

B186

EASTERN   AVENUE

POL

ROMFORD

Ravensbourne

SOUTHEND

29

ROAD

A127   Southend-on-Sea 18

CHADWELL
HEATH

EASTERN AVE W

A12

EMERSON
PARK

Upminster
Hall

CRANHAM

AA

H A V E R I N G

B187

B186

Romford
Stadium

AVENUE

Ingrebourne

Oldchurch
Hospital H

UPR   HORNCHURCH   RD

Upminster
Windmill

OODMAYES

HORNCHURCH

A124

UPMINSTER

b

Valence
House

WOOD   LANE

B1421

BECONTREE

Mayesbrook
Park

ELM
PARK

A125

Ingrebourne

B186

A R K I N G

DAGENHAM

Beam

M25

GREATER LONDON
ESSEX

stbury
ouse

RIPPLE   ROAD

A13   NEW   ROAD

SOUTH
HORNCHURCH

arking
wer Stn

Ford Motor
Works

Rainham
Hall NT

RAINHAM

SOUTH
OCKENDON

B1335

Rainham Marshes

AVELEY

Southend-on-Sea 20   A13

016

Erith Marshes

A13

30

a

THAMESMEAD

Erith Reach

Aveley Marshes

Mar Dyke

ARTERIAL ROAD   W. THURROCK

A1012

BBEY WOOD

BELVEDERE

COLDHARBOUR

Crayford
Ness

LONDON RD

A13

31

WEST
THURROCK

SOUTH
STIFFORD

Tilbury 3   A126

ERITH

A126   LONDON   ROAD

PURFLEET

D   E   F

GREATER LONDON SOUTH-WEST

0   1   2   3   4
MILES

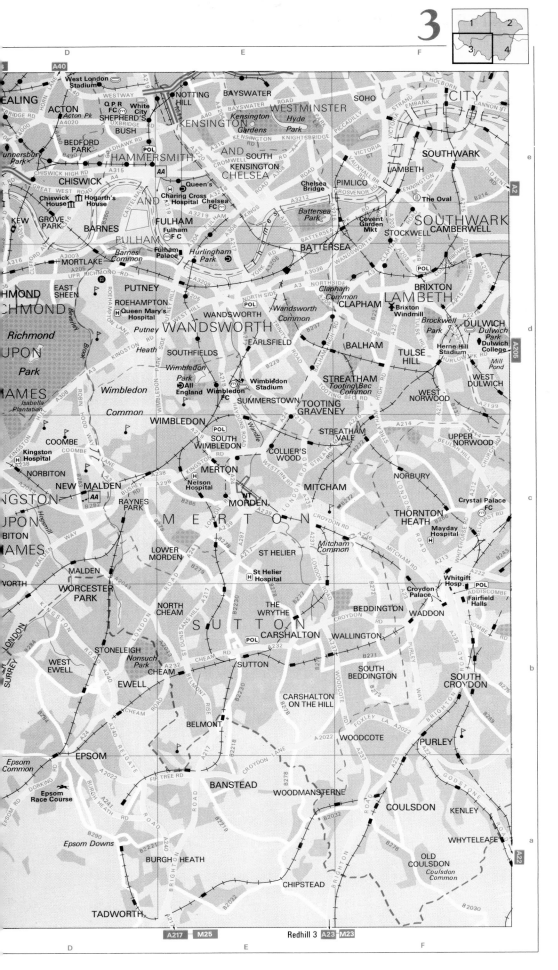

1 2
3 4

D E F

A40

West London
Stadium
BAYSWATER
NOTTING
HILL
WESTWAY
ACTON Q.P.R
FC
White
City
SHEPHERD'S
BUSH
UXBRIDGE RD
WESTMINSTER
SOHO
CITY
Acton Pk
A4020
KENSINGTON
Kensington
Gardens
Hyde
Park
PICCADILLY
STRAND
EMBANK
CANNON ST
EALING
BEDFORD
PARK
POL
AND
Knightsbridge
SOUTHWARK
e
HAMMERSMITH
SOUTH
KENSINGTON
CROMWELL
RD
LAMBETH
A2
CHISWICK
AA
Queen's
CHELSEA
Chelsea
Bridge
PIMLICO
GROSVENOR
The Oval
Chiswick
House
Hogarth's
House
Charing Cross
Hospital
Chelsea
FC
Battersea
Park
SOUTHWARK
FULHAM
KINGS
Covent
Garden
Mkt
CAMBERWELL
KEW
GROVE
PARK
BARNES
AND
FULHAM
Fulham
FC
BATTERSEA
Stockwell
BRIXTON
MORTLAKE
Barnes
Common
Fulham
Palace
Hurlingham
Park
YORK
RD
A3036
POL
LAMBETH
EAST
SHEEN
PUTNEY
Clapham
Common
CLAPHAM
Brixton
Windmill
DULWICH
RICHMOND
ROEHAMPTON
Queen Mary's
Hospital
POL
Wandsworth
Common
Brockwell
Park
Dulwich
Park
Dulwich
College
Richmond
Park
WANDSWORTH
EARLSFIELD
BALHAM
Herne Hill
Stadium
d
UPON
SOUTHFIELDS
TULSE
HILL
WEST
DULWICH
Mill
Pond
THAMES
Wimbledon
Park
Wimbledon
Stadium
STREATHAM
A205
Isabella
Plantation
All
England
Wimbledon
FC
SUMMERSTOWN
Tooting Bec
Common
WEST
NORWOOD
Wimbledon
Common
TOOTING
GRAVENEY
COOMBE
POL
SOUTH
WIMBLEDON
STREATHAM
VALE
UPPER
NORWOOD
Kingston
Hospital
COLLIER'S
WOOD
NORBURY
NORBITON
MERTON
Nelson
Hospital
MITCHAM
Crystal
Palace
FC
c
NEW MALDEN
AA
MORDEN
THORNTON
HEATH
KINGSTON
RAYNES
PARK
MERTON
CROYDON RD
Mayday
Hospital
UPON
LOWER
MORDEN
Mitcham
Common
THAMES
ST HELIER
Whitgift
Hosp
POL
MALDEN
WORCESTER
PARK
NORTH
CHEAM
THE
WRYTHE
BEDDINGTON
Croydon
Palace
Fairfield
Halls
WADDON
WEST
EWELL
STONELEIGH
Nonsuch
Park
CARSHALTON
WALLINGTON
SUTTON
SOUTH
CROYDON
b
EWELL
CHEAM
POL
SUTTON
CARSHALTON
ON THE HILL
SOUTH
BEDDINGTON
BELMONT
WOODCOTE
PURLEY
EPSOM
BANSTEAD
WOODCOTE
Epsom
Common
Epsom
Race Course
WOODMANSTERNE
COULSDON
KENLEY
WHYTELEAFE
a
Epsom Downs
BURGH HEATH
CHIPSTEAD
OLD
COULSDON
Coulsdon
Common
A22
TADWORTH

A217 M25 Redhill 3 A23 M23

D E F

GREATER LONDON SOUTH-EAST

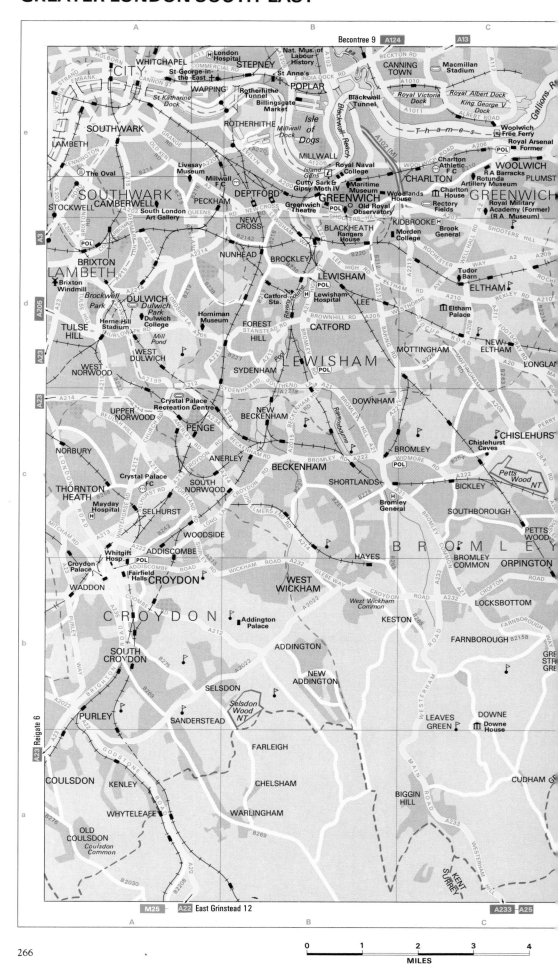

MILES

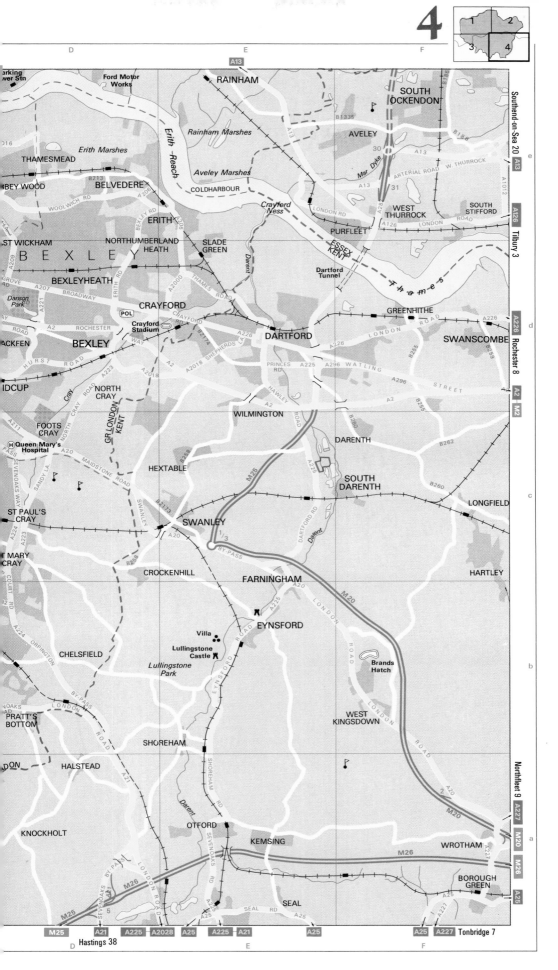

A13

RAINHAM

SOUTH
OCKENDON

AVELEY

B1335

Erith Marshes

Rainham Marshes

30

Mar Dyke

THAMESMEAD

ARTERIAL ROAD W. THURROCK

Aveley Marshes

B213

31

BEY WOOD

BELVEDERE

COLDHARBOUR

A13

A1012

ERITH

Crayford
Ness

WEST
THURROCK

SOUTH
STIFFORD

WOOLWICH RD

BEXLEY RD

A206

ROAD

ST WICKHAM

NORTHUMBERLAND
HEATH

SLADE
GREEN

Darent

LONDON RD

A126

B E X L E Y

A207
BROADWAY

ERITH RD

PURFLEET

ESSEX
KENT

BEXLEYHEATH

A2000

THAMES ROAD

Dartford
Tunnel

Thames

Danson
Park

A221

CRAYFORD

POL

GREENHITHE

A226

Crayford
Stadium

LONDON

ROAD

A207

ROCHESTER

A2

CRAYFORD

B214

DARTFORD

A226

B235

SWANSCOMBE

B259

ACKFEN

BEXLEY

A2

WAY

A2018 SHEPHERDS

A225 A296 WATLING

A2

B235

IDCUP

HURST   ROAD

A223

A2018

PRINCES
RD

A296

STREET

Cray

A211

GR LONDON
KENT

NORTH
CRAY

B258

WILMINGTON

HAWLEY
ROAD

A226

DARENTH

B262

FOOTS
CRAY

MAIDSTONE ROAD

M25

B260

H Queen Mary's
Hospital

A20

HEXTABLE

SOUTH
DARENTH

LONGFIELD

SANDY LA

SWANLEY

DARTFORD RD

St PAUL'S
CRAY

B2173

SWANLEY

Darent

A20

HARTLEY

T MARY
CRAY

B258

1/3

BY-PASS

CROCKENHILL

FARNINGHAM

LONDON

ORPINGTON

CHELSFIELD

A224

Villa

EYNSFORD

A225

M20

Lullingstone
Castle

EYNSFORD ROAD

Brands
Hatch

Lullingstone
Park

BY-PASS

LONDON ROAD

PRATT'S
BOTTOM

LONDON

ROAD

SHOREHAM

WEST
KINGSDOWN

DON

HALSTEAD

A21

SHOREHAM RD

2

A20

M20

Darent

KNOCKHOLT

OTFORD

KEMSING

SEVENOAKS RD

WROTHAM

M25

SEVENOAKS BY PASS

M26

M26

A227

BOROUGH
GREEN

LONDON ROAD

5

SEAL RD

SEAL

A25

A227

Southend-on-Sea 20 A13

A26

Tilbury 3

A26 Rochester 8

A2

M2

c

b

Northfleet 9 A227

M20

M26

A25

a

d

e

CENTRAL LONDON WEST

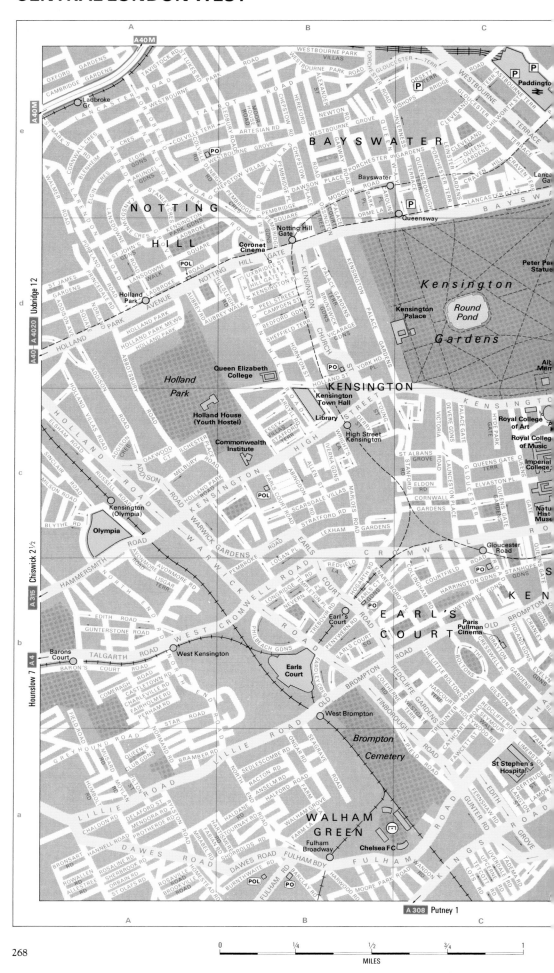

0   ¼   ½   ¾   1
MILES

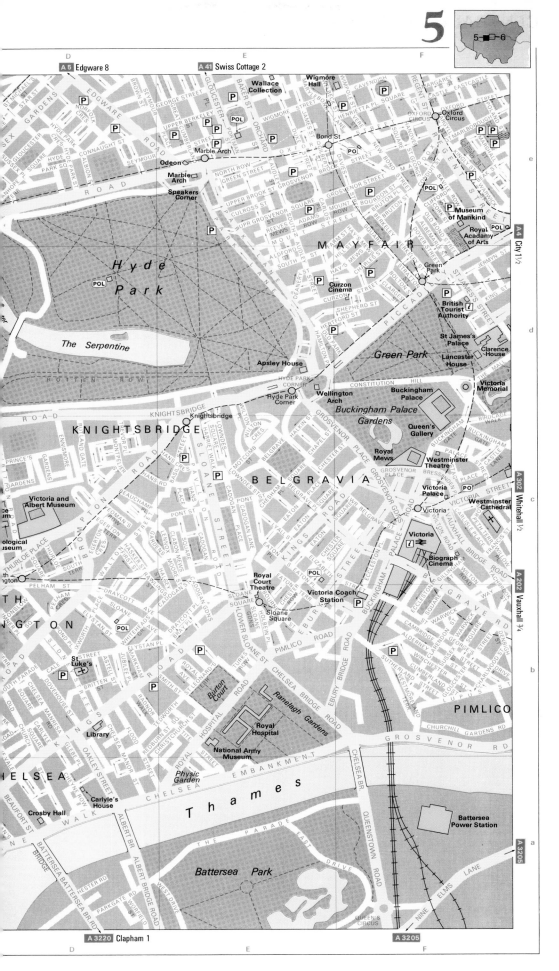

D   E   F

Wigmore
Hall

Wallace
Collection

P   P

POL

Oxford
Circus

Oxford
Circus

e

Baker St

Bond St

P

PO

Marble Arch

Odeon

Marble
Arch

Speakers
Corner

P

POL

Museum
of Mankind

P   POL

Royal
Acadamy
of Arts

A 4 City 1½

M A Y F A I R

P   Green
Park

*Hyde
Park*

POL

Curzon
Cinema

P

P

British
Tourist
Authority i

d

The Serpentine

Apsley House

Green Park

St James's
Palace

Lancaster
House

Clarence
House

HYDE PARK
CORNER

Hyde Park
Corner

Wellington
Arch

CONSTITUTION   HILL

Buckingham
Palace

Victoria
Memorial

Knightsbridge

Knightsbridge

*Buckingham Palace
Gardens*

Queen's
Gallery

BIRDCAGE
WALK

K N I G H T S B R I D G E

Royal
Mews

Westminster
Theatre

B E L G R A V I A

Victoria
Palace

PO

A 302 Whitehall ½

c

Victoria and
Albert Museum

Westminster
Cathedral

P

P

Victoria
i

Victoria

Biograph
Cinema

A 202 Vauxhall ¾

ological
Museum

PELHAM ST

POL

Royal
Court
Theatre

Victoria Coach
Station

POL

P

T O N

POL

Sloane
Square

PIMLICO   ROAD

P   b

St
Luke's

P

P

*Burton
Court*

*Ranelagh
Gardens*

P I M L I C O

Library

Royal
Hospital

CHURCHILL GARDENS RD

National Army
Museum

G R O S V E N O R   RD

*Physic
Garden*

C H E L S E A   EMBANKMENT

Battersea
Power Station

E L S E A

Carlyle's
House

CHELSEA BR

A 3205   a

Crosby Hall

T h a m e s

ALBERT BR

THE   PARADE

Battersea   Park

CENTRAL LONDON EAST

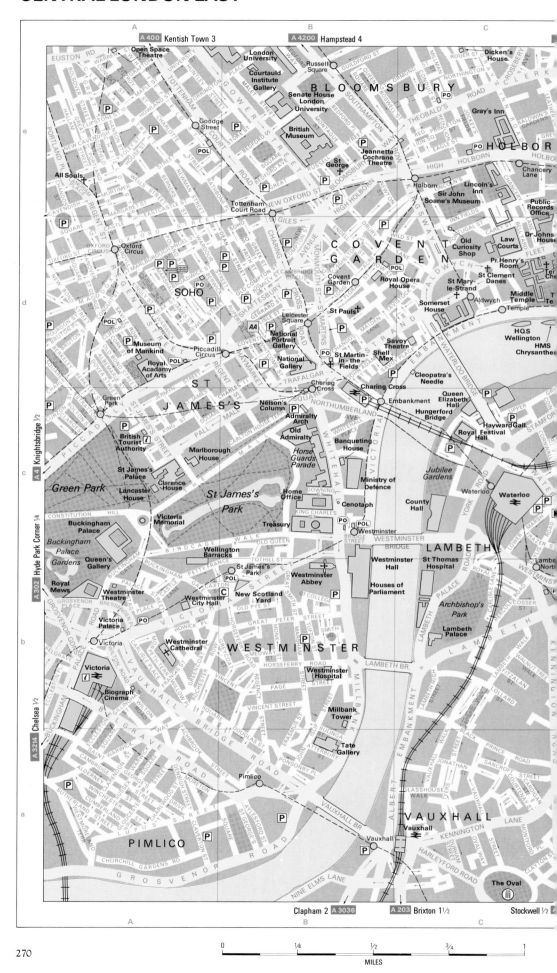

MILES

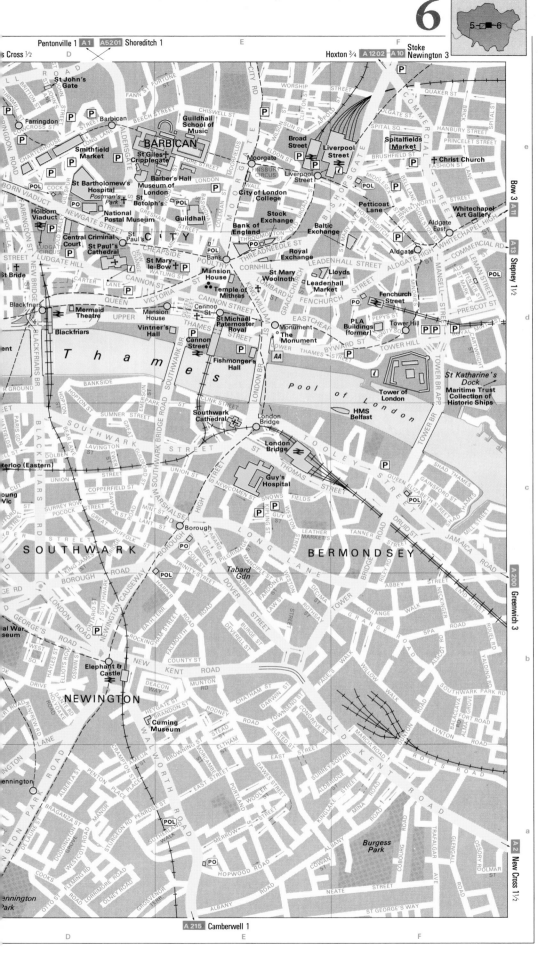

Bow 3 A11

A13 Stepney 1½

A200 Greenwich 3

A2 New Cross 1½

St John's
Gate
Farringdon
Barbican
Smithfield
Market
St Bartholomew's
Hospital
Postman's
Park
National
Postal Museum
Holborn
Viaduct
Central Criminal
Court
St Paul's
Cathedral
St Bride
Blackfriars
Blackfriars
Mermaid
Theatre
Vintner's
Hall
Mansion
House

Guildhall
School of
Music
BARBICAN
St Giles
Cripplegate
Barber's
Hall
Museum of
London
St
Botolph's
Guildhall
City of London
College
CITY
St Paul's
St Mary-
le-Bow
Mansion
House
Temple
of Mithras
Cannon
St
St Michael
Paternoster Royal
Cannon
Street
Fishmonger's
Hall

Moorgate
Broad
Street
Liverpool
Street
Liverpool
Street
Stock
Exchange
Bank of
England
Royal
Exchange
Bank
St Mary
Woolnoth
Baltic
Exchange
Lloyds
Leadenhall
Market
Fenchurch
Street
PLA
Buildings
(former)
Monument
The
Monument

Spitalfields
Market
Christ Church
Petticoat
Lane
Whitechapel
Art Gallery
Aldgate
East
Aldgate
Tower Hill
Tower of
London
HMS
Belfast
St Katharine's
Dock
Maritime Trust
Collection of
Historic Ships

T h e   T h a m e s
P o o l   o f   L o n d o n

Southwark
Cathedral
London Bridge
London
Bridge
Guy's
Hospital
Waterloo (Eastern)
Young
Vic
Borough

S O U T H W A R K
NEWINGTON
Elephant &
Castle
Cuming
Museum

B E R M O N D S E Y

Burgess
Park

al War
seum

A215 Camberwell 1

D

E

F

271

LOOE

Looe Cornwall

About 200 to 300 sharks a year are caught by anglers off Looe. They cause havoc with fishing-nets 10-20 miles offshore, but do not come close to shore and are no threat to bathers.

The town consists of two resorts, East and West Looe, joined by an eight-arched Victorian bridge across the River Looe.

West Looe is built around the Church of St Nicholas, erected some time before 1336. The tower has a campanile belfry, and in the early 19th century contained a "Scold's Cage" in which nagging women were placed. The Jolly Sailor Inn dates back to the 16th century.

St Mary's Church in East Looe has a 13th-century tower which used to be whitewashed. It is a landmark for sailors.

The Old Guildhall in East Looe was built in the late 16th century. Today it houses a museum which contains old punch-bowls, documents, a pillory, stocks and other items of local history.

Looe Island, about half a mile offshore, has the ruins of a medieval monastery.

Information Tel. 2072 (summer); 2255 (winter).
Location On the A387, 20 m. W of Plymouth.
Parking East Looe: Station Road; Buller Quay, off Fore Street; Church End. West Looe: Millpool, off Polperro Road; The Quay (all cps).
District council Caradon (Tel. Liskeard 43818).
Population 4,500.
E-C Thur.
Police Station Road, East Looe (Tel. 2233).
Casualty hospital Passmore Edwards, Liskeard (Tel. Liskeard 42137).
Post offices Fore Street, East Looe; The Quay, West Looe.
Public library Sea Front Court, East Looe.
Places to see Museum, Old Guildhall; Woolly Monkey Sanctuary, Murrayton, 4 m. E.
Shopping East Looe: Fore Street; Buller Street; Higher Market Street. West Looe: The Quay.
AA 24 hour service
Tel. Plymouth 69989.

Lossiemouth Grampian

While scores of Scottish herring ports have declined, Lossiemouth remains busy. Its progressive fishermen were the first to use the steam drifter, and in 1921 pioneered the Danish seine net in Britain.

Lossiemouth is also an RAF base and a holiday resort with extensive, safe sandy beaches on both sides of the town. To the west lies the twin community of Branderburgh.

Information Tel. 3388.
Location On the A941, 5 m. N of Elgin.
Parking Gregory Place; Pitgaveny

RAMSAY MACDONALD

Britain's first Labour prime minister, James Ramsay MacDonald (1866-1937), was born in Lossiemouth at No. 1 Gregory Place. An inscribed stone marks the cottage. A labourer's son, MacDonald became a pupil teacher in the town before leaving for London in 1888. He formed the first Labour Government in 1924.

Street (both car parks).
District council Moray (Tel. Elgin 3451).
Population 6,340.
E-C Thur.
Police Clifton Road (Tel. 2022).
Casualty hospital Dr Gray's, High Street, Elgin (Tel. Elgin 3131).
Post office James Street.
Public library Town Hall.
Places to see Birthplace of Ramsay MacDonald, Gregory Place.
Shopping Queen Street.
AA 24 hour service
Tel. Aberdeen 51231.

Lostwithiel Cornwall

The small market town and touring centre in the Fowey Valley was the 13th-century capital of Cornwall. The Earls of Cornwall had their stronghold at Restormel Castle, 1 mile north. This is the best-preserved castle of its period in the county.

In its medieval hey-day, Lostwithiel was also a stannary town, where tin from local mines was brought to be taxed and assayed. The stannary offices and county treasury were in the 13th-century Old Duchy Palace in Quay Street.

Until the 16th century, the river was navigable up to Lostwithiel bridge, and there are remains of quays in this area.

The parish church of St Bartholomew was built in the 13th century. Its spire, with an octagonal, windowed base called a lantern, was added about 100 years later.

Lostwithiel contains many other fine buildings – among them Georgian houses in Fore Street, the 18th-century grammar school in Queen Street, and the Guildhall of 1740. The wall of the 17th-century Malt House in North Street has a plaque recording the issue of a 3,000 year lease on the property in 1652.

Information Tel. 872672.
Location On the A390, 6 m. S of Bodmin.
Parking Cattle Market; The Quay

(both car parks).
District council Borough of Restormel (Tel. St Austell 4466).
Population 2,100.
E-C Wed.
Police Queen Street (Tel. 872248).
Casualty hospital Passmore Edwards, Liskeard (Tel. Liskeard 42137).
Post office Queen Street.
Public library Municipal Buildings, Fore Street.
Places to see Restormel Castle; Old Duchy Palace; Boconnoc, 3 m. E.
Shopping Fore Street.
Event Silver Band Gala Week (July).
Trade and industry Agriculture.
AA 24 hour service
Tel. Plymouth 669989.

Loughborough Leics.

Bells made in Loughborough have rung round the world since 1858 when the bell-foundry of John Taylor moved to the town from Oxford. They have cast many famous bells, including Great Paul for St Paul's Cathedral in London.

Bells are a recurring motif in the town. Queen's Park has a 150 ft Carillon Tower, built in 1923 as a memorial to the dead of the First World War. The tower contains a small museum.

The tower of the parish church of All Saints has a peal of ten bells, and contains a memorial to the bell-founding Taylor family. The church has a 19th-century appearance, because of extensive restoration work carried out by Sir Gilbert Scott in 1862. But in fact much of the building dates from the 14th century.

The aisles have windows dating from about 1300, and the oak roof of the nave is carried on beams which spring from carved musician angels resting on stone supports.

The Old Rectory is a 13th and 14th-century building with a gabled front. In 1962 the 19th-century additions were demolished and the partially roofed remains opened as a museum.

The striking Italianate town hall in the Market Place was built in 1855, but extensively restored inside after a fire in 1972.

Loughborough University of Technology is a major teaching and research centre covering 140 acres and

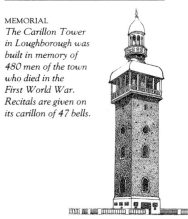

MEMORIAL
The Carillon Tower in Loughborough was built in memory of 480 men of the town who died in the First World War. Recitals are given on its carillon of 47 bells.

272

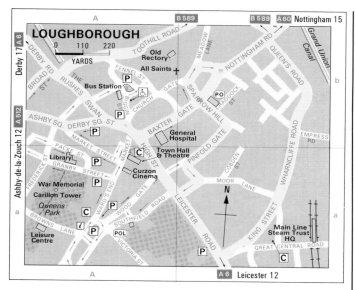

LOUGHBOROUGH

0   110   220
YARDS

Old Rectory
All Saints
Bus Station
General Hospital
Town Hall & Theatre
Curzon Cinema
Library
War Memorial
Carillon Tower
Queens' Park
Leisure Centre
PO
POL
Main Line Steam Trust HQ

Derby 17 A 6
Ashby-de-la-Zouch 12 A 512

A 6 Leicester 12

---

incorporating a specially designed village for its students.

The Education Department of the University specialises in training students to teach physical education.

Loughborough's links with the age of steam are preserved by the Main Line Steam Trust, based at Central Station. Steam locomotives run from here to Quorn and Birstall, a distance of about 10 miles.

Information Tel. 30131.
Location On the A6, 12 m. N of Leicester.
Parking Granby Street; Derby Square; Biggin Street; Ashby Square; Packe Street; Market Place; Leicester Road (all car parks).
District council Borough of Charnwood (Tel. 63151).
Population 47,600.
E-C Wed. **M-D** Thur., Sat.
Police Southfields Road (Tel. 31111).
Casualty hospital Leicester Royal Infirmary, Leicester (Tel. Leicester 541414).
Post office (Bb) Sparrow Hill.
Theatre (Aa) Charnwood, Town Hall, Market Place (Tel. 31914).
Cinema Curzon 1, 2, 3 and 4 (Aa), Cattle Market (Tel. 212261).
Public library (Aa) Granby Street.
Places to see Carillon Tower (Aa); Old Rectory (Ab); Main Line Trust Steam Railway (Ba).
Town trails Tourist Information Centre, John Storer House, Ward's End.
Shopping Market Place; Charnwood Precinct; High Street; Swan Street.
Trade and industry Engineering; hosiery and knitwear; pharmaceutical and scientific equipment.
AA 24 hour service Tel. Leicester 20491.

Louth Lincolnshire

The 295 ft spire of the parish church of St James pinpoints Louth from miles around, as it rises from the vast plain of the Lincolnshire fens. The Poet Laureate, John Betjeman, has called the church "one of the last great medieval Gothic masterpieces". Its beautiful spire was built between 1501 and 1515. The rest of the church is mainly 15th century.

The intricate network of streets is largely made up of a variety of Georgian and early-Victorian architecture. Mercer Row, Westgate and Bridge Street are particularly fine.

At the western end of the town, Thorpe Hall is an impressive 17th-century house. In Louth Park are the remains of a Cistercian abbey, founded in 1139 and dissolved in 1536.

Alfred, Lord Tennyson was educated at the local grammar school, and Parkers, a booksellers in the Market Place, published his first work, *Poems by Two Brothers*, in 1827.

Information Tel. 602391.
Location On the A16, 16 m. S of Grimsby.
Parking Cannon Street; Eastgate (2); Northgate; Kidgate; Queen Street; Eve Street; Bridge Street; Newmarket (all car parks).
District council East Lindsey (Tel. 601111).
Population 13,300.
E-C Thur. **M-D** Wed., Fri. and Sat.
Police Eastgate (Tel. 604744).
Casualty hospital County, High Holme Road (Tel. 601131).
Post office Eastgate.
Theatre Little, Newmarket (Tel. 603549).
Cinema Playhouse, Cannon Street (Tel. 603333).
Public library Upgate.
Places to see Abbey ruins; Museum, Enginegate; St James's Church.
Shopping Eastgate; Mercer Row; Cornmarket; Market Place.
Event May Fair.
AA 24 hour service Tel. Lincoln 42363.

MAJESTIC SPIRE *The soaring hexagonal spire of St James's Church, Louth, is one of the most beautiful in England. It was completed in 1515.*

Lowestoft Suffolk

Wide, sandy beaches, and the inland lakes and rivers of the Broads, have made Lowestoft a major resort.

Fishing was the town's main industry from the middle of the last century until recently. There are guided tours of the harbour and the fish market, and often a trawler is available for viewing. An 18th-century smoke house is still in use in Raglan Street.

The main part of the port, which has a dry dock and shipyard, lies up-river and is used mainly by grain and timber ships. The outer harbour is the home of the yacht club and the Lowestoft lifeboat station which was founded in 1801, 23 years before the establishment of the Royal National Lifeboat Institution.

Cobbled steps known as The Scores lead down the cliffs to the site of the original beach village, now an industrial estate. Sparrow's Nest, named after one of the founders of the lifeboat station, is a park with a theatre and other entertainments. It includes a maritime museum, at Bowling Green Cottage. At Carlton Colville, 2 miles south-west, is the East Anglia Transport Museum. Working exhibits include trams and a narrow-gauge railway.

Oulton Broad, one of the finest stretches of inland water in the country, offers almost every type of boat for hire, coarse angling, sailing regattas and motor-boat races.

Lowestoft was the birthplace of Thomas Nash (1567-1601), the poet and dramatist, and of the composer Benjamin Britten (1913-76).

Information The Esplanade (Tel. 65989).
Location On the A12, 10 m. S of Great Yarmouth.
Parking Nicholas Everitt Park; Kirkley Cliff; Pakefield Road; Links Road; Belvedere Road; Clifton Road; St Peter's Street; All Saints Road (all car parks).
District council Waveney (Tel. 62111).
Population 55,200.
E-C Thur. **M-D** Fri., Sat.
Police (Bb) Old Nelson Street (Tel. 62121).
Casualty hospital General, Lowestoft Road, Gorleston (Tel. Great Yarmouth 56222).
Post office (Aa) London Road North.
Theatres Sparrow's Nest (Tel. 3318); South Pier Pavilion **(Aa)** (4793).
Cinemas Seagull Theatre, Morton Road (Tel. 62863); Marina **(Ab)**, The Marina (4186).
Public library (Ab) Clapham Road.
Places to see Maritime Museum; Sparrow's Nest; Transport Museum, Chapel Road, Carlton Colville.
Shopping London Road North; High Street; Market Triangle.
AA 24 hour service
Tel. Norwich 29401.

LUDLOW CASTLE *The 11th–16th-century fortress is now an impressive red-stone ruin.*

Ludlow Salop

In Tudor times the border town of Ludlow was the capital of the Welsh Marches. It was guarded by the massive red-stone fortress which still stands on high ground overlooking the River Teme. The castle was begun in the late 11th century.

The 135 ft high tower of the glorious cathedral-like Church of St Laurence dominates the town. The church was begun in 1199, and some early fragments can still be seen.

The Angel Hotel in Broad Street is a splendid coaching inn. Other outstanding buildings include the 16th-century Feathers Hotel, the 13th-century Reader's House and the 18th-century Hosyer's Almshouses. The Butter Cross, built in 1743, houses a display that traces Ludlow's history. A collection of over 30,000 fossils may be viewed by appointment at the County Museum Natural Science Department in Old Street.

Information Tel. 3857.
Location On the A49, 11 m. N of Leominster.
Parking Castle Street; Lower Galdeford; Upper Galdeford; Linney; Station Street (all car parks). Corve Street; Broad Street; Mill Street; High Street; Bull Ring.
District council South Shropshire (Tel. 2381).
Population 7,500.
E-C Thur. **M-D** Mon., Fri., Sat.
Police Lower Galdeford (Tel. 2222).
Casualty hospital East Hamlet (Tel. 2201).
Post office Corve Street.
Public library Old Street.
Places to see Castle; Feathers Hotel, Bull Ring; The Reader's House, Churchyard; Hosyer's Almshouses, College Street.
Town trails Available from Shropshire County Museum Services, Old Street, Ludlow.
Shopping Corve Street; High Street; King Street; Bull Ring; Broad Street.
Event Ludlow Festival (June or July).
Trade and industry Agricultural implements; tourism; antiques.
Sport Horse racing, Bromfield.
AA 24 hour service
Tel. Birmingham (021) 550 4858.

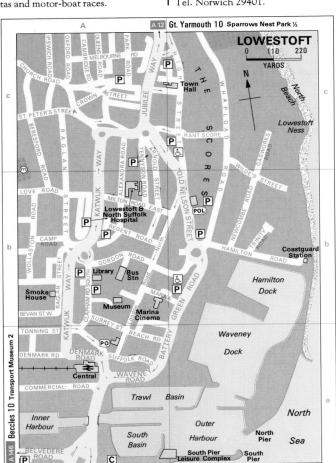

Map of Lowestoft:

Gt. Yarmouth 10 Sparrows Nest Park ½

LOWESTOFT

0   110   220
YARDS

Key map features: IPSWICH ROAD, OXFORD ROAD, CAMBRIDGE RD, QUEENS ROAD, PARK ROAD, MELBOURNE RD, CHURCH ROAD, ST PETER'S STREET, CROWN STREET, JUBILEE WAY, HIGH STREET, THE SCORES, WHAPLOAD ROAD, Town Hall, BERESFORD ROAD, RAGLAN STREET, KATWIJK WAY, ALEXANDRA ROAD, MILTON ROAD EAST, ARNOLD STREET, OLD NELSON STREET, GRANT SCORE, WILDE'S STREET, NEWCOMBE ROAD, GASWORKS ROAD, North Beach, Lowestoft Ness, LOVE ROAD, CAMP ROAD, WOLLASTON ROAD, GORDON ROAD, REGENT ROAD, HAMILTON ROAD, Coastguard Station, Lowestoft & North Suffolk Hospital, POL, Library, Bus Stn, Smoke House, BEVAN ST W., Museum, Marina Cinema, MARINA, Hamilton Dock, TONNING ST, SURREY ST, BEACH RD, BATTERY GREEN ROAD, Waveney Dock, DENMARK RD, DENMARK ROAD, SUFFOLK ROAD, WAVENEY ROAD, PO, Central, COMMERCIAL ROAD, Trawl Basin, Inner Harbour, South Basin, Outer Harbour, North Pier, South Pier Leisure Complex, South Pier, North Sea, BELVEDERE ROAD

Beccles 10 Transport Museum 2
A146
A12 Ipswich 44

ARCHITECTURAL TREASURE *The half-timbered Tudor and Georgian brick buildings of Broad Street, Ludlow, make it one of the handsomest streets in England. Lord Nelson was made a burgess of the borough at the Angel in 1802.*

Luton Bedfordshire

The prosperity of Luton, founded on the airport and the production of motor cars, trucks, electrical goods and hats, is reflected in the Arndale Centre, the largest covered shopping complex in Britain.

The town also has some impressive links with the past. St Mary's Church, built from the 12th to the 14th centuries, has a splendid chequer-patterned tower built of black knapped flint and white limestone. Luton Museum and Art Gallery includes collections devoted to lace-making and hat-making.

Luton Hoo, a house originally built in 1767 by Robert Adam for the 3rd Earl of Bute but reconstructed after a fire in 1843, stands in a 1,500 acre park. It houses the Wernher family's magnificent art collection and other treasures, including mementoes of the Russian Imperial Family.

Information Tel. 32629.
Location On the A6, 30 m. N of London.

Parking Bus Station; Library Road; Central, Cheapside; Market, Nelson Street; Guildford Street; Regent Street; Inner Ring Road; Crawley Road (all car parks).
District council Borough of Luton (Tel. 31291).
Population 164,000.
M-D Mon.–Sat. (not Wed.).
Police Buxton Road (Tel. 31122).
Casualty hospital Luton and Dunstable, Dunstable Road (Tel. 53211).
Post office Dunstable Road.
Theatre Library Theatre (**Ab**), St George's Square (Tel. 21628).
Cinemas ABC (**Aa**), George Street (Tel. 27311); Odeon, Dunstable Road (20341).
Public library (Ab) St George's Square.
Places to see Museum and Art Gallery; Luton Hoo, 2 m. S.
Shopping Arndale Centre.
Sport FA League football, Luton Town FC, Kenilworth Road.
AA 24 hour service
Tel. Hatfield 62852.

Lyme Regis Dorset

The town acquired the suffix Regis (meaning "of the king") when Edward I used its harbour in the 13th century as a base for his wars against the French. Four centuries later, in 1685, the Duke of Monmouth landed there to lead his ill-fated rebellion against James II. But within 100 years, Lyme had become a peaceful, fashionable resort. It was a favourite with the novelist Jane Austen (1775-1817) who had a seafront cottage.

Lyme Regis has five small beaches and a 14th-century breakwater called The Cobb. The coastal scenery includes Golden Cap, at 617 ft the highest cliff on the south coast.

The Philpot Museum contains the fossilised remains of an ichthyosaurus, a 30 ft long aquatic reptile of 140 million years ago. It was found near Lyme Regis, in cliffs that are a never-ending source of fossils.

St Michael's Church, built about 1500, contains a carved 17th-century pulpit and a chained Bible.

Charmouth, 2½ miles east, is a holiday resort with Regency houses and an old inn, the Queen's Armes, where Catherine of Aragon, Henry VIII's first wife, stayed in 1501.

UMBRELLA COTTAGE *An unusual roof by a roadside in Lyme Regis.*

Information Tel. 2138.
Location On the A3052, 10 m. W of Bridport.
Parking Monmouth Beach; Hill Road; Broad Street (2); Cobb Gate (all car parks).
District council West Dorset (Tel. Dorchester 65211).
Population 3,450.
E-C Thur.
Police Hill Road (Tel. 2603).
Casualty hospital Lyme Regis, Pound Road (Tel. 2254) for minor accidents. For major casualties: Weymouth and District, Melcombe Avenue, Weymouth (Tel. Weymouth 72211).
Post office Broad Street.
Theatre Marine, Church Street (Tel. 2394).
Cinema Regent, Broad Street (Tel. 2053).
Public library Silver Street.
Places to see Philpot Museum, Bridge Street; Aquarium, The Cobb.
Shopping Broad Street.
Event Regatta (Aug.).
AA 24 hour service
Tel. Yeovil 27744.

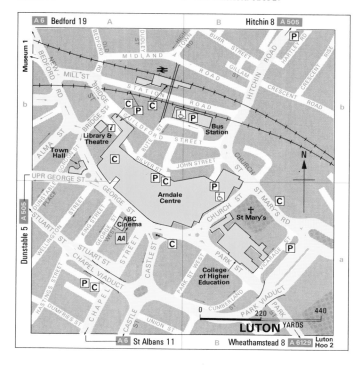

Lymington Hampshire

The sheltered harbour at Lymington is one of the busiest yacht havens on the south coast. It is also the terminal for a ferry service to the Isle of Wight.

Lymington old town is a place of cobbled streets and Georgian houses. The Church of St Thomas the Apostle, partly 13th century, has a fine cupola-topped tower built in 1670.

Information Tel. 75244.
Location On the A337, 18 m. E of Bournemouth.
Parking St Thomas Street; Belmore Lane; Emsworth Road; Quay Street (all car parks).
District council New Forest (Tel. Lyndhurst 3121).
Population 38,700.
E-C Wed. **M-D** Sat.
Police Southampton Road (Tel. 75411).
Casualty hospital Lymington and District, Southampton Road (Tel. 74271).
Post office High Street.
Cinema Centre, New Street (Tel. 72337).
Public library Cannon Street.
Shopping High Street; Queen Street; New Street; St Thomas Street.
Trade and industry Boat-building; agriculture; light engineering.
Car ferry To Yarmouth, I.o.W. (Tel. 73301).
AA 24 hour service
Tel. Southampton 36811.

Lytham St Annes Lancs.

A large windmill next to the old lifeboat house provides the family resort of Lytham St Annes with a notable landmark. Built in 1805, it was gutted by fire in 1918 but has recently been restored.

Lytham has golden sands, beautiful gardens and four golf courses, including the Royal Lytham and St Annes, where major tournaments are played.

Information Tel. 725610.
Location On the A584, 7 m. S of Blackpool.
Parking Off East Beach (2); Outer Promenade (2); South Promenade (2); North Promenade; Pier (2); Orme Road (all car parks).
District council Borough of Fylde (Tel. 721222).
Population 39,700.
E-C Wed.
Police Bannister Street (Tel. 736222).
Casualty hospital Victoria Hospital, East Park Drive, Blackpool (Tel. Blackpool 34111).
Post offices Clifton Street; Clifton Drive.
Cinema Studios 1, 2 and 3, St Georges Road (Tel. 726235).
Public library Clifton Street.
Places to see Windmill; Motor Museum.
Shopping Clifton Street; St Annes Square.
AA 24 hour service
Tel. Blackpool 44947.

Mablethorpe Lincolnshire

The terraced promenade at Mablethorpe, which gives access to miles of sandy beach for summer holiday-makers, is also the low-lying town's defence against the sea in winter gales. Tree stumps that appear on the sands at very low tides are all that remain of a village and forest that was engulfed by the sea in 1289.

Information Tel. 2496.
Location On the A52, 15 m. E of Louth.
Parking Mablethorpe: High Street; Queen's Park; Quebec Road (2); Sherwood; Seacroft; North End (all car parks). Sutton-on-Sea: Broadway; High Street; Sandilands (all car parks).
District council East Lindsey (Tel. Louth 601111).
Population 7,460.
E-C Wed. (not in summer).
M-D Mon. (summer), Thur.
Police Victoria Road (Tel. 2222).
Casualty hospital County Hospital, High Holme Road, Louth (Tel. 601131).
Post offices Wellington Road, Mablethorpe. High Street, Sutton-on-Sea.
Theatre The Dunes, North Promenade (Tel. 2496).
Cinema The Bijou, Quebec Road (Tel. 7040).
Public libraries Victoria Road, Mablethorpe. Broadway, Sutton-on-Sea.
Town trails Available from Information Bureau, Central Promenade, Mablethorpe.
Shopping High Street and Victoria Road, Mablethorpe. High Street, Sutton-on-Sea.
AA 24 hour service
Tel. Lincoln 42363.

Macclesfield Cheshire

Mills dating from the 18th and 19th centuries can be seen in the steep streets of this silk-manufacturing town overlooking the Bollin Valley. The 13th-century Church of St Michael stands so high above the town that on one side 108 steps must be climbed to reach it. Tombs with effigies in the church date from the 15th century onwards.

The West Park Museum contains a collection of Egyptian antiquities, and a gallery of Victorian paintings.

Gawsworth Hall, 3 miles south-west of the town, was built mainly in the 15th century. It was the home of Mary Fitton, Maid of Honour to Elizabeth I and according to some authorities the "Dark Lady" of Shakespeare's sonnets.

Information Tel. 21955.
Location On the A523, 12 m. W of Buxton.
Parking Churchill Way; Park Green; Waters Green; Great King Street (3);

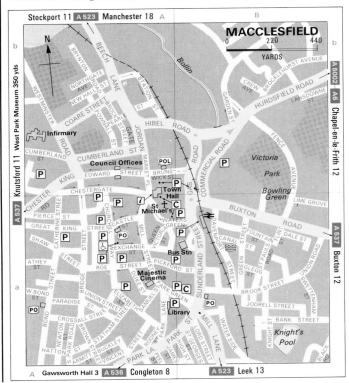

MILL TOWN *A modern industrial town has grown around Macclesfield's silk mills, but above the town winding cobblestone streets climb steeply between moss-covered walls and the picturesque cottages that look down on the Bollin Valley.*

Preston Street; Wellington Street; Commercial Road; Westminster Road; Church Street West; Roe Street (2); Park Lane; Pickford Street; Brunswick Street (all cps).
District council Borough of Macclesfield (Tel. 21955).
Population 46,800.
E-C Wed. **M-D** Tues., Fri., Sat.
Police (Ab) Brunswick Street (Tel. 21966).
Casualty hospital (Ab) Macclesfield Infirmary, Cumberland Street (Tel. 21000).
Post office (Aa) Castle Street.
Cinema Majestic **(Aa)**, Mill Street (Tel. 22412).
Public library (Aa) Park Green.
Places to see West Park Museum and Art Gallery; Gawsworth Hall, 3 m. SW.
Shopping Mill Street; Chestergate; Sunderland Street; Grosvenor Centre; Market Place.
Events May Fair (Apr./May); Carnival (May, bi-annually); Motor Show, Adlington Hall (June); Wakes Fair (Oct.)
AA 24 hour service
Tel. Manchester (061) 485 6299.

Maidenhead Berkshire

In Edwardian times, Maidenhead was a favourite spot for the fun-loving younger generation, and a popular place of residence for London's theatre folk. The old town has been encircled by modern development, but on the riverside Maidenhead still retains its old-world charm.

The stone bridge over this stretch of the Thames was built in 1777 to replace a wooden structure of 1280.

The railway bridge, known as the Sounding Arch because of its echo, was built in 1838 by Isambard Kingdom Brunel, the railway engineer. Its two arches, each spanning 128 ft, are the widest ever constructed in brick.

Information Tel. 25657.
Location On the A4, 6 m. W of Slough.
Parking Grove Road; Boulter's Lock; West Street; Broadway; Stafferton Way; Crown Lane; Park Street; Market Street; Cookham Road (all car parks).
District council Royal Borough of Windsor and Maidenhead (Tel. Maidenhead 33155).
Population 49,000.
E-C Thur. **M-D** Fri., Sat.
Police (Bb) Bridge Road (Tel. 39922).
Casualty hospital Wexham Park Hospital, Wexham Street, Slough (Tel. Slough 34567).
Post office (Aa) High Street.
Cinema ABC **(Ba)**, Bridge Avenue (Tel. 23750).
Public library (Ba) St Ives Road.
Places to see Henry Reitlinger Fine Arts Museum, Guards' Club Road; Courage Shire Horse Centre, Maidenhead Thicket.
Shopping High Street; Queen Street; King Street; Market Street; Nicholson's Walk.
Events Swan Upping (July); Regatta (Aug.); Knowl Steam Fair (Aug.).
Trade and industry Publishing; light engineering.
AA 24 hour service
Tel. Reading 581122.

SKINDLES HOTEL *In Edwardian times the hotel was a favourite riverside rendez-vous of the wealthy.*

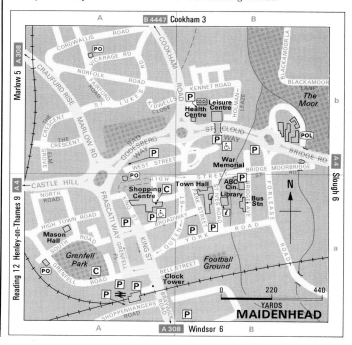

MAIDENHEAD

Maidstone Kent

The county town of Kent stands on the rivers Medway and Len, in the heart of the rich farmland nicknamed "The Garden of England", and at the foot of the North Downs.

From Saxon times it was the site of the "shire moot", or county assembly, and the first recorded trial in England was held at Penenden Heath, now a recreation ground.

Maidstone's geographical position made it, from the Middle Ages onwards, the natural market centre through which fruit and vegetables from the surrounding countryside were shipped to feed the population of London; and this role continues today. The area is also the main source in England of hops for brewing.

Weaving and related crafts expanded in Maidstone during the 16th century, after Flemish refugees from religious persecution settled there. Until the 19th century, Maidstone was also famous for its linen thread. But the industry declined and the flax fields were turned over to hops, while the water-driven textile mills – such as Barcham Green's Mill at Tovil – were converted to make paper, still a major local industry.

From before AD 975 until the 16th century, the manor of Maidstone belonged to the Archbishops of Canterbury. They built a country residence there, the Manor House or Archbishop's Palace, beside the Medway. The present building dates from the 14th century, though it was extensively altered by later owners. Its rooms are now used for public and private meetings.

Next to the palace is the Church of All Saints, which was begun in 1395 and has one of the widest naves in England – 93 ft. In the same group of buildings are the 14th-century College of Secular Canons, now the Kent Music School, and, across Bishop's Way, the early-15th-century Archbishop's Stables, which contain a carriage museum.

Other medieval buildings in Maidstone include the 14th-century bridge over the Len in Mill Street, and the 15th-century Corpus Christi Hall in Earl Street, originally the headquarters of a religious guild and later the grammar school.

In the 15th century, Mote Park, on the edge of the town centre, was the home of the powerful Woodville family. Anthony Woodville, Lord Rivers, was the patron of the printer William Caxton, while his sister Elizabeth became the queen of the Yorkist Edward IV. Mote House was rebuilt in the 18th century, and is now a Cheshire Home for the disabled.

Chillington Manor House in St Faith's Street belonged to the Wyatt family, and is now the town museum and art gallery. The Wyatts also owned Allington Castle, on the outskirts of the town, which was built in the 13th century on a site occupied since Roman times. It has been restored and now belongs to the Carmelite Order, but it is open to the public. Boughton Monchelsea Place, a 16th-century manor house 3 miles south of Maidstone, was a third Wyatt home, and is preserved as a museum.

The essayist William Hazlitt was born in Maidstone in 1778, though he left at the age of two. His father was minister of the Unitarian Chapel, which stands in an arcade off the High Street.

Information Tel. 673581.
Location On the A20, 8 m. S of Rochester.
Parking King Street; Medway Street; Wheeler Street; Museum Street; Waterside; Mill Street; College Road; Fairmeadow; Brunswick Street; Mote Road; Maryland (all car parks).
District council Borough of Maidstone (Tel. 671361).
Population 72,300.
E-C Wed. **M-D** Tues.
Police Palace Avenue (Tel. 64141).
Casualty hospital (Bb) West Kent General, Marsham Street (Tel. 65411).
Post office (Bb) King Street.
Theatre Hazlitt **(Ab)**, Earl Street (Tel. 58611).
Cinema Granada 1, 2 and 3 **(Ba)**, Lower Stone Street (Tel. 52628).
Public library (Ab) St Faith's Street.
Places to see Carriage Museum **(Ba)**; Allington Castle; Archbishop's Palace **(Aa)**; Chillington Manor House Museum and Art Gallery **(Ab)**; Boughton Monchelsea Place, 3 m. S.
Shopping Week Street; High Street; New Stoneborough Shopping Centre.
Event Kent County Agricultural Show (July).
AA 24 hour service
Tel. 55353.

Maldon Essex

The wide reaches of the Blackwater estuary have made Maldon a natural base for yachtsmen, and at least half-a-dozen clubs now flourish in the town. Boat-building has been an important industry at Maldon for many decades, and the local fishing smacks still line up with their catches at the Marine Parade. The 13th-century Church of All Saints has the only triangular church tower in Britain.

OLD CRAFT *Some of the Thames sailing barges, which used to carry coastal trade, are berthed at Hythe Quay, Maldon.*

Information Tel. 54477.
Location On the A414, 10 m. E of Chelmsford.
Parking White Horse; Butt Lane; Marine Parade (all car parks).
District council Maldon (Tel. 54477).
Population 15,250.
E-C Wed. **M-D** Thur., Sat.
Police West Square (Tel. 52255).
Casualty hospital Chelmsford and Essex, London Road, Chelmsford (Tel. Chelmsford 83331).
Post office High Street.

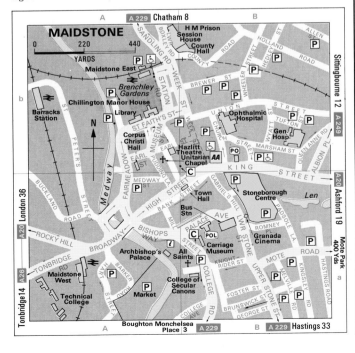

Cinema Embassy, High Street
(Tel. 53168).
Public library St Peter's Room, High
Street.
Places to see Moot Hall; Plume
Library, St Giles's Hospital ruins,
Spital Road.
Town trails Available from Planning
Officer, Maldon District Council,
Market Hill.
Shopping High Street.
Event Barge Match (June/July).
AA 24 hour service
Tel. Chelmsford 61711.

Malmesbury Wiltshire

A charter granted in 924 by King
Edward, son of Alfred the Great, is
the basis of Malmesbury's claim to be
the oldest borough in England. The
town perches on a hill above the
River Avon, spanned along this
stretch by six bridges.

The pride of Malmesbury is the
magnificent nave of a 12th-century
Benedictine abbey church – all that
remains of an abbey founded in the
7th century. The nave survived the
Dissolution of 1539 to become the
parish church. Its outstanding features include the 15th-century
screens and the musicians' gallery
above the arcade.

In the 11th century a monk called
Elmer broke his legs while attempting
to fly with home-made wings from
the roof of the original abbey – an
exploit commemorated in a window
of the church.

Information Tel. 2143.
Location On the A429, 16 m. W of
Swindon.
Parking Cross Hayes; Horsefair;
Market Cross; Station Yard (all car
parks).
District council North Wiltshire
(Tel. Chippenham 2821).
Population 2,550.
E-C Thur.
Police Burton Hill (Tel. 2222).
Casualty hospital Malmesbury
Hospital, Burton Hill (Tel. 3358).
Post office High Street.
Public library Cross Hayes.
Places to see Abbey; Museum in
Cross Hayes; Almshouses; Market
Cross.
Shopping High Street; The Triangle.
AA 24 hour service
Tel. Swindon 21446.

Malton N. Yorks.

Prize-winning, thoroughbred race-
horses have galloped in training across the gentle turf of Langton Wold
for almost 200 years. But, at heart,
Malton is essentially a farming town,
and its livestock market is one of the
biggest in the North of England.

The Romans built a fort where the
town now stands as they advanced
north nearly 2,000 years ago. The
Roman Museum in the Market Place
contains many finds from the camp.

Six miles west of the town stands
Castle Howard, the largest house in

MEMORABLE GLASS *Great Malvern Priory is second only to York Minster in its collection of 15th-century stained glass. The north transept window, a gift of Henry VII, is noted for its glorious yellows.*

Yorkshire, designed by Sir John Vanbrugh about 1700 for the 3rd Earl of
Carlisle.

Information Tel. 4011.
Location On the A64, 18 m. NE of
York.
Parking Wentworth Street (cp).
District council Ryedale (Tel. 4011).
Population 4,150.
E-C Thur. **M-D** Tues., Fri., Sat.
Police Old Maltongate (Tel. 2424).
Casualty hospital Malton Hospital,
Middlecave Road (Tel. 3041).
Post office Wheelgate.
Cinema Studio 1, Yorkersgate
(Tel. 3173).
Public library St Michael Street.
Places to see Roman Museum.
Shopping Wheelgate; Yorkersgate.
AA 24 hour service
Tel. York 27698.

Malvern H. & W.

Pure spring water from the Malvern
Hills turned Malvern into a spa in
Victorian times, and more than a
million bottles of the water are still
sold throughout the world every year.

Six Malverns nestle on the flanks of
the hills – Great, Little and North
Malvern, together with West Malvern, Malvern Wells and Malvern
Link.

Great Malvern is a place of steep
streets and Georgian and Victorian
buildings. Its great glory is its priory
church, founded in 1085 but mainly
15th century in fabric.

Little Malvern lies beneath the
Herefordshire Beacon, which is topped by an Iron Age fort begun about
300 BC. On these slopes the poet
William Langland (*c.* 1340-1400) is
said to have dreamed his *Vision of
Piers Plowman*.

Little Malvern also has a priory,
founded about 1150, of which the
church and refectory survive. Wynd's
Point, behind the priory, was the last

home of the Stockholm-born singer
Jenny Lind (1820-87), known as the
Swedish Nightingale.

St Wulstan's churchyard, on the
road to Malvern Wells, contains the
grave of the composer Sir Edward
Elgar (1857-1934), who composed
much of his music while walking on
the Malvern Hills.

West Malvern lies beyond North
Hill and the Worcestershire Beacon
(1,394 ft), the highest point of the
hills. North Malvern keeps its old
stocks and whipping-post.

Malvern Link was probably named
after the practice of linking extra
horses to stagecoaches to pull them up
the steep hill to Great Malvern.

Information Tel. 4700.
Location On the A449, 8 m. S of
Worcester.
Parking Great Malvern: Edith Walk;
Priory Road; Victoria Road. Malvern
Link: Victoria Park Road (all car
parks).
District council Malvern Hills
(Tel. 2700).
Population 30,200.
E-C Wed. (Great Malvern); Thur.
(Malvern Link). **M-D** Fri.
Police Victoria Road (Tel. 61616).
Casualty hospital Royal Infirmary,
Castle Street, Worcester
(Tel. Worcester 27122).
Post office Abbey Road.
Theatres Malvern Festival, Grange
Road (Tel. 3377/8); Winter
Gardens, Grange Road (66266).
Cinema Winter Gardens Cinema,
Grange Road (Tel. 3377/8).
Public library Graham Road.
Places to see Museum, Abbey Road;
Malvern Priory; Iron Age hill-fort;
Little Malvern Court.
Shopping Great Malvern: Church
Street; Belle Vue Terrace. Malvern
Link: Worcester Road.
Event Shaw/Elgar Festival (May).
AA 24 hour service
Tel. Worcester 51070.

MANCHESTER Greater Manchester

The industrial capital of the North

Cotton and the Industrial Revolution created Manchester in the 18th century. The damp climate prevented the fine cotton threads breaking while being spun, and machinery revolutionised the textile industry founded in the 14th century by Flemish weavers. In 1894 the opening of the Manchester Ship Canal made the city a port, 36 miles from the sea.

Manchester's history has been notable for its social reforms, a tradition which has been carried into the 20th century with slum clearance, smokeless-zone regulations and sweeping redevelopment of the city centre. But Manchester is proud of its origins, and is still unmistakably a Victorian city.

The heart of modern Manchester is Piccadilly, a great square which was almost totally destroyed by bombing in the Second World War. Hotels, shops and the towering Piccadilly Plaza building loom over the square, but its centre is a green oasis of lawns and flower beds where the roar of the encircling traffic is reduced to a whisper.

In contrast to Piccadilly, the area bounded by Princess Street, Mount Street and Lower Mosley Street carries a strong reminder that Manchester was a Victorian city. The **Town Hall**, covering nearly 2 acres, stands facing Albert Square and is surmounted by a clock-tower 281 ft 6 in. tall. The building was completed in 1877 to the design of Alfred Waterhouse (1830-1905) and is in Gothic style. Above the Lord Mayor's entrance, in Princess Street, is a carving of Edward III, whose introduction of Flemish weavers into England laid the foundation of the city's traditional industry.

Inside the Town Hall are statues of men who played an important role in Manchester's history, including John

PORT OF MANCHESTER *The Manchester Ship Canal was built to link the city's textile industry with the sea. It also opened the way for the growth of other industries. Today the port is the third-busiest in Britain, bringing raw materials to the factories and exporting their goods.*

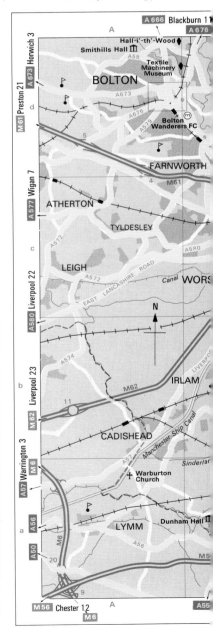

Bright (1811-89), who was MP for Manchester in 1847 and 1852; Richard Cobden (1804-65), who was closely associated with Bright as an opponent of the Corn Laws, and several other prominent members of the Anti Corn Law League.

Hall of words and music

The league opposed the law which banned the import of cheap foreign wheat. Their headquarters was the **Free Trade Hall**, in Peter Street, built in 1843. The Anti Corn Law League was disbanded in 1846 when the Corn Laws were repealed, and the hall was later used by the Athenaeum Society whose first chairman was Charles Dickens.

A new hall was built in 1856, and it was here that the orchestra founded by Sir Charles Hallé (1819-95) gave its first concert in 1857. Second World War bombing almost totally destroyed the hall, but it was rebuilt

VIOLENT REPRESSION *The demand for political reform in Britain reached a bloody peak in 1819, when troops dispersed a meeting at St Peter's Field with sabres drawn. Eleven people died and many more were injured in what became known as "The Peterloo Massacre". The cartoonist George Cruikshank (1792-1878) portrayed his own cynical version of the incident.*

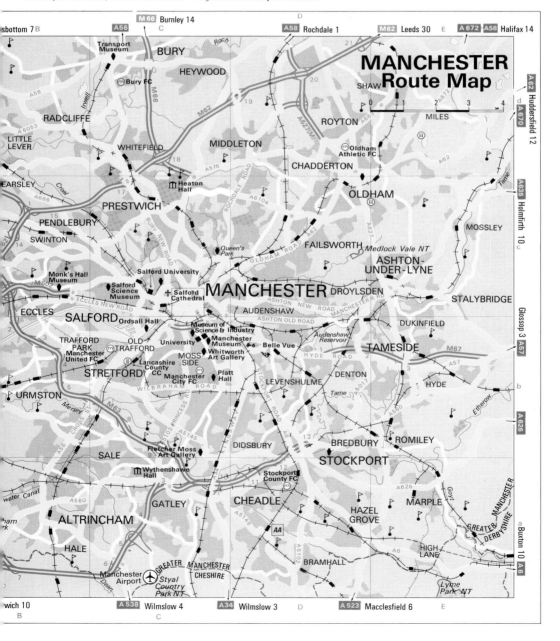

in 1951 in its original Palladian style.

The Free Trade Hall is still the home of the Hallé Orchestra, which gained international repute in the 1950s and 1960s under the leadership of Sir John Barbirolli (1899-1970).

Massacre and reform

St Peter's Square is on the site of St Peter's Field where, in 1819, a black page was written in Manchester's history. High unemployment, intolerable working conditions and widespread poverty had led to strikes and riots. Manchester was still unrepresented in Parliament, and on August 16, 1819, 50,000 people assembled in St Peter's Field to press for political reform. The meeting was broken up by mounted troops in a sabre charge.

Eleven people died and hundreds were injured, and the event became known as the "Peterloo Massacre"– the Battle of Waterloo had been fought four years earlier. The incident strengthened the hands of the reformers, who finally achieved some success with the introduction of the Factory Act of 1819. The voice of the people can still be heard near where the Peterloo victims died; an area close to St Peter's Square has been set aside for the use of public speakers.

The Manchester radicals were supported by John Edward Taylor (1791-1844) who founded the *Manchester Guardian* newspaper in 1821. The newspaper became the instrument of radicalism, and its influence was felt on a national scale. Its greatest editor was C. P. Scott (1846-1932), who edited the paper from 1872 until 1929.

First free library

Some of the earliest examples of printed words can be seen in the **John Rylands University Library**. John Rylands (1801-88) was a weaving tycoon and public benefactor. After his death his widow founded the library, purchasing books through his legacies, as a memorial to him. It was opened in 1900.

In 1972 the John Rylands Library was merged with the Manchester University Library, but is still housed in the Gothic-style building in Deansgate which was its original

CITY GREEN *Only the buildings in the background reveal that these lawns and flower beds are in the city centre – Piccadilly.*

home. The library's collection includes a copy of the Gutenberg Bible; more than 60 books printed by William Caxton; first editions of Greek, Latin and English classics, and manuscripts in more than 50 languages dating from 3000 BC to the present day.

ARTISTRY IN WOOD *The carved bench ends in Manchester Cathedral were installed by Bishop Stanley about 1505-10.*

Another of Manchester's benefactors was Humphrey Chetham (1580-1653), who bequeathed funds for founding a school for the poor and for a public library. The school, **Chetham's Hospital**, was opened in 1656. It now operates as the Chetham School of Music, developing the talents of musically gifted children. **Chetham's Library** was the first free library in Europe. It contains printed books and manuscripts, including a collection of works of the 16th–18th centuries. Manchester Grammar School was founded in 1515 by Hugh Oldham, Bishop of Exeter, a Lancashire man. The modern school's academic record is among the best in Britain.

Manchester's **Central Library** has been a favourite meeting place for Mancunians since it was opened in 1934. The circular building is one of the largest municipal libraries in England, having a stock of more than 9 million books. In contrast to the nearby Town Hall the library has classical lines, with a portico of Corinthian columns and Tuscan columns around the upper storey. Inside there is a domed reading-room, and the Shakespeare Hall has a stained-glass window showing the playwright surrounded by some of his characters. The tiny Library Theatre, seating 308, is housed in the basement and stages repertory productions.

Biggest room in the world

Manchester's newest and most revolutionary theatre is in the **Royal Exchange** building in St Ann's Square. The building was opened in 1921 as the city's cotton exchange, replacing an earlier one in Market Street. The floor space of the main hall covers about 1 acre, which earned it the claim when built of "the biggest room in the world". The roof has three glass domes and is supported on giant marble columns. Cotton trading ceased in 1968, and the

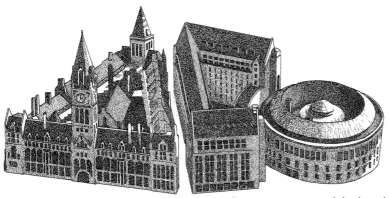

CONTRAST IN STYLES *The Gothic Town Hall, its 1938 extension and the classical Central Library form a block of buildings that show the changing styles of Manchester's architecture over a period of 60 years.*

theatre, which opened in 1976, now occupies the hall. The complete theatre is a steel capsule weighing 100 tons. Because the floor was unable to bear the weight, the structure was suspended from the marble columns.

The theatre has a seating capacity of 740. The stage is in the centre of the auditorium and is used for "theatre-in-the-round" productions and musical concerts.

Medieval Manchester

At the junction of Victoria Street and Cateaton Street stands **Manchester Cathedral**, a 15th-century building in Perpendicular Gothic style. It is dedicated to St Mary, St Denys and St George, and was given cathedral status in 1847. A tower was added in 1868, enhancing the striking majesty of the church, but its chief glory is its early-16th-century carved woodwork – particularly the canopied choir stalls. A side chapel is dedicated to the Manchester Regiment, and contains the regiment's old colours.

St Ann's Church dates from 1709-12. It overlooks St Ann's Square, dating from the same period and now an elegant part of the city's shopping area. **Barton Arcade**, a Victorian thoroughfare with an iron-framed glass roof, connects the square with Deansgate.

An even-older shopping place, the medieval **Old Shambles**, was largely destroyed by bombing in the Second World War, but the 14th-century half-timbered Wellington Inn has survived.

Galleries of English art

Manchester has a wealth of art galleries, seven municipally controlled and one administered by the university. The **City Art Gallery**, in Mosley Street, was originally the headquarters of the Royal Manchester Institution for the promotion of Literature, Science and the Arts, and was opened in 1829. The building was designed by Sir Charles Barry, the architect of the Houses of Parliament. Since becoming a public gallery in 1882 it has constantly added to its fine collection of paintings, specialising in the development of English art from the 16th century to the present day.

There are also some early-Italian, Flemish and Dutch paintings and works by 19th-century French Impressionists. Sculptures include a bronze bust of C. P. Scott, the former *Manchester Guardian* editor, by Sir Jacob Epstein.

The adjoining annexe to the gallery, the **Athenaeum**, contains ceramics, silver and glassware. The **Fletcher Moss Art Gallery** contains a selection of paintings by British artists, including Thomas Rowlandson, J. M. W. Turner, Augustus John and L. S. Lowry. There is also a display of 19th-century English domestic silver and porcelain.

A rich collection of paintings, drawings and sculpture of the last 100 years is shown in the **Queen's Park**

GLASS UMBRELLA *Shoppers in Barton Arcade have been protected from the weather by this elegant roof since 1871.*

Art Gallery. There are numerous paintings by Victorian artists such as Lord Leighton, G. F. Watts and Sir John Millais. A collection of works by war artists of the First World War contrasts vividly with the gentler subjects chosen by some of their contemporaries.

Victorian dresses are among those displayed in the **Gallery of English Costume** in Platt Hall. The Georgian building makes a fitting setting for an exhibition that covers the changing

ART CENTRE *Sir Charles Barry, architect of the Houses of Parliament, designed the City Art Gallery.*

styles of everyday clothing of the last 350 years. Platt Fields Park, adjoining the house, was once noted for its public orators – the Manchester equivalent of London's Speakers' Corner.

Houses of distinction

Royal Lancastrian pottery, English delft and Staffordshire pottery are displayed in the library of **Wythenshawe Hall**. The house is of architectural interest, parts of it dating from the 16th century. It has a distinctive frontage, the black-and-white half-timber on two projecting wings being herringbone in pattern. Elizabethan silver, 17th-century furniture, oil paintings and armour are also exhibited in the house.

Heaton Hall is an art treasure in itself. It was designed by James Wyatt (1746-1813) in 1772, and is notable for its superbly decorated interior. The rooms are furnished with 18th and 19th-century furniture.

MANCHESTER

MAN OF MUSIC *Sir John Barbirolli conducted the Hallé Orchestra for 27 years. This sculpture by Byron Howard is in the Town Hall.*

MUSICAL HERITAGE *For more than 120 years, music has replaced the voices of angry men in Manchester's Free Trade Hall.*

In the Music Room an organ built in 1790 is still in use.

Spacious parklands surround both Wythenshawe Hall and Heaton Hall. Both have children's playgrounds, lawns and woodlands. At one end of the lake in Heaton Park is a fragment of Manchester's old town hall, which stood in King Street until 1912.

Manchester University's own art collection is housed in the **Whitworth Art Gallery**. It includes English water-colours, Japanese woodcuts, textiles, and contemporary paintings and sculptures.

The **Manchester Museum** is also part of the university. A geological gallery occupies most of the ground floor, and there are large galleries dedicated to zoology, entomology, botany, archaeology and ethnology.

The university buildings were designed by Alfred Waterhouse, designer of Manchester Town Hall, in 1869. Later additions were made by his son, Paul. The building replaced the university's premises where it started life as the Owens College. John Owens (1790-1846) was a Manchester merchant who left money in his will for the founding of a college where there would be no test of religious opinions. The college opened in 1851 and became part of the Victoria University in 1880. It became a separate university in 1903.

Many structures have joined Waterhouse's buildings over the years, reflecting the styles of the periods in which they were built, and ranging from the Edwardian Metallurgy Building to the concrete Mathematics Building erected in the 1960s.

Industrial heritage

A city that has its roots in the Industrial Revolution is a natural place to find a museum of science and technology. The **North Western Museum of Science and Industry** in Grosvenor Street was opened in 1969, and is the largest of its kind in north-west England.

A large part of the museum is devoted to textile machinery, with the emphasis on cotton spinning, and the allied trades such as calico printing and dyeing. The development of steam power is represented by exhibits ranging from a one-third scale model of Newcomen's first engine to a modern steam turbine.

Engineering exhibits include machine tools, railway locomotives and an atmospheric gas engine. The second motor-car engine built by Henry Royce is in the museum; Henry Royce (1863-1933) built his first car, a 10 hp model, in 1904 at the Cooke Street premises of his electrical engineering business. He formed the partnership with C. S. Rolls in 1906.

Historic transport

The Industrial Revolution brought two historic transport systems to Manchester, the Liverpool to Manchester Railway and the Manchester Ship Canal. The railway opened in 1830 and was the world's first commercially successful line. It was built by George Stephenson (1781-1848) whose locomotive *Rocket* heralded the railway age. The Manchester terminus of the railway is Liverpool Road Station, which now handles only goods traffic. The Manchester Ship Canal enables sea-going vessels of up to 15,000 tons to sail almost to the city centre. The canal was opened in 1894 and runs the 36 miles from Manchester to Eastham on the Mersey Estuary. At Barton the canal is crossed by a branch of the Bridgewater Canal, using a swing aqueduct built in 1893. It is a bridge carrying water instead of a roadway, and pivots

to allow ships using the ship canal to pass underneath.

Manchester has been the birthplace of several people who became public figures. David Lloyd George (1863-1945), although of Welsh parentage, was born there. He was Britain's Prime Minister from 1916 until 1922. Another Mancunian, Emmeline Pankhurst (1858-1928), fought militantly for women's rights and suffered imprisonment for her efforts.

Manchester-born writers include the historical novelist William Harrison Ainsworth (1807-96) and Thomas De Quincey (1785-1859), who wrote *Confessions of an Opium-eater*. Only the home of Emmeline Pankhurst, 62 Nelson Street, still stands.

Britain's second-busiest airport, at Ringway, is a fitting reminder that two Mancunians, Captain Sir John Alcock and Sir Arthur Whitten Brown, were the first men to fly the Atlantic Ocean, in 1919. In addition, Manchester was a place of study for several men whose researches led to revolutionary discoveries. John Dalton (1766-1844) provided the first insight into the understanding of atomic theory while teaching at New College; his pupil James Joule (1818-89) gave his name to a unit of electrical energy. In 1906 Professor Ernest

ATOMIC PIONEER *A mural by Ford Maddox Brown (1821-93) in the Town Hall shows the Manchester schoolmaster John Dalton collecting marsh gases. His research led to the understanding of atomic matter.*

Rutherford (1871-1937) proved Dalton's theories while at Manchester University.

Sporting scenes

Mancunians support two professional football teams – Manchester City and Manchester United. Manchester City play at the Maine Road Stadium, and United at Old Trafford – and near by is the other Old Trafford, home of the Lancashire County Cricket Club and a traditional venue for Test Matches.

Manchester also has its own Boat Race, rowed between Manchester and Salford Universities on the River Irwell.

The industrial area of Manchester spreads north of the city, taking in the cotton-spinning towns such as Bolton and Blackburn. But between the towns are flat-topped heights running north to south above rivers and motorways, and here are the unspoiled acres of the Forest of Rossendale, the Cliviger Moors, Turton Moor and Pendle Hill. Ancient pathways climb wooded hillsides to Tudor farmhouses and old stone churches, and Celtic outposts lie atop majestic pikes – and all within a few miles of the bustling city.

Information Tel. Manchester (061) 236 1606/2035 or 247 3694.

Location On the A6, 200 m. NW of London.

Parking Church Street; Gartside Street; King Street West; Cateaton Street; York Street; Aytoun Street; Great Bridgewater Street; Great Ducie Street; Little Peter Street; Liverpool Road; Pritchard Street; Store Street; Thompson Street; Travis Street; Watson Street; Whitworth Street West; High Street; Market Place; Smithfield; Bridge Street; Faulkner Street; Nicholas Street; Portland Street; Wood Street; George Street; Mary Street; Julia Street (all car parks).

District council City of Manchester (Tel. 061 236 3377).

Population 448,900.

M-D Daily.

Police (Aa) Bootle Street (Tel. 061 872 5050).

Casualty hospital Royal Infirmary, Oxford Road (Tel. 061 273 3300).

Post office (Bb) Spring Gardens.

Theatres Library Theatre **(Ba)**, St Peter's Square (Tel. 061 236 7110); Palace Theatre **(Ba)**, Oxford Street (061 236 7671); Royal Exchange **(Bb)**, St Ann's Square (061 833 9833); University Theatre, Devar Street (061 273 5696).

Cinemas Odeon Film Centre **(Ba)**, Oxford Street (Tel. 061 236 8264); Studios 1–4, Oxford Road (061 236 2437); Studios 6–9 **(Ab)**,

Deansgate House, Deansgate (061 834 3580).

Public library (Ba) St Peter's Square.

Places to see City Art Gallery **(Ba)**, Mosley Street; Queen's Park Gallery **(RCc)**, Harpurhey; Heaton Hall **(RCc)**, Heaton Park; Gallery of English Costume, Rusholme; Fletcher Moss Art Gallery **(RCa)**, Didsbury; Wythenshawe Hall **(RCa)**, Northenden; Manchester Museum **(RCb)**, The University; Free Trade Hall **(Aa)**, Peter Street; Chetham's Hospital **(Bc)**, Victoria Street; North Western Museum of Science and Industry, Grosvenor Street; John Rylands University Library **(Ab)**, Deansgate; Town Hall **(Ba)**.

Town trails Available from the Tourist Information Centre, Town Hall.

Shopping Deansgate; Market Street; King Street; Arndale Centre.

Events Ideal Home Exhibition (May); Lord Mayor's Parade (June); Manchester Show (July).

Trade and industry Textiles; engineering; chemicals; electronics.

Sport FA League football: Manchester City FC **(RCb)**, Maine Road; Manchester United FC **(RCb)**, Old Trafford. Cricket, Lancashire County CC **(RCb)**, Old Trafford. Greyhound racing, White City.

AA 24 hour service
Tel. 061 485 6299.

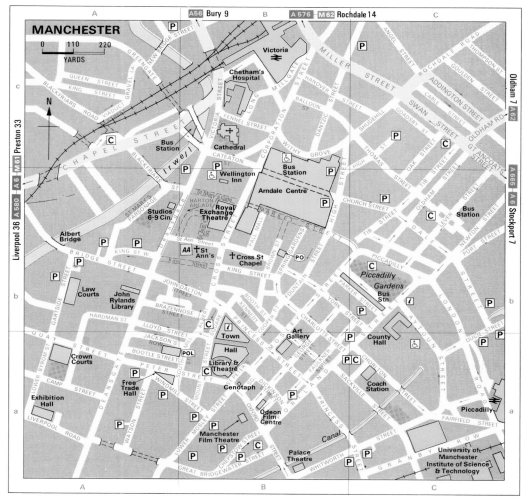

Mansfield Nottinghamshire

The centre oak of Sherwood Forest stood in Westgate, Mansfield, until the 1940s when it had to be felled. A plaque now marks the spot. The forest, legendary home of Robin Hood, was broken up by the enclosures of the last 200 years, and most of what remains stands east of the town.

The parish church of St Peter and St Paul has Saxon stonework in the tower. A huge coat of arms looks down on the market place from the 18th-century Moot Hall, now a bank.

Mansfield is now a market town, a dormitory for surrounding collieries, and a centre of light industry and hosiery manufacturing.

Information Tel. 26983.
Location On the A61, 14 m. N of Nottingham.
Parking Clumber Street; Station Road; Church Lane; Chesterfield Road; Toothill Lane (all car parks).
District council Mansfield (Tel. 22561).
Population 58,900.
E-C Wed. **M-D** Mon., Thur., Fri. and Sat.
Police Station Street (Tel. 22622).
Casualty hospital Mansfield and District General, West Hill Drive (Tel. 22515).
Post office Church Street.
Theatre Civic, Leeming Street (Tel. 23882/22561).
Cinema ABC 1, 2 and 3, Leeming Street (Tel. 23138).
Public library Westgate.
Places to see Sherwood Visitor Centre; Newstead Abbey, 2 m. S.
Shopping Four Seasons Shopping Centre, Westgate; Market Square; Stockwell Gate.
Trade and industry Metal-box manufacture; hosiery; engineering.
Sport FA League football, Mansfield Town FC, Field Mill.
AA 24 hour service Tel. Nottingham 787751.

Margate Kent

Nine miles of sandy beach and the Dreamland family park make Margate, with its easy access from London, a day-tripper's paradise.

Many Regency and Victorian buildings survive from the town's early days as a resort. There are also a few reminders of an earlier past, including the Tudor House, now a museum, smugglers' caves and a grotto inlaid with shells said to have been placed there more than 2,000 years ago.

There is a 3½ mile cliff walk to Birchington, where the Powell-Cotton Museum displays stuffed wild animals in natural tableaux.

Information Tel. 20241.
Location On the A28, 16 m. NE of Canterbury.
Parking Dane Hill Row; Duke Street; Winter Gardens; Hawley Street; Trinity Hill; Market Street; Mill Lane; St John's Road; Marine Drive; Zion Place; Wellington Gardens;

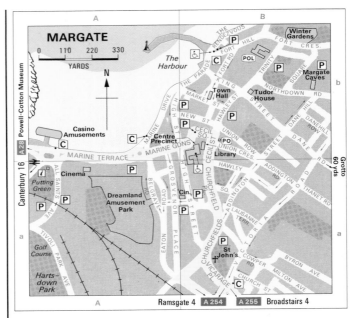

Booth Place (all car parks).
District council Thanet (Tel. Thanet 25511).
Population 53,300.
E-C Thur. **M-D** Thur.
Police (Bb) Fort Hill (Tel. Thanet 25566).
Casualty hospital Kent and Canterbury, Ethelbert Road, Canterbury (Tel. 66877).
Post office (Bb) Cecil Square.
Theatres Winter Gardens and Queens Hall **(Bb)**, Fort Crescent (Tel. 21348/22795); Lido, Ethelbert Crescent, Cliftonville (23456).
Cinemas Dreamland 1, 2 and 3 **(Aa)**, Marine Terrace (Tel. Thanet 27822); Plaza **(Ba)**, High Street (20058); Carlton, St Mildred's Road, Westgate (32019); New Parade, The Parade (22099).
Public library (Bb) Cecil Square.
Places to see Caves **(Bb)**; Grotto; Powell-Cotton Museum; Tudor House; Salmestone Grange; Drapers Windmill; Lifeboat House; Aquarium.
Shopping Northdown Road, Cliftonville; Station Road, Birchington; High Street, The Centre and Cecil Square, Margate; Station Road and St Mildred's Road, Westgate.
AA 24 hour service Tel. Thanet 81226.

Market Harborough
Leicestershire

A broad triangle with chequered paving is the site of the market, which gives the town its name. Markets have been held there since 1204.

Overlooking the town – and the countryside for miles around – is the 14th-century Church of St Dionysius, with a tower and spire soaring to 161 ft. There are many fine Georgian buildings in the town, including the Three Swans Inn with its 18th-century wrought-iron sign.

SCHOOL AND MARKET *Built in 1614, the Old Grammar School, Market Harborough, once sheltered a butter market.*

Information Tel. 62649.
Location On the A6, 15 m. SE of Leicester.
Parking Coventry Road; Bowden Lane; Fairfield Road; Northampton Road; St Mary's Road (all car parks).
District council Harborough (Tel. 67000).
Population 15,900.
E-C Wed. **M-D** Tues., Sat.
Police Leicester Road (Tel. 62251).
Casualty hospital Market Harborough Hospital, Coventry Road (Tel. 64756).
Post office St Mary's Road.
Theatre Harborough, Church Square (Tel. 63673).
Public library Adam and Eve Street.
Places to see Old Grammar School; Market Place; Canal Basin.
Shopping The Square; High Street; Northampton Road.
Event Carnival (June).
AA 24 hour service Tel. Leicester 20491.

Marlborough Wiltshire

The town straddles the former stagecoach route from London to Bath, beside the River Kennet. It is the commercial centre of a large area of rural Wiltshire.

The broad High Street is lined with

GEORGIAN ELEGANCE *Broad, sloping, Marlborough High Street is lined on its north side by colonnaded Georgian shops with tile-hung fronts.*

Georgian buildings and has a Perpendicular church at both ends – St Mary's, which has a Norman doorway, and St Peter's. Behind, there are alleys with half-timbered cottages.

Marlborough College, established in 1843, stands beside Castle Mound, where Stone Age and Roman remains have been found.

On the downlands around Marlborough are many prehistoric remains, including the Iron Age hillfort of Barbury Castle, 4 miles northwest. The White Horse, 1 mile southwest beside the A4, was cut in 1804.

Information Tel. Devizes 4911.
Location On the A4, 12 m. S of Swindon.
Parking Hyde Lane; George Lane (both car parks); High Street; London Road.
District council Kennet (Tel. Devizes 4911).
Population 5,770.
E-C Wed. **M-D** Wed., Sat.
Police George Lane (Tel. 52311).
Casualty hospital Princess Margaret, Okus Road, Swindon (Tel. Swindon 36231).
Post office High Street.
Public library High Street.
Places to see Marlborough College; Barbury Castle hill-fort; White Horse, beside A4.
Shopping High Street.
AA 24 hour service
Tel. Swindon 21446.

Marlow Buckinghamshire

Thames-side Marlow is lively yet delightfully rural, with a foaming weir downstream and wooded hills upstream. The oldest building is the Old Parsonage which, together with the adjoining deanery, was once part of a great 14th-century house. It contains fine panelled rooms and decorated windows. Remnantz, in West Street, was the home of the Royal Military Academy until it moved to Sandhurst in 1812.

West Street has many literary associations. The poet Shelley (1792-1822) wrote his *Revolt to Islam* in a house next to Sir William Borlase's School in 1817-18, while his wife Mary wrote *Frankenstein*. The poet T. S. Eliot (1888-1965) lived in West Street for a time after the First World War.

Information Tel. High Wycombe 26100.
Location On the A4155, 4 m. S of High Wycombe.
Parking Oxford Road; Pound Lane; Dean Street; Chapel Street; Crown Lane; Institute Road (all car parks).
District council Wycombe (Tel. High Wycombe 26100).
Population 14,100.
E-C Wed.
Police Dean Street (Tel. 2414).
Casualty hospital Wycombe Cottage Hospital, Alexander Road (Tel. High Wycombe 26161).
Post office High Street.

Cinema Regal, Station Road (Tel. 2323).
Public library Institute Road.
Shopping High Street; West Street; Spittal Street.
AA 24 hour service
Tel. Reading 581122.

Marple Greater Manchester

The Peak Forest and Macclesfield canals, which meet in Marple, helped the town to develop as a centre of the cotton industry in the 19th century. Cotton has gone, but the canals remain as quiet byways for pleasure-boating and as monuments to the engineers who built them.

Information Tel. Manchester (061) 427 7011.
Location On the A626, 5 m. E of Stockport.
Parking Chadwick Street; The Hollins; Brabyns Row; Derby Street; Memorial Park; Cross Lane (all car parks).
District council Metropolitan Borough of Stockport (Tel. 061 480 4949).
Population 23,900.
E-C Wed.
Police Memorial Park (Tel. 061 480 7979).
Casualty hospital Stockport Infirmary, Wellington Road South, Stockport (Tel. 061 480 7441).
Post office Stockport Road.
Cinema Regent, Stockport Road (Tel. 061 427 5951).
Public library Memorial Park.
Shopping Market Street; The Hollins; Stockport Road.
AA 24 hour service
Tel. 061 485 6299.

Maryport Cumbria

Fascinating reminders of the past abound in the old coal and iron port, whose pits are now closed and whose docks are used only by the local fishing fleet. Some relics of the old port are displayed at the Maritime Museum in Senhouse Street.

Fletcher Christian, leader of the mutiny on the *Bounty*, was born near the town.

Information Tel. 3738.
Location On the A596, 6 m. N of Workington.
Parking Mill Street; Eaglesfield Street.
District council Allerdale (Tel. Cockermouth 823741).
Population 11,600.
E-C Wed. **M-D** Fri.
Police Eaglesfield Street (Tel. 2601).
Casualty hospital Ewanrigg Road (Tel. 2634).
Post office High Street.
Theatre Civic Hall, Lower Church Street (Tel. 2652).
Public library Lawson Street.
Shopping Senhouse Street.
AA 24 hour service
Tel. Carlisle 24274.

MARLOW *The outstanding feature of the riverside town is its suspension bridge, built in 1831. Its arch provides a splendid frame for the 19th-century Church of All Saints, with its soaring spire.*

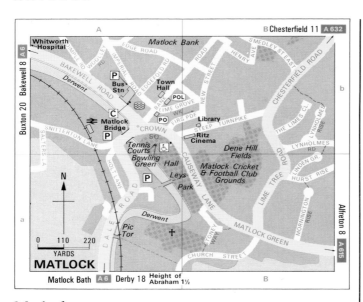

Map labels:
Chesterfield 11 A 632 · Buxton 20 · Bakewell 8 A 6 · Whitworth Hospital · Matlock Bank · SMEDLEY ST · EDGE ROAD · BAKEWELL ROAD · Derwent · Bus Stn · Town Hall · POL · Matlock Bridge · LIME GROVE · PO · Library · Ritz Cinema · STEEP TURNPIKE · CHESTERFIELD ROAD · LYNHOLMES CL · Tennis Courts · Bowling Green · Hall · CROWN SQ. · Dene Hill Fields · Matlock Cricket & Football Club Grounds · LYNHOLMES RD · SNITTERTON LANE · SALTERS LA · HOLT LANE · DALE ROAD · Leys Park · CAUSEWAY LANE · LIME TREE ROAD · HURST RISE · LINDEN GR · MORNINGTON RISE · Alfreton 8 A 615 · Pic Tor · Derwent · STONEY WAY · MATLOCK GREEN · CHURCH STREET · N · 0 110 220 YARDS · **MATLOCK** · Matlock Bath A 6 · Derby 18 · Height of Abraham 1½

Matlock Derbyshire

The town of Matlock is strung out along the narrow valley of the River Derwent, beneath wooded hills that rise up to Derbyshire's Peak District.

In Victorian times Matlock Bath was famous for its thermal water, which wells up from underground at a constant 20°C (68°F). The Pavilion, at which the waters were taken, is now an entertainments centre. Along this stretch of the river a Venetian Fête takes place every summer.

North of Matlock Bath is Matlock Dale, which is sandwiched between the 750 ft summit of the Heights of Abraham and the 380 ft High Tor. The Heights of Abraham were named after their likeness to the cliffs which General Wolfe scaled to capture Quebec in 1759. They are crowned by the Victoria Prospect Tower, which commands breathtaking views of the surrounding hills and dales. There are two huge caverns in the Heights, the Great Rutland and Great Masson, both of which were worked by the Romans for lead.

Information Tel. 55082.
Location On the A6, 11 m. SW of Chesterfield.
Parking Bakewell Road; Station Yard; Olde English Road; Bank Road; Edgefold Road; Matlock Bath Pavilion (all car parks).
District council West Derbyshire (Tel. 3461).
Population 20,800.
E-C Thur. **M-D** Tues., Fri.
Police (Ab) Bank Road (Tel. 3215).
Casualty hospital Whitworth Hospital, Bakewell Road (Tel. 3846).
Post office (Ab) Bank Road.
Cinema Ritz **(Bb)**, Causeway Lane (Tel. 2121).
Public library (Bb) Steep Turnpike.
Places to see Great Rutland and Great Masson Caverns; Victoria Prospect Tower; Riber Castle Wildlife Park; Lead Mining Museum.
Town trails Available from the Arkwright Society, c/o Tawney House, Matlock.
Shopping Causeway Lane; Firs Parade; Crown Square; Dale Road; Smedley Street; North and South Street.
Event Venetian Fête and Illuminations (Aug.-Oct.).
AA 24 hour service
Tel. Nottingham 787751.

Melrose Borders

The bitter wars that ravaged the Scottish borders for centuries did irreversible damage to Melrose Abbey. But even in ruins it remains beautiful.

David I founded the abbey in 1136. It was badly damaged by Richard II of England in 1385 – after which it was rebuilt, only to be ravaged again by the English in 1545. The abbey as it stands today was preserved by the money of the Duke of Buccleuch and the energy of Sir Walter Scott in 1822.

MATLOCK BATH *In Victorian times the riverside area of Matlock was a spa noted for its warm springs.*

Information Tel. 2555.
Location On the A6091, 5 m. SE of Galashiels.
Parking Buccleuch Street; St Dunstans; Palma Place (all car parks).
District council Ettrick and Lauderdale (Tel. Galashiels 4751).
Population 2,200.
E-C Thur.
Police High Street (Tel. 2602).
Casualty hospital Peel Hospital, Clodenfords, By Galashiels (Tel. Galashiels 2295).
Post office Buccleuch Street.
Public library Market Square.
Places to see Melrose Abbey; Abbotsford House, 2 m. E.
Shopping High Street; Buccleuch Street.
AA 24 hour service
Tel. Edinburgh (031) 225 8464.

Melton Mowbray Leics.

This old town has long been renowned for fox-hunting, pork pies and Stilton cheese.

It is the unofficial centre of English fox-hunting, the meeting place of the boundaries of the Quorn, Cottesmore and Belvoir hunts. The pork-pie industry, which began in 1831, produces pies noted for their hand-raised crust and chopped pork.

HOME OF STILTON

Stilton cheese, a speciality of Melton Mowbray, derives its blue veining and characteristic flavour from the action of the mould *Penicillium Roqueforti*. Each cheese takes four months to mature. Stilton is named after the Huntingdonshire village where it used to be sold. It has never been made there.

Blue-green veins marble the creamy body of fully ripe Stilton cheese.

The parish church of St Mary, in the town centre, is a splendid 12th–14th-century building, with a 100 ft tower. Near by is the Maison Dieu, or Bede House, an almshouse dating from the 17th century.

Information Tel. 69946.
Location On the A607, 15 m. NE of Leicester.
Parking Thorpe End; Chapel Street; Wilton Road; Scalford Road; Mill Street (all car parks).
District council Mowbray Borough Council (Tel. 67771).
Population 23,600.
E-C Thur. **M-D** Tues., Sat.
Police Leicester Road (Tel. 3676).
Casualty hospital Leicester Royal Infirmary, Leicester (Tel. 541414).
Post office Windsor Street.
Theatre The Theatre, Leisure Centre (Tel. 69280).
Cinema Regal, King Street (Tel. 62251).
Public library Wilton Road.
Places to see Anne of Cleves House; Melton Carnegie Museum; Bede House, Burton Street.
Shopping Market Place; Nottingham Street; Sherrard Street.
AA 24 hour service
Tel. Leicester 20491.

Merthyr Tydfil Mid Glam.
The Industrial Revolution transformed the market town of Merthyr Tydfil into one of the world's great iron-working centres. Iron was worked in the area as early as the 16th century. Then, in the late 18th century, there was an explosive development of the industry which turned Merthyr into the largest town in Wales by 1801. But before the end of the century, heavy industry was moving to the coastal ports, and Cardiff, Newport and Swansea had all overtaken Merthyr.

Kier Hardie (1856-1915), the first leader of the Parliamentary Labour Party, was the town's MP from 1900 until his death.

Information Tel. 3201.
Location On the A470, 12 m. N of Pontypridd.
Parking College; Castle; Eastern By-Pass; Swan Street (all car parks).
District council Borough of Merthyr Tydfil (Tel. 3201).
Population 53,800.
E-C Thur.
Police Swan Street (Tel. 2541/4).
Casualty hospital Prince Charles (Tel. 71111).
Post office John Street.
Cinemas Studios 1 and 2, High Street (Tel. 3877); Scala, St John Street (3877).
Public library High Street.
Places to see Cyfarthfa Castle Art Gallery and Museum.
Town trails Available from Merthyr Tydfil Heritage Trust, Joseph Parry Cottage, 4 Chapel Row, Georgetown.
Shopping St Tydfil's Shopping Precinct, High Street.
AA 24 hour service
Tel. Cardiff 394111.

Merton see London

Middlesbrough Cleveland
The opening in 1830 of an extension to the Stockton and Darlington railway transformed a tiny village of 40 people into a town of 40,000 in 40 years. Middlesbrough's prosperity was founded on coal shipped through its docks from the South Durham field. Later, with the discovery of ore in the Cleveland hills, came iron and steel.

The town's best-known landmark, the Transporter Bridge across the Tees, was opened in 1911 and built to replace a river ferry.

Information Tel. 245750.
Location On the A66, 15 m. E of Darlington.
Parking Gurney Street; Watson Street; Yew Street; Monkland Street; Atkinson Street; Blake Street; Station Street; Cleveland Centre.
District council Borough of Middlesbrough (Tel. 245432).
Population 149,400.
E-C Wed. **M-D** Tues., Sat.
Police (Ba) Emily Street (Tel. 248184).
Casualty hospital Middlesbrough General, Ayresome Green Lane (Tel. 83133).
Post office (Ba) Corporation Road.
Theatre Little, The Avenue (Tel. 85181).
Cinemas ABC (Aa), Linthorpe Road (Tel. 247400); Odeon (Ba), Corporation Road (242888).
Public library (Ba) Victoria Square.
Places to see Transporter Bridge; Captain Cook Birthplace Museum, Stewart Park, Marton; Dorman Museum.
Shopping Linthorpe Road; Cleveland Centre.
Sport FA League football, Middlesbrough FC, Ayresome Park; Yorkshire County cricket, Acklam Park.
AA 24 hour service
Tel. 246832.

Middleton G. Manch.
Cotton and silk were the town's main industries during its 19th-century expansion, but they have now given way to engineering, plastics, tobacco and chemicals. Norman parts remain in St Leonard's Church, which was rebuilt in the 16th century.

Information
Tel. Manchester (061) 643 6291.
Location On the A664, 6 m. N of Manchester.
Parking Limetrees Road (2); Silk Street; Old Hall Street; Park Road; Suffield Street (2); Market Street (2); Chapel Street; East View (all car parks).
District council Metropolitan Borough of Rochdale (Tel. Rochdale 47474).
Population 51,700.
E-C Tues. **M-D** Fri., Sat.
Police Oldham Road (Tel. Rochdale 47401).
Casualty hospital Rochdale Infirmary, Whitehall Street, Rochdale (Tel. Rochdale 40952).
Post office Manchester New Road.
Cinema Palace, Manchester Old Road (Tel. 061 643 2852).
Public library Long Street.
Shopping Arndale Shopping Centre.
AA 24 hour service
Tel. 061 485 6299.

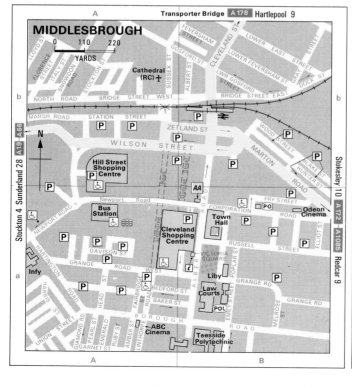

MIDDLESBROUGH

Transporter Bridge A178 Hartlepool 9

Milford Haven Dyfed

The town is less than 200 years old, but the 20 mile long Haven has had a long and eventful history. Henry II used it to launch his invasion of Ireland in 1171, and in 1485 Henry Tudor landed there on his way to Bosworth Field and the crown. Nelson described it as one of the finest natural harbours in the world.

The town was founded in 1793 by Sir William Hamilton, husband of Nelson's mistress, Emma. At first it was a whaling port, then a dockyard. Since 1960 it has become a major oil port, with huge refineries fed by supertankers from all over the world.

Information
Tel. Haverfordwest 4551.
Location On the A4076, 22 m. S of Fishguard.
Parking Market Square; Manchester Square; Robert Street; Spike's Lane (all car parks).
District council Preseli (Tel. Haverfordwest 4551).
Population 13,900.
E-C Thur. **M-D** Fri.
Police Charles Street (Tel. 2351/2).
Casualty hospital Withybush General, Fishguard Road, Haverfordwest (Tel. Haverfordwest 4545).
Post office Hamilton Terrace.
Theatre Torch, St Peter's Road (Tel. 5267).
Cinema Empire, Stratford Road (Tel. 3223).
Public library Hamilton Terrace.
Shopping Hamilton Terrace; Charles Street.
AA 24 hour service Tel. Cardiff 394111.

Millport Strathclyde

Great Cumbrae is an island in the Firth of Clyde, and Millport, its only town, has sweeping sandy beaches and many seaside amusements.

At nearby Keppel is a Marine Biology Station with an aquarium of sea creatures from the Firth.

Information Tel. Largs 673765.
Location On the A860, 4 m. SW of Largs.
Parking Clifton Street (cp); College Street; Cardiff Street; Guildford Street; Stuart Street.
District council Cunninghame (Tel. Irvine 74166).
Population 1,350.
E-C Wed.
Police Millburn Street (Tel. 316).
Casualty hospital Lady Margaret, Millport (Tel. 307).
Post office Guildford Street.
Public library Glasgow Street.
Places to see Marine Biology Station, Keppel; Garrison House Museum.
Shopping Guildford Street; Stuart Street.
Event Cumbrae Week (June).
Car ferry Cumbrae Slip to Largs (Tel. Gourock 34568).
AA 24 hour service Tel. Glasgow (041) 812 0101.

Milton Keynes Bucks.

Since 1971 the new town of Milton Keynes (designated in 1967) has been the home of the Open University. Three centres provide facilities for leisure and sporting activities.

There are Norman churches at Bradwell, Castlethorpe and Little Linford. Chicheley Hall, on the A422, is an 18th-century mansion. (See also Bletchley.)

Information Tel. 678361.
Location On the A5, 15 m. SE of Northampton.
Parking Silbury Boulevard; Midsummer Boulevard; Saxon Gate; Seklow Gate (all car parks).
District council Borough of Milton Keynes (Tel. 679200).
Population 107,000.
M-D Tues., Thur., Sat.
Police North Eight Street, Central Milton Keynes (Tel. 606438).
Casualty hospital Northampton General, Cliftonville, Northampton (Tel. Northampton 34700).
Post office 74 Midsummer Arcade.
Theatres Jennie Lee, Bletchley Leisure Centre, Princes Way, Bletchley (Tel. 77251); Stantonbury, Purbeck, Stantonbury (314466); Woughton Campus, Chaffron Way, Coffee Hall (660392).
Cinemas Electra, St Johns Street, Newport Pagnell (Tel. Newport Pagnell 611146); Studio, Queensway, Bletchley (73121).
Public library Silbury Boulevard, Wolverton.
Places to see Chicheley Hall; Cowper Museum, Olney; Bradwell Abbey; Peace Pagoda.
Nature trails Available from City Information and Homefinders Centre, Saxon Gate.
Shopping Central Milton Keynes: Silbury Arcade; Midsummer Arcade; Acorn Walk; Crown Walk; Eagle Walk.
Event Olney Pancake Race (Shrove Tuesday).
AA 24 hour service Tel. Hatfield 62852.

Minehead Somerset

Every May Day a colourful hobby horse dances down to Minehead quay, accompanied by accordion and drum. The custom commemorates either an ancient fertility rite or is a re-enactment of a legendary occasion when a horse's mask frightened Viking pirates from the town. Minehead has safe beaches and attractive parks. Quay Town huddles by a 17th-century harbour.

Information Tel. 2624.
Location On the A39, 24 m. NW of Taunton.
Parking Quay West; Martlet Road; North Road; Parade Avenue; Alexandra Road (all car parks).
District council West Somerset (Tel. Williton 32291).
Population 11,200.
E-C Wed.

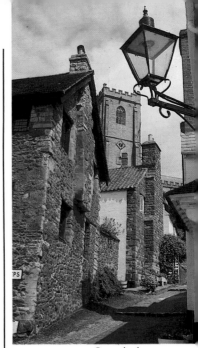

HILLSIDE CHURCH *Steps lead up to Minehead's parish church of St Michael, perched on North Hill, above the town.*

Police Townsend Road (Tel. 3361).
Casualty hospital Minehead Hospital, The Avenue (Tel. 3377).
Post office Park Street.
Cinema Regal 1 and 2, The Avenue (Tel. 2439).
Public library Bancks Street.
Places to see Dunster Castle, 2 m. E.
Shopping The Parade; Friday Street; The Avenue; Park Street.
Event Hobby Horse (May).
AA 24 hour service Tel. Taunton 73363.

Mold Clwyd

Prehistoric burial mounds ring Mold, the administrative capital of Clwyd. The busy little town holds four markets a week: two for livestock (Mondays and Fridays) and two street markets. Mold's most famous son is Daniel Owen (1836-95), a novelist highly esteemed for his mastery of the Welsh language.

Information Tel. Holywell 710710.
Location On the A494, 12 m. W of Chester.
Parking Clayton Road; Earl Road; New Street (2); King Street (all car parks).
District council Borough of Delyn (Tel. Holywell 710710).
Population 8,600.
E-C Thur. **M-D** Wed., Sat.
Police King Street (Tel. 2321).
Casualty hospital Wrexham, Rhosddu Road, Wrexham (Tel. Wrexham 51041).
Post office Earl Road.
Theatre Theatr Clwyd, Soughton Road (Tel. 55114).
Public library Daniel Owen Centre.
Shopping High Street; Daniel Owen Precinct.
AA 24 hour service Tel. Llandudno 79066.

FORTIFIED BRIDGE *Monmouth's 13th-century bridge over the River Monnow is the only fortified bridge left in Britain, and one of the few in Europe. The gateway astride it has served as guardhouse, watchtower and prison.*

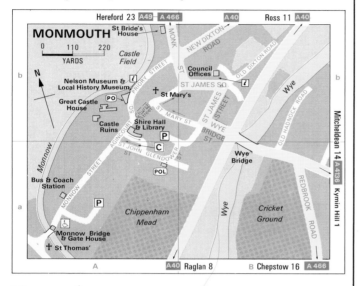

Monmouth Gwent

The Romans founded Monmouth as the military station of Blestium. From Norman times the castle was the stronghold from which the Welsh were subdued in the lands between the Severn and the Wye. It was the birthplace in 1387 of the future Henry V, whose statue is on the 18th-century Shire Hall. The castle was largely destroyed during the Civil War, but part of the great hall remains. In 1673 the 1st Duke of Beaufort built Great Castle House on the site, incorporating stones from the ruins.

The town developed markets in both agricultural produce and live-stock, and these are still held. Monmouth was also a stopping-place for coaches between London and South Wales. Several coaching inns and

PIONEER *A statue of C. S. Rolls (1877-1910), co-founder of Rolls-Royce and aviation pioneer, stands in Agincourt Square, Monmouth. Rolls was born at nearby Rockfield.*

Georgian houses date from this era. Modern Monmouth is a touring centre for the Wye Valley.

The parish church at Dixton, consecrated between 1066 and 1070, still bears traces of Saxon work.

The Naval Temple of 1800, on top of the 800 ft hill the Kymin, commemorates English admirals. Nelson visited it in 1802, and his own deeds are commemorated in the Monmouth Museum in the Market Hall.

Information Tel. 3899.
Location On the A466, 20 m. S of Hereford.
Parking Glendower Street; Monnow Street (both car parks).
District council Monmouth (Tel. Pontypool 2311).
Population 7,500.
E-C Thur. **M-D** Fri., Sat.
Police (Aa) Glendower Street (Tel. 2321).
Casualty hospital Nevill Hall, Brecon Road, Abergavenny (Tel. Abergavenny 2091).
Post office (Ab) Priory Street.
Public library (Ab) Shire Hall.
Places to see Monmouth Museum (Ab); Castle ruins (Ab); Great Castle House (Ab); Naval Temple, Kymin, off Staunton Road (A4136).
Shopping Monnow Street.
Event Monmouthshire Show (Aug.).
AA 24 hour service Tel. Newport 62559.

Montgomery Powys

A population of about 1,000 made Montgomery the smallest of the former boroughs in England and Wales. The town stands beneath the ruins of Montgomery Castle, built by Henry III to command the approach to central Wales.

Montgomery has changed little since the 18th century. Broad Street, the central square, is lined by Georgian shops and houses that open on to cobbled pavements. In St Nicholas churchyard is the Robber's Grave, burial place of John Davies who was hanged for highway robbery in 1821. He claimed to be innocent, and said, that as proof, no grass would grow on his grave for a generation – and none did.

Information Tel. Welshpool 2828.
Location On the B4385, 9 m. S of Welshpool.
Parking Broad Street; square behind Town Hall; Arthur Street.
District council Montgomery (Tel. Welshpool 2828).
Population 1,000.
E-C Sat. **M-D** Thur.
Police Chirbury Street (Tel. 222).
Casualty hospital Victoria Memorial, Salop Road, Welshpool (Tel. Welshpool 3133).
Post office Broad Street.
Public library Arthur Street.
Places to see Castle; Offa's Dyke.
Shopping Broad Street.
AA 24 hour service Tel. Cardiff 394111.

Montrose Tayside

The royal burgh stands on a spit jutting out into the mouth of the River South Esk. The spit encloses a 4 sq. mile tidal lagoon known as The Montrose Basin, which is used for sailing. Fishing and cargo trade with the Continent once brought the town wealth, but recently the servicing of North Sea oil rigs has brought new prosperity. The centre of Montrose is dominated by a 220 ft steeple built in 1832. From it, "Big Peter", a 300-year-old bell, rings a 10 o'clock curfew each night. The Scots hero, the Marquis of Montrose (1612-50), was born in Castle Place.

Information Tel. 2000.
Location On the A92, 25 m. NE of Dundee.
Parking Baltic Street; Western Road; Murray Lane (all car parks).
District council Angus (Tel. Forfar 65101).
Population 10,900.
E-C Wed. **M-D** Fri.
Police George Street (Tel. 2222).
Casualty hospital Montrose Infirmary, Bridge Street (Tel. 2020).
Post office Bridge Street.
Public library High Street.
Places to see Montrose Museum and Art Gallery, Panmure Place.
Shopping High Street.
AA 24 hour service Tel. Dundee 25585.

Morecambe Lancashire

With neighbouring Heysham (pronounced Heesham), Morecambe is one of the "lungs" of Lancashire. Its wide bay and spacious beaches have attracted holidaymakers from the industrial towns of northern England since the beginning of the century, and today they draw visitors from all parts of Britain.

Most of the traditional seaside entertainments are in Morecambe. Funfairs, amusement arcades and theatres overlook the broad promenade where illuminations light up the seafront from August to mid-October. Marineland, on the stone jetty, claims to be Europe's first oceanarium and has a well-stocked aquarium and performing dolphins.

At Heysham Head there is a holiday park and go-kart racing. Away from the bustle, Heysham village has a church dating from the 7th century. Beyond the headland, Half Moon Bay nestles against the arm of Heysham harbour.

At low tide it is possible to walk across the bay from Hest Bank to Grange-over-Sands, on the estuary of the River Kent, a distance of about 8 miles. Walkers must be accompanied by an official guide as there are fast-flowing channels to ford, but the journey is worthwhile, especially for naturalists. The riverlets and creeks teem with marine life, preyed upon by flocks of oystercatchers and other wading birds.

LOCAL DELICACY *Morecambe Bay's extra-large shrimps are caught by small trawlers called nobbies.*

Information Tel. 414110.
Location On the A589, 4 m. W of Lancaster.
Parking Moneyclose Lane; Barrows Lane; Marine Road Central; Central Drive (2); Market Street; Pedder Street; Matthias Street; Marine Road East; Coastal Road (all car parks).
District council Lancaster City Council (Tel. 417120).
Population 41,200 (includes Heysham).
E-C Wed. **M-D** Mon. (summer only), Tues. and Thur.
Police (Ba) Poulton Square (Tel. 411534).
Casualty hospital Royal Lancaster Infirmary, South Road, Lancaster (Tel. Lancaster 65944).
Post office (Aa) Victoria Street.
Theatres Palace, Sandylands Promenade (Tel. 410601); Central Pier **(Bb)**, Marine Road (410039).
Cinema Empire 1, 2, 3 **(Aa)**, Marine Road Central (Tel. 412518).
Public library (Aa) Central Drive.
Places to see St Peter's Church, Heysham; Leighton Moss Bird Sanctuary; Carnforth Railway Museum, 5 m. N.
Shopping Arndale Shopping Centre; Euston Road; West End; Regent Road.
Events Preston to Morecambe Vintage Car Rally (July); Agricultural Show (July).
AA 24 hour service
Tel. Manchester (061) 485 6299.

Morley see Leeds

Motherwell and Wishaw Strathclyde

The fiery glare of steel furnaces lights the night sky above what is unashamedly an industrial town of the latter part of the 19th century. Until 1850 history had scarcely touched the tiny villages lying in forest and pastureland in the valley of the Clyde above Glasgow. When William Cobbett travelled through the area in 1832, he described its rural beauty "as the place of all places in Scotland that I should like to live at". However, by 1914 the farmers had gone, and Motherwell and Wishaw had the largest steel works in Britain. The metal for the hulls of the two great Cunard sister ships, *Queen Mary* and *Queen Elizabeth*, was forged there.

Motherwell takes its name from *Modyrwaile* (the well, or pool, of the Virgin Mary). The site is marked by a plaque in Ladywell Road. Wishaw, originally Waygateshaw, means "the gate in the wood".

Information Tel. 66166.
Location On the A721, 13 m. SE of Glasgow.
Parking Motherwell: Menteith Road; Hope Street; High Road; Scott Street; Brandon Street. Wishaw: Hill Street; Kenilworth Avenue; Graham Street; Glasgow Road; Belhaven Terrace (all car parks).
District council Motherwell (Tel. 66166).
Population 61,500.
E-C Wed. **M-D** Tues., Fri.
Police Windmillhill Street, Motherwell (Tel. 66144); Stewarton Street, Wishaw (Wishaw 72592).
Casualty hospital Strathclyde Hospital, Crawford Street, Motherwell (Tel. 64661).
Post office Brandon Parade, Motherwell.
Theatre Civic Centre, Airbles Road, Motherwell (Tel. 66166).
Cinema Classic, Kirk Road (Tel. Wishaw 72117).
Public libraries Hamilton Road, Motherwell; Main Street, Wishaw.
Places to see Dalzell House.
Shopping Motherwell: Windmillhill Street; Menteith Road; Brandon Street. Wishaw: Main Street.
Sport Scottish League football, Motherwell FC, Fir Park.
AA 24 hour service
Tel. Glasgow (041) 812 0101.

Mountain Ash Mid Glam.

The colliery town in the Cynon Valley played a major role in the industrial growth of South Wales and was once famous for its choir. Depression hit the town hard in the 1930s, but since the war new industries such as cloth-weaving and carpet-making have considerably reduced unemployment.

Prehistoric graves are scattered among the surrounding hills.

Information Tel. Aberdare 875161.
Location On the A4224, 5 m. S of Merthyr Tydfil.
Parking Oxford Street; Miskin Road (both car parks). Oxford Street.
District council Borough of Cynon Valley (Tel. 875161).
Population 26,200.
E-C Thur.
Police High Street (Tel. 473781).
Casualty hospital Mountain Ash General (Tel. 472212).
Post office Knight Street.
Public library Duffryn Road.
Shopping Commercial Street; Oxford Street.
Trade and industry Electrical engineering; textiles.
AA 24 hour service
Tel. Cardiff 394111.

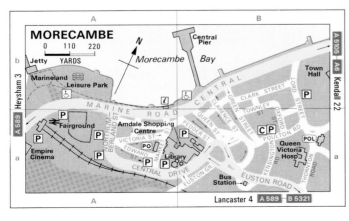

PRIORY RUINS *Wenlock Priory was founded in 680 by Merewald, King of Mercia. The Danes destroyed it in about 874, and two centuries later it was rebuilt by Leofric, husband of Lady Godiva. The present ruins date from the 11th and 13th centuries.*

N

Much Wenlock Salop

Half-timbered buildings and black-and-white cottages line the streets of Much Wenlock, a town that can trace its history back to Saxon days. The ruins of a priory, dissolved in 1540, rise from well-kept lawns.

The town claims some of the credit for the revival of the Olympic Games. The physical-education pioneer Dr William Penny Brookes, who was born there, held Olympic Games at Much Wenlock in 1850. Ten years later the Games were opened to all England. Dr Brookes, who founded the Olympian Society, died in 1895, aged 86. The following year the first International Olympiad was held in Athens. The people of Much Wenlock claim that much of the credit for re-founding the Games given to Baron Pierre de Coubertin, really belonged to Dr Brookes. The doctor did leave one undisputed achievement: the introduction of physical education into Britain's schools.

Information Tel. Bridgnorth 3358.
Location On the A458, 13 m. SE of Shrewsbury.
Parking St Mary's Road; Back Lane; High Street (all car parks).
District council Bridgnorth (Tel. Bridgnorth 5131).
Population 2,450.
Police Smithfield Road (Tel. 727333).
Casualty hospital Bridgnorth Infirmary, Northgate, Bridgnorth (Tel. Bridgnorth 2641).
Post office High Street.
Public library High Street.
Places to see Wenlock Priory; Guildhall; Museum.
Shopping High Street.
AA 24 hour service Tel. Stoke-on-Trent 25881.

Musselburgh Lothian

The town suffered during the centuries of strife between Scotland and England. The English burned most of it in 1544, and again in 1547. Upstream from the A1 bridge that crosses the River Esk is a stone bridge of unknown date. It was certainly used as far back as 1314 by Edward II's forces when he was retreating from Bannockburn.

In the autumn the town's fishermen take "Walks of Thanksgiving" for their catches.

Information Tel. 031 665 6597 (summer); 031 665 3711.
Location On the A1, 6 m. E of Edinburgh.
Parking Ladywell Way (2); Millhill (all car parks). Mall Avenue; High Street; Newbigging.
District council East Lothian (Tel. Haddington 4161).
Population 18,800.
E-C Thur.
Police High Street (Tel. 031 665 2583).
Casualty hospital Royal Infirmary, Lauriston Place, Edinburgh (Tel. 031 229 2477).
Post office High Street.
Theatre Brunton, Ladywell Way (Tel. 031 665 2240).
Public library Bridge Street.
Places to see Tolbooth; Inveresk Gardens; Pinkie House.
Shopping High Street.
Events Honest Toun's Festival (July).
Trade and industry Manufacture of wire, paper; coal-mining.
Sport Horse racing, Linkfield Road.
AA 24 hour service Tel. 031 225 8464.

MUSSELBURGH TOLBOOTH *The 16th-century tower was partly constructed from an ancient chapel destroyed by the English. Its clock was given to the town in 1498 by Dutch traders.*

Nairn Highland

This town on the Moray Firth was once a prosperous herring fishing port, based on its Fishertown district. The industry died in the 1930s, with the loss of its overseas markets, and Nairn is now a thriving family resort and agricultural centre of the Highlands. With safe, sandy beaches and sunny climate, it has been dubbed the "Brighton of the North". Recently industries connected with North Sea oil have brought added prosperity.

Nairn was given a royal charter by Alexander I early in the 12th century. Before the Battle of Culloden in 1746 the Duke of Cumberland stayed in the town and spent his 25th birthday in a house in the High Street, which is marked by an inscription.

In 1645 the Marquis of Montrose led Charles I's troops to victory over the Covenanters, Scottish Presbyterian opponents of the established Church, and flew the royal standard from the Boath Doocot (dovecot) that stands 3 miles east of the town.

Rait Castle, 3 miles south, was the 13th-century home of the Comyns, who in 1424 intended to slaughter the Macintoshes at a banquet there, but were killed by their guests instead.

Information Tel. 52753.
Location On the A96, 16 m. NE of Inverness.
Parking East Beach Road; Millbank Street; King Street; Court House Lane; Watson's Place; Riverside; Harbour Street; Cumming Street; Marine Road (all car parks).
District council Nairn (Tel. 52056).
Population 10,400.
E-C Wed.
Police King Street (Tel. 52222).
Casualty hospital Town and County Hospital, Cawdor Road (Tel. 52101).
Post office Cawdor Street.
Cinema Regal, King Street (Tel. 53287).
Public library Viewfield House.
Places to see Fishertown Museum, King Street; Museum, Viewfield House; Cawdor Castle and village, 5 m. S.
Shopping High Street; Cawdor Street; Leopold Street.
Events Golf Week (May); Nairn Games (Aug.); Nairnshire Farmers' Show (Aug.).
AA 24 hour service Tel. Aberdeen 51231.

Nantwich Cheshire

Salt springs made Nantwich prosperous in Roman times, and salt continued to be produced throughout the Middle Ages. In 1583 a great fire devastated the town, which was rebuilt in Elizabethan style. Buildings from this period include houses in Welsh Row and almshouses of 1638.

The restored Church of St Mary has a 14th-century chancel and choir stalls, and a beautifully carved roof.

CHURCHE'S MANSION *The house survived the Nantwich fire of 1583.*

Information Tel. 63914.
Location On the A51, 4 m. SW of Crewe.
Parking Hospital Street (2); Beam Street; Welsh Row (2); Water Lode (all car parks).
District council Borough of Crewe and Nantwich (Tel. Crewe 583191).
Population 12,000.
E-C Wed. **M-D** Thur., Sat.
Police Beam Street (Tel. 65515).
Casualty hospital Leighton Hospital, Middlewich Road, Crewe (Tel. Crewe 55141).
Post office Pepper Street.
Theatre Civic Hall, Beam Street (Tel. 64031).
Public library Beam Street.
Places to see Churche's Mansion.
Shopping High Street.
AA 24 hour service
Tel. Manchester (061) 485 6299.

Neath W. Glamorgan

Industrial development in the west and unspoiled valleys in the east make Neath a town of marked contrasts. In or near the town are the ruins of a castle, an abbey and a church, all dating from the 12th century, and the old Roman station of Nidum.

Information Tel. 4121.
Location On the B4434, 9 m. NE of Swansea.
Parking Fairfield Way; Gnoll Park Road; Victoria Gardens; Prince of Wales Drive (all car parks).
District council Borough of Neath (Tel. 4121).
Population 26,600.
E-C Thur. **M-D** Wed., Sat.
Police Windsor Road (Tel. 55321).
Casualty hospital Neath General, Westbourne Road (Tel. 4161).
Post office Windsor Road.
Cinema Talk of the Abbey, Windsor Road (Tel. 3333).
Public library Victoria Gardens.
Shopping Windsor Road; Queen Street; Orchard Street; Wind Street.
Sport Rugby football, Neath RFC, Gnoll Ground.
AA 24 hour service
Tel. Swansea 55598.

Nelson Lancashire

The town's name was taken from the Nelson Inn, a public house named after the admiral and around which the town grew in the 19th century.

Nelson developed as a textile centre out of the parishes of Great and Little Marsden. Bronze Age and Roman artefacts have been found in the area.

Information Tel. 67731.
Location On the A56, 26 m. E of Preston.
Parking Netherfield Road; Broadway; Cuba Street; New Brown Street; Every Street (all car parks).
District council Borough of Pendle (Tel. 67731).
Population 30,400.
E-C Tues. **M-D** Wed., Fri. and Sat.
Police Hibson Street (Tel. 62374).
Casualty hospital Burnley General, Casnet Avenue, Burnley (Tel. Burnley 25071).
Post office Manchester Road.
Public library Market Square.
Shopping Manchester Road; Leeds Road; Arndale Centre.
AA 24 hour service
Tel. Manchester (061) 485 6299.

Newark-on-Trent Notts.

The riverside wall and fine towered gatehouse of a 12th-century castle still stand. The impressive parish church of St Mary Magdalene has a soaring 240 ft west spire, a tremendous 15th-century east window in the chancel, and beautiful screenwork.

The Clinton Arms Hotel, where W. E. Gladstone, later to become Prime Minister, made his first election speech in 1832, overlooks the market place.

Information Tel. 78962.
Location On the A46, 17 m. SW of Lincoln.
Parking London Road; Lombard Street; King's Road; Appleton Gate; St Mark's Lane; Beast Market Hill (all car parks).
District council Newark (Tel. 705111).
Population 24,100.
E-C Thur. **M-D** Wed., Fri., Sat.
Police (Bb) Appleton Gate (Tel. 703242).
Casualty hospital (Ba) Newark Hospital, London Road (Tel. 73841).
Post office (Bb) Kirk Gate.
Theatre The Palace **(Bb)**, Appleton Gate (Tel. 71636).
Cinema Savoy Studios 1, 2, 3 and 4 **(Bb)**, Middle Gate (Tel. 704199).
Public library (Bb) Castlegate.
Places to see Newark Castle remains **(Ab)**; Air Museum, Winthorpe Airfield; Folk Museum, Millgate.
Town trails Available from the library.
Shopping Market Square; Carter Gate; Middle Gate; Stodman Street; Bridge Street; Kirk Gate; St Mark's Shopping Precinct.
AA 24 hour service
Tel. Nottingham 787751.

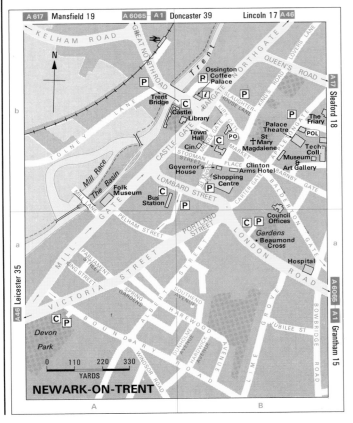

ELIZABETHAN HAVEN *Storms shifted the course of the Ouse from its outlet to the sea at Seaford in 1570, and the busy port of Newhaven grew up on the new estuary.*

Newbury Berkshire

In the 15th century England's first true factory, employing more than 1,000 wool weavers, was established in the town by John Winchcombe, known as Jack of Newbury. The north-gable end of Jack's house still stands in Marsh Lane. The Cloth Hall, a beautiful three-storeyed Jacobean building, is now the town museum. The 14th-century gatehouse is all that remains of Donnington Castle, 2 miles north of the town.

The racecourse, east of the town, has meetings the year round.

Information Tel. 30267/42400.
Location On the A34, 20 m. SW of Reading.
Parking Park Way (3); Pelican Lane; Northbrook Street/West Street; Northcroft Lane; Market Street (2); Cheap Street; Bartholomew Street; Wharf Road (2) (all car parks).
District council Newbury (Tel. 42400).
Population 26,400.
E-C Wed. **M-D** Thur., Sat.
Police Mill Lane (Tel. 31000).
Casualty hospital Royal Berkshire, Craven Road, Reading (Tel. Reading 85111).
Post office Cheap Street.
Theatre The Windmill, Bagnor (Tel. 46044).
Cinema ABC, Park Way (Tel. 41291).
Public library Carnegie Road.
Places to see Museum, Wharf Street; Donnington Castle ruins.
Shopping Northbrook Street; Market Place; The Mall Precinct.
Event Agricultural Show (Sept.).
Sport Horse racing, Newbury Racecourse.
AA 24 hour service Tel. Reading 581122.

Newcastle-under-Lyme Staffordshire

A mound and part of a wall in Queen Elizabeth Park are all that now remain of the Norman castle which gave the town its name.

Set in open country, Newcastle is an attractive residential town with modern industries and a university (Steele). However, it retains several old buildings, including the 18th-century Guildhall and the Pork Shop, a former coaching inn.

Still a thriving market centre, Newcastle was once the main trading centre of north Staffordshire.

Information Tel. 618125.
Location On the A34, 2 m. W of Stoke-on-Trent.
Parking Hick Street; Goose Street; Brunswick Street; Midway; King Street; Corporation Street; Brook Lane (all car parks).
District council Borough of Newcastle-under-Lyme (Tel. 610161).
Population 72,900.
E-C Thur. **M-D** Mon., Fri. and Sat.
Police Merrial Street (Tel. 616222).
Casualty hospital North Staffordshire Royal Infirmary, Prince's Road, Stoke-on-Trent (Tel. Stoke-on-Trent 49144).
Post office The Ironmarket.
Theatre Victoria, Hartshill (Tel. 615962).
Cinema Savoy, High Street (Tel. 616565).
Public library The Ironmarket.
Shopping High Street; The Ironmarket; Merrial Street.
Trade and industry Electronics; electrical engineering; coal mining; commerce; clothing.
AA 24 hour service Tel. Stoke-on-Trent 25881.

Newhaven E. Sussex

The town is a cross-Channel port that handles both passengers and cargo, and it also has a fishing fleet, boat-building yards and an extensive yacht marina.

The parish church of St Michael was begun in the 12th century, and has a heavily beamed roof supported by timber columns.

Close to the swing bridge over the harbour is the 17th-century Bridge Hotel, in which King Louis Phillippe of France stayed after fleeing from the revolution of 1848.

Information Tel. 5712.
Location On the A259, 9 m. E of Brighton.
Parking Lower Place; Chapel Street; Woolgars Passage; South Lane; Bay View Road; Railway Road (all car parks).
District council Lewes (Tel. Lewes 71600).
Population 9,900.
E-C Wed.
Police South Way (Tel. 5801).
Casualty hospital Royal Sussex, Eastern Road, Brighton (Tel. Brighton 606611).
Post office High Street.
Public library Church Hill.

Shopping High Street; Bridge Street.
Car ferry To Dieppe (Tel. 4131).
AA 24 hour service Tel. Brighton 695231.

Newmarket Suffolk

For nearly 400 years Newmarket has been the headquarters of British horse racing, breeding and training. The town is surrounded by a heath where horses can be seen exercising.

The first formal link with racing began in 1605 when James I began hunting in the neighbourhood. Spring and autumn races were held to coincide with his visits. Charles I, Charles II and succeeding monarchs continued the royal patronage.

In 1683 a great fire almost destroyed the town. The only house built before that date still standing today is one in Palace Street said to have belonged to Nell Gwynne, mistress of Charles II.

Newmarket has two courses – the July and the Rowley Mile, which, with a length of 1¼ miles and a width of 176 ft, is the longest and widest straight in the world.

The National Stud, on the Heath, is a 500 acre farm administered by the Horse-race Betting Levy Board.

JOCKEY CLUB *The original headquarters of the controlling body of British racing, in Newmarket High Street. The club was founded in 1750 in a Newmarket coffee house.*

Information Tel. 61216.
Location On the A1304, 13 m. E of Cambridge.
Parking Fred Archer Way (2); All Saints Road; Church Lane; Grosvenor Yard (all car parks).
District council Forest Heath (Tel. Mildenhall 71600).
Population 16,200.
E-C Wed. **M-D** Tues., Sat.
Police Vicarage Road (Tel. 2211).
Casualty hospital West Suffolk Hospital, Hardwick Lane, Bury St Edmunds (Tel. Bury St Edmunds 63131).
Post office High Street.
Public library The Rookery.
Places to see Jockey Club; Nell Gwynne's Cottage, Palace Street.
Shopping High Street; Rookery Shopping Precinct.
Trade and industry Light engineering; caravan manufacture.
Sport Horse racing, The Racecourse.
AA 24 hour service Tel. Cambridge 312302.

NEWCASTLE UPON TYNE Tyne & Wear

A "canny" town on bustling Tyneside

The commercial and industrial capital of England's North-East region takes its name from the "new castle" built by the Normans on the site of a Roman fort. Tynesiders call it "canny Newcassel", meaning orderly and pleasant. For this they must thank three men – the architect John Dobson, a builder named Richard Grainger and a town clerk, John Clayton. Between 1825 and 1840 these men planned and built one of the finest town centres in England, sparing Newcastle the ugliness of indiscriminate building that marred other industrial cities of the period. The city's modern planners have added other fine buildings, including a new Civic Centre and Newcastle University. They have also planted trees in the city centre – something that Dobson, Grainger and Clayton omitted to do.

The elegance of Newcastle's town centre is remarkable, because it was built at a time when most Victorian architects were obsessed with the Gothic Revival. John Dobson's and Richard Grainger's designs were in the Classical style, with gently curving streets that showed to advantage the graceful colonnaded façades of their buildings.

Dobson's masterpiece is the porticoed **Central Station** in Neville Street, one of the great monuments to the railway age. It was opened in 1850 by Queen Victoria and when completed in 1865 it covered 17 acres and had 2 miles of platforms. Near the station, in Westgate Road, is a statue of George Stephenson (1781-1848), the railway pioneer, who was born in the village of Wylam, 8 miles west of the city.

From Westgate Road, Grainger Street sweeps uphill to converge with Grey Street at **Grey's Monument.** This 133 ft high memorial commemorates Earl Grey (1764-1845), MP for Northumberland for more than 20 years and the Prime Minister who master-minded the Reform Bill of 1832 which gave seats in Parliament to the new towns created by the Industrial Revolution. Near by is

Eldon Square which was built by Dobson and Grainger between 1825 and 1831. The square is now the focal point of a vast shopping and recreation centre designed to serve the whole of the North-East region.

Fountains and pools

Newcastle's **Civic Centre** was opened in 1968, and received a Civic Trust Award in 1969. It is built round a quadrangle with lawns, fountains and pools.

The Council Chamber is an elliptical building joined to the main block. Directly above it is a square tower

surmounted by a copper-clad lantern and decorated with castles and sea-horses from the city's coat of arms. The tower contains a carillon of 25 bells which play traditional tunes during the day.

The River Tyne is crossed at Newcastle by six bridges, the most prominent being the "coat-hanger" suspension bridge erected in 1928 to carry the A1 road into the city. Less than a mile up-river is the two-tiered High Level Bridge carrying a railway line on its upper deck and a roadway on the lower. Between these two nestles the swing bridge designed by William Armstrong in 1876. The King Edward VII railway bridge (1906) and the Redheugh road bridge (1900) span the river west of the city.

SWANS IN FLIGHT *A bronze sculpture by David Wynne rises from a pool in the Civic Centre quadrangle.*

BAGPIPE MUSEUM

The world's only bagpipe museum is housed in Black Gate, a fortified gatehouse which was once part of the castle. More than 100 sets of bagpipes from all parts of the world are on show. Naturally Northumbrian pipes have pride of place. These are blown by a bellows tucked under the piper's arm, unlike Scottish pipes, which are blown by mouth. The museum also contains recordings and a pipe-maker's workshop.

Northumbrian small-pipes of the 17th to 19th centuries. The bellows can be seen on the bottom right instrument.

CEREMONIAL WAY *The approach to the Civic Centre is lined with torches which are lit on special occasions.*

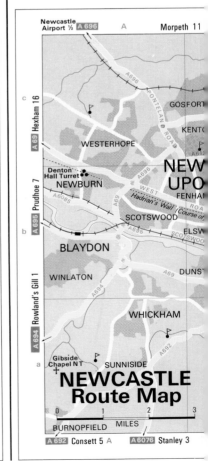

NEWCASTLE Route Map

RAINBOW OF STEEL *The great arch of Newcastle's famous landmark carries the road to the city high above the River Tyne.*

The 100-year-old swing bridge below turns on a central pivot to allow ships to pass up and down the river.

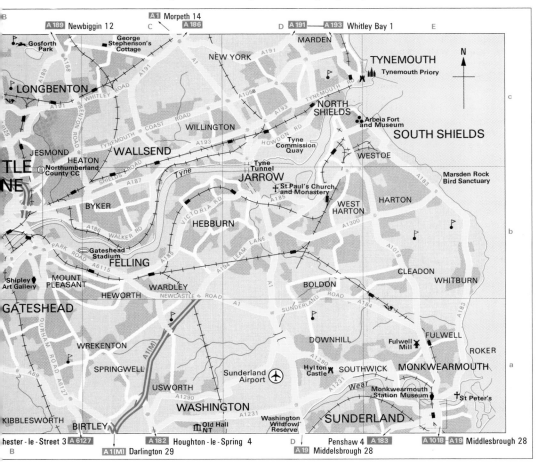

REGENCY GRANDEUR *Leazes Terrace, recently restored by Newcastle University, was built between 1829-34 by Richard Grainger to the design of Thomas Oliver.*

HERITAGE OF SCIENCE AND ENGINEERING

The past achievements of Newcastle are recorded in an impressive display of exhibits in the Museum of Science and Engineering. Among the original exhibits is a steam locomotive built by George Stephenson in 1830 for the Killingworth Colliery. The museum also has working models of marine and stationary steam engines. Ship models include the liner RMS *Mauretania* and the battleship HMS *Nelson*, both built on Tyneside.

A reconstruction of Turbinia, the world's first steam-turbine-driven boat, which was built by Sir Charles Parsons in 1894, is in the museum.

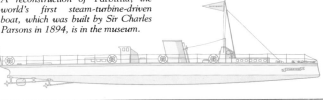

The first Tyne bridge was built by the Romans, who also erected a fort to guard it. A wooden fort built in 1080 was replaced by a stone castle in the 12th century. Only the Keep, the 13th-century Black Gate and parts of the south wall remain.

The 82 ft high **Keep** was restored by John Dobson in 1811. The basement was used as the county gaol until 1812. **Black Gate** guarded the only level approach to the castle.

The City Walls were built during the reigns of Edward I and Edward II. Part of the **West Wall** has been restored, and in the East Wall the **Plummer Tower** houses 18th-century furnishings and the **Sallyport Tower** is used as a meeting room.

On the eastern outskirts of the city, at Denton Burn, is the easternmost surviving stretch of Hadrian's Wall, which once snaked 73 miles across the width of England. At Heddon-on-the-Wall there is a 100 yd well-preserved section of the wall, and at Benwell a causeway crosses the Vallum (the southern ditch).

Quayside

From the 15th to the 19th centuries the Quayside and adjoining streets were the centre of Newcastle's commercial and civic life. The **Guildhall** was built in 1658. Inside are a 17th-century courtroom and the Merchant Adventurers' Court. Merchants lived in the timbered 16th-century houses which still stand in Sandhill. The **Customs House** dates from 1766 and **Trinity House** has an early-18th-century chapel and courtyard. At the corner of Sandgate and Milk Market a granite fountain marks the spot where John Wesley preached in 1742. A street market is held on the Quayside every Sunday. Running up from the Quayside are the chares, narrow lanes, which have survived from the medieval city.

St Nicholas's Cathedral has a rare, 15th-century "crown spire" sur-

MUSEUM OF ANTIQUITIES

The museum is part of Newcastle University's Department of Archaeology and contains a collection of prehistoric, Roman and Anglo-Saxon antiquities. It dates from 1813 and is one of the largest and oldest collections in Britain.

There are Bronze Age relics, Roman jewellery, sculptured stones from Hadrian's Wall, a scale model of the wall and a reconstruction of the pagan Temple of Mithras found at Carrawburgh beside the wall.

A Stone Age deer-horn harpoon and a 3rd-century carving of Mithras.

mounted by an open lantern supported by flying buttresses. Inside, the cathedral is mainly 14th century with fine woodwork and monuments. There is a cenotaph to Admiral Lord Collingwood, Nelson's second-in-command at Trafalgar, who was born in Newcastle in 1748.

In 1644, during the Civil War, St Nicholas's was saved from destruction by the Mayor, Sir John Marley. A Scottish army, besieging the city, had threatened to fire on the church, but Sir John thwarted them by placing Scottish prisoners in the tower.

The Roman Catholic **Cathedral of St Mary** was built in Gothic style in 1844 by Augustus Pugin, who assisted Barry in the design of the Houses of Parliament. The city's oldest church is St Andrew's, which is mainly 13th and 14th century with some 12th-century masonry in the tower and porch.

Museums and art galleries

One of the oldest collections of antiquities in Britain is housed in the Museum of the University and Society of Antiquities. The **Hatton Art Gallery** has a collection of European paintings of the 14th–18th centuries and some modern English paintings and drawings.

The **Hancock Museum** is devoted to natural history and contains specimens of plants and animals thought to have been brought to this country by the explorer Captain Cook. A bird collection was once the property of the 19th-century zoologist John Hancock.

An interesting collection of 16th–18th-century furniture, arms and armour is displayed in the **John G. Joicey Museum**. The building dates from the late 17th century and was an almshouse until 1934.

The **Laing Art Gallery** was built in 1901 and is a fine example of the Edwardian Baroque style. Its collection of oil-paintings includes works by Reynolds, Constable, Landseer and Lowry; among the water-colours are works by Turner, Gainsborough and Rowlandson.

Information Tel. 610691.
Location On the A1, 12 m. NW of Sunderland.
Parking Archbold Terrace; Claremont Road; Leazes Lane; Leazes Park; Terrace Place; Blandford Street; Castle Leazes; Cattle Market; Railway Street; Queen Street; Greenmarket; New Bridge Street; Melbourne Street; Quayside; The Close; Dean Street; Percy Street; Northumberland Road; Morden Street; Blenheim Street; Scotswood Road (all car parks).
District council City of Newcastle upon Tyne (Tel. 28520).

Population 192,500.
M-D Tues., Thur., Sat. and Sun.
Police (Bb) Market Street (Tel. 323451).
Casualty hospital Westgate Road (Tel. 38811).
Post office (Ba) St Nicholas Street.
Theatres Theatre Royal **(Bb)**, Grey Street (Tel. 322061); Newcastle Playhouse **(Bc)**, Barras Bridge (323421).
Cinemas ABC **(Bc)**, Haymarket (Tel. 323345); Tyneside Film Theatre **(Bb)**, Pilgrim Street (321507); ABC 1 and 2 **(Aa)**, Westgate Road (323232); Odeon **(Bb)**, Pilgrim Street (323248); Studios 1, 2, 3 and 4 **(Aa)**, Waterloo Street (326198).
Public library (Bb) Princess Square.
Places to see Museum of Antiquities **(Bc)**, Hatton Art Gallery **(Bc)**, The Quadrangle, University; Mining Engineering Museum **(Bc)**, University; Hancock Museum **(Bc)**, Great North Road; John G. Joicey

Museum **(Ca)**, City Road; Laing Art Gallery **(Bb)**, Higham Place; Museum of Science and Engineering **(Bd)**, Exhibition Park; Bagpipe Museum, Black Gate **(Ba)**; The Keep **(Ba)**, Castle Garth; Black Friars Priory ruins **(Aa)**, Friars Street; Greek Museum **(Bc)**, University; Plummer Tower Museum **(Bb)**, Croft Street.
Town trails Available from City Information Service, Central Library.
Shopping Eldon Square Shopping Centre; Northumberland Street; Market Street; Pilgrim Street; Grainger Street; Percy Street; Newgate Street; Bigg Market.
Event "Hoppings" Fair (June).
Sport FA League football, Newcastle United FC, St James's Park; Horse racing, Gosforth Racecourse, High Gosforth Park.
Car ferry To Esjberg (Tel. 78115).
Motorail Tel. 26262.
AA 24 hour service Tel. 610111.

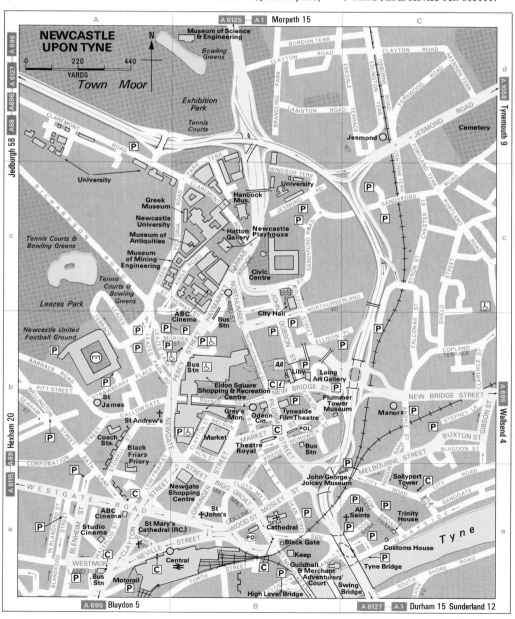

Newport Gwent

In the 5th century Newport was known as Gwynllyw, after the warrior who ruled it. He became a Christian, founded a church and was canonised. The Normans later built the church which is now the cathedral. It is dedicated to Gwynllyw, whose name is now rendered as Woolos. It still retains much of the original interior.

Not far from the cathedral stand the ruins of a 15th-century castle, on a site controlling the river crossing and next to Newport Bridge. The outstanding feature of the ruins is the riverside Gothic arch which forms a watergate and preserves the groove of the original portcullis.

In 1521 Newport was described as a borough "whereunto very great ships may resort and have good harbour", and three centuries later, at the onset of the Industrial Revolution, it became the outlet for the coal and iron industries of Monmouthshire. Its importance increased dramatically.

Today, Newport is well served by road and rail, and it exports not only the products of South Wales industry but also those of the Midlands. Modern dockyard equipment has made it one of Britain's major timber-importing centres. Access to its two deep-water docks is by one of the largest sea locks in the country – 100,000 sq. ft.

The outstanding collection in the town museum is the archaeological remains from the Romano-British town of Venta Silurum (Caerwent) which lies 10 miles east of the town.

A bust in the museum commemorates the poet W. H. Davies (1871-1940) who was born in the town.

Modern murals depicting the history of Newport decorate the central hall of the Civic Centre. The subjects, ranging from the first Celtic settlement to the building of the New George Street Bridge in the 1960s, were painted in 1961-4 by the German artist Hans Feibusch.

There is another mural on the main roundabout of the Old Green Interchange scheme. Created in relief-mosaic and concrete by Kenneth Budd in 1971-5, this illustrates mid-19th-century scenes in the history of the prosperous Monmouthshire Railway and Canal Company.

A mosaic in John Frost Square commemorates the Chartist Riots of 1839.

In the High Street, near the old west gate, is Murenger House, an Elizabethan timber-fronted building with lattice windows.

On the outskirts of the town is Tredegar House, a superb 17th-century brick house, incorporating part of a Tudor building. It was the home of the Morgan family, local landowners and industrialists, from the 15th century until 1951.

Information Tel. 842962.
Location On the M4, 13 m. NE of Cardiff.
Parking Park Square; Kingsway (2); Cambrian Road (2); Hill Street; Upper Dock Street; Godfrey Road; Canal Parade (2); Mountjoy Road (all car parks).
District council Borough of Newport (Tel. 65491).
Population 105,400.
E-C Thur. **M-D** Wed.
Police (Ab) Civic Centre (Tel. 62292).
Casualty hospital Royal Gwent, Cardiff Road (Tel. 52244).
Post office (Bb) High Street.
Theatre Dolman **(Ba)**, Kingsway Centre (Tel. 51338).

Cinemas ABC **(Ab)**, Bridge Street (Tel. 54326); Odeon, Clarence Place (58344); Studios 1 and 2, Clarence Place (58776).
Public library (Ba) John Frost Square.
Places to see Civic Centre murals **(Ab)**; Tredegar House and country park; Cathedral **(Aa)**; Castle ruins **(Bb)**; Museum and Art Gallery **(Ba)**; Transporter Bridge.
Shopping Kingsway Centre; Commercial Street; High Street.
Sport FA League football, Newport County FC, Somerton Park.
AA 24 hour service Tel. 62559.

Newport Isle of Wight

The position of Newport at the centre of the island and at the navigable head of the River Medina has made it a natural market place for the island's mixed agriculture since Saxon days.

On the south-west outskirts of the town is Carisbrooke Castle, a powerful fortress with a Norman keep and moat. The gatehouse was added in the 14th century.

In November 1647 friends took Charles I to the castle, hoping that they would win the governor over to the royal cause. Charles soon discovered he was a prisoner, not a guest, and made two unsuccessful attempts to escape. He finally left the island in November 1648, on the way to his trial and execution in London.

The County Club and Guildhall of Newport were the work of John Nash (1752–1835), who designed London's Regent Street.

Information Tel. 524343.
Location On the A3020, 5 m. S of Cowes.
Parking Lugley Street; Chapel Street; Orchard Street; Barton Road (2); Furrlongs; St John's Road; Town Lane; Royal Exchange; Carisbrooke High Street; Medina Avenue (all car parks).
District council Borough of Medina (Tel. 522493).
Population 23,600.

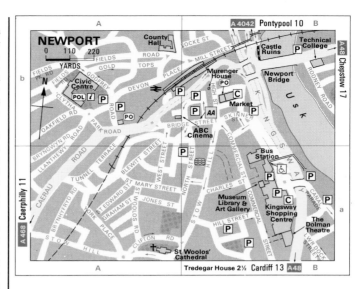

NEWPORT TRANSPORTER BRIDGE *The bridge, built in 1906, carries cars and passengers across the lower Usk in a carriage suspended from a trolley.*

CARISBROOKE CASTLE *Charles I was held prisoner in this Isle of Wight fortress before his trial and execution in 1649.*

E-C Thur. **M-D** Tues.
Police High Street (Tel. 528000).
Casualty hospitals St Mary's, Parkhurst (Tel. 524081); Royal IoW, Ryde (Ryde 63311) (24 hours).
Post office High Street.
Theatres Apollo, Pyle Street (Tel. 527267); Medina Community, Fairlee Road (527020).
Cinemas Savoy, Town Lane (Tel. 528468); Studio One, High Street (527169).
Public library Orchard Street.
Places to see Carisbrooke Castle and Museum; Roman villa.
Shopping High Street; Pyle Street.
Trade and industry Brewing; joinery; agriculture; boat-building.
AA 24 hour service Tel. 522653.

Newquay Cornwall

Cornwall's principal holiday resort has ten beaches of firm, golden sand. The most sheltered is Towan. The others are more open to the Atlantic surf, which attracts international surfing champions to the town – but all are safe for bathing if care is taken.

Settlement of the site dates back 3,000-4,000 years, as shown by the numerous Bronze Age barrows in the area. For centuries Newquay was a fishing village that depended for its livelihood on pilchards.

In the mid-16th century, and again in the mid-19th century, Newquay shared in the Cornish mining boom, producing silver as well as lead and copper. Old shaft entrances can still be seen on the cliffs.

From about 1850 until the early 1880s Newquay was a thriving port. Long rowing-boats, known as gigs, competed each other to land a pilot on an incoming cargo ship. Throughout the summer there are organised races for gigs around a 6 mile course in the bay.

Trenance Gardens, behind the town, have a wealth of flowering plants and trees, and a zoo.

Trerice Manor, 3 miles south-east, is a gabled Elizabethan house.

Information Tel. 71345.
Location On the A3059, 16 m. N of Truro.

Parking St Michael's Road; Mount Wise; Fistral Beach; Porth Beach; Fore Street; Sydney Road; Trenance; St George's Road; Belmont Place; Albany Road; Tolcarne Road; Atlantic Road; Tregunnel Hill (all car parks).
District council Borough of Restormel (Tel. St Austell 4466).
Population 16,000.
E-C Wed. (not in summer).
Police (Ba) Tolcarne Road (Tel. 2263).
Casualty hospital Newquay and District, St Thomas Road (Tel. 3883).
Post office (Ba) East Street.
Theatres Cosy Nook **(Aa)**, Towan Promenade (Tel. 3365); Newquay **(Aa)**, St Michael's Road (3379); Lane Theatre, Lane (6945).
Cinemas Camelot **(Aa)**, The Crescent (Tel. 4222); Astor, Narrowcliff (2023).
Public library (Aa) Marcus Hill.
Places to see Huer's House **(Ab)**; Trerice Manor, 3 m. SE; Ancient burial mounds, Barrowfields; Zoological Gardens, Trenance.
Shopping Fore Street; Bank Street; East Street; Cliff Road.
AA 24 hour service Tel. Truro 76455.

HUER'S HOUSE, NEWQUAY *A huer – a lookout for pilchards – would call through a horn from the watchtower on Towan Head when he sighted a shoal.*

Newton Abbot Devon

The age of steam turned Newton Abbot into a railway-workshop town like Crewe and Swindon, and swept away many of its old buildings. The railway boom lasted less than 100 years, though Newton Abbot has remained an important junction. The town now relies mainly on tourists, attracted by the moors on one side and the sea on the other.

The town's name derives from the 13th century when it was the "new town" of William de Brewer, abbot of Torre Abbey.

Forde House, in the town centre, has seven magnificent plastered ceilings, and Bradley Manor includes a great hall with a fine beamed roof dating from 1419.

Information Tel. 66629.
Location On the A380, 6 m. NW of Torquay.
Parking Marlborough Street; Sherborne Road; Osborne Street; Newfoundland Way; Cricket Field Road (all car parks).
District council Teignbridge (Tel. 67251).
Population 20,900.
E-C Thur. **M-D** Wed., Sat.
Police Baker's Hill (Tel. 4444).
Casualty hospital Torbay Hospital, Torquay (Tel. Torquay 64576).
Post office Market Square.
Cinema Alexandra, Market Street (Tel. 5368).
Public library Bank Street.
Shopping Market Precinct; Queen Street; Courtenay Street.
Event Cheese and Onion Fair (Sept.).
Trade and industry Agricultural engineering; clay works.
Sport Horse racing, Kingsteignton Road.
Motorail Tel. 66490.
AA 24 hour service Tel. Torquay 25903.

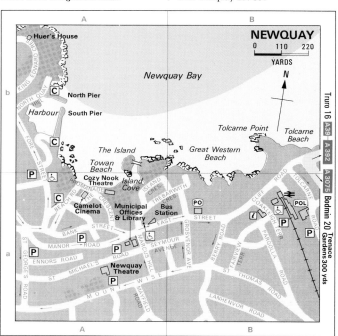

NEWQUAY

Newtown Powys

The ancient market town of Cedewain was renamed Newtown in medieval times, and the diversity of the local architecture suggests that it has been trying to become a new town ever since. Tudor, Gothic, Jacobean, Georgian, Victorian, Edwardian and modern buildings crowd together in this gentle loop of the River Severn. Scarcely two blocks are alike.

Robert Owen (1771-1858), the mill owner and social reformer whose ideas inspired the Co-operative movement, was born and died in Newtown. He is buried in the old churchyard of St Mary's beside the river.

Information Tel. Welshpool 2043.
Location On the A483, 14 m. SW of Welshpool.
Parking Back Lane; Short Bridge Street; Severn Square (all car parks).
District council Montgomery (Tel. Welshpool 2828).
Population 9,350 (includes Llanllwchaiarn).
E-C Thur. **M-D** Tues., Sat.
Police Park Lane (Tel. 25704).
Casualty hospital Montgomery County Hospital, Llanfair Road (Tel. 27722).
Post office Short Bridge Street.
Cinema Regent, Broad Street (Tel. 26372).
Public library Park Street.
Places to see Textile Museum, Commercial Road.
Shopping High Street; Broad Street; Market Street; Market Hall; Ladywell Shopping Precinct.
AA 24 hour service Tel. Cardiff 394111.

Northallerton N. Yorks.

Domesday Book baldly described Northallerton as "a waste", but its name suggests it was Aelfhere's, or Alfred's, farm or town in Saxon days. Robert Bruce burned the town to the ground as he harassed England in 1318. Since then Northallerton has been a staging post on the long coaching route to the North, and a railway town. Its weekly livestock market and street market draw large crowds from the surrounding plain of the North Riding.

Information Tel. 6101.
Location On the A167, 16 m. SE of Darlington.
Parking High Street; Bullamoor Road; Lascelles Road (all car parks).
District council Hambleton (Tel. 6101).
Population 9,600.
E-C Thur. **M-D** Wed.
Police Racecourse Lane (Tel. 3131).
Casualty hospital Friarage Hospital, Bullamoor Road (Tel. 6111).
Post office High Street.
Cinema Lyric, North End High Street (Tel. 2019).
Public library Thirsk Road.
Shopping High Street.
AA 24 hour service Tel. Middlesbrough 246832.

Northampton Northants.

A great fire destroyed Northampton in 1675, but it was rebuilt in such a spacious, well-planned way that Daniel Defoe (1661-1731) called it "the handsomest and best built town in all this part of England".

Boot, shoe and leather manufacturing became major industries in the late 18th century. Their importance to the town is reflected in the Central Museum and Art Gallery, which displays Roman sandals, Queen Victoria's wedding slippers and Margot Fonteyn's ballet pumps. The strangest item is a huge boot worn by an elephant which was taken across the Alps in 1959 in a re-enactment of Hannibal's crossing.

The rebuilding of Northampton after the fire took place around a massive market square, one of the largest in the country. The main streets which radiate from it recall the town's medieval trades: among them are Gold Street and Sheep Street.

Five fine churches survived the fire. The Church of the Holy Sepulchre, built about 1100 in imitation of the original in Jerusalem, is one of only four round churches in the country.

Delapre Abbey, a mainly 17th-century house, incorporates the remains of a medieval nunnery and now houses the County Records Office. Two of the few secular buildings to survive the fire were Haselrigg House, built in 1662, and Welsh House, built in 1595 – a relic of the days when Welsh drovers brought their cattle to Northampton market.

Abington Park Museum and the Regimental Museum occupy a manor house that was originally medieval but was greatly altered in the 17th and 18th centuries. Shakespeare's granddaughter once lived in it.

Information Tel. 22677.
Location On the A45, 14 m. SW of Kettering.

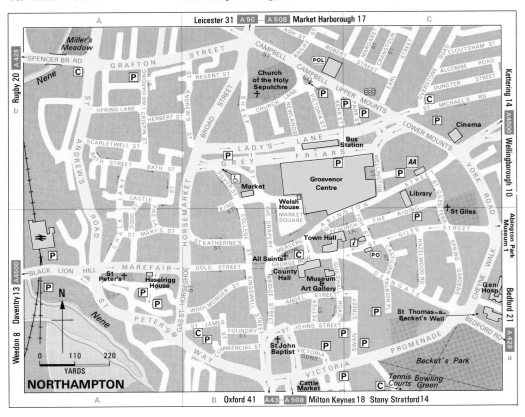

MEMORIAL TO A QUEEN *The Eleanor Cross outside Northampton is one of 12 erected by Edward I to the memory of his wife, who died in 1290.*

DEVIL IN A BOOT *An old pub sign in Northampton Museum depicts the 14th-century legend of Sir John Schorne, who imprisoned the Devil in a boot.*

Parking Grey Friars; The Riding; Upper Mounts; Commercial Street; Albion Place; Campbell Square; Lady's Lane; Wellington Street; Lower Mounts; Victoria Promenade; St John's Street (all car parks).
District council Borough of Northampton (Tel. 34881).
Population 145,400.
M-D Wed., Fri. and Sat.
Police (Bb) Campbell Square (Tel. 33221).
Casualty hospital (Ca) General, Cliftonville (Tel. 34700).
Post office (Ca) St Giles Street.
Theatre The Royal Theatre Repertory Theatre, Guildhall Road (Tel. 32533).
Cinemas ABC 1, 2 and 3 **(Cb)**, Abington Square (Tel. 35839); Studio, Lings Forum (233711).
Public library (Cb) Abington Street.
Places to see Central Museum **(Ba)**; Abington Park Museum.
Shopping Market Square; Gold Street; Abington Street; St Giles Street; Bridge Street; The Drapery; Grosvenor Centre; Sheep Street; Peacock Way; Weston Favell Centre.
Sport FA League football, Northampton Town FC, Abington Avenue. County cricket, Wantage Road.
AA 24 hour service Tel. 66241.

North Berwick Lothian

Some of Scotland's finest golf courses are in and around North Berwick. It also has fine sands, and is a centre for sailing and fishing. The town is overlooked by North Berwick Law, a 613 ft volcanic crag, topped by the ruins of a watchtower built during the Napoleonic Wars, and an arch made from the jawbone of a whale.

Offshore, in the Firth of Forth, is the 350 ft high Bass Rock, a nature reserve where gannets breed. The ruins of Tantallon Castle, the stronghold of the Earls of Angus, built in 1375, stand on a headland with sheer cliffs on three sides.

Information Tel. 2197.
Location On the A198, 13 m. NW of Dunbar.
Parking Quality Street; Kirk Ports; Law Road (2) (all car parks). Marine Parade; High Street.
District council East Lothian (Tel. Haddington 4161).
Population 5,390.
E-C Thur.
Police High Street (Tel. 3585 or Haddington 4101).
Casualty hospital Roodlands Hospital, Hospital Road, Haddington (Tel. Haddington 3182).
Post office Westgate.
Cinema Playhouse, High Street (Tel. 2422).
Public library School Road.
Places to see Bass Rock Nature Reserve; Tantallon Castle, 3 m. E.
Shopping High Street.
AA 24 hour service Tel. Edinburgh (031) 225 8464.

Northwich Cheshire

The Latin motto in Northwich's coat of arms says simply *Sal est Vita* (Salt is Life), for Northwich sits above Cheshire's vast rock-salt beds.

Salt has been exploited in the town since Roman times. Today solution mining produces over 4,000 million gallons of brine a year and 75 per cent of the salt extracted from it goes to the chemical industry.

At Anderton, on the northern outskirts of the town, the unique boat-lift opened in 1875 raises and lowers boats of up to 100 tons the 50 ft between the River Weaver and the Trent and Mersey Canal.

Information Tel. 41510.
Location On the A533, 18 m. NE of Chester.
Parking Bapons Quay Road; Leicester Street; Tabley Street; Albion Road; Crum Hill; Applemarket Street; Brockhurst Street; Chester Way; London Road (all car parks).
District council Vale Royal (Tel. 74477).
Population 17,100.
E-C Wed. **M-D** Tues., Fri., Sat.
Police Chester Way (Tel. 3541/6).
Casualty hospital Leighton Hospital, Crewe (Tel. Crewe 55141).

Post office Witton Street.
Cinema Regal, London Road (Tel. 3130).
Public library Witton Street.
Places to see Salt Museum, London Road.
Shopping High Street; Witton Street.
AA 24 hour service Tel. Manchester (061) 485 6299.

BOATS FIRST *A road bridge over the River Weaver at Northwich swings aside to let boats pass.*

Norwich see page 304

Nottingham see page 308

Nuneaton Warwickshire

A wealthy order of Benedictine nuns set up a priory beside the River Anker in the middle of the 12th century, and the town that grew up alongside took the name Nuneaton (the nun's farmstead by the river). The priory ruins can be seen near the parish church of St Mary.

Coal was being mined near the town in the 14th century, and it was an important local industry 400 years later. The arrival of the railways in 1847 led to the development of Nuneaton as a textile and engineering town.

Information Tel. 384027.
Location On the A444, 9 m. N of Coventry.
Parking Broad Street; Newtown Road; Chapel Street; Church Street; Wheat Street; Pool Bank Street; Victoria Street; Heron Way; Bondgate; Back Street; Dugdale Street; Princes Street (all car parks).
District council Nuneaton Borough Council (Tel. 326211).
Population 71,500.
E-C Thur. **M-D** Sat.
Police Vicarage Street (Tel. 328431).
Casualty hospital Manor Hospital, Manor Court Road (Tel. 384201).
Post office Church Street.
Theatre Arts Centre, Pool Bank Street (Tel. 327359).
Cinema Ritz, Abbey Street (Tel. 382808).
Public library Church Street.
Shopping Market Place; Bridge Street; Church Street; Heron Way; Queens Road; Abbey Street; Newdegate Street.
AA 24 hour service Tel. Birmingham (021) 550 4858.

OLD BOY *Nelson attended King Edward VI School. His statue stands near by.*

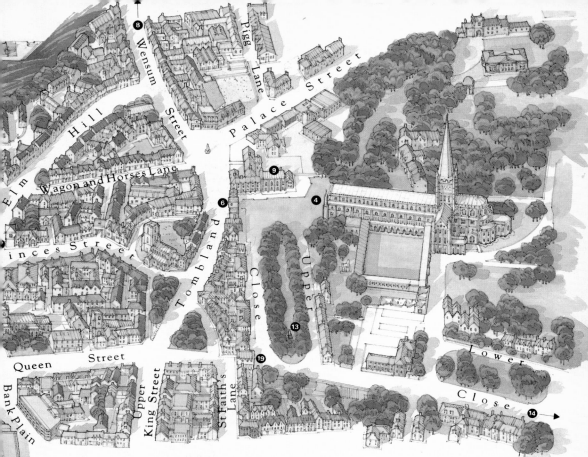

A LOOK AROUND
NORWICH
Norfolk

East Anglia's flourishing capital

Enchanting Norwich: a truly English city watched over by the gleaming spire of its dignified cathedral and wrapped in the shimmering thread of the River Wensum . . . a city shaped by 1,000 years of history, from the ageless beauty of Cathedral Close to the stark modernity of Anglia Square.

The name of Norwich appears on coins minted during the reign of King Athelstan, at the beginning of the 10th century AD. At the time of the Norman Conquest the city was one of the largest in England, with a population of 5,500.

The city flourished under the Nor-mans, attracting many craftsmen and becoming a major centre for the lucrative wool trade by the end of the 14th century. Then, as now, the surrounding countryside was exceptionally fertile and, in medieval times, the Rivers Wensum and Yare provided a convenient export route to the sea. The prospering city also had its share of problems. There was a bloody riot in 1272, when the citizens fought with the cathedral monks who tried to impose tolls on the annual fair held at Tombland. In 1349 the "Black Death" claimed an estimated 2,000 people – roughly one-third of the entire population – and in 1381 Norwich was captured and its mayor was killed by rebels during the Peasants' Revolt. The insurgents were eventually defeated by an army under the warrior-bishop Henry le Despenser, who is remembered by a splendid decorated screen behind the altar which he gave to the cathedral.

Civil strife flared up in the city again in 1549. A rebel army of 20,000 yeoman farmers, protesting against the enclosure of common land, was routed by the Earl of Warwick, and the rebel leader, Robert Kett from nearby Wymondham, was hanged from the walls of **Norwich Castle**.

CAR-MAKER'S CAR *An 1898 Panhard-Levassor at Strangers' Hall belonged to C. S. Rolls.*

PEACEFUL HAVEN *Norwich Cathedral Close is one of the largest in Britain. Standing near the River Wensum, and less than 20 miles from the sea, it provides a haven for seagulls driven inland by winter gales.*

Towards the end of the 16th century the population of Norwich was increased by many settlers from the Netherlands, who did much to revive the textile industry. These and other settlers from Europe are recalled in the name of the **Strangers' Hall**, a large and rambling mansion in Charing Cross.

The earliest parts of the Strangers' Hall date from 1320 and, 600 years later, the house became a museum of domestic life. The rooms are decorated and furnished in many styles, from Tudor to Victorian. Exhibits range from costume to traditional tradesmen's signs. In the coach house, the splendid Lord Mayor's coach stands beside a car originally owned by the Hon. C. S. Rolls, one of the founders of Rolls-Royce Ltd.

Oldest Christian effigy

The **cathedral** was started in 1096 by Herbert de Losinga, the first Bishop of Norwich. Norfolk flints formed the core of the building, but the beautiful white stone of the exterior came from Caen, in Normandy, reaching Norwich by way of Great Yarmouth and the River Wensum. On the last stage of its journey the stone was shipped along a short canal dug to link the cathedral to the river. The little canal was used for 300 years, and its course is now followed by a lane which runs from Lower Close to **Pull's Ferry**.

Inside the cathedral, the nave roof is a superb work of art. It was embellished between 1465 and 1510 and has bosses painted with biblical scenes telling the story of mankind from the Creation right through to the Last Judgment. The roof can be studied closely through a series of mirrors on wheels. Similar bosses, portraying everything from saints and musicians to grotesque creatures, may be seen in the cloisters, one of the largest in any English cathedral. They were rebuilt after being burned during the riot of 1272.

Set in the wall near **St Luke's Chapel** is a stone effigy dating from about 1100. It may represent Herbert de Losinga, Pope Gregory I or St Peter, and is possibly the oldest Christian effigy in England. St Luke's and St Saviour's chapels both contain paintings by unknown 14th-century Norwich painters that rival Italian works of the same period.

The cathedral spire was added by Bishop James Goldwell at the end of the 15th century. Its topmost point is 315 ft above the ground – the highest land in Norfolk is only 329 ft above sea-level – and only Salisbury, among British cathedrals, is taller.

Nurse Edith Cavell, executed by the Germans in 1916 for helping Allied prisoners to escape from occupied Brussels, is buried in a simple grave close to the South Door. Juliana of Norwich, a 15th-century mystic, is commemorated in the cathedral every year on May 8. Her theological treatise *XVI Revelations of Divine Love*

CASTLE AND MARKET *Rows of brightly striped awnings stand like neat furrows in a field of colour below the castle. The market is held daily, except Sundays, as it has been since Norman times.*

PULL'S FERRY *In the 18th century a ferry plied the Wensum at this point, and took its name from the ferryman. The gateway was built in the 15th century to guard the entrance to the small canal leading to the cathedral.*

was the first book to be written in English by a woman.

The **Cathedral Close** runs down to the river and has many fine buildings. The main entrances from Tombland are **St Ethelbert Gate** and the **Erpingham Gate**, opposite the cathedral's west front. This gate is carved with many figures and was the gift of Sir Thomas Erpingham in 1420. He commanded the archers at the Battle of Agincourt, and was immortalised by Shakespeare in *King Henry V*. Inside the gates, beside the cathedral, is **King Edward VI School**; near by stands a statue of its most famous pupil, Lord Nelson.

Norwich school paintings

Norwich Castle dates from the early part of the 12th century. The original walls were made of Caen stone, like the cathedral, but they were refaced with Bath stone in 1834-9. The huge keep – one of the largest in the country – is now a museum and houses a fascinating variety of exhibits. They include the world's finest collection of Lowestoft porcelain, weapons, natural history and archaeological items, and many works by John Crome (1768-1821), John Cotman (1782-1842) and other artists of what became known as the Norwich

school. From 1220 to 1887 the castle was the county gaol, and in the dungeons are the death masks of prisoners executed there.

The River Wensum formed a natural line of defence for only part of Norwich, and the city was given the additional protection of walls 20 ft high at the end of the 14th century. There were ten fortified gateways with a series of towers between them. The remains are seen at their best on Carrow Hill, where a 50 yd section of wall climbs steeply to the **Black Tower**. At the foot of the hill, on either side of the river, are the remains of boom towers built to guard against attacks by water. Cargo ships and pleasure craft now moor a little higher upstream. The riverside walk from **Carrow Bridge** to the Cathedral Close is one of the best in Norwich. It passes Pull's Ferry, the ruined **Cow Tower** and the 14th-century **Bishop Bridge**.

The city's museums include **St Peter Hungate**, rebuilt between 1430 and 1460. It was saved from demolition in 1902, and now houses a collection of religious arts and crafts.

The Bridewell, a museum of Norwich trades and industries, illustrates weaving, boots and shoes, ironwork and brewing. The building, which dates from the 14th century, was used as a "bridewell", or prison, from 1583 to 1828. Near by is the unique and charming **Mustard Shop**. Entering the shop is like stepping back into the Victorian past. There is a small "mustard museum" at the back of the shop.

Like the cathedral and castle, a lively open-air market has been a feature of Norwich life since Norman times. At one end of the square stands the **Church of St Peter Mancroft**, a fine example of Perpendicular architecture. Bells that celebrated the defeat of the Spanish Armada in 1588 still peal from its tower. Opposite is the **Guildhall**, built at the start of the 15th century and much restored in the 19th century.

Among prized possessions preserved in the Guildhall is a Spanish admiral's sword presented to the city by Nelson after the victory off Cape St Vincent in 1797.

The third side of the square is flanked by the **City Hall**, opened by George VI in 1938. Together with the cathedral and the noble 19th-century **Roman Catholic Cathedral of St John the Baptist**, the Hall's 202 ft tower dominates the city skyline.

Elm Hill has perhaps more atmosphere than any other Norwich thoroughfare. Named after a great elm that once stood at its top, the cobble-paved hill runs down between timber-framed and pastel-coloured buildings housing art galleries, antique shops, picture-framers and a pottery. An unexpected feature is a brass-rubbing centre. In Magdalen Street is **Gurney Court**, birthplace in 1780 of Elizabeth Fry the Quaker and prison reformer. Off Magdalen Street, Anglia Square is dominated by the concrete-and-glass headquarters of HM Stationery Office.

NORWICH CANARIES

Immigrant weavers from the Netherlands who settled in Norwich in the 16th century are said to have brought their pet canaries with them. Canary breeding became a local hobby, and by the 18th century the Norwich canary was recognised as a distinct breed, prized for its song and colour. The Norwich football team is nicknamed "The Canaries".

A case of Norwich canaries is displayed in the Bridewell Museum.

Information Tel. 20679.
Location On the A11, 43 m. N of Ipswich.
Parking Bethel Street; Malthouse Road; St Giles Street; Duke Street; Elm Hill; Ber Street; Surrey Street; St Andrew's Street; St Saviours Lane; Market Avenue; Mountergate; Rouen Road; St Swithins Road; Westwick Street; Cattle Market Street; Theatre Street; Golden Dog Lane; Bishopgate; St Crispins Road; Queens Road (all car parks).
District council City of Norwich (Tel. 22233).
Population 122,300.
E-C Thur. **M-D** Mon. to Sat.
Police (Aa) Bethel Street (Tel. 21212).
Casualty hospital St Stephen's Road

(Tel. 28377).
Post office (Bb) Bank Plain.
Theatres Maddermarket Theatre **(Bb)**, St John's Alley (Tel. 20917); Theatre Royal **(Aa)**, Theatre Street (28205); Puppet Theatre, Whitefriars (29921).
Cinemas ABC **(Cb)**, Prince of Wales Road (Tel. 23312); Noverre **(Aa)**, Theatre Street (26402); Odeon, Anglia Square (21903); Cinema City, St Andrew's Street (22047).
Public library (Aa) Bethel Street.
Places to see Assembly House **(Aa)**, Theatre Street; St Peter Hungate Museum **(Bb)**, Elm Hill; Bridewell Museum **(Bb)**, Bridewell Alley; Castle and Museum **(Bb)**, Castle Meadow; Guildhall **(Bb)**, Market Place; St Andrew's and Blackfriars'

Halls, St Andrew's Street; Strangers' Hall **(Ab)**, Charing Cross; Royal Norfolk Regiment Museum, Mousehold Heath; Cathedral **(Cb)**.
Town trails Available from Communication Counsel Ltd, 63 Caernarvon Road, Norwich.
Shopping London Street; St Giles Street; Exchange Street; St Andrew's Street; Bank Plain; Upper King Street; Prince of Wales Road; Bedford Street; Castle Street; Castle Meadow; Red Lion Street; Brigg Street; The Walk; Anglia Square; St Stephen Street; Pottergate; St Benedict's Street; Dove Street.
Event Lord Mayor's Parade (July).
Sport FA League football, Norwich City FC, Carrow Road.
AA 24 hour service Tel. 29401.

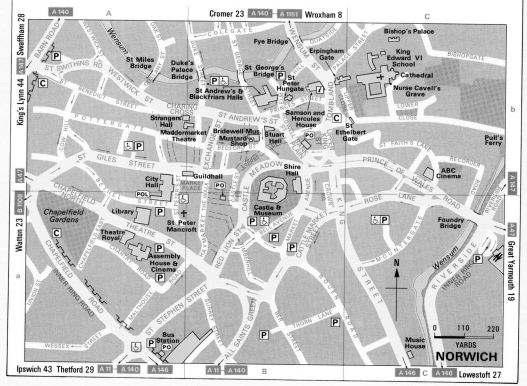

NORWICH

NOTTINGHAM Nottinghamshire

City of lace and legend

Versatile Nottingham – city of lace and Robin Hood, home of the Luddites, the bicycle and ready-rolled cigarettes – has played a decisive role in the history of Britain. Two events at Nottingham were the starting point for revolutions – one political, the other industrial. They were the raising of Charles I's standard in 1642, and the introduction of Richard Arkwright's spinning machine 125 years later. Nottingham received its first charter from Henry II in 1155, and was made a city in 1897.

When Charles I fled from London to assemble an army against his rebellious Parliament he raised his standard at **Nottingham Castle**, a fortress that has stood on a rock above the town for 900 years.

Charles was not the castle's first royal visitor. Edward III lived there for a time, Edward IV proclaimed himself king from the castle, and it was from there that Richard III set out to his defeat on Bosworth Field in 1485. Charles's association with the castle was no happier than Richard's, for less than 300 men rallied to his standard. During the Civil War that followed, the castle was held by Parliamentarian forces under Colonel Hutchinson, and after the war it was demolished by order of Parliament.

In 1674 the 1st Duke of Newcastle bought the site and built the mansion house that stands today. But Nottingham Castle's stormy days were still not over. The defeat of the Reform Bill in 1831 started riots in the town. The Nottingham townspeople were strongly in favour of the reform of Parliament, but the Duke of Newcastle at that time opposed it, so the rioters vented their fury on the castle and set it on fire. It remained an empty shell for 44 years, and then was

LUDDITE LEADER *Ned Ludd was depicted as an idiot boy in woman's clothing by an unknown 19th-century cartoonist.*

acquired by the town and restored as a museum and art gallery.

Hero of Sherwood

Outside the castle stands a bronze statue of **Robin Hood**, the legendary outlaw of Sherwood Forest. In the 12th century the forest to the north of Nottingham covered some 200 sq. miles, and it was from here that the

PEOPLE'S HERO *Fact or fiction, Nottingham honours Robin Hood with a statue outside the castle.*

folklore hero is said to have carried on his feud with the Sheriff of Nottingham. In fact, Nottingham did not have its own sheriff until 1449, and Robin may have been one of several outlaws of the 12th to 14th centuries who continued to resist the Norman and Plantagenet kings.

Revolution – and revolt

Nottingham was deeply involved in the Industrial Revolution. Richard Arkwright set up his first spinning mill there, using his spinning frame, in 1769; James Hargreaves introduced his spinning jenny in 1770; and in 1809 a lace-making machine, invented by John Heathcoat of Loughborough, arrived.

Since the 17th century, a thriving cottage industry of hosiery and knitwear had existed, using the stocking frame invented by William Lee in 1589. But it could not compete with the new sophisticated inventions, and the cottagers were barely able to scrape a living. In 1811 they banded together and destroyed many of the new machines that had caused their misery. The gangs became known as Luddites, after their leader Ned Ludd who was probably an imaginary character.

Nottingham's knitting and lace industries grew in the 19th century, and Nottingham lace is still world renowned.

CAUSE AND CURE *Players made cigarettes in 1877, Boots cough lozenges followed ten years later.*

TRADITIONAL FAIR *In October each year Nottingham holds its Goose Fair. The origin of the fair is not known, but it is believed to derive from medieval times, when geese were sold in Nottingham market.*

In 1877 John Player opened a small plant to make ready-rolled cigarettes; half a century later the firm had grown into a national manufacturer.

A lawyer named Frank Bowden bought a small workshop in Raleigh Street in 1887 and set up the Raleigh Bicycle Company, where 12 men made three bicycles a week. Twenty years later it was producing 50,000 bicycles a year.

About the same time that Bowden was starting his business, the Boots family opened a chemist's shop in Goosegate. Ninety years later "Boots the Chemists" had grown into Britain's largest chain of chemist shops.

Tradition of sport

Nottingham has three of the oldest sporting clubs in Britain. The **Trent Bridge** cricket ground was opened in 1838 and is the home of the County Cricket Club. Nottingham Forest Football Club was established in 1865, and Notts County Football Club, established in 1862, is the oldest Football League club in England.

Information Tel. 40661.
Location On the A60, 16 m. E of Derby.
Parking Broad Marsh; Fletcher Gate;

Trinity Square; Victoria Centre; Mount Street; Queensbridge Road; St James's Terrace; Pilcher Gate; Hanley Street; Maid Marian Way; Cumberland Place; Stoney Street; Chaucer Street (all car parks).
District council City of Nottingham (Tel. 48571).
Population 271,000.
E-C Mon. **M-D** Mon. to Sat.
Police (Bc) North Church Street (Tel. 45544).
Casualty hospital Queen's Medical Centre, University Hospital, Derby Road (Tel. 70011).
Post office (Bb) Queen Street.

ANCIENT INN *The Trip to Jerusalem is said to have been used by Crusaders journeying to the Holy Land.*

Theatres Playhouse (**Ab**), Wellington Circus (Tel. 45671); Theatre Royal (**Ac**), Theatre Square (42328); Co-operative Arts Theatre (**Bb**), George Street (46096).
Cinemas ABC (**Ab**), Chapel Bar (Tel. 45260); Odeon (**Ab**), Angel Row (47766); Classic (**Ab**), Market Street (44749); Nottingham Film Theatre, Broad Street (46095); Savoy, Derby Road (42580).
Public library (Ab) Angel Row.
Places to see Castle Museum and Brewhouse Yard Museum (**Aa**), Castle Rock; Castlegate Museum (**Aa**); Natural History Museum, Wollaton Hall; Industrial Museum, Wollaton Park; Midland Group Art Gallery (**Bb**), Carlton Street.
Shopping Upper and Lower Parliament Street; Market Street; King Street; Clumber Street; Chapel Bar; Angel Row; Long Row; Pelham Street; High Street; South Parade; Victoria Centre; Broadmarsh Shopping Centre.
Sport Nottingham County CC, Trent Bridge. FA League football: Notts County FC, Meadow Lane; Nottingham Forest FC, City Ground. National Water Sport Centre, Holme Pierrepont.
AA 24 hour service Tel. 787751.

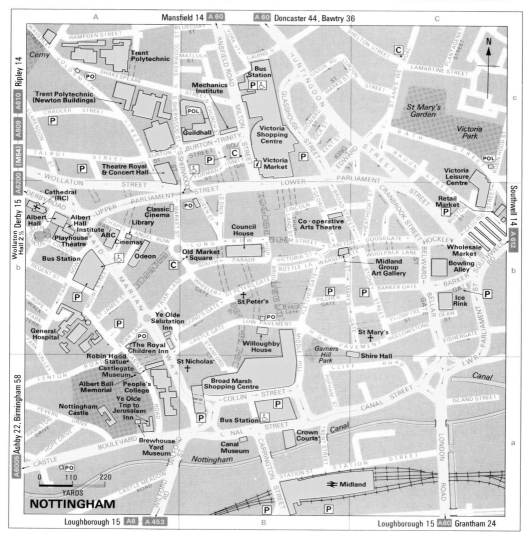

Oakham Leicestershire

Uninterrupted centuries of hunting and farming have rolled over the vales around Oakham, and history has left it largely untouched. For centuries Oakham was the county town of Rutland, England's smallest county, until Rutland was merged with Leicestershire in 1974.

On the eastern edge of the town is the largest man-made lake in Britain, Rutland Water. It is as big as Windermere, with a 24 mile perimeter. A half-mile wide dam, 110 ft high, blocks off the water of the River Gwash. The reservoir not only supplies water, but also provides fishing and sailing, and there are picnic areas round its shore.

Oakham probably got its name from a Saxon lord, Occa. Only a 12th-century banqueting hall, built by Walkelin de Ferrers, remains of the medieval castle; it is now used as a courtroom. It contains more than 200 horseshoes, given over the centuries by monarchs and peers visiting the lord of the manor.

Rutland County Museum is housed in an indoor riding school of 1796, built for the local militia. It contains fascinating displays of agricultural vehicles and machinery, and an exhibition of folk life dating back to prehistoric times.

Beside Station Road stand the original 16th-century buildings of Oakham School, founded in 1584. It is now one of the largest, independent co-educational schools in the country with 500 boys and 400 girls.

Titus Oates (1649-1705), fabricator of the Popish Plot in 1684, was born at Oakham. Nine-year-old Jeffery Hudson, the town's celebrated 18 in. high dwarf, was "served" to Charles I and his queen, Henrietta, in a cold pie when the king was hunting from nearby Burley on the Hill in 1628. The delighted Henrietta made Jeffery her page. He died in 1682.

GREAT HALL *The 12th-century banqueting hall of Oakham Castle is the finest of its period still standing.*

Information Tel. 2918.
Location On the A606, 11 m. W of Stamford.
Parking Church Street; Brooke Road; Westgate; Burley Road; Market Square; South Street (all car parks).
District council Rutland (Tel. 2577).
Population 8,510.
E-C Thur. **M-D** Wed., Sat.
Police Station Road (Tel. 2626).
Casualty hospital Leicester Royal Infirmary, Leicester (Tel. Leicester 541414).
Post office Market Square.
Cinema County, High Street (Tel. 2019).
Public library Catmos Street.
Places to see Castle; County Museum; Oakham School; Rutland Farm Park.
Shopping High Street; Melton Road; Mill Street; Church Street; Market Place.
Trade and industry Agriculture; clothing; boots and shoes; light engineering.
AA 24 hour service
Tel. Leicester 20491.

Oban Strathclyde

The tourist industry of the Western Islands largely revolves around this port, which runs steamer services to Mull, Iona, Coll, Tiree, Barra, South Uist, Colonsay and Lismore, and also provides access to the breathtaking mountains, lochs and forests of the Western Highlands.

In the mid-18th century it consisted of a few fishermen's and farmers' cottages, and an inn where Dr Johnson and Boswell stayed in 1773. Sir Walter Scott, who visited the town in 1814 and included local scenes in his poem *The Lord of The Isles* (1815), was partly responsible for popularising Oban, and by the end of the 19th century it had grown into a thriving resort with large hotels.

The harbour, protected from the Atlantic by the island of Kerrera, is always a lively scene as fishing boats unload their catches. Fish auctions take place on the Railway Pier, and ferries carry passengers in and out.

The ancient art of glass-making is shown in the workshops of Oban Glass on the Lochavullin Industrial Estate, and at the top of Soroba Road there are demonstrations of spinning and weaving in a tweed-mill.

The major event of the year is Games Day (also known as The Argyllshire Gathering), which takes place on the last Thursday in August. Top pipers and athletes take part.

Overlooking the town is the curious

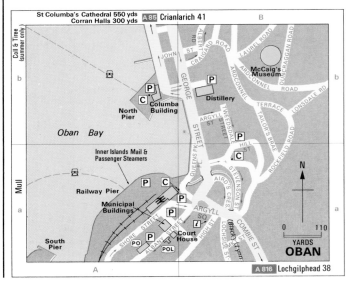

BUSY PORT *The Western Highlands rise up beyond Oban, a major port for steamer services to the Western Islands. Fishing boats, excursion steamers, car ferries and yachts make the harbour one of the liveliest in Scotland.*

McCaig's Tower, an unfinished granite structure reminiscent of the Colosseum in Rome. It was built in the 1890s by a local banker, both as a memorial to his family and to provide work for the unemployed of the town.

The 15th-century ruin of Dunollie Castle stands on a rocky promontory at the mouth of Oban Bay. Founded in the 7th century, it was the principal seat of the MacDougalls, from whom it passed to the Stewarts and later the Campbells. It was abandoned in 1750. Near by is the little granite Cathedral of St Columba, built this century by Sir Giles Gilbert Scott.

On the island of Kerrera stands 16th-century Gylen Castle, another stronghold of the MacDougalls. Three miles north of Oban is 13th-century Dunstaffnage Castle, which has 10 ft thick walls.

Information Tel. 63122.
Location On the A85, 38 m. NW of Inveraray.
Parking Albany Street; Corran Halls; Tweeddale Street; Glencruitten Road; Longsdale Road; Lochavullin Road; Pulpit Hill; North Pier (all car parks).
District council Argyll and Bute (Tel. 64211).
Population 7,830.

E-C Thur. **M-D** Tues.
Police (Aa) Albany Street (Tel. 62213).
Casualty hospital West Highland Hospital, Polvinister Road (Tel. 62544).
Post office (Aa) Albany Street.
Theatre Corran Halls, Corran Esplanade (Tel. 64211).
Cinema Phoenix, Albany Terrace (Tel. 62444).
Public library Corran Esplanade.
Places to see McCaig's Tower **(Bb)**; McCaig Museum, Corran Esplanade; Gylen Castle, Kerrera; Dunstaffnage Castle, 3 m. N off A85.
Shopping George Street; High Street.
Event Games Day (Aug.).
Trade and industry Tourism; fishing; whisky distilling.
Car ferry To Lismore, Lochaline, Craignure, Coll and Colonsay (Tel. 2285).
AA 24 hour service
Tel. Glasgow (041) 812 0101.

Okehampton Devon

Set in the very heart of Devon, Okehampton is a market town selling the agricultural produce of the surrounding area, and a touring centre for exploring Dartmoor. Two of the moor's highest points, High Willhays and Yes Tor, both over 2,000 ft, lie south, within walking distance.

The town site was occupied in the Iron Age – there are remains of a fort on a ridge to the south-east. The Saxons also had a settlement there, and the parish church occupies the site of their church.

Modern Okehampton was founded by a Norman knight, Baldwin de Brionne, 20 years after the Conquest, on a site between the East and West Okehampton rivers. The Normans built a castle on high ground beside the Exeter to Cornwall road, in the valley of the West Okement. In its day it was one of the most powerful castles in the country, but after one of its later owners, a Courtenay, was beheaded in the reign of Henry VIII, it fell into decay. Substantial ruins survive. The keep is late Norman, the rest 14th century.

A fire in 1842 destroyed the 15th-century parish church, except for the tower which was incorporated into its successor; this has windows by William Morris, the Victorian designer. In Fore Street a 14th-century chantry chapel to St James contains a splendid pulpit of 1626.

The handsome town hall of 1685 was originally built as a town house, and was converted to its present use in the 1820s. Opposite is a Georgian inn, the White Hart.

Oaklands, north of the town, is a pink-sandstone manor built in 1820 in the Grecian style, but with a strangely contrasting ornate lodge.

South-west lies Meldon Viaduct, which carries the railway line over a 160 ft deep, strikingly beautiful ravine.

The great stretch of scrubland on a hillside between the town and Meldon was once Okehampton Park, the medieval hunting ground of the Courtenay family.

At Sticklepath, a village 4 miles east, is a Museum of Rural Industry housed in a 19th-century forge. Its massive old machinery, mostly wooden, which made agricultural tools, has been lovingly preserved.

Information Tel. 2901.
Location On the A30, 23 m. W of Exeter.
Parking Market Street; Mill Road.
District council West Devon (Tel. 2901).
Population 4,000.
E-C Wed. **M-D** Sat.
Police George Street (Tel. 2201).
Casualty hospital Okehampton and District, East Street (Tel. 2188).
Post office George Street.
Cinema Carlton, Park Row (Tel. 2167).
Public library North Street.
Places to see Castle; Town Hall; Museum of Rural Industry, 4 m. E; Dartmoor Museum, West Street; Watermill and Museum, Mill Road.
Shopping Red Lion Precinct; The Arcade; West Street; Fore Street.
AA 24 hour service
Tel. Exeter 32121.

Oldham G. Manch.

In the 19th-century hey-day of the cotton industry, the mills of Oldham each year spun millions of yards of yarn. The industry flourished in Oldham because the town stands on the western slopes of the Pennines, where the damp atmosphere prevented cotton fibre from drying out and snapping when being spun and woven.

Through this area almost 2,000 years ago the Romans built a road from Manchester to York, traces of which still remain. Cloth-making was flourishing in the town by the early 1600s, and by the middle of the following century the woollen trade was well established. But during the 1790s, mechanised spinning and weaving caused cotton to supplant wool as the main industry.

Oldham was in the forefront of the fight for parliamentary reform, and in 1832 the radical William Cobbett was elected as its first MP. In 1900 Oldham became the first parliamentary seat of another great political figure, Sir Winston Churchill. The composer Sir William Walton was born in the town in 1902.

The Central Art Gallery is noted for its collection of outstanding water-colours. Works of contemporary British art include Jacob Epstein's bust of Sir Winston Churchill. The Local Interest Centre has a museum devoted to relics of Oldham's past.

The impressive town hall is a neo-Classical building of 1841-2. Oldham parish church, standing opposite, dates from the early 19th century.

At Chadderton, to the west, is Foxdenton Hall, a handsome manor house built at the end of the 17th century by Alexander Radclyffe, a member of the family who owned this and earlier houses on the site from the 13th century until 1960. Foxdenton Hall, a symmetrical building in classical Renaissance style, is set in an attractive small park with a lake.

Information Tel. Manchester (061) 678 4654.
Location On the A62, 7 m. NE of Manchester.
Parking Hobson Street; Bow Street; Bradshaw Street; Coronation Street; Gas Street; Greaves Street; New Radcliffe Street; Silver Street; Ashcroft Street; Wick Street (all car parks).
District council Metropolitan Borough of Oldham
(Tel. 061 624 0505).
Population 95,500.

CHURCHILL *The Central Art Gallery, Oldham, contains a bust of Sir Winston Churchill by Jacob Epstein.*

TOWN AND COUNTRY *The huge mills which brought prosperity to Oldham in the age of cotton rear up below the foothills of the Pennines, less than a mile from the town centre. Cotton no longer dominates Oldham, but the mills remain to house the new industries which have taken the place of textiles.*

E-C Tues. **M-D** Mon., Fri. and Sat.
Police Barn Street
(Tel. 061 624 0444).
Casualty hospital Oldham and District General, Rochdale Road
(Tel. 061 624 0420).
Post office St Peter's Precinct.
Theatres Coliseum, Fairbottom Street (Tel. 061 624 2829); Grange Arts Centre, Rochdale Road
(061 624 8012).
Cinemas Odeon, Union Street
(Tel. 061 624 1328); Roxy, Hollinwood (061 681 1441).
Public library Union Street.
Places to see Central Art Gallery; Local Interest Centre; Foxdenton Hall, Chadderton; Castleshaw Roman camp.
Shopping Yorkshire Street; High Street; St Peter's Precinct; Chadderton Precinct; Tommyfield Market; Market Hall.
Trade and industry Textiles; electronics; engineering; boatbuilding.
Sport FA League football, Oldham Athletic FC, Boundary Park; Rugby League football, Oldham RLFC, Watersheddings.
AA 24 hour service
Tel. 061 485 6299.

Ormskirk Lancashire

Much of the land around Ormskirk was waterlogged moorland until 200 years ago. Drained, it became a rich source of vegetable and cereal crops, and the town developed as a market.

The Church of St Peter and St Paul has both a spire and a separate tower, alleged to have been added in 1540 to house the bells from Burscough Priory after its dissolution. The ruins of the priory, which dates from the 12th century, are 2 miles to the north-east.

Burscough Street still has some fine Georgian houses, though many have been demolished.

Scarisbrick Hall, 3 miles north-west of the town, was rebuilt in neo-Gothic style in the 19th century. It was formerly the home of the Scarisbrick family, who were mainly responsible for draining the moorland. The hall is now a school, and is not open to the public.

Rufford Old Hall, 5 miles north, is an outstanding half-timbered medieval mansion. It houses a museum of Lancashire folk life.

Information Tel. 77177.
Location On the A570, 13 m. NE of Liverpool.
Parking Moor Street; Aughton Street; Burscough Street; Moorgate; Park Road; Southport Road; Derby Street West (all car parks).
District council West Lancashire
(Tel. 77177).
Population 36,700.
E-C Wed. **M-D** Thur., Sat.
Police Derby Street (Tel. 76971).
Casualty hospital Ormskirk and District General Hospital, Wigan Road (Tel. 75471).
Post office Aughton Street.
Cinema Pavilion, Moorgate
(Tel. 72269).
Public library Burscough Street.
Places to see Burscough Priory, 2 m. NE; St Peter and St Paul Parish Church; Martinmere Wildfowl Centre, 5 m. NE; Rufford Old Hall, 5 m. N.
Shopping Moor Street; Church Street; Burscough Street; Aughton Street.
AA 24 hour service
Tel. Liverpool (051) 709 7252.

DOUBLE-HEADED EAGLE *The crest on 17th-century Llwyd Mansion in Oswestry was granted to the Lloyd family by the Holy Roman Emperor.*

Oswestry Salop

For centuries English and Welsh fought for possession of Oswestry until, in 1535, Henry VIII's Act of Union made the town officially part of England. However, Welsh is still widely spoken there.

The area – beneath the foothills of the Welsh mountains – was settled in the Bronze Age. At Old Oswestry, north of the town, are the remains of a vast Iron Age hill-fort, one of the most elaborate examples of its kind in the world. It was occupied from about 550 BC until AD 75, when the Romans overran it. Two banks and ditches originally protected the hill. Later, a third bank was added, and finally an enormous double rampart, enclosing the whole. There is evidence of reoccupation during the Middle Ages.

The town's name is probably a corruption of Oswald's Tree, referring to Oswald, a Christian king killed here in 642 by Penda, the pagan king of Mercia. But there are two versions of the origin of Oswald's Tree. One story is that Oswald erected a wooden cross or "tree" before his battle with Penda. The other has it that the dead king's body was hung from a tree.

Another legend tells how an angel flew off with part of Oswald's dismembered body and dropped it. On the spot where it fell a spring welled up, and is now known as King Oswald's Well. The parish church is dedicated to St Oswald. Much rebuilt, it still has some 13th-century stonework.

In the 8th century, Wat's Dyke and, later, Offa's Dyke were built to mark the border of Anglo-Saxon Mercia with Welsh territory. Remains of both lie west of the town.

The Normans built a motte-and-bailey castle here soon after the Conquest to keep down the increasing Welsh raids.

In 1559 plague killed nearly one-third of the inhabitants of Oswestry. The Croeswylan Stone, or Cross of Weeping, marks the spot to which the market was shifted during the affliction.

Three great fires between the 13th and 18th centuries and the ravages of the Civil War combined to destroy much of the town. Oswestry was Royalist, but was taken and held by the Parliamentarians who, after the war, destroyed the castle. Only frag-

ments of it now remain, on a grassy hilltop which provides fine views from the centre of the town.

Many old buildings were demolished when Oswestry became a railway headquarters in 1860. One that escaped was 17th-century Llwyd Mansion, the town's best half-timbered building. On its side is a double-headed eagle crest, granted to the Lloyd family by the Holy Roman Emperor for distinguished service during the Crusades. Oswestry School, in Upper Brook Street, was founded in 1407 and is believed to be the oldest secular school in the country. Oswestry is also a centre for fishing in the rivers of the nearby Welsh valleys, pony trekking in the hills and rambling along Offa's Dyke.

Wilfred Owen (1893-1918), the First World War poet, and Sir Walford Davies (1869-1941), Master of the King's Musick, were both born in the town.

Six miles north, just inside the Welsh border, is the beautifully preserved Chirk Castle, completed in 1310 and inhabited continuously since – at present by the descendants of Sir Thomas Myddelton, a 17th-century Lord Mayor of London. The castle, which has five round towers, contains state rooms open to the public, with fine tapestries, paintings and furniture on display. The entrance gates, made in 1719-21 by two Welsh smiths, Robert and John Davies, are among the best wrought-iron work in Britain. A moated castle at Whittington, 2 miles north-east, was built during the reign of Henry III.

The bridge over the River Ceiriog, in Chirk village, marks the border with Wales, and provides a splendid view of the 100 ft high Chirk Aqueduct, which carries the Shropshire Union Canal.

Information Tel. 4411.
Location On the A483, 16 m. S of Wrexham.
Parking English Walls; Salop Road; Oak Street; Castle Street (all cps).
District council Borough of Oswestry (Tel. 4411).
Population 12,000.
M-D Wed.
Police Park Street (Tel. 3222).
Casualty hospital Oswestry and District, Upper Brook Street (Tel. 4511).
Post office Willow Street.
Cinema Regal, Salop Road (Tel. 4043).
Public library Arthur Street.
Places to see Old Oswestry Iron Age fort; King Oswald's Well, Maserfield; Croeswylan Stone, Morda Road; Llwyd Mansion; Chirk Castle, 6 m. N on A483; Llanrhaedar Waterfall, 8 m. NW.
Shopping Church Street; Willow Street; The Cross; Bailey Street.
Event Oswestry Show (July).
Trade and industry Agriculture; light industry.
AA 24 hour service
Tel. Shrewsbury 53003.

Oundle Northamptonshire

Old buildings of soft grey limestone dignify the centre of Oundle, which has been the market town for the surrounding valleys since Saxon times.

The graceful 208 ft spire of the parish church rises from an old-world cluster of stone houses divided by narrow alleys and courtyards. Dating from Norman times, the church has a 15th-century porch and contains 14th-century screenwork.

Oundle School was re-endowed in 1556 by William Laxton, a citizen of the town who became a grocer and eventually Lord Mayor of London.

One of the most interesting old inns, the Talbot Hotel, was rebuilt in 1626 with stone from Fotheringhay Castle, scene of the execution of Mary, Queen of Scots in 1587. Sparse remains of the castle lie about 4 miles north-east of the town.

Oundle is surrounded on three sides by the River Nene, and has become a holiday yachting centre.

Two miles north-east stands Cotterstock Hall, a 17th-century E-shaped manor house with fine gardens. Here the English poet and dramatist John Dryden (1631-1700) wrote many of his *Fables*, in an attic in the south front.

LATHAM'S HOSPITAL *These unspoiled 17th-century almshouses contribute to the tranquillity of Oundle.*

Information Tel. Rushden 58631.
Location On the A605, 12 m. SW of Peterborough.
Parking St Osyth's Lane (cp); Market Place; West Street; New Street.
District council East Northamptonshire (Tel. Rushden 58631).
Population 3,900.
E-C Wed. **M-D** Thur.
Police Glapthorne Road (Tel. 2222).
Casualty hospital Kettering and District General Hospital, Rothwell Road, Kettering (Tel. Kettering 81141).
Post office New Street.
Theatres Victoria Hall, West Street (Tel. 2269); Stahl, West Street (3930).
Public library Glapthorne Road.
Places to see Oundle School; Latham's Hospital; Cotterstock Hall, 2 m. NE; Lyveden New Bield, 4 m. SW off A427; Fotheringhay Castle ruins, 4 m. NE.
Shopping Market Place; West Street.
AA 24 hour service
Tel. Leicester 20491.

Oxford Oxfordshire

England's first seat of learning

Centuries of patient learning among Gothic towers and cloisters have given Oxford a quiet timelessness that neither the bustle of its modern city nor the clangour of its sprawling car industry can spoil. Oxford is all echoing quadrangles, wide streets and beautiful buildings, of which no fewer than 653 are listed as of historic or architectural merit. There is an air of antiquity about the city; a lasting quality that insists that the more things change, the more Oxford will remain what it always has been: one of the great centres of European learning.

Saxon ox-drovers were the first to found a settlement where the city stands today, fording the Thames near **Christ Church Meadow**. They probably received some hospitality from the scholarly inhabitants of a priory near the river.

One day in 872, according to legend, King Alfred stepped ashore near the ford, and met by chance a group of clerics. He engaged with them in a scholarly discussion that went on for days, and in this way the University of Oxford was said to have been founded.

But Henry II was the actual founder. In 1167, when he discovered that the exiled Archbishop Thomas Becket had found refuge in France, he ordered all English students on the Continent to return home at once. Perhaps the legend of Alfred inspired them, for many went to Oxford to try to re-create the style of learning they had discovered in Europe.

Strife and distrust between the townsfolk and students caused the university to close in 1209. Its members dispersed, some back to the Continent, some to Reading, others to a small Fenland town called Cambridge, where they founded a new university.

Students killed

The Oxford traders and merchants felt the pinch when the students' business went, and in 1214 invited them back again. A chancellor was appointed with disciplinary power over the students, but the clashes between townspeople and students were renewed. During a two-day riot in 1355 many students died. The King's Commissioners imprisoned the mayor and 200 townsfolk, and gave the chancellor dictatorial powers over the town.

At first, students rich and poor simply arrived at Oxford and took lessons from masters of arts. Later there were formal debates, but it was many cen-

THE ASHMOLEAN MUSEUM

Britain's oldest public museum houses one of the finest art collections in the country, Renaissance sculptures, a department of antiquities that illustrates the art of the great Mediterranean civilisations, fascinating relics of British history and many other treasures.

Ornament made for Alfred the Great.

turies before examinations and degrees were officially set up, and a tutorial system adopted.

University College was founded in 1249 when William of Durham gave money to support ten masters of arts. **Balliol** was established in 1263 after John de Baliol had insulted the Bishop of Durham by calling him names. As a penance he agreed to finance students at Oxford.

The following year the Lord High Chancellor of England, Walter de Merton, founded **Merton**, the first residential college.

Merton still straddles the old city wall, and some of its original buildings survive. Merton has one of the oldest libraries in England, built between 1371 and 1379. The original 13th-century stained-glass windows can still be seen in the college chapel. Merton also gave Oxford one of its characteristics, the quadrangle.

The remarkable Robert of Eglesfield, a not-very-rich Cumbrian landowner, was chaplain to Philippa, Edward III's wife. He founded **Queen's College** in her honour in 1341. Eglesfield ordained that his scholars should number 12 like the Apostles, should sit on three sides of an oblong table to symbolise the Last Supper, wear blood-red robes to signify the Crucifixion, and study theology.

Eglesfield's extravagant scheme outran his pocket. In 1349 the Black Death nearly wiped out the college, and there were never more than eight fellows until the end of the 15th century. It struggled along until centuries later the sale of property in Southampton made it prosperous.

William of Wykeham, Bishop of

Winchester, developed the concept of the quadrangle brilliantly when he founded **New College** in 1379. Much of the original building survives, a splendid example of English Perpendicular architecture.

Lincoln was founded in 1427, and is the college where John Wesley taught from 1729 to 1735. **All Souls** was founded in 1438 as a memorial to Henry V and the heroes of Agincourt. Its fine medieval hall is still intact. **Magdalen** (pronounced Maudlin) was established by William of Waynflete, Bishop of Winchester, in 1458. Its great Gothic bell-tower was finished in 1509, and stands like a sentinel beside the Magdalen Bridge.

Victims of the Reformation

Cardinal Wolsey began building **Christ Church**, or Cardinal's College as he called it, in 1525, four years before his fall from power. Typically, he lavished huge sums of money on it. His great hall, 115 ft long, 40 ft wide and 50 ft high, with its elaborate hammer-beam roof, is magnificent.

Sir Christopher Wren (1632–1723) added **Tom Tower** over Wolsey's gate in 1682. Each evening, at five minutes past nine, Great Tom, the bell in the tower, tolls its curfew.

The Reformation was a serious threat to Oxford, where the teaching was carried out by religious orders. But Henry VIII ordered the dissolution only of the Oxford monasteries, not the colleges. The only major casualty of the Dissolution was the library founded by Duke Humfrey, the youngest brother of Henry V. All the manuscripts were dispersed or

TRADITIONAL TRANSPORT *The time-honoured method of propulsion for university students around traffic-congested Oxford is the bicycle.*

A KEY TO THE UNIVERSITY

Modern Oxford is a thriving industrial city, but at its heart lie the ancient buildings which are the home of England's oldest university. Here the bustle of the factories is left behind in the quiet cloisters and quadrangles of colleges that have remained unchanged for hundreds of years. The key, below, identifies the buildings which can be seen in the aerial view of the city centre, left.

1 Magdalen	12 Brasenose
2 Merton	13 Lincoln
3 Corpus Christi	14 Hertford
4 St Edmund Hall	15 Clarendon Building
5 Queen's	16 Bodleian Library
6 University	16 Bodleian Library
7 Oriel	17 Sheldonian Theatre
8 New	
9 All Souls	18 Exeter
10 Radcliffe Camera	19 Manchester College
11 St Mary the Virgin Church	20 Wadham
	21 Trinity

DUKE HUMFREY'S LIBRARY *Founded in 1444, the library is now part of the great Bodleian Library and contains some of its rarest manuscripts.*

REYNOLDS' WINDOWS *The windows depicting the Virtues in New College antechapel were designed by the artist Sir Joshua Reynolds (1723–92).*

PREHISTORY PRESERVED *The University Museum houses giant skeletons of prehistoric animals and major geological and mineral collections.*

destroyed, and even the bookshelves were sold.

But Humfrey's vision of a great library was not lost. In 1598 one of Elizabeth I's diplomats, Sir Thomas Bodley, began restoring it, and it was reopened in 1603. The **Bodleian Library**, one of the world's greatest, now includes the Radcliffe Camera, a circular building built as a library in 1737, and the New Bodleian building completed in 1940. A copy of every new book published in Britain is sent to the library, which contains more than 3 million volumes.

Oxford saw the Reformation's bloodier side. At **St Mary's Church** in 1555 three Protestant martyrs were tried. They were Thomas Cranmer, Archbishop of Canterbury and spiritual leader of the Reformation, Nicholas Ridley, Bishop of London, and the Protestant preacher Hugh Latimer. All were condemned to death for heresy. They were the most notable victims of the 283 martyrs of Queen Mary's short and bloody reign. Latimer and Ridley died together horribly in the flames at a site in Broad Street opposite Balliol College, which then formed part of the city walls. A few months later, Cranmer followed them to the stake.

Oxford's role in the political affairs of the nation has been strikingly ambiguous. It was both the effective birthplace of Parliament and the last permanent outpost of the absolute rule of monarchy.

Royalist garrison

In 1258 the determined, French-born knight Simon de Montfort (1208–1265), Earl of Leicester, led 23 fellow barons to the city where they signed the Provisions of Oxford. This order forced upon Henry III a powerful council of citizens to control the affairs of the kingdom he had failed to rule. Seven years later the council met at Westminster Hall as the first English Parliament.

Four centuries later another king, Charles I, losing his control of the people, headed forlornly for Oxford. His Cavalier troops had fought an indecisive battle with the Roundhead supporters of Parliament at Edgehill, north-west of Banbury. Christ Church became the king's home for more than three years as he wrestled with Parliament. In 1645 the Roundheads finally besieged the city. Charles was trapped, but he escaped in disguise. A month later he ordered the Royalist garrison in Oxford to surrender.

Another revolution shook Oxford in the late 19th century. In 1870, when the dons still had to be celibate, the university opened examinations to women for the first time. There was great opposition. In 1873 Annie Rogers topped the lists in the local examinations and later became one of Oxford's first women tutors. **Lady Margaret Hall** and **Somerville College** began as hostels for women students in 1879. Their opponents did not give in easily, but by 1894 all degree examinations were open to women. It was not until 1920, however, that women were finally admitted to full membership of the university and enabled to acquire degrees.

By then Oxford was in the middle of another revolutionary change: the establishment of the motor-car industry by William Morris, later Lord Nuffield, who founded Morris Motors Ltd.

Since then the complex at Cowley, in the south-east of the city, has expanded steadily and is now part of British Leyland. Remarkably, the vast influx of machinery, industrial workers and road transporters has had little effect on the city's august calm.

River carnival

The Thames at Oxford is known as the Isis, from its Latin name *Tamesis*. Each May the river is like a Venetian carnival when colleges row against each other in Eights Week. Crews try to bump the boat in front of them. The leading crew at the end of four days wins the title Head of the River.

University-degree ceremonies and concerts are still held in the semicircular **Sheldonian Theatre**, built in 1669 to the design of Christopher Wren, then Professor of Astronomy at the university.

A new university college, Green College, was opened in 1981.

Oxford gave the world another historic moment on May 6, 1954. At the

---

FOUNDER OF A MOTOR-CAR EMPIRE

The city of dreaming spires seems an unlikely setting for the birth of a major British industry – yet it was in Oxford that a car-manufacturing empire originated. In 1913 William Morris (1877–1963), a farmer's son, began building the first two-seater Morris-Oxford cars. Six years later he formed Morris Motors Ltd, and by the 1920s the four-seater Morris Cowley had displaced the Ford Model T as the biggest-selling car in Britain. In 1952 Morris Motors merged with Austin as the British Motor Corporation, now part of British Leyland. Morris, who was made Viscount Nuffield in 1938, donated millions of pounds to medical research and founded Nuffield College.

William Morris, Viscount Nuffield.

Lord Nuffield's first car, the 1913 Morris Oxford.

Iffley Road track a young medical student, Roger Bannister, became the first man to run a mile in under four minutes.

Information Tel. 726871/2.
Location On the A40, 56 m. NW of London.
Parking Westgate; Castle Street; Old Greyfriars Street; Gloucester Green; Oxpens Road; Station Car Park; St Clement's Street; Worcester Street (all car parks).
District council City of Oxford (Tel. 49811).
Population 98,500.
E-C Thur. **M-D** Daily.
Police (Ba) St Aldate's (Tel. 49881).
Casualty hospital John Radcliffe, Headington (Tel. 64711).

Post office (Bb) St Aldate's.
Theatres Apollo **(Ab)**, George Street (Tel. 44544); Playhouse **(Ab)**, Beaumont Street (47133).
Cinemas ABC 1, 2 and 3 **(Ab)**, George Street (Tel. 44607); ABC **(Ab)**, Magdalen Street (43067); Phoenix 1 and 2, Walton Street (54909); Penultimate Picture Palace, Jeune Street (723837).
Public library Westgate.
Places to see University Colleges (35); Christ Church Cathedral **(Bb)**; Ashmolean Museum **(Ac)**; St Aldate's; Bodleian Library **(Bb, Bc)**; Divinity School **(Bb)**; History of Science Museum **(Bb)**; Modern Art Museum **(Bb)**; Radcliffe Camera **(Bb)**; Rhodes House **(Bc)**; Sheldonian Theatre **(Bb)**; Museum

of Oxford **(Bb)**; University Museum **(Bc)**; Sheldonian Theatre; Botanic Gardens; Pitt Rivers Museum.
Shopping Magdalen Street; George Street; Broad Street; Cornmarket Street; Queen Street; High Street; Westgate Shopping Centre.
Events Eights Week (May); May Morning (May 1); The Encaenia – honorary degree ceremony (June).
Trade and industry Motor manufacture; light industry; mechanical engineering; printing.
Sport FA League football, Oxford United FC, Osler Road, Headington; Rugby football, Oxford University RFC, Iffley Road; Greyhound racing/speedway racing, Oxford Stadium, Cowley.
AA 24 hour service Tel. 40286.

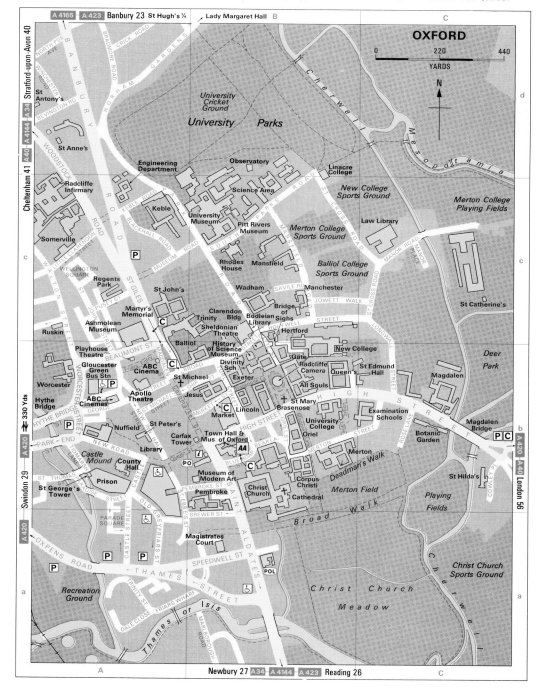

P

Paisley Strathclyde

The Paisley shawl was Paisley's best-known product in the 19th century. The industry died long ago, but a priceless collection of these garments survives in the town's museum.

Paisley grew up around an abbey, founded in 1163. It was rebuilt in the 15th century and has been rebuilt and renovated several times since.

The Gothic-style Thomas Coats Memorial Church of 1894 is an outstanding and unusual church with a crown spire.

Information
Tel. Glasgow (041) 889 5400.
Location On the A726, 7 m. SW of Glasgow.
Parking Gilmour Street Station; New Street; Cochran Street; Bank Street; Skye Crescent; Glasgow Road; Storie Street; Washington Road; Mill Street; New Sneddon Street; Oakshaw Street; School Wynd; Saucel Street; Stow Street; Wallneuk Street; Orchard Street; Christie Street; Glen Street (all car parks).
District council Renfrew (Tel. 041 889 5400).
Population 82,500.
E-C Tues. **M-D** Mon.
Police Mill Street (Tel. 041 889 1113).
Casualty hospital Royal Alexandra Infirmary, Neilston Road (Tel. 041 887 9111).
Post office County Square.

PAISLEY SHAWL *The pattern of the shawl originated in Kashmir, and was first copied in Paisley in 1770 from garments sent home by Scottish troops.*

Cinema Kelburne, Glasgow Road (Tel. 041 889 3938).
Public library High Street.
Places to see Paisley Abbey; Museum and Art Gallery, High Street.
Shopping High Street; Causeyside Street; Gilmour Street Piazza.
Sport Scottish League football, St Mirren FC, St Mirren Park.
AA 24 hour service
Tel. 041 812 0101.

Peebles Borders

The rushing Tweed at Peebles is celebrated for its salmon, and the town's coat of arms bears the motto "Against the stream they multiply". The quiet town has attracted several writers, including Robert Louis Stevenson and John Buchan.

Peebles was also the birthplace of William and Robert Chambers, 19th-century founders of the Edinburgh firm of Chambers, publishers of encyclopaedias and dictionaries.

The town takes its name from a Celtic word, *pebyll* (tent). It was a camping site of the Gadeni, an early nomadic tribe.

STRONGHOLD *Neidpath Castle, 1 mile west of Peebles, has walls more than 11 ft thick and still retains its 14th-century tower.*

Information Tel. 20153; (summer 20138).
Location On the A72, 19 m. W of Galashiels.
Parking Greenside (N end of Cuddy Bridge); Kingsmeadows (S end of Tweed Bridge); Venlaw Road; School Brae; Tweed Brae (all car parks).
District council Tweeddale (Tel. 20153).
Population 6,710.
E-C Wed.
Police High Street (Tel. 20637).
Casualty hospital Peel Hospital, Cloverfords, Galashiels (Tel. Galashiels 2295).
Post office Eastgate.
Public library High Street.
Places to see Neidpath Castle; Chambers Institution; Kailzie Gardens, 2 m. SW; Traquair House, 6 m. SE.
Town trails Available from Ian Jenkins, Peebles Civic Society, 1 South Park Drive.
Shopping High Street; Northgate; Old Town; Eastgate.
AA 24 hour service
Tel. Edinburgh (031) 225 8464.

NATURAL DEFENCES *A headland surrounded on three sides by water provided a magnificent, ready-made defensive site for Pembroke Castle.*

Pembroke Dyfed

One of the most impressive and best preserved Norman castles in Britain dominates this small capital town of South Pembrokeshire.

Set just outside the Pembrokeshire Coast National Park, the town is in a region sometimes known as "Little England beyond Wales". There the English-speaking people who settled after the Norman Conquest gave their towns English names, and built fortifications to cut off the area from Welsh-speaking Wales.

Standing stones and burial mounds in the area give evidence of prehistoric occupation. But Pembroke began to develop only in the late 11th century around the castle. In 1109 Gilbert Strongbow became its commander and was created Earl of Pembroke, and in 1457 it was the birthplace of Henry Tudor, who became Henry VII and founded the House of Tudor. During the Civil War the town's mayor changed sides from Cromwell to the Royalists, and in 1648 Parliamentary guns damaged the castle. The town then suffered a period of decline until 1814, when the Royal Naval dockyard was removed from Milford Haven to Pembroke Dock, 2 miles north-west. This brought prosperity to the town.

The oldest part of the castle is the

keep, which dates from 1200. It is 75 ft high, with walls up to 19 ft thick at the base, and is unusual in being circular and roofed. Below the north wall is the Wogan, a huge cavern opening on to the river, that was probably used for taking in stores.

Pembroke has three fine old churches. The most ancient is Monkton Priory Church, first recorded in 1098 but probably founded as early as the 6th century. It has an impressively high chancel, a "leper's squint", through which sick monks could watch the service from outside, and an ancient holy-water stoup.

St Mary's, built in the 13th and 14th centuries, retains much original work, including its massive Norman tower and some excellent Early English mouldings. St Michael's, also founded in the 13th century, preserves a splendid vaulted roof in the north vestry.

Since 1814 more than 250 warships – and three royal yachts for Queen Victoria – have been built at Pembroke Dock. Boat cruises run from Hobbs Point up and down Milford Haven past the Martello Towers, giant oil tankers and refineries.

Information Tel. Tenby 2402.
Location On the A477, 10 m. W of Tenby.
Parking Pembroke: The Quay; Long Entry; Commons Road; Station Road; St Michael's Square (all car parks). Pembroke Dock: Meyrick Street; Upper and Lower Meyrick

Street; Commercial Row; Gordon Street; Albion Square (all car parks).
District council South Pembrokeshire (Tel. 683122).
Population 15,600.
E-C Wed. **M-D** Fri. (Pembroke Dock).
Police Water Street, Pembroke Dock (Tel. 682222).
Casualty hospital South Pembrokeshire Hospital, Fort Road, Pembroke Dock (Tel. 682114).
Post offices Main Street, Pembroke; Dimond Street, Pembroke Dock.
Cinemas Haggars, Main Street, Pembroke (Tel. 682855); Palace, Queen Street, Pembroke Dock (684355).
Public libraries Wesley Schoolroom, Pembroke; Meyrick Street, Pembroke Dock.
Places to see Pembroke Castle; Pembrokeshire Motor Museum; Gypsy Caravan Museum.
Shopping Pembroke: Main Street. Pembroke Dock: Dimond Street; Meyrick Street.
Event Fair (Oct.).
AA 24 hour service
Tel. Cardiff 394111.

Penarth S. Glamorgan

A long Victorian esplanade adds an air of sedateness to this resort on high ground south of Cardiff. Penarth first a fishing village, then a coal-exporting port. It now earns most of its living from tourism, and the harbour is now filled in.

Strong currents run off its shingle beach, which is backed by cliffs up to 100 ft high; but there are two indoor sea-water pools for swimmers.

Landscaped gardens sloping down to the sea, and flower-filled gardens in the town have earned the resort the name of "Garden by the Sea".

Turner House Art Gallery, part of the National Museum of Wales, contains some fine paintings, including works by Gustave Courbet (1819-77), the French landscape painter.

About 5 miles offshore is Flat Holm island, where it is believed the knights who murdered Thomas Becket are buried. Adjacent Steep Holm island is a nature reserve.

Information Tel. 707201.
Location On the A4160, 4 m. S of Cardiff.
Parking Esplanade; Victoria Road; Windsor Road (all car parks).
District council Vale of Glamorgan (Tel. Barry 730311).
Population 23,000.
E-C Wed.
Police Windsor Road (Tel. 702428).
Casualty hospital Cardiff Royal Infirmary, Newport Road, Cardiff (Tel. Cardiff 492233).
Post office Albert Road.
Public library Stanwell Road.
Places to see Turner House Art Gallery; St Augustine's Church.
Shopping Windsor Road; Stanwell Road; Cornerswell Road.
AA 24 hour service
Tel. Cardiff 394111.

Penrith Cumbria

Only 5 miles from Ullswater, Penrith is the northern gateway to the Lake District. The old streets on its perimeter are narrow, because that made them easy to defend against raiders from over the Border who pillaged the town until the 17th century. The open spaces of Sandgate and Dockray, in the town centre, were there to protect cattle during raids.

The town was probably the capital of Owain Caesarius, King of Cumbria from 920 to 937. The Giant's Grave, a stone monument in the parish churchyard, is said to mark his grave.

The ruins of Penrith Castle stand in the public park. The castle was built in 1397-9 and was later enlarged by the Earl of Westmorland, to whom Richard II gave the town in 1398.

Towering above the town is 937 ft high Penrith Beacon, whose summit yields superb views of Ullswater.

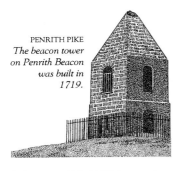

PENRITH PIKE
The beacon tower on Penrith Beacon was built in 1719.

Information Tel. 64671 (summer).
Location On the A66, 20 m. S of Carlisle.
Parking Southend; Princes Street; Blue Bell Lane; Friargate; Market Square; St Andrew's View; Burrowgate; Crown Square; Castle Hill Road (all car parks).
District council Eden (Tel. 64671).
Population 12,200.
E-C Wed. **M-D** Tues., Sat.
Police Hunter Lane (Tel. 64355).
Casualty hospital Cumberland Infirmary, Port Road, Carlisle (Tel. Carlisle 23444).
Post office Crown Square.
Theatre Penrith Playhouse, Castlegate (Tel. 65557).
Cinema The Regent, Old London Road (Tel. 62400).
Public library Portland Place.
Places to see Penrith Castle, Castle Park; Penrith Beacon, Beacon Edge; The Giant's Grave, St Andrew's churchyard; Plague Stone, Bridge Lane; Lowther Wildlife Park, 4 m. S.
Shopping Great Dockray; Devonshire Street; Middlegate.
AA 24 hour service
Tel. Carlisle 24274.

Penzance Cornwall

One of the mildest climates in Britain has given Penzance some of the most beautiful gardens in the country. Acacias, palms and banana trees grow in the open in the town's Morrab Gardens. Two miles west of the town, Trengwainton Gardens, owned by the National Trust, has many plants that cannot be grown in the open elsewhere in England.

The town stands on Mount's Bay, with its 4 miles of sandy beaches and the island of St Michael's Mount.

Chapel Street, leading away from the harbour, is lined by Regency and Georgian town houses and fishermen's cottages. It also contains the Museum of Nautical Art.

The Natural History and Antiquarian Museum in Penlee House specialises in local archaeology, and includes Bronze and Stone Age relics.

On St Michael's Mount there is a castle which incorporates part of a 12th-century Benedictine priory. The island is accessible on foot at low tide by a cobbled causeway.

Information Tel. 2341/2207.
Location On the A30, 8 m. W of Hayle.
Parking The Harbour; Penalverne; St Anthony's Gardens; Well Fields; Union Street; Wherrytown (cps).
District council Penwith (Tel. 2341).
Population 19,500.
E-C Wed. **M-D** Tues., Thur.
Police (Ab) Penalverne Drive (Tel. 2395).
Casualty hospital West Cornwall, St Clare Street (Tel. 2382).
Post office (Bb) Market Jew Street.
Cinema Savoy **(Ab)**, Causewayhead (Tel. 3330).
Public library (Ab) Morrab Road.
Places to see Geological Museum **(Ab)**, St John's Hall; Morrab Gardens **(Aa)**; Museum of Nautical Art **(Bb)**, Chapel Street; Penlee House Museum **(Ab)**, Penlee Park; St Michael's Mount; Egyptian House **(Ab)**, Chapel Street; Trengwainton Gardens, 2 m. W.
Shopping Causewayhead; Market Jew Street; Alverton Street.
Car ferry To Isles of Scilly (Tel. 2009).
Heliport Service to Isles of Scilly (Tel. 3871).
AA 24 hour service
Tel. Truro 76455.

THE MINERS' FRIEND

Davy's lamp sprang from his discovery that a filter of fine wire mesh stopped gas igniting.

The scientist Sir Humphry Davy (1778-1829) was born in Penzance. His invention of the miners' safety lamp in 1815 saved many lives. Davy's statue stands outside the Market Hall.

REGENCY WHIMSY *Nothing in Egypt ever looked anything like the "Egyptian" House in Chapel Street, Penzance.*

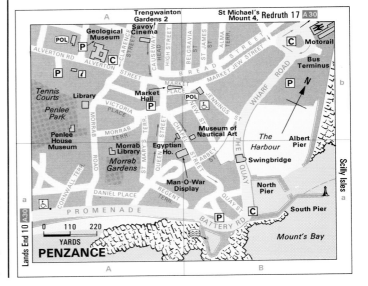

PENZANCE

Perth see page 322

Peterborough Cambs.

The glory of Peterborough is its cathedral, one of the finest Norman buildings in the country. Today the city is a manufacturing and commercial centre, but its history goes back nearly 6,000 years: excavations have revealed the site of a thatched hut dating from about 3700 BC.

The Romans built the town of Durobrivae and a 27 acre fortress (now beneath Thorpe Wood golf course), and developed local pottery into a major industry.

Modern Peterborough began with a monastery dedicated to St Peter in 656. The Danes sacked this in 870, but 100 years later the Bishop of Winchester built another. Fire destroyed it in 1117, and the core of the present cathedral was built on the site as an abbey church between 1118 and 1258. The nave, built in 1194-7, has 11 bays and massive piers, built from the local cream-coloured Barnack stone. The high wooden roof is decorated with 13th-century paintings.

In the nave is a painting of Old Scarlett, a 16th-century gravedigger, who buried Catherine of Aragon, Henry VIII's first wife, and Mary, Queen of Scots, in the cathedral.

Fronting Cathedral Square is the Great Gate, originally Norman with later additions. The chancel of the 14th-century Chapel of St Thomas of Canterbury stands left of the gate.

The impressive old Butter Cross (known as the Guildhall) dates from 1671. Next to it is Peterborough's ancient parish church of St John the Baptist. It was built in 1402-7 with stone from the nave of the Chapel of St Thomas of Canterbury.

Longthorpe Tower is a three-storey building of about 1300, and contains the best-surviving examples of English medieval wall-paintings.

The 16th-century Customs House is surmounted by a light which guided vessels to a wharf on the River Nene.

The Town Museum is notable for its collection of carved bonework and straw marquetry made by prisoners during the Napoleonic Wars.

Information Tel. 63141.
Location On the A15, 19 m. N of Huntingdon.
Parking Craig Street; Lincoln Road; Bourges Boulevard (2); Brook Street; Bishops Road; Cattle Market (cps).
District council City of Peterborough (Tel. 63141).
Population 88,300.
E-C Thur. **M-D** Tues., Wed., Fri. and Sat.
Police (Ba) Bridge Street (Tel. 62231).
Casualty hospital Thorpe Road (Tel. 67451).
Post office (Ab) Church Street.
Theatre Key Theatre **(Ba)**, Embankment Road (Tel. 52439).
Cinemas ABC 1, 2 and 3 **(Bb)**, Broadway (Tel. 43504); Odeon **(Bb)**, Broadway (43319).
Public library (Bb) Broadway.
Places to see Museum and Art Gallery **(Aa)**, Priestgate; Guildhall **(Bb)**, Cathedral Square; Longthorpe Tower, 2 m. E on A47.
Town trails Available from Information Centre, Town Hall.

Shopping Cowgate; Long Causeway; Broadway; Bridge Street; Queensgate.
Event East of England Show (July).
Trade and industry Engineering; building materials.
Sport FA League football, Peterborough FC, London Road.
AA 24 hour service Tel. Cambridge 312302.

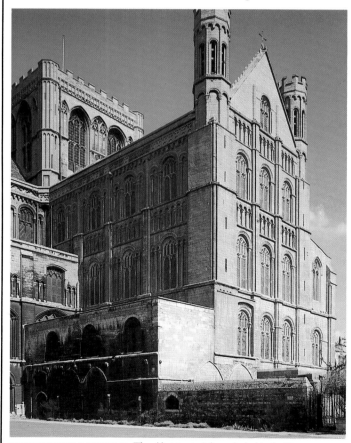

PETERBOROUGH CATHEDRAL *The oldest part of the cathedral is the Norman arm to the south of the central tower. The lower of its three tiers of windows contains some 19th-century stained glass by William Morris.*

PERTH Tayside

The fair city of Scotland's kings

The compact city of Perth lies beside the River Tay amid countryside which still justifies Sir Walter Scott's description of it as "the most varied and most beautiful" in Scotland. During the Middle Ages, Perth was a meeting place of the Scottish parliament and a home of Scotland's kings. But the ravages of war and of the followers of the 16th-century reformer John Knox have left few of its ancient buildings intact, and today's "fair city" is largely a creation of the 18th and 19th centuries.

HIGHLAND SENTINEL *The traditionally dressed Highlander, one of a pair flanking the entrance to Perth's Salutation Hotel, is a 19th-century ship's figurehead. It occupies a niche in the façade, originally designed for a classical statue.*

When a band of rebels acting on behalf of the Earl of Atholl murdered the poet-king James I in Perth in 1437, they also robbed the city of its chance to become Scotland's permanent capital.

During the previous three centuries, monarchs from Alexander I onwards had held councils in Perth. James I chose the city as his seat of government and as the home of the new parliament he was trying to create on the English pattern.

The king, a prolific law-giver, had many enemies among the nobles whose powers he had reduced. When he rode to spend the Christmas of 1436 in Perth he was warned by an old woman as he reached the Forth: "An (if) ye pass this water ye shall never return again alive." James ignored the warning, crossed the river, and continued his journey.

Stabbed 16 times

Six weeks later, rebels led by Sir Robert Graham galloped into the cloisters of the **Blackfriars Monastery** at midnight. The king had been playing chess with his family in the royal lodgings there. The conspirators forced their way in and James was struck down with 16 stab wounds in the chest.

His distraught widow fled with her six-year-old son, James II, to the safety of Edinburgh, which has been Scotland's capital ever since.

St John's Kirk is the only visible reminder of Perth's illustrious medieval past. The church was consecrated in 1243, though much of the present building dates from the 15th century. There is some fine stained glass of the Renaissance, and a priceless collection of old pewter and silver sacramental dishes.

A wave of destruction

The church pulpit is one of the birthplaces of Scotland's Calvinism. John Knox made straight for Perth after his long exile on the Continent ended in 1559, and his first rousing sermon, preached in St John's Kirk, launched the Reformation in Scotland amid a wave of destruction.

The Mass, thundered Knox, was idolatry. The congregation responded by smashing the high altar under a rain of stones. Then Knox's followers swarmed into the streets, gutting the monasteries of Greyfriars, Blackfriars and Charterhouse, leaving only their outer walls. The new order was to be seen as well as heard.

The damage inflicted on Perth during the Reformation compounded that done earlier by a series of invaders who had smashed their way into the city – Edward I and Edward III of England, William Wallace and Robert Bruce. The Roundheads of Oliver Cromwell took the destruction further in 1651, when they drove out the Royalist forces who had held the city since 1644.

The same year saw the last coronation at Scone Abbey, 1 mile northwest, original home of the Stone of Destiny, on which the early Scots kings were crowned. The stone itself, linked by legend to the Old Testament story of Jacob, had been captured by Edward I in 1297 and taken to England, where it remains, underneath the Coronation Chair in Westminster Abbey.

Historical mystery

However, Charles II, who was trying to rally the Scots against Cromwell, revived a tradition by having himself crowned at Scone in 1651. He was to face nine years of exile until the Restoration.

FAIR CITY *The spire of St Matthew's dominates the Perth skyline. For about 200 years St John's Kirk (right) was divided into three separate churches, but it was reunified in 1923-6 as a memorial to the dead of the First World War.*

ABERDEEN ANGUS *Cattle buyers from all over the world come to Perth for locally raised beef bulls.*

Scone Palace, now the home of the Earls of Mansfield, has fine collections of furniture and porcelain.

Perth's former county buildings in Tay Street stand opposite the site of Gowrie House, a seat of the Earls of Gowrie in the 16th and 17th centuries, and the scene of a historical mystery.

In the summer of 1600, James VI of Scotland (later James I of England) was hunting at Falkland when he was invited to Gowrie House by Alexander Ruthven, the earl's brother. The king told the Duke of Lennox he was going to Perth "because there is a man there with a pitcher full of gold". It seemed a strange reason for a king to leave the hunting field. The events at the house were even stranger.

"Treason, treason"

The king's friends followed him there, but on asking for him were told that James had left suddenly to return to Falkland. As they rode away from the house, the king himself appeared at a window of a turret shouting: "Treason, treason! Help! Help!" The nobles rushed back and in a skirmish Alexander Ruthven and the Earl of Gowrie were killed. Was it a conspiracy by Gowrie and his brother to capture the king and carry him off? Or was it a plot by the king to avenge himself on Gowrie, whose father, 18 years earlier, had held James a prisoner for a year at the Gowrie castle of **Huntingtower,** 2 miles west of Perth? The mystery remains unsolved.

Royalty may have flirted with Perth for centuries, but the city's prosperity has come from the surrounding countryside. Buyers come from all over the world to buy thoroughbred Shorthorn and Aberdeen Angus bulls.

Perth lies between two parklands, the **South Inch** and the **North Inch**.

MAID'S HOME *The house of the Fair Maid of Perth, heroine of Scott's novel, was rebuilt in 1893.*

Bonnie Prince Charlie drilled his troops on the North Inch in 1745, and stayed at the 17th-century **Salutation Hotel** in South Street.

The **Fair Maid of Perth's House,** in Curfew Row, stands on the site of the 14th-century home of Catherine Glover, the "Fair Maid" of Sir Walter Scott's novel and Bizet's opera.

Information Tel. 22900.
Location On the A9, 21 m. W of Dundee.
Parking Mill Street (3); Scott Street; King's Place; Marshall Place; King Street; Thimblerow; West Mill Street (2); Canal Street; Charles Street; Victoria Street; Elibank Street; Leonard Street; Carpenter Street (all car parks).
District council Perth and Kinross (Tel. 21161).
Population 42,000.
E-C Wed., Sat. **M-D** Fri.
Police (Ab) Barrack Street (Tel. 21141).
Casualty hospital Perth Royal Infirmary, Tullylumb (Tel. 23311).
Post office South Street **(Ba).**
Theatre Perth Theatre **(Ba),** High Street (Tel. 21031).
Cinema Playhouse **(Ab),** Murray Street (Tel. 23126).
Public library Kinnoull Street.
Places to see Balhousie Castle and Black Watch Museum **(Ab);** Branklyn Garden, 1½ m. E on A85; Scone Palace, 1 m. N off A93; Huntingtower Castle, 2 m. W off A85; Elcho Castle; Fair Maid of Perth's House **(Bb);** Museum and Art Gallery **(Bb);** St John's Kirk **(Ba).**
Town trails Available from Tourist Information Centre, Marshall Place, Perth (Tel. 22900).
Shopping High Street; St John

John Buchan (1875-1940), who was born in the manse, 20 York Place, Perth, combined the careers of novelist and statesman. His thriller *The 39 Steps* was first filmed by Alfred Hitchcock in 1935. Below, a still from the film shows Robert Donat as the hero, Richard Hannay.

John Buchan – he became Lord Tweedsmuir.

Street; George Street; Scott Street; South Street; Methven Street.
Events Aberdeen Angus Bull Sales (Feb. and Oct.); Music Festival (Mar.); Festival of Arts (May); Highland Games (Aug.); Agricultural Show (Aug.).
Trade and industry Insurance; whisky blending/bottling.
Sport Horse racing, Scone Park. Scottish League football, St Johnstone FC, Muirton Park.
AA 24 hour service Tel. Dundee 25585.

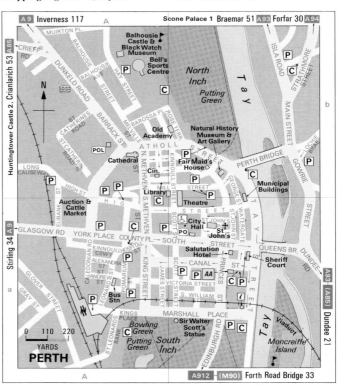
PERTH

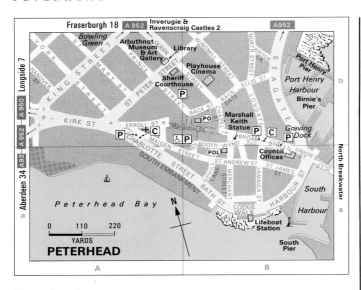

Fraserburgh 18 `A 952` Inverugie & Ravenscraig Castles 2 `A952`

Longside 7 `A 950` `A 952` `A92` Aberdeen 34

Bowling Green
York Street
Arbuthnot Museum & Art Gallery
Library
Windmill Street
Queen Street
Prince Street
Hanover Street
St Mary St
King Street
St Peter Street
Playhouse Cinema
Sheriff Courthouse
Back Street
Chapel Street
North Brook St
Seagate
Ellis St
Port Henry Pier
Port Henry Harbour
Birnie's Pier
KIRK ST
ERROLL ST
Marischal St
Maiden St
Charlotte Street
Bath Street
SOUTH EMBANKMENT
BOOTH WYND
St Andrew St
Merchant St
Jamaica St
Longate
Broad St
PO
Marshall Keith Statue
POL
Council Offices
St James St
Harbour St
Union Bridge St
Graving Dock
North Breakwater
South Harbour
LODGE WALK
Lifeboat Station
Peterhead Bay
South Pier
N
0 110 220
YARDS
PETERHEAD

A   B

Peterhead Grampian

Red granite of the type used to build Peterhead's massive harbour walls has also been used in the many handsome buildings in the town. The harbour was a whaling station in the 19th century, and later a herring port. It is now one of Scotland's biggest fishing ports, and is a base for the North Sea oil industry. It has a fishing fleet of about 80 vessels.

Information Tel. Ellon 20730, or Banff 2419/2789.
Location On the A952, 18 m. SE of Fraserburgh.
Parking South Road; Threadneedle Street; Broad Street (all car parks).
District council Banff and Buchan (Tel. Banff 2521).
Population 16,950.
E-C Wed. **M-D** (fish) Harbour, Mon. to Sat., 8.30 a.m.
Police (Ba) Merchant Street (Tel. 2571).
Casualty hospital Cottage Hospital, Links Terrace (Tel. 2316).
Post office (Bb) Marischal Street.
Cinema Playhouse **(Bb)**, Queen Street (Tel. 3494).
Public library (Ab) St Peter Street.
Shopping Marischal Street; Chapel Street; Drummer's Corner Complex .
AA 24 hour service
Tel. Aberdeen 51231.

Peterlee Durham

A local hero's name was given to this new town. Peter Lee (1864-1935), who was a miner when only ten, rose to be President of the International Federation of Miners.

The town was founded in 1950 as a dormitory for the local coalfield and a social and shopping centre. Mining has since declined, and Peterlee is now attracting new industry.

Information Tel. 864450.
Location Off the A1086, 10 m. NW of Hartlepool.
Parking St Cuthbert's Road; Town Centre Shopping Precinct; Bede Way; Surtees Road (all car parks).

District council Easington (Tel. Easington 270501).
Population 22,800.
E-C Wed.
Police Yoden Way (Tel. 862621).
Casualty hospital St Hilda's, Friar Street, Hartlepool (Tel. Hartlepool 66155).
Post office The Broadclose.
Cinema Fair World Cinema Centre, Sunderland Road, Horden (Tel. 864344).
Public library Burnhope Way.
Shopping Town Centre Shopping Precinct; Upper Yoden Way; The Broadclose; The Upper Broadclose.
AA 24 hour service
Tel. Middlesbrough 246832.

Petworth W. Sussex

The imposing gateway and walls of the 17th-century Petworth House gaze down on a country town of cobbled streets and charming old buildings. The 320 ft long frontage of the house looks across a lake and parkland laid out by "Capability" Brown in the late 18th century. The house contains woodcarvings by Grinling Gibbons and paintings by Van Dyck, Gainsborough and Turner. Petworth Church was restored in 1827 by Sir Charles Barry.

Information Tel. 42241.
Location On the A272, 14 m. NE of Chichester.
Parking Saddler's Row (car park).
District council Chichester (Tel. Chichester 784255).
Population 2,980.
E-C Wed.
Police Grove Street (Tel. 42222).
Casualty hospital St Richards, Spitalfield Lane, Chichester (Tel. Chichester 788122).
Post office East Street.
Public library High Street.
Places to see Petworth House; Bignor Roman Villa, 5½ m. S.
Shopping High Street; Market Square.
AA 24 hour service
Tel. Guildford 72841.

Pickering N. Yorks.

An ancient market town on the edge of the North Yorkshire moors, Pickering was founded as a Celtic settlement in 270 BC. Its ruined 12th-century castle was once a hunting lodge for medieval kings; but only the chapel, postern gate, dungeon and three towers remain. Among fine old buildings in the town is the Black Swan where cock-fights were held.

MARTYRDOM OF ST EDMUND *Superb 15th-century religious paintings decorate the walls of Pickering parish church.*

Information Tel. 73791.
Location On the A170, 17 m. E of Scarborough.
Parking Eastgate; Ropery; New Bridge Street (all car parks).
District council Ryedale (Tel. Malton 4011).
Population 5,940.
E-C Wed. **M-D** Mon.
Police Malton Road (Tel. 72112).
Casualty hospital Scarborough General, Scalby Road, Scarborough (Tel. Scarborough 68111).
Post office Market Place.
Cinema Castle, Burgate (Tel. 72622).
Public library Market Place.
Places to see Castle ruins; Beck Isle Museum (Easter-Oct.); North Yorkshire Moors Railway (Easter-Oct.).
Town trails Available from Tourist Information Bureau, the Station.
Shopping Market Place; Hungate.
AA 24 hour service
Tel. York 27698.

Pitlochry Tayside

Few towns in Britain are set in such magnificent scenery as Pitlochry, "the Centre of the Highlands". Mountains, lochs, rivers and woodlands surround it. There are good fishing in the River Tummel, boating on Loch Faskally, and pony-trekking in the hills and glens.

Information Tel. 2215.
Location On the A9, 27 m. NW of Perth.
Parking Atholl Road; Ferry Road; Rie-achan Road (all car parks).
District council Perth and Kinross (Tel. Perth 21161).
Population 2,610.
E-C Thur.
Police Atholl Road (Tel. 2222 or Perth 21141).
Casualty hospital Irvine Memorial, Nursing Home Brae (Tel. 2052).

Post office Atholl Road.
Theatre Pitlochry Festival, Port-na-Craig (Tel. 2680).
Cinema Regal, West Moulin Road (Tel. 2560).
Public library Atholl Road.
Places to see Blair Castle, 7 m. NW.
Shopping Atholl Road; Bonnethill Road.
AA 24 hour service
Tel. Dundee 25585.

Plymouth see page 326

Pontefract see Wakefield

Pontypool Gwent
To the west of the town lie the industrial valleys of South Wales; to the east the fertile Usk Valley.

For centuries, Pontypool has been part industrial and part agricultural. A Japanese-type lacquer-ware was produced in the town from the 17th to 19th centuries. Known as Pontypool Japan Ware, it is now much prized by collectors.

Information Tel. 2471.
Location On the A472, 9 m. N of Newport.
Parking Glantorvaen Road; Crane Street; Trosnant Street; Park Road; Riverside; Rosemary Lane; High Street (all car parks).
District council Borough of Torfaen (Tel. Pontypool 2471).
Population 36,800.
E-C Thur. **M-D** Wed., Fri. and Sat.
Police Glantorvaen Road (Tel. 4711).
Casualty hospital Nevill Hall, Brecon Road, Abergavenny (Tel. Abergavenny 2091).
Post office Osborne Road.
Cinema Scala, Osborne Road (Tel. 56038).
Public library Hanbury Road.
Shopping Market Street.
AA 24 hour service
Tel. Newport 62559.

Pontypridd Mid Glamorgan
The rattle of anchor chains may seem a far cry from a Welsh valley, but it was in this town that the gigantic ships' chains were made for such liners as the *Queen Mary*, and the *Queen Elizabeth*. The chainworks, established at Ynysyngharad beside the Glamorgan Canal in 1816, is still in business. A slender, 18th-century stone bridge crosses the Taff in a single 140 ft span. It was built by William Edwards, a local self-taught engineer.

Information Tel. 407811.
Location On the A470, 12 m. NW of Cardiff.
Parking Sardis Road; Rhondda Road; Taff Street; Berw Road; East Street (all car parks).
District council Borough of Taff-Ely (Tel. 407811).

Population 33,000.
E-C Thur. **M-D** Wed., Sat.
Police St Catherine's Street (Tel. 404351).
Casualty hospital East Glamorgan General, Church Village, Newtown Llantwit (Tel. Newtown Llantwit 204242).
Post office Broadway.
Cinema White Palace, Sardis Road (Tel. 402503).
Public library Library Road.
Shopping Taff Street.
AA 24 hour service
Tel. Cardiff 394111.

Poole Dorset
The heart of Poole is a 15 acre area beside the harbour crammed with buildings of historic interest. There are 80 houses, a church, six pubs, the old Guildhall, the Custom House, 30 shops, and other buildings, all maintained or restored to harmonise with one another.

Fine parks, a magnificent harbour, gently sloping sandy beaches and the unspoiled scenery of the countryside add to the charm of Poole.

The town developed as a port in the 13th century, on one of the largest shallow-water anchorages in Britain. It became a base for pirates, then fishermen, and in the 18th and 19th centuries for timber trading with Newfoundland. It is still used commercially – by coasters – but is primarily a centre for leisure craft of all types. The town itself has grown into a busy commercial and industrial centre as well as a resort.

On the quayside the Town Cellars, a group of 15th-century warehouses, contain a maritime museum. The nearby lifeboat museum has models, paintings, documents and other relics

illustrating 150 years of the Royal National Lifeboat Institution.

The 18th-century Guildhall and medieval Scaplen's Court both serve as museums of local history.

In the middle of the harbour lies Brownsea Island, which is owned by the National Trust. In 1907 it became the birthplace of the Boy Scout movement when Lord Baden-Powell held a camp there for about 20 boys. The island, which is covered by heath and woodland, has a nature reserve.

Some of Britain's finest gardens are near Poole, including Compton Acres and Upton Country Park.

Information Tel. 5151.
Location On the B3369, 5 m. W of Bournemouth.
Parking Kingland Road; Hill Street; Old Orchard; Serpentine; Seldown Lane; Towngate; Newfoundland Drive (all cps); The Quay.
District council Borough of Poole (Tel. 5151).
Population 118,900.
E-C Wed.
Police Civic Centre (Tel. Bournemouth 22099).
Casualty hospital Poole General, Longfleet Road (Tel. 5100).
Post office (Ba) High Street.
Theatre and cinema (Bb) Poole Arts Centre (Tel. 85222).
Public library (Bb) High Street.
Places to see Guildhall Museum **(Aa)**; Scaplen's Court Museum **(Aa)**; Maritime Museum **(Aa)**; Compton Acres Gardens.
Shopping High Street; Arndale Centre.
Sport Speedway, Wimborne Road; Greyhound racing, Wimborne Road.
Car ferry To Studland and Swanage.
AA 24 hour service
Tel. Bournemouth 25751.

POOLE map

PLYMOUTH Devon

City of the great adventurers

For more than 700 years, Plymouth's fortunes have been linked with the sea. Here began the voyages of the Elizabethan sailors Hawkins, Raleigh, Frobisher and Sir Francis Drake, who is said to have finished his game of bowls on The Hoe before turning his attention to defeating the Spanish Armada.

The Pilgrim Fathers sailed from Plymouth in 1620, as did the explorer and map-maker James Cook in 1772. Much of Plymouth's present livelihood comes from the sea. The naval dockyard at Devonport, founded in 1691, is the largest in Britain. The city is a major holiday centre and a base for touring the countryside of Devon and Cornwall.

RAIL LINK *Plymouth is linked to Cornwall by Brunel's superb Royal Albert Bridge across the Tamar.*

Plymouth in the Middle Ages was the "littel fishe towne" of Sutton, at the mouth of the River Ply, and belonged to the monks of Plympton Priory, 4 miles east. It was not until 1231 that the present name was first used.

During the 14th and 15th centuries the town was caught up in the wars with France, and was several times raided by Bretons. Defences were built around the port, which is still known as **Sutton Harbour.**

Most of these fortifications have disappeared, though their existence is commemorated in **The Barbican**, a street beside Sutton Harbour which has given its name to the surrounding old district of narrow, cobbled alleys and quays.

Defences were also put up on what is now **Drake's Island** in Plymouth Sound. They have been added to over the centuries, and the island was garrisoned until the end of the Second World War. It is now a youth adventure centre, and may be visited by boat from Sutton Harbour.

Few buildings survive from Sutton's days as a monastic port. The "mother church" of St Andrew, on the western edge of the Barbican district, was founded in the 12th century and rebuilt in the 15th century and again after being destroyed by air-raids.

Adjoining the churchyard is another 15th-century building, the Prysten (or priests') House. The doorway contains a memorial to Americans captured by the British during the war of 1812.

GIANT OGGIE *Men called oggieaters collect for charity with a box shaped like an oggie, a kind of pastry.*

In Southside Street, on land which forms part of a distillery where Plymouth gin is made, is all that remains of a **Dominican friary** (Blackfriars) – the 16th-century refectory. It is open to the public, and is said to be the place where the Pilgrim Fathers assembled before boarding the *Mayflower.*

In 1439, Plymouth was freed from monastic rule and became the first English town to be granted a charter by Act of Parliament.

Port of Drake and Raleigh

Plymouth's life as a naval base began about a century later, not so much from government choice as because it was the port from which Drake, Raleigh and the other Elizabethan naval heroes sailed.

Tudor houses in the Barbican district bear witness to the city's prosperity in the 16th century. The **Elizabethan House** in New Street, once a merchant's home, has been turned into a museum of costume and furniture.

Mount Edgcumbe House, which stands in 800 acres of parkland just across the Tamar and can be reached by foot or car ferry, also dates from the Tudor period.

Plymouth is dominated by the voyage of the Pilgrim Fathers, who are commemorated by the steps in Sutton Harbour which now bear their ship's name, and by the **Mayflower Stone** in New Street.

In the 17th century, Plymouth withstood a two-year siege by Royalist troops. Following the Restoration, Charles II ordered the building of a **citadel** to keep the town in order, and work began on it in 1666.

It stands on the eastern edge of The Hoe (high place), on the site where, according to tradition, Drake played his famous game of bowls. Its high

THE OLD AND THE NEW *The green sward of ancient Plymouth Hoe lies beside the Sound and stretches inland to the modern city centre, which arose from the ashes left by a devastating bombing raid in March 1941.*

PRIESTS' HOME *The 15th-century Prysten House was built by Plympton Priory for Augustinian priests.*

ramparts look out over Plymouth Sound. Close by lies the **Marine Biological Association aquarium.**

At the end of the 17th century, the opening of the Royal Naval Dockyard in what is now Devonport began a new era of prosperity for Plymouth. The docks can be visited.

Smeaton's Tower, on Plymouth Hoe, was from 1759 to 1882 the top section of the Eddystone Lighthouse. It was taken down and re-erected on The Hoe when its foundations began to crumble. From its summit the present Eddystone Light can be seen on a clear day, 14 miles out to sea.

The **City Art Gallery and Museum,** in Drake Circus, contains portraits by Sir Joshua Reynolds and exhibitions devoted to the life of pre-historic man on Dartmoor.

Information Tel. 264850/1.
Location On the A38, 15 m. S of Tavistock.
Parking Mayflower Street (3); Notte Street; Cornwall Street (2); Market Square; New George Street; Western Approach (2); Union Street; Royal Parade (2); Whimple Street; Millbay Road; Vauxhall Street; Mayflower Street; Market Way; Regent Street; Charles Street; Lockyer Street; Madeira Road (2); Derry's Cross (all car parks).
District council City of Plymouth (Tel. 668000).
Population 243,900.
E-C Wed. (smaller shops only).
M-D Mon. to Sat.
Police (Bb) Charles Cross

NONCHALANT DRAKE *The Armada in Sight, 1588, a painting by John Lucas (1849-1923), shows Drake finishing a game of bowls before engaging with the Spanish fleet.*

A statue honouring Drake the circumnavigator stands on Plymouth Hoe.

(Tel. 21345).
Casualty hospital Plymouth General, Freedom Fields (Tel. 668080).
Post office (Ba) St Andrew's Cross.
Theatres Hoe, Hoe Park (Tel. 668000); Athenaeum **(Aa)**, Derry's Cross (266104); Theatre Royal **(Aa)**, Royal Parade (669595); Palace, Union Street (25622).
Cinemas ABC **(Aa)**, Derry's Cross (Tel. 663300); Drake **(Aa)**, Derry's Cross (27074); Belgrave, Belgrave Road, Mutley Plain (662423).
Public library (Bb) Drake Circus.
Places to see Aquarium; Barbican and Mayflower Memorial; Citadel; Elizabethan House Museum; Blackfriars Refectory **(Ba)**; Guildhall **(Ba)**; City Museum and Art Gallery **(Bb)**, Drake Circus; Prysten House **(Ba)**; Smeaton's Tower; Mount Edgcumbe House and Park (Cremyll ferry from Stonehouse or Torpoint car ferry from Devonport); Saltram House, 2 m. E.
Town trails Available from Tourist

Information Bureau, Civic Centre.
Shopping Armada Way; Mayflower Street; Cornwall Street; Market Avenue; New George Street; Raleigh Street; Royal Parade; The Pannier Market.
Events Music Week (June); Saltram Fayre (July); Navy Days (Aug.).
Trade and industry Shipbuilding; marine, mechanical and electrical engineering; tourism.
Sport FA League football, Plymouth Argyle FC, Home Park.
Car ferries To Brittany (Tel. 21321); to Torpoint (812233).
Motorail Tel. 21300.
AA 24 hour service Tel. 669989.

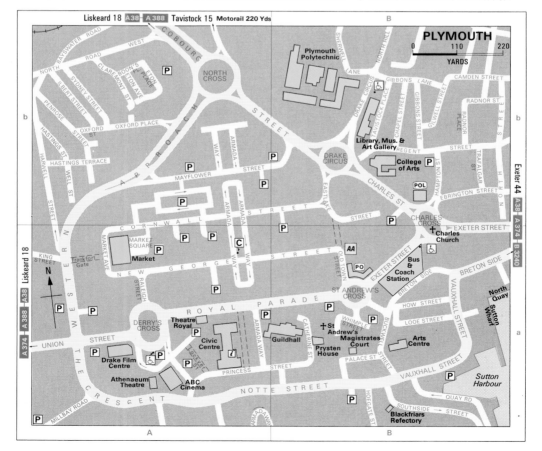

Port Glasgow Strathclyde

Before the Clyde was deepened in the late 18th century Port Glasgow, once a fishing village called Newark, was the harbour for Glasgow. It declined as a port in the 19th century, but became important as a ship-building centre.

Newark Castle, once the home of the Maxwell family, is a 15th-century turreted mansion beside the river.

COMET *A replica of Britain's first commercially successful steamboat, built in 1812, is in Port Glasgow.*

Information Tel. 41291.
Location On the A8, 3 m. E of Greenock.
Parking William Street; Fore Street (both car parks).
District council Inverclyde (Tel. Greenock 24400).
Population 22,600.
E-C Wed.
Police King Street (Tel. Greenock 24444).
Casualty hospital Inverclyde Royal, Larkfield Road, Greenock (Tel. Greenock 33777).
Post office Princes Street.
Public library King Street.
Places to see Newark Castle; *Comet* replica, Shore Street.
Shopping Princes Street.
AA 24 hour service
Tel. Glasgow (041) 812 0101.

Porthcawl Mid Glamorgan

Like several other coastal towns in South Wales, Porthcawl grew up as a coal port in the 19th century and, when trade declined, developed into a holiday resort. Its dock, built in 1831, was closed in 1906. Only the outer tidal basin and breakwater remain, and these are now used by pleasure cruisers and private craft.

The town is built on a low, limestone headland. With its three protected sandy bays, vast caravan site and funfair, it is now the leading resort in South Wales. It is a centre for shark fishing and surfing. The golf course is one of the finest in Wales.

Two miles north-west is the lost town of Kenfig. Sandstorms engulfed it during the Middle Ages, and it now lies buried beneath the dunes. The sparse ruins of Kenfig Castle can still be seen poking out of the sand.

Kenfig Pool is less than a mile from the sea but, locked in by dunes, it is the largest freshwater lake in all Glamorgan.

Information Tel. 6639.
Location On the A4106, 11 m. SE of Port Talbot.
Parking Eastern Promenade; Hillsboro Place; Mackworth Road; Lias Road; Newton Beach; Rest Bay (all car parks).
District council Borough of Ogwr (Tel. Bridgend 62141).
Population 15,600.
E-C Wed.
Police John Street (Tel. 5411).
Casualty hospital Bridgend General, Quarella Road, Bridgend (Tel. Bridgend 62166).
Post office John Street.
Theatre Grand Pavilion, Esplanade (Tel. 6996).
Cinema Cinema Two, Trecco Bay (Tel. 2103).
Public library Church Place.
Places to see Kenfig Castle ruins, 2 m. NW.
Shopping John Street; New Road Shopping Precinct.
AA 24 hour service
Tel. Swansea 55598.

Porthmadog Gwynedd

The seaport and holiday town of Porthmadog owes its existence to the imagination and energy of a 19th-century MP, William Alexander Maddocks, who reclaimed from the sea the land on which it stands. The mile-long embankment, which encloses about 5,000 acres of the Glaslyn estuary, cost £100,000, and almost ruined Maddocks.

Porthmadog became the port from which slate quarried at Blaenau Ffestiniog was exported. It was carried to the town by a narrow-gauge railway. This was abandoned in the 1940s, but in 1954 local volunteers began restoring the line, which now carries thousands of holidaymakers through some of the finest scenery in Wales.

Information Tel. 2327.
Location On the A487, 14 m. E of Pwllheli.
Parking Heol-y-Parc; Lombard Street; Madoc Street (all car parks).
District council Dwyfor (Tel. Pwllheli 3131).
Population 3,900.
E-C Wed. (winter only).
Police High Street (Tel. 2226).
Casualty hospital Madoc Memorial, Garth Road (Tel. 2255).
Post office Bank Place.
Cinema Coliseum, High Street (Tel. 2108).
Public library Snowdon Street.
Places to see Festiniog narrow-gauge railway; Gwynedd Maritime Museum.
Shopping High Street.
AA 24 hour service
Tel. Cardiff 394111.

Port Talbot W. Glamorgan

The town was named after the Talbot family who pioneered its industrial development in the 19th century.

The port has the biggest tidal harbour in Britain, built to serve the growing industrialisation, which includes a vast steel-rolling mill and a petroleum chemical plant. A sports and entertainment centre, the Afan Lido, dominates Port Talbot's seafront and 3 mile long beach.

Margam Abbey, south-west of the town, was founded in 1147 by Robert, Earl of Gloucester. Parts of it remain, including the chapter house, and there is a museum on the site.

Information Tel. 883141.
Location On the A48, 7 m. E of Swansea.
Parking Aberafan Centre; Princess Margaret Way; Scarlet Avenue; Llewelyn Street; St Mary's Church (all car parks).
District council Borough of Afan (Tel. 883141).
Population 47,300.
E-C Thur. **M-D** Tues., Sat.
Police Station Road (Tel. 883101).
Casualty hospital Neath General, Westbourne Road, Neath (Tel. Neath 4161).
Post office Station Road.
Cinema Plaza, Talbot Road (Tel. 882856).
Public library Commercial Road.
Shopping Aberafan Shopping Centre.
AA 24 hour service
Tel. Swansea 55598.

Prestatyn Clwyd

This modern family resort stands on an ancient site. New Stone Age farmers lived on it about 3000 BC. There the Romans built a fort, and manned it from the 2nd to 4th centuries AD. And it was the Romans who opened up, near by at Meliden, the Talar Goch lead mine, which has been worked almost continuously ever since. Prestatyn was also the starting point of the great dyke built by Offa, King of Mercia, in the 8th century to mark the boundary between the English and Welsh.

Strife often erupted along the frontier. Henry II built Prestatyn Castle after making peace with Owain Gwynedd, King of North Wales, in 1157. But the peace was short lived. The Welsh resumed their plundering raids in 1165 and Henry returned to Wales, where, two years later, the rival chieftains united against the English for the first time. Bad weather forced Henry's forces back, and Owain captured and razed the castle.

Information Tel. 2484 (summer).
Location On the A548, 13 m. N of Denbigh.
Parking King's Avenue; Station Road; Fern Avenue, off High Street; Nant Hall Road (2); Beach Road East (2); Beach Road West; Victoria Road West; Bastion Road (all car parks).

District council Borough of
Rhuddlan (Tel. Rhyl 4752).
Population 16,400.
E-C Thur. **M-D** Tues., Fri.
Police Victoria Road (Tel. 2341).
Casualty hospital Glan Clwyd,
Bodelwyddan
(Tel. St Asaph 583910).
Post office King's Avenue.
Theatre Royal Lido, Bastion Avenue
(Tel. 4768).
Cinema Scala, High Street
(Tel. 4365).
Public library Nant Hall Road.
Places to see Welsh Motor Museum.
Shopping High Street.
AA 24 hour service
Tel. Llandudno 79066.

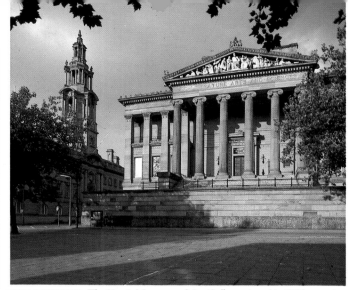

PRIDE OF PRESTON *The Harris Museum and Art Gallery, opened in 1893, contains
an outstanding collection of British paintings.*

Presteigne Powys

In Georgian times the border town of
Presteigne lay on the main route from
London to Aberystwyth, and 30 of
the older buildings in the town were
once coaching inns. The Duke's
Arms still retains the toll-window
where coach passengers paid their
fares, and tracks worn by coach
wheels can be seen in the courtyard.
The half-timbered Radnorshire Arms
has a "priest hole" – a secret hiding
place for Catholic priests – dating
from Tudor times.

The Saxon name for Presteigne was
Presthemede (the household of
priests), and the Welsh name for the
town is Llanandras. This derives from
the parish church of St Andrew,
which dates from the 14th century.

In the tower there is a carillon with
a mechanism believed to be unique in
Britain. It was built in 1726 and was
restored to full working order in 1968.
It can be seen by arrangement with
the rector.

Information Tel. 279 (Tues. and
Wed. only).
Location On the B4362, 14 m. W of
Leominster.
Parking Hereford Street; Broad
Street; High Street; St David's Street.
District council Radnor
(Tel. Llandrindod Wells 3737).
Population 1,520.
E-C Thur.
Police Harper Street (Tel. 222).
Casualty hospital Hereford General,
Nelson Street, Hereford
(Tel. Hereford 2561).
Post office High Street.
Shopping High Street.
Event Vintage Car Rally (Oct.).
AA 24 hour service
Tel. Newport 62559.

Preston Lancashire

One of the most decisive battles of
the Civil War was fought at Preston
in 1648 when Cromwell's army
routed 20,000 Scots, allies of Charles
I, in three hours. Nearly 100 years
later, in 1745, Preston was captured
by Bonnie Prince Charlie on his
march south from Scotland.

In 1786 John Horrocks set up the
first of Preston's cotton mills. And

another Preston man, Sir Richard
Arkwright (1732-92), invented the
spinning frame, which revolutionised
the textile industry.

The Temperance Movement was
founded in Preston by a local man,
Joseph Livesay, who published England's first newspaper for abstainers,
the *Preston Temperance Advocate*, in
1834. It is said that the word teetotal
came from a stammering friend of
Livesay's when he tried to take the
pledge of "t-t-total abstinence".

Information Tel. 54881.
Location On the A59, 10 m. W of
Blackburn.
Parking St George's, Lune Street;
Central Bus Station; Market Hall;
Avenham Lane; Syke Street; Glover
Street; Ringway (westbound);
Tenterfield Street/Ringway
(eastbound); Church Street; Chapel
Yard; Hill Street; Lancaster Road;
Saul Street; Trinity Square; Butler
Street (all car parks).
District council Borough of Preston

(Tel. 54881).
Population 86,900.
E-C Thur. **M-D** Mon., Wed., Fri.
and Sat.
Police (Bb) Lawson Street
(Tel. 54811).
Casualty hospital Preston Royal
Infirmary, Deepdale Road
(Tel. 54747).
Post office (Ba) Market Street.
Theatres The Playhouse **(Ab)**,
Market Street West (Tel. 52288);
Charter Theatre, Guild Hall **(Ba)**,
Lancaster Road (21721).
Cinemas ABC (Aa), Fishergate
(Tel. 55566); Odeon 1 and 2 **(Ba)**,
Church Street (55122).
Public library (Ba) Market Square.
Places to see Harris Museum and Art
Gallery **(Ba)**, Market Square.
Shopping St George's Shopping
Centre; St John's Centre; Fishergate.
Event Pace-egging (Easter).
Sport FA League football, Preston
North End FC, Deepdale.
AA 24 hour service
Tel. Manchester (061) 485 6299.

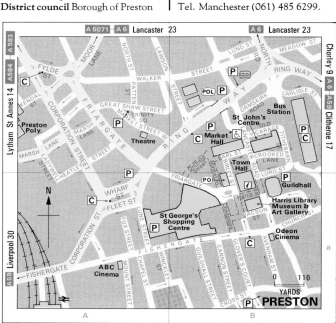

PORTSMOUTH Hampshire

The city where the British Navy was born

The island on which much of modern Portsmouth now stands was just squelchy saltings outside a small port in 1415 when Henry V issued the order that effectively founded the British Navy. The warrior king had massed his knights and foot troops at Porchester Castle, on the northern edge of the harbour. He sent men to commandeer all the ships they could find along the south coast in readiness for the invasion of France. There was no room to embark an army at Portsmouth, so the first assembled royal fleet met at Southampton, and from there carried Henry V to France and his triumph at Agincourt. Eighty years later, Henry VII fortified the sea walls at Portsmouth and built behind them the first permanent dry dock in England. In 1540, Henry VIII expanded it into the first royal dockyard. Portsmouth has been England's chief naval station ever since.

STEPS TO VICTORY *A. C. Gow's romanticised version of Nelson's departure.*

The fortress, at the harbour mouth opposite Gosport, was considerably strengthened and extended by Sir Bernard de Gomme, Charles II's Dutch-born engineer of castles. The bastions on either side of the Sally Port were lengthened to take a total of 28 guns. Portsmouth became the strongest fortress in Britain.

Behind these walls for the next 250 years rested the world's greatest navy. Towering, 100-gun, wooden ships of the line; steam-powered ironclads; great aircraft carriers and the swift, sophisticated super-ships of the nuclear age have all cut their way along Spithead to Portsmouth, home to great admirals and countless heroes.

Early on the afternoon of Saturday, September 14, 1805, the most famous of these, Vice-Admiral Viscount Nelson, took his last walk on English soil. Nelson walked through cheering crowds and boarded his barge to be rowed out to **HMS Victory** from Southsea Beach, not as was believed (and shown in A. C. Gow's painting above) from the Sally Port at the entrance to Portsmouth Harbour. Five weeks later he had smashed the Franco-Spanish fleet at Trafalgar and was dead.

The battered *Victory* returned in December with Nelson's body, and was refitted at Chatham. It was retired from service in 1824 and became the flagship of Portsmouth Command. It now stands in dry dock at the Naval Dockyard, still the flagship of Portsmouth Command, and one of Britain's great tourist attractions.

The city has several literary ties. Sir Arthur Conan Doyle (1859-1930) practised as a doctor at Bush Villas, Elm Grove, Southsea, and wrote his first Sherlock Holmes story, *A Study in Scarlet*, there. H. G. Wells (1866-1946) worked as a drapery assistant in a shop at the corner of King's Road and St Paul's Road. Rudyard Kipling (1865-1936) spent six miserable childhood years lodging with a woman in Campbell Road, Southsea, while his parents were in India. Nevil Shute Norway lived in Portsmouth from 1933 to 1939 and set up the Airspeed factory for aircraft, fuselage and spare parts. The actor Peter Sellers was born in Southsea in 1925.

Portsmouth was the birthplace of Isambard Kingdom Brunel (1806-59) the engineering genius, and the eccentric philanthropist Jonas Hanway (1712-86), the man who introduced the umbrella to the streets of London.

Neighbouring Southsea is one of the south coast's most successful resorts, with a 2 mile promenade backed by open parkland. There are magnificent views of **Spithead**, constantly filled with ships and yachts.

Southsea Castle is kept as a museum, and also serves as a lighthouse station. Near Clarence Pier is one of the anchors from the *Victory*, and Nelson's statue stands in Pembroke Gardens, facing the beach where he embarked for Trafalgar.

Work is being carried out to raise the *Mary Rose*, a warship built for Henry VIII which sank in 1545 off Spithead. A museum will display the ship and contents at Eastney.

Information Tel. 834092/3.
Location On the A3, 8 m. SE of Fareham.
Parking Portsmouth: Melbourne Place; White Swan Road; Mary Rose Street; Greetham Street; Paradise Street; Clarendon Street. Southsea: Long Curtain Road; Clarence Parade (2); Clarence Esplanade (2); Southsea Esplanade; Melville Road;

OLD PORTSMOUTH *Broad Street is one of several Georgian streets nestling behind the 15th-century defensive wall that still protects the harbour mouth.*

THE PAY CLERK'S SON WHO BECAME A GREAT NOVELIST

On February 7, 1812, the wife of John Dickens, a navy pay clerk, gave birth to a son at No. 387 Mile End Terrace, Commercial Road. The son, Charles, was destined to become one of the most widely read writers in the English language.

The Dickens family moved six months after Charles's birth, and in 1901 the road was renumbered and the house became No. 393 Commercial Road. It is now a museum and contains personal relics of Dickens and an extensive library of his works, including several first editions. The house is furnished in the style of the early 19th century.

Charles Dickens died in 1870 and is buried in Westminster Abbey.

An ink-well is among Dickens's relics.

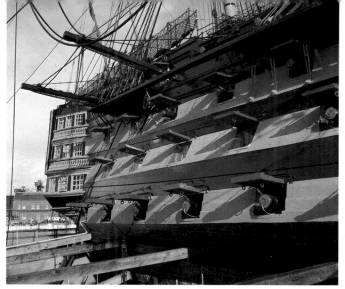

FIRE POWER *Victory's guns could fire a broadside every 80 seconds. At Trafalgar they devastated the French ships with shattering blasts at point-blank range.*

Public library (Cb) Guildhall Square.

Places to see HMS *Victory* **(Ac)**, Royal Naval Museum, Dockyard; Charles Dickens Birthplace Museum, Old Commercial Road; City Museum and Art Gallery **(Ba)**, Museum Road; Cumberland House Museum and Aquarium, Eastern Parade; Round Tower and Point Battery **(Aa)**, Portsmouth Point; Royal Marines Museum, Eastney Barracks, St Georges Road; Southsea Castle Museum, Clarence Esplanade; Eastney Pumping Station and Gas Engine House, Henderson Road; Fort Widley, Portsdown Hill Road.

Shopping Tricorn Shopping Centre, off Marketway; Commercial Road; Arundel Street; Charlotte Street; London Road; Palmerston Road, Southsea; High Street, Cosham.

Events Navy Days (Aug.).

Sport FA League football, Portsmouth FC, Fratton Park, Milton; Greyhound racing, Tipnor Stadium.

Car ferries To Cherbourg (Tel. 815231); to St Malo (827701); to Isle of Wight (327744); to Channel Islands (755111); to Le Havre (815231); Hovercraft to Isle of Wight (829988).

AA 24 hour service Tel. Southampton 36811.

Ferry Road; Marmion Road; Ashby Place (all car parks).

District council City of Portsmouth (Tel. 822251).

Population 179,400.

E-C Mon., Wed.

M-D Thur., Fri., Sat.

Police (Cb) Winston Churchill Avenue (Tel. 822222).

Casualty hospital Queen Alexandra, Cosham (Tel. Cosham 79451).

Post office (Cc) Slindon Street.

Theatre Kings Theatre, Albert Road, Southsea (Tel. 828282).

Cinemas ABC, Commercial Road (Tel. 823538); Salon, Festing Road, Southsea (732163); Odeon, London Road (661539); Classic, High Street, Cosham (Cosham 376635); Classic, Fratton Road (822933).

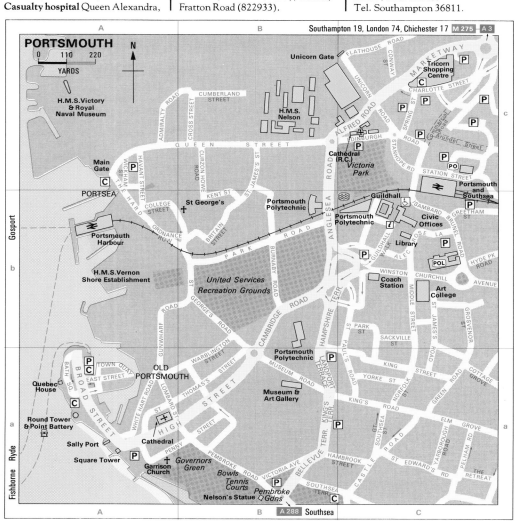

Prestonpans Lothian

Salt-pans, in which sea water was evaporated to obtain salt, gave the town its name. They were in use from the 12th to the early 18th centuries. But the town owes its fame to Bonnie Prince Charlie's one real victory in the rebellion of 1745. His army routed a force led by Sir John Cope in less than 15 minutes.

Scotland's National Mining Museum at Prestongrange includes a restored Cornish beam engine used for pumping at Prestonpans colliery from 1874 to 1954.

Information Tel. 031 665 6597 (summer); 031 665 3711.
Location On the A198, 7 m. W of Haddington.
Parking High Street; Ayres Wynd; New Street.
District council East Lothian (Tel. Haddington 4161).
Population 7,620.
E-C Wed.
Police New Street (Tel. 810250 or Haddington 4101).
Casualty hospital Roodlands General, Hospital Road, Haddington (Tel. Haddington 3182).
Post office Ayres Wynd.
Public library West Loan.
Shopping High Street.
AA 24 hour service Tel. 031 225 8464.

Prestwich see Manchester

Prestwick Strathclyde

During the Second World War, Prestwick was the terminal for the transatlantic air-ferry service. Today it is Scotland's international airport.

The town was known to travellers of a different kind long before the aerodrome was opened in 1935, for the ruined Church of St Nicholas has been a landmark for mariners since the 12th century. Prestwick is also a holiday resort; its sandy beach is part of the 6 mile stretch in Ayr Bay. There are three golf clubs; the first British Open Championship was held at Prestwick Golf Club in 1860.

Information Tel. 79234.
Location On the A719, 3 m. N of Ayr.
Parking North Esplanade; Central Esplanade; Bellevue Road; Station Road (all car parks).
District council Kyle and Carrick (Tel. Ayr 81511).
Population 13,400.
E-C Wed.
Police Main Street (Tel. 78587).
Casualty hospital Ayr County Hospital, Holmston Road, Ayr (Tel. Ayr 81991).
Post office The Cross.
Public library Kyle Street.
Places to see Bruce's Well, Maryborough Road.
Shopping Main Street.
AA 24 hour service Tel. Glasgow (041) 812 0101.

Pudsey see Leeds

Pwllheli Gwynedd

Edward the Black Prince gave Pwllheli and the neighbouring town of Nefyn to his friend Nigel de Loryng in 1349. It was a fine gift. The town has a spectacular beach and a natural harbour, and lies in beautiful countryside with the ranges of Snowdonia in the background.

For centuries it was a small market town where farmers of the Lleyn Peninsula sold their livestock, and where a small community of fishermen and boatbuilders lived. The Victorian rush to the seaside and the boom in bathing gave Pwllheli the chance to sell its great natural asset, the 5 miles of sandy beach fringing Cardigan Bay. Now thousands flock to Pwllheli each year to enjoy the sunny climate, fine sailing, fishing and excellent walking. Near the town is one of the biggest holiday camps in Britain.

Information Tel. 3000.
Location On the A497, 9 m. SW of Criccieth.
Parking Penlan Street; Station Square; Lower Cardiff Road; Penrhydliniog; Sand Street (all car parks).
District council Dwyfor (Tel. 3131/6; 3371/4).
Population 4,000.
E-C Thur. **M-D** Mon., Wed.
Police Ala Road (Tel. 2277).
Casualty hospital Bryn Beryl, Caernarvon Road (Tel. 2231).
Post office Lower Cardiff Road.
Cinema Town Hall Cinema, Penlan Street (Tel. 3131).
Public library Upper Ala Road.
Shopping High Street; Gaol Street; Penlan Street.
Event Agricultural Show (July).
AA 24 hour service Tel. Llandudno 79066.

R

Ramsey Isle of Man

Every June, thousands of visitors flock to Ramsey to see the Isle of Man T.T. (Tourist Trophy) motor-cycle races. The course, which snakes over the hills west of the town, is used again each September for the Manx Grand Prix races.

In 1313 Robert Bruce landed at Ramsey, captured the island from the English and held it, for a short time, for Scotland. Although the island is self-governing, it has been ever since a possession of the British Crown.

Ramsey, the second largest town on the island after Douglas, clusters round the mouth of the River Sulby where it enters the Irish Sea. It has safe sand-and-shingle beaches, sea angling and sailing.

Behind the Old Harbour is Mooragh Park, where palm trees fringing a 12 acre boating lake give a tropical-lagoon atmosphere.

Ten miles south of Ramsey, the harbour town of Laxey is dominated by its giant waterwheel, the largest in the world. It was built in 1854 to pump water from the lead mines beneath Snaefell mountain and was christened *Lady Isabella*, after the wife of the island's Lieutenant-Governor. The wheel is 72 ft 6 in. in diameter, has a circumference of 217 ft and revolves at a rate of two revolutions per minute.

VICTORIAN RETREAT *When the Victorians discovered Pwllheli many of them settled in the new resort, building houses roofed with the blue-grey slate of Wales.*

Information Tel. 812228.
Location On the A3, 15 m. NE of Douglas.
Parking Bircham Avenue; Peel Street (both car parks).
Local authority Ramsey Town Commissioners (Tel. 812228).
Population 5,370.
E-C Wed. **M-D** Mon.
Police Parliament Street (Tel. 812234).
Casualty hospital Ramsey Cottage Hospital, Bowring Road (Tel. 813254).
Post office Court Row.
Public library Town Hall, Parliament Square.
Places to see Curraghs Wild Life Park, 6 m. W; Laxey Wheel, Laxey; Grove Rural Life Museum, Andreas Road; Albert Tower, Hairpin Corner.
Shopping Parliament Street; St Paul's Square Precinct.
Events Round I.O.M. Offshore Yacht Race (May); Tourist Trophy (first two weeks in June); Manx Grand Prix (first two weeks in Sept.).
AA 24 hour service
Tel. Liverpool (051) 709 7252.

BOATS AT WORK AND AT PLAY *Ramsgate's Royal Harbour has a modern yacht marina, crowded in summer, and is still used by cargo vessels and fishing boats.*

Ramsgate Kent

The opening in 1969 of the hovercraft terminal at Pegwell Bay, 1 mile to the south, has restored Ramsgate as a Channel port, a role which it has had on and off since Roman times.

The Jutish leaders Hengist and Horsa landed near Ramsgate in AD 449, an event commemorated by the replica of a longship on the clifftop at Pegwell Bay. In AD 597 came St Augustine, the first Christian missionary sent from Rome to the Anglo-Saxons. A Celtic cross on Minster Road commemorates his landfall.

But Ramsgate is best known as a seaside resort, one of those which sprang up with the vogue for sea-bathing in the 19th century. Sandy, south-facing beaches are sheltered by chalk cliffs, and along the Esplanade are amusement parks and a pavilion.

Most of Ramsgate's buildings date from the 19th century or later, but the Church of St Lawrence is part Norman, and Queen's Court, in Cavendish Place, is 17th century.

The Roman Catholic church of St Augustine, in St Augustine Road, was dedicated in 1851. It is the work of Augustus Welby Pugin. His son Edward designed St Augustine Abbey in 1860. Augustus Pugin's house, The Grange, stands on the West Cliff. He died there in 1852.

The parish church of St George, built in 1827, has a stained-glass window commemorating the 1940 Dunkirk evacuation.

Information
Tel. Thanet 51086.
Location On the A253, 4 m. S of Margate.
Parking Albion Place; Hardres Street; Harbour Parade; Cavendish Street; Church Road; Cannon Road; Meeting Street; Queen Street (all car parks).
District council Thanet (Tel. Thanet 25511).

Population 39,700.
E-C Thur. **M-D** Fri.
Police (Bb) Cavendish Street (Tel. Thanet 25516).
Casualty hospital Victoria Hospital, London Road, Deal (Tel. Deal 2122).
Post office (Bb) High Street.
Theatre Granville, Victoria Parade (Tel. Thanet 51750).
Cinemas Classic **(Bb)**, King Street (Tel. Thanet 51081); Kings **(Bb)**, Market Place (Thanet 52524).
Public library (Ab) Guildford Lawn.
Places to see Local History Museum, Library; Viking ship, Pegwell Bay.
Trail Harbour Trail available from Thanet District Council.
Shopping Queen Street; King Street; Harbour Street; High Street; Argyle Centre.
Car ferry To Calais (Tel. Thanet 54761). To Dunkirk (Tel. Thanet 583371).
AA 24 hour service
Tel. Thanet 81226.

STATIONS OF THE CROSS *St Veronica wipes the face of Jesus, number VI of the Stations of the Cross as shown in St Augustine's Church, Ramsgate.*

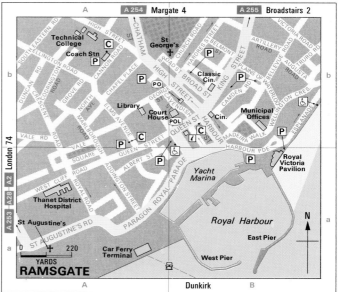

Rawtenstall Lancashire

Textiles and footwear are the traditional industries of this moorland town, which stands on the southern fringes of the Forest of Rossendale, just north of Greater Manchester. Over the last decade extensive land reclamation and landscaping have removed many of its dark terraces of mill-town dwellings.

Information Tel. Rossendale 217777.
Location On the A681, 18 m. N of Manchester.
Parking Kay Street; Newchurch Road; Bacup Road; Bank Street; South Street (all car parks).
District council Borough of Rossendale (Tel. Rossendale 217777).
Population 22,200.
E-C Tues. **M-D** Thur., Sat.
Police Lord Street
(Tel. Rossendale 215242).
Casualty hospital Bury General, Walmersley Road, Bury
(Tel. Manchester (061) 764 2444).
Post office Kay Street.
Cinema Unit Four, Bacup Road
(Tel. Rossendale 213123).
Public library Haslingden Road.
Shopping Bank Street; The Centre Shopping Precinct.
AA 24 hour service
Tel. Manchester (061) 485 6299.

Reading Berkshire

The market centre, railway junction and university town of Reading began its rapid expansion in the 19th century. But its history as a settlement stretches back more than 2,000 years. The Romans had farms and villas in the area, and relics of their occupation are in Reading Museum.

RELICS OF RURAL ENGLAND

The vanished world of pre-tractor England, when the horse dominated the countryside, lives on in the Museum of English Rural Life at Reading. Ploughs and churns are among the thousands of items preserved, together with nearly 300,000 photographs.

A butter churn of the mid-19th century.

Nineteenth-century Dorset plough.

Henry I founded a Benedictine abbey at Reading in 1121. Its 13th-century inner gateway in Abbey Street is now a museum.

Information Tel. 55911.
Location On the A33, 17 m. NE of Basingstoke.
Parking Chatham Street; Inner Distribution Road; Castle Street; King Street; Queens Road; Forbury (3); Station Hill; King's Meadow Road; Caversham Road; Great Knolly's Street. Caversham: George Street (all car parks).
District council Borough of Reading (Tel. 55911).
Population 123,700.
E-C Six-day trading. **M-D** Mon., Wed., Fri. and Sat.
Police (Ba) Civic Centre
(Tel. 585111).
Casualty hospital (Ca) Royal Berkshire, Craven Road (Tel. 85111).
Post office (Bb) Friar Street.
Theatre The Hexagon **(Ba)**, Civic Centre (Tel. 56215).

Cinemas ABC **(Bb)**, Friar Street
(Tel. 53931); ABC, London Road
(61465); Odeon **(Ba)**, Cheapside
(57887).
Public library (Bb) Blagrave Street.
Places to see Abbey ruins **(Cb)**; Museum and Art Gallery **(Bb)**, Blagrave Street. University: Museum of English Rural Life; Cole Collection (Zoology); Ure Museum of Greek Archaeology.
Shopping Butts Shopping Centre; Friar Street; Friar's Walk; West Street; Market Place; Butter Market; Gun Street; Minster Street; Oxford Road.
Trade and industry Electronics; printing; brewing; engineering.
Sport FA League football, Reading FC, Norfolk Road; Speedway racing, Bennet Road.
Motorail Tel. 595911.
AA 24 hour service Tel. 581122.

Redbridge see London

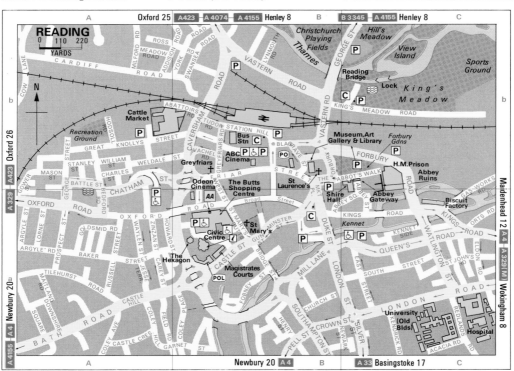

Redcar Cleveland

This is a lively seaside resort with extensive sands. In Coatham Amusement Park, Redcar possesses the largest indoor funfair in the north-east. It also has the best known racecourse in that part of England. The Zetland Museum on The Promenade contains the oldest lifeboat in Britain, the *Zetland*, built in 1800.

Information Tel. 471921 or 472162.
Location On the A1042, 9 m. NE of Middlesbrough.
Parking Esplanade; Lord Street; Ridley Street; Wilton Street; Beach Grove (all car parks).
District council Borough of Langbaurgh
(Tel. Eston Grange 468141).
Population 84,900.
E-C Wed.
Police France Street off Lord Street (Tel. 483333).
Casualty hospital Middlesbrough General, Ayresome Green Lane, Middlesbrough
(Tel. Middlesbrough 83133).
Post office Cleveland Street.
Cinema Regent, Esplanade
(Tel. 482094).
Public library Coatham Road.
Places to see Zetland Museum; Sir William Turner Hospital, Kirkleatham.
Shopping High Street; Station Road.
Sport Horse racing, West Dyke Road.
AA 24 hour service
Tel. Middlesbrough 246832.

Redditch H. & W.

The town grew up around a Cistercian abbey founded on the banks of the River Arrow in 1138 and dissolved exactly four centuries later. The abbey ruins have been partially excavated.

Beside the ruins is the Forge Mill, an old watermill which has been restored, and is now a museum.

Information Tel. 60806.
Location On the A441, 14 m. S of Birmingham.
Parking Ringway; Station Way; Church Road; William Street; Plymouth Road (all car parks).
District council Redditch
(Tel. 64252).
Population 63,400.
E-C Wed. **M-D** Tues. to Sat.
Police Grove Street (Tel. 68181).
Casualty hospital Selly Oak, Raddlebarn Road, Birmingham
(Tel. 021 472 5313).
Post office Church Road.
Theatre Palace, Alcester Road
(Tel. 68484).
Cinema Classic, Unicorn Hill
(Tel. 62572).
Public library Market Place.
Places to see Abbey ruins; Forge Mill.
Shopping Kingfisher Centre; Royal Square; Unicorn Hill; Market Place.
Events Water Fiesta (July); Carnival (Sept.).
Trade and industry Manufacture of needles; light engineering for the

motor and aerospace industries.
AA 24 hour service
Tel. Birmingham (021) 550 4858.

Redruth see Camborne

Reigate Surrey

Modern development has obliterated much of historical interest in this town on the edge of the North Downs. But the quaint 18th-century Old Town Hall, the 16th-century Old Sweep's House in Slipshoe Street, the timber-framed, tile-hung house, La Trobes, in High Street, and other old buildings still survive.

Information Tel. 42477.
Location On the A25, 6 m. E of Dorking.
Parking Bell Street; Bancroft Road; Upper West Street; High Street (all car parks).
District council Borough of Reigate and Banstead (Tel. 42477).
Population 52,600.
E-C Wed.
Police Reigate Road
(Tel. Redhill 65040).
Casualty hospital Redhill General, Earlswood Common, Redhill
(Tel. Redhill 65030).
Post office Bell Street.
Cinema Majestic, Bancroft Road
(Tel. 42943).
Public library London Road.
Shopping High Street; Bell Street.
AA 24 hour service
Tel. Crawley 25685.

Renfrew Strathclyde

The county town of the former Renfrewshire is part of the heavily industrialised conurbation which sprawls along the River Clyde west of Glasgow. The title of Baron Renfrew is held by the Prince of Wales as heir apparent to the Scottish throne.

Information
Tel. Glasgow (041) 886 3344.
Location On the A737, 6 m. W of Glasgow.
Parking Muir Street; High Street; Broadloan (all car parks).
District council Renfrew
(Tel. 041 889 5400).
Population 21,900.
E-C Wed. **M-D** Sun.
Police Inchinnan Road
(Tel. 041 886 1113).
Casualty hospital Royal Alexandra Infirmary, Neilston Road, Paisley
(Tel. 041 887 9111).
Post office Canal Street.
Public library Paisley Road.
Places to see Argyll Stone, Blythe Road.
Shopping High Street; Bell Street; Hairst Street; Canal Street.
Car ferry To N. Side Yoker
(Tel. 041 959 8842).
Trade and industry Boiler-making; furniture; oil refining; engineering.
AA 24 hour service
Tel. 041 812 0101.

Rhondda Mid Glamorgan

The two Rhondda valleys – Fawr (large) and Fach (small) – were once heavily wooded, sparsely populated and extremely beautiful. Intensive coal-mining in the 19th century brought a huge increase in population, and strings of villages along the valley sides.

Demand for steam coal declined in the 1920s, and now the Rhondda is a residential area and also an expanding light-industrial area.

Information Tel. Tonypandy 434551.
Location On the A4058, 8 m. N of Pontypridd.
Parking Tonypandy: Dunraven Street. Porth: Hannah Street. Treorchy: Station Road. Ferndale: Rhondda Road (all car parks).
District council Borough of Rhondda
(Tel. Tonypandy 434551).
Population 81,700.
E-C Thur.
Police Maindy Road, Ton Pentre
(Tel. Tonypandy 434222).
Casualty hospital East Glamorgan, Church Village, Nr Pontypridd (Tel. Newtown Llantwit 4242).
Post offices Tonypandy: Dunraven Street. Porth: Porth Street. Treorchy: High Street. Ferndale: High Street.
Theatre and cinema Parc and Dare, Station Road, Treorchy (Tel. Treorchy 773112).
Cinema Plaza, Dunraven Street, Tonypandy (Tel. Tonypandy 432214).
Public library Station Road, Treorchy.
Shopping Tonypandy: Dunraven Street. Porth: Hannah Street. Treorchy: High Street. Ferndale: High Street.
Event Rhondda Festival (Aug./Sept.).
Trade and industry Light engineering; textiles; electronic components.
AA 24 hour service
Tel. Swansea 55598.

Rhyl Clwyd

There is nothing sedate about Rhyl, with its giant funfair, bathing-beauty contests, amusement arcades and variety shows. In summer, holidaymakers from Lancashire and Cheshire flock from over the border to enjoy these, and the miles of safe, flat sandy beaches.

Information Tel. 31515/6.
Location On the A548, 12 m. E of Colwyn Bay.
Parking East Parade; Splash Point; West Parade (2); West Kinmel Street; Wellington Road; High Street; Brighton Road; Greenfield Place; Quay Street (2); Marine Drive; Garford Road (all car parks).
District council Borough of Rhuddlan (Tel. 4752).
Population 22,700.
E-C Thur. (except summer).

Police Wellington Road
(Tel. 55661).
Casualty hospital Glan Clwyd
Hospital, Bodelwyddan (Tel.
St Asaph 583910).
Post office Water Street.
Theatres Coliseum, West
Promenade (Tel. 51126); Gaiety,
East Promenade (51251); Little, Vale
Road (2229).
Cinemas Astra 1, 2 and 3, High
Street (Tel. 53856); Plaza, High
Street (53442).
Public library Wellington Road.
Places to see Rhuddlan Castle ruins,
3 m. S.
Shopping High Street; Queen Street.
Events Manchester-Rhyl Cycle Race
(Apr.); Festival Week (end May-
early June); Milk Week (Aug.).
AA 24 hour service
Tel. Llandudno 79066.

Richmond N. Yorks.

The ruins of a great Norman castle
look down from a hilltop on the market town of Richmond. The castle
was built in the 11th century to guard
the valley of the River Swale. Its
massive keep is 100 ft high and its
walls are among the oldest-surviving
military walls in the country.

The town is an attractive blend of
twisting alleyways and open spaces.
In the great cobbled market place is
Holy Trinity Church, one of the most
curious churches in Britain. Until
1971 there were shops beneath its
north aisle, and one half of it is now
the museum of the Green Howards
Regiment. The other half is still used
for services.

Off the market place is a Georgian
theatre of 1788. One mile south-east
of the town lies Easby Abbey, founded in the mid-12th century. The remains of its infirmary and fine refectory are well preserved.

Information Tel. 3525.
Location On the A6108, 13 m. SW
of Darlington.
Parking Victoria Road/Hurgill Road;
Nuns Close (both car parks).
District council Richmondshire
(Tel. 4221).
Population 7,700.
E-C Wed. **M-D** Sat.

Police l'Anson Road
(Tel. 2245/3055).
Casualty hospital Duchess of Kent
Military Hospital, Horne Road,
Catterick Garrison (Tel. 833731).
Post office Queens Road.
Theatre Georgian, Victoria Road
(Tel. 3021).
Cinema The Zetland, Victoria Road
(Tel. 3161).
Public library Dundas Street.
Places to see Green Howards
Museum; Richmond Castle; Grey
Friars Tower; Easby Abbey, 1 m. SE.
Shopping Finkle Street; King Street;
Market Place.
Events Richmondshire Festival
(May/June); Scorton Feast (Aug.).
AA 24 hour service
Tel. Middlesbrough 246832.

Richmond upon Thames
see London

Rickmansworth Herts.

The rivers Colne, Gade and Chess
meet near Rickmansworth, once a
small market town but now chiefly a
residential district.

The winding High Street has a
number of Georgian buildings, including Basing House, once the home
of William Penn, the 17th-century
founder of Pennsylvania, USA.

Moor Park Mansion, 1 mile south-
east of the town, was designed in
Palladian style about 1720 by the
Venetian architect Giacomo Leoni.
It is now a golf clubhouse.

Information Tel. 76611.
Location On the A412, 21 m. NW of
London.
Parking Park Road; Talbot Road (2);
Northway; High Street; Bury Lane
(2) (all car parks).
District council Three Rivers
(Tel. 76611).
Population 29,400.
E-C Wed.
Police Rectory Road
(Tel. Watford 44444).
Casualty hospital Peace Memorial
Hospital, Hempstead Road, Watford
(Tel. Watford 25611).
Post office High Street.
Public library High Street.

Places to see Moor Park Mansion;
Aquadrome/Grand Union Canal.
Shopping High Street; Moneyhill
Parade; Berry Lane, Mill End; New
Road, Croxley Green.
AA 24 hour service
Tel. 01 954 7373.

Ringwood Hampshire

The River Avon, famed for its trout,
flows through this market town of old
cottages, several of them thatched.
There is good riding and walking on
the surrounding heathland.

The Duke of Monmouth was
brought to Ringwood in 1685 after his
defeat at the Battle of Sedgemoor and
held for two days at a house in West
Street, now called Monmouth
House, before being taken to London
for execution.

The attractive parish church in the
main square was rebuilt in the 19th
century, in Early English style.

Information Tel. 2212/2613.
Location On the A31, 11 m. NE of
Bournemouth.
Parking Meeting House Lane (cp).
District council New Forest
(Tel. Lyndhurst 3121).
Population 11,810.
E-C Mon., Thur. **M-D** Wed.
Police Christchurch Road
(Tel. 3378).
Casualty hospital Poole General,
Longfleet Road, Poole
(Tel. Poole 5100).
Post office Southampton Road.
Public library Christchurch Road.
Shopping Christchurch Road; High
Street; Southampton Road; Meeting
House Lane.
AA 24 hour service
Tel. Southampton 36811.

Ripon N. Yorks.

A rare Saxon crypt, reputedly built
for St Wilfrid in 672, lies beneath the
nave of Ripon Cathedral. The crypt is
now a strongroom in which ancient
silver and other church treasures from
all parts of Yorkshire are displayed.
The cathedral retains features from
every period of English church building, including a splendid 13th-
century western front and a grand
16th-century Gothic nave.

At 9 p.m. every evening in the
market square the city Wakeman
blows his horn – a custom known as
Setting the Watch. This dates back
more than 1,000 years, and used to
announce that the city was then in
the Wakeman's care for the night.

The 14th-century half-timbered
Wakeman's House in the square,
once the hornblower's official residence, is now a local-history museum
(and tourist information centre).

About 2 miles south-west of Ripon,
in a lovely wooded valley, lie the
magnificent ruins of Fountains
Abbey, a vast Cistercian abbey begun
in 1134 and dissolved in 1539. It
stands by the River Skell, which con-
verges with the Ure at Ripon.

MILITARY CHURCH *The regimental museum of the Green Howards occupies part of a
church that dominates the cobbled market place of Richmond.*

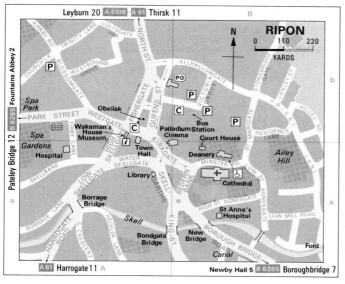

N **RIPON**
0   110   220
YARDS

Fountains Abbey 2

B 6265

Pateley Bridge 12

Church Lane; School Lane (all car parks).
District council Metropolitan Borough of Rochdale (Tel. 47474).
Population 92,700.
E-C Tues. **M-D** Wkdys, except Tues.
Police The Holme (Tel. 47401).
Casualty hospital Rochdale Infirmary, Whitehall Street (Tel. 40952).
Post office The Esplanade.
Theatre Gracie Fields Theatre, Hudson Walk (Tel. 30149).
Cinema ABC, The Butts (Tel. 45954).
Public library The Esplanade.
Places to see Rochdale Museum, Sparrow Hill; Pioneers Museum, Toad Lane.
Shopping Drake Street; Yorkshire Street; Market Way Precinct.
Sport FA League football, Rochdale AFC, Spotland, Wilbutts Lane; Rugby League, Rochdale Hornets RFC, Milnrow Road.
AA 24 hour service
Tel. Manchester (061) 485 6299.

Rochester see page 338

Romsey Hampshire

The River Test, one of England's finest trout and salmon streams, attracts anglers from all parts of the world to this ancient market town.

Romsey's development followed that of its abbey, said to have been founded by Edward, son of Alfred the Great, in AD 907. The abbey church, mostly Norman, is all that remains. Inside is the Romsey Psalter, a 15th-century illuminated manuscript.

In the Market Place is a statue of the former Prime Minister, Lord Palmerston (1784-1865), who was born and died at Broadlands House, 1 mile south. The house, which stands in 400 acres of parkland landscaped by "Capability" Brown, was the home of Lord Mountbatten.

Information Tel. 515117.
Location On the A31, 8 m. NW of Southampton.
Parking Broadwater Road; Church Street; Love Lane; Portersbridge Street; Newton Lane off Bell Street (all car parks).
District council Test Valley (Tel. Andover 3621).
Population 12,900.
E-C Wed. **M-D** Fri., Sat.
Police The Hundred (Tel. 512161).
Casualty hospital Southampton General Hospital, Tremona Road, Shirley, Southampton (Tel. Southampton 777222).
Post office Church Street.
Public library Station Road.
Places to see King John's House; Romsey Abbey; Broadlands, 1 m. S.
Shopping Market Place; The Hundred; Bell Street; Church Street.
Trade and industry Beer bottling; jam-making; basket-making; tourism.
AA 24 hour service
Tel. Southampton 36811.

RIPON CATHEDRAL *The great east window, more than 50 ft high, is supported by gabled buttresses.*

Information Tel. 4625 summer; Harrogate 65912.
Location On the A61, 11 m. N of Harrogate.
Parking Allhallowgate/Queen Street; Blossomgate (both car parks).
District council Borough of Harrogate (Tel. Harrogate 68954).
Population 12,000.
E-C Wed. **M-D** Thur.
Police North Street (Tel. 2222).
Casualty hospital (Aa) Ripon and District, Firby Lane (Tel. 2546).
Post office (Bb) Finkle Street.
Cinema Palladium **(Aa)**, Kirkgate (Tel. 2266).
Public library (Aa) Skellgarths.
Places to see Cathedral **(Ba)**; Town Hall (civic regalia); Wakeman's House Museum **(Ab)**; Newby Hall, 5 m. SE.
Town trails Available from Tourist Information Centre, Wakeman's House, or Tourist Information Centre, Royal Baths Assembly Rooms, Crescent Road, Harrogate.
Shopping Market Place; Kirkgate; Fishergate; North Street; Westgate.
Sport Horse racing, The Racecourse.
AA 24 hour service
Tel. York 27698.

Rochdale G. Manch.

Wool brought early prosperity to this town set in a wooded valley below the Pennine moors. Later Rochdale was

renowned for its cotton, but the industry is now declining. The huge Gothic-style town hall was opened in 1871.

Rochdale was the birthplace of John Bright (1811-89), the celebrated Liberal opponent of the Corn Laws. The singer Gracie Fields was also born in the town, in 1898. She died in 1979.

Blackstone Edge, 2 miles east, is considered to be one of the best-preserved Roman roads in Britain, and there are Roman and Bronze Age relics from the surrounding area in Rochdale Museum.

Information Tel. 52110.
Location On the A58, 13 m. NE of Manchester.
Parking Hunters Lane; Smith Street; The Esplanade (2); St Mary's Gate; Penn Street; Drake Street; Yorkshire Street; High Street; Eastgate Street;

ROCHDALE'S PIONEERS

The Co-operative Movement started in 1844 when a group of Rochdale working men opened a shop in Toad Lane. They called themselves the Rochdale Society of Equitable Pioneers. The shop sold goods at ordinary prices and the members shared the profits.

The original shop of the Rochdale Pioneers is now a museum devoted to the Co-operative Movement.

ROCHESTER Kent

The fortress city that guards the Medway

The ancient cathedral city on the lower reaches of the River Medway is a major port and an industrial and commercial centre – part of the Medway Towns complex which also includes Strood, Chatham and Gillingham. Rochester's older buildings are clustered around the cathedral and in the High Street, where they were confined by the medieval walls. The city is closely associated with the novelist Charles Dickens, and features more often in his books than any other place, apart from London.

MEDWAY SENTINEL *The 125 ft high keep of Rochester Castle, built in 1126, is one of the finest examples of Norman military building in England.*

There has been a settlement at Rochester since before Roman times, and its Celtic name *Durobruae* means "the bridges of the stronghold".

The crossing over the Medway, on the route from Dover and Canterbury to London, gave the site its early strategic importance.

The Romans built a walled city, and traces of their defences can be seen in The Esplanade and in Eagle Alley, where they were incorporated into Saxon and medieval fortifications.

The Saxons re-fortified Rochester about AD 600. Four years later the Church of St Andrew was founded as the mother church of England's second bishopric after Canterbury, which had been established by St Augustin seven years earlier.

The site on which the apse of this church stood is marked by a brass strip on the floor of the present cathedral.

Though heavily restored, **Rochester Cathedral** is predominantly Norman. It stands between the High Street and Boley Hill, and was originally the hub of a group of ecclesiastical buildings which included a monastery, a monastic school and the bishop's palace.

Unique column figures

The Saxon church was sacked by the Vikings and its reconstruction was begun about 1077 by Bishop Gundulph, the Norman military and ecclesiastical architect who also built the White Tower in the Tower of London. **Gundulph's Tower**, a shell which stands on the north side of the cathedral, is from this period.

Building went on in the following century, but was several times interrupted by fire, and the main body of the church was completed in the period 1179-1240. The wooden ceiling of the nave is 15th century. The tower and spire were rebuilt in 1904.

The Norman west door is guarded by two column-figures, unique in England, which may represent Henry I and his queen or, as some think, King Solomon and the Queen of Sheba.

The cathedral library contains ancient manuscripts and documents, including a copy of Miles Coverdale's English version of the Bible, printed in 1535.

The monastery which Bishop Gundulph founded was largely destroyed during the Reformation, but the ruins of the chapter house and cloisters can still be seen in the cathedral precincts. Three of the 15th-century monastery gateways survive – **Prior's Gate**, which once formed part of King's School, **Sextry Gate**, which is also known as Deanery Gate, and **College** or **Chertsey's Gate**, which was the home of John Jasper in Dickens's *Edwin Drood*.

Place of pilgrimage

Beside the cathedral is the narrow **Pilgrim's Passage**, used by visitors to the tomb of St William of Perth, who was murdered in Rochester in 1201. Various miracles were attributed to him, and his grave became a place of pilgrimage which rivalled the shrine of Thomas Becket at Canterbury.

ADMIRAL'S LEGACY *Admiral Sir Cloudesley Shovell's coat of arms decorates the clock of the old Corn Exchange he had built for the city in 1706.*

St Nicholas's Church, near the cathedral, was built by the townspeople in 1423 after they had quarrelled with the monks and had been barred from the cathedral. The church was rebuilt in 1624, and now contains the diocesan offices.

Rochester Castle, which stands between the cathedral precincts and the river, was also begun by Bishop Gundulph shortly after the Norman Conquest, on a site which had been fortified by the Romans and the Saxons. The five-storey keep was added in 1126, and is little altered. Its walls are in some places 13 ft thick, and it contains a banqueting hall and a chapel. There are fine views from the top. The rest of the castle is largely ruined, and the bailey has been laid out as a park.

Below Castle Hill, on The Esplanade, is the **Bridge Chapel**, built in 1387 and restored in 1879 and again in 1937. It is now the board-room of the Bridge Wardens, a trust formed in 1391 to administer the vital crossing over the Medway.

Mentioned by Dickens

The 400-year-old **Royal Victoria and Bull Hotel**, close to the bridge, is mentioned in *Pickwick Papers*. Mr Pickwick was supposed to have stayed there, in either room 11 or room 17. The inn has a colonnaded yard.

Watts Charity, at 97 High Street, was founded in 1579 to house poor travellers, and is open to visitors. It was established by Richard Watts, who lived at Satis House in Boley Hill – now part of King's School. Founded in 604, this is one of Britain's oldest public schools.

A "Satis House" is mentioned by Charles Dickens in *Great Expectations*, but it is not Watts's mansion. The author's description more closely resembles **Restoration House**, a Tudor building in Maidstone Road opposite The Vines, a public park which was once the monastery vineyard. Charles II is reputed to have stayed at Restoration House on his return to England in 1660.

Rochester Guildhall Museum, in the High Street, was built in 1687. It is a red-brick building supported by columns, and the space underneath it was formerly the market place. The city's early charters are displayed inside. There are 23 municipal charters in all, making one of the finest collections in the country.

South of the town, the M2 motorway sweeps across the Medway on a cantilevered bridge. Beside it stands Fort Borstal, built in the 19th century to defend the area during the Napoleonic Wars. In 1902 it became a juvenile reformatory, which gave its name to the Borstal system.

Information Tel. Medway 43666.
Location On the A229, 8 m. N of Maidstone.
Parking Corporation Street (2); Blue Boar Lane; Epaul Lane; Almon Place; Lower High Street; The Common;

EASTGATE HOUSE *The 16th-century mansion on the main street houses the Charles Dickens Centre, and its grounds contain Dickens's chalet, formerly at Gads Hill Place.*

King Street; Union Street (all car parks).
District council Borough of Rochester upon Medway (Tel. Medway 77890).
Population 52,500.
E-C Wed. **M-D** Fri., Sat.
Police (Aa) Cazeneuve Street (Tel. Medway 41566).

Casualty hospital Medway, Windmill Road (Tel. Medway 46111).
Post office (Ba) Eastgate.
Theatre Medway Little Theatre, High Street (Tel. Medway 42096).
Public library (Ab) Northgate.
Places to see Castle **(Ab)**; Guildhall Museum **(Ab)** ; Eastgate House Charles Dickens Centre **(Aa)**; Restoration House **(Aa)** ; Watts Charity Hospital **(Aa)**; King's School **(Aa)**; Fort Borstal; Corn Exchange **(Ab)**.
Town trails Available from Tourist Information Centre, High Street.
Shopping High Street.
Events Dickens Festival (May/June); Admiralty Court and Admiral's Cruise (July).
Trade and industry Heavy machinery; shipping; board and paper-making.
AA 24 hour service Tel. Maidstone 55353.

ANCIENT CATHEDRAL *The stones of Rochester Cathedral are worn and dark with history – most of the building dates from between 1179 and 1240.*

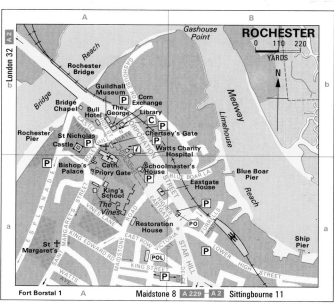

Ross-on-Wye H. & W.

Few people have made as great a mark on a town as John Kyrle (1637-1724) did on Ross. Kyrle introduced a public water supply to the town and laid out the Prospect Gardens. He also reconstructed and gave pinnacles to the unsafe 14th-century spire of the Church of St Mary, donated a great tenor bell to the church, and built a causeway to Wilton Bridge. The poet Alexander Pope praised him as the "Man of Ross", the name by which he has been known ever since. Kyrle's house, now two shops, still stands in the Market Square. The gateway to the Prospect Gardens, which provide superb views of the surrounding hills, is dedicated to him, and there is a walk named after him leading from an arch in the gardens. The gabled, sandstone almshouse in Church Street dates from 1575.

Information Tel. 62768.
Location On the A40, 11 m. NE of Monmouth.
Parking Henry Street; Brook End Street; Wilton Road; Millpond Street; Kyrle Street; Edde Cross Street (all car parks).
District council South Herefordshire (Tel. 64411).
Population 7,200.
E-C Wed. **M-D** Thur., Fri., Sat.
Police Old Maids Walk (Tel. 62345).
Casualty hospital Cottage Hospital, Gloucester Road (Tel. 62022).
Post office Gloucester Road.
Cinema Roxy, Broad Street (Tel. 62398).
Public library Market Square.
Places to see Market House, Market Square; Almshouse, Church Street.
Town trails Available from the Information Centre, Broad Street.
Shopping High Street; Broad Street; Gloucester Road.
Trade and industry Toolmaking; chemicals.
AA 24 hour service
Tel. Worcester 51070.

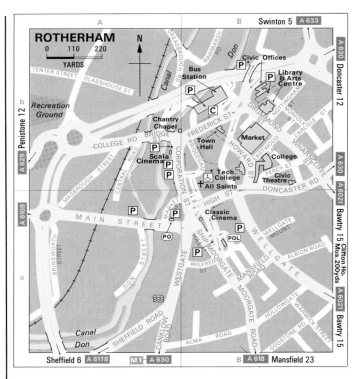

(map: ROTHERHAM)

Rotherham S. Yorks.

The Saxons had a market at Rotherham, and William the Conqueror gave the manor to his half-brother the Earl of Mortain. Rotherham's development into a busy industrial town began in the early 19th century with the discovery of coal and the development of the iron and steel industry by Joshua Walker and his family. Walker built Clifton House, now the town's museum.

At the heart of the town is the magnificent 15th-century parish church of All Saints.

Information Tel. 2121.
Location On the A630, 6 m. NE of Sheffield.
Parking Effingham Street; Greasbrough Road (via A630/Bridge Street); Nottingham/Norfolk Streets; Corporation Street (2); Market Street; Main Street; Wellgate; Moorgate Street (cps).
District council Borough of Rotherham (Tel. 2121).
Population 82,000.
E-C Thur. **M-D** Mon., Fri., Sat.
Police (Ba) Moorgate (Tel. 71121).
Casualty hospital Rotherham and District General, Moorgate Road (Tel. 62222).
Post office (Aa) Main Street.
Theatre Civic **(Bb)**, Doncaster Gate (Tel. 77150).
Cinemas Classic **(Ba)**, High Street (Tel. 2402); Scala **(Ab)**, Corporation Street (2316).
Public library (Bb) Walker Place.
Places to see Clifton House Museum; Roman fort, 1½ m. SW.
Shopping All Saints' Square; Howard Street; College Street; High Street; Bridgegate; Corporation Street; Effingham Street; Westgate.
Sport FA League football, Rotherham United FC, Millmoor Ground.
AA 24 hour service
Tel. Sheffield 28861.

Rothesay Strathclyde

The principal town of the Isle of Bute in the Firth of Clyde, Rothesay is a holiday resort and the island terminus for car ferries from Wemyss Bay on the mainland. Fine Victorian buildings surround the harbour, busy with small boats and holiday yachts that explore the Kyle of Bute straits to the north. The Bute Museum, in Stuart Street, illustrates the island's wildlife and contains archaeological finds.

The ruins of 11th-century Rothesay Castle, destroyed by Parliamentarians, stand in the town.

PASTORAL PEACE *The market town of Ross-on-Wye presents a peaceful image of rural England. The graceful spire of its parish church rises from timbered houses, trees and water meadows to sketch its reflection in the Wye.*

Information Tel. 2151.
Location On the A844, on the Isle of Bute in Firth of Clyde.
Parking Bridge Street; Chapel Hill Road (both car parks).
District council Argyll and Bute (Tel. Lochgilphead 2127).
Population 6,120.
E-C Wed.
Police High Street (Tel. 2121).
Casualty hospital Victoria Cottage Hospital, High Street (Tel. 3938).
Post office Bishop Street.
Public library Stuart Street.
Places to see Rothesay Castle; Bute Natural History Museum.
Town trails Available from Miss D. Marshall, The Museum, Stuart Street; or Information Centre, the Pier.
Shopping Montague Street; Victoria Street.
Car ferries To Wemyss Bay (Tel. Gourock 34567 or Rothesay 2707).
AA 24 hour service Tel. Glasgow (041) 812 0101.

Rothwell Northamptonshire

Shoe-making is the main industry in this ancient hillside town. The unusually long parish church of the Holy Trinity is 13th century, and retains original Norman work.

The fine Market House was built by Sir Thomas Tresham in 1577. He lived at nearby Rushton Hall, now a school for the blind. In the grounds is Triangular Lodge, where conspirators in the Gunpowder Plot of 1605 sometimes met.

Information Tel. Kettering 85211.
Location On the A6, 4 m. NW of Kettering.
Parking Bell Hill; Squire Hill; Market Hill (all car parks).
District council Borough of Kettering (Tel. 85211).
Population 6,400.
E-C Thur. M-D Mon.
Police London Road, Kettering (Tel. Kettering 83433).
Casualty hospital General, Rothwell Road, Kettering (Tel. Kettering 81141).
Post office Bridge Street.
Public library Market Hill.
Places to see Jesus Hospital; Manor House; Triangular Lodge at Rushton, 2 m. NE; Rushton Hall 2 m. NE.
Shopping High Street; Bridge Street.
AA 24 hour service Tel. Northampton 66241.

Royston Hertfordshire

The town grew up soon after the Norman Conquest around the intersection of the Roman road, Ermine Street, and the prehistoric trackway, the Icknield Way. A Lady Roisia erected a cross there, and the settlement started its existence as Roisia's Town. The Royse Stone, of Millstone Grit, brought by an ice sheet in the Ice Age, is still at the crossroads in the town centre.

Information Tel. Letchworth 6500.
Location On the A10, 14 m. SW of Cambridge.
Parking Baldock Street; The Warren; Melbourn Road; Market Hill (all car parks).
District council North Hertfordshire (Tel. Letchworth 6500).
Population 11,800.
E-C Thur. M-D Wed., Sat.
Police Priory Lane (Tel. 42222).
Casualty hospital Addenbrookes Hospital, Hills Road, Cambridge (Tel. Cambridge 45151).
Post office Baldock Street.
Cinema Priory, Melbourn Street (Tel. 43133).
Public library Market Hill.
Places to see Old Palace.
Shopping High Street; Angel Pavement Shopping Precinct; Melbourn Street.
Trade and industry Engineering; metal refining; flour milling.
AA 24 hour service Tel. Hatfield 62852.

Rugby Warwickshire

The home of Rugby public school is surrounded by lovely old villages and crossed by a peaceful meandering canal used for pleasure boating.

A granite plaque on a wall beside Rugby School Close commemorates "the exploit of William Webb Ellis", the pupil who originated rugby football in 1823. The school's most celeb-rated headmaster was Dr Thomas Arnold (1795-1842). He initiated many distinctive features of English public-school education, and lives on in the pages of Thomas Hughes's Tom Brown's Schooldays (1857).

Information Tel. 2687/71813.
Location On the A428/A426, 12 m. E of Coventry.
Parking Chapel Street; Gas Street; James Street; Little Church Street; Little Elborow Street; North Street; Bath Street; Westway (all car parks).
District council Rugby (Tel. 77177).
Population 59,500.
E-C Wed. M-D Mon., Fri. and Sat.
Police Newbold Road (Tel. 74831).
Casualty hospital St Cross Hospital, Barby Road (Tel. 72831).
Post office (Ba) North Street.
Theatre Rugby Theatre (Bb), Henry Street (Tel. 32488).
Public library (Aa) St Matthew's Street.
Places to see Rugby School (Ba); Miranda's shop (oldest building in Rugby), Chapel Street; Gilbert's rugby shop and museum, St Matthew's Street.
Shopping Regent Street; North Street; Church Street; Market Place.
Trade and industry Engineering; cement; agriculture.
Sport Rugby football, Rugby RFC, Webb Ellis Road.
AA 24 hour service Tel. Birmingham (021) 550 4858.

CLOSE PLAY Rugby football began on Rugby School Close, when William Webb Ellis carried the ball instead of kicking it in a soccer match.

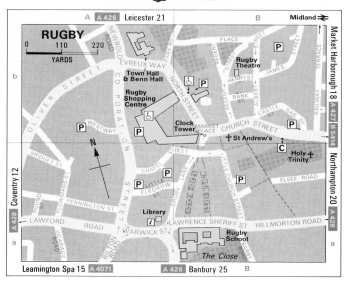

Runcorn Cheshire

In the 10th century Alfred the Great's daughter, Aethelfleda, governor of Mercia, built a fort at a site on the River Mersey named Runckhorn. The Normans made the settlement a dependent manor of the Barony of Halton.

The town's industrial growth began in the late 18th century when a barge dock was built on the newly completed Manchester-Liverpool canal system. Quarrying became important, and Runcorn sandstone was used for many local buildings and docks. By the end of the 19th century, however, chemicals dominated the town's industry.

In 1964 Runcorn was designated a New Town, and since then its planned growth has attracted town planners from all over the world.

Today, 900 years after the Conquest, local-government reorganisation has once more absorbed Runcorn into Halton.

Information Tel. 76776 or 69656.
Location On the A533, 14 m. SE of Liverpool.
Parking Princess Street; High Street; Bridgewater Street; Wellington Street; Shopping City (all car parks).
District council Borough of Halton (Tel. Liverpool (051) 424 2061).
Population 64,100.
E-C Wed. **M-D** Tues., Thur., Sat.
Police Shopping City (Tel. 713456).
Casualty hospital Warrington District General, Lovely Lane (Tel. Warrington 35911).
Post office High Street.
Cinema City Cinemas, Shopping City (Tel. 717144).
Public libraries Egerton Street; Shopping City.
Town trails Available from Information Centre, Church Street.
Shopping Shopping City.
Event Carnival (June).
Trade and industry Chemicals; salt; engineering; brewing.
AA 24 hour service
Tel. Liverpool (051) 709 7252.

TRIBUTE *The Kennedy Memorial stands on the slopes of Runnymede meadows.*

Runnymede Surrey

It was in a meadow at Runnymede, in 1215, that the feudal barons forced King John to put his seal to Magna Carta, or Great Charter, which promised liberty for his subjects.

A memorial to Magna Carta presented by the American Bar Association, stands in the meadow at the foot of Cooper's Hill. At the top is another memorial, commemorating the 20,000 Commonwealth airmen of the Second World War who died with no known grave. A third memorial, near by, is to President John F. Kennedy.

Since 1974, Runnymede has been the name of the district council that administers Egham with Chertsey.

Egham, which lies east of the meadow, was a crossing place over the Thames and a coaching stop on the old Exeter Road, which climbs up Egham Hill. At the top of the hill is the great red pile of the Royal Holloway College, which was opened in 1886 as a women's college of London University.

Chertsey, just downstream from Egham, grew up round a Benedictine abbey founded in 666. It was dissolved in 1538, and only a few fragments now remain in a field north of the parish church of St Peter. Windsor Street has several handsome 18th-century town houses. The Cedars contains the town museum.

On the slopes of 240 ft high St Ann's Hill, part of which is a public park, stand some of the garden buildings erected in the 18th century by the politician Charles James Fox (1749-1806), including a Gothic-style tea-room.

Information Tel. Weybridge 45500.
Location On the A30, 5 m. SE of Windsor.
Parking Chertsey: Guildford Street; Heriot Road; Guildford Road. Egham: High Street; Hummer Road; Church Road; Station Road; Windsor Road; Runnymede Pleasure Grounds (all car parks).
District council Runnymede (Tel. Weybridge 45500).
Population 71,000.
E-C Chertsey (Wed.). Egham (Thur.).
Police High Street, Egham (Tel. 33781/2).
Casualty hospital Guildford Road, Chertsey (Tel. Ottershaw 2000).
Post offices Guildford Street, Chertsey. Station Road, Egham.
Public libraries Guildford Street, Chertsey. High Street, Egham.
Places to see Museum, Windsor Street, Chertsey. Literary Institute Museum, High Street, Egham.
Shopping Guildford Street, Chertsey. High Street, Egham.
AA 24 hour service
Tel. Guildford 72841.

Ruthin Clwyd

The Maen Huail ("Huail Stone") in the market square of this old market town is where King Arthur is said to have had Huail, his rival in love, beheaded. Also in the square is the old courthouse and prison, dated 1401, and now a bank. From its eaves projects a sawn-off gibbet, which was last used in 1679, for a Franciscan priest, Charles Mahoney.

The ruins of Ruthin's 13th-century castle stand beside a 19th-century Gothic castle, now a hotel.

Nantclwyd House, in Castle Street, is a half-timbered 14th–16th-century mansion (not open to the public).

Information Tel. 2201.
Location On the A494, 12 m. SW of Mold.
Parking Clwyd Street; Dog Lane; Rhos Street; Park Road (all cps).
District council Glyndŵr (Tel. 2201).
Population 4,400.
E-C Thur. **M-D** First Tues. in month.
Police Record Street (Tel. 2041).
Casualty hospital Glanclwyd Hospital, Farm Lane, Bodelwyddan (Tel. St Asaph 583910).
Post office St Peter's Square.
Public library Clwyd Street.
Places to see Church of St Peter; Christ's Hospital; Ruthin School; Ruthin Gaol (now Record Office and Library), Clwyd Street.
Town trails Available from Record Office, Clwyd Street.
Shopping St Peter's Square; Clwyd Street; Well Street.
AA 24 hour service
Tel. Llandudno 79066.

POWER AND GLORY *The cooling towers of a power station across the Mersey contrast sharply with the spire of Runcorn's Church of All Saints.*

Ryde Isle of Wight

The Victorians made the Isle of Wight a holiday island, and nowhere is their influence more apparent than in Ryde.

Bay-windowed houses line the streets that climb steeply from the seafront, and elegant hotels stand back from the wide, tree-lined esplanade. The town hall, in Lind Street, has a colonnaded façade and a handsome clock-tower.

The town faces across The Solent towards Portsmouth, and the half-mile long pier – built in 1813 – is the island's main entry point for passenger ferries. There is a modern hoverport close to the pier entrance, and the journey between Ryde and Southsea was the world's first scheduled hovercraft service.

Ryde's 5 miles of sandy beach is particularly spacious at low tide, and the Esplanade has attractive gardens.

ROOFTOPS OF RYE *The quarterboy standing above the town is one of two which strike the quarters of a 16th-century clock on St Mary's Church.*

Information Tel. 62905/62581.
Location On the A3054, 7 m. E of Newport.
Parking Lind Street; George Street; Esplanade; Garfield Road; St Thomas' Street; Broadway Crescent (all car parks).
District council Borough of Medina (Tel. Newport I.o.W. 522493).
Population 24,300.
E-C Thur.
Police (Aa) Station Road (Tel. 62222).
Casualty hospital Royal Isle of Wight County Hospital, Swanmore Road (Tel. 63311).
Post office (Ab) Union Street.
Theatre Esplanade Pavilion (Bb) (Tel. 63465).
Cinema Commodore 1, 2 and 3 (Aa), Star Street (Tel. 64930).
Public library (Aa) George Street.
Shopping Union Street; High Street.
Car ferry Fishbourne to Portsmouth (Tel. Wootton Bridge 882432).
AA 24 hour service
Tel. Newport I.o.W. 522653.

Rye E. Sussex

In Elizabethan times the port of Rye was heavily armed with cannon, but such defences were useless against the town's ageless enemy, the sea. Silting of the harbour was a constant problem, and as the sea receded it left the town high and dry. It is now some 2 miles inland.

Many of Rye's streets have Elizabethan buildings, some with Georgian frontages. One example is the bow-fronted Apothecary's Shop in the High Street.

The town's best-known inn, the Mermaid, dates from the 15th and 16th centuries. In the 18th century it was a favourite haunt of smugglers, and it is said that they sat at the tables with loaded pistols in open defiance of the Customs men.

Near the Mermaid is Lamb House, an 18th-century mansion which, in 1898, became the home of the American author Henry James, who

lived there until his death in 1916.

In the 14th century, Rye was a walled town with four gates. The Land, or North Gate, is the only survivor. The gate was closed by a portcullis on its northern side – the grooves in the gateway can still be seen – and by heavy oak gates on the southern side.

The remains of the seaward defences are represented by the Ypres Tower, so-called because it was the residence of a John de Ypres in 1430.

In front of Ypres Tower is the Gun Garden, the site of Rye's main artillery defences in Tudor times.

South of Rye is Camber Castle, which suffered the same fate as the town – it was left stranded by the receding sea. The castle, built about 1540, was abandoned in 1642.

Information Tel. 2293.
Location On the A259, 12 m. NE of Hastings.
Parking Udimore Road; Wish Street; Ferry Road; Cinque Ports Street; Rope Walk; Bedford Place; Fishmarket Road (all car parks).
District council Rother (Tel. Bexhill-on-Sea 216321).
Population 4,300.
E-C Tues. **M-D** Thur.
Police Cinque Ports Street (Tel. 2112).
Casualty hospital Royal East Sussex Hospital, Cambridge Road, Hastings (Tel. Hastings 434513).
Post office Cinque Ports Street.
Public library Lion Street.
Places to see Ypres Tower Museum, Gun Garden Steps; Lamb House; Camber Castle, 2 m. S on A259; Art Gallery, Ockman Lane; Rye Town Model, foot of Mermaid Street.
Town trails Available from Tourist Information Centre, Ferry Road.
Shopping High Street; Cinque Ports Street.
Event Musical Festival (Sept.).
AA 24 hour service
Tel. Maidstone 55353.

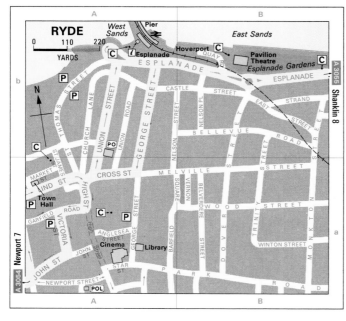

S

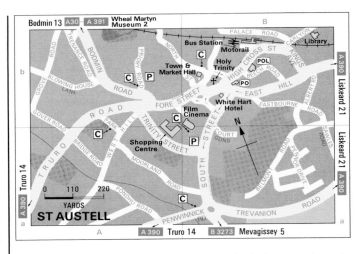

Bodmin 13 · A30 · A 391 · Wheal Martyn Museum 2
Bus Station · Motorail · Library
Town & Market Hall · Holy Trinity · POL
White Hart Hotel
Film Cinema
Shopping Centre
Truro 14 · A 390
0 110 220 YARDS
ST AUSTELL
Liskeard 21 · A 390
A 390 · Truro 14 · B 3273 · Mevagissey 5

Saffron Walden Essex

The autumn-flowering crocus which gave the town the first part of its name was cultivated locally on a wide scale until the end of the 18th century. The flower is purple, but it makes a yellow dye for cloth. It was also used as a source of perfume, a flavouring for food and a medicine to treat catarrh and nervous ailments.

The plant is still privately grown, but the saffron now sold commercially is imported.

Saffron was expensive in the Middle Ages, as it is today, and the prosperity it helped to bring Walden is evident from the many medieval buildings in the streets around the Market Square.

Farming and woollen cloth were the other sources of the town's wealth. Agriculture still thrives, but cloth-making has yielded to engineering, printing and agrochemical research.

Saffron Walden has been settled since prehistoric times, and there are three earthworks near the town.

The Norman Mandeville family built Walden Castle in the 12th century. Only the ruins of the keep re-main, and next to them is the town museum. The Mandevilles also founded a priory at Audley End, 1 mile west. It was dissolved in the reign of Henry VIII, and the land eventually passed to the Earl of Suffolk, who began the present mansion on the site in 1603. The house was substantially restored by Robert Adam in the 18th century.

The huge church of St Mary the Virgin, set back from Church Street, was reconstructed between 1450 and 1526, and the spire was added in 1832. The church, nearly 200 ft long, is one of the finest in Essex.

Saffron Walden's central streets still follow the grid established in the Middle Ages. One of the best-preserved buildings from this period is a 15th-century house, now a youth hostel, on the corner of Myddylton Place. In the High Street, there are late-Georgian houses.

The largest turf maze in England, with a path which twists and turns for about 1 mile, is preserved at the eastern end of the Common. It was probably constructed in the Middle Ages.

Information Tel. 24282.
Location On the A130, 13 m. SE of Cambridge.
Parking Common Hill; Fairycroft Road; Catons Lane; Market Square; Debden Road (all car parks).
District council Uttlesford (Tel. 23124).
Population 12,500.
E-C Thur. **M-D** Tues., Sat.
Police East Street (Tel. 23131).
Casualty hospital Radwinter Road (Tel. 22464).
Post office High Street.
Public library Corn Exchange, Market Square.
Places to see Castle Museum; Audley End House, 1 m. W; Ring Hill Iron Age fort, 1½ m. W; Town Hall; The Maze, off Chaters Hill.
Shopping High Street; Market Place; George Street; King Street.
AA 24 hour service
Tel. Chelmsford 617111.

LIVELY PLASTERWORK *Legendary figures, foliage and designs decorate the overhanging gables of the medieval houses in Church Street, Saffron Walden.*

St Albans see page 348

St Andrews see page 350

St Austell Cornwall

The white "mountains" on the northern fringes of the town are spoil-heaps of sand from the china-clay quarries. The clay is used in making porcelain, paper, medicines and cosmetics, and is shipped all over the world. The Wheal Martyn China Clay Museum records the history of the industry on a site that was one of the most complete and best preserved clay works of the last century. The works have been restored to their original state and include four kilns and a 35 ft water-wheel, the largest in operation in south-west England.

St Austell stands on a steep slope, and a network of narrow streets spreads out from the Town and Market Hall, an Italianate granite building put up in 1844.

The parish church has a 15th-century tower of local yellow stone. It is heavily carved near the top, and niches contain sculpted stone figures. Inside, there is a sharp curve in the central aisle, possibly a deliberate feature but more probably the result of difficulties encountered in the building.

The White Hart Hotel is an 18th-century inn, possibly earlier, which displays an oil-painting by Augustus John, and four by John Nash.

The former Quaker Meeting House, built in 1829, is in Georgian style.

St Austell has given its name to the bay which lies 2 miles south of the town centre. It stretches from Black Head in the west to Gribbin Head in the east, and is an area of sandy beaches, cliffs and small villages. Porthpean, at the western end of the bay, is a former pilchard-fishing centre, while Duporth is a more modern resort. Charlestown has a small harbour, once used to ship china clay, and is now a haven for yachtsmen.

At Crinnis and Par there are pleasure beaches, and Par is also the harbour through which china clay is now exported. Polkerris, at the eastern end of the bay, is another former pilchard-fishing village.

Information Tel. Newquay 71345.
Location On the A390, 13 m. SW of Bodmin.
Parking South Street; Priory, off Bodmin Road; White Hart, on East Hill (all car parks).
District council Borough of Restormel (Tel. 4466).
Population 30,700.
E-C Thur. **M-D** Wed. (in summer).
Police (Bb) High Cross Street (Tel. 2313).
Casualty hospital City Hospital, Infirmary Hill, Truro (Tel. Truro 74242).
Post office (Bb) High Cross Street.

Cinema Film Centre, Aylmer Square **(Bb)** (Tel. 3750).
Public library (Bb) Carlyon Road.
Places to see Market Hall **(Bb)**; Wheal Martyn Museum, 2 m. N.
Shopping Fore Street; Aylmer Square.
Motorail Tel. 5671.
AA 24 hour service Tel. Truro 76455.

St Helens Merseyside

The glass industry in St Helens began in the 18th century due to the availability of coal, sand and good transport. The Pilkington Glass Factory now dominates the town, named after a much-rebuilt 14th-century church.

St Helens became a coal-mining area as far back as the 16th century, when pits were sunk at Sutton Heath. The Sankey Navigation Canal, built in 1762 to transport coal from St Helens to the River Mersey, was the first artificial waterway completed in Britain for 200 years but has now been partly filled in.

The Rainhill trials in which Stephenson's first steam engine, *The*

HISTORY OF GLASS *Relics in the Pilkington Glass Museum, St Helens, include Roman, German and English ware.*

Rocket, proved an all round winner took place in St Helens in 1830.

The conductor Sir Thomas Beecham (1879-1961) was born in the town.

Information Tel. 24061.
Location On the A58, 12 m. NE of Liverpool.
Parking Birchley Street; Chalon Way; Tontine; Bridge Street; Water Street; Birchley Street; King Street; St Mary's (all car parks).
District council Metropolitan Borough of St Helens (Tel. 24061).
Population 98,800.
E-C Thur. **M-D** Mon.-Sat. (closed Thur. afternoon).
Police College Street (Tel. 22222).
Casualty hospital St Helens, Marshalls Cross Road (Tel. 26633).
Post office Bridge Street.
Theatre Theatre Royal, Corporation Street (Tel. 28467).
Cinema ABC, Bridge Street (Tel. 23392).

Public library Gamble Institute.
Places to see Pilkington Glass Museum, Prescot Road; St Helens Museum, Lincoln House, Corporation Street.
Shopping Bridge Street; St Mary's Arcade; Church Street; Duke Street; Baldwin Street.
Event St Helens Show (July).
Sport Rugby League, Knowsley Road; Haydock Park Racecourse.
AA 24 hour service Tel. Liverpool (051) 709 7252.

St Helier Jersey

In 1204, Philip II of France marched into Rouen and snatched the Dukedom of Normandy from the vacillating King John. All that was left to the English was a small part of Normandy, a handful of islands scattered among the shoals between the Cotentin Peninsula and the north coast of Brittany. More than 750 years later the people of the Channel Islands, of which St Helier, capital of Jersey, is the largest town, remain loyal to the monarch while prizing their independence from Westminster.

The heart of St Helier, the Royal Square, was once the market place. Chestnut trees border the square lined by the Royal Court House and the States Chamber, meeting place of the island parliament.

In 1781, when all Europe was in arms against Britain, the French tried to capture Jersey. The invading troops, who landed at La Rocque, were routed by the local militia, led by 24-year-old Major Francis Peirson, who died in the battle that saved the island. A public house in Royal Square, where he fell, is named after him.

On a rocky outcrop to the west of St Helier Harbour stands Elizabeth Castle, named after Elizabeth I by Sir Walter Raleigh when he was Governor of Jersey (1600-3). The 19-year-old Charles II, proclaimed king in Jersey after his father was executed, fled to the castle in September 1649. From Elizabeth Castle he reigned over the last fragment of his dominions until February 1650, when he sailed for Holland and ten years of exile.

He left in Elizabeth Castle one of the great Royalists, Sir George Carteret. Sir George stubbornly resisted Cromwell and the Commonwealth until an invading force took the castle on December 15, 1651. Charles did not forget. After the Restoration he rewarded Sir George by the grant of a province in America. Carteret called it New Jersey.

St Helier's other fortress, Fort Regent, stands above the harbour. Built in 1806-14, it is now a sports and entertainment centre.

Most of St Helier was built in the 19th century when, after the defeat of Napoleon at Trafalgar and Waterloo, the island became a favourite retreat of the British. In this century its liberal tax laws have made it a haven for the wealthy. Its recent growth as a financial centre makes this a major industry, alongside tourism and agriculture.

Since the grim five years of German Occupation (1940-5), when the Channel Islands were the only British territory occupied by the Nazis, recovery has been remarkable.

(All tel. nos.: Jersey Central.)
Information Tel. 78000.
Parking Cheapside; Victoria Avenue; Sand Street; La Route du Fort (3); Green Street; Belmont Road; Minden Place; Pier Road; Elizabeth Lane; Midvale Road; Nelson Street; Snow Hill; The Weighbridge (all car parks).
Population 20,000. **E-C** Thur.
Police Rouge Bouillon (Tel. 75511).
Casualty hospital (Ab) General Hospital, Gloucester Street (Tel. 71000).
Post office (Aa) Broad Street.
Theatre Opera House **(Ab)**, Gloucester Street (Tel. 22165).
Cinemas Odeon **(Bb)**, Bath Street (Tel. 24166); Ciné de France, St Saviour's Road (71611).
Public library (Aa) Royal Square.
Places to see Fort Regent **(Aa)**, Pier Road; Mont Orgueil Castle, Gorey; Elizabeth Castle, St Aubin's Bay; Museums at la Hougue Bie; German Military Underground Hospital, St Peter's Valley; Zoological Park, Trinity; St Peter's Bunker and Occupation Museum, St Peter; Jersey Motor Museum, St Peter; Battle of Flowers Museum, St Ouen; Tropical Gardens, St Ouen; Jersey Museum and Barreau Art Gallery **(Aa)**, Pier Road.
Shopping King Street, Queen Street, Bath Street, West's Centre and Halkett Street precincts; The Parade; Colomberie; Halkett Place.
Event Battle of Flowers (Aug.).
Car ferries To Guernsey, Weymouth and Portsmouth (Tel. 77122); to France (74458).
AA service 0900-1900 hours (Tel. 23344).

THE APPEAL OF ST IVES *The attractions of the resort are various – a town of painted cottages and steep, winding ways that beg to be explored; a typically Cornish harbour and clean white beaches for bathing and surfing.*

St Ives Cornwall
The narrow, winding ways and coloured stone cottages of this former pilchard fishing port have inspired countless artists since James McNeill Whistler and Walter Sickert first depicted its charms in the 19th century.

St Ives is named after St Ia, who is said to have arrived from Ireland in a coracle in the 6th century and built a chapel on the "Island", the headland at the western limit of St Ives Bay. The fishermen's chapel of St Nicholas now stands on the supposed site, by the remains of an ancient British settlement.

The town's best-known artist, the sculptress Barbara Hepworth (1903-75), is commemorated by a collection of her work in the Trewyn Studio, and her figure of *Our Lady and Child* in the 15th-century parish church.

(All tel. nos.: Penzance.)
Information Tel. 796297
Location On the B3306, 10 m. N of Penzance.
Parking Trenwith; The Island; The Station; Porthmeor Beach; Barnoon;

Porthgwidden (all car parks).
District council Penwith (Tel. 2341).
Population 11,000.
E-C Thur.
Police Wills Lane (Tel. 795305).
Casualty hospital Edward Hain Memorial (Tel. 795044).
Post office Tregenna Place.
Cinema The Royal, Royal Square (Tel. 796843).
Public library Gabriel Street.
Places to see Barbara Hepworth Museum, Trewyn Studio; Cinematographic Museum, Fore Street; Leach Pottery, High Stennack; Barnoon Hill; Museum, Wheal Dream.
Shopping Tregenna Place; Tregenna Hill; Fore Street; High Street; The Wharf.
Event Feast Monday celebration (Feb.).
AA 24 hour service
Tel. Truro 76455.

St Neots Cambridgeshire
Benedictine monks founded a priory near the River Great Ouse in the 10th century and named it after St Neot, a Saxon holy man who is said to have been a spiritual adviser to King Alfred. Neot's bones were brought to the priory – possibly stolen – from the church near Bodmin in Cornwall where they were originally buried. The priory was destroyed after the Dissolution of the Monasteries in 1539, and only the foundations remain.

The market town which grew up around the priory has a large square. The wooden vault of the 15th-century Church of St Mary is ornately carved with angels, animals and birds.

Information Tel. Huntingdon 72458.
Location On the A45, 9 m. S of Huntingdon.
Parking Riverside Park; River Terrace; Tebbutts Road; Market Square; Priory Lane (all car parks).

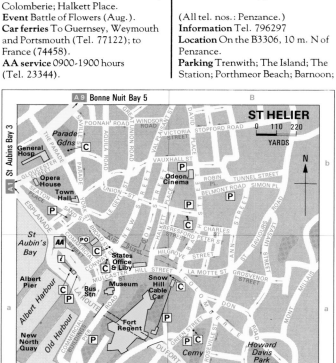

District council Huntingdon
(Tel. Huntingdon 52181).
Population 21,200.
E-C Tues. **M-D** Thur.
Police Dovehouse Close
(Tel. 73131).
Casualty hospital Bedford General,
Kempston Road, Bedford
(Tel. Bedford 55122).
Post office New Street.
Public library Huntingdon Street.
Shopping High Street; New Street.
AA 24 hour service
Tel. Cambridge 312302.

St Peter Port Guernsey

Approached from the sea, St Peter
Port can be seen rising behind its
magnificent harbour. The town, at
least 1,000 years old, climbs the hillside and vanishes over the skyline.
Cobbled streets and quaint, steep
steps wander upwards between buildings that seem to stand on each
other's rooftops.

The Town Church, which stands
below tiers of white-fronted buildings, is the finest church in the Channel Islands. It was founded in the
12th century and still retains its chancel from the period. Opposite, flanking the southern arm of the harbour,
is Castle Cornet, which in 1651 became the last Royalist stronghold to
surrender to Parliament during the
Civil War.

In the parish of St Andrew's there is
an unusual church, the Little Chapel
at Les Vauxbolets. It was built in the
1920s from pieces of broken china by
a monk, Brother Deodat.

There are always many boats in the
harbour: yachts, passenger-carrying
launches, cargo steamers, fishing
smacks and locally built schooners. In
the 18th century the harbour was
often crowded with ships of a different kind – the private warships built
in the shipyards at Havelot, La Piette
and Les Banques which provided
Guernsey with its chief industry –
privateering. Since the Second
World War Guernsey has prospered
from tomatoes and tourism.

Guernsey, as one of the Channel
Islands, is part of the last remnant of
the great Dukedom of Normandy that
belonged, long before 1066 and the
Battle of Hastings, to the Conqueror's grandfather. Through this
historic link the islands belong to the
English Crown, but they are independent of Parliament at Westminster,
an independence which the islanders
defend as vigorously as they protest
their loyalty to the monarch.

The island still governs itself under
a system that dates back to the days of
the Normans. A Lieutenant-
Governor represents the crown, and
the States, the elected parliament,
meets under the chairmanship of the
Bailiff, who combines the roles of
Speaker and head of the judiciary.

In Union Street there is a pillar-box
on the site of the first post-box
erected in the British Isles, in 1853.
Pillar-boxes were introduced from
France by the novelist Anthony Trol-
lope (1815-82) who was a post office
surveyor.

Since 1945 tourism has boomed in
Guernsey, and now more than
350,000 visitors travel there each
summer. In addition, wealthy Britons
have settled there permanently to
take advantage of the island's serenity
– and its low rates of tax.

(All tel. nos.: Guernsey.)
Information Tel. 23552.
Parking The Bordage; Upland Road;
Calerie Battery; Truchot Street;
Victoria Pier; Albert Pier; South
Esplanade; Mignot Plateau (all cps).
Population 14,900.
E-C Thur. **M-D** Daily.
Police (Bb) St James Street
(Tel. 25111).
Casualty hospital Princess Elizabeth,
Le Vauquiedor (Tel. 25241).
Post office (Bb) Smith Street.
Theatres Little **(Ba)**, off Clifton
(Tel. 22422); Beau Séjour Leisure
Centre, La Butte (Tel. 27211).
Cinemas Gaumont 1 and 2 **(Bb)**, St
Julian's Avenue (Tel. 20022); Beau
Séjour Leisure Centre, La Butte
(Tel. 28555).
Public library (Ba) Market Street.
Places to see Guernsey Museum
(Ab); Hauteville House; Victoria
Tower **(Ab)**; Aquarium; Motor
Museum; Château des Marais at
Bouet (Ivy Castle).
Shopping High Street; Mill Street;
Market Street.
Events Notre Dame Music Festival
(July/Aug.); Battle of Flowers (Aug.).
Car ferries To Weymouth,
Portsmouth and Jersey (Tel. 24742).
AA service 0900-1900 hours
(Tel. 22984).

ROMANTIC EXILE

For 15 years St Peter Port was the
home in exile of the French
Romantic poet, novelist and
dramatist Victor Hugo (1802-
85). An opponent of the Emperor
Napoleon III, he fled to Guernsey
in 1855. He spent most of his
exile in Hauteville House, which
is open to the public. There he
wrote his novel *The Toilers of the
Sea* (1866), which portrays the
islanders among whom he made
his home.

*Victor
Hugo's
statue, by
Jean
Boucher,
stands in
Candie
Gardens.*

ST ALBANS Hertfordshire

Cathedral city by a Roman's shrine

Nearly 2,000 years ago St Albans was one of the largest Roman towns in Britain. The Romans called the town Verulamium. It was there, about AD 209, that a Roman soldier was put to death for sheltering a Christian priest. The soldier's name was Alban, and he was later canonised as Britain's first Christian martyr. By the early 5th century, when the Romans left Britain, there was a shrine on the execution spot. Verulamium crumbled, but some time later the Saxons occupied the site. Then, in the 8th century, they built an abbey there – dedicated to St Alban. By the 11th century the abbey had given its name to the town which grew up around it.

The Roman town of Verulamium is west of the city centre, on the banks of the River Ver. The town was a "municipium", where the citizens had the same rights as those of Rome.

A hypocaust, or heating system for a suite of baths, survives and is housed in a special building in **Verulamium Park**. Sections of the town's 3rd-century walls, and the remnants of a street of shops also survive.

Verulamium Museum contains plans and a model of the town as it was in the 3rd century; the finest collection of Roman decorated wall-plaster in Britain; well-preserved mosaics, with shell, lion and sea-god motifs; a ceiling with bird paintings; pottery, glassware, jewellery and coins; and a large collection of tools.

Hilltop shrine

St Albans' first abbey was built on the site of St Alban's shrine, on a hill above Verulamium. The first Norman abbot, Paul de Caen, demolished the Saxon monastery in 1077 and built a new one, but in the course of the Dissolution of the Monasteries, in 1539, nearly all the buildings were destroyed. Only the abbey church – which became the parish church – and its great gateway were left intact, though part of another gate, the **Waxhouse Gate**, still survives.

The church, now the **cathedral**, is 550 ft long – one of the longest in Britain.

The surviving Norman sections of the cathedral are the tower, transepts, choir and eastern bays of the nave. In the 13th century the building was extended westwards to its present length, and in the 14th century the Lady Chapel was added to the east side. From the Dissolution until 1870 this chapel served as the local grammar school.

Some of the most notable features of the cathedral include the massive Norman piers in the nave, decorated with 13th and 14th-century paintings; the great arches of the tower soaring to more than 100 ft; and the ancient pillars in the transepts, probably taken from the original Saxon abbey. There are fine Norman decorations on the doorway of the south transept. The reconstructed marble base of St Alban's shrine, with its carved scene of the martyrdom, is overlooked by the superbly decorated 15th-century watching chamber for the monk who guarded the shrine. Near by is the 14th-century brass of Abbot Thomas de la Mare. It was in de la Mare's time, about 1365, that the abbey gateway was erected.

In 1877 the abbey became a cathedral, and St Albans was made a city.

Oldest inn

A footpath from the cathedral leads to **Ye Old Fighting Cocks,** which is tucked away beside the River Ver. The octagonal timber-framed inn, where cock-fighting was once held, claims to be the oldest inhabited licensed house in England. Medieval, but of unknown date, it was once a fishing lodge for the abbey's monks.

In the 10th century the Saxon abbot Ulsinus established three churches in the town – St Michael's, St Peter's and St Stephen's.

Some Saxon work survives inside St Stephen's, but St Peter's was virtually rebuilt in the 15th century and was twice restored in the 19th century. It contains a monument of 1723 to Edward Strong, Sir Christopher Wren's master mason in the building of St Paul's Cathedral.

St Michael's Church was built in 948 over the ruins of the Roman forum, or market place. It retains its original Saxon nave and chancel walls, and 12th-century Norman aisles. Inside are 14th-century brasses, a superb Jacobean carved pulpit and a monument to Sir Francis Bacon (1561-1626), the statesman and writer, who was Lord Verulam and Viscount St Albans.

Bacon's family home was **Gorhambury**, 2 miles west of the city. It was there that he retired in 1621 after being impeached for bribery and stripped of his office of Lord Chancellor. He lived in the 16th-century manor house that now stands in ruins in the park. There he devoted himself to the scientific and philosophical writings which have made him famous. The present house, built in the 18th century, is the home of the Earl of Verulam. It contains many relics of the Bacon family, and is open to the public on Thursdays during the summer.

Almshouses

The red-brick **Pemberton Almshouses**, opposite St Peter's Church, were founded in 1627 by Roger Pemberton, member of a prominent local family. An arrowhead in the gate recalls a legend that Pemberton built the almshouses in atonement for accidentally killing a widow with an arrow while hunting.

Sarah Jennings, wife of the 1st Duke of Marlborough, was born in the city. She is remembered by the **Marlborough Almshouses** in Hatfield Road, which she built in 1733. The duchess often stayed in the town while her husband, John Churchill, the 1st Duke of Marlborough and victor of Blenheim in 1704, was fighting on the Continent. The Churchill family dominated the city's politics for many years.

The **Clock Tower** at the junction of French Row and High Street dates from the early 15th century. It was originally a curfew tower, the clock being a Victorian addition.

Opposite the Clock Tower, in the High Street, is a plastered arch which

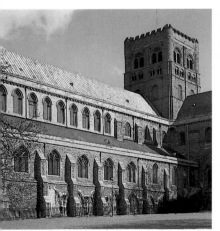

NORMAN ABBEY *The red-brick tower of St Albans Abbey was built with materials taken from Verulamium.*

CLOCK TOWER *The 77 ft high tower has a curfew bell of 1335.*

ABBEY GATEWAY *The gateway was the principal entrance to the monastery and its church. It was the town gaol for many years, until 1868.*

WHERE MONKS FISHED *Fishpool Street takes its name from a fishpond that lay near by in medieval times. The Georgian fronts lining the raised pavements cover much older structures, among them pilgrims' hostels.*

leads to the cathedral. This is all that remains of a 15th-century gateway to the abbey, known as the **Waxhouse Gate**, where candles and tapers were made and sold to pilgrims visiting St Alban's shrine.

French Row, which runs down to the Clock Tower, is a medieval street, now open to pedestrians only. It takes its name from the French soldiers, recruited by the barons to fight King John, who were quartered there in 1216. The 15th-century Fleur-de-Lys Inn in French Row incorporates some of the timber of an earlier inn where King John of France was kept prisoner after being captured at the Battle of Poitiers in 1356.

The town played a major role in the Wars of the Roses. In 1455 Yorkists defeated Lancastrians in St Peter's Street and took Henry VI prisoner. Six years later the Lancastrians turned the tables at **Bernard's Heath**, 1 mile north of the city centre, and released the king.

Holywell Hill, which runs south from the High Street, is an attractive street of Georgian buildings. It was once lined by medieval inns, the finest surviving example of which is the 15th-century White Hart.

Medieval meeting place

In Romeland, in front of the abbey's great gate, is a public garden which was a public meeting place in medieval times. During the Peasants' Revolt of 1381, rioting townsfolk burned court rolls and other documents there; and in 1555 George Tankerfield, a Protestant baker, was burned there at the stake as a heretic.

There are two other museums in St Albans in addition to the one at Verulamium. The **City Museum** has folk-life and natural-history displays and the Salaman collection of craftsmen's tools. **St Albans Organ Museum** is a private collection of fairground and mechanical organs which is open to the public on Sundays.

Information Tel. 64511.
Location On the A6, 10 m. N of Barnet.
Parking Drovers Way; Bricket Road; Keyfield; Hart Road; Civic Centre; Russell Avenue; Adelaide Street (all car parks).
District council City of St Albans (Tel. 66100).
Population 50,900.
E-C Thur. **M-D** Wed., Sat.
Police (Ba) Victoria Street (Tel. 54681).
Casualty hospital Normandy Road (Tel. 52211).
Post office (Bb) St Peters Street.
Theatre Abbey Theatre, Holywell Hill (Tel. 57861).
Cinema Odeon 1, 2 and 3 **(Ca)**, London Road (Tel. 53888).
Public library (Bb) Victoria Street.
Places to see Verulamium Museum, St Michael's Street; City Museum **(Bb)**, Hatfield Road; Clock Tower **(Ba)**, French Row; Roman Theatre, Hypocaust, Verulamium; Organ Museum, 320 Camp Road; Salisbury

ROMAN HERITAGE

The Roman theatre at Verulamium is the only known example in Britain that has a stage instead of an amphitheatre. It probably seated 6,000 spectators.

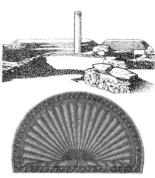

A 2nd-century Roman mosaic in the Verulamium Museum has a shell motif made up of two shades of Purbeck marble.

Hall, London Colney, 4 m. SE.
Town trails Available from Tourist Information Centre, Chequer Street.
Shopping St Peters Street; Market Place; High Street; George Street; Chequer Street; Catherine Street; Heritage Close.
Event Carnival (Aug.).
AA 24 hour service
Tel. Hatfield 62852.

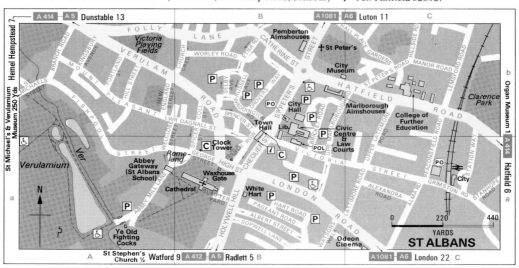

ST ANDREWS Fife

A seat of learning and the home of golf

An ancient town steeped in history, with the oldest university in Scotland and a ruined 12th-century castle; a touring centre for the Central Highlands, Edinburgh and a wealth of historic sites; a holiday centre in its own right, with a mile of golden beach, sailing, fishing and most other traditional seaside recreations; the home of golf and of the most famous course in the world – St Andrews is all of these.

The town is named after the patron saint of Scotland, the first of Christ's disciples and the brother of St Peter. The saint's life is shrouded in mystery, and the story that in the 11th century a Greek monk named Regulus, or Rule, removed St Andrew's bones from the monastery where they were buried and brought them to Scotland is almost certainly a legend. Nevertheless, it was a potent one. The supposed relics were believed to effect miraculous cures, and brought pilgrims flocking to St Andrews.

St Rule's Church, of which the tower still stands on the clifftop, was built about 1130.

The **cathedral** was begun 30 years later. When consecrated in 1318 it was 355 ft long – Scotland's largest. In 1559 the townspeople, inflamed by the anti-Catholic preaching of John Knox, leader of the Scottish Reformation, stripped the building.

During the life of the cathedral St Andrews was the ecclesiastical centre of Scotland, and a great priory adjoined the cathedral. The wall that surrounded the entire precincts remains almost intact. The **Pends**, two Gothic arches, probably 14th century, are all that survive of the gatehouse that led to the priory.

Site of a martyrdom

The ruined **castle**, which stands on a rock near the cathedral, was founded in 1200 as the archbishop's palace and stronghold. Destroyed in the wars between Scotland and England, it was rebuilt in the late 14th century.

In 1546 the Catholic Archbishop Beaton, who had strongly fortified the castle against attack by Henry VIII, had the Reformation leader George Wishart burned at the stake outside the castle. The initials GW, carved in stone, show the site of his martyrdom. Wishart's friends were determined to avenge him. Disguised as workmen they entered the castle, overcame the guard and stabbed Beaton to death in his bedchamber. They then hung his body from a window. The Reformers held the castle for nearly a year, but were later defeated by a French force from the sea.

Among the prisoners taken by the French was John Knox, who was sent to the galleys for 19 months.

Much of the castle was demolished in the 17th century to provide stones for repairing the harbour.

Other medieval remains include the aisle of **Blackfriars Chapel**, which stands in the grounds of 19th-century Madras College, and the ruins of **Greyfriars Monastery**, which can still be seen in the street called Greyfriars Gardens.

University colleges

St Andrews University was founded in 1410. **St Salvator's College**, the present centre of university life, was added in 1450 by Bishop Kennedy, one of the young James III's regents. In the chapel is a pulpit from which John Knox preached.

A girls' school now stands on the site of **St Leonard's College**, added in 1512 by Archbishop Stewart. Its library is a restored 16th-century mansion in which Mary, Queen of Scots once lived.

The third college, **St Mary's**, was founded in 1537 by Archbishop Beaton, and since 1579 has been the university's theological college. A spreading oak dominates its quadrangle, which also contains a thorn tree reputed to have been planted by Mary, Queen of Scots.

Adjoining St Mary's quadrangle is the university library building, founded by James VI in the early 17th century. The library of nearly half a million volumes, including many valuable ancient books, is now housed in new premises in North Street. Part of the old library comprises the Old Parliament Hall, where the Scottish Parliament sat in 1645 and 1646.

ANCIENT UNIVERSITY *Stone houses cluster around the spired tower of St Salvator's Chapel, part of St Salvator's College, which was founded in 1450 and is now one of the main centres of the university.*

CATHEDRAL BY THE SEA *The ruins of a 12th-century cathedral rise from the clifftops. On the right, St Rule's Tower.*

The laws governing golf are drawn up in the clubhouse of the Royal and Ancient Golf Club.

BIRTHPLACE OF MODERN GOLF

The rules of golf were first drawn up at the Royal and Ancient Golf Club, founded at St Andrews in 1754. The 18-hole round also originated there. On the Old Course (below) the world's greatest golfers have competed for the Open and many other championships.

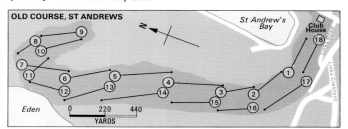

OLD COURSE, ST ANDREWS

After the Reformation the university, and the town, declined.

In the 19th century, however, the town's fortunes revived – largely through the initiative of Hugh Lyon Playfair, provost from 1842 until 1861. He widened streets, had new university and public buildings erected, and improved the harbour.

During term-time the students wear a traditional scarlet gown, which lends colour to the town's old streets. The Kate Kennedy Procession in April is a pageant of historical figures from the university's past. Kate Kennedy is said to have been Bishop Kennedy's niece, and to have given oatmeal to poor students.

Executioner's axe

The 19th-century **Town Hall** contains several relics, including an executioner's axe and a stone dated 1565 from the tolbooth that the town hall replaced.

Spanning the west end of South Street is the grim West Port, built in 1589 – the main entrance to the old city and the best surviving example of a burgh port, or gate, in Scotland.

There are four full-length golf courses on the links north-west of the town. The **Old Course**, dating back to the 15th century, is the oldest golf course in the world.

In the Byre Theatre, St Andrews has one of the few repertory theatres in Scotland. The theatre was originally housed in a converted cowshed, or byre, and opened in 1933. It now occupies a new building which has become a training ground for some of Britain's leading actors.

Information Tel. 72021.
Location On the A91, 13 m. S of Dundee.
Parking Argyle Street; Murray Place; City Road; Doubledykes Road; Old Station Road; St Nicholas Street; Woodburn Place (all car parks).
District council North East Fife (Tel. Cupar 53722).
Population 11,300.
E-C Thur.
Police (Bb) North Street (Tel. 72222).
Casualty hospital Cottage Memorial Hospital, Abbey Walk (Tel. 74197).
Post office (Ba) South Street.
Theatre Byre **(Ca)**, Abbey Street (Tel. 72544).
Cinema New Picture House **(Bb)**, North Street (Tel. 73509).
Public library (Ba) Church Square.
Places to see Castle (including bottle dungeon) **(Cb)**; Cathedral ruins and St Rule's Tower **(Cb)**; Queen Mary's House **(Cb)**; The Pends **(Cb)**; Town Hall **(Ba)**; South Court **(Cb)**; West Port **(Aa)**.
Shopping South Street; Market Street; North Street; Church Street; Bell Street.
Events Kate Kennedy Procession (Apr.); Rotary International Golf Tournament (June); Lammas Market (Aug.); St Andrew's Day (Sept.).
AA 24 hour service
Tel. Dundee 25585.

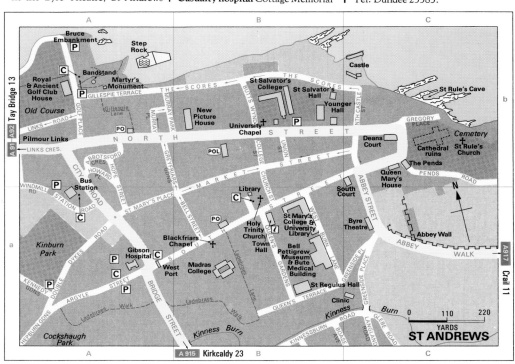

ST ANDREWS

PLEASURE AND BUSINESS *Yachts ride at anchor in Salcombe harbour, which is also the picturesque base for a lively commercial fleet of lobster and crab catchers.*

Salcombe Devon

Devon's most southerly resort stands near the Kingsbridge Estuary, with its deep, sheltered harbour and winding creeks and inlets. Palms and other Mediterranean trees grow in its exceptionally mild climate, and the whitewashed houses add to its southern atmosphere.

A museum on the Custom House Quay traces Salcombe's history as a fishing and boat-building port.

At Sharpitor, 1½ miles south-west, there is a 6 acre garden with rare shrubs and plants, and the Overbeck Museum devoted to ships and ship-building.

Information Market Street
(Tel. 2736).
Location On the A381, 28 m. SE of Plymouth.
Parking Shadycombe Road; Gould Road; Fore Street; South Sands Road (all car parks).
District council South Hams
(Tel. Totnes 864499).
Population 2,400.
E-C Thur.
Police Onslow Road (Tel. 2107).
Casualty hospital South Hams Hospital, Plymouth Road, Kingsbridge
(Tel. Kingsbridge 2349).
Post office Fore Street.
Public library Cliff House, Cliff Road.
Places to see Museum, Custom House Quay; Overbeck Museum and gardens, Sharpitor, 1½ m. SW.
Shopping Fore Street.
Events Town Regatta (Aug.); Yacht Club Regatta (Aug.).
AA 24 hour service
Tel. Torquay 25903.

Sale Greater Manchester

The opening in 1849 of the railway line between Altrincham and Manchester transformed Sale from a small agricultural community into a residential district.

Most of Sale's churches and chapels are Victorian or later, but St Martin's at Ashton-upon-Mersey is 18th century and has a hammer-beam roof.

Information
Tel. Manchester (061) 872 2101.
Location On the A56, 6 m. SW of Manchester.

Parking Sibson Road; Broad Road; Curzon Road; Springfield Road; Ashton Lane; York Road (all car parks).
District council Metropolitan Borough of Trafford
(Tel. 061 872 2101).
Population 57,800.
E-C Wed.
Police Tatton Road
(Tel. 061 872 5050).
Casualty hospital Wythenshawe Hospital, Southmoor Road, Wythenshawe (Tel. 061 998 3070).
Post office Washway Road.
Theatre Civic, Sale Town Hall
(Tel. 061 973 2253).
Cinema Odeon, Washway Road
(Tel. 061 973 2247).
Public library Tatton Road.
Shopping School Road; off Town Square.
Event Sale Festival (May).
AA 24 hour service
Tel. 061 485 6299.

Salford Greater Manchester

Although it merges with Manchester, Salford is a city in its own right. Salfordians take pride in the fact that their charter of 1230 is about 80 years older than that of their larger neighbour. Salford has its own university and a Roman Catholic cathedral, St John's, completed in 1855. The boroughs of Eccles, Swinton and Pendlebury and the Urban Districts of Irlam and Worsley were joined to Salford in 1974.

Information
Tel. Manchester (061) 794 4711.
Location On the A57, 2 m. W of Manchester.
Parking Ellor Street; Pendleton Way (2); Rossall Way; Mulberry Road; George Street; Lower Broughton Road (all car parks).
District council City of Salford
(Tel. 061 794 4711).
Population 98,000.
E-C Wed. **M-D** Salford: Mon., Wed., Fri. and Sat. Eccles: Tues., Thur., Sat. Swinton and Pendlebury: Tues., Fri. and Sat.
Police The Crescent, Salford
(Tel. 061 736 5877).
Casualty hospital Salford Royal Hospital, Chapel Street
(Tel. 061 834 8656).
Post offices Chapel Street, Salford; Church Street, Eccles; Liverpool Road, Irlam; Chorley Road, Swinton; St Ouen Centre, Walkden, Worsley.
Theatre Salford Players Theatre, Liverpool Street
(Tel. 061 737 5961).
Cinemas The Carlton Twins, Cross

LOWRY'S SALFORD

The grim industrial architecture of Salford that fascinated the Manchester-born painter L. S. Lowry (1887-1976) is gradually disappearing through redevelopment. But many of the backgrounds to his pictures of matchstick-like figures scurrying to and from work like an army of ants can still be seen in the city. Salford Art Gallery in Peel Park contains the largest collection of Lowry's work in the country.

Detail from Coming from the Mill, *painted by Lowry in 1930.*

CRADLE OF LEARNING *Salford University is a mere baby among universities. It was founded only in 1967, but its modern buildings have reshaped the skyline above Peel Park, and its students make a lively addition to the community.*

Lane (Tel. 061 736 1651); The New Princes, Monton Road, Monton, Eccles (061 789 3426); Unit Four, Bolton Road, Walkden, Worsley (061 790 9432).
Public libraries Peel Park, Salford; Church Street, Eccles; Chorley Road, Swinton.
Places to see Mining Museum, Salford; Ordsall Hall, Salford; Salford Cathedral.
Shopping Precincts in Salford, Eccles, Swinton, Worsley and Irlam.
AA 24 hour service
Tel. 061 485 6299.

Salisbury see page 354

Saltburn Cleveland
When the resort was founded in the mid-19th century, its first streets were built of white brick and named after jewels. Much of this original Victorian elegance still remains.

Two miles west and linked to Saltburn by a fine sandy beach is the smaller resort of Marske, noted for its Jacobean hall, the finest 17th-century house in Cleveland. The hall is now a Cheshire Home.

Information Tel. Redcar 471921 or Eston Grange 468141.
Location On the A174, 14 m. E of Middlesbrough.
Parking Saltburn: Boating Lake; Lower Promenade. Marske: Stray (all car parks).
District council Borough of Langbaurgh
(Tel. Eston Grange 468141).
Population 20,000.
E-C Tues.
Police 08.30-17.30 hrs: Windsor Road (Tel. 3383). Lord Street, Redcar (Tel. Redcar 483333).
Casualty hospital Middlesbrough General, Ayresome Green Lane, Middlesbrough
(Tel. Middlesbrough 83133).
Post office Station Road.
Public library Windsor Road.
Places to see Marske Hall; Miniature Railway.
Town trails Available from Saltburn YHA, Riftswood Hall, Victoria Road, Saltburn, or Langbaurgh Town Hall, Fabian Road, Eston.
Shopping Station Street; Milton Street; Dundas Street.
AA 24 hour service
Tel. Middlesbrough 246832.

Sandown-Shanklin IOW
These twin resorts on sheltered Sandown Bay are connected by a promenade and a 6 mile long stretch of sands. Both provide all the traditional seaside entertainments and are popular for family holidays.

Shanklin, built on the clifftops, has held the annual sunshine record more often than any other resort in Britain. The Old Village has thatched cottages overgrown with honeysuckle and roses. Its Crab Inn dates from the early 17th century. The poet John Keats lived there during the early 19th century, while writing part of *Endymion*. Keats Green, on the clifftop, commemorates his stay. Shanklin Chine is a deep cleft in the cliffs, cool with running water and green foliage.

A museum of geology in Sandown displays a number of rare fossils found on the island.

Information Sandown
(Tel. 403886); Shanklin (2942).
Location On the A3055, 10 m. SE of Newport.
Parking Sandown: St Johns Road; Culver Parade; Fort Street; The Barracks; New Road, Lake. Shanklin: Esplanade (2); Orchardleigh Road; Landguard Road; Osborne Road; Chine Avenue (all car parks).
District council South Wight
(Tel. Newport 523627).
Population 16,900.
E-C Wed.
Police Landguard Road, Shanklin (Tel. 2211).
Casualty hospital Royal Isle of Wight County Hospital, Swanmore Road, Ryde (Tel. Ryde 63311).
Post offices Beachfield Road, Sandown. Regent Street, Shanklin.
Theatres Sandown Pier Pavilion (Tel. 2295); Shanklin Theatre, Steephill Road (2739); Shanklin Pier Theatre (2232).
Cinemas The Queens, Albert Road, Sandown (Tel. 403478); Regal, High Street, Shanklin (2272).
Public libraries High Street, Sandown. Victoria Avenue, Shanklin.
Places to see Geology Museum, High Street, Sandown.
Shopping Shanklin: High Street; Regent Street. Sandown: High Street.
Events Regattas (Aug.).
AA 24 hour service
Tel. Newport, IOW, 522653.

Sandwich Kent
Visitors to this charming old town, set 2 miles inland, may well be surprised to learn that it was once, with Dover, Hythe, Romney and Hastings, one of Britain's Cinque Ports—a medieval federation of five seaports for the defence of the south coast.

From the 16th century the River Stour silted up, and Sandwich became a market town.

The town is full of interesting old buildings, including the mainly 14th–15th-century Church of St Clement, reached from Church Street; Fisher Gate, a 14th-century gateway on the quay; the 16th-century Barbican, a former blockhouse, by the toll bridge; and the Guildhall of 1579, which contains the town's treasures, including medieval silver maces. The village of Wingham, 5 miles west, has half-timbered houses in a wide, tree-lined main street.

Information Tel. 613305.
Location On the A258, 6 m. NW of Deal.
Parking The Quay; Strand Street; Moat Sole (all car parks).
District council Dover
(Tel. Dover 206090).
Population 4,200.
E-C Wed. **M-D** Thur.
Police Guildhall (Tel. Thanet 581724).
Casualty hospital Victoria Hospital, London Road, Deal (Tel. Deal 2122).
Post office King Street.
Public library Market Street.
Places to see Guildhall; Richborough Castle.
Shopping King Street; Market Street.
Sport Royal St George's golf course.
AA 24 hour service
Tel. Thanet 81226.

Sandy Bedfordshire
The rich soil deposited by the River Ivel, a tributary of the Ouse, has made the town a market-gardening centre since the early 17th century. The Royal Society for the Protection of Birds has a 104 acre reserve 1 mile east of Sandy, on the Potton road.

Information Tel. Ampthill 402051.
Location On the B1042, 8 m. E of Bedford.
Parking High Street (car parks).
District council Mid-Bedfordshire
(Tel. Ampthill 402051).
Population 8,000.
E-C Thur. **M-D** Fri.
Police Station Road, Biggleswade (Tel. Biggleswade 312222).
Casualty hospital Bedford General Hospital, Kempston, Bedford (Tel. Bedford 55122).
Post office High Street.
Public library Market Square.
Places to see The Lodge.
Shopping Market Square; High Street.
Event Carnival (July).
AA 24 hour service
Tel. Hatfield 62852.

SALISBURY Wiltshire

City of the soaring spire

Long before the Romans came to Britain an Iron Age camp stood on a hill a few miles south of Stonehenge. The Romans strengthened it and called the place Serviodunum. Then the Normans built a castle and a cathedral on the site and called it Sarum. Bishop Herbert Poore found that Sarum was not big enough to accommodate the authority of both Church and castle, and decided to build a new cathedral to the south. The bishop died before he could carry out his plan, but his brother Richard, who succeeded him, began to build the new cathedral in 1220. Around it grew a community which was called New Sarum and is known today as Salisbury.

Bishop Richard Poore completed the **cathedral** in the remarkably short time of 38 years and, as a result, it is built largely in a single style, unlike many other medieval English cathedrals. The tower and spire, a combined height of 404 ft, the tallest in England, were added in 1334.

The west front, the last part of the building to be completed, is the most lavishly decorated. Its rows of statues in niches are Victorian replacements of the originals.

Inside, graceful columns of Purbeck stone line the high-vaulted nave and the many windows add to the airy, yet dignified, atmosphere of the interior. The nave is rich in monuments, tombs and effigies. The oldest tomb is that of William Longespée, Earl of Salisbury, who was buried in the cathedral in 1226. He was a witness at the sealing of Magna Carta by King John, his half-brother, in 1215, and is supposed to have brought back to Salisbury the copy which is now in

the cathedral library. It is one of only four surviving originals of the document.

In the north aisle of the nave there is a clock dating from 1386 and claimed to be the oldest working clock in the world. It has no dial, and chimes the hours.

Beneath the spire is a brass plate, set into the floor and engraved "AD 1737 the centre of the tower". It marks the result of a check made 50 years after Sir Christopher Wren had discovered that the spire was leaning 29½ in. off centre. Wren's solution was to straighten it with iron tie-rods. When these were replaced in 1951 it was found that the spire had moved no further.

The **chapter house,** which is octagonal and has a graceful central column, is decorated around its walls with 60 scenes from the Old Testament involving about 130 carved figures – splendid examples of the medieval stonecutters' art.

Walled close

The cathedral was built before the town, and so Church authorities had to build houses for the clergy. These were contained within a walled square – the largest and finest **cathedral close** in Britain. It is entered through medieval gateways, and many of the buildings inside, such as the Bishop's Palace and the Deanery, are also medieval.

Some private residences in the close date from later periods. **Malmesbury House**, built during the 15th or 16th century, has a façade added in 1719. **Mompesson House** was built in 1701 for Charles Mompesson, a rich Wiltshire merchant. The house is open to the public and has fine rooms furnished and decorated in 18th-century style.

South of the cathedral stands the **Bishop's Palace,** built in the 13th century. The view of the cathedral from the palace gardens was portrayed by John Constable in a famous painting now in the Victoria and Albert Museum. The palace was considered sufficiently isolated by Charles II to use for his court during the Great Plague of 1665. Today it is used by boys of the cathedral choir school.

Ancient inns

Outside the walls of the close the city streets were laid out in a grid pattern. In most of them can be seen timbered houses and inns, overhanging gables and bow-windowed shops. Among the outstanding black-and-white half-timbered buildings are the 15th-century **House of John A'Port** in Queen Street, the National Trust's 16th-century **Joiners' Hall** in St Ann Street, a 15th-century inn, the Haunch of Venison and a 14th-

SOARING GRACE *The slender spire of Salisbury Cathedral rises higher than any other in England. But its central piers stand on* *foundations a mere 5-6 ft down in swampy ground. A testimonial to the skill – and faith – of medieval masons.*

century inn, the Rose and Crown.

Salisbury has a large market square and a modern shopping precinct, the Old George Mall, which blends unobtrusively with the older buildings around it.

The city's churches are almost as old as the cathedral. St Thomas's dates from 1238, and with its tower and cap spire is far enough away from the cathedral not to be dominated by it. St Martin's chancel dates from 1230.

Salisbury lies by four rivers – the Avon, Nadder, Bourne and Wylye – which converge south of the town. Their branches and backwaters interlace the city and its surrounding parks and gardens. The Avon is navigable in some parts.

The original Norman cathedral was dismantled when Bishop Poore made his move south, and only the foundations remain. The hilltop is now called **Old Sarum.** Today it is a place of grassy mounds and excavations.

Until the Reform Bill of 1832 Old Sarum was one of the so-called "rotten boroughs" because it returned two MPs to Parliament with an electorate of only ten people. One MP was Wil-

POULTRY CROSS *The 15th-century cross was originally the centre of poultry sales in Salisbury.*

ORNATE FAÇADE *Rows of statues in niches decorate the splendid west front of Salisbury Cathedral.*

liam Pitt the Elder (1708-78), who became Prime Minister.

The **Salisbury and South Wilts Museum,** in King's House, The Close, exhibits many finds from Stonehenge, together with pottery from Old Sarum and the surrounding district, a Roman mosaic pavement, and a collection of English pottery, china and glass.

Information Tel. 4956.
Location On the A30, 23 m. NW of Southampton.
Parking College Street; Salt Lane; Market Place; Brown Street; Culver Street; Churchill Way East; New Street; Cathedral Close; Crane Bridge Road; Churchill Way West (all car parks).
District council Salisbury (Tel. 6272).
Population 35,400.
E-C Wed. **M-D** Tues., Sat.
Police Wilton Road (Tel. 29631).
Casualty hospital Salisbury General Infirmary, Fisherton Street (Tel. 6212).
Post office (Ab) Castle Street.
Theatres City Hall **(Ab)**, Fisherton Street (Tel. 4432); Playhouse **(Ab)**, Malthouse Lane (20333).
Cinemas Odeon **(Ab)**, New Canal (Tel. 22080); St Edmund's Art Centre, Bedwin Street (20379).
Public library (Ab) Market Place.
Places to see Cathedral **(Aa)**; Bishop's Palace **(Aa)**, Cathedral Close; Mompesson House **(Aa)**, Cathedral Close; Salisbury and South Wilts Museum **(Aa)**, King's House, The Close; Old Sarum, 2 m. N; Wilton House, 3 m. W.
Shopping High Street; Castle Street;

MATRON'S COLLEGE *Bishop Seth Ward built these almshouses for clergymen's widows in the 17th century.*

New Canal; Winchester Street; Queen Street; Catherine Street; Old George Mall; Blue Boar Row.
Event Salisbury Festival (Sept.).
Trade and industry Brewing; light engineering; agricultural supplies.
Sport Horse racing, Netherhampton Road.
AA 24 hour service
Tel. Bournemouth 25751.

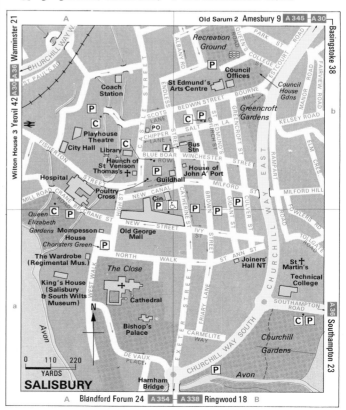

SALISBURY

Scarborough N. Yorks.

The headland on which the seaside resort of Scarborough stands has been occupied on and off since the Bronze Age. The earliest visible remains are those of a Roman signal station, built on the cliff about AD 370. It was one of five such stations along this stretch of coast. From them, watch was kept for northern sea raiders, and if any were sighted warning signals were sent to Roman garrisons inland.

The Normans built a large castle on the headland. Its massive square keep, completed in 1158, is 80 ft high in parts. The keep still stands, as do the barbican, or outer defence, and the curtain wall, whose towers date from the 13th century.

The castle survived many sieges until, like so many other British strongholds, it was severely damaged by the Parliamentarians during the Civil War and partly demolished by them after the war, in 1649.

It was about this time that Scarborough developed as a spa. A Mrs Farrow claimed that water from the stream flowing across South Sands should be drunk to cleanse the stomach and blood, and to cure asthma, scurvy, jaundice, leprosy, melancholy and other ills.

In the next century the first bathing machine appeared at Scarborough, and local people claim it was invented there. In any event, people flocked to the town's sandy bays to take dips in the North Sea.

Today the town is one of the largest resorts along the east coast of Britain. Conferences are held throughout the year, and the large shopping centre is always busy.

Only commercial vessels, mostly fishing vessels and ships unloading timber, use the old inner harbour; pleasure craft use the outer.

The 19th-century Church of St Martin-on-the-Hill, in Albion Road, contains much pre-Raphaelite work, including a chancel roof by William Morris and Philip Webb, and glass and murals by Sir Edward Burne-Jones, Dante Gabriel Rossetti and Ford Madox Brown.

St Mary's Church, in St Mary's churchyard, was severely damaged during the Civil War, but retains its medieval arcades, piers and south-aisle chapels.

The town has several literary associations. The poet Wordsworth was married in Brompton Church, 9 miles south-west, in 1802. Anne Brontë, who often visited the town with her sister Charlotte, died there in 1849 and is buried in St Mary's churchyard.

In Sandside, behind the old inner harbour, is King Richard III House, a medieval building which was refaced in Elizabethan times, where the king is reputed to have stayed in 1483. It is now a café.

Princess Street is the best preserved street in the Old Town and has some fine Georgian and Victorian houses.

The Three Mariners Inn, in Quay Street, built in 1300 and once the haunt of smugglers, is now the Fishermen's Craft Centre.

The town is an angling centre, and the September fishing festival is a national highlight, attracting anglers from all over the country.

Another successful festival, held in the same month, is the Scarborough Cricket Festival, in which the country's top players take part.

The resort is a children's delight, with a pleasure lake, The Mere, across which a quarter-size model of the *Hispaniola* from Robert Louis Stevenson's *Treasure Island* can be sailed to an island with treasure, pirates and a stockade; Marineland, with dolphins and sea lions; Land of the Dinosaurs, with life-size models; amusement park; naval battles between the ships of the world's smallest manned navy, in Peasholm Park; a miniature railway and many other attractions.

On the southern outskirts of the town is Oliver's Mount, a 500 ft hill that gives splendid views across the

GARDENS BY THE SHORE *At South Bay, Scarborough, beautiful gardens sweep down to the sandy beaches that stretch on either side of the headland. The town itself has nearly 400 acres of parkland.*

ROTUNDA MUSEUM *The ancient past of north-east Yorkshire comes to life in Scarborough's town museum.*

bay. Part of the winding road to the top is sometimes used for motor-cycle racing.

Information Tel. 72261/73333.
Location On the A165, 7 m. N of Filey.
Parking Westwood; St Thomas Street; Falconer's Road; St Nicholas Cliff; Market Way; North Street; Vernon Road; Quay Street; Eastborough; Castle Road; Esplanade; The Spa; Seacliff; Scalby Mills; Burniston Road; Royal Albert Drive; Albion Road; Brook Square;

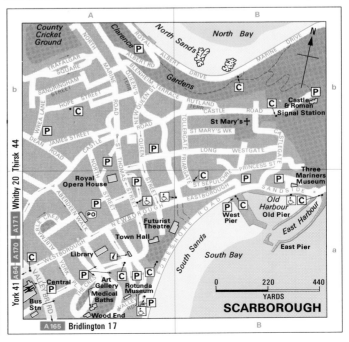

THE SITWELLS OF WOODEND

Woodend, Scarborough, was the family home of the most gifted English literary family of the 20th century, the Sitwells. All three, Sir Osbert (1892-1969), Sir Sacheverell (born 1897) and Dame Edith (1887-1964), became poets, critics and authors of distinction. The house is now occupied by the town's Natural History Museum.

A detail of a painting by John Singer Sargent (1856–1925) shows Edith and Sacheverell Sitwell with their parents, Sir George and Lady Ida.

Foreshore Road; Friars Way (all car parks).
District council Borough of Scarborough (Tel. 72351).
Population 43,100.
E-C Wed. **M-D** Thur.
Police Northway (Tel. 63333).
Casualty hospital Scarborough General, Scolby Road (Tel. 68111).
Post office (Aa) Aberdeen Walk.
Theatres Spa, Grand Hall and Theatre, Esplanade (Tel. 72351); Futurist Theatre **(Aa)**, Foreshore Road (60644); Opera House **(Aa)**, St Thomas Street (69999).
Cinemas Odeon, Westborough (Tel. 61725); Elvenhome, Aberdeen Walk (74077); Hollywood Plaza, North Marine Road (60188).
Public library (Aa) Vernon Road.
Places to see Castle **(Bb)**; Natural History Museum **(Aa)**; Three Mariners Museum **(Ba)**; Roman signal station **(Bb)**; Rotunda Museum of Archaeology **(Aa)**, Museum Terrace.
Town trails Available from the Tourist Information Centre, St Nicholas Cliff.
Shopping Westborough; Newborough; Eastborough; Falsgrave.
Sport County cricket, and Cricket Festival (Sept.), North Marine Road.
AA 24 hour service
Tel. York 27698.

Scunthorpe Humberside
The exploitation of the vast ironstone beds, the largest in Europe, that surround Scunthorpe has changed its face with dramatic rapidity. In 1860 it was a huddle of five sleepy villages; today it is a densely populated industrial dynamo that produces about 18 per cent of all British steel. Despite this, it has many attractive parks and open spaces.

The Borough Museum and Art Gallery in Oswald Road illustrates the geology, natural history and folk life of the region from Stone Age times, and includes finds from the Roman Villa at nearby Winterton.

The much-restored St Lawrence's Church at Frodingham, one of the five original villages, retains its 12th-century tower and nave, which has a fine oak roof.

Normanby Hall, 4 miles north, is an outstanding Regency building of 1825-9 and contains some fine examples of Regency furniture.

Information Tel. 60161.
Location On the A1077, 23 m. NE of Doncaster.
Parking Dunstall Street; Mary Street (2); West Street (2); Manley Street; Carlton Street; High Street East; Winterton Road; Home Street (all car parks).
District council Borough of Scunthorpe (Tel. 62141).
Population 63,400.
E-C Wed. **M-D** Fri., Sat.
Police Laneham Street (Tel. 843434).
Casualty hospital Scunthorpe General, Cliff Gardens (Tel. 843481).
Post office Oswald Road.
Theatre Civic, Laneham Street (Tel. 840883).
Cinemas Studios 5,6 and 7, Oswald Street (Tel. 842352); Scunthorpe Film Theatre, The Precinct (60190).
Public library The Precinct.
Places to see Roman Villa, Winterton, 5 m. N, on A1077; Normanby Hall, 4 m. N, on B1430.
Shopping Ashby High Street; High Street; The Precinct.
Sport FA League football, Scunthorpe United FC, Doncaster Road.
AA 24 hour service
Tel. Hull 28580.

Seaford E. Sussex
The town was a bustling port until 1579 when the course of the River Ouse was diverted, causing it to enter the Channel at what is now Newhaven and left Seaford harbour literally high and dry. It was from the early 19th century that Seaford began to develop as a seaside resort.

The town has a high proportion of retired people as residents, as well as eight private schools. It is secluded from the industries of the area, which are concentrated around Newhaven.

Most of the town's buildings are 19th century or later, but the Church of St Leonard is part-Norman, with a 15th-century tower. The churches at East Blatchington and Bishopstone, on the outskirts of Seaford, are part-Saxon, part-Norman.

The downlands around the town make good walking country, with fine views of the Seven Sisters cliffs. There are the remains of a pre-Roman camp on Seaford Head, half a mile south-east.

Information The Downs, Sutton Road (Tel. 892224).
Location On the A259, 3 m. E of Newhaven.
Parking Dane Road; Weir Street (2); Crouch Lane; Seafront; Sutton Road (all car parks).
District council Lewes (Tel. Lewes 71600).
Population 17,800.
E-C Wed. **M-D** Sat.
Police Church Street (Tel. 892241).
Casualty hospital King's Drive, Eastbourne (Tel. Eastbourne 21351).
Post office Church Street.
Public library Sutton Park Road.
Places to see Seaford Museum, Pelham Road; Martello Tower; Seaford Head, pre-Roman camp, ½ m. SE.
Town trails Available from Tourist Information Centre, The Downs, Sutton Road.
Shopping Broad Street; High Street.
AA 24 hour service
Tel. Brighton 695231.

Seaham Durham
Lord Londonderry had the harbour built in 1828 to ship coal. Seaham has suffered from the decline of the Durham coalfields, but three local mines still operate, beneath the North Sea. The original village stands on a limestone cliff. Its church is late Saxon, and Roman stones have been used in the walls. The font is 12th century.

Lord Byron stayed at Seaham Hall, after his marriage to Anne Milbanke in 1815. The poet termed the coast "dreary", but there are good views of the cliffs and sea from the promenade.

Information Tel. Easington 270501.
Location On the B1287, 14 m. NE of Durham.
Parking Adelaide Row; Church Street; North Terrace (car parks); South Railway Street; St John's Square.
District council Easington (Tel. Easington 270501).
Population 21,100.
E-C Wed.
Police North Terrace (Tel. 812255).
Casualty hospital New District General, Kayll Road, Sunderland (Tel. Sunderland 56256).
Post office Adelaide Row.
Cinema Fairworld, South Terrace (Tel. 813936).
Public library St John's Square.
Shopping Church Street.
Event Seaham Show (Sept.).
Trade and industry Coal-mining; engineering; furniture.
AA 24 hour service
Tel. Newcastle upon Tyne 610111.

Selby N. Yorks.

Although only a small market town, Selby has one of the most magnificent churches in England. The church was built for Selby Abbey about 1100. At the Dissolution of the Monasteries it became the parish church, and so avoided the fate of the other great Yorkshire abbeys, such as Fountains and Rievaulx, which now stand in ruins.

The Market Cross was put up in 1790, and there are several 18th-century houses, including Corunna House in Ousegate.

Selby may have been the birthplace in 1068 of Henry I. His mother, Queen Matilda, is said to have been staying there while William the Conqueror put down a revolt by the Saxons of Yorkshire.

NORMAN MASTERPIECE *Selby Abbey has stood for 900 years, surviving both the Dissolution of the Monasteries and a great fire in 1906.*

Information Tel. 705101.
Location On the A63, 14 m. S of York.
Parking Millgate; Thornden Buildings (Public Park); New Lane; Audus Street; Harper Street (all car parks); Micklegate; Market Place; Park Street; Church Hill.
District council Selby (Tel. 705101).
Population 10,700.
E-C Thur. **M-D** Mon.
Police New Lane (Tel. 702596).
Casualty hospital Selby and District War Memorial Hospital, Doncaster Road (Tel. 702664).
Post office Micklegate.
Cinema Ritz, Scott Road (Tel. 703434).
Public library Abbey Yard.
Places to see Selby Abbey.
Shopping Gowthorpe; Market Place; Finkle Street; Micklegate.
Trade and industry Coal-mining; agriculture-related industries.
AA 24 hour service Tel. York 27698.

Selkirk Borders

Cloth has been woven in Selkirk for more than 350 years, but before that the town was famous for its shoes, and the inhabitants are still

SIR WALTER SCOTT *A statue of the novelist stands in Selkirk, outside the courtroom over which he presided in the early 19th century.*

nicknamed "souters", or shoemakers.

Selkirk stands on the edge of Ettrick Forest, rising on a hillside from the River Ettrick, a salmon and trout stream which flows into the Tweed.

It is a touring and angling centre, and thousands of visitors flock to Selkirk each June to watch the Common Riding, a colourful ceremony celebrating the town's past, in particular the townsmen's heroic role at the Battle of Flodden in 1513, when they defended the defeated James IV to the last.

The novelist Sir Walter Scott was Sheriff of Selkirk from 1800 to 1832. His home, Abbotsford, 3 miles northeast of the town, off the road to Melrose, is a museum. He is buried at Dryburgh Abbey, 5 miles to the east.

Information Tel. 20054 (summer); St Boswells 3301 (winter).
Location Off the A7, 12 m. N of Hawick.
Parking Scott's Place; Chapel Street; Bannerfield Housing Estate (all car parks).
District council Ettrick and Lauderdale (Tel. Galashiels 4751).
Population 5,420.
E-C Thur., Sat.
Police Scott's Place (Tel. 21701).
Casualty hospital Cottage Hospital, Halliday's Park (Tel. 20746).
Post office Market Place.
Public library Ettrick Terrace.
Places to see Museum of Ironmongery, off Market Place; Abbotsford, 3 m. NE.
Shopping High Street; Market Place.
Event Common Riding (June).
AA 24 hour service Tel. Edinburgh (031) 225 8464.

Sevenoaks Kent

Not even the constant stream of south-bound traffic can destroy the distinctive character and charm of Sevenoaks with its half-timbered façades, steep gables and mellow bricks.

The town was first mentioned in 1114, in a record of churches, as Seovenaca. In 1450 Jack Cade's Kentish rebels defeated an army led by Henry VI. The rebels later dispersed when the people of London refused to support them, and Cade was hunted down and killed.

Inside the 600-year-old parish church of St Nicholas is a memorial to the poet John Donne, rector of Sevenoaks from 1616 to 1631.

South-east of Sevenoaks is Knole, one of the largest houses in England, with 365 rooms and 52 staircases, standing in a vast deer park. It dates mainly from the late 15th century and belonged to the Sackville family until the National Trust took over in 1946.

Information Tel. 59711; 50305 (summer).
Location On the A25, 18 m. W of Maidstone.
Parking London Road; High Street; South Street; Hitchen Hatch Lane; St John's Hill; St James Road; Bradbourne Park Road; Blighs Road; Buckhurst Lane (all car parks).
District council Sevenoaks (Tel. 59711).
Population 17,100.
E-C Wed. **M-D** Wed., Sat.
Police London Road (Tel. 58161).
Casualty hospital Sevenoaks Hospital, St John's Hill (Tel. 55155).
Post office South Park.
Cinema Focus 1, 2 and 3, London Road (Tel. 54456).
Public library The Drive.
Places to see Knole House.
Shopping High Street; London Road.
Event Sevenoaks Three Arts Festival (June/July).
AA 24 hour service Tel. Maidstone 55353.

Sheerness Kent

There has been a dockyard at Sheerness since 1665, when Samuel Pepys, the diarist, supervised its construction. Much of the present dockyard, however, was designed by the architect John Rennie in 1812. The Royal Navy moved out from Sheerness in 1960, and it is now a thriving commercial port handling imports of vehicles in particular. Sheerness is also a holiday resort with a 1½ mile long promenade and a sand-and-shingle beach.

The town was badly damaged by fire in 1827, and the cottages that sprang up in replacement make it one of the most Victorian towns in the county.

The Royal Fountain Inn stands opposite the pier where Lord Nelson's body was landed after Trafalgar in 1805.

Queenborough, to the south-east, has a harbour popular with yachtsmen and a Guildhall of 1793 containing magnificent regalia.

Information Tel. Sittingbourne 24381.
Location On the A249, 7 m. N of Sittingbourne.
Parking Beach Street; Bridge Road; Cross Street; Rose Street; Russell Street (all car parks).
District council Swale (Tel. Sittingbourne 24381).
Population 11,500.
E-C Wed. **M-D** Tues.
Police Cross Street (Tel. 661451).
Casualty hospital Medway Hospital, Windmill Road, Gillingham

(Tel. Medway 46111).
Post office Broadway.
Theatre Little Theatre, Meyrick Road (Tel. 665700).
Cinema Images, Wood Street (Tel. 661851).
Public library Trinity Road.
Shopping High Street; Broadway.
Car ferry To Flushing (Tel. 664981).
AA 24 hour service
Tel. Maidstone 55353.

Sheffield see page 360

Sheffield see page 360

Shepton Mallet Somerset

In the Middle Ages, Shepton Mallet was famed for its woollen cloth and stockings. Now the town is best known for cider, cheese, gloves and shoes, and as the home of the Bath and West Agricultural Show, held each June. In the square are the remains of the 15th-century Shambles – the meat market.

The Church of St Peter and St Paul has a 16th-century carved barrel ceiling, and a stone pulpit from the same period. Several 17th and 18th-century houses survive in the town.

Information Tel. Wells 73026 or 72552.
Location On the A361, 6 m. E of Wells.
Parking Old Market Road; Rectory Road; Park Street (all cps).
District council Mendip (Tel. Wells 73026).
Population 6,300.
E-C Wed. **M-D** Fri.
Police Commercial Road (Tel. 2387).
Casualty hospital Wells and District Cottage Hospital, Bath Road, Wells (Tel. Wells 73154).
Post office Town Street.
Theatre/cinema The Centre (Tel. 3544).
Public library Market Place.
Places to see Museum, High Street; Market Cross; The Shambles.
Shopping High Street.
Events Royal Bath and West Show (June); Mid-Somerset Agricultural Show (Aug.); Carnival (Nov.).
AA 24 hour service
Tel. Yeovil 27744.

Sherborne Dorset

The county's historical and architectural gem, Sherborne has a medieval abbey church, two castles and five public schools.

The Church of St Mary the Virgin, built of golden Ham Hill stone, was founded in the 8th century as a cathedral, and a Saxon doorway still stands in the largely 15th-century reconstruction. Norman arches support a roof of 15th-century fan vaulting.

Sherborne School was rebuilt in 1550 on the site of the cathedral school which King Alfred reputedly attended. The 12th-century Old Castle was partly demolished by the Parliamentarians in 1645. The present

MELLOW STONEWORK *Much of Sherborne's main thoroughfare, Cheap Street, is built of the same golden Ham Hill stone that forms its abbey. The street contains some fine medieval buildings that add to the town's architectural interest.*

Sherborne Castle – a mansion not a fortress – was built in 1594 by Sir Walter Raleigh.

Information Tel. 2923.
Location On the A30, 5 m. E of Yeovil.
Parking Coldharbour; Newland Street; Acreman Street; Long Street (all car parks); Newland Street; Digby Road.
District council West Dorset (Tel. Dorchester 65211).
Population 7,600.
E-C Wed. **M-D** Thur.
Police Digby Road (Tel. 2101).
Casualty hospital Yeatman Hospital, Hospital Lane (Tel. 3991).
Post office Cheap Street.
Public library Hound Street.
Places to see Sherborne Abbey; Sherborne Castle; Sherborne School; Old Castle.
Shopping Cheap Street.
Trade and industry Agriculture; engineering.
AA 24 hour service
Tel. Yeovil 27744.

SHERBORNE'S PRIDE *The abbey church of St Mary the Virgin is the finest of the many medieval buildings in the town.*

Sheringham Norfolk

Because Sheringham has no harbour, the fishing boats are hauled up the beach and the lifeboat is launched by a tractor. A sail-powered lifeboat is preserved in its shed by the shore.

The town, which sits on the curving hump of East Anglia, is also a holiday resort. Victorian and Edwardian hotels look out north over a beach of sand and shingle.

Information Tel. 824329 (summer); Cromer 513811 (winter).
Location On the A149, 27 m. N of Norwich.
Parking Station Yard; Morris Street; Cliff Road (all car parks).
District council North Norfolk (Tel. Cromer 513811).
Population 5,500.
E-C Wed. **M-D** Sat.
Police Weybourne Road (Tel. 822121).
Casualty hospital Cromer Hospital, Mill Road, Cromer. (Tel. Cromer 513571).
Post office Station Road.
Theatre Little Theatre, Station Road (Tel. 822347).
Public library New Road.
Places to see North Norfolk Railway; Sheringham Hall, 2m. W off the A148; Felbrigg Hall, 4 m. SE.
Shopping Station Road; Church Street.
AA 24 hour service
Tel. Norwich 29401.

Shoreham-by-Sea
W. Sussex

The busy harbour of Shoreham, at the mouth of the River Adur, is the South Coast port nearest to London. The wide Adur estuary is ideal for small-boat sailors.

The town dates from Roman times, and was a ship-building centre in the 14th century. Much of its history is recorded in the Marlipins Museum, a 12th-century building of chequered flint and stone.

Information Tel. 4438.
Location On the A259, 5 m. E of Worthing.
Parking North Street; Wide Water; Beach Green; Old Fort; Little High Street; Ship Street; Middle Street; Tarmount Lane; Riverside (all car parks).
District council Adur (Tel. 5566).
Population 20,800.
E-C Wed. **M-D** Sat.
Police Ham Road (Tel. 4521).
Casualty hospital Worthing General Hospital, Lyndhurst Road, Worthing (Tel. Worthing 205111).
Post office Brunswick Road.
Theatre Shoreham Community Centre, Pond Road (Tel. 4686).
Public library St Mary's Road.
Places to see Marlipins Museum, High Street.
Shopping High Street; Ham Road; East Street; Brunswick Road.
AA 24 hour service
Tel. Brighton 695231.

SHEFFIELD South Yorkshire

City of silver and steel

Sheffield grew on seven hills, divided by wooded valleys. These surroundings helped the city to become the steel capital of Britain. For the hills yielded iron ore, the woods provided charcoal, and the rivers powered the mills. Gritstone from the nearby moors was used to make the grinding wheels. But it was the discovery of coal locally, and Benjamin Huntsman's invention of a process for making a hard steel with a uniform quality that revolutionised industry in Sheffield. About the same time, Thomas Boulsover began to fuse silver to copper, and gave the city its other main product – Sheffield Plate.

People have lived in the Sheffield area since prehistoric times. At Wincobank, in the north-eastern suburbs of the city, the ramparts of an Iron Age hill-fort stand on the summit of a steep hill above the River Don. It was built by the Celtic Brigantes tribe in the 1st century AD, possibly to withstand the northward advance of the Roman legions.

Five centuries later, the Saxons founded a settlement beside the River Sheaf, which they called Scafeld. It was at Dore, 6 miles south-west, that

King Egbert of Wessex received the submission of King Eanred of Northumbria in 829 and so became the first Saxon overlord of all England. A stone on the green at Dore, now a suburb of Sheffield, records the event.

Sheffield retained its Saxon lord for some years after the Conquest, but early in the 12th century it passed to William de Lovetot, a Norman. He founded the parish church – which today is the **cathedral** – and built **Sheffield Castle**, of which only fragments remain.

Mary, Queen of Scots spent 14 years imprisoned in the castle and its dependent buildings. The castle park once extended beyond the present Manor Lane, where the remains of

STEEL CITY *Sheffield lies in the shadow of the south Pennine slopes, surrounded by the hills and moors that provided the raw materials for its steelworks. Twentieth-century development has changed the city's heart, but Victorian suburbs, built in the flourishing years of its cutlery industry, still spread like an apron before it.*

Sheffield Manor still stand. Beside them is the Turret House, an Elizabethan building, which may have been built to accommodate the captive queen. A room, believed to have been the queen's, has an elaborate plaster ceiling and overmantel, with heraldic decorations.

Famous knives

During the Civil War, Sheffield changed hands several times, finally falling to the Parliamentarians, who demolished the castle in 1648. Castle Market now occupies the site, but part of the walls have been preserved.

Sheffield's cutlery trade is nearly as old as its castle. Smiths and cutlers are recorded there in the 14th century. Chaucer, in his *Canterbury Tales*, mentions a "Sheffield thwitel", a knife, carried by the miller in the Reeve's Tale. By the time of Elizabeth I, the town was famous for its knives, scissors, scythes and shears. In the reign of her successor, James I, the Company of Cutlers in Hallamshire was established by Act of Parliament, "for the good order and government of the makers of knives, sickles, sheers and other cutlery". It still fulfils this role today, and its head, the

GEORGIAN HEAVEN *Paradise Square was developed in the 18th century and retains the simple elegance of the period. At one time the square was a meeting ground for preachers. John Wesley drew a great crowd there in 1779.*

Master Cutler, is second only to the Lord Mayor in Sheffield.

The Industrial Revolution brought large-scale steel-making to Sheffield in the 18th century. Much of the medieval town was swept away to be replaced in some part by Georgian elegance, but also by Victorian squalor.

Sheffield city centre has been largely rebuilt in recent years, but among the modern glass and concrete some of the best old buildings have been retained. These include the cathedral and the **Cutlers' Hall** which face one another across Church Street.

The present Cutlers' Hall, built in 1832, is the third to stand on the site. It contains many fine rooms in the Classical style, including the banqueting hall, where the annual Cutlers' Feast has been held for nearly 350 years.

A new industry

In 1773, Sheffield was granted its own Assay Office for approving silver and its own mark – a crown. The Cutlers' Hall contains a collection of silver comprising at least one piece bearing the Sheffield crown for each year since the Assay Office was opened. Since 1904 the office has been authorised to assay gold, on which its mark is the York rose.

Sheffield Plate, which gave the town a new industry in the middle of the 18th century, was based on the discovery by Thomas Boulsover, a Sheffield cutler, of a method of fusing a thin layer of silver to an ingot of copper alloy. The plated ingot could then be rolled and treated as a single

metal. The new material found a market among the expanding middle classes. They could have tableware and cutlery that looked like silver, at a fraction of its cost.

Modern silver plating is done by electrolysis, and the old Sheffield Plate, made by Boulsover's method, is now valuable and highly prized by collectors.

MAN OF STEEL

Benjamin Huntsman (1704-76) evolved a method of producing cast steel by heating steel with charcoal in enclosed earthen crucibles. His steel was of uniform high quality, hard and ideal for the making of cutting tools. When he had perfected his invention Huntsman offered it to the cutlers of Sheffield. But they were not interested because Huntsman's hard steel was difficult to work, so he exported his output to France.

Soon, however, competition from French cutlery forced the Sheffield cutlers to change to the new material. The story goes that an ironfounder named Walker disguised himself as a tramp and went to Huntsman's foundry at Handsworth, 4 miles east of the city, seeking shelter. He was allowed to warm himself by the furnace, and during the night watched the process.

Huntsman had not patented his invention, and once the secret was known the making of crucible-cast steel was carried out in Sheffield on a large scale. By 1835 the town was the centre of tool-steel manufacture in Britain.

BOTANICAL GARDENS *Eighteen acres of neat lawns and flower beds lie within easy reach of the city centre. The conservatories were built in the style of the Great Conservatory at Chatsworth House, Derbyshire. An aviary and aquarium add further interest to the gardens, leased to the city by the Sheffield Town Trust.*

The **City Museum** has the finest collection of Sheffield Plate in the world. It also has a collection of cutlery, including examples by Sheffield and European craftsmen from the 16th century onwards.

The city has two art galleries: **Mappin Art Gallery** contains English paintings, including works by Turner, Constable and Gainsborough. The **Graves Art Gallery** has eight display rooms housing British and European oil-paintings and English watercolours. There are also examples of Chinese, Indian, African and Islamic art, and a collection of Chinese ivories.

The **York and Lancaster Regimental Museum** shows the history of the regiment from 1758 to the present day with weapons, uniforms, photographs and medals. Seven Victoria Crosses are on display.

Until 1914, the Cathedral of St Peter and St Paul was the parish church of Sheffield. Its origins go back to the 12th century, but it was largely rebuilt about 1435, when the tower and crocketed spire were added. A new nave was built in 1805 and extended in 1880.

History in glass

The 16th-century Lady Chapel contains alabaster figures of some of the Earls of Shrewsbury, whose chapel it was until 1617.

In the north transept window is glass which is believed to be part of a 14th-century Jesse window made in Spain. The Chapter House has modern stained-glass windows depicting the city's history and the Canterbury pilgrims.

The cathedral had a new entrance porch added on the south side in the 1960s. It is a modern interpretation of the Perpendicular style, with glass and stainless-steel doors.

Another city-centre landmark is the **Town Hall**, which was opened in 1897 and extended in 1910 and 1923. It has a 193 ft high tower surmounted by the figure of Vulcan – the blacksmith of the gods – the symbol of the city's main industries.

Soaring even higher than the Town Hall is the 255 ft **Arts Tower** of Sheffield University's Western Bank site, which includes nine lecture theatres in its 19 storeys.

Sheffield Medical School, founded in 1828, is the oldest of the schools and colleges brought together in 1897 to form University College, Sheffield. This became a university in 1905. Today it has 70 departments, many specialising in science.

Rare plants

Sheffield is one of the most fortunate cities in Britain for open space. It stands on the eastern border of the Peak District National Park, part of which actually lies within the city boundary. Sheffield's own open spaces total 8,000 acres. They range from Blacka Moor, a stretch of wild moorland on the edge of the Derbyshire Hills, to the **Botanical Gardens**, where rare plants in carefully tended beds surround elegant conservatories.

In **Meersbrook Park**, on the south side of the city, a timber-framed yeoman's house of the late 15th century is preserved as a museum of domestic life of the period. It is set in gardens planted with herbs and flowers typical of the time when it was built. The house, called **Bishops' House**, is said to have been the home of the brothers John and Geoffrey Blythe. John was Bishop of Salisbury from 1494 to 1499, and his brother was Bishop of Lichfield and Coventry from 1503 to 1533.

Beauchief Abbey, about 4 miles south-west of the city centre, was founded in 1175 by Robert Fitzranulph, in atonement for his part in

---

A STEELWORKS POWERED BY WATER

The story of the Industrial Revolution in Sheffield can be seen in the **Abbeydale Industrial Hamlet**, where a complete water-powered steelworks of the late 18th century has survived intact. From 1712 until 1933, the Abbeydale works made scythes, hay-knives and other agricultural tools. Today, the complete process can still be followed, from the making of the steel to the grinding of the finished product. Most impressive is the tilt forge where the scythes were formed under tilt hammers driven by huge waterwheels turned by the River Sheaf. Water power was used throughout the life of the works, except in times of drought, when a steam engine was used.

Also on the site are workmen's cottages, a manager's house, a coach-house and a warehouse, where an illustrated history of industrial development in the Sheffield area is on show.

Although the works ceased production in 1933, the furnace was relit during the Second World War to make high-quality steel.

A number of working days are held each year, when some of the furnaces are lit and the forges are

Tilt hammers were driven by huge waterwheels. The hammers struck 126 blows a minute as the wheel turned twice.

once again manned by craftsmen.

Another 18th-century factory, the **Shepherd Wheel** grinding works, is preserved in Whiteley Wood, north of Abbeydale. It has two grinding shops and is still in working order. The tenant of the works in 1794 was a Mr Shepherd, from whom the wheel takes its name, but there was a wheel there as early as 1584.

The old forge was built in 1785. Skilled craftsmen made scythes there, by welding three pieces of metal under the tilt hammers.

the plot to murder Thomas Becket, Archbishop of Canterbury. Only the western tower of the 12th-century abbey still stands.

Information Tel. 734760/1/4.
Location On the A61, 22 m. SW of Doncaster.
Parking Blonk Street; Campo Lane (2); Pond Street; Arundel Gate; Matilda Way; Wellington Street; Charter Row; Leopold Street; Eyre Lane; Union Lane (2); Rockingham Lane (2); Broad Street; Wheel Hill (2); Young Street; Boston Street; Furnival Square; Charles Street (2); Holly Street; Carver Street (2); Surrey Street; Tudor Street; Earl Way (all car parks).
District council City of Sheffield (Tel. 26444).
Population 477,100.
E-C Thur. **M-D** Mon., Tues., Wed., Fri. and Sat.
Police (Cc) Snig Hill (Tel. 78522).
Casualty hospitals Royal Hallamshire, Glossop Road (Tel. 26484) Mon., Tues., Thur., Fri. and Sun. Northern General, Herries Road (387253) Wed. and Sat. Accident and emergency service Ansafone (739444).
Post office (Cb) Fitzalan Square.
Theatres Crucible **(Bb)**, Norfolk Street (Tel. 79922); Lantern Theatre, Kenwood Park Road (51857); Library Theatre **(Bb)**, Surrey Street (734716); Merlin Theatre, Meadowbank Road

BISHOPS' HOUSE *The name of the 15th-century house is of recent origin; there is no evidence that it was ever occupied by bishops. It is now a museum.*

(51638); Montgomery, Surrey Street (20455); University Drama Studio, Glossop Road (78555); Lyceum, Tudor Place (754944).
Cinemas ABC **(Bc)**, Angel Street (Tel. 24620); Cineplex **(Bb)**, Charter Square (760778); Classic **(Cb)**, Fitzalan Square (25624); Gaumont Twin **(Bb)**, Barkers Pool (77962).
Public library (Bb) Surrey Street.
Places to see Cathedral **(Bc)**; City Museum; Cutlers' Hall **(Bb)**; Graves and Mappin Art Galleries **(Bb)**; York and Lancaster Regimental Museum; Abbeydale Industrial Hamlet; Beauchief Abbey; Shepherd Wheel; Bishops' House; Botanical Gardens; Kelham Island Industrial Museum;

Sheffield Manor and Turret House.
Shopping High Street; Angel Street; Castle Street; Exchange Street; Haymarket; Fargate Precinct; Pinstone Street; The Moor Precinct; Barkers Pool; Church Street; Castle Square (underground concourse); Attercliffe Road; Ecclesall Road South.
Events Lord Mayor's Parade (June); Sheffield Show (Sept.).
Sport County cricket, Yorkshire CC, Abbeydale Park. FA League football: Sheffield United FC, Bramall Lane; Sheffield Wednesday FC, Hillsborough. Greyhound racing, Owlerton Stadium, Penistone Road. Speedway racing Owlerton Stadium.
AA 24 hour service Tel. 28861.

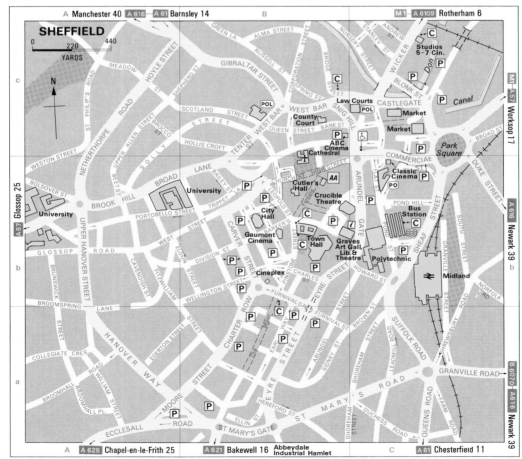

Shrewsbury Salop

The old county town of Shrewsbury (pronounced Shrozebury) can be seen from a distance rising clear of the surrounding countryside.

Its narrow streets branch off from two main thoroughfares, as in Roman towns. Shrewsbury may have been founded by Britons who abandoned the Roman city of Viroconium, the remains of which can be seen at Wroxeter, 5 miles south-east.

A castle commanding the approach to Shrewsbury was built soon after the Norman Conquest, but the present structure dates chiefly from about 1300.

Parts of the old town walls, including a 13th-century tower, also survive. Ten bridges connect the town to the opposite bank of the Severn.

St Chad's Church (1792), in St Chad's Terrace, is one of the few round churches in Britain. Statues commemorate two great men associated with the town: Charles Darwin (1809-82), born and educated in Shrewsbury, and Robert Clive (1725-74) – Clive of India. Clive was MP for Shrewsbury, from 1761 until his death, and was mayor in 1762.

Information Tel. 52019.
Location On the A5, 12 m. W of Telford.
Parking Barker Street (2); Riverside (2); Greyfriars; Belmont Place; Frankwell; Raven Meadows; St Mary's Place; Princess Street; Abbey Foregate; Kingsland Bridge (all car parks).
District council Borough of Shrewsbury and Atcham (Tel. 52255).
Population 59,900.
E-C Thur. **M-D** Wed., Fri. and Sat.
Police Monkmoor Road (Tel. 53971).
Casualty hospital Copthorne Hospital, Mytton Oak Road (Tel. 52244).
Post office (Bb) St Mary's Street.
Theatre (Bb) Music Hall, The Square (Tel. 52019).
Cinema (Bb) Empire, Mardol (Tel. 62257).

TUDOR SHREWSBURY *The Abbot's House of 1450, in Butcher Row, is an outstanding example of the well-preserved, black-and-white, half-timbered houses that make Shrewsbury one of the finest Tudor towns in England.*

Public library (Bb) Raven Meadows.
Places to see Abbot's House **(Bb)**; Castle **(Bb)**; Charles Darwin's birthplace; Clive House Museum **(Ba)**; Longden Coleham Pumping Station Museum **(Ba)**; Lion Hotel **(Ba)**; Ireland's Mansion **(Bb)**; Owen's Mansion **(Bb)**; Old Market Hall **(Bb)**; Rowley's House **(Ab)**; Viroconium Roman city, 5 m. SE.
Town trails Available from Tourist Information Centre, The Square.
Shopping Mardol; Pride Hill; Castle Street; High Street; Riverside Shopping Precinct.
Trade and industry Agriculture;

engineering.
Sport FA League football, Shrewsbury Town FC, The Gay Meadow.
AA 24 hour service Tel. 53003.

Sidmouth Devon

The River Sid trickles to the sea between cliffs of warm pink rock which shelter the town. For hundreds of years Sidmouth was a tiny fishing village. In the 19th century it became a smart seaside resort, and its Regency villas and Victorian cottages have kept their charm.

Information Tel. 6441 (summer); 6551 (winter).
Location On the B3175, 15 m. SE of Exeter.
Parking The Ham; Manor Road; Temple Street; Church Street (all car parks).
District council East Devon (Tel. 6551).
Population 12,400.
E-C Thur.
Police Temple Street (Tel. 2674).
Casualty hospital Victoria Cottage Hospital, All Saints Road (Tel. 2482).
Post office Vicarage Road.
Theatre Manor Pavilion, Manor Road (Tel. 4413).
Cinema Radway, Radway Place (Tel. 3085).
Public library Blackmore Drive.
Town trails Available from

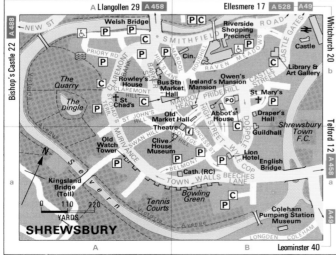

SHREWSBURY

Sidmouth Town Council, Sidmouth Museum or local shops.
Shopping Fore Street; High Street.
AA 24 hour service
Tel. Exeter 32121.

Sittingbourne Kent

The town's position on Milton Creek off the Swale waterway and its ample supply of water make it an ideal site for the paper-making industry. Since 1840 it has expanded rapidly as an industrial centre. Delightful villages and orchards lie round about.

Information Tel. 24381.
Location On the A2, 11 m. E of Rochester.
Parking Bell Road; St Michael's Road (2); Station Street; Central Avenue; Pembury Street; Avenue of Remembrance (all car parks).
District council Swale (Tel. 24381).
Population 33,600.
E-C Wed. **M-D** Fri.
Police Central Avenue (Tel. 72121).
Casualty hospital Medway Hospital, Windmill Road, Gillingham (Tel. Medway 46111).
Post office Central Avenue.
Public library Central Avenue.
Places to see Court Hall, Milton; Sailing Barge Museum, Crown Quay Lane.
Shopping High Street; Forum Shopping Precinct off High Street.
AA 24 hour service
Tel. Maidstone 55353.

Skegness Lincolnshire

The 9th Earl of Scarborough began planning Skegness as a holiday town in 1877. By 1881 its 1,843 ft long pier had been built, and holidaymakers were pouring into the town. Today it has a holiday camp, swimming-pools and 34 acres of seafront gardens, but no pier. This was destroyed in the gales of January 1978.

Information Tel. 4821 (summer).
Location On the A52, 23 m. NE of Boston.
Parking Wainfleet Road; Richmond Drive; Central Grand Parade; Seaview, North Parade; Beresford Avenue (all car parks).
District council East Lindsey (Tel. Louth 60111).
Population 14,450.
E-C Thur. **M-D** Fri., Sat. (daily in summer).
Police Park Avenue (Tel. 2222).
Casualty hospital Dorothy Avenue (Tel. 2401).
Post office Roman Bank.
Theatres Arcadia, Drummond Road (Tel. 3102); Embassy, Grand Parade (2263); Festival Pavilion, Tower Esplanade (4267); Pier, Grand Parade (4267/3128).
Cinema Tower, Lumley Road (Tel. 3938).
Public library Roman Bank.
Places to see Church Farm Museum, Church Road; Lifeboat, South Parade; Gibraltar Point Nature

SKEGNESS

IS SO BRACING

Illustrated Guide from Secretary Advancement Association
Skegness or any LNER Enquiry Office.

CELEBRATED POSTER *John Hassall's railway poster of 70 years ago is still used to advertise Skegness.*

Reserve, 3 m. S.
Shopping Roman Bank; High Street; Lumley Road; Drummond Road.
AA 24 hour service
Tel. Lincoln 42363.

Skelmersdale and Up Holland Lancashire

The industrial town which grew up around the coal mines in the 19th century is being rebuilt and enlarged, and will eventually have a population of 70,000. Up Holland, which is linked to its larger neighbour in the new town development scheme, is a centre of the brick industry.

Information Tel. Ormskirk 24933.
Location On the A577, 3 m. SE of Ormskirk.
Parking Skelmersdale: Northway; Southway; Westgate; Birkrig; Birleywood. Upholland: Hall Green; Tithebarn Street (all car parks).
District council West Lancashire (Tel. Ormskirk 77177).
Population 43,500.
E-C Up Holland: Wed. **M-D** Tues. – Sat.
Police The Concourse, Skelmersdale (Tel. 24101).
Casualty hospital Ormskirk and District General, Wigan Road, Ormskirk (Tel. Ormskirk 75471).
Post office The Concourse.
Cinema Focus, Town Centre, Skelmersdale (Tel. 25041).
Public library The Concourse.
Shopping Concourse Shopping Precinct; Sandy Lane Shopping Centre.
Places to see Beacon Park, Tawd Valley Park, Town Centre.
Town trails Beacon Park Nature Trail; Tawd Valley Park, available from Information Office, The Concourse.
Trade and industry Metal production; light engineering.
AA 24 hour service
Tel. Liverpool (051) 709 7252.

Skipton N. Yorks.

Sheep graze on the surrounding hills before being brought for sale in the town's market. Skipton's atmosphere is that of a farming community, and factories and mills have done little to change this.

At the top of the High Street stands an 11th-century castle, rebuilt in the 14th and 17th centuries.

Information Tel. 2304.
Location On the A65, 22 m. W of Harrogate.
Parking High Street; Coach Street; Keighley Road (2); Cavendish Street; Newmarket Street (all car parks).
District council Craven (Tel. 2304).
Population 13,200.
E-C Tues. **M-D** Mon., Wed., Fri. and Sat.
Police Otley Road (Tel. 3377).
Casualty hospital Airedale General Hospital, Eastburn, Keighley (Tel. Steeton 52511).
Post office Swadford Street.
Theatre Little Theatre, Clifford Street.
Cinemas Regals 1 and 2, Keighley Road (Tel. 2161); Plaza, Sackville Street (3417).
Public library High Street.
Places to see Castle, The Bailey; Craven Museum, Town Hall; Broughton Hall, 3½ m. W.
Shopping High Street; Keighley Road; Swadford Street.
Event Skipton Gala (June).
AA 24 hour service
Tel. Leeds 38161.

Sleaford Lincolnshire

The elaborately decorated west front of a 12th-century parish church dwarfs the other buildings in Sleaford Market Place. Its 144 ft stone spire is one of the oldest in England.

Mounds beside Castle Causeway are all that remain of the 12th-century castle where, in 1216, King John was taken with a fatal fever. He died at Newark, in Nottinghamshire.

Information Tel. 303456.
Location On the A15, 17 m. SE of Lincoln.
Parking Carre Street (2); Church Lane; Eastgate; Jermyn Street; Market Place; Westgate (2); Watergate (all car parks).
District council North Kesteven (Tel. 303241).
Population 8,500.
E-C Thur. **M-D** Mon.
Police Kesteven Street (Tel. 302420).
Casualty hospital Grantham and Kesteven District, Manthorpe Road, Grantham (Tel. Grantham 5232).
Post office Southgate.
Cinema Picturedrome, Southgate (Tel. 303187).
Public library Watergate.
Shopping Southgate Shopping Precinct, Market Place.
Trade and industry Seeds; malting.
AA 24 hour service
Tel. Nottingham 787751.

Slough Berkshire

In the 1930s Sir John Betjeman strongly disapproved of the planning decisions which established 850 factories and a new town in what was previously the rural area of Slough in the Thames Valley. He wrote:

"Come, friendly bombs, and fall on Slough.

It isn't fit for humans now."

For all Sir John's pique, Slough turned out open and airy, if modern. There are 533 acres of parkland within its boundaries, and extensive opportunities for sport and recreation.

The village of Upton, now part of Slough, has a Norman church and a graveyard with ancient yews. It is claimed by some to have inspired the 18th-century poet Thomas Gray's *Elegy written in a Country Churchyard.* Others suggest Stoke Poges where there is a monument to the poet.

BACKYARD ASTRONOMER

The astronomer Sir William Herschel (1738-1822) made the first true map of the universe with the aid of a telescope he built in his garden at Slough. A monument in Windsor Road commemorates his achievement.

Herschel's giant telescope had a 48 in. mirror.

Information Town Hall, Bath Road (Tel. 23881).
Location On the A4, 29 m. W of London.
Parking Wellington Street (3); Brunel Way; Herschel Street (2); Burlington Road; Hatfield Road; The Grove; Sussex Place; Yeovil Road; Malton Avenue (all car parks).
District council Borough of Slough (Tel. 23881).
Population 87,000.
E-C Wed. **M-D** Tue., Thurs., Fri., Sat.
Police Windsor Road (Tel. 31282).
Casualty hospital Wexham Park Hospital, Wexham Road (Tel. 34567).
Post office Queensmere, High Street.
Theatre Fulcrum Leisure Centre, Queensmere (Tel. 38669).
Cinema Granada, Windsor Road (Tel. 21212).
Public library High Street.
Places to see Cliveden, 4 m. NW; Thomas Gray Monument, Stoke Poges.
Shopping Queensmere Shopping Centre, off High Street; High Street.

Event Slough Festival of Arts (May–June).
AA 24 hour service
Tel. Reading 581122.

Solihull W. Midlands

Some fine timber-framed Tudor buildings still survive in the High Street and elsewhere in the modern centre of Solihull.

Malvern Hall, in Brueton Avenue, is a 16th-century house now used as a school. Chester House at Knowle, 3 miles south of Solihull, is a timber framed building with parts dating from the mid-15th century. It is now used as a branch library.

St Alphege's Church has a 13th-century chancel and a 168 ft tower and spire.

Information Tel. Birmingham (021) 705 6789 (ext. 505).
Location On the A41, 7 m. SE of Birmingham.
Parking Warwick Road; Poplar Road; Lode Lane; Church Hill Road; George Road; Station Road; Homer Road (all car parks).
District council Metropolitan Borough of Solihull (Tel. 021 705 6789).
Population 111,500.
E-C Wed.
Police Homer Road (Tel. 021 705 7611).
Casualty hospital Solihull Hospital, Union Road (Tel. 021 705 6741).
Post office Drury Lane.
Theatre Library, Homer Road, (Tel. 021 705 0060).
Cinema Solihull, High Street,
Solihull (Tel. 021 705 0398).
Public library Homer Road.
Places to see Malvern Hall, Brueton Avenue; Chester House, Knowle, 3 m. S; Packwood House, near Lapworth, 6 m. S.
Shopping High Street; Mell Square Precinct.
Trade and industry Motor vehicles; light engineering.
AA 24 hour service
Tel. 021 550 4858.

Southampton see page 370

Southend-on-Sea Essex

Big, brash and noisy, Southend has been a day-tripper's delight for nearly a century – since the first Thames paddle-steamers thrashed down river to land Londoners at what was then the world's longest pleasure pier.

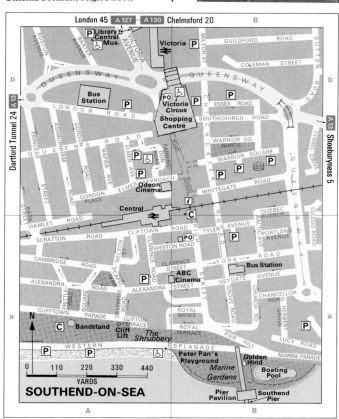

SOUTHEND-ON-SEA

Southend-on-Sea is actually on the Thames Estuary, and when the tide goes out it leaves a vast expanse of mud stretching about a mile from the seafront in places. So Southend's 1¼ mile long pier was essential for the steamers when it was built in 1889. The trippers now arrive by road or rail, and the pier, now shortened by fire, is used only by the lifeboat. Near the pier is a full-size replica of Drake's *Golden Hind.* Fun and frivolity stretch all the way along the seafront, culminating in the Kursaal amusement park.

Away from the hustle of the seafront can be found the Southend of an earlier age. Less than 2 miles inland from the pier entrance is Prittlewell, once a village from which the town grew. The name Southend means the south end of Prittlewell.

Prittlewell Priory dates back to the 12th century. Set in acres of park-

END OF AN ERA *Southend Pier is now only a gaunt memorial to the golden age of the day trippers.*

land, it now houses the South-East Essex Museum, devoted to local and natural history.

Southchurch Hall, a few minutes' walk from the Kursaal amusement park, is a moated, timber-framed manor house of the early 14th century and furnished in Tudor style.

To the west of the pier the Esplanade runs at the foot of the cliffs of Westcliff, and a lift climbs the steep face to the ornamental gardens. Further west is Old Leigh, a fishing village where the cockle boats can be seen unloading.

Transport of the modern age can be seen at Southend Airport, and in the appropriately named Aviation Way is the Historic Aircraft Museum, containing some 30 aircraft.

Information Tel. 44091 or 49451.
Location On the A13, 20 m. SE of Chelmsford.
Parking Baxter Avenue; Milton Street; London Road; Elmer Avenue; Warrior Square; Essex Street; Clarence Road; Richmond Avenue; Great Eastern Avenue; Baltic Avenue; Chancellor Road (all car parks).

District council Southend-on-Sea (Tel. 49451).
Population 156,700.
E-C Wed. **M-D** Thur., Fri. and Sat.
Police Victoria Avenue (Tel. 41212).
Casualty hospital Southend General, Prittlewell Chase, Westcliff-on-Sea (Tel. 48911).
Post office (Ba) Weston Road; Victoria Circus Precinct.
Theatres Palace, London Road, Westcliff-on-Sea (Tel. 42564); Cliffs Pavilion, Westcliff Parade (351135).
Cinemas ABC **(Ba)** Alexandra Street (Tel. 44580); Odeons 1 and 2 **(Ab)**, Elmer Approach (44434); Classics 1 and 2, London Road, Westcliff-on-Sea (42773).
Public library (Ab) Victoria Avenue.
Places to see Central Museum **(Ab)**; Historic Aircraft Museum; Prittlewell Priory and Museum; *Golden Hind* and Waxworks Museum **(Ba)**; Southchurch Hall.
Shopping High Street; Southchurch Road; London Road; Victoria Circus Precinct; Hamlet Court Road; Leigh Broadway.
Trade and industry Engineering.
Sport FA League football, Southend United FC, Victoria Avenue; Greyhound racing, Grainger Road; County cricket, Southchurch Park.
AA 24 hour service Tel. Chelmsford 61711.

South Molton Devon

This ancient sheep and cattle-market town on the edge of Exmoor dates back to the 12th century. Until the middle of the 19th century it thrived as a centre of the wool trade.

A plaque on the Guildhall (1740-3) commemorates Hugh Squier (1625-1710), a local farmer's son who became a wealthy London merchant before he was 30 and built and endowed the town's grammar school in 1684.

South Molton Museum, housed in a 17th-century building, contains several fascinating exhibits, including 18th-century wig-making tools, cider press and a wooden fire engine.

The parish church of St Mary Magdalene, approached along an avenue of limes, was built in the 1430s and preserves its original stone pulpit with carvings of five of the apostles.

There are many fine Georgian houses, particularly in East Street.

Henry Williamson (1895-1977), author of *Tarka the Otter* and *Dandelion Days,* lived at Shallowford House, just outside the town.

Information Tel. 2378.
Location On the A361, 12 m. SE of Barnstaple.
Parking The Square; Central (both car parks).
District council North Devon (Tel. Barnstaple 72511).
Population 3,410.
E-C Wed. **M-D** Thur.
Police North Road (Tel. 2221).
Casualty hospital North Devon District Hospital, Raleigh Park, Barnstaple (Tel. Barnstaple 72577).
Post office The Square.
Public library East Street.
Places to see Borough Museum.
Town trails Available from Information Centre, East Street.
Shopping The Square; East Street; South Street.
AA 24 hour service Tel. Barnstaple 45691.

Southport Merseyside

In the late 18th century an enterprising innkeeper named William Sutton built the first sea-bathing house on the beach at Southport, and thus founded a new seaside resort. Dignified, restful, noted for its gardens and golf courses, the town stands in marked contrast to boisterous Blackpool a few miles away. The pier, just under ¾ mile long and served by an electric railway, begins inland by crossing an 86 acre marine lake, on which yacht, canoe and dinghy races are held. Flanking the lake are some of the attractive gardens for which Southport is famed. Hesketh Park is one of the most splendid open spaces in the north. Victoria Park is the annual venue of the international three-day Southport Flower Show.

THE CONTINENTAL LOOK *Southport's main thoroughfare, Lord Street, is a mile-long, tree-shaded boulevard, lined with flower gardens, cafes and many fine shops.*

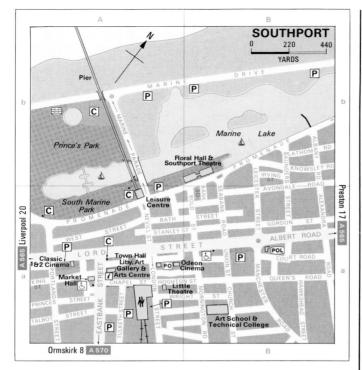

Thatched cottages surround the parish church of St Cuthbert, built in the early 18th century. It contains some fine wood-carving.

The Botanic Gardens Museum contains an outstanding collection of Liverpool porcelain, together with Victoriana, local water-colours and a section devoted to British birds. Steamport is a transport museum that displays steam locomotives, buses and tramcars. The Atkinson Art Gallery has a good collection of 19th and 20th-century English paintings and sculpture.

About 5 miles east of Southport, the Martin Mere Wildfowl Sanctuary provides a haven for geese and many other water-birds.

Southport is probably second only to St Andrews, Scotland, as a centre for British golf. The town has five 18-hole courses, including the famous Royal Birkdale where major tournaments such as the British Open are held.

Information Tel. 33133 or 40404; or 33333 (evenings and weekends).
Location On the A565, 20 m. N of Liverpool.
Parking Tulketh Street; West Street; London Street; Marine Drive (Sea Wall); Esplanade; Derby Road; Kingsway; King Street; Anchor Street; Union Street (all car parks).
District council Metropolitan Borough of Sefton
(Tel. Liverpool (051) 922 4040).
Population 89,700.
E-C Tues., **M-D** Daily, except Sun.
Police (Ba) Albert Road
(Tel. 38000).
Casualty hospital General Infirmary, Scarisbrick New Road (Tel. 42901).
Post office (Aa) Lord Street.
Theatres Southport **(Bb)**,

Promenade (Tel. 40404); Little **(Aa)**, Hoghton Street (30521); Floral Hall **(Bb)**, Promenade (40404); Arts Centre **(Aa)**, Lord Street (40011).
Cinemas Classics 1 and 2 **(Aa)**, Lord Street (Tel. 30627); ABC, Lord Street (32797); Odeon **(Aa)**, Lord Street (35582).
Public library (Aa) Lord Street.
Places to see Botanic Gardens Museum, Churchtown; Atkinson Art Gallery, Lord Street; Steamport Transport Museum, Derby Road; Southport Zoo, Princes Park; Ainsdale National Nature Reserve, 3 m. S off A565; Martin Mere Wildfowl Sanctuary, 5 m. E.
Shopping Lord Street; Chapel Street; Eastbank Street; London Street; Tulketh Street; King Street; Churchtown; High Park; Birkdale; Hillside; Ainsdale.
Events Southport Flower Show (Aug.); Southport Music and Drama Festival (Sept.).
Sport County cricket, Trafalgar Road. Royal Birkdale Golf Club.
AA 24 hour service
Tel. 051 709 7252.

South Shields Tyne & Wear
This growing port at the mouth of the River Tyne is a town of remarkable contrasts. It is both ancient and modern, and its busy docks are a short bus ride from its holiday attractions – a sandy beach, wide promenades and flower-decked gardens. The Romans used South Shields as a granary for legions campaigning in the north and stationed along Hadrian's Wall. The grain was shipped into the town and stored in granaries, at least nine of which can be traced at the Roman fort.

In the 19th century, South Shields

boomed as a port, shipping coal from the Durham fields. The coast trade has declined, and the docks which stretched for 3 miles along the Tyne are now a major centre for importing timber from Scandinavia.

Information Tel. 554321 or 557411.
Location On the A183, 11 m. E of Newcastle upon Tyne.
Parking Mile End Road; Thomas Street; North Street; Coronation Street; Pollard Street; Marsden; South Promenade; Trow Quarry; Pier Parade; Harbour Drive (all car parks).
District council Borough of South Tyneside (Tel. 554321).
Population 87,200.
E-C Wed. **M-D** Mon., Sat.
Police Keppel Street (Tel. 568011).
Casualty hospital Ingham Infirmary, Westoe Road (Tel. 560221).
Post office Keppel Street.
Cinemas ABC, Ocean Road (Tel. 561503); Focus, Mile End Road (560819).
Public library Catherine Street.
Places to see Roman Fort Museum, Baring Street; Museum and Art Gallery, Ocean Road.
Shopping King Street; Prince Edward Road; Frederick Street; Boldon Lane.
AA 24 hour service
Tel. Newcastle upon Tyne 610111.

Southwark see London

Southwold Suffolk
Domesday Book records Southwold as an important fishing port. But in the following centuries a shingle bar built up across the harbour mouth and stifled any chance of the town developing as a major port.

Now it is a small resort at the mouth of the River Blyth, with a brewery that produces a renowned ale which is still delivered by horse and dray.

In 1672 the English and French fleets clashed with the Dutch under de Ruyter in Sole Bay, just offshore. The battle was bloody but indecisive, and many bodies were washed ashore. Six 18 lb. cannons standing on the cliff were provided in 1745 for the defence of the town as the result of a petition to George II.

"SOUTHWOLD JACK"
Services at St Edmund's Church begin after the carved-oak man-at-arms strikes a bell.

LANDMARK *A gleaming lighthouse, topped by a golden weathervane, forms a distinctive landmark above Southwold's contrasting red-brick and flint cottages.*

Once the home of Maurice Johnson, founder of the Gentlemen's Society, it is now a natural-history museum.

The Church of St Mary and St Nicholas, in Church Street, was built in 1284, but its architecture spans the succeeding centuries. Among its outstanding features are the 15th-century timber roof carried on supports carved as angels, and a brass chandelier of 1766.

Information Tel. 5468.
Location On the A16, 20 m. N of Peterborough.
Parking Church Gate; Winfrey Avenue; Broad Street; Vine Street; Sheep Market; Albion Street (all car parks).
District council South Holland (Tel. 3272).
Population 18,200.
E-C Thur. **M-D** Tues., Sat.
Police Sheep Market (Tel. 2233).
Casualty hospital Johnson Hospital, Priory Road (Tel. 2386).
Post office Sheep Market.
Cinema Gemini, London Road (Tel. 3077).
Public library Victoria Street.
Places to see Museum, Broad Street; Ayscoughfee Hall; Springfields gardens.
Town trails Available from Information Centre, Ayscoughfee Hall.
Shopping High Street; Sheep Market; Market Place.
Event Spalding Flower Parade (May).
AA 24 hour service
Norwich 29401.

Information Tel. 722366.
Location On the A1095, 15 m. S of Lowestoft.
Parking Pier; Ferry Road; Harbour Quay; Gardner Road; The Common (all car parks).
District council Waveney (Tel. Lowestoft 62111).
Population 1,800.
E-C Wed. **M-D** Mon., Thur.
Police Station Road (Tel. 722666).
Casualty hospital District General, Lowestoft Road, Gorleston (Tel. Great Yarmouth 600611).
Post office High Street.
Theatre St Edmund's Hall, Cumberland Road (Tel. 722389, summer only).
Public library North Green.
Places to see Museum, Victoria Street; Sutherland House; Lifeboat Museum; Old Water Tower.
Shopping High Street; East Street; Queen Street.
Events Trinity Fair (May); Model Yacht Regatta (Aug.).
AA 24 hour service
Tel. Norwich 29401.

Spalding Lincolnshire

In late spring a sea of tulips and daffodils washes round this Fenland town, where more than half Britain's bulbs are grown. Each May thousands of visitors come to see the Flower Parade and visit Springfields, a colour-splashed 30 acre garden of spring flowers and roses.

The Spalding Gentlemen's Society Museum, in Broad Street, commemorates the second-oldest antiquarian society in the country, founded in 1710 and numbering among its members the scientist Sir Isaac Newton and the poet Alexander Pope. It has a fine library built up by gifts from its members, together with manuscripts, coins and porcelain.

Ayscoughfee Hall, in Churchgate, is a restored 15th-century mansion.

TULIP TOWN *A tulip gatherer on the town sign symbolises Spalding's association with the flower industry. The open book depicts the Gentleman's Society.*

Spennymoor Durham

Coal has been mined in the area since the 17th century, and the ironworks were the largest in Europe when they opened in 1892. But the Depression and the national coal strike in 1926 brought economic disaster to Spennymoor. A programme of modernisation has been carried out, and industrial estates have been developed.

The village of Kirk Merrington, 2 miles south and 600 ft above sea level, has a fine Norman church and offers good views of the Wear Valley and Cleveland Hills.

Information Tel. 816166.
Location On the A688, 5 m. S of Durham.
Parking behind Parkwood Precinct; Clarence Street; Silver Street; Church Street; Princess Street.
District council Sedgefield (Tel. 816166).
Population 20,600.
E-C Wed. **M-D** Sat.
Police Dundas Street (Tel. 814411).
Casualty hospital Bishop Auckland General, Cockton Hill Road (Tel. Bishop Auckland 604040).
Post office Parkwood Precinct.
Public library Cheapside.
Shopping High Street; Parkwood Precinct; Cheapside.
AA 24 hour service
Tel. Middlesbrough 246832.

SOUTHAMPTON Hampshire

A front-line port for 1,000 years

According to legend it was at Southampton that King Canute ordered the waves to retreat; that he did not succeed is evident in the fact that, in the 1,000 years since, it has been one of Britain's leading seaports. Southampton has always been a front-line port, both as a jumping-off point for English armies and as a target for invaders. The Romans had a port there called Clausentum. It was William the Conqueror's port for his ships coming from Normandy, and Richard the Lionheart sailed from there on his Crusades. In 1338 the French sacked the town, and Edward III returned the visit in 1346 when his armies embarked at Southampton for the invasion of France and their victory at Crécy.

In the two World Wars, more than 10 million troops left Southampton for the battlefields of France, and in the Second World War the town was heavily bombed. But there was a time when the town enjoyed a period of peace and tranquillity. This was when the Georgians, obsessed with the medicinal benefits of sea-bathing, made Southampton a spa. It lasted for nearly 50 years, until the Prince Regent transferred his affections to Brighton and society went with him.

The 8 mile stretch of Southampton Water runs inland from The Solent to where the rivers Test and Itchen converge to form a wide peninsula. On this broad arrowhead are grouped Southampton's docks. From here sail craft of all kinds: liners to America, cruise ships to the Mediterranean, car ferries to Europe, and hovercraft and hydrofoils to the Isle of Wight.

At the tip of the peninsula, the **Eastern Docks** include the Ocean Dock which was home to the world's greatest liners. The *Mauretania*, *Queen Mary* and *Queen Elizabeth* berthed at the dock, and today it is the home of *Queen Elizabeth II*, possibly the last of the Atlantic greyhounds.

The **Western Docks** extend along the River Test and include the King George V Graving Dock, the largest in the world when it was opened up in 1933. It can take vessels of up to 100,000 tons gross.

Royal Pier

The original pier on the Western Esplanade was opened by the Duchess of Kent and her daughter, Princess Victoria, in 1833. It was built of timber, but was replaced by the present cast-iron structure several years later. When it was erected, Royal Pier was the largest pleasure pier in the South of England, and had a concert pavilion and horse-drawn tramway to the pierhead. Royal Pier is now closed as it is no longer safe.

Historic quay

Outside the West Gate in Western Esplanade is the **Mayflower Memorial**, a tall stone column standing near the spot where the Pilgrim Fathers embarked for America in 1620. The park opposite the memorial occupies the site of the old West Quay where the *Mayflower* was moored. The quay

is one of the best viewing points for the constant movement of ships using the docks.

In Norman times the northern entrance to Southampton was **Bargate**, which later served as the town's guildhall and court house. It now

houses a museum which displays an embroidered tapestry depicting the story of Southampton during the Second World War.

It was at Bargate, it is said, that Shakespeare presented his new plays to his patron, the Earl of Southampton, and in *Henry V* the playwright told of the plot against the king by Richard of Cambridge, who was executed just outside Bargate.

The original walls and towers of Southampton were built by the Normans, but the only surviving section, in Western Esplanade, is the wall erected after the devastating French attack in 1338.

The **towers**, however, remain; **Polymond** at the north-east corner of the wall, **Catchcold** at the north-west, **Wind Whistle** on the western side and **God's House Tower** in the south. God's House, or Hospital, was founded in 1185 and contains a Norman chapel.

Civic Centre

The **Guildhall** and **Art Gallery** were built of Portland stone in the 1930s. There is a 182 ft high clock-tower with a peal of bells.

The Art Gallery is part of the Civic Centre group of buildings and specialises in British paintings, including works by Edward Burne-Jones, L. S. Lowry and Graham Sutherland. Works by continental masters, nota-

THE DEPARTURE OF THE MAYFLOWER *A copy of the painting by A. Forestier which depicts the scene on West Quay as the* Mayflower *sets out on her journey to America. The ship later called at Plymouth, from where the last leg of the journey began.*

QUEEN OF THE SEAS *Tugs bustle around the* Queen Elizabeth II *as she leaves the Ocean Terminal and heads towards the sea.*

bly Renoir and Van Dyck, are also among the exhibits.

Although Southampton was made a city in 1964 it has no cathedral. Its main church is St Mary's, in St Mary's Street. It was built in the late 19th century and considerably restored in 1956 as it was bombed during the Second World War. The church's peal of bells inspired the song *The Bells of St Mary's*.

Southampton's oldest church is St Michael's, in Castle Way. The tower is Saxon, with a spire added in the 19th century. The church has a rare 12th-century font imported from Tournai in France.

Holy Rood stands at the corner of Bernard Street and High Street, and was damaged beyond restoration during the air-raids of 1940. But the 600-year-old tower has been preserved as a memorial to the men of the Merchant Navy who were killed during the Second World War.

The **Tudor House** is a typical building of the 16th century, with half-timbered walls, overhanging gables, mullioned windows and oak-panelled rooms. The garden is laid out in Tudor style and in it there is a 16th-century bronze cannon made for Henry VIII.

God's House Tower Museum is devoted to archaeological finds including prehistoric, Roman, Saxon and medieval relics. The oldest items on show are hand-axes dating from the Stone Age and animal bones from the Ice Age.

In medieval times Southampton was a port for the export of wool, and the 14th-century **Wool House** is now the city's maritime museum. The roof is of Spanish chestnut, and carved on the beams are the names of French prisoners of war who were confined there during the 18th century.

The museum traces the history of merchant shipping, and the walls are lined with models of ships from the past to the present day.

In Marlands Hall, Kings Bridge Lane, is Southampton's latest museum, dedicated to R. J. Mitchell who designed the Spitfire, the fighter-plane that helped to win the Battle of Britain. Mitchell built his first Spitfire in Southampton, and one of the thousands built is on display. In the late 1920s the designer built a series of seaplanes which captured for Britain the coveted Schneider Trophy. Mitchell's Supermarine S6B, which won the event in 1931 with a speed of 340 mph, was the forerunner of the Spitfire and is in the museum.

Titanic remembered

A white-marble sculpture in **East Park** recalls a sad moment in Southampton's history. It is dedicated to the engineers of the *Titanic* who died when the liner struck an iceberg in 1912, four days after leaving Ocean Dock on her maiden voyage across the Atlantic.

There are several ancient taverns in the city, especially in the High Street. The Dolphin, built in 1432 and rebuilt in 1760, has elegant bow windows. The Star is late Georgian and, like the Dolphin, was once a coaching inn. Southampton's oldest tavern, the Red Lion, is also in the High Street. It dates from the 12th century, and may have been the "courtroom in Southampton" which Shakespeare mentions in *Henry V*.

Information Tel. 23855.
Location On the A27, 13 m. S of Winchester.
Parking Portland Terrace; Eastgate Street; Southbrook Road; Gloucester Square; College Street; Grosvenor Square; Rockstone Place; Western Esplanade; Lime Street; Town Quay; West Park Road; Havelock Road; Commercial Road; Wyndham Place; Kings Park Road; Amoy Street; Wilton Avenue (all car parks).
District council City of Southampton (Tel. 23855).
Population 204,400.
E-C Mon., Wed. **M-D** Thur., Fri. and Sat.
Police (Ab) Civic Centre (Tel. 34234).
Casualty hospital General, Tremona Road, Shirley (Tel. 777222).
Post office (Aa) High Street.
Theatres Guildhall **(Ab)**, Civic Centre (Tel. 32601); Mountbatten Theatre **(Bb)**, East Park Terrace (29381); Nuffield Theatre, University Road (555028).
Cinemas ABC 1, 2 & 3 **(Ab)**, Above Bar (Tel. 23536); Gaumont **(Ab)**, Commercial Road (29772); Odeon **(Ab)**, Above Bar (22243).

TUDOR HOUSE *Within the half-timbered walls are rooms furnished in the style of the period.*

Public library (Ab) Commercial Road.
Places to see Bargate Museum **(Aa)**, High Street; Guildhall Art Gallery **(Ab)**, Civic Centre Road; God's House Tower Museum **(Aa)**, Winkle Street; Tudor House **(Aa)**, Bugle Street; Maritime Museum **(Aa)**, Town Quay; Town Walls; R. J. Mitchell Museum **(Ab)**, Marlands Hall.
Shopping Above Bar Street; Shirley Shopping Precinct; Bedford Place.
Town trails Available from the Southampton Tourist Guides Association. (Tel. 23855).
Sport FA League football, Southampton FC, The Dell, Milton Road.
Car ferries To Le Havre, Cherbourg (Tel. 34444); to Isle of Wight (22042); Hydrofoil to Cowes (27599).
AA 24 hour service Tel. 36811.

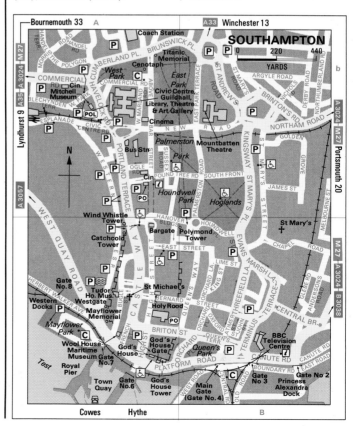

Stafford Staffordshire

The centre of Stafford retains its medieval street pattern, built around the ancient market square. Many of the original half-timbered buildings have now disappeared, but some fine examples remain. The most outstanding is the 16th–17th-century, many-gabled High House, which sheltered Charles I and Prince Rupert for three nights in 1642. In the same street, Greengate, is the Tudor Swan Hotel. George Borrow (1803-81), the travel writer, worked at the inn as an ostler and described it in *Romany Rye*.

The 12th–15th-century parish church of St Mary lost much of its medieval stone and wood when it was restored in the 1840s. But it retains its 13th-century nave and tower, and a fine Norman font.

Izaak Walton (1593-1683), author of *The Compleat Angler*, who was born in Eastgate Street, was baptised at this font. There is also a bust to him in the north aisle.

A cottage at Shallowford, 5 miles north-west of Stafford, where Walton once lived, is now a museum dedicated to his life and works.

The William Salt Library, in Eastgate Street, is a fine 18th-century house containing a large collection of pictures, maps, manuscripts and other items illustrating the history of the borough and county.

Shugborough Hall, 5½ miles south-east of the town, is a neo-Classical building of 1693 and later the ancestral home of the Earls of Lichfield. Apart from containing outstanding collections of silver, glass, porcelain, paintings and furniture, it houses the Staffordshire County Museum, devoted to crafts, industries, agriculture and costumes. In the grounds are a Doric temple and a Chinese house.

South-east of Stafford begins Cannock Chase, 30,000 acres of wild parkland, once the hunting ground of royalty and now one of the most extensive leisure areas in the Midlands.

Information Tel. 3181.
Location On the A34, 18 m. S of Stoke-on-Trent.
Parking Bridge Street; South Walls (2); North Walls (2); Chell Road (2); Broad Street; Tenterbanks (2); Earl Street (2) (all car parks).
District council Borough of Stafford (Tel. 3181).
Population 55,500.
E-C Wed. **M-D** Tues., Fri. and Sat.
Police (Bb) Eastgate Street (Tel. 58151).
Casualty hospital Stafford General Infirmary **(Ab)**, Foregate Street (Tel. 58251).
Post office (Aa) Chetwynd House, Greengate Street.
Theatres The Gate House, and The Cabin, both in Borough Hall **(Bb)**, Eastgate Street (Tel. 53595).
Cinemas Astra **(Aa)**, The Green (Tel. 51277); Picture House **(Aa)**, Bridge Street (58291).
Public library (Aa) The Green.
Places to see The Castle; High House **(Aa)**, Greengate Street; Chetwynd House **(Aa)**; William Salt Library **(Bb)**; Museum and Art Gallery **(Aa)**.
Shopping Greengate Street; Bridge Street; Princess Street Precinct; Sheridan Centre, Gaolgate Street.
AA 24 hour service
Tel. Stoke-on-Trent 25881.

Staines Surrey

The Roman road from London to the West Country crossed the Thames and Colne rivers at what is now Staines. The Romans called the set-tlement there *Ad Pontes* (at the bridges), and ever since their days it has been a staging post on the route to the west.

Among the town's notable 19th-century buildings are the Flemish-style Town Hall in the Market Place, the stone bridge over the Thames, and the Church of St Mary, which has a 17th-century base to its tower.

The London Stone, by the river, was put in place in 1285 to mark the western limit of the capital's jurisdiction over the Thames.

Information Tel. 51499.
Location On the A308, 6 m. SE of Windsor.
Parking South Street; Bridge Street; Kingston Road; Thames Street (all car parks).
District council Borough of Spelthorne (Tel. 51499).
Population 53,800.
E-C Thur. **M-D** Wed., Sat.
Police London Road (Tel. 50261).
Casualty hospital Ashford Hospital, London Road, Ashford (Tel. Ashford 51188).
Post office High Street.
Cinema ABC, 1, 2 and 3, Clarence Street (Tel. 53316).
Public library Oast House, Kingston Road (moving to Elmsleigh Centre in October, 1982).
Places to see Town Hall and Museum, Market Square; London Stone; Church of St Mary.
Shopping High Street, Elmsleigh Centre.
Events Staines Regatta (July); Swan Upping (July).
AA 24 hour service
Tel. Guildford 72841.

Stamford Lincolnshire

Stamford was an early Anglo Saxon settlement, and later was taken over by the Danes. The Normans built a castle beside the river, and in 1215 Earl Warenne assembled the barons and an army of 2,000 there to march on Runnymede in order to force King John to agree to Magna Carta.

Stamford became a prosperous wool town and an important religious centre in the Middle Ages. There were four monasteries and priories, four friaries, six religious hospitals and 14 parish churches in the town. Five of these early churches remain. There are also many fine medieval, 17th and 18th-century buildings in the local grey stone, making Stamford one of the most elegant towns in the Midlands. Six churches stand in 1 sq. mile. St Mary's has a magnificent 13th-century spire; All Saints has a spire standing 152 ft; St Martin's and St John's are both fine examples of English Perpendicular architecture; and St George's was enlarged in 1449 by Sir William Bruges, first Garter King of Arms. The sixth church, St Michael's, collapsed while being restored in 1832, and the present church was built on the site four years later. Browne's Hospital, found-

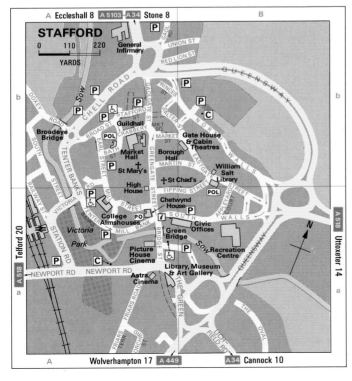

STAFFORD
0 110 220
YARDS

A Eccleshall 8   A 5103   A 34   Stone 8   B

General Infirmary
UNION ST
RED LION ST
QUEENSWAY
PRINCES
P
C
GAOLGATE STREET
STAFFORD ST
CRABBERY
Guildhall
MKT ST
MARKET
Gate House & Cabin Theatres
Broadeye Bridge
CHELL ROAD
SOW
DOXEY ROAD
BROAD ST
EARL STREET
BATH ST
SALTER ST
Market Hall
Borough Hall
GREENGATE ST
St Mary's
MARTIN
EASTGATE ST
William Salt Library
High House
St Chad's
TIPPING STREET
POL
Chetwynd House
PO
College Almshouses
SOUTH
WALLS
APPLEYARD STREET
A 518 Uttoxeter 14
Civic Offices
Green Bridge
Recreation Centre
SOW
N
QUEENSWAY
Victoria Park
MILL BANK
BRIDGE ST
Picture House Cinema
Library, Museum & Art Gallery
Astra Cinema
STATION RD
RAILWAY ST
TENTER BANKS
VICTORIA RD
Telford 20
A 518
NEWPORT RD
NEWPORT RD
THE GREEN
FRIARS TERR
FRIARS RD
ORCHARD ST
LICHFIELD RD
THE OVAL
A Wolverhampton 17   A 449   A 34   Cannock 10

BURGHLEY ALMSHOUSES *Benedictine monks from Peterborough founded a hospital in Stamford in the 11th century. It was enlarged by Lord Burghley in the 16th century for the poor and aged of the town.*

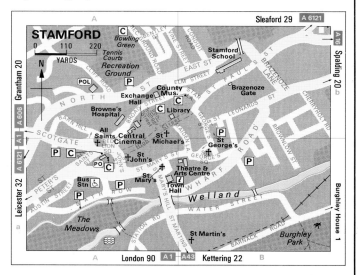

STAMFORD map with references: Sleaford 29 A 6121; Grantham 20; A 606; A 1; A 6121; Leicester 32; Bowling Green; Tennis Courts; Recreation Ground; NORTH; SCOTGATE; Stamford School; A 16; Spalding 20; County Mus.; Brazenoze Gate; Exchange Hall; Browne's Hospital; Library; All Saints Central Cinema; St Michael's; St George's; St John's; Theatre & Arts Centre; Bus Stn; St Mary's; Town Hall; Welland; Water Street; The Meadows; St Martin's; Burghley Park; Burghley House 1; London 90 A 1 A 43 Kettering 22

Parking Town Centre Precinct; Thorneyholme Terrace; Scott Street; Royal Road (all car parks).
District council Derwentside (Tel. Consett 505211).
Population 41,200.
E-C Wed. **M-D** Thur.
Police Thorneyholme Terrace (Tel. 32144).
Casualty hospital Shotley Bridge General, Consett (Tel. Consett 503456).
Post office Clifford Road.
Theatre Civic Hall, Town Centre (Tel. 32164).
Cinema Civic Hall, Town Centre (Tel. 32164).
Public library High Street.
Places to see North of England Open Air Museum, 2 m. E.
Shopping Town Centre Precinct.
Trade and industry Coal-mining; engineering; clothing.
AA 24 hour service
Tel. Newcastle upon Tyne 610111.

Stevenage Hertfordshire

The new town of Stevenage is a large, well-planned, post-war extension of Old Stevenage, a market town which dates back to the 7th century. It was then called Stithenac, meaning "strong oak".

In the old town is the 12th–15th-century flintstone Church of St Nicholas, which still has a Norman tower. Alleyne's Grammar School, now a comprehensive, was founded in 1558 and retains the timber-framed room that constituted the original school.

The Six Hills, south of the town, are round barrows that were probably Romano-British burial places.

Information Tel. 56133/3344.
Location On the A1(M), 5 m. S of Letchworth.
Parking Lytton Way (2); Danesgate (2); Swingate; Silkin Way; Danestrete; Fairlands Way (2); St George's Way (3). Old Town: Primett Road; Church Lane (2) (all car parks).
District council Borough of Stevenage (Tel. 56133).
Population 74,400.
E-C Mon., Wed. **M-D** Thur.
Police Lytton Way (Tel. 2323).
Casualty hospital Lister Hospital, Corey's Mill Lane (Tel. 4333).
Post office Town Square.
Theatre Gordon Craig Theatre, Leisure Centre, Lytton Way (Tel. 54568).
Cinema ABC 1 and 2, The Forum, St George's Way (Tel. 3267).
Public library Southgate.
Places to see Museum, St George's Way; Knebworth House, 1 m. S.
Town trails Available from the Museum.
Shopping Town Centre Precinct; High Street.
Trade and industry Electronics; light engineering; furniture.
AA 24 hour service
Tel. Hatfield 62852.

ed in the 15th century by a rich wool merchant of the town, is one of England's outstanding medieval almshouses.

In 1552, the manor of Stamford was inherited by William Cecil, Elizabeth I's favourite adviser, who became the first Lord Burghley. His parents and grandparents had lived in the town. Cecil began building Burghley House, 1 mile south of the river in 1553. It is regarded as the biggest and grandest surviving building of the Elizabethan age.

Stamford was the birthplace of Sir Malcolm Sargent (1895-1967), the orchestral conductor. He is buried in the town cemetery.

Information Tel. 4444.
Location On the A1, 14 m. NW of Peterborough.
Parking North Street; Scotgate; Bath Row; St Leonards Street; Wharf Road (all car parks).
District council South Kesteven (Tel. Grantham 5591).
Population 16,200.
E-C Thur. **M-D** Fri.
Police (Ab) North Street (Tel. 52222).
Casualty hospital Peterborough District, Thorpe Road, Peterborough (Tel. Peterborough 67451).
Post office (Aa) All Saints' Place.
Theatre Arts Centre **(Ba)**, St Mary's Street (Tel. 3203).
Cinema Central **(Ab)**, Broad Street (Tel. 3179).

Public library (Ab) High Street.
Places to see County Museum **(Ab)**, Broad Street; Browne's Hospital **(Ab)**, Broad Street; Brewery Museum, All Saints' Street; Brasenose Gate **(Bb)**, St Paul's Street; Burghley House, 1 m. S.
Shopping High Street; Ironmonger Street; Broad Street; St Mary's Street.
Events Burghley Park Horse Trials (Sept.).
Trade and industry Engineering; plastics; bricks and tiles.
AA 24 hour service
Tel. Leicester 20491.

Stanley Durham

The Romans had a cattle camp at Stanley in the 2nd and 3rd centuries AD, from which they supplied their forts at Newcastle and South Shields. Stanley remained a tiny village until the 18th century, when high-grade coal was discovered in the area.

Occupying a 200 acre site around 19th-century Beamish Hall, 2 miles east of the town, is the North of England Open Air Museum. There, the past is re-created through buildings fitted with period furniture and machinery, a 19th-century railway station with locomotive and coaches, and an electric tramway.

Information Tel. Consett 505211.
Location On the A6076, 9 m. NW of Durham.

STIRLING Central

The war-scarred rock at the crossroads of Scotland

Perched high on a crag commanding the crossings of the upper Forth, where the Highlands meet the Lowlands, Stirling has played a vital role in its country's tumultuous history. For centuries, warring factions fought for possession of its great Rock. Yet the town was more than "the Striveling", or place of strife, from which it takes its name. It was long the virtual capital of Scotland and the site of the royal palace, and it now has a fine heritage of buildings steeped in history.

The first-known inhabitants of the area were Middle Stone Age people of 4000-2000 BC. There is also evidence of Bronze Age occupation, and between 300 BC and AD 300 Iron Age settlers built defensive works, traces of which survive.

In the 1st century AD the Roman Antonine Wall passed within 10 miles, but there is no evidence of Roman fortification of the Rock.

In the 11th century a castle was built on the heights, and in the 12th century Alexander I of Scotland granted Stirling a royal charter, which entitled it to hold weekly markets and set up merchant guilds. It thus developed into a town of both strategic importance and wealth.

The **castle** figured prominently in the wars of Scottish succession during the 13th and 14th centuries, passing back and forth between Scots and English. But from 1342 the castle stayed in Scottish hands. With the accession of the Stewart kings in 1370 it became again a royal residence. The Stewarts built most of the castle as it now stands. In the 16th century Mary of Guise, mother of Mary, Queen of Scots and Regent of Scotland, built new town defences.

Mary, Queen of Scots married her second husband, Lord Darnley, secretly in Stirling Castle in 1565, and the following year their son, James VI of Scotland (James I of England), was baptised in the Chapel Royal there. When James departed for England in 1603 the life of the castle as a royal residence came to an end.

In 1745, on his march south, Bonnie Prince Charlie forced the town to surrender, but not the castle which withstood his siege.

Landmarks of Stirling's past

The castle remains the finest example of Renaissance architecture in Scotland. Most of the main buildings date from the 15th and 16th centuries. The palace was built by James V in the 16th century; much of the ornate stonework was cut by French masons. The upper rooms of the palace house the **Museum of the Argyll and Sutherland Highlanders.**

The **King's Knot**, a group of raised banks, designed by a 17th-century landscape gardener, lies in a field below the castle. Jousting was once held here, and the **Ladies Rock** in the cemetery was used as a vantage point.

On the castle esplanade, **Stirling Castle Visitor Centre** offers, with its multi-screen theatre and exhibition, a good picture of Stirling's history.

At the head of Broad Street is **Mar's Wark**, the ruins of a once magnificent town house, built between 1570 and 1572 by the Earl of Mar, Regent of Scotland, but never completed. In 1589 James VI and his bride, Princess Anne of Denmark, stayed there until their rooms in the castle were completed. The building subsequently became a workhouse. Beside Mar's Wark stands the large 15th-century **Church of the Holy Rude**. It was here in 1567, after Mary had abdicated, that the infant James was crowned James VI of Scotland. John Knox, the Scottish Protestant reformer, preached the sermon. The oldest parts of the church, the nave and lower section of the tower, were built about 1460. The open timber roof is a rare example of its kind.

Old market place

South of the church stands **Cowane's Hospital**, or Guildhall, built for the support of "12 decayed Gild Breithers" with money left by John Cowane, a wealthy local merchant who died in 1633. It contains old relics and a statue of its founder.

In the centre of Broad Street, flanked by cannon, stands the **Mercat Cross**. The street was once Stirling's market place. The town **tolbooth** faces Broad Street. It has an attractive clock-tower pavilion roof, and was built in 1704 by Sir William Bruce, tutor to the Adam brothers.

Stirling Gallery, in Baker Street, houses an art gallery and Scottish craft shop. It is supported by the Scottish Arts Council and promotes the work of Scottish artists.

Stirling's **Auld Brig**, or Old Bridge,

SYMBOLIC LAMPS *Reversed 4s, sign of Stirling's ancient guild, decorate the lamps outside the Guildhall.*

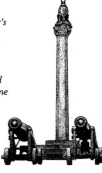

GUARDED CROSS *Cannon flank Stirling's Mercat Cross, which stands in the centre of Broad Street. For centuries all public events were celebrated there. The unicorn, one of the royal beasts of Scotland, is the only surviving part of the original cross, which was restored in 1891.*

TUMULTUOUS PAST *Warfare, intrigues and killings marked Stirling Castle for 700 years until 1745, when Bonnie Prince Charlie tried – and failed – to take it.*

was built across the Forth in 1415. Every Scottish king from James I (1406-37) to Charles II (1660-85) crossed the river over these medieval arches. Pedestrians can still use the Old Bridge, but traffic is routed over a modern bridge just downstream.

Ruined abbey

Beside the river lie the remains of **Cambuskenneth Abbey**, an Augustinian abbey founded by David I in the 11th century. The abbey was dissolved during the Reformation and fell into ruin as its stones were used for new buildings, such as Mar's Wark. James III and his queen, Margaret of Denmark are buried in the abbey.

Argyll's Ludging (lodging), in Irvine Place, is the finest example of 17th-century domestic architecture to survive in Scotland. The mansion was built by William Alexander, the 1st Earl of Stirling, in 1630, but it takes its name from Archibald Campbell, 1st Marquis of Argyll. He bought the mansion in 1655 and extended it. Later it became a military hospital and is now a youth hostel.

On Abbey Craig, 1 mile north, is the **Wallace Monument**, a 220 ft tower completed in 1869. A bronze statue of the 13th-century patriot surmounts the door, and in the Tower Hall is Wallace's two-handed sword—5 ft 4 in. in length. The hall also contains busts of other noted

THE STIRLING HEADS *This medallion of a woman is one of 56 carved about 1540 for the ceiling of the king's presence chamber in Stirling Palace.*

Scotsmen, including Robert Bruce, Robert Burns, Sir Walter Scott and Thomas Carlyle. The top of the tower is reached by a climb of 246 steps.

Standing at the central crossroads of Scotland's main highways, Stirling is a perfect centre for touring. Edinburgh, St Andrews and the southern Highlands are all within easy reach.

Information Tel. 5019.
Location On the A9, 27 m. NE of Glasgow.
Parking Albert Hall; George Street; Morris Terrace; Goosecroft (2); Station; Castle Esplanade; Guildhall; Johnston Avenue; Pitt Terrace (all car parks).
District council Stirling (Tel. 3131).
Population 38,600.
E-C Wed. **M-D** Thur.
Police (Aa) Viewfield Place

(Tel. 3161).
Casualty hospital Stirling Royal Infirmary, Livilands Gate (Tel. 3151).
Post office (Bb) Murray Place.
Theatre MacRobert Arts Centre, University of Stirling (Tel. 61081).
Cinema (Aa) Allan Park Leisure Centre (Tel. 4137).
Public library (Bb) Corn Exchange Road.
Places to see Stirling Castle and Regimental Museum **(Ac)**; Argyll's Ludging **(Ab)**; Mar's Wark **(Ab)**; Stirling Gallery **(Bb)**; Stirling Castle Visitor Centre **(Ac)**; Smith Art Gallery and Museum **(Ab)**; Cambuskenneth Abbey; Wallace Monument, 1 m. N; Bannockburn Monument, 2 m. S; Cowane's Hospital; Safari Park, 5 m. NW; Doune Castle, 8 m. NW.
Town trails Available from Tourist Information Centre, 41 Dumbarton Road.
Shopping King Street; Thistle Centre; Port Street; Murray Place; Barnton Street.
Event District Festival (May/ June).
Trade and industry Agricultural marketing and engineering; concrete; cigarettes; insulation materials; insurance.
Motorail Tel. 3812 or Falkirk 24922.
AA 24 hour service
Tel. Glasgow (041) 812 0101.

CREATOR OF A NATION

In 1314 King Robert Bruce routed the army of Edward II at Bannockburn, 2 miles south of Stirling, and achieved nationhood for Scotland. The National Trust for Scotland has built a rotunda around the Borestone, where Robert is said to have set his standard, and erected a bronze statue of him there.

Scotland's hero looks down on the field of Bannockburn.

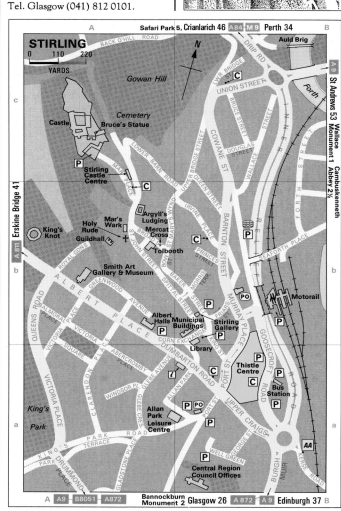

Stockport G. Manch.

The landed gentry of Cheshire built themselves fine houses around the market place of Stockport in the Middle Ages. The charm of the old town can still be seen in the streets that wind around the hilltop market on the south bank of the River Mersey.

Soft water tumbling down from the hills of the Peak District made Stockport an ideal centre for the development of the cotton-spinning trade, and the town expanded rapidly in the 19th century. It also enjoyed a reputation for manufacturing fine silk hats. Today, office development and engineering have largely replaced the old textile crafts.

The town has a superb railway viaduct, built in 1839-40. It has 22 arches and is more than 100 ft high. Near by is another remarkable piece of civil engineering: a large shopping precinct covering a stretch of the River Mersey.

Stockport Grammar School, founded in 1487, is one of the oldest schools in Britain.

The Borough of Stockport leases nearby Lyme Park, home of the Legh family for six centuries, from the National Trust. The house, which dates from Elizabethan times, contains fine period furniture, tapestries and other works of art. The house is surrounded by 1,300 acres of parkland where red deer roam.

Information
Tel. Manchester (061) 480 0315.
Location On the A6, 6 m. SE of Manchester.
Parking Bridge Street; Great Underbank; St Petersgate (2); John Street (2); Edward Street; Daw Bank; Great Egerton Street; Norbury Street (all car parks).
District council Metropolitan Borough of Stockport (Tel. 061 480 4949).
Population 136,500.
E-C Thur. **M-D** Fri., Sat.
Police Lee Street (Tel. 061 480 7979).
Casualty hospital Infirmary, Wellington Road South (Tel. 061 480 7441).
Post office Chestergate.
Theatres Garrick, Wellington Road South (Tel. 061 480 5866); Davenport, Buxton Road, Davenport (061 483 3801).
Cinemas Classic, Wellington Road South (Tel. 061 480 2244); Ritz, Piccadilly (061 480 4281); Davenport, Buxton Road, Davenport (061 483 3801).
Public library Wellington Road South.
Places to see Art Gallery, Wellington Road South; Vernon Park Museum, Turncroft Lane; Bramall Hall, 3 m. S; Lyme Hall, 7 m. SE.
Shopping Merseyway Precinct; Market Hall; Princes Street.
Sport FA League football, Stockport County FC, Edgeley Park.
AA 24 hour service
Tel. Manchester (061) 485 6299.

Stockton-on-Tees Clev.

On the afternoon of September 27, 1825, George Stephenson's *Locomotion No. 1* pulled a string of coaches and wagons from Darlington into Stockton Station. The world's first passenger railway had been born. And, with it, Stockton turned from a quiet market town into a busy industrial centre. Today it is a vast borough embracing townships on both sides of the River Tees.

Stockton High Street is claimed to be the broadest in the country. A market dating back to the early 14th century is held in it twice weekly.

It was in the High Street that the chemist John Walker invented and sold the friction match in 1827. However, he failed to patent his invention and made little money from it.

Another famous Stockton man was Thomas Sheraton (1751-1806), the furniture designer, who was born in the town and spent his early life there as a journeyman cabinet-maker.

Preston Hall Museum, just outside Stockton on the road to Yarm, contains one of the finest collections of arms and armour in the country, a period street and period rooms, a toy museum and a transport museum, and relics of John Walker.

Information Tel. 62200.
Location On the A66, 4 m. SW of Middlesbrough.
Parking Castle Centre; Riverside; Leeds Street; Parliament Street; Tower Street (all car parks).
District council Borough of Stockton-on-Tees (Tel. 62200).
Population 154,600.
E-C Thur. **M-D** Wed., Sat.
Police The Square (Tel. 607114).
Casualty hospital North Tees General Hospital, Hardwick Road (Tel. 62122).
Post office High Street.
Theatres Forum Theatre, Town Centre, Billingham (Tel. 552663); Billingham Players Theatre, Belasis Avenue, Billingham (551981).
Cinemas Classic 1, 2 and 3, Dovecot Street (Tel. 66048); Odeon, High Street (67832).
Public library Church Road.
Places to see Preston Hall Museum, Preston Park.
Shopping High Street; Castle Centre.
AA 24 hour service Tel. 607215.

Stoke-on-Trent
see page 378

Stonehaven Grampian

The former county town of Kincardineshire, Stonehaven is a fishing port and holiday resort backed by rolling farmland and woods. Whisky is manufactured in the Glenury Royal Distillery, founded in 1824 by Captain Robert Barclay-Allardice and "Mr Windsor" – the Prince Regent, later George IV.

The 15th-century tolbooth behind the harbour was a storehouse, later used as a courtroom and prison. It is now a museum and restaurant.

At the southern end of Market Square, a plaque marks the birthplace of Robert Thomson (1822-73), who in 1845 invented the pneumatic tyre. Thomson also pioneered the dry dock and the use of electricity in mines. A veteran-car rally is held each June in his honour.

On New Year's Eve, at the stroke of midnight, Stonehaven stages its Fireball Ceremony, in which the inhabitants parade in the High Street swinging fireballs made from wire-netting packed with rags and set alight. The ritual, which dates back to pagan times, is said to ward off evil spirits.

In June, the town holds a Feeing Market, a modern revival of an old fair at which farm servants were hired. Now it is a festival of Scottish music and dancing.

There are several castles in the Stonehaven area, the most spectacular of which stands on a sea-girt rock at Dunnottar, 1½ miles south. It was built in the 14th century, and was the last castle in Scotland to fall to Cromwell's troops, in 1652.

Information Tel. 62806 (summer); 62001 (winter).
Location On the A94, 15 m. S of Aberdeen.
Parking Beach Road; Promenade; Market Square (all car parks).
District council Kincardine and Deeside (Tel. 62001).
Population 7,300.
E-C Wed.
Police Dunnottar Avenue (Tel. 62963).
Casualty hospital Arduthie Hospital, Auchinblae Road (Tel. 62022).
Post office Allardice Street.
Public library Arduthie Road.
Places to see Tolbooth Folk Museum, Old Pier; Dunnottar Castle, 1½ m. S; Fetteresso Castle, 1 m. W.
Shopping Market Square; High Street.
Events Fireball Ceremony (New Year's Eve); Feeing Market (June); Veteran Car Rally (June).
AA 24 hour service
Tel. Aberdeen 51231.

Stornoway Western Isles

When the Norsemen were raiding the rugged outer isles of the Hebrides in the 11th century they found a settlement already existed in the 2 mile long natural harbour at Stornoway, on the island of Lewis. Many of them stayed, mixing with the native Celts, and created Stornoway, the only town in the Western Isles. Gaelic, the language of the Celts, is still spoken, and can be seen on shops and road signs.

Stornoway is the base of the Harris Tweed industry. To be legally marketed as Harris Tweed, the cloth must be made from pure Scottish wool, spun, dyed and finished in the Outer

STOURPORT-ON-SEVERN *The dock basins of the 18th-century Staffordshire and Worcestershire Canal were once busy with commercial craft, but today they are used only by pleasure boats, and Stourport has become a holiday town.*

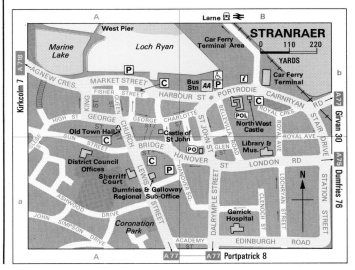

Hebrides and hand-woven by the islanders in their own homes.

Stornoway is a busy fishing port, and the large, safe harbour also provides a base for yachtsmen and sea-anglers.

Information Tel. 3088.
Location On the A866, 37 m. NE of Tarbert.
Parking Cromwell Street; Ferry Road; Shell Street; South Beach (all car parks).
District council Western Isles Islands Council (Tel. 3773).
Population 5,970.
E-C Wed.
Police Church Street (Tel. 2222).
Casualty hospital Goathill Road (Tel. 2500).
Post office Francis Street.
Cinema Galaxy, in Seaforth Hotel, James Street (Tel. 2740).
Public library Keith Street.
Places to see Lews Castle.
Shopping Cromwell Street; Bayhead Street; Francis Street.
Car ferry To Ullapool (Tel. Gourock 33755).

Stourport-on-Severn
Hereford & Worcester

The town is sometimes known as the Venice of the Midlands, because it stands at the junction of the rivers Severn and Stour and the Staffordshire and Worcestershire Canal. It owes its existence to the building of the canal in the 18th century. Before that it was a quiet village, but afterwards it became a busy inland port.

The town has several fine red-brick Georgian houses. The iron bridge over the Severn dates from 1870.

Information Tel. 2866.
Location On the A451, 4 m. S of Kidderminster.
Parking Raven Street; New Street; Vale Road (all car parks).
District council Wyre Forest (Tel. 77211).
Population 19,100.
E-C Wed.
Police Bewdley Road (Tel. 2255).
Casualty hospital General, Bewdley Road, Kidderminster (Tel. Kidderminster 3424).
Post office High Street.
Public library Worcester Street.

Shopping High Street.
AA 24 hour service Tel. Birmingham (021) 550 4858.

Stowmarket Suffolk

Roads converge on this little country town from all directions – a fact reflected in its name, for the Anglo-Saxon word *stow* means "meeting place". The market was added later.

Abbot's Hall, on the site of an old monastic building, is now an open-air museum of rural life. Dr Thomas Young, who was tutor to the poet John Milton, lived at Stowmarket. Dr Young is buried in the central aisle of the parish church of St Peter and St Mary, and an old portrait of him hangs in the church.

Information Tel. 2060.
Location On the A1308, 12 m. NW of Ipswich.
Parking Bury Street; Ipswich Street; Milton Road; Iliffe Way (all car parks).
District council Mid-Suffolk (Tel. Eye 341).
Population 10,900.
E-C Tues. **M-D** Thur., Sat.
Police Violet Hill Road (Tel. 2318).
Casualty hospital Ipswich Hospital, Ivry Street, Ipswich (Tel. Ipswich 212477).
Post office Ipswich Street.
Theatre and cinema Regal, Ipswich Street (Tel. 2825).

Public library Church Walk.
Places to see Museum of East Anglian Life, Abbot's Hall, Crowe Lane.
Shopping Bury Street; Ipswich Street; Tavern Street; Station Road.
AA 24 hour service Tel. Norwich 29401.

Stranraer D. & G.

The main ferry service from Scotland to Northern Ireland runs out of Stranraer, a natural port at the head of Loch Ryan, which is sheltered from the sea by the Rhinns of Galloway.

The town is also a popular holiday resort with safe bathing, yachting and good fishing.

The 16th-century Castle of St John was one of the headquarters of Graham of Claverhouse, fanatical persecutor of the Protestant Covenanters in the late 17th century. Many Presbyterians died in its dungeons.

A house on the seafront, called North West Castle, was built by the Arctic explorer Sir John Ross (1777-1856). His expeditions to find the North-West Passage to the Pacific led to the discovery in 1831 of the North Magnetic Pole. His house is now a hotel.

Information Tel. 2595.
Location On the A75, 25 m. W of Newton Stewart.
Parking Market Street, Portrodie; Hanover Square; North Strand Street (all car parks).
District council Wigtown (Tel. 2151).
Population 10,170.
E-C Wed. **M-D** Wed.
Police (Bb) Portrodie (Tel. 2112).
Casualty hospital Garrick Hospital **(Ba)**, Edinburgh Road (Tel. 2323).
Post office (Ba) Hanover Street.
Public library (Ba) London Road.
Places to see Castle of St John **(Ab)**; Wigtown District Museum **(Ba)**.
Shopping George Street; Charlotte Street; Hanover Street; Castle Street.
Car ferry To Larne (Tel. 2262).
AA 24 hour service Tel. Glasgow (041) 812 0101.

STOKE-ON-TRENT Staffordshire

The city that grew on clay

Known in popular imagination as the Potteries, the city of Stoke-on-Trent was created in 1910 from a federation of six towns. Even today, however, each of the six original towns – Tunstall, Burslem, Hanley (the principal shopping centre), Stoke-upon-Trent, Fenton and Longton – maintains its individual personality. Among the celebrated figures the Potteries have produced are Josiah Wedgwood, founder of English pottery, and the novelist Arnold Bennett, who made the area widely known as the fictional "Five Towns".

Pottery was first made in the area about 3,500 years ago, in the Bronze Age. Cremation urns of this period are on display at the **City Museum** in Broad Street, Hanley. There is also a collection of Roman pottery, including lampholders and cooking pots from a garrison established in about AD 50 at Trent Vale. Excavations at Trent Vale have uncovered a perfectly preserved Roman pottery kiln. Two medieval pottery kilns dating from about 1300 have been found at Sneyd Green, and medieval pottery has been unearthed at Burslem. But pottery was no more important in the area than in any other part of Britain until the 17th century. It was then that North Staffordshire potters began to take advantage of the vast local supplies of marl clay, coal and water, and nearby deposits of iron, copper and lead, for the oxides used in glazing.

The greatest single figure in the gradual development of Staffordshire pottery from cottage craft to major industry was Josiah Wedgwood (1730-95). He is best known today for his blue Jasper ware ornamented with Classical white designs, but he was most successful in his lifetime for the crockery he brought to the masses – tasteful, yet simple and cheap. Wedgwood was also a scientist, and was made a Fellow of the Royal Society for his invention of the pyrometer, which measures extreme heat.

World's largest potteries

Today, the Wedgwood Group employs about 8,000 people and is one of the largest potteries in the world. With two other famous Stoke firms, Spode and Royal Doulton, it produces more than three-quarters of

Britain's pottery, bone china, earthenware, sanitary fittings, floor and wall tiles and electrical porcelain. Stoke exports ceramics to more than 140 markets throughout the world.

A mixture of china clay from Cornwall, ball clay from Devon and Dorset, flint from Essex or France and ground stone has largely replaced marl clay. In the unique English bone china, more than half the mixture is burned, powdered animal bone. The bone gives the china both transparency and strength.

Most of the major companies provide guided tours around their works and have museums illustrating the history of their wares.

There is a memorial tablet to Wedgwood in the 19th-century Church of

St Peter ad Vincula, and a bronze statue of him facing the railway station.

The City Museum has one of the finest collections of pottery and porcelain in the world, including outstanding examples of Egyptian, Roman, Greek, Persian, Chinese and Japanese ware. The museum also contains Epstein bronzes, English 18th and 19th-century water-colours, glass, coins, costume and archaeological and natural-history exhibits.

Potteries in fiction

The novelist Arnold Bennett (1867-1931) was born in Hanley, and in *The Old Wives' Tale, Clayhanger* and other novels he fictionalised the Potteries of his youth as the "Five Towns". In Waterloo Road is the house he lived in for seven years before leaving the district for London and journalism in 1889.

The Mitchell Memorial Youth Centre in Broad Street, Hanley, and the **Spitfire Museum,** in Bethesda Street, commemorate Reginald Mitchell (1895-1937), the designer of the Spitfire aircraft, who was born at Talke, a nearby village. After

THE LIVING PAST *The Gladstone Pottery Museum, in Longton, is Britain's last surviving early-Victorian pottery. There the visitor can see craftsmen shaping pots in the original workshops and firing them in bottle ovens.*

JASPER WARE
Blue pottery ornamented with Classical white designs brought fame to the 18th-century Stoke craftsman Josiah Wedgwood.

ARNOLD BENNETT

The novelist Arnold Bennett, who immortalised Stoke in his novels of the "Five Towns", was born Enoch Arnold Bennett in Hope Street, Hanley, in 1867. Bennett left Stoke when he was 21 and never lived there again, but all his best-known works are set there. The "Five Towns" of *Clayhanger, The Old Wives' Tale, The Card* and other Bennett novels are (with their real names in brackets): Knype (Stoke), Bursley (Burslem), Hanbridge (Hanley), Longshaw (Longton), and Turnhill (Tunstall). Bennett died in London in 1931.

A cartoon of Bennett having his hair cut, from one of his scrapbooks now in Stoke City Museum.

studying at Hanley High School, Mitchell became an apprentice engineer in Fenton and then a teacher, before joining Supermarine Aviation at Southampton in 1916. It was there in the 1930s that he designed the Spitfire fighter, which played a major part in winning the Battle of Britain.

Oldest house

The oldest house in the city is **Ford Green Hall,** in Ford Green Road, Smallthorne. This is an Elizabethan half-timbered manor house of about 1580, with brick wings added in 1734. The furnishings include a rare 16th-century shop counter with a sliding top, an Elizabethan four-poster bed which has a secret panel, and a scold's bridle worn by nagging women as a punishment. Outside is a dovecot.

Trentham Gardens, 3½ miles south of the city centre, comprises 700 acres of formal gardens, pleasure gardens, woodland and parkland. At the heart of the estate are the Italian Gardens, originally laid out by "Capability" Brown, which overlook the mile-long waters of Trentham Lake.

Information Tel. 48241.
Location On the A50, 36 m. NE of Shrewsbury.
Parking Stoke: South Wolfe Street; Kingsway; Spark Street; Vale Street. Hanley: Clough Street; Meigh Street (2); Birch Terrace; Bryan Street; Hinde Street; Broad Street. Burslem: Navigation Road; Chapel Lane. Tunstall: Rathbone Street. Longton: Baths Road; Bennett Precinct; Cooke Street (all car parks).
District council City of Stoke-on-Trent (Tel. 48241).
Population 252,350.
E-C Thur. (Hanley town centre, six-day trading). **M-D** Wed., Fri., Sat.

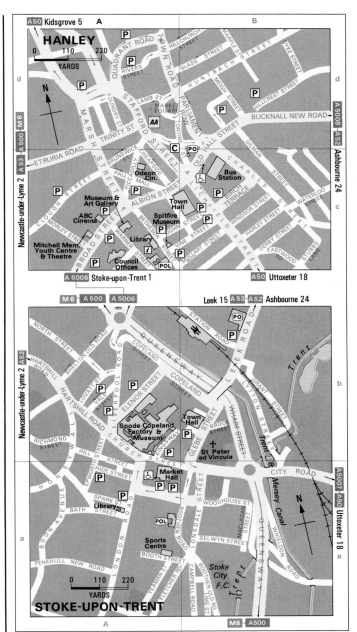

Police South **(Aa)**: Boothen Road, Stoke (Tel. 46611); North **(Ac)**: Bethesda Street, Hanley (29551).
Casualty hospital North Staffordshire Royal Infirmary, Princes Road, Hartshill (Tel. 49144).
Post offices Leek Road **(Bb)**, Stoke; Tontine Street **(Bc)**, Hanley.
Theatres Mitchell Memorial **(Ac)**, Broad Street, Hanley (Tel. 268161); Victoria, Hartshill (615962); Repertory, Beresford Street, Shelton (44784).
Cinemas ABC **(Ac)**, Broad Street, Hanley (Tel. 22320); Odeon Film Centre **(Ac)**, Piccadilly, Hanley (25311); Regional Film Theatre, College Road, Shelton (411188); Plaza, Fenton (319003).
Public library (Ac) Bethesda Street, Hanley.
Places to see City Museum and Art Gallery **(Ac)**, Hanley; Spitfire Museum **(Ac)**, Hanley; Ford Green Hall, Smallthorne; Chatterley Whitfield Mining Museum, 3 m. N off A527; Gladstone Pottery Museum, Longton; Wedgwood Pottery, Barlaston. By prior arrangement only: Spode Pottery **(Ab)**, Church Street, Stoke; Royal Doulton Pottery, Nile Street, Burslem; Trentham Gardens, 3½ m. S on A34.
Town trails Available from Director of Environmental Services, Unity House, Hanley.
Shopping All town centres. Principal shopping centre: Hanley (Market Square, Piccadilly).
Events Stoke Festival (Oct. – April).
Trade and industry Pottery; coal mining; tyres; engineering.
Sport FA League football: Stoke City FC, Boothen Old Road, Stoke; Port Vale FC, Hamil Road, Burslem.
AA 24 hour service Tel. 25881.

A LOOK AROUND
STRATFORD-UPON-AVON
Warwickshire

Birthplace of William Shakespeare

England's greatest dramatist and poet William Shakespeare dominates Stratford-upon-Avon, and has made it Britain's biggest tourist centre after London. Even so, the town has managed to retain its identity as a small, delightfully mellow, old market community in the rural heart of England. With its memorable buildings, broad streets, meadow-flanked river and canal bright with boats, it would be a rewarding place to visit even without its links with Shakespeare. Many package-tour pilgrims snatch only a fleeting impression of the town's character as they are hustled between Shakespeare's Birthplace, his grave, the riverside theatre and Anne Hathaway's Cottage. It is the visitor with time to linger and explore who sees Stratford at its best.

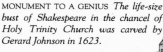

MONUMENT TO A GENIUS *The life-size bust of Shakespeare in the chancel of Holy Trinity Church was carved by Gerard Johnson in 1623.*

William Shakespeare was born in Henley Street on or about April 23, 1564. His father, John Shakespeare – or Shakspere, according to the parish records – was a glover and wool dealer who later became the town's bailiff, or mayor. His mother, Mary Arden, was the daughter of a yeoman farmer from the nearby village of **Wilmcote.** Her home, complete with cider-mill, dovecot and other outbuildings housing old farm implements, dates from the early 16th century and has been owned by the Shakespeare Birthplace Trust since 1930. Mary married John Shakespeare in 1557. Documents show that her husband had been living in Henley Street for at least five years before the wedding.

Their house in Henley Street was sold in 1847 to what later became the Shakespeare Birthplace Trust. The price was £3,000. Only 41 years earlier the building had changed hands for £210. Posters advertising the sale described the house as "the most honoured monument of the greatest genius that ever lived".

More than 500,000 people visit **Shakespeare's Birthplace** every year. Its rooms are furnished with items typical of middle-class homes in the time of Shakespeare. An unusual feature of the kitchen is a 17th-century "baby-minder", fitted to keep small children away from the huge fireplace with its roasting spits and cast-iron pots. Upstairs, the room in which the playwright is believed to have been born has a window engraved with the signatures of notable visitors, including the novelist Sir Walter Scott and the Victorian actor Sir Henry Irving.

William's desk

The part of the building which John Shakespeare used for his business, and which later became an inn, is now a museum containing documents, rare books, portraits, and the desk young William is said to have worked at as a schoolboy. The garden is planted with many of the trees, flowers and herbs mentioned in Shakespeare's works.

Shakespeare was almost certainly educated at **Stratford Grammar School,** which was at least 250 years old when it was re-founded by Edward VI in 1553. It still stands in Church Street and may be visited by organised parties during the Easter and summer holidays, after a written application has been granted. Beneath the school, under the room where Shakespeare would have attended lessons, is the old **Guildhall,** used in

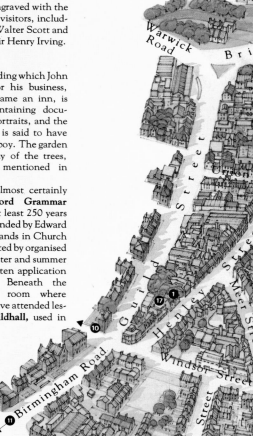

SHAKESPEARE'S BIRTHPLACE *The half-timbered building in Henley Street where the dramatist was born in 1564 has been furnished in the style of the time.*

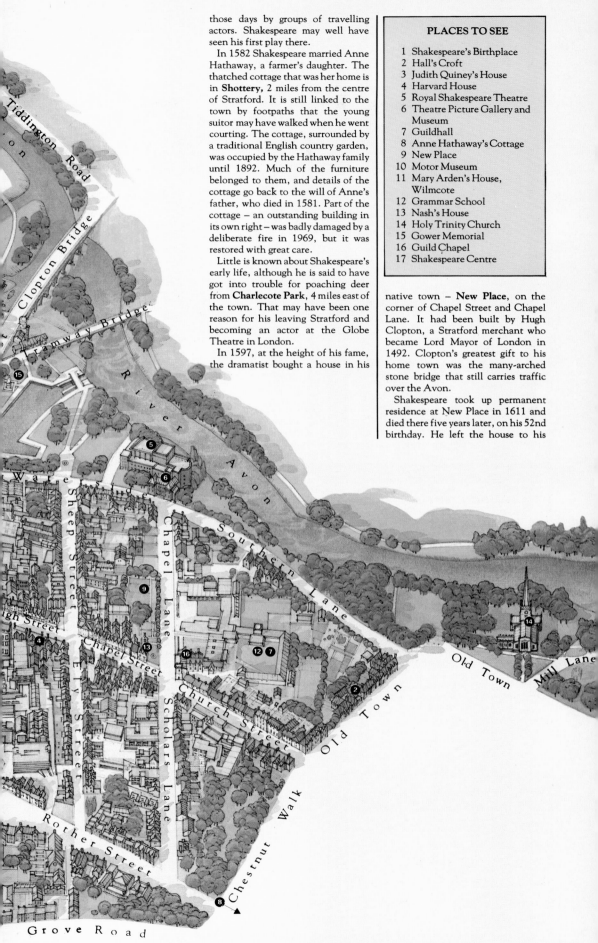

those days by groups of travelling actors. Shakespeare may well have seen his first play there.

In 1582 Shakespeare married Anne Hathaway, a farmer's daughter. The thatched cottage that was her home is in **Shottery,** 2 miles from the centre of Stratford. It is still linked to the town by footpaths that the young suitor may have walked when he went courting. The cottage, surrounded by a traditional English country garden, was occupied by the Hathaway family until 1892. Much of the furniture belonged to them, and details of the cottage go back to the will of Anne's father, who died in 1581. Part of the cottage – an outstanding building in its own right – was badly damaged by a deliberate fire in 1969, but it was restored with great care.

Little is known about Shakespeare's early life, although he is said to have got into trouble for poaching deer from **Charlecote Park,** 4 miles east of the town. That may have been one reason for his leaving Stratford and becoming an actor at the Globe Theatre in London.

In 1597, at the height of his fame, the dramatist bought a house in his

PLACES TO SEE

1 Shakespeare's Birthplace
2 Hall's Croft
3 Judith Quiney's House
4 Harvard House
5 Royal Shakespeare Theatre
6 Theatre Picture Gallery and Museum
7 Guildhall
8 Anne Hathaway's Cottage
9 New Place
10 Motor Museum
11 Mary Arden's House, Wilmcote
12 Grammar School
13 Nash's House
14 Holy Trinity Church
15 Gower Memorial
16 Guild Chapel
17 Shakespeare Centre

native town – **New Place,** on the corner of Chapel Street and Chapel Lane. It had been built by Hugh Clopton, a Stratford merchant who became Lord Mayor of London in 1492. Clopton's greatest gift to his home town was the many-arched stone bridge that still carries traffic over the Avon.

Shakespeare took up permanent residence at New Place in 1611 and died there five years later, on his 52nd birthday. He left the house to his

ON THE BANKS OF THE AVON *Beyond a bend in the meadow-lined river rises the spire of Holy Trinity Church, where Shakespeare was baptised and where he, his wife Anne and his eldest daughter Susanna and her husband are buried.*

Like Stratford in general, Holy Trinity has much to offer in addition to its memories of the dramatist. There are fine examples of 15th-century wood-carving, superb stained-glass windows and several ornate tombs, the most outstanding of which is that of Joyce Clopton and her husband, the Earl of Totnes, who was James I's Master of Ordnance. Carved guns, cannonballs and barrels of powder indicate his office.

Before Shakespeare died, his elder daughter Susanna and her husband, John Hall, lived in what is known as **Hall's Croft,** one of the town's most memorable Tudor houses, owned by the Shakespeare Birthplace Trust. It is seen at its best from the spacious walled garden. John Hall was an eminent local doctor, and the house contains fascinating insights into 16th and early-17th-century medicine. The Halls' daughter Elizabeth, Lady Barnard, brought the playwright's direct line to an end when she died in 1670.

Although it had long been famous as Shakespeare's birthplace, Stratford did not stage a festival in honour of its famous son until 1769. It was organised by David Garrick, the actor-manager commemorated by the name of an old public house in High Street.

The first Shakespeare Memorial Theatre, opened in 1879, was destroyed by fire in 1926; its replacement was completed six years later. It is now known as the **Royal Shakespeare Theatre,** and is renowned for the quality of its productions. The adjoining **Theatre Picture Gallery and Museum** houses costumes worn by leading actors and actresses, relics of Henry Irving, David Garrick, Dame Ellen Terry, Sarah Siddons and other celebrated theatrical figures. It also displays paintings by Sir Joshua Reynolds, George Romney and other noted artists.

The lofty **Gower Memorial,** near the theatre, was unveiled in 1888. Beneath a seated figure of Shakespeare are life-size statues of Hamlet, Lady Macbeth, Falstaff and Henry V, symbolising, respectively, philosophy, tragedy, comedy and history.

---

elder daughter, Susanna, but it eventually passed back to the Clopton family, was completely rebuilt in 1702 and then demolished in 1759.

However, the foundations have been uncovered and now form part of the garden beside **Nash's House,** another of Stratford's impressive timber-framed buildings. This takes its name from Thomas Nash, husband of Elizabeth Hall, Shakespeare's grand-daughter. The house is now a museum which tells Stratford's story since prehistoric times and paints a picture of the England that Shakespeare knew.

Behind Nash's House are the **Knott Garden,** with herbs and flowers laid out in intricate patterns, and the **Great Garden,** with lawns that are shaded by a mulberry tree said to have been grown from a cutting of one planted by Shakespeare.

The playwright was buried in the Collegiate Church of the **Holy Trinity,** an old riverside church dating in part from the 13th century and approached down an avenue of limes. The north door has a sanctuary knocker: any fugitive who reached it could claim sanctuary for 37 days. In the chancel, a bust of Shakespeare, quill in hand, is set in the wall above his gravestone. Above the bust is a carving of the Shakespeare coat of arms with its motto *Non Sans Droict* (Not Without Right). The

gravestone bears the words:
*"Good frend for Jesus sake forbeare
To digg the dust encloased heare
Bleste be ye man yt spares thes stones
And curst be he yt moves my bones."*

Parish records

The now-broken font in which Shakespeare was baptised can be seen, as can a copy of the parish register recording his baptism and burial. There are also monuments to Shakespeare's wife Anne and his eldest daughter and her husband, who are all buried in the church.

PRODUCTIONS TO REMEMBER *The Royal Shakespeare Theatre, built on the riverside in 1932, stages consistently outstanding productions of Shakespeare that draw audiences from all over the world.*

The Guild of the Holy Cross, an influential religious brotherhood known to have existed before 1269, gave Stratford its grammar school, Guildhall and other buildings. The **Guild Chapel,** founded in the 13th century, stands beside the school. The nave, tower and porch were rebuilt about 1496 by Hugh Clopton. Many leading citizens of the past are depicted in the chapel's stained-glass windows.

Flames of damnation

Inside, the wall at the western end of the nave bears the remains of a "doom" – a mural depicting Judgment Day. Fortunate souls are shown ascending to Heaven, while sinners are being tormented by devils and cast into the flames of eternal damnation. The chapel, for which a £50,000 restoration appeal was launched in 1976, is used by the grammar school for daily services during term time. On the other side of the school is another legacy of the Guild of the Holy Cross – a row of almshouses built to house old or sick members of the guild.

Some of Stratford's architectural treasures, such as the Shrieve's House in Sheep Street and Mason's Court in Rother Street, are still used as private dwellings, and cannot be visited. Others are now used as shops, offices, hotels and inns. **Judith Quiney's House,** where Shakespeare's younger daughter lived after marrying Thomas Quiney, is the town's information centre. The Falcon Hotel, where the Shakespeare Club was formed in 1824, has panelling from New Place, its former neighbour.

In 1927 a mural depicting a legendary story, Tobias and the Angel, believed to date from the mid-16th century, was discovered in the White Swan, a 15th-century hotel at the top of Rother Street.

Harvard House, a 16th-century building in High Street, is a place of pilgrimage for many American visitors. It was the home of Katherine Rogers, a butcher's daughter who married Robert Harvard of London. Their son, John, who studied at Cambridge, emigrated to America, where he founded Harvard University. In 1910, through the efforts of the novelist Marie Corelli, the building was bought and restored by a wealthy benefactor from Chicago and became the property of Harvard University.

American interest in Shakespeare's home town has always been great, and in 1887, the year of Queen Victoria's Golden Jubilee, George W. Childs of Philadelphia gave the town a **clock-tower and drinking fountain.** It stands in Rothermarket and was unveiled by the Shakespearian actor Henry Irving. The fountain bears an inscription from the Bard's *Timon of Athens:* "Honest water which ne'er left man i' the mire."

The **Shakespeare Centre,** flanking the garden of the dramatist's birthplace, was built as the headquarters of

CARS FROM THE PAST

The Stratford Motor Museum, in Shakespeare Street, houses a superb collection of vintage cars and motor-cycles. The cars include Rolls-Royces, Lagondas and Mercedes. The museum, once a church, is atmospherically fitted out with old petrol pumps and motoring signs, and a replica of a 1920's garage. A gallery upstairs contains pictures by noted motoring artists.

The polished aluminium 1926 Rolls-Royce Phantom 1 was built for a prime minister of Hyderabad, India.

the Shakespeare Birthplace Trust and as a study centre. It was opened in 1964, to commemorate the 400th anniversary of Shakespeare's birth. An extension, completing the original premises, was added in 1981.

Each year, on October 12, the Mop Fair fills the streets of the town with stalls, sideshows and merrymaking crowds. The old tradition of roasting an ox has died out, but there is usually a pig-roast. The fair is the only surviving one of several that were once held under charters granted by King John and Henry III. The town's weekly market has been held since the 12th century, a privilege originally given by Richard I.

Information Tel. 293127.
Location On the A34, 20 m. NW of Banbury.
Parking Windsor Street; Rother Street; Bridgeway; Arden Street (all car parks).
District council Stratford-upon-Avon (Tel. 67575).
Population 20,900.
E-C Thur. **M-D** Fri.
Police (Ab) Rother Street (Tel. 68711).
Casualty hospital (Aa) Alcester Road (Tel. 5831).
Post office (Bb) Bridge Street.
Theatres Royal Shakespeare **(Ba)** (Tel. 292271); The Other Place, Southern Lane (292271); Heritage **(Bb)** (69285).
Cinema Picture House **(Aa),** Greenhill Street (Tel. 292622).
Public library (Ab) Henley Street.
Shopping Wood Street; Bridge Street; High Street; Henley Street; Sheep Street.
Events World homage to Shakespeare (Apr.); Mop Fair (Oct.).
Trade and industry Agriculture; market gardening; fruit canning.
AA 24 hour service
Tel. Birmingham (021) 550 4858.

STRATFORD-UPON-AVON

A46 Warwick 8 B
Birmingham 24 · A34
Banbury 20 · A422 · A34 Oxford 39
Stratford-Upon-Avon Canal
0 110 220 YARDS
Mary Arden's House
Alcester 8 · A422
Motor Mus.
Shakespeare Centre
Shakespeare's Birthplace
Library
Bus Station
Clopton Bridge
Gower Memorial
Heritage Theatre
Judith Quiney's House
Bancroft Gardens
Picture House Cinema
Hosp.
Harvard House
Town Hall
Nash's House
New Place
Picture Gallery
Royal Shakespeare Theatre
Theatre Gardens
Avon
Mason's Court
Knott & Great Gardens
Guild Chapel Guildhall
Alms-houses
Grammar School
POL
Firs Gdn
Mason Croft
Hall's Croft
CHESTNUT WALK
A A439 Evesham 14
Holy Trinity Church 200yds

Street Somerset

In the early 19th century James Clark hit upon the idea of lining slippers with sheepskin. His brainwave transformed Street from a tranquil sheep-farming community into a busy town, and the shoe firm he founded now employs about one-third of Street's population.

The countryside around the town is good for walking, and there are fine views of the Mendip and Quantock Hills from Ivythorn Hill, 2 miles south, a 90 acre wooded estate owned

THE STORY OF SHOES

A museum housed in Clark Brothers' shoe factory, Street, traces the history of shoe-making since the firm was founded in the 1830s. On display are materials, tools, benches, machines and photographs. One section illustrates footwear of the past, right back to Roman times.

Shoes that were apparently hand-sewn could be produced by the Keats-Clark machine, patented in 1863. The lady's boot of 1840 is made of camlet cloth and leather.

by the National Trust. On Windmill Hill, south-east of the town, stands a monument to Admiral Lord Hood (1724-1816).

Information Tel. Wells 73026.
Location On the A361, 2 m. SW of Glastonbury.
Parking Farm Road/Orchard Road; Strode Road; Vestry Road; Goswell Road; Church Road (all car parks).
District council Mendip (Tel. Wells 73026).
Population 8,800. **E-C** Wed.
Police Oakfield Road, Frome (Tel. Frome 62211).
Casualty hospital Wells and District Cottage Hospital, Bath Road, Wells (Tel. Wells 73154).
Post office High Street.
Theatre Strode Theatre, Church Road (Tel. 42846).
Cinema Maxime, Leigh Road (Tel. 42028).
Public library Leigh Road.
Places to see Shoe Museum; Ivythorn Manor, 2 m. S.
Shopping West End; Crispin Centre.
AA 24 hour service
Tel. Yeovil 27744.

Stretford Greater Manchester

Manchester United Football Club and Lancashire County Cricket Club are both based in Stretford – at Old Trafford. The town, which developed after the opening of the Manchester Ship Canal in 1894, includes a large part of Manchester docks within its boundaries. Britain's first industrial estate was established at Trafford Park, in 1897.

Information
Tel. Manchester (061) 872 2101.
Location On the A56, 5 m. SW of Manchester.
Parking Broady Street; Newton Street; Lacy Street (all car parks).
District council Metropolitan Borough of Trafford (Tel. 061 872 2101).
Population 47,600.
E-C Wed.
Police Talbot Road (Tel. 061 872 5050).
Casualty hospital Park Hospital, Moorside Road, Davyhulme, Urmston (Tel. 061 748 4022).
Post office Kingsway.
Theatre Stretford Children's Theatre, Sydney Street (Tel. 061 865 0278).
Public library Kingsway.
Places to see Trafford Park; Longford Hall Park.
Shopping Arndale Centre.
Event Stretford Pageant (June).
Sport FA League football, Manchester United FC, Old Trafford, Warwick North. Lancashire County Cricket Club, Old Trafford.
AA 24 hour service
Tel. 061 485 6299.

Stromness Orkney

Visitors who travel by ferry to Orkney get their first view of Stromness as they round the island of Hoy. It is a harbour busy with fishing boats, with gabled houses at the water's edge and narrow, flagstoned streets leading into a warren of passages.

A plaque at Logan's Well records the visits of Hudson's Bay Company ships between 1670 and 1891, the visit of Captain Cook's *Resolution* and *Discovery* in 1780 and the *Erebus* and *Terror* of Sir John Franklin's 1845 Arctic expedition.

In the 18th century, Stromness was the home of John Gow, a pirate who ended his days on the gallows in London. Sir Walter Scott based his novel *The Pirate* on Gow's adventures.

Information Tel. 850 716.
Location On the A965, 15 m. W of Kirkwall.
Parking The Quay (cp).
District council Orkney (Tel. Kirkwall 850 3535).
Population 1,650.
E-C Thur. **M-D** Wed.
Police North End Road (Tel. 850 222).
Casualty hospital Balfour Hospital, New Scapa Road, Kirkwall

(Tel. Kirkwall 2763).
Post office Victoria Street.
Public library Hellihole.
Places to see Pier Art Centre Museum, Alfred Street.
Shopping Victoria Street; Dundas Street.
Events Gala Week (July); Boat Championships (Sept.).
Car ferry To Scrabster (Thurso) (Tel. 850 655).

Stroud Gloucestershire

The narrow old streets of Stroud climb steep hillsides on a site where five Cotswold valleys meet. Cloth-mills, powered by fast-flowing streams, were operating in the area in the early 16th century, and by the 1820s there were more than 150 of them. Stroud-water scarlet, a cloth used for military uniforms, was renowned throughout the world. Today, only four mills remain, but these produce fine-quality cloth.

Information Council Offices, High Street (Tel. 4252).
Location On the A46, 10 m. S of Gloucester.
Parking London Road; Parliament Street; Merrywalks; Church Street; Union Street (all car parks).
District council Stroud (Tel. 6321).
Population 20,900.
E-C Thur. **M-D** Wed., Fri. and Sat.
Police Parliament Street (Tel. 6311).
Casualty hospital Stroud General Hospital, Trinity Road (Tel. 2283).
Post office Russell Street.
Theatre Cotswold Playhouse, Parliament Street (Tel. 3664).
Public library Lansdown.
Places to see George Room Gallery; Museum, Lansdown; Old Town Hall.
Shopping George Street; Russell Street; King Street; High Street.
Event Stroud Show (July).
AA 24 hour service
Tel. Gloucester 23278.

Sudbury Suffolk

Weaving is still carried on in the ancient town of Sudbury, once the largest of East Anglia's woollen centres. The silk for the Princess of Wales' wedding dress was made at a local mill. Sudbury was a busy river port on the Stour when the great English painter Thomas Gainsborough was born there in 1727.

The centre of the town is Market Hill. Below it lie the medieval Anchor Inn and the 15th-century Salters Hall, with its fine oriel windows.

Information Public Library, Market Hill (Tel. 72092 or 76029).
Location On the A134, 15 m. NW of Colchester.
Parking North Street; Station Road (2); Stour Street (all car parks).
District council Babergh (Tel. Hadleigh 822801).
Population 9,900.
E-C Wed. **M-D** Thur., Sat.
Police Acton Lane (Tel. 72345).

The portrait and landscape painter Thomas Gainsborough (1727-88) was born in Sudbury at 46 Sepulchre Street, since renamed after him. He left the town at 14 to study in London. Among his celebrated portraits are those of George III and Dr Johnson.

Gainsborough's birthplace is now an art gallery and museum.

Casualty hospital West Suffolk, Hardwick Lane, Bury St Edmunds (Tel. Bury St Edmunds 63131).
Post office East Street.
Theatre Quay, Quay Lane (Tel. 74745).
Cinema Gainsborough, East Street (Tel. 72776).
Public library Market Hill.
Places to see Gainsborough's House, Gainsborough Street; Sudbury Museum, Station Road; Melford Hall, 3 m. N; Kentwell Hall, 3 m. N.
Shopping Market Hill; North Street.
AA 24 hour service
Tel. Chelmsford 61711.

Sunbury-on-Thames
Surrey

This riverside town was a fashionable suburb of London as long ago as the 17th century, and many of the fine houses built then and later still stand on the river banks.

Kempton Park, an estate dating from the 17th century, is best known for its racecourse laid out in 1889.

Information Tel. 51499.
Location On the A308, 5 m. E of Staines.
Parking Staines Road West (2); Thames Street; Fordbridge Road; Green Street (all car parks).
District council Borough of Spelthorne (Tel. Staines 51499).
Population 39,000.
E-C Thur.
Police Staines Road East (Tel. 89561).
Casualty hospital Ashford Hospital, London Road, Ashford (Tel. Ashford 51188).
Post office Staines Road West.
Public library Staines Road West.
Shopping Staines Road West; Sunbury Cross Shopping Centre; Thames Street, Lower Sunbury.
Sport Horse racing, Kempton Park.
AA 24 hour service
Tel. Guildford 72841.

Sunderland Tyne & Wear

At the head of the River Wear stands the industrial dynamo called Sunderland – one of the world's great shipbuilding towns, a famous coal-mining and glass-manufacturing centre, and a busy port.

In Monkwearmouth, the area north of the river, the ancient St Peter's Church, built in 674, was the home of the Venerable Bede (about 673-735), who through his monumental history of the English Church is known as the Father of English History. St Peter's was rebuilt in 1872-5, but the original Saxon west tower and wall survive.

In the early 18th century, Sunderland's quays, workshops and warehouses grew in number and activity, and by the mid-19th century it had become a major port for the export of coal brought down the river by barges and, more importantly, the greatest ship-building centre in the world, turning out merchant sailing vessels at speed.

The shipyards have dwindled to two, but each can produce ships of up to 160,000 tons – a greater tonnage than the entire output of the river a century ago.

The Wear Bridge, erected in 1927-9, succeeded a famous one built in 1796, the second-ever bridge of cast iron and at that time the biggest in the country.

Ryhope Pumping Station is one of the finest industrial monuments in the north-east. Its enormous gleaming beam-engines, built in the 1860s, pumped 3 million gallons of water a day for nearly 100 years to supply drinking water to Sunderland.

Information Tel. 76161.
Location On the A19, 12 m. SE of Newcastle upon Tyne.
Parking Bedford Street; Green Street; High Street West (2); Park Lane; Burdon Road; Boughton Street; The Green; Paley Street (2); West Wear Street; Lambton Street; Nile Street; The Rink; Tavistock Place; Reynoldson Street; Tatham Street; Chester Road; Hind Street; Low Road (all car parks).
District council Borough of Sunderland (Tel. 76161).
Population 196,100.
M-D Daily.
Police (Ab) Gillbridge Avenue (Tel. 76155).
Casualty hospital New District General, Kayll Road (Tel. 56256).
Post office (Bb) Market Square.
Theatres Empire **(Ab)**, High Street West (Tel. 42517); Royalty Theatre, The Royalty (72669).
Cinemas ABC 1 and 2 **(Aa)**, Holmeside (Tel. 74148); Odeons 1, 2 and 3 **(Ba)**, Holmeside (74881); Fairworld 1 and 2, Concord, Washington (462711).
Public library (Ba/Bb) Borough Road.
Places to see Central Museum **(Ba/Bb)**; Monkwearmouth Station Museum; Ryhope Pumping Station.
Shopping High Street West; Fawcett Street; Market Square; Holmeside.
Events Carnival (Aug.); Houghton Feast (Oct.).
Trade and industry Ship-building; coal-mining; engineering; clothing.
Sport FA League football, Sunderland FC, Roker Park.
AA 24 hour service
Tel. Newcastle upon Tyne 610111.

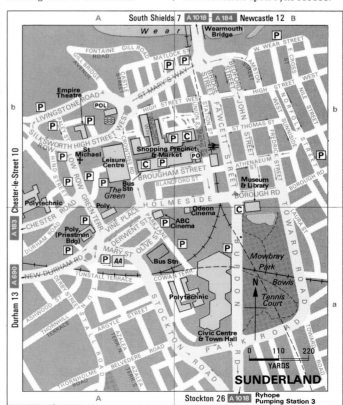

SUNDERLAND

Sutton see London

Sutton Coldfield
see Birmingham

Sutton-in-Ashfield Notts.
This industrial town on the western edge of Sherwood Forest was once a village in woods abounding with ash trees. The Norman family of de Sutton built the parish church, which has much of its original architecture.

Information Tel. Mansfield 559111.
Location On the A615, 18 m. NW of Nottingham.
Parking Idlewells Precinct; New Street; Church Street; Stoney Street; Priestsic Road; Market Place (Mon., Tues., Wed.) (all car parks).
District council Ashfield (Tel. Mansfield 52181).
Population 41,300.
E-C Wed. **M-D** Fri., Sat.
Police Church Street (Tel. Mansfield 553333).
Casualty hospital Mansfield General, West Hill Drive, Mansfield (Tel. Mansfield 22515).
Post office Brook Street.
Public library Devonshire Mall.
Shopping Idlewells Precinct.
AA 24 hour service
Tel. Nottingham 787751.

Swadlincote Derbyshire
Until the 18th century Swadlincote was a hamlet, without even a church of its own. Then local clay and coal turned it into a pottery town. Workshops and kilns were well established by 1795. The arrival of the railway in the mid-19th century speeded the growth of the town to its present size.

Information
Tel. Burton upon Trent 217701.
Location On the B586, 7 m. SE of Burton upon Trent.
Parking Belmont Street; Church Street (both car parks).
District council South Derbyshire (Tel. Burton upon Trent 215361).
Population 23,400.
E-C Wed. **M-D** Fri., Sat.
Police Civic Way (Tel. Burton upon Trent 215361).
Casualty hospital District Hospital Centre, Belvedere Road, Burton upon Trent (Tel. Burton upon Trent 66333).
Post office Midland Road.
Public library Civic Way.
Shopping High Street; Market Street.
AA 24 hour service
Tel. Nottingham 787751.

Swaffham Norfolk
An Anglo-Saxon tribe called the Swaefas settled in this fertile part of Norfolk and gave their name to Swaffham. In the 14th and 15th centuries the town had a flourishing sheep and wool trade, centred on its great wedge-shaped market place. The Market Cross was built by Horace Walpole (1717-97), 4th Earl of Orford.

Information Tel. 21513.
Location On the A47, 15 m. SE of King's Lynn.
Parking Market Place; Theatre Street; Station (all car parks).
District council Breckland (Tel. Attleborough 452884).
Population 4,780.
E-C Thur. **M-D** Sat.
Police Westacre Road (Tel. 21222).
Casualty hospital Queen Elizabeth Hospital, Gayton Road, King's Lynn (Tel. King's Lynn 66266).
Post office Lynn Street.
Public library The Pightle.
Places to see Market Cross.
Shopping Market Place; Lynn Street.
AA 24 hour service
Tel. Norwich 29401.

Swanage Dorset
Stonework and street furnishings brought from London in the 19th century are an intriguing feature of Swanage. The façade of the Town Hall came from the Mercers' Hall, Cheapside, designed by a student of Sir Christopher Wren in 1670; and the clock-tower near the pier was originally erected at the end of London Bridge in honour of the Duke of Wellington.

A safe, sandy beach lines the sweeping bay, said to be the scene of a naval battle in 877 in which King Alfred defeated a Danish fleet.

Information The White House, Shore Road (Tel. 2885).
Location On the A351, 10 m. SE of Wareham.
Parking Broad Road; Central, off King's Road; De Moulham Road; Victoria Avenue (all car parks).
District council Purbeck (Tel. Wareham 6561).
Population 8,650.
E-C Thur.
Police Argyle Road (Tel. 2004).
Casualty hospital General Hospital, Queen's Road (Tel. 2282).
Post office King's Road.
Theatre The Mowlem, Shore Road (Tel. 2239).
Cinema The Mowlem, Shore Road (Tel. 2239).
Public library High Street.
Places to see Town Hall, High Street; Wellington clock-tower, Seafront.
Shopping High Street; Station Road; Institute Road.
Event Annual Regatta and Carnival Week (end July and early Aug.).
AA 24 hour service
Tel. Bournemouth 25751.

Swansea W. Glamorgan
The City of Swansea is the second largest in Wales, after Cardiff. Its name derives from Sweyn's Ey (the island of Sweyn). Sweyn was a Viking pirate who chose this site, where the River Tawe enters Swansea Bay, as a base for plundering the coast.

In about 1330 Bishop Henry de Gower built a castle – or, rather, a fortified manor house – at Swansea. It was severely damaged in the early 15th century by the Welsh rebel

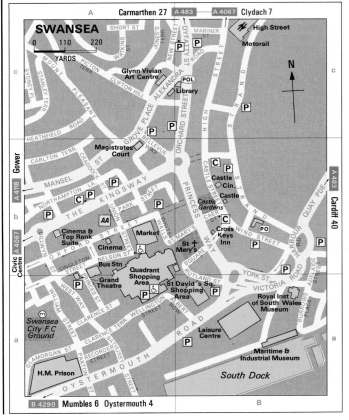

WHERE A POET GREW UP

Swansea featured largely in the work of Welsh poet Dylan Thomas (1914-53), who spent his first 20 years in the town. A memorial to him stands in Cwmdonkin Park.

Thomas's birthplace, 5 Cwmdonkin Drive, is close to the park where his memorial stands.

leader Owain Glyndwr, and was demolished by the Parliamentarians in 1647, during the Civil War. The ruins today consist of a large tower and some domestic buildings.

In the 18th century the docks, established in 1306 for ship-building, were developed for the exporting of Welsh coal, copper and iron ore.

Since the Second World War a spacious new city centre, with wide streets and oases of greenery, has grown up on the ashes of the old, which was severely bombed in 1941.

At Oystermouth there is a ruined 13th-century castle; the hall, main apartments and chapel still stand. In the village churchyard is the grave of Thomas Bowdler (1754-1825), whose expurgated edition of Shakespeare gave the language the term "bowdlerise".

Information Tel. 468321.
Location On the A48, 40 m. W of Cardiff.
Parking Adelaide Street; Garden Street; Mariner Street; Northampton Lane; North Dock; Park Street East; Park Street West; Pell Street; Picton Lane; Rialto; Strand Row; Trinity Place; Worcester Place; Weavers; St David's Square; Oystermouth Road; Orchard Street; The Kingsway; New Street; Dyfatty Street; Strand; Little Wind Street; Grove Place; Princess Street (all car parks).
District council City of Swansea (Tel. 50821).
Population 167,800.
M-D Weekdays, except Thur. afternoons.
Police (Bc) Alexandra Road (Tel. 52222).
Casualty hospital Singleton Hospital, Sketty Park Lane (Tel. 20566).
Post office (Bb) Wind Street.
Theatres (Aa) Grand, Singleton Street (Tel. 55141); Dylan Thomas Theatre, Gloucester Place (466757).
Cinemas Castle, Worcester Place (Tel. 53433); Odeon **(Bb)**, The

Kingsway (52351); Studio 1, 2 and 3, St Helen's Road (460996).
Public library (Ac) Alexandra Road.
Places to see Brangwyn Hall; Guildhall; Castle **(Bb)**, Castle Street; Glynn Vivian Art Centre, Alexandra Road; Museum, Quay Parade; Royal Institution of South Wales Museum **(Ba)**, Gloucester Place; Maritime and Industrial Museum **(Ba)**, South Dock; Oystermouth Castle, 3 m. SW on A4067.
Town trails Tourist Information Centre, Old Bus Station, Singleton Street.
Shopping The Quadrant; The Kingsway; Oxford Street; High Street.
Trade and industry Light and medium manufacturing, such as clothing; tourism; shipping.
Sport FA League football, Swansea City FC, Vetch Field; Rugby football, Swansea RFC, St Helen's Ground.
Car ferry To Cork (Tel. London (01) 734 4681).
AA 24 hour service Tel. 55598.

Swindon Wiltshire

The initials GWR, standing for Great Western Railway, stamped themselves indelibly on the town's history from the middle of the last century, turning Swindon from an agricultural settlement into an industrial centre and the largest town in Wiltshire.

In 1835 it became a station on the GWR London to Bristol line, and a few years later was chosen as the site of a locomotive works. When other lines were built, Swindon became a major junction. In the hey-day of steam, the locomotive works were among the largest in the world, covering 320 acres and employing 12,000 workers. These had their own specially designed village, maintained today by the council because of its historical interest.

The Great Western Railway Museum, housed in a former Wes-

leyan chapel, displays famous locomotives, signalling equipment and other railway relics, and has a room devoted to the 19th-century engineer Isambard Kingdom Brunel, who established the GWR.

The town art gallery contains paintings by Graham Sutherland, Ben Nicholson and other modern artists, including one by L. S. Lowry.

Information Tel. 30328 or 26161.
Location Off the M4, 3½ m NW from Junction 15.
Parking Queen Street; John Street; Granville Street; Princes Street; Rolleston Street; Henry Street; Villett Street; Fleming Way; Carlton Street; Brunel Centre; Spring Gardens; Prospect Place; Bath Road; Devizes Road; The Planks; Market Street; Cheltenham Street; County Ground (all car parks).
District council Borough of Thamesdown (Tel. 26161).
Population 91,100.
M-D Mon. and Fri.
Police (Bb) Fleming Way (Tel. 28111).
Casualty hospital Princess Margaret, Okus Road (Tel. 36231).
Post office (Bb) Fleming Way.
Theatres Wyvern Theatre and Arts Centre **(Ba)**, Theatre Square (Tel. 24481); Arts Centre, Devizes Road (26161 ext. 3133).
Cinema ABC **(Ba)**, Regent Street (Tel. 22838).
Public library (Ba) Regent Circus.
Places to see Great Western Railway Museum and Railway Village **(Ab)**, Faringdon Road; Art Gallery and Museum, Bath Road; Richard Jeffries Museum, Marlborough Road, Coate.
Shopping Brunel Shopping Centre; Faringdon Road; Fleet Street; The Parade; Regent Street; Commercial Road; Victoria Road; Wood Street; High Street; Devizes Road.
Sport FA League football, Swindon Town FC, Shrivenham Road.
AA 24 hour service Tel. 21446.

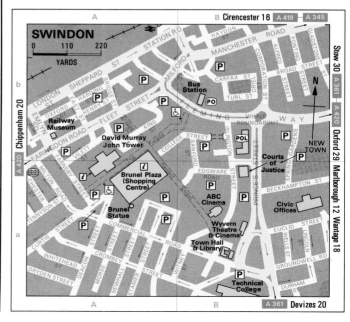

T

Tameside G. Manch.

A number of small Lancashire and Cheshire towns and villages were combined to form this new borough in 1974. It is centred on the old market town of Ashton-under-Lyne on the north bank of the River Tame.

The Manor of Ashton was owned by the Assheton family from the 14th century; under-Lyne either refers to the Pennine uplands once known as Lyme or to the county boundary or line.

Ashton was one of the first planned towns in England since the Middle Ages. From the 1790s, the western part was laid out on a gridiron pattern, a feature still visible today.

Tameside also absorbed the former cotton towns of Stalybridge, Hyde, Mossley and Duckinfield, the former hatting town of Denton, Langdendale, and the Manchester suburbs of Audenshaw and Droylsden.

Information Tel. Manchester (061) 330 8355.
Location On the A627, 6 m. E of Manchester.
Parking Ashton-under-Lyne: Albion Street; Gas Street; Church Street (2); Henrietta Street; Mill Lane; Adam Street. Hyde: Union Street (2); Water Street; Clarendon Street. Stalybridge: Trinity Street (2); Newton Street; Lees Street; Castle Street (all car parks).
District council Borough of Tameside (Tel. 061 330 8355).
Population 205,900.
E-C Tues. **M-D** All other weekdays.
Police Manchester Road, Ashton-under-Lyne (Tel. 061 330 8321).
Casualty hospital Tameside General Hospital, Fountain Street, Ashton-under-Lyne (Tel. 061 330 8373).
Post offices Ashton-under-Lyne: Warrington Street. Hyde: Market Street. Stalybridge: Trinity Street.
Theatres Hyde Festival Theatre, Corporation Street, Hyde (no telephone); Tameside Theatre, Oldham Road, Ashton-under-Lyne (Tel. 061 308 3223).
Cinemas Metro, Old Street, Ashton-under-Lyne (Tel. 061 330 1993); Tameside Theatre, Oldham Road, Ashton-under-Lyne (061 308 3223); Theatre Royal, Corporation Street, Hyde (061 368 2206); Palace, Market Street, Stalybridge (061 338 2156).
Public libraries Ashton-under-Lyne:

Old Street. Stalybridge: Trinity Street. Hyde: Union Street.
Shopping Ashton-under-Lyne: Mercian Way Precinct; Market Square. Hyde: Civic Square; Hyde Precinct. Stalybridge: Market Street; Melbourne Street; Grosvenor Street.
AA 24 hour service
Tel. Manchester (061) 485 6299.

Tamworth Staffordshire

The Saxon Kingdom of Mercia was ruled from Tamworth in the 8th century, and in AD 913 Aetheflaed, daughter of King Alfred, established a fortress there. A Norman castle was built on the site, at the junction of the rivers Tame and Anker, by William the Conqueror's Royal Champion, Robert de Marmion.

In 1834 Sir Robert Peel, the MP for Tamworth, made a pre-election speech to his constituents in which he outlined his plans for political reform. The speech became known as the Tamworth Manifesto, and was the forerunner of modern electioneering addresses.

Information Tel. 4222.
Location On the A453, 7 m. SE of Lichfield.
Parking Bolebridge Street; Spinning School Lane; Marmion Street; Castle car park; Ankerside; Orchard Street; Hollow Way; Mill Lane; Albion Street; Lower Gungate; Hospital Street; Church Lane; Fazely Road (all car parks).
District council Borough of Tamworth (Tel. 4222).
Population 64,300.
E-C Wed. **M-D** Tues. and Sat.
Police Spinning School Lane (Tel. 61001).
Casualty hospital Hospital Street (Tel. 3771).
Post office Lower Gungate.
Cinema Palace, Lower Gungate (Tel. 57100).
Public library Corporation Street.
Places to see Norman castle and Museum, Market Street.
Shopping Market Square; Middle Entry Shopping Precinct; The Precinct.
AA 24 hour service
Tel. Stoke-on-Trent 25881.

Taunton Somerset

History has left its mark on Taunton in its many fine buildings and pleasant streets, though it is a history that was often bloody and cruel. It was the scene of bitter struggles during the Civil War of 1642-9, and in 1685 Judge Jeffreys held a "Bloody Assize" in the castle when 508 supporters of the Duke of Monmouth's rebellion were condemned to death.

The Norman castle retains part of its keep, which has walls 13 ft thick. The great hall where Judge Jeffreys presided is 120 ft long.

The gabled and half-timbered Tudor House in Fore Street bears the date 1578. It was the home of Sir

ROMAN MOSAIC *A well-preserved Roman floor found at Low Ham, about 12 miles north-east, is in the Somerset County Museum in Taunton.*

William Portman, who took the Duke of Monmouth to London for his trial after the rebellion. It is believed that Judge Jeffreys was entertained there during the "Bloody Assize".

The Church of St Mary Magdalene was built between 1488 and 1514, but it was considered unsafe in 1862 and was dismantled and rebuilt to the original design. The 163 ft high tower of red Quantock sandstone faces Hammet Street, a completely Georgian thoroughfare with white-porticoed houses. The tower of St James's Church, though smaller than its neighbour, is similar in style.

Georgian architecture abounds in the High Street, blending with the 16th-century Municipal Buildings in nearby Corporation Street, which were originally a grammar school. At one end of the High Street is Vivary Park, with a gateway that is a riot of Victorian decorative ironwork.

Taunton takes its name from the River Tone, which flows through the centre of the town. The surrounding Blackdown, Quantock and Brendon Hills shelter the town and the rich Vale of Taunton Deane.

The warm climate and fertile soil of the vale are responsible for Taunton's best-known product – cider. The Taunton Cider Company's headquarters is just outside the town at Norton Fitzwarren. At Bradford-on-Tone,

TELEPHONE MUSEUM

A fascinating history of the telephone service can be seen in Taunton's British Telecom Museum. The oldest telephone dates from 1877.

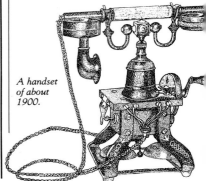

A handset of about 1900.

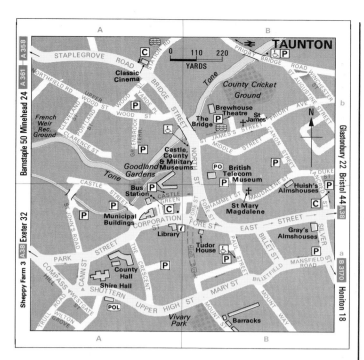

DEVON LADY *An effigy of Judge John Glanville's wife is on their 17th-century tomb in St Eustachius Church, Tavistock.*

about 3 miles south-west of Taunton on the A38, is Sheppy's Farm, where cider-making by traditional methods can be seen each autumn.

Information Tel. 74785.
Location On the A38, 11 m. S of Bridgwater.
Parking Belvedere Road; Canon Street; Castle Green; Castle Street; Coal Orchard; Duke Street; Greenbrook Terrace; Victoria Gate; Kilkenny; Paul Street; Priory Bridge Road; Silver Street; The Crescent; Wood Street (all car parks).
District council Borough of Taunton Deane (Tel. 85166).
Population 35,300.
E-C Thur. **M-D** Tues., Sat.
Police (Aa) Shuttern, Upper High Street (Tel. 87911).
Casualty hospital Taunton and Somerset, East Reach (Tel. 73444).
Post office (Bb) North Street.
Theatre Brewhouse Theatre and Arts Centre, Coal Orchard (Tel. 83244).
Cinema Classics 1 and 2, Station Road (Tel. 72291).
Public library Corporation Street.
Places to see Castle **(Ab)**, including County Museum and Somerset Light Infantry Museum; British Telecom Museum **(Bb)**, North Street; Tudor House **(Ba)**, Fore Street; St Margaret's Hospital, East Reach; Shire Hall **(Aa)**; Gray's Almshouses **(Ba)**, East Street; Municipal Buildings **(Aa)**, Corporation Street.
Shopping High Street; North Street; East Street; Bridge Street; Station Road; Fore Street.
Events Festival (July); Carnival (Oct.); Music Drama Festival (Nov.).
Trade and industry Agriculture; electronic and optical instruments; cider.
Sport Somerset County Cricket, St James's Street.
AA 24 hour service Tel. 73363.

Tavistock Devon

One of England's greatest heroes, Sir Francis Drake, was born on the borders of Tavistock in 1542 and baptised in the parish church. His birthplace, Crowndale Farm, is 1 mile south-west of the town. A statue to him stands outside the school in Plymouth Road, Tavistock.

The town, the largest in west Devon, grew up around a great Benedictine abbey founded in 974. In 1281, Tavistock became a stannary town – the administrative centre for the tin-mining industry based on Dartmoor. It also developed into a prosperous woollen centre.

The abbey was devastated in the 16th century during Henry VIII's Dissolution of the Monasteries, and all that remains are three gates, part of the church cloister, a dining hall and a tower. After the Dissolution the town became the property of the Russell family, who later became Dukes of Bedford.

From the 1790s until 1901, when the seams were exhausted, some of the biggest copper mines in the world were worked just outside the town. Today Tavistock is an agricultural market town, shopping centre and touring centre for Dartmoor.

The River Tavy, one of the fastest-flowing rivers in England, runs through the town.

Information Tel. 2938 or 5911.
Location On the A386, 15 m. N of Plymouth.
Parking Whitchurch Road; Pixon Lane; Market Street; Plymouth Road; Brook Street; Bedford Square (all car parks).
District council West Devon (Tel. 5911).
Population 10,000.
E-C Wed. **M-D** Fri.
Police Bedford Square (Tel. 2217).
Casualty hospital Spring Hill (Tel. 2233).
Post office Abbey Place.
Public library Market Road.
Places to see Abbey, Abbey Place; Town Hall, Bedford Square.
Town trails Available from Dartmoor National Park Information Centre, Bedford Square.
Shopping Bedford Square; Duke Street; West Street; Brook Street.
Event Goose Fair (Oct.).
AA 24 hour service Tel. Plymouth 669989.

GATEWAY TO A NATIONAL PARK *The market town of Tavistock stands on the south-western edge of Dartmoor.*

Teignmouth Devon

The quays along the River Teign shipped the Dartmoor granite which was used to build London Bridge in 1831. Now they handle timber and ball clay (the staple material of the English pottery industry) which is quarried up-river.

Teignmouth (pronounced Tin-muth) started to develop as a holiday resort in the 18th century, and its early visitors included the novelists Fanny Burney and Jane Austen, and the poet John Keats. There are many Regency buildings on the Sea Front, and in the streets behind.

Across the Teign Estuary, the village of Shaldon is sheltered by the red-sandstone headland of The Ness.

The main beach at Teignmouth is sandy, and there is a rocky cove reached by tunnel through The Ness.

Information Tel. 6271.
Location On the A379, 8 m. N of Torquay.
Parking The Lower Point; The Point; Eastcliff; Brunswick Street; Lower Brook Street; Teign Street (all car parks).
District council Teignbridge (Tel. Newton Abbot 67251).
Population 13,300.
E-C Thur.
Police Carlton Place (Tel. 2433).
Casualty hospital Mill Lane (Tel. 2161).
Post office Den Road.
Theatre Carlton Theatre, The Den (Tel. 4252).
Cinema Riviera, The Den (Tel. 4624).
Public library Fore Street.
Places to see Aquarium, The Den; Museum, French Street.
Town trails Available from Tourist Information Centre, The Den.
Shopping Bank Street; Wellington Street; Regent Street; Teign Street.
Events Flower Show (July); Carnival (July); Regatta (Aug.).
AA 24 hour service Tel. Torquay 25903.

Telford Salop

Britain's newest new town is being built over an area of 30 sq. miles and takes in the towns of Wellington, Oakengates, Ironbridge, Dawley and Hadley.

Beneath the wooded slopes of the 1,334 ft Wrekin, where Telford is growing, more than a million trees, bushes and shrubs will be planted to justify the planners' description of the future town as a "forest city".

Telford was named in honour of the Scottish-born civil engineer Thomas Telford (1757-1834), who was County Surveyor of Shropshire. He designed many of the county's bridges, tunnels and other buildings. He was also responsible for much of the work on the Holyhead Road (A5). This follows the line of the Roman Watling Street, through Oakengates and Wellington.

At the south-west corner of the town, the River Severn rushes through a limestone gorge. On its banks, in 1709, Abraham Darby (c. 1677-1717) discovered how to smelt iron using coke instead of charcoal, a technical achievement which helped to launch the Industrial Revolution.

The role which the villages of Coalbrookdale and Ironbridge played in early industrial development is traced on sites in the gorge, now run by the Ironbridge Gorge Museum Trust. One of these sites, at Blists Hill, has trams and steam engines, and preserves a section of the Coalport Canal. It also houses a recreated 18th-century village, including cottages, shops and workshops. At Coalbrookdale are the Darby foundry and other iron-founding relics.

It was in the gorge that Richard Trevithick (1771-1833) made the steam engine that in 1804 became the first to run on rails.

The towns and villages which make up Telford still have many buildings which pre-date the Industrial Revolution. At Madeley, 16th-century Madeley Court was the home of

Abraham Darby the Elder. The church was designed by Telford.

Information Tel. 505051.
Location On the M54, 16 m. E of Shrewsbury.
Parking Telford: Town Centre. Wellington: Regent Street; Princess Street; Grooms Alley; Belmont Hall. Oakengates: Hadley Road; New Street. Ironbridge: High Street; Waterloo Street; The Wharfage. Dawley: Station Road; King Street; New Street. Hadley: Manse Road (all car parks).
District council Wrekin (Tel. Telford 505051).
Population 103,800.
E-C Mon.
Police Victoria Road, Wellington (Tel. Telford 44383).
Casualty hospital Royal Shrewsbury, Mytton Oak Road, Shrewsbury (Tel. Shrewsbury 52244).
Post office Walker Street, Wellington.
Theatre Oakengates Town Hall, Limes Walk, Oakengates (Tel. Telford 612718).
Cinema Clifton, Bridge Road, Wellington (Tel. Telford 3439).
Public library Walker Street, Wellington.
Places to see Coalbrookdale Museum; The Iron Bridge; Blists Hill Open Air Museum; Coalport China Works Museum; Buildwas Abbey.
Shopping Telford Centre.
AA 24 hour service Tel. Stoke-on-Trent 25881.

Tenby Dyfed

The remains of a 13th-century Norman castle overlook Tenby's old fishing harbour. The castle stands on the site of a Welsh fort called *Dinbych-y-Pysgod* (Little Fort of the Fish).

In his *Tour through Great Britain* of 1724 Daniel Defoe described Tenby as "the most agreeable town on all the south coast of Wales, except Pembroke".

The heart of Tenby, set on a headland fringed by four sandy beaches, is packed tightly inside medieval town walls. Shops almost touch across the narrow streets. St Catherine's Rock, just offshore, is topped by a fort built in 1869. Caldy Island, 2½ miles away, has a medieval church which con-

MONUMENT TO A REVOLUTION *The Iron Bridge, near Telford, was built in 1779 by Abraham Darby III. He used the iron-smelting process, invented by his grandfather, that fostered the Industrial Revolution.*

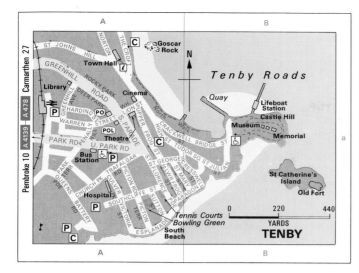

Carmarthen 27 A 478 A 4139 Pembroke 10

ST JOHNS HILL
Town Hall
GREENHILL
Library
GREENHILL ROAD
ROCKY PARK
DEER PARK
HARDING
PO
WARREN STREET
PARK RD
POL
Theatre
U. PARK RD
Bus Station
QUEENS
CHURCH PK
Hospital
SOUTHCLIFFE
PICTON BATTERY
VICTORIA
ESPLANADE
South Beach

Goscar Rock
C
N
Tenby Roads
Quay
Lifeboat Station
Castle Hill
Museum
Memorial
a
St Catherine's Island
Old Fort
Tennis Courts
Bowling Green

0   220   440
YARDS
TENBY

William Caxton, the father of English printing, is believed to have been born in Tenterden. Smallhythe Place, a 15th-century house at Smallhythe, was the home of the actress Ellen Terry for 25 years, until her death in 1928. It is now a theatrical museum that includes some of her costumes.

Information Tel. 3752/2271.
Location On the A28, 11 m. N of Rye.
Parking Bridewell Lane; Recreation Ground Road; Station Road (all car parks).
District council Borough of Ashford (Tel. Ashford 34241).
Population 6,200.
E-C Wed. **M-D** Fri.
Police Oaks Road (Tel. Ashford 25789).
Casualty hospital William Harvey, Kennington Road, Ashford (Tel. Ashford 33331).
Post office Ashford Road.
Public library The Pebbles, High Street.
Places to see Ellen Terry Museum, Smallhythe.
Shopping High Street.
AA 24 hour service
Tel. Maidstone 55353.

tains an Ogham Stone. Ogham was a form of script used by Irish Celts in about the 6th century. The monks of a modern monastery on the island produce Caldy Abbey perfume.

Tenby was the birthplace of the portrait painter Augustus John (1878-1961) and of the mathematician Robert Recorde (1510-58), who invented the = sign.

Information Tel. 2402.
Location On the A478, 10 m. E of Pembroke.
Parking Lower Park Road; Upper Park Road; Station; Southcliffe Street (2); Norton; The Croft; Crackwell Street; Battery Road (all car parks).
District council South Pembrokeshire (Tel. Pembroke 683122).
Population 4,800.
E-C Wed. **M-D** Weekdays.
Police (Aa) Warren Street (Tel. 2303/4).
Casualty hospital Trafalgar Road (Tel. 2040).
Post office (Aa) Warren Street.
Theatre De Valence Pavilion **(Aa)**, Upper Frog Street (Tel. 2730).
Cinema Royal Playhouse **(Aa)**, White Lion Street (Tel. 2093).
Public library (Aa) Greenhill Avenue.
Places to see Museum, Castle Hill **(Ba)**; St Catherine's Fort **(Ba)**; Caldy Island Monastery.
Shopping High Street; Tudor Square; Warren Street; Upper Frog Street.
AA 24 hour service
Tel. Cardiff 394111.

Tenterden Kent

In the 7th century, monks from Minster Abbey in Thanet made a denne, or clearing in a forest, which became known as "Tentwardene" – the denne of the Thanet people. In those days, Tenterden was almost on the coast, and it had a port at Smallhythe, on the River Rother, 2 miles south. The port died when the Rother was diverted to drain Welland and Romney marshes.

Tenterden is now a market town with one of the most attractive main streets in the south of England – wide, tree-lined and full of Georgian houses and shops with bow windows, porticoed doorways and shiplapped-timber frontages. The 15th-century parish church of St Mildred is dedicated to the second Abbess of Minster Abbey, and has a 100 ft tower.

A TOUCH OF THE SEA *The ship-builder's craft, called shiplapping, was often used to clad houses in Kent during the Georgian period. This one, at Tenterden, is one of many in the town.*

Tewkesbury Glos.

The valley where the Avon and Severn meet is the setting for Tewkesbury. There, in 1471, during the Wars of the Roses, the Yorkists won a great battle, when Edward IV confirmed his claim to be king, and 18-year-old Edward, the Lancastrian Prince of Wales, was slain.

Tewkesbury's pride is the abbey church of St Mary the Virgin, which the townspeople saved from destruction at the Dissolution of the Monasteries. In 1539 they collected £453, and bought the church from Henry VIII to keep it for the parish. It has the largest Norman tower still in existence, 46 ft square and 148 ft high, beneath which the young Prince Edward lies buried. The superb high altar is a 13 ft 6 in. long slab of Purbeck marble consecrated in 1239. In the nave a decorated, vaulted ceiling is supported by 14 Norman pillars, and opposite the choir stands one of the oldest organs still in use in Britain. Its pipework dates from 1610.

Information Tel. 295027 (summer); 294639 (winter).
Location On the A38, 11 m. N of Gloucester.
Parking St Mary's Lane; Gander Lane; Spring Gardens; Swilgate; Oldbury Road; Gloucester Road (all car parks).
District council Borough of Tewkesbury (Tel. 295010).
Population 9,600.
E-C Thur. **M-D** Wed., Sat.
Police Barton Street (Tel. 293930).
Casualty hospital Barton Road (Tel. 293303).
Post office High Street.
Theatre and cinema Roses Theatre, Sun Street (Tel. 295074).
Public library High Street.
Places to see Museum, Barton Street; John Moore Museum, Church Street; Abbey Mill, Mill Street.
Town trails Available from Information Centre, Barton Road.
Shopping High Street; Church Street; Barton Street.
Events Carnival Week (July); Mop Fair (Oct.).
AA 24 hour service
Tel. Gloucester 23278.

PARISH CHURCH *Tewkesbury Abbey has cathedral-like dimensions.*

OLD AND OLDER *Thame High Street is a study in architectural styles. Smart Georgian houses stand side by side with medieval cottages.*

Thame Oxfordshire

The wide High Street of this market town has largely escaped the attentions of developers, in this century at least, and timber-framed, medieval buildings rub shoulders with brick-built Georgian houses displaying elegant porches and fanlight windows. The 15th-century Birdcage Inn in Cornmarket once had a wooden cage on the forecourt to hold miscreants caught on market-days.

The parish church of St Mary contains many brasses, and in the 13th-century chancel there is the magnificent 16th-century tomb of Lord Williams of Thame and his wife.

Some of the materials from a Cistercian abbey, dissolved in 1539, were used to build Thame Park, an 18th-century mansion south of the town. Part of the house retains much of the 16th-century Abbot's Lodging.

Information Tel. 2834/2036.
Location On the A418, 10 m. SW of Aylesbury.
Parking Cattle Market, North Street; High Street; Upper High Street (not Tues.) (all car parks).
District council South Oxfordshire (Tel. Wallingford 35351).
Population 8,500.
E-C Wed. **M-D** Tues.
Police Park Street (Tel. 2121).
Casualty hospital John Radcliffe II, Headington, Oxford (Tel. Oxford 64711).
Post office High Street.
Public library Rooks Lane.
Shopping High Street; Cornmarket.
Event Thame Show (Sept.).
Trade and industry Agriculture; light engineering.
AA 24 hour service
Tel. Oxford 40286.

Thetford Norfolk

When the Danes conquered East Anglia in the 9th century, they made Thetford their capital. Later, it was the See of the Bishops of East Anglia until 1091. Everywhere in the town are reminders of its past, the most prominent being the ruins of the 12th-century priory, Castle Hill with its Iron Age earthworks, and a Norman castle mound.

The rivers Thet and Little Ouse meet in the centre of the town, and a three-way bridge spanning the junc-

RADICAL WRITER *A gilded bronze statue of Thomas Paine stands in front of Thetford's 17th-century King's House.*

tion leads to a river promenade. By Spring Walk stands a house built as a pump-room in 1818, when Thetford made an unsuccessful attempt to become a spa.

Medieval and Georgian buildings can be seen in almost every street. One of them, the 15th-century Ancient House, is Thetford's museum of local history. The Church of St Mary the Less is part Saxon, part Norman.

Thetford was the birthplace in 1737 of Thomas Paine, author of *The Rights of Man* and supporter of the American and French revolutions.

Information Tel. 2599.
Location On the A11, 12 m. N of Bury St Edmunds.
Parking Bury Road; Pike Lane; Tanner Street (2); Bridge Street; Market Place; Earls Street; St Nicholas Street; School Lane; Lime Kiln Lane; Bainham Cross (all car parks).
District council Breckland (Tel. Attleborough 452884).
Population 19,600.
E-C Wed. **M-D** Tues., Sat.
Police Norwich Road (Tel. 4314).
Casualty hospital West Suffolk, Hardwick Lane, Bury St Edmunds (Tel. Bury St Edmunds 63131).
Post office Market Place.
Cinema Palace Cinema, Guildhall Street (Tel. 2279).
Public library Raymond Street.
Places to see Ancient House Museum, White Hart Street; Castle Hill earthworks, Castle Lane; Priory ruins, Water Lane; Redcastle Norman earthworks, Brandon Road; King's House, King Street.
Shopping King Street; Tanner Street; Guildhall Street; Riverside Walk.
AA 24 hour service
Tel. Norwich 29401.

Thornton Cleveleys
Lancashire

This combination of two towns straddles the strip of land bounded by the River Wyre to the east and the Irish Sea to the west.

On the coastal side it is the northernmost point of almost 15 miles of highly developed holiday coast dominated by Blackpool. Inland there is an 18th-century windmill, Marsh Mill, which was in use until 1922.

Information Tel. Cleveleys 853378 (summer); Fleetwood 71141.
Location On the A587, 5 m. N of Blackpool.
Parking Derby Road; River Road; Rough Lea Road; Promenade (all car parks).
District council Borough of Wyre (Tel. Poulton-le-Fylde 882233).
Population 26,100.
E-C Wed.
Police Fleetwood Road North (Tel. Cleveleys 856822).
Casualty hospital Victoria Hospital, Whinney Heys Road, Blackpool (Tel. Blackpool 34111).
Post office Rossell Road.
Public library Victoria Road.
Places to see Marsh Mill, on A585.
Shopping Victoria Road.
Trade and industry Chemicals.
AA 24 hour service
Tel. Blackpool 44947.

Thurso Highland
The most northerly town on the Scottish mainland lies in a broad, sandy bay on the Pentland Firth.

In the 19th century, flagstones from local quarries were exported to pave streets in towns and cities as far distant as Canada and Australia.

The ruined Old St Peter's Kirk, near the harbour, was founded in the 13th century by Gilbert Murray, Bishop of Caithness.

Information Tel. 2371.
Location On the A836, 20 m. W of John o' Groat's.
Parking Riverside Road (2); Ormlie Road; Grove Lane; Mansens Lane; High Street; Janet Street; Princes Street (all car parks).
District council Caithness (Tel. Wick 3761).
Population 9,100.
E-C Thur. **M-D** Tues. and Thur.
Police Olrig Street (Tel. 3222).
Casualty hospital Ormlie Road (Tel. 3263).
Post office Sinclair Street.
Cinema Picture House, Sir George Street (Tel. 2784).
Public library Davidson's Lane.

HARALD'S TOWER
The Norse earl, Harald Ungi, killed in 1196, is buried beneath the tower at Thurso.

Places to see Folk Museum, Town Hall.
Shopping Rotterdam Street; Traill Street; Olrig Street; Princes Street.
Car ferry Scrabster to Stromness, Mainland, Orkney (Tel. 2052).
AA 24 hour service
Tel. Aberdeen 51231.

Tilbury Essex
The long landing-stage at Tilbury and the flat marshlands beyond have been a first close-up view of England for millions of travellers in the past 100 years. The largest ocean-going liners have been able to moor at the 1,142 ft quay at any stage of the tide. Now that the great passenger-carrying trade has declined, Tilbury's 5 miles of docks have become London's major port for container ships. Since 1963, the Dartford-Purfleet Tunnel has improved the town's access to the south of England.

Henry VIII built a fort at Tilbury to guard the Thames Estuary, and it was there in 1588 that Elizabeth I gathered the army that was to repel a Spanish invasion should the navy fail to defeat the Armada at sea. She told her soldiers: "I have the body of a weak and feeble woman, but I have the heart and stomach of a king and I think foul scorn that any prince should dare to invade the borders of my realm. Rather than any dishonours shall grow by me, I will myself take up arms."

Information Tel. Grays Thurrock 5122.
Location On the A128, 4 m. E of Grays.
Parking Quebec Road; Dunlop Road; Dock Road (all car parks).
District council Borough of Thurrock (Tel. Grays Thurrock 5122).
Population 8,000.
E-C Wed.
Police Civic Square (Tel. Grays Thurrock 2541).
Casualty hospital Orsett Hospital, Rowley Road, Orsett (Tel. Grays Thurrock 891100).
Post office Calcutta Road.
Public library Civic Square.
Places to see Tilbury Fort Museum; Thurrock Riverside Museum, Civic Square; Coalhouse Fort, East Tilbury.
Shopping Civic Square; Dock Road; Calcutta Road.
AA 24 hour service
Tel. Chelmsford 617111.

Tiverton Devon
Textiles have been the basis of Tiverton's prosperity since the 13th century. They still are, but the mills and other factories are hidden on the fringes of the town, and Tiverton keeps the air of a market town. Around it is farming land, with rich red soil, rounded hills, wooded valleys and high-banked lanes.

Tiverton grew up as a settlement in the 9th century, close to where the River Lowman joins the River Exe. There are reminders of earlier inhabitants in the prehistoric earthworks on Exeter Hill, half a mile south of the market place.

The pink-sandstone castle in the town, built in the 12th to 14th centuries, was once the home of the Courtenay family, Earls of Devon.

The Church of St Peter was consecrated in 1073 and enlarged and altered during the 15th and 16th centuries. On the outside there are 16th-century carvings of ships built in the reign of Henry VIII.

One of Tiverton's assets during the Middle Ages was its supply of fresh drinking water, which still bubbles up from Coggan's Well in Fore Street. Here, twice a year, the mayor proclaims the opening of the town fair, and every seven years, in September, an ancient stream is "perambulated" and claimed by the townsfolk.

Old Blundell's School was built in 1604 by a local wool merchant. The original building in Station Road is preserved by the National Trust, and on its lawn – known as the "Ironing Box" – John Ridd fought Robin Snell in R. D. Blackmore's novel *Lorna Doone*. The school moved to more extensive premises in Blundells Road in 1882.

Tiverton Museum is devoted mainly to social history, and includes farm wagons and railway items.

Knightshayes Court was built in the 19th century for the Heathcoat-Amories, descendants of John Heathcoat, who founded the town's modern textile industry in 1816.

The Grand Western Canal, 11 miles long, has been restored and carries tourists in horse-drawn barges during the summer.

Information Tel. 256295.
Location On the A373, 15 m. N of Exeter.
Parking Newport Street; Fore Street (2); Wellbrook Street; Blundells Road; Westexe South; Canal Hill; William Street (all car parks).
District council Mid Devon (Tel. 255255).
Population 16,500.
E-C Thur. **M-D** Tues., Fri., Sat.
Police The Avenue (Tel. 252323).
Casualty hospital William Street (Tel. 253251).
Post office Bampton Street.
Cinema Tivoli, Fore Street (Tel. 252157).
Public library Angel Hill.
Places to see Museum, St Andrew Street; St Peter's Church; Castle; Knightshayes Court, 2 m. N; Exeter Hill earthworks.
Town trails Available from Mid Devon District Council Offices, St Peter Street, or Museum.
Shopping Gold Street; Bampton Street; Fore Street; Market Precinct.
Events Proclamation of the Fair (first Thur. in June and Oct.).
AA 24 hour service
Tel. Exeter 32121.

Todmorden W. Yorks.

Until 1888 the county boundary between Yorkshire and Lancashire cut this old cotton town in half, and ran through the middle of the Town Hall.

Todmorden stands in beautiful scenery on the edge of the Pennines and at the junction of three sweeping valleys that lead to Burnley, Halifax and Rochdale. One of the town's finest buildings is Todmorden Old Hall, which has a chimneypiece of 1603.

TODMORDEN *Mill stacks rise from the old cotton town beside the Pennines.*

Information Tel. 4811.
Location On the A646, 24 m. NE of Manchester.
Parking School Lane; Halifax Road; Union Street South; Rise Lane; Dalton Street; Oxford Street; Fielden Square; Blind Lane (all car parks).
District council Metropolitan Borough of Calderdale (Tel. Halifax 65701).
Population 14,660.
E-C Tues. **M-D** Wed., Fri. and Sat.
Police Burnley Road (Tel. 2104).
Casualty hospital Halifax Royal Infirmary, Free School Lane, Halifax (Tel. Halifax 57222).
Post office Brook Street.
Theatre Hippodrome, Halifax Road (Tel. 4875).
Public library Strand, Rochdale Road.
Places to see Todmorden Old Hall; Town Hall.
Shopping Halifax Road; Burnley Road; Water Street; Dale Street.
AA 24 hour service
Tel. Bradford 724703.

Tonbridge Kent

The River Medway branches into several easily fordable streams at Tonbridge, and this made the town strategically important from early times. A Norman castle guarded the crossing. Its ruins include a magnifi-

cent gatehouse added in the 13th century.

Tonbridge public school was founded in 1553 by Sir Andrew Judde, a local man who became Lord Mayor of London. Its old boys include Kent and England cricketer Colin Cowdrey. Frank Woolley, another great Kent and England batsman, was born in Tonbridge in 1887.

The town's fine houses include the 15th-century house of the Portreeve (mayor) in East Street, and the 16th-century Chequers Inn in the High Street.

Information Tel. 353241.
Location On the A26, 5 m. N of Tunbridge Wells.
Parking The Slade; Vale Road (3); The Botany; St Stephens Street (2); Priory Street (2); Medway Wharf Road; Lamberts Yard; River Lawn Road; Bradford Street; Kinnings Row; Lower Castle Field (all car parks).
District council Tonbridge and Malling (Tel. West Malling 844522).
Population 30,300.
E-C Wed. **M-D** Sat.
Police Pembury Road (Tel. 352211).
Casualty hospitals Kent and Sussex Hospital, Mount Ephraim, Tunbridge Wells (Tel. Tunbridge Wells 26111); Pembury Hospital, Pembury, Nr Tunbridge Wells (Pembury 3535).
Post office High Street.
Cinema Carlton, The Botany (Tel. 353929).
Public library Avebury Avenue.
Places to see Tonbridge Castle.
Shopping High Street; Quarry Hill Parade; Shipbourne Road; York Parade; Angel Lane.
AA 24 hour service
Tel. Maidstone 55353.

Torbay see page 396

Totnes Devon

According to a local legend, Brutus, the great-grandson of Aeneas of Troy, sailed up the River Dart and founded both Totnes and the British race. There is a rock in Fore Street on which he reputedly stood while studying the site.

Totnes was settled and fortified by the Saxons, and then by the Normans

who built the castle on its steep mound to defend the crossing over the Dart. The Church of St Mary dates from the 15th century; but a church has stood on this site since Norman times.

Two gateways remain from the medieval town, and there are many 16th–18th-century houses in the main street, which climbs a steep hill from the river. The 17th-century Guildhall contains a small collection of local relics, including Saxon coins minted in Totnes in the 10th century.

There is a larger museum in Fore Street, in a house built in 1575. One section is devoted to the development of computers since the pioneering work done by Charles Babbage (1792-1871), who studied for a time at the King Edward VI school in Totnes.

Totnes has a thriving boatyard, and a quay through which timber is imported. In summer it is the starting-point for pleasure-steamers to Dartmouth, and a touring centre.

The ruins of Berry Pomeroy Castle, 2 miles east of the town, include an incomplete Tudor mansion built in the keep.

Information Tel. 863168.
Location On the A385, 6 m. W of Paignton.
Parking North Street; South Street (2); Steamer Quay (2); Leechwell Street; Cistern Street (all car parks). Warland Road; Babbage Road; Station Road.
District council South Hams (Tel. 864499).
Population 5,600.
E-C Thur. **M-D** Tues., Fri.
Police Ashburton Road (Tel. 862222).
Casualty hospital Totnes and District Hospital, Bridgetown (Tel. 863146).
Post office Fore Street.
Public library High Street.
Places to see Castle; Elizabethan House Museum, Fore Street; Guildhall; Costume Museum; Motor Museum; Berry Pomeroy Castle, 2 m. E; Dartington Hall, 1 m. N.
Town trails Available from Tourist Information Office, The Plains (summer); Elizabethan House Museum, Fore Street; Guildhall.
Shopping Fore Street; High Street.
AA 24 hour service
Tel. Torquay 25903.

Tower Hamlets
see London

Tring Hertfordshire

There is a twice-weekly market in this small country town, set among the beechwoods and chalk hills of the Chilterns. The Rothschild zoological collection at the corner of Akeman and Park Streets is part of the Natural History section of the British Museum. It includes exhibits of rare fish, birds and insects – among them fleas clad in tiny human clothes.

Four reservoirs north of the town,

MEDIEVAL GATE
The restored East Gate in Totnes.

which were constructed to supply the Grand Union Canal, are now a bird sanctuary and nature reserve. At Pitstone, 3 miles north-east, is a restored 17th-century windmill owned by the National Trust.

Information Tel. 2193.
Location On the A41, 7 m. E of Aylesbury.
Parking High Street; Akeman Street; Frogmore Street (all car parks).
District council Dacorum (Tel. Hemel Hempstead 60161).
Population 10,700.
E-C Wed. **M-D** Mon., Fri.
Police High Street (Tel. 2140 and Berkhamsted 71551).
Casualty hospital Hemel Hempstead General, West Herts Wing, Hillfield Road, Hemel Hempstead (Tel. Hemel Hempstead 93141).
Post office High Street.
Theatre Pendley Arts Centre, Station Road (Tel. 2483).
Public library Akeman Street.
Places to see Zoological Museum, Akeman Street; Whipsnade Zoo, 5 m. NE; Pitstone Windmill, 3 m. NE.
Shopping High Street; Western Road; Miswell Lane; Dolphin Square; Frogmore Street.
Trade and industry Light engineering; plastics; agriculture.
Event Shakespeare Festival (Aug.).
AA 24 hour service Tel. 01 954 7373.

Troon Strathclyde

They say you can play golf on a different course each day for a week at Troon, and still have a few left over for another visit. Five of the town's courses are of championship standard. But Troon is more than just a golfers' paradise. The resort has an old harbour that serves a small fishing fleet and incorporates a modern marina, a busy shipyard, and miles of sandy beach flanking two bays that are ideal for bathing and sailing.

Information Tel. 315131.
Location On the A759, 8 m. N of Ayr.
Parking Academy Street (3); South Beach; Portland Street (2); Ayr Street; Templehill (all car parks).
District council Kyle and Carrick (Tel. Ayr 81511).
Population 14,100.
E-C Wed.
Police Portland Street (Tel. 313100).
Casualty hospital Ayr County Hospital, Holmston Road, Ayr (Tel. Ayr 81991).
Post office Church Street.
Public library South Beach.
Places to see Dundonald Castle, 4 m. NE.
Shopping Church Street; Portland Street; Ayr Street.
Event Scottish Boat Show (Oct.).
Trade and industry Shipbuilding; shipbreaking; hosiery.
AA 24 hour service Tel. Glasgow (041) 812 0101.

RARE TOWERS *Truro Cathedral, built between 1880 and 1910, was the first English Protestant cathedral constructed since St Paul's, London, in 1675. It is also notable for its unusual spire-topped towers.*

Trowbridge Wiltshire

The administrative county town of Wiltshire has been a centre of the weaving trade since the 14th century, and one mill still makes the West of England cloth that is used for suits.

Trowbridge is a good base from which to tour the Wiltshire Downs and the Cotswolds. There are fine 18th-century stone houses, built by prosperous merchants, in Fore and Roundstone streets.

The interior of the Church of St James was restored in the 19th century, but follows the style of the lavishly decorated church endowed by a wealthy cloth-maker in 1483. The spire dates from an earlier church built in the 14th century. A former rector, George Crabbe (1754-1832), who wrote the poem on which Benjamin Britten's opera *Peter Grimes* is based, is buried in the chancel.

The Town Hall has on its front wall a plaque commemorating Sir Isaac Pitman (1813-97), inventor of the shorthand system which bears his name. He was born in a house in Nash Yard, now demolished.

Information Tel. 63111.
Location On the A361, 12 m. SE of Bath.
Parking Castle Street; Duke Street; Broad Street; Court Street; Church Street (all car parks).
District council West Wiltshire (Tel. 63111).
Population 23,000.
E-C Wed. **M-D** Tues., Fri. and Sat.
Police Polebarn Road (Tel. 63101).
Casualty hospital Trowbridge and District Hospital, Seymour Road (Tel. 2558).
Post office Roundstone Street.
Cinema Europa Cinema 1 and 2, Castle Place (Tel. 63554).
Public library Hill Street.
Places to see Town Hall; Museum, Civic Hall.
Shopping Castle Place Shopping

Precinct; Silver Street; Fore Street.
AA 24 hour service Tel. Bath 24731.

Truro Cornwall

Cornwall's only city, Truro, is the administrative centre for the county and so claims to be the county town, a claim also made by Bodmin because the assizes are held there.

Truro Cathedral, which was completed in 1910, incorporates part of the 16th-century parish church. It blends well with the surrounding Georgian streets, of which Lemon Street is one of the best preserved. The former Assembly Rooms, built in 1772, are in High Cross.

The County Museum and Art Gallery illustrates Cornish archaeology, geology, wildlife and crafts, and contains drawings and paintings by Rubens, Canaletto and other artists.

Information Tel. 74555.
Location On the A39, 11 m. N of Falmouth.
Parking Moorfield, off Calenick Street; Lemon Quay; St Clement Street (all car parks).
District council Carrick (Tel. 78131).
Population 16,200.
E-C Thur. **M-D** Wed.
Police Tregolls Road (Tel. 76211).
Casualty hospital Royal Cornwall City Hospital, Infirmary Hill (Tel. 74242).
Post office High Cross.
Theatre City Hall, Boscawen Street (Tel. 74555).
Cinema Plaza, Lemon Street (Tel. 2894).
Public library Pydar Street.
Places to see Cathedral; County Museum and Art Gallery, River Street; City Hall; Assembly Rooms.
Shopping Boscawen Street; High Cross; St Clement Street.
AA 24 hour service Tel. 76455.

TORBAY Devon

Holiday playground where tigers once roamed

The 22 miles of coast from St Mary's Bay to Maidencombe are crowded in summer with holidaymakers, for Torbay is Devon's most popular tourist region. Beaches of all shapes and sizes are strung around the bay, and there are others beyond the headlands of Hope's Nose to the north and Berry Head to the south.

The cliffs are mainly of yellow-white limestone, with a few of red sandstone. Some are fashioned into weird shapes by the action of wind and sea. But the coastal scenery is saved from harshness by the lush, sub-tropical vegetation which flourishes in the mild climate.

Three towns make up the Torbay area. Brixham, the most southerly, is a commercial fishing port and a favourite spot for painters, as well as a holiday centre.

Paignton is a family resort, while Torquay is grander, with Victorian terraces, luxury hotels and shops, and a harbour frequented by pleasure boats and ocean-going yachts.

Brixham

In the 18th century, local fishermen developed the trawl – a net dragged on or near the bottom of the sea – and the town's trawling fleet was the world's first.

Trawling is still the main industry, and catches are sold in the fish market beside the stone harbour. Torbay sole – really a variety of flounder – is a fine fish and a feature of local hotel and restaurant menus.

The harbour was enlarged and deepened in 1916, when the 800 yd sea wall was completed, but the inner area is more than 300 years older. William of Orange landed there in 1688 on his way to claim the throne. A plaque marks the spot where he stepped ashore, and his statue gazes landwards by the water's edge.

All Saints Church, near the harbour, has a carillon which plays *Abide with Me* and other hymn tunes written by the Rev. H. F. Lyte, the vicar of Lower Brixham from 1823 to 1847.

The town's history is largely that of its seamen and fishermen, but the area has been inhabited for more than 20,000 years. The **Windmill Hill Cave**, discovered in 1858, has relics of Stone Age man and prehistoric animals. The town museum in the High Street has other local finds.

On **Berry Head**, on the southern fringe of Brixham, there are remains of an Iron Age fort of about 500 BC beneath a rampart built during the Napoleonic Wars.

Paignton

The town has a history which is almost as long as that of its neighbours, but most of it is well buried. Modern Paignton grew up after the opening of the railway from Exeter in 1859.

There are miles of hotels and guest houses along the esplanade, and a well-stocked zoo, an aquarium and a pleasure pier.

The Church of St John was established in Saxon times on the site of a Bronze Age settlement. It has a Norman west door and font, but most of the present building dates from the 15th century. The church's Kirkham Chantry, from this period, has a carved stone screen and vaulted ceiling.

The Kirkham family, who built the chantry, were local landowners. Their 15th-century home in Paignton, **Kirkham House**, is now open to the public.

The Bishops of Exeter had a palace at Paignton until the 16th century. It has now disappeared, apart from one house beside the church, named **Coverdale Tower** after Miles Coverdale (1488-1568), translator of the Bible and Bishop of Exeter from 1551 to 1553.

The 100-room **Oldway Mansion**, in ornate gardens beside the Torquay Road, is a building of pale pink stone modelled partly on Versailles and partly on the Paris Opera House. Oldway was started in 1873 by the American sewing-machine millionaire Isaac Singer and continued by his son, Paris Singer, who set up home there with the dancer Isadora Duncan (1878-1927) shortly before the First World War. The mansion now contains municipal offices, but the hall and ballroom are open to the public.

The rail link which brought Paignton prosperity is partially preserved by the **Torbay Steam Railway**, which operates a line from the town to Kingswear using Great Western Region locomotives. **Torbay Aircraft Museum**, 1½ miles east off the A385, has 20 complete aeroplanes, and many other exhibits.

Torquay

Some 40,000 years ago, Stone Age man sheltered in **Kent's Cavern**, two parallel caves 1 mile north-east of the present harbour. Layers of limestone, deposited by water dripping through the rock, have preserved fragments of bones from the sabre-toothed tigers and the bears they fought, among the red, green and white stalactites and stalagmites.

In the 12th century, monks from Prémontré in northern France founded **Torre Abbey**, and acquired the fishing rights in Torbay. They built the quay which eventually gave the settlement its name. The remains of the abbey stand in a park on the

YACHTSMEN'S HAVEN *Torquay harbour, which bustles with pleasure craft throughout the year, is protected by wooded hills and massive breakwaters.*

seafront, beside an 18th-century house which contains an art gallery and museum. The abbey's tithe barn was, in 1588, the prison of sailors from the Armada, who were captured as the sea-battle raged across the mouth of Torbay. It is still called the "Spanish Barn".

At the opening of the 19th century another European war, with Napoleon, laid the foundation of Torquay's modern development. The navy used the bay as an anchorage and the village as a supply base, and the families of naval officers began to move into the district.

The local landowners, the Palk family, extended the harbour and started to construct a town. It quickly became a fashionable resort for wealthy people who were prevented from going abroad by the war. Architects employed by the Palks laid out streets and terraces of houses on the hillsides, imposing on Torquay the pattern it has today.

Since 1914, Torquay's growth has slowed down, but it is still spreading. Babbacombe, 2 miles north-east, has been swallowed up. It has a rack-and-pinion railway running down the cliffs to the sea, and a model village.

Cockington, 2 miles inland between Torquay and Paignton, is a hamlet of thatched cottages. Its manor house is Elizabethan, and there is a 14th-century forge in the centre of the village.

Compton Castle, 4 miles west of Torquay, is a fortified manor house, built in 1320 and extended during the two following centuries. It once belonged to Sir Humphrey Gilbert (1539-83), step-brother to Sir Walter Raleigh. Sir Humphrey founded the first British colony in North America, on Newfoundland, in 1583. He was lost at sea on the return voyage to England.

Information Tel. Brixham 2861; Paignton 558383; Torquay 27428.
Location On the A379, 8 m. S of Teignmouth.
Parking Brixham: Central Multistorey, Breakwater; Freshwater; Shoalstone; Berry Head. Paignton: Colin Road; Victoria Multi-storey; Clennon Valley; Preston Gardens; Goodrington Park; South Sands; Cliff Park Road; Roundham Road. Torquay: The Terrace; Lower Union Lane; The Beacon; North Quay; Shedden Hill; Anstey's Cove; Brunswick Square; Stentiford Hill; Cockington; Meafoot Road; Hampton Avenue (all car parks).
District council Borough of Torbay (Tel. Torquay 26244).
Population 115,600.
E-C Brixham: Wed. Paignton: Wed. Torquay: Wed.
Police Brixham: Rea Barn Road (Tel. 2231). Paignton: Southfield Road (555201). Torquay **(Ac)**: South Street (22293).
Casualty hospital Torbay Hospital, Lawes Bridge (Tel. 64567).
Post offices Brixham: New Road. Paignton: Torquay Road. Torquay **(Cb)**: Fleet Street.
Theatres Brixham Theatre, New Road, Brixham (Tel. 2829). Festival, Eastern Esplanade, Paignton (558641); Palace Avenue Theatre, Paignton (558367). Babbacombe, Babbacombe Downs Road, Torquay (38385); Princess **(Ba)**, Torbay Road, Torquay (27527).
Cinemas Regent, Paignton (Tel. 559017); Torbay, Torbay Road, Paignton (559544); Colony **(Bc)**, Union Street, Torquay (22146); Odeon **(Bb)**, Abbey Road, Torquay (22324).
Public libraries Brixham: Market Street. Paignton: Courtland Road. Torquay **(Bc)**: Lymington Road.
Places to see Brixham: Aquarium; Museum; Berry Head Country Park; Harbour. Paignton: Oldway Mansion; Torbay Aircraft Museum; Torbay Steam Railway. Torquay: Aquarium **(Ca)**; Babbacombe Model Village; Cockington Village; Kent's Cavern; Natural History Museum; Torre Abbey and Gardens **(Ab)**.
Shopping Brixham: Fore Street; Middle Street. Paignton: Victoria Street; Hyde Road; Torquay Road; Palace Avenue; Winner Street. Torquay: Union Street; Fleet Street; Castle Circus; Strand; Torwood Street; Victoria Parade.
Events Paignton Children's Week (Aug.); Torbay Carnival (July); Babbacombe Regatta (July).
Trade and industry Tourism; fishing (Brixham).
Sport FA League football, Torquay United FC, Plainmoor.
AA 24 hour service Tel. Torquay 25903.

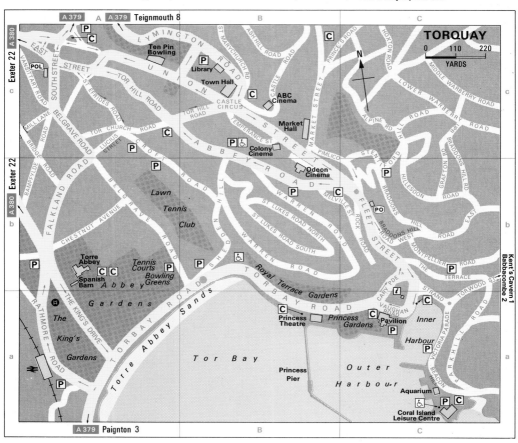

THE PANTILES *The oldest street in Tunbridge Wells is a colonnaded shopping centre that derives its name from the baked tiles with which it was paved in 1700. These were later replaced with Purbeck flagstones.*

Tunbridge Wells Kent

In 1606 Lord North found that water from a spring in Kent contained iron and other minerals. Thus, the spa of Tunbridge Wells was born.

Henrietta Maria, wife of Charles I, recuperated there after the birth of the future Charles II in 1630. She was forced to camp in a field because accommodation was scarce, but soon after this seal of royal approval buildings began to appear.

In 1678 the Church of King Charles the Martyr (Charles I) was begun. This modest brick building with a wooden cupola reveals inside a sumptuous Baroque plaster ceiling.

During the 18th century celebrities flocked to the spa, presided over by the famous dandy Beau Nash (1674-1762), from Bath. It had so many royal visitors then, and later, that in 1909 it was granted the prefix "Royal" to its name.

Waters are still sometimes dispensed in summer from the Bath House portico on the Pantiles.

In London Road is Thackeray's House, where the novelist wrote his essay *Tunbridge Toys* in 1860. The house is not open to the public.

Information Tel. 26121.
Location On the A26, 14 m. E of East Grinstead.
Parking Crescent Road; Goods Station Road; Victoria Road (3); Beech Street; John Street; Varney Street; Mount Pleasant Avenue; Vale Road; Eridge Road; Little Mount Sion; Warwick Road; Monson Road; Major Yorks Road (all car parks).
District council Tunbridge Wells (Tel. 26121).
Population 44,800.
E-C Wed. **M-D** Wed.
Police (Bb) Crescent Road (Tel. 26242).
Casualty hospital Kent and Sussex **(Ab)**, Mount Ephraim (Tel. 26111).
Post office (Ba) Vale Road.
Theatre Assembly Hall **(Bb)**, Crescent Road (Tel. 30613).
Cinema Classic 1, 2 and 3 **(Ba)**, Mount Pleasant Road (Tel. 23135).
Public library (Bb), Mount Pleasant Road.
Places to see Municipal Museum and Art Gallery **(Bb)**.
Shopping Calverley Road; Camden Road; The Pantiles; Mount Pleasant.
AA 24 hour service
Tel. Maidstone 55353.

Turriff Grampian

The first skirmish in the Civil War took place at Turriff when a band of Covenanters, Presbyterian extremists, was routed by a Royalist force in May 1639. The incident became known as "The Trot of Turriff". The old parish church, founded in the 11th century, has a double belfry and a bell bearing the date 1559.

Delgatie Castle, the home of the Clan Hay, lies 2 miles north-east of the town. Its keep is 14th century, but most of the castle is 16th century.

Information Tel. 3417.
Location On the A947, 12 m. S of Banff.
Parking High Street; The Square; Cheyne's Lane; Crown Street (all car parks).
District council Banff and Buchan (Tel. Banff 2521).
Population 3,600.
E-C Wed. **M-D** Tues., Thur.
Police The Square (Tel. 2222).
Casualty hospital Chalmers Hospital, Clunie Street, Banff (Tel. Banff 2567).
Post office High Street.
Public library The Square.
Places to see Delgatie Castle (by appointment only).
Shopping High Street; Main Street.
AA 24 hour service
Tel. Aberdeen 51231.

Tynemouth Tyne & Wear

Sheer cliffs overlook clean golden sands at this resort where the River Tyne meets the sea. On the clifftops stand the ruins of an 11th-century priory and a 14th-century castle.

The Old Watch House, the museum of Tynemouth's Volunteer Life Brigade, contains relics of ships wrecked on the treacherous Black Midden rocks at the river mouth.

Information Tel. Wallsend 627371.
Location On the A193, 9 m. E of

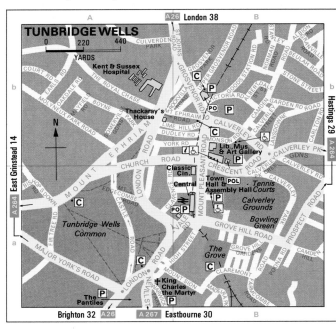

TUNBRIDGE WELLS

Newcastle upon Tyne.
Parking Front Street; Spanish Battery Point; Oxford Street; Pier Road (2); East Street; Sea Banks; Grand Parade (4); Beverley Terrace (all car parks).
District council Borough of North Tyneside
(Tel. North Shields 575544).
Population 60,000.
E-C Wed.
Police Upper Pearson Street, North Shields
(Tel. North Shields 575533).
Casualty hospital Tynemouth Victoria Jubilee Infirmary, Hawkeys Lane, North Shields
(Tel. North Shields 574101).
Post office Saville Street, North Shields.
Theatre Priory Theatre, Percy Street (Tel. North Shields 575186).
Public library Northumberland Square.
Places to see Tynemouth Priory and Castle, Prior's Haven; Old Watch House Museum, Prior's Haven.
Shopping Tynemouth: Front Street. North Shields: Bedford Street; Saville Street; Preston Grange Shopping Centre.
AA 24 hour service
Tel. Newcastle upon Tyne 610111.

Tywyn Gwynedd
The home of the Talyllyn narrow-gauge railway lies on the edge of the Snowdonia National Park, and offers fine walking inland as well as seaside pleasures on its long stretch of sands.

The railway was opened in 1865 to carry locally quarried slate. After the quarries closed in 1951 the railway continued to operate.

The Railway Museum, next to Wharf Station, illustrates the history of Britain's narrow-gauge railways.

St Cadfan's parish church, which was founded in the 6th century, contains the earliest existing example of written Welsh – the 7th-century St Cadfan's Stone, or Tywyn Stone.

Information Tel. 711017.
Location On the A493, 20 m. SW of Dolgellau.
Parking Promenade; Corbett Square; Corbett Avenue; National Street; Neptune Street; Swimming Pool, rear of High Street; Gwalia Road (all car parks).
District council Meirionnydd (Tel. Dolgellau 422341).
Population 4,600.
E-C Wed.
Police High Street (Tel. 710311).
Casualty hospital Aberdovey Road (Tel. 710411).
Post office High Street.
Cinema Tywyn Cinema, Corbett Square (Tel. 710260).
Public library Neptune Road.
Places to see Bryn Castell, 2 m. E; Narrow-gauge Railway Museum, Wharf Station.
Shopping High Street.
AA 24 hour service
Tel. Cardiff 394111.

U

Uttoxeter Staffordshire
In Uttoxeter market a kiosk records the occasion in 1780 when Dr Samuel Johnson, then aged 70, did penance for his boyhood refusal to look after his father's bookstall. Johnson stood bareheaded in the rain for several hours on the site of the stall. A ceremony recalling the incident is held every September.

Uttoxeter's market has been held since the town was granted a charter by Henry III in 1251. Half-timbered buildings surround the market square. The tower and spire of the parish church are medieval.

PENANCE *A plaque in Uttoxeter market shows Dr Johnson's act of penance for boyhood disobedience.*

Information Tel. 2341.
Location On the A518, 12 m. SE of Stoke-on-Trent.
Parking The Maltings Shopping Precinct; Carter Street; Smithfield Road; Fairfield Road; Oldfield Road (all car parks).
District council East Staffordshire (Tel. Burton upon Trent 45369).
Population 10,000.
E-C Thur. **M-D** Wed., Sat.
Police Balance Street (Tel. 2222).
Casualty hospital District Hospital Centre, Belvedere Road, Burton upon Trent
(Tel. Burton upon Trent 66333).
Post office Carter Street.
Public library High Street.
Shopping The Maltings Shopping Precinct.
Events Carnival (July); Samuel Johnson Ceremony (Sept.).
Sport Horse racing, Uttoxeter Racecourse, 2 m. E on B5017.
AA 24 hour service
Tel. Stoke-on-Trent 25881.

V

Ventnor Isle of Wight
A winding road descends sharply into Ventnor in a series of hair-pin bends, amid Victorian villas clinging to the hillside and verandahed hotels perched on shelf-like ledges. Behind the town the green slopes of St Boniface Down rise to 787 ft, the island's highest point, which shelters Ventnor against the cold winds from the north.

The sandy beach is sheltered by jutting cliffs to the east and west. Along the Undercliff, a 6 mile ledge formed by landslides, grow palms, myrtle and cork trees. The effect is continental, and Ventnor likes to call itself the Madeira of England. At the western end of the Undercliff is St Catherine's Point, which has a lighthouse open to the public. At nearby Niton the Buddle Inn dates from the 14th century. Bonchurch, east of Ventnor, is an old village with a Norman church, and Victorian villas where Dickens and Thackeray stayed.

The unmistakable influence of the Victorians is everywhere apparent in Ventnor, from the pier to the parks and ornamental gardens. For today's holidaymakers there are boating and paddling-pools, amusement arcades, discos, summer shows and a night club.

Information Tel. 853625 (summer); Shanklin 2942 (winter).
Location On the A3055, 5 m. SW of Shanklin.
Parking High Street; The Grove; Alpine Road; Dudley Road; Wheelers Bay; Ventnor Botanic Gardens; East Cliff; Shore Road (all car parks).
District council Borough of South Wight
(Tel. Newport I.o.W. 523627).
Population 7,900.
E-C Wed.
Police Church Street (Tel. 852055).
Casualty hospital Royal Isle of Wight County Hospital, Swanmore Road, Ryde (Tel. Ryde 63311).
Post office Church Street.
Public library High Street.
Places to see Appuldurcombe House, Wroxall, 3 m. N; Smuggling Museum; Botanic Gardens.
Shopping High Street; Pier Street.
Events Horticultural Flower Show (Easter, Summer Bank Hol.); Crab Fair (June); Carnival (Aug.).
AA 24 hour service
Tel. Newport I.o.W. 522653.

W

Wakefield W. Yorks.

Weaving and the wool trade were established at Wakefield soon after the Norman Conquest, and the town was the capital of Yorkshire's woollen industry for more than 700 years. But when the factory age arrived, the wool trade moved north to Leeds and Bradford. Cloth manufacture still plays a part in Wakefield's life, but the town has diversified into chemicals and engineering.

CHAPEL ON A BRIDGE *Wakefield's medieval Chantry Chapel stands on a 600-year-old, nine-arched bridge which spans the River Calder.*

The cathedral-church of All Saints stands on a green bank in the city centre where the old streets of Kirkgate, Warrengate, Northgate and Westgate meet. Parts of the nave and chancel date from the 14th century, and its lovely 247 ft spire is the tallest in Yorkshire.

Wakefield is renowned for its mystery plays, performed in the city for more than 600 years. They tell of the people's work and play, and of the comfort religion gave them. It is probable that even-earlier plays gave the city its name – the field of the wake-play or festival.

The city of Wakefield incorporates the old towns of Pontefract and Castleford. Above Pontefract rise the ruins of one of England's most famous castles. Richard II died there in 1400 – possibly murdered – shortly after being deposed. It changed hands three times in the Civil War, and was partly demolished in 1649.

Information Tel. 370211.
Location On the A61, 10 m. S of Leeds.
Parking Upper Warrengate; Garden Street (3); Tavora Street; Borough Road; York Street; Drury Lane; Smyth Street; Denby Dale Road; Marsh Way; Almshouse Lane (all car parks).
District council Metropolitan City of Wakefield (Tel. 370211).
Population 60,500.
E-C Wed. **M-D** Mon., Thur., Fri. and Sat.
Police (Ab) Wood Street (Tel. 375831).
Casualty hospital Pinderfields General Hospital,
Aberford Road (Tel. 375217).
Post office (Bb) Providence Street.
Theatre Pussycat Theatre, Doncaster Road.
Cinema ABC 1, 2 and 3 **(Ba)**, Kirkgate (Tel. 373400).
Public library (Ab) Drury Lane.
Places to see Chantry Chapel; cathedral-church; Art Gallery **(Ab)**, Wentworth Terrace; Museum **(Ab)**, Wood Street; Pontefract Castle.
Town trails Available from Chief Planning Officer, Wakefield Metropolitan District Council.
Shopping Pedestrianised precinct.
Sport Rugby League football, Wakefield Trinity, Belle Vue; Horse racing, Pontefract (June, July, Aug., Sept. and Oct.).
AA 24 hour service
Tel. 377957.

Wallasey Merseyside

The town sits on the north-eastern tip of the Wirral peninsula and offers splendid views across one of Europe's busiest seaways, the Mersey estuary. A seafront promenade links it with the nearby resort of New Brighton. There is a regular ferry service from Seacombe to Liverpool.

Information Tel. Liverpool (051) 625 9441; 051 639 0929 (summer).
Location On the A551, 5 m. W of Liverpool.
Parking Wallasey: Liscard, St Albans Road; Rappart Road. New Brighton: Kings Parade (all car parks).
District council Metropolitan Borough of Wirral (Tel. 051 638 7070).
Population 90,000.
E-C Wed.
Police Manor Road (Tel. 051 709 6010).
Casualty hospital Arrowe Park Hospital, Arrowe Park Road, Upton (Tel. 051 678 7111). Minor injuries: Victoria Central, Mill Lane (051 638 7000).
Post office Liscard Village.
Theatre Floral Pavilion, Victoria Gardens (Tel. 051 639 4360).
Cinemas Unit 4, King Street (Tel. 051 639 2833); Phoenix, Wallasey Village (051 639 9429).
Public library Earlston Road.
AA 24 hour service
Tel. 051 709 7252.

Wallingford Oxfordshire

The ford across the River Thames which gave the town its name was one of the most important in Saxon England. Remains of the earthworks the Saxons built to guard the crossing are in Kine Croft, off the High Street.

Only ruins remain of the Norman castle, demolished by order of Oliver Cromwell in 1652 after his troops had taken 65 days to capture it. Modern Wallingford is a market town, a centre of malt production and a riverside resort. The 17th-century Town Hall, which stands on stone pillars, contains portraits by Gainsborough.

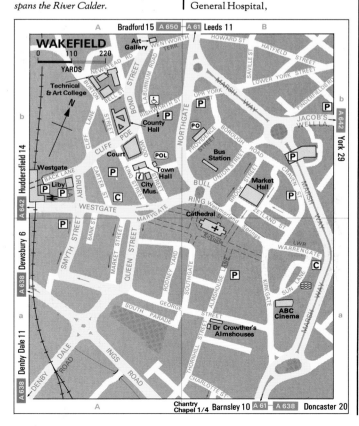

WAKEFIELD

Bradford 15 A 650 A 61 Leeds 11

Huddersfield 14 · A 642 · Dewsbury 6 · A 638 · Denby Dale 11 · A 638

York 29 · A 642

Chantry Chapel 1/4 · Barnsley 10 A 61 A 638 Doncaster 20

The 900 ft long bridge over the river incorporates some of the original 13th-century stonework.

Information Tel. 35351.
Location On the A329, 12 m. SE of Oxford.
Parking Cattle Market, New Road; St Albans, High Street; Goldsmiths Lane; Thames Street (all car parks).
District council South Oxfordshire (Tel. 35351).
Population 6,300.
E-C Wed. **M-D** Fri.
Police Reading Road (Tel. 36242).
Casualty hospital Wallingford Community Hospital, Reading Road (Tel. 35577).
Post office Market Place.
Theatres Corn Exchange, Market Place (Tel. 37106); Kine Croft Theatre Centre, Goldsmiths Lane (35419).
Public library High Street.
Places to see Wallingford Castle; Anglo-Saxon fort, Kine Croft.
Shopping St Mary's Street; St Martin's Street; Market Place.
AA 24 hour service
Tel. Oxford 40286.

Wallsend Tyne & Wear

Towering 200,000 ton oil tankers are built in Wallsend's modernised shipyard. They are launched into the Tyne near the slipway where, in 1907, local ship-builder Sir George Hunter built the liner *Mauretania*.

Stone paving set in some roads traces out the boundaries of the Roman camp of Segedunum, now buried beneath the town. The camp marked the limit of Hadrian's Wall, and this gave the town its name.

Information
Tel. North Shields 627371.
Location On the A193, 4 m. E of Newcastle upon Tyne.

Parking Forum Shopping Centre; High Street East (2) (all car parks).
District council North Tyneside (Tel. North Shields 627371).
Population 44,700.
E-C Wed.
Police Alexandra Street (Tel. 625422).
Casualty hospital Tynemouth Victoria Jubilee Infirmary, Hawkeys Lane, North Shields (Tel. North Shields 574101).
Post office Station Road.
Theatre Wallsend Young People's Theatre (Tel. 629547).
Public library Ferndale Avenue.
Places to see Fragment of Roman wall in Richardson Dees Park; Holy Cross Church ruins, Burns Closes.
Shopping High Street; Forum Shopping Precinct.
AA 24 hour service
Tel. Newcastle upon Tyne 610111.

Walsall W. Midlands

The diversity of Walsall's industry has given it the name "The Town of 100 Trades". The magnificent Garman-Ryan Art Collection in the Central Library was donated to the town in 1973 by the widow of the sculptor Sir Jacob Epstein.

Information Tel. 21244.
Location On the A461, 9 m. NW of Birmingham.
Parking Hatherton Street; Lower Hall Lane; High Street (2); George Street; Lower Rushall Street (3); Walhouse Road; Ward Street; Day Street; Green Lane; Freer Street; St Pauls Street (all car parks).
District council Metropolitan Borough of Walsall (Tel. 21244).
Population 178,900.
E-C Thur. **M-D** Tues., Fri., Sat.
Police (Ab) Green Lane (Tel. 38111).
Casualty hospital General,

Wednesbury Road (Tel. 28911).
Post office (Bb) Darwall Street.
Cinema ABC **(Ab)**, Townsend Bank (Tel. 22444).
Public library (Bb) Lichfield Street.
Places to see Garman-Ryan Art Collection, Central Library **(Bb)**; Lock Museum, Walsall Street, Willenhall.
Shopping High Street; Old Square; Digbeth Square; Park Street.
Trade and industry Leather goods; locks; metal casting; printing.
Sport FA League football, Walsall FC, Hillary Street.
AA 24 hour service
Tel. Birmingham (021) 550 4858.

Waltham Forest
see London

Walton and Weybridge
Surrey

In the Domesday Survey, Walton was described as "Waletona" and had a church, two mills and a fishery. Henry VIII married his fifth bride, Catherine Howard, at Oatlands Palace, Weybridge, which was demolished in 1650.

In 1907 Weybridge became the home of the world's first motor-racing track, built on the Brooklands estate. It was also Britain's first aerodrome, and the world's oldest air-travel booking office still survives there.

Information Tel. Walton-upon-Thames 28844.
Location On the A3050, 18 m. SW of London.
Parking Walton: Drewitt's Court, Bridge Street; Ashley Road; Hepworth Way; Hersham Road; New Zealand Avenue. Weybridge: Monument Hill; Churchfield Road; Oatlands Village; York Road (all car parks).
District council Borough of Elmbridge (Tel. Walton-upon-Thames 28844).
Population 49,200.
E-C Wed.
Police New Zealand Avenue (Tel. Walton-upon-Thames 46464).
Casualty hospital St Peter's Hospital, Guildford Road, Chertsey (Tel. Ottershaw 2000).
Post offices Walton: Hersham Road. Weybridge: High Street.
Cinema Odeon, High Street (Tel. Walton-upon-Thames 20870).
Public libraries Walton: Hersham Road. Weybridge: High Street.
Places to see Claremont House, Esher; Weybridge Museum, Church Street; Elm Grove.
Shopping Walton: High Street; The Centre. Weybridge: High Street.
Sport Steeplechasing and Flat Racing, Sandown Park.
AA 24 hour service
Tel. 01 954 7373.

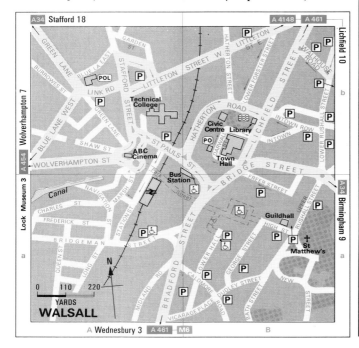

WALSALL

Wandsworth see London

Wantage Oxfordshire

Romans, Saxons and Normans all flourished at Wantage, and it became a prosperous market town. However, little survives from those earliest days; most of the town dates from the 17th and 18th centuries.

The Church of St Peter and St Paul contains the tombs of some members of the Fitzwaryn family, into which Dick Whittington – thrice Lord Mayor of London – married.

ALFRED THE GREAT
A statue of the Saxon king, who was born in Wantage in AD 849, stands in the town square.

Information Tel. 3456.
Location On the A417, 15 m. SW of Oxford.
Parking Limborough Road; Portway/Church Street (car parks).
District council Vale of White Horse (Tel. Abingdon 20202).
Population 8,800.
E-C Thur. **M-D** Wed., Sat.
Police Church Street (Tel. 3254).
Casualty hospital John Radcliffe, Headington, Oxford (Tel. Oxford 64711).
Post office Market Place.
Public library The Cloisters.
Places to see Wantage Museum, Church Street; White Horse, Uffington (6 m. W).
Shopping Market Place.
AA 24 hour service
Tel. Reading 581122.

Ware Hertfordshire

The busy High Street of Ware has gabled and straight-fronted houses dating from the 16th century onwards. Close by, in Bluecoat Yard, is the 15th-century Place House, home of the Bluecoat School between 1674

and 1761. Part of a 14th-century priory is now used as council offices.

Ware has one special association with royalty, for it was here that Lady Jane Grey – England's nine-day Queen – was proclaimed in 1553. The town was also immortalised in verse by William Cowper when he wrote of John Gilpin's ride to Ware in his ballad *The diverting history of John Gilpin.*

Information Tel. 61261.
Location On the A1170, 3 m. NE of Hertford.
Parking Amwell End; Kibes Lane; High Street; Church Street; Coronation Road (all car parks).
District council East Hertfordshire (Tel. Bishops Stortford 55261).
Population 14,200.
E-C Thur. **M-D** Tues.
Police Ware Road, Hertford (Tel. Hertford 57711).
Casualty hospital County Hospital, Hertford (Tel. Hertford 52275).
Post office High Street.
Public library High Street.
Places to see Scott's Grotto, Scotts Road.
Shopping High Street.
AA 24 hour service
Tel. Hatfield 62852.

Wareham Dorset

The early Britons settled on the site where the town now stands, so did the Romans, but it was the Saxons who developed the town and named it Wareham (town by the weir). Wareham was the centre of conflict between the Saxons and the invading Danes, who sailed into Poole Harbour and up the River Frome.

During the Civil War the town changed hands constantly between Roundheads and Royalists, and suffered heavily as a result. Then, in 1762, fire destroyed many buildings. Wareham's architecture, therefore, is mostly Georgian, but some older relics remain. The Town Walls were originally ancient British earthworks, later reinforced by the Romans. The

section known as Bloody Bank was the scene of executions by the order of Judge Jeffreys after the Monmouth Rebellion in 1685.

The 8th-century St Martin's Church contains a fine effigy of Lawrence of Arabia, who lived in Clouds Hill cottage, 7 miles northwest of Wareham. The sculpture is the work of Eric Kennington, and was completed in 1939. St Mary's Church, overlooking the quay, contains the stone coffin of Edward the Martyr (d. 978).

Information Tel. 6561.
Location On the A351, 10 m. W of Poole.
Parking The Quay; Rempstone Centre; Streche Road; St John's Hill; Church Green; Howard's Lane (all car parks).
District council Purbeck (Tel. 6561).
Population 4,600.
E-C Wed. **M-D** Thur.
Police Worgret Road (Tel. 2222).
Casualty hospital Poole General, Longfleet Road, Poole (Tel. Poole 5100).
Post office North Street.
Cinema Rex, West Street (Tel. 2778).
Public library South Street.
Places to see Art Gallery, South Street; Museum, St John's Hill; Town Walls.
Shopping North Street; West Street; South Street; Rempstone Centre; East Street.
AA 24 hour service
Tel. Bournemouth 25751.

Warminster Wiltshire

Much of Warminster's past is retained in its wealth of houses, shops and inns built in the 18th and 19th centuries. Many of the houses are of local stone, and three fine old inns are survivors of the days when Warminster was a coaching centre.

The 14th-century Minster Church contains an organ originally built for Salisbury Cathedral. Warminster School, built in 1707, was attended by Dr Thomas Arnold – later headmaster of Rugby School. The doorway on the school house was designed by Wren for Longleat House, but was later removed to its present site.

Longleat House, 4 miles southwest, the seat of the Marquis of Bath, was built in 1567-80. There are fine state rooms and collections of paintings, furniture and books. There is a safari park in the grounds.

In the 16th century, Warminster was a wool town. Today it is a military centre – site of the School of Infantry and the workshops of the Royal Electrical and Mechanical Engineers.

Information Tel. 216611.
Location On the A36, 21 m. NW of Salisbury.
Parking Station Road; Sambourne Road; Weymouth Street; Emwell Street (all car parks).

QUIET WATERS *Barges once thronged the River Lea at Ware, plying between the town's maltings and London. Several 18th-century inns had gardens running down to the river, and summer-houses at the water's edge.*

District council West Wiltshire
(Tel. Trowbridge 63111).
Population 15,000.
E-C Wed. M-D Fri.
Police Station Road (Tel. 213303).
Casualty hospital The Avenue
(Tel. 212076).
Post office Market Place.
Theatre Athenaeum Arts Centre,
High Street (Tel. 213891).
Cinema Regal, Weymouth Street
(Tel. 212112).
Public library Portway.
Places to see Dewey Museum, High
Street.
Shopping Market Place, High Street;
Three Horseshoes Shopping Mall.
AA 24 hour service
Tel. Bath 24731.

Warrington Cheshire

This town was once the "beer capital
of Britain", for more beer was brewed
in and around Warrington than anywhere else in the country. Today
prosperity derives mainly from engineering, metal products, including
wire work, and light industry.

The town's medieval street pattern
survived redevelopment in the 18th
century. A few buildings of this
period survive in the town centre.
One of the finest, Bank Hall, built in
1750, is now the Town Hall. It was
designed by James Gibbs.

The parish church of St Elphin,
mentioned in Domesday Book in
1086, was rebuilt in the 14th century.
Its 281 ft spire was added in 1860.

The Municipal Museum and Art
Gallery is devoted to local history,
and its exhibits trace Warrington's
history from Stone Age times.

THE DORMOUSE *A window in All Saints
Church, Daresbury, near Warrington,
is dedicated to Lewis Carroll.*

Information Tel. 36501.
Location On the A57, 18 m. E of
Liverpool.
Parking Legh Street; Academy Way;
Orford Street; Dial Street; Knutsford
Road (all car parks).
District council Borough of
Warrington (Tel. 35961).
Population 135,600.
E-C Thur. M-D Weekdays, except
Thur.
Police Arpley Street (Tel. 52222).
Casualty hospital Warrington
District General, Lovely Lane
(Tel. 35911).
Post office Springfield Street.
Cinemas ABC, Bridge Foot
(Tel. 35635); Odeon, Buttermarket
Street (32825).

Public library Museum Street.
Places to see Regimental Museum of
South Lancashire and Lancashire
Regiment, O'Leary Street; Municipal
Museum and Art Gallery, Bold
Street; Allied Breweries and Greenall
Whitley accept visitors by
appointment.
Nature trail Available from Head
Ranger, Risley Moss, Ordnance
Avenue, Birchwood, Warrington
(Tel. 824339).
Shopping Bridge Street; Horsemarket
Street; Sankey Street; Buttermarket
Street; Bank Street; Golden Square
Shopping Centre.
Events Festival (May); Walking Day
(July); Rush-bearing Holiday, Lymm
(Aug.).
Trade and industry Engineering;
metal products; chemicals; soap;
brewing; vodka distilling; light
industry.
Sport Rugby League, Warrington
RFC, Wilderspool Stadium.
AA 24 hour service
Tel. Liverpool (051) 709 7252.

Warwick see page 406

Watford Hertfordshire

Most of the surviving buildings of old
Watford are grouped round the flint-
built parish church of St Mary. The
parish registers date from 1539.

Cassiobury Park, on the western
edge of the town centre, belonged to
the Earls of Essex. Their mansion no
longer exists, but the grounds are a
public park through which the tiny
River Gade and the Grand Union
Canal both flow.

Information Tel. 26400.
Location On the A412, 20 m. NW of
London.
Parking Beechen Grove; Derby
Road; Station Road; Wellington
Road; Platts Avenue; Exchange
Road; Roslyn Road; Eastcourt Road;
Gartlet Road; High Street;
Hempstead Road (all car parks).
District council Borough of Watford
(Tel. 26400).
Population 74,300.
E-C Wed. M-D Tues., Fri. and Sat.
Police Shady Lane (Tel. 44444).
Casualty hospital Hempstead Road
(Tel. 25611).
Post office Market Street.
Theatres Palace Theatre, Clarendon
Road (Tel. 25671); Pump House
Theatre, Local Board Road (22792).
Cinemas Empire, Merton Road
(Tel. 24088); Odeon, High Street
(24884).
Public library Hempstead Road.
Shopping High Street; The Parade,
Market Street; Queens Road; Charter
Place.
Event Whitsun Carnival (May).
Trade and industry Printing;
engineering; light industries.
Sport FA League football, Watford
FC, Vicarage Road.
AA 24 hour service
Tel. 01 954 7373.

Wellingborough
Northamptonshire

The River Nene flows through Wellingborough and provides an attractive leisure area for the town.

Cromwell stayed at an inn, now the
Hind Hotel, on his way to the Battle
of Naseby in 1645.

All Hallows, the 14th-century parish church, contains examples of
medieval craftsmanship, and 20th-
century St Mary's, designed by Sir
Ninian Comper, has a fine ceiling.

Information Tel. 229777.
Location On the A45, 10 m. NE of
Northampton.
Parking Oxford Street; High Street;
Commercial Way; Arndale Centre
(all car parks).
District council Borough of
Wellingborough (Tel. 229777).
Population 43,900.
E-C Thur. M-D Wed., Fri., Sat.
Police Midland Road (Tel. 76011).
Casualty hospital Kettering and
District, Rothwell Road, Kettering
(Tel. 81141).
Post office Midland Road.
Cinema Palace 1, 2 and 3, Gloucester
Place (Tel. 222184).
Public library Pebble Lane.
Shopping Arndale Centre; Market
Street; Sheep Street; Midland Road.
Trade and industry Footwear;
engineering; printing.
AA 24 hour service
Tel. Northampton 66241.

Wells Somerset

England's smallest city has one of its
finest cathedrals. The magnificent
building which dominates Wells was
started in the late 12th century after
the Bishop of Bath transferred his
headquarters to Wells.

The 13th-century west front was
erected as a backing for nearly 400
statues of saints, angels and prophets,
many of which were destroyed by
Puritans in the 17th century.

The astronomical clock in the
north transept was made in 1392, and
is one of the oldest working clocks in
the world. It has a dial more than 6 ft
across, and moving models of knights
that joust every quarter-hour.

South of the cathedral lies the fortified, moat-ringed Bishop's Palace,
one of the oldest inhabited houses in

CATHEDRAL GATE *A medieval gateway, called the Bishop's Eye, straddles
the approach to the Bishop's Palace in
Wells from the town's market place.*

CAPITAL OF THE MENDIPS *The city of Wells lies protected by the Mendip Hills, and in the shadow of its glorious cathedral. Since the 12th century it has been the seat of the Bishop of Bath and Wells.*

England. Its outer walls date back to 1206. Sometimes the swans on the moat ring the bell by the bridge for food, as their ancestors were taught to do by a Victorian bishop's daughter.

In a yard behind the 16th-century Crown Hotel it is said that the persecuted Quaker William Penn (1644–1718), who founded Pennsylvania in the USA, preached to a vast crowd before being arrested.

Information Tel. 72552 or 73026.
Location On the A39, 21 m. SW of Bath.
Parking Market Place (2); Town Hall Buildings; South Street; Chamberlain Street (all car parks).
District council Mendip (Tel. 73026).
Population 8,400.
E-C Wed. **M-D** Wed., Sat.
Police (Aa) Glastonbury Road

CHORISTER'S SEAT *A carved misericord in Wells Cathedral.*

(Tel. 73481).
Casualty hospital Bath Road (Tel. 73154).
Post office (Bb) Market Place.
Theatre Little Theatre **(Ab)**, Chamberlain Street (Tel. 72933).
Cinema Regal **(Aa)**, Priory Road (Tel. 73195).
Public library (Bb) Union Street.
Places to see Cathedral Library and Green **(Bb)**; Wells Museum **(Bb)**; Wookey Hole Caves, 2 m. NW.
Shopping High Street; Market Place; Broad Street; Sadler Street.
AA 24 hour service
Tel. Bristol 298531.

Welshpool Powys

The wide streets of Welshpool are lined with handsome Georgian houses, interspersed here and there with earlier, timbered buildings.

Overlooking the town is Powis Castle, a Welsh border fortress that has been continuously inhabited by the Powis family for the past 500 years, except the years of Cromwell's Commonwealth. It is now owned by the National Trust.

The castle gardens, constructed in 1722, are superb – four terraces of ornamental trees, hedges and statues falling dramatically to a lawn 100 ft below the castle. A Douglas fir in the gardens, almost 200 ft high, is one of the tallest trees in Britain.

A narrow-gauge steam and diesel railway – opened in 1903 and run since 1963 by a preservation society – runs between Sylfaen, 3 miles west, and Welshpool.

The town's market dates back to 1263 and holds the largest livestock sales in Wales. The Powysland Museum, founded in 1874, illustrates local archaeology and history.

Information Tel. 2043.
Location On the A483, 19 m. W of Shrewsbury.
Parking Berriew Street; Church Street (both car parks).
District council Montgomery (Tel. 2828).
Population 7,300.
E-C Thur. **M-D** Mon.
Police Severn Street (Tel. 2345).
Casualty hospital Victoria Memorial Hospital, Salop Road (Tel. 3133).
Post office Severn Street.
Cinema Pola Cinema, Berriew Street (Tel. 2145).
Public library Church Bank.
Places to see Powis Castle; Powysland Museum; Welshpool and Llanfair Light Railway.
Shopping Broad Street; High Street.
Event Montgomery County Agricultural Show (end of May).
AA 24 hour service
Tel. Llandudno 79066.

Welwyn Garden City
Hertfordshire

Sir Ebenezer Howard (1850-1928) founded Welwyn Garden City in 1920, 17 years after his first "garden city" was established at Letchworth.

The playwright George Bernard Shaw (1856-1950) lived at Shaw's Corner in the village of Ayot St Lawrence, 2 miles west. His house, left to the National Trust, is preserved as a museum.

Information Tel. 31212.
Location On the A1000, 6 m. W of Hertford.
Parking Church Road; Shoplands; The Campus; College Way; Stonebank; Broadwater Road; Peartree Lane; Cole Green Lane; Hollybush Lane; Bridge Road (all car parks).
District council Welwyn Hatfield (Tel. 31212).
Population 40,500.
E-C Wed.
Police The Campus (Tel. 24472).
Casualty hospital Queen Elizabeth II Hospital, Howlands (Tel. 28111).
Post office Howardsgate.
Theatres Campus West, The Campus (Tel. 21106); Barn Theatre, Handside Lane (24300).
Cinema Embassy, Parkway (Tel. 22456).
Public library The Campus.
Places to see Roman bathhouse,

WELLS map labels: Wooky Hole Caves 2 · Bath 21 A39 · Bristol 21 · Radstock 12 B 3139 · A 371 · Shepton Mallet 5 · Cheddar 8 A 371 · Glastonbury 6

GARDEN CITY *Wide streets, large gardens and generous open spaces were the basis of Sir Ebenezer Howard's plan for Welwyn Garden City. The town stands on a site that was farmland in 1920.*

Welwyn, 2 m. NW; Shaw's Corner, Ayot St Lawrence, 2 m. W.
Shopping Howardsgate; Parkway.
AA 24 hour service
Tel. Hatfield 62852.

West Bromwich
W. Midlands
The name Bromwich means "broom village", and where the town now stands was once broom-covered heathland. Coal-mining began in the late 18th century and led to industrialisation, and today West Bromwich pulsates with heavy engineering.

The Oak House is a Tudor building of about 1500, with a Jacobean wing added in 1635. The restored Manor House, which has a great hall dating from 1290–1310, is now an inn.

Information
Tel. Birmingham (021) 569 2463.
Location On the A41, 5 m. NW of Birmingham.
Parking John Street; Temple Street; Walsall Street (2); New Paradise Street (2); West Bromwich Ringway (all car parks).
District council Borough of Sandwell (Tel. 021 569 2200).
Population 154,900.
E-C Wed. **M-D** Mon., Thur., Fri. and Sat.
Police New Street (Tel. 021 553 2971).
Casualty hospital Sandwell General, Lyndon (Tel. 021 553 1831).
Post office High Street.
Cinema Kings, Sandwell Centre (Tel. 021 553 0192).
Public library High Street.
Places to see Oak House, Oak Road; Manor House, off Hall Green Road; Art Gallery and Museum, Holyhead Road, Wednesbury.
Shopping Sandwell Centre; Kings Square; High Street.
Sport FA League football, West Bromwich Albion FC, The Hawthorns, Birmingham Road.
AA 24 hour service
Tel. 021 550 4858.

Westbury Wiltshire
Georgian houses surround the market place at Westbury – a testimony to the town's prosperity after centuries as a weaving and cloth-making

centre. It was also renowned for the quality of its gloves.

Overlooking the town from Bratton Down, 1½ miles to the north-east, is Wiltshire's best-known white horse. The figure was cut into the chalk in 1778 over an earlier, smaller horse, which legend says commemorated King Alfred's victory over the Danes at the Battle of Ethandun, 3 miles away, in 878.

Information Tel. Trowbridge 63111.
Location On the A350, 5 m. S of Trowbridge.
Parking Bratton Road; High Street; Warminster Road (all car parks).
District council West Wiltshire (Tel. Trowbridge 63111).
Population 7,330.
E-C Wed.
Police Station Road (Tel. 822171).
Casualty hospital Westbury and District Hospital, The Butts (Tel. 823616).
Post office Edward Street.
Public library Edward Street.
Places to see White Horse and Bratton Castle hill-fort, 1½ m. NE; Phillips Countryside Museum, Brokerswood, 2 m. W.
Shopping High Street; Market Place.
Trade and industry Cement production; engineering.
AA 24 hour service
Tel. Bath 24731.

Weston-super-Mare Avon
The Victorians began building this seaside town on the Bristol Channel around an old fishing village. Today it is one of the biggest and busiest resorts on the west coast.

Steep Holm, an island 5 miles offshore, is a nature reserve that is now a memorial to Kenneth Allsop, the writer, television personality and naturalist. It is the only place in Britain where the wild paeony grows. To visit it, write to Kenneth Allsop Memorial Island, Milborne Port, Sherborne, Dorset.

Information Tel. 26838.
Location On the A370, 21 m. SW of Bristol.
Parking Grove Park Road; Knightstone Road; South Road; Upper Church Road; Marine Parade (7); Locking Road; Carlton Street; High Street (all car parks).
District council Woodspring (Tel. 31701).
Population 58,000.
E-C Thur.
Police (Ba) Walliscote Road (Tel. 25411).
Casualty hospital (Bb) General Hospital, The Boulevard (Tel. 25211).
Post office (Ab) Post Office Road.
Theatres Knightstone, Knightstone Causeway (Tel. 29075); Playhouse, High Street (23521).
Cinema Odeon Film Centre **(Bb)**, The Centre (Tel. 21784).
Public library The Boulevard.
Places to see Woodspring Museum **(Bb)**, Burlington Street; Railway Museum, Bridgwater Road; Model Village, Marine Parade; Worlebury Hill Iron Age camp, Weston Woods, 1 m. N.
Shopping High Street; Dolphin Square; Meadow Street.
Events International Hockey Festival (Apr.); Carnival (July); County Cricket Festival (Aug.).
AA 24 hour service
Tel. Bristol 298531.

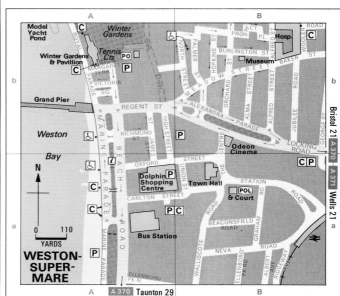

WARWICK Warwickshire

A county town in the heart of England

Above the tree-fringed River Avon rise the majestic walls and turrets of Warwick Castle. Seen from across the river the castle forms a bluff sentinel guarding the town beyond, where narrow streets cluster together behind a wooded ridge. It is a view thought by the novelist Sir Walter Scott to be unsurpassed in England. Warwick is a medieval walled town which barely survived a disastrous fire in 1694. But out of the ashes arose fine Queen Anne houses and a church tower, to blend with the gabled and timber-framed buildings that escaped the flames. Outside the walls, modern Warwick has spread with dignity, combining town and country in the heart of England's shires.

HIDDEN SALLY-PORT *To the right of the large opening of 1800, lies a gate, out of sight, used by defenders in the Civil War to counter-attack the enemy.*

Warwick Castle was built in the 14th century on the site of a Norman castle which William the Conqueror gave to Henry de Newburgh, and with it the title of Earl of Warwick. For nearly 1,000 years the castle remained the seat of the Earls of Warwick.

The castle's history, and its fortunes, fluctuated with the rise and fall of its owners over the centuries. The Beauchamp family were responsible for most of the fortifications visible today. **Caesar's Tower** was completed in 1356, and was almost immediately used to house French prisoners taken in the Battle of Poitiers. It is built on solid rock and towers 147 ft above the ground. At the top of the tower is a parapet from which stones, boiling pitch and quicklime could be dropped on attackers.

Bear Tower and **Clarence Tower** are the remains of an unfinished tower built for artillery by Richard III.

During the 16th century the castle fell into poor condition, while the title of Earl of Warwick changed hands several times. It was granted to John Dudley in 1547, who lost it, and his head, when he tried to put Lady Jane Grey on the throne in place of Mary Tudor.

Early in the 17th century the castle passed to Sir Fulke Greville, and his successors were granted the earldom in 1759. The title has remained with the Greville family ever since.

Baronial splendour

Warwick Castle has two faces – the grim, forbidding walls and towers with their dungeons and trappings of war, and the grandeur of its state apartments. The dungeon below Caesar's Tower has a grisly display of torture instruments, and inscriptions carved on the wall show that Royalist soldiers were held there during the Civil War. A collection of arms and armour in the **Armoury** includes a helmet said to have belonged to Oliver Cromwell, and the sword of Guy of Warwick. Sir Guy was a Saxon knight who, according to legend, vanquished attacking Danes by slaying their giant, Colbrand.

The state apartments, all overlooking the river, are dominated by the Great Hall – a room of baronial splendour. It is 62 ft long, 45 ft wide and 40 ft high. The floor, of red-and-white Venetian marble, was laid in 1830. The room is notable for its furnishings, paintings and suits of armour. The armour includes a tiny suit said to have been made for the Earl of Leicester's son, who died at a young age in 1584. A chilling relic in the Great Hall is the death mask of Oliver Cromwell.

Panelled rooms

The focal point of the state dining room is Van Dyck's portrait of Charles I, clad in armour and mounted on a white horse. Above a white-marble fireplace is a Rubens picture of two lions, which are said to have killed their keeper while the artist was at work.

A series of drawing rooms are named after their styling: the Red Drawing Room is panelled in red and gold; the Cedar Drawing Room has Lebanese cedarwood panelling; and the Green Drawing Room is painted in green picked out with gold. Beyond the drawing rooms is the Queen Anne Bedroom, which contains the bed used by the queen at Windsor. It was presented to the Earl of Warwick by George III.

The smallest room is the Blue Boudoir, with wall coverings of blue damask. A silver-and-enamel clock opposite the fireplace belonged to France's Queen Marie Antoinette, who was guillotined in 1793 during the French Revolution.

Medieval streets

The most interesting building to survive the fire of 1694 is the **Lord Leycester Hospital.** The group of buildings date from the 12th to 16th centuries and have been used as a guildhall, council chamber and grammar school. In 1571 Robert Dudley, Earl of Leicester, founded the hospital, or almshouses, for those wounded in the service of the queen and her successors. The accommodation was for a Master and 12 Brethren, and some ex-servicemen occupy it today.

The tiny courtyard is surrounded by Elizabethan gables and a half-timbered building with an overhanging gallery. Next to the hospital is the **West Gate**, part of the original medieval wall; and above it is the hospital's chapel, founded in 1123, rebuilt in 1383 and again in 1863.

At the other end of the High Street is the **East Gate**, dating from the 15th century. On top of the gate is **St Peter's Chapel**, also 15th century but greatly rebuilt and restored.

Other Tudor buildings in Warwick can be found in Mill Street, Bridge End and Castle Street. There, in the middle of the street, is the black-and-

CASTLE-TOP VIEW *Warwick below the ramparts of its castle is a panorama of medieval and Georgian buildings, pierced by the pinnacle tower of St Mary's Church. The old town lies inside 12th-century walls, parts of which remain.*

white fronted **Oken's House**. It was the home of Thomas Oken, Warwick's 16th-century bailiff and a public benefactor. The house now contains a doll museum with a collection of a few hundred antique dolls.

Collegiate church

St Mary's Church is believed to date back to pre-Norman times. It was made a collegiate church by Roger, Earl of Warwick, in 1123, which gave it similar status to a cathedral. The fire of 1694 destroyed the nave and tower, but much of the medieval building survived, including Earl Roger's crypt.

The **Beauchamp Chapel** was built to house the tomb of Richard Beauchamp, who died in 1439.

The tomb is one of the finest of the medieval period in Britain. Purbeck marble was used for the base, and Beauchamp's effigy lies with hands raised towards the figure of Our Lady in the vaulted roof. A cage of hoops and bars around the effigy was designed to support a velvet pall. Close by is the tomb of Ambrose Dudley, who was made Earl of Warwick by Elizabeth I when the Beauchamp line died out. Ambrose's brother Robert, Earl of Leicester, is also buried in the Beauchamp Chapel, next to his third wife Lettice Knollys. She was the mother of the Noble Impe, the child who died in infancy, whose tomb is in the chapel.

The nave and tower of St Mary's were built by Sir William Wilson, a local architect, between 1698 and 1704. The 174 ft high tower stands on arches straddling the road and is in Gothic style. It has a peal of ten bells which play a tune every three hours.

Stocks and a dungeon

Warwickshire's County Museum is housed in the **Market Hall**, built in 1670. It was built in arches to provide under-cover space for stalls, but in the 19th century the archways were railed off and the area was used for the stocks. These were on wheels, and the culprit was made to pull them into the railed space before being locked in them. The stocks were used as a punishment for drunkenness as late as 1872. The railings were removed in 1879 and the archways filled by windows and doors.

A branch of the County Museum, displaying folk life and costume, is in the 17th-century **St John's House**. On the first floor is the museum of the Royal Warwickshire Regiment. The gardens are laid out in Jacobean style and are entered by a pair of wrought-iron gates dating from about 1700.

Some of the best examples of Warwick's rebirth in the 18th century can be seen in Northgate Street. Buildings in the Classical style line one side, including the **Shire Hall**.

The hall contains two octagonal courtrooms, a shape continued in the grim building next door – the County Gaol. The dungeon, dating from 1680, is 21 ft in diameter with a

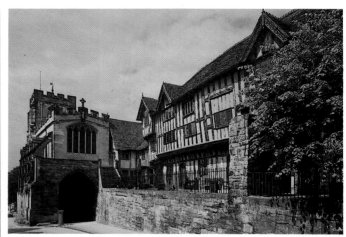
SOLDIERS' HOME *Lord Leycester's Hospital has served as almshouses for disabled or aged soldiers for more than 400 years. From the terrace a stone staircase leads to the hospital chapel, St James's, built on the West Gate which was part of the town wall.*

stone-vaulted roof through which a single grating allowed light and air to enter. The prisoners, as many as 50 or more, were shackled to a single chain connected to posts and running up the entrance steps to be secured at a point outside the door. The groove worn by the chain can still be seen in the top step leading to the dungeon.

As the entrance to the dungeon is through the dock in the courtroom, it is rarely open to the public.

Information Tel. 492212.
Location On the A41, 20 m. NW of Banbury.
Parking The Butts; Theatre Street; New Street; Castle Lane; Castle Hill; Puckerings Lane; Linen Street; West Rock; Priory Road (all car parks).
District council Warwick (Tel. Leamington Spa 27072).
Population 21,900.
E-C Thur. **M-D** Sat.
Police (Ab) Priory Road

(Tel. 492121).
Casualty hospital Lakin Road (Tel. 495321).
Post office (Ab) Old Square.
Public library (Ab) Church Street.
Places to see Warwick Castle **(Aa/Ba)**, Castle Lane; West Gate and Lord Leycester Hospital **(Aa)**, High Street; Doll Museum **(Aa)**, Oken's House, Castle Street; County Museum **(Ab)**, Market Place; St John's House Museum **(Bb)**, St John's; Warwickshire Yeomanry Museum **(Bb)**; East Gate, Smith Street.
Town trails Available from Tourist Information Centre, Jury Street.
Shopping High Street; Jury Street.
Events Mayor Making (May); Carnival (June); Arts Week (July); Mop Fair (Oct.).
Sport Horse racing, Warwick Racecourse, Hampton Road.
AA 24 hour service
Tel. Birmingham (021) 550 4858.

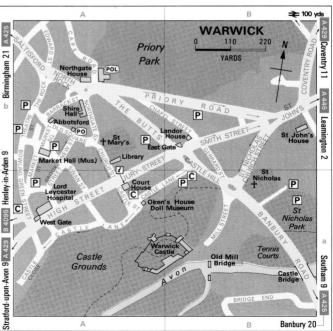

Weymouth Dorset

When George III dipped a royal toe into the waters of Weymouth Bay in 1789 he became the first reigning monarch to take up sea-bathing, and ensured the future prosperity of this ancient town. A statue of the king on the Esplanade was erected in 1810 to celebrate the 50th year of his reign.

Wealthy Georgians followed George III's example, and descended upon the town in droves. The results of their patronage can be seen along the Esplanade and in the streets behind: terraces of porticoed houses, bow-fronted shops and inns and the elegant St Mary's Church with its Classical-style clock-tower. The Gloucester Hotel was formerly Gloucester Lodge, George III's summer home between 1789 and 1805.

The broad promenade curves gently around a sandy beach to the harbour, which took on a new role with the coming of the railway in 1857. The line was extended along the harbour quay, and Weymouth became a major port for services to Cherbourg and the Channel Islands.

In the centre of the Esplanade stands the brightly painted Queen Victoria Jubilee Clock-Tower, looking like a miniature version of London's Big Ben tower.

The Town Bridge crosses the River Wey, linking the two old settlements of Melcombe Regis and Weymouth which now form the modern town. On the south side of the harbour, in Trinity Street, are two early-17th-century cottages which have been made into a museum, and an inn of the same period. The rooms are furnished in Elizabethan style. Further south are the remains of Sandsfoot Castle, a blockhouse built to the command of Henry VIII in 1541.

The Isle of Portland, which shelters Weymouth harbour, is a plateau of rock joined to the mainland by a narrow causeway of shingle which is part of the 18 mile stretch of Chesil Beach. Portland stone, which has been quarried for centuries, is a superb limestone that has been used for major buildings the world over. They include St Paul's Cathedral, London, and the United Nations headquarters in New York.

Portland harbour has been a naval base since 1872. Beyond the harbour the limestone rock rises to a height of 496 ft above Portland Bill.

At the tip of Portland Bill is the lighthouse, which can be visited at certain times, and an older lighthouse of 1869 which is now a bird observatory. Portland's museum of local history is in the 17th-century Avice's Cottage, which Thomas Hardy described in his novel *The Well-Beloved*.

Information Tel. 72444.
Location On the A354, 8 m. S of Dorchester.
Parking Weymouth: Preston Road; Radipole Park Drive; Abbotsbury Road; Pavilion; Governors Lane; Nicholas Street. Portland: Portland Bill; Weymouth Road; Fortuneswell. Melcombe Regis: Commercial Road (all car parks).
District council Borough of Weymouth and Portland (Tel. 785101).
Population 46,300.
E-C Wed. **M-D** Thur. (Weymouth).
Police Dorchester Road, Weymouth (Tel. 963011).
Casualty hospital Weymouth and District, Melcombe Avenue (Tel. 72211).
Post office (Aa) St Thomas Street, Weymouth.

SEA-BATHING MONARCH *A seafront statue commemorates George III, who popularised Weymouth as a resort.*

Theatre Pavilion **(Ba)**, Esplanade (Tel. 783225).
Cinema Classic **(Ab)**, Gloucester Street (Tel. 785847).
Public library (Ab) Westwey Road.
Places to see Portland Castle; Sandsfoot Castle; Bow and Arrow Castle; Portland Museum; Weymouth Local History Museum **(Ab)**, Westham Road.
Shopping St Mary Street; St Alban Street; St Thomas Street.
Events Navy Days (July); Carnival (Aug.).
Car ferry To Guernsey, Jersey and Cherbourg (Tel. 73344).
AA 24 hour service
Tel. Bournemouth 25751.

Whickham Tyne & Wear

The hilltop town, a suburb of Gateshead overlooking the Tyne, has grown from a village since the Second World War. Its Church of St Mary has a Norman chancel arch and a 13th-century tower. The former Rectory, now a hospital, dates from 1713.

South-west of Whickham, beside the River Derwent, is the Gibside Chapel and the ruins of Gibside Hall – all that remains of the 18th-century estate of the Bowes family.

Information Tel. Gateshead 884112.
Location On the B6316, 4 m. SW of Gateshead.
Parking St Mary's Green (3); Broom Lane (all car parks).
District council Metropolitan Borough of Gateshead (Tel. Gateshead 771011).
Population 31,600.
E-C Wed.
Police Whickham Highway (Tel. 882921).
Casualty hospital Queen Elizabeth Hospital, Sheriff Hall, Gateshead (Tel. Low Fell 878989).
Post office Front Street.
Public library St Mary's Green.
Places to see Hollinside Manor; Chase Park windmill.
Shopping Front Street; St Mary's Green Shopping Centre; Fellside Road.
AA 24 hour service
Tel. Newcastle upon Tyne 610111.

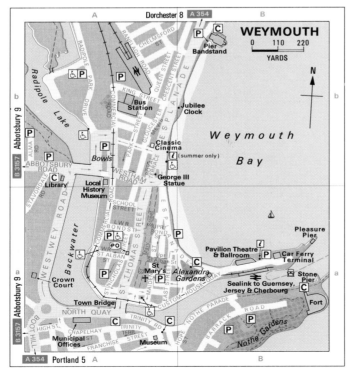

WHITBY *Fishermen's houses descend in tiers to the harbour's edge. In the last century the port was a prosperous whaling base.*

Whitby N. Yorks.

The gaunt sandstone ruins of a 13th-century abbey stand on the East Cliff, overlooking the mouth of the River Esk and the fishing harbour.

In the narrow streets and steep alleys of the old town beside the river, fishermen mend the nets outside their cottages, and craft shops sell jewellery made from jet, a form of fossilised wood found on Whitby beach.

Whitby reached its hey-day as a port in the 18th century, when the town had a whaling fleet and was a base for coal-ships plying the North Sea. On these colliers, the navigator and map-maker James Cook (1728-79) first learned the art of seamanship. For nine years he lived in Whitby, at a house in Grape Lane now marked with a plaque. The ships he commanded on his epic voyages to the South Seas, the *Endeavour* and the *Resolution*, were built locally.

Whitby still has a fishing fleet, but the port has declined and the town has become a holiday resort and tourist centre for the North York Moors and Cleveland Hills.

Whitby Abbey was founded in AD 657 by St Hilda or Hild (614-80), and in AD 664 it was the meeting place of the Synod of Whitby, at which the churches in England decided to follow Roman, rather than Celtic, usages. At this time the abbey was the home of Caedmon, the first English Christian poet, who is commemorated by a cross of 1898 in the yard of St Mary's Church. The present abbey ruins date from the 13th century, and their eerie atmosphere provided part of the setting for Bram Stoker's novel *Dracula*, published in 1897.

St Mary's Church, reached by 199 steps, has a Norman tower. The 18th-century carved interior is like the 'tween-decks area of a wooden ship, reflecting the main occupation of the local craftsmen whose work it is.

The western area of Whitby has grown up since the Victorian era. There is a clifftop walk and, at Pannett Park, a museum with a large collection of fossils and a display devoted to Captain Cook.

Mulgrave Castle, 4 miles northwest, was built in the 18th century and is the home of the Marquis of Normanby.

Information Tel. 602674.
Location On the A174, 20 m. N of Scarborough.
Parking Church Street (2); New Quay Road; Abbey Lane; Cliff Street; Royal Crescent/Crescent Avenue; North Terrace; St Hilda's Terrace Back (all car parks).
District council Borough of Scarborough
(Tel. Scarborough 72351).
Population 13,800.
E-C Wed. **M-D** Sat.
Police (Aa) Spring Hill
(Tel. 603443).
Casualty hospital Whitby Hospital **(Aa)**, Spring Hill (Tel. 604851).
Post office (Aa) Baxtergate.
Theatre Spa **(Ab)**, off North Terrace (Tel. 602124).
Cinema Empire **(Aa)**, Station Square (Tel. 603194).
Public library (Aa) Windsor Terrace.
Places to see Whitby Abbey **(Bb)**; Captain Cook's House **(Ba)**; Museum, Pannett Park **(Aa)**.
Shopping Baxtergate; Flowergate; Skinner Street; Church Street.
AA 24 hour service
Tel. Middlesbrough 246832.

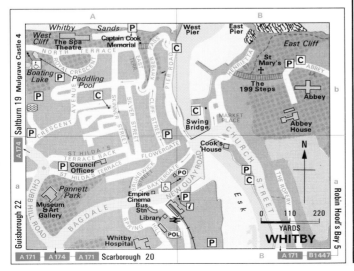

Whitehaven Cumbria

Less than 200 years ago Whitehaven was the port second to London. Coal from local mines, some of them extending 4 miles under the sea, was exported to Ireland and Europe, and tobacco was shipped in from Virginia. The port declined when the railway age opened up Liverpool and the Mersey in the early 1800s.

The town was developed in the 17th and 18th centuries by the Lowther family, along lines inspired by Sir Christopher Wren's plans for rebuilding London after the Great Fire of 1666. Many of the elegant buildings of that period have been preserved – particularly in Lowther Street, near the Civic Hall. The Church of St James, in Queen Street, was built in 1752-3 by Carlisle Spedding, a mining engineer. It has the finest Georgian interior in the country.

Whitehaven witnessed a bizarre episode in 1778, during the American War of Independence. The Scottish-born adventurer John Paul Jones, who had been apprenticed as a seaman at Whitehaven, sailed into the harbour in a ship of the American Navy and destroyed three boats.

In the harbour, built in the 17th century, the last coal-fired dredger working in Britain can be seen.

Information Tel. 3111.
Location On the B5345, 7 m. S of Workington.
Parking Swingpump Lane; Queen Street; Hicks Lane; Church Street; West Strand (all car parks). Disc parking: Duke Street; George Street; Lowther Street; Church Street.
District council Borough of Copeland
(Tel. Cleator Moor 810391).
Population 26,700.
E-C Wed. **M-D** Thur., Sat.
Police Scotch Street (Tel. 2616).
Casualty hospital West Cumberland Hospital, Hensingham (Tel. 3181).
Post office Lowther Street.
Theatre Civic Hall, Lowther Street (Tel. 2778).
Cinema Gaiety, Tangier Street (Tel. 3012).
Public library Lowther Street.
Places to see Museum and Art Gallery, Market Place; Whitehaven Castle; Egremont Castle, 3 m. SE.
Town trails Available from Tourist Information Centre, Market Place, Whitehaven, Cumbria LA28 7JG.
Shopping Lowther Street; King Street; Market Place; Duke Street; Church Street.
Sport Rugby League, Whitehaven RLFC, Recreation Ground.
AA 24 hour service
Tel. Carlisle 24274.

Whitley Bay Tyne & Wear

Fresh, clean breezes off the North Sea make Whitley Bay a bright, invigorating town, popular as a holiday resort for the workers of industrial Tyneside. An electric railway runs in a circular route from the town through the Newcastle suburbs and back along the Tyne. It is packed in the morning and evening with workers from the shipyards and the city offices travelling to and from Whitley Bay's residential area.

Holidaymakers flock each summer to Whitley Bay's mile-long beach of clean, flat sands. There are golf courses, parks, rugged coast to the north and a variety of seaside entertainments. At the north end of the bay, St Mary's Island can be reached at low tide.

GUIDING LIGHT *A lighthouse stands on St Mary's Island, Whitley Bay.*

Information Tel. 524494.
Location On the A193, 2 m. N of Tynemouth.
Parking The Link; Eastbourne Gardens; Bournemouth Gardens (all car parks).
District council Metropolitan Borough of North Tyneside
(Tel. North Shields 513131).
Population 37,000.
E-C Wed.
Police Laburnum Avenue
(Tel. North Shields 575533).
Casualty hospital Victoria Jubilee Infirmary, Hawkeys Lane, North Shields (Tel. North Shields 574101).
Post office Park Avenue.
Theatre Playhouse, Marine Avenue (Tel. 523505).
Cinemas Classic, Cauldwell Lane (Tel. 525540); Playhouse Theatre.
Public library Park Road.
Shopping Whitley Road.
AA 24 hour service
Tel. Newcastle upon Tyne 610111.

Whitstable Kent

The Romans knew Whitstable for its oysters. Today it is a holiday resort and yachtsman's paradise. Its old harbour, rebuilt in 1832, was the port of departure for the first steamboat to sail from England to Australia, in 1837. It was the world's first harbour to be served by a railway, which in 1830 connected it with Canterbury, 7 miles inland.

West of the town lies Seasalter, once the centre of an ancient salt-making industry, and east is Tankerton. Both offer safe bathing.

The glorious sunsets that blaze above the Isle of Sheppey have long been a source of attraction for artists.

The village of Chestfield, just inland, contains some beautifully preserved oast houses.

Information Tel. 272233.
Location On the A290, 7 m. N of Canterbury.
Parking Tankerton Road; Harbour Street; Victoria Street; Gladstone Road; Marine Crescent; Middle Wall (all car parks).
District council City of Canterbury (Tel. Canterbury 51755).
Population 27,900.
E-C Wed. **M-D** Thur., Sat.
Police Bexley Street (Tel. 262584).
Casualty hospital Kent and Canterbury General, Ethelbert Road, Canterbury
(Tel. Canterbury 66877).
Post office High Street.
Cinema Oxford, Oxford Street (Tel. 272736).
Public library Oxford Street.
Shopping High Street; Oxford Street; Tankerton Road.
AA 24 hour service
Tel. Thanet 81226.

Wick Highland

Visitors will hear no Gaelic spoken in this ancient little fishing port; most of the people are descendants of the Norsemen who landed in their long-ships centuries ago. The name, Wick, is a Norse word meaning "bay".

The town lies on the River Wick, which flows into the North Sea at the centre of a low-lying bay. To north and south are spectacular cliffs.

Wick was an important sea-fishing centre for centuries, but in modern times the industry has declined. In 1960 a glassworks was established in the town. Its hand-blown glass of modern design has achieved an international reputation.

Just over 1 mile south-east lies the Castle of Old Wick, a 12th–14th-century ruined tower known to seafarers as the Auld Man o' Wick.

Information Tel. 2596.
Location On the A9, 17 m. S of John o' Groats.
Parking Louisburgh Street; Riverside Road; Scalesburn Road (all car parks).
District council Caithness (Tel. 3761).
Population 8,000.
E-C Wed.
Police Bridge Street (Tel. 3551).
Casualty hospital Bignold Hospital, George Street (Tel. 2434).
Post office Market Square.
Cinema Pavilion, High Street (Tel. 2035).
Public library Sinclair Terrace.

CLIFFTOP RUINS *Girnigoe Castle, with Sinclair Castle in the foreground, stands on the cliffs near Wick.*

THE SEARCH FOR WIGAN PIER

Wigan's famous pier is a hump on the bank of the Leeds and Liverpool Canal, where coal from local collieries was once loaded into barges. It is likely that no one outside the town would ever have heard of the pier if a music-hall comedian had not been hissed off the stage of the Wigan Hippodrome. The comedian, George Formby senior, a local man, took his revenge by making fun of the pier in his act. This was easy, because the original meaning of the word pier – a solidly built landing place – had been taken over by the Victorian seaside industry and applied to fanciful structures of iron and wood

projecting far out to sea, and carrying places of entertainment such as theatres and dance halls. Beside these glamorous complexes, the humble hump on the canalside at Wigan became an object of ridicule. Outsiders who came to look for the pier not unnaturally failed to find it. One unsuccessful searcher was George Orwell, whose book *The Road to Wigan Pier* brought renewed fame to the town in 1937. By then the railways had taken the coal traffic from the canals and the pier was disused, except as a starting place for occasional pleasure trips; and as Wigan's equivalent to "Lovers' Lane".

The Duke of Gloucester arriving at Wigan Pier after a barge trip in the 1930s.

Deserted and forgotten, the site of Wigan's music-hall joke is now marked only by a grassy hump on the canal side.

Places to see Caithness Glass Factory; Castle of Old Wick, 1 m. SE.
Shopping Bridge Street; High Street.
AA 24 hour service
Tel. Aberdeen 51231.

Widnes Cheshire
For centuries, Widnes was a collection of small villages with a ferry across the Mersey at Runcorn Gap. Sometimes, at low tide, it was possible to ford the river. Then in 1845 the Runcorn Gap and St Helens Railway Company completed the world's first railway, canal and dock complex there. Coal from Lancashire and salt from Cheshire were brought in, and these formed the basis of a thriving alkali industry.

Information
Tel. Liverpool (051) 424 2061.
Location On the A568, 7 m. SW of Warrington.
Parking Lacey Street; Albert Road; Tomas Street; Caldwell Street; Moon Street; Cross Street; Denton Street (all car parks).
District council Halton (Tel. 051 424 2061).
Population 54,400.
E-C Thur. **M-D** Mon., Fri. and Sat.
Police Kingsway (Tel. 051 424 7431).
Casualty hospital Whiston Road Hospital, Warrington Road, Prescot (Tel. 051 426 1600).
Post office Widnes Road.
Cinema Empire, Widnes Road (Tel. 051 424 2100).
Public library Victoria Square.
Shopping Albert Road; Widnes Road; Hypermarket.
Sport Widnes RLFC, Naughton Park.
AA 24 hour service
Tel. 051 709 7252.

Wigan Greater Manchester
Contrary to a widespread belief, this great industrial town is not a product of the 19th century, but an ancient settlement which received a royal charter in 1246. Many centuries earlier, the Romans had built a fort there.

Coal was mined in the area, and Wigan itself was a thriving weaving and market town by 1400. Four-hundred years later, it was also a pewter-manufacturing and clock-making centre.

The construction of the Leeds and Liverpool Canal, linking Wigan to Liverpool in 1779, brought the Industrial Revolution to the town. The famous Wigan Pier is a loading point on this canal.

The coal-mining that, with ironworking, engineering and textiles, was long one of Wigan's main industries, ceased with the closing of the last big colliery in 1967. The town museum contains displays illustrating this and other industries of the past.

In 1974 Wigan merged with the neighbouring borough of Leigh and several urban and rural districts to become part of the new county of Greater Manchester.

The medieval parish church of All Saints was rebuilt in the 19th century, and has fine stained glass by William Morris and some interesting 14th-century monuments. In the Civic Centre is a display of town regalia, including some items of locally made pewter.

A monument in Wigan Lane marks the site of a battle in 1651 when Royalist supporters of Charles I were defeated by a Parliamentarian army.

Mesnes Park forms an oasis of greenery in the centre of the town, and Haigh Hall, a 19th-century mansion that was once the home of the

Earls of Crawford and Balcarres, has extensive grounds containing much woodland and a small zoo.

The town is a thriving centre for sport. Its Rugby League teams are famous, and each April the annual Six-mile Road Race attracts competitors from all parts of Britain.

Information Tel. 44991.
Location On the A49, 11 m. SW of Bolton.
Parking Station Road (4); Harrogate Street; Crompton Street; Wallgate; Brick Kiln Lane; Mesnes Terrace (2); Hope Street; Hallgate; Dorning Street (all car parks).
District council Metropolitan Borough of Wigan (Tel. 44991).
Population 79,500.
E-C Wed. **M-D** Fri., Sat.
Police Harrogate Street (Tel. 449181).
Casualty hospital Royal Infirmary, Wigan Lane (Tel. 44000).
Post office Wallgate.
Theatre Wigan Little Theatre, Crompton Street (Tel. 42561).
Cinema ABC, Station Road (Tel. 42376).
Public library Rodney Street.
Places to see Wigan Hall; Powell Museum, Station Road; Haigh Hall; Turnpike Gallery, Leigh Library, Leigh; Hindley Museum, Market Street, Hindley.
Town trails Available from The Warden, Teachers' Centre, Warrington Lane, Wigan.
Shopping Market Street; Wallgate; Mesnes Street; Market Hall; Wigan Centre Arcade; Standishgate.
Sport FA League football: Wigan Athletic AFC, Springfield Park. Rugby League: Wigan RLFC, Central Park; Leigh RLFC, Hilton Park.
AA 24 hour service
Tel. Liverpool (051) 709 7252.

Wigtown D. & G.

This quiet town overlooking the salt-ings, marshes and sands of Wigtown Bay was once a flourishing seaport. But silt blocked its harbour in 1914, and since then it has developed as a touring centre for the neighbouring peninsula of The Machars.

In the large, central square stand two town crosses – the Old Cross of 1748, topped by a sundial, and one of 1816, erected to celebrate the victory at Waterloo.

In 1685 two female Covenanters – Scottish Presbyterians persecuted by Charles II – were drowned at the stake by the rising tide on Wigtown sands. A post marks the site of their death, and a memorial to them and other Covenanter martyrs stands on Windyhill, a viewpoint behind the town.

About 3 miles north-west is the Bronze Age Torhouse Stone Circle – 19 standing stones forming a ring 60 ft across. The ruined Baldoon Castle, 1 mile south-west, was the setting for Scott's novel *The Bride of Lammermoor*.

There is sea-fishing in the bay, for tope, skate, wrasse and conger eel. The area is rich in birdlife, and at-tracts both birdwatchers and wildfowlers. Greylag and pinkfoot geese, ducks and waders winter on the marshes; and in July scoters assemble on the saltings.

Information Tel. Newton Stewart 2431.
Location On the A714, 7 m. S of Newton Stewart.
Parking North Main Street; South Main Street (both car parks).
District council Wigtown (Tel. Stranraer 2151).
Population 1,015.
E-C Wed.
Police Duncan Park (Tel. 3200).
Casualty hospital Garrick Hospital, Edinburgh Road, Stranraer (Tel. Stranraer 2323).
Post office South Main Street.
Public library The School.
Places to see Museum, Main Street.
Shopping Main Street.
AA 24 hour service
Tel. Glasgow (041) 812 0101.

Wilmslow Cheshire

North of Wilmslow lie the outskirts of Manchester, and the town is large-ly a residential suburb of the city. It is surrounded on three sides by open country, and the River Bollin flows through the town to meet the River Dean at Twinnies Bridge.

In South Drive a gipsy caravan has been preserved as a memorial to its owner, the Reverend G. Bramwell Evans, who was the naturalist and broadcaster "Romany".

Information Tel. 522275.
Location On the A34, 12½ m. S of Manchester.
Parking South Drive (2); Church Street; Water Lane; Broadway (all car parks).

District council Macclesfield Borough (Tel. Macclesfield 21955).
Population 30,200.
E-C Wed. **M-D** Fri.
Police Green Lane (Tel. 522215).
Casualty hospital Macclesfield Infirmary, Cumberland Street, Macclesfield (Tel. Macclesfield 21000).
Post office Hawthorn Lane.
Theatre Public Hall, Church Street (Tel. 523356).
Cinema Rex, Alderley Road (Tel. 522266/530179).
Public library South Drive.
Town trails Available from Information Centre, South Drive.
Shopping Grove Street; Water Lane; Alderley Road.
AA 24 hour service
Tel. Manchester (061) 485 6299.

Wilton Wiltshire

The carpets which have made Wilton, former capital of Saxon Wessex, world renowned are woven at the Royal Wilton Carpet Factory beside the Bath Road. The factory was given its royal charter by William III in 1699. Wilton is the centre of the sheep trade for the area – although the fleeces are not used for carpets – and three fairs are held each year.

An 18th-century market-house stands on the town square, from which a series of ruined arches leads to the restored Gothic church. Wilton House, home of the Earls of Pembroke, stands on the site of an abbey founded by Alfred the Great. The house was largely destroyed by fire in 1647, and rebuilt by Inigo Jones. It contains fine furniture and paintings, including works by Rubens, Van Dyck and Tintoretto, and a collection of 7,000 model soldiers. In the

WILTON WEAVE *Wilton carpet is woven with continuous threads which create an exceptionally thick pile.*

gardens are several fine cedar trees, and a Palladian bridge built in 1737.

Information Tel. Salisbury 4956.
Location On the A30, 4 m. W of Salisbury.
Parking Market Place; South Street (both car parks).
District council Salisbury (Tel. Salisbury 6272).

Population 4,000.
E-C Wed. **M-D** Thur.
Police Wilton Road, Salisbury (Tel. Salisbury 29631).
Casualty hospital Salisbury General Hospital, Fisherton Street, Salisbury (Tel. Salisbury 6212).
Post office West Street.
Public library South Street.
Places to see Wilton House, Minster Street; Royal Wilton Carpet Factory, Bath Road.
Shopping Market Square; North Street; West Street; South Street.
Events Sheep Fairs (Aug., Sept. and Oct.).
AA 24 hour service
Tel. Bournemouth 25751.

Wimborne Minster Dorset

The twin-towered, grey-and-brown chequered Minster Church of St Cuthberga gave the town the second part of its name. The first part comes from the River Wim, now called the Allen, which flows into the Stour on the outskirts.

The Minster, which may stand on the site of the nunnery founded by St Cuthberga around AD 700, embraces almost every style of architecture from Norman to late Gothic. It is faithfully reproduced in a model of the town, which is displayed off West Row.

In the streets around the square there are several old inns and hotels, and Wimborne is a good touring base for the surrounding countryside, vividly depicted in the writings of Thomas Hardy (1840-1928). He lived at 16 Avenue Road between 1880 and 1883.

In one of his poems he celebrates the Minster's most eye-catching feature, the "jack-o-clock" or "quarter jack", a figure of a grenadier on the West Tower, which strikes the quarter-hours with a hammer.

Information Tel. 886116 (summer); 886201.
Location On the A31, 9 m. NW of Bournemouth.
Parking Poole Road; Park Lane; King Street; Old Road; Westfield Road; Hanham Road; Allenview Road (all car parks).
District council Wimborne (Tel. 886201).
Population 5,600.
E-C Wed. **M-D** Tues., Fri.
Police Hanham Road (Tel. Broadstone 696262).
Casualty hospital Poole General, Longfleet Road, Poole (Tel. Poole 5100).
Post office East Street.
Public library Crownmead.
Places to see Model Town, West Row; Priest's House Museum, High Street; Merley Tropical Bird Gardens, 1½ m. S; Badbury Rings, 3 m. NW.
Shopping The Square; High Street; East Street; Crownmead.
AA 24 hour service
Tel. Bournemouth 25751.

ANCIENT GATEWAY *Winchelsea's Strand Gate is one of three in the town dating from the 13th century. The house to the left of the gate, Tower Cottage, was once owned by the actress Ellen Terry (1847-1928).*

Winchelsea E. Sussex

The town was described as "ancient" 600 years ago when, with neighbouring Rye, it joined the original Cinque Ports; and the adjective ancient is part of its official title. Edward I laid out Winchelsea on its present hilltop site in the 13th century, to replace the original town which was eventually engulfed by the sea. He followed Roman traditions of design, so the walls, of which three gatehouses remain, formed a rectangle. Whitewashed and weather-boarded cottages face each other across avenues built on a grid pattern.

Winchelsea continued as a port until the 15th century, when it had a population of some 6,000. Then the harbour silted up and the sea receded. Now, with a population of some 600, it is a town by virtue of its history rather than its size; it is the smallest town in England. Around the town, bumps and hollows in the fields mark the site of the streets and abandoned houses.

The 14th-century Church of St Thomas Becket stands on a green at the centre of the grid of streets. Only the chancel, side chapels and ruined transepts remain – all else was destroyed by the French in the 14th and 15th centuries.

South of the church, in Friars Road, are the remains of a Franciscan friary, dissolved in the 16th century. Stones from this and other religious buildings in Rye were used to build Camber Castle, now a ruin. An 18th-century windmill stands in a field to the west of the town. Below the mill can be seen traces of St Leonard's Church, which once stood outside the town walls. The 14th-century Court Hall contains a museum which traces the history of the Cinque Ports.

A house in Friars Road, marked with a plaque, was the home of the novelist and critic Ford Madox Ford (1873-1939).

Information Tel. Rye 2293.
Location On the A259, 3 m. SW of Rye.
Parking Street parking only: High Street; Rectory Lane; North Street; Back Lane.
District council Rother (Tel. Bexhill-on-Sea 216321).
Population 600.
E-C Wed. **M-D** Fri. (summer only).
Police Castle Street (Tel. 2112).
Casualty hospital Rye, Winchelsea and District Memorial Hospital, Playden, Rye (Tel. Rye 2109).
Post office High Street.
Public library Castle Street.
Places to see Court Hall Museum, High Street; Camber Castle ruins, 2 m. E; The Armoury, Castle Street; The Well House, Castle Street; Strand Gate, Strand Hill.
Town trails County Planning Department, East Sussex County Council, Southover House, Southover Road, Lewes, East Sussex.
Shopping High Street.
AA 24 hour service
Tel. Maidstone 55353.

Winchester see page 414

Windermere Cumbria

The Lake District's busiest tourist centre was a tiny farming hamlet until the railway arrived in 1847. Now holidaymakers, walkers and climbers fill many of its guest houses in summer, and hotels have spread over the surrounding countryside.

The focal point in the mountainous scenery is the lake itself, more than 10 miles long and England's largest. Pleasure steamers, yachts and rowing boats ply its surface, and fishermen probe in its depths for pike, perch and the salmon-like char. The lake has been the scene of several water-speed record attempts. In 1930 Sir Henry Seagrave was killed there while attacking the world record.

Orrest Head, 784 ft, easily reached by a footpath which starts opposite the railway station, gives fine views of the lake and Belle Isle, a landscaped island estate with a round 18th-century mansion.

The 15th century parish church of St Martin's, in the suburb of Bowness, has several chained books.

The Baddeley Clock, on Lake Road, was erected in 1907 to commemorate a local fell guide, Mountford John-Byrde Baddeley, described as "the thorough guide".

Information Tel. 4561.
Location On the A591, 5 m. SE of Ambleside.
Parking Broad Street; British Rail car park (both car parks).
District council South Lakeland (Tel. Kendal 24007).
Population 8,600. **E-C** Thur.
Police Lake Road, Bowness (Tel. 4941).
Casualty hospital Westmorland County Hospital, East View, Kendal (Tel. Kendal 22641).
Post office Crescent Road.
Cinema Royalty, Lake Road, Bowness (Tel. 3364).
Public library Ellerthwaite.
Places to see Belle Isle; Steamboat Museum, Rayrigg Road.
Town trails Tourist Information Centre, Victoria Street.
Shopping Crescent Road; Main Street.
AA 24 hour service
Tel. Carlisle 24274.

WINDERMERE STEAMBOAT MUSEUM

The steam launch *Dolly*, built about 1850 and claimed to be the oldest mechanically powered boat in the world, is one of 11 old steamboats preserved by the museum. *Dolly* was salvaged from the bed of Ullswater in 1962 after lying there for almost 70 years.

Dolly, restored Victorian splendour.

WINCHESTER Hampshire

England's first capital city

King Alfred the Great made Winchester – the old Roman city of Venta Belgarum – the capital of Saxon England in the 9th century. It remained the national capital for 200 years after the Norman Conquest, sharing the honour with London. A magnificent Norman cathedral, one of the longest cathedrals in Europe, dominates the city, which today is an agricultural market centre. The surrounding streets contain fine buildings from every period since the early 12th century.

KING ALFRED THE GREAT *A bronze statue of the founder of the English nation stands in the city that was his capital.*

It took 300 years to complete **Winchester Cathedral**, which the Normans established on the site of Alfred's Saxon church. The cathedral, set in spacious lawns that enhance its splendour, is 556 ft long.

Building began in 1079, and the early-Norman work can be seen in the 11th-century transepts and crypt and the 12th-century tower. The masonry of the nave is Norman, but in the 14th century it was remodelled and encased with stonework in the Perpendicular style. This is continued in the presbytery and the Lady Chapel.

The retrochoir, or area behind the high altar, was added in about 1200. It has clustered columns of Purbeck stone, and rib and panel vaulting. The lancet windows contain restored 13th-century glass from Salisbury Cathedral.

The cathedral's many treasures include a black-marble Norman font, medieval wall-paintings and fine 19th-century stained glass. Wood carvings abound, particularly in the choir and presbytery. The nave screen is a 19th-century replica of the 14th-century choir stalls.

Winchester Cathedral is dedicated to the Holy Trinity and St Peter, St Paul and St Swithun, a 9th-century Bishop of Winchester. When St Swithun died in 862 he was buried, at his own request, in the churchyard where the rain would fall on him. But on July 15, 971 his remains were re-buried inside the cathedral. According to legend, this so angered the bishop that he made it rain for 40 days – giving rise to the tradition that if it rains on July 15, St Swithun's Day, it will rain for 40 days. There is a shrine to the saint in the retrochoir. In the presbytery is the tomb of William Rufus, the Norman king killed while hunting in the New Forest in 1100, and on top of the presbytery screens are 16th-century mortuary chests containing the bones of pre-Norman kings, including Canute.

Historic hall

Among the ancient buildings lining the Cathedral Close are the 13th-century **Deanery**, the 17th-century **Pilgrims' School** and the **Pilgrims' Hall**, which has a 14th-century hammer-beam roof.

Izaak Walton (1593-1683), author of the *Compleat Angler*, died at 7 Dome Alley, a cul-de-sac in the Cathedral Close. His burial stone and a memorial window are in the south transept of the cathedral.

Castle Hall, in Castle Street, is all that survives of a 13th-century castle built by Henry III on the site of a Norman fortress. Cromwell's forces destroyed the rest in 1645. Henry V received the envoys of France in the castle in 1415 before launching the campaign that culminated in his victory at Agincourt; Sir Walter Raleigh was sentenced to death there in 1603; and Judge Jeffreys held a "Bloody Assize" there after the Monmouth Rebellion in 1685.

On the west wall hangs a representation of King Arthur's **Round Table** which is believed to date back to 1230–1300. It was re-painted and the Tudor-rose motif added in 1522 when Henry VIII entertained the Emperor Charles V in the city.

Winchester College was founded in 1382 for poor scholars by Bishop William of Wykeham, one of the later architects of the cathedral. The pupils of the school are known as Wykehamists, after the founder.

The college stands close to **Kingsgate**, one of the medieval gateways to the old walled town, and is bounded by streets of charm and character, such as Kingsgate Street with its bow-fronted buildings.

Latin inscription

The medieval college buildings have been added to or altered over the centuries. The chapel was restored, and its tower rebuilt, in the 19th century. A detached building known as "School", built in 1687, bears a Latin inscription inside which means "Learn, leave or be licked". The College War Cloister was built to commemorate Wykehamists killed in the two World Wars. New Hall, in the Warden's Garden, was completed in 1960.

Jane Austen (1775-1817) died in a house in College Street. This is a private residence and cannot be visited. However, Jane Austen's house at Chawton, on the A31 north-east of Winchester, can be visited. Her tomb is in the cathedral.

Next to the Cathedral Close lie the ruins of 12th-century **Wolvesey Castle**, former residence of the Bishops of Winchester and another victim of the Civil War. Near the ruins stands the surviving wing of the **Bishops' Palace** which Christopher Wren built in 1674. This, the residence of today's bishops, incorporates a Tudor chapel that was part of the castle.

The black gowns and ruffed capes of the pensioners of the **Hospital of St Cross** are a familiar sight in Winchester. The hospital, in St Cross Road, is a group of almshouses founded by Bishop Henry de Blois in 1136. It is the oldest charitable institution still functioning in England. The hospital's Norman Chapel of St Cross has a squat tower resembling that of the cathedral. Another charitable foundation, the Order of Noble Poverty

WINCHESTER CATHEDRAL *This masterpiece of Norman architecture is one of the longest cathedrals in Europe.*

MAGNIFICENT BIBLE *An illuminated letter B from the 12th-century Winchester Bible, in the cathedral library, shows Christ casting out the Devil and the harrowing of Hell.*

started by Cardinal Beaufort in 1445, has purple robes for its pensioners.

Street of contrasts

A bronze **statue of King Alfred**, erected in 1901, gazes down from the High Street towards the medieval Westgate. High Street is a street of contrasts, from shop-fronts of the 1970s to the **Gothic High Cross**, a market cross of the 15th century. The **Old Guildhall**, dating from 1713, is now a bank. It has a domed turret with a curfew bell which is rung at 8 p.m. each day.

Winchester's ancient history is brought to life in the **City Museum**, which contains prehistoric, Roman and Saxon finds.

The **Westgate Museum** is housed on top of the 13th-century Westgate of the city. Its exhibits include armour and weapons, and Tudor and Elizabethan weights and measures.

City Mill, by the River Itchen which runs through the city, was built

PRIORY GATE *This picturesque 15th-century archway is the main access through the medieval walls that surround Cathedral Close. The gate adjoins the gabled and half-timbered Cheyney Court, parts of which are 16th century.*

TRADITIONAL REFRESHMENT *Visitors to the Hospital of St Cross almshouses may still ask for the traditional Wayfarer's Dole of bread and ale.*

on the site of a medieval mill in 1774. It is now used as a youth hostel. The **House of Godbegot**, in the High Street, is an impressive Tudor timber-framed house that is now two shops.

Information Tel. 68166 (Mon.-Fri.); 65406 (weekends).
Location On the A333, 13 m. N of Southampton.
Parking Middle Brook Street (2); Chesil Street; Colebrook Street; Jewry Street; Tower Street; Worthy Lane (2); Lower Brook Street; Sussex Street (all car parks).
District council City of Winchester (Tel. 68166).
Population 30,600.
E-C Thur. **M-D** Wed., Fri. and Sat.
Police (Cc) North Walls (Tel. 68100).
Casualty hospital (Ab) Royal Hampshire County Hospital, Romsey

Road (Tel. 63535).
Post office (Cb) Middle Brook Street.
Theatre Theatre Royal **(Bc)**, Jewry Street (Tel. 4127).
Cinema Studios 1, 2 and 3, **(Bc)**, North Walls (Tel. 2592).
Public library (Bc) Jewry Street.
Places to see Castle Hall **(Bb)**; Cathedral and Close **(Bb)**; City Cross **(Bb)**; City Mill **(Cb)**; City Museum **(Bb)**; Godbegot House **(Bb)**; Guildhall Picture Gallery **(Cb)**; Hyde Abbey Gatehouse **(Bc)**; Royal Greenjackets Museum **(Ab)**; Royal Hampshire Regiment Museum **(Bb)**; Westgate Museum **(Bb)**; Winchester College **(Ba)**; St Cross Hospital.
Shopping St George's Street; High Street; Jewry Street; The Broadway; City Road.
AA 24 hour service
Tel. Southampton 36811.

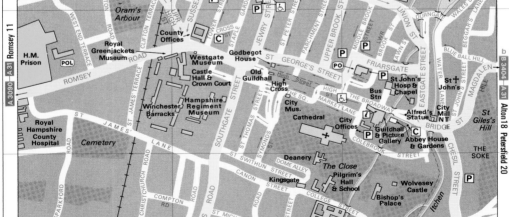

WINDSOR Berkshire

The home of England's monarchs

The town owes its existence and much of its livelihood to the great royal castle which sprawls its stone bulk across a dozen acres of chalk bluff above the River Thames. William the Conqueror began building the castle 900 years ago. It soon became a royal residence and England's kings and queens have lived in it ever since, altering and adding to it to create a monument to their tastes and interests. Beneath its walls the mellow old town stands like a faithful servant, a royal borough whose name the royal family has borne since 1917.

BOROUGH SEAL *The 13th-century Seal of Windsor includes the badge of Queen Eleanor, wife of Edward I.*

Most of the royal hunting forest that stretched across southern Berkshire in medieval times has long since disappeared, but the 4,800 acre Great Park at Windsor is a reminder of its former importance. The park has tracts of woodland separated by walks and drives, formal gardens, farms and cottages. Within its boundaries is the Long Walk, a 3 mile long, tree-lined avenue which runs from the castle to a statue of George III on horseback, known as the Copper Horse, and Virginia Water, a large artificial lake, beside which stand Roman ruins brought from North Africa in 1816.

The **Home Park**, which runs up to the castle ramparts, includes the Queen's private gardens.

Victoria and Albert

In the southern section of the park are the formal gardens of **Frogmore House**, and the **mausoleum** in which Queen Victoria lies beside her beloved Prince Albert.

When William the Conqueror (reigned 1066-87) came to Windsor shortly after the Norman invasion of 1066, he stayed in a Saxon hunting lodge on the fringe of the great forest.

William was planning a defensive ring of fortresses around London, at one day's marching distance from the capital, and a cliff up-river from the lodge provided an ideal site.

Work on William's castle began in 1070, and followed the customary Norman pattern of a central mound, topped with a wooden fort, and earthen ramparts enclosing an open area called a bailey.

By 1110, Henry I (1100-35) had built himself a house in the securest part of the castle's defensive stockade, and was holding court there. Henry II (1154-89) added the first solid stone defences, including the lower half of the **Round Tower**, and employed the first of the chain of royal builders whose work is partly preserved today. Henry III (1216-72) added the D-shaped towers called **Henry III, Salisbury, Garter** and **Curfew** in 1227.

In the 16th century, Elizabeth I (1558-1603) retreated to Windsor to avoid the plague which was sweeping London. She cleared and replaced many ancient wooden buildings in the upper ward. In the 17th century, Windsor was caught up in the general unrest which led to the Civil War and the execution in 1649 of Charles I, who was buried in **St George's Chapel**. This was begun by Edward IV (1461-83) and completed during the reign of Henry VIII (1509-47), who shares a tomb in the chapel with Jane Seymour, his third and favourite wife.

Windsor and the Georges

After the restoration of the monarchy in 1660, Charles II (1660-85) modernised the castle in the French style. He commissioned the Italian artist Antonio Verrio to paint the ceilings and walls of many of the

HORSESHOE CLOISTER *Built in 1478 to house St George's Chapel priests.*

SEAT OF MAJESTY *Windsor Castle has been the home of British kings and queens for nearly 900 years. Its present shape owes* much to George IV, who added the distinctive crown to Henry II's Round Tower and doubled its height.

rooms with elaborate pictures which were a suitable background to his lavish way of life. The castle was neglected by George I and George II, and only three of Verrio's works remain.

When George III came to the throne in 1760, he restored Windsor's status as a royal family home. His son, George IV, who ruled England as regent from 1811 until 1820, and as king until 1830, shared his father's enthusiasm for Windsor.

To celebrate the victory at Waterloo in 1815 he began the **Waterloo Chamber** on the site of an enclosed courtyard. The vast room is decorated with pictures of the soldiers and statesmen who had helped to bring about Napoleon's downfall. George IV was the last monarch to make major changes at Windsor. He altered the whole outline of the castle, and the familiar views it presents are little altered since his day.

New Windsor

When Henry I moved his court from Old Windsor to the castle in 1110, he gave the signal for the development of the new town.

This spread south from the castle gates to the **Church of St John** and, eventually, westwards to engulf the village of Clewer beside the Thames.

If the treasures of the castle are not enough, Windsor has two museums. One, devoted to the town's history, is in the 17th-century **Guildhall** completed by Sir Christopher Wren. The other, in **Combermere Barracks**, displays the uniforms and arms of the Household Cavalry regiments.

Clewer parish church, 1 mile from the castle, is Windsor's oldest surviving building. It was largely completed before the end of the 11th century, and parts are 150 years older than the most ancient sections of the castle. It has a Saxon font, and a tomb with Saxon lettering.

Windsor parish church, off the High Street, was established by 1168, but was extensively rebuilt in 1820. Its treasures include 16th-century plate, and registers which record the burial of Charles I.

The area between Church Lane and Castle Hill, off the High Street, was in medieval times the site of Windsor's market. Most of the buildings along the narrow, cobbled streets were put up in the 17th and 18th centuries, but some, like the Three Tuns Hotel, built in 1518, are older. Burford Lodge, in St Alban's Street, was in the 17th century the home of Nell Gwynne, mistress of Charles II.

Some of Windsor's best Regency houses are in Adelaide Square, while there are attractive Victorian buildings in Queen's Terrace. **Windsor Bridge**, built in 1821, links the town to Eton across the Thames.

Information Tel. 52010 (summer).
Location On the B3022, 3 m. S of Slough.
Parking Stovell Road; Victoria Street (3); Charles Street; Central Station;

Gas Board Site, Goswell Road; King Edward VII Avenue; River Street; Romney Lock Road, Datchet Road; Riverside Station (all car parks).
District council Royal Borough of Windsor and Maidenhead (Tel. Maidenhead 33155).
Population 29,200.
E-C Wed. **M-D** Sat.
Police (Aa) Alma Road (Tel. 51371).
Casualty hospital Heatherwood, London Road, Ascot (Tel. Ascot 23333).
Post office (Ab) Peascod Street.

Theatre Theatre Royal **(Ab)**, Thames Street (Tel. 53888).
Cinema ABC **(Bb)**, Thames Street (Tel. 63888).
Public library (Aa) St Leonard's Road.
Places to see Household Cavalry Museum **(Aa)**, St Leonard's Road; The Guildhall **(Bb)**, High Street; Windsor Castle **(Bb)**, Castle Hill.
Shopping King Edward Court; Thames Street; High Street; Peascod Street; St Leonard's Road.
AA 24 hour service Tel. Reading 581122.

EVIL BE TO HIM WHO EVIL THINKS

Edward III founded the Order of the Garter in 1348 as a reward for chivalry. Its motto is said to derive from an occasion when Edward picked up the garter of the Countess of Salisbury and rebuked his amused courtiers with the words *"Honi soit qui mal y pense"*. Each year, on the third Monday in June, the Garter Knights parade to St George's Chapel.

Garter robes – the insignia of the highest order of chivalry in the land.

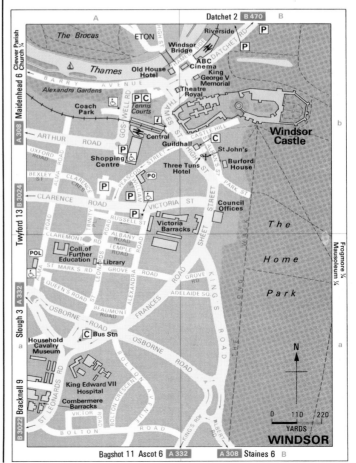

Winsford Cheshire

Britain's only rock salt mine is at Winsford. Today the mine is 600 ft deep and produces around 1.8 million tons of salt a year. During the Second World War it was used as a bomb-proof store for strategic raw materials, such as cotton and rubber.

Winsford combines two ancient towns – Over and Wharton – which face one another on either side of the River Weaver at its highest navigable point. Both were mentioned in Domesday Book, and Over has a borough charter of 1300. The 14th-century Church of St Chad, at Over, has a priest's chamber over the south door and part of a Saxon cross incorporated in a pillar in the chancel. In the hey-day of the salt industry, vessels of up to 120 tons visited the town. The river is now mainly used by pleasure craft. Upstream, the river expands into Bottom Flash, a lake and a marina with boats for hire.

At Vale Royal, on the northern boundary of the town, are the remains of a Cistercian monastery founded by Edward I in 1277 and the largest ever built in England. (The ruins are not open to the public.)

Information Tel. Northwich 74477.
Location On the A54, 4 m. S of Northwich.
Parking Station Road; Dean Drive (2); Church Street (all car parks).
District council Vale Royal (Tel. Northwich 74477).
Population 27,300.
E-C Wed. **M-D** Thur., Sat.
Police High Street (Tel. 2222).
Casualty hospital Leighton Hospital, Middlewich Road, Crewe (Tel. Crewe 55141).
Post office Dingle Walk.
Theatre Civic Hall, Dene Drive (Tel. 2944).
Public library Queen's Parade.
Places to see Church of St Chad, off Swanlow Lane.
Shopping Town Centre Shopping Precinct; High Street.
AA 24 hour service
Tel. Manchester (061) 485 6299.

Wirksworth Derbyshire

From Roman times until the early 19th century, Wirksworth, a town of winding alleys and narrow, zigzag streets, was a mining centre for lead and calamine.

The parish church of St Mary is an impressive and beautiful building which contains a rare, carved Saxon coffin lid of AD 800 and a Norman font. Gell's Almshouses and the near-by grammar school were both founded about 1580.

Every May thousands of visitors watch the town's well-dressing ceremonies – a thanksgiving for water dating back many centuries.

George Eliot set her novel *Adam Bede* in the Wirksworth area, and a later novelist, D. H. Lawrence, lived at Mountain Cottage in Middleton, 1½ miles north-west.

Information Library (Tel. 3173).
Location On the B5025, 4 m. S of Matlock.
Parking Market Place; Barmote Croft (both car parks).
District council West Derbyshire (Tel. Matlock 3461).
Population 5,500.
E-C Wed., Sat. **M-D** Tues.
Police Bank Road, Matlock (Tel. Matlock 3215).
Casualty hospital Whitworth Hospital, Bakewell Road, Matlock (Tel. Matlock 3846).
Post office Church Street.
Public library Town Hall.
Places to see Gell's Almshouses; Moot Hall; Old Manor House; Babington House; Hopton Hall, 2 m. SW.
Town trails Available from Civic Society, or Corner Bookshop in St John's Street.
Shopping Market Place; St John's Street; Dale End; Coldwell Street.
Event Well-dressing Festival (May); Clipping the Church (Sept.).
Trade and industry Limestone quarrying; mining.
AA 24 hour service
Tel. Nottingham 787751.

Wisbech Cambridgeshire

The Brinks, two rows of impeccable houses lining the River Nene in Wisbech, are among the finest examples of Georgian architecture in England. Peckover House, built on the North Brink in about 1722, is the town's most outstanding building. Presented to the National Trust in 1943 by the Peckover family, local bankers, it reflects their wealth in its rococo wood and plasterwork interior decoration. A plaque on a building on the South Brink commemorates it as the birth-place in 1838 of Octavia Hill, co-founder of the National Trust.

Once 4 miles from the sea, Wisbech is now 11 miles inland, as the result of land reclamation, but it is still a busy port. Ships of up to 1,500 tons can navigate the Nene.

The Rose and Crown Hotel, which dates from about 1600, has fine Tudor work and a graceful 18th-century staircase; and the Old Market and Norfolk Street contain good Georgian buildings. A Regency house at the centre of the town embodies the remains of successive castles from Norman times.

Near this house stands the Wisbech and Fenland Museum, established in 1835. It illustrates local history, and also contains the manuscript of Charles Dickens's *Great Expectations*, donated to the museum by his friend Chauncey Hare Townshend.

The parish church of St Peter and St Paul includes Norman work and a monument by Joseph Nollekens, the 18th-century sculptor.

Among flower beds beside the river rises a 68 ft high memorial by Sir Gilbert Scott to Thomas Clarkson (1760-1846), a locally born campaigner against slavery.

Information Tel. 3263/64009.
Location On the A47, 14 m. SW of King's Lynn.
Parking West Street; Old Market; Market Square; Church Terrace; Chapel Road; Horsefair (all car parks).
District council Fenland (Tel. March 2471).
Population 17,300.
E-C Wed. **M-D** Thur., Sat.
Police Lynn Road (Tel. 2112).
Casualty hospital North Cambridgeshire Hospital, The Park (Tel. 5781).
Post office Bridge Street.
Theatres Angles Theatre, Alexandra Road (Tel. 5587); Empire, Blackfriars Road (3532) (films 3 days a week).
Cinema Unit 1, Hill Street (Tel. 61224).
Public library Ely Place.
Places to see Peckover House; Wisbech and Fenland Museum.
Shopping Market Place; High Street.
Event Rose Fair (second Sat. in July).
AA 24 hour service
Tel. King's Lynn 3731.

Witney Oxfordshire

The Witan, or council of Saxon kings, established the significance of Witney when they chose the village as a meeting place in the 10th and 11th centuries. Later, the main London to Gloucester road was built through Witney and contributed to its economic prosperity in the Middle Ages. The town has been producing wool, cloth and blankets since the 13th century, as well as being the traditional market for the surrounding countryside.

The town centre, west of the river, was laid out by the Bishop of Winchester in the early 13th century, and is a good example of medieval town planning. Market Square, which lies at the junction of the two main streets, contains the Butter Cross, a medieval marketing and meeting place. This has a steeply gabled roof surmounted by a clock-turret added in 1683.

Opposite the Butter Cross, the 18th-century Town Hall is built above a piazza.

Market Square widens into Church Green, which is dominated by the tower and spire of the 13th-century Church of St Mary. Pollarded lime trees and Georgian houses surround the green. Many of these houses, built for master weavers or trades-men, contain "turries", or cross passages, which lead to employees' cottages at the rear.

In the High Street is the 18th-century Blanket Hall, built by the Witney Blanket Weavers Company for weighing and measuring locally made blankets.

On the road to Woodstock and Bicester lies Woodgreen, an 18th-century residential suburb. This contains some of the best Georgian houses in the town, as well as a 19th-

NORTH BRINK, WISBECH *No two of the Georgian houses that overlook the River Nene are alike, yet they blend perfectly to form one of the most outstanding rows of Georgian architecture in the country.*

century blanket warehouse converted into flats, all grouped round a small green.

About half a mile east of Market Square, off the B4022 road to Oxford, is the hamlet of Cogges where an ancient manor house and farm were opened as an agricultural museum in 1978. Part of the manor dates from the 13th century.

Information Tel. 4379.
Location On the A4095, 12 m. W of Oxford.
Parking Welch Way; Market Square (both car parks). Church Green; Market Square; Butter Cross.
District council West Oxfordshire (Tel. 3051).
Population 14,100.
E-C Tues. **M-D** Thur., Sat.
Police Welch Way (Tel. 3913).
Casualty hospital John Radcliffe II, Headington, Oxford (Tel. Oxford 64711).
Post office Market Square.
Cinema Palace Cinema, Market Square (Tel. 3147).
Public library Welch Way.
Places to see Butter Cross, Market Square; Cogges Manor Farm Museum, ½ m. E off the B4022.
Shopping High Street; Market Square; Corn Street.
Events Witney Feast Fair (Sept.); Trade Fair (June, biennially).
AA 24 hour service
Tel. Oxford 40286

Woking Surrey

Modern Woking is a thriving commuter town for London. Old Woking, now a village, was a market town in the 17th century. It still retains several interesting houses in its main street, including the 17th-century Manor House. The parish church of St Peter has a Norman north wall and a 13th–15th-century west tower.

At Pyrford, east of the town centre, stands St Nicholas's Church, which has changed little since the Normans built it. On the south wall of the nave are simple outline wall-paintings dating from 1200, beneath which are even-earlier paintings in colour.

In Oriental Road stands the onion-domed Shah Jehan Mosque, built in 1889, the first of its kind in England. The mosque was financed largely by the Begum Shah Jehan, the immensely rich ruler of Bhopal State in India, following her visit to Woking that year. It points exactly towards the Muslim holy city of Mecca, and was aligned after bearings had been taken by a P & O Line captain.

Information Tel. 5931.
Location On the A320, 7 m. N of Guildford.
Parking Victoria Way (2); Brewery Road; Cawsey Way; Heathside Crescent (all car parks).
District council Borough of Woking (Tel. 5931).
Population 81,400.

E-C Wed. **M-D** Tues., Fri., Sat.
Police Guildford Road (Tel. 61991).
Casualty hospital Royal Surrey County Hospital, Farnham Road, Guildford (Tel. Guildford 71122).
Post office Market Square.
Theatre Rhoda McGaw Theatre, Centre Halls, Town Square (Tel. 69765).
Cinemas ABC, Chobham Road (Tel. 61020); Film Theatre, Centre Halls, Town Square (69765).
Public library Town Square.
Places to see Old Hall; Hoe Place; Sutton Place, 5¾ m. S; Pyrford Place.
Shopping Commercial Way; Wolsey Walk; Cawsey Way; Mercia Walk; Middle Walk; Town Square; Market Square.
Trade and industry Commerce; light engineering; agriculture.
AA 24 hour service
Tel. Guildford 72841.

Wokingham Berkshire

The prosperity of Wokingham grew up round the silk trade, which was probably introduced by French Protestant refugees in Tudor times. Silk stockings, hat bands and cravats were made at Wokingham until the late 18th century.

Wokingham, today mainly a commuter town for Reading, Bracknell and London, has several half-timbered cottages and Georgian houses. In the 17th-century Olde Rose Inn in the Market Place, the poet Alexander Pope, the essayist Dean Swift and the dramatist John Gay each wrote verses to "Sweet Molly Mog", the landlord's daughter.

The restored 15th-century parish church retains its original octagonal font, and Lucas Hospital, built in 1663, has some fine stained glass.

Information Tel. 783185.
Location On the A321, 8 m. SE of Reading.
Parking Denmark Street; Rose Street; Easthampstead Road; Elms Road; Cockpit Path (all car parks).
District council Wokingham (Tel. 786833).
Population 24,300.
E-C Wed. **M-D** Tues., Thur., Fri. and Sat.
Police Rectory Road (Tel. 781212).
Casualty hospital Royal Berkshire, Craven Road, Reading (Tel. Reading 85111).
Post office Broad Street.
Theatre Wokingham Theatre, Norrey's Avenue (Tel. Crowthorne 3501).
Cinema Ritz, Easthampstead Road (Tel. 780633).
Public library Broad Street.
Places to see Town Hall; Lucas Hospital, Luckley Road; Rose Street; Stratfield-Saye, 6 m. SW; Caesar's Camp, 4 m. SE; Easthampstead Park, 2 m. SE.
Shopping Market Place; Peach Street; Denmark Street.
AA 24 hour service
Tel. Reading 581122.

Wolverhampton W. Mid.

Huge local deposits of coal and iron-stone provided the impetus for Wolverhampton's transformation from a quiet country town to "the capital of the Black Country". The first part of Wolverhampton's name comes from Wulfruna, sister of King Edgar of Mercia. In 994 she re-founded a monastery near the site of the present Church of St Peter. This was built in the 13th century, and its tower added 200 years later.

The art gallery, by St Peter's Gardens, contains a collection of British and American paintings of the 18th to 20th centuries.

Information Tel. 27811.
Location On the A41, 15 m. NE of Birmingham.
Parking Birch Street; Bell Street; Pipers Row; School Street; Garrick Street; North Street; Wulfruna Street; Skinner Street; Church Street; Cleveland Street; Fold Street; Temple Street (2); Pitt Street; St James's Square; Tower Street; Bilston Street; St Mary's Street; Bath Avenue; Church Lane; Faulkland Street; Fryer Street (2); Railway Drive; Peel Street; Stanhope Street; Walsall Street (all car parks).
District council Metropolitan Borough of Wolverhampton (Tel. 27811).
Population 252,400.
E-C Thur. **M-D** Tues., Wed., Fri. and Sat.
Police (Ab) Red Lion Street (Tel. 27851).
Casualty hospital Royal Hospital, Cleveland Road (Tel. 51532).
Post office (Bb) Lichfield Street.
Theatre Grand **(Bb)**, Lichfield Street (Tel. 25244).

Cinemas ABC **(Ba)**, Garrick Street (Tel. 22917); Odeon **(Aa)**, Skinner Street (20364).
Public library (Ba) Snow Hill.
Places to see Art Gallery **(Bb)**, Lichfield Street; Bantock House Museum, Merridale Road; Moseley Old Hall, 4 m. N; Wightwick Manor, 3 m. W.
Town trails Available from the Planning Department, Civic Centre, St Peter's Square.
Shopping Darlington Street; Queen Square; Lichfield Street; Victoria Street; Cleveland Street; Garrick Street; Market Street; Princess Street; King Street; Queen Street; Wulfrun Shopping Centre; Mander Shopping Centre.
Sport FA League football, Wolverhampton Wanderers FC, Molineux Grounds; Horse racing, Dunstall Park.
AA 24 hour service
Tel. Birmingham (021) 550 4858.

SEA POWER *The 18th-century watermill at Woodbridge was operated by the tide. It has been restored, and its machinery can be seen working.*

Woodbridge Suffolk

The River Deben cuts a swathe around Woodbridge and, along its banks, quays and boatyards bear witness to the town's history of ship-building, rope and sail-making.

Both Edward III, in the 14th century, and Sir Francis Drake, in the 16th century, used Woodbridge-built ships as fighting vessels.

Boat-building is flourishing again, and the town has developed into a yachting centre.

Information Tel. 3789.
Location Off the A12, 9 m. NE of Ipswich.
Parking New Street; Hamblin Road; Station Road; Theatre Street (all car parks).
District council Suffolk Coastal (Tel. 3789).
Population 7,200.
E-C Wed. **M-D** Thur.
Police Grundisburgh Road (Tel. 3377).
Casualty hospital Ipswich General, Ivry Street, Ipswich (Tel. Ipswich 212477).
Post office Cumberland Street.
Cinema Woodbridge Cinema, Quay Street (Tel. 2174).
Public library New Street.
Places to see Shire Hall; Seckford Almshouses; Tide Mill.
Shopping Church Street; Thoroughfare; Market Hill.
AA 24 hour service
Tel. Norwich 29401.

Woodstock Oxfordshire

Glove-making was once Woodstock's chief industry, but the town now prospers more from the tourists who flock to Blenheim Palace. Sir John Vanbrugh designed the palace for John Churchill, 1st Duke of Marlborough. It was largely paid for by the nation in gratitude for his victory over the French and Bavarians at Blenheim in 1704.

Sir Winston Churchill was born there in 1874, and is buried in Bladon churchyard, 1½ miles to the south. The park surrounding the palace was landscaped in the 18th century by "Capability" Brown.

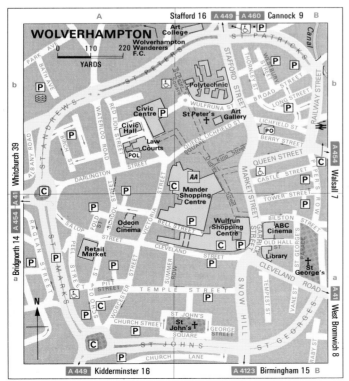

Information Tel. 811038 (summer).
Location On the A34, 8 m. NW of Oxford.
Parking Hensington Road (car park).
District council West Oxfordshire (Tel. Witney 3051).
Population 2,000.
E-C Wed.
Police Hensington Road (Tel. 811311).
Casualty hospital John Radcliffe II, Headington (Tel. Oxford 64711).
Post office Park Street.
Public library Town Hall, Market Place.
Places to see Blenheim Palace; Oxfordshire County Museum, Fletchers House, Park Street; Harrison's Lane.
Shopping Oxford Street; High Street; Market Street.
Event Woodstock Fair (Oct.).
AA 24 hour service
Tel. Oxford 40286.

Worcester see page 422

Workington Cumbria

The Georgian elegance of cobbled Portland Square, and the ruins of 14th century Workington Hall, where Mary Queen of Scots stayed in 1568, are almost all that now remain of old Workington.

The deep-water port is used for the freight of railway lines made in the steelworks and coal.

Information Tel. 2122.
Location On the A596, 8 m. W of Cockermouth.
Parking John Street (2); Washington Street; William Street; Upton Street (all car parks).
District council Allerdale (Tel. Cockermouth 823741).
Population 27,600.
E-C Thur. **M-D** Wed., Sat.
Police Nook Street (Tel. 2422).
Casualty hospital West Cumberland, Whitehaven (Tel. Whitehaven 3181).
Post office Finkle Street.
Theatre Carnegie Theatre, Finkle Street (Tel. 2122).
Cinema Ritz, Murray Road (Tel. 2505).
Public library New Oxford Street.
Places to see Helena Thompson Museum, Park End Road; Portland Square; Workington Hall.
Shopping Murray Road; Oxford Street; Finkle Street.
Sport Rugby League, Speedway, Derwent Park; Greyhound racing, Lonsdale Park.
AA 24 hour service
Tel. Carlisle 24274.

Worksop Nottinghamshire

The town is a good centre for touring Sherwood Forest and the Dukeries – a group of neighbouring estates which were owned by the Dukes of Kingston, Newcastle and Portland.

Worksop's twin-towered parish church of St Cuthbert and St Mary is part of a former 12th-century priory, and has splendid Norman work and a 13th-century Lady Chapel. The 14th-century gatehouse still stands.

The rebuilding of Worksop Manor was begun in 1763, but it was never completed. Exhibits in the town museum include two Bronze Age decorated beakers found in nearby Clumber Park, the former estate of the Duke of Newcastle which is now owned by the National Trust.

Information Tel. 475531.
Location On the A57, 18 m. SE of Sheffield.
Parking Potter Street; Castle Street; Memorial Avenue; Central Avenue; Bridge Place; Gateford Road; Lead Hill; Newgate Street (all car parks).
District council Bassetlaw (Tel. 475531).
Population 37,000
E-C Thur. **M-D** Wed., Fri. and Sat.
Police Potter Street (Tel. 475171).
Casualty hospital Victoria Hospital, Watson Road (Tel. 472831).
Post office Ryton Street, Victoria Square.
Cinema Studios 1, 2 and 3, Carlton Road (Tel. 472352).
Public library Memorial Avenue.
Places to see Museum, Memorial Avenue; Priory Gatehouse; Worksop Manor; Clumber Park, 3 m. SE.
Shopping Netherholme Shopping Precinct, Bridge Street; Bridge Place; Potter Street; Newgate Street.
AA 24 hour service
Tel. Nottingham 787751.

Worthing W. Sussex

The largest town in West Sussex was a small fishing village in 1798 when Princess Amelia, youngest daughter of George III, came to stay. Her visit gave Worthing the royal seal of approval, and over the following 14 years rapid building created the centre of today's resort.

The area has been inhabited since the Stone Age, but the name Worth-ing is Saxon – it means "belonging to Weoro's people". The town includes the former villages of Broadwater and Tarring. Broadwater Church preserves two intricately carved late-Norman arches. In the cemetery are the graves of two 19th-century authors, W. H. Hudson (1841-1922) and Richard Jeffries (1848-87).

The Archbishops of Canterbury built a palace at Tarring in the 13th century. One stone building survives, and is used as a school. A row of 15th-century cottages in the High Street contains a folk museum.

Cissbury Ring, on the northern edge of Worthing golf course, is an Iron Age camp used from 300 BC.

Information Tel. 39999.
Location On the A24, 14 m. W of Brighton.
Parking Graham Road; Grafton; High Street (2); Teville Gate; Chapel Road; Town Hall; Lyndhurst Road; Beach House; Brighton Road (all car parks).
District council Borough of Worthing (Tel. 37111).
Population 91,670.
E-C Wed. **M-D** Sat.
Police (Ab) Union Place (Tel. 31821).
Casualty hospital Worthing Hospital **(Bb)**, Lyndhurst Road (Tel. 205111).
Post office (Ab) Chapel Road.
Theatres Connaught **(Ab)**, Union Place (Tel. 35333); Pavilion **(Aa)**, Marine Parade (202221); Assembly Hall, Stoke Abbot Road (202221).
Cinemas Odeon **(Aa)**, Liverpool Gardens (Tel. 35016); Dome **(Aa)**, Marine Parade (200461).
Public library (Ab) Richmond Road.
Places to see Cissbury Ring, 4 m. N; Tarring Cottages Folk Museum, Tarring; Museum and Art Gallery.
Shopping Montague Street precinct; Guildbourne Centre, Chapel Road; Teville Gate precinct; Warwick Street; South Street.
AA 24 hour service
Tel. Brighton 695231.

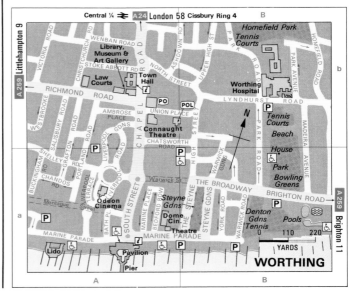

WORTHING

WORCESTER Hereford & Worcester

Cathedral city where a king lies buried

Sauce and fine china have carried Worcester's name around the world; and glove-making, a local craft since the 13th century, is still carried on alongside such modern industries as engineering and printing. The city centre has many splendid medieval buildings, crowned by the cathedral beside the River Severn. There are also carefully preserved reminders of Worcester's 19th-century industrial history.

The city is set amid rich farmland of meadows, apple and cherry orchards and hopfields. Agriculture has always played an important part in its economic life.

In medieval times, the eastern boundary of Worcester was marked by defences which ran parallel to City Walls Road. These have been excavated, and Worcester's oldest buildings lie between them and the river front. The oldest church is **St Helen's** in Fish Street, established in AD 680, rebuilt many times, most recently in 1880, and now used to store ecclesiastical and secular records.

Dominating the city is the **cathedral**, founded as a Saxon monastery by St Oswald in 983. It stands on high ground, on the eastern bank of the Severn, with its out-buildings extending to the edge of the river and the city stretching away behind it. The earliest part of the present building, the Norman crypt, was constructed by St Wulstan, the only Saxon bishop to keep his office after the invasion of 1066. It was built for the safe keeping and worship of saints' relics. On each anniversary of St Wulstan's death on January 19,

1095, services are held in it. The circular chapter house, one of the first of its kind, was built about 1120, and 50 years later the west end of the nave was reconstructed.

The great tower was added in the 14th century, when much of the rest of the cathedral was rebuilt. Prince Arthur's Chantry, an elaborately carved chapel, was built in 1504 by Henry VII in memory of his son Arthur, who had died at Ludlow. It is remarkable for its fine tracery, heraldry and sculptures. Worcester Cathedral is the burial place of King John, who died in 1216. Above his tomb in the choir is the oldest royal effigy in England. It is made of Purbeck marble and was once painted and bejewelled. The tomb was opened in the 18th century, and the king's remains were found wrapped in an embroidered robe and monk's cowl.

The cathedral library, over the south aisle of the nave, contains a large collection of early manuscripts, including fragments of an 8th-century Gospel and deeds of land from the same period.

A monastery grew up around the

cathedral and was dissolved in 1540, but some of the buildings remain. Among them are the refectory, which is part of the King's School, the cloisters, a circular chapter house and the 14th-century **Edgar Tower**. The massive gateway of the tower, which formerly led to the priory, is still in use. South of the cathedral, across College Green, is the site of Worcester Castle, built in the 11th century and never more than a fortified enclosure.

The **Commandery**, just outside the old city walls in Sidbury, was founded in 1085 as a hospital by St Wulstan. It was rebuilt in the 15th century, and has a great hall with mural paintings. Charles II used it as his headquarters during the Battle of Worcester in 1651. The Royalist forces were defeated, and their commander, the Duke of Hamilton, died of his wounds in the Commandery.

Friar Street and its continuation, New Street, contain several 15th and 16th-century houses. Among them is **Nash House**, a four-storey, half-timbered Elizabethan building.

Another, **Greyfriars**, was put up about 1480 as a hostelry for travellers, and is one of the few buildings of the friars to survive in the city after the Dissolution of the Monasteries. It contains some early fireplaces, panelling and furniture of the period. Also in Friar Street is the **Tudor House**, a 500-year-old timber-framed building which has been turned into a folk museum, depicting life in the city from Elizabethan times. It includes a

---

MAJESTIC CATHEDRAL *The massive bulk of Worcester Cathedral, built between the 11th and 14th centuries, rises beside the River Severn, above the rooftops of a city that attractively mingles the medieval and the modern.*

ROYAL TOMB *The marble effigy on King John's tomb in the cathedral choir was carved two years after his death in 1216.*

Stuart room and a kitchen with a cast-iron cooking range. **King Charles's House**, a half-timbered building in New Street, was built in 1577. It was partly destroyed by fire in the 18th century, but the remainder has been restored and is used as a restaurant. The king hid in the house after his defeat in the battle outside the city walls, and fled through the back door as Parliamentary troops entered at the front.

Charles II and his father, Charles I, are commemorated by statues on the façade of the **Guildhall** in High Street, designed in 1721 by Thomas White, a pupil of Sir Christopher Wren. Oliver Cromwell's head is depicted, too, nailed by the ears above the doorway, in illustration of the city's unswerving loyalty to the Stuarts. The whole frontage is one of the finest examples of early Georgian architecture in the country. Inside the building is a beautifully decorated Queen Anne assembly room and a collection of armour, including some left on the field after the Battle of Worcester. Civil War relics are also on display at the **City Museum** in Foregate Street, next to the 19th-century Shire Hall. One section of the museum is devoted to the Worcestershire Regiment raised in 1694,

and the county's Yeoman Cavalry, formed exactly 100 years later. Apart from the usual uniforms and weapons, the exhibits include three Victoria Crosses and captured German and Japanese relics of the Second World War.

Worcester's porcelain industry was started in 1751 by Dr John Wall and a group of local businessmen. Their factory soon produced its own successful lines of Chinese blue-printed ware and, later, richly ornamented ware. The present factory of the **Worcester Royal Porcelain Company** in Severn Street is open to visitors by appointment.

The **Lea & Perrins** sauce factory in Midland Road was founded in 1825 by two local men, and they first made their celebrated Worcestershire sauce five years later.

The city is the home of the world's oldest surviving newspaper, *Berrow's Worcester Journal*, founded in 1690. Every third year the cathedral is the setting for Europe's oldest music festival, the Three Choirs Festival, which it has shared with Gloucester and Hereford since 1719.

The composer Sir Edward Elgar (1857-1934) was born at **Broadheath**, 4 miles north-west of Worcester, in a house which is now a museum containing proofs of his musical scores, photographs and personal mementoes. The composer's father owned a music shop in the city, and Elgar trained as a pianist and violinist before turning to composing. Some of his best-known works are regularly performed at the city's Three Choirs Festival.

Worcester has one of the oldest racecourses in the country. In summer, county cricket is played on the attractive ground across the river from the cathedral. Boat excursions,

through the green and wooded local countryside, start from Worcester Bridge. **Digles Basin**, where the river meets the Worcester-Birmingham Canal, is a busy junction on the inland waterways network.

Information Tel. 23471.
Location On the A38, 8 m. NE of Great Malvern.
Parking Croft Road; Farrier Street; City Walls Road (2); Blackfriars Square; Bull Entry; Queen Street; Providence Street; St Martin's Gate; St Paul's Street; Tallow Hill; Clare Street; Parell's Row; George Street; Lowesmoor Place; Copenhagen Street; King Street; Commandery Road; New Road (all car parks).
District council City of Worcester (Tel. 23471).
Population 74,200.
E-C Thur. **M-D** Mon., Sat.
Police (Ba) Deansway (Tel. 22222).
Casualty hospital Worcester Royal Infirmary, Castle Street (Tel. 27122).
Post office (Bb) Foregate Street.
Theatre Swan (**Ab**), The Moors (Tel. 27322).
Cinema Odeon 1, 2, 3, (**Bb**), Foregate Street (Tel. 24733).
Public library (Bb) Foregate Street.
Places to see Cathedral (**Ba**); City Museum and Art Gallery (**Bb**); Commandery (**Ba**); Edgar Tower (**Ba**); Greyfriars (**Ba**); Guildhall (**Ba**); King Charles's House (**Bb**); King's School (**Ba**); Royal Porcelain Works (**Ba**); Dyson Perrins Museum; Shire Hall (**Bb**); Tudor House (**Ba**); Spetchley Park, 3 m. E.
Shopping Foregate; The Cross; High Street; The Shambles; Pump Street; Angel Street; Angel Place.
Sport Horse racing, Pitchcroft.
AA 24 hour service Tel. Worcester 51070.

WORCESTER WARE

The Dyson Perrins Museum has the finest and most comprehensive collection of Worcester porcelain in the world. It is based on the collections of the late Dyson Perrins and the Worcester Royal Porcelain Company, whose factory in Severn Street is adjacent to the museum.

Two vases dating from about 1770 were possibly made by Dr Wall, the founder of the porcelain company.

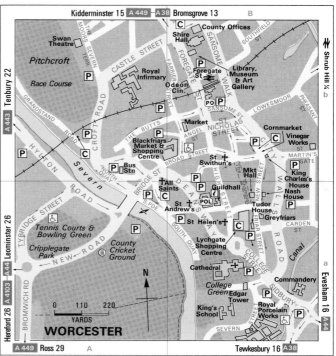

WORCESTER

Wrexham Clwyd

The industrial and commercial capital of North Wales lies just across the border from England, on land fought over by English and Welsh for many centuries.

Its name, usually said to derive from a mixture of Latin and Anglo-Saxon meaning "the hamlet of the king", suggests that its origins were English rather than Welsh. And Offa's Dyke, the boundary between the Anglo-Saxons and Welsh in the 8th century, runs 4 miles west of the town, so that when the dyke was made, Wrexham was part of Anglo-Saxon Mercia. Wrexham has been the market centre for a large rural area since the early 14th century. Its cattle sales – held every Monday – provide the raw material for its oldest industry, the tanning of leather.

During the 19th century, Wrexham's prosperity was built on coal, steel, brick-making, leather manufacture and brewing. Britain's first lager brewery was opened by a German immigrant in Wrexham in the 1880s, and for many years Wrexham Lager was the only draught beer available on British ships as, unlike traditional ales, it is unaffected by the motion of the sea.

The Church of St Giles was built in the 15th century after its predecessor had been destroyed by fire. The pinnacled tower, 136 ft high, is one of the "Seven Wonders of Wales".

The churchyard contains the grave of Elihu Yale (1648-1721), the American-born son of a local man. Yale became Governor of Madras in India, and eventually settled in Britain with the fortune he had acquired in the East. In 1718, he donated books and paintings to help to raise money for the collegiate school of Connecticut in the USA. This was the origin of today's Yale University. The tower of Yale University's chapel is modelled on the tower of St Giles's.

Wrexham and the surrounding villages are a stronghold of two Welsh traditions – Nonconformism and choral singing. Rhosllannerchrugog, a former mining village 3 miles south, has two choirs and has been the site of the National Eisteddfod.

The coal industry has declined, and only one pit in the area is still working. But new industries, such as chemicals and textiles, have taken the place of coal.

There is attractive mountain scenery to the west, and the River Dee loops round the town to the east and south. National Hunt racing takes place at Bangor-on-Dee, 4 miles south-east. Gresford, 3 miles north, has a part-15th-century church with a peal of 12 bells which is another of the "Seven Wonders of Wales".

Erddig Hall, 2 miles south of Wrexham, is a 17th-century mansion in a 1,900 acre estate. It has been extensively restored by the National Trust to show what life was like on a country squire's estate 300 years ago. The estate buildings include working

ARTISTRY IN IRON *The wrought-iron gates of St Giles's Church, Wrexham, were made in the 18th century by two local craftsmen, the Davies brothers.*

bakeries, joiners' shops and a smithy. In the mansion there are displays of household bills and accounts, as well as the paintings and fine furniture usually associated with stately homes.

Information Tel. 364611.
Location On the A525, 12 m. S of Chester.
Parking Regent Street; Chester Street; Hill Street; Town Hill; Smithfield Road; Market Street; Lambpit Street; St George's Crescent (all car parks).
District council Borough of Wrexham Maelor (Tel. 364611).
Population 40,300.
E-C Wed. **M-D** Mon.
Police (Bb) Bodhyfryd (Tel. 53111).
Casualty hospital (Bb) Wrexham and East Denbighshire War Memorial Hospital, Rhos Ddu Road (Tel. 51041).
Post office (Ab) Egerton Street.
Theatre Little Theatre **(Aa)**, Hill Street (Tel. 51091).
Cinemas Hippodrome **(Bb)**, Henblas Street (Tel. 364479); The Vogue **(Ba)**, High Street (262269).
Public library (Bb) Rhos Ddu Road.
Places to see Erddig Hall, 2 m. S.
Town trails Available from County Planning Officer, Clwyd County Council, Shire Hall, Mold, Clwyd.
Shopping Regent Street; High Street; Beast Market; Lord Street; Bank Street.
Sport FA League football, Wrexham FC, Racecourse Ground, Mold Road.
AA 24 hour service
Tel. Llandudno 79066.

Wymondham Norfolk

A great fire swept through Wymondham in 1615, destroying most of its medieval buildings. Among the few buildings that survived was one which is now one of the oldest inns in the country, the 14th-century Green

LEATHER TOWN *A shoe-repair sign in a Wrexham street recalls the leather industry that once made the town prosper.*

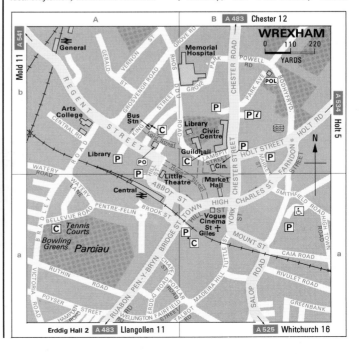

ANCIENT TRADE *A wood-turner on Wymondham's town sign symbolises the trade that has been the town's staple business for the past 800 years.*

Dragon, in Church Street. It once belonged to the local Benedictine abbey, founded in 1107.

The abbey church of St Mary and St Thomas was shared by the monks and the townspeople. The sharing led to feuds, and in about 1400 the monks built an octagonal bell-tower at the east end of the church. Fifty years later the citizens built a square one at the west end, and a roof-high wall was built across the nave. Both towers and the nave, with a magnificent hammer-beam roof, survive.

In 1549 Robert Kett, lord of the manor of Wymondham, and his brother, William, led a rebellion of townspeople protesting against the enclosure of common land and what they considered to be other high-handed actions. They marched on Norwich and took the city. When the rebellion was stamped out, the brothers were executed.

Information Middleton Street (Tel. 603302).
Location On the A11, 9 m. SW of Norwich.
Parking Market Place; Market Street; Chandlers Hill; Central Hill; The Fairland (all car parks).
District council South Norfolk (Tel. Long Stratton 31122).
Population 9,800.
E-C Wed. **M-D** Fri.
Police Avenue Road (Tel. 602303).
Casualty hospital Norfolk and Norwich Hospital, St Stephens Road, Norwich (Tel. Norwich 28377).
Post office Middleton Street.
Cinema Regal, Friarscroft Lane (Tel. 602025).
Public library Church Street.
Places to see Market Cross; Old Manor House; The Bridewell; The Chapel of St Thomas Becket; Abbey Church of St Mary and St Thomas of Canterbury.
Shopping Market Place; Market Street; Middleton Street; Fairland Street.
AA 24 hour service Tel. Norwich 29401.

Yeovil Somerset

The many old buildings in Yeovil owe their mellow appearance to the honey-coloured Ham limestone quarried from Hamdon Hill, 4 miles west of the town.

An Iron Age fort stands on the 426 ft Hamdon Hill, which provides panoramic views across the fertile valley of the River Yeo. Nearby 16th-century Montacute House, built of Ham stone, is one of the finest mansions in the south-west; it contains beautiful furnishings and is surrounded by lovely gardens.

The former coach house and stables of Hendford Manor Hall contain Yeovil Museum, which specialises in Roman remains from the nearby Westland and Lufton Manor sites and in local history; the museum also contains a collection of firearms.

The 14th-century Church of St John the Baptist has a stately nave with lofty arches and windows that admit such a flood of light that the church has long been called "The Lantern of the West". The church also has a fine timbered roof.

With two livestock markets, Yeovil serves a large and prosperous agricultural area that concentrates on dairy farming. Westland Helicopters, part of an aircraft company founded in the First World War, is one of the world's largest helicopter manufacturers, and the town has also been a glove and leather-making centre for centuries.

It was on glove-making that Yeovil first built its prosperity. Sheepskins from flocks grazing on the Dorset downland provided high-quality material for gloves, clothes and shoe-uppers. The trade has survived despite the arrival of man-made materials, and Yeovil still produces gloves for fashion shops all over the world.

The Fleet Air Arm Museum, at the Royal Navy Air Station, Yeovilton, to the north, portrays the development of naval aviation from the airships and man-lifting kites of the early years of the century to the high-speed strike aircraft of today. Beside the museum stands Concorde 002, the British-built prototype of the world's first supersonic airliner.

East Coker, 2 miles south, is one of the prettiest villages in Somerset. The poet T. S. Eliot (1888-1965), whose ancestors came from the village, is buried in the churchyard. A plaque in the church commemorates William Dampier (1652-1715), who after a career as a pirate became a captain in the Royal Navy and an early explorer of Australia.

Information Tel. 22884 or 5272.
Location On the A30, 42 m. W of Salisbury.
Parking Old Station Road; Stars Lane; Petters Way; Huish (2); Salthouse Lane; Peter Street; Earle Street; Vicarage Street; Vincent Place; Court Ash; North Lane (all car parks).
District council Yeovil (Tel. 5272).
Population 27,300.
E-C Thur. (but some six-day trading). **M-D** Mon., Fri.
Police Horsey Lane (Tel. 5291).
Casualty hospital (Ab) Yeovil District, Higher Kingston (Tel. 5122).
Post office (Aa) King George Street.
Theatre Johnson Hall Civic Theatre **(Aa)** (Tel. 22884).
Cinema Classic **(Ab)**, Court Ash Terrace (Tel. 23663).
Public library (Aa) King George Street.
Places to see Montacute House, 4 m. W; Yeovil Museum, Hendford Manor Hall **(Aa)**; Fleet Air Arm Museum, Royal Naval Air Station, Yeovilton.
Shopping Middle Street; High Street; Princes Street.
Event Yeovilton Air Day (Aug.).
AA 24 hour service Tel. 27744.

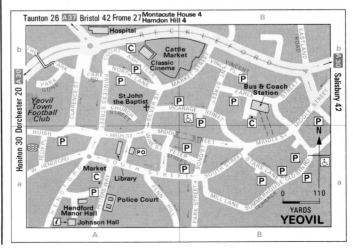

THE MINSTER *England's largest Gothic church dates from the 13th to 15th centuries – but retains the Anglo-Saxon name for a large church. It is the fourth cathedral to stand on the site.*

Goodramgate

Ogleforth

Chapter House

11

12

Minster Yard

College St

6

Minster Yard

Deangate

9

Low Petergate

High Petergate

Church Street

Newgate

St Leonards Pl.

Duncombe Place

Stonegate

14

Sampson's Square

St

Parliament

5

Museum Street

Blake Street

Davygate

New Street

Market Street

7

1

Lendal

Coney Street

10

River Ouse

A LOOK AROUND
YORK
North Yorkshire

England's "Eternal City"

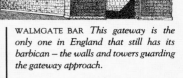

For almost 2,000 years York has played a leading role in England's history. Even without its crowning glory – a cathedral of breathtaking grandeur – it would be a city of outstanding beauty, interest and ageless charm. Its character is rich and colourful enough to be appreciated on the shortest of strolls down narrow streets little changed since the Middle Ages. The broad scope of York's appeal is perhaps best illustrated in its museums, where exhibits range from a meteorite 200 million years older than Earth to the prototype of the latest 150 mph railway locomotive.

York evolved from Eboracum, a Roman city and military base established at the end of the 1st century AD. Substantial traces of the Roman city have survived, the most spectacular being the base of the **Multangular Tower** which formed the western corner of the legionary fortress.

York later became a Saxon settlement before falling to Viking invaders from Denmark in 867, when it was called Jorvik. In 1973, when the vaults of a bank were being deepened in Coppergate – "gate" is the old Norse word for street – many links with the Viking city were discovered. They included three timber buildings – miraculously preserved in the wet, peaty subsoil – and numerous examples of Scandinavian craftsmanship.

After the Norman Conquest in 1066, northern England rose in rebellion against the invaders, but William the Conqueror crushed the uprising and built two wooden castles to guard the River Ouse at York. The one on the east bank was burned during a riot in 1190, but its stone replacement, **Clifford's Tower**, still stands near the Castle Museum.

The Middle Ages brought York a

SIGN OF LEARNING *Minerva, Goddess of Wisdom, above a former bookshop.*

period of relative peace and prosperity. One of the most notable legacies of the period is the **Merchant Adventurers' Hall**, built by the oldest and most powerful of the city's many guilds. The oldest parts of the hall date from the 14th century, and the medieval atmosphere is enhanced by walls hung with banners.

Charles I made York his northern headquarters in 1639, and the Parliamentarians laid siege to the city five years later. After the battle of Marston Moor, fought 6 miles west of the city in 1644, the garrison surrendered. But fortunately the terms included a promise that the puritanical victors would not desecrate the Minster or any of the city's many churches.

The 19th century saw the birth of modern York and the meteoric career of George Hudson, a far-sighted local draper who was three times Lord Mayor of York. Hudson cashed in on the railway boom, and became manager of the York and North Midland Railway Company. He made his native city a leading centre for the new

PLACES TO SEE

1 Multangular Tower
2 York Heritage Centre
3 Clifford's Tower
4 Merchant Adventurers' Hall
5 King's Manor, courtyard only
6 The Minster
7 Yorkshire Museum
8 Castle Museum
9 Holy Trinity Church
10 Guildhall and Mansion House
11 Treasurer's House
12 St William's College
13 The Shambles
14 Stonegate

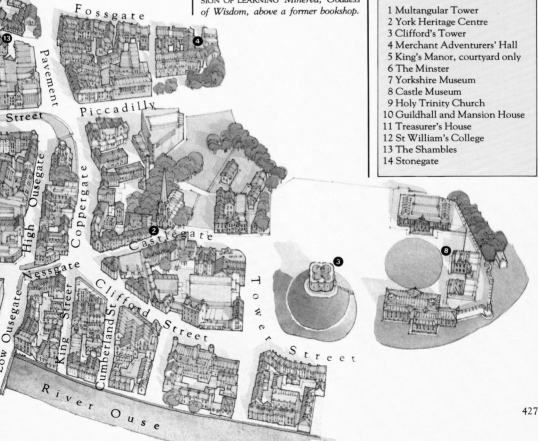

form of transport and became one of the wealthiest men in England. York also became rich, but Hudson fell from grace when irregularities in some of his business deals were discovered. He died in 1871, and Hudson Street was renamed Railway Street. Exactly a century later the controversial "Railway King" was forgiven. His portrait now hangs in the elegant 18th-century **Mansion House** – the lord mayor's official residence – and George Hudson Street is back on the map.

York's ancient traditions as a seat of learning were revived when a university was opened in 1963. Attractive buildings on a 190 acre site, open to the public, are grouped round an artificial lake with a fountain as its focal point. In the city centre, buildings used by the university include **King's Manor**, where the Council of the North met in Tudor times.

Oldest stained glass

York is dominated by the great **Minster**, 524 ft long and 249 ft wide across the transepts. A wooden church stood on the site in Saxon times. Stone buildings followed after the Norman Conquest, but the present Minster was started by Archbishop Walter de Grey in the early years of the 13th century. The

ACT OF MERCY *A 15th-century window in All Saints' Church, North Street, shows water being given to the poor. It is one of six "acts of mercy" panels.*

234 ft central tower was finished about 250 years later.

The Minster's treasures include more than 100 stained-glass windows, which span 800 years. The second window on the left, as the visitor enters through the nave's west door, has what is said to be the oldest glass in England, dating from about 1150. The stone choir screen is carved with figures of all England's rulers from William I to Henry VI.

In 1967, serious weaknesses were found at the base of the 20,000 ton central tower. Rescue work on the foundations revealed a rich and varied hoard of archaeological treasures, including Roman walls and carved Saxon stones. The **Undercroft** is now a spellbinding museum encompassing

STREET OF SLAUGHTER *Butchers' stalls once lined The Shambles – the word became a term for a scene of carnage.*

the whole of the Minster's history.

The **York Heritage Centre** is perhaps the ideal starting point for anyone planning to explore the city. It is housed in the former Church of St Mary, and uses models, paintings, embroidered panels and an audio-visual display to illustrate York's history since before the Roman invasion of AD 71.

The **Yorkshire Museum** stands in spacious gardens on the banks of the River Ouse. It includes a collection of pottery and porcelain, and the fossilised remains of an ichthyosaur and a plesiosaur – large sea reptiles from 160 million years ago – unearthed at Whitby in the 19th century. Ruins in the museum gardens include parts of the city walls, St Mary's Abbey and the Multangular Tower.

York's **Castle Museum** occupies two Classical 18th-century buildings originally built as prisons for debtors and women. The size and scope of the collection is quite astonishing, ranging from ornate Victorian truncheons to farm machinery, and rooms deco-

rated and furnished in Jacobean, Georgian and Victorian styles. Most remarkable of all, however, are Alderman's Walk, Kirkgate, and Princess Mary Court – full-scale reconstructions of three cobbled streets, flanked by picturesque buildings, which transport visitors straight back to the colourful age of gaslight and the Hansom cab.

Elsewhere in the museum is the condemned cell where Dick Turpin spent his last night before going to the gallows in 1739. Generally portrayed as a gallant rogue, Turpin was in fact a cold-blooded killer. His legendary ride to York on Black Bess was actually made 60 years earlier by another highwayman, William Nevison. He, too, was hanged at York in 1684. Turpin's grave may be seen in **St George's Churchyard**.

More than half of York's 50 medieval churches have been demolished. The survivors include All Saints, with its beautiful lantern tower built in the 19th century as a replica of the original. In ancient times a light was hung in the tower to guide travellers through the Forest of Galtres, to the north of York. Down by the Ouse, in North Street, another All Saints is renowned for its 14th and 15th-century stained glass. In Goodramgate, Holy Trinity dates from 1250 and has quaint box-pews as well as a two-tier pulpit.

History of England

The 15th-century **Guildhall** was devastated by fire during an air-raid in 1942, but the building has been restored. The colourful, and in many cases grotesque, carvings in the timber roof are copies of the originals, but genuine 15th-century craftsmanship may be seen in the inner chamber which survived the blaze.

One of the city's loveliest buildings is the 17th–18th-century **Treasurer's House**, close to the cathedral and surrounded by a peaceful walled

---

BRITAIN'S RAILWAY HERITAGE ON DISPLAY

The National Railway Museum at York is one of the world's largest. Special displays cover such subjects as royal trains and the history of Britain's railways from the horse-drawn days to the present. Locomotives spanning the ages include the *Agenoria* of 1829 and *Mallard*, the fastest of all steam-powered locos, which reached 126 mph in 1938.

Journey's end – steam locomotives of all ages lie at rest in the museum.

garden. Its last private owner gave it to the National Trust in 1930, and the rooms have a wealth of period furniture. Near by, the east end of the Minster overlooks **St William's College**, built in 1453 for the Minster's Chantry priests. An early-Georgian doorway leads to a picturesque quadrangle, where carved figures can be seen on the beams beneath the roof eaves. The college is named after William Fitzherbert, who became Archbishop of York in 1153.

The Shambles and **Stonegate**, both closed to traffic, are among the best-preserved medieval streets in Europe. Keen eyes will notice details, such as the carved devil under the eaves of a former printing shop in Stonegate.

A narrow passage leads from Stonegate to the **Twelfth-century House**, a restored remnant of a Norman dwelling including a stone-faced wall and a window. The house is the oldest in York of which substantial traces remain.

The 260 acre heart of the city is still almost completely surrounded by its 13th-century walls, with gates set into them at irregular intervals. A complete circuit on foot along the walls, a distance of almost 3 miles, takes between one and two hours, but is rewarded by superb views over a city whose importance was perfectly summarised by George VI. "The history of York," he said, "is the history of England."

PAINTED WAGON *The gipsy caravan in Castle Museum was made in Leeds in 1897. It is called a "Leeds wagon".*

Information Tel. 21756.
Location On the A19, 24 m. NE of Leeds.
Parking Union Terrace; St John's; Paragon Street; Bootham Row; Monk Bar; Foss Bank; Haymarket; Kent Street; St George's Field; Bishophill; Trinity Lane; Nunnery Lane; Esplanade; Marygate; Castle; Heworth Green; North Street; Tanner Row; Leeman Road (all car parks).
District council City of York (Tel. 59881).

Population 99,800.
E-C Wed. **M-D** Weekdays.
Police Fulford Road (Tel. 31321).
Casualty hospital Wigginton Road (Tel. 31313).
Post office (Ab) Lendal.
Theatres Arts Centre **(Ab)**, Micklegate (Tel. 27129); Theatre Royal **(Ac)**, St Leonard's Place (23568).
Cinemas ABC **(Bb)**, Piccadilly (Tel. 24356); Odeon, Blossom Street (23040).
Public library (Ac) Museum Street.

Town trails Available from Tourist Information Centre, De Grey House, Exhibition Square.
Shopping Bridge Street; Coney Street; Market Street; Feasegate; New Street; Blake Street; Davygate; Parliament Street; Micklegate; Colliergate; Church Street; Stonegate.
Sport FA League football, York City FC, Bootham Crescent Stadium; Horse racing, York Racecourse, Knavesmire.
Motorail Tel. 53022.
AA 24 hour service Tel. 27698.

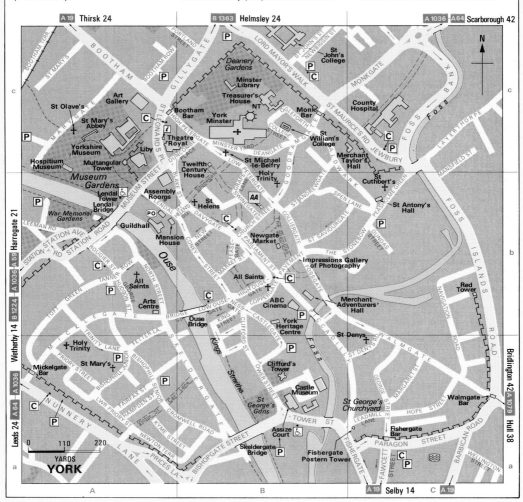

Glossary of architectural and historical terms

Angel beam A carving, usually of an angel, on the end of a hammerbeam.

Anglo-Saxon The architectural period of the 10th and 11th centuries. The best surviving examples are churches, such as the Church of St Lawrence at Bradford on Avon, Wilts. Saxon windows are recognised by a thick, central pillar.

Apse The semicircular end of a church behind the chancel.

Art nouveau A movement in architecture, furniture and decorative design started in the late 19th century to break away from imitations of the past, and characterised by the use of curves and flowing lines. The pioneer of art nouveau in architecture in Britain was Charles Mackintosh (1868-1928).

Artifact Any object fashioned by man.

Ashlar Stone masonry cut to give smooth faces and clean, square edges.

Bailey The space within the outer walls of a castle.

Barbican A fortified outer tower defending the entrance to a castle.

Baroque An architectural style of the 17th century typified by lavish and exuberant decorations such as foliage, shells, figures, arms and musical instruments.

Barrow An earthen burial mound. There are two main types; the long barrow of the Neolithic Age, or late Stone Age, and the round barrow of the Bronze Age.

Bas-relief A carved design which projects from the material from which it is formed.

Bastion A projecting fortification on a castle wall. Usually placed at intervals to give fire-cover to all parts of the outer wall.

Battlements A parapet of square-toothed pattern. A defensive feature on castle walls, but often used decoratively on church towers.

Box-pew Enclosed wooden seating in a church. Introduced in the Georgian period.

Broach spire A spire which rises directly from a tower without a parapet.

Bronze Age The period from about 2000 BC to 600 BC when metal replaced stone as a material for tools. Bronze is an alloy of copper and tin.

Canopy A hood over a doorway, window, altar or pulpit.

Cantilever A supporting beam, such as in a bridge or a roof, secured at one end only.

Capital The carved or moulded head of a column supporting a superstructure.

Carayatid A column in the form of a female figure.

Chamber Structure containing the buried dead in a barrow and usually built of stone, timber or turf.

Chancel The eastern end of a church, beyond the nave, in which the altar is placed.

Chantry chapel A chapel inside, or attached to, a church and used for saying Mass for the soul of the person to whom the chapel is dedicated.

Chapter house Administrative building for a monastery or cathedral.

Choir The part of a church where divine service is sung.

Classicism Revival of the Greek and Roman styles of architecture, particularly the use of columns and pediments, begun in the 1750s (see also Palladian).

Clerestory Upper storey of a church nave, above the aisle roofs, and containing windows.

Coffering Recessed panels in ceilings, usually decorative, but sometimes used to reduce the weight of the structure.

Colonnade A row of columns along a building or group of buildings.

Column Structural pillar of which there are three main styles: Doric, with clean lines and a plain head; Ionic, with carved or moulded head representing rams' horns; and Corinthian, which has an elaborately carved head with foliage designs.

Communion rail A low, balustered railing in front of a church altar.

Corbel Stepped projection from a wall giving support to a structure above, such as a balcony.

Crocket A carving representing foliage on Gothic spires and canopies.

Crypt The underground space beneath the chancel of a church, originally used as a burial chamber and occasionally with an altar.

Cupola A small, dome-roofed structure surmounting the roof of a building.

Curtain wall The outer wall of a medieval castle.

Decorated The architectural style of the 13th and 14th centuries which followed the Early English period. Recognised by large windows with tracery work in the frames, and an abundance of decorative carvings on gables and arches. Wells Cathedral is a notable example of this style.

Dolmen The exposed stone burial chamber of a barrow, where the earth covering has disappeared.

Dormer An upright window projecting from a pitched roof.

Early English The architectural style of the 12th century, following the Norman period. Tall, graceful buildings, such as Lincoln Cathedral, replaced the squat, bulky style of the previous period.

Earthwork Protective rings of ditches surrounding settlements built in prehistoric times, before the Romans came. The ditches were armed with sharpened stakes, and the removed earth was built up to form a protective bank.

Edwardian The trend in architecture and design during the reign of Edward VII (1901-10). The Victorian style continued to flourish, but art nouveau influenced decoration.

Elizabethan The architectural style of the second half of the 16th century, covered by the reign of Elizabeth I (1558-1603). Increased prosperity led to the building of many large houses in brick, often in H or E shapes. The period was also notable for timber-framed buildings – the framework was usually oak, and the spaces were filled with brick, tiles or lath-and-plaster. The exposed timbers were sometimes lavishly carved, but the black-and-white chequered effect was a Victorian embellishment.

Folly A building with no apparent use. Most were built by 18th and 19th-century landowners to embellish the landscape of their estates. The commonest forms were fake castles, classical temples and mock-Gothic ruins.

Font Water receptacle in a church used for christening ceremony.

Frieze A horizontal band of sculpture around the upper part of a wall.

Gallery Upper floor over part of the area of a church or theatre.

Gargoyle Grotesque carving on church eaves, usually on the end of a water spout. Intended to ward off evil spirits.

Gatehouse The tower over the fortified entrance to a castle or walled town.

Gazebo A structure designed to overlook a view, often a balcony, tower or summerhouse.

Georgian The era in architecture and design which began with the accession of George I in 1714 and lasted until 1810 when the Regency period began. In architecture the period saw the beginning of the Classical revival in large houses and public buildings. Smaller buildings were of simple lines and well-proportioned.

Gothic The architectural style introduced from France in the 12th century. Typified by pointed arches, flying buttresses and rib vaulting. The style was revived in churches and public buildings during the Victorian period.

Hammerbeam A timber bracket projecting from a wall to support roofing beams. The best-known example of a hammerbeam roof is in Westminster Hall, London.

Henge A circle of wooden or stone

uprights built in the late Neolithic Age as ceremonial sites.

Hill-fort A fortified hilltop settlement (see Earthwork) of the Iron Age.

Hypocaust Under-floor chambers in Roman houses and baths which distributed warm air from a furnace through hollow tiles set in the walls.

Iron Age The period following the Bronze Age and extending to about AD 43. During this period, iron replaced bronze for cutting tools and weapons.

Jacobean The period of James I's reign (1603-25). Houses typified by large casement windows and carved oak interiors. During this period, Inigo Jones (1573-1652) introduced the Palladian style to Britain with his Queen's House at Greenwich and the Banqueting House in Whitehall.

Jesse window A medieval stained-glass window depicting the genealogical tree of Christ springing from the root of Jesse, father of David.

Keep The inner defensive tower of a Norman castle.

Keystone The wedge-shaped stone at the centre of an arch which locks the surrounding stones in place.

Lancet window A tall, narrow window with a sharply pointed arch. Typical of Early English church architecture.

Lectern Reading desk in a church, often in the shape of an eagle with the Bible resting on its outspread wings.

Linen-fold A decorative carving on wood in imitation of draped or folded cloth.

Lintel A horizontal beam supporting the wall above a window or doorway.

Lychgate A roofed gateway at the entrance to a churchyard. The name comes from the Anglo-Saxon *lich*, meaning "corpse". The gate marks the division between consecrated and unconsecrated ground, and it was there that bearers stopped with the coffin to await the priest.

Mausoleum A magnificent and stately tomb, usually for the burial of members of a noble family. The name derives from the tomb of Mausolos at Halicarnassus, Turkey, dating from the 4th century BC.

Megalithic A structure of large stones, such as a henge or a chamber in a barrow.

Misericord A hinged seat in a choir stall which, when lifted, gave support for the occupant while standing during long services. The underside was often ornately carved.

Motte An artificial mound on which the Normans, and later builders, erected a castle.

Nave The central body of a church running from the west door to the transepts.

Neolithic Age The latter part of the Stone Age when man began to farm the land, using flint tools. The period extended from about 4000 BC to 2000 BC and immediately preceded the Bronze Age.

Niche Recess in a wall for a statue, in churches usually a saint.

Norman The architectural style which began with the Norman Conquest of 1066 and lasted until the end of the 12th century. The style, sometimes called Romanesque, is typified by rounded arches and deeply set doorways often carved with chevron or foliage designs.

Oratory A small chapel used for prayer, or a Roman Catholic church.

Oriel window An upper-floor bay window supported by corbels.

Palladian A style of architecture based on that of the Italian architect Andrea Palladio (1508-80). It was introduced into England by Inigo Jones in 1619 with the building of the Queen's House, Greenwich. It was revived in the 18th century by Colen Campbell (1673-1729) and Lord Burlington (1694-1753). The style is characterised by the use of columns, porticoes and ornate pediments.

Pantile A roofing tile of S-shaped section.

Pargetting Exterior plasterwork on buildings and usually decorated with designs of foliage, figures or geometric patterns.

Parvise A room above a church porch.

Pediment Triangular-shaped roof end, or a decorative mounting above doors and windows in Classical architecture. Where the pediment has the central portion opened out it is called a broken pediment.

Peel tower A 16th-century fortified tower built on the English side of the border with Scotland as a defence against sudden raids.

Perpendicular Style which followed the decorated period with a return to comparative simplicity. An emphasis on straight verticals and horizontals, large windows and fan-vaulted ceilings.

Pier A solid masonry support, also the area of a wall between windows.

Pilaster A shallow pier projecting from a wall. Largely used for decoration in the Classical revival.

Pinnacle Ornamental structure surmounting a tower or steeple and usually conical or pyramidal.

Plinth Projecting base of a wall or column. Also base of a statue or a tomb.

Porch The covered entrance to a building.

Portcullis Grid-shaped gate which could be raised and lowered at the entrance to a castle.

Portico A colonnaded and roofed entrance to a building, often with a pediment.

Pulpit A raised and enclosed platform in a church from which the priest or minister delivers his sermon.

Queen Anne A mixture of Baroque and Classical styles which began in the reign of William III and Mary II (1689-1702) and continued in the reign of Queen Anne (1702-14).

Refectory The dining hall in a convent or monastery.

Regency A continuation of the Georgian period, but with a more delicate style of interior decoration influenced largely by Robert Adam (1728-92).

Renaissance Meaning "rebirth", it began in Italy in the 14th century as a return to the Roman standards and styles of art and architecture. The movement came to England during the Tudor period.

Reredos A wood or stone ornamental screen behind a church altar.

Rood screen A wooden or stone-carved screen separating the nave and choir in a church, and surmounted by or incorporating a rood or cross.

Rose window Circular window with tracery resembling a rose; a feature of Gothic architecture.

Rotunda A circular building, usually with a domed roof.

Sedilia Seats for the clergy built into the wall on the south side of a chancel.

Stuart The period of the Stuart kings, and Cromwell's Commonwealth, which began in 1603 and ended in 1688.

Stucco A plaster finish on the faces of buildings made to look like stonework. Used extensively by John Nash (1752-1835) in the Regency period.

Tile-hanging A wall covering of overlapping tiles hung vertically. A feature of Elizabethan architecture; slate-hanging follows the same principle.

Tracery The ornamental carvings in the framework of Gothic windows, and in vaulted roofs.

Transept The north and south arms of a church leading off from the nave and the chancel.

Tudor The transitional period in the 16th century between the Gothic style and the Classical style. Brick became the new building material.

Tuscan One form of Classical architecture in which the columns are plain and straight sided.

Tympanum The space between the lintel of a doorway and the arch above it.

Undercroft A vaulted basement sometimes found in monasteries. Often below the church, such as in Westminster Abbey.

Vaulting An arched ceiling or roof. Types of vaulting range from the simple arch of the barrel vault of the Norman period to the intricately carved fan-vaulting of the Perpendicular period.

Victorian During the reign of Queen Victoria (1837-1901) the Gothic style of architecture was revived in churches and public buildings. The grandiose cathedrals and town halls were counter-balanced, however, by the mass building of squalid houses in the industrial areas which rapidly became slums.

Voussoirs The wedge-shaped stones used to make an arch.

Weather-boarding Overlapping timber boards used to face a building. It is also called clapboarding or ship-lapping because of its resemblance to the construction of a wooden ship's hull. Common in Kent and Essex.

ACKNOWLEDGMENTS

Credits on each page are arranged column by column from top to bottom. Work commissioned by Reader's Digest is shown in *italics*

The photographs in this book are by the following photographers:

3 *Neil Holmes* **5** *Neil Holmes* **6** *Neil Holmes* **7** *Neil Holmes* **8** *Patrick Thurston* **11** *Philip Llewellin* **12** *Philip Llewellin* **13** *C. M. Dixon* **14** Patrick Thurston **15** Trevor Wood; John Donat Photography **17** Patrick Thurston; *Julian Plowright* **18** Kenneth Scowen **19** Martyn F. Chillmaid **20** *Chris Morris* **21** Patrick Thurston **22** Pix Photos Ltd; Scottish Tourist Board **23** *Philip Llewellin* **24** Pix Photos Ltd **26** Pix Photos Ltd; John Topham Picture Library **28** British Tourist Authority **30** Mansell Collection; Reproduced by permission of The American Museum in Britain, Bath **31** British Tourist Authority **32** Patrick Thurston **33** The Trustees, The Cecil Higgins Art Gallery, Bedford **35** Susan Griggs **36** *Clive Coote;* Pix Photos Ltd **37** *Antony Howarth* **38** John Topham Picture Library **39** Clive Coote **40** Patrick Thurston **41** Robert Harding Associates **42** Airviews Ltd, Manchester Airport; *Ric Gemmell;* City of Birmingham **45** Susan Griggs **46** Northern Picture Library **47** Derek Widdicombe **49** Patrick Thurston **50** *Reader's Digest* **51** *Malcolm Aird* **52** Patrick Thurston **53** Trevor Wood **54** *Clive Coote;* Spectrum Photography **55** Clive Coote; Robert Harding Associates **56** Colin Molyneux **58** *Reader's Digest* **59** Susan Griggs **60** Trevor Wood; Michael Holford **61** Kenneth Scowen **62** Patrick Thurston **63** Patrick Thurston **64** San Francisco Maritime Museum; The National Maritime Museum, London; Susan Griggs; *Christopher Drew* **67** Patrick Thurston **68** *Eric Meacher* **69** Patrick Thurston **70** Aerofilms Ltd **71** Colin Molyneux **73** *Michael Hardy* **74-75** Cambridge University Collection (Copyright Reserved) **76** Susan Griggs **78** Sonia Halliday **80** *Philip Llewellin; Mike Wells* **81** *Philip Llewellin* **82** Colin Molyneux; Colin Molyneux **85** Susan Griggs **86** Michael Holford **87** *Malcolm Aird; Malcolm Aird;* The Marconi Co. Ltd **88** Patrick Thurston **89** Patrick Thurston; Mary Evans Picture Library; Cheltenham Art Gallery and Museum Service; Howard C Moore, Woodmansterne Ltd **90** Wales Tourist Board **91** Patrick Thurston **92** Patrick Thurston **93** Michael Holford **94** Michael Holford **95** Clive Friend FIIP, Woodmansterne Ltd; A. F. Kersting **96** Susan Griggs **97** Pix Photos Ltd; Susan Griggs **98** Trevor Wood **99** Malcolm Aira **100** Susan Griggs **102** *Clive Coote* **103** Picturepoint – London **104** *Colin Molyneux* **105** *Colin Molyneux* **106** *Colin Molyneux; Colin Molyneux; Colin Molyneux;* **107** *Colin Molyneux; Colin Molyneux* **108** Patrick Thurston **109** Patrick Thurston; Mary Evans Picture Library; Christopher Drew **110** Trevor Wood; Susan Griggs **112** Susan Griggs **113** A. F. Kersting **114** Susan Griggs **115** Patrick Thurston **116** *Clive Coote;* Franklin A. Barrett, Derby Museum **118** Spectrum Colour Library **119** Malcolm Aird **120** Martyn F. Chillmaid; By permission of the Board of the British Library; Mansell Collection **121** Susan Griggs; Susan Griggs **122** *Malcolm Aird; John Perkins* **123** C. M. Dixon **125** *Reader's Digest* **126** Patrick Thurston **127** Scottish Tourist Board **128** Northern Picture Library; *Ric Gemmell* **129** *Ric Gemmell;* Mary Evans Picture Library **131** *Mike Taylor* **133** John Bethell **134** John Bethell; Trevor Wood; *Reader's Digest* **135** *Reader's Digest* **136** Susan Griggs **137** *Reader's Digest* **139** Trevor Wood **140** Trevor Wood; Scottish Tourist Board **142** Malcolm Aird; Spectrum Colour Library **143** John Garrett **144** Patrick Thurston **145** Susan Griggs; Martyn F. Chillmaid **147** John Topham Picture Library **148** *Ian Yeomans* **149** *Colin Molyneux* **150** *John Perkins* **151** *Clive Coote* **152** *Julian Plowright* **154** Susan Griggs **155** Bruce Coleman Ltd **158** City of Glasgow District Council **159** Glasgow Museums and Art Galleries; Hunterian Art Gallery, University of Glasgow, Mackintosh Collection; Hunterian Art Gallery, University of Glasgow, Mackintosh Collection; *Penny Tweedie* **160** Susan Griggs **161** Burrell Collection, Glasgow Art Gallery **162** Patrick Thurston **164** *Clive Coote; Clive Coote* **165** Mary Evans Picture Library; *Malcolm Aird* **166** Trevor Wood; Great Yarmouth News Agency **167** Trevor Wood **168** Kenneth Scowen; Scottish Tourist Board **169** Mary Evans Picture Library **170** *Clive Coote; Penny Tweedie* **172** *Clive Coote; Clive Coote* **173** *Clive Coote* **175** *Antony Howarth* **177** *Penny Tweedie* **178** Gilbert Odd; J. Allan Cash Ltd **179** *Philip Llewellin* **180** Aerofilms Ltd **182** Ann Ronan Picture Library; Mary Evans Picture Library **183** Kenneth Scowen **184** Picturepoint – London; John Hedgecoe, Daily Telegraph Colour Library **185** Mary Evans **186** *Ian Yeomans* **187** Ernest J. Cooke; Scottish Tourist Board **188** Ernest J. Cooke; Chris Morris **190** Susan Griggs **191** Malcolm Aird **192** Ernest J. Cooke **193** Stanley Gibbons; Mary Evans Picture Library **195** Trevor Wood **196** *Clive Coote; Clive Coote;* Mary Evans Picture Library **197** *Clive Coote* **198** Ernest J. Cooke **199** Mary Evans Picture Library; Peter Baker Photography **200** Nigel Trotter, Daily Telegraph Colour Library **203** J. Allan Cash Ltd; British Tourist Authority **204** Susan Griggs **205** A. F. Kersting **206** Leeds City Council; Susan Griggs **207** Lucinda Lambton/Vision International **208** *Mike St Maur Sheil* **209** *Mike St Maur Sheil* **210** Susan Griggs **211** Patrick Thurston **212** Susan Griggs **214** Susan Griggs; Susan Griggs **216** Susan Griggs **217** *Reader's Digest;* Sonia Halliday **218** Picturepoint – London **219** Detail from G. Stubbs 'Horse frightened by a Lion', The Walker Art Gallery, Liverpool; Rex Features Ltd **220** *Adam Woolfit;* Picturepoint – London; National Portrait Gallery **222** Patrick Thurston **224** John Bethell; Cam Culbert **225** Cam Culbert; Michael Holford **226** British Tourist Authority; Brecht-Einzig Ltd **227** Reproduced by kind permission of F. Warne (Publishers) Ltd from their publication 'The Armorial Bearings of the Guilds of London'; British Tourist Authority **228** John Bethell **229** John Bethell **230** John Bethell; Neil Holmes; British Tourist Authority **231** Andrew Lawson **232** John Bethell; British Tourist Authority **233** Susan Griggs; British Tourist Authority; British Tourist Authority **234** Andrew Lawson; National Portrait Gallery; *Neil Holmes;* Andrew Lawson; *Neil Holmes* **235** Clive Friend FIIP, Woodmansterne Ltd; The William Morris Gallery, Walthamstow **236** A. F. Kersting **238** John Bethell; Pitkin Pictorials Ltd **239** John Watney **240** Michael Holford **241** Ronald Sheridan's Photo Library; *Creative Collection Ltd* **242** *Clive Coote;* Michael Holford **243** National Trust **244** Cam Culbert **245** Susan Griggs; Susan Griggs **246** Cam Culbert **247** Michael Holford **248** *Mike Freeman;* John Bethell **249** John Bethell **250** *Eric Meacher;* Susan Griggs **251** *Christopher Drew;* John Bethell **252** Andrew Lawson; Patrick Thurston; Andrew Lawson **253** *Patrick Thurston* **254** Neil Holmes **256** Tony Duffey, All-Sport Photographic Ltd **257** Patrick Eagar; The Cooper-Bridgeman Library **272** Northern Scotland Newspapers; National Portrait Gallery **273** Peter Baker Photography **274** Patrick Thurston **275** John Sims **277** British Tourist Authority **279** Peter Baker Photography **280** *Reader's Digest* **281** Mansell Collection **282** *Mike St Maur Sheil; Mike St Maur Sheil* **283** *Mike St Maur Sheil* **284** *Mike St Maur Sheil; Mike St Maur Sheil* **287** John Sims; *Peter Keen* **288** *Penny Tweedie* **290** Patrick Thurston **291** Chris Morris **292** Patrick Thurston **293** *Patrick Thurston* **294** Gerald Wilkinson **295** S. & O. Mathews; Ronald Sheridan's Photo Library **296** British Tourist Authority **297** British Tourist Authority **298** Ian Howes **300** Colin Molyneux **301** John Bethell **303** John Bethell; Northampton Museums and Art Gallery; Gerald Wilkinson **305** *Trevor Wood* **306** *Trevor Wood; Trevor Wood* **307** *Trevor Wood* **308** City of Nottingham; Mansell Collection; *Ric Gemmell* **309** Patrick Thurston **310-11** Ernest J. Cooke **312** *Sefton Samuels* **313** *Martyn F. Chillmaid* **314-15** Aerofilms Ltd **315** *Ashmolean Museum, Oxford; Adam Woolfit* **316** Howard C. Moore, Woodmansterne Ltd; British Leyland UK Ltd; Sonia Halliday; British Leyland UK Ltd; Trevor Wood **318** Ernest J. Cooke, Paisley Museum and Art Galleries **318-19** Airviews Ltd **320** National Trust **321** Michael Holford **322** *Patrick Thurston; Patrick Thurston* **323** *Patrick Thurston;* Still from the film *The 39 Steps*, courtesy of The Rank Organisation; Robert Harding Associates **324** C. M. Dixon **326** Daily Telegraph/Westair; *Philip Llewellin* **327** Art Gallery of New South Wales **329** *Clive Coote* **330** Mike St Maur Sheil; Barnaby's Picture Library **331** Barnaby's Picture Library **332** *Clive Coote* **333** Sonia Halliday; Picturepoint – London **336** R. Jemmett **337** J. Allan Cash Ltd **338** Peter Baker Photography **339** R. Jemmett **340** Pix Photos Ltd **341** Mansell Collection **342** Sefton Samuels Photo Library; Barnaby's Picture Library **343** Picturepoint – London **344** John Bethell **345** Pilkington Glass Museum **346-7** British Tourist Authority **348** Michael Holford **349** John Bethell; Michael Holford **350** *John Perkins* **351** *John Perkins* **352** Malcolm Aird; Salford Museum and Art Gallery **353** Chris Morris **354** Michael Holford **355** John Bethell; John Bethell **356** Patrick Thurston **357** The Cooper-Bridgeman Library **358** *Clive Coote* **359** Martyn F. Chillmaid **360-1** *Mike St Maur Sheil* **361** *Mike St Maur Sheil* **362** *Mike St Maur Sheil;* Patrick Thurston **363** *Mike St Maur Sheil* **364** Patrick Thurston **365** *Michael Newton* **366** Ann Ronan Picture Library; Ann Ronan Picture Library **366-7** R. Jemmett **367** Patrick Thurston **369** *Mike Taylor;* Martyn F. Chillmaid **370** City of Southampton; City of Southampton **373** R. Jemmett **374** John Bethell **375** Scottish Tourist Board **377** Clive Coote **378** *Mike Hewton;* Clive Coote **379** *Michael Hardy* **380** Philip Llewellin **382** John Bethell; *Julian Plowright* **383** Stratford Motor Museum **385** Malcolm Aird; R. Jemmett **387** Robert Harding Associates **388** Somerset County Museum **389** *Patrick Thurston* **390** R. Jemmett **391** Trevor Wood **392** John Bethell; R. Jemmett **394** Susan Griggs **395** *Julian Plowright* **396** Aerofilms Ltd **398** R. Jemmett; The Cooper-Bridgeman Library **402** John Bethell **403** Sonia Halliday **404** R. Jemmett **405** John Bethell **406** R. Jemmett **407** John Bethell **409** Robert Harding Associates **411** Evening Post and Chronicle, Wigan; Sefton Samuels **412** *Malcolm Aird* **413** Pix Photos Ltd **414** *Reader's Digest;* Sonia Halliday **415** *Chris Morris* **416** Malcolm Aird **419** Gerald Wilkinson **420** R. Jemmett **422** Robert Harding Associates **423** Dyson Perrins Museum Trust **424** Colin Molyneux **425** R. Jemmett **426** John Bethell **428** Sonia Halliday; Patrick Thurston; Jarrold Colour Publications.

Cartography by:
The Cartographic Department, Publications Division of the Automobile Association.

All maps in the book are based on aerial photography by:
Aerofilms Ltd; BKS Surveys Ltd; Cartographical Services (Southampton) Ltd; Department of the Environment-Fairey Surveys Ltd; Meridan Airmaps Ltd; Scottish Development Department. End-paper map prepared by: Fairey Surveys Ltd.

The publishers also acknowledge their indebtedness to the following books and journals which were consulted for reference:

Berkshire by Ian Yarrow (Robert Hale); *Blue Plaques on Houses of Historical Interest* (Greater London Council); *The Buildings of England* by Nikolaus Pevsner (Penguin); *Castles and Historic Places in Wales* (Wales Tourist Board); *Chambers's Encyclopaedia* (Pergamon); *The Companion Guide to Kent and Sussex* by Keith Spence (Collins); *The Companion Guide to London* by David Piper (Collins); *The Companion Guide to the Coast of North East England* by John Seymour (Collins); *The Companion Guide to the West Highlands of Scotland* by W. H. Murray (Collins); *The Concise Oxford Dictionary of English Place-Names* by E. Ekwall (Oxford University Press); *Cumbria* by John Parker (Bartholomew); *Devon and Cornwall* by Denys Kay-Robinson (Bartholomew); *A Dictionary of Arts and Artists* by Peter and Linda Murray (Penguin); *The Dictionary of National Biography* (Oxford University Press); *Discover Unexpected London* by Andrew Lawson (Elsevier-Phaidon); *Discovering Castles in England and Wales* by J. Kinross (Shire); *Encyclopaedia Britannica* (Encyclopaedia Britannica); *Guide to London Museums and Galleries* (HMSO); *Heart of England* by Louise Wright and James Priddey (Robert Hale); *Historic Houses, Castles and Gardens in Great Britain and Ireland* (ABC); *Illustrated Road Book of England and Wales* (Automobile Association); *Illustrated Road Book of Scotland* (Automobile Association); *The King's England Series* by Arthur Mee (Hodder and Stoughton); *London* (Michelin); *London Shopping Guide* by Elsie Burch Donald (Penguin); *London Street Names* by Gillian Bebbington (Batsford); *The Municipal Year Book* Editor, W. A. C. Roope (Municipal Journal); *Museums and Galleries in Great Britain and Ireland* (ABC); *National Trust atlas of places to visit* (Bartholomew); *The National Trust Guide* Editors, Robin Fedden and Rosemary Joekes (Jonathan Cape); *Nicholson's Guides to the Waterways* (Robert Nicholson); *The Oxford Companion Guide to Sports and Games* Editor, John Arlott (Oxford University Press); *The Oxford Companion to Ships and the Sea* Editor, Peter Kemp (Oxford University Press); *The Oxford Literary Guide to the British Isles* by Dorothy Eagle and Hilary Carnell (Oxford University Press); *The Penguin Guide to London* by F. R. Banks (Penguin); *Red Guides* (Ward Lock); *Shell Guide to Britain* Editor, Geoffrey Boumphrey (Ebury Press); *Shell Guide to England* Editor, John Hadfield (Michael Joseph); *Shell Guides to the Counties of England* (Faber); *Shopping in London* (British Tourist Authority); *Sussex* by John Burke (Batsford); *Time Out's Book of London* (Time Out); *Town Plans* (Automobile Association); *The Travellers Guides* Editor, Sean Jennett (Darton, Longman and Todd); *Victorian Cities* by Asa Briggs (Penguin); *What's Where in London with BP* by Denys Parsons (Kenneth Mason); *Who's Who* (Adam and Charles Black).

Paper, printing and binding by
Hale Paper Company Ltd, London;
Jarrold and Sons Ltd, Norwich; Mullis Morgan Ltd, London;
Vantage Photosetting Co. Ltd, Southampton; Winter and Co. Ltd, Huntingdon

01-039-2

Mileage chart

The distances shown are the shortest routes along classified roads and motorways between principal towns in Great Britain. The mileage chart towns are shown on the map, right. Their position in relation to the main road system and the other towns in the book can be seen on the map inside the front cover.

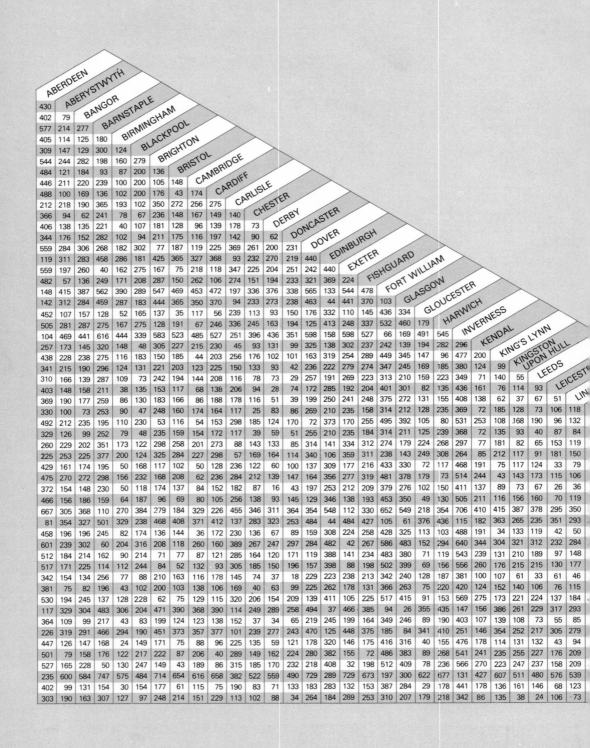